Let's Go writers travel on your budget.

"Guides that penetrate the veneer of the holiday brochures and mine the grit of real life."

—*The Economist*

"The writers seem to have experienced every rooster-packed bus and lunar-surfaced mattress about which they write."

—*The New York Times*

"All the dirt, dirt cheap."

—*People*

Great for independent travelers.

"The guides are aimed not only at young budget travelers but at the independent traveler; a sort of streetwise cookbook for traveling alone."

—*The New York Times*

"Flush with candor and irreverence, chock full of budget travel advice."

—*The Des Moines Register*

"An indispensible resource, *Let's Go*'s practical information can be used by every traveler."

—*The Chattanooga Free Press*

Let's Go is completely revised each year.

"Only *Let's Go* has the zeal to annually update every title on its list."

—*The Boston Globe*

"Unbeatable: good sightseeing advice; up-to-date info on restaurants, hotels, and inns; a commitment to money-saving travel; and a wry style that brightens nearly every page."

—*The Washington Post*

All the important information you need.

"*Let's Go* authors provide a comedic element while still providing concise information and thorough coverage of the country. Anything you need to know about budget traveling is detailed in this book."

—*The Chicago Sun-Times*

"Value-packed, unbeatable, accurate, and comprehensive."

—*Los Angeles Times*

Let's Go Publications

Let's Go: Alaska & the Pacific Northwest 2001
Let's Go: Australia 2001
Let's Go: Austria & Switzerland 2001
Let's Go: Boston 2001 **New Title!**
Let's Go: Britain & Ireland 2001
Let's Go: California 2001
Let's Go: Central America 2001
Let's Go: China 2001
Let's Go: Eastern Europe 2001
Let's Go: Europe 2001
Let's Go: France 2001
Let's Go: Germany 2001
Let's Go: Greece 2001
Let's Go: India & Nepal 2001
Let's Go: Ireland 2001
Let's Go: Israel 2001
Let's Go: Italy 2001
Let's Go: London 2001
Let's Go: Mexico 2001
Let's Go: Middle East 2001
Let's Go: New York City 2001
Let's Go: New Zealand 2001
Let's Go: Paris 2001
Let's Go: Peru, Bolivia & Ecuador 2001 **New Title!**
Let's Go: Rome 2001
Let's Go: San Francisco 2001 **New Title!**
Let's Go: South Africa 2001
Let's Go: Southeast Asia 2001
Let's Go: Spain & Portugal 2001
Let's Go: Turkey 2001
Let's Go: USA 2001
Let's Go: Washington, D.C. 2001
Let's Go: Western Europe 2001 **New Title!**

Let's Go *Map Guides*

Amsterdam
Berlin
Boston
Chicago
Florence
Hong Kong
London
Los Angeles
Madrid
New Orleans
New York City
Paris
Prague
Rome
San Francisco
Seattle
Sydney
Washington, D.C.

Coming Soon: *Dublin* and *Venice*

AUSTRIA & SWITZERLAND 2001

Nathaniel V. Popper editor
Rebecca L. Schoff associate editor

researcher-writers
Emily Griffin
Glenn Kinen
Kristin E. Meyer
Diana P. Moreno

Filip Wojciechowski map editor

Macmillan

HELPING LET'S GO If you want to share your discoveries, suggestions, or corrections, please drop us a line. We read every piece of correspondence, whether a postcard, a 10-page email, or a coconut. Please note that mail received after May 2001 may be too late for the 2002 book, but will be kept for future editions. **Address mail to:**

Let's Go: Austria & Switzerland
67 Mount Auburn Street
Cambridge, MA 02138
USA

Visit Let's Go at **http://www.letsgo.com,** or send email to:

feedback@letsgo.com
Subject: "Let's Go: Austria & Switzerland"

In addition to the invaluable travel advice our readers share with us, many are kind enough to offer their services as researchers or editors. Unfortunately, our charter enables us to employ only currently enrolled Harvard students.

Published in Great Britain 2001 by Macmillan, an imprint of Macmillan Publishers Ltd, 25 Eccleston Place, London, SW1W 9NF, Basingstoke and Oxford.
Associated companies throughout the world
www.macmillan.com

Published in the United States of America by St. Martin's Press.

ISBN: 0-333-90117-7
First edition
10 9 8 7 6 5 4 3 2 1

Let's Go: Austria & Switzerland is written by Let's Go Publications, 67 Mount Auburn Street, Cambridge, MA 02138, USA.

Printed in the USA on recycled paper with biodegradable soy ink.

ADVERTISING DISCLAIMER All advertisements appearing in Let's Go publications are sold by an independent agency not affiliated with the editorial production of the guides. Advertisers are never given preferential treatment, and the guides are researched, written, and published independent of advertising. Advertisements do not imply endorsement of products or services by Let's Go, and Let's Go does not vouch for the accuracy of information provided in advertisements.

If you are interested in purchasing advertising space in a Let's Go publication, contact: Let's Go Advertising Sales, 67 Mount Auburn St., Cambridge, MA 02138, USA.

ABOUT LET'S GO

FORTY-ONE YEARS OF WISDOM

As a new millennium arrives, *Let's Go: Europe*, now in its 41st edition and translated into seven languages, reigns as the world's bestselling international travel guide. For over four decades, travelers criss-crossing the Continent have relied on *Let's Go* for inside information on the hippest backstreet cafes, the most pristine secluded beaches, and the best routes from border to border. In the last 20 years, our rugged researchers have stretched the frontiers of backpacking and expanded our coverage into Asia, Africa, Australia, and the Americas. This year, we've introduced a new city guide series with titles to San Francisco and our hometown, Boston. Now, our seven city guides feature sharp photos, more maps, and an overall more user-friendly design. We've also returned to our roots with the inaugural edition of *Let's Go: Western Europe.*

It all started in 1960 when a handful of well-traveled students at Harvard University handed out a 20-page mimeographed pamphlet offering a collection of their tips on budget travel to passengers on student charter flights to Europe. The following year, in response to the instant popularity of the first volume, students traveling to Europe researched the first full-fledged edition of *Let's Go: Europe*, a pocket-sized book featuring honest, practical advice, witty writing, and a decidedly youthful slant on the world. Throughout the 60s and 70s, our guides reflected the times. In 1969 we taught travelers how to get from Paris to Prague on "no dollars a day" by singing in the street. In the 80s and 90s, we looked beyond Europe and North America and set off to all corners of the earth. Meanwhile, we focused in on the world's most exciting urban areas to produce in-depth, fold-out map guides. Our new guides bring the total number of titles to 51, each infused with the spirit of adventure and voice of opinion that travelers around the world have come to count on. But some things never change: our guides are still researched, written, and produced entirely by students who know first-hand how to see the world on the cheap.

HOW WE DO IT

Each guide is completely revised and thoroughly updated every year by a well-traveled set of nearly 300 students. Every spring, we recruit over 200 researchers and 90 editors to overhaul every book. After several months of training, researcher-writers hit the road for seven weeks of exploration, from Anchorage to Adelaide, Estonia to El Salvador, Iceland to Indonesia. Hired for their rare combination of budget travel sense, writing ability, stamina, and courage, these adventurous travelers know that train strikes, stolen luggage, food poisoning, and marriage proposals are all part of a day's work. Back at our offices, editors work from spring to fall, massaging copy written on Himalayan bus rides into witty, informative prose. A student staff of typesetters, cartographers, publicists, and managers keeps our lively team together. In September, the collected efforts of the summer are delivered to our printer, who turns them into books in record time, so that you have the most up-to-date information available for your vacation. Even as you read this, work on next year's editions is well underway.

WHY WE DO IT

We don't think of budget travel as the last recourse of the destitute; we believe that it's the only way to travel. Living cheaply and simply brings you closer to the people and places you've been saving up to visit. Our books will ease your anxieties and answer your questions about the basics—so you can get off the beaten track and explore. Once you learn the ropes, we encourage you to put *Let's Go* down now and then to strike out on your own. You know as well as we that the best discoveries are often those you make yourself. When you find something worth sharing, please drop us a line. We're Let's Go Publications, 67 Mount Auburn St., Cambridge, MA 02138, USA (email: feedback@letsgo.com). For more info, visit our website, www.letsgo.com.

HOW TO USE THIS BOOK

Welcome to Let's Go: Austria & Switzerland 2001! We're here to help you find close encounters with all things Swiss and Austrian, from high culture to goats.

THE ORGANIZATION OF THIS BOOK

The book begins with the **Essentials** section, which contains vital practical information you will need before and during your trip. After Essentials, the book is divided into two halves for the two countries. The Austria half precedes the Switzerland half (in the middle, a few pages are devoted to Liechtenstein).

THE "MEAT": Each half begins with a chapter providing a general introduction to the history, culture, and people of the nation. The rest of the chapters in **Austria** have been divided up by *Bundesländer*, and are ordered clockwise from the capital, Vienna. In a few cases the strict lines of the *Länder* were overridden by logistics of transportation. The Salzkammergut, actually in Upper Austria, was placed in the Salzburger Land chapter because Salzburg is the main access point for the resort area. The Hohe Tauern National Park chapter includes portions of a number of *Länder* because of the shape of the park. In **Switzerland,** the coverage begins with the capital Bern and the Bernese Oberland, and spirals out clockwise in geographical groupings.

APPENDIX. The appendix contains useful **conversions,** a pronunciation guide and a handy **phrasebook** for German, French, and Italian (sorry, no Romansch, see p. 389), along with temperature, holidays, and distance charts. There is also a table with phone code guides for major cities (also see Phone Codes, below).

A FEW NOTES ABOUT LET'S GO FORMAT

RANKING ESTABLISHMENTS. In each section (accommodations, food, etc.), we list establishments in order from best to worst. Our absolute favorites are so denoted by the highest honor given out by Let' s Go, the Let's Go thumbs-up (☒).

PHONE CODES AND TELEPHONE NUMBERS. The **phone code** for each region, city, or town appears opposite the name of that region, city, or town, and is denoted by the ☎ icon. **Phone numbers** in text are also preceded by the ☎ icon.

GRAYBOXES AND WHITEBOXES. Grayboxes at times provide wonderful cultural insight, at times simply crude humor. In any case, they're usually amusing, so enjoy. **Whiteboxes,** on the other hand, provide important practical information, such as warnings (☒), helpful hints, and further resources (☒).

UNIQUE AND USEFUL SECTIONS. The 2001 guide has added explanatory sections on the recent political developments in each country that might raise questions in some travelers' minds (see p. 68, p. 295). We have focused on expanding the outdoors coverage, adding new hikes nearly everywhere, as well as regional outdoor intros that explain accommodations and transportation options for popular outdoor regions. Our Vienna coverage has been overhauled to make the sights section more accessible; sights are now grouped under headers that identify the nearest *Platz* (square) or landmark, with directions under each header.

A NOTE TO OUR READERS The information for this book was gathered by *Let's Go* researchers from May through August of 2000. Each listing is based on one researcher's opinion, formed during his or her visit at a particular time. Those traveling at other times may have different experiences since prices, dates, hours, and conditions are always subject to change. You are urged to check the facts presented in this book beforehand to avoid inconvenience and surprises.

CONTENTS

CONTENTS

MAPS

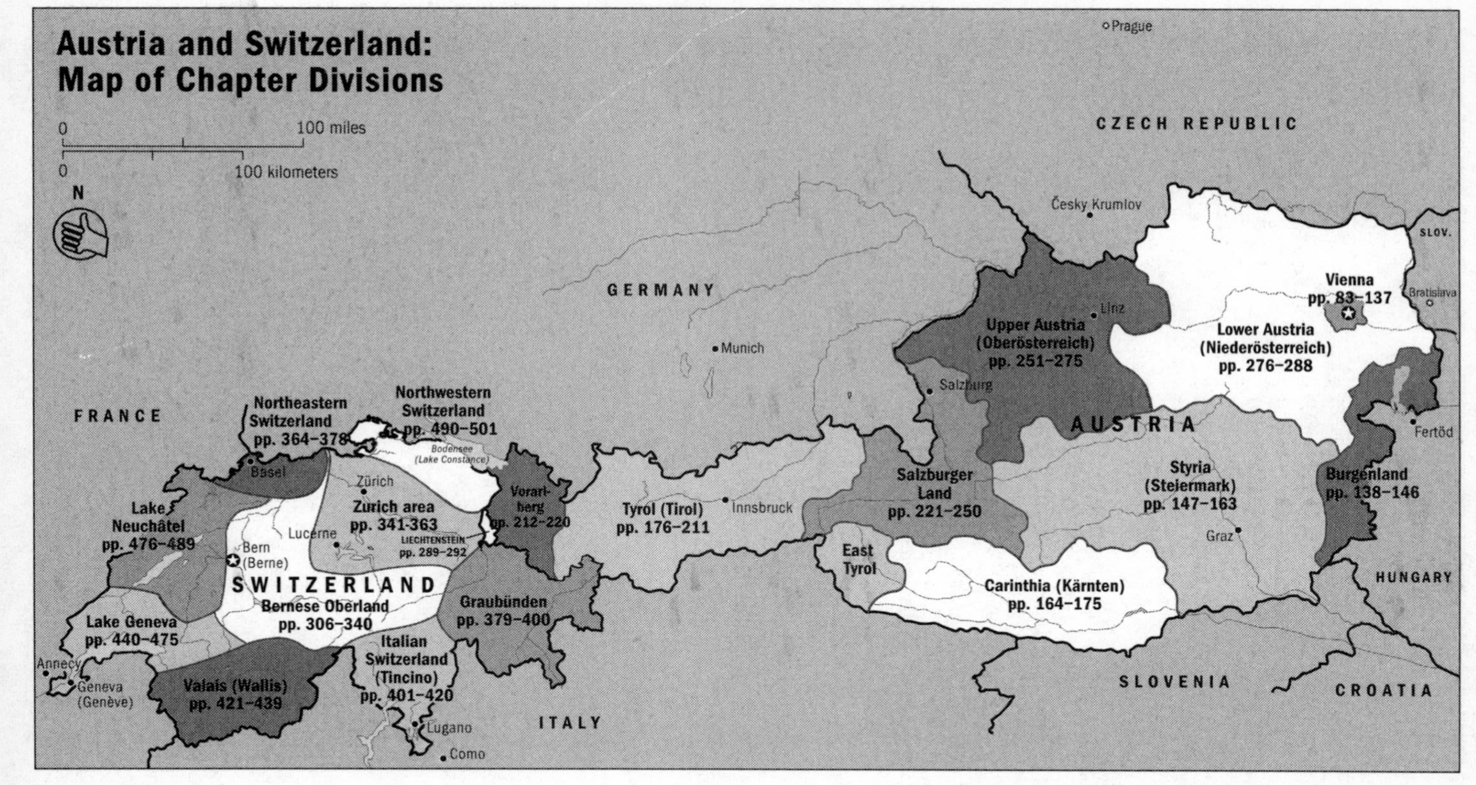
Austria and Switzerland:
Map of Chapter Divisions
0
100 miles
0
100 kilometers
N
Prague
CZECH REPUBLIC
Česky Krumlov
SLOV.
GERMANY
Munich
Linz
Vienna
pp. 83–137
Bratislava
Upper Austria
(Oberösterreich)
pp. 251–275
Lower Austria
(Niederösterreich)
pp. 276–288
Salzburg
AUSTRIA
Fertöd
FRANCE
Northeastern
Switzerland
pp. 364–378
Northwestern
Switzerland
pp. 490–501
Bodensee
(Lake Constance)
Basel
Zürich
Zurich area
pp. 341–363
Vorarlberg
pp. 212–220
Tyrol (Tirol)
pp. 176–211
Innsbruck
Salzburger
Land
pp. 221–250
Styria
(Steiermark)
pp. 147–163
Burgenland
pp. 138–146
Lake
Neuchâtel
pp. 476–489
Lucerne
LIECHTENSTEIN
pp. 289–292
Bern
(Berne)
SWITZERLAND
Bernese Oberland
pp. 306–340
Graz
East
Tyrol
Carinthia (Kärnten)
pp. 164–175
HUNGARY
Graubünden
pp. 379–400
Lake Geneva
pp. 440–475
Italian
Switzerland
(Tincino)
pp. 401–420
Annecy
Geneva
(Genève)
Valais (Wallis)
pp. 421–439
Lugano
Como
ITALY
SLOVENIA
CROATIA

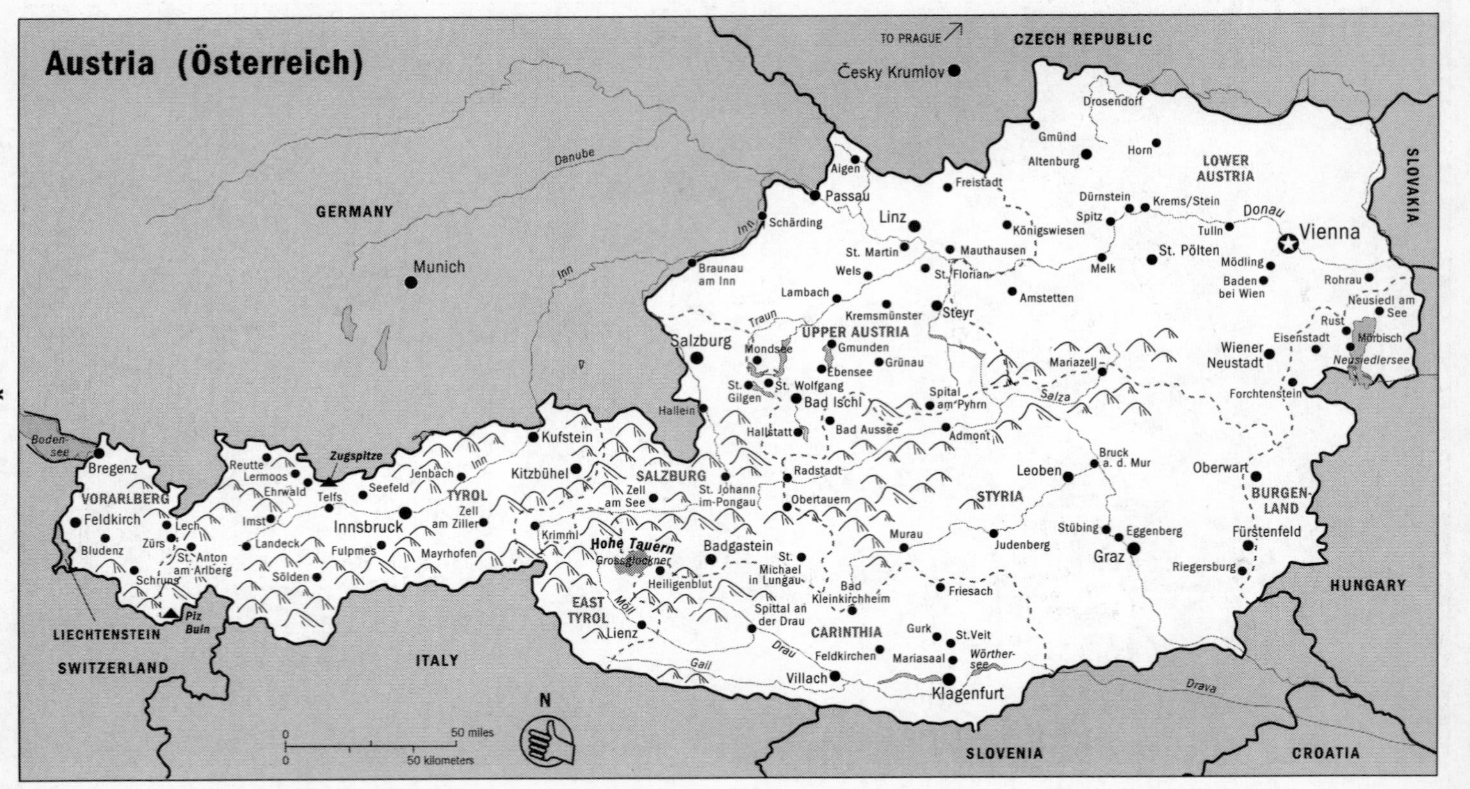
Austria (Österreich)
TO PRAGUE
CZECH REPUBLIC
Česky Krumlov
SLOVAKIA
GERMANY
Munich
Danube
Inn
Drosendorf
Gmünd
Horn
Altenburg
LOWER AUSTRIA
Aigen
Freistadt
Passau
Dürnstein
Krems/Stein
Schärding
Linz
Spitz
Donau
Tulln
Vienna
Königswiesen
St. Martin
Mauthausen
Melk
St. Pölten
Mödling
Braunau am Inn
Wels
St. Florian
Baden bei Wien
Rohrau
Lambach
Amstetten
Kremsmünster
Steyr
Neusiedl am See
Traun
UPPER AUSTRIA
Rust
Salzburg
Mondsee
Gmunden
Eisenstadt
Mörbisch
Wiener Neustadt
Grünau
Neusiedlersee
Ebensee
Mariazell
St. Gilgen
St. Wolfgang
Spital am Pyhrn
Forchtenstein
Salza
Hallein
Bad Ischl
Bad Aussee
Hallstatt
Admont
Boden-see
Kufstein
Bruck a. d. Mur
Oberwart
Bregenz
Reutte
Zugspitze
Lermoos
Jenbach
Kitzbühel
SALZBURG
Radstadt
Leoben
BURGEN-LAND
Seefeld
Ehrwald
St. Johann im-Pongau
Zell am See
VORARLBERG
Telfs
TYROL
Obertauern
STYRIA
Zell am Ziller
Feldkirch
Lech
Imst
Innsbruck
Stübing
Eggenberg
Fürstenfeld
Krimml
Zürs
Landeck
Hohe Tauern
Murau
Judenberg
Bludenz
St. Anton am Arlberg
Fulpmes
Mayrhofen
Badgastein
Graz
Grossglockner
St. Michael in Lungau
Riegersburg
Schruns
Sölden
Heiligenblut
Friesach
Bad Kleinkirchheim
HUNGARY
EAST TYROL
Möll
Spittal an der Drau
Piz Buin
CARINTHIA
LIECHTENSTEIN
Lienz
Gurk
St.Veit
Drau
Feldkirchen
Mariasaal
Wörther-see
Gail
SWITZERLAND
ITALY
Villach
Klagenfurt
Drava
N
0
50 miles
0
50 kilometers
SLOVENIA
CROATIA

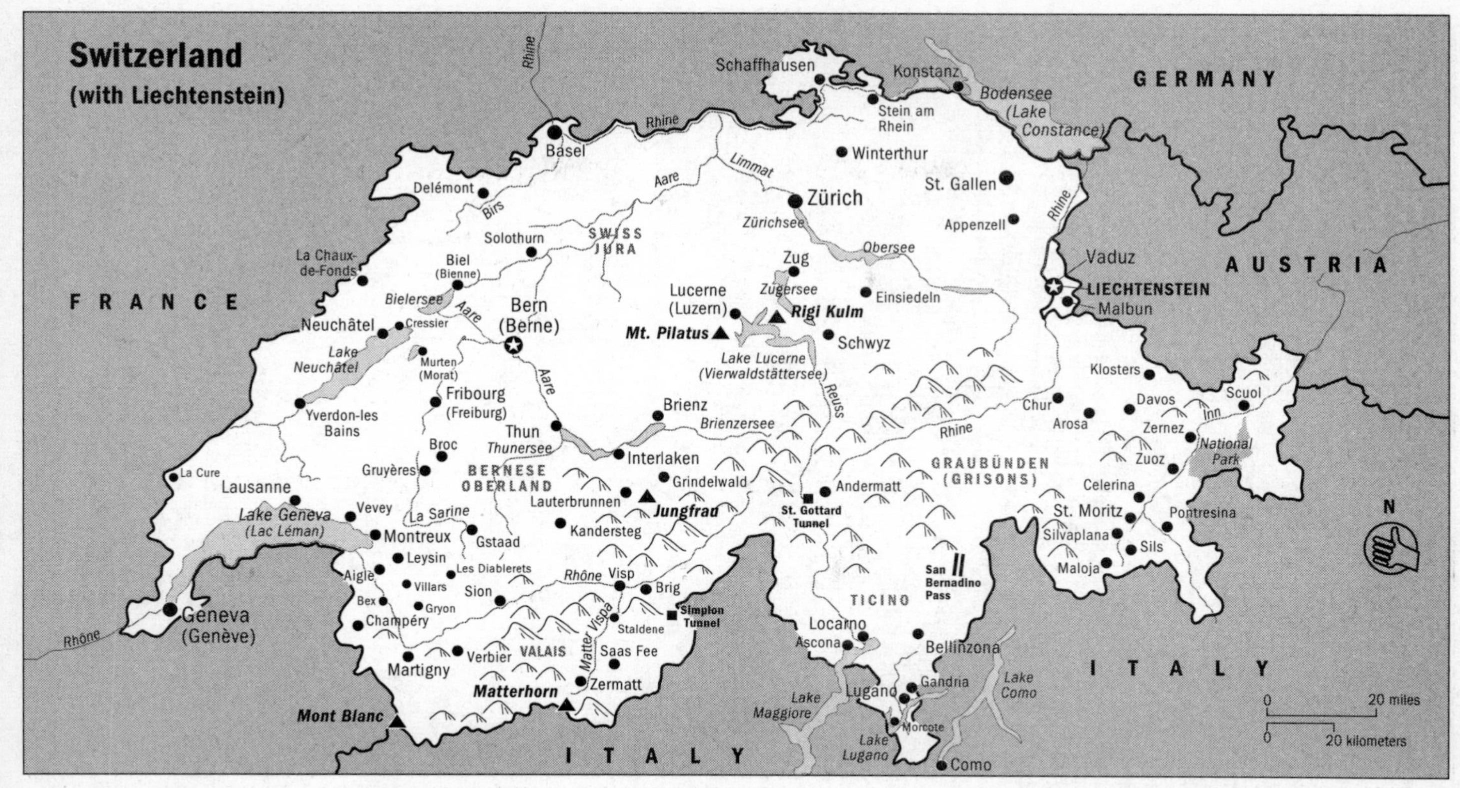

Switzerland
(with Liechtenstein)
FRANCE
GERMANY
AUSTRIA
ITALY
ITALY
ITALY
Rhine
Rhine
Rhine
Rhine
Rhône
Rhône
Basel
Schaffhausen
Konstanz
Bodensee (Lake Constance)
Stein am Rhein
Winterthur
St. Gallen
Appenzell
Zürich
Zürichsee
Obersee
Limmat
Aare
Aare
Aare
Birs
Delémont
Solothurn
SWISS JURA
La Chaux-de-Fonds
Biel (Bienne)
Bielersee
Bern (Berne)
Neuchâtel
Cressier
Lake Neuchâtel
Murten (Morat)
Fribourg (Freiburg)
Yverdon-les Bains
Thun
Thunersee
Broc
Gruyères
BERNESE OBERLAND
La Cure
Lausanne
Lake Geneva (Lac Léman)
Vevey
La Sarine
Montreux
Gstaad
Leysin
Les Diablerets
Aigle
Villars
Bex
Gryon
Sion
Champéry
Geneva (Genève)
Martigny
Verbier
VALAIS
Matterhorn
Mont Blanc
Zermatt
Saas Fee
Matter Vispa
Staldene
Visp
Brig
Simplon Tunnel
Kandersteg
Lauterbrunnen
Jungfrau
Grindelwald
Interlaken
Brienz
Brienzersee
Lucerne (Luzern)
Mt. Pilatus
Lake Lucerne (Vierwaldstättersee)
Zug
Zugersee
Rigi Kulm
Schwyz
Einsiedeln
Reuss
Andermatt
St. Gottard Tunnel
Vaduz
LIECHTENSTEIN
Malbun
Klosters
Chur
Arosa
Davos
Scuol
Inn
Zernez
National Park
Zuoz
GRAUBÜNDEN (GRISONS)
Celerina
St. Moritz
Pontresina
Silvaplana
Sils
Maloja
San Bernadino Pass
TICINO
Locarno
Ascona
Bellinzona
Lugano
Gandria
Morcote
Lake Maggiore
Lake Lugano
Lake Como
Como
N
0
20 miles
0
20 kilometers

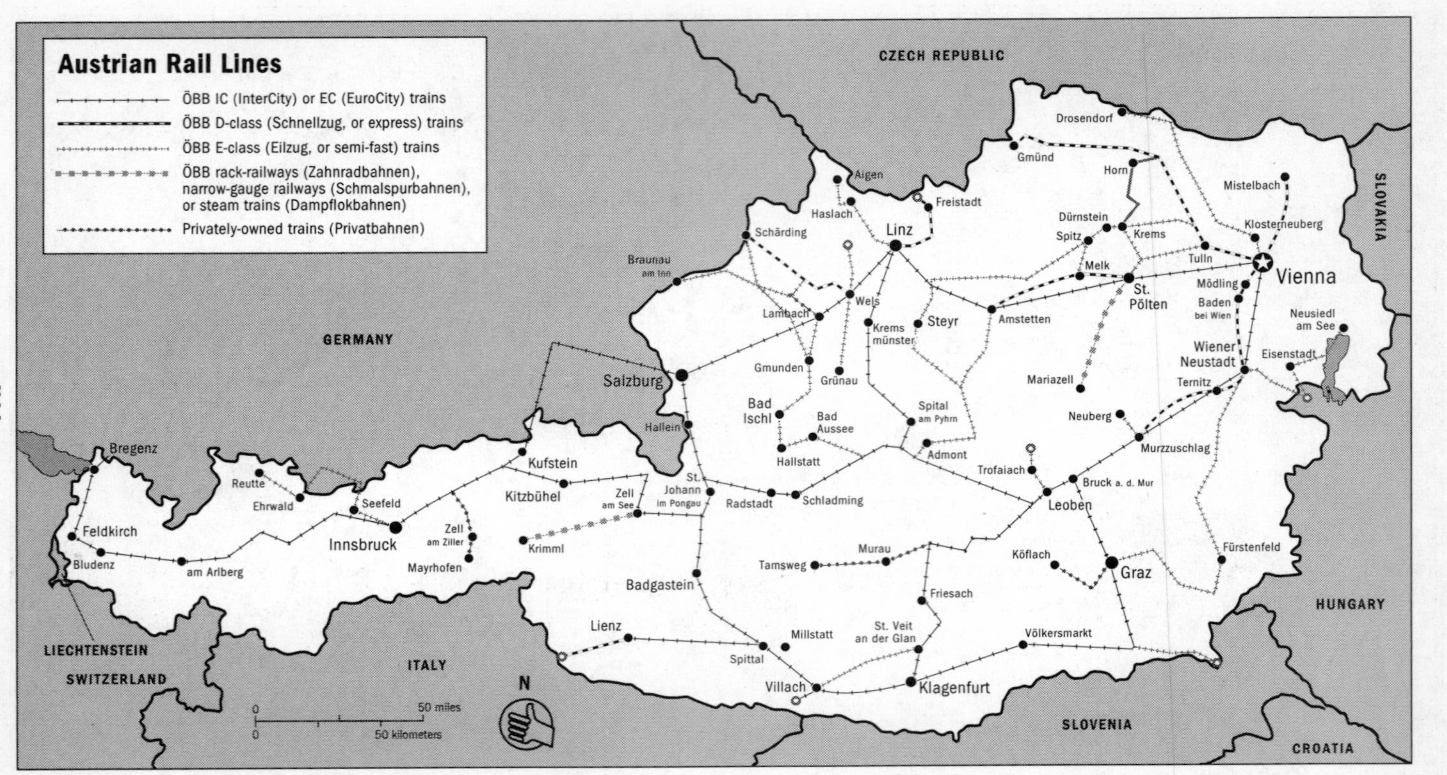

Austrian Rail Lines
ÖBB IC (InterCity) or EC (EuroCity) trains
ÖBB D-class (Schnellzug, or express) trains
ÖBB E-class (Eilzug, or semi-fast) trains
ÖBB rack-railways (Zahnradbahnen), narrow-gauge railways (Schmalspurbahnen), or steam trains (Dampflokbahnen)
Privately-owned trains (Privatbahnen)
CZECH REPUBLIC
SLOVAKIA
GERMANY
HUNGARY
ITALY
SLOVENIA
CROATIA
SWITZERLAND
LIECHTENSTEIN
Vienna
Mistelbach
Klosterneuberg
Drosendorf
Gmünd
Horn
Dürnstein
Krems
Spitz
Tulln
Melk
St. Pölten
Mödling
Baden bei Wien
Neusiedl am See
Eisenstadt
Wiener Neustadt
Ternitz
Mariazell
Neuberg
Murzzuschlag
Amstetten
Steyr
Linz
Freistadt
Aigen
Haslach
Schärding
Braunau am Inn
Wels
Lambach
Krems münster
Gmunden
Grünau
Salzburg
Bad Ischl
Bad Aussee
Hallstatt
Spital am Pyhrn
Admont
Hallein
St. Johann im Pongau
Radstadt
Schladming
Trofaiach
Bruck a. d. Mur
Leoben
Graz
Köflach
Fürstenfeld
Murau
Tamsweg
Friesach
St. Veit an der Glan
Völkersmarkt
Klagenfurt
Villach
Millstatt
Spittal
Badgastein
Lienz
Kufstein
Kitzbühel
Zell am See
Krimml
Zell am Ziller
Mayrhofen
Innsbruck
Seefeld
Reutte
Ehrwald
Bregenz
Feldkirch
Bludenz
am Arlberg
N
0
50 miles
0
50 kilometers

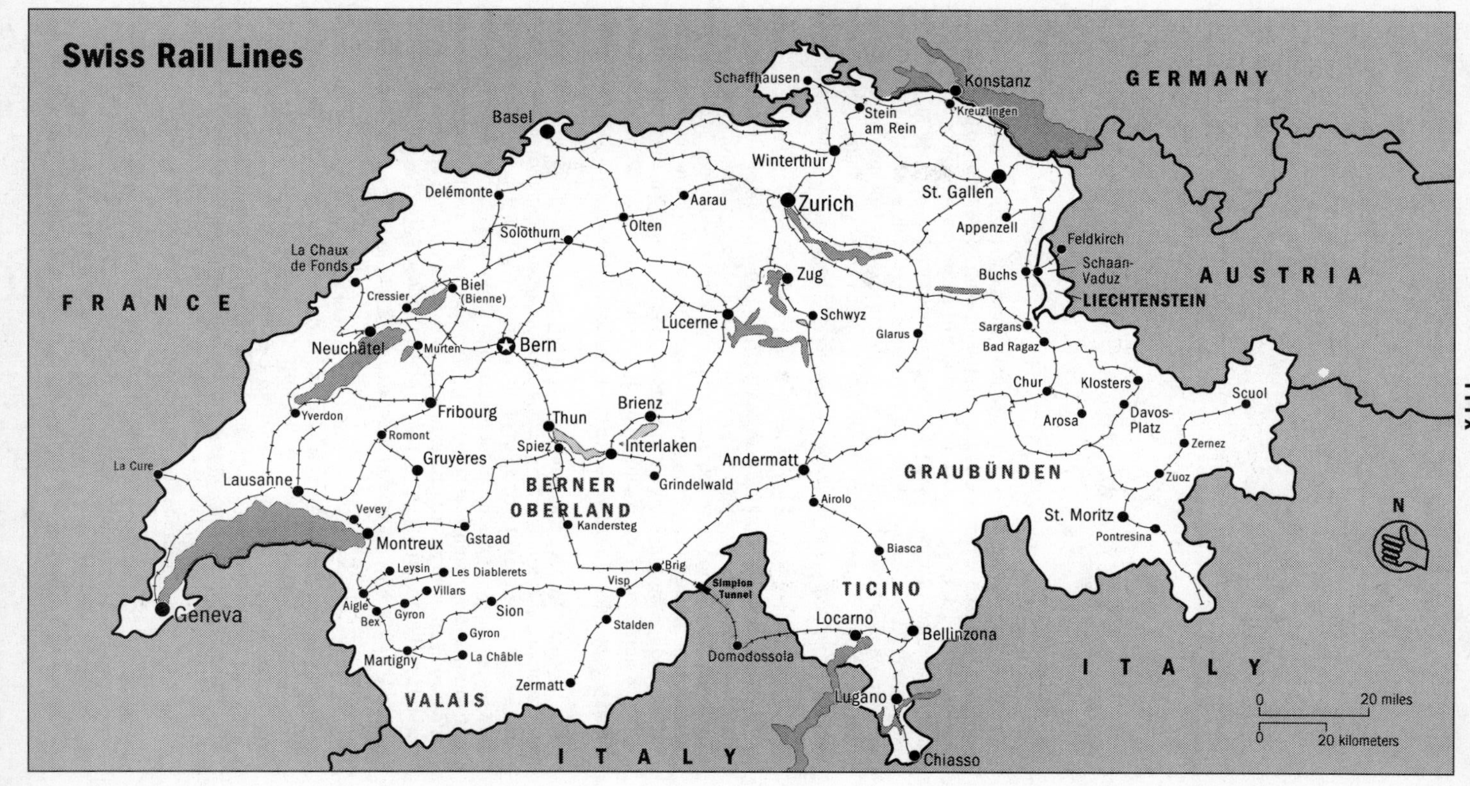
Swiss Rail Lines
GERMANY
FRANCE
AUSTRIA
LIECHTENSTEIN
ITALY
ITALY
Schaffhausen
Konstanz
Stein
am Rein
Kreuzlingen
Basel
Winterthur
St. Gallen
Zurich
Delémonte
Aarau
Olten
Appenzell
Solothurn
Feldkirch
La Chaux
de Fonds
Schaan-
Vaduz
Buchs
Zug
Biel
(Bienne)
Cressier
Schwyz
Lucerne
Sargans
Glarus
Bad Ragaz
Neuchâtel
Murten
Bern
Chur
Klosters
Scuol
Brienz
Arosa
Davos-
Platz
Thun
Fribourg
Yverdon
Romont
Zernez
Spiez
Interlaken
Gruyères
Andermatt
La Cure
GRAUBÜNDEN
Zuoz
Lausanne
BERNER
OBERLAND
Grindelwald
Airolo
Vevey
St. Moritz
Kandersteg
Montreux
Gstaad
Pontresina
Biasca
Leysin
Les Diablerets
Brig
Villars
Visp
Simplon
Tunnel
TICINO
Aigle
Bex
Gyron
Sion
Geneva
Stalden
Locarno
Gyron
Bellinzona
Martigny
La Châble
Domodossola
Zermatt
VALAIS
Lugano
Chiasso
N
0
20 miles
0
20 kilometers

RESEARCHER-WRITERS

Emily Griffin *Lake Geneva, Lake Neuchâtel, Northeastern, Northwestern and Central Switzerland*

A veteran of *Let's Go: USA 2000*, Emily fearlessly showed us the same urban-rust-belt mettle and more (once the authorities finally let her in). Her finely-trained eye quickly summarized the sedate *See*-side cities of Switzerland, mercilessly uncovering the not-so-sedate night life that even the Swiss didn't know they had. While Emily showed sympathy for the bears in the pit, she showed none for slovenly proprietors. Somehow, even after long days and late nights out researching, she still managed to turn in the cleanest prose we'd ever seen—so accurate it was ready for the publisher as soon as it arrived.

Glenn Kinen *Tyrol, Vorarlberg, Salzkammergut, Hohe Tauern National Park, and Stryria*

Armed with dry wit, a philosophical bent, and a backpack full of nineteenth-century novels, Glenn braved the wilds of rural Austria. Proving immune to deceptive cuteness, he sent back God's truth, tell-it-like-it-is accounts of everything from park officials to Austrian Hooters (the restaurant chain, really). When doors were literally slammed in his face, Glenn forged on to discover welcoming new accommodations. He found the Dachstein Ice Caves a little slippery, but conquered our coverage of Alpine villages. Trust Glenn to tell you why it's worth the trip.

Kristin E. Meyer *The Jungfrau Region, Wallis, Italian Switzerland, Graubünden, Appenzell*

Even when Switzerland snowed on her in mid-summer, the irrepressible and irresistible Kristin ruthlessly burned through her itinerary. She adapted to the extremes of the Swiss backpacking universe with an enthusiasm like sunshine and determination that didn't fade with the fair weather. Hardcore, hang-gliding outdoorswoman by day, discerning social maven by night, Kristin charmed everyone she met, getting the local word on the favorite nightspots. Her sparklingly fresh coverage blazes new trails for any reader who can keep up with her pace.

Diana P. Moreno *Vienna, Burgenland, Lower Austria, Linz, Salzburg, Carinthia, Graz*

For Diana heading to Vienna was less a departure than a homecoming. And from the first moments, she showed herself to be an insider, moving beyond the commonplace to capture illustrative cultural tales and evocative descriptions. While she was tempted to act like a true Viennese and linger over her steaming mélange at Café Central, she managed to tear herself away, and make tracks up the Danube. She overcame less-than-friendly hostesses with her accustomed graciousness and sweetness, turning a smile even when times turned tough.

Rebecca S. Tinio *Editor, Munich*

David A. Boyajian, Aram Yang *Researcher-Writers, Munich.*

ACKNOWLEDGMENTS

A&S THANKS: Alice Farmer, who played the Einstein to our universe, the suspenders to our pants, the string to our bikini, the polka-dots to our pantaloons, . well, thanks. Filip, without whom we, and countless others, would be lost. Alex and Marc, for taking out our appendix, Matt for conversations. Nora, for letting us steal office supplies. We like Campo sandwiches. Allie and Emmie who made it so that we didn't have to do practically nothing. Thanks Nick, Kaya, Kate, Ankur, and Anne C. for making it what it is.

NATHANIEL POPPER THANKS: One scholar who pulled her head out of the middle ages and gave herself over (even missing Thursday Tango) to a baby that didn't even respond with tinny, pre-recorded declarations of love (yeah, Aunt B). Thanks for doing the work when I couldn't, for handing me me binmoculars when I didn't want to lose my angle on the ternimal in the shurberry. Teddy, thanks for being there when I wasn't. To the axis boys and girl who made the whole summer a fun trip to the bathroom. Thanks Nora, Sarah, Mica and Alex for never leaving, Lucy for leaving with me. Nina and Angela, yeah. Ilan for a vacation. Ann, for lessons in life and more. MP, JP, LP, SP, from whom I came.

REBECCA SCHOFF THANKS: Papageno, best of editors, for being dedicated but not anal, learned but never Harvardian, for being damn good company. . . and for introducing me to Dylan. Thanks to Marc, *il mio professore*, and to Matt, for putting up with my Diplododon, and for understanding fondue. Love to Team Germany for administering the smack, you cavmen. To *mon secretaire*, Alex, thanks for the help with French. To Beth, for dishing news, and Nora, for being Nora. To friends and family, who learned to dial the office number first, thanks for keeping close.

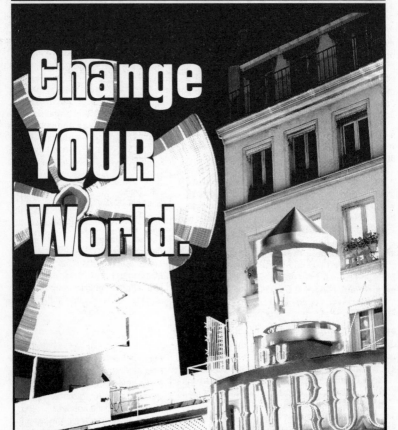

DISCOVER AUSTRIA AND SWITZERLAND

The ubiquitous bells of Austria and Switzerland, whether they hang from the neck of milk chocolate- and cheese- producing cows, or from the towers of famed 13th-century churches, call to the traveler in everyone. The cool, forested valleys, and the narrow, cobblestoned streets through which these bells echo are a testament to the diversity of spaces Austria and Switzerland offer up for exploration. World-class cities like Vienna, Salzburg, and Zurich showcase many of Europe's most prized artistic, musical, and architectural treasures. Nearby stratospheric peaks, reflected in almost unnaturally blue lakes, serve as beacons toward unparalleled natural adventures, ranging from time-tested mountain-climbing and glacier skiing to cutting-edge adventure sports like paragliding and canyoning. The incredible array of man-made and natural attractions in Austria and Switzerland is complemented by a dense network of perfectly coordinated trains, and carefully tended budget accommodations allowing the budget traveler to experience everything right on schedule.

FACTS AND FIGURES

CAPITAL OF AUSTRIA: Vienna

POPULATION: 8,120,000

LIFE EXPECTANCY: Men 74.3; Women 80.8

LAND AREA: 83,858km^2 (32,378mi.^{2})

LANGUAGE: German

RELIGION: 85% Catholic, 6% Protestant

CAPITAL OF SWITZERLAND: Bern

POPULATION: 7,444,000

LIFE EXPECTANCY: Men 75.8, Women 82.3

LAND AREA: 41,290km^2 (15,938mi.^{2})

LANGUAGES: German, French, Italian, and Romansch

RELIGION: 48% Catholic, 44% Protestant

WHEN TO GO

The best time to visit the Alpine states of Austria and Switzerland depends on what you're looking for. November to March is peak season for skiing, and July and August are the favorite months for hikers. Lodgings tend to be slightly more expensive during these times, and rooms can be harder to come by if you don't have a reservation. The cheapest time to go is in the shoulder season (May/June, September/October) when there is the added benefit of milder weather. However, many mountain towns in Graubünden and Walais in Switzerland, and a few towns in Tyrol in Austria shut down in May and June between skiing and hiking seasons so that the hostel owners can take a break from providing vacation for others. For a temperature chart, see p. 507. If you're a music or theater fan, be aware that the Vienna State Opera, the Vienna Boys' Choir, and major theaters throughout Austria and Switzerland don't have any performances during July and August.

CULTURE IN A BOX

Thanks to the imperious Habsburgs and the smart banking of the Swiss the two nations have collected quite a stash of masterworks in their museums. **Vienna** reigns supreme on the two-dimensional front: one of the four largest art collections in the world was amassed by the ever-aesthetic Habsburgs, now stored in the **Kunsthistorisches Museum**

(p. 124). The **Österreichische Galerie** assembles, among other pieces, great works from the Viennese artistic explosion at the beginning of the twentieth century, including Klimt's "The Kiss" (p. 124). To see where art was made—rather than stored—head to the under-touristed **Mozarts Wohnhaus** (p. 228) in **Salzburg.** On the way to Salzburg take a virtual flight to the stars and back at the **Ars Electronica** in **Linz** (p. 267). In Switzerland, be sure not to miss the **Kunsthaus Zürich** (p. 349), which thoughtfully juxtaposes unusual works by well-known masters with cutting-edge new art, or the **Oskar Reinhart collections** in **Winterthur** (p. 353) where the houses that hold the museum are as beautiful as the Daumier's and Picasso's contained within. Though not painted by trained artists, the inspiring works in **Collection de l'Art Brut** (p. 459) demonstrate unexpected wells of artistic potential making a trip to **Lausanne** worthwhile in themselves; also moving is the **International Red Cross Museum** in nearby **Geneva** (p. 451).

CULTURE WITH A DOOR AND LOCKS

Centuries of serfdom, feudalism, and imperial power-mongering left their mark on the landscape of Austria and Switzerland with crumbling castles, elaborate palaces, and medieval inner cities. In Austria, explore the ruins of **Burg Dürnstein** (p. 278), where Richard the Lionheart was held for ransom, hike up to **Burg Hochosterwitz** (p. 167) along spiraling outer fortifications, or shiver in the *Hexenzimmer* (Witches' Room) of **Burg Kronegg** in Riegersburg (p. 153), built on a barren cliff of volcanic rock. If you're looking for something a little more ornate, the **Benediktinerstift** of Melk (p. 281) takes the prize for ecclesiastical Baroque splendor in Austria, with an honorable mention going to the warm, gilt-wood library of **St. Gallen** (p. 371) in Switzerland. Vienna and Salzburg hold the lion's share of Austria's palaces—among the most impressive are **Lustschloß Hellbrunn** (p. 233), which boasts hilarious *Wasserspiele* (water games) in its gardens, and the delicate, mirrored, yellow **Schloß Schönbrunn** (p. 118). The Italianate **Schloß Porcia** in Spital an der Drau (p. 172) can be visited for its arcaded staircases, or for the ghostly countess who is said to haunt them. In Switzerland, the **Château de Chillon** in Montreux (p. 465) is the subject of a famous poem by Lord Byron, but other equally fascinating (though less-lauded) châteaux have stories of their own to share: don't miss the **Castello di Montebello** in Bellinzona (p. 405) with its working drawbridge, **Schloß Thun** (p. 312) with its tower darkened by a tale of defenestration, or the three châteaux that face off with each other on the hills surrounding **Sion** (p. 421). For the complete medieval experience, visit the towns of **Stein** (p. 274) and **Rust** (p. 140) in Austria, or follow the labyrinthine streets of Switzerland's **Bern** (p. 304).

THE BEATEN PATH...

You'll discover pretty quickly that the backpacker's world is a small one; large, centrally-located hostels in strategic locations throughout Austria and Switzerland serve as magnets for the footloose and fancy-free. If you want to follow the beaten path and go with the partying crowd, Switzerland's backpacker mecca is in **Interlaken** (p. 318), which boasts a dizzying aggregation of hostels and young, English-speaking travelers all year round looking for adrenaline rushes of all sorts. Other Swiss hotspots are **Zermatt** (p. 421), **Zurich** (p. 341), **Montreux** (p. 462), and **Geneva** (p. 439). In Austria, nothing can touch **Vienna** and its vast array of accommodations (p. 80) for backpacker-congregating, though **Innsbruck** (p. 174) and **Salzburg** (p. 215) put up a good fight.

...AND THE ROAD LESS TRAVELED

If you didn't come to Europe to hear American pop music, and hang out with the same English-speaking backpackers every night, head for the handful of smaller, more personal backpacker resorts/hostels hidden in the hills. Switzerland has the greater number of these getaways, including the backpacker's Nirvana, a.k.a. **Swiss Alp Retreat** in Gryon (p. 473), the super-friendly **Hiking Sheep Guesthouse** in Leysin (p. 472), the tiny but home-like **Baracca Backpacker** in Aurigeno (p. 411), as well as the adventure-oriented **Swiss Adventure Hostel** in Boltigen (p. 315). Austria has the **Treehouse** hostel in Grünau (p. 240), the gorgeous **Schloß Röthelstein** in Admont (p. 159), and just about any place in **Hallstatt** (p. 235). This small cache of hostels that have made a name for themselves for good reason: they are more service-oriented than mainstream hostels, they give you the opportunity to get to know both the owners and the countryside well, without paying any more. Privatzimmer are widespread option for experiencing the warmth of Austrian and Swiss hospitality and a down comforter away from the crowds.

LET'S GO PICKS

BEST PLACE TO THROW YOURSELF OFF A CLIFF: If the many bungee options in **Interlaken** (p. 323) do not sate your appetite head to **Val Verzasca** (p. 411) for the highest bungee jump in the world.

NICEST PEOPLE THIS SIDE OF THE ALPS: Andi and Joy, owners of **Pension Sinilill** (p. 254) tell stories of Austrian swimming championships and Philipino cock-fighting on their warm hearth. If you need more love go to **Haus Wolf** (p. 179) where Frau Wolf charms guests with motherly advice, smiles, and baskets and baskets of bread.

BEST NAME FOR THE GOAT ON OUR COVER: Personally, we like Ziggy, but you decide–send us an email.

BEST PLACE TO TREAT YOUR SWEET TOOTH: Be dazzled and nearly blinded by the colorful extravagance of the fruity and chocolate-y pastries at **Puntschella Café-Restaurant** (p. 396), the home of the Engadiner Torte.

BEST PLACE TO PRETEND YOU'RE HEIDI: Enjoy fresh cheese and milk at a mountain hut on the hike from **Saas Fe** to **Hannig** (p. 431).

BEST PLACE TO TEST YOUR MULTILINGUAL CAPABILITIES: Hike for 5 hours on the stunning **Panorama Hochweg** (p. 401) from Italian-speaking Soglio to German-speaking Maloja or St. Moritz.

BEST OPERA WITHOUT RED VELVET: Every July and August the **Bregenzer Festspiel** (p. 210) stages world-class opera, floating on the Bodensee.

BEST LIGHTING EFFECTS IN A BATHROOM: The pissoir at the **Hotel Goldener Löwe** (p. 158) illuminates (so that you can let the waterfall on the wall inspire you). You get less help in the bathroom at the **Funny Farm** (p. 321), where the only light is a black light (wear lots of white–the only other light comes from the disco ball on the ceiling).

MOST WORTHWHILE WAIT: Wait a few hours for dirt-cheap standing room tickets at Vienna's superior **Staatsoper** (p. 126). Your feet may hurt, but your eyes and ears will love you forever.

BEST BUS RIDE ON EARTH: Spend five hours with your face smooshed up against the window of the public bus on the ride down the **Großglocknerstraße** (p. 250).

SUGGESTED ITINERARIES

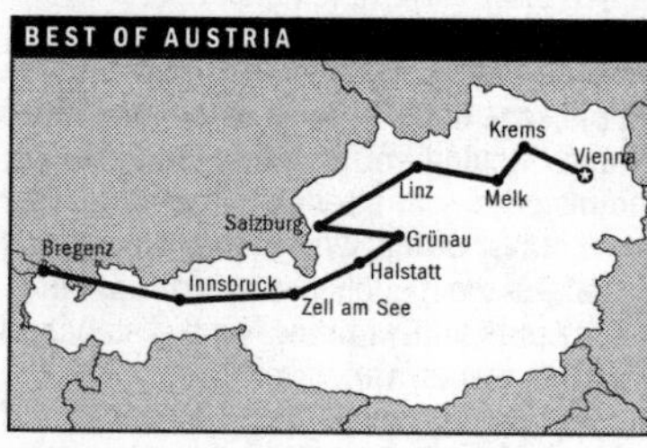

BEST OF AUSTRIA (MIN. 2 WEEKS)
If you want to move across Austria, seeing both the mountains in the west and the cities in the east, Munich is a good middle point from which to begin and end. From Munich go to **Bregenz** (p. 207) and spend two days poking around the rolling hills of the Bregenzerwald. Take a train ride through gorgeous Alpine scenery on the way to **Innsbruck** (p. 174). After checking out the museums in the morning and mountains at midnoon you'll understand why this was the Hapsburg's favorite city. Explore the Hohe Tauern National Park from **Zell am See** (p. 253). Take one daytrip to the Krimml Waterfalls, and the next day to wind down the serpentine Großglocknerstraße–so beautiful you might think it is tempting you to sin. Head just north to the hills of the Salzkammergut–*the* getaway for Austrians in the know. **Hallstatt** (p. 235), balanced between cliffs and a lake, is of historical interest as a cradle of European civilization, and of immediate interest for its stunning hiking and ice caves. To see the glory of rural Austria with no pretension, take one of the Salzkammergut's ubiquitous buses to **Grünau** (p. 240), where the

Treehouse Hostel will happily put you up for the night. While it may be crowded, the **Salzburg** (p. 215) of Maria von Trapp and Mozart is worth seeing. Spend a day exploring the streets that are preserved in much the same condition as when these two luminaries were around. Don't forget the oft-forgotten but very accessible **Linz** (p. 263), Austria's third largest city. The technological and industrial leader of Austria has a progressively modern atmosphere to complement preserved wonders like the oldest church in Austria and the largest church in Austria. Allow yourself time to go to the nearby Kremsmünster Abbey, the oldest order in Austria, with expansive grounds. Make your way over to **Melk** (p. 279), with its unmistakable yellow abbey perched high on a hill. Save an afternoon for the Renaissance courtyard, Romanesque fortress, and Gothic chapel at Schloß Schallaburg, only 5km away. The imposing ruins of Schloß Dürnstein loom over the valley as you make your way along the Danube river, past Krems/Stein, to **Vienna** (p. 80) itself, the Imperial headquarters of romance. The magic of Strauss's waltzes and the thunder of Beethoven symphonies resonate through Vienna's magnificent Baroque buildings. From the stately Staatsoper to the glittering Musikverein, the majestic Hofburg to Otto Wagner's simple Kirche am Steinhof, Vienna's attractions will leave you with enough sensory stimulation to last until your next vacation, at least.

BEST OF SWITZERLAND

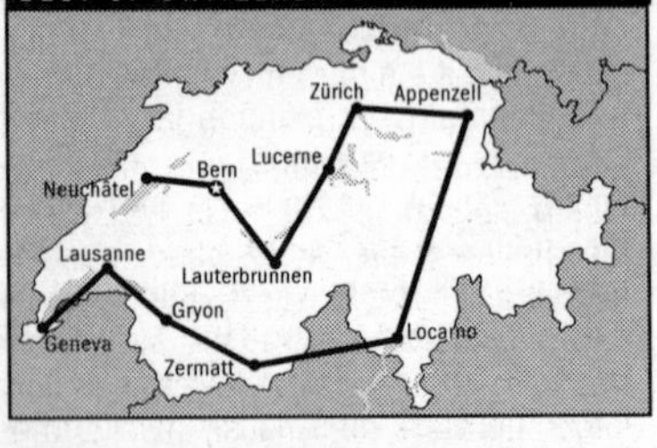

Zürich
Appenzell
Bern
Lucerne
Neuchâtel
Lausanne
Lauterbrunnen
Gryon
Geneva
Zermatt
Locarno

BEST OF SWITZERLAND (MIN. 2 WEEKS) Spend your first day strolling the quiet squares around John Calvin's Cathédrale de St. Pierre in **Geneva** (p. 439) to get a sense for the diversity of this international city (the home of countless world organizations), a symbol of the diversity of the quadrilingual, tri-ethnic nation. To look for inspiration of the sort that T.S. Eliot and Charles Dickens found in Switzerland scoot around the lake to **Lausanne** (p. 454). Recline on the relaxed waterfront after a sobering look at the collection in the *Collection de l'Art Brut* (if you time it right, you can also catch the nearby Montreux Jazz Fest in early July). For a first taste of those mountains you've been seeing over the lakes, enter the welcoming confines of the Swiss Alp Retreat hostel in **Gryon** (p. 473) for a night. Dive into the full splendor of the mountains in **Zermatt** (p. 421). The number of hikes and ski trails within walking distance of the town is unparalleled: give yourself a couple of days to explore. To warm up from the Zermatt snow that falls even in August, head for the Mediterranean climate and atmosphere of **Locarno** (p. 406). The calm waters of warm Lago Maggiore suffuse the *città vecchia* with its tranquility (it might be worthwhile to head to one of two sprawling, villa-cum-hostels in Lugano for the night). Get back into hiking mode as you take the train to **Appenzell** (p. 373). Near this tiny town are cattle trails that will take you into the Switzerland of childhood imagination, the Switzerland where the quiet mountain passes are shared between hikers, bell-laden cows, and their gentle, lederhosen-laden owners. A short train ride to **Zurich** (p. 341) will get you back into the beat of the city. Ulrich Zwingli and the DaDa'ists each fomented their own revolution in this city, though the placid lake, and quiet, sprawling *Altstadt* would never betray this. If you only visit one museum in Switzerland, make it Zurich's innovative Kunsthaus (art museum). Nearby **Lucerne** (p. 354) gives you all that you would want from a city in a package small enough to explore in two days. Moving south, through the highly touristed city of Interlaken, head into the mountains of the Jungfrau region. Staying in one of the hostels in **Lauterbrunnen** (p. 329) puts you within walking distance of all the towns and trails that cover the mountainous region. The compact capital city of **Bern** (p. 304), should take at least two days to unravel. As dictated by the atmosphere, move at a leisurely pace as you window-shop along arcaded streets, buy farm-grown produce at the open market outside the Parliament, feed the bears in the *Bärengraben,* and take a dip in the brisk Aare River. Finish your tour in the well-rounded **Neuchâtel** (p. 476) which looks as good as the food tastes.

HIKING THE ALPS

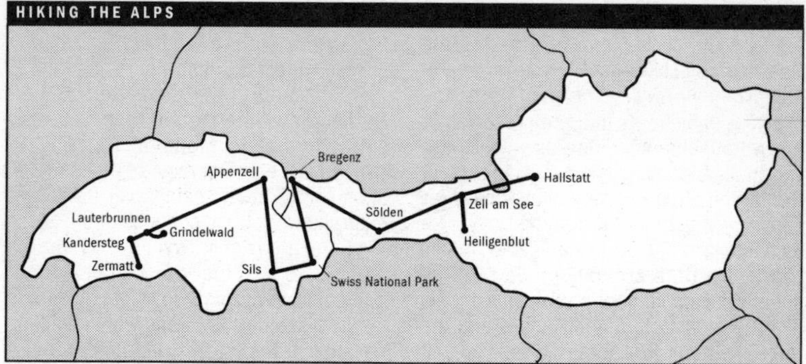

HIKING THE ALPS (MIN. 2 WEEKS) Full of towering mountains, Switzerland and Austria are a hiker's paradise. Each of the hiking regions offers unique pleasures; read on and decide which area suits your interests, or give yourself a smorgasbord of hiking by tracing the following route.

Test out your trail legs on the paths that extend from **Zermatt** (p. 421) in every direction. The carless, but bustling town's most exciting hikes lead to spectacular and varied views of the unmistakable Matterhorn. Moving to central Switzerland, oft-forgotten **Kandersteg** (p. 335) has memorable hikes to glaciers and high lying glacial lakes—be ready for drama. In Lauterbrunnen, just a bit northeast, there are a number of great hostels to crash in after strenuous days on the trails of the **Jungfrau region** (p. 324). The cliff walled valleys of the region allow very level hikes and very steep hikes, but little in between. These hikes tend to be more social than in other areas thanks to the many mountain villages in this populated region. To get completely away from any hints of a resort hit up rustic **Appenzell** (p. 373). The hikes, a short train ride away, are more consistently difficult, but there is a warm, wooden guesthouse at the end of almost every trail pulling you along. Heading south to Graubünden, the wildest canton in the country, doesn't give much more warm weather, but it does bring more splendid isolation in the **Swiss National Park** (p. 387). Even the normal trails in the park can be killers, but there is more wildlife, and unbroken silence than almost anywhere in the two countries combined (it is one of the only areas in Switzerland where cows are not allowed). Also in Graubünden is the **Upper Engadine** (p. 395) valley. While towns like St. Moritz and Sils are more famous for their skiing, Sils in particular has easy access to wonderfully tranquil, flat hikes that meander along the banks of the many lakes in the valley.

Just over the border in Austria, **Bregenz** (p. 207) and its surrounding hills provide fantastic walks through rolling hills and rustic towns where wooden shingles never went out of style. Things get a bit more wild and dramatic as you enter the mountainous Alpine territory of the **Ötztal** (p. 202). The valley is easily accessible from Sölden, which gives access to trails that stretch up the untouristed silent valley above. As you move eastward, you'll run into the **Hohe Tauern National Park** (p. 249), home to 246 glaciers and 304 mountains over 3000m. The largest national park in Europe has countless paths leading through meadows, along glaciers, and up to the roaring Wasserfallwinkel. The towns of Zell am See and Lienz offer rewarding hiking on their own, but also serve as good, larger bases for exploring the park. If you're interested in being in the middle of the park, among the mountains, stay in Heiligenblut, which lies in the shadow of the Großglockner, Austria's highest mountain. Finish up your tour in the **Salzkammergut's** Halstatt (p. 235). Some of the easiest and most rewarding hiking leaves from this precariously placed town; hikes that lead past waterfalls, rivers, and lush foliage that sometimes looks more tropical than Alpine.

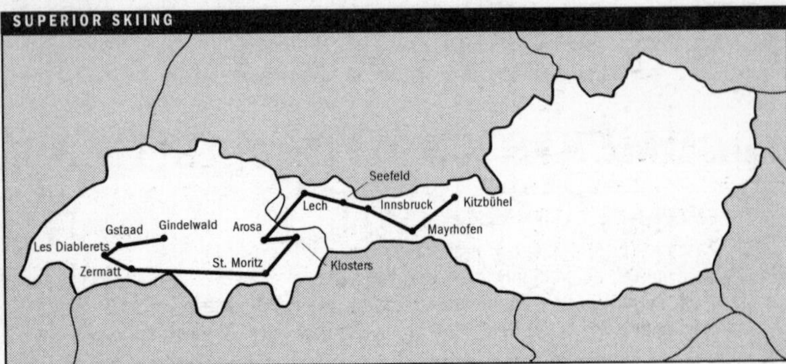

SUPERIOR SKIING (MIN. 3 WEEKS) You could land just about anywhere in Switzerland or western Austria in the winter and have a fabulous skiing experience (there are fewer places where you could land in the summer and do the same thing, but it's possible). It's important to differentiate between the snowbound hotspots—many give you a great deal for your money and the chance of glimpsing some famous faces. One good place to start is **Kitzbühel** (p. 189), where downhill skiing itself started in 1892—plan carefully so that you are either in or not in town for the gigantic Hahnenkamm World Cup race. On your way west stop in **Mayrhofen** (p. 196), or tiny Hintertux, where even August finds skiers on the glacier. Medieval **Innsbruck** (p. 174), home of the 1964 and 1976 Winter Olympics, had the games for good reason. Shuttles take you right from the *Altstadt* to snow covered mountains (even in the summer). You can hide away in **Lech** (p. 201) with the celebrities seeking refuge from the larger resorts, and find excellent skiing as well. If you're looking to party *apres-ski* hightail it over to happening **Arosa** (p. 381) in eastern Switzerland, where hostel beds come complete with affordable ski passes at a disco-inclusive hostel. More travelled, **St. Moritz** (p. 397) and **Klosters** (p. 386) are familiar names in any skiing household, particularly the royal families of Britain and Hollywood. Ostentatious St. Moritz is the hub of an extensive skiing network that encompasses a number of smaller towns, while Klosters provides more understated class. When you're ready for some serious skiing, take the cog railway up to **Zermatt** (p. 421), the hedonistic ski paradise in southwestern Switzerland, where you will once again be able to go from the trails to the slopes in summer. French Switzerland does its best to compete, with *Les Diablerets* where snowboarders and a younger crowd is welcomed with open arms. As you move north, back into German Switzerland, you'll run across thriving **Gstaad/Saanen** (p. 337), an international jet-set magnet. The tiny towns of **Wengen** (p. 331) and **Grindelwald** (p. 326), in the Jungfrau region serve as gateways to some of the finest powder and the most breathtaking panoramas known to humankind.

ESSENTIALS

DOCUMENTS AND FORMALITIES

ENTRANCE REQUIREMENTS

Passport (p. 8). Required for all foreign visitors.
Visa (p. 9). Required only for a continuous stay of more than 3 months.
Work Permit (p. 9). Required to work in Austria or Switzerland.
Driving Permit (p. 45). Required for all those planning to drive.

EMBASSIES AND CONSULATES

CONSULAR SERVICES IN AUSTRIA

All foreign embassies in Austria are based in Vienna. For a complete listing, look in the Vienna telephone book under *Botschaften* (embassies) or *Konsulate* (consulates). The first number in each address tells you in which district of Vienna they can be found.

Australia: Embassy, IV, Mattiellistr. 2 (☎(01) 512 8580; austemb@xpoint.at; www.australian-embassy.at).

Canada: Embassy, I, Laurenzerberg 2 (☎(01) 531 3830 00; fax 531 3833 21; vienn@dfait-maeci.gc.ca).

Ireland: Embassy, III, Landstrasser Hauptstr. 2, Hilton Center 16th floor (☎(01) 715 42460; irishemb@vienna.at).

New Zealand: Embassy, New Zealand Embassy in Berlin, Germany has responsibility for Austria, Friedrichstr. 60, 10117 Berlin (☎(030) 206 210; fax 206 21114; nzemb@t-online.de); **Consulate: Vienna,** XIX, Springsiedelg. 28 (☎318 8505; bbolt@cso.at).

South Africa: Embassy, XIX, Sandg. 33 (☎(01) 320 6493; fax 320 649318; saemb-vie@ins.at).

UK: Embassy, III, Jauresg. 12 (☎(01) 716 130; fax 716 1329 00; britem@netway.at; www.britishembassy.at).

US: Embassy, IX, Boltzmanng. 16 (☎(01) 31339; fax 310 0682; www.usembassy-vienna.at).

CONSULAR SERVICES IN SWITZERLAND

Nearly all foreign embassies in Switzerland are located in Bern, southeast of the Kirchenfeldbrücke.

Australia: Consulate, Geneva 56 Rue de Moillebeau, 1209 Geneva (☎(022) 84129; fax 733 5664; mission.austrlia@ties.itu.int).

Canada: Embassy, Kirchenfeldstr. 88 (☎(031) 357 3200; fax 357 3210; bern@dfait-maeci.gc.ca).

Ireland: Embassy, Kirchenfeldstr. 68 (☎(031) 352 1442; fax 352 1455).

New Zealand: Embassy, New Zealand Embassy in **Berlin, Germany** has responsibility for Switzerland, Friedrichstr. 60, 10117 Berlin (☎(030) 206 210; fax (030) 206 21114; nzemb@t-online.de); **Consulate: Geneva,** 2 Chemin des Fins, 1218 Grand Saconnex (☎(022) 939 0350; fax (022) 929 0374; mission.nz@itu.ch).

South Africa: Embassy, Alpenstr. 29 (☎(031) 350 1313; fax 350 1311; ambassador@southafrica.ch; www.southafrica.ch).

UK: Embassy, Thunstr. 50 (☎(031) 359 7700; fax 359 7701; information@british-embassy-berne.ch; website www.british-embassy-berne.ch).

US: Embassy, Jubiläumstr. 93 (☎(031) 357 7011; fax 351 7344).

AUSTRIAN CONSULAR SERVICES ABROAD

Australia: Embassy, 12 Talbot St., Forrest, Canberra ACT 2603 (☎(02) 629 51533; fax 623 96751; austria@dynamite.com.au); **Consulates** in Adelaide, Brisbane, Melbourne, and Sydney.

Canada: Embassy, 445 Wilbrod St., Ottawa, ON KIN 6M7 (☎(613) 789 1444; fax 789 3431; embassy@austro.org; www.austro.org); **Consulates** in Montréal, Toronto, and Vancouver.

Ireland: Embassy, 15 Ailesbury Court Apts., 93 Ailesbury Rd., Dublin 4 (☎(01) 269 4577 or 269 1451; fax 283 0860).

New Zealand: Consulate, Consular General, 22-4 Garrett St., Wellington (☎(04) 499 6393).

South Africa: Embassy, P.O.Box 95572, Waterkloof, Pretoria 0145 (☎(012) 462 483; fax 461 151; autemb@mweb.co.az); during the sessions of Parliament (Jan.-June), the embassy is based in Cape Town, Standard Bank Centre, 1001 Main Tower, Hertzog Blvd., Cape Town 8001. **Consulates** in Cape Town, and Johannesburg.

UK: Embassy, 18 Belgrave Mews West, London SW1 X 8HU (☎(020) 7235 3731; fax 344 0292; embassy@austria.org.uk; www.austria.org.uk); **Consulate** in Edinburgh.

US: Embassy, 3524 International Court NW, Washington, D.C. 20008-3035 (☎(202) 895-6700; fax 895-6750); **Consulates** in Chicago, Los Angeles, and New York.

SWISS CONSULAR SERVICES ABROAD

Australia: Embassy, 7 Melbourne Ave., Forrest, Canberra ACT 2603 (☎(02) 627 33977; fax 627 33428; swiemcan@dynamite.com.au); **Consulates** in Melbourne, and Sydney.

Canada: Embassy, 5 Marlborough Ave., Ottawa, ON KIN 8E6 (☎(613) 235 1837; fax 563 1394; vertretung@ott.rep.admin.ch); **Consulates** in Montréal, Toronto, and Vancouver.

Ireland: Embassy, 6 Ailesbury Rd., Ballsbridge, Dublin 4 (☎(01) 218 6382; fax 283 0344; vertretung@dub.rep.admin.ch).

New Zealand: Consulate, 22 Panama St., Wellington (☎(04) 472 1593; fax 499 6302).

South Africa: Embassy, P.O. Box 2289, Pretoria 0001 (☎(012) 436 707; fax 436 771; swiempre@cis.co.az; during the sessions of Parliament (Jan.-June), the embassy is based in Cape Town, P.O. Box 1546, Cape Town 8000 (☎(021) 418 3669; fax 418 1569); **Consulates** in Cape Town, and Johannesburg.

UK: Embassy, 16-18 Montague Place, London W1H 2BQ (☎(020) 761 66000; fax 772 47001; vertretung@lon.rep.admin.ch); **Consulate** in Manchester.

US: Embassy, 2900 Cathedral Ave. NW, Washington, D.C. 20008-3499 (☎(202) 745-7900; fax 387-2564; wwww.swissemb.org); **Consulates** in Chicago, San Francisco, New York, Houston, Los Angeles, and Atlanta.

PASSPORTS

REQUIREMENTS. Citizens of Australia, Canada, New Zealand, South Africa, and the US need valid passports to enter Austria and Switzerland and to reenter their own country, and can stay 3 months without a visa. If you apply for a visa, make sure your passport is valid for at least a few months longer than the visa, or you could face a fine upon returning with an expired passport. Citizens of Ireland and the UK can stay as long as they please.

PHOTOCOPIES. Be sure to photocopy the page of your passport with your photo, passport number, and other identifying information, as well as any visas, travel insurance policies, plane tickets, or traveler's check serial numbers. Carry one set of copies in a safe place, apart from the originals, and leave another set at home. Consulates also recommend that you carry an expired passport or an official copy of your birth certificate in a part of your baggage separate from other documents.

LOST PASSPORTS. If you lose your passport, immediately notify the local police and the nearest embassy or consulate of your home government. A replacement may take weeks, and may be valid for only a limited time. Any visas stamped in your old passport will be lost. In an emergency, ask for immediate temporary traveling papers that will permit you to reenter your home country. Your passport is a public document belonging to your nation's government. You may have to surrender it to a foreign government official, but if you don't get it back in a reasonable amount of time, inform the nearest mission of your home country.

NEW PASSPORTS. File any new passport or renewal applications well in advance of your departure date. Most passport offices offer rush services for a steep fee. Citizens living abroad who need a passport or renewal should contact the nearest consular service of their home country.

Australia: Info ☎131 232; passports.australia@dfat.gov.au; www.dfat.gov.au/passports. Apply for a passport at a post office, passport office (in Adelaide, Brisbane, Canberra, Darwin, Hobart, Melbourne, Newcastle, Perth, or Sydney), or overseas diplomatic mission. Passports AUS$128 (32-page) or AUS$192 (64-page); valid for 10 years. Children AUS$64 (32-page) or AUS$96 (64-page); valid for 5 years.

Canada: Canadian Passport Office, Department of Foreign Affairs and International Trade, Ottawa, ON K1A 0G3 (☎(613) 994-3500 or (800) 567-6868; www.dfait-maeci.gc.ca/passport). Applications available at passport offices, Canadian missions, and post offices. Passports CDN$60; valid for 5 years (non-renewable).

Ireland: Pick up an application at a *Garda* station or post office, or request one from a passport office. Then apply by mail to the Department of Foreign Affairs, Passport Office, Molesworth St., Dublin 2 (☎(01) 671 1633; fax 671 1092; www.irlgov.ie/iveagh), or the Passport Office, Irish Life Building, 1A South Mall, Cork (☎(021) 27 25 25). Passports IR£45; valid for 10 years. Under 18 or over 65 IR£10; valid for 3 years.

New Zealand: Send applications to the Passport Office, Department of International Affairs, P.O. Box 10526, Wellington, New Zealand (☎(0800) 225 050 or (4) 474 8100; fax (4) 474 8010; passports@dia.govt.nz; www.passports.govt.nz). Standard processing time is 10 working days. Passports NZ$80; valid for 10 years. Children NZ$40; valid for 5 years. 3 day "urgent service" NZ$160; children NZ$120.

South Africa: Department of Home Affairs. Passports are issued only in Pretoria, but all applications must still be submitted or forwarded to the nearest South African consulate. Processing time is 3 months or more. Passports around SAR80; valid for 10 years. Under 16 around SAR60; valid for 5 years. For more information, check out http://usaembassy.southafrica.net/VisaForms/Passport/Passport2000.html.

United Kingdom: Info ☎(0870) 521 0410; www.open.gov.uk/ukpass/ukpass.htm. Get an application from a passport office, main post office, travel agent, or online (for UK residents only) at www.ukpa.gov.uk/forms/f_app_pack.htm. Then apply by mail or in person at a passport office. Passports UK£28; valid for 10 years. Under 15 UK£14.80; valid for 5 years. The process takes about 4 weeks; faster service (by personal visit to the offices listed above) costs an additional £12.

United States: Info ☎(202) 647-0518; www.travel.state.gov/passport_services.html. Apply at any federal or state courthouse, authorized post office, or US Passport Agency (in most major cities); see the "US Government, State Department" section of the telephone book or a post office for addresses. Processing takes 3-4 weeks. New passports US$60; valid for 10 years. Under 16 US$40; valid for 5 years. Passports may be renewed by mail or in person for US$40. Add US$35 for 3-day expedited service.

VISAS AND WORK PERMITS

Citizens of Australia, Canada, Ireland, New Zealand, South Africa, the UK, and the US do not need visas to visit Austria or Switzerland. For more detailed information about which nationalities require visas, visit either the Austrian Embassy website (www.bmaa.gv.at/embassy/uk/index.html.en) or the Swiss Embassy website

ONE EUROPE. The idea of European unity has come a long way since 1958, when the European Economic Community (EEC) was created in order to promote solidarity and cooperation between its six founding states. Since then, the EEC has become the European Union (EU), with political, legal, and economic institutions spanning 15 member states: Austria, Belgium, Denmark, Finland, France, Germany, Greece, Ireland, Italy, Luxembourg, the Netherlands, Portugal, Spain, Sweden, and the UK.

What does this have to do with the average non-EU tourist? Well, 1999 established **freedom of movement** across 14 European countries–the entire EU minus Denmark, Ireland, and the UK, but plus Iceland and Norway. This means that border controls between participating countries have been abolished, and visa policies harmonized. While you're still required to carry a passport (or government-issued ID card for EU citizens) when crossing an internal border, once you've been admitted into one country, you're free to travel to all participating states. Britain and Ireland have also formed a **common travel area,** abolishing passport controls between the UK and the Republic of Ireland, meaning that the only times you'll see a border guard within the EU are traveling between the British Isles and the Continent–and of course, in and out of Denmark. For more important consequences of the EU for travelers, see The Euro (see p. 15) and European Customs (see p. 11).

(www.swissemb.org). Admission as a visitor does not include the right to work, which is authorized only by a work permit, and studying in Austria or Switzerland requires a special visa (see Alternatives to Tourism, p. 56).

IDENTIFICATION

When you travel, always carry two or more forms of identification on your person, including at least one photo ID; a passport combined with a driver's license or birth certificate is usually adequate. Many establishments, especially banks, may require several IDs in order to cash traveler's checks. Never carry all your forms of ID together; split them up in case of theft or loss. It is useful to bring extra passport-size photos to affix to the various IDs or passes you may acquire along the way.

STUDENT AND TEACHER IDENTIFICATION. The **International Student Identity Card (ISIC),** the most widely accepted form of student ID, provides discounts on sights, accommodations, food, and transport. The ISIC is preferable to an institution-specific card (such as a university ID) because it is more likely to be recognized (and honored) abroad. All cardholders have access to a 24-hour emergency helpline for medical, legal, and financial emergencies (in North America call (877) 370-ISIC, elsewhere call US collect +1 (715) 345-0505), and US cardholders are also eligible for insurance benefits (see Insurance, p. 23). Many student travel agencies issue ISICs, including STA Travel in Australia and New Zealand; Travel CUTS in Canada; USIT in the Republic of Ireland and Northern Ireland; SASTS in South Africa; Campus Travel and STA Travel in the UK; Council Travel (www.counciltravel.com/idcards/default.asp) and STA Travel in the US (see p. 35). The card is valid from September of one year to December of the following year and costs AUS$15, CDN$15, or US$22. Applicants must be degree-seeking students of a secondary or post-secondary school and must be of at least 12 years of age. Because of the proliferation of fake ISICs, some services (particularly airlines) require additional proof of student identity, such as a school ID or a letter attesting to your student status, signed by your registrar and stamped with your school seal.

The **International Teacher Identity Card (ITIC)** offers the same insurance coverage as well as similar but limited discounts. The fee is AUS$13, UK£5, or US$22. For more info, contact the **International Student Travel Confederation (ISTC),** Herengracht 479, 1017 BS Amsterdam, Netherlands (☎ +31 (20) 421 28 00; fax 421 28 10;

istcinfo@istc.org; www.istc.org). The **International Student Travel Confederation** issues a discount card to travelers who are 25 years old or under, but are not students. This one-year **International Youth Travel Card** (IYTC; formerly the GO 25 Card) offers many of the same benefits as the ISIC. Most organizations that sell the ISIC also sell the IYTC (US$22).

NATIONAL TOURIST OFFICES ABROAD

Austria and Switzerland are old pros at tourism. Before visiting either country, contact the national tourist office in your country, which can provide copious information for planning your trip, ranging from help with a specific itinerary to personalized information for travelers with specific concerns.

AUSTRIAN NATIONAL TOURIST OFFICES

The international website for Austrian tourism is www.experienceaustria.com.

South Africa: Johannesburg, Private Bag X18, Parklands 2121 (☎(11) 442 7235; fax 788 2367; oewjnb@mweb.co.za).

Australia and New Zealand: Sydney, 1st Floor, 36 Carrington Street, Sydney NSW 2000 (☎ (2) 929 93621; fax 929 93808; oewsyd@world.net).

UK and Ireland: London, 14 Cork Street GB-London W1X 1PF (☎(020) 762 90461; fax 749 96038; info@anto.co.uk).

US and Canada: New York, 500 Fifth Ave., Suite 800, PO Box 1142, New York, NY 10108-1142 (☎(212) 944-6880; fax 730-4568; info@oewnyc.com).

SWISS NATIONAL TOURIST OFFICES

The international website for Swiss tourism is www.myswitzerland.com.

Australia and New Zealand: Sydney, Swissair Building Level 8, 33 Pitt Street, (☎(02) 923 13744; fax 925 16531).

UK: London, Swiss Centre, Swiss Court, London W1V 8EE (☎(020) 785 11710; fax 785 11720).

US and Canada: New York, 608 Fifth Ave., New York, NY 10020 (☎(212) 757-5944; fax 262-6116; info.usa@switzerlandtourism.ch); additional offices in Chicago (☎(312) 332-9900), San Francisco (☎(415) 362-2260), and Los Angeles (☎(310) 640-8900). In **Canada** call toll free (☎(800) 100 200 30) to be transferred to New York.

CUSTOMS

GETTING IN. Austria and Switzerland prohibit or restrict the importation of firearms, explosives, ammunition, fireworks, booby traps, controlled drugs, most plants, lottery tickets, most animals, and pornography. They don't look keenly on items manufactured from protected species (e.g. ivory or fur), either. To avoid hassles about prescription drugs, ensure that your bottles are clearly marked and carry a copy of the prescription. Upon entering Austria or Switzerland, you'll have to declare certain items (such as cigarettes, wine, per-

EUROPEAN CUSTOMS As well as freedom of movement of people within the EU (see p. 10), travelers can also take advantage of the freedom of movement of goods. This means that there are no customs controls at internal EU borders (i.e., you can take the blue customs channel at the airport), and travelers are free to transport whatever legal substances they like as long as it is for their own personal (non-commercial) use—up to 800 cigarettes, 10L of spirits, 90L of wine (60L of sparkling wine), and 110L of beer. You should also be aware that duty-free was abolished on June 30, 1999 for travel between EU member states; however, travelers between the EU and the rest of the world still get a duty-free allowance when passing through customs.

fume, etc.) brought with you from abroad and pay a duty on the value of those articles that exceed the allowance established by Austria or Switzerland's customs service. Keeping receipts for purchases made abroad will help establish values when you return. It is wise to make a list, including serial numbers, of any valuables that you carry with you from home; if you register this list with customs before your departure and have an official stamp it, you will avoid import duty charges and ensure an easy passage upon your return.

GOING HOME. Upon returning home, you must declare all articles acquired abroad and pay a duty on the value of articles that exceed the allowance established by your country's customs service. Goods and gifts purchased at duty-free shops abroad are not exempt from duty or sales tax at your point of return; you must declare these items as well. "Duty-free" merely means that you are eligible to receive a tax refund in the country of purchase.

FURTHER RESOURCES

Australia: Australian Customs National Information Line (in Australia call (01) 30 03 63, from elsewhere call +61 (2) 6275 6666; www.customs.gov.au).

Canada: Canadian Customs, 2265 St. Laurent Blvd., Ottawa, ON K1G 4K3 (☎(800) 461-9999 (24hr.) or (613) 993-0534; www.revcan.ca).

Ireland: Customs Information Office, Irish Life Centre, Lower Abbey St., Dublin 1 (☎(01) 878 8811; fax 878 0836; taxes@revenue.iol.ie; www.revenue.ie/customs.htm).

New Zealand: New Zealand Customhouse, 17-21 Whitmore St., Box 2218, Wellington (☎(04) 473 6099; fax 473 7370; www.customs.govt.nz).

South Africa: Commissioner for Customs and Excise, Privat Bag X47, Pretoria 0001 (☎(012) 314 9911; fax 328 6478; www.gov.za).

United Kingdom: Her Majesty's Customs and Excise, Passenger Enquiry Team, Wayfarer House, Great South West Road, Feltham, Middlesex TW14 8NP (☎(020) 8910 3744; fax 8910 3933; www.hmce.gov.uk).

United States: US Customs Service, 1330 Pennsylvania Ave. NW, Washington, D.C. 20229 (☎(202) 354-1000; fax 354-1010; www.customs.gov).

MONEY

COSTS

Though Austria and Switzerland are not the cheapest destinations, there are ways to travel in them on a budget. If you stay in hostels and prepare most of your own food, expect to spend anywhere from $30 to $65 (45-100SFr; 400-850AS) per person per day in Switzerland, slightly less in Austria. **Accommodations** start at about $16 (25SFr) per night for a hostel in Switzerland, and $10 (150AS) in Austria, while a basic sit-down meal usually costs around $12.

CURRENCY AND EXCHANGE

The unit of currency in Austria is the **Schilling,** abbreviated as **AS, ÖS,** or, within Austria, simply **S.** Each *Schilling* is subdivided into 100 **Groschen (g).** Coins come in 2, 5, 10, and 50g, and 1, 5, 10, and 20AS denominations. Bills come in 20, 50, 100, 500, 1000, and 5000AS amounts.

The Swiss monetary unit is the **Swiss Franc (SFr),** which is divided into 100 *centimes* (called *Rappen* in German Switzerland). Coins are issued in 5, 10, 20, and 50 *centimes* and 1, 2, and 5SFr; bills come in 10, 20, 50, 100, 500, and 1000SFr denominations. Currency exchange is easiest at ATMs, train stations, and post offices, where rates are close to bank rates but where commissions are smaller.

The currency chart below is based on August 2000 exchange rates between local currency and US dollars (US$), Canadian dollars (CDN$), British pounds (UK£), Irish pounds (IR£), Australian dollars (AUS$), New Zealand dollars (NZ$), South African Rand (SAR), and European Union euros (EUR€). Check a large newspaper or the web (e.g. finance.yahoo.com or www.bloomberg.com) for the latest exchange rates.

AUSTRIAN SCHILLING	
US$1 = 15.06 (AS/ÖS/ATS)	10AS = US$.66
CDN$1 = 10.13AS	10AS = CDN$.99
UK£1 = 22.69AS	10AS = UK£.44
IR£1 = 17.47AS	10AS = IR£.57
AUS$1 = 8.80AS	10AS = AUS$1.14
NZ$1 = 6.76AS	10AS = NZ$1.48
SAR1 = 2.17AS	10AS = SAR4.60
1SFR = 8.81AS	10AS = SFR1.13
1DM = 7.04AS	10AS = DM1.42
L1000= 7.11AS	10AS = L1407.14
1Kč = .39AS	10AS = Kč25.72
1FT = .53AS	10AS = FT189.70
EUR€1 = 13.76AS	10AS = EUR €.73

SWISS FRANC	
US$1 = 1.71 (SFR/CHF)	1SFR = US$.58
CDN$1 = 1.15SFR	1SFR = CDN$.87
UK£1 = 2.57SFR	1SFR = UK£.39
IR£1 = 1.98SFR	1SFR = IR£.50
AUS$1 = 1.00SFR	1SFR = AUS$1.00
NZ$1 = .77SFR	1SFR = NZ$1.30
SAR1 = .25SFR	1SFR = SAR4.06
10AS = 1.14SFR	1SFR = AS8.81
1DM = .80SFR	1SFR = DM1.25
1F = .24SFR	1SFR = F4.20
L1000 = .81SFR	1SFR = L1239.40
EUR€1 = 1.56AS	1SFR = EUR €.64

As a general rule, it's cheaper to convert money in Austria or Switzerland than at home. It's wise to bring enough foreign currency to last for the first 24-72 hours of a trip to avoid being penniless after banking hours or on a holiday. Better yet, bring an ATM card and find the machine quickly—you'll be able to zip through the airport and start your vacation without languishing in lines. Travelers from the US can get foreign currency from the comfort of home: **International Currency Express** (☎(888) 278-6628) delivers foreign currency or traveler's checks overnight (US$15) or second-day (US$12) at competitive exchange rates.

Currency exchange kiosks and change machines should be your last resort when you need local funds, since their unfavorable rates and hefty commissions will cripple your resources. Banks, post offices, and small train stations often have better rates, but ATMs and credit cards are your best bet, since you'll profit from their low corporate rates (see p. 16). The only hitch to ATMs is the transaction fee that some banks charge—be sure to check what the fee is with your bank at home. If you need to change cash or traveler's checks, take the time to compare the rates offered by different banks and kiosks (*Wechselstube* in German, *bureau de change* in French, *cambio* in Italian). A good rule of thumb is only to go to banks or kiosks with at most a 5% margin between their buy and sell prices. Since you lose money with each transaction, convert in large sums (unless the rate is disadvantageous).

THE EURO. Since 1999, the official currency of 11 members of the European Union–Austria, Belgium, Finland, France, Germany, Ireland, Italy, Luxembourg, the Netherlands, Portugal, and Spain–has been the **euro.** (As of January 2001, Greece will be admitted as well.) But you shouldn't throw out your francs, pesetas, and Deutschmarks just yet; actual euro banknotes and coins won't be available until January 1, 2002, and the old national currencies will remain legal tender for six months after that (though July 1, 2002).

While you might not be able to pay for a coffee and get your change in euros yet, the currency has some important–and positive–consequences for travelers hitting more than one euro-zone country. For one thing, money-changers across the euro-zone are obliged to exchange money at the official, fixed rate (see below), and at no commission (though they may still charge a small service fee). So now you can change your guilders into escudos and your escudos into lire without losing fistfuls of money on every transaction. Second, euro-denominated travelers checks allow you to pay for goods and services across the euro-zone, again at the official rate and commission-free.

The exchange rate between euro-zone currencies was permanently fixed on January 1, 1999 at 1 EUR = 1.96DM (German marks) = 6.56F (French francs) = 1936.27L (Italian liras) = 13.76AS (Austrian schillings). For more info, see www.europa.eu.int.

TRAVELERS' CHECKS

Travelers' checks are one of the safest and least troublesome means of carrying funds, since they can be refunded if stolen. Several agencies and banks sell them, usually for face value plus a small percentage commission. **American Express** and **Visa** are the most widely recognized. If you're ordering checks, do so well in advance, especially if you are requesting large sums. You can get travelers' checks in most currencies, including Swiss Francs and euros (no one offers Schillings).

Each agency provides refunds if your checks are lost or stolen, and many provide additional services, such as toll-free refund hotlines in the countries you're visiting, emergency message services, and stolen credit card assistance.

In order to collect a **refund for lost or stolen checks,** keep your check receipts separate from your checks and store them in a safe place or with a traveling companion. Record check numbers when you cash them, leave a list of check numbers with someone at home, and ask for a list of refund centers when you buy your checks. Never countersign your checks until you are ready to cash them, and always bring your passport with you when you plan to use the checks.

American Express: Call (800) 251 902 in Australia; in New Zealand (0800) 441 068; in the UK (0800) 521 313; in the US and Canada (800) 221-7282. Elsewhere call US collect +1 (801) 964-6665; www.aexp.com. In **Austria,** call (0800) 206 840; in **Switzerland,** call (0800) 550 100. American Express travelers' checks are available in 10 currencies, including Swiss francs and euros (for Austria since they don't offer Austrian Schillings). Checks can be purchased for a small fee (1-4%) at American Express Travel Service Offices, banks, and American Automobile Association (AAA) offices (see p. 45). American Express offices cash their checks commission-free, but often at slightly worse rates than banks. *Cheques for Two* can be signed by either of 2 people.

Citicorp: In the US and Canada call (800) 645-6556; in Europe, the Middle East, or Africa call the UK +44 (020) 7508 7007; elsewhere call US collect +1 (813) 623-1709. Traveler's checks available in 7 currencies at 1-2% commission.

Thomas Cook MasterCard: In the US and Canada call (800) 223-7373; in the UK call (0800) 62 21 01; in Austria call (0800) 296 266, in Switzerland call (0800) 550 130. Checks available in 13 currencies including Swiss Francs at 2% commission. Thomas Cook offices and *Sparkasse* banks in Austria will cash Thomas Cook travelers' checks commission-free.

Visa: In the US call (800) 227-6811; in the UK call (0800) 89 50 78; in Austria call (0800) 296 102; in Switzerland call (0800) 558 450.

CREDIT CARDS

Credit cards and debit cards are generally accepted in Austria and Switzerland, though smaller businesses and accommodations may refuse them, particularly in Austria, where the retail credit card rates are the highest in Europe. Major credit cards such as **MasterCard** (a.k.a. EuroCard or Access in Europe) and **Visa** (a.k.a. Carte Bleue or Barclaycard) can be used to obtain cash advances in Schillings or Swiss francs from some associated banks and teller machines instantly. Credit card companies get the wholesale exchange rate, which is generally 5% better than the retail rate used by banks and other currency exchange establishments. **American Express** cards also work in some ATMs, as well as at AmEx offices and major airports. As an extra bonus, many credit cards offer an array of other services, from insurance to emergency assistance.

However, transaction fees for all credit card advances (up to US$10 per advance, plus 2-3% extra on foreign transactions after conversion) tend to make credit cards a more costly way of withdrawing cash than ATMs or traveler's checks, and not all banks will be willing to let you buy Schillings or Swiss francs on credit. In an emergency, however, the transaction fee may prove worth the cost. To be eligible for an advance, you'll need to get a **Personal Identification Number (PIN)** from your credit card company (see **Cash (ATM) Cards,** below).

It is also a good idea to call your credit card company and let them know that you will be using your card abroad, as some companies initiate security measures, such as freezing cards, when spending patterns change.

CREDIT CARD COMPANIES. **Visa** (US ☎(800) 336-8472) and **MasterCard** (US ☎(800) 307-7309) are issued in cooperation with banks and other organizations. **American Express** (US ☎(800) 843-2273) has an annual fee of up to US$55. AmEx cardholders may cash personal checks at AmEx offices abroad, access an emergency medical and legal assistance hotline (24hr.; in North America call (800) 554-2639, elsewhere call US collect +1 (202) 554-2639), and enjoy American Express Travel Service benefits (including plane, hotel, and car rental reservation changes; baggage loss and flight insurance; mailgram and international cable services; and held mail). The **Discover Card** (in US call (800) 347-2683, elsewhere call US +1 (801) 902-3100) offers small cashback bonuses on most purchases, but it may not be readily accepted in Austria and Switzerland.

CASH (ATM) CARDS

Cash or debit cards—often called ATM (Automated Teller Machine) cards—can be used throughout Austria and Switzerland. ATMs get the same wholesale exchange rate as credit cards. Despite these perks, do some research before relying too heavily on automation. There is often a limit on the amount of money you can withdraw per day (usually about US$500, depending on the type of card and account), and computer networks sometimes fail. Also, many banks charge a fee of $1-5 for each withdraw—check with your bank before leaving.

PLEASE SIR, MAY I HAVE SOME MORE All automatic teller machines require a 4-digit **Personal Identification Number (PIN),** which credit cards in the United States do not always carry. You must ask your credit card company to assign you one before you leave. Without a PIN, you will be unable to withdraw cash with your credit card abroad. There are no letters on the keypads of European ATMs, so work out your PIN numerically: ABC correspond to 2; DEF to 3; GHI to 4; JKL to 5; MNO to 6; PQRS to 7; TUV to 8; and WXYZ to 9. If you punch the wrong code into an ATM 3 times it will eat your card. If you lose your card, call for help at the following toll-free numbers, all of which have English-speaking operators: **MasterCard** (Austria ☎(0800) 21 8235; Switzerland (0800) 89 7092); **Visa** (Austria ☎(0600) 6704; Switzerland ☎(0800) 892 733); **American Express** (call the US collect +1 (301) 731-5724).

The two major international money networks are **Cirrus** (US ☎(800) 424-7787) and **PLUS** (US ☎(800) 843-7587). To locate ATMs around the world, call the above numbers, or consult www.visa.com/pd/atm or www.mastercard.com/atm. Look for signs reading "Bankomat" with a green or blue "B," and compare the symbols on the back of your card with those above the machine to find out which machines your card will work in.

Visa TravelMoney is a system allowing you to access money from any Visa ATM, common throughout Austria and Switzerland. You deposit an amount before you travel (plus a small administration fee), and you can withdraw up to that sum. The cards, which give you the same favorable exchange rate for withdrawals as a regular Visa, are especially useful if you plan to travel through many countries. Check with your local bank to see if it issues TravelMoney cards.

GETTING MONEY FROM HOME

AMERICAN EXPRESS. Cardholders can withdraw cash from their checking accounts at any of AmEx's major offices and many representative offices (up to US$1000 every 21 days; no service charge, no interest). AmEx also offers "Express Cash" at any of their ATMs or offices in Austria and Switzerland. Express Cash withdrawals are automatically debited from the cardholder's checking account or line of credit. Green card holders may withdraw up to US$1000 in any seven-day period (2% transaction fee; minimum US$2.50, maximum US$20). To enroll in Express Cash, cardmembers may call (800) 227-4669 in the US; elsewhere call the US collect +1 (336) 668-5041.

WESTERN UNION. Travelers from the US, Canada, and the UK can wire money abroad through Western Union's international money transfer services. In the US, call (800) 325-6000; in Canada, (800) 235-0000; in the UK, (0800) 833 833; in Austria call 0660 8066, in Switzerland call the office in Zurich at 512 223 358. The rates for sending cash are generally US$10-11 cheaper than with a credit card, and the money is usually available at the place you're sending it to within an hour. To locate the nearest Western Union location, consult www.westernunion.com.

FEDERAL EXPRESS. Some people choose to send money abroad in cash via FedEx to avoid transmission fees and taxes. In the US and Canada, call (800) 463-3339; in the UK, (0800) 123 800; in Ireland, (800) 535 800; in Australia, 13 26 10; in New Zealand, (0800) 733 339; and in South Africa, (021) 551 7610. While FedEx is reasonably reliable, note that this method is illegal and somewhat risky.

US STATE DEPARTMENT (US CITIZENS ONLY). In dire emergencies only, the US State Department will forward money within hours to the nearest consular office, which will then disburse it according to instructions for a US$15 fee. Contact the Overseas Citizens Service, American Citizens Services, Consular Affairs, Room 4811, US Department of State, Washington, D.C. 20520 (☎(202) 647-5225; nights, Sundays, and holidays 647-4000; http://travel.state.gov).

TIPPING AND BARGAINING

There is technically no need for tipping in Switzerland, as gratuities are already automatically factored into prices; in Austria, menus will say whether service is included (*Preise inclusive* or *Bedienung inclusiv*); if it is, you don't have to tip. If it's not, leave a tip up to about 10%. However, it is considered polite in both Austria and Switzerland to round up your bill to the nearest 5 or 10 Schillings or 1 or 2 Francs as a nod of approval for good service; tell the waiter or waitress how much you want back from the money you give. If you just say "*Danke*," the waiter/waitress will most likely assume that you intend for him/her to keep the change. Austrian restaurants expect you to seat yourself, and servers will not bring the bill until you ask them to do so. Say "*Zahlen bitte*" (TSAHL-en BIT-uh) to settle your accounts. Don't leave tips on the table. Be aware that some restaurants charge for each piece of bread that you eat during your meal.

Don't expect to bargain in shops or markets in Austria and Switzerland, except at flea markets. Most prices are fixed. If you are concerned about getting ripped off by taxi drivers or shopkeepers, get a few price quotes for the route or purchase so you know what range is reasonable.

TAXES

No taxes are added to purchases made in **Switzerland.**

In **Austria,** there is a 20% to 34% value added tax (VAT) on all books, clothing, souvenir items, art items, jewelry, perfume, cigarettes, alcohol, etc. Tourists must pay this tax at the time of purchase, but may get the tax refunded later if the amount of purchase is 1000AS (US$95) or greater at a particular store. To get the refund, fill out the Austrian Form U-34, available at most stores, and an ÖAMTC quick refund form to get a check at the airport or train station. Make sure the store affixes their store identification stamp to the forms at the time of purchase. When you leave the country, go to the VAT or Customs office (located in the airport or train station) to get your form validated. To get the form validated, you must have the (unused) items on your person. They will issue you a check for the amount of the refund, which can be cashed at bank tellers in the airport or train station.

Make sure you have your unused purchases and the Austrian U-34 form on your person at the airport or train station so you can get the form validated and your taxes back!

SAFETY AND SECURITY

GENERAL SAFETY TIPS. Austria and Switzerland are relatively safe countries, so most safety and security concerns can be resolved by using common sense. In general, safety means not looking like a target. Tourists are particularly vulnerable to crime because they often carry large amounts of cash and are not as street savvy as locals. The gawking camera-toter is a more obvious target than the low-profile traveler, so avoid unwanted attention by trying to blend in. Familiarize yourself with your surroundings before setting out; if you must check a map on the street, duck into a cafe or shop. Also, carry yourself with confidence, as an obviously bewildered bodybuilder is more likely to be harassed than a stern and confident 98-pound weakling. If you are traveling alone, be sure that someone at home knows your itinerary and never admit that you're traveling alone. When you arrive in a new city, find out what areas to avoid from tourist information or the manager of your hostel. Stick to busy, well-lit streets. Whenever possible, *Let's Go* warns of unsafe neighborhoods and areas, such as drug hangouts. The American Society of Travel Agents provides extensive informational resources at their website (www.astanet.com) where there is a section on *Travel Safety*.

EMERGENCY TELEPHONE NUMBERS	Police: Austria, **133.** Switzerland, **117.** Ambulance: Austria and Switzerland, **144.** Fire: Austria, **122.** Switzerland, **118.**

SELF DEFENSE. There is no sure-fire way to avoid all the threatening situations you might encounter when you travel, but a good self-defense course will give you concrete ways to react to unwanted advances. Impact, Prepare, and Model Mugging can refer you to local self-defense courses in the US (☎(800) 345-5425) and Vancouver (☎(604) 878-3838). Workshops (2-3hr.) start at US$50; full courses run US$350-500. Both women and men are welcome.

DRIVING SAFELY. Driving in Austria and Switzerland is a pleasant but expensive proposition. The roads are well maintained with the money drivers pay for the right to drive here (they won't even let you on the Autobahn in Switzerland without a permit sticker). Be sure to observe the speed limit and don't drive drunk—

TRAVEL ADVISORIES. The following government offices provide travel information and advisories by telephone, by fax, or via the web:

Australian Department of Foreign Affairs and Trade: ☎(2) 626 11111; www.dfat.gov.au.

Canadian Department of Foreign Affairs and International Trade (DFAIT): In Canada call (800) 267-6788, elsewhere call +1 (613) 944-6788; www.dfait-maeci.gc.ca. Call for their free booklet, *Bon Voyage...But.*

New Zealand Ministry of Foreign Affairs: ☎(04) 494 8500; fax 494 8511; www.mft.govt.nz/trav.html.

United Kingdom Foreign and Commonwealth Office: ☎(020) 723 84503; fax 723 84545; www.fco.gov.uk.

US Department of State: ☎(202) 647-5225, auto faxback (202) 647-3000; http://travel.state.gov. For *A Safe Trip Abroad,* call (202) 512-1800.

the Austrian and Swiss police will not hesitate to take away your license and your car if you have any alcohol in your blood. If you decide to drive a car, learn local driving signals and wear a seatbelt. Children under 40lbs. should ride only in a specially designed carseat, available for a small fee from most car rental agencies. Study route maps before you hit the road; depending on the region, some roads have poor (or nonexistent) shoulders, few gas stations, and roaming animals. Twisty mountains roads may be closed in winter but, when open, require particular caution. Learn the **Alpine honk:** when going blind around an abrupt turn, stop and give the horn a toot before proceeding. Shift to low gear, drive slowly, brake occasionally, and *never ever* pass anyone, no matter how slow they're going.

If you plan on spending a lot of time on the road, you may want to bring spare parts. For long drives in desolate areas invest in a cellular phone and a roadside assistance program (see p. 45). Be sure to park your vehicle in a garage or well-traveled area, and use a steering wheel locking device in larger cities. Try not to leave valuable possessions—such as radios or luggage—in it while you are away. If your tape deck or radio is removable, hide it in the trunk or take it with you. If it isn't, at least conceal it under something else. Similarly, hide baggage in the trunk—although savvy thieves can tell if a car is heavily loaded by the way it sits on its tires. **Sleeping in your car** is one of the most dangerous (and often illegal) ways to get your rest, second only to sleeping in the open. If your car breaks down, wait for the police to assist you.

Let's Go does not recommend **hitchhiking** under any circumstances, particularly for women—see **Getting Around,** p. 39, for more information.

PROTECTING YOUR VALUABLES. Although Austria and Switzerland have low crime rates, thieves are happy to relieve ignorant tourists of their money. Be on the alert, particularly in crowds. Beware of classic scams: sob stories that require money, distractions that allow enough time to steal your bag, and little kids with big newspapers. To prevent easy theft, don't keep all your valuables (money, important documents) in one place. **Photocopies** of important documents allow you to recover them in case they are lost or filched. Carry one copy separate from the documents and leave another copy at home. Label every piece of luggage both inside and out. **Don't carry your wallet or money in your back pocket.** Never count your money in public and carry as little as possible. If you carry a purse, buy a sturdy one with a secure clasp, and carry it crosswise on the side, away from the street with the clasp against you. Secure packs with small combination padlocks which slip through the two zippers. A **money belt** is the best way to carry cash; you can buy one at most camping supply stores. A nylon, zippered pouch with a belt that sits inside the waist of your pants or skirt combines convenience and security. A **neck pouch** is equally safe, though less accessible. Refrain from pulling it out in public; if you must, be very discreet. Avoid keeping anything precious in a waist-pack: your valuables will be highly visible and easy to steal. Keep some money separate from the rest to use for emergencies or in case of theft.

In public, watch your belongings at all times. Beware of con artists and **pickpockets** on the street and on public transportation (although neither Austria nor Switzerland has a big problem with street crime). On buses and trains, keep your bag close to you: don't check your baggage on trains, don't trust anyone to "watch your bag for a second," and don't ever put it under your seat in train compartments. If you take a **night train,** either lock your bag to the luggage rack or use it as a pillow. In your hostel, if you can't lock your room, lock your bag in lockers or at the train station (you'll need your own **padlock**).

DRUGS AND ALCOHOL. Drugs could easily ruin a trip. Every year thousands of travelers are arrested for trafficking or possession of drugs or for simply being in the company of a suspected user. Marijuana, hashish, cocaine, and narcotics are illegal in Austria and Switzerland, and the penalties for illegal possession of drugs, especially for foreigners, range from stern to severe. You may be imprisoned or deported, and a meek "I didn't know it was illegal" will not suffice. It is not unknown for a dealer to increase profits by first selling drugs to tourists and then turning them in to the authorities for a reward. Even such reputedly liberal cities as Vienna, Salzburg, and Zurich take an officially dim view of mussed-up tourists. The worst thing you can possibly do is carry drugs across an international border—you could not only end up in prison but also be hounded by a "Drug Trafficker" stamp on your passport for the rest of your life. If you are arrested, all your home country's consulate can do is visit, provide a list of attorneys, and inform family and friends. Remember that you are subject to the laws of the country in which you travel, not to those of your home country, and it is your responsibility to familiarize yourself with these laws before leaving. Police officers, members of the *Polizei* or *Gendarmerie*, typically speak little English.

Imbibing **alcohol** in Austria and Switzerland is generally trouble-free—beer is more common than soda, and a lunch without wine or beer would be unusual. In Switzerland, you must be 16 to drink legally. Each Austrian province sets a legal minimum drinking age; typically, anyone over 18 can drink whatever he or she wishes, and drinking beer is often legal at younger ages. In Switzerland you can only be arrested for being drunk in public if you cause danger or harm to others.

HEALTH

Common sense is the simplest prescription for good health while you travel. Travelers complain most often about their feet and guts, so take precautionary measures: drink lots of fluids to prevent dehydration and constipation, wear sturdy, broken-in shoes and clean socks, and use talcum powder to keep your feet dry.

BEFORE YOU GO

Preparation can help minimize the likelihood of contracting a disease and maximize the chances of receiving effective health care in the event of an emergency. Make sure you get a statement and prescription from your doctor if you'll be carrying insulin, syringes, or prescription medicine. Leave all medication in original, labeled containers. What is legal at home may not be legal abroad; check with your doctor or the appropriate foreign consulate to avoid nasty surprises. For minor health problems, bring a compact **first-aid kit,** including bandages, aspirin or other pain killer, antibiotic cream, a thermometer, a Swiss army knife with tweezers, moleskin, decongestant for colds, motion sickness remedy, medicine for diarrhea or stomach problems (Pepto Bismol tablets or liquid and Immodium), sunscreen, insect repellent, and burn ointment.

In your **passport,** write the names of any people you wish to be contacted in case of a medical emergency, and also list any **allergies** or medical conditions you would want doctors to be aware of. Allergy sufferers might want to obtain a full supply of any necessary medication before the trip. Matching a prescription to a foreign equivalent is not always easy, safe, or possible. Carry up-to-date, legible prescriptions or a statement from your doctor stating the medication's trade name, manufacturer, chemical name, and dosage. While traveling, be sure to keep all medication with you in your carry-on luggage.

IMMUNIZATIONS. Take a look at your immunization records before you go. Travelers over two years old should be sure that the following vaccines are up to date: MMR (for measles, mumps, and rubella); DTaP or Td (for diphtheria, tetanus, and pertussis); OPV (for polio); HbCV (for haemophilus influenza B); and HBV (for hepatitis B). Check with a doctor for guidance through this maze of injections.

USEFUL ORGANIZATIONS AND PUBLICATIONS. The US **Centers for Disease Control and Prevention** (**CDC;** ☎(877) FYI-TRIP; www.cdc.gov/travel), which is an excellent source of information for travelers, maintains an international fax information service. The CDC's comprehensive booklet *Health Information for International Travelers*, an annual rundown of disease, immunization, and general health advice, is free on the website or US$22 via the Government Printing Office (☎(202) 512-1800). The **US State Department** (http://travel.state.gov) compiles Consular Information Sheets on health, entry requirements, and other issues for various countries. For quick information on health and other travel warnings, call the **Overseas Citizens' Services** (☎(202) 647-5225; after-hours 647-4000), contact a US passport agency or a US embassy or consulate abroad, or send a self-addressed, stamped envelope to the Overseas Citizens' Services, Bureau of Consular Affairs, #4811, US Department of State, Washington, D.C. 20520. For information on medical evacuation services and travel insurance firms, see http://travel.state.gov/medical.html. The **British Foreign and Commonwealth Office** also gives health warnings for individual countries (www.fco.gov.uk).

For detailed information on travel health, including a country-by-country overview of diseases, try the **International Travel Health Guide,** Stuart Rose, MD (Travel Medicine, US$20; www.travmed.com). For general health info, contact the **American Red Cross** (☎(800) 564-1234).

MEDICAL ASSISTANCE ON THE ROAD. Medical care in Austria and Switzerland is generally excellent. Most doctors and pharmacists speak at least some English. If you are concerned about being able to access medical support while traveling, contact one of two services: The *MedPass* from **Global Emergency Medical Services (GEMS),** 2001 Westside Dr., #120, Alpharetta, GA 30004, USA (☎(800) 860-1111; fax (770) 475-0058; www.globalems.com), provides 24-hour international medical assistance, support, and medical evacuation resources. The **International Association for Medical Assistance to Travelers** (**IAMAT;** US ☎(716) 754-4883, Canada ☎(416) 652-0137, New Zealand ☎(03) 352 2053; www.sentex.net/~iamat) has free membership, lists English-speaking doctors worldwide, and offers detailed info on immunization requirements and sanitation. If your regular **insurance** policy does not cover travel abroad, you may wish to purchase additional coverage (see p. 23).

Those with medical conditions (diabetes, allergies to antibiotics, epilepsy, heart conditions) may want to obtain a stainless-steel **Medic Alert ID tag** (first year US$35, $15 annually thereafter), which identifies the condition and gives a 24-hour collect-call number. Contact the Medic Alert Foundation, 2323 Colorado Ave, Turlock, CA 95382, USA (☎(800) 825-3785; www.medicalert.org). Diabetics can contact the **American Diabetes Association,** 1660 Duke St., Alexandria, VA 22314 (☎(800) 232 3472), to receive copies of the article "Travel and Diabetes" and a diabetic ID card, which carries messages in 18 languages explaining the carrier's diabetic status.

ENVIRONMENTAL HAZARDS

Heat exhaustion and dehydration: Heat exhaustion, characterized by dehydration and salt deficiency, can lead to fatigue, headaches, and wooziness. Avoid it by drinking plenty of fluids, eating salty foods (e.g. crackers), and avoiding dehydrating beverages (e.g. alcohol, coffee, tea, and caffeinated soda). Continuous heat stress can eventually lead to heatstroke, signaled by a rising temperature, severe headache, and cessation of sweating. Victims should be cooled off with wet towels and taken to a doctor.

Sunburn: If you're prone to sunburn, bring sunscreen with you (it's often more expensive and hard to find when traveling), and apply it liberally and often to avoid burns and risk of skin cancer. If you are planning on spending time near water, in the desert, or in the snow, you are at risk of getting burned, even through clouds. If you get sunburned, drink more fluids than usual and apply calamine or an aloe-based lotion.

Hypothermia and frostbite: A rapid drop in body temperature is the clearest sign of overexposure to cold. Victims may also shiver, feel exhausted, have poor coordination or slurred speech, hallucinate, or suffer amnesia. *Do not let hypothermia victims fall asleep,* or their body temperature will continue to drop and they may die. To avoid hypothermia, keep dry, wear layers, and stay out of the wind. When the temperature is below freezing, watch out for frostbite. If skin turns white, waxy, and cold, do not rub the area. Drink warm beverages, get dry, and slowly warm the area with dry fabric or steady body contact until a doctor can be found.

High altitude: Allow your body a couple of days to adjust to less oxygen before exerting yourself. Note that alcohol is more potent and UV rays are stronger at high elevations.

TRANSMITTED DISEASES

Many diseases are transmitted by insects—mainly mosquitoes, fleas, ticks, and lice. Be aware of insects in wet or forested areas, especially while hiking and camping. **Mosquitoes** are most active from dusk to dawn. **Ticks**—responsible for Lyme and other diseases—can be particularly dangerous in rural and forested regions. **Tick-borne encephalitis** is a viral infection of the central nervous system transmitted during the summer by tick bites (primarily in wooded areas). Symptoms range from nothing at all to headaches and flu-like symptoms to swelling of the brain (encephalitis). **Lyme disease** is a bacterial infection carried by ticks and marked by a circular bull's-eye rash of 2 in. or more. Later symptoms include fever, headache, fatigue, and aches and pains. Antibiotics are effective if administered early. Transmitted through the saliva of infected animals, **rabies** is fatal if untreated. If you are bitten, wash the wound thoroughly, seek immediate medical care, and try to have the animal located.

AIDS, HIV, STDS

AIDS and HIV are only as common in Austria and Switzerland as in the rest of Western Europe. Nonetheless, for more detailed information on **Acquired Immune Deficiency Syndrome (AIDS)** in the two countries, call the **US Centers for Disease Control's** 24-hour hotline at (800) 342-2437, or contact the **Joint United Nations Programme on HIV/AIDS (UNAIDS),** 20 Av. Appia 20, CH-1211 Geneva 27, Switzerland (☎+41 (22) 791 3666, fax 791 4187). Council's brochure, *Travel Safe: AIDS and International Travel,* is available at all Council Travel offices and on their website (www.ciee.org/Isp/safety/travelsafe.htm).

Sexually transmitted diseases (STDs) such as gonorrhea, chlamydia, genital warts, syphilis, and herpes are easier to catch than HIV and can be just as deadly. **Hepatitis B** and **C** are also serious STDs (see **Other Infectious Diseases,** above). Though condoms may protect you from some STDs, oral or even tactile contact can lead to transmission. Warning signs include swelling, sores, bumps, or blisters on sex organs, the rectum, or the mouth; burning and pain during urination and bowel movements; itching around sex organs; swelling or redness of the throat; and flu-like symptoms. If these symptoms develop, see a doctor immediately.

WOMEN'S HEALTH

Women traveling in unsanitary conditions are vulnerable to **urinary tract** and **bladder infections,** common bacterial diseases that cause a burning sensation and painful and sometimes frequent urination. To try to avoid these infections, drink plenty of vitamin-C-rich juice and plenty of clean water, and urinate frequently, especially right after intercourse. Untreated, these infections can lead to kidney infections, sterility, and even death. If symptoms persist, see a doctor.

FURTHER READING: WOMEN'S HEALTH

Handbook for Women Travellers, Maggie and Gemma Moss (US$15).
Adventures in Good Company: The Complete Guide to Women's Tours and Outdoor Trips, by Thalia Zepatos (US$17).

Since **tampons, pads,** and reliable **contraceptive devices** are sometimes hard to find when traveling and your preferred brand will rarely be available, you should consider bringing supplies with you. Women considering an **abortion** abroad should contact the **International Planned Parenthood Federation (IPPF),** Regent's College, Inner Circle, Regent's Park, London NW1 4NS (☎(020) 7487 7900; fax 7487 7950; www.ippf.org), for more information.

INSURANCE

Travel insurance generally covers four basic areas: medical/health problems, property loss, trip cancellation/interruption, and emergency evacuation. Although your regular insurance policies may well extend to travel-related accidents, you may consider purchasing travel insurance if the cost of potential trip cancellation/interruption or emergency medical evacuation is greater than you can absorb. Prices for travel insurance purchased separately generally run about US$50 per week for full coverage, while trip cancellation/interruption may be purchased separately at a rate of about US$5.50 per US$100 of coverage.

Medical insurance (especially university policies) often covers costs incurred abroad; check with your provider. **US Medicare** does not cover foreign travel. **Canadians** are protected by their home province's health insurance plan for up to 90 days after leaving the country; check with the provincial Ministry of Health or Health Plan Headquarters for details. **Homeowners' insurance** (or your family's coverage) often covers theft during travel and loss of travel documents (passport, plane ticket, railpass, etc.) up to US$500.

ISIC and **ITIC** (see p. 10) provide basic insurance benefits, including US$100 per day of in-hospital sickness for up to 60 days, US$3000 of accident-related medical reimbursement, and US$25,000 for emergency medical transport. Cardholders have access to a toll-free 24-hour helpline for medical, legal, and financial emergencies overseas (US and Canada ☎(877) 370-4742, elsewhere call US collect +1 (713) 342-4104). **American Express** (US ☎(800) 528-4800) grants most cardholders automatic car rental insurance (collision and theft, but not liability) and ground travel accident coverage of US$100,000 on flight purchases made with the card.

EU citizens traveling to Austria or Liechtenstein should attain a **E111 form** for reimbursement in case you need emergency medical care, or hospitalization.

INSURANCE PROVIDERS. **Council** and **STA** (see p. 35) offer a range of plans that can supplement your basic coverage. Other private insurance providers in the **US and Canada** include: **Access America** (☎(800) 284-8300); **Berkely Group/Carefree Travel Insurance** (☎(800) 323-3149; www.berkely.com); **Globalcare Travel Insurance** (☎(800) 821-2488; www.globalcare-cocco.com); and **Travel Assistance International** (☎(800) 821-2828; www.worldwide-assistance.com). Providers in the **UK** include **Campus Travel** (☎(01865) 258 000) and **Columbus Travel Insurance** (☎(020) 7375 0011). In **Australia,** try **CIC Insurance** (☎ 9202 8000).

PACKING

Pack according to the extremes of climate you may experience and the type of travel you'll be doing. **Pack light:** a good rule is to lay out only what you absolutely need, then take half the clothes and twice the money. The less you have, the less you have to lose (or store or carry on your back). Don't forget the obvious things: no matter when you're traveling, it's always a good idea to bring a rain jacket (Gore-Tex is a miracle fabric that's both waterproof and breathable), a warm

USEFUL THINGS TO BRING:

First-aid kit: moleskin (for blisters), medications, vitamins (see Health, p. 20).
Laundry supplies, such as a travel clothesline and small carton of detergent.
Shower supplies: towel, shampoo, slippers for the shower, soap.
Personal hygiene supplies: deodorant, tampons, razors, tweezers, condoms.
Sealable plastic bags (for damp clothes, food, shampoo, and other spillables).
Money belt for carrying valuables; small calculator for currency conversion.
Useful items: travel alarm clock, pocketknife, water bottle, needle and thread, safety pins, umbrella, sunscreen, sunglasses, sun hat, insect repellent, padlock, earplugs, flashlight, compass, string, electrical tape (for repairing tears).

jacket or wool sweater, and sturdy shoes and thick socks. If you plan to be doing a lot of hiking, see Outdoors, p. 29. Even casual hikers should bring water-proof **hiking boots;** pavement-pounding city-types should wear well-cushioned **sneakers.** Break in your shoes before you leave. A double pair of socks—light silk or polypropylene inside and thick wool outside—will cushion feet, keep them dry, and help prevent blisters. Remember that wool will keep you warm even when soaked through, whereas wet cotton is colder than wearing nothing at all. You may also want to add one dressier outfit beyond the jeans and t-shirt uniform, and a nicer pair of shoes if you have room. Be prepared for sudden weather shifts.

LUGGAGE. If you plan to cover most of your itinerary by foot, a sturdy **frame backpack** is unbeatable. (For the basics on buying a pack see p. 29). Toting a **suitcase** is fine if you plan to live in one or two cities and explore from there, but a very bad idea if you're going to be moving around a lot. In addition, a small backpack, rucksack, or courier bag will be very useful as a **daypack** for sight-seeing expeditions; it doubles as an airplane **carry-on.**

SLEEPSACK. Some youth hostels require that you have your own sleepsack or rent one of theirs. Save cash by making your own sleepsack: fold a full size sheet in half the long way, then sew it closed along the open long side and one of the short sides.

ELECTRIC CURRENT. In Europe electricity is 220V AC (240 V in Britain and Ireland), enough to fry any 110V North American appliance. You can get an adapter (which changes the shape of the plug) and a converter (which changes the voltage) at a hardware store. **Americans** and **Canadians** should buy an **adapter** and a **converter.** Don't make the mistake of using only an adapter. **New Zealanders** and **South Africans** (who both use 220V at home) as well as **Australians** (who use 240/250V) won't need a converter, but will need a set of adapters to use anything electrical.

CONTACT LENSES. Machines which heat-disinfect contact lenses will require a small converter (about US$20) to 220V. Consider switching temporarily to a chemical disinfection system, but check with your lens dispenser to see if it's safe to switch; some lenses may be damaged by a chemical system. Contact lens supplies may be expensive and difficult to find; bring enough for your entire vacation.

FILM. Film in Austria and Switzerland costs about the same as anywhere else, generally around US$5 for a roll of 24 color exposures. If you're not a serious photographer, you might consider bringing a **disposable camera** rather than an expensive permanent one. Always pack film and cameras in your carry-on luggage.

FURTHER READING: PACKING

The Packing Book, by Judith Gilford. Ten Speed Press (US$9).
Backpacking One Step at a Time, Harvey Manning. Vintage (US$15).

PACKING LIGHT, THE AUSTRIAN WAY In the summer of 1870, when the air was clean and all snow came from clouds, Austrian climbing legend Hermann von Barth took to the hills of the Karwendel Range in Tyrol and climbed no fewer than 88 peaks, 12 of which were first-ever ascents. His luggage consisted simply of a drinking cup, binoculars, smelling salts, a lighter, a can of paint and a paintbrush to paint his name on each peak, and a bottle of poison in case he fell and wasn't able to rescue himself. He never fell.

ACCOMMODATIONS

Like most things Austrian and Swiss, accommodations in these countries are usually clean, orderly, and expensive. Always ask if your lodging provides a **guest card** *(gästekarte)*. Guest cards generally grant discounts to local sports facilities, hiking excursions, town museums, and public transportation. In Austria, the 10AS tax that most accommodations slap on bills funds these discounts—take advantage of them to get your money's worth.

Most local tourist offices distribute extensive listings (the *Gastgeberverzeichnis*), and many will reserve a room for a small fee. National tourist offices can also supply more complete lists of campsites and hotels. Be aware that *Privatzimmer* and *Pensionen* may close their doors without notice; it's best to call ahead.

HOSTELS

A HOSTELER'S BILL OF RIGHTS. Unless we state otherwise, you can expect that every hostel has: no lockout, no curfew, a kitchen, free hot showers, secure luggage storage, and no key deposit.

Hostels (*Jugendherbergen* in German, *Auberges de Jeunesse* in French, *Ostelli* in Italian) are the hubs of the gigantic backpacker subculture that rumbles through Europe every summer, providing innumerable opportunities to meet travelers from all over the world. Hostels generally offer dorm-style accommodations, often in single-sex large rooms with bunk beds, although some hostels do offer private rooms for families and couples. They sometimes have kitchens and utensils for your use, bike or moped rentals, storage areas, and laundry facilities. There can be drawbacks: some hostels close during certain daytime "lock-out" hours, have a curfew, don't accept reservations, impose a maximum stay, or, less frequently, require that you do chores. In Austria and Switzerland, a dorm bed in a hostel averages around US$12-20. Check out the **Internet Guide to Hostelling** (www.hostels.com), which provides a directory of hostels from around the world in addition to oodles of information about hosteling and backpacking worldwide. **Eurotrip** (www.eurotrip.com/accommodation/accommodation.html) has information and reviews on budget hostels and several international hostel associations.

Both Austria and Switzerland have branches of **Hostelling International (HI).** In Switzerland the *Schweizer Jugendherbergen* (SJH or Swiss Youth Hostels) runs the 63 HI hostels in Switzerland. The SJH has a comprehensive website that contains contact information for all member hostels, and allows you to make reservations at many of them (www.youthhostel.ch). Austria has two HI organizations that operate together as the *Österreicher Jugendherbergsverband-Hauptverband* (OJH). Non-HI members can stay in all of these hostels but are usually charged a $5 surcharge—check out their website at www.oejvh.or.at. Because of the rigorous standards of the national organizations, the SJH and OJH hostels are usually as clean as any hotel. While the clientele of the hostels varies, HI hostels tend to be oriented toward families and school groups.

LOCAL HI ORGANIZATIONS. To join HI, contact one of the following organizations:

Australian Youth Hostels Association (AYHA), 422 Kent St., Sydney NSW 2000 (☎(02) 926 11111; fax 926 11969; www.yha.org.au). AUS$49, under 18 AUS$14.50.

Hostelling International-Canada (HI-C), 400-205 Catherine St., Ottawa, ON K2P 1C3 (☎(800) 663-5777 or (613) 237-7884; fax 237-7868; info@hostelling-intl.ca; www.hostellingintl.ca). CDN$25, under 18 CDN$12.

An Óige (Irish Youth Hostel Association), 61 Mountjoy St., Dublin 7 (☎(1) 830 4555; fax 830 5808; anoige@iol.ie; www.irelandyha.org). IR£10, under 18 IR£4.

Youth Hostels Association of New Zealand (YHANZ), P.O. Box 436, 173 Cashel St., Christchurch 1 (☎(03) 379 9970; fax 365 4476; info@yha.org.nz; www.yha.org.nz). NZ$40, ages 15-17 NZ$12, under 15 free.

Hostels Association of South Africa, 3rd fl. 73 St. George's St. Mall, P.O. Box 4402, Cape Town 8000 (☎(021) 424 2511; fax 424 4119; info@hisa.org.za; www.hisa.org.za). SAR50, under 18 SAR25, lifetime SAR250.

Scottish Youth Hostels Association (SYHA), 7 Glebe Crescent, Stirling FK8 2JA (☎(01786) 891 400; fax 891 333; www.syha.org.uk). UK£6, under 18 UK£2.50.

Youth Hostels Association (England and Wales) Ltd., Trevelyan House, 8 St. Stephen's Hill, St. Albans, Hertfordshire AL1 2DY, UK (☎(01727) 855 215; fax 844 126; www.yha.org.uk). UK£12, under 18 UK£6, families UK£24.

Hostelling International Northern Ireland (HINI), 22-32 Donegall Rd., Belfast BT12 5JN, Northern Ireland (☎(01232) 324 733; fax 439 699; info@hini.org.uk; www.hini.org.uk). UK£7, under 18 UK£3.

Hostelling International-American Youth Hostels (HI-AYH), 733 15th St. NW, #840, Washington, D.C. 20005 (☎(202) 783-6161 ext. 136; fax 783-6171; hiayhserv@hiayh.org; www.hiayh.org). US$25, under 18 free.

Many HI hostels also accept reservations via the **International Booking Network** (Australia ☎(02) 926 11111; Canada ☎(800) 663-5777; England and Wales ☎(1629) 581 418; Northern Ireland ☎(1232) 324 733; Republic of Ireland ☎(01) 830 1766; NZ ☎(09) 379 4224; Scotland ☎(541) 553 255; US ☎(800) 909-4776) for a nominal fee. The HI webpage (www.iyhf.org) has information on the IBN as well as the web addresses and phone numbers of all national associations and can be a great place to begin researching hostelling in a specific region. Other comprehensive hostelling websites include www.hostels.com and www.eurotrip.com/accommodation.

Switzerland also has the smaller, more informal **Swiss Backpackers (SB)** organization. As might be guessed from the fact that the name of the organization is english, SB is an organization of 28 hostels that appeal to the young, foreign traveler interested in socializing. The neon-colored, all-English website lists the hostels and also has a wealth of general information on backpacking, and specific information on adventure activities in Switzerland (www.backpacker.ch).

OTHER ACCOMMODATIONS

DORMS. Some **colleges and universities** (see Vienna: Accommodations, p. 95), open their residence halls to travelers when school is not in session—some do so even during term-time. These dorms are often close to student areas—good sources for information on things to do, places to stay, and possible rides out of town—and are usually very clean. Rates tend to be low, and many offer free local calls. *Let's Go* lists colleges that rent dorm rooms among the accommodations for appropriate cities. College dorms are popular with many travelers, especially those looking for long-term lodging, so reserve ahead.

HOTELS. Hotels are expensive in Austria (singles 200-350AS; doubles 400-800AS) and exorbitant in Switzerland (singles 50-75SFr; doubles 80-150SFr). Switzerland has set the international standard for hotels; even 1-, 2-, and 3-star accommodations tend to be nicer than their counterparts in other countries.

The cheapest hotel-style accommodations have **Gasthof** or **Gästehaus** in the name; **Hotel-Garni** also means cheap. Continental breakfast *(Frühstück)* is almost always included.

PRIVATE ROOMS AND PENSIONS. Renting a **private room** *(Privatzimmer)* in a family home is an inexpensive and friendly way to house yourself. Such rooms generally include a sink with hot and cold running water and use of a toilet and shower. Many places rent private rooms only for longer stays, or they may levy a surcharge (10-20%) for stays of less than 3 nights. *Privatzimmern* start at 25 to 60SFr per person in Switzerland. In Austria, rooms range from 250 to 400AS a night. Slightly more expensive, pensions *(Pensionen)* are similar to the American and British notion of a bed-and-breakfast. Generally, finding rooms for only one person might be difficult, especially for 1-night stays, as most lodgings have rooms with double beds *(Doppelzimmer)*; single travelers can get these rooms if they pay a bit more. Continental breakfast is *de rigueur;* in classier places, meat, cheese, and an egg will grace your plate and palate. Contact the local tourist office for a list of private rooms.

YMCA AND YWCAS. Not all **Young Men's Christian Association (YMCA)** locations offer lodging; those that do are often located in urban downtowns, which can be convenient but a little gritty. YMCA rates are usually lower than hotel rates but higher than hostel rates and may include the use of TV, air conditioning, pools, gyms, access to public transportation, tourist information, safe deposit boxes, luggage storage, daily housekeeping, multilingual staff, and 24-hour security. Many YMCAs accept women and families (group rates often available), and some will not lodge people under 18 without parental permission. There are several ways to make a reservation, all of which must be made at least two weeks in advance and paid for in advance with a traveler's check, US money order, certified check, Visa, or Mastercard in US dollars. Visit www.ymca.net.

HOME EXCHANGE AND RENTALS. Home exchange offers the traveler the opportunity to live like a native in various types of homes (houses, apartments, condominiums, villas, even castles in some cases), and to cut down dramatically on accommodation fees—usually only an administration fee is paid to the matching service. Once you join or contact one of the exchange services listed below, it is then up to you to decide with whom you would like to exchange homes (remember—they will be living in your house while you live in theirs). Most companies have pictures of members' homes and information about the owners (some will even ask for your photo!). A great site listing many exchange companies can be found at www.aitec.edu.au/~bwechner/Documents/Travel/Lists/HomeExchangeClubs.html. In order to assist you with exchanging your home with another person or family that suits your living habits, most companies offer personalized matching services. **Home rentals** are more expensive than exchanges, but they can be cheaper than comparably serviced hotels. Both home exchanges and rentals are ideal for families with children, or travelers with special dietary needs; you often get your own kitchen, maid service, TV, and telephones.

Intervac International Home Exchange, www.intervac.com. For **Austria,** contact Hans and Ingeborg Winkler, Pestalozzistr. 5, A-9100 Völkermarkt (☎/fax (0423) 23838; hwinkler@asn-klu.ac.at); **Intervac Switzerland,** Oberdorfstr. 7, CH-9524 Zuzwil (☎/fax (071) 944 2779; farewell@blackpoint.ch). You must pay for each catalogue you receive and for listing your home in a catalogue.

The Invented City: International Home Exchange (US ☎(800) 788-CITY, elsewhere call US +1 (415) 252-1141; www.invented-city.com), or surf www.aitec.edu.au/~bwechner/Documents/Travel/Lists/HomeExchangeClubs.html. For US$75, you get your offer listed in 1 catalog and unlimited access to the club's database containing thousands of homes for exchange.

ESSENTIALS

CAMPING AND THE OUTDOORS

CAMPING

Camping can be one of the most inexpensive ways of touring Austria and Switzerland. Be prepared, though, these sites are not isolated areas; they are large plots with many camper vans and cars. Camping in Austria and Switzerland is less about getting out into nature and more about having a cheap place to sleep. Most sites are open in the summer only, but some sites are specifically set aside for winter camping. In Switzerland, prices average 6-9SFr per person, 4-10SFr per tent site. In Austria, prices run 50-70AS per person and 25-60AS per tent (plus 8-9.50AS tax if you're over 15), seldom making camping substantially cheaper than hosteling.

HIKING

Austria and Switzerland are renowned for their hiking, with paths ranging from simple hikes in the foothills of the Swiss Jura and Carinthia to ice-axe-wielding expeditions through the glaciers of the Berner Oberland and the Zillertal Alps. Nearly every town and city in the two countries has a series of trails in its vicinity which the tourist office will be able to tell you about.

Hiking trails are marked by signs indicating the time to nearby destinations, which may not bear any relation to your own expertise and endurance. ("Std." is short for *Stunden*, or hours.) Usually trails will also be marked with either a red-white-red marker, or a blue-white-blue marker. The blue marker, or any trail marked *"Für Geübte"* means that mountaineering equipment is needed, while the red markers line paths that require no more than sturdy boots and hiking poles. Most mountain hiking trails and mountain huts are only open from late June to early September because of snow in the higher passes.

Free **hiking** maps are available from even the most rinky-dink of tourist offices, but for lengthy hikes every hiker should have a topographic map of no more than 1:50,000 scale. In Austria and Switzerland two companies make these maps: **Freytag-Berndt** or **Kümmerly-Frey** (maps around US$10). These maps are readily available in kiosks, bookstores, and tourist offices all over Austria and Switzerland and from **Pacific Travellers Supply,** 12 W. Anapamu St., Santa Barbara, CA 93101 (☎(805) 963 4438). The Austrian National Tourist Office publishes the pamphlet *Hiking and Backpacking in Austria*, with a complete list of Freytag-Berndt maps and additional tips.

Contact the following organizations for information on hiking and the mountain huts which they administrate:

Swiss Alpine Club (SAC). Membership costs 126SFr, and as a bonus you'll receive the titillating publication *Die Alpen*. Contact the SAC, Sektion Zermatt, Haus Dolomite, CH-3920 Zermatt, Switzerland (☎(028) 672 610).

OVERNIGHT HIKING IN AUSTRIA AND SWITZERLAND

Be aware that camping in the backcountry is not standard practice in Austria and Switzerland as it is in America; in fact, camping overnight in public areas is forbidden in both countries. Travelers planning **overnight hikes** will have to stay in the mountain huts that abound in Swiss and Austrian outdoor areas. Mountain huts, which are run by the Alpine clubs in both countries, are quite developed, and many have simple mattresses and hot water. Swiss and Austrian Alpine Club huts are open to all, but members get discounts. Prices are usually 25-35SFr in Switzerland and 200-300AS in Austria. Sleeping in one of these huts is safer for the environment than camping out, and it is generally safer for you—when you leave, you are expected to list your next destination in the hut book, thus alerting search-and-rescue teams if a problem should occur.

FURTHER READING: HIKING

100 Hikes in the Alps, by Vicky Spring (US$15).
Walking Austria's Alps, by Jonathan Hurdle (US$11).
Walking Switzerland the Swiss Way, by Marcia and Philip Lieberman. The "Swiss Way" refers to hiking hut-to-hut (US$13).
Downhill Walking in Switzerland, by Richard and Linda Williams (US$12).
Swiss-Bernese Oberland, by Philip and Loretta Alspach (US$17).
Walking Easy in the Austrian Alps and *Walking Easy in the Swiss Alps,* by Chet and Carolee Lipton (US$11).

Österreichischer Alpenverein (ÖAV) maintains most of the mountain huts across Tyrol and throughout Austria. Third-party insurance, accident provision, travel discounts, and a wealth of maps and mountain information are also included with membership. For information, contact the Österreichischer Alpenverein, Willhelm-Greil-Str. 15, A-6010 Innsbruck (☎(0512) 587 828; fax 588 842). Membership (US$55, students under 25 US$40; one-time fee US$10) also includes use of some of the huts operated by the Deutscher Alpenverein (German Alpine Club).

Touristenverein "Die Naturfreunde," Viktoriag. 6, A-1150 Vienna (☎(01) 892 3534), also operates a network of cottages in rural and mountain areas.

WILDERNESS SAFETY

Stay warm, stay dry, and stay hydrated. The vast majority of life-threatening wilderness situations result from a breach of this simple dictum. On any hike, however brief, you should pack enough equipment to keep you alive should disaster befall. This includes raingear, hat and mittens, a first-aid kit, a reflector, a whistle, high energy food, and extra water. Dress in warm layers of **synthetic materials** designed for the outdoors, or **wool.** Pile fleece jackets and Gore-Tex raingear are excellent choices. Never rely on **cotton** for warmth. This "death cloth" will be absolutely useless should it get wet. Make sure to check all equipment for any defects before setting out, and see Camping and Hiking Equipment, below, for more information.

Check **weather forecasts** and pay attention to the skies when hiking. Weather patterns can change suddenly. Don't hike when visibility is low. Whenever possible, let someone know when and where you are going hiking, either a friend, your hostel, a park ranger, or a local hiking organization. Do not attempt a hike beyond your ability—you may be endangering your life. Of particular concern in Austria and Switzerland is **glacier hiking.** Never hike over glaciers alone. Snow-covered crevasses in glaciers have swallowed many an unsuspecting hiker. See Health, p. 20, for information about outdoor ailments such as heatstroke, hypothermia, giardia, rabies, and insects, as well as basic medical concerns and first-aid.

For more information, consult *How to Stay Alive in the Woods,* by Bradford Angier (Macmillan, US$8).

CAMPING AND HIKING EQUIPMENT...

Purchase equipment before you leave so that you'll know exactly what you have and how much it weighs. Spend some time examining catalogues and talking to knowledgeable salespeople. Camping equipment is generally more expensive in Australia, New Zealand, and the UK than in North America.

Sleeping Bag: Most good sleeping bags are rated by "season," or the lowest outdoor temperature at which they will keep you warm ("summer" means 30-40°F at night and "four-season" or "winter" often means below 0°F). Sleeping bags are made either of down (warmer and lighter, but more expensive, and miserable when wet) or of synthetic material (heavier, more durable, and warmer when wet). Prices vary, but might range from US$80-210 for a summer synthetic to US$250-300 for a good down winter bag. For **sleeping bag pads** you can choose from foam pads (US$10-20) or air mattresses (US$15-50). Both types cushion your back and neck and insulate you from the ground. Therm-A-Rest brand self-inflating sleeping pads are part foam and part air-mattress that partially inflate upon unrolling, US$45-80. Bring a **"stuff sack"** or plastic bag to store your sleeping bag and keep it dry.

Backpack: If you intend to do a lot of hiking, you should have a frame backpack. **Internal-frame packs** mold better to your back, keep a lower center of gravity, and can flex to allow you to hike difficult trails that require a lot of bending and maneuvering (external-frame packs are the skeletal ancestors of internal frame packs). Make sure your pack has a strong, padded hip belt, which transfers the weight from the shoulders to the legs. Any serious backpacking requires a pack of at least 3000 cubic inches (12,000cc). Sturdy backpacks cost anywhere from US$125-420. Before you buy any pack, try it on and imagine carrying it, full; insist on filling it with something heavy and walking around the store to get a sense of how it distributes weight before committing to buy it. A **waterproof backpack cover** will prove invaluable. Otherwise, plan to store all of your belongings in plastic bags inside your backpack.

Boots: Be sure to wear hiking boots with good **ankle support** regardless of the terrain you are hiking in. Your boots should fit snugly and comfortably over a pair of wool socks and a thin liner sock. Breaking in boots properly before setting out requires wearing them for several weeks; doing so will spare you from painful and debilitating blisters. If you're planning on doing any serious hiking your boots should be waterproof, with Gore-Tex or a similar fabric. In addition, the fewer seams a boot has the more waterproof it will be–the best hiking boots are solid leather–flashy boots with different fabrics allow for many seams through which water can leak.

Tent: The best tents are free-standing (with their own frames and suspension systems), set up quickly, and only require staking in high winds. Low-profile dome tents are the best all-around. Good 2-person tents start at US$90, 4-person at US$300. Seal the seams of your tent with waterproofer, and make sure it has a rain fly. Other tent accessories include a **battery-operated lantern,** a **plastic groundcloth,** and a **nylon tarp.**

Other Necessities: Raingear in two pieces, a top and pants, is far superior to a poncho. Three-layer Gore-Tex is more waterproof and breathable than two-layer, but the difference will be negligible for casual hikers. **Synthetic materials,** like polypropylene tops, socks, and long underwear, along with a pile jacket, will keep you warm even when wet. When camping in autumn, winter, or spring, bring along a **"space blanket,"** which helps you to retain your body heat and doubles as a groundcloth (US$5-15). Plastic **canteens** or water bottles keep water cooler than metal ones do, and are virtually shatter- and leak-proof. Large, collapsible **water sacks** will significantly improve your lot in primitive campgrounds and weigh practically nothing when empty. Bring **water-purification tablets** (iodine) for when you can't boil water, unless you are willing to shell out money for a portable water-purification system. Though most campgrounds provide campfire sites, you may want to bring a small metal grate or grill of your own. For those places that forbid fires or the gathering of firewood (virtually every organized campground in Europe), you'll need a **camp stove.** The classic Coleman stove starts at about US$40. Purchase a fuel bottle and fill it with propane to operate it. A **first aid kit, Swiss Army knife, insect repellent, calamine lotion,** and **waterproof matches** or a **lighter** are other essential camping items.

...AND WHERE TO BUY IT

The mail-order/online companies listed below offer lower prices than many retail stores, but a visit to a local camping or outdoors store will give you a good sense of the look and weight of certain items.

Campmor, P.O. Box 700, Upper Saddle River, NJ 07458 (US ☎(888) 226-7667; elsewhere call US +1 (201) 825-8300; www.campmor.com).

Discount Camping, 880 Main North Rd., Pooraka, South Australia 5095, Australia (☎(08) 826 23399; www.discountcamping.com.au).

Eastern Mountain Sports (EMS), 327 Jaffrey Rd., Peterborough, NH 03458, USA (☎ (888) 463-6367 or (603) 924-7231; www.shopems.com).

L.L. Bean, Freeport, ME 04033 (US and Canada ☎(800) 441-5713; UK ☎(0800) 962 954; elsewhere, call US +1 (207) 552-6878; www.llbean.com).

Mountain Designs, P.O. Box 1472, Fortitude Valley, Queensland 4006, Australia (☎(07) 325 28894; www.mountaindesign.com.au).

Recreational Equipment, Inc. (REI), Sumner, WA 98352, USA (☎(800) 426-4840 or (253) 891-2500; www.rei.com).

YHA Adventure Shop, 14 Southampton St., London, WC2E 7HA, UK (☎(020) 783 68541). The main branch of one of Britain's largest outdoor equipment suppliers.

CAMPERS AND RVS

Many North American campers harbor a suspicion that traveling with a **camper** or **recreational vehicle** (RV) is not "real camping." The stigma is not as prevalent in Europe, where RV camping, or "caravanning," is both popular and common. European RVs are smaller and more economical than the 40-foot Winnebagos of the American road. Renting an RV will always be more expensive than camping or hosteling, but the costs compare favorably with the price of staying in hotels and renting a car (see Rental Cars, p. 50) and the convenience of bringing along your own bedroom, bathroom, and kitchen makes it an attractive option for some, especially older travelers and families with small children.

It is not difficult to arrange an RV rental from overseas, although you will want to begin gathering information several months before your departure. Rates vary widely by region, season (July and August are the most expensive months), and type of RV. It always pays to contact several different companies to compare vehicles and prices (see p. 47).

FURTHER INFORMATION: CAMPING AND RVS.

Camping Your Way through Europe, Carol Mickelsen (US$15).

Exploring Europe by RV, Dennis and Tina Jaffe (US$15).

Great Outdoor Recreation Pages, www.gorp.com.

The Caravan Club, East Grinstead House, East Grinstead, West Sussex, RH19 1UA, UK (☎(01342) 326 944; fax 410 258; www.caravanclub.co.uk). Produces one of the most detailed English-language guides to campsites in Europe.

SKIING

Western **Austria** is one of the world's best skiing regions. The areas around Innsbruck and Kitzbühel in Tyrol are saturated with lifts and runs. Skiers swoosh down some glaciers into the summer in the Ötztal, the Dachstein in the Salzkammergut, and Hintertux near Mayerhofen, among other places. High season normally runs from mid-December to mid-January and from February to March. Tourist offices provide information on regional skiing and can suggest budget travel agencies that offer ski packages.

Contrary to popular belief, **skiing in Switzerland** is often less expensive than in the US if you avoid the pricey resorts. Ski passes (valid for transportation to, from, and on lifts) run 30-50SFr per day and 100-300SFr per week. A week of lift tickets, equipment rental, lessons, lodging, and *demi-pension* (half-board—breakfast plus one other meal, usually dinner) averages 475SFr. Summer skiing is no longer as prevalent as it once was, but it's still available in a few towns like Zermatt, Saas Fee, and Les Diablerets.

With peaks between 3000 and 30,000m, the Alpine vertical drop is ample—1000 to 2000m at all major resorts. For mountain country, winter **weather** in the Austrian Alps is moderate, thanks to lower elevation and distance from the ocean. Daytime temperatures in the coldest months (Jan. and Feb.) measure around -7°C (20°F). Humidity is low, so snow on the ground stays powdery longer.

KEEPING IN TOUCH

MAIL

Austria and Switzerland have rapid, efficient postal systems. Letters take 1 to 3 days within Switzerland and 1 to 2 days within Austria. Airmail from North America takes 4 to 5 days to either country. Mark all letters and packages "mit flugpost" or "par avion." In all cases, include the postal code if you know it; those of Swiss cities begin with "CH," Austrian with "A."

SENDING MAIL TO AUSTRIA AND SWITZERLAND. Mark envelopes "airmail" or "par avion" to avoid having letters sent by sea.

Australia: Allow 4-7 days for regular **airmail** to Austria and Switzerland. Postcards cost AUS$1, letters up to 50g cost AUS$1.50; packages up to 0.5kg AUS$13, up to 2kg AUS$46. **EMS** can get a letter to the two countries in 3-5 days for AUS$32. www.auspost.com.au/pac.

Canada: Allow 4-7 days for regular **airmail** to Austria and Switzerland. Postcards and letters up to 20g cost CDN$0.95; packages up to 0.5kg CDN$8.50, up to 2kg CDN$28.30. www.canadapost.ca/CPC2/common/rates/ratesgen.html#international.

Ireland: Allow 3-4 days for regular airmail to Austria and Switzerland. Postcards and letters up to 25g cost IR£0.32. Add IR£2.30 for Swiftpost International. www.letterpost.ie.

New Zealand: Allow 5-9 days for regular airmail to Austria and Switzerland. Postcards NZ$1.10. Letters up to 20g cost NZ$1.80-6; small parcels up to 0.5kg NZ$13.20, up to 2kg NZ$41.70. www.nzpost.co.nz/nzpost/inrates.

UK: Allow 3-5 days for airmail to Austria and Switzerland. Letters up to 20g cost UK£0.36; packages up to 0.5kg UK£2.67, up to 2kg UK£9.42. UK Swiftair delivers letters a day faster for UK£2.85 more. www.royalmail.co.uk/calculator.

US: Allow 4-8 days for regular **airmail** to Austria and Switzerland. Postcards/aerogrammes cost US$0.55/0.60; letters under 1 oz. US$1. Packages under 1 lb. cost US$7.20; larger packages cost a variable amount (around US$15). **US Express Mail** takes 2-3 days and costs US$19/23 (0.5/1 lb.). **US Global Priority Mail** delivers small/large flat-rate envelopes to Austria and Switzerland in 3-5 days for US$5/9. http://ircalc.usps.gov.

Additionally, **Federal Express** (Australia ☎ 132 610; US and Canada ☎ (800) 247-4747; New Zealand ☎ (0800) 733 339; UK ☎ (0800) 123 800) handles express mail services from most of the above countries to Austria and Switzerland; for example, they can get a letter from New York to Austria and Switzerland in 2 days for US$25.50. Rates among non-US locations are prohibitively expensive (London to Vienna, for example, costs upwards of US$56). By **US Express Mail,** a letter from New York would arrive within four days and would cost US$1.

RECEIVING MAIL IN AUSTRIA AND SWITZERLAND. There are a few ways to arrange pick-up of letters sent to you by friends and relatives while you are abroad:

General Delivery: Mail can be sent to Austria and Switzerland through **Poste Restante** (the international phrase for General Delivery; *Postlagernde Briefe*) to almost any city or town with a post office. Address *Poste Restante* letters to: Katie SCHULTZ, *Postlagernde Briefe,* A-1010 Vienna, Austria. In Switzerland use the same formula, though the postal code will be preceded by a CH. The mail will go to a special desk in the central post office, unless you specify a post office by street address or postal code. As a rule, it is best to use the largest post office in the area, and mail may be sent there regardless of what is written on the envelope. It is usually safer and quicker to send mail express or registered. When picking up your mail, bring a form of photo ID, preferably a passport. There is generally no surcharge; if there is a charge, it generally does not exceed the cost of domestic postage. If the clerks insist that there is nothing for you, have them check under your first name as well. *Let's Go* lists post offices in the **Practical Information** section for each city and most towns.

American Express: AmEx's travel offices throughout the world offer a free **Client Letter Service** (mail held up to 30 days and forwarded upon request) for cardholders who contact them in advance. Address the letter in the same way shown above. Some offices will offer these services to non-cardholders (especially AmEx Travelers' Cheque holders), but call ahead to make sure. *Let's Go* lists AmEx office locations for most large cities in **Practical Information** sections; for a complete, free list, call (800) 528-4800.

Surface mail is by far the cheapest and slowest way to send mail. It takes 1 to 3 months to cross the Atlantic and 2 to 4 to cross the Pacific, appropriate for sending large quantities of items you won't need to see for a while. When ordering books and materials from abroad, always include 1 or 2 **International Reply Coupons (IRCs)**, a way of providing the postage to cover delivery. IRCs should be available from your local post office and those abroad (US$1.05).

SENDING MAIL HOME FROM AUSTRIA AND SWITZERLAND. For **airmail** transit times see Sending Mail to Austria and Switzerland, above. To send a postcard or letter under 250g from Switzerland to an international destination within Europe costs 1.10SFr first class and .90SFr second class, and to any other international destination via airmail costs 1.80SFr first class and 1.10SFr second class. Domestically, postcards require .90SFr first class and .70SFr second class.

To send a postcard or letter under 250g from Austria to an international destination within Europe costs 7AS, and to any other international destination via airmail costs 13AS. **Aerogrammes,** printed sheets that fold into envelopes and travel via airmail, are available at post offices. It helps to mark "mit luftpost" if possible, though "par avion" is universally understood. Most post offices will charge exorbitant fees or simply refuse to send aerogrammes with enclosures. **Surface mail** is by far the cheapest and slowest way to send mail. It takes 1 to 3 months to cross the Atlantic and 2 to 4 to cross the Pacific—good for items you won't need to see for a while, such as souvenirs or other articles you've acquired along the way that are weighing down your pack.

TELEPHONES

CALLING AUSTRIA OR SWITZERLAND FROM HOME. To call Austria or Switzerland from home, dial:

1. The international prefix for your home country. **International access codes** include: Australia 0011; Ireland 00; New Zealand 00; South Africa 09; UK 00; US 011. Country codes and city codes are sometimes listed with a zero in front (e.g., 033), but after dialing the international access code, drop successive zeros (with an access code of 011, e.g., 011 33).
2. 43 (for Austria) or 41 (for Switzerland).
3. The city code minus the 0 (see the city's **Phone Code** box) and local number.

CALLING HOME FROM AUSTRIA OR SWITZERLAND. A **calling card** is probably your best and cheapest bet. Calls are billed either collect or to your account. **To obtain a calling card** from your national telecommunications service before you leave home, contact the appropriate company below. Ask your calling card provider for directions on calling home with their calling card.

Australia: Telstra **Australia Direct** (☎132 200)

Canada: Bell Canada **Canada Direct** (☎(800) 565-4708)

Ireland: Telecom Éireann **Ireland Direct** (☎(800) 250 250)

New Zealand: Telecom New Zealand (☎(0800) 000 000):

South Africa: Telkom South Africa (☎09 03)

UK: British Telecom **BT Direct** (☎(800) 345 144)

US: AT&T (☎(888) 288-4685), **Sprint** (☎(800) 877-4646), or **MCI** (☎(800) 444-4141).

To **call home with a calling card** or to make a **collect call,** contact the operator for your service provider in Austria and Switzerland by dialing the appropriate toll-free access number:

AT&T: Austria (☎(022) 903 011) Switzerland (☎(0800) 890 011).

Sprint: Austria (☎(0800) 200 236) Switzerland (☎(0800) 890 978).

MCI WorldPhone Direct: Austria (☎(022) 903 012) Switzerland (☎(0800) 890 222).

Canada Direct: Austria (☎(0800) 200 217) Switzerland (☎(0800) 558 330).

BT Direct: Austria (☎(0800) 200 209) Switzerland (☎(0800) 552 544).

Telecom New Zealand Direct: Austria (☎(022) 903 064) Switzerland (☎(0800) 556 411).

Telkom South Africa Direct: Austria (☎(022) 903 027) Switzerland (☎(0800) 558 535).

Wherever possible, use a calling card for international phone calls, as the long-distance rates for national phone services are often exorbitant. You can usually make direct international calls from pay phones, but if you aren't using a calling card you may need to drop your coins as quickly as your words. Where available, **prepaid phone cards** and occasionally **major credit cards** can be used for direct international calls, but they are still less cost-efficient.

If you dial direct, first insert the appropriate amount of money or a prepaid card, then dial the country code and number you want to call (61 (Australia), 353 (Ireland), 64 (New Zealand), 27 (South Africa), 44 (UK), 001 (US and Canada)). The expensive alternative to dialing direct or using a calling card is using an international operator to place a **collect call.** An English-speaking operator from your home nation can be reached by dialing the provider for your country with the phone numbers listed above.

CALLING WITHIN AUSTRIA AND SWITZERLAND. The simplest way to call within the country is to use a pay phone. Most pay phones in Switzerland, and more and more in Austria, accept only **prepaid phone cards** and not coins. Phone cards are available at kiosks, post offices, or train stations. Phone rates are highest in the morning, lower in the evening, and lowest on Sunday and late at night. Dial the city code (refer to the phone code box in each city's Practical Information) before each number when calling from outside the city; within the city, dial only the actual number.

EMAIL AND INTERNET

Internet access is widespread in Austria and Switzerland. You can check your email from cybercafés, which *Let's Go* lists in the Practical Information section for each city, and sometimes from universities, libraries, and hostels. Though limited free access is sometimes available in bookstores and libraries, regular Internet access isn't cheap; in Switzerland the standard price is 12SFr per hour, in Austria it is 50-100AS. For a complete listing of cybercafés in Austria and Switzerland, visit cybercaptive.com or netcafeguide.com.

Free, web-based email providers include Hotmail (www.hotmail.com), RocketMail (www.rocketmail.com), and Yahoo! Mail (www.yahoo.com). Almost every Internet search engine has an affiliated free email service.

GETTING THERE

BY PLANE

When it comes to airfare, a little effort can save you a bundle. If your plans are flexible enough to deal with the restrictions, courier fares are the cheapest. Tickets bought from consolidators and standby seating are also good deals, but last-minute specials, airfare wars, and charter flights often beat these fares. The key is to hunt around, to be flexible, and to ask persistently about discounts. Students, seniors, and those under 26 should never pay full price for a ticket.

DETAILS AND TIPS

Timing: Airfares to Austria and Switzerland peak between July and August; holidays are also expensive periods during which to travel. During ski season, it may be cheaper to fly to a non-skiing destination, like Paris or Frankfurt, and then take the train. Midweek (M-Th morning) round-trip flights run US$40-50 cheaper than weekend flights, but the latter are generally less crowded and more likely to permit frequent-flier upgrades. Return-date flexibility is usually not an option for the budget traveler; traveling with an "open return" ticket can be pricier than fixing a return date when buying the ticket and paying later to change it.

Route: Round-trip flights are by far the cheapest; "open-jaw" tickets (arriving in and departing from different cities) are pricier but reasonable alternatives. Patching one-way flights together is the least economical way to travel, though frequently student travel agencies will allow you to do this for no extra charge. Student tickets will also frequently allow free, lengthy lay overs in hub cities (Paris, London, Frankfurt). Flights between capital cities or regional hubs will offer the most competitive fares.

Boarding: Whenever flying internationally, pick up tickets for international flights well in advance of the departure date and confirm by phone within 72hr. of departure. Most airlines require that passengers arrive at the airport at least two hours before departure. One carry-on item and two pieces of checked baggage is the norm for non-courier flights. Consult the airline for weight allowances.

Fares: Fares from the US to Austria and Switzerland vary tremendously depending on airfare wars and special deals. For a round-trip ticket during peak season, expect to spend anywhere from US$400-$1000; $200-400 during off-season. It's worth extra effort to find bargain fares!

BUDGET AND STUDENT TRAVEL AGENCIES

A knowledgeable agent specializing in flights to Austria and Switzerland can make your life easy and help you save too, but agents may not spend the time to find you the lowest possible fare—they get paid on commission. Students and under-26ers holding **ISIC and IYTC cards** (see Identification, p. 10), respectively, qualify for big discounts from student travel agencies. Most flights from budget agencies are on major airlines, but in peak season some may sell seats on chartered aircraft.

STA Travel (www.sta-travel.com). A student and youth travel organization with over 240 offices worldwide. Ticket booking, travel insurance, railpasses, and more. STA has offices in 18 **US** states, call (800) 777-0112 for locations. For the location of 40 branches in the **UK,** call (0171) 938 4711. In **South Africa,** call (012) 342 5292 for information on 9 branches. Call 1 300 135 541 in **Australia** and (0800) 800 272 in **New Zealand.** The website has a listing of all the offices worldwide along with online reservations.

Campus/Usit Youth and Student Travel (www.usitcampus.co.uk) is the main budget travel agency for Britain, Ireland, and New Zealand. For offices in the **UK,** call 441 71 437 7767, in **Ireland,** the number is ☎353 1602 1600, and in **New Zealand,** call (649) 379 4224.

Council Travel (www.counciltravel.com). Call (800) 2-COUNCIL for over 60 offices in the **US.**

Travel CUTS (Canadian Universities Travel Services Limited) (www.travelcuts.com) has 61 offices in **Canada**, call (416) 614-2887 for locations. Call (0207) 255 2082 for 3 offices in the **UK**

Wasteels (www.wasteels.dk/uk). Danish chain specializes in train tickets, but also has youth plane tickets. One office in the **UK** at Victoria Station, London, UK SW1V 1JT (☎ (0171) 834 7066; fax 630 7628). Sells the Wasteels BIJ tickets, which are discounted (30-45% off regular fare) 2nd-class international point-to-point train tickets with unlimited stopovers (must be under 26); sold only in Europe.

COMMERCIAL AIRLINES. The commercial airlines' lowest regular offer is the **APEX** (Advance Purchase Excursion) fare, which provides confirmed reservations and allows "open-jaw" tickets. Generally, reservations must be made 7 to 21 days in advance, with 7- to 14-day minimum and up to 90-day maximum-stay limits, and hefty cancellation and change penalties (fees rise in summer). Book peak-season APEX fares early, since by May you will have a hard time getting the departure date you want.

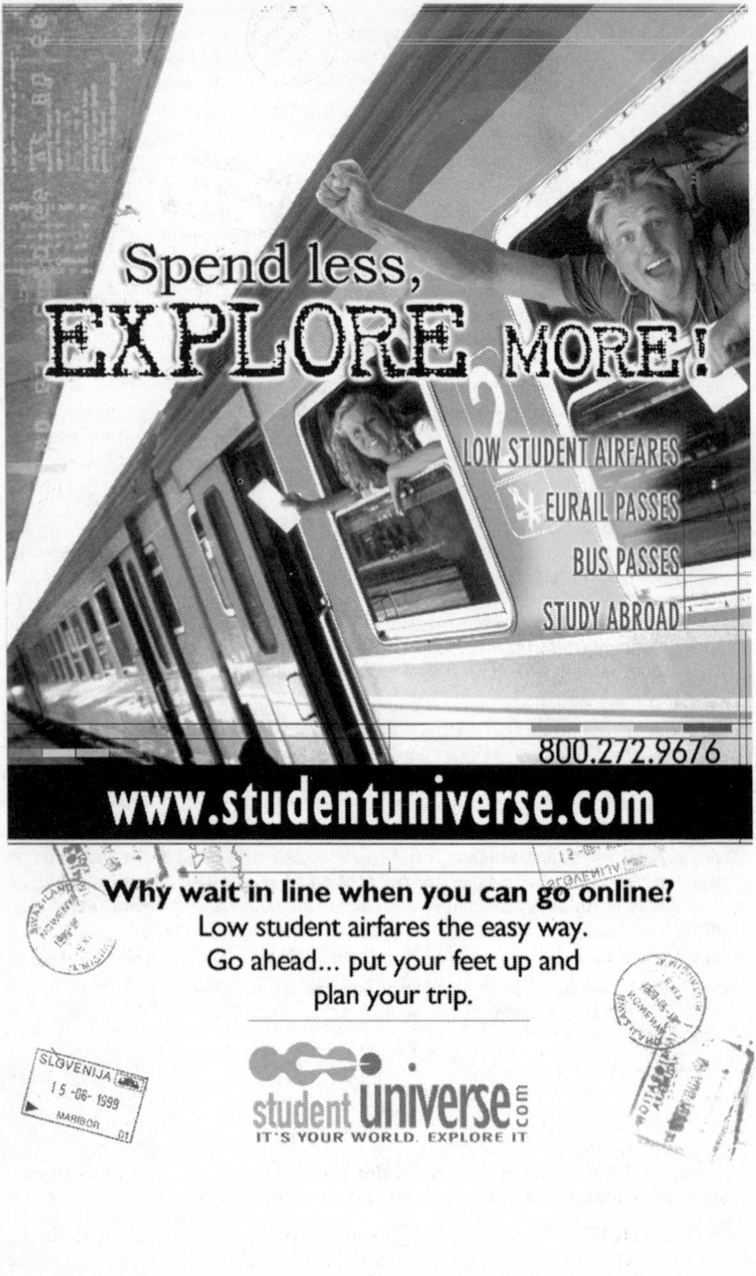
Spend less,
EXPLORE MORE!
LOW STUDENT AIRFARES
EURAIL PASSES
BUS PASSES
STUDY ABROAD
800.272.9676
www.studentuniverse.com
Why wait in line when you can go online?
Low student airfares the easy way.
Go ahead... put your feet up and
plan your trip.
student universe.com
IT'S YOUR WORLD. EXPLORE IT
SLOVENIJA
15-06-1999
MARIBOR

Although APEX fares are probably not the cheapest possible fares, they will give you a sense of the average commercial price, from which to measure other bargains. Specials advertised in newspapers may be cheaper but have more restrictions and fewer available seats. For cheap commercial flights in the **US,** check **Icelandair** (☎(800) 223-5500; www.icelandair.com). They have stopovers in Iceland for no extra cost on most transatlantic flights. New York to Frankfurt from May-Sept. is US$470-710; Oct.-May US$370-$425. For last-minute offers, subscribe to their email Lucky Fares. In the **UK** check **buzz** (☎(0870) 240 7070; www.buzzaway.com), a subsidiary of KLM. Tickets from London to Vienna run from UK£50-80. Tickets can not be changed or refunded. Also try **EasyJet** in the UK (☎(0870) 600 0000; www.easyjet.com). Flights from London to Geneva, and Zurich are UK£47-136. Online tickets available. **Aer Lingus** in Ireland (☎(01) 886 8888; www.aerlingus.ie) has return tickets from Dublin, Cork, Galway, Kerry, and Shannon to Munich and Zürich from IR£102-240.

The most popular carriers to Austria and Switzerland are Austrian Air, Swiss Air, and Lufthansa.

OTHER CHEAP ALTERNATIVES

AIR COURIER FLIGHTS

TRAVELING FROM NORTH AMERICA. Round-trip courier fares from the US to Western Europe run about US$200-500. Most flights leave from New York, Los Angeles, San Francisco, or Miami in the US; and from Montreal, Toronto, or Vancouver in Canada. The first four organizations below provide their members with lists of opportunities and courier brokers worldwide for an annual fee (typically US$50-60). While no courier companies fly to Austria or Switzerland, the following are the largest companies with flights to Western Europe: **Air Courier Association** (☎(800) 282-1202; www.aircourier.org), one-year membership costs US$64. **Global Courier Travel,** has a searchable online database (www.globalcouriertravel.com); one year membership is US$40, 2 people US$55. **International Association of Air Travel Couriers (IAATC)** (☎(561) 582-8320; fax 582-1581; www.courier.org), membership is US$45-50. **NOW Voyager** (☎(212) 431-1616; fax 219-1753; www.nowvoyagertravel.com), costs US$50. **Worldwide Courier Association** (☎(800) 780-4359, ext. 441; www.massiveweb.com), is US$58.

FROM THE UK, IRELAND, AUSTRALIA, AND NEW ZEALAND. Although the courier industry is most developed from North America, there are limited courier flights in other areas. The minimum age for couriers from the **UK** is usually 18. **Brave New World Enterprises,** P.O. Box 22212, London SE5 8WB (guideinfo@nry.co.uk; www.nry.co.uk/bnw); publishes a directory of all the companies offering courier flights in the UK (UK£10, in electronic form UK£8). The **International Association of Air Travel Couriers** (see above) often offers courier flights from London to Budapest. **Global Courier Travel** (see above) also offer flights from London and Dublin to continental Europe. **British Airways Travel Shop** (☎(0870) 606 1133; www.british-airways.com/travelqa/booking/travshop/travshop.shtml) arranges some flights from London to destinations in continental Europe (specials may be as low as UK£60; no registration fee). From **Australia** and **New Zealand, Global Courier Travel** (see above) often has listings from Sydney and Auckland to London and occasionally Frankfurt.

CHARTER FLIGHTS. Charters are flights a tour operator contracts with an airline to fly extra loads of passengers during peak season. Charters can sometimes be cheaper than flights on scheduled airlines, some operate nonstop, and restrictions on minimum advance-purchase and minimum stay are more lenient. However, charter flights fly less frequently than major airlines, make refunds particularly difficult, and are almost always fully booked. Schedules and itineraries may also change or be cancelled at the last moment (as late as

48 hours before the trip, and without a full refund), and check-in, boarding, and baggage claim are often much slower. As always, pay with a credit card if you can, and consider traveler's insurance against trip interruption.

Discount clubs and **fare brokers** offer members savings on last-minute charter and tour deals. Study their contracts closely; you don't want to end up with an unwanted overnight layover. **Travelers' Advantage,** Stamford, CT (☎(800) 259-2691; www.travelersadvantage.com; US$60 annual fee includes discounts, newsletters, and cheap flight directories), specializes in European travel and tour packages.

STANDBY FLIGHTS. To travel standby, you will need considerable flexibility in the dates and cities of your arrival and departure. Companies that specialize in standby flights don't sell tickets but rather the promise that you will get to your destination (or near your destination) within a certain window of time (anywhere from 1-5 days). You may only receive a monetary refund if all available flights which depart within your date-range from the specified region are full, but future travel credit is always available.

Carefully read agreements with any company offering standby flights, as tricky fine print can leave you in the lurch. To check on a company's service record, call the Better Business Bureau of New York City (☎(212) 533-6200). It is difficult to receive refunds, and clients' vouchers will not be honored when an airline fails to receive payment in time.

TICKET CONSOLIDATORS. Ticket consolidators, popularly known as **"bucket shops,"** buy unsold tickets in bulk from commercial airlines and sell them at discounted rates. The best place to look is in the Sunday travel section of any major newspaper, where many bucket shops place tiny ads. Call quickly, as availability is typically extremely limited. Not all bucket shops are reliable establishments, so insist on a receipt that gives full details of restrictions, refunds, and tickets, and pay by credit card. For more information, check the website Consolidators FAQ (www.travel-library.com/air-travel/consolidators.html) or the book *Consolidators: Air Travel's Bargain Basement*, by Kelly Monaghan (Intrepid Traveler, US$8).

ONCE THERE

TOURIST INFORMATION AND TOWN LAYOUTS. The **Swiss National Tourist Office** and the **Austrian National Tourist Office** publish a wealth of information about tours and vacations; every single town has a tourist office. To simplify things, all offices are marked by a standard "i" sign (green in Austria, blue in Switzerland). *Let's Go* lists tourist offices in the Practical Information section of each city. The staff may or may not speak English—the skill is not a requirement in smaller towns; we'll try and let you know whether they do or don't. Tourist offices are good for free maps. In Swiss cities, look for the excellent **Union Bank of Switzerland maps,** which have very detailed streets and sites.

One thing to keep in mind is that Austrian and Swiss creativity in naming small towns is pretty meager. Many towns, even within the same state or province, have the same names (Gmünd or Stein, for instance). Most Austrian and Swiss train stations have luggage storage, currency exchange, and bike rentals (at a discount if you have a train ticket for that day or a valid railpass). The **post office** is often next door to the train station, even in larger cities. Most towns are small enough that all sights are within walking distance. Public transportation is usually pretty good, too. Buy local public transport tickets from *Tabak* stands, which sell them for reduced rates. Most ticket validation is based on the honor system, and many tourists interpret that as a free ride. Though certainly a tempting budget option, **Schwarzfahren** (i.e. riding without a ticket) can result in big anti-budget fines, and playing "dumb tourist" probably won't work.

GETTING AROUND

Fares on all modes of transportation are either one-way ("single") or round-trip ("return"). "Period returns" require you to return within a specific number of days; "day return" means you must return on the same day. Unless stated otherwise, *Let's Go* always lists one-way fares.

BY TRAIN

Given that trains are likely to be your preferred mode of transportation in Austria and Switzerland, it is fortunate that European trains are generally comfortable, convenient, and reasonably swift. In fact, the train can get you places throughout Austria and Switzerland where a car cannot. European trains retain the charm and romance that their North American counterparts lost generations ago. Second-class travel is pleasant, and compartments, which seat 2-6, are excellent places to meet fellow travelers. Trains, however, are not always safe; lock your compartment door (if possible) and keep your valuables on your person at all times. Non-smokers probably won't be comfortable in smoking compartments, which tend to be very, very smoky. Get your stuff together a few stops early since trains pause only a few minutes before zipping off. For longer trips, make sure that you are on the correct car, as trains sometimes split at crossroads. Towns in parentheses on schedules require a train switch at the town listed immediately before the parenthesis. "Salzburg—Attnang-Puchheim—(Bad Ischl—Hallstatt)" means that in order to get to Bad Ischl or Hallstatt, you have to disembark at Attnang-Puchheim and pick up a different train. You might want to ask if your route requires a changing trains, as the schedules are sometimes as decipherable as dolphin squeaks.

The **Österreichische Bundesbahn** (ÖBB), Austria's federal railroad, is one of Europe's most thorough and efficient. The ÖBB prints the yearly *Fahrpläne Kursbuch Bahn-Inland*, a compilation of all rail, ferry, and cable-car transportation schedules in Austria. The massive compendium is available at any large train station, along with its companion tomes, the *Kursbuch Bahn-Ausland* for international trains, and the *Internationales Schlafwagenkursbuch* for sleeping cars. You can also consult the ÖBB website at www.oebb.at/index.html (in German only), or call (01) 93 00 00 (in German only).

Getting around Switzerland is also a snap. Federal **(SBB, CFF)** and private railways connect most towns and villages, with trains running in each direction on an hourly basis. **Schnellzüge** (express trains) speed between metropoli, while **Regionalzüge** chug into podunk cowtowns. The national telephone number for rail information is ☎0 900 300 300 and has operators who speak English, German, French, and Italian, but it costs 1.19SFr per minute. Check the website for the federal railway system at www.sbb.ch (available in French, German, Italian, and English versions), or email them at railinfo@sbb.ch (answered only Monday through Friday). Be aware that sometimes only private train lines go to remote tourist spots; therefore Eurail and SwissPasses might not be valid. Yellow signs announce departure times *(Ausfahrt, départ, partenze)* and platforms *(Gleis, quai, binario)*. White signs are for arrivals *(Ankunft, arrivé, arrivo)*. On major Austrian lines, make reservations at least a few hours in advance.

Even with a railpass, you are not guaranteed a seat unless you make a **reservation** US$11; they are advisable during the busier holiday seasons and often required on major lines. Also, while many high-speed or quality trains (e.g., EuroCity and InterCity) are included in a railpass, a supplement (also US$11) is required to ride certain international trains. For overnight travel, a tight, open bunk called a **couchette** is an affordable luxury (about US$28). Both seat and couchette reservations can be made by your local travel agent or in person at the train station (reserve at least a few hours in advance for seats; at least a few days for couchettes).

RAIL TICKETS AND DISCOUNTS

You can purchase **individual tickets** at every train station in Austria and Switzerland, at Bahn-Total service stations, at the occasional automat, and from the conductor for a small surcharge. Over 130 stations accept the major credit cards as well as American Express Traveler's Cheques and Eurocheques.

In Austria, children under 6 travel free, while children ages 6-12 receive a 50% discount. In Switzerland, travelers under 16 travel free with a parent with the Swiss Family Card (see p. 42). When traveling without a parent, children up to sixteen years have a 50% discount on all the offers of the Swiss Travel System.

For tourists under 26, **BIJ** tickets (Billets Internationals de Jeunesse; a.k.a. **Wasteels, Eurotrain,** and **Route 26**) are a great alternative to railpasses. Available for international trips within Europe as well as most ferry services, they knock 20-40% off regular second-class fares. Tickets are good for 60 days after purchase and allow a number of stopovers along the normal direct route of the train journey. Issued for a specific international route between two points, they must be used in the direction and order of the designated route and must be bought in Europe. The equivalent for those over 26, **BIGT** tickets provide a 20-30% discount on 1st- and 2nd-class international tickets for business travelers, temporary residents of Europe, and their families. Both types of tickets are available from European travel agents, at Wasteels or Eurotrain offices (usually in or near train stations), or directly at the ticket counter. For more info, contact **Wasteels,** Laupenstrasse 19, Bern 3008, ☎(031) 381 1555, fax (031) 381 3230, or check www.wasteels.dk/uk/ for the Wasteels nearest you.

RAILPASSES

Ideally, a railpass allows you to jump on any train in the specified zone, go wherever you want whenever you want, and change your plans at will for a set length of time. In practice, it's not so simple; you must still wait to pay for supplements, seat reservations, and couchette reservations, as well as have your pass validated when you first use it. More importantly, railpasses don't always pay off. For ballpark estimates, consult the **DERTravel** or **RailEurope** railpass brochure for prices of point-to-point tickets. The brochures should be available in most travel agencies. DER-Travel brochures can be ordered online at www.dertravel.com. You can also get prices of point-to-point tickets from the federal railways themselves (see p. 39). Add them up and compare with railpass prices.

SINGLE-NATION RAILPASSES

NATIONAL RAILPASSES. The domestic analogs of the Eurailpass (see p. 42), national railpasses are valid either for a given number of consecutive days or for a specific number of days within a given time period. National railpasses are the way to go if you're going to be covering long distances within Austria or Switzerland. Nearly all are sold either through RailEurope or at local train stations (contact www.raileurope.com for more info, or dial 1-800-4EURAIL). Consider the following options:

Austrian Railpass: Sold worldwide, this pass is valid for 3 days of unlimited train travel in a 15-day period on all Austrian Federal Railway lines, state, and private rail lines in Austria, also grants a 40% discount on bicycle rental in over 130 railway stations and 50% discount on DDSG steamers between Passau and Linz and 20% on steamers between Melk, Krems, and Vienna. You can purchase up to 5 additional rail days. 1 adult, 2nd class $104, each additional day $16. Travelers ages 6-12 travel at half price. The card itself has no photo, so you must carry a valid ID in case of inspections.

VORTEILS card Senior: The ÖBB offers a discount card for women over 60 and men over 65 called the Vorteils Card Senior, available in train stations and most travel agencies. Holders get 50% off train fares, 25% off selected steamers, currency exchange at half the charge, and various other benefits. Good in Austria for 1 year. 350AS, requires a photo and proof of age. Call 01 93000 36457 for more information. Operators speak German only.

VORTEILS card Schüler: Offers similar benefits as the Vorteils Card Senior, only for students. Good in Austria for one year. 250AS, requires a photo and an ISIC card for non-Austrian students. Call 01 93000 36457 for more information. Operators speak German only.

VORTEILScard Behinderte: Offers similar benefits as the Vorteils Card Senior for travelers with disabilities. Good in Austria for 1 year. 250 AS, requires identification and proof of status, no photo necessary. Call 01 93000 36457 for more information. Operators speak German only.

Swiss Transfer Ticket: Good for a one-day trip from any entry point (airport or border crossing) to any single destination within Switzerland, and the return trip back to the border, within a period of one month. Second class costs $71.

Swiss Card: Offers the same round trip as the Swiss Transfer Ticket, plus 50% off unlimited rail and bus tickets within the period of the month between your entry and departure. 1 person, 2nd-class costs $104.

SwissPass: Sold worldwide, this pass offers unlimited rail travel for a certain number of consecutive days: choose between 4 days, 8 days, 15 days, 21 days, or 1 month, 1st or 2nd class. In addition to rail travel, it entitles you to unlimited urban transportation in 36 cities, unlimited travel on certain private railways and lake steamers, and 25% discounts on excursions to most mountaintops. 1 adult, second class 4 day-passes start at US$160, 8 days at $220, 15 days at $265, 21 days at $305, and 1 month at $345.

Swiss Saver Pass: Offers the same benefits as the SwissPass at a 15% discount for groups of two or more adults traveling together.

Swiss Flexipass: This pass entitles you to any 3-9 days unlimited rail travel within a 1-month period, 1st or 2nd class, with the same benefits as the SwissPass. Second class adult passes for 3 days start at US$156, 4 days at $184, 5 days at $212, 6 days at $240, 7 days at $261, 8 days at $282, 9 days at $303.

Swiss Saver Flexipass: Offers the same benefits as the Swiss Flexipass at a 15% discount for groups of two or more adults traveling together.

Swiss Family Card: This card allows children under 16 to travel free if accompanied by at least one parent and holder of a SwissPass, Swiss Flexipass, Swiss Transfer Ticket, or Swiss Card. Available free of charge in conjunction with any of these offers.

EURO DOMINO. Like the Interrail Pass (see p. 43), the Euro Domino pass is available to anyone who has lived in Europe for at least six months; it differs in that it is only valid in one country (which you designate upon buying the pass). It is available for 29 European countries, including Austria and Switzerland. Reservations must still be paid for separately. The Euro Domino pass is available for first- and second-class travel (with a special rate for under 26ers), for three to eight days of unlimited travel within a one-month period. Euro Domino is not valid on Eurostar or Thalys trains. **Supplements** for many high-speed trains are included, though you must still pay for **reservations** where they are compulsory. The pass must be bought within your country of residence and can be found at travel agents and major train stations. Below is a sample of prices for Austria and Switzerland:

EURO-DOMINO PASS (SWITZ.)	**3 days**	**5 days**	**8 days**
2nd class	165 SFr	204 SFr	261 SFr
2nd class youth (under 26)	128 SFr	157 SFr	200 SFr
EURO-DOMINO PASS (AUSTRIA)	**3 days**	**5 days**	**8 days**
2nd class	1350 AS	1626 AS	2040 AS
2nd class youth (under 26)	1020 AS	1244 AS	1580 AS

MULTINATIONAL RAILPASSES

EURAILPASS. Eurail is **valid** in most of Western Europe: Austria, Belgium, Denmark, Finland, France, Germany, Greece, Hungary, Italy, Luxembourg, the Netherlands, Norway, Portugal, the Republic of Ireland, Spain, Sweden, and Switzerland. It is **not valid** in the UK. Standard **Eurailpasses,** valid for a consecutive given number of days, are most suitable for those planning on spending extensive time on trains every few days. **Flexipasses,** valid for any 10 or 15 (not necessarily consecutive) days in a two-month period, are more cost-effective for those traveling longer distances less frequently. **Saverpasses** provide first-class travel for travelers in groups of two to five (prices are per person). **Youthpasses** and **Youth Flexipasses** provide parallel second-class perks for those under 26. For more information, check the Eurail website at www.raileurope.com.

EURAILPASSES	**15 days**	**21 days**	**1 month**	**2 months**	**3 months**
1st class Eurailpass	US$554	US$718	US$890	US$1260	US$1558
Eurail Saverpass	US$470	US$610	US$756	US$1072	US$1324
Eurail Youthpass	US$388	US$499	US$623	US$882	US$1089

EURAIL FLEXIPASSES	**10 days in 2 months**	**15 days in 2 months**
1st class Eurail Flexipass	US$654	US$862
Eurail Saver Flexipass	US$556	US$732
Eurail Youth Flexipass	US$458	US$599

Passholders receive a timetable for major routes and a map with details on possible ferry, steamer, bus, car rental, hotel, and Eurostar discounts. Passholders often also receive reduced fares or free passage on many bus and boat lines.

EUROPASS. The Europass is a slimmed-down version of the Eurailpass: it allows five to 15 days of unlimited travel in any two-month period within France, Germany, Italy, Spain, and Switzerland. **First-Class Europasses** (for individuals) and **Saverpasses** (for people traveling in groups of 2-5) range from US$348/296 per person (5 days) to US$728/620 (15 days). **Second-Class Youthpasses** for those ages 12-25 cost US$233-513. For a fee, you can add **additional zones** (including Austria/Hungary): $60 for one associated country, $100 for two. Plan your itinerary before buying a Europass: it will save you money if your travels are confined to three to five adjacent Western European countries, or if you only want to go to large cities, but would be a waste if you plan to make lots of side-trips. If you're tempted to add many rail days and associated countries, consider a Eurailpass.

SHOPPING AROUND FOR A EURAIL OR EUROPASS. Eurailpasses and Europasses are designed by the EU itself and are purchasable only by non-Europeans almost exclusively from non-European distributors. These passes must be sold at uniform prices determined by the EU. However, some travel agents tack on a US$10 handling fee, and others offer certain bonuses with purchase, so shop around. Also, keep in mind that pass prices usually go up each year, so if you're planning to travel early in the year, you can save cash by purchasing before January 1 (you have three months from the purchase date to validate your pass in Europe).

It is best to buy your Eurail- or Europass before leaving; only a few places in major European cities sell them, and at a marked-up price. Once in Europe, you'd probably have to use a credit card to buy over the phone from a railpass agent in a non-EU country (one on the North American East Coast would be closest) who could send the pass to you by express mail. Eurailpasses are non-refundable once validated; if your pass is completely unused and invalidated and you have the original purchase documents, you can get an 85% refund from the place of purchase. You can get a replacement for a lost pass only if you have purchased insurance on it under the Pass Protection Plan (US$10). Eurailpasses are available through travel agents, student travel agencies like STA and Council (see p. 35), and **Rail Europe,** 500 Mamaroneck Ave., Harrison, NY 10528 (US ☎(888) 382-7245, fax (800) 432-1329; Canada ☎(800) 361-7245, fax (905) 602-4198; UK ☎(0990) 848 848; www.raileurope.com) or **DER Travel Services,** 9501 W. Devon Ave. #301, Rosemont, IL 60018 (US ☎(888) 337-7350; fax (800) 282-7474; www.dertravel.com).

INTERRAIL PASS. If you have lived for at least six months in one of the European countries where InterRail Passes are valid, they prove an economical option. There are eight InterRail **zones:** A (Great Britain, Northern Ireland, Republic of Ireland), B (Norway, Sweden, and Finland), C (Germany, Austria, Denmark, and Switzerland), D (Croatia, Czech Republic, Hungary, Poland, and Slovakia), E (France, Belgium, the Netherlands, and Luxembourg), F (Spain, Portugal, and Morocco), G (Greece, Italy, Slovenia, and Turkey, including a Greece-Italy ferry), and H (Bulgaria, Romania, Yugoslavia, and Macedonia).

Under 26 InterRail Card: allows either 14 days or one month of unlimited travel within one, two, three or all of the eight zones; the cost is determined by the number of zones the pass covers (UK£159-259). If you buy a ticket including the zone in which you have claimed residence, you must still pay 50% fare for tickets inside your own country.

FURTHER READING AND RESOURCES ON TRAIN TRAVEL.

Rail schedules: bahn.hafas.de/bin/db.w97/query.exe/en. A testament to German efficiency, with minute-by-minute itineraries and connection information.

Point-to-point fares: www.raileurope.com/us/rail/fares_schedules/index.htm. Allows you to calculate whether buying a railpass would save you money.

European Railway Servers: home.wxs.nl/~grijns/timetables/time.html and mercurio.iet.unipi.it/home.html. Links to rail servers throughout Europe.

Info on rail travel and railpasses: www.eurorail.com; www.raileuro.com.

Thomas Cook European Timetable, updated monthly, covers all major and most minor train routes in Europe. In the US, order it from Forsyth Travel Library (US$28; ☎(800) 367-7984; www.forsyth.com; order@forsyth.com). In Europe, find it at any Thomas Cook Money Exchange Center. Alternatively, buy directly from Thomas Cook (www.thomascook.com).

Guide to European Railpasses, Rick Steves. Available online and by mail. US ☎(425)771-8303; fax (425)771-0833; www.ricksteves.com). Delivery $8.

On the Rails Around Europe: A Comprehensive Guide to Travel by Train, Melissa Shales. Thomas Cook Ldt. (US$18.95).

Eurail and Train Travel Guide to Europe. Houghton Mifflin (US$15).

Europe By Eurail 2000, Laverne Ferguson-Kosinski. Globe Pequot Press (US$16.95).

Over 26 InterRail Card: provides unlimited second-class travel in Austria, Bulgaria, Croatia, Czech Republic, Denmark, Finland, Germany, Greece, Hungary, Republic of Ireland, Luxembourg, the Netherlands, Norway, Poland, Romania, Slovakia, Slovenia, Sweden, Turkey, and Yugoslavia inclusive for either 15 days (UK£215) or one month (UK£275).

Passholders receive **discounts** on rail travel, Eurostar journeys, and most ferries to Ireland, Scandinavia, and the rest of Europe. Most exclude **supplements** for high-speed trains. For info and ticket sales in Europe contact **Student Travel Center,** 24 Rupert St., 1st fl., London W1V 7FN (☎(020) 74 37 81 01; fax 77 34 38 36; www.student-travel-centre.com). Tickets are also available from travel agents or main train stations throughout Europe.

EUROPEAN EAST PASS. This pass is good for 5 days of 1st class, unlimited travel in a 1 month period, as well as various discounts on steamers and private railways within Austria, the Czech Republic, Hungary, Poland, and Slovakia. It also includes a 40% discount on bike rentals in over 130 railstations. You can purchase up to 5 days additional travel. Adult $205, each additional day $23.

BY BUS

Just like the railroads, the bus networks of Austria and Switzerland are very extensive, efficient, and comfortable; it may be difficult to negotiate the route you need, but short-haul buses can reach rural areas inaccessible by train. Bus stations are usually adjacent to the train station. The efficient **Austrian system** consists mainly of orange BundesBuses that generally complement the train system, serving mountain areas inaccessible by train rather than duplicating long-distance, inter-city routes already covered by rail. They cost about the same as trains, but no railpasses are valid. Buy tickets at a ticket office at the station or from the driver. For buses in heavily touristed areas during high season (such as the Großglocknerstraße in summer), you should probably make reservations. All public buses are non-smoking. Anyone can buy discounted tickets, valid for one week, for any particular route. A *Mehrfahrtenkarte* gives you 6 tickets for the price of 5. The Seniorenausweis (see p. 51) is valid on buses. Trips can be interrupted under certain conditions, depending on your ticket—be sure to ask. Small, regional bus schedules are available for free at most post offices. For more bus information, call (0222) 71101 within Austria (from outside Austria dial 1 instead of 0222), available 7am-8pm.

In **Switzerland**, PTT **Post Buses,** a barrage of banana-colored coaches delivered to you expressly by the Swiss government, connect rural villages and towns, picking up the slack where trains fail to go. SwissPasses are valid on many buses, Eurailpasses are not. Even with the SwissPass, you might have to pay a bit extra (5-10SFr) if you're riding one of the direct, faster buses. In cities, public buses transport commuters and shoppers alike to outlying areas. Buy tickets in advance at automatic machines, found at most bus stops. The system works on an honor code and inspections are infrequent, but expect to be hit for 30-50SFr if you're caught riding without a valid ticket. *Tageskarten*, valid for 24 hours of free travel, run 2-7.50SFr, but most Swiss cities are small enough to cover on foot.

BY CAR

Cars offer speed, freedom, access to the countryside, and an escape from the town-to-town mentality of trains. Unfortunately, they also insulate you from the esprit de corps of rail traveling. Although a single traveler won't save by renting or leasing a car, 3 or 4 usually will. As a rule, it is cheaper to rent in Germany than in Austria or Switzerland. Before setting off, know the laws of the countries in which you'll be driving (e.g., no right turn on red allowed anywhere in Austria or Switzerland). The **speed limit** in Austria is 50km per hour (31mph) within cities unless otherwise indicated; outside towns, the limit is 130kph (81mph) on highways and 100kph (62mph) on all other roads. The speed limits are 50kph in cities, 80kph on open roads, and 120kph on highways in Switzerland. In Austria and Switzerland, all people in every car must wear **seat belts;** the fine for not wearing a belt is 40SFr in Switzerland, 300AS in Austria. Driving under the influence of alcohol is a serious offense—fines begin at 700SFr (5000AS) and rise rapidly from there; violators may also lose their licenses. The legal **blood-alcohol limit** in Switzerland is .08 percent—slightly lower than in most American states.

The **Association for Safe International Road Travel** (ASIRT) can provide more specific information about road conditions. It is located at 11769 Gainsborough Rd., Potomac, MD 20854 (☎(301) 983-5252; fax 983-3663; asirt@erols.com; www.asirt.org). ASIRT considers road travel (by car or bus) to be relatively safe in both Austria and Switzerland. Austrian and Swiss highways are excellent. With armies of mechanized road crews ready to remove snow at a moment's notice, roads at altitudes of up to 1500m generally remain open throughout winter. (Mountain driving does present special challenges, however; see p. 18). Many small Austrian and Swiss towns forbid cars to enter all together; others forbid only visitors' cars, require special permits, or restrict driving hours. EU citizens driving in Austria and Switzerland don't need any special documentation—registration and license will suffice. All cars must carry a first-aid kit and a red emergency triangle. All passengers in both countries must wear seatbelts, and children under 12 may not sit in the front passenger seat unless a child's seatbelt or a special seat is installed. Emergency phones are located along all major highways. The Austrian Automobile, Motorcycle, and Touring Club (ÖAMTC; ☎(1) 711 997) provides an English-language service and sells a set of 8 detailed road maps, far superior to the tourist office's map (open daily 7am-6pm). The Swiss Touring Club, 4 Chemin de Blandonnet, 1214 Vernier (☎(022) 417 272; fax (022) 417 2020; www.tcs.ch) operates road patrols that assist motorists in need; dial 140 for help.

FOR ROADSIDE ASSISTANCE

In Switzerland, call ☎140.

In Austria call, ☎120

DRIVING PERMITS: INTERNATIONAL DRIVING PERMIT (IDP). If you plan to drive a car while in **Austria,** you must have an International Driving Permit (IDP) in addition to your driver's license. Most car rental agencies in **Switzerland** don't require the permit, but it may be a good idea to get one anyway, in case you're in a situation (e.g. an accident or being stranded in a smaller town) where the police do not know English. Information on the IDP is available from local automobile clubs and printed in ten languages, including French, Italian, and German.

Your IDP is valid for one year, and it must be issued in your own country before you depart; AAA affiliates cannot issue IDPs valid in their own country. You must be 18 years old to receive the IDP. A valid driver's license from your home country must always accompany the IDP. The IDP application needs to include one or two photos, a current local license, an additional form of identification, and a fee.

Australia: Contact your local Royal Automobile Club (RAC) or the National Royal Motorist Association (NRMA) if in NSW or the ACT (☎(08) 942 14444; www.rac.com.au/travel). Permits AUS$15.

Canada: Contact any Canadian Automobile Association (CAA) branch office or write to CAA, 1145 Hunt Club Rd., #200, K1V 0Y3. (☎(613) 247-0117; www.caa.ca/CAAInternet/travelservices/internationaldocumentation/idptravel.htm). Permits CDN$10.

Ireland: Contact the nearest Automobile Association (AA) office or write to the UK address below. Permits IR£4. The Irish Automobile Association, 23 Suffolk St., Rockhill, Blackrock, Co. Dublin (☎(01) 677 9481), honors most foreign automobile memberships (24hr. breakdown and road service ☎(800) 667 788; toll-free in Ireland).

New Zealand: Contact your local Automobile Association (AA) or their main office at Auckland Central, 99 Albert St. (☎(9) 377 4660; www.nzaa.co.nz). Permits NZ$8.

South Africa: Contact the Travel Services Department of the Automobile Association of South Africa at P.O. Box 596, 2000 Johannesburg (☎(11) 799 1400; fax 799 1410; http://aasa.co.za). Permits SAR28.50.

UK: To visit your local AA Shop, contact the **AA Headquarters** (☎(0990) 448 866), or write to: The Automobile Association, International Documents, Fanum House, Erskine, Renfrewshire PA8 6BW. To find the location nearest you that issues the IDP, call (0990) 500 600 or (0990) 448 866. For more info, see www.theaa.co.uk/motoringandtravel/idp/index.asp. Permits UK£4.

US: Visit any American Automobile Association (AAA) office or write to AAA Florida, Travel Related Services, 1000 AAA Drive (mail stop 100), Heathrow, FL 32746 (☎(407) 444-7000; fax 444-7380). You don't have to be a member to buy a permit ($10). AAA Travel Related Services (☎(800) 222-4357) provides road maps, travel guides, emergency road services, travel services, and auto insurance.

CAR INSURANCE. Some credit cards cover standard insurance (that is, up to the deductible on collision insurance, allowing their customers to decline the collision damage waiver) for a rental car if you pay with your credit card—but usually only cards at the gold and platinum level. Check with your credit card company to see what they offer before you rent. If you have car insurance on your own car, check with your insurer to have your insurance applied to your rental car. Non-Europeans could check with their national motoring organization (like AAA or CAA) for international coverage. If you rent, lease, or borrow a car, you will need an International Insurance Certificate (green card) to prove that you have liability insurance. Obtain it through the car rental agency; most include coverage in their prices. If you lease a car, you can obtain a green card from the dealer. Some travel agents offer the card; it may also be available at border crossings. Even if your insurance at home does cover you abroad, you will still need a green card to certify this to foreign officials. If you have a collision abroad, the accident will show up on your domestic records if you report it to your insurance company.

ACQUIRING SOME WHEELS

RENTING A CAR. To rent a car in Austria, you must be at least 19 for most companies and carry both an International Driver's Permit and a valid driver's license that you have had for at least 1 year (see p. 45). Most Austrian companies restrict travel into Hungary, the Czech Republic, Poland, and Slovakia. Rental taxes are high (21%). In Switzerland, the minimum rental age is 21 but also varies by company. You must possess a valid driver's license that you have had for at least one year (foreign licenses are valid). In both countries, drivers under 25 must often pay a daily "young driver" fee. Rates for all cars rented in Switzerland and Austria include an obligatory annual road toll, called a *vignette*, 40SFr and 70 AS per week, respectively.

You can rent a car from a US-based firm (Alamo, Avis, Budget, or Hertz) with European offices, from a European-based company with local representatives (Europcar), or from a tour operator (Auto Europe, Europe By Car, and Kemwel Holiday Autos) that will arrange a rental for you from a European company at its own rates. Multinationals offer greater flexibility, but tour operators often strike better deals. Expect to pay US$200-300 per week, plus tax, for a teensy car. Reserve ahead and pay in advance if at all possible. It is always significantly less expensive to reserve a car from the US than from Europe. Always check if prices quoted include tax, unlimited mileage, and collision insurance. Ask about discounts and check the terms of insurance, particularly the size of the deductible (for more info see p. 46). Ask airlines about special fly-and-drive packages; you may get up to a week of free or discounted rental.

Car rental in Austria and Switzerland is available with the following agencies:

Auto Europe, 39 Commercial St., P.O. Box 7006, Portland, ME 04112 (US and Canada ☎(888) 223-5555 or (207) 842-2000; fax (207) 842-2222; www.autoeurope.com).

Avis (US and Canada ☎(800) 331-1084; UK ☎(0990) 900 500; Australia ☎(800) 225 533; New Zealand ☎(0800) 655 111; www.avis.com).

Budget (US ☎(800) 472-3325; Canada ☎(800) 527-0700; UK ☎(0800) 181 181; Australia ☎132 727; www.budgetrentacar.com).

Europe by Car, One Rockefeller Plaza, New York, NY 10020 (US ☎(800) 223-1516 or (212) 581-3040; fax 246-1458; info@europebycar.com; www.europebycar.com).

Europcar, 145 av. Malekoff, 75016 Paris (☎(01) 450 008 06); US ☎(800) 227-3876; Canada ☎(800) 227-7368; www.europcar.com).

Hertz (US ☎(800) 654-3001; Canada ☎(800) 263-0600; UK ☎(0990) 996 699; Australia ☎969 82555; www.hertz.com).

Kemwel Holiday Autos (US ☎(800) 576-1590; www.kemwel.com).

LEASING. For longer than 17 days, leasing can be cheaper than renting; it is often the only option for those ages 18 to 21. The cheapest leases are agreements to buy the car and then sell it back to the manufacturer at a prearranged price. As far as you're concerned, though, it's a lease and doesn't entail enormous financial transactions. Leases generally include insurance coverage and are not taxed. The most affordable ones usually originate in Belgium, France, or Germany. Expect to pay around US$1100-1800 (depending on size of car) for 60 days. Contact **Auto Europe, Europe by Car,** or **Kemwel Holiday Autos** (see above) before you go.

BY AIR

No air deals can compare with railpass bargains in Austria and Switzerland, so flying across Europe on regularly scheduled flights can devour your budget, but if you are short on time (or flush with cash) you might consider it. Student travel agencies sell cheap tickets, and budget fares are frequently available in the spring and summer on high-volume routes between northern Europe and resort areas in Italy, Greece, and Spain; consult budget travel agents and local newspapers. The Air Travel Advisory Bureau in London (☎(0171) 636 5000; www.atab.co.uk) can also point the way to discount flights.

In addition, a number of European airlines offer coupon packets that considerably discount the cost of each flight leg. Most are only available as tack-ons to their transatlantic passengers, but some are available as stand-alone offers. Most must be purchased before departure, so research in advance.

Europe by Air: US ☎(888) 387-2479; Australia ☎(02) 928 56888; New Zealand ☎(09) 309 8094; Israel ☎(03) 549 333; www.europebyair.com. Coupons good on 16 partner airlines to 130 European cities in 27 countries. Must be purchased prior to departure; available only to non-European residents. US$99 each, excluding airport tax.

Alitalia: US ☎(800) 223-5730; www.alitaliausa.com. "Europlus," available to North Americans who fly into Milan or Rome on Alitalia, allows passengers to tack on 3 coupons good for flights to 48 airports in Europe. US$299; each additional ticket US$100.

Austrian Airlines: US ☎(800) 843-0002; www.austrianair.com/specials/visit-europe-fares.html. "Visit Europe," good to cities served by AA and partner airlines, is available in the US to Austrian Airlines transatlantic passengers (3 min., 6 max.). US$100 each.

Lufthansa: US ☎(800) 399-5838; www.lufthansa-usa.com. "Discover Europe" is available to US travelers booked on a transatlantic Lufthansa flight. Special deals vary but usually include up to 6 flights to 100 cities within Europe for around $89.

SAS: US ☎(800) 221-2350; www.flysas.com/airpass.html. One-way coupons for travel within Scandinavia, the Baltics, or all of Europe US$75-225. Most are available only to transatlantic SAS passengers, but some United and Lufthansa passengers also qualify.

BY BICYCLE

Today, biking is one of the key elements of the classic budget Eurovoyage. With the proliferation of mountain bikes, you can do some serious natural sightseeing. May, June, and September are prime biking months in Austria and Switzerland, for leisurely or hard-core bicycling. Many airlines will count your bike as your second free piece of luggage; a few charge extra (US$60-110 one-way). Bikes must be packed in a cardboard box with the pedals and front wheel detached; many airlines sell bike boxes at the airport (US$10). Most ferries let you take your bike for free or for a nominal fee, and you can always ship your bike on trains. For more info on cycles and trains, see the Swiss Federal Railway's website (http://s26282.sbb.ch/pv/velobahn_e.htm). Renting a bike beats bringing your own if your touring will be confined to one or two regions. Some youth hostels rent bicycles for low prices. *Let's Go* lists bike rental shops for most cities and towns. In Switzerland and Austria most train stations rent bikes and often allow you to drop them off elsewhere.

For info about touring routes, consult national or local tourist offices. The **Touring Club Suisse,** Cyclo Tourisme, chemin Riantbosson 11-13, CH-1217 Meyrin (☎ (022) 785 1222; fax 785 1262), will send you information, maps, brochures, route descriptions, and mileage charts. In Austria, **www.radtouren.at** maintains a wonderful list of long distance bike routes (many not open to cars) throughout Austria.

If you're planning on doing long distance touring, you'll need **panniers** in which you can pack your luggage, a good **helmet** (US$25-50) and a good U-shaped **Citadel** or **Kryptonite lock** (from US$30). For equipment, **Bike Nashbar,** 4111 Simon Rd., Youngstown, OH 44512 (US ☎(800) 627-4227; www.nashbar.com), beats all competitors' offers and ships anywhere in the US or Canada. Take some reasonably challenging day-long rides at home to prepare yourself before you leave, and have your bike tuned up by a reputable shop. Wear visible clothing, drink plenty of water (even if you're not thirsty), and use the international signals for turns. Know how to fix a modern derailer-equipped mount and change a tire; practice on your own bike. A few simple tools and a good bike manual will be invaluable.

MCI WORLDCOM
WORLDPHONE
1-800-888-8000
J. L. SMITH

BY MOPED AND MOTORCYCLE

Motorized bikes don't use much gas, can be put on trains and ferries, and are a good compromise between the high cost of car travel and the limited range of bicycles. However, they're uncomfortable for long distances, dangerous in the rain, and unpredictable on rough roads and gravel. Always wear a helmet and never ride with a backpack. If you've never been on a moped before, twisting alpine roads are not the place to start. Expect to pay about US$20-35 per day; try auto repair shops and remember to bargain. Motorcycles are more expensive and normally require a license, but are better for long distances. **Bosenberg Motorcycle Excursions,** Mainzer Str. 54, 55545 Bad Kreuznach, Germany (☎(49) 671 67312; www.bosenberg.com, Bosenberg@compuserve.com) arranges tours in Austria and Switzerland; they also rent motorcycles (Apr.-Oct.). Before renting, ask if the quoted price includes tax and insurance, or you may be hit with an unexpected additional fee. Avoid handing your passport over as a deposit; if you have an accident or mechanical failure, you may not get it back until you cover all repairs. Pay ahead of time instead. *Europe by Motorcycle*, by Gregory Frazier (Arrowstar Publishing; US$20), is helpful for planning your itinerary and making arrangements.

BY THUMB

HITCHHIKERS BEWARE. *Let's Go* strongly urges you to consider seriously the risks before hitching. We do not recommend it as a safe means of transportation, and none of the information presented here is intended to do so.

No one should hitch without careful consideration of the risks involved. Not everyone can be an airplane pilot, but any bozo can drive a car. Hitching means entrusting your life to a random person who happens to stop beside you on the road and risking theft, assault, sexual harassment, and unsafe driving. The choice, however, remains yours. In Austria and Switzerland, men and women traveling in groups and men traveling alone might consider hitching (called "autostop") beyond the range of bus or train routes. If you're a woman traveling alone, don't hitch. It's just too dangerous. A man and a woman are a safe, viable combination, while 2 men will have a harder time, and 3 will go nowhere. If you do decide to hitch, consider where you are; where one stands is vital. Experienced hitchers pick a spot outside of built-up areas, where drivers can stop, return to the road without causing an accident, and have time to look over potential passengers as they approach. Hitching (or even standing) on superhighways is usually illegal: one may only thumb at rest stops or at the entrance ramps to highways. In the Practical Information section of many cities, we list tram or bus lines that take travelers to strategic points for hitching out.

Finally, success will depend on what one looks like. Successful hitchers travel light and stack their belongings in a compact but visible cluster. Most Europeans signal with an open hand, rather than a thumb; many write their destination on a sign in large, bold letters and draw a smiley-face under it. Drivers prefer hitchers who are neat and wholesome. No one stops for anyone wearing sunglasses. Safety issues are always imperative, even for those who are not hitching alone. Safety-minded hitchers avoid getting in the back of a 2-door car and never let go of their backpacks. They will not get into a car that they can't get out of again in a hurry. If they ever feel threatened, they insist on being let off, regardless of where they are. Acting as if they are going to open the car door or vomit on the upholstery will usually get a driver to stop. Hitchhiking at night can be particularly dangerous; experienced hitchers stand in well-lit places and expect drivers to be leery of nocturnal thumbers (or open-handers).

Most large cities in Austria and Switzerland offer a **ride service** (listed as Mitfahrzentrale in the Practical Information), a cross between hitchhiking and the ride boards common at many universities, which pairs drivers with riders. The fee varies according to destination. Riders and drivers can enter their names on the Internet through the Taxistop website (www.taxistop.be), but be aware that not all of these organizations screen drivers and riders; ask in advance.

SPECIFIC CONCERNS

WOMEN TRAVELERS

Women travelers will likely feel safer in Austria and Switzerland than just about anywhere in the world—violent crime is generally rare. Unlike in some parts of southern Europe, catcalls and whistling are not acceptable behaviors in Austria and Switzerland. Still, women exploring on their own inevitably face some additional safety concerns, but it's easy to be adventurous without taking undue risks. If you are concerned, you might consider staying in hostels which offer single rooms that lock from the inside or in religious organizations that offer rooms for women only. Stick to centrally located accommodations and avoid solitary late-night treks or metro rides. Generally, the less you look like a tourist, the better off you'll be. Dress conservatively, especially in rural areas. Wearing a conspicuous wedding band may help prevent unwanted overtures. Some travelers report that carrying pictures of a "husband" or "children" is extremely useful to help document marriage status. Even a mention of a husband waiting back at the hotel may be enough in some places to discount your potentially vulnerable, unattached appearance.

In cities, you may be harassed no matter how you're dressed. Your best answer to verbal harassment is no answer at all; feigned deafness, sitting motionless and staring straight ahead at nothing in particular will do a world of good that reactions usually don't achieve. The extremely persistent can sometimes be dissuaded by a firm, loud, and very public "Go away!"

When traveling, always carry extra money for a phone call, bus, or taxi. Hitching is never safe for lone women, or even for 2 women traveling together. Choose train compartments occupied by other women or couples. Look as if you know where you're going (even when you don't) and consider approaching older women or couples for directions if you're lost or feel uncomfortable. Don't hesitate to seek out a police officer or a passerby if you are being harassed. *Let's Go: Austria & Switzerland* lists emergency numbers (including rape crisis lines) in the Practical Information listings of most cities. Memorize the emergency numbers in the places you visit. Carry a whistle or an airhorn on your keychain, and don't hesitate to use it in an emergency. An IMPACT Model Mugging self-defense course will not only prepare you for a potential attack, but will also raise your level of awareness of your surroundings as well as your confidence (see **Self Defense,** p. 19). Women also face specific health concerns when traveling (see **Women's Health,** p. 22).

TRAVELING ALONE

There are many benefits to traveling alone, among them greater independence and challenge. As a lone traveler, you have greater opportunity to interact with the residents of the region you're visiting. Without distraction, you can write a great travel log in the grand tradition of Mark Twain, John Steinbeck, and Charles Kuralt. On the other hand, any solo traveler is a more vulnerable target of harassment and street theft. Lone travelers need to be well-organized and look confident at all times. Try not to stand out as a tourist and be especially careful in deserted or very crowded areas. If questioned, **never admit that you are traveling alone.** Maintain regular contact with someone at home who knows

FURTHER READING: WOMEN TRAVELERS

A Journey of One's Own: Uncommon Advice for the Independent Woman Traveler, Thalia Zepatos. Eighth Mountain Press (US$17).

Adventures in Good Company: The Complete Guide to Women's Tours and Outdoor Trips, Thalia Zepatos. Eighth Mountain Press (US$17).

Active Women Vacation Guide, Evelyn Kaye. Blue Panda Publications (US$18).

Travelers' Tales: Gutsy Women, Travel Tips and Wisdom for the Road, Marybeth Bond. Traveler's Tales (US$8).

A Foxy Old Woman's Guide to Traveling Alone, Jay Ben-Lesser. Crossing Press. (US$11).

More Women Travel: Adventures, Advice & Experience. Miranda Davies and Natania Jansz. Penguin Books (US$16.95).

your itinerary. A number of organizations supply information for solo travelers, and others find travel companions. Here are a few to get started:

Connecting: Solo Traveler Network, P.O. Box 29088, 1996 W. Broadway, Vancouver, BC V6J 5C2, Canada (☎(604) 737-7791; info@cstn.org; www.cstn.org). Bi-monthly newsletter features going solo tips, single-friendly tips, and travel companion ads. Annual directory lists holiday suppliers that avoid single supplement charges. Advice and lodging exchanges facilitated between members. Membership US$25-35.

Travel Companion Exchange, P.O. Box 833, Amityville, NY 11701 (☎(631) 454-0880 or (800) 392-1256 in the US; www.whytravelalone.com). Publishes the pamphlet "Foiling Pickpockets & Bag Snatchers" (US$4.70) and "Travel Companions," a bi-monthly newsletter for single travelers seeking a travel partner (subscription US$48).

FURTHER READING: TRAVELING ALONE

Traveling Solo, Eleanor Berman. Globe Pequot (US$17).

The Single Traveler Newsletter, P.O. Box 682, Ross, CA 94957 (☎(415) 389 0227). 6 issues US$29.

OLDER TRAVELERS

Seniors often qualify for hotel and restaurant discounts as well as discounted admission to many tourist attractions. If you don't see a senior citizen price listed, ask and you may be delightfully surprised. In Switzerland, women over 62 and men over 65 qualify as seniors, and women over 60 and men over 65 get senior status in Austria. A **Seniorenausweis** (Senior Citizen Identification Card) entitles holders to a 50% discount on all Austrian federal trains, Post Buses, and BundesBuses, and the card works as an ID for discounted museum admissions. The card costs about 350AS, requires a passport photo and proof of age, and is valid for one calendar year. It is available in Austria at railroad stations and major post offices, as well as the main train station in Zurich. Both National Tourist Offices offer guides for senior citizens. Many discounts require proof of status, so prepare to be carded. Agencies for senior group travel are growing in enrollment and popularity. Here are a few of them:

Elderhostel, 75 Federal St., Boston, MA 02110, USA (☎(617) 426-7788 or (877) 426-8056; registration@elderhostel.org; www.elderhostel.org). Offers culture, history, and nature courses in Austria and Switzerland of varying lengths throughout the spring, summer, and fall. Must be 55 or over (spouse can be of any age).

The Mature Traveler, P.O. Box 50400, Reno, NV 89513, USA (☎(775) 786-7419, credit card orders (800) 460-6676). Deals, discounts, and travel packages for the 50+ traveler. Subscription $30.

Walking the World, P.O. Box 1186, Fort Collins, CO 80522, USA (☎(970) 498-0500; fax 498-9100; walktworld@aol.com; www.walkingtheworld.com), organizes trips for 50+ travelers to Switzerland.

FURTHER READING: OLDER TRAVELERS

No Problem! Worldwise Tips for Mature Adventurers, Janice Kenyon. Orca Book Publishers (US$16).

A Senior's Guide to Healthy Travel, Donald L. Sullivan. Career Press. (US$15).

Unbelievably Good Deals and Great Adventures That You Absolutely Can't Get Unless You're Over 50, Joan Rattner Heilman. Contemporary Books (US$13).

Have Grandchildren, Will Travel. Pilot Books (US$10).

Doctor's Guide to Protecting Your Health Before, During, and After International Travel. Pilot Books (US$10).

Europe the European Way: A Traveler's Guide to Living Affordably in the World's Great Cities. Globe Piquot Press (US$14).

GAY AND LESBIAN TRAVELERS

As Austria and Switzerland are conservative countries with limited tolerance for homosexuality, public displays of affection can attract unfriendly attention. On the other hand, Geneva, Zurich, and Vienna have a wide variety of homosexual organizations and establishments, from biker and Christian groups to bars and barber shops. Though these services can be difficult to find, tourist offices sometimes have info; otherwise check the local listings. The German word for gay is *schwul;* for lesbian, *lesben* (LEZ-ben) or *lesbisch* (LEZ-bisch). Bisexual is *bisexual* or simply *bi* (bee). In French, *homosexuelle* can be used for both men and women, but the preferred terms are *gai* (GEH) and *lesbienne* (les-bee-YENN).

The age of consent in Austria is 18 for gay men, 14 for lesbians. Homosexuelle Initiative (HOSI) is a nation-wide organization with offices in most cities that provides information on gay and lesbian establishments, resources, and supports as well as publishing warnings about aggressively intolerant areas and establishments. HOSI Wien, II, Novarag. 40, Vienna (☎/fax (01) 216 66 04), publishes Austria's leading gay and lesbian magazine, the "Lambda-Nachrichten," quarterly. A number of smaller and alternative organizations operate throughout the country. The age of consent in Switzerland is 16. Switzerland has a nationwide lesbian, gay, and bisexual information hotline, the **Rainbowline** ☎(084) 880 5080. There are several gay working groups in the larger cities, such as **Homosexuelle Arbeitsgruppe Dialogai,** headquartered in Geneva, av. Wendt 57, mailing address: Case Postale 27, CH-1211, Geneva 7 (☎(022) 340 0000; fax 340 0398), formed a partnership with l'Aide Suisse contre le Sida (ASS), an organization that works against AIDS. Several gay publications are available in centers and bookshops. **Dialogai Info** provides information on French Switzerland, articles, interviews, and more. For information about organizations, centers, and other resources in specific cities, consult the city's Practical Information section; for information on bars and nightclubs, see the individual Sights and Entertainment sections. Listed below are contact organizations, mail-order bookstores, and publishers that offer materials addressing some specific concerns.

Gay's the Word, 66 Marchmont St., London WC1N 1AB (☎(020) 7278 7654; sales@gaystheword.co.uk; www.gaystheword.co.uk). The largest gay and lesbian bookshop in the UK, with both fiction and non-fiction titles. Mail-order service available.

Giovanni's Room, 345 S. 12th St., Philadelphia, PA 19107, USA (☎(215) 923-2960; fax 923-0813; www.queerbooks.com). An international lesbian/feminist and gay bookstore with mail-order service (carries many of the publications listed below).

International Gay and Lesbian Travel Association, 4331 N. Federal Hwy., #304, Fort Lauderdale, FL 33308, USA (☎(954) 776-2626; fax 776-3303; www.iglta.com). An organization of over 1350 companies serving gay and lesbian travelers worldwide.

International Lesbian and Gay Association (ILGA), 81 rue Marché-au-Charbon, B-1000 Brussels, Belgium (☎/fax +32 (2) 502 2471; www.ilga.org). Not a travel service; provides political information, including homosexuality laws of individual countries.

RESOURCES FOR GAY AND LESBIAN TRAVELERS

Spartacus International Gay Guide. Bruno Gmunder Verlag. (US$33).

Damron Men's Guide, Damron Road Atlas, Damron's Accommodations, and *The Women's Traveller.* Damron Travel Guides (US$14-19). For more info, call US ☎(415) 255-0404 or (800) 462-6654 or check their website (www.damron.com).

Ferrari Guides' Gay Travel A to Z, Ferrari Guides' Men's Travel in Your Pocket, Ferrari Guides' Women's Travel in Your Pocket, and *Ferrari Guides' Inn Places.* Ferrari Guides (US$14-16). For more info, call ☎(602) 863-2408 or (800) 962-2912 or try www.q-net.com.

The Gay Vacation Guide: The Best Trips and How to Plan Them, Mark Chesnut. Citadel Press (US$15).

Gayellow Pages ($US 16). Call ☎(212) 674-0120, gayellow@banet.net or check the website at http://gayellowpages.com.

TRAVELERS WITH DISABILITIES

Austria and Switzerland are relatively accessible to travelers with disabilities (*behinderte Reisende*). Tourist offices can offer info about which sights, and services are wheelchair-accessible. Disabled visitors to Austria may want to contact the Vienna Tourist Board, Obere Augartenstr. 40, A-1025 Vienna (☎(01) 21114; fax 216 8492, www.info.wien.at), which offers booklets on accessible Vienna hotels and a general guide to the city for the disabled. The Austrian National Tourist Offices in New York and Vienna offers many pages of listings for wheelchair-accessible sights, museums, and lodgings in Vienna—ask for the booklet "Wien für Gäste mit Handicaps." With 3 days' notice, the Austrian railways will provide a wheelchair for the train. The international wheelchair icon or a large letter "B" indicates access. In Switzerland, disabled travelers can contact Mobility International Schweiz, Hard 4, CH-8408 Winterthur (☎(052) 222 6825; fax 222 6838). Most Swiss buildings and restrooms have ramps. The Swiss Federal Railways have adapted most of their train cars for wheelchair access, and InterCity and long-distance express trains have wheelchair compartments. The Swiss National Tourist Office publishes a fact sheet of "Travel Tips for the Disabled."

Cities, especially Vienna, Zurich, and Geneva, publish mounds of information for handicapped visitors. *Let's Go* tries to indicate which budget accommodations have wheelchair access. In general, those with disabilities should inform airlines and hotels of their disabilities when making arrangements for travel; some time may be needed to prepare special accommodations. Call ahead to restaurants, hotels, parks, and other facilities to find out about the existence of ramps, the widths of doors, the dimensions of elevators, etc.

Rail is probably the most convenient form of travel for disabled travelers in Austria and Switzerland, but you have to be willing to ask for assistance. Many trains have a special compartment reserved for disabled travelers. Guide-dog owners should inquire as to the specific quarantine policies of each destination country. At the very least, they will need to provide a certificate of immunization against rabies. Hertz, Avis, and National car rental agencies have hand-controlled vehicles at some locations. The following organizations provide information or publications that might be of assistance:

USEFUL ORGANIZATIONS

Mobility International USA (MIUSA), P.O. Box 10767, Eugene, OR 97440, USA (☎(541) 343-1284 voice and TDD; fax 343-6812; info@miusa.org; www.miusa.org). Sells *A World of Options: A Guide to International Educational Exchange, Community Service, and Travel for Persons with Disabilities* (US$35).

Moss Rehab Hospital Travel Information Service (☎(215) 456-9600 or (800) CALL-MOSS; netstaff@mossresourcenet.org; www.mossresourcenet.org). An information resource center on travel-related concerns for those with disabilities.

Society for the Advancement of Travel for the Handicapped (SATH), 347 Fifth Ave., #610, New York, NY 10016 (☎(212) 447-7284; www.sath.org). An advocacy group that publishes the quarterly travel magazine *OPEN WORLD* (free for members, US$13 for nonmembers). Also publishes a wide range of info sheets on disability travel facilitation and destinations. Annual membership US$45, students and seniors US$30.

TOUR AGENCIES

Directions Unlimited, 123 Green Ln., Bedford Hills, NY 10507, USA (☎(914) 241-1700 or (800) 533-5343; www.travel-cruises.com). Specializes in arranging individual and group vacations, tours, and cruises for the physically disabled.

Flying Wheels Travel Service, 143 W. Bridge St., Owatonne, MN 55060 (☎(800) 535-6790; fax 451-1685). Arranges trips for groups and individuals in wheelchairs or with other sorts of limited mobility.

FURTHER READING: DISABLED TRAVELERS

Resource Directory for the Disabled, Richard Neil Shrout. Facts on file (US$45).

Wheelchair Through Europe, Annie Mackin. Graphic Language Press (☎(760) 944-9594; niteowl@cts.com; US$13).

The Diabetic Traveler, P.O. Box 8223 RW, Stamford, CT (☎(203) 327-5832). A short quarterly offering advice on flying, eating abroad, and visiting extreme climates. A subscription (US$18.95) includes a list of organizations worldwide.

Global Access (www.geocities.com/Paris/1502/disabilitylinks.html) has specific links for disabled travelers in Switzerland, as well as general links.

TRAVELERS WITH CHILDREN

Family vacations often require that you slow your pace and always require that you plan ahead, but that doesn't mean they can't be done cheaply. Austria and Switzerland are decidedly family-friendly, offering transportation discounts and a plethora of attractions. Children under 6 travel free on Austrian trains, and children 6-12 for half-price. The **Swiss Family Card** (see **Railpasses,** p. 41) lets children under 16 travel free with at least 1 parent holding a valid ticket. Children under 16 travel alone at half price. Make sure car rental companies provide a car seat for younger children.

When deciding where to stay, the special needs of young children can limit your choice of accommodations; once you decide on a *Pension* or *Privatzimmer*, call ahead and make sure it's child-friendly. *Let's Go* notes which accommodations are particularly family-oriented. Virtually all museums and tourist attractions also have a children's rate. Children under 2 generally fly for 10% of the adult airfare on international flights (this does not necessarily include a seat). International fares are usually discounted 25% for children from 2 to 11. Make sure each child, no matter how young, has a valid passport. Underschedule yourself with free days for unexpected emergencies. Check with your family doctor to be sure your child's immunizations are up to date. It's even a good idea to schedule a well-child checkup if it's been a while since the last one. Consider taking along useful equipment, such as a baby carrier or stroller. Be sure that your child carries some sort of ID in case of an emergency or if he/she gets lost, and arrange a reunion spot in case of separation when sight-seeing.

FURTHER READING: TRAVELERS WITH CHILDREN

Backpacking with Babies and Small Children, Goldie Silverman. Wilderness Press (US$10).

Take Your Kids to Europe, Cynthia W. Harriman. Globe Pequot (US$17).

How to Take Great Trips with Your Kids, Sanford and Jane Portnoy. Harvard Common Press (US $10).

Have Kid, Will Travel: 101 Survival Strategies for Vacationing With Babies and Young Children, Claire and Lucille Tristram. Andrews and McMeel (US$9).

Adventuring with Children: An Inspirational Guide to World Travel and the Outdoors, Nan Jeffrey. Avalon House Publishing ($15).

Trouble Free Travel with Children, Vicki Lansky. Book Peddlers (US$9).

MINORITY TRAVELERS

Although Austria and Switzerland are predominantly Caucasian, they are quite tolerant of minority travelers, particularly in larger cities. The majority of minority travelers will likely never encounter any difficulty, though the further you venture out into the countryside, the more likely it is that you will encounter the occasional odd stare. Villagers are notoriously curious, so don't be surprised or offended if old women linger in their windows to catch a glimpse of you. In recent years, a growing population of foreign workers (particularly Turks) has felt the sting of Swiss anxiety about economic recession, but physical confrontations are rare—Austrians and Swiss tend to be much too mild-mannered to provoke violence or hurl insults. Anti-Semitism is not a large problem in either country. For more information on the concerning political developments in each country see **Haider and Austria's Swing to the Right,** p. 68, and **Switzerland Today,** p. 295.

RELIGIOUS CONCERNS

Despite the overwhelmingly Christian population of Austria and Switzerland, serious religious intolerance is uncommon and unauthorized. While the predominance of Catholics and Protestant churches make it simple for anyone of those faiths to find a place to worship or attend services, the same task can be challenging for those of other religions and faiths. Locating religious communities outside the mainstream is easiest in large cities, as is attending services in English. The following list of organizations and websites may be helpful in planning ahead:

Buddhist communities have centers in Vienna (Fleischmarkt 16, 1st fl., A-1010 Vienna; ☎(01) 513 3880; bodhidharma.zendo@blackbox.at), Innsbruck (An der Furt 18, II., A-6020 Innsbruck; ☎/fax (0512) 367113; aldo.deutsch@uibk.ac.at), and Salzburg (Schlossstr. 38, A-5020 Salzburg; ☎/fax (62) 747 516; sunyata@magnet.at).

Hindu temples can be found in Switzerland, including a Swami temple in Bern (Verein Murugan Temple, Looslistr. 21A, 3027 Bern; ☎(031) 992 2098) and a Shiva temple in Zurich (Sivan Temple, Wehntalerstr. 293, 8046 Zurich; ☎(01) 371 0242).

Jehovah's Witnesses can check out www.watchtower.org for more information.

Jewish visitors to Vienna can contact The Jewish Welcome Service (☎(01) 533 8891). The Federation of Austrian Jewish Communities (Seitenstetteng. 4, Postfach 145, A-1010 Vienna; ☎(01) 531 040; fax 530 4108) is a good resource for information elsewhere in Austria. Switzerland has its own version, the Federation of Swiss Jewish Communities (SIG) (Gotthardstr. 65, Postfach 564, 8027 Zurich; ☎(01) 201 5583; fax (01) 202 1672, sig-fsce@bluewin.ch). Or consult *The Jewish Travel Guide,* which lists synagogues, kosher restaurants, and Jewish institutions in over 100 countries, available in Europe from Vallentine Mitchell Publishers, Newbury House 890-900, Eastern Ave., Newbury Park, Ilford, Essex IG2 7HH, UK (☎(020) 859 98866; fax (020) 859 90984) and in the US ($16.95 + $4 S&H) from ISBS, 5804 NE Hassallo St., Portland, OR 97213 (☎(800) 944-6190).

Mormon temples can be found in Switzerland, including in Zollikofen, near Bern (Tempelstr., Ch-3052 Zollikofen; ☎(031) 911 0912). Contact www.spin.ch/~hlt-chur/schweiz.html for more information. For Austria, go to www.ettl.co.at/mormon/english/.

Muslims can turn to www.islam.ch (available in German, French, or Italian) for information and addresses throughout Switzerland. For Austria, www.angelfire.com/nm/nourmedia offers Islamic news specific to Austria.

DIETARY CONCERNS

The dairy-based cuisine in Austria and Switzerland is not particularly vegan-friendly, but the growing health- and environmentally-conscious movements in both countries mean more options for vegetable-eaters. Vegans will likely have difficulty outside of large cities, but ovo-lacto vegetarians can enjoy many traditional meatless dishes. *Let's Go* lists vegetarian and vegetarian-friendly restaurants under Food listings in each city or town. Tourist offices list hotels and restaurants that serve vegetarian, organically grown, or whole food. In addition, locating vegetarian restaurants in major cities can be done on the Internet. Visit www.vrg.org/travel/ for suggestions, reviews, and links to specific vegetarian restaurants. The European Vegetarian Union maintains the webpage www.ivu.org/evu/. Contact the **North American Vegetarian Society,** P.O. Box 72, Dolgeville, NY 13329 (☎(518) 568-7970; navs@telenet.net; www.navs_online.org).

Travelers who keep kosher should contact synagogues in larger cities for information on kosher restaurants. The Swiss National Tourist Office distributes the pamphlet *The Jewish City Guide of Switzerland* (published by Spectrumpress International, Spectrum-House, Tanegg., 8055 Zurich), which lists synagogues, rabbis, butchers, kosher hotels, and restaurants, along with other useful information and phone numbers for kosher and Jewish travelers. Kosher food may not be available outside of large cities. When preparing your trip, it might be helpful to consult the **Jewish Travel Guide,** which lists synagogues, kosher restaurants, and Jewish institutions in Austria and Switzerland (see Religious Concerns, p. 55).

ALTERNATIVES TO TOURISM

For an extensive listing of "off-the-beaten-track" and specialty travel opportunities, try the **Specialty Travel Index,** 305 San Anselmo Ave., #313, San Anselmo, CA 94960, USA (☎(888) 624-4030 or (415) 455-1643; www.spectrav.com; US$6). **Transitions Abroad** (www.transabroad.com) publishes a bimonthly on-line newsletter for work, study, and specialized travel abroad.

STUDY ABROAD

There is a plethora of study abroad programs in both Austria and Switzerland. In **Austria,** there are summer or year-long academic programs associated with American Universities in Vienna, Salzburg, Innsbruck, and Bregenz. You can study anything from architecture to social work to Vienna's psychologists. German language programs are available for study abroad in both Austria and Switzerland. In **Switzerland,** there are summer and winter sessions for universities in Geneva and Zurich. The University of Delaware organizes a summer-long Swiss Hospitality Program. One resource if you're considering studying abroad is www.studyabroadlinks.com. In addition, there are walking, bicycling, and hiking programs that can be arranged for students visiting both countries.

If you plan to study abroad in Switzerland for more than 3 months, you need to fill out a residency permit and receive authorization from Swiss authorities. To study in Austria, citizens of non-EU countries must have visas. All foreigners must have valid study permits. Most US universities will arrange permits for students.

UNIVERSITIES

Most American undergraduates enroll in programs sponsored by US universities. However, if your German is already good, local universities can be much cheaper than an American university program, though it can be hard to receive academic credit. Schools that offer study abroad programs to foreigners are listed below.

Webster University in Geneva and Vienna, contact: Study Abroad Office, Webster University, 470 E. Lockwood, St. Louis, MO, USA 63119 (☎(314) 968-6988 or (800) 984-6857; fax (314) 968-7119; worldview@webster.edu. More than 400 students from 65 countries come here to pursue full degree programs or summer and semester sessions in a range of concentrations and electives. All courses are taught in English and are fully accredited.

American Institute for Foreign Study, College Division, River Plaza, 9 West Broad St., Stamford, CT 06902, USA (☎(800) 727-2437, ext. 5163; www.aifsabroad.com). Organizes programs for high school and college study in universities in Austria.

Beaver College Center for Education Abroad, 450 S. Easton Rd., Glenside, PA 19038, USA (☎(888) 232-8379; www.beaver.edu/cea). Operates programs in Austria. Costs range from $1900 (summer) to $20,000 (full-year).

Central College Abroad, Office of International Education, 812 University, Pella, IA 50219, USA (☎(800) 831-3629 or (515) 628-5284; studyabroad.com/central). Offers semester- and year-long programs in Austria. US$25 application fee.

School for International Training, College Semester Abroad, Admissions, Kipling Rd., P.O. Box 676, Brattleboro, VT 05302, USA (☎(800) 336-1616 or (802) 258-3267; www.sit.edu). Semester- and year-long programs in Switzerland run US$9500-12,900.

International Association for the Exchange of Students for Technical Experience (IAESTE), 10400 Little Patuxent Pkwy. #250, Columbia, MD 21044, USA (☎(410) 997-3068; www.aipt.org). 8- to 12-week programs in Austria and Switzerland for college students who have completed 2 years of technical study. US$50 application fee.

LANGUAGE SCHOOLS

Programs are run by foreign universities, independent international or local organizations, and divisions of the local universities. Programs vary in cost tremendously, and may or may not include lodging, daytrips, and cultural activities.

University of Geneva Summer Courses, contact: Mr. Gerard Benz, University of Geneva, summer courses, rue de Candolle 3, CH-1211 Geneva 4, Switzerland (☎(22) 750 7434; fax 750 7439; bisatti@uni2a.unige.ch). Teaches French language and civilization at all levels and offers excursions to Geneva and its surroundings. Tuition for a 3-week summer course SF470. Minimum age 17.

Wiener Internationale Hochschulkurse, contact: Magister Sigrun Anmann-Trojer, Wiener Internationale Hochschulkurse, Universität, Dr. Karl Lueger-Ring 1, A1010 Wien, Austria by mail, www.univie.ac.at/wihok (☎(01) 405 1254; fax (01) 405 1254 10). Offers German courses for beginners and advanced students, as well as lectures on German and Austrian literature, music, linguistics, and Austrian culture, including exposure to the Vienna waltz and choir singing. Tuition for a 4-week summer course 4600AS, accommodations 5500AS.

FURTHER READING: STUDY

Academic Year Abroad. Institute of International Education Books (US$45).
Vacation Study Abroad. Institute of International Education Books (US$40).
Peterson's Study Abroad Guide. Peterson's (US$30).
Also see www.language-learning.net.

WORK

Austria has strict work restrictions. If you are a citizen of an EU country, you do not need a work permit for employment in Austria. Otherwise, you need to obtain a work permit before leaving your country of origin. Of course, as a stroke of bureaucratic genius, this is virtually impossible for casual and seasonal work. Expect to pay 16% of your salary to mandatory health and Social Security programs (except for au pairs). To find employment in Austria, German-speakers can contact the state-run employment office *Arbeitmarktservice*. There are no private employment offices in Austria. The easiest jobs for foreigners to find are in the hotel and agriculture industries. Also, English teachers and au pairs are always in demand.

Switzerland has equally strict immigration policies that can make it very difficult for foreigners to find work. A free booklet entitled *Living and Working in Switzerland* can be obtained from any Swiss embassy for full information on their policies. A residence permit covers both the right to live and work in Switzerland. Do not attempt to find employment there without a permit, as ski resorts have been known to hire police solely for the purpose of checking visas. Employers may be fined 3000SFr for hiring illegal workers. One job you don't (usually) need a permit for is busking—street musicians in Bern can do quite well by the end of the day—but check with the local police for authorized areas.

Swiss hotels hire foreign workers for their summer and winter tourist seasons. It's worth it to start looking for a job early: April/May for the summer season and September/October for the winter season. Writing ahead to places can save you grief later. Fluency in German will be helpful, sometimes necessary, in finding a job. Tourist offices may also be of help.

If you are interested more in a rural experience than in making money, a job in the agriculture industry might be suited to you. One-third of summer farm hands are foreign workers. The hours are long but room and board is generally included. In general, expect to work very hard, long hours. The Swiss hold very high standards for cleanliness and productivity but are willing to pay high wages in return.

AU PAIR

Accord Cultural Exchange, 750 La Playa, San Francisco, CA 94121, USA (☎(415) 386-6203); www.cognitext.com/accord). US$40 application fee.

InterExchange, 161 Sixth Ave., New York, NY 10013 (☎(212) 924-0446; fax 924-0575; www.interexchange.org). Participants must speak the local language.

Childcare International, Ltd., Trafalgar House, Grenville Pl., London NW7 3SA (☎(020) 890 63116; fax 890 63461; www.childint.co.uk). UK£100 application fee.

TEACHING ENGLISH

International Schools Services, Educational Staffing Program, P.O. Box 5910, Princeton, NJ 08543, USA (☎(609) 452-0990; www.iss.edu). Recruits teachers and administrators for American and English schools in Austria and Switzerland. US$150 application fee.

Office of Overseas Schools, US Department of State, Room H328, SA-1, Washington, D.C. 20522 (☎(202) 261-8200; fax 261-8224; www.state.gov/www/about_state/schools/). Keeps a comprehensive list of schools abroad and agencies that arrange placement for Americans to teach abroad.

AGRICULTURE

Willing Workers on Organic Farms (WWOOF), For **Austria:** contact Hildegard Gottlieb, Langeg. 155, 8511 St. Stefan ob Stainz, Austria, ☎/fax (03) 463 82270. For **Switzerland:** WWOOF, Postfach 59, 8124 Maur, Switzerland (fairtours@gn.apc.org or wwoof@dataway.ch; www.phdcc.com/sites/wwoof or www.dataway.ch/~reini/wwoof/). Membership (350 AS + 2 International Reply Coupons to receive list of farms) allows you to receive room and board at a variety of organic farms in Austria and Switzerland in exchange for your help on the farm.

VOLUNTEER

Volunteer jobs are readily available, and many provide room and board in exchange for labor. You can sometimes avoid high application fees by contacting the individual workcamps directly.

Service Civil International Voluntary Service (SCI-IVS), 814 NE 40th St., Seattle, WA 98105, USA (☎/fax (206) 545-6585; www.sci-ivs.org). Arranges placement in workcamps in Austria and Switzerland for those 18+. Registration fee US$65-150.

Volunteers for Peace, 1034 Tiffany Rd., Belmont, VT 05730, USA (☎(802) 259-2759; www.vfp.org). Arranges placement in workcamps in Austria and Switzerland. Annual *International Workcamp Directory* US$20. Registration fee US$200. Free newsletter.

FURTHER READING: ALTERNATIVES TO TOURISM.

International Jobs: Where they Are, How to Get Them, Eric Koocher. Perseus Books (US$17).

How to Get a Job in Europe, Robert Sanborn. Surrey Books (US$22).

Work Abroad: The Complete Guide to Finding a Job Overseas, Clayton Hubbs. Transitions Abroad (US$16).

International Directory of Voluntary Work, Louise Whetter. Vacation Work Publications (US$16).

Teaching English Abroad, Susan Griffin. Vacation Work (US$17).

Overseas Summer Jobs 2001, Work Your Way Around the World, and *The Directory of Jobs and Careers Abroad.* Peterson's (US$17-18 each).

FURTHER RESOURCES

THE INTERNET

Almost every aspect of budget travel is accessible via the web. Even if you don't have internet access at home, seeking it out at a public library or at work would be well worth it: within 10min. at the keyboard, you can make a reservation at a hostel, get advice on travel hotspots or experiences from other travelers who have just returned from Austria and Switzerland, or find out exactly how much a train between cities costs.

Listed here are some budget travel sites to start off your surfing; other relevant web sites are listed throughout the book. Because website turnover is high, use search engines (such as www.yahoo.com) to strike out on your own. But in doing so, keep in mind that most travel web sites simply exist to get your money.

Switzerland has a comprehensive web network. Even in the smallest towns, everything is online. Business, tourist offices, hostels, and individuals in the smallest villages have great user-friendly websites. Austria is a bit behind Switzerland, but is still fairly up-to-date. It is definitely worth your time to search the Internet for Austrian and Swiss websites before you go; they can be helpful both in planning your vacation and learning more about Austrian and Swiss culture in general.

WWW TIPS

The **domain** for many Swiss webpages is .ch; Austria's is .at.

Swiss Search Engines: Try www.search.ch or www.sear.ch.

Austrian Search Engines: Try www.search.at or www.suchmaschine.at.

LEARNING THE ART OF BUDGET TRAVEL

How to See the World: www.artoftravel.com. A compendium of great travel tips, from cheap flights to self defense to interacting with local culture.

Rec. Travel Library: www.travel-library.com. A fantastic set of links for general information and personal travelogues.

Shoestring Travel: www.stratpub.com. An e-zine focusing on budget travel.

INFORMATION ON AUSTRIA AND SWITZERLAND

CIA World Factbook: www.odci.gov/cia/publications/factbook/index.html. Tons of statistics on the geography, government, economy, and people of Austria and Switzerland.

Foreign Language for Travelers: www.travlang.com. Provides free online translating dictionaries and lists of phrases in French, German, and Italian (among others).

Geographia: www.geographia.com. Info on the highlights, culture, and people of Austria and Switzerland.

Atevo Travel: www.atevo.com/guides/destinations. Detailed introductions, travel tips, and suggested itineraries.

Columbus Travel Guides: http://www.travel-guides.com/navigate/world.asp. Helpful practical information.

TravelPage: www.travelpage.com. Links to official tourist office sites throughout Austria and Switzerland.

PlanetRider: www.planetrider.com/Travel_Destinations.cfm. A subjective list of links to the "best" websites on the culture and tourist attractions of Austria and Switzerland.

Youth Hostel Listings: The official hostel webpages for Austria (www.jgh.at) and Switzerland (www.jugendherberge.ch) give an overview of all hostels at a glance.

AND OUR PERSONAL FAVORITE...

Let's Go: www.letsgo.com. Our recently revamped website features photos and streaming video, info about our books, a travel forum buzzing with stories and tips, and links that will help you find everything you could ever want to know about Austria and Switzerland.

TRAVEL BOOK PUBLISHERS AND BOOKSTORES

Hippocrene Books, Inc., 171 Madison Ave., New York, NY 10016 (☎(212) 685-4371; orders (718) 454-2366; www.netcom.com/~hippocre).

Hunter Publishing, 130 Campus Dr., Edison, NJ 08818, USA (☎(800) 255-0343; www.hunterpublishing.com). Quality maps.

Rand McNally, 150 S. Wacker Dr., Chicago, IL 60606, USA (☎(800) 234-0679 or (312) 332-2009; www.randmcnally.com), publishes road atlases (each US$10).

Adventurous Traveler Bookstore, 245 S. Champlain St., Burlington, VT 05401, USA (☎(800) 282-3963 or (802) 860-6776; www.adventuroustraveler.com).

Bon Voyage!, 2069 W. Bullard Ave., Fresno, CA 93711, USA (☎(800) 995-9716, from abroad (209) 447-8441; www.bon-voyage-travel.com). They specialize in Europe but have titles pertaining to other regions as well. Free catalog.

Travel Books & Language Center, Inc., 4437 Wisconsin Ave. NW, Washington, D.C. 20016 (☎(800) 220-2665 or (202) 237-1322; www.bookweb.org/bookstore/travelbks). Over 60,000 titles from around the world.

AUSTRIA (ÖSTERREICH)

AUSTRIAN SCHILLING

US$1 = 15.06 (AS/ÖS/ATS)	**10AS = US$.66**
CDN$1 = 10.13AS	**10AS = CDN$.99**
UK£1 = 22.69AS	**10AS = UK£.44**
IR£1 = 17.47AS	**10AS = IR£.57**
AUS$1 = 8.80AS	**10AS = AUS$1.14**
NZ$1 = 6.76AS	**10AS = NZ$1.48**
SAR1 = 2.17AS	**10AS = SAR4.60**
1SFR = 8.81AS	**10AS = SFR1.13**
1DM = 7.04AS	**10AS = DM1.42**
L1000= 7.11AS	**10AS = L1407.14**
1Kč = .39AS	**10AS = Kč25.72**
EUR€1 = 13.76AS	**10AS = EUR€.73**

PHONE CODES The **country code** for Austria is 43. International calls from Austria require the prefix 00 or, from Vienna only, 900.

Although the mighty Austro-Hungarian Empire crumbled during World War I, Austria remains a complex, multiethnic country with a fascinating political and cultural history. At the peak of Habsburg megalomania, the Austrian empire was one of the largest empires in history, encompassing much of Europe from Poland and Hungary in the east to the Netherlands in the west. The complex constellation of identities present within the empire continues today in the diverse constitutions of the nine provinces, or *Bundesländer*, of present-day Austria. Clockwise from the northeast, Austria's provinces are: Vienna *(Wien)*, Burgenland, Styria *(Steiermark)*, Carinthia *(Kärnten)*, Tyrol *(Tirol)*, Vorarlberg, Salzburg, Upper Austria *(Oberösterreich)*, and Lower Austria *(Niederösterreich)*. Each province was once an independent region that became part of the Habsburg lands by marriage, treaty, or trade, and each retains deep-rooted identities and unique dialects.

Austria owes its contemporary fame and fortune to the meeting of its history with the overpowering Alpine landscape that hovers over the remnants of Austria's tumultuous past. The mention of Austria evokes images of onion-domed churches set against snow-capped Alpine peaks, lush meadows of mustard flowers surrounding mighty castles, and 10th-century monasteries towering over the majestic Danube. Forests and meadows cover two thirds of Austria's total land area, and much of the land is studded with mountains. Western Austria, especially Tyrol, is particularly studly. Its highpoint—and Austria's—is the *Großglockner*, at 3797m (12,457 ft.). The mountains generate year-round tourism: Alpine sports dominate the winter scene, while lakeside frolicking draws visitors in the warmer months. The blue-green Danube, Europe's longest river, has been central to Austrian industry and aristocracy since the country's beginning: both ruling families of early Austria, the Babenbergs and the Habsburgs, set up residences on its shores. Now, river cruises showcase their ruined castles as well as the thriving vineyards whose magic potion made the Middle Ages bearable.

Vienna, once the imperial headquarters and now the country's capital, majestically straddles the river, holding treasures from both imperial times and the period at the turn of the 20th century when Vienna led the world's charge toward modernism in revolutionary figures like Sigmund Freud and Gustav Klimt. The mix between stately Baroque architecture and the modern urban landscape is a fitting metaphor for the exciting, unstable nature of this city at the crossroads of eastern and western Europe.

A BRIEF HISTORY OF AUSTRIA

IN THE BEGINNING

80,000 BC The first *Homo Sapiens* venture into the Danube river valley.

23,000 BC The statuette now known as Venus of Willendorf is carved.

500 BC Celts establish the kingdom of Noricum in present-day Austria, and mine "white gold" (salt).

15 BC-AD 488 Roman troops under Caesar Augustus conquer and occupy Noricum, establishing settlements at Carnuntum and Vindobona (present-day Vienna).

AD 375-800 The Romans abandon Noricum. Various Germanic tribes, followed by Huns, Slavs, Avars, and Magyars sweep through the area during the great Tribal Migration.

Beginning in Paleolithic times, nomadic hunter-gatherers roamed through what is now Austria for thousands of years, gradually becoming more settled as they began to farm, domesticate stock animals, and mine Austria's rich salt deposits. 6km-thick glaciers crawled north, carving out the alpine valleys that tourists enjoy today, and making room for greater habitation of Austrian lands. The 25,000 year old carved-stone fertility goddess Venus of Willendorf (which is so valuable that the Natural History Museum in Vienna displays only a copy) bears witness to the level of civilization. By 6000 BC, even the remotest areas of Austria were part of a vigorous commercial network that linked mining centers and agricultural communities, as the recent discovery of the hunter-trader Ötzi (see below) has proved.

As economic opportunities moved beyond salt, more aggressive peoples wanted a share of the wealth. Around 500 BC, the **Celts** took control of the salt mines and established the kingdom of **Noricum,** which developed a relatively affluent economy based on a thriving salt and iron trade. In turn, the **Romans** conquered their Austrian neighbors to secure the Danube frontier against marauding Germanic tribes in 15 BC. Christianity came to Austria via the Roman soldiers, while legions, traders, and missionaries came via Roman roads along the Danube and across the Alps. One of the first Roman military posts was Vindobona, at the present site of Vienna.

Germanic raids finally forced Romans to retreat from Noricum in the 5th century. Over the next three centuries, during the *Völkerwanderung* (tribal migration), various peoples, including the Huns, Ostrogoths, and Langobards romped through the Austrian territories, but none established any lasting settlement. Eventually, three groups divided the region: the **Slavs** in the southwest, the **Bavarians** in the north, and the **Alemanni** in the south. In what would become a recurring pattern, the nobles from Bavaria concentrated on converting the population to Christianity in an attempt to establish law and order and create a power-base. The result of their efforts was the creation of the Archbishopric of Salzburg, which has remained Austria's ecclesiastical center.

FROZEN IN TIME On September 19, 1991, hikers accidentally discovered the deep-frozen corpse of a middle-aged man in a glacier, 10,000 feet above sea level, along the Austro-Italian border. The dead man, nicknamed Ötzi the Iceman after the Ötztal valley where he was found, lived approximately 5,300 years ago, but his body was perfectly preserved in the ice. Ötzi's appearance has been a boon to prehistoric research, but the question of who owned his body was hotly debated for several years. Although he was found by Austrians, his resting place was just within the Italian border. In 1998, Ötzi was put on display in Bolzano, Italy, where he lies behind bulletproof glass at -6° Celsius and 98% humidity. The Italians appreciate their oldest resident, not least because of brisk trade in chocolate Ötzis, Ötzi ice cream, Ötzi pizza, Ötzi wine, and Ötzi sausage throughout Bolzano.

HOLY ROMANS AND HAPSBURGS (900-1740)

The lands currently known as Austria first fell to imperialism in the 9th century when **Charlemagne,** founder of the Holy Roman Empire, turned his eyes east in hopes of heading off Avar invaders on the frontiers of his empire. Charlemagne was the first to make Austria the barrier and meeting point between eastern and western Europe that it remains today. When he died, Charlemagne's kingdom collapsed and its eastern regions were overrun by marauding tribes. The German king Otto regained control of the Holy Roman Empire only after conquering one of these tribes, the Magyars.

While much of Austria was held by a number of small lords at this time the first notion of Austria as a unique entity was expressed when Otto named Margrave Liutpoldus (a.k.a. Leopold of Babenberg, see A Rose by Another Name? p. 64) duke of the Empire's eastern territories in 976. Leopold, a Bavarian lord, was nonetheless the first ruler Austria calls its own. During his reign, Austria gained its name: *Ostarrichi* (Old High German for *Österreich*), that is, "Eastern (in German, *Öst*) Realm" of the Empire.

The **Babenbergs,** who served as the Dukes of the Eastern Realm for the next 270 years, claimed Vienna as their home. From Vienna they concentrated on stabilizing the frontiers but also on extending their protectorate by shrewdness and strategic marriages. By founding monasteries and abbeys, as well as importing German-speaking settlers, the Babenbergs built up a core of loyal subjects that supported them in their political maneuvering between the Holy Roman Emperor and the Pope. Pragmatically, they supported whichever side benefitted them the most. One case of this occured when Duke Leopold V captured **Richard the Lionheart** on his way home from crusading, and rather than giving Richard over to the Holy Roman Emperor, who had put a price on the head of the English king, returned Richard to England for hard, cold silver (see Dürnstein, p. 278).

Unfortunately for the dynasty, the last Babenberg died childless, leaving the country fragmented during a 19-year *Interregnum*. The major contestants for the Austrian lands were the Bohemian King Ottokar II and the new Holy Roman Emperor, the Swiss nobleman **Rudolf of Habsburg.** Rudolf had a surprisingly small plot of land in Switzerland before he beat out Ottokar in the Battle of Marchfeld in 1278, claiming the Austrian lands, and laying the foundation for 6 centuries of Habsburg dynastic rule in Austria. Like their Babenberg predecessors, the Habsburgs made every effort to increase their property by means of treaties and marriages, with memorable success (though they lost their original Swiss holdings after a farmer's revolution). Gradually, the Habsburgs accumulated the various regions that make up modern Austria and then some. **Rudolf the Founder's** short rule (1358-1365) was marked by his acquisition of the Earldom of Tirol, as well as the founding of the University of Vienna. After **Friedrich III** was elected Emperor of the Holy Roman Empire the Imperial Crown was passed down through the Hapsburg line until the collapse of the Empire in the 19th century. Friedrich expanded the direct claims of the Hapsburg family by strategically betrothing his son, **Maximilian I,** to the heiress of the powerful Burgundian kingdom, giving the Hapsburgs control of much of western Europe, including the Netherlands.

798 Bavarian nobles establish the Archbishopric of Salzburg as Austria's ecclesiastical headquarters.

803 Charlemagne marks Austrian lands as the eastern frontier (Ostmark) of the Holy Roman Empire.

955 Emperor Otto I defeats the Magyars, winning back the Austrian territories in the Battle of Lechfeld.

976 Marchio Liutpoldus, the first Babenberg, receives control of portions of present day Austria.

996 The name Austria (*Ostarrichi*) appears for the first time in an official document.

1246 After the death of the last Babenberg duke, Ottokar II of Bohemia rules Austria for 26 years.

1278 Holy Roman Emperor Rudolf von Habsburg defeats Ottokar, beginning more than 600 years of Habsburg rule in Austria.

1452 Friedrich III is crowned Holy Roman Emperor by the Pope in Rome, subsequently claiming the imperial throne as the hereditary right of the Habsburgs.

A ROSE BY ANOTHER NAME?

Medieval history celebrates Austria's two major ruling families: the Babenbergs (976-1246) and the Hapsburgs (1278-1918). Unfortunately for the history books, the Babenbergs were not actually named Babenberg, but rather Poppon; furthermore, their family seat was not the Castle Babenberch in Bamberg, Germany, but a nameless castle somewhere in German Swabia. The name Babenberg was an invention of the 12th-century historian Otto von Freising, himself a Poppon, who found the name of his ancestor Poppo von Grabfeld (that is, Poppo "of the Cemetary") unsuitable for his patriotic purposes. He casually renamed the dynasty "Babenberg," which later historians adopted and embellished with individual heroic epithets, such as Ernst the Brave and Leopold the Glorious. This relatively harmless deception quickly became an integral part of Austrian history, with the result that historians today still refer to the "Babenbergs" without a second thought.

1496 Philipp the Handsome, Friedrich III's grandson, marries Juana of Aragon (daughter of Ferdinand and Isabella of Spain).

1527 Phillip's son Ferdinand is crowned King of Bohemia and Hungary, founding the Danube Monarchy.

Mid-16th century The Protestant Reformation reaches Austria, followed by the Catholic Counter-Reformation.

1618-1648 Austria is involved in the Thirty Years War between Catholics and Protestants.

1683 The Ottoman Turks surround and besiege Vienna. The Austrians drive the Turks out of Hungary.

1701-1714 Austria fights France in the War of Spanish Succession.

Maximilian is credited with the adaptation of Ovid's couplet: *"Bella gerant alii, tu felix Austria nube."* (Let other nations go to war; you, lucky Austria, marry—an early riff on "Make love, not war.") Maximilian's son **Philipp** married into the Spanish royal house, endowing his son, **Charles V,** with a vast empire that encompassed Austria, the Netherlands, Spain, Burgundy, Spanish America, and Italian and Mediterranean possessions. The Habsburg Empire reached the height of its power during Charles' reign. It seems the power was too much for Charles who gave the Austrian empire and the Imperial crown to his brother **Ferdinand** (and the Spanish possesions to his son Phillip) before retiring to the woods to become a monk in 1556. Ferdinand, despite not knowing German, Czech, or Hungarian, managed to add Bohemia and Hungary to the Hapsburg possesions thanks to another crafty marriage planned long before by Maximillian.

The massive Habsburg ship hit rough waters in the 16th and 17th centuries, when Martin Luther's Protestant **Reformation** swept through the Empire. By the time **Ferdinand II** assumed control of the Hapsburg empire in 1619, somewhere near nine tenths of the population of Austria had been converted from Catholocism to Protestantism--most of the converted being peasants. But Ferdinand II, inspired by his Jesuit education, made Austria the first battleground of the Catholic **Counter-Reformation.** Resistance by protestant, Bohemian nobles in Prague to Ferdinand's plans touched off Europe's Thirty Years War (1618-1648). A larger cause of the war was the unresolved and pervading sense of fragmentation within the monstrous empire. In the war the Austrian Imperial troops promptly (and forcibly) converted most of the peasants back to Catholicism and chased Protestants in the upper classes off to a sympathetic, protestant Germany. With the Treaty of Westphalia that ended the war, the Habsburgs forfeited vast tracts of territory. While Austria was recuperating, the Ottoman Turks repeatedly besieged Vienna until the French **Prince Franz Eugene** came with a Christian relief army and drove them out. Eugene was given Schloss Belvedere in Vienna in thanks for his work (see p. 118). Eugene again came through for the Hapsburgs when he led their troops to victory over the French in the **War of Spanish Succession,** which ended with a treaty giving Spain to France, while the Habsburgs gained Belgium, Sardinia, and parts of Italy.

CASTLES CRUMBLE (1740-1900)

What the Hapsburgs gained in land they sacrificed in stability. This huge empire, with no dominant ethnic group and a series of foreign leaders began to crumble in the 18th century. When Maria Theresa ascended the throne in 1740 (thanks to the Pragmatic Sanction passed by her father, which allowed Hapsburg succesion through the female line) her European neighbors were eager to see Habsburg power diminished. King **Friedrich the Great** of Prussia snatched Silesia (now southwest Poland), one of the Habsburg's most prosperous provinces; Maria Theresa spent the rest of her life unsuccessfully maneuvering to reclaim it. In the **War of Austrian Succession** between 1740 and 1748, Maria Theresa maintained her rule with help from the Hungarians, and through the battles Maria Theresa came to be loved by the Austrian people as their *Landesmutter* (mother of the people). She didn't, however, do such a good job looking after the well-being of her own children. She married her daughter Marie Antoinette to the French Prince Louis XVI, a marriage that ended with no small amount of blood spilled under the guillotine during the **French Revolution.** The French Revolutionaries who killed Maria Theresa's daughter soon declared war on Maria Theresa's son, **Joseph II,** who by that time, in 1792, was ruling Austria. Showcasing the military genius of young commander General **Napoleon Bonaparte,** the Republic of France wrested possession of Belgium and most of Austria's remaining Italian territories from the Hapsburgs. Napoleon's troops even invaded Vienna, where Napoleon took up residence in Maria Theresa's favorite palace, Schönbrunn (p. 118), and married her granddaughter.

1740 Thanks to the Pragmatic Sanction, Maria Theresa is crowned Empress of Austria, Queen of Hungary and Bohemia. During her reign, Austria loses several territories to Prussia.

1780 Josef II abolishes serfdom and grants freedom of religion.

1804 Napoleon's troops occupy Vienna. The Holy Roman Empire of the German Nation is officially dissolved and the former Holy Roman Emperor becomes Emperor Franz I of Austria.

1815 The Congress of Vienna, made up of representatives from 200 states, duchies, and independent cities, establishes a political system that maintains peace in Europe for the next 40 years.

AUSTRIA

Napoleon's success led to the establishment of the much smaller, but much more Austrian, Hapsburg empire. In 1804, **Franz II** renounced his claim to the now-defunct Holy Roman crown and proclaimed himself Franz I, Emperor of Austria. During the Congress of Vienna, which redrew the map of Europe after Napoleon's defeat, Austrian Chancellor **Clemens Wenzel Lothar von Metternich** (like so many other Austrian leaders, a foreigner, from Germany) masterfully orchestrated the re-consolidation of Austrian power. For the rest of the century, Metternich's foreign policy for Austria was dictated by a desire to maintain monarchic stability throughout Europe. Austria feared the crumbling of the Ottoman Empire to the south, and the resulting creation of the new indpendent Slavic states in the Balkans. Metternich rightly believed that the independence of these states would encourage the Slavic people in the Hapsburg Empire—Slavs represented half of the Hapsburg population—to fight for their own independence. Metternich pushed the other great powers in Europe to mobilize against any threats to the Ottoman Empire.

In order to maitain stability within Austria Metternich introduced harshly repressive social policies. The people responded to these policies by moving inwards, and focusing on non-political issues. In Austria, as elsewhere in Europe, the first half of the 19th century was marked by immense technological progress. This progress led to the rise of an introverted middle class, satirized in the character Papa Biedermeier, by poet Ludwig Eichro-

1848 The so-called "Storm Year" witnesses workers' revolutions throughout the Europe and the Danube-Monarchy. Disheartened, Emperor Ferdinand abdicates in favor his nephew Franz Josef.

cht. The term **Biedermeier** came to label the bourgeois, domestic culture that flourished in this time (see p. 76).

As Metternich's fears became realized with the slow disintegration of the Ottoman empire, domestic resistance to Austria's repressive social policies increased. Resistance came to a head in early 1848. Working together, students and workers built barricades, took control of the imperial palace, and demanded a constitution and freedom of the press. Ethnic rivalries and political differences divided the revolutionary forces, however, and the government was able to suppress the worker's revolution and a Hungarian rebellion. The epileptic emperor **Ferdinand I** paid the price for the renewed stability; he was pressured to abdicate in favor of his nephew, **Franz Josef I,** whose 68-year reign was one of the longest in history.

1867 To resist Prussian aggression, Emperor Franz Josef agrees to the dual monarchy of Austria-Hungary.

Austria's position in Europe continued to shift throughout Franz Josef's life. Austria and Prussia vied for control of the German Empire. Under **Otto von Bismarck,** Prussia dominated European politics, and defeated Austria in 1866 at the battle of Königgrätz, creating a Germany "without the participation of the Austrian empire." The Austrian fall from power continued in 1867, when the Hungarian parliament voted to end the Austrian Empire, and form the dual **Austro-Hungarian Empire** over which Franz Josef was only the titular ruler. Still, non-German speakers were marginalized within the new empire, until 1907, when the government ceded basic civil rights to all peoples in the Empire and accepted universal male suffrage. But these concessions to the Slavic elements of the empire came too late. Burgeoning nationalist sentiments, especially among the Serbia-inspired South Slavs, led to severe divisions within the multinational Austro-Hungarian Empire. Tired and disheartened after half a century on the throne, the suicide of his only son, and the murder of his wife, Franz Josef wanted to maintain *Ruhe und Ordnung* (peace and order), but he could not stop the tide of modernity.

THE RISE OF THE REPUBLIC (1900-2000)

1914 The heir to the Austrian throne, Franz Ferdinand is murdered in Sarajevo by a Serbian nationalist on June 28. One month later, Austria-Hungary declares war on Serbia, triggering World War I.

1916 Emperor Franz Joseph dies and is succeeded by his grandnephew Charles I.

1918 The Austro-Hungarian empire collapses; the first Republic of Austria is established and the Habsburgs lose the Austrian throne.

As the now-free Slavic states of the Ottoman Empire—and particularly Serbia—agitated the Slavic elements within the Austro-Hungarian Empire, Franz Josef had to either quiet these forces or quietly relinquish claims to the Slavic half of his Empire. When **Franz Ferdinand,** the heir to the imperial throne, and his wife Sophie were assassinated by a young Serbian nationalist named Gavrilo Prinzip in Sarajevo in 1914, Franz Josef had an excuse to attack the Serbians. Austria's declaration of war against Serbia set off a chain reaction that pulled most of Europe into the conflict: Russia hurried to support Serbia, Germany to support Austria, and France to support its Entente partner, Russia. Franz Josef died during the war in 1916 leaving the throne to his reluctant grandnephew **Charles I** (see Charlie's Last Stand, below) who struggled in vain to preserve the Habsburg inheritance (going so far as to initiate secret negotiations with the French). Despite his valiant efforts and those of the army, declarations of independence by the Empire's non-German peoples and the desperate maneuvering of Viennese intellectuals ensured the demise of the monarchy. On November 11, 1918, Charles finally got the peace he had striven for, but only after liberals declared the first **Republic of Austria,** ending the 640-year-old Habsburg dynasty.

CHARLIE'S LAST STAND Contrary to popular history, Charles I, the last emperor of the Austro-Hungarian empire, did not abdicate. Leaders of the Republic were willing to let him remain Emperor as long as he signed an agreement renouncing all political involvement. Charles signed (in pencil), but in Feldkirch, on the Swiss border, he composed the Feldkircher Manifest, which nullified all agreements he had signed since October 1918. The Austrians banned him from the country, so Charles mounted a campaign to reclaim the Hungarian throne, but, alas, the Hungarians arrested and deported him to England. Within a year, Charles died of tuberculosis on the island of Madeira.

Between 1918 and 1938, Austria had its first, bitter taste of parliamentary democracy. After the Entente that ended the first World War forbade a unified *Deutsch-Österreich*, the shrunken Austrian state became the **First Republic,** consisting of the German-speaking lands of the former Habsburg empire minus those granted to Italy, Czechoslovakia, and Hungary. The Republic suffered massive inflation, unemployment, and near economic collapse, but by the mid-1920s, the Austrian government had stabilized the currency and established economic relations with neighboring states. Still, violent internal strife between political parties weakened the Republic's already shaky democratic foundation. In 1933, the weak coalition government gave way to **Engelbert Dollfuss's** declaration of martial law. In order to protect Austria from Hitler, Dollfuss entered an ill-fated alliance with fascist Italy. Two years later, just as Mussolini and Hitler made peace, Austrian Nazis assassinated Dollfuss. His successor, **Kurt Schuschnigg,** was also ultimately unable to maintain Austrian independence in the face of Nazi pressure.

1920s Social Democrats and Christian Socialists struggle for domination of the new parliamentary democracy.

1933 Chancellor Dollfuss dissolves Parliament and declares martial law in an effort to protect Austria from Hitler.

1935 Dollfuss is murdered by Nazis.

The end of the First Republic was the Nazi annexation of Austria. On March 9, 1938, hoping to stave off a Nazi invasion, Schuschnigg called a referendum against unity with Germany, but Hitler demanded Schuschnigg's resignation. On March 12, the new Nazi chancellor invited German troops into Austria, where they met no resistance. Although Goebbels' propaganda wildly exaggerated the enthusiasm of Austrians for Hitler (as did a phony referendum in April, in which 99% of Austrians approved of annexation), many Austrians wanted to believe the **Anschluß** (union with Germany) would make their future brighter. When the Nazis marched into Vienna on March 14, thousands turned out to cheer them on. Disappointment quickly set in, as Austria lost both its name (it became the "Ostmark," then merely the "Alpine district") and its self-respect. Aside from individual resistance fighters, cooperation with the Nazis and anti-Semitism became the rule in Austria, though disillusionment with empty Nazi promises of peace and prosperity soon grew. While WWII raged, tens of thousands of Jews, among them many of Austria's leading intellectuals, artists, and writers, were forced to emigrate or sent to concentration camps, along with political and religious dissidents, handicapped persons, Gypsies, and homosexuals. Only a few thousand came home alive.

1938 Chancellor Schuschnigg calls for a plebiscite against annexation by Nazi Germany. Hitler forces Schuschnigg to resign. German troops invade Austria and the country is absorbed into the Nazi German empire as the "Ostmark" (Eastern Province).

1941 Deportations of Austrian Jews begins.

1943 Allied powers publish the Moscow Declaration stating that Austria was a victim of Nazi aggression.

After Soviet troops brutally "liberated" Vienna in 1945, Austria was divided into 4 zones of occupation by Allied troops in order to re-establish an Austrian government. By April 1945, a provisional government was established with 75-year old **Karl Renner**

1945 Vienna is liberated by Soviet troops and a provisional Austrian government is formed under Karl Renner.

as president. In November, the National Assembly declared Austria's independence from Germany (Wir sind kein zweiter deutscher Staat; wir sind nichts anders als Österreicher—We are not a second German state; we are nothing but Austrians). During the Allied occupation, the Soviets tried to make Austria Communist, but finally settled for stripping their sector of anything that could be moved. The immediate post-war period was a time of general political, economic, and psychological chaos throughout Austria, but most Austrians rejoiced in their new-found independence and eagerly grasped their second chance at creating a democracy. Despite Russian plundering and severe famines in the late 1940s, the Marshall Plan helped to jump-start the Austrian economy, laying the foundation for Austria's present prosperity. In 1955, after Stalin died, Austria was able to convince the four powers to allow Austria complete sovereignty after it pledged to be neutral in the **State Treaty** of that year.

1955 The State Treaty is signed and Allied troops withdraw, restoring Austria's independence. Austria declares absolute neutrality.

The State Treaty, along with the Federal Constitution, which was restored in 1945 from the First Republic, formed the basis for the nation, which is frequently referred to as the **Second Republic.** These documents provide for a president (head of state) who is elected for six-year terms, a chancellor (head of government), usually the leader of the strongest party, a bicameral parliamentary legislature, and strong provincial governments. Until very recently the government has been dominated by two parties, the Social Democratic Party (SPÖ), and the People's Party (ÖVP). The rigidness of the two party system has raised questions of corruption and paternalism, many of which came out in the recent election of the Freedom Party (see current events). The two parties have built up one of the world's most successful industrial economies, with enviably low unemployment and inflation rates, as well as a generous, comprehensive welfare state. Austria has emerged as a progressive, social democratic welfare state. The success of the nation's transformation was questioned in 1986 when it was alleged that Kurt Waldheim, the president-elect, had lied about his past in the German army during World War II. The US was particularly strident in its criticism, placing Waldheim on its "watch-list," effectively preventing Waldheim from entering the United States.

1995 Austria joins the European Union.

1998 Austria assumes the six-month presidency of the EU.

During the 1990s, Austria has moved toward closer European integration. In 1994 **Thomas Klestil,** the current President, was elected on a platform of integration. In 1995 the country was accepted into the European Union (EU), and the Austrians accepted membership through a national referendum. Unlike some EU countries Austria also joined the Economic and Monetary Union (EMU), which inaugurated the euro, a common European currency, on January 1, 1999. (All prices in Austria should be listed in both Schillinge and euros, though the euro will not circulate until 2002.) Things have been calm until recently.

HAIDER AND AUSTRIA'S SWING TO THE RIGHT

Austria has recently been plastered over front pages internationally, thanks to the gains made by the far-right **Freedom Party** in 1999's elections. This party is infamous primarily for its leader **Jörg Haider,** who assumed the reigns of the then-powerless party in 1986. Haider entered the public eye for his anti-immigrant stance, and his many remarks that have been seen as Nazi-sympathetic. In leading his party to power Haider called the Nazi camps "punishment camps" rather than concentration camps.

He has called for Austrian military members who fought for the Nazis to have pride in their work. He has demanded a complete ban on immigration, playing off Austrian fears of the influx of immigrants from Eastern Europe. In the November 1999 elections, Haider's party claimed 27 percent of the vote, second among all parties, effectively breaking up the traditional two-party lock that the Social Democratic Party and People's Party had held on the country's politics since WWII. The Social Democratic Party, which has ruled the country for decades, came in first with 33 percent of the vote but refused to form a coalition with Haider's party; consequently Haider's Freedom Party formed a coalition government with the conservative People's Party in February, 2000. **Wolfgang Schlüssel** of the People's Party is the Chancellor of the new government while six of the government's 12 cabinet posts are held by Freedom Party members.

Though Haider does not have a post in the new federal government—he remains governor of the province of Carinthia—the new government was met by fierce protests both domestically and internationally. In Vienna, 100,000 protestors turned out on the day that the Freedom Party government was sworn in. At the same time the 14 other nations of the **European Union** synchronizedly levied unprecendented political sanctions against Austria that essentially cut off official political contact between these nations and Austria; in addition, the United States recalled its ambassador for "consultation." The Belgian Foreign Minister went so far as to call traveling to Austria "immoral." Haider confirmed some fears of his detractors when he asked that ethnic Germans who were expelled from Czeckoslovakia after WWII be compensated in the same way that Holocaust victims have been compensated.

But in addition to the reasons discussed in "Does Haider Represent the People?" (see below), there are other reasons to reconsider the condemnation of the EU. Haider and his party have made serious efforts to distance themselves from Haider's offensive comments. Haider himself has apologized repeatedly for the insensitivity of his comments, though these efforts have been mitigated by further questionable comments. Still, when the new government was entering office, Haider and the new chancellor **Schlüssel** also signed the declaration, "Responsibility for Austria" which stated that the new government would work "for an Austria in which xenophobia, anti-Semitism, and racism have no place." In addition, Haider resigned from his post as president of the Freedom Party three weeks after the new government took power in February to dispel questions about his role in the government, though this has been called a purely political move by many.

DOES HAIDER REPRESENT THE PEOPLE?

While Jörg Haider's rise gives reason for the traveler to pause before visiting Austria, careful consideration should be given to the actual circumstances before plans are changed. The most important knowledge for travelers is an understanding of why Haider's party is so popular with the people. Two primary reasons have been given for the people's swing toward Haider's party—neither of the reasons are related to Haider's racist views. Two thirds of the people who voted for Haider explained that it was because of his desire and ability to break up the two-party system of the Social Democratic and the People's Party that has ruled Austria since WWII. The *Proporz* system that these two parties established meant that many government contracts and jobs were awarded on the basis of connections to the major parties; Haider's third party broke this monopoly. The other major reason given for Haider's success is his support for cuts to public spending and privatization of the many large companies that are still owned by the government (including the telephone company and the largest tobacco company). The Freedom Party's success—still only 27 percent of the vote—should thus not be seen as an endorsement by the Austrian people of Haider's racist comments. In fact the 1999 elections were not seen as either influential or decisive by the Austrian people; the election had the lowest voter turnout in Austria's post-war history.

These developments have led many of the European nations to reconsider their sanctions against Austria. In May 2000, six of the 14 nations announced that they would consider dropping all sanctions against Austria. Many critical of the European response to the Austrian situation have claimed that the sanctions were only pushed through in the first place because the liberal Social Democratic parties that rule in a majority of the European nations wanted to protect themselves from challenges by extreme parties in their own countries. The two nations who have been most strident in their criticism—France and Belgium—have ruling Social Democratic parties that feel threatened politically by far-right domestic parties.

CULTURE AND CUSTOMS

PEOPLE

Austrians are fiercely proud of their culture, history, and principles. Following the pattern established by their beloved Emperor Franz Joseph, Austrians live on average about 77 years. The great emphasis they place on education is responsible for over 99% literacy throughout the country. Comprehensive welfare ensures few homeless people; unemployment hovers at around 7%. Ethnically, the Austrian people embody the idea of the "melting pot," for although 99% of Austria's 8 million people call themselves German, nearly every Austrian has genealogical ties to at least one of the countless ethnic groups once encompassed by the Habsburg empire. As befits the erstwhile stronghold of the Counter-Reformation, 78% of Austrians are Roman Catholic. 5% are Protestant, while 17% belong to Muslim, Jewish, Baptist and other religious denominations.

Austrians are as impressed as any tourist by the beauty of their country, and they actively appreciate it by taking extensive *Wanderungen* (hikes). They often spend summer vacations on the lakes of Carinthia and the Salzkammergut, and ski the winters away in Tirol and Vorarlberg. In fact, it was a Moravian Austrian, Matthias Zdarsky, who invented skiing near the end of the 19th century.

LANGUAGE

Although German is the official language of Austria, common borders with the Czech Republic, Slovakia, Hungary, Italy, Slovenia, Liechtenstein, and Switzerland make speaking more than one language imperative for most Austrians. In addition to foreign languages, however, the German spoken in Austria differentiates itself by accent and vocabulary from that of other German-speaking countries—interestingly, Austrian German is related to the Bavarian dialect. German-speakers don't need to be too worried about being understood: all Austrians speak High German, but as the inhabitants of each region speak a particular dialect, it is helpful to know some general peculiarities of Austrian German. As a result of the international connections of the Habsburg Empire, there are lots of French, Italian, Czech, Hebrew, and Hungarian words mixed in to the German, for example *Babuschka* for old woman. One easy way to recognize familiar words in Austrian German is to remember that Austrians add a diminutive '*erl*' (instead of the High German '*chen*' or '*lein*') to a lot of words; store clerks may ask if you want a *Sackerl* (a small bag), waiters might inquire if you would like a *bisserl* (a little bit) more of this or that, and a young girl is called a *Mäderl.* Something else to watch out for is that many vegetables have unique names in Austrian German: the German *Kartoffel* (potato) becomes *Erdapfel*, tomatoes are *Paradeiser*, corn is not *Mais* but *Kukuruz*, and green beans are *Fisoln.* Austrians mean "this year" when they say *heuer* and January when they say *Jänner.* If you get to know an Austrian well, chances are they'll say *Baba!* for goodbye.

FOOD AND DRINK

Just as the Austrians and their language are ethnically jumbled, many of the most famous Austrian dishes are foreign in origin: *Gulasch* is Hungarian, *Knödel* (dumplings) are Bohemian, and the archetypal Austrian dish, *Wienerschnitzel*, probably originated in Milan. Immigrants continue to influence Austrian cooking,

FROTHY FACTS The first historical documentation of beer is over 6,000 years old, as a staple food of the Sumerian people. In the Babylonian epic *Gilgamesh*, soldiers of the realm were paid in beer. More than 20 recipes for the fermentation of beer appear in ancient Egyptian scrolls, but the Teutonic tribes will go down in history for creating the celebrated mix of hops, barley, malt, yeast, and water that greases the wheels of the Western world today. There are few, if any, places in the world that provide a better opportunity to sample traditional brews than Austria. If you saunter up to a bar in Austria and simply order "ein Bier," you're likely to get a **Shankbeir,** a fairly mild, frothy beverage with a sharp hops aftertaste, served in a standard bar mug (*Schankglas).* If, however, an Austrian joins you at the bar, he/she will probably request "ein Pils," which is a native staple slightly stronger than Shankbier, served in a tulip glass. The ultra-dark beer in a tall tumbler is simply called **Dunkel**–it can stand on its own feet. For a more carbonated beer, try a **Weizenbier,** either "Kristall" or "Hefetrüb," or venture into the unknown with a **Bockbier,** a strong, full-bodied, dark amber beer consumed mostly at Christmas and Easter. This heavy brew was originally called "liquid bread," so that drinking it would not violate religious fasts. An Austrian custom, imported from Bavaria centuries ago, dictates that a rather special ritual be performed on the earliest brew of the season in order to ensure its quality: when the first keg is filled, old wives from the town must dance around the barrel and spit into its frothy content to bless the remainder of the brewing year. If you decide to sample some of a brewery's first yield, be sure to ask for your **Stein ohne Schleim** (without slime).

AUSTRIA

and Turkish dishes like *Dönerkebab* are on their way to becoming an integral part of Austrian cuisine. In addition, each region of Austria contributes traditional dishes to the national cuisine, such as Carinthian *Kasnudeln* (large cheese- or meat-filled pasta squares) or Salzburger *Nockerl* (a mountain of sweetened, baked egg whites). Most of Austria's culinary inventions appear on the dessert cart. *Tortes* commonly contain *Erdbeeren* (strawberries) and *Himbeeren* (raspberries). Don't miss *Marillen Palatschinken*, a crepe with apricot jam, or *Kaiserschmarrn*, the *Kaiser's* favorite (pancake bits with a plum compote). Austrians adore the sweet dessert *Knödeln*, especially *Marillenknödel* (sweet dumplings with a whole apricot in the middle), though the typical street-stand dessert is the *Krapfn*, a hole-less doughnut usually filled with jam. The pinnacle of Austrian baking, however, are the twin delights of *Sacher Torte* (a rich chocolate cake layered with marmalade) and *Linzer Torte* (a light yellow cake with currant jam).

Loaded with fat, salt, and cholesterol, traditional Austrian cuisine is a cardiologist's nightmare but a delight to the palate. Staple foods are simple and hearty, centering around *Schweinefleisch* (pork), *Kalbsfleisch* (veal), *Wurst* (sausage), *Ei* (egg), *Käse* (cheese), *Brot* (bread), and *Kartoffeln* (potatoes). Austria's most renowned dish, *Wienerschnitzel*, is a meat cutlet (usually veal or pork) fried in butter with bread crumbs. Although *Schnitzel* is Austria's most famous meat dish, its most scrumptious is *Tafelspitz*, beautifully cooked boiled beef. Soups are also an Austrian speciality; try *Gulaschsuppe* (gulasch soup) and *Frittatensuppe* (pancake strips in broth). Recently, vegetarianism has gained popularity in Vienna, and even meaty dishes are showing the influence of a lighter, vegetable-reliant style. Vegetarians should look for *Spätzle* (a homemade noodle often served with melted cheese), *Steinpilze* (enormous mushrooms native to the area), *Eierschwammerl* (tiny yellow mushrooms), or anything with the word "Vegi" in it. Supermarket connoisseurs should have a blast with Austrian staples: yogurt (rich, almost dessert-like); the cult favorite Nutella (a chocolate-hazelnut spread); *Almdudler* (a lemonade-like soft drink); *Semmeln* (very cheap, very fresh rolls); the original *Müesli* (granola of the gods); and all kinds of chocolate, including Milka (you can't miss the purple cow) and Ritter Sport.

In the afternoon, Austrians flock to *Café-Konditoreien* (cafe-confectioners) to nurse the national sweet tooth with *Kaffee und Kuchen* (coffee and cake). You will discover pastries to suit every taste in Austria. While drinking a *Mélange*, the

EAT THE MENÜ, BABY! If you're trying to pinch pennies but not starve in the process, eating the *Menü* is the way to go. In Austria, a *Menü*, much like a *prix-fixe* meal, is a three-course meal served only for lunch. Most *Menüs* cost between 55-85AS for soup, an entree, and dessert (drinks not included). The same meal would cost double for dinner, so get into the habit of eating a large *Menü* lunch to save money and still savor Austrian cuisine. To save even more money carry a water bottle so that you don't have to buy micro-sized drinks at macro-prices, and buy picnic supplies at the supermarket rather than purchasing meals.

classic Viennese coffee with frothed cream and a hint of cinnamon, nibble on a heavenly *Mohr im Hemd*, a chocolate sponge cake topped with hot whipped chocolate, or just about anything with *Mohn* (poppyseed) in it. If you get the chance, try some steam-cooked *Buchteln* with vanilla sauce or poppy seeds.

Of course, you've got to have something to wash all that down. The most famous Austrian wine is probably *Gumpoldskirchen* from Lower Austria, the largest wine-producing province. *Klosterneuburger*, produced in the eponymous district near Vienna, is both reasonably priced and dry. Austrian beers are outstanding. *Ottakringer* and *Gold Fassl* flow from Vienna breweries, *Stiegl Bier* and *Augustiner Bräu* from Salzburg, *Zipfer Bier* from upper Austria, and *Gösser Bier* from Styria. Austria imports a great deal of Budweiser beer, but theirs is *Budvar*—the original Bohemian variety, not the chintzy American imitation.

THE ARTS

THE SOUND OF MUSIC

Austrian music occupies a central position in the Western Classical tradition, primarily due to the unique constellation of Austrian composers, including Haydn, Mozart, Schubert, and Beethoven, who essentially invented "classical music" as we know it today. Yet Austria is in many ways also the birthplace of modern music, having sheltered many of those who challenged the rules of classical composition, including luminaries like Gustav Mahler and Arnold Schönberg. Austria is where Western Classical music was done and undone.

THE CLASSICAL ERA. Toward the end of the 18th century, Vienna was a musical madhouse. Composers hung out in salons, made fun of each other, and listened to themselves play music they wrote. The whole thing fed on itself: the more music was written, the more people wanted to write music. The product of all this compositional brilliance (and competition) is now described as "Viennese Classicism."

One of the early stalwarts amidst this musical melee was **Christoph Willibald Gluck** (1714-1787), who composed many of his best-known operas in Vienna, including *Alceste* and early versions of *Orfeo*, while at the same time acting as *Kapellmeister* for the court of Empress Maria Theresa (see p. 65). A staunch opponent of Italian opera factions, Gluck defended the use of German in song and promoted German operas by such illustrious contemporaries as Carl von Weber and Wolfgang Amadeus Mozart. Through his friendships with younger musicians and his own pioneering approach, Gluck influenced later Romantic composers.

The first master musician of Viennese Classicism is **Josef Haydn** (1732-1809). Born into the family of a poor wheelwright in Rohrau (Lower Austria), Haydn began his career as a chorister in the cathedral of St. Stephen in Vienna before working for the princes of Esterházy (see Eisenstadt, p. 136). He soon became the conductor of the court orchestra and one of the most celebrated composers in Europe. Haydn created a variety of new musical forms that led to the shaping of the sonata and the symphony, structures that dominated musical doctrines throughout the 19th century. Fifty-two piano sonatas, 24 piano and organ concertos, 104 symphonies, and 83 string quartets provide rich and abundant proof of his pioneering productivity. He wrote the imperial anthem,

Gott erhalte Franz den Kaiser, in order to rouse patriotic feeling during the Napoleonic wars. After WWI, Germany adopted the melody of *Gott erhalte* for its new anthem *Deutschland über Alles*.

The work of **Wolfgang Amadeus Mozart** (1756-1791) represents the pinnacle of Viennese Classicism. Born in Salzburg, Mozart was the quintessential child prodigy, playing violin and piano by age four, composing simple pieces by five, and performing at Europe's imperial courts by age six. At 13, Mozart became *Konzertmeister* of the Salzburg court, but as he grew he increasingly disliked the town's narrow bourgeois atmosphere. In 1781 the *Wunderkind* finally fled Salzburg for Vienna, where he produced his first mature concerti, his best-known Italian operas, including *Don Giovanni* and *La Nozze di Figaro*, and the beloved and shamefully overwhistled string showpiece, *Eine kleine Nachtmusik*. In his later years (that is, his early thirties) he began to have difficulty supporting himself and his family, but this was never because he was not producing music—it's just that what he produced didn't always sell. Throughout his life, Mozart wrote with unprecedented speed, creating 626 works of all kinds during his 35 years, always jotting down music without preliminary sketches or revisions. Mozart's overwhelming emotional power found full expression in his final work, the (unfinished) *Requiem*, which he continued composing until the last hours before his death, fulfilling his bitter aside to favorite student Franz Süssmayr: "You see, I *have* been writing this Requiem for myself." Although many people have postulated mysterious reasons for the genius's demise, most historians agree that Mozart died of kidney failure. He was buried in an unmarked paupers' grave. However, within a few decades of his death, Mozart was recognized once more as a master, who in Tchaikovsky's words was "the culmination of all beauty in music."

Only **Ludwig van Beethoven** (1770-1827) could compete with Mozart for the devotion of the Viennese. Born into a family of Flemish musicians in Bonn, he lived in Vienna all his adult life and died there too. Beethoven was an innovator in a music scene steeped in tradition. His gifts were manifest in his piano sonatas, string quartets, overtures, and concertos, but shone most intensely in his nine epoch-shattering symphonies. His *Ninth Symphony* had an enormous cultural impact, in part because of his introduction of singers to the symphonic form—a chorus and four soloists sing the text to Friedrich Schiller's *Ode to Joy*. Beethoven's *Fidelio*, which premiered May 23, 1814 at the Kärntnertortheater in Vienna, is regarded as one of the greatest German operas. Due to increasing deafness, the composer could maintain contact with the world only through a series of conversational notebooks, which provide an extremely thorough, though one-sided, record of his conversations (including his famous emotional outpouring, the *Heiligenstadt Testament*, written in Vienna's 19th district). Music historians locate Beethoven somewhere between Viennese Classicism and Romanticism.

THE ROMANTIC ERA. The music of **Franz Schubert** (1797-1828) is the soul of Romanticism. Born in the Viennese suburb of Lichtenthal in 1797, Schubert began his career as a chorister in the royal imperial Hofkapelle and later made his living teaching music. Mainly self-taught, he composed the *Unfinished Symphony* and the *Symphony in C Major*, which are now considered masterpieces but were virtually unknown during his lifetime. His lyrical genius was more readily recognized in his *Lieder*, musical setting of poems by Goethe, Schiller, and Heine. Through his compositions, the *Lied* became a serious work in the tradition of Viennese Classicism. *Die schöne Müllerin* and the quietly despairing *Winterreise* frame Schubert's finest and most mature creative period. These great song cycles were made famous during musical soirées called "Schubertiade," which spawned a new trend of domestic social gatherings in Biedermeier Vienna, featuring chamber music, readings, and alcohol (see p. 63 and p. 76). This burst of creativity was cut short by his early death at the age of 32. Coincidentally, he died the year after Beethoven did, and was buried next to him. Despite the brevity of Schubert's career, his genius for pure melody was a catalyst for later musical innovations by (among others) Schumann, the Strausses, and Gustav Mahler.

Like Beethoven, **Johannes Brahms** (1833-1897) straddled musical traditions. In his home near the Karlskirche in Vienna, Brahms composed his Hungarian Dances, piano concertos, and numerous symphonies, all of which were first performed by the Vienna Philharmonic. Despite his own Romantic compositions, Brahms is often regarded as a classicist who used his position in the Viennese *Musikverein* and his status as a major composer to oppose Romanticism and the musical experiments of his arch-rival, Wagner. In the process, Brahms became the grand old man of the Viennese music scene. Although he was rigorously formalistic in his music, Brahms demonstrated the Viennese delight in the lighter things in life. When a well-wisher approached him in the opera house and asked the great composer for a momento of their meeting, he penned the opening bars of the Blue Danube Waltz on her fan and wrote underneath: "Unfortunately not by your Johannes Brahms."

THE NINETEENTH CENTURY. Beginning with **Johann Strauss the Elder** (1804-1849), the Strauss family kept Vienna on its toes for much of the 19th century. Johann Sr. composed mostly waltzes and showy pieces, including the famous *Radetzkymarsch*, which is still played every New Year by the Vienna Philharmonic. Largely responsible for the "Viennese Waltz," **Johann Strauss the Younger** (1825-1899) shone in his youth as a brilliant violinist and savvy cultural entrepreneur. The waltz became popular during the Congress of Vienna (p. 63), offering a new exhilaration that broke free from older, more stiffly formal dances. The quick step allowed for more intimate physical contact as partners whirled about the room, arm in arm, constantly on the verge of falling down or getting intoxicatingly dizzy. Richard Wagner, of all people, noted admiringly on a visit to the city that Viennese waltzing was "more potent than alcohol." Sensing the trend, Johann became its master, eventually writing the *Blue Danube* and *Tales from the Vienna Woods*, two of the most recognized waltzes of all time, thereby earning the title, "King of the Waltz." In his spare time he managed to knock off some popular operas as well, *Die Fledermaus* being his most celebrated. His brothers, Josef (1827-1870) and Eduard (1835-1916) also worked as conductors and composers.

Anton Bruckner (1824-1896) is famous for his massively orchestrated symphonies. Born and bred in the Danube valley, Bruckner sang as a choirboy and became organist at the monastery of St. Florian before moving to Vienna in 1868 at age 44 to write his most renowned compositions, including the Third, Fourth, and Seventh Symphonies. **Hugo Wolf** (1860-1903) is little-known in the English-speaking world, due mainly to the fact that his chosen form, the *Lied*, is not an established genre in the average concert repertoire. Wolf perfected the *Lied* as a dramatic symphonic miniature, in which music and words are indissolubly linked. He frequently set poems by Goethe, Eichendorff, and Mayreder to music, creating such masterful collections as the *Mörike Lieder* (1888) and the *Italienisches Liederbuch* (1890). A key figure in the development of Austrian classical music, Wolf's *Lieder* rank among some of the loveliest and most evocative music ever composed in Vienna. As a direct precursor to the Second Viennese experiments of Arnold Schönberg, **Gustav Mahler's** (1860-1911) music incorporates fragments and deliberately inconclusive segments which read like nostalgic remnants of a once certain and orderly world. Mahler employed unusual instrumentation and startling harmonic juxtapositions. His Eighth Symphony, often called *Symphony of Thousand*, requires an orchestra and two full choruses. Mahler's music hides formalist experimentation beneath a deeply moving emotional beauty. His works form an integral part of the *fin de siècle* Viennese avant-garde.

THE MODERN ERA. While Mahler destabilized the conventions of composition, **Arnold Schönberg** (1874-1951) broke away from traditional harmony altogether. Originally a devotee of Richard Wagner, Schönberg rejected compositional rules that require music to be set in a tonal key, and pursued what is generally called atonality but which Schönberg himself preferred to think of as pantonality, or the disappearance of any dominant tone. Some of his most famous works are *Pierre Lunaire* and the string piece *Verklärte Nacht.* **Anton von Webern** (1883-1945) stud-

FALCO! Somewhere between the 12-tone system of Schönberg and the sweeping harmonics of Brahms, Falco bursts into the spectrum of Austrian musical achievements. Attempting to reconcile an artistic quest for the self with the nationalistic and naturalistic intellectual bent of the era, his rockin' *Amadeus* permeated the subconscious of radio listeners across the globe in the 80s. The song took as its subject Wolfgang Amadeus Mozart, and attempted, in the infamous "historical breakdown," to reconcile the classical past with the rock'n'roll present. History goes something like: Mozart, then Falco, nothing in between. Sadly, Falco died in a car crash in the Dominican Republic in February 1998. For a nostalgic reexamination of Falco's talent, seek out *The Remix Collection*, a compendium of his greatest hits.

ied under Schönberg, eventually adopting and expanding the latter's 12-tone system. Webern's music is incredibly sparse, a sharp contrast to the lush, opulent, often overwritten music of his contemporaries. Webern drifted into obscurity and depression as the Nazis took over. While fleeing the Nazis, Webern was accidentally shot by U.S. troops in Salzburg. **Alban Berg** (1885-1935), another student of Schönberg's, was a perfectionist who completed very few works because of his obsession with ideal expression. Berg wrote using the 12-tone system, but also using complex chromaticism—technically within the traditional tonal system but obscuring it. His work employed classical styles and motifs but always set with and against atonality. Like Schönberg and Webern, he suffered under the Nazis as a creator of "degenerate art" and died young, in 1935.

VISUAL ART AND ARCHITECTURE

Landlocked in the middle of Europe and rolling with cash, the Habsburgs married into power and bought into art. In keeping with the cosmopolitan nature of their empire and outlook, the imperial family pursued a cultural policy that decidedly favored foreign artists over their own native sons and daughters. With the popularity of Baroque palaces and churches in the 17th- and 18th-centuries, however, the empire's artists began to develop a distinct, graceful architectural style that still dominates the old centers of former Habsburg towns across Central and Eastern Europe. Around the turn of the 20th century, Austrian artists finally got fed up with traditionalism and foreign decadence and decided to stir up the coals a bit. (See Vienna: Sights, p. 105 for more discussion of art and architecture.)

GOLDEN ARCHES. Austria's past as an outpost of the Roman empire is still visible in the ruins of **Carnuntum** and **Vindobona** (Vienna). The influence of such classical remains is to be seen in the Romanesqe art and architecture of the early Middle Ages throughout Austria; for example, in the Riesentor of Vienna's **Stephansdom** (see p. 106) and the cycle of frescoes in the **Nonnberg Abbey** near Salzburg (see p. 227). Ordinarily this influence takes the form of semi-circular arches, columns, and delicate metalwork, but the builders of the 8th-century **Martinskirche** of Linz actually "borrowed" Roman tombstones to fill in the walls (see p. 266). The elaborate enamel **Verduner Altar**, by the master Nicholas of Verdun, at Stift Klosterneuberg (see p. 133), is witness to the richness of art under the Babenburgs (976-1246), but if it isn't rich enough for your blood, check out the tenth-century **Imperial Crown** of the Holy Roman Emperor, encrusted with cabuchons and gold filigree, its shape echoing those Roman arches.

GOTHIC TRANSCENDENCE. Austrian architecture got over the Romanesque arches as the French Gothic style spread across Europe. The inventions of flying buttresses, pointed arches, and groin vaults all meant that walls could be thinner, vaults could be higher, and windows up in the stratosphere could flood the whole space with light. The vast fourteenth-century additions to the **Stefansdom** in Vienna also show the delicate tracery and stained glass work typical of the period. Sculpture reached new heights with the intricate carvings of **Anton Pilgram** (see p. 106) and the altarpieces of **Albrecht Altdorfer** (see p. 269). And don't forget Austria's castles: these stern fortresses-cum-palaces, exemplified by **Festung Hohensalzburg** (see p. 227) and **Burg Hochosterwitz** (see p. 167), combined the medieval desire for imposing beauty with the practical goal of imposing power.

BAROQUE EXTRAVAGANCE. With fluidly ornate forms orchestrated into a succession of grand entrances, dreamy vistas, and overwrought, cupid-covered facades, the Baroque invokes what was then the most popular art form in Europe, music. The turbulent swell of Haydn or Beethoven is incarnated in stone and mortar. Austria's preeminent Baroque architects were Johann Bernhard Fischer von Erlach, Johann Prandtauer, and Lukas von Hildebrandt. **Johann Bernard Fischer von Erlach,** born in Graz to a sculptor father, drew up the plans for Vienna's Schönbrunn and Hofburg palaces. His best works, however, were ecclesiastical in nature, including the **Trinity** and **Collegienkirche** in Salzburg and the ornate **Karlskirche** in Vienna. **Prandtauer** was a favorite of the Church. His yellow Benedictine abbey at **Melk** perches on rocky cliffs over the Danube. **Lukas von Hildebrandt** shaped Austria's more secular side. After battering the Turks, Prince Eugène of Savoy (see p. 63) got him to revamp his newest acquisition, the Belvedere palace. Hildebrandt's penchant for theatricality shows up in the palace's succession of pavilions and grand views of Vienna; stone sphinxes dotting his ornamental gardens allude to Eugene's victory over the Ottomans.

THE RINGSTRAßE STYLE. The political and aesthetic conservatism of nineteenth-century Austria is showcased by the neo-historical reproductions along the **Ringstraße,** the broad circular boulevard that demarcates Vienna and that was authorized in 1857 by Emperor Franz Josef to replace fortified medieval walls. The street has distinctly authoritarian roots. During the Revolution of 1848, rebels barricaded themselves inside the old city wall. After quashing the rebellion, unnerved generals of the Habsburg military insisted the wall be razed and the grand boulevard built in its place. The leafy, tree-lined *Ringstraße* was built exceptionally wide not merely for beauty's sake, but also with the intention of preventing barricades and giving the imperial army ready access to subversive behavior in any part of the city. Emperor Franz Josef lined the boulevard with centers of bourgeois constitution and culture: a university, a parliament building, and a civic theater. Architects designed each building in a different historical style deemed symbolic of its function. The neo-gothic *Rathaus* celebrates the civic strength of the *Bürgermeister* and their medieval town halls; the early baroque style of the *Burgtheater* recalls the 17th-century golden era of the theatrical arts, while the stately Renaissance design of the *Universität* evokes the cult of rationalism and science.

BIEDERMEIER. Between Napoleon and the foundation of the republic, Austria developed a large, dissatisfied middle class. Since political expression and social critique were virtually impossible during this era, artistic expression was funneled into a narrow channel of naturalistic and applied art centered around the family circle and domestic ideals, dominated by genre, landscape, and portrait painting. The *Biedermeier* period (see history, p. 65) is remembered today primarily as a furniture style, but it was also an artistic movement with limited crossover into literature, characterized by a predilection for symmetries, technique, naturalism, and harmonious detail. *Biedermeier* architecture is exemplified by the well-ordered dignity of the **Dreimäderlhaus** at Schreyvogelgasse 10 in Vienna; and the best of the period's furniture is on view in the **Beidermeier Room** of the *Österreichisches Museum für Angewandte Kunst* (see p. 125).

JUGENDSTIL (A.K.A. ART NOUVEAU). In the early years of the 20th century, Vienna's artistic community was racked by disagreement. In 1897, the "young" artists split from the "old," as proponents of *Jugendstil* modernism took issue with the Viennese Academy's rigid conservatism and traditional symbolism. The idea was to leave behind prevailing artistic conventions and formulate a new way of seeing the world. **Gustav Klimt** (1862-1918) and his followers founded what is known as the **Secession** movement. They aimed to provide the nascent Viennese avant-garde with an independent forum in which to show their work and to encourage contact with foreign artists. In their revolt against the calcified artistic climate of the old-guard Künstlerhaus, Secessionists sought to create space and appreciation for new artistic styles. The effect of this freedom might be seen in Klimt's own later paintings, such as The Kiss, which combine naturalistic portraits with abstractly patterned backgrounds. Their trademark style was Art Nouveau. Josef Maria Olbrich's **Secession Building** (see p. 116) was a reaction to the backward-looking conservative architecture of the Ringstraße. The composer Richard Wagner's idealization of the *Gesamtkunstwerk* (all-encompassing work of art) was an important subtext of Secessionist aesthetic ambitions. Their fourteenth exhibition was their crowning glory, an attempted synthesis of all major artistic media, featuring **Max Klinger's** Beethoven statue, Klimt's allegorical tribute to the composer, Josef Hoffmann's interior, and Mahler's music.

Once the *Jugendstil* fever broke, ornamentation was firmly streamlined, and a new ethic of function over form gripped Vienna's artistic elite. Vienna's guru of architectural modernism, **Otto Wagner,** cured the city of its "artistic hangover." His Kirche am Steinhof (see p. 120) and Postsparkasse (see p. 116) enclose fluid *Jugendstil* interiors within stark, delineated structures. Wagner frequently collaborated with his student **Josef Maria Olbrich,** notably on the Majolicahaus (see p. 116) and the Karlsplatz Stadtbahn (see p. 116). Wagner's admirer **Josef Hoffmann** founded the **Wiener Werkstätte** in 1903, drawing on Ruskin's English art and crafts movement and Vienna's new brand of streamlined simplicity. Its influence later resonated in the **Bauhaus** of Weimar Germany.

Adolf Loos, Hoffmann's principal antagonist, strongly opposed such attention to luxury. Loos once said, "Ornamentation is criminal," setting himself against the Baroque grandeur that Imperial Vienna supported. Thanks to this opposition, few examples of his work reside in his native city. His indictment of the Ringstraße, entitled *Potemkin City*, affiliated him with the early Secessionist movement, but his notorious **Goldman and Salatsch building** (1909-1911) in the Michaelerplatz went a step beyond their aesthetic toward a more starkly functional architecture.

EXPRESSIONISM. **Oskar Kokoschka** and **Egon Schiele** revolted against art, seeking to present the frailty, neuroses, and sexual energy formerly concealed behind the Secession's aesthetic surface. Kokoschka is often considered (though never by himself) the founder of Viennese **Expressionism.** Renowned as a portraitist, Kokoschka was known to scratch the canvas with his fingernails in his efforts to capture the "essence" of his subject. Schiele, like the young Kokoschka, paints with a feverish intensity in line and color. His paintings are controversial even today, for their depictions of tortured figures seemingly destroyed by their own bodies or by debilitating sexuality. His figures are twisted, gnarled, and yet oddly erotic. **František Kupka** studied at the Vienna academies at the same time as Kokoschka and Schiele, but soon left for France to study Pointillism. Kupka became one of the early pioneers of abstract art.

URBAN SOCIALISM. In the 1920s and early 1930s, the **Social Democratic** administration built thousands of apartments in large **municipal projects,** their style reflecting the newfound assertiveness of the workers' movement. The most outstanding project of the era is the **Karl-Marx-Hof** (see p. 119). The huge structure, completed in 1930, extends over 1km and consists of 1600 apartments clustered around several courtyards. The Austrian Socialist party fought a pitched battle with rightist rioters in this apartment complex just before the outbreak of World War II. **Friedensreich Hundertwasser** (translation: Peaceful Hundredwaters; given name: Friedrich Stowasser) began with big brush strokes and bright colored canvas and moved on to plastic material. A builder of buildings, he designed KunstHaus Wien (see p. 120) and the Hundertwasser House (see p. 119), which attempt to make architecture organic and to bring natural life back into the "desert" of the city.

The structures created by American-trained architect **Hans Hollein** recall the sprawling abandon of his training ground while maintaining the Secessionists' attention to craftsmanship and elegant detail. His exemplary contribution to Viennese **postmodern** architecture is the **Haas House** (see p. 106), completed in

1990. Controversy has surrounded the building ever since sketches were published in the mid-80s, mainly because it stands opposite Vienna's landmark, St. Stephen's Cathedral. Examples of modern interior design are the **Restaurant Salzamt** (I, Ruprechtspl. 1) and **Kleines Café** (see p. 102), both by **Hermann Czech.**

LITERATURE

EARLY EXAMPLES. In the Roman settlement Vindobona, **Marcus Aurelius** wrote his *Meditations*, starting a long tradition of Viennese immigré (and emigré) artists. A collection of poetry dating from around 1150 and preserved in the abbey of Vorau in Styria marks the earliest known Austrian literature in German. Apart from sacred poetry, the courtly style known as *Minnesang* developed in the 12th and 13th centuries culminated in the lyrical works of minstrel **Walther von der Vogelweide.** On a more epic scale, the **Nibelungenlied,** which dates from around 1200, is one of the most impressive heroic epics in German (it is also the primary source for Richard Wagner's *Ring of the Nibelungen* opera cycle). The **Codex Buranas,** compiled ca. 1240, survived to provide Austrian sources for Carl Orff's "Carmina Burana." **Emperor Maximilian I** (1459-1519), nicknamed "The Last Knight," provided special support for theater and the dramatic arts during his reign. Splendid operas and pageants frequently involved the whole of the imperial court and led to popular religious drama that has survived in the form of rural **passion plays.**

THE CLASSICAL WRITERS. Born in Vienna in 1801, **Johann Nestroy** wrote biting comedies and satires lampooning social follies. Although his name is not readily recognized by Anglophones, Nestroy is one of the canonical figures of German drama, famous for such plays as *Der Talisman* and *Liebesgeschichten und Heiratssachen*, as well as the *Tannhäuser* on which Wagner based his famous opera. Often called Austria's greatest novelist, **Adalbert Stifter** wrote around the same time period as Nestroy but concerned himself much more with classical *Bildungs-roman* themes and descriptions of nature. Many of his short stories and novels, such as *Der Condor* (1840), *Die Mappe meines Urgroßvaters* (1841), and *Der Nachsommer* (1857), belong to the canon of German literature.

A classicist with a more lyrical style, **Franz Grillparzer** penned plays about the conflict between a life of thought and a life of action. Grillparzer worked as a clerk in the Austrian bureaucracy and wrote some of his most critically acclaimed plays, such as *The Waves of the Sea and Love* (1831) in his spare time. Most of Grillparzer's fame came posthumously, when interest grew in his published work and the beautifully composed *Der arme Spielmann* was discovered.

FIN DE SIÈCLE. Around 1890, Austrian literature rapidly transformed in the heat of the "merry apocalypse" atmosphere that permeated society at the turn of the century (see p. 66). The literature dating from this second heyday of Austrian culture is legendary. The satires of **Karl Kraus** tried to awaken the conscience of the collapsing empire, while **Sigmund Freud** analyzed its dreams. **Arthur Schnitzler** heated up its stage with bedroom scenes (including the one that was later adapted into the Stanley Kubrick movie *Eyes Wide Shut*), while **Hugo von Hofmannsthal** staged its death with reconceptualizations of medieval and Baroque tragedies. The cafe provided the backdrop for the *fin de siècle* literary landscape. Like many popular institutions of its time, the relaxed elegance of the Viennese cafe was part fantasy, part imaginative camouflage of an ugly and best ignored reality. Vienna faced severe shortages of both housing and firewood, and the cafe was the only place where many people could relax in relative comfort and warmth. Some even had their mail addressed to them at their habitual cafe. At the Cafe Griensteidl, **Hermann Bahr**—lyric poet, critic, and one-time director of the *Burgtheater*—loosely presided over a pioneer group known as **Jung Wien** (Young Vienna), which rejected the **Naturalism** of Emile Zola in favor of a psychological realism aimed at capturing the subtlest nuances of the Viennese atmosphere. Hofmannsthal walked a tightrope between Impressionism and verbal decadence, creating such exquisite pieces of drama as *Yesterday* (1891) and *Everyman* (1911) while at the same time collaborating with Richard Strauss to write librettos for, among other things, *Der Rosenkavalier*. Schnitzler, a playwright and colleague of Freud, was the first German to write stream-of-consciousness prose. He skewered Viennese aristocratic decadence in dramas and essays, and shocked contemporaries by portraying the complexities of erotic relationships in many of his plays, including his famous *Merry-Go-Round* (1897).

Many of Austria's literary titans, such as **Marie von Ebner-Eschenbach** and **Franz Kafka,** lived within the Habsburg protectorate of Bohemia. Ebner-Eschenbach is often called the greatest female Austrian writer, known for her vivid individual portraits and her defense of women's rights. Prague was a major literary center around the turn of the century, in dialogue with the literary scene in Vienna. Kafka often traveled to Vienna to drink coffee at the Herrenhof Café and swap story ideas with other writers. No one else could master the surrealism of Kafka's writing, however, most famously demonstrated in *The Metamorphosis*, a bizarre and disorienting tale in which the narrator comes to terms with his unexpected transformation—into an insect. No less dehumanizing is *The Trial*, in which Kafka explores the impersonal power of the bureaucratized modern world.

The collapse of the Austro-Hungarian monarchy marked a major turning point in the intellectual and literary life of Austria. Novelists **Robert Musil** and **Joseph Roth** concerned themselves with the consequences of the empire's breakdown. Roth's novels, *Radetzkymarsch* and *Die Kapuzinergruft*, romanticize the former empire. He is most famous for his unfinished work in 3 volumes *Der Mann Ohne Eigenschaften (The Man Without Qualities)*.

THE 20TH CENTURY. By WWI, the cult of despair had replaced the cult of art. **Georg Trakl's** Expressionist works epitomize the early 20th-century fascination with death and dissolution. "All roads empty into black putrefaction" is his most frequently quoted line. At the outbreak of WWI, Trakl served on the front; he eventually ended his life with a large dose of cocaine in an army hospital.

Other Prague-born greats such as **Franz Werfel** *(The Forty Days of Musa Dagh)* and **Rainer Maria Rilke** shaped Austrian literature between the wars. Werfel's works investigate the dark side of the human psyche. In addition to his essays and stories, Rilke is most famous for his lyric poetry cycles the *Duino Elegies* and *Sonnets to Orpheus*. After WWII, Rilke's poetry and Kafka's oppressive parables of a cold world became the models for a new generation of writers. These artistic movements owe their fascination with the unconscious to the new science of psychoanalysis and its most famous proponent, **Sigmund Freud.** Freud is best known for his theories of sexual repression, particularly applicable for bourgeois society, and his theories of the unconscious, which recast the literary world forever.

Austrian literature today is still affected and informed by its literary tradition, but there is plenty of innovation as well. **Ingeborg Bachman's** stories and novels left an important legacy for Austrian feminism. One of the stalwarts of modern Austrian writing, **Thomas Bernhard** wrote *Holzfäller* (Woodcutters) and *Wittgenstein's Nephew*. In short, literature in Austria still thrives, and will continue to as long as people are still upset enough to write.

GETTING TO KNOW AUSTRIA (READING TIPS).

Vienna: Its Musical Heritage (1968). Egon Gartenberg.
Fin-de-Siecle Vienna (1961). Carl Schorske.
The Fall of the House of Habsburg (1963). Edward Crankshaw.
The World of Yesterday (*Die Welt von Gestern*; 1943). Stefan Zweig.
The Metamorphosis (*Die Verwandlung*; 1915). Franz Kafka.
Eyes Wide Shut (*Die Traumspiele;* 1900). Arthur Schnitzler.
The Classic Art of Viennese Pastry (1997). Christine Berl.

VIENNA (WIEN)

From its humble origins as a Roman camp along the Danube, Vienna became the cultural heart of Europe for centuries, prodding fledgling musicians, writers, artists, philosophers, and politicians to greatness or, at least, infamy. It was not without reason that home-grown satirist Karl Kraus once dubbed Vienna—birthplace of psychoanalysis, atonal music, functionalist architecture, Zionism, and Nazism—a "laboratory for world destruction." From the glory days of the Habsburg dynasty under Maximilian I and Maria Theresia to *fin-de-siècle* Vienna's feverish brilliance, Vienna has rivaled Paris, London, and Berlin in significance, thanks to its inspired musicians (including Mozart, Beethoven, Schubert, Strauss, and Brahms), vast imperial wealth, and impeccable taste in Baroque art, architecture, and decor. At the height of its artistic ferment at the turn of the century, during the smoky and caffeine-permeated days of the great cafe culture, the Viennese were already self-mockingly referring to their city as the "merry apocalypse." That nervous atmosphere of disruption and disintegration was the reaction of a civilization staring down its own dissolution. Vienna's smooth veneer of waltz music and *Gemütlichkeit* concealed a darker reality expressed by Freud's theories, Kafka and Musil's dark fantasies, and Mahler's deathly beautiful music.

SUGGESTED ITINERARIES

ONE DAY Wake yourself up with a cup of coffee and a pastry at **Café Central** (p. 101), then hit the *innere Stadt,* starting with a climb up the tower of **Stephansdom** in the center of the city (p. 106). Wander along the **Ringstraße** (p. 114), which circles Vienna's medieval first district and showcases such architectural triumphs as Wagner's Jugendstil *Postsparkasse* and the *Burgtheater,* with access to the **Hofburg** (p. 110) and elaborate **public gardens** (p. 118). Indulge in a late afternoon dessert at **Hotel Sacher** (p. 102), before visiting Klimt's controversial *Beethoven Frieze* in the **Secession Building** (p. 116). Then refuel near the **Naschmarkt** (p. 117) for the nightlife in the **Bermuda Dreiecke** (p. 130).

THREE DAYS Spend your first day as above, then discover how art was "made and unmade" in Vienna's world-class art **museums,** especially the *Kunsthistorisches Museum* (p. 123) and the completely curvilinear *Kunsthaus Wien* (p. 124). Eat a bite-sized lunch at Kafka's favorite restaurant, **Trzesniewski** (p. 98). Then explore outside the Ring: tour **Schloß Belvedere** (p. 118), which holds more *fin-de-siecle* wonders, and linger in yet another cafe (trust us). Take one evening to see an opera at the **Staatsoper** (p. 126), (and a few hours of an afternoon if you want to snag one of the super-cheap standing room tickets). Venture into the **Wienerwald** (Vienna Woods) for a vineyard visit and taste new wine in the *Heurigen* (wine gardens) nestled in the suburbs of Vienna (p. 103). On your last evening, watch Vienna sparkle from the **Donauturm** (p. 122).

FIVE DAYS Tackle three of your days as above, only take more time to explore the different neighborhoods within the Ring–seek out the Vienna of the past near Judenplatz, Am Hof and Freyung (p. 108), where there are **Roman ruins** and medieval gems like **Maria am Gestade,** a chapel perched on a former tributary of the Danube. If you're in town on Sunday, enjoy a mass sung by the **Vienna Boys' Choir** (p. 128). Then take a daytrip to steam along the **Danube** between Krems and Melk (p. 274). Back in Vienna, spend almost a full day at the delicate **Schloß Schönnbrunn** (p. 118), then (window) shop the upscale "Kaiserlich und Königlich" stores in **Kohlmarkt** (p. 107). As a final fling, return to the heart of Vienna for the spectacular evening tour of the **Stephansdom.**

Vienna has a reputation for living absent-mindedly in this grand past; for being a museum city. The city does have a way of sitting quietly as you enjoy its streets, overflowing with Baroque flourishes, sinuous art nouveau facades, and cafes with pooling light and worn, nicotine-stained velvet sofas. Postmodern architecture and ecological fantasies by Friedensreich Hundertwasser share space with calmly domestic *Biedermeier* apartment buildings. But as the last fringes of the Iron Curtain have been drawn back, Vienna has tried to revitalize its political, cultural, and economical life through connections with the former Communist bloc—to reestablish itself as the gateway to Eastern Europe. In 1998, when Austria held the European Union's (E.U.) presidency, Vienna threw a "celebration between E and U" festival, referring not only to Vienna's role as a truly central-European city easily accessible to the former Communist Bloc, but also to the city's fusion of "E" (a term for classical, traditional music) and "U" (popular and modern). In this effort Vienna is attempting to reconnect with its turn-of-the-century identity as a place where experimentalism thrives, where rules of genre, style, and structure are made and unmade in everything from music to contemporary film and art.

PHONE CODES	The **city code** for Vienna is 0222 for calls placed from within Austria, 1 for calls from abroad.

GETTING THERE

BY PLANE. Vienna's airport is the **Wien-Schwechat Flughafen** (☎700 7222 31, departure info ☎700 7221 84), home of **Austrian Airlines** (☎1789 or 176 676 30; www.aua.com; open M-F 8am-7pm, Sa-Su 8am-5pm). There is a daily flight to and from **New York** and frequent flights to **London, Rome,** and **Berlin,** among other places. Travelers under 25 qualify for discounts if tickets are bought 2 weeks in advance. Student travelers ages 25 and 26 also qualify.

The **airport** is far from the city center (18km), but easily accessible by public transportation. The cheapest way to reach the city is to take train S7 "Flughafen/Wolfsthal" which stops at the Wien Mitte (30min., every half hr. 5:03am-9:36pm, 38AS; Eurail not valid). There is also train service every day between Wien Nord or Wien Mitte and the airport (every half hr. 5:03am-10:24pm, 38AS). The heart of the city, Stephansplatz, is an easy metro ride from **Wien Mitte** on the orange U3 line.

A more convenient option is taking the **Vienna Airport Lines Shuttle Bus** (☎ 930 0023 00; www.oebb.at/regional/wien/wien4.html). Buses leave the airport for the City Air Terminal downtown (at the Hilton opposite "Wien Mitte" station) every 20 minutes from 6:30am to 11:10pm, and every 30 minutes from midnight to 6am (70AS). Buses leave from the airport for Südbahnhof and Westbahnhof every 30 minutes from 8:55am to 7:25pm and every hour from 8:20pm-8:25am. Similarly, buses travel to the airport from the city stations. By far the easiest but also the most expensive way to and from the airport is by private airport shuttle services, such as **JetBus** (☎700 7387 79), which are located just outside the baggage claim and deliver passengers to any address in the city for 160AS per person. Call 1 day in advance to arrange pick-up for a return trip. Parties of 3 or more get discounts when booking a return trip.

BY TRAIN. Vienna has 2 main train stations with international departures. For general train information, call 1717 (24hr.) or check www.bahn.at.

Westbahnhof, XV, Mariahilferstr. 132. An easy ride on the orange U3 line to and from the city center, at Stephansplatz. The station primarily sends trains **west,** domestically to **Salzburg** (3hr., every hr., 430AS), **Linz** (2hr., every hr. 4:24am-11:25pm, 290AS), **Innsbruck** (6hr., every 2hr. 5:04am-11:25pm, 660AS), **Bregenz** (8hr., 5 per day 5:04am-10:15pm, 810AS). Internationally to **Zurich** (9¼hr., 3 per day 7:17am-9:15pm, 1122AS), **Amsterdam** (14½hr., 1 per day 7:17pm, 2276AS), **Paris** (14hr., 2 per day 8:47am, 8:21pm, 2096AS), **Hamburg** (9½hr., 2 per day 10:17am, 7:45pm, 2328AS), and **Munich** (4½hr., 5 per day 5:47am-3:47pm, 788AS). There are a few trains east and north; to **Berlin Zoo** (11hr, 1 per day 9:19pm, 1678AS), and **Budapest** (3-4hr., 6 per day 8:25am-6pm, 420AS). The Westbahnhof train **information counter** is open daily 7:30am-8:40pm.

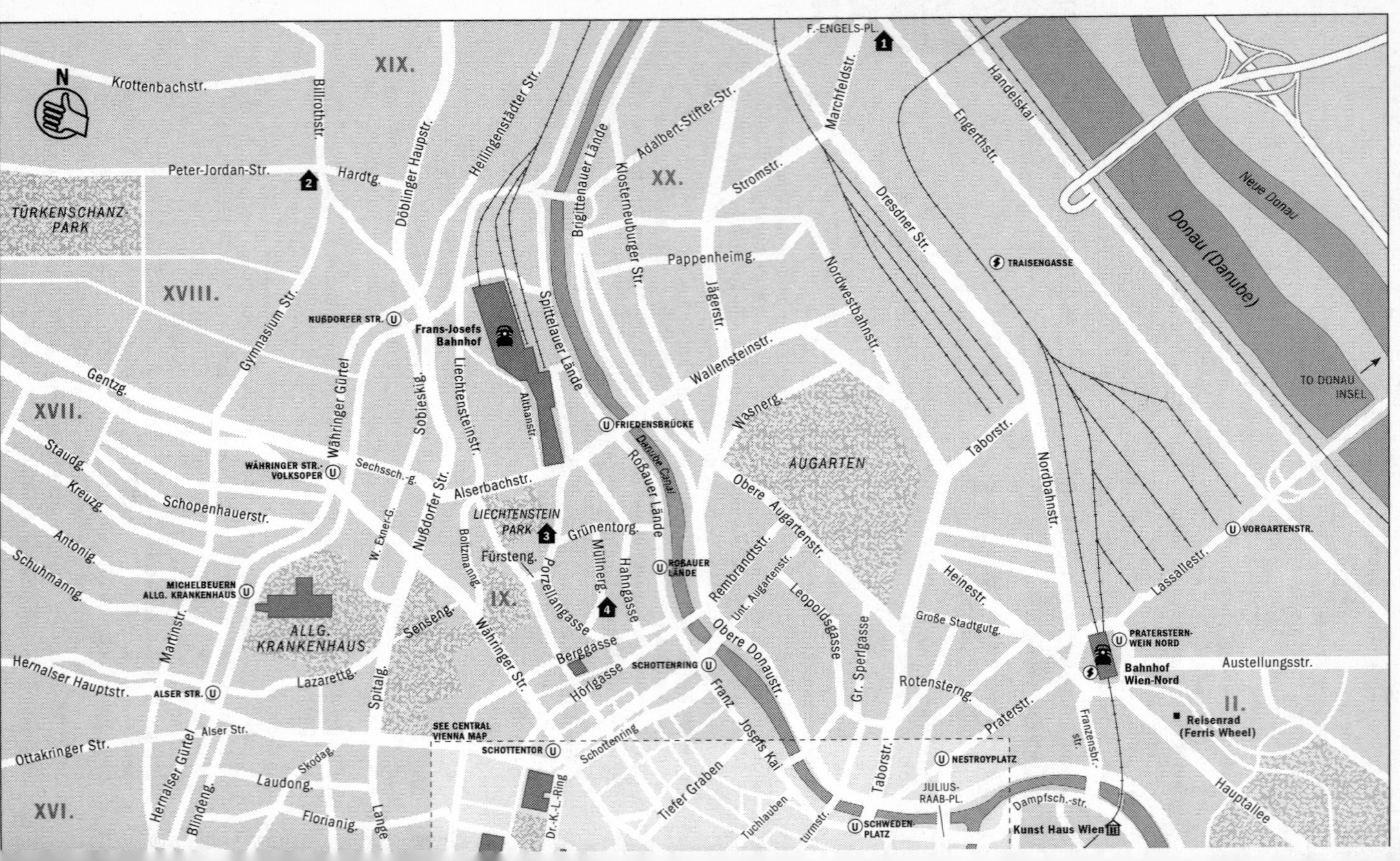

N
Krottenbachstr.
XIX.
F.-ENGELS-PL.
Billrothstr.
Peter-Jordan-Str.
Hardtg.
Döblinger Haupstr.
Heiligenstädter Str.
Brigittenauer Lände
Adalbert-Stifter-Str.
Marchfeldstr.
Handelskai
Engerthstr.
Neue Donau
Donau (Danube)
TÜRKENSCHANZ PARK
XX.
Stromstr.
Klosterneuburger Str.
Pappenheimg.
Dresdner Str.
TRAISENGASSE
XVIII.
Gymnasium Str.
NUSSDORFER STR.
Frans-Josefs Bahnhof
Spittelauer Lände
Jägerstr.
Nordwestbahnstr.
Wallensteinstr.
TO DONAU INSEL
Gentzg.
Währinger Gürtel
Sobieskig.
Liechtensteinstr.
Althanstr.
XVII.
FRIEDENSBRÜCKE
Wasnerg.
Taborstr.
Staudg.
WÄHRINGER STR.-VOLKSOPER
Sechssch.-g.
Nußdorfer Str.
Alserbachstr.
Danube Canal
Roßauer Lände
AUGARTEN
Nordbahnstr.
Kreuzg.
Schopenhauerstr.
LIECHTENSTEIN PARK
Grünentorg.
Obere Augartenstr.
VORGARTENSTR.
Antonig.
W. Exner-G.
Boltzmanng.
Fürsteng.
Müllnerg.
Hahngasse
ROSSAUER LÄNDE
Rembrandtstr.
Unt. Augartenstr.
Leopoldsgasse
Heinestr.
Lassallestr.
Schuhmanng.
MICHELBEUERN ALLG. KRANKENHAUS
IX.
Porzellangasse
Senseng.
Währinger Str.
Große Stadtgutg.
PRATERSTERN-WEIN NORD
ALLG. KRANKENHAUS
Martinstr.
Obere Donaustr.
Gr. Sperlgasse
Berggasse
Bahnhof Wien-Nord
Austellungsstr.
Hernalser Hauptstr.
ALSER STR.
Lazarettg.
Spitalg.
Hörlgasse
SCHOTTENRING
Franz Josefs Kai
Rotensterng.
Praterstr.
II.
Reisenrad (Ferris Wheel)
Alser Str.
SEE CENTRAL VIENNA MAP
Franzensbr.-str.
Ottakringer Str.
SCHOTTENTOR
Schottenring
NESTROYPLATZ
Skodag.
Hernalser Gürtel
Laudong.
Dr.-K.-L.-Ring
Tiefer Graben
Taborstr.
JULIUS-RAAB-PL.
Hauptallee
XVI.
Blindeng.
Florianig.
Lange
Tuchlauben
turmstr.
SCHWEDEN-PLATZ
Dampfsch.-str.
Kunst Haus Wien

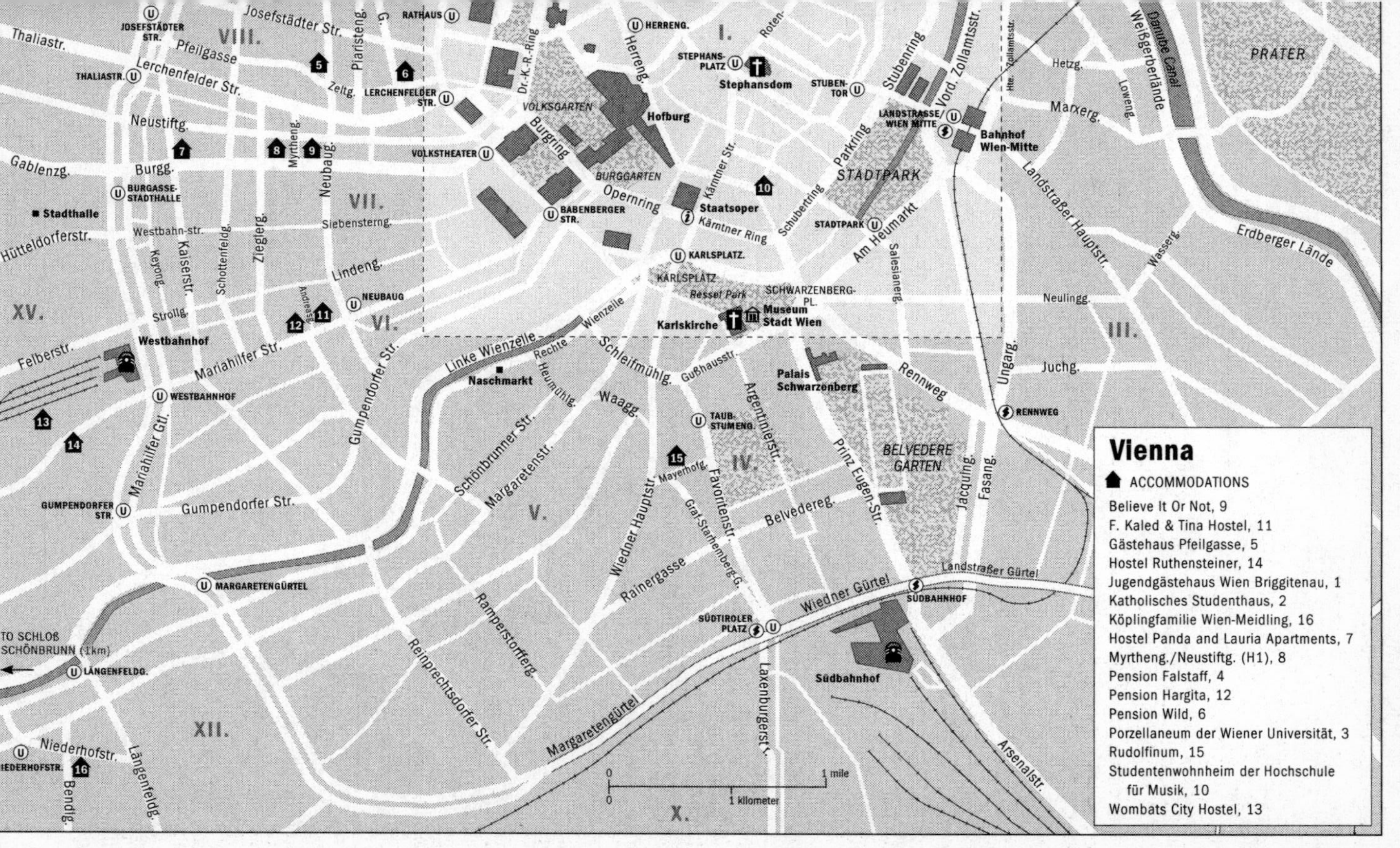
Vienna
ACCOMMODATIONS
Believe It Or Not, 9
F. Kaled & Tina Hostel, 11
Gästehaus Pfeilgasse, 5
Hostel Ruthensteiner, 14
Jugendgästehaus Wien Briggitenau, 1
Katholisches Studenthaus, 2
Köplingfamilie Wien-Meidling, 16
Hostel Panda and Lauria Apartments, 7
Myrtheng./Neustiftg. (H1), 8
Pension Falstaff, 4
Pension Hargita, 12
Pension Wild, 6
Porzellaneum der Wiener Universität, 3
Rudolfinum, 15
Studentenwohnheim der Hochschule für Musik, 10
Wombats City Hostel, 13
PRATER
Danube Canal
Weißgerberlände
Erdberger Lände
Landstraßer Hauptstr.
STADTPARK
Stephansdom
Hofburg
Staatsoper
Karlskirche
Museum Stadt Wien
Palais Schwarzenberg
BELVEDERE GARTEN
Südbahnhof
Westbahnhof
Naschmarkt
Stadthalle
Bahnhof Wien-Mitte
VOLKSGARTEN
BURGGARTEN
Ressel Park
Prinz Eugen-Str.
Wiedner Gürtel
Landstraßer Gürtel
Margaretengürtel
Wiedner Hauptstr.
Mariahilfer Str.
Mariahilfer Gtl.
Linke Wienzeile
Rechte Wienzeile
Gumpendorfer Str.
Josefstädter Str.
Lerchenfelder Str.
Thaliastr.
Kaiserstr.
Arsenalstr.
Rennweg
Favoritenstr.
Schönbrunner Str.
Margaretenstr.
Reinprechtsdorfer Str.
Laxenburgerstr.
TO SCHLOß SCHÖNBRUNN (1km)
0
1 mile
1 kilometer

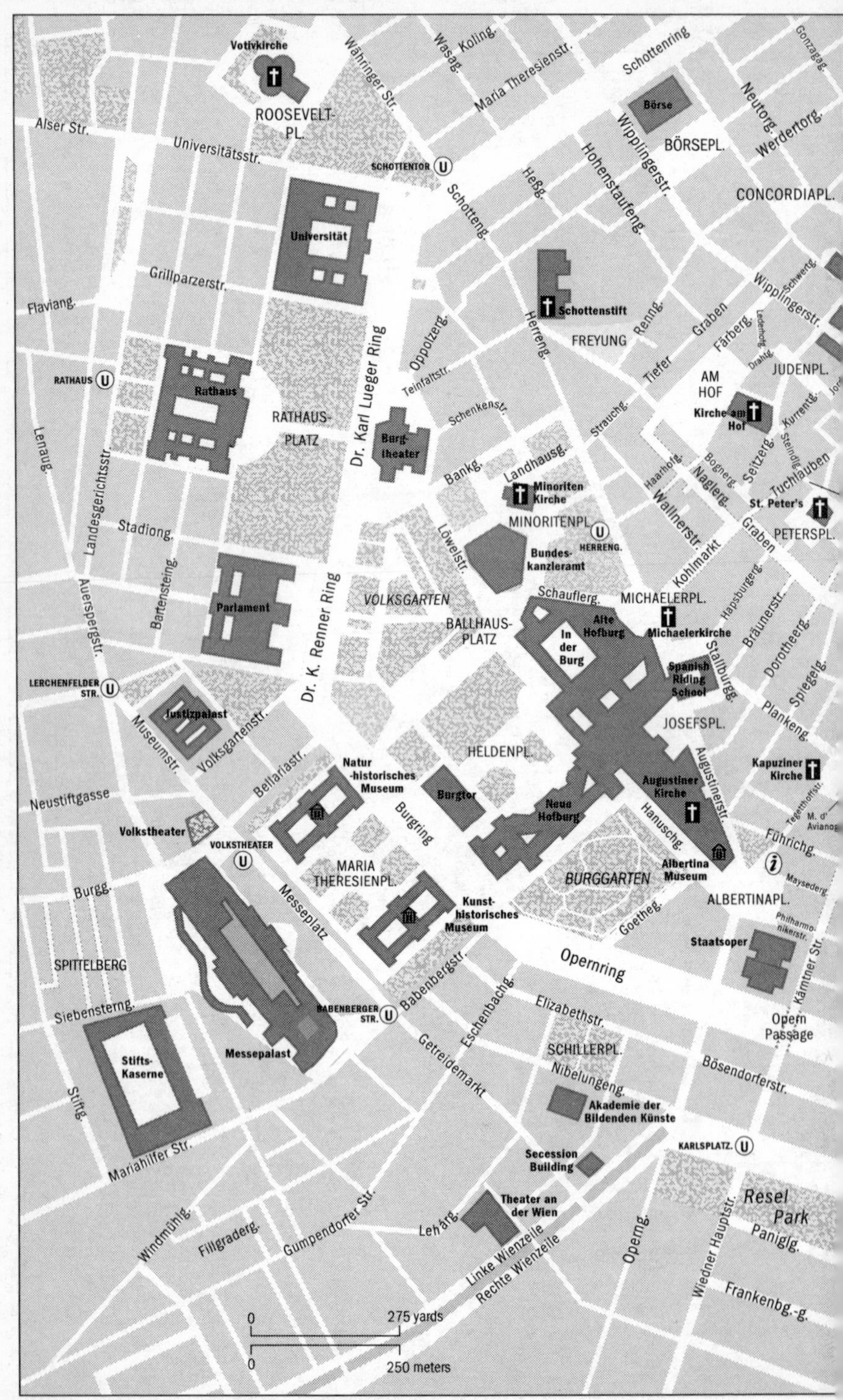

Votivkirche
ROOSEVELT-PL.
Alser Str.
Universitätsstr.
Währinger Str.
Wasag.
Koling.
Maria Theresienstr.
Schottenring
Börse
BÖRSEPL.
Neutorg.
Werdertorg.
Gonzagag.
CONCORDIAPL.
SCHOTTENTOR
Schotteng.
Heßg.
Hohenstaufeng.
Wipplingerstr.
Universität
Grillparzerstr.
Flaviang.
Schottenstift
Herreng.
FREYUNG
Renng.
Tiefer
Graben
Färberg.
Wipplingerstr.
Schwertg.
JUDENPL.
AM HOF
Kirche am Hof
Oppolzerg.
Teinfaltstr.
Dr. Karl Lueger Ring
RATHAUS
Rathaus
RATHAUS-PLATZ
Burg-theater
Schenkenstr.
Strauchg.
Lenaug.
Landesgerichtsstr.
Bankg.
Landhausg.
Minoriten Kirche
Haarhofg.
Naglerg.
Bognerg.
Seitzerg.
Kurrentg.
Steindlg.
Tuchlauben
Wallnerstr.
St. Peter's
PETERSPL.
Graben
Stadiong.
MINORITENPL.
HERRENG.
Bundes-kanzleramt
Löwelstr.
Kohlmarkt
Auerspergstr.
Bartensteing.
Parlament
Dr. K. Renner Ring
VOLKSGARTEN
Schauflerg.
MICHAELERPL.
Habsburgerg.
Bräunerstr.
BALLHAUS-PLATZ
Alte Hofburg
In der Burg
Michaelerkirche
Dorotheerg.
Stallburgg.
Spanish Riding School
Spiegelg.
LERCHENFELDER STR.
Justizpalast
Volksgartenstr.
Museumstr.
JOSEFSPL.
Plankeng.
HELDENPL.
Bellariastr.
Natur-historisches Museum
Augustinerstr.
Kapuziner Kirche
Neustiftgasse
Burgtor
Augustiner Kirche
Neue Hofburg
Hanuschg.
Tegetthoffstr.
Burgring
Volkstheater
VOLKSTHEATER
Führichg.
Albertina Museum
MARIA THERESIENPL.
BURGGARTEN
Maysederg.
Burgg.
Messeplatz
ALBERTINAPL.
Kunst-historisches Museum
Goetheg.
Philharmonikerstr.
Staatsoper
SPITTELBERG
Opernring
Kärntner Str.
Babenbergstr.
Eschenbachg.
Elizabethstr.
Siebensterng.
BABENBERGER STR.
Opern Passage
Messepalast
Getreidemarkt
SCHILLERPL.
Stifts-Kaserne
Nibelungeng.
Bösendorferstr.
Stiftg.
Akademie der Bildenden Künste
Mariahilfer Str.
KARLSPLATZ
Secession Building
Theater an der Wien
Resel Park
Windmühlg.
Fillgraderg.
Gumpendorfer Str.
Lehárg.
Wiedner Hauptstr.
Paniglg.
Operng.
Linke Wienzeile
Rechte Wienzeile
Frankenbg.-g.
0
275 yards
0
250 meters

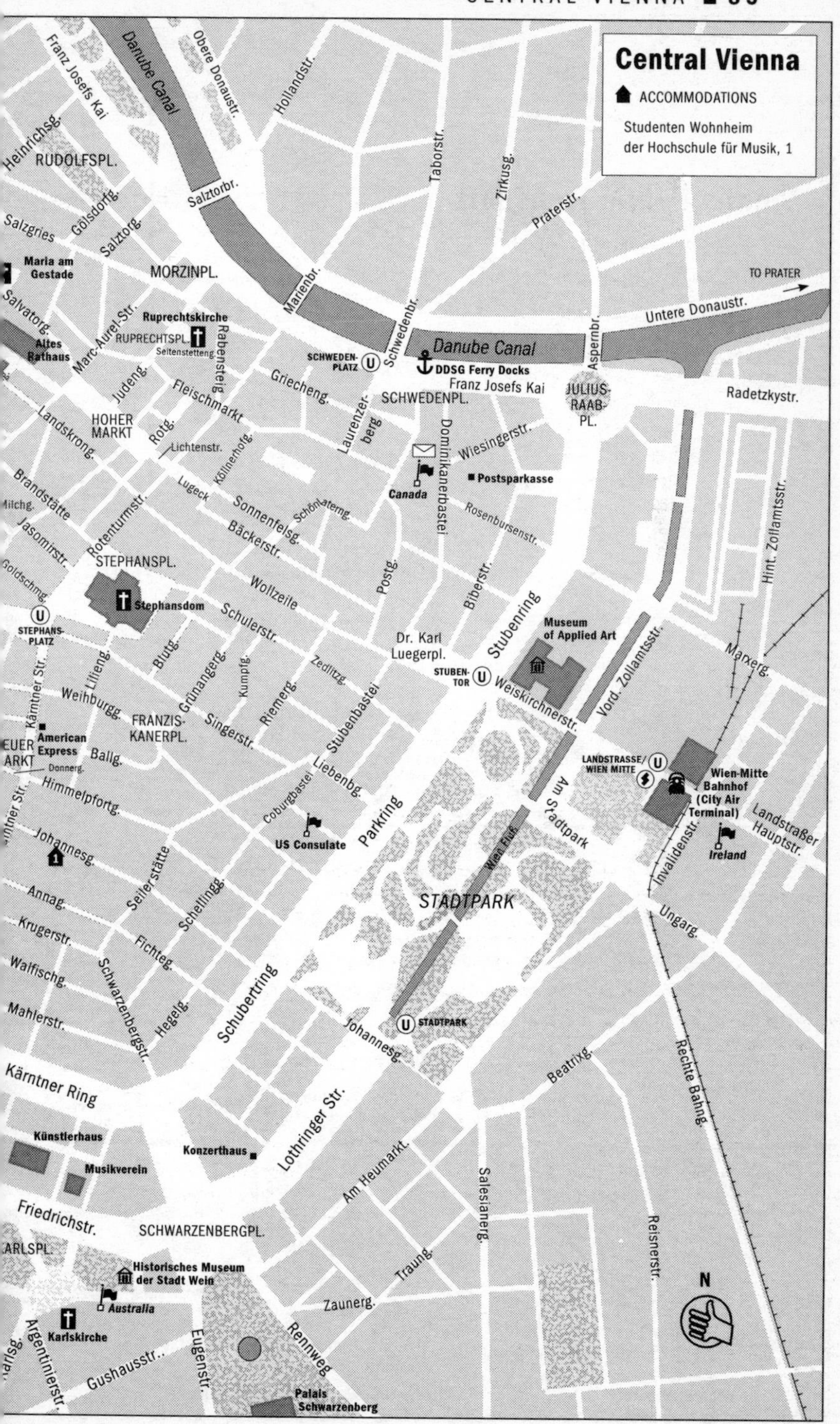

Central Vienna
ACCOMMODATIONS
Studenten Wohnheim der Hochschule für Musik, 1
Danube Canal
Franz Josefs Kai
Obere Donaustr.
Hollandstr.
Taborstr.
Zirkusg.
Praterstr.
TO PRATER
Untere Donaustr.
Heinrichsg.
RUDOLFSPL.
Salztorbr.
Salzgries
Gölsdorfg.
Salztorg.
Maria am Gestade
MORZINPL.
Marienbr.
Schwedenbr.
Aspernbr.
Salvatorg.
Ruprechtskirche
RUPRECHTSPL.
Seitenstetteng.
Rabensteig
Altes Rathaus
Marc-Aurel-Str.
SCHWEDEN-PLATZ
DDSG Ferry Docks
SCHWEDENPL.
JULIUS-RAAB-PL.
Radetzkystr.
Judeng.
Fleischmarkt
Griecheng.
Laurenzerberg
Landskrong.
HOHER MARKT
Rotg.
Lichtenstr.
Köllnerhofg.
Dominikanerbastei
Wiesingerstr.
Canada
Postsparkasse
Brandstätte
Lugeck
Sonnenfelsg.
Schönlaterng.
Rosenbursenstr.
Jasomirstr.
Rotenturmstr.
Bäckerstr.
STEPHANSPL.
Wollzeile
Postg.
Biberstr.
Hint. Zollamtsstr.
Stephansdom
Schulerstr.
Stubenring
Museum of Applied Art
STEPHANS-PLATZ
Dr. Karl Luegerpl.
Vord. Zollamtsstr.
Marxerg.
STUBEN-TOR
Weiskirchnerstr.
Zedlitzg.
Blutg.
Lilieng.
Grünangerg.
Kumpfg.
Riemerg.
Weihburgg.
FRANZIS-KANERPL.
Singerstr.
Stubenbastei
Kärntner Str.
American Express
Ballg.
Donnerg.
LANDSTRASSE/ WIEN MITTE
Wien-Mitte Bahnhof (City Air Terminal)
Liebenbg.
Himmelpfortg.
Coburgbastei
Parkring
Am Stadtpark
Landstraßer Hauptstr.
Johannesg.
US Consulate
Invalidenstr.
Ireland
Wien Fluß
Seilerstätte
Annag.
Schellingg.
STADTPARK
Ungarg.
Krugerstr.
Fichteg.
Walfischg.
Schwarzenbergstr.
Schubertring
Hegelg.
Mahlerstr.
STADTPARK
Johannesg.
Rechte Bahng.
Beatrixg.
Kärntner Ring
Lothringer Str.
Künstlerhaus
Konzerthaus
Musikverein
Am Heumarkt
Salesianerg.
Friedrichstr.
SCHWARZENBERGPL.
Reisnerstr.
Historisches Museum der Stadt Wein
Traung.
Australia
Zaunerg.
N
Karlskirche
Eugenstr.
Rennweg
Argentinierstr.
Gushausstr.
Palais Schwarzenberg

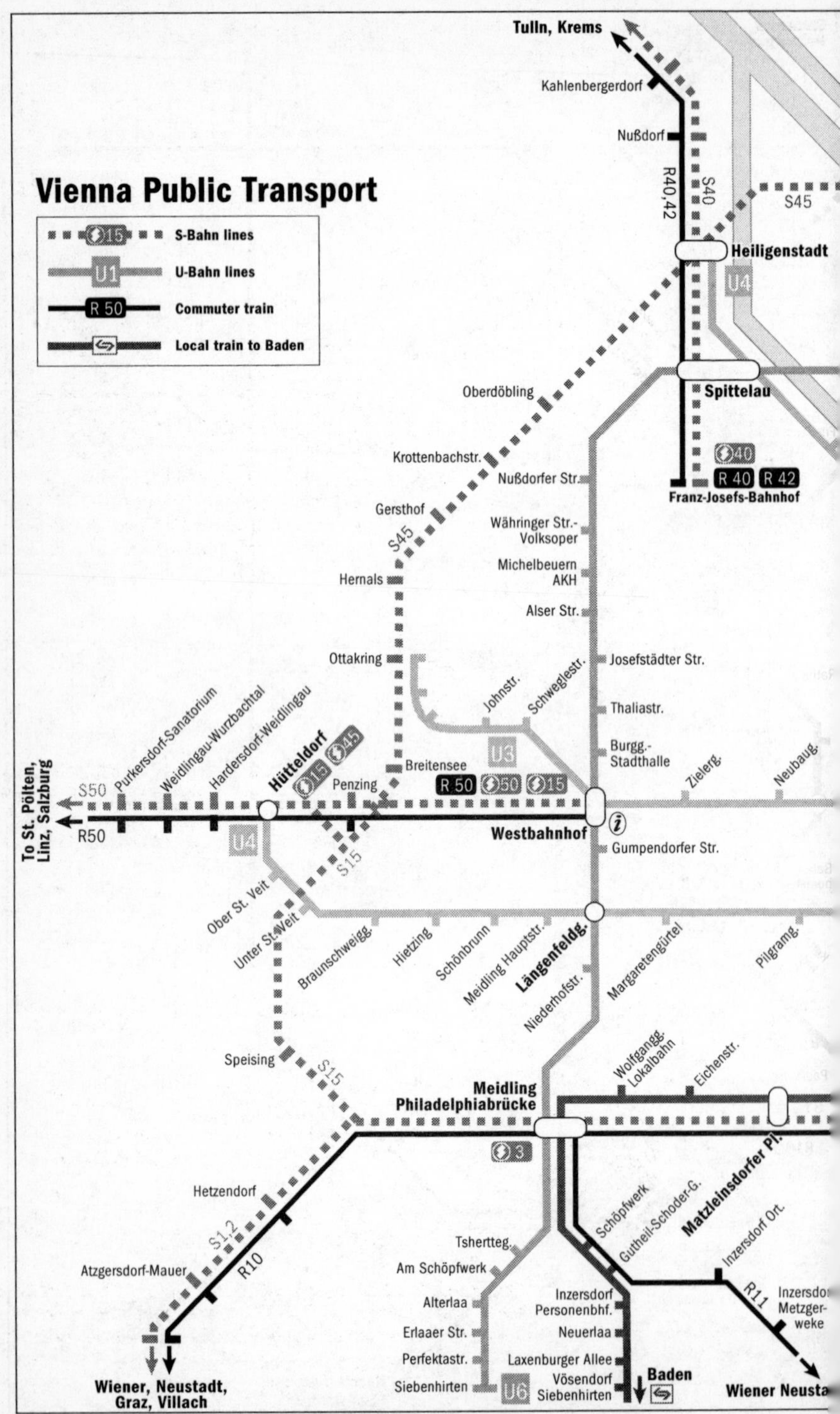

Vienna Public Transport
S-Bahn lines
U-Bahn lines
Commuter train
Local train to Baden
Tulln, Krems
Kahlenbergerdorf
Nußdorf
R40,42
S40
S45
Heiligenstadt
U4
Spittelau
Franz-Josefs-Bahnhof
R 40
R 42
Oberdöbling
Krottenbachstr.
Nußdorfer Str.
Gersthof
Währinger Str.-Volksoper
Michelbeuern AKH
Hernals
Alser Str.
Ottakring
Josefstädter Str.
Johnstr.
Schweglerstr.
Thaliastr.
U3
Burgg.-Stadthalle
Zieglerg.
Neubaug.
Purkersdorf-Sanatorium
Weidlingau-Wurzbachtal
Hardersdorf-Weidlingau
Hütteldorf
Breitensee
Penzing
R 50
S50
R50
To St. Pölten, Linz, Salzburg
Westbahnhof
Gumpendorfer Str.
S15
Ober St. Veit
Unter St. Veit
Braunschweigg.
Hietzing
Schönbrunn
Meidling Hauptstr.
Längenfeldg.
Margaretengürtel
Pilgramg.
Niederhofstr.
Speising
Wolfgangg. Lokalbahn
Eichenstr.
Meidling Philadelphiabrücke
Matzleinsdorfer Pl.
Hetzendorf
S1,2
R10
Atzgersdorf-Mauer
Tshertteg.
Am Schöpfwerk
Schöpfwerk
Gutheil-Schoder-G.
Inzersdorf Ort.
R11
Inzersdorf Personenbhf.
Alterlaa
Erlaaer Str.
Neuerlaa
Perfektastr.
Laxenburger Allee
Siebenhirten
U6
Vösendorf Siebenhirten
Baden
Wiener, Neustadt, Graz, Villach
Inzersdo Metzger-weke
Wiener Neusta

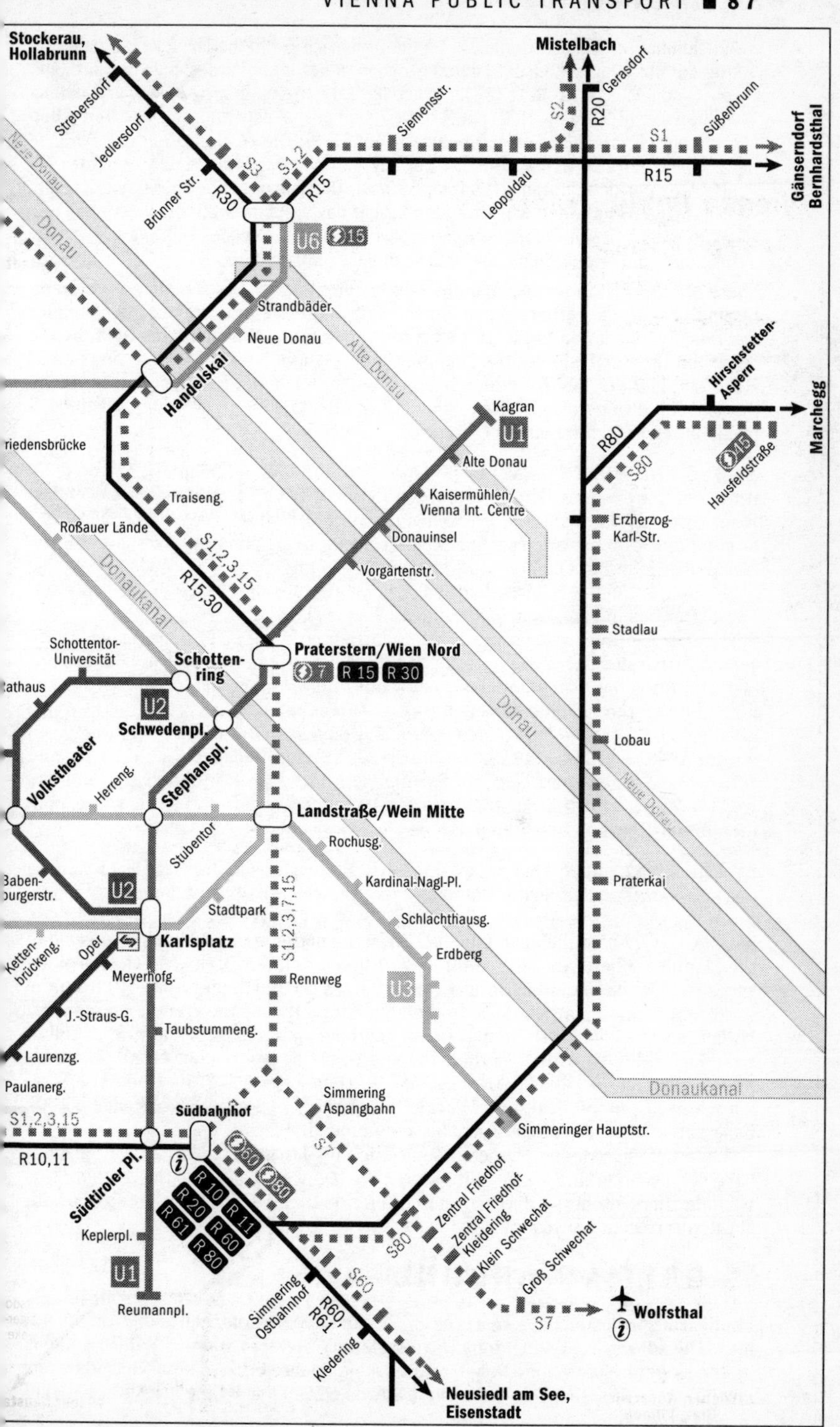
Stockerau, Hollabrunn
Mistelbach
Gänserndorf Bernhardsthal
Marchegg
Neusiedl am See, Eisenstadt
Wolfsthal
Strebersdorf
Jedlersdorf
Brünner Str.
Siemensstr.
Leopoldau
Gerasdorf
Süßenbrunn
S1
R15
S2
R20
S3
S1,2
R30
U6
15
Strandbäder
Neue Donau
Alte Donau
Donau
Handelskai
Kagran
U1
Alte Donau
Kaisermühlen/ Vienna Int. Centre
Donauinsel
Vorgartenstr.
Hirschstetten-Aspern
R80
S80
Hausfeldstraße
Erzherzog-Karl-Str.
Stadlau
Lobau
Praterkai
riedensbrücke
Traiseng.
Roßauer Lände
S1,2,3,15
R15,30
Donaukanal
Praterstern/Wien Nord
7
R 15
R 30
Schottentor-Universität
Schottenring
Rathaus
U2
Schwedenpl.
Volkstheater
Stephanspl.
Herreng.
Landstraße/Wein Mitte
Stubentor
Rochusg.
Kardinal-Nagl-Pl.
Schlachthausg.
Erdberg
U3
Babenbergerstr.
Stadtpark
Karlsplatz
Kettenbrückeng.
Oper
Meyerhofg.
J.-Straus-G.
Laurenzg.
Paulanerg.
Taubstummeng.
S1,2,3,7,15
Rennweg
Simmering Aspangbahn
Simmeringer Hauptstr.
Südbahnhof
S1,2,3,15
R10,11
Südtiroler Pl.
S7
60
80
R 10
R 11
R 20
R 60
R 61
R 80
Zentral Friedhof
Zentral Friedhof-Kledering
Klein Schwechat
Groß Schwechat
S80
S60
Keplerpl.
Reumannpl.
Simmering Ostbahnhof
R60, R61
Kledering
S7

Südbahnhof, X, Wiedner Gürtel 1a. On the D tram—to get to the city take the tram (dir. Nußdorf) to "Opera/Karlspl." From the station, trains leave for destinations **south** and **east,** domestically to **Graz** (2¾hr., every hr. 6:04am-10:34pm, 310AS), and **Villach** (5hr., every hr. 6:04am-10:34pm, 470AS). International departures include **Berlin Östbahnhof** (9¼hr., 1 per day 10:55am, 1160AS), **Prague** (4½hr., 3 per day 6:55am-2:55pm, 524AS), **Rome** (14hr., 2 per day 7:34am, 7:36pm, 1352AS), **Venice** (9-10hr., 3 per day 7:34am-10:34pm, 880AS), **Bratislava** (1hr., 3per day 10:15am-10:15pm, 166AS), and **Krakow** (7-8hr., 2 per day 9:25am, 9:25pm, 496AS), as well as to other cities in **Poland, Germany, Russia, Turkey, Greece,** and **Spain.** The Südbahnhof train **information counter** is open daily 6:30am-9:20pm.

There are three stations that handle mostly commuter trains. The largest is **Franz-Josefs Bahnhof,** IX, Althamstr. 10, on the D tram line. There are also two smaller stations: **Bahnhof Wien Mitte,** in the center of town, and **Bahnhof Wien Nord,** by the Prater on the north side of the Danube Canal. Bahnhof Wien Nord is the main S-Bahn and U-Bahn link for trains heading north, but most Bundesbahn trains go through the other stations. Some regional trains (Krems, for example) also leave from **Spittelau,** located on the U4 and U6 subway lines.

VIENNA

BY BUS AND BOAT. Travel by bus in Austria is seldom cheaper than travel by train; compare prices before you buy a ticket. **City bus terminals** are located at Wien Mitte/Landstr., Hütteldorf, Heiligenstadt, Floridsdorf, Kagran, Erdberg, and Reumannpl. Domestic **BundesBuses** run from these stations to local and international destinations. (Ticket counter open M-F 6am-5:50pm, Sa-Su 6am-3:50pm.) Many international bus lines also have agencies in the stations, each with different hours. For bus information, call BundesBus at ☎71101 (7am-7pm).

The Danube River also carries boats to farther points. The famous **Donaudampffschiffahrtsgesellschaft Donaureisen** (DDSG), I, Friedrichstr. 7 (☎588 800; fax 588 804 40; info@ddsg-blue-danube.at; www.ddsg-blue-danube.at), organizes cruises up and down the Danube, hitting the cities of Melk, Spitz, Dürnstein, and Krems/Stein (see p. 274). The DDSG also operates **Hydrofoils** to **Bratislava** (1¾hr., between May and Sept. 9:30am, 240AS, round-trip 370AS) and **Budapest** (5-6hr., June and July 8am, Aug. 9am and 1pm780AS, round-trip 1100AS). Eurail and ISIC holders get 20% off travel within Austria, children 10-15 travel at 50% off regular fare, children under 10 travel free with a parent.

BY CAR. Traveling to Vienna by car is fairly simple; the capital city lies on numerous *Autobahn* routes. From the **west,** take A1, which begins and ends in Vienna. From the **south,** take A2, A21, or A3 (the latter two cross A2, which runs directly into the city). From the **east,** take A4. From the **north,** take A22, which runs along the Danube. There are also a number of much smaller highways that provide access to Vienna, including Routes 7 and 8 from the north and Route 10 from the south. An economical, but less predictable alternative to the train is **ride-sharing. Mitfahrzentrale Wien,** VIII, Daung. 1a, off Laudong., pairs drivers and riders. Call to see which rides are available, then, to meet your ride from Schottentor, take tram #43 to "Skodag." and walk down Skodag. to Daung. (☎ 408 2210. Open M-F 8am-noon and 2-7pm, Sa-Su 1-3pm.) A ride to **Salzburg** costs 210AS, to **Prague** 450AS. Reservations two days in advance are recommended.

While Let's Go does not recommend hitching, **hitchhikers** headed for Salzburg have been seen taking U4 to "Hütteldorf"; the highway leading to the *Autobahn* is 10km farther. Hitchers traveling south often ride tram #67 to the last stop and wait at the rotary near Laaerberg.

GETTING AROUND

Public transportation in Vienna is extensive and dependable; call 58000 for general info. The **subway** (U-Bahn), **tram** (Straßenbahn), **elevated train** (S-Bahn), and **bus** systems operate under one ticket system. A single fare is 22AS if purchased from a machine on a bus, 19AS if purchased in advance from a machine in a station, ticket office, or tobacco shop *(Tabak* or *Trafik)*. This ticket permits you to travel to any single destination in the city and switch from bus to U-Bahn to tram to S-Bahn, as long as your travel is uninterrupted. This bit's tricky: to validate a ticket, punch it in the machine immediately upon entering the first vehicle of your journey. This action records the time and date of your trip, and you should not stamp the ticket again when you switch trains. A ticket stamped twice or not stamped at all is invalid, and plain clothes inspectors may fine you 560AS plus the ticket price for freeloading *(Schwarzfahren)*. Other ticket options (available at the same places as pre-purchased single tickets) are a **24-hour pass** (60AS), a **3-day "rover" ticket** (150AS), a **7-day pass** (155AS; valid from M 9am to the following M 9am), or an **8-day pass** (300AS; valid any 8 days, not necessarily consecutive; valid also for several people traveling together). The **Vienna Card** (210AS) offers free travel on the public transportation system for 72 hours, as well as substantial discounts at museums, sights, and events, and is especially useful for non-students.

If you are traveling with a child over 6 years old, a bicycle, or a dog, you must buy a half-price ticket (11AS) for your companion. Children under 6 always ride free, and, on Sundays and school holidays, anyone under 15 rides free. (The pocket map available at the tourist offices lists official holidays.) You can take bicycles on all underground trains, but the U6 line only allows bikes on the middle car, which is marked with a bicycle symbol.

All regular trams and subway cars stop running between 12:30am and 5am. **Nightbuses** pick up the slack (every 30min.) along most tram, subway, and major bus routes. In major hubs like Schottentor, some of the buses leave from slightly different areas than their daytime counterparts. "N" signs with yellow cat eyes designate night bus stops (15AS; day transport passes not valid). A complete night bus schedule is available at bus info counters in U-Bahn stations.

The **public transportation information line** has live operators that give public transportation directions to any point in the city (☎790 9105; open M-F 6:30am-6:30pm, Sa-Su 8:30am-4pm). **Information stands** (marked with an "i") in many stations also provide detailed instructions. The staff can explain how to purchase tickets and can provide an indispensable free pocket map of the U-Bahn and S-Bahn systems. A comprehensive map of Vienna's public transportation is 15AS. Stands in the U-Bahn at Karlspl., Stephanspl., and the Westbahnhof are the most likely to have information in English (open M-F 6:30am-6:30pm, Sa-Su and holidays 8:30am-4pm). Other stands are located at Praterstern, Philadelphiabrücke, Landstr., Floridsdorf, Spittelau, and Volkstheater (open M-F 6:30am-6:30pm). Website www.wiennet.at/efa calculates the shortest route between two points (commonly known as a "line").

Taxis: (☎31300, 40100, 60160, 81400, or 91091). Stands at Westbahnhof, Südbahnhof, and Karlspl. in the city center. Accredited taxis have yellow and black signs on the roof. Rates generally 27AS plus 14AS per km. 26AS surcharge for taxis called by radiophone; 27AS surcharge Sundays, holidays, and nights (11pm-6am); 13AS surcharge for luggage over 20kg, 26AS for over 50kg.

Car Rental: Avis, I, Opernring 3-5 (☎587 6241). Open M-F 7am-6pm, Sa 8am-2pm, Su 8am-1pm. **Hertz,** (☎700 72661), at the airport. Open M-F 7:15am-11pm, Sa 8am-8pm, Su 8am-11pm.

Auto Repairs: If your car needs fixing, call **ÖAMTC** (☎120) or **ARBÖ** (☎123).

Parking: In the 1st district, parking is allowed M-F 9am-7pm for 1½hr. Buy a voucher (6AS per 30min.) at a *Tabak* and display it, with the time, on the dashboard. It's easiest to park cars outside the *Ring* and walk into the city center. Garages line the Ringstr., including 2 by the Opera House, 1 at Franz-Josef Kai, and 1 at the Marek-Garage at Messepalast. In districts VI through IX, parking is permitted M-F 9am-8pm for 2hr. **Parking cards** (50AS) enable all-day parking there and can be purchased either from a *Tabak* or the machine on the street. Avoid parking illegally, unless a 300AS-2,000AS parking ticket won't phase you.

Bike Rental: At Wien Nord and the Westbahnhof. 150AS per day, 90AS with a train ticket from the day of arrival. Elsewhere in the city, including Donauinsel, rentals average 60AS per hr. **Pedal Power,** II, Ausstellungsstr. 3 (☎729 7234; fax 729 7235; office@pedalpower.co.at; www.pedalpower.co.at) rents bikes for 60AS per hr., 300AS per half day, 395AS for 24hr. with delivery. They also offer bike tours of the city (180-280AS). Discounts available for students and Vienna Card holders. Open May-Sept. 8am-8pm. Pick up *Vienna By Bike* at the tourist office for details on the bicycle scene.

CRIME IN THE CITY. Vienna is a metropolis with crime like any other; use common sense, especially after dark. Karlsplatz is home to many pushers and junkies. Also beware of the city's small skinhead population. Avoid areas in the 5th, 10th, and 14th districts, as well as Landstraßer Hauptstr. and **Prater Park,** after dark. Vienna's Red Light District covers sections of the Gürtel.

ORIENTATION

Vienna's layout reflects its history. The city is divided into 23 **districts** *(Bezirke)*. The first is the *innere Stadt*, or *Innenstadt* (city center), and the rest of the districts radiate out from it like the spokes of a wheel. The *Innenstadt* is defined by the **Ringstraße,** once the site of the old city fortifications and now a massive automobile artery, on three sides, with the Danube Canal on the fourth. The Ringstraße (or "Ring") consists of many different segments, each with its own name: Opernring, Kärntner Ring, Dr.-Karl-Lueger-Ring, etc. This fragmentation occurs because of the tendency of Austrian streets to change names after a few blocks.

Many of Vienna's major attractions are in the first district (the *innere Stadt*) and immediately around the Ringstraße, including the **Kunsthistorisches Museum,** the **Rathaus,** and the **Burggarten.** At the intersection of the **Opernring, Kärntner Ring,** and **Kärntnerstraße** stands the **Staatsoper** (Opera House), near the **tourist office** and the **Karlsplatz** U-Bahn stop. Districts two through nine spread out from the city center following the clockwise, one-way traffic of the Ring. The remaining districts expand from yet another ring, the **Gürtel** ("belt"). Like the Ring, this major two-way thoroughfare has numerous segments, including Margaretengürtel, Währinger Gürtel, and Neubaugürtel. Street signs indicate the district number in Roman or Arabic numerals, and postal codes correspond to the district number: 1010 for the first district, 1020 for the second, 1110 for the eleventh, etc. *Let's Go* includes district numbers for establishments before the street address.

DISTRICT NAMES AND NUMBERS: Moving in a roughly clockwise direction, Vienna's 23 districts are: I, **innere Stadt;** II, **Leopoldstadt;** III, **Landstraße;** IV, **Wieden;** V, **Margareten;** VI, **Mariahilf;** VII, **Neubau;** VIII, **Josefstadt;** IX, **Alsergrund;** X, **Favoriten;** XI, **Simmering;** XII, **Meidling;** XIII, **Hietzing;** XIV, **Penzing;** XV, **Rudolfsheim Fünfhaus;** XVI, **Ottakring;** XVII, **Hernals;** XVIII, **Währing;** XIX, **Döbling;** XX, **Brigittenau;** XXI, **Floridsdorf;** XXII, **Donaustadt;** XXIII, **Liesing.**

PRACTICAL INFORMATION

TOURIST OFFICES

Main Tourist Office: I, Am Albertinapl. (www.info.wien.at). Follow Operngasse up 1 block from the Opera House. The newly enlarged tourist office still serves hordes with an assortment of brochures, including a free map of the city. The brochure *Youth Scene* provides vital information for travelers of all ages. The office books 300-400AS rooms for a 40AS fee plus a 1-night deposit. Open 9am-7pm. **Branch Offices:**

Westbahnhof, open 7am-10pm daily. **Airport,** open 8:30am-9pm daily.

Highway exit "Wien Auhof," off A1. Open Easter Week to Oct. 8am-10pm daily, Nov.-Mar. 10am-6pm.

Highway exit "Zentrum," off A2, XI, Trierstr. 149. Open July-Sept. 8am-10pm; Oct. and Easter Week to June 9am-7pm.

North Danube Island, open May-Sept. 10am-6pm.

Vienna International Airport, in arrival hall. Open 8:30am-9pm.

Jugend-Info Wien (Vienna Youth Information Service): Bellaria-Passage (☎1799; jiw@blackbox.at), in the underground passage at the Bellaria intersection. Enter at the "Dr.-Karl-Renner-Ring/Bellaria" stop (trams #1, 2, 46, 49, D, or J) or at the "Volkstheater" U-Bahn station. Hip staff has information on cultural events, housing, and employment opportunities and sells discount youth concert and theater tickets. Get the indispensable *Jugend in Wien* brochure here. Open M-Sa noon-7pm.

Österreichisches Verkehrsbüro (Austrian National Travel Office): 4, Margaretenstrasse 1. (☎587 2000; oeinfo@oewwien.via.at; www.austria-tourism.at.) Open M-W, F 10am-5pm, Th 10am-6pm.

Ökista, IX, Türkenstr. 8 (☎401 480), specializes in student travel, such as tickets, passes, and discounts. Open M-F 9am-7:30pm.

Embassies and Consulates: Complete list of consular services can be found in Essentials (see p. 7). Generally, each country's embassy and consulate are located in the same building, listed under *"Botschaften"* or *"Konsulate"* in the phone book. Contact consulates for assistance with visas and passports and in emergencies.

VIENNA

FINANCIAL AND COMMUNICATION SERVICES

Currency Exchange: ATMs are your best bet. Nearly all accept Cirrus, Eurocard, MC, and Visa (see p. 16). **Banks** and **airport exchanges** use the same official rates. Minimum commission 65AS for travelers' checks, 10AS for cash. Most are open M-W and F 8am-12:30pm and 1:30-3pm, Th 8am-12:30pm and 1:30-5:30pm. **Train station** exchanges offer long hours and a 50AS charge for changing up to US$700 of travelers' checks. The 24hr. exchange at the **main post office** has excellent rates and an 80AS fee to change up to $1100 in travelers' checks. The **24hr. bill exchange** machines in the *Innenstadt* have horrible rates. The **casino,** 41 Kärntnerstr., has slightly better rates (open 3pm-4am). The only place in Vienna that will accept credit cards to buy AS is **Rieger Bank,** Kohlmarkt 3, down Graben from the Stefansdom (open M-F 9am-7pm, Sa 9am-6pm, Su 9:30am-4:30pm).

American Express: I, Kärntnerstr. 21-23, P.O. Box 28, A-1015 (☎51540), down the street from Stephanspl. Cashes AmEx and Thomas Cook (3% commission) checks, sells theater, concert, and other tickets, and holds mail for 4 weeks for AmEx members. Open M-F 9am-5:30pm, Sa 9am-noon. For 24hr. refund service, call (0800) 206 840.

Bookstores: Shakespeare & Company, I, Sterng. 2 (☎535 5053; fax 535 5053 16; bookseller@shakespeare.co.at; www.ping.at/members/shbook). Eclectic and intelligent. Great British magazine selection. Open M-F 9am-7pm, Sa 9am-5pm. The **British Bookshop,** I, Weihburgg. 24 (☎512 1945; fax 512 1026), has an extensive collection of travel books. Open M-F 9am-6:30pm, Sa 10am-5pm. **Comic-Treff Steiner,** VI, Barnabitengasse 12 (☎586 7627). One of Vienna's best comicbook stores. Open M-F 10am-7pm; Sat 10am-2pm.

Internet Access: Libro, XXII, Donauzentrum (☎202 5255), provides free access at 6 terminals. Open Su-F 7am-7pm, Sa 9am-5pm. **Jugend-Info des Bundesministeriums,** I, Franz-Josefs-Kai 51 (☎533 7030). Free access at 2 PCs. Open M-F 11am-6pm. The **National Library,** I, Neue Burg 1 (☎53 41 00), in Heldenpl. at the Hofburg, has 2 terminals and long lines. 50AS per 30min. Open M-Sa 10am-4pm, Su 10am-1pm. **Public Internet terminal** in Stephansplatz U-bahn station, by "Kärtnerstr." exit (10AS).

English Language Radio: Blue Danube radio, 103.8FM. Mixes classical, oldies, and mainstream music with news updates every hr. until 7pm in English, French, and German, including the BBC World Service. "What's on in Vienna" airs at 1pm.

Post Offices: Hauptpostamt, I, Fleischmarkt 19. Vast structure containing exchange windows, phones, faxes, and mail services. Open 24hr. Address *Poste Restante* to "REED, Carol; Postlagernde Briefe; Hauptpostamt; Fleischmarkt 19; A-1010 Wien." Branches throughout the city and at the train stations; look for the yellow signs with the trumpet logo. **Postal Codes:** In the 1st district A-1010, in the 2nd A-1020, in the 3rd A-1030, and so on, to the 23rd A-1230.

OTHER SERVICES

Bisexual, Gay, and Lesbian Organizations: The bisexual, gay, and lesbian community in Vienna, though small, is more integrated than in other Austrian cities. For the gay goings on around town, pick up either the monthly Viennese magazine (in German) called **Extra Connect,** the free monthly publication **Bussi** at any gay bar, cafe, or club, or consult the straight **Falter** newspaper, which lists gay events under a special heading. The following organizations also sponsor events and offer help in Vienna:

Rosa Lila Villa, VI, Linke Wienzeile 102 (☎586 8150), is a favored resource and social center for Viennese homosexuals and visitors to the city. Friendly staff speaks English and provides counseling, information, a library, and nightclub listings (see Nightlife, p. 130). Open M-F 5-8pm.

Homosexuelle Initiative Wien (HOSI), II, Novarag. 40 (☎216 6604; fax 585 4159). Lesbian group and phone network W at 7pm. Youth group Th at 8pm. Prints a political newspaper, *Lambda Nachrichten.* Open Tu 6-8pm (includes phone counseling), Th 7-9pm (for youth). cafe open Su 5-10pm.

Lesbischwul und Transgender Referat (☎588 015 890; efisher@mail.zserve.tuwien.ac.at) is a gay student counseling group. Open F 4-6pm.

Laundromat: Schnell und Sauber, VII, Westbahnhofstr. 60 (☎524 6460); U6 to "Burgg. Stadthalle." 6kg wash 60AS. Spin-dry 10AS. Detergent included. Open 24hr. **Münzwäscherei Karlberger & Co.,** III, Schlachthausg. 19 (☎798 8191). Wash 90AS per 7kg, dry 10AS. Soap 10AS. Open M-F 7:30am-6:30pm. Many hostels offer laundry facilities (50-60AS).

Public Showers and Toilets: At **Westbahnhof,** in Friseursalon Navratil downstairs from subway passage. Well maintained. 30min. shower 54AS, with soap and towel 66AS (10AS extra for either on Su). Showers are also available at **Jörgerbad,** XVII, Jörgerstr. 42-44, and at the airport. There are toilets in most U-bahn stations (1-5AS), and a special *Jugendstil* toilet in Graben. (Requires a 1AS or 5AS coin to open. 9am-7pm.)

Snow Reports: In German for Vienna, Lower Austria, and Styria (☎1583); for Salzburg, Upper Austria, and Carinthia (☎1584); for Tyrol and the Voralberg (☎1585).

Luggage Storage: Lockers are 30-50AS per 24hr. at all train stations. Adequate for sizable backpacks. **Luggage watch** 30AS. Open 4am-1:15am.

Lost Property: Fundbüro, IX, Wasag. 22 (☎313 449 211 or 9217). For items lost on public transportation, call 790 9435 00. Open M-F 8am-noon. For items lost on trains, call 580 0329 96 (Westbahnhof) or 580 0356 56 (Südbahnhof).

EMERGENCIES

Emergencies: Police, ☎133. **Ambulance,** ☎144. **Fire,** ☎122. Alert your embassy of any emergencies or legal problems.

Poison Control: ☎406 4343. Open 24hr.

Medical Assistance: Allgemeines Krankenhaus, IX, Währinger Gürtel 18-20 (☎404 0019 64). **Emergency care,** ☎141. **24hr. pharmacy,** ☎1550. Consulates offer lists of English-speaking physicians, or call **Fachärzte Zugeck** (☎512 1818; open 24hr.).

Crisis Hotlines: All hotlines can find English speakers. **House for Threatened and Battered Women:** ☎545 4800, 202 5500, or 408 3880. 24hr. emergency hotline. **Rape Crisis Hotline:** ☎523 2222. Open M 10am-6pm, Tu 2-6pm, W 10am-2pm, Th 5-9pm. **24hr. immediate help:** ☎71719. **Psychological Counsel Hotline:** ☎319 3566 or 402 7838. Open M-F 8pm-8am, Sa-Su 24hr. **English-language "Befrienders" Suicide Hotline:** ☎713 3374. Open 9:30am-1pm and 6:30-10pm.

ACCOMMODATIONS AND CAMPING

One of the few unpleasant aspects of visiting Vienna is the hunt for cheap rooms during peak tourist season (June-Sept.). Write or call for reservations at least 5 days in advance. Otherwise, plan on calling from the train station between 6 and

9am during the summer to put your name down for a reservation. If your choice is full, ask to be put on a waiting list, or ask for suggestions—don't waste time tramping around. A list of budget accommodations in Vienna is available at almost every tourist office. Those unable to find a hostel bed should consider a *Pension*. One-star establishments are generally adequate and are most common in the 7th, 8th, and 9th districts. Singles start around 350AS, doubles around 500AS. The summer crunch for budget rooms is slightly alleviated in July, when university dorms are converted into makeshift hostels. Bear in mind that these "dorms" are singles and doubles, not dormitories, and are priced accordingly.

If you're staying for a longer period of time, try **Odyssee Reisen und Mitwohnzentrale,** VIII, Laudong. 7. They find apartments for 225-350AS per person per night. A week costs about 1200AS, and a month starts at 2000AS. They charge 20% commission on each month's rent. Bring your passport to register. (☎402 6061. Open M-F 10am-2pm and 3-6pm.) Otherwise, visit either *Österreichische Hochschülerschaft* at Rooseveltpl. 5 or the bulletin boards on the first floor of the *Neues Institut Gebäude* (NIG building) on Universitätstr. 7 near the *Votivkirche*.

HOSTELS AND DORMITORIES

Hostel Ruthensteiner (HI), XV, Robert-Hamerlingg. 24 (☎893 4202 or 843 2796; fax 893 2796; hostel.ruthensteiner@telecom.at; www.hostelruthensteiner.com), is 5min. from the Westbahnhof and about a 10min. ride from the city center. Exit Westbahnhof at the main entrance, turn right and head to Mariahilferstr. Turn right again and continue until Haidmannsg. Turn left, then take the first right on Robert-Hammerlingg., and continue to the middle of the block. This top-notch hostel not only offers exceptional value and extremely knowledgeable, English-speaking staff, but also spotless rooms and a beautiful sun-filled oasis of ivy. Breakfast 29AS. Showers and sheets (except for 10-bed rooms) included. Snack bar open all day. Lockers and kitchen available. Net access from 20AS. 4-night max. stay. Reception 24hr. Phone or email reservations recommended, but owners often hold beds for spontaneous travelers. "The Outback" summer dorm 125AS; 10-bed dorms 145AS; 3- to 5-bed dorms 169AS; doubles 470AS.

Wombats City Hostel, 15, Grangasse 6 (☎897 2336; fax 897 2577; wombats@chello.at; www.womabats.at). U3/U4 to "Westbahnhof." Take the "Außer Mariahilferstr." exit. Turn right and head down Mariahilferstr. Take 6th right at Rosinagaße. Walk up until Granfasse (2nd left). While right next to the train tracks and near a number of auto-body shops, this superb modern hostel compensates with in-the-know staff and a pub. Breakfast 35AS. Coin-operated laundry. Internet access. No curfew or lockout. 164 beds in 2-, 4-, and 6-bedrooms. All with showers. 175-245AS per person.

Believe It Or Not, VII, Myrtheng. 10, Apt. #14 (☎526 4658). From Westbahnhof, take U6 (dir.: Heiligenstadt) to "Burgg./Stadthalle," then bus #48A (dir.: Ring) to "Neubaug." Walk back on Burgg. 1 block and take the first right on Myrtheng. (15min.). From Südbahnhof, take bus #13A (dir.: Skodag./Alerstr.) to "Kellermanng." Walk 2 blocks to your left on Neustiftg. and turn left on Myrtheng. Ring the bell. A converted apartment, this sociable hostel has a **kitchen** and 2 co-ed bedrooms full of bunks. The caretaker kicks you out (10:30am-12:30pm) to clean. Reception 8am until early afternoon–call early. No curfew. Reservations recommended. 160AS; Nov.-Easter 110AS.

Myrthengasse (HI), VII, Myrtheng. 7, across the street from Believe it or Not, and **Neustiftgasse (HI),** VII, Neustiftg. 85 (☎523 6316; fax 523 5849; hostel@cello.at). These simple, Swedish-modern hostels, under the same management, are a 20min. walk from the *Innenstadt*. Breakfast and sheets included. Lockers and keys provided. Lunch or dinner 65AS. **Laundry** 50AS. Reception at Myrtheng. 7am-11:30pm. Lockout 9am-2pm. Curfew 1am. Reservations recommended; accepted only by fax or email. From Jan. 1-Mar.18 and Oct. 29-Dec. 23, 4- to 6-bed dorms with shower 170AS; 2-bed dorms 200AS. Rest of the year 4- to 6-bed dorms with shower 185AS; 2-bed dorms with shower 215AS. Non-member surcharge 40AS.

Hostel Panda, VII, Kaiserstr. 77, 3rd fl. (☎522 5353). From Westbahnhof, take tram #5 to "Burgg." From Sudbahnhof, take tram #18 to "Westbahnhof," then tram #5 to "Burgg." Housed in an old-fashioned, semi-*Jugendstil* Austrian apartment building, this fun and eclectic hostel has 18 mattresses packed into 2 co-ed dorms with huge ceilings and Chinese lanterns. **Kitchen** and TV. Bring lock for lockers. Dorms 160AS; Nov.-Easter 110AS. 50AS surcharge for 1-night stays.

Hostel Zöhrer, IX, Skodag. 26 (☎406 0730; fax 408 0409; infor@zoehrer.com, www.zoehrer.com). From Westbahnhof take tram #5 to "Laudongaße." Walk back and turn on second right at Daungaße. Walk 1 block to Skodagaße. From Südbahnhof take bus #13a to "Alserstr., Skodag." Caring staff manage this well-located hostel. Breakfast, kitchen, and shower included. Lockout 11am-2pm. No curfew. Reservations recommended. 6- to 8- bed dorms 170AS; double 460AS; triple 690AS.

Kolpingfamilie Wien-Meidling (HI), XIII, Bendlg. 10-12 (☎813 5487; fax 812 2130). Take U6 to "Niederhofstr." Head right on Niederhofstr. and take the 4th right onto Bendlg. This well-lit, modern hostel has 202 beds. While not too exciting inside or out, it's close to the U-bahn. Breakfast 55AS. Sheets included. Showers in all rooms, baths in some. Reception 6am-midnight. Check-out 9am. Lockout midnight-4am. 8- and 10-bed dorms 150AS; 4- and 6- bed dorms 95AS. Non-members add 40AS.

Schloßherberge am Wilhelminenberg (HI), XVI, Savoyenstr. 2 (☎485 8503, ext. 700; fax 485 8503, ext. 702; SHB@wigast.com). Take U6 to "Thaliastr.," then tram #46 (dir.: Joachimsthalerpl.) to "Maroltingerg." (or take tram #44 from Schottentor to "Wilhelminenstr."). Then (in both cases) take bus #146B or #46B to "Schloß Wilhelminenberg." Enter the palace gates and follow the signs to the hostel (2min.). Beware that nightlife will be difficult from here, as the last bus is at 11:45pm. Breakfast, sheets, and showers included. **Laundry** 65AS. Keycard 25AS. Reception 7am-11pm. Lockout 9am-2pm. Curfew midnight. Reserve at least 2 days in advance. 164 impeccable 4-bed dorms with bathrooms and balconies, 225AS. Some singles also available (540AS).

Jugendgästehaus Wien Brigittenau (HI), XX, Friedrich-Engels-Pl. 24 (☎332 8294 or 330 0598; fax 330 8379; oejhv-wien-jgh-brigiltneu@oejhv.or.at). 25min. from city center. Take U1 or U4 to "Schwedenpl.," then tram N to "Floridsdorferbrücke/Friedrich-Engels-Pl." Follow the signs. It's the large green building behind the tram stop across the street and to the left of the tracks. This roomy hostel with exceptional facilities for the disabled is unfortunately distant from the city center. Breakfast, lockers, and sheets included. Internet access. Lunch and dinner 65AS. 5-night max. stay. Reception 24hr. Lockout 9am-1pm. Reservations by fax or phone. 24-bed dorms 145AS; 4-bed dorms 180AS; 2-bed dorms with bath 210AS per person. Non-member surcharge 40AS. Reduction of 15AS Jan. 1-Mar. 13 and Nov. 1-Dec. 23.

Turmherberge Don Bosco, III, Lechnerstr. 12 (☎713 1494). Take U3 to "Kardinal-Nagl-Pl.," then take the exit facing the park. Walk to the other side of the park and turn right on Erdbergstr. Lechnerstr. is the 2nd left. The cheapest beds in town are here in a bare former bell tower (ca.1950s) which is hot in summer–though separate quarters for guys and girls help keep things cool. Curfew 11:45pm. Open Mar.-Nov. 80AS per person.

Jugendgästehaus Hütteldorf-Hacking (HI), XIII, Schloßbergg. 8 (☎877 0263; fax 877 02 632; jgh@wigast.com). From Karlspl., take U4 to "Hütteldorf," take the Hadikg. exit, cross the footbridge, and follow signs to the hostel (10min.). Weary backpackers take bus #53B from the side of the footbridge opposite the station to the hostel. From Westbahnhof, take S50 to "Hütteldorf." 35min. from the city center, this secluded hostel with sunny green grounds has great views of the city, and has a playground area for the kids. Also popular with high school groups. Lunch and dinner 65-72AS. Breakfast included. Free luggage storage. Keycard 25AS. Reception 7am-11:45pm. Lockout 9:30am-3:30pm. Curfew 11:45pm. Discounts for groups of 18 or more. 2-, 4-, 6-, and 8-bed rooms, one room with 22 beds, some doubles with showers, 175AS. Add 35AS for rooms with showers or for one of the few singles. Non-members add 40AS. MC, Visa.

HOTELS AND PENSIONS

Check the hostels section for good singles deals as well. The prices are higher here, but you pay for convenient reception hours, no curfews, and no lockouts.

Lauria Apartments, VII, Kaiserstr. 77, Apt. #8 (☎522 2555). From Westbahnhof, take tram #5 to "Burgg." From Sudbahnhof, take tram #18 to "Westbahnhof" then tram #5 to "Burgg." A lovely building, close to city center and Westbahnhof. Fully equipped **kitchens.** Sheets and TV included. 2-night min. for reservations. Dorms 160AS; singles and student-bunk twins 480AS; doubles 530AS, with shower 700AS; student-bunk triples 600AS; triples 700AS, 800AS; quads 850AS, 940AS. Credit cards accepted except for dorm beds.

Pension Kraml, VI, Brauerg. 5 (☎587 8588; fax 586 7573). Take U3 to "Zierierg." exit onto Otto-Bauerg. Take 1st left, then 1st right. From Südbahnhof, take bus #13A to Esterhazyg. and walk up Brauerg. Situated near the *Innenstadt* and the Naschmarkt, Kraml has large airy rooms, a kind staff, and a lounge with cable TV, all for a low price. Breakfast buffet 40AS. 38 beds. Singles 310AS; doubles 560AS, with shower 640AS, with bath 760AS; triples 720AS, with shower 930AS. Apartment with bath 1120-1250AS for 3-5 people.

Pension Wild, VIII, Langeg. 10 (☎406 5174; fax 402 2168; info@Pension-wild.com; www.pension-wild.com). Take U2 to "Lerchenfelderstr.," and take the 1st right onto Langeg. From Südbahnhof, take bus #13A (dir.: Alserstr./Skodag.) to "Piaristeng." Turn left onto Lerchenfelderstr., and left again onto Langeg. 15min. walk from the city center. While the rooms are rather expensive, a friendly, English-speaking staff run this cheerfully decorated hostel with a laid back atmosphere. Breakfast and shower included. **Kitchen** access. Reception 7am-10pm. Reservations by fax recommended. 35 beds. Singles 490-690AS; doubles 590-990AS; triples 1030-1230AS.

VIENNA

Pension Hargita, VII, Andreasg. (☎526 1928; fax 526 0492). Take U3 to "Neubaug." then head down Mariahilferstr., away from the city center to Andreasg. This *Pension* offers amicable service, and a prime location. Breakfast 40AS. Reception 8am-10pm. Singles 400AS, with shower 450AS; doubles 600AS, 700AS, with bath 800-900AS.

Pension Reimer, IV, Kircheng. 18 (☎523 6162; fax 524 3782), is centrally located and has huge, comfortable rooms that are cleaned constantly, but the hallway and staircase are not well lit. Breakfast included. Singles 500AS, in winter 470AS. Doubles 740AS, with bath 860AS; in winter 680AS, 810AS. Credit cards accepted for long stays only.

F. Kaled and Tina, VII, Mariahilferstr. 72, 3rd fl. (☎523 9013; fax 526 2513). Take U3 to "Neubaug." or follow Mariahilferstr. away from the center, to just past the intersection with Neubaug. This new *Pension* is located in a "happening" neighborhood on a busy shopping avenue, right above a fairly prominent sex shop. 2-night min. stay. Reservations by phone or fax. Singles 500AS; doubles with bath 700AS; triples 950AS.

Pension Falstaff, IX, Müllnerg. 5 (☎317 9127; fax 317 91864). Take U4 to "Roßauer Lände." Cross Roßauer Lände, head down Grünentorg., and take the 3rd left onto Müllnergasse. Breakfast included. Reception 7:30am-9pm. Singles 390AS, with shower 500AS; doubles 670-760AS. Extra bed 250AS. 10% reduced rate for stays of 1 week or more in off-season; 15% for 2 weeks, 30% for more than 1 month. 100AS reduction Nov. 1-March 30 (excluding Christmas and Jan.). Credit cards accepted.

Pension Amon, VII, Daung. 1 (☎/fax 405 0194). Take tram #5 from Westbahnhof or #13 from Südbahnhof to Alserstr. and Skodag. Walk down Skodag. and turn left onto Daung. The *Pension* is colorful and pleasant, though its neighborhood is not. Reception 24hr. **Kitchen.** Reservations by fax or phone. Singles with shower 400AS; doubles with shower 700AS. Credit cards accepted.

UNIVERSITY DORMITORIES

From July through September, many university dorms become hotels, usually with singles, doubles, and a few triples and quads. These rooms don't have much in the way of character, but showers and sheets are standard, and their cleanliness and relatively low cost suffice for most budget travelers, particularly for longer stays.

Porzellaneum der Wiener Universität, IX, Porzellang. 30 (☎317 72820; fax 317 72830). From Südbahnhof, take tram D (dir.: Nußdorf) to "Fürsteng." From Westbahnhof, take tram #5 to "Franz-Josefs Bahnhof," then tram D (dir.: Südbahnhof) to

"Fürsteng." 10min. from the Ring. Sheets included. Reception 24hr. Reservations recommended. 177 beds. Singles 190AS; doubles 380AS; quads 760AS.

Rudolfinum, IV, Mayerhofg. 3 (☎505 5384; fax 505 5385 450). Take U1 to "Taubstummeng." for rock 'n' roll and MTV. More serious guests watch CNN. Large rooms in a great location. Breakfast included. **Kitchen** available by prior arrangement. **Laundry** facilities 65AS. Reception 24hr. Singles 270AS; doubles 480AS; triples 600AS.

Gästehaus Pfeilgasse, VIII, Pfeilg. 6 (☎40174; fax 401 7620; acahot@academia-hotels.co.at). Take U2 to "Lerchenfelderstr.," go right, then right again on Lange Gasse, and left on Pfeilg. Breakfast included. Reception 24hr. Reservations recommended. Singles 270AS; doubles 480AS; triples 600AS. Credit cards accepted.

Katholisches Studentenhaus, XIX, Peter-Jordanstr. 29 (☎/fax 347 47312). From Westbahnhof, take U6 (dir.: Heiligenstadt) to "Nußdorferstr.," then bus #35A or tram #38 to "Hardtg." and turn left. From Südbahnhof, take tram D to "Schottentor" then tram #38 to "Hardtg." Enjoy the laid-back atmosphere of the 19th district. Showers and sheets included. Reception closes at 10pm. Call ahead. Singles 250AS; doubles 400AS.

Studentenwohnheim der Hochschule für Musik, I, Johannesg. 8 (☎514 8448; fax 514 8449). Walk 3 blocks down Kärnterstr. away from the Stephansdom and turn left onto Johannesg. Fabulous location and inexpensive meals. Breakfast and showers included. Reception 24hr. Reduction for groups larger than 20. Singles 430AS, with bath 490AS; doubles 760AS, 940AS; triples 840AS; quads 1000AS; quints 1250AS. Apartment also available (includes 2 double rooms, bathroom, kitchen, living room). 350AS per person, 500AS per person for single occupancy, 1200AS for entire apartment.

CAMPING

Wien-West, Hüttelbergstr. 80 (☎914 2314; fax 911 3594). Take U4 to "Hütteldorf," then bus #14B or 152 (dir.: Campingpl.) to "Wien West." This convenient campground, 8km from the city center, is crowded but grassy and pleasant. **Laundry** machines, grocery stores, wheelchair accessible, and **cooking facilities.** Reception 7:30am-9:30pm. Closed Feb. Electricity 40AS. 75AS per person in July-Aug, 68AS rest of the year, ages 4-15 yrs 40AS, tent 40-45AS, camper 63-70AS. In July and Aug. 2- and 4-person cabins available for 250AS and 400-440AS.

Aktiv Camping Neue Donau, XXII, Am Kleehäufel 119 (☎/fax 202 4010, west2@vie.at), is 4km from the city center and adjacent to Neue Donau beaches. Take U1 to "Kaisermühlen" then bus #91a to "Kleehäufel." Showers included. **Laundry,** supermarket, **kitchen.** Handicapped access. Open May 14-Sept. 10. Electricity 40AS. July-Aug. 75AS, children 40AS, camper 70AS, tent 45AS. May, June, and Sept. 48AS, children 40AS, camper 63AS, tent 40AS.

Campingplatz Schloß Laxenburg (☎ 223 6713 33; fax 223 6739 66), at Münchendorfer Str., Laxenburg, is 15km from Vienna, but extremely popular and beautifully situated near the Gumpoldskirchen vineyards. Facilities include a restaurant, **boat rental,** heated **pool,** children's pool, and supermarket. Open April 1-Oct. 31. Electricity 40AS. July-Aug. 82AS per person, ages 4-15 yrs. 40AS; caravans 70AS; tents 45AS. Rest of season 75AS, children 40AS; caravans 63AS; tents 40AS.

FOOD

"Here the people think only of sensual gratifications."
—Washington Irving, 1822

In a world full of uncertainty, the Viennese believe that the least you can do is face things with a full stomach. Food is not mere fuel for the body; it is an aesthetic, even philosophical experience that begins when you wish someone *"Mahlzeit"* and ends with one of Vienna's renowned sublime desserts and chocolates—unbelievably rich, and priced for patrons who are likewise blessed. Most residents, however, maintain that the sumptuous treats are worth every *Groschen.* Unless you buy your sin wholesale at a local bakery, *Sacher Torte, Imperial Torte,* and even *Apfelstrudel* can cost up to 50AS.

Most places close Saturday afternoons and all of Sunday (on the first Sa of every month, most shops close at 5 or 6pm). In general, restaurants stop serving after 11pm.

Vienna's restaurants are as varied as its cuisine. *Gästehäuser*, *Imbiße* (food stands), and *Beisln* serve inexpensive meals that stick to your ribs and are best washed down with copious amounts of beer. *Würstelstände*, found on almost every corner, provide a quick, cheap lunch (a sausage runs 27AS or so). The restaurants near **Kärntnerstraße** are generally expensive—a better bet is the neighborhood north of the university and near the *Votivkirche* (take U2 to "Schottentor"), where **Universitätsstraße** and **Währingerstraße** meet. cafes with cheap meals also line **Burggasse** in the 6th district. The area radiating from the **Rechte** and **Linke Wienzeile** near Naschmarkt (take U4 to "Kettenbrückeg.") houses a range of cheap restaurants, and the **Naschmarkt** itself contains open-air stands where you can purchase aromatic delicacies (bread and a variety of ethnic food) to sample while shopping at Vienna's premier flea market (weekends only; see p. 117). Almost all year long, **Rathausplatz** hosts food stands tied into whatever the current festival happens to be. At Christmas time, **Christkindlmarkt** offers hot food and spiked punch amid vendors of Christmas charms, ornaments, and candles. From the end of June through July, the film festival, **Festwochen,** brings international foodstuffs to the stands behind the seats of the films (stands open 11am-11pm). The open-air **Brunnenmarkt** (take U6 to "Josefstädterstr." then walk up Veronikag. 1 block and turn right) is cheap and cheerful. *Bäckereien* (bakeries) are everywhere.

As always, supermarkets provide building blocks for cheap, solid meals. The lowest prices can be found on the shelves of **Billa, Hofer,** and **Spar.** More expensive chains include **Julius Meinl, Ledi, Mondo, Renner,** and **Zielpunkt.** Travelers can buy kosher groceries at the **Kosher Supermarket,** Hollandstr. 10 (☎216 9675). To join the legions of Viennese conquering the summer heat, seek out the **Italeis** or **Tichy** ice cream vendors.

SACHER SCANDAL Austria takes its desserts very seriously. *Linzer Torte* is extremely important to the residents of Linz, and the whole country has a love affair with *Apfelstrudel,* but things work a little differently in Vienna, where *Sacher Torte* reigns supreme. It is one of the country's most famous cakes, but it is not clear who deserves credit for this celebrated dessert. While legend praises Franz Sacher as the originator of the confection Prince von Metternich loved, Café Demel doesn't agree—its proprietors claim the original recipe. Demel sued the Hotel Sacher, and the suit has resulted in bankruptcy, the sale of Demel to a corporation, and the suicide of Sacher's general manager. It's probably safest to stick to *Strudel.*

RESTAURANTS

INSIDE THE RING

Bizi Pizza, I, Rotenturmstr. 4 (☎513 3705) One block up Rotenturmstr. from Stephanspl. The best deal in the city center, Bizi will whip up a fresh food that rivals Italy's best for a pittance (pasta 65-75AS, whole pizza 60-75AS, salad bar 39-69AS). Open daily 11am-11:30pm. **Branches** with same hours at Franz-Josefs-Kai (☎535 7913), Mariahilferstr. 22-24 (☎523 1658), and X, Favoritenstr. 105 (☎600 5010).

Café Ball, I, Ballg. 5 (☎513 1754), near Stephanspl. off Weihburgg. This charming cafe has candlelit tables and friendly staff. Listen to opera music as you enjoy Italian dishes with an Austrian touch average 90AS. Open M-Sa 11am-1am, Su noon-midnight.

Brezelg'wölb, I, Lederhof 9 (☎/fax 533 8811), near Am Hof, off Drahtgasse. Nestled in a tiny cobblestone-paved sidestreet, this old-fashioned Backstube popular with students serves excellent hearty Viennese cuisine in a quiet setting. Don't leave without glancing at the rare piece of the intact medieval city wall in the courtyard—the rest was torn down to build the Ringstraße. Reservations recommended in the evening, but lunch is a sure bet (around 100AS). Open daily 11:30am-1am, hot food until midnight.

La Crêperie, I, Grünangerg. 10 (☎512 5687), off Singerstr. near Stephanspl. The sensual decor of this restaurant complements the light, scrumptious crepes, both sweet and savory (60-250AS). Try the *Himbeer* (raspberry) soda. Open 11:30am-midnight.

Margaritaville, I, Bartensteing. 3 (☎405 4786). Take U2 to "Lerchenfelderstr." and walk across the triangular green to Bartensteing. Enjoy creative Mexican food, most notably the *Fajita Lupita,* at this sizzling joint with a tiny outdoor garden. Entrees 90-250AS. Open M-Sa 6pm-2am (hot food until 1am), Su 6pm-midnight.

Rosenberger Markt, I, Mayserderg. 2 (☎512 3458), behind the Sacher Hotel. This large and chaotic subterranean buffet offers a gargantuan selection of decent food at reasonable prices. Food stations include salad, fruit salad, waffle, antipasto, potato, and pasta bars. You pay by the size of your plate, not by weight, so pile high. Salads 29-64AS, waffles 55AS, vegetable dishes 24-64AS. Open 10:30am-11pm.

Levante, I, Wallnerstr. 2 (☎533 2326; fax 535 5485). Walk down the Graben away from the Stephansdom, turn left on Kohlmarkt, and right on Wallnerstr. This Greek-Turkish restaurant features street-side dining and lots of vegetarian dishes, though they are not always prepared to perfection. Entrees 80-150AS, sandwiches 40AS. **Branches** at I, Wollzeile 19 (off Rotenturm, take U3 or U1 to "Stephanspl."); Mariahilferstr. 88a; and VIII, Josefstädterstr. 14 (take U2 to "Rathaus"). All open 11:30am-11:30pm.

Maschu Maschu, I, Rabensteig 8 (☎533 2904). This hole-in-the-wall joint serves filling and super-cheap Israeli *falafel* (38AS) and *schwarma,* outdoors in summer. Open M 11am-midnight, Tu 11am-1am, W 11am-2am, Th 11am-3am, F-Su 11am-4am.

Trzesniewski, I, Dorotheerg. 1 (☎512 3291; fax 513 9565), 3 blocks down the Graben from the Stephansdom. A famous stand-up restaurant, this unpronounceable establishment has been serving petite open-faced sandwiches for over 80 years. They are 10AS per dainty slice–you'll want 5-6 of them for a solid lunch. Favorite toppings include salmon, onion, paprika, and egg. This was Franz Kafka's favorite place to eat. Open M-F 8:30am-7:30pm, Sa 9am-5pm. **Branches** at VI, Mariahiferstr. 95 (☎596 4291); and III, Hauptstr. 97 (☎712 9964) in Galleria.

Inigo, I, Bäckerstr. 18 (☎512 7451). This contemporary diner, across from Vienna's Jesuit church, was founded by a Jesuit priest as part of a socio-economic reintegration program. It provides transit employment, training, and social work for 17 people who are long-term unemployed. Menu includes eclectic international dishes, many whole wheat and vegetarian options, and a salad bar. Try the delicious, original *Schweinekotlett Gorgonzola* (108AS). Entrees 60-110AS, salad 22-58AS. Open M-Sa 8:30am-midnight, Su and holidays 10am-4pm. In July and Aug., closed Sa-Su.

OUTSIDE THE RING

OH Pot, OH Pot, IX, Währingerstr. 22 (☎319 4259). Take U2 to "Schottentor." This adorable joint serves amazingly good Spanish food at rock-bottom prices. Try one of their filling namesake "pots" (82-110AS), which are stew-like concoctions in veggie and meat varieties. Terrific *Empanadas* (57AS). Open M-F 11am-midnight, Sa-Su 6pm-midnight.

Hunger Künstler, VI, Gumpendorfstr. 48 (☎587 9210) Exceptional food in a laid-back candlelit atmosphere. Try the Sinatspätzle (baby dumplings covered in spinach, cream and cheese) and you will never become a "hunger artist." Entrees average 90AS. Open Su-Sa 11am-2am.

Tunnel, VIII, Florianig. 39 (☎42 3465). Take U2 to "Rathaus," then, with your back to the *Rathaus,* head right on Landesgerichtstr. and left on Florianig. Pronounced "Too-nehl," this is a student crowd paradise, dark and smoky with funky paintings, heavy tables, and the occasional divan. Tunnel is a popular place prized for its dilapidated hipness, live nightly music, and affordable food. Daily lunch *Menüs* 45AS. Choose between Italian, Austrian, and Middle Eastern dishes, with many vegetarian options (45-125AS). Some of the cheapest beer in Vienna (0.50L *Gösser* 27AS), good pizza (55-85AS), and a breakfast menu (28AS) until 11:30am. Open daily 10am-2am.

Blue Box, VII, Richterg. 8 (☎523 2682). Take U3 to "Neubaug.," turn onto Neubaug., and take your 1st right onto Richterg. Blue Box leads a double life, restaurant by day, night club by, well, night, as indicated by the decor–an orange chandelier, blue leather couches, and not much light. Dishes are fresh, flamboyant, and very original, often centering around themes. DJs pick music to match the meals. A great place to come for a late (or really late) breakfast (until 5pm). Choose from Viennese, French, or vegetarian cuisine. Entrees from 53-116As. Open Tu-Su 10am-2am, M 6pm-2am.

Zum Mogulhof, VII, Burgg. 12 (☎526 2864). The best Indian food served amidst crimson carpets and velvet wallpaper–indulgence that won't strain your wallet. Vegetarian and meat dishes average 90As. Open daily 11:30am-2:30pm and 6:00-11:30pm.

Café Willendorf, VI, Linke Wienzeile 102 (☎587 1789). Take U4 to "Pilgramg." and look for the big pink building which also houses the Rosa Lila Villa, Vienna's gay and lesbian center. This cafe, bar, and restaurant with a leafy outdoor terrace serves creative vegetarian fare for under 100AS. Mixed crowd and a warm community atmosphere. Open daily 6pm-2am; meals until midnight.

Elsäßer Bistro, IX, Währingerstr. 32 (☎319 7689). U2 to "Schottentor." Within the palace that houses the French Cultural Institute–walk in the garden and follow your nose for an extravagant meal. Wonderful food, with prices hovering around 120AS, and beautiful French wines. Open M-F 11am-3pm and 6-11pm. Kitchen closes 1hr. earlier.

Café Nil, VII, Siebensterng. 39 (☎526 6165). Take tram #49 from the *Volksgarten* three stops away from the *innere Stadt* to reach this serene and low-key incense-scented Middle Eastern cafe. Enjoy tasty dishes, all pork-free and many vegetarian (54-105AS). Open daily 10am-midnight. Breakfast until noon, Sa until 3pm.

Schnitzelwirt, VII, Neubaug. 52 (☎523 3771). Take U2 or U3 to "Volkstheater," then bus #49 to "Neubaug." You'll find every kind of *Schnitzel* (65-125AS) imaginable here. It's not gourmet, but servings are guaranteed to be so big they go over the edge of the plate. If you can't finish it, ask for paper to wrap it up in. Open M-Sa 10am-11pm.

Fischerbräu, XIX, Billrothstr. 17 (☎369 5941). Take U6 to "Nußdorfer Str." then walk up Währinger Gürtel, left on Döblinger Hauptstr., and left on Billrothstr. Popular spot for young locals. The leafy courtyard and jazz music perfectly complement the home-brewed beer (large 40AS), delicious veal sausage (60AS), and chicken salad (87AS). Open M-Sa 4pm-1am, Su 11am-1am. Jazz brunch Su noon-3pm.

Amerlingbeisl, VII, Stiftg. 8 (☎526 1660). Take U2 to "Babenbergerstr." or U3 to "Neubaug." Halfway between the stops on Mariahilferstr., turn onto Stiftg. After a couple of blocks you'll hit a cluster of outdoor restaurants. Walk past the first to reach Amerlingbeisl in a bamboo courtyard roofed with grape vines. Eat vegetarian food while listening to the grape leaves rustle. Occasional live music. Entrees 58-113AS, late breakfast 58-130AS. Open daily 9am-2am (hot food served until 1am).

Stomach, IX, Seeg. 26 (☎310 2099). Take tram D to "Fürsteng." then walk down Porzellang. to Seeg. and turn right. This sophisticated establishment serves 1st-class Austrian cooking with a Styrian kick (130-230AS). Eat your beautifully cooked food inside or outside in a lovely courtyard. Twenty-something crowd. Open W-Sa 4pm-midnight, Su 10am-10pm. Reservations recommended.

Restaurant am Radetzkyplatz, III, Radetzkypl. 1 (☎712 5750), is a mellowed old Austrian pub with 150 years of beer to its credit (0.50L 30AS). Well-worn bar railings testify to its popularity. Sit outside under an awning and enjoy robust servings and veggie options (70-175AS). Open daily 8am-11pm.

Vegetasia, III, Ungarg. 57 (☎713 8332) on the #O tram line. A vegetarian nirvana, this cozy Taiwanese vegetarian restaurant offers tofu, *seitan,* and soy-delights artfully disguised as beef, chicken, and fish. Open daily 11:30am-3pm and 5:30-11:30pm.

Hatam, IX, Währingerstr. 64 (☎310 9450). Take tram #38, 40, or 41 to "Spitalg." for Persian food at good prices. Try their *gorme sabse* (spiced eggplant dish with rice) or grab a *Döner* to go (40-60AS). Entrees 75-165AS. Open daily 11:30am-11:30pm.

University Mensa, IX, Universitätsstr. 7 (☎427 729 ext.841), on the 7th fl. of the university building, between U2 stops "Rathaus" and "Schottentor." Visitors can ride the old-fashioned *Pater Noster* elevator (no doors and it never stops; you have to jump in and out, so say your prayers) to the 6th floor and take the stairs up. There isn't much atmosphere but the food is cheap. Typical cafeteria meals 40-60AS. Open M-F 11am-2pm.

Other inexpensive student cafeterias serve their constituents at: **Music Academy,** I, Johannesg. 8 (☎512 9470). Open M-F 7:30am-3pm. Eat while listening to budding musicians. Food served 11am-2pm; in July and Aug. and weekends 7:30-10am. **Academy of Applied Art,** I, Oskar-Kokoschka-Pl. 2 (☎718 6695). Open M-Th 8:30am-6pm, F 8:30am-3pm. **Academy of Fine Arts,** I, Schillerpl. 3 (☎58 81 6138). Open M-F 9am-5pm. Closed June to early Sept. **Afro-Asiatisches Institut,** IX, Türkenstr. 3, near Schottentor. Open M-F 11:30am-2:30pm. **Vienna Technical University,** IV, Wiedner Hauptstr. 8-10 (☎586 6502). Open M-F 11am-3pm. **Catholic University Students' Community,** I, Ebendorferstr. 8 (☎408 3585). *Menü* 33-40AS. Open M-F 11am-2pm. **Economics University,** IX, Aug. 2-6 (☎310 5718). Open M-Th 7:30am-7:30pm, F 7:30am-6:30pm; July-Aug. M-F 7:30am-3:30 pm.

VIENNA

COFFEEHOUSES AND KONDITOREIEN

"Who's going to start a revolution? Herr Trotsky from Café Central?"
—Austrian general quoted on the eve of the Russian Revolution

There is an unwritten rule for the Vienna coffeehouse: the coffee matters, but the atmosphere matters more. The 19th-century coffeehouse was a haven for artists, writers, and thinkers who flocked to soft, brooding interiors to flee badly heated, telephone-less apartments. In the coffeehouses, they surrounded themselves with dark wood and dusty velvet, ordered a cup of coffee, and stayed long into the night composing operettas, writing books, and cutting into each other's work. The bourgeoisie followed suit, and the coffeehouse became the living room of the city. A grand coffeehouse culture arose. Peter Altenberg, "the café writer," scribbled lines, Oskar Kokoschka grumbled alone, and exiles Lenin and Trotsky played chess. Theodor Herzl made plans here for a Zionist Israel, and Kafka came from Prague to visit the Herrenhof. Karl Kraus and a circle of minor writers baited Hugo von Hofmannsthal and Arthur Schnitzler. The original literary cafe, just before the "merry apocalypse," *fin de siècle* culture rose, was **Café Griensteidl.** After it was demolished in 1897, the torch passed first to **Café Central** and then to **Café Herrenhof.** Cafes still exist under all these names, but only Café Central looks like it used to. Adolf Loos, pioneer of 20th-century Minimalist architecture, designed the interior of the **Museum Café** in smooth, spacious lines. Unfortunately, coffeehouse culture now rests partway in the past. Tourists visit Café Central as if it were a museum, but the best places succumb to a noble, comfortable decrepitude as they resist both tourist hordes and renovations.

VIENNESE COFFEE CULTURE Vienna's time-honored coffeehouse culture is arguably more famous than the Boys' Choir or the Ringstraße. There is, however, considerably more to mastering the finer points of Viennese coffee-drinking than ordering a *café latte,* as many a visitor has discovered with chagrin. Here is a quick reference guide to some of the most common and enticing Viennese coffees:

Melange: espresso-like coffee with hot milk, optional whipped cream and cinnamon
Kaisermelange: a regular *Melange* with an egg yolk mixed in
Mokka: strong black coffee, much like espresso
Kapuziner: small *Mokka* with cream, sprinkled with cocoa, chocolate, or cinnamon
Piccolo: black coffee served in a tiny cup with or without whipped cream
Verlängerter: weak coffee with cream
Fiaker: black coffee with rum
Pharisäer: black coffee with rum, sugar, and whipped cream
Mazagran: cold coffee with rum or maraschino liqueur, served over ice cubes
Wiener Eiskaffee: chilled black coffee and vanilla ice cream, with whipped cream
Maria Theresia: coffee with orange liqueur and whipped cream

Viennese coffee is distinct, not quite as strong as an espresso, but with more kick than your average Dripmaster. The quintessential Viennese coffee is the *Melange*, and you can order every kind of coffee as a *Kleiner* (small) or *Grosser* (large), *Brauner* (brown, with a little milk), or *Schwarzer* (black). Whipped cream is *Schlag* (short for *Schlagobers*); if you don't like it, say *"ohne Schlag, bitte."* Choosing your coffee is an art form in Vienna (see Viennese Coffee Culture above). Opulent pastries complete the picture: *Apfelstrudel*, cheesecakes, tortes, *Buchteln* (warm cake with jam in the middle), *Palatschinken*, *Krapfen*, and *Mohr im Hemd* have all helped place Vienna on the culinary map. The *Konditoreien*, no less traditional, focus their attention on delectables rather than coffee. These pastries are something of a national institution—Switzerland may have its gold reserves, but Austria could back its currency with its world-renowned *Sacher Torte*. To see a menu, ask for a *Karte*.

Most cafes also serve hot food, but don't order food and coffee together (except pastries), unless you want to be really gauche. Coffee may seem expensive (30-40AS), but when you realize that you're actually paying to linger for hours and read newspapers, the price suddenly seems much more reasonable. The most serious dictate of coffeehouse etiquette is that you linger. The waiter (often outfitted with black bow tie) will serve you as soon as you sit down, and then leave you to sip, read, and brood. He's known as *Herr Ober* in Austria, not as a *Kellner*. Newspapers and magazines, many in English, are neatly racked for patrons. When you are ready to leave, just ask to pay: *"Zahlen bitte!"*

INSIDE THE RING

Café Hawelka, I, Dorotheerg. 6 (☎512 8230), off Graben, 3 blocks down from the Stephansdom. With its dusty wallpaper, dark wood, and old red-striped velvet sofas, the Hawelka is shabby and glorious. Josephine and Leopold Hawelka put this legendary cafe on the map when they opened it in 1937–Leopold received an award from the Austrian government and Josephine a visit from Falco. *Buchteln* (served fresh from the oven at 10pm) 35AS. Melange 37AS. Open M and W-Sa 8am-2am, Su 4pm-2am.

Café Central, I (☎533 3763 26), at the corner of Herreng. and Strauchg. inside Palais Fers. Café Central has unfortunately surrendered to tourists because of its fame, but this mecca of the cafe world is definitely worth a visit. Oh, they serve coffee, too, at elegant tables in an arcade court. Live piano 4-7pm. Open M-Sa 8am-8pm. Su 10am-6pm.

Demel, I, Kohlmarkt 14 (☎535 1717). 5min. from the Stephansdom down Graben. The most luxurious Viennese *Konditorei*, Demel's was confectioner to the imperial court until the empire dissolved. All of the chocolate is made fresh every morning. A fantasy of mirrored rooms, cream walls, and a display case of legendary desserts. Waitresses in convent-black serve the divine confections that every visit to Vienna should include (40-50AS). Don't miss the *crème-du-jour*. Open daily 10am-7pm.

Cafe Griensteidl, I, Michaelerpl. 6 (☎535 2693). Down the street from Cafe Central toward the Hofburg. Vienna's first literary cafe where intellectuals wrote, read, and debated until it was closed in 1897 for refurbishment. Almost a century later, it was reopened and still maintains its literary air with a couple of bookshelves and an excellent selection of international newspapers. Open daily 8am-11:30pm.

TIME FOR DECAF? The aura of legend that surrounds Café Central is well earned by the list of luminaries it claims as the regulars of its heyday. Theodor Herzl, Sigmund Freud, Karl Kraus, and Vladimir Ilych Ulianov (better known by his pen name, Lenin) hung out there, along with Leon Trotsky, who played chess. Alfred Polgar published an essay entitled *Theorie de Café Central,* in which he wrote: "It is a place for people who know how to abandon and be abandoned for the sake of their fate, but do not have the nerve to live up to this fate. It is a true asylum for people who have to kill time so as not to be killed by it...a first-aid station for the confused...all their lives in search of themselves and all their lives in flight from themselves..."

Hotel Sacher, I, Philharmonikerstr. 4 (☎512 1487). Behind the opera house. This historic sight has served world-famous **Sachertorte** (50AS) in red velvet opulence for years. During the reign of Franz Josef, elites invited to the Hofburg would make late reservations at the Sacher (the emperor ate quickly, Elisabeth was always dieting, and as nobody dared eat after the imperial family had finished, all the guests left hungry and had a real dinner later at Sacher). Today you won't catch many Viennese there. While it's still exceedingly elegant, casual is fine—you won't be the only tourist there. Open 8am-11:30pm. (Also see **Sacher Scandal** p. 97, and Sights: Hotel Sacher, p. 113.)

Gelateria Hoher Markt, I, Hoher Markt, just off Rotenturmstr. Expatriate Italians flock here to sample all 23 mouth-watering *gelato* flavors. Open daily Mar.-Oct. 9am-11pm.

Café Bräunerhof, I, Stallburgg. 2 (☎512 38 93). This delightfully shabby cafe's location—on a small alley near the Hofburg—has left it virtually untouched by tourists. Hosts many readings and piano concerts. You can order bread, *Käse* and *Schinken,* or Austrian salad from a menu lined with Peter Altenberg prose (36-65AS). Open M-F 7:30am-8:30pm, Sa 7:30am-6pm, Su 10am-6pm.

Café Prückel, I, Stubenring 24 (☎512 4339). High-ceilinged and spacious, this artsy cafe has developed a noble slouch over time. Prückel hosts numerous readings and performances, patronized by art students from the MAK (Museum of Applied Arts) down the street. Open daily 9am-10pm, kitchen open noon-8pm.

Kleines Café, I, Franziskanerpl. 3. Turn off Kärtnerstr. onto Weihburg. and follow it to the *Franziskanerkirche*. This tiny, cozy cafe, designed by architect Hermann Czech, features green paneling, a low-vaulted ceiling, art exhibits, nightclub posters, and tables spilling out into the courtyard. The salads here are minor works of art, costing on average 65AS. Open M-Sa 10am-2am, Su 1pm-2am.

Café MAK, I, Stubenring 3-5 (☎714 0121), inside the Museum für Angewandte Kunst. Take tram #1 or 2 to "Stubenring." Light, bright, white, and very tight at night, this cafe feels like a display case in the museum, but the people are stunning and the furniture is *Bauhaus* but funkier. Peek through glass walls into the museum, or dine outside among sunflowers. The cafe gets rowdy with students after 10pm and hosts techno-rave parties on Sa in July. Open Tu-Su 10am-2am (hot food until midnight).

Café Museum, I, Opernring 21 (☎586 5202), near the Opera. Head away from the *Innenstadt* to the corner of Operng. and Friedrichstr. Built in 1899 by Adolf Loos, in a plain, spacious style with striking curves, this cafe once attracted a crowd of cabaret artists, painters, and famous musicians including Lehár, Berg, Musil, Kokoschka, and Schiele. Once known as "Café Nihilism," the place lost much of its importance (and a number of its clientele) after the bloody 1918 revolution. It now attracts a mixed bag of artists, lawyers, students, and chess players. Open daily 8am-midnight.

Café Alt Wien, I, Bäckerg. 9 (☎512 5222) is a bohemian, nicotine-stained place behind the Stephansdom. Smoky red sofas and layers of avant-garde posters set the mood. Open M-Th 10am-2am, F-Su 10am-4am.

Hotel Imperial, I, Kärnter Ring 16 (☎501 1031 89; fax 501 1035 5). From the opera, turn left onto the Ring and walk 5min. This elegant, chandeliered cafe, with a lovely flower-hung courtyard, serves its own insignia-stamped, marzipan-filled *Imperial Torte* (50AS), which some prefer to the rival *Sachertorte.* Karl Kraus became a regular here after deciding Café Central was too noisy, and brought Hugo von Hofmannsthal, Rainer Maria Rilke, Peter Altenberg, and Franz Werfel with him. Freud occasionally came here and was not above having an informal psychoanalytic consultation at his table. Trotsky played chess here, too. Open daily 7am-11pm.

Café Opera Zum Peter, I, Riemberg. 9 (☎512 8981). A low-key, opera-mad crowd lingers here among walls plastered with a hodgepodge of autographed photos, posters, and pictures of opera performers and performances. Open M-F 8am-2am, Sa 7pm-2am.

Waldland, I, Peterspl. 11 (☎533 4156). This tiny *Konditorei* bakes everything imaginable topped with poppyseed *(Mohn)* and honey and serves it in a charming setting. Decadent cookies, cakes, rolls, pastries (30-50AS). Open M-F 9am-6pm, Sa 9am-1pm.

OUTSIDE THE RING

Café Sperl, VI, Gumpendorferstr. 11 (☎586 4158). 15min. from the Westbahnhof. Take U2 to "Babenbergstr.," walk one block on Getreidemarkt, and turn right on Gumpendorferstr. Built in 1880, Sperl is one of Vienna's oldest and most beautiful cafes. Though some of the original trappings were removed during renovations, the *fin de siècle* atmosphere remains. Franz Lehár was a regular here; he composed operettas at a table by the entrance. This luxurious cafe is also the former home of Vienna's *Hagenbund,* an Art Nouveau group excluded from the Secession. Coffee 40-60AS; cake 35-45AS. Open M-Sa 7am-11pm, Su 3-11pm; July-Aug. closed Su.

Café Savoy, VI, Linke Wienzeile 36, is a scruffy *fin de siècle* cafe with dark wood and decrepit gold trim. Check yourself out in the gigantic mirror as you step inside. A large gay and lesbian crowd moves in to make this a lively nightspot on weekends. Open M-F 5pm-2am, Sa 9am-6pm and 9pm-2am.

Café Rüdigerhof, V, Hamburgerstr. 20 (☎586 3138). In a 1902 building designed by students of Otto Wagner, this *Jugendstil* cafe is adorned with floral patterns and leather couches, with a large outside garden. Soups (35-45AS), omelettes, and meat and fish dishes (30-100AS). Open daily noon-10:30pm; garden open for drinks until midnight.

Café Drechsler, VI, Linke Wienzeile 22 (☎587 8580), near Karlspl. Head down Operng. and continue on Linke Wienzeile. This is *the* place to be the morning after the night before. Early birds and night owls roost in this less-than-fresh cafe over pungent cups of *Mokka.* Great lunch menu (60-90AS). Open M-F 3am-8pm, Sa 3am-6pm.

Café Stein, IX, Währingerstr. 6 (☎319 7241; fax 319 7241 2), near Schottentor, has chrome seats outside to see and be seen, and clustered tables indoors in the smoky red-brown and metallic interior. Intimate and lively, at night it transforms into "Stein's Diner," when DJs appear. Billiards and **Internet access** (65AS per 30min. 5-11pm; present ID at the bar). Breakfast until 8pm. Open M-Sa 7am-1am, Su 9am-1am. **Stein's Diner** in the basement open M-Sa 7pm-2am.

Kunsthaus Wien Café, III, Untere Weißgerberstr. 13 (☎712 0497). Situated in an overgrown courtyard in Hundertwasser's Kunsthaus museum (see p. 124 for directions), this cafe serves drinks in an undulating atmosphere. Open daily 10am-midnight.

Berg das Café, IX, Bergg. 8 (☎319 5720). Take U2 to "Schottentor" and take a right off Währingerstr. onto Bergg. A super-swank gay cafe/bar by night and casual hang-out by day, this place is always crowded. Wonderful food, desserts, and music in a relaxed atmosphere make this a delightful place for anyone. It recently merged with nearby gay and lesbian bookstore **Das Löwenherz,** so you can browse during the day while you drink your *Melange.* Plenty of English titles. Open daily 10am-1am.

Alte Backstube, VIII, Langeg. 34 (☎406 1101). Around the corner from Theater in der Josefstadt, this popular after-theater cafe/restaurant functioned as a bakery from 1701 until 1963. The cafe serves Austrian dishes, coffees and pastries, but more interestingly, it is also a **museum of bakery art.** On display are the original baking ovens, 300-year-old bakers' equipment, articles, photos, and all sorts of baked-goods devotionalia. Open Sept. to mid-July Tu-Sa 10am-midnight, Su 4pm-midnight.

Das Frauencafé, VIII, Lange Gasse 11, (☎406 3754). Near U6 station "Lerchenfelderstr." Vienna's sole **women-only** cafe has a relaxed atmosphere. Open Tu-Sa 5pm-2am.

HEURIGEN (WINE TAVERNS)

Created by imperial edict in the early 18th century, *Heurigen,* marked by a hanging branch of evergreen at the door, sell new wine and snacks. The wine, also called *Heuriger,* is young wine from the most recent harvest and has typically been grown and pressed by the *Heuriger* owner himself. Good *Heuriger* wine is generally white, fruity, and full of body (try *Grüner Veltliner* or *Riesling*). *Heuriger* is ordered by the *Achtel* or the *Viertel* (eighth or quarter liter respectively, about 25AS per *Viertel*). *G'spritzer* (wine and soda water) is a popular drink; patrons often order a bottle of wine and water to mix themselves.

VIENNA

Half of the pleasure of visiting a *Heuriger*, however, comes not from the wine but from the atmosphere. The worn picnic benches and old shade trees provide an ideal spot to contemplate, converse, or listen to *Schrammelmusik* (sentimental, wine-lubricated folk songs played by elderly musicians who inhabit the *Heuriger*). Drunken patrons often take the matter into their own hands and begin belting out verses praising the *Bäckchen* (cheeks) of girls in the Wachau. A *Heuriger* generally serves simple buffets (grilled chicken, salads, pickles) that make for enjoyable and inexpensive meals. Those looking for some traditional fare should order *Brattfett* or *Liptauer*, a spicy soft paprika-flavored cheese for your bread.

At the end of August or the beginning of September in **Neu stift am Walde,** now part of Vienna's 19th district, the *Neustifter Kirchtag mit Winzerumzug* rampages through the wine gardens: local vintners march in a 500m-long procession through town, carrying a large crown adorned with gilt nuts. After the **Feast of the Martins** on November 11, the wine from last year's crop becomes "old wine," no longer proper to serve in the *Heurigen*. The Viennese do their best to spare it this fate by consuming the beverage in Herculean quantities before the time's up. Grab a *Viertel* to help them in their monumental task.

VIENNA

Heurigen cluster together in the northern, western, and southern Viennese suburbs, where the grapes grow. The *Heurigen* are each open for only a couple of months during the year—stroll along the street and look for the evergreen branches. The most famous region, **Grinzing,** is found in the 19th district of Vienna, and produces strong wine, perhaps to distract the touristy clientele from the high prices. *Heurigen* in Grinzing (incidentally Beethoven's favorite neighborhood) are unfortunately well known to tour bus operators. You'll find better atmosphere and prices among the hills of **Sievering, Neustift am Walde** (both in the 19th district), and **Neuwaldegg** (in the 17th). Authentic, charming, and jolly *Heurigen* abound on Hochstr. in **Perchtoldsdorf,** just southwest of the city. To reach Perchtoldsdorf, take U4 to "Hietzing" and tram #6 to "Rodaun." Walk down Ketzerg. until Hochstr. and continue for a few minutes to reach the *Heurigen* area. True *Heuriger* devotees should make the trip to **Gumpoldskirchen,** a celebrated vineyard village with bus and train connections to Vienna and Mödling, and on the S-bahn line from Südbahnhof. Most vineyard taverns are open 4pm to midnight.

Heuriger Josef Lier, XIX, Wildgrubeng. 44 (☎320 2319). Take tram #38 from Schottentor to the end of the line; walk up the Grinzigerstiege to the *Heiligenstädter Friedhof* (cemetery), and follow the road uphill to the left (5min. from the cemetery). Set right into the vineyards, this *Ur-Heuriger* recalls the times before electric-powered grape presses and mass commercialism. The place boasts clambering roses and a panoramic view of Vienna from the natural beauty of the Vienna Woods. Only one white and one red wine are sold here—Josef Lier's own, from the vineyards you're sitting in. The dishes are equally *Alt-Wiener* and equally excellent—boiled eggs, pickles, *Liptauer,* and *Wurst. G'spritzer* 18AS. Quarter liter 24AS. Open W-F from 3pm, Sa-Su from noon.

Buschenschank Heinrich Niersche, XIX, Strehlg. 21 (☎440 21 46). Take U1 to "Währingerstr./Volksoper" then tram #41 to "Pötzleing." or bus #41A to "Pötzleindorfer Höhe." Walk uphill one block and turn right on Strehlg. On a small side street hidden from tourists, the beautiful garden overlooks the fields of Grinzing—an oasis of green grass, cheerful voices, and relaxation in a neighborly atmosphere. *Weiße G'spritzter* (white wine with soda water) 18AS. Open Su-M and W-Sa 3pm-midnight.

Weingut Heuriger Reinprecht, XIX, Cobenzlg. 22 (☎32 0147 10). Take U4 to "Heiligenstadt" then bus #38A to "Grinzing." This *Heuriger* embodies the stereotype, with endless picnic tables under an ivy-laden trellis, and *Schrammel* musicians strolling from table to table. Despite the many tourists here, don't be surprised to hear whole tables of nostalgic Austrians break into song on their own. There's quite a bottle opener collection near the entryway. *Viertel* 30AS. Open Mar.-Nov. 3:30pm-midnight.

Zum Krottenbach'l, XIX, Krottenbachstr. 148 (☎440 1240). Take U6 to "Nußdorferstr." then bus #35A (dir.: Salmannsdorf) to "Kleingartenverein/Hackenberg." With a terraced garden on the fertile slope of Untersievering, this *Heuriger* offers a comfortable spot for savoring the fruit of the vine. *Viertel* about 30AS. Open daily 3pm-midnight.

Weingut Helm, XXI, Stammersdorferstr. 121 (☎292 1244). Take tram #31 from Schottenring to the last stop, turn right by the *Würstelstand,* then turn left. The family who owns and staffs this establishment keeps it low-key and friendly. Their garden tables are shaded by enormous old trees. Open Tu-Sa 3pm-midnight.

Franz Mayer am Pfarrplatz Beethovenhaus, XIX, Pfarrpl. 2 (☎371 287). Take U4 to "Heiligenstadt" then bus #38A to "Fernsprechamt/Heiligenstadt." Walk up the hill and head right onto Nestelbachg. Beethoven used to stay in the *Heuriger* when it offered guest quarters. Festive patios. Somewhat pricey at 38AS per *Viertel.* Open M-F 4pm-midnight, Su and holidays 11am-midnight. Live music 7pm-midnight.

SIGHTS

Vienna's streets are by turns startling, *gemütlich,* scuzzy, and grandiose. Expect contrasts around every corner: the expanse of the Ringstraße and the narrow confines of a cobblestone courtyard, the curling ornamentations of a Baroque palace, and the spare lines of a Socialist public apartment building. To wander on your own in an organized manner, grab the brochure *Vienna from A to Z* (with Vienna Card discount 50AS; available at the tourist office). Whatever you do, don't miss the **Hofburg, Schloß Schönbrunn, Schloß Belvedere,** or any of the buildings along the **Ringstraße.** Those ensnared by the flowing tendrils of *Jugendstil* architecture can find plenty turn-of-the-century examples of it in Vienna—ask the tourist office for the *Art Nouveau in Vienna* pamphlet, which contains photos and addresses of *Jugendstil* treasures throughout town.

The range of available **tours** is overwhelming—walking tours, ship tours, bike tours, tram tours, and more. There are 57 themed walking tours alone, detailed in the brochure *Walks in Vienna,* which is provided by the tourist office. Tours are 130AS; some require admission fees to sites. All are worthwhile, but "Vienna in the Footsteps of *The Third Man,*" which takes you into the sewers and the graffiti-covered catacomb world of the Wien River's underground canals, is one of the most unusual and exciting (bring your own flashlight). Tours on turn-of-the-century "old-timer" **trams** run May to October. (☎790 9440 26. 1½hr. 200AS. Departs from Karlspl. near the Otto Wagner Pavilion Sa-Su 9:30, 11:30am, and 1:30pm.) The drivers of legendary **Fiaker,** horse-drawn carriages, are happy to taxi you wherever your heart desires, but be sure to agree on the price before you set out, usually around 400AS for 20min. Official *Fiaker* stands can be found in Stephanspl., Albertinapl., Heldenpl., and at the corner of Graben and Kohlmarkt. Contact **Vienna-Bike,** IX, Wasag. (☎319 1258), for **bike rental** (60AS) or a 2- to 3-hour **cycling tour** (280AS). **Bus tours** are given by **Vienna Sightseeing Tours,** III, Stelzhamerg. 4/11 (☎712 4683) and **Cityrama,** I, Börgeg. 1 (☎53413). Tours start at 200AS. For a quick do-it-yourself tour, take tram #1 or 2 around the Ring. For a longer, walking tour, walk the city's Platzs in the order listed below following the second set of directons (for each Platz directions are given first by public transportation, and second from the Platz just described).

INSIDE THE RING

The **First District,** *die Innenstadt* or *innere Stadt* (inner city), Vienna's social and geographical epicenter, is enclosed on 3 sides by the massive **Ringstraße** and on the northern side by the **Danube Canal.** With the mark of master architects on everything from palaces and theaters to tenements and toilet bowls, the *innere Stadt* is a gallery of the history of aesthetics, from Romanesque to *Jugendstil.*

STEPHANSPLATZ

Take U1 or U3 to "Stephansplatz."

Right at the heart of Vienna, this square in the shadow of the massive **Stephansdom** teems with activity. It is a prime location for people watching—suited professionals, political demonstrators, and camera-toting tourists, all throng the square while students in period costumes sell tickets to Strauss or Mozart evenings.

A BAD PACT WITH THE DEVIL In the sixteenth century, during the construction of the North Tower of the Stephansdom, a young builder named Hans Puchsbaum wished to marry his master's daughter. The master, rather jealous of Hans's skill, agreed on one condition: Hans had to finish the entire North Tower on his own within a year. Faced with this impossible task, Hans despaired until a stranger offered to help him. The good Smaritan required only that Hans abstain from saying the name of God or any other holy name. Hans agreed, and the tower grew by leaps and bounds. One day the young mason spotted his love in the midst of his labor, and, wishing to call attention to his progress, he called out her name, "Maria!" With this invocation of the Blessed Virgin, the scaffolding collapsed and Hans plummeted to his death. Rumors of a satanic pact spread, and work on the tower ceased, leaving it in its present condition.

STEPHANSDOM. Affectionately known as "Der Steffl", Stephansdom (St. Stephen's Cathedral) is Vienna's most treasured symbol, fascinating viewers with its Gothic intensity and smoothly tapered **South Tower.** Modernist architect Adolf Loos wrote of it, "We have the most solemn church in the world. It is not a dead place of inventory that we have taken from our fathers. This building tells us our history. Every generation has worked on it, each in their own language."

The oldest sections of the cathedral, the Romanesque **Riesentor** (Giant Gate) and **Heidentürme** (Towers of the Heathens), were built during the reign of King Ottokar II when Vienna was a Bohemian protectorate (see p. 63). Habsburg Duke Rudolf IV later ordered a complete Gothic retooling and thus earned the sobriquet "the Founder." The **North Tower** was originally intended to be as high and graceful as the South Tower, but construction ceased after a spooky tragedy (see **A Bad Pact with the Devil,** above). Take the elevator up the North Tower *(open Apr.-Sept. 9am-6pm; Oct.-Mar. 8am-5pm; elevator ride 40AS)* for a view of the Viennese sprawl, or climb the 343 steps of the South Tower for a 360-degree view, as well as a close-up encounter with the gargoyles *(open 9am-5:30pm; 30AS).*

Inside, some of the important pieces include the early 14th-century Albertine choir and the Gothic organ loft by **Anton Pilgram,** so delicate that Pilgram's contemporaries warned him that it would never bear the organ's weight. Pilgram replied that he would hold it up himself and carved a self-portrait at the bottom, bearing the entire burden on his back. The **high altarpiece** of the Stoning of St. Stephen is just as stunning. (*Tours of the cathedral in English M-Sa at 10:30am and 3pm, Su and holidays 3pm; 40AS. Spectacular evening tour July-Sept. Sa 7pm; 100AS.)*

Downstairs in the **catacombs,** the skeletons of thousands of plague victims line the walls. The lovely **Gruft** (vault) stores all of the Habsburg innards. (*Tours M-Sa 10, 11, 11:30am, 2, 2:30, 3:30, 4, and 4:30pm, Su and holidays 2, 2:30, 3:30, 4, and 4:30pm. 50AS.)* Everyone wanted a piece of the rulers—the Stephansdom got the entrails, the Augustinerkirche got the hearts, and the Kapuzinergruft (on Neuer Markt) got the remainder. High above it all hangs the **bell** of the Stephansdom, the world's heaviest free-ringing bell (the whole bell moves, not just the clapper). The original bell, cast in 1711 from the metal of captured Turkish cannons, was smashed during WWII much to the grief of the Viennese. A series of photographs inside chronicles the painstaking process of reconstruction. The new bell has been ringing in the New Year since 1957.

HAAS HAUS. This controversial modern building, just opposite the cathedral at Stephansplatz 12, reflects the Stephansdom in its post-modern façade of glass and aluminum. The view is even better from inside the Haus, which has a restaurant on the top floor. Primarily a shopping center, the Haus, which opened in 1990 amid rumors of bureaucratic bribery, is considered something of an eyesore by most Viennese (much to the dismay of postmodern architect Hans Hollein).

NEAR PETERSPLATZ

Take U1 or U3 to "Stephansplatz." Take Graben away from the Stephansdom for two blocks. Petersplatz is on the right.

This tiny square off Graben is home to the Peterskirche and a good landmark from which to explore the Fußgängerzone that spreads from the intersection of Graben and Kohlmarkt off the southwest corner of Peterskirche.

PETERSKIRCHE. Charlemagne founded the first version of this church in the 8th century. Town architects just couldn't resist tinkering with the structure throughout the ages. The Baroque ornamentation was completed in 1733, with Rottmayer on fresco duty.

GRABEN. Now closed off to any traffic except that of feet and horses, this boulevard was once a moat surrounding the Roman camp that became Vienna. The city was able to rid itself of the old moat by financing its removal with part of the huge ransom the Austrians received for releasing the kidnapped Richard the Lionheart (see **Holding a Grudge,** p. 278). The landscape of Graben now shows the debris of Baroque, *Biedermeier* and *Jugendstil* efforts, the last of which include the **Ankerhaus** (#10) and the red-marble **Grabenhof** by Otto Wagner. One of the most interesting (and interactive) sights is the underground *Jugendstil* public toilet complex, designed by Adolf Loos. The **Pestsaüle** (Plague Column) in the square's center was built in 1693, in gratitude for the passing of the Black Death. According to the inscription, the monument is "a reminder of the divine chastisement of plagues richly deserved by this city." The Viennese had ways of dealing with guilt complexes (and phallic symbols) long before Freud.

KOHLMARKT. This second leg of the *Fußgängerzone* starts at the end of Graben, just past Peterskirche, and is home to upscale shops marked "K.U.K." (Kaiserlich und Königlich), indicating that they once earned the Habsburg seal of approval.

VIENNA

HOHER MARKT, RUPRECHTSPLATZ, MORZINPLATZ

Take U1 or U3 to "Stephansplatz." Walk down Rotenturmstr. and turn left onto Lichtenst., which runs into Hoher Markt. Or, take Milchg. out of Petersplatz, turn right and go about three blocks on Tuchlauben. Hoher Markt is on the right, just after the intersection with Wipplingerstr. Judeng. runs from Hoher Markt to Ruprechtspl. and Morzinpl.

These three squares lie just north of Petersplatz. Hoher Markt is the oldest square in town, offering largely historical attractions, while Ruprechtsplatz is home to a slew of cafes and bars in Vienna's hottest nightlife district, known as the **Bermuda Dreiecke** (see Nightlife, p. 130), as well as Vienna's oldest church. Morzinplatz is a grassy plot along the Danube with a dark history of its own.

HOHER MARKT. Once both market and execution site, Hoher Markt was the heart of the Roman encampment, Vindobona. It still boasts **Roman ruins** beneath the shopping arcade on the south side of the square *(25AS, open Sa-Su 11am-1pm).* Fischer von Erlach's **Vermählungsbrunnen** (Marriage Fountain), depicting the union of Mary and Joseph, is now the square's centerpiece. The square's biggest draw, however, is the corporate-sponsored *Jugendstil* **Ankeruhr** (clock). Built in 1914 by Franz Matsch, the magnificent mechanical timepiece has 12 3m-tall historical figures, ranging from Emperor Marcus Aurelius to Maria Theresia to Joseph Haydn, which rotate past the old Viennese coat of arms, accompanied by music of their time period. *(One figure per hr. At noon, all the figures appear in succession.)* Take a peek under the bridge to see depictions of Adam, Eve, an angel, and the Devil.

RUPRECHTSKIRCHE. Overlooking the Danube on Ruprechtspl., the Romanesque Ruprechtskirche is the oldest church in Vienna. The present church, dating from the 13th century, was built on the site of a Carolingian church of AD 740 and one of the gates of the Roman settlement. Maria Theresia donated the well-clad skeleton of an early Christian martyr that lives in a glass case in the corner.

STADTTEMPEL. Almost hidden away in Ruprechtsplatz, the Stadttempel (City Temple) was built in 1826 following an imperial regulation that Jewish and Protestant places of worship should not have conspicuous sheet fronts. Although a sign of intolerance at the time of its decree, the regulation saved the synagogue from greater persecution. The *Stadttempel* is the only synagogue of Vienna's 94 temples to escape Nazi destruction during *Kristallnacht* on November 9-10, 1938. The *Stadttempel* was spared because it stood on a residential block, concealed from the street. The torching of neighboring buildings damaged the synagogue, but it has been restored to its original *Biedermeier* elegance. Today, an armed guard patrols the synagogue as a precaution against repeats of a 1983 terrorist attack, which killed 3 people. *(Seitenstetteng. 2-4. Bring your passport. Open Su-F. Free.)*

MORZINPLATZ. This now quiet, residential square once held the Hotel Metropole, headquarters of the Gestapo, where many Viennese were tortured for speaking against the Anschluß. The hotel was demolished in 1945 and in its place stands **The Monument to the Victims of Fascism.**

NEAR JUDENPLATZ

Take U1 or U3 to "Stephansplatz" and walk down Graben. When Graben ends go right and then continue in the same direction as Graben on Bognerg.; then turn right on Seitzerg. and continue in the same direction on Kurrentg. Or, from Hoher Markt, walk down Wipplingerstr. and turn left on Jordang.

Judenplatz is the site of the city's first Jewish ghetto, established in the Middle Ages. Wipplingerstraße, which runs east-west along this pretty square's north side, offers a number of architectural sights.

JUDENPLATZ. The focal point of the square is a statue of Jewish playwright Gotthold Ephraim Lessing (1729-81). Originally erected in 1935, the statue was torn down by Nazis and a new model was returned to the spot in 1982. The square has an outdoor exhibit about the *Stadttempel* (see Ruprechtsplatz, above) and viewable excavations of a synagogue built in 1294 and burned down in a 1421. House #2, **Zum grossen Jordan,** bears a 16th-century relief and a Latin inscription commemorating this medieval purge of Vienna's Jews.

MARIA AM GESTADE. A short stroll down Schwertg. (right off Wipplingerstr., passing Judenplatz on your left) brings you to a gem of a Gothic church with an extraordinarily graceful spire of delicately carved stone, which depicts the Virgin's heavenly crown. The church's cramped position on the very edge of the old medieval town caused the nave's crookedness. The steep steps from the west door leading to **Tiefergraben,** a former tributary of the Danube, explain the name "Am Gestade," meaning "by the riverbank."

BÖHMISCHE HOFKANZLEI (BOHEMIAN COURT CHANCELLORY). Walking down Wipplingerstr. toward Hoher Markt, you encounter the impressive Baroque façade of the Court Chancellory designed by Fischer von Erlach and now the seat of Austria's Constitutional Court.

ALTES RATHAUS. Directly across the street from the Court Chancellory, the *Altes Rathaus* (Old Townhall) was occupied from 1316 to 1885, when the government moved to the Ringstr. The building is graced by another Donner fountain depicting the myth of Andromeda and Perseus. The *Altes Rathaus* is also home to the **Austrian Resistance Museum,** chronicling anti-Nazi activity during World War II (see Austrian Graffiti, below), and temporary exhibits. *(Friedrich-Schmidt-Pl. ☎52550. Open M, W, Th 9am-5pm. Free. Tours M, W, and F 1pm.)*

AM HOF, FREYUNG, MINORITENPLATZ

Take U1 or U3 to "Stephansplatz" and walk down Graben. When Graben ends go right and then continue in the same direction as Graben on Bognerg. Am Hof will be on the right; Freyung, straight ahead; and Minoritenplatz, to the left (take Strauchg. off Freyung). Or, from Judenplatz, take Drahtg., which runs into Am Hof.

AUSTRIAN GRAFFITI Scratched into the stones near the entrance of the Stephansdom is the mysterious abbreviation "O5." It's not a sign of hoodlums up to no good, but rather a reminder of a different kind of subversive activity. During World War II, "O5" was the secret symbol of Austria's resistance movement against the Nazis. The capital letter "O" and the number "5," for the fifth letter of the alphabet, form the first two letters of "Oesterreich"—meaning Austria. Recently the monogram has received new life. Every time alleged Nazi collaborator and ex-president of Austria Kurt Waldheim attends mass, the symbol is highlighted in chalk. Throughout the city, "O5"'s have also been appearing, drawn on the sides of buildings and on flyers, in protest against the Freedom Party of Jörg Haider's anti-immigrant policies.

AM HOF. The grand courtyard, Am Hof, hosts a weekend **market** *(open Sa-Su 11am-1pm)*. The Babenbergs used this square as the ducal seat when they moved the palace in 1155 from atop Leopoldsberg (in the *Wienerwald*) to the present site. What was once a medieval jousting square now houses the **Kirche am Hof** (Church of the Nine Choirs of Angels; built 1386-1662). In the middle of the square looms the black **Mariensäule** (Column to Mary), erected by Emperor Ferdinand III to thank the Virgin Mary for her protection when the Protestant Swedes threatened Vienna during the Thirty Years' War. Emperor Franz II proclaimed his abdication as Holy Roman Emperor in 1806 from the terrace (see p. 65). But Am Hof was in use long before the Habsburgs, as evidenced by more **Roman ruins.**

FREYUNG. Just west of Am Hof, Freyung is an uneven square with the **Austriabrunnen** (Austria fountain) in the center. Freyung, meaning sanctuary, got its name from the **Schottenstift** (Monastery of the Scots) just behind the fountain, where fugitives could claim asylum in medieval times. Freyung was also used for public executions in the Middle Ages, but now, the annual **Christkindl markt** held here each year before Christmas blots out such unpleasant memories. Three major art galleries flank Freyung: the museum in Schottenstift, the **Kunstforum,** and **Palais Harrach.** A glass-roofed passage leads from Freyung to the Italianate **Palais Ferstel,** which houses one of Vienna's most cherished coffee houses, **Café Central** (see **Time for Decaf?,** p. 101), but it previously served as the National Bank of Austria and the Stock Exchange. Palais Ferstel is just one of the palaces bordering **Herrengaße** (Lord's Lane), which were once occupied by the nobility of the Habsburg court.

MINORITENPLATZ. Go down Herreng. from Freyung, and take a right on Landhausgasse to reach this peaceful square which shelters the 14th-century **Minoritenkirche.** The church's tower was destroyed during the Turkish siege of Vienna in 1529. A mosaic copy of da Vinci's *Last Supper*, commissioned by Napoleon and purchased by Franz I, adorns the north wall of the church. On the south side of the square stands the **Bundeskanzleramt** (Federal Chancery), where the Congress of Vienna met in 1815 and where Chancellor Engelbert Dollfuss was assassinated in 1934 (see p. 66).

MICHAELERPLATZ

Take U3 to "Herreng." Take a right onto Herreng., which leads into Michaelerplatz. Or, from Minoritenplatz, go back up Landhausg., and take a right onto Herreng.

Herreng., Kohlmarkt, and Schauflerg. all meet in this prominent square, which is dominated by the neo-Baroque, half-moon-shaped **Michaelertor,** the spectacular main gate of the Hofburg (see below). In the middle of Michaelerpl. lie more excavated foundations of the Roman military camp called **Vindobona,** where Marcus Aurelius penned his *Meditations*.

MICHAELERKIRCHE. Michaelerplatz is named for this church occupying the block between Kohlmarkt and Habsburgerg. Leopold "the Glorious" Babenberg purportedly founded the church in gratitude for his safe return from the Crusades. The church's Romanesque foundation dates back to the early 13th century, but construction continued until 1792, as attested by the Baroque embellishment over the Neoclassical doorway. *(Open May-Oct. M-Sa 10:30am-4:30pm, Su 1-5pm. 25AS.)*

LOOSHAUS. On the corner of Kohlmarkt and Herrengasse stands the *Looshaus*, constructed by Adolf Loos in 1910-11. Emperor Franz-Josef branded it "the house without eyebrows," as a result of the shocking lack of window pediments customary on Viennese buildings. Offended by the building's modernity, the old emperor never again used the Michaelerplatz entrance to the Hofburg.

CAFÉ GRIENSTEIDL. On the opposite corner, a reconstructed Café Griensteidl invites nostalgic visitors to imagine themselves drinking coffee alongside *Jung Wien* writers Arthur Schnitzler, Hermann Bahr, and Hugo von Hofmannsthal. The original cafe was demolished in 1897 and the authors moved down the street to Café Central, but Griensteidl was reconstructed in 1990 (see Cafés, p. 101).

HOFBURG

Take tram #1 or 2 from anywhere on the Ringstr. to Heldenplatz, or enter through the Michaelertor, which is in Michaelerplatz.

A massive reminder of the Habsburgs' 700-year reign, the sprawling, grandiose **Hofburg** was the winter residence of the emperors. Construction on the original fortress began in 1279, but it didn't become the official dynastic seat until the mid-16th century. Over the centuries, the Hofburg experienced periods of neglect when various emperors chose to live in other palaces, such as Schönbrunn and Klosterneuburg, but it remained the symbol of the family's power. As few Habsburgs were willing to live in their predecessors' quarters, hodge-podge additions and renovations continued until the end of the family's reign in 1918, by which time the palace had become a mini-city. Today, the complex houses several museums, the **Österreichische Nationalbibliothek** (Austrian National Library), the performance halls of the **Lippizaner stallions** and the **Vienna Boys' Choir,** a convention center, and the offices of the Austrian President. It also includes the **Burggarten** and the **Volksgarten** (see Parks and Gardens, p. 121). The Hofburg is divided into several sections, including **In der Burg,** the **Alte Burg, Heldenplatz,** the **Neue Burg, Stallburg, Josefsplatz,** and **Albertina.**

IN DER BURG. If you come through the Michaelertor, you'll first enter the courtyard called In der Burg (within the fortress). The central monument to Emperor Franz II isn't too exciting, but on your left you'll find the more visually stimulating red and black striped **Schweizertor** (Swiss Gate), erected in 1552 and named for the Swiss mercenaries who guarded it under Empress Maria Theresia. Here street musicians take advantage of wonderful acoustics to play melodies of the old Empire, adding to the personal soundtrack of your visit in the hope of a few schillings in return. This section of the Hofburg contains the entrances to the **Kaiserappartements** and the **Hofsilber und Tafelkammer.** *(Imperial apartments 80AS; combined admission to Silver and Porcelain Collection 95AS. Open daily 9am-4:30pm.)*

Kaiserappartements (Imperial Apartments). On the right side of the Michaelortor is the entrance to the imperial apartments. Once the private quarters of Emperor Franz Josef (1830-1916) and Empress Elisabeth (1838-1898). Neither of them spent much time in the Hofburg (or with each other, for that matter), so the rooms are disappointingly lifeless. Amid all the Baroque trappings, the two most personal items seem painfully out of place: Emperor Franz Josef's military field bed and Empress Elisabeth's wooden gym bear mute testimony to lonely lives (See Unforgettable Empress, above). Franz Josef's rooms are unelectrified—he didn't approve of the advances of the Industrial Age, although Sisi did manage to convince him to install running water for her bathtub.

Hofsilber und Tafelkammer (Court Silver and Porcelain Collection), on the ground floor opposite the ticket office, displays examples of the outrageously ornate cutlery that once adorned the Imperial table.

UNFORGETTABLE EMPRESS An anarchist murdered the Empress of Austria in 1898. Today, Austria remembers Empress Elisabeth (better known as Sisi) not for her untimely death, but for her legendary beauty. When she married Franz Josef in 1854, the 16-year-old Bavarian princess was considered by some to be the most gorgeous woman in Europe. Love, however, did not flourish—even in the hundreds of rooms of the Hofburg and Schönbrunn palaces, the imperial couple could not get far enough away from each other. Franz Josef built the Hermes Villa in the Wienerwald (Vienna Woods) for his wife's private residence. There, she unhappily wrote: "Love is not for me. Wine is not for me. The first makes me ill. The second makes me sick." In other poems, she complained about her duties as Empress, disparaged her husband, and labeled her children bristle-haired pigs. Over a century later, this melancholy, tight-lipped, beautiful woman is plastered on postcards and in guide books, and immortalized in various musicals and plays. A plaque on a statue of her in the Volksgarten dubs her the "unforgettable Empress Elisabeth."

ALTE BURG. Behind the Schweizertor lies the **Schweizerhof,** the inner courtyard of the Alte Burg (Old Fortress), which stands on the same site as the original 13th-century palace. The Alte Burg houses the **Weltliche und Geistliche Schatzkammer** (Secular and Sacred Treasury), and the **Burgkapelle.**

Burgkapelle, at the top of the stairs on the right of the Schweizertor. This Gothic chapel is where the heavenly voices of the **Wiener Sängerknaben** (Vienna Boys' Choir) grace Mass-goers on Sundays (except in July-Aug.; see p. 128).

Weltliche und Geistliche Schatzkammer, entrance beneath the steps to Burgkapelle, right of the Schweizertor. In this treasury are stashed the Habsburg jewels, the crowns of the Holy Roman and Austrian Empires, Imperial christening robes, and an elaborate cradle presented by the city of Paris in 1811 to the infant son of Napoleon. Besides these sparklers, the treasury also contains a "horn of a unicorn" (really an 8ft long Narwahl's horn) and the tooth reported to have belonged to John the Baptist. (*Open daily except Tu 10am-6pm. 80AS, senior and students 50AS. English tours, one per day, 30AS.)*

HELDENPLATZ. Reachable through arches in the far side of In der Burg (opposite the Michaelertor), Heldenplatz (Heroes' Square) is an enormous park-cum-parking lot at the feet of the Neue Burg, which is the large semi-circular wing attached to the southwest side of Alte Burg. On March 15, 1938, the square was filled with a jubilant crowd cheering Adolf Hitler's proclamation of Austria's Anschluß. Later in the war, the square, planted with potatoes to feed the starving populace, showed Austria's inability to pick the right heroes in 1938. The equestrian statues (both done by Anton Fernkorn) depict two of Austria's great military commanders: Prince Eugene of Savoy and Archduke Charles, whose horse rears triumphantly on its hind legs with no other support, a feat of sculpting never again duplicated. Poor Fernkorn went insane, supposedly due to his inability to recreate the effect.

NEUE BURG. Built between 1881 and 1926, the Neue Burg (New Fortress) is the youngest wing of the palace, but as the Empire ended in 1918, no Habsburg ever inhabited the place. Still, when the setting sun gives the stones of this Neo-classical monolith a golden sheen, power and grace seem to emanate from it. The double-headed golden eagle crowning the roof symbolizes the double empire of Austria-Hungary. Planned in 1869, the Neue Burg's design called for twin palaces across Heldenplatz, both connected to the Kunsthistorisches and Naturhistorisches Museums by arches spanning the Ringstraße. WWI put an end to the Empire and its grand designs. Today, the Neue Burg houses Austria's largest working library, the **Österreichische Nationalbibliothek** (Austrian National Library), and the **Reichskanzleitrakt,** as well as the fantastic **Völkerkunde Museum** (see Museums, p. 123), and three branches of the **Kunsthistorisches Museum,** for all three see Museums, p. 124).

Österreichische Nationalbibliothek contains millions of books and an outstanding little museum of papyrus, scriptures, and musical manuscripts. The main reading room is open to the public; anyone can request books for in-library use with a picture ID. *(Entrance on Heldenpl. ☎534 10 397. Open May 7-Oct. 26 M-Sa 10am-4pm, Th until 7pm, Su and holidays 10am-1pm; Nov.-April M-Sa 10am-1pm. Museum admission May-Nov. 60AS, students 40AS; Nov.-April 40AS.)*

Reichskanzleitrakt (State Chancellery Wing), the building attached to the Neue Burg, opposite the Alte Burg. Despite the demise of the Habsburg dynasty, the Hofburg continues an association with the Austrian government. The architecture is perhaps most notable for the labors of Hercules, a group of buff statues said to have inspired the 11-year-old Arnold Schwarzenegger, then on his first visit to Vienna, to pump up.

STALLBURG (PALACE STABLES). Attached to the northeast side of the Alte Burg (to the left of the Michaelertor, if you are facing it from the outside) is the Renaissance Stallburg, the famous digs of the Royal Lipizzaner stallions and the **Spanische Reitschule** (Spanish Riding School; see Hot to Trot, below). The cheapest way to get a glimpse of the famous steeds is to watch them train. *(Mid-Feb. to June and Nov. to mid-Dec. Tu-F 10am-noon; Feb. M-Sa 10am-noon, except when the horses tour. Tickets sold at the door at Josefspl., Gate 2, from about 8:30am. 100AS, children 30AS. No reservations.)* For a more impressive (and more expensive) display, you can try to attend a **Reitschule performance,** but sold-out performances require you to reserve tickets months in advance. *(☎533 9032; fax 535 0186. Apr.-June and Sept. Su 10:45am, W 7pm; Mar. Su 10:45am; 1½hr. Write to: Spanische Reitschule, Hofburg, A-1010 Wien. If you reserve through a travel agency, expect at least a 22% surcharge. Reservations only; no money accepted by mail. Tickets 250-900AS, standing room 200AS.)* You can also learn about the Lipizzaner's history and training at the **Lipizzaner Museum** (see Museums, p. 126).

JOSEFSPLATZ. Just south of Stallburg, this courtyard is named after the large statue of Emperor Josef II in the center. The modest emperor would no doubt be appalled at his statue's chest-baring Roman garb, but the sculptor probably couldn't bring himself to depict the decrepit hat and patched-up frock coat the emperor favored. The square contains the ticket entrance for the **Stallburg,** and, behind the statue, the entrance to the **Prunksaal** (Grand Hall). Maintained by the Nationalbibliothek, the Prunksaal is marked by a small plaque next to very modest doors. All architectural restraint stops at the doors, however, as the imposing staircase suggests. Inside, the hall is immensely Baroque, glittering with gilded

HOT TO TROT The Royal Stables, some of the best Renaissance buildings in Vienna, were built as a residence for the Archduke Maximilian in the mid-16th century and were later converted to the stables of the Lipizzaner horses, known for their snowy-white coats and immense physical strength and grace. The Lipizzaners descend from an equine breed ordered by the Austrian Emperor while in Lipizza, Italy, which is now in Slovenia, but was once part of the Spanish lands annexed by the Habsburgs in the late 16th century. Breeders mixed Arab and Berber genes, and once the stud line had been established, the Lipizzaners were imported to Vienna to dance in the heyday of highly stylized Renaissance horsemanship. Despite their fame, the Lipizzaners' survival has been tenuous over the centuries. The horses ran from the French in the Napoleonic wars, and they barely survived the poverty that ensued after WWI and the breakup of the Empire. During WWII, they escaped destruction in a safe haven in Czechoslovakia. In 1945, US General Patton flagrantly violated his own orders to stay put by leading a madcap Eastern push to prevent the Russians from reaching the four-legged treasures first. In the early 1980s, an epidemic virus in the stud killed upwards of thirty brood mares; today, stud farmers worry that the decreasing number of Lipizzaners may lead to health problems resulting from inbreeding. Recently, UN peace keepers ran across starving Lipizzaners near Banja Luca in Bosnia, prompting the Lipizzaner Society to start a fund-raiser to save the beasts from an ugly death.

wood, frescoes, and marble pillars. Begun in 1723, the Prunksaal is the secular counterpart of Fischer von Erlach's magnificent Karlskirche (see p. 116). Though just a part of the Nationalbibliothek, this impressive room is the largest Baroque library in Europe. Multi-media exhibits in the free, functional part of the library on Heldenpl. give three-dimensional tours of the hall. Wander through the floor-to-ceiling bookcases that house more than 200,000 leather-bound books, and pay your respects to the 16 marble statues of various Habsburg rulers, including one of library founder Charles VI. *(☎534 100. Prunksaal open June-Oct. M-Sa 10am-4pm, Su 10am-1pm; Nov.-May M-Sa 10am-noon. Closed first 3 weeks of Sept. 60AS.)*

AUGUSTINERKIRCHE. In a wing attached to the south side of the **Prunksaal,** on the left side of Josefsplatz if you are facing it from the outside. Glorious High Masses are held each Sunday in this 14th-century Gothic church. Eighteenth-century renovations (and some Napoleonic flourishes) have altered the interior. The Augustinerkirche witnessed the wedding of Maria Theresia and Franz Stephan and is now the final resting place of the hearts of the Habsburgs, which are stored in the **Herzgrüftel** (Little Heart Crypt). *(Mass 11am. Free to the public. Church open M-Sa 10am-6pm, Su 11am-6pm.)*

ALBERTINA. Further south along Augustinerstr., past Augustinerkirche, is this southernmost wing of the Hofburg, which was once inhabited by Maria Christina (Maria Theresia's favorite daughter) and her hubby Albert. Originally part Augustinian monastery, and part 18th-century palace, today the Albertina houses a film museum and the celebrated **Collection of Graphic Arts** with its array of old political cartoons and drawings by Dürer, Michelangelo, da Vinci, Raphael, Cezanne, and Schiele. *(☎53483. Open Tu-Sa 10am-5pm. 70AS.)*

VIENNA

NEAR NEUER MARKT

Take U1 or U3 to "Stephanspl." Walk down Kärntnerstr., away from the Stephansdom. Turn right on Donnergasse, which leads into Neuer Markt. Or, from Albertina, walk down Tegetthoffstr., which runs into Neuer Markt.

The spectacular Neuer Markt is centered around George Raphael Donner's **Donnerbrunnen,** a graceful embodiment of the Danube surrounded by 4 gods, who represent her tributaries. The streets radiating from it connect pedestrians to some of the most famous sights in Vienna. Parallel to Neuer Markt and running south into that giant on the Ringstraße, the **Staatsoper,** Kärntnerstr. is one of Vienna's grand boulevards, lined with chic cafes and boutiques. Street musicians play everything from Peruvian folk to Neil Diamond.

KAPUZINERKIRCHE (CHURCH OF THE CAPUCHIN FRIARS). On the southwest corner of Neuer Markt. Within its pale orange, 17th-century façade lies the **Kaisergruft** (Imperial Vault), a series of subterranean rooms filled with coffins, including the remains (minus heart and entrails—see Augustinerkirche above, and Stephansdom, p. 106) of all the Habsburg rulers since 1633. Empress Maria Theresia rests next to beloved husband Franz Stephan of Lorraine in an ornate Rococo sepulcher surrounded by cherubim and a dome. Maria Theresia was crushed by the death of her husband and visited his tomb frequently. When she got old, the Empress had an elevator installed. On her last trip, the elevator stalled 3 times, prompting the empress to exclaim that the dead did not want her to leave. She was entombed a week later. *(Open 9:30am-4pm. Imperial Vault 40AS, students 30AS.)*

HOTEL SACHER. At the end of Kärntnerstr, across from the rear of the Opera, stands the flag-bedecked Hotel Sacher. This legendary institution once served magnificent dinners over which the elite discussed affairs of state. The hotel's *chambres separées* provided discreet locations where the elite conducted affairs of another sort. In one of its elegant suites, John Lennon and Yoko Ono awed the public by holding a press conference while naked in bed—all of course in the name of peace. Although you may still be able to spot a celebrity or two, the crowds flock to Hotel Sacher to get their hands on its renowned chocolate dessert, the Sacher torte (see **Sacher Scandal,** p. 97; and Coffeehouses: Hotel Sacher, p. 102).

MONUMENT GEGEN KRIEG UND FASCHISMUS. This Memorial Against War and Fascism, sculpted by Alfred Hrdlicka in 1988 and located behind Hotel Sacher on Albertinapl., graphically commemorates the suffering caused by WWII.

THE RINGSTRAßE

Trams #1 and 2 run along the Ringstr., and the U-bahn has stops on opposite sides of the Ring at U2: "Schottentor" and U3: "Stubentor." Or, from Neuer Markt, take Donnergasse out of the Markt and turn right on Kärnterstraße, which will lead you roughly to the middle of the Ring, at the Staatsoper.

The Ringstraße defines the boundaries of the inner city, and is an attraction in itself. Freud used to walk the circuit of the Ring every day during his lunch break. It took him 2 hours at a brisk pace. This 57m-wide, 4km-long boulevard was commissioned by Emperor Franz Josef in 1857 to replace the city fortifications that had encircled Vienna's medieval center since the last siege by the Ottoman Turks in 1683, separating the old town from the suburban districts. The military, still uneasy in the wake of the revolution attempted 9 years earlier, demanded that the 1st district be surrounded by fortifications; the erupting bureaucratic bourgeoisie, however, argued for the removal of all formal barriers and for open space within the city. Imperial designers reached a compromise: the walls would be razed to make way for the Ringstraße, a peace-loving, tree-studded spread of boulevard and, at the same time, a sweeping circle designed for the efficient transport of troops. This massive architectural commitment attracted participants from all over Europe. Urban planners put together a grand scheme of monuments dedicated to staples of Western culture: religion, scholarship, commerce, politics, and art. In total, 12 giant public buildings were erected along the Ring; counter-clockwise from Schottenring, they are the **Börse,** the **Votivkirche,** the **Universität,** the **Rathaus,** the **Burgtheater,** the **Parlament,** the **Kunsthistorisches Museum** and **Naturhisorisches Museum,** the **Staatsoper,** the **Museum für angewandte Kunst,** and the **Postsparkasse,** each built in the appropriate Historicist style (See Visual Art and Architecture, p. 75).

STARCH OR NO STARCH? The Habsburgs habitually strolled around Vienna with a full retinue of bodyguards. These casual jaunts were supposedly incognito—the emperor demanded that his subjects pretend not to recognize the imperial family. On one of these walks in 1853, a Hungarian insurrectionist leapt from nearby bushes and attempted to stab the emperor. Franz Josef's collar was so heavily starched, however, that the knife drew no blue blood, and the crew of bodyguards dispatched the would-be assassin before he could strike again. Saved by his starch, but still afraid of ambush, Franz Josef began the building of the wide open Ringstraße.

SCHOTTENRING. The first stretch of the Ring extending south from the Danube Canal, called Schottenring, leads past the Italianate **Börse** (stock exchange) to Schottentor, which is surrounded by university cafes, bookstores, and bars. Across Universitätsstr. rise the twin spires of the **Votivkirche,** a neo-Gothic wonder surrounded by rose gardens, that is home to a number of expatriate religious communities. Franz Josef's brother Maximilian commissioned the church as a gesture of gratitude after the Emperor survived an assassination attempt near the spot in 1853 (see **Starch or no Starch?** above).

KARL-LUEGER RING. The next stretch of the Ring runs from the university to Rathausplatz. **Universität Wien** was founded in 1365, but by the 19th century the original building had long become too small. The massive new building was built in the Italian Renaissance style which celebrated the beginning of the "Golden Age" of science. The professors, however, had hoped for a more modern building which would suggest the continuance of that Golden Age. Inside the university is a tranquil courtyard lined with busts of famous departed professors.

DR. KARL-RENNER RING. Rathausplatz and Parlament mark off this section of the Ring. The **Rathaus** (town hall), with fluted arches and red geraniums in the windows, is meant to honor the Flemish burghers who pioneered the idea of town halls and civic government in Europe. The Viennese, just emerging from imperial constraints through the strength of the growing bureaucratic middle class, sought to imbue their city hall with the same sense of budding freedom and prosperity. There are art exhibits inside, and the city holds outdoor festivals out front on the **Rathausplatz,** which is the inner city's largest square. Opera buffs will enjoy the free nightly Music Film Festival held during July and August (see p. 129). *(Free tours W at 1pm; meet at the blue Information booth outside.)* Across the street from the Rathaus is the **Burgtheater** (Imperial Court Theater), which has seen the premieres of some of the most famous operas and plays by Austrians, including Mozart's *La Nozze di Figaro*. Inside, frescoes by Gustav Klimt, his brother, and his partner Matsch depict the interaction between drama and history through the ages. Klimt used contemporary faces as models for the audience members; notables of the day sent him baskets of fruit and tasteful presents in hopes of being covertly included in one of the murals. *(Performance season runs from Sept.-June. Tours July-Aug. M, W, and F 1, 2, and 3pm; Sept.-June on request. 50AS.)* Next to Rathausplatz is the **Parlament.** Decked out with winged chariots, a grand ramp leading to its columned façade and an imposing statue of wise Athena, the *Parlament* tries to invoke the great democracies of ancient Greece. After a shaky start, the Parlament now houses the Austrian National and Federal Councils. *(Tours mid-Sept. to mid-July M-F at 11am and 3pm; mid-July to mid-Sept. M-F 9, 10, 11am, 1, 2, and 3pm; Easter holidays 11am and 3pm.)*

BURGRING. On Burgring, opposite the Hofburg, stand two of Vienna's largest and most comprehensive museums, the **Kunsthistorisches Museum** (Museum of Art History) and the **Naturhistorisches Museum** (Museum of Natural History) on either side Maria-Theresien-Platz (see Museums, p. 124 and p. 126). When construction was complete, the builders realized with horror that Apollo, patron deity of art, stood atop the Naturhistorisches Museum, and Athena, goddess of science, atop the Kunsthistorisches. Tour guides claim that each muse is situated intentionally to look down on the appropriate museum. In the center of the square, a huge statue immortalizes the throned Empress Maria Theresia, surrounded by her key statesmen and advisers. The statue purportedly faces the Ring so that the Empress may extend her hand to the people. She holds a copy of the Pragmatic Sanction, which granted women the right to succeed to the Austrian throne (see p. 65).

OPERNRING/KÄRNTNERRING. Runs from the Burggarten (see Parks and Gardens, p. 121) to Schwarzenbergstr., marked by an equestrian statue, the **Schwarzenberg Denkmal.** The largest feature of Opernring is the **Staatsoper** (State Opera). Built in 1869 by and for the opera adoring public, the Staatsoper had first priority during the construction of the Ringstraße. Due to a mistake in laying the foundation, however, the builders had to cut a full story from the building's height. When Franz Josef saw the building, he agreed with the consensus that it was "a little low." The two architects wanted so badly to impress that the lukewarm reactions drove one to suicide and caused the other to die two months later "of a broken heart." The emperor was so shocked that for the rest of his life, whenever he was presented with something he responded, *"Es ist sehr schön, es hat mich sehr erfreut"* (It's very beautiful, it pleases me very much). Over the years, the Viennese became very attached to their flagship building and their collective heart broke when Allied bombs destroyed the Staatsoper in 1945. Vienna meticulously restored the exterior and re-opened the building in 1955, with a slightly redesigned auditorium inside. Today, the Staatsoper is still at the heart of Viennese culture (see **Masters of the House,** p. 127). If you can't make it to a performance, at least **tour** the gold, crystal, and red velvet interior. *(Tours July-Aug.: 10, 11am, 1, 2, and 3pm;*

Sept.-Oct. and May-June: 1, 2, and 3pm; Nov.-Apr.: 2 and 3pm. 60AS, students 45AS.) Seeing an opera is cheaper, though (see Staatsoper: standing room tickets, p. 126).

SCHUBERTRING/STUBENRING. From Schwarzenbergstr. to the Danube Canal, Schubertring borders the **Stadtpark** (see Parks and Gardens, p. 121). The **Postsparkasse** (Post Office Savings Bank), near the end of Stubenring and down a little side street, is Otto Wagner's greatest triumph of function over form, and the most contemporary of the Ringstraße monuments. A bulwark of modernist architecture, the building raises formerly concealed elements of construction, like the thousands of symmetrically placed metallic bolts on the rear wall, to a position of exaggerated significance. The distinctly Art Nouveau interior is open during banking hours free of charge. *(George-Coch-Pl. 2. Open M-W and F 8am-3pm, Th 8am-5:30pm.)*

OUTSIDE THE RING

As the city expands beyond the Ring in all directions, the distance between notable sights also expands. But what the area outside the Ring gives up in accessibility, it makes up for in the varied attractions it offers. Some of Vienna's most famous modern architecture is not surprisingly found outside the Ring, where 20th-century designers found more space to build. At the same time, this modern sprawl of Vienna is also home to a number of startlingly beautiful Baroque palaces and parks that were once beyond the city limits.

NEAR KARLSPLATZ

Take U1, U2, or U4 to "Karlspl." Or, from the Staatsoper, walk about 2 blocks down Kärntnerstraße. Karlsplatz is on the left side after the intersection with Rechte Weinzeile.

Once a central gathering place for the Viennese, Karlsplatz is now isolated behind a major traffic artery, but it is home to Vienna's most impressive Baroque church, the **Karlskirche,** and is surrounded by the ornate **Musikverein** and several major museums, including the **Secession,** the **Künstlerhaus,** and the garish **Kunsthalle.**

KARLSKIRCHE. Situated in the center of the gardens where the **Naschmarkt** (see p. 117) was held until the 1890s, the Karlskirche is an eclectic masterpiece, combining a Neoclassical portico with a Baroque dome and towers on either side. Two massive columns, covered with spiraling reliefs depicting the life of St. Carlo Borromeo, to whom the church is dedicated, frame the central portion of the church. The interior of the church is overwhelmingly beautiful, with colorful ceiling frescoes and a sunburst altar. Designed by Fischer von Erlach and completed by his son, Johann Michael, this imposing edifice was constructed in 1793 to fulfil a vow Emperor Charles VI made during a plague epidemic in 1713. In front of the church, a reflecting pool and modern sculpture designed by Henry Moore connect it to the 20th century. *(Church open M-Sa 9-11:30am and 1-5pm, Su 1-5pm. Free.)*

RESSELPARK. The park opposite Karlskirche, named for Josef Ressel (the Czech gentleman who invented the propeller), is peaceful and shady, ringed by museums. The **Historisches Museum der Stadt Wien** stands to the left of the Karlskirche (see Museums, p. 125). The blocky yellow and blue **Kunsthalle** stands out at the opposite end of the park (see p. 125). Above one side of the park, a terrace links the *Jugendstil* **Karlsplatz Stadtbahn Pavilions,** designed in 1899 by Otto Wagner (see **Artistic Transportation,** below).

SECESSION BUILDING. Northwest of Resselpark, across Friedrichstr. at No. 12, is the nemesis of the tradition-bound Künstlerhaus, the Secession Building. Its white walls, restrained decoration, and gilded dome (hence the nickname the "Golden Cabbage") are meant to clash with the Historicist Ringstraße. Otto Wagner's pupil Josef Olbrich built this *fin de siècle* monument to accommodate artists who broke with the rigid, state-sponsored Künstlerhaus. The inscription above the door reads: *"Der Zeit, ihre Kunst; der Kunst, ihre Freiheit"* (To the age, its art; to art, its freedom). The Secession exhibits of

1898-1903 were led by Gustav Klimt and attracted cutting-edge European artists. His painting, *Nuda Veritas* (Naked Truth), became the icon of a new aesthetic ideal. Oscar Wilde's *Salomé* and paintings by Gauguin, Vuillard, van

ARTISTIC TRANSPORTATION Otto Wagner, even more than Adolf Loos, is the architect responsible for Vienna's *Jugendstil* face. The graceful, gold-edged pavilions that grace Vienna's subway system are part of a series Wagner produced when the system was redesigned at the turn of the century. All of the U6 stations between Längenfeldg. and Heiligenstadt are also Wagner's work. His attention to the most minute details on station buildings, bridges, and even lampposts give the city's public transportation an elegant coherence. Wagner's two arcades in Karlspl. are still in use: one functions as a cafe, and the other as an exhibition hall.

Gogh, and others created an island of modernity amid an ocean of Habsburgs and Historicism. The exhibition hall remains firmly dedicated to the cutting edge *(See Museums,* p. 125, *for more details).*

MAJOLICAHAUS. This colorful wonder of an apartment building is at Linke Wienzeile 40. From the Secession Building, head away from Karlsplatz, down Friedrichstr., which runs into Linke Wienzeile. The acclaimed *Jugendstil* Majolicahaus was a collaborative effort by Wagner and Olbrich. The wrought-iron spiral staircase is by Josef Hoffmann, founder of the Wiener Werkstätte, a communal arts-and-crafts workshop and key force in the momentum of *Jugendstil*. The Majolicahaus's golden neighbor, the **Goldammer** building, is another Wagnerian mecca.

NASCHMARKT. To the West of Karlsplatz, along Linke Wienzeile, is the beginning of the Naschmarkt, a colorful, multi-ethnic food bazaar that moved from the Karlspl. to its present location in the 1890s. During the week, the Naschmarkt, which derives its name from the German verb *naschen* (to nibble), presents a dazzling array of fresh fruits and vegetables laid out in front of bakeries, cafes, *Wurst* vendors, and cheese and spice shops. On Saturdays, the Naschmarkt becomes a massive flea market, where shrewd bargainers can acquire anything from loose junk to traditional Austrian clothing. Come before 11am and walk to the end of the square for the cheapest prices from local farmers. *(Open M-F 7am-6pm, Sa 7am-1pm.)*

THEATER AN DER WIEN. Further down Linke Wienzeile, opposite the Naschmarkt, stands the theater that hosted the premiere of Mozart's *Die Zauberflöte* once upon a time (see p. 128). The name of the street and the theater commemorate the Wien river, which used to flow freely through Vienna, but is now almost completely buried under city streets.

MUSIKVEREIN. Step across Lothringerstr. opposite Karlspl. to view the acoustically miraculous Musikverein, home of the Wiener Philharmoniker (Vienna Philharmonic Orchestra). The modest exterior of the building conceals the brilliance of the **Grosser Saal** inside, where the crème de la crème of the international music world performs. Standing room concert tickets offer an inexpensive way to admire both the music and the golden caryatids that line the hall (see p. 127).

SCHWARZENBERGPLATZ

Take tram #71 to "Schwarzenbergpl." Or, facing the Künstlerhaus on Karlsplatz, turn right on Friedrichstr, which leads into the middle of Schwarzenbergpl.

Schwarzenbergplatz, marked by the illuminated **Hochstrahlbrunnen** (Tall Fountain), is an elongated square with an unsavory military history. During the Nazi era, the occupied city renamed the square "Hitlerplatz," and when the Russians brutally liberated Vienna, they renamed it "Stalinplatz" and erected an enormous **Russen Heldendenkmal** (Russian Heroes' Monument), a concrete colonnade behind a column bearing the figure of a Russian soldier, with a quotation from Stalin inscribed in the base. The Viennese have attempted to destroy the monstrosity three times, but the product of sturdy Soviet engineering refuses to be demolished. Vienna's disgust with their Soviet occupiers is further evident in their nickname for an anonymous Soviet soldier's grave: "Tomb of the Unknown Plunderer." When it is windy and raining the water from the fountain is mighty enough to cover the view of the offending monument. Across the street from Schwarzenbergpl., on the Ring, **Café Schwarzenberg** is one of the poshest meeting-places in the city.

PALAIS SCHWARZENBERG. Behind the Hochstrahlbrunnen. Its present location on a traffic island makes it hard to believe that Palais Schwarzenberg, designed in 1697 by Fischer von Erlach's rival architect, Lukas von Hildebrandt, was once the center of a neighborhood preferred by Vienna's nobility. The palace is now a swank hotel, where, rumor has it, daughters of the super-rich gather annually to meet young Austrian noblemen at the grand debutante ball. If you're not a hotel guest, the palace is off limits.

SCHLOß BELVEDERE

Take tram D to "Schwarzenberg," tram #71 one stop past Schwarzenbergpl., or walk up Prinz-Eugen-Str. from Südbahnhof. Walking southeast from Schwarzenbergpl. (away from the city center), you'll find Belvedere just beyond the Schwarzenberggarten, which is next to Beleved-ere's own gardens.

Designed by Lukas von Hildebrandt, Belvedere was originally the summer residence of **Prince Eugène of Savoy,** Austria's greatest military hero (see Unpopular Hero, p. 119). His distinguished career began when he routed the Ottomans in the late 17th century. After Eugene's death without heirs in 1736, his cousin sold off his possessions and Empress Maria Theresia snatched up the palace as a showroom for the Habsburgs' art collection and opened the extensive formal gardens to the public. Though the imperial art moved to the Kunsthistorisches Museum in the 1890s, Archduke Franz Ferdinand lived in the Belvedere until his 1914 assassination. The grounds of the Belvedere, stretching from the Schwarzenberg Palace to the Südbahnhof, now contain 3 spectacular sphinx-filled gardens (see p. 121) and an equal number of excellent museums (see p. 124).

SCHLOß SCHÖNBRUNN

Take U4 to "Schönbrunn."

From its humble beginnings as a hunting lodge, Schönbrunn, named after a "beautiful brook" on the property, was destroyed twice before Fischer von Erlach conceived a plan for a palace to make Versailles look like a gilded outhouse. Construction began in 1696, but the cost was so prohibitive that the project was slowed down considerably until, three emperors later in 1740, Maria Theresia inherited the project and created the Rococo palace that became her favorite residence. Its cheery yellow color has been named *"Maria Theresien gelb"* after her. When Napoleon conquered Vienna, he shared Maria Theresia's fondness for the place and promptly moved in. Tours of some of the palace's 1500 rooms reveal the elaborate taste of her era. Both the Grand (44 rooms) and the Imperial (22 rooms) tours give you access to the **Great Gallery** where the Congress of Vienna danced the night away after a long day of dividing up the continent and the **Hall of Mirrors** where the 6-year-old Mozart played. But upon reaching the **Ceremonial Hall** decorated with paintings of Joseph II's wedding to Isabella of Parma, those with cheaper Imperial Tour tickets are shown the exit. Those with Grand Tour tickets can enjoy the more sumptuous pleasures of the palace such as the **Millions Room** with its exquisite Oriental miniatures and rosewood paneling and Maris Theresia's bedroom with its original decadent red velvet bed cover protected behind glass. (*Apartments open daily Apr.-Oct. 8:30am-5pm; Nov.-Mar. 8:30am-4:30pm. Imperial Tour 95AS, students 85AS. Grand Tour 125AS, students 110AS. Audio-guides included.*)

THE GARDENS. Even more impressive than the palace itself are the classical gardens behind it. Designed by Emperor Josef II, the gardens extend nearly 4 times

UNPOPULAR HERO Though Prince Eugene of Savoy was publicly lionized for his military exploits (see p. 64), his appearance was most unpopular at court—Eugene was a short, ugly, impetuous man. The Belvedere summer palace (originally only the **Untere** (Lower) **Belvedere**), ostensibly a gift from the emperor in recognition of Eugene's military prowess, was more likely intended to get Eugene out of the imperial hair. Eugene's military exploits, however, had left him with a larger bank account than his Habsburg neighbors (a fact that didn't help their relationship), and he decided to improve upon his new home. The result is the **Obere** (Upper) **Belvedere,** which was designed as a place to throw bacchanalian parties. The building has one of the best views of Vienna. Eugene's *pièce de resistance* was a rooftop facsimile of an Ottoman tent, which called undue attention to Eugene's martial glory.

the length of the palace. They include an encyclopedic orchestration of various elements, ranging from a sprawling zoo to the massive stone **Neptunbrunnen** (Neptune fountain) and bogus **Roman ruins.** Edging the geometric flower beds, the trees have been carefully pruned to create the effect of a vaulted arch. At one end of the garden is the **Palmenhaus,** an enormous greenhouse of tropical plants and the **Schmetterlinghaus** (Butterfly House), an enclosure where soft-winged beauties fly free in the tropical environment. There is also a **maze** in whose center two stones, activated by a Master of Feng Shui, emanate energy-giving harmony. To enter this domain of power you must pay an entrance fee *(30AS, students 20AS).* The compendium is crowned by the **Gloriette,** an ornamental temple serenely perched upon a hill with a beautiful view. If you're feeling indulgent, drink a somewhat pricey *Melange* in the temple's new cafe. In summer, open-air opera is performed in the park. *(Park open 6am-dusk. Free.)* Built to amuse Maria Theresia's husband in 1752, the **Schönbrunn Tiergarten** (zoo) is the world's oldest menagerie, but as the oldest it's not necessarily the best. Skip it unless you have brought a little one along who may be amused. *(Zoo open daily May-Sept. 9am-6:30pm; Feb. and Oct. 9am-5pm; Nov.-Jan. 9am-4:30pm; Mar. and Oct. 9am-5:30pm; Apr. 9am-6pm. 95AS, students 45AS, children 30AS.)*

ALONG THE DONAUKANAL

The Danube Canal cuts a semi-circle into the city south of the river, extending beyond the *innere Stadt.* Much of the area inside of the semi-circle is now taken up by parks (see Parks and Gardens, p. 121), but the outside edge of the canal provided building space for some of Vienna's great 20th-century architects to experiment with populist public architecture.

KARL-MARX-HOF. The most famous example of public housing built during the interwar years by the Austrian Social Democratic Republic set, Karl-Marx-Hof illustrates the ideology and aesthetic of *"Rot Wien"* (Red Vienna, the socialist republic from 1918 until the Anschluß). The "palace for the people" stretches out for a full kilometer and encompasses over 1600 identical orange-and-pink apartments, with common space and courtyards to garnish the urban-commune atmosphere. The Social Democrats used this structure as their stronghold during the civil war of 1934, until army artillery shelled the place and broke down the resistance. *(Take U4 or 6 to "Heiligenstadt." XIX, Heiligenstadterstr. 82-92.)*

HUNDERTWASSER HAUS. Friedensreich Hundertwasser (translation: Peace-filled Hundredwaters; given name: Friedrich Stowasser), who was a Fantastic Realist and environmental activist, designed Hundertwasser Haus in opposition to the aesthetic of *Rot Wien* (see Karl-Marx-Hof, above). Completed in 1985, the multi-colored building with 50 apartments makes both an artistic and a political statement. Hundertwasser included trees and grass in the undulating balconies as a means of bringing life back to the urban "desert" that the city had become; trees sticking out of windows, oblique tile columns, and free-form color patterns all contribute to the eccentricity of this blunt rejection of architectural orthodoxy. Hundertwasser created what he called a "Window Bill of Rights," which guaranteed everyone living within a building he designed the ability to decorate the area around their window for as long a space as their arm could reach. Architectural politics aside, this place is fun, bordering on insane—Hundertwasser's design team must have included droves of finger-painting toddlers. The Viennese have nicknamed it the "Bowling Pin House." Despite hordes of visitors, Hundertwasserhaus remains a private residence, where tenants decorate their window spaces as they see fit. *(At the corner of Löweng and Kegelg take tram N from Schwedenpl. to "Hetzg.")*

KUNST HAUS WIEN. Another Hundertwasser project, just 3 blocks away at Untere Weißgerberstr. 13, the Kunst Haus is a museum devoted to the architect's graphic art (see Museums, p. 124) on the lower floors and controversial contemporary artists above (Robert Mapplethorpe and Annie Lennox have both exhibited here). A cafe built along the lines of a Hundertwasser blueprint is inside (see Cafes, p. 103).

MÜLLBRENNEREI (GARBAGE INCINERATOR). Behind the "Spittelau" U-Bahn station. Hundertwasser devotees may also want to check out his huge jack-in-the-box of a trash dump. It has a high smokestack topped by a golden disco ball. He also designed a ferry that cruises the Danube under the auspices of the DDSG.

OTHER SIGHTS

KIRCHE AM STEINHOF. High on a hill in northwest Vienna, Wagner's church embodies another approach to architecture for the people. Commissioned for the inmates of the state mental hospital in 1907, this light, cheerful church combines streamlined symmetry and Wagner's signature functionalism with a Byzantine influence. The white walls are tiled for easy cleaning, the holy water in the basins by the door runs continuously for maximum hygiene, all corners are rounded to avoid injuries, and the pews are widely spaced to give nurses easy access to unruly patients. The church faces north-south, in order to allow patients to enjoy the maximum amount of daylight through the stained-glass windows, designed by Koloman Moser, a vanguard member of the Secession. Above the altar, bright gold mosaics of holy figures seem to levitate. *Jugendstil* sculptor Lukasch fashioned the statues of Leopold and Severin poised upon each of the building's twin towers. The people of Vienna were shocked by Wagner's breaks with tradition and declared, "That crazy church belongs out there with the crazy people." *(Take U2 or U3 to "Volkstheater" then bus #48A. XIV, Baumgartner Höhe 1. ☎ 910 6020 031. Open M-F 8am-3pm, Sa 3-4pm. 40AS, students 20AS. Guided tours (in German only) 40AS. Call ahead.)*

THE ZENTRALFRIEDHOF. The Viennese like to describe the **Zentralfriedhof** (Central Cemetery) as half the size of Geneva but twice as lively. The phrase is meant not only to poke fun at Vienna's rival but also to illustrate Vienna's healthy attitude toward death. In bygone days, the phrase "a beautiful corpse" was a common way of describing a dignified funeral in Vienna. Death doesn't get any better than it does at the Zentralfriedhof. The **Dr. Karl-Lueger-Kirche** marks the center of the cemetery, with the graves of the famous, infamous, and unknown spreading out from it in a grid. The tombs in this massive park (2km^2 with its own bus service) memorialize the truly great along with the ones who wanted to be so considered.

Tor II (2nd gate) is the main gate to the cemetery, and the place to pay respects to your favorite Viennese decomposer: beyond it are Beethoven, Wolf, Strauss, Schönberg, Moser, and an honorary monument to Mozart, whose true resting place is an unmarked paupers' grave in the **Cemetery of St. Mark,** III, Leberstr. 6-8. St. Mark's deserves a visit not just for sheltering Mozart's dust, but also for its *Biedermeier* tombstones and the wild inundation of lilac blossoms that flower everywhere for 2 weeks in spring.

Tor I leads to the **Jewish Cemetery** and Arthur Schnitzler's burial plot. The state of the Jewish Cemetery mirrors the fate of Vienna's Jewish population—many of the headstones are cracked, broken, lying prone, or neglected because the families of most of the dead are gone from Austria. Various structures throughout this portion of the burial grounds memorialize the millions slaughtered in Nazi death camps.

Tor III leads to the Protestant section and the new Jewish cemetery. To the east of the Zentralfriedhof is the melancholy **Friedhof der Namenlosen** on Alberner Hafen, where the nameless corpses of people fished out of the Danube are buried. This little cemetery (separate from the Zentralfriedhof) is accessible by bus #6A from the terminus of tram #71. *(The main entrance to Zentralfriedhof is at XI, Simmeringer Hauptstr. 234. Take tram #71 from Schwarzenbergpl., or tram #72 from Schlachthausg. The tram stops 3 times, at each of the gates. Bus #6A also services the other gates. You can also take S-7 to "Zentralfriedhof," which stops along the south-west wall of the cemetery. ☎ 76041. 38AS. Open May-Aug. 7am-7pm; Mar.-Apr. and Sept.-Oct. 7am-6pm; Nov.-Feb. 8am-5pm.)*

GARDENS AND PARKS

The Viennese have gone to great lengths to brighten the urban landscape with patches of green. The Habsburgs opened and maintained the city's primary public gardens throughout the last 4 centuries; the areas became public property after WWII. There are several parks along the Ring, including the **Stadtpark, Resselpark, Burggarten,** and **Volksgarten,** and in nearly every suburb of the city. The gardens of **Schloß Schönbrunn** and **Schloß Belvedere** (see p. 118) are particularly beautiful. During food shortages after WWII, the city distributed plots of land in sections of the 14th, 16th, and 19th districts to citizens to let them grow their own vegetables. These community *Gärten* still exist, full of roses and garden gnomes.

ALONG THE RING. Vienna's *Innenstadt* is demarcated on 3 sides by the Ringstraße and on the fourth by the Danube Canal. Just south of the Ring, the canal branches into the tiny **Wien River,** which flows to the southwest, passing through *Innenstadt* along the Linke Wienzeile, where it hides beneath the city streets, and, eventually reappears near Schloß Schönbrunn. On its merry way, the Wien, replete with ducks and lilies, bisects the **Stadtpark** (City Park; take U4 to "Stadtpark"), which snuggles up to Parkring. Established in 1862, this area was the first municipal park outside the former city walls. The sculpted vegetation, with one of Vienna's most photogenic monuments, the gilded **Johann-Strauss-Denkmal,** in the center, provides a soothing counterpoint to the central bus station and nearby Bahnhof Wien-Mitte/Landstr.

Clockwise up the Ring, past the Staatsoper, lie the **Burggarten** (Palace Gardens), a quiet park with monuments to such Austrian notables as Mozart, Emperor Franz Josef, and Emperor Franz I, Maria Theresia's husband. The **Babenberger Passage** leads from the Ring to the marble **Mozart Denkmal** (1896), which depicts the composer standing on a pedestal surrounded by instrument-toting cherubim, with reliefs from his operas and portraits of his father and sister on the sides. Reserved for the imperial family and members of the court until 1918, the Burggarten is now a favorite for lounging students, young lovers, and hyperactive dogs. The Burggarten borders Heldenplatz, across from the Kunsthistorisches Museum and behind the Hofburg, which abuts the **Volksgarten,** once the site of a defensive bastion destroyed by Napoleon's troops. In the center of the park, the **Temple of Theseus** can be found in the midst of the formal arrangement of roses and trees. Its columns and roof browned by neglect provide a cool shaded spot to sit. At the North side of the Garden a stark, white statue of Empress Elisabeth sits on a throne, her melancholy eyes looking down on a simple goldfish pond. The statue was placed here shortly after her assassination with a plaque reading "The People of Austria erected this monument to their unforgettable Empress Elisabeth in steadfast love and loyalty" (See **Unforgettable Empress,** p. 111).

AUGARTEN. The Augarten, on Obere Augartenstr., northeast of downtown Vienna in Leopoldstadt, is Vienna's oldest public park. To reach the park, take tram #31 up from Schottenring or tram N to "Obere Augartenstr." and head left down Taborstr. Originally a formal French garden, the Augarten was given a Baroque face-lift and opened to the public by Kaiser Josef II in 1775. Today, the Augarten is no longer as fashionable as it was in the days of Mozart and Strauss, due primarily to the daunting WWII **Flaktürme** (concrete anti-aircraft towers) that dominate the central portion of the park. The sturdy construction of these and other *Flaktürme* in parks around the city has thwarted repeated demolition attempts (the walls of reinforced concrete are up to 5m thick). Despite the dampening influence of the towers, children play soccer in fields of flowers. Buildings located within the Augarten include the headquarters for the **Wiener Porzellanmanufaktur** (Vienna China Factory), founded in 1718, and the **Augartenpalais,** now a boarding school for the Vienna Boys' Choir.

PRATER. For many nostalgic Viennese, the symbol of their city is the **Prater,** a park extending southeast from the Wien Nord Bahnhof/Praterstern. The park was a private game reserve for the Imperial Family until 1766, and the site of the World Expo in 1873. Squeezed into a riverside woodland between the Donaukanal and the river proper, the park is surrounded by ponds, meadows, and stretches of forest. But the Prater is most famous for its old-school amusement park, with the stately wooden 65m-tall **Riesenrad** *(Giant Ferris Wheel; 50AS; ride lasts 20min.).* The wheel, which provides one of the greatest views of Vienna, is best known for its cameo role in *The Third Man.* Locals cherish this wheel of fortune, and when it was destroyed in WWII, the city built an exact replica, which has been turning since 1947. The area near U1: "Praterstern" is the actual amusement park, which contains various rides, arcades, restaurants, and casinos. Entry to the complex is free, but each attraction charges admission *(generally 40AS).* The garish thrill machines and wonderfully campy spookhouse rides are packed with children during the day, but the Prater becomes less wholesome after sundown, due to the proliferation of seedy peep shows. *(Open May-Sept. 9am-midnight; Oct.-Nov. 3 10am-10pm; Nov. 4-Dec. 1 10am-6pm.)*

VIENNA

ON THE DANUBE. The Danube's spring floods were problematic once settlers moved outside the city walls, so the Viennese stretch of the Danube was diverted into canals (and the sewer-like structures documented in *The Third Man*) from 1870 to 1875 and again from 1972 to 1987. One of the side benefits of this restructuring was the creation of new recreational areas, ranging from new tributaries (including the **Alte Donau** and the **Donaukanal**) to the **Donauinsel,** a narrow island stretching for kilometers. The Donauinsel is devoted to bike paths, soccer fields, swimming areas, barbecue plots, boats, discos, and summer restaurants. The northern shore of the island, along the Alte Donau, is lined with beaches and bathing areas. *(Take U1 (dir.: Kagran) to "Donauinsel" or "Alte Donau." Open May-Sept. M-F 9am-8pm, Sa-Su 8am-8pm. Beach admission is roughly 50AS.)* To catch a view of Vienna sparkling at her best, go after sundown to **Donaupark** and take the elevator up to the revolving restaurant in the **Donauturm** (Danube Tower), near the UN complex. *(Take the U1 to "Kaisermühlen/Vienna International Center" and follow signs to the park. Tower open daily April-Sept. 9:30am-midnight; Oct.-March 10am-10pm. 60AS.)* The whole area celebrates during the annual open-air **Donauinsel Fest,** which stages jazz and rock concerts and fireworks displays, in late June (see **Festivals,** p. 129).

IN THE SUBURBS. Vienna's outlying suburbs shelter somewhat wilder parks than the tame enclaves in the center of the city. Nearly every district has public gardens tucked away somewhere, like the **Türkenschanz Park,** in the 18th district, which attracts a plethora of leashed dachshunds. The garden is famous for its Turkish fountain, pools, and peacocks. In summer, feed ducks or gaze in rapture at the water lilies. In winter, come for sledding or ice-skating. *(Take bus #40A or #10A, and enter the park anywhere along Gregor-Mendel-Str., Hasenauerstr., or Max-Emmanuelstr.)*

West of the 13th district is the **Lainzer Tiergarten** (Lainz Game Preserve). Once an exclusive hunting preserve for the royals, this enclosed space has been a nature park and reserve since 1941. Along with paths, restaurants, and spectacular vistas, the park encloses the **Hermes Villa.** This erstwhile retreat for Empress Elisabeth houses exhibitions by the Historical Museum of Vienna, most recently one about the unhappy empress herself. *(Take U4 (dir.: Hütteldorf) to "Hietzing," change to streetcar #60 to "Hermesstr.," then take bus #60B to "Lainzer*

Tor." Open Tu-Su and holidays 10am-6pm, Oct.-Mar. 9am-4:30pm. Villa admission 50AS, students and seniors 20AS; family card 75AS.)

The 14th, 17th, 19th, and 20th districts peter off into well-tended forests that invite *Spaziergänger* (people out for a stroll) and hikers alike. The **Pötzleindorfer Park,** at the end of tram line #41 (dir.: Pötzleindorfer Höhe) from Schottentor, overlaps the lower end of the *Wienerwald* (Vienna Woods). Wild deer roam through overgrown meadows and woodland.

WIENERWALD. Far to the north and west of Vienna sprawls the forested hills of the Wienerwald (Vienna Woods), which extends all the way past Baden bei Wien to the first foothills of the Alps. The woods are known for their excellent *Heuriger* and divine new wines (see p. 103). There are countless ways to enter the Wienerwald, by tram #38 to "Grinzing," tram D to "Nußdorf," tram #43 to "Neuwaldegg," etc. One of the most famous and most easily accessible routes is via **Kahlenberg** and **Leopoldsberg,** 2 hills north of Vienna which provide a great view of the city and direct entrance to the woods. **Kahlenberg** (484m) is the highest point of the rolling Wienerwald, and affords spectacular views of Vienna, the Danube, and distant Alps. The Turks besieged Vienna from here in 1683, and Polish king Jan Sobieski celebrated his liberation of the city from Saracen infidels in the small **Church of St. Joseph.** *(Open May-Oct. Sa noon-6pm, Su and holidays 9am-6pm.)* Just off the central square of Kahlenberg stands the trusty **Stefania Warte** tower; catch the views from part of the river valley's old fortifications. *(Take U4 to "Heiligenstadt" then bus #38A to "Kahlenberg," or hike up the steep 1km-long Nasen Weg from the Kahlenbergdorf S-Bahn station.)*

The area around Kahlenberg, Cobenzl, and Leopoldstadt is criss-crossed with *Wanderwege* (hiking paths) marked by colored bars blazed on tree trunks. Kahlenberg and its country cemetery are within easy walking distance of the wine-growing districts of **Nußdorf** and **Grinzing.** You can follow in an early Pope's footsteps and hike over to the **Leopoldskirche,** a renowned pilgrimage site. It's 1km east of Kahlenberg on **Leopoldsberg** (425m), site of a Babenberg fortress destroyed by the Turks in 1529. Leopoldsberg is named for St. Leopold III of the royal Babenberg family, and offers all-encompassing views of the surrounding city and river valleys. *(You can also take bus #38A from Kahlenberg to Leopoldsberg; 20min.)* **Klosterneuburg,** a decadently Baroque monastery town founded by Leopold (see p. 133), is only a 1½-hour hike from Leopoldsberg.

MUSEUMS

Vienna owes its vast selection of masterpieces to the acquisitive Habsburgs as well as to the city's own crop of art schools and world-class artists (see p. 75). Though painting and architecture dominate most museums, Vienna's treasures are as diverse as the former imperial Habsburg possessions. The vast array of venues can boggle the mind, so take it one step at a time and plan your attack strategy. An exhaustive list is impossible to include here, but the tourist office's free *Museums* brochure lists all opening hours and admission prices. All museums run by the city of Vienna are **free on Friday** morning before noon (except on public holidays); they are marked in the brochure with a coat of arms. Individual museum tickets usually cost 20-80AS, discounted with the **Vienna Card** (though student or senior citizen discounts are usually comparable; see p. 88). If you're going to be in town for a long time, investing in the **Museum Card** (issued through the *Verein der Museumsfreunde*) will save you a bundle on museum entrance fees (ask at a museum ticket window). In 2000, the **Messepalast,** originally the imperial barracks, was under construction to become in 2001 the **MuseumsQuartier** (Museumsplatz 1-5, ☎523 5881, www.mqw.at). This modern complex, which will interrupt the continuity of 19th-century architecture on the Ringstraße, will combine a number of collections now scattered in different venues. The MuseumsQuartier will house the **Leopold Museum** (rumored to hold one of Austria's most significant art collections including a number of valuable Schieles), the **Museum of Modern Art**—currently split between Palais Liechtenstein and 20er Haus—and a new **Kunsthalle** (a venue for temporary exhibits) to replace the one on Karlsplatz. The MuseumsQuartier is scheduled to open in the Summer of 2001.

ART MUSEUMS

Österreichische Galerie (Austrian Gallery), III, Prinz-Eugen-Str. 27 (☎795 570), in the Belvedere Palace behind Schwarzenbergpl. (see p. 118). Walk up from the Südbahnhof or take tram D, #566, 567, 666, 668, or 766 to "Prinz-Eugen-Str." The collection is split into 2 parts. The **Upper Belvedere** (built in 1721-22 by Hildebrandt) houses Austrian Art and other European art of the 19th and 20th centuries. If you can get past the crowds, catch a glimpse of Klimt's *The Kiss* in its golden decadence. In the lesser trafficked areas of the museum linger in front of the violent portraits by the Expressionists Kokoschka and Schiele. Use the same ticket to enter the **Lower Belvedere,** which contains the **Baroque Museum**'s extensive collection of sculptures by Donnere, and Maulbertsch, as well as Messerschmidt's busts, which are studies in human expression ranging from the comical to the tortured. David's majestic portrait of Napoleon on horseback is also here, as is the **Museum of Medieval Austrian Art,** with its Romanesque and Gothic sculptures and altarpieces. Both Belvederes are open Tu-Su 10am-6pm. Admission until 5:30pm. English guided tours at 11am. 60AS, students 40AS. Audio guide included for collection in Upper Belvedere.

Kunsthistorisches Museum (Museum of Fine Arts; ☎52 5240), take U2 to Babenbergerstr., U2/U3 to Volkstheater or tram 1, 2, D, J. Across from the Burgring and Heldenpl. on Maria Theresia's right. The KHM houses the world's 4th-largest art collection, including vast amounts of 15th- to 18th-century Venetian and Flemish paintings. The works by Brueghel are unrivaled, and the museum possesses entire rooms of Rembrandt, Rubens, Titian, Van Dyck, and Velàzquez. Must-sees include Vermeer's *Art of Painting* (room 24) and Raphael's *Madonna in the Meadow* (room 4). Ancient and classical art, including an Egyptian burial chamber, are also well represented. The museum building itself should not be overlooked. The walls above the arches leading to the museum cafe were painted by Klimt in the Historicist style he would later attack. Open Tu-Su 10am-6pm. Picture gallery also open Th until 9pm. During the summer, Easter, and Christmas, English guided tours are offered at 11am and 3pm (30AS). 120AS, students and seniors 80AS. Audio guide included for special exhibition when present. Small **branches** of the museum reside in the Neue Burg (Same hours as the picture gallery. 60AS, students and seniors 30AS):

Ephesos Museum, exhibits the massive finding of an Austrian excavation of Classical ruins from Ephesus in Turkey, including an ancient Greek temple and statues.

Hofjagd- und Rustkammer (Arms and Armor Collection), the second-largest collection of arms and armor in the world.

Sammlung alter Musikinstrumente (Ancient Musical Instruments Collections) which includes Beethoven's harpsichord and Mozart's piano with a double keyboard.

Museum Moderner Kunst (Museum of Modern Art; ☎317 6900; museum@MMK-SLW.or.at; www.MMKSLW.or.at) is split between 2 locations. The 1st is in **Palais Liechtenstein,** IX, Fürsteng. 1. Take tram D (dir.: Nußdorf) to "Fürsteng." The palace, surrounded by a manicured garden, holds Central Europe's largest collection of 20th-century masters including Magritte, Motherwell, Picasso, Miró, Kandinsky, Pollock, Warhol, and Klee in opulent Baroque surroundings. The 2nd location is the **20er Haus** (☎799 6900), III, Arsenalstr. 1, opposite the Südbahnhof. Its large, open *Bauhaus* interior provides the perfect setting for the substantial collection of ground-breaking 60s and 70s work—Keith Arnnat and Larry Poons among them—alongside contemporary artists. It sits in a large sculpture garden stocked with pieces by Giacometti, Moore, and others. Both collections will move in summer 2001 to the new MuseumsQuartier (see above). Open Tu-Su 10am-6pm; until 8pm on Th. 60AS, students 40AS. Ticket for both locations 80AS, students 60AS. Wheelchair accessible.

Kunst Haus Wien, III, Untere Weißgerberstr. 13 (☎712 0491; see p. 120). Take U1 or U4 to "Schwedenpl.," then bus N to "Radetzkypl." This museum, built by Hundertwasser, displays much of his work, including his environmental machines (the "plant water purification plant," for instance). The building itself is one of Hundertwasser's greatest achievements. It notably lacks straight lines, which Hundertwasser called "the Devil's work." The floor bends and swells, creating (in Hundertwasser's words) "a melody for the feet." The Kunst Haus also hosts exhibits of contemporary art from around the world. Open daily 10am-7pm. 95AS, students 70AS; M half price.

Österreichisches Museum für Angewandte Kunst (a.k.a. the MAK; Austrian Museum of Applied Art), I, Stubenring 5 (☎712 8000). Take U3 to "Stubentor." A museum dedicated to the beauty and ingenuity of design, from the smooth curves of Thonet bentwood chairs to the intricate detail of Venetian glass. The rooms themselves were designed by some of the brightest stars of the contemporary Viennese art scene: Observe the exquisite carpets displayed above and below, a single stream of light entering a room, or a darkened hallway with only the sleek silhouettes of the chair collection visible. For Klimt lovers, *The Embrace* is a special highlight. Open Tu-W and F-Su 10am-6pm, Th 10am-9pm. 90AS, students 45AS.

Akademie der Bildende Kunst (Academy of Fine Arts), I, Schillerpl. 3 (☎588 162 25 or 588 162 28), From Karlspl. turn left onto Friedrichstr., then right on Operng. take a left on Lungeng. Famous for having rejected Hitler's application, the Academy holds an excellent and manageable collection which includes impressive works by Peter Paul Rubens. But the centerpiece is Hieronymus Bosch's *The Last Judgment,* placed in a dim room to amplify its effect on the viewer. Open Tu-Su 10am-4pm. 50AS, students 20AS.

Kunsthalle Wien, Moving in Summer 2001 from Karlspl. to the MuseumsQuartier (see p. 116). Take U3 to "Volkstheater." Thematic exhibitions of international contemporary artists using everything from sculpture to film. Open daily 10am-6pm, Th 10am-10pm. 80AS, students 60AS.

Secession Building, I, Friedrichstr. 12 (☎587 5307), on the western side of Karlspl. (see p. 116). With crisp white walls and a "Golden Cabbage" adorning its roof, the Secession Building stands out in the Viennese landscapes. Although the commitment to new art is evident here, and the museum continually changes its exhibits of contemporary artists, the main attraction is almost 100 yrs old, Klimt's controversial *Beethoven Frieze.* This impressive, 30m-long work is his visual interpretation of Beethoven's *Ninth Symphony.* Pick up the English brochure for excellent commentary on the work's symbolism. Open Tu-Su 10am-6pm, Th until 8pm. 60AS, students 40AS. See also p. 116.

Künstlerhaus, I, Karlspl. 5 (☎587 9663). Once the home of the Viennese artistic establishment, this museum now invites temporary exhibits, usually of contemporary and non-European art. The theater hosts numerous **film festivals.** Open daily 10am-6pm, Th until 9pm. 90AS, students 60AS.

Palais Surreal, Josefspl. 5 (☎512 2549). Take U3 to "Herreng." The Baroque palace of the Pallavicini family now houses a small but renowned collection of Surrealist sculptures by Dalí, including a wobbly work called "Space Elephant," and ethereal sculptures done in glass. Open 10am-6pm. 90AS, students and elderly 50AS.

OTHER MUSEUMS

Museum für Völkerkunde, I, (☎534 300), in the Neue Burg on Heldenpl. (see p. 111). Take U2 or U3 to "Volkstheater." Collected here are Benin bronzes, Chinese demon paper kites, West African Dan heads, and a Japanese Doll Festival. The focal point, however, is undoubtedly the crown of Montezuma, still drawing a crowd of protesters wishing its return to Mexico. Open Apr.-Dec. W-M 10am-4pm. 50AS, students 30AS, free entry on May 16, Oct. 26, Dec. 10 & 24.

Historisches Museum der Stadt Wien (Historical Museum of the City of Vienna), IV, Karlspl. 5 (☎505 8747), to the left of the Karlskirche (see p. 116). This amazing collection of historical artifacts and paintings documents Vienna's evolution from a Roman encampment, through the Turkish siege of Vienna, to the subsequent 640 years of Habsburg rule. Don't miss the memorial rooms to Loos and Grillparzer, the *fin de siècle* art, or the temporary exhibitions on all things Viennese. Open Tu-Su 9am-6pm. 50AS, students 25AS.

Jüdisches Museum (Jewish Museum), I, Dorotheerg. 11 (☎535 0431). Jewish culture and history told through a variety of media from the traditional objects-in-a-glass-case presentation, to fragments of texts stamped into the museum walls, to ever elusive holograms. Temporary exhibits focus on prominent Jewish figures and contemporary Jewish art. Open Su-F 10am-6pm, Th until 8pm. 70AS, students 40AS.

Bestattungsmuseum (Undertaker's Museum), IV, Goldeg. 19 (☎501 9542 27). As Viennese as the waltz, the perfect funeral has its special place here. This museum displays a morbidly fascinating if somewhat comical exhibit, including coffins with alarms (should the body decide to rejoin the living) and Josef II's proposed reusable coffin. Open M-F noon-3pm by appointment only. Free.

Sigmund Freud Haus, IX, Bergg. 19 (☎319 1596), near the Votivkirche. Take U2 to "Schottentor," then walk up Währingerstr. to Bergg. Sorry folks, the famed couch is not here, but this former Freud home provides lots of photos and documents, including the young Freud's report cards and circumcision certificate. Open July-Sept. 9am-6pm; Oct.-June 9am-4pm. 60AS, students 40AS.

Lippizaner Museum, I, Reitschulg. 2 (☎526 4184). If you ever liked horses, this is the place for you. What used to be the imperial pharmacy now serves as a museum dedicated to the imperial horses, featuring paintings, harnesses, video clips, and a small viewing window through which you can glimpse the stables. Open daily 9am-6pm. 50AS, students 35AS, tour 20AS. Call ahead to arrange an English tour.

Naturhistorisches Museum (Natural History Museum; ☎52177), opposite the Kunsthistorisches Museum. Although the museum could benefit from more hands-on exhibits, it has a substantial collection of dinosaur skeletons and meteorites plus giant South American beetles. Two of its star attractions are man-made: a spectacular floral bouquet comprised of gemstones and a copy of the fascinating Stone-Age beauty *Venus of Willendorf* (the original is locked in a vault). Open W 9am-9pm, Th-M 9am-6:30pm, admission until 5:30pm; in winter, 1st floor only 9am-3pm. 30AS, students 15AS.

ENTERTAINMENT

TO EVERYTHING THERE IS A SEASON. Beware that Vienna's biggest cultural draws, the **Staatsoper** (State Opera), the **Wiener Philharmoniker** (Vienna Philharmonic), the **Wiener Sängerknaben** (Vienna Boys' Choir), and the **Lipizzaner Stallions** have no performances in Vienna during July and August.

While Vienna offers all the standard entertainments in the way of theater, film, and festivals, the heart of the city beats to music. All but a few of classical music's marquee names lived, composed, and performed in Vienna. Mozart, Beethoven, and Haydn wrote their greatest masterpieces in Vienna, creating the **First Viennese School;** a century later, Schönberg, Webern, and Berg teamed up to form the **Second Viennese School.** Every Austrian child must learn to play an instrument during schooling, and the Vienna **Konservatorium** and **Hochschule** are world-renowned conservatories. All year, Vienna has performances ranging from the above-average to the sublime, with many accessible to the budget traveler.

OPERA

Staatsoper, Opernring 2, is Vienna's premier opera (See Masters of the House, p. 127), performing about 300 times a year, nearly every night from Sept. to June. There are three ways to get tickets:

Standing-room tickets: The cheapest way to enjoy the opera. 500 are available for every performance, though they are limited to 1 per person and can be bought only right before the perfomance. The tickets are not half bad but your feet can get a bit sore after 4 hours of Wagner. While the box office opens 1hr. before the curtain, those with the desire (and the stamina) should start lining up at least 1½ hr. before curtain (2-3hr. in tourist season and for more popular productions) in order to get orchestra tickets—the side views from the balconies are limited. The earlier you get there, the better your view will be. The standing line forms inside the side door on the western side of the Opera (by Operng.). Once you get your precious ticket, hurry to secure yourself a space on the rail and tie a scarf around it to reserve your spot. Balcony 30AS, orchestra 50AS. Formal dress not necessary, but no shorts.

Box office tickets in advance: The more secure ticket option—also easier on the feet–is to purchase tickets through the official ticket offices, which are reachable by fax, phone, or in person, and charge no fees above the ticket price. The main ticket office is the Bundestheaterkasse, I, Hanuschgasse 3, around the corner from the opera. (☎513 1313; fax 514 4429 69; Open M-F 8am-6pm, Sa-Su 9am-noon.) There is also a ticket office inside the Staatsoper, open during the same hours, which, in addition to tickets, offers tours of the building year round. Seats range from 120 to 2,150AS, depending on location.

MASTERS OF THE HOUSE "Too many notes, dear Mozart," observed Josef II after the premiere of *Die Entführung aus dem Serail (The Abduction from the Seraglio)*. "Only as many as are necessary, Your Majesty," was the genius's reply. The Hapsburgs may be forgiven this critical slip, for they have provided invaluable support of opera. The Hapsburg emperors gave Austria an operatic tradition to rival Italy's by commissioning such masterpieces as Mozart's *Le nozze di Figaro*. Emperor Franz Josef commissioned the **Hofoper** (Court Opera House), today's **Staatsoper** (State Opera House), the first edifice built on the Ringstraße. The design of the building was criticized by many Viennese, causing one architect to commit suicide and the other to have a heart attack before the curtain went up for the first performance (Mozart's *Don Giovanni*) in 1869. Gustav Mahler became Director of the Opera in 1897, and in 1919, composer Richard Strauss and director Franz Schalk took control. Much of the old opera house was destroyed during a bombing in 1945, but it was the first public building to be reconstructed, before even St. Stephen's cathedral. It reopened on November 5, 1955, with a production of Beethoven's *Fidelio*. The Staatsoper remains one of the five great opera houses of the world.

Tickets by the Internet: The main ticket office, the Bundestheaterkasse, also maintains a multi-lingual website (www.bundestheater.at) that allows you to purchase tickets in advance, see the seating plan, and check out the season schedule. It's better used as a source of information than as a means of buying your tickets, however, because they charge a hefty commission (20% of your ticket price).

Volksoper, IX, Währingerstr. 78, specializes (but not exclusively) in lighter comedic opera, operettas, and occasional musicals in their own beautiful venue. Box office tickets are available through Bundestheaterkasse and its website (see Staatsoper, above).

Wiener Kammeroper (Chamber Opera; ☎513 0100), offers performances of Mozart's operas in an open-air theater in the Schönbrunner Schloßpark during the summer as part of the **Klangbogen** festival (☎42717). Pick up a brochure at the tourist office.

ORCHESTRAS

Wiener Philharmoniker (Vienna Philharmonic Orchestra) plays in the **Musikverein;** Austria's–perhaps the world's–premier concert hall. Constructed in 1867, the building is a concert hall of unparalleled acoustic perfection. The *Musikverein's* program is essentially conservative, although it occasionally includes contemporary classical music. Musikverein, I, Bösendorferstr. 12 is on the northeast side of Karlsplatz. Tickets to Philharmoniker concerts are mostly on a subscription basis and tend to sell out well in advance, but there are three ways to get them, and it's worth the trouble:

Musikverein box office tickets in advance: You can contact the box office of the Musikverein in person or by letter. **Standing room tickets** are available from the Musikverein, but even they must be bought in advance just as a seat. Open Sept.-June M-F 9am-7:30pm, Sa 9am-5pm. Write Gesellschaft der Musikfreunde, Bösendorferstr. 12, A-1010 Wien for more information.

Bundestheaterkasse tickets in advance: As with the Staatsoper, tickets to the Philharmoniker are offered through the Bundestheaterkasse (see Staatsoper, above, for hours and information).

Tickets by the Internet: The Philharmoniker maintains its own website (www.wienerphilharmoniker.at) which provides a full schedule, and sells tickets not only to the subscription performances at the Musikverein, but also provides links to sites selling tickets to its performances on tour and at festivals throughout the country. Budget travelers beware of Internet commissions!

Wiener Symphoniker (Vienna Symphony Orchestra), Vienna's second fiddle, is frequently on tour but plays some concerts at the grand, late-19th-century Konzerthaus, III, Lothringerstr. 20, just around the corner and across the river Wien from the Musikverein. They focus on 20th-century classical music, including some ultra-modern, experimental works. The season runs from Sept.-June. Get tickets and

PREPUBESCENT PRODIGIES The 500-year-old Wiener Sängerknaben (Vienna Boys' Choir) functions as Austria's "ambassador of song" on their extensive international tours. Dressed in sailor suits, they export great works of music to the entire world. Emperor Maximilian I founded the group in 1498, and Franz Schubert was a chorister, and Anton Bruckner held the post of organist and music teacher. Today, the choir provides a forum where Mozart, Hadyn, Schubert, and Bruckner, not to mention Beethoven's gorgeous Mass in C Op 86, can be heard as they were originally meant to be performed–sung by the clear sweet voices of a boys' choir.

information from the Konzerthaus box office. (☎712 1211; fax 712 2872; ticket@konzerthaus.at; www.konzerthaus.at. Open M-F 9am-7:45pm, Sa 9am-1pm; June 20-Sept. 30 9am-1pm.)

CHORAL MUSIC

Wiener Sängerknaben (Viennese Boys' Choir) main showcase is mass every Sunday at 9:15am (mid-Sept. to June only) in the **Burgkapelle** (Royal Chapel) of the Hofburg (U3 "Herrengasse"). There are three ways to get tickets to these masses:

Reserve tickets (70-380AS) at least 2 months in advance; write to Hofmusikkapelle, Hofburg, A-1010 Wien, but do not enclose money. You will be sent a slip and you can pick up tickets at the Burgkapelle on the Friday before mass from 11am-noon or on the Sunday of the mass by 9am.

Unreserved seats are sold in small quantity the Friday before mass from 4-6pm (get in line a half hr. to hr. early), maximum 2 per person.

Standing room is free, despite rumors to the contrary, but you have to arrive before 8am to have a chance.

The lads also perform every Friday at 3:30pm at the **Konzerthaus** (see Wiener Symphoniker, above) during May, June, September, and October. For tickets (390-430AS), contact *Reisebüro Mondial*, Faulmanng. 4, A-1040 Wien (☎588 0414 1; fax 587 1268; ticket@mondial.at).

Sunday High Masses also occur in the major churches of the city (Augustinerkirche, Michaelerkirche, Stephansdom) and, while they don't include the Boys' Choir, they are glorious–and free–musical experiences. They are also, of course, worship services, so respect of the worshippers is required (beginning at 10 or 11am, all year round).

Wiener Singakademie bills itself as the oldest concert choir in Europe. Brahms was their director for the 1863-1864 season, and they have worked with some of the greatest conductors of choral music, including Mahler, Strauss, Solti, Furtwängler, and Gardiner. They perform in the Konzerthaus. See Wiener Symphoniker, above, for ticket info.

THEATER

In the past few years, Vienna has made a name for itself as a city of musicals, with productions of such Broadway and West End favorites as *Les Misérables*, or the long-running home-grown favorite *Elisabeth*, a creative interpretation of the late empress's life. Take U1, U2, or U4 to "Karlspl." and just off the Ring you'll find the **Theater an der Wien,** VI, Linke Wienzeile 6, Vienna's top venue for musicals, which once produced musicals of a different sort, hosting in its 18th-century edifice the premieres of Beethoven's *Fidelio* and Mozart's *Die Zauberflöte* (The Magic Flute). The nearby **Raimund Theater** also shows popular musicals. Tickets for either venue can be bought at the box offices for each theater, or over the phone. (☎588 3031 3. Box office open 10am-1pm, 2-6pm. Tickets 310-1200AS.)

Vienna's English Theatre, VIII, Josefsg. 12 (☎402 1260 0), presents English-language drama. (Box office open M-F 10am-5pm. Tickets 190-490AS, student rush 100AS.) The **International Theater,** IX, Porzellang. 8 (☎319 6272; tickets 250-350AS, under 26 140AS), is another English-language venue. **WUK,** IX, Währingerstr. 59 (☎401 2110), is a workshop and cultural center that puts on dance, concerts, and readings. The most respected German language theaters are the **Burgtheater,** and **Akademietheater.** You can buy tickets for both at the **Bundestheaterkasse** (see Opera, above).

FILMS

Films in English usually play at **Burgkino,** I, Opernring 19 (☎587 8406; last show usually around 8:30pm, Sa around 11pm; also shows *The Third Man* every other weekend), **Top Kino,** VI, Rahlgassel 1 (☎587 5557; open 3pm-10:30pm), at the intersection of Gumpendorferstr.; and **Haydnkino** (☎587 2262; last show usually around 9:30pm), on Mariahilferstr. 57 near the U3 stop "Neubaug." More and more theaters show movies in English or with subtitles—in the newspaper films listed as 'OF' after the title are shown in the original language, films listed as O.m.U. are shown in the original language with subtitles. **Votivkino,** Währingerstr. 12 (☎317 3571), near Bergg. and Schottentor, is an art-house popular with the university crowd and shows all films with German subtitles. **Artis Kino, Filmcasino,** and **Stadtkino** also show subtitled art and foreign films. **Künstlerhauskino,** I, Karlspl. 5 (☎505 4328), hosts art house film festivals. Prices for shows range from 70-120AS; be warned—you pay for the row you sit in. On Monday, all seats are discounted to 70AS. In summer, there are several **open-air cinemas** in the *Augarten* park (all shows at 9:30pm; 90AS). From Schottenring, take tram #31 to "Gaußpl." Ask at the tourist office for details on occasional free movies in the *Volksgarten.* While Vienna hosts a full-sized film festival in August (see Festivals, p. 129), the rest of the year the Austrian **Filmmuseum,** Augustinerstr. 1 (☎533 7054 0), shows a rotating program of classic and avant-garde films.

VIENNA

FESTIVALS

Vienna hosts an array of important annual festivals, mostly musical. The **Vienna Festival** (mid-May to mid-June) has a diverse program of exhibitions, plays, and concerts. (☎589 2222; fax 589 2249; kartenbuer@festwochen.at; www.festwochen.or.at.) Of particular interest are the celebrated orchestras and conductors joining the party. The Staatsoper and Volkstheater host the annual **Jazzfest Wien** during the first weeks of July, featuring many famous acts. For information, contact Jazzfest Wien (☎503 5647; www.jazzfestwien.at). While other big guns take summer siesta, Vienna has held the **Klangbogen** (☎42717) every summer since 1952, featuring excellent concerts across Vienna, including **Wiener Kammeroper** (Chamber Opera; ☎513 0100), performances of Mozart's operas in an open-air theater in the Schönbrunner Schloßpark. Pick up a brochure at the tourist office. From the end of July to the beginning of August, the **Im-Puls Dance Festival** (☎523 55 58; www.impuls-tanz.wien.at) attracts some of the world's great dance troupes and offers seminars to enthusiasts. Some of Vienna's best parties are thrown by the parties (political, that is). The Social Democrats host a late-June **Danube Island Festival,** which draws millions of party goers annually, while the Communist Party holds a **Volkstimme Festival** in mid-August. Both cater to impressionable youngsters with free rock, jazz, and folk concerts. In mid-October, the annual city-wide film festival, the **Viennale,** kicks off. In past years, the program has featured over 150 movies from 25 countries. One final free treat not to be missed is the **Rathausplatz Music Film Festival** in July and August, in the Rathausplatz at dusk. Filmed operas, ballets, operettas, and concerts enrapture the audience.

WINTER FESTIVITIES

The Viennese don't let long winter nights go to waste. Christmas festivities begin in December with **Krampus** parties. *Krampus* (Black Peter) is a hairy devil that accompanies St. Nicholas on his rounds and gives bad children coal and sticks. On December 5th, people in *Krampus* suits lurk everywhere, rattling their chains and chasing passersby, while small children nibble marzipan *Krampus* effigies.

As the weather gets sharper, huts of professional *Maroni-* (chestnut) roasters and *Bratkartoffeln-* (potato pancake) toasters pop up everywhere. Cider, punch, red noses, and *Glühwein* (a hot, spicy mulled wine) become ubiquitous on sidewalks. **Christmas markets** *(Christkindlmärkte)* open around the city. The somewhat tacky **Rathausplatz Christkindlmarkt** is probably the best known of the yule marketplaces, offering, among other things, excellent *Lebkuchen* (a spicy, very strong gingerbread-like cake), *Langos* (a Hungarian round bread soaked in hot oil, garlic, and onions), and beeswax candles (open 9am-9pm). **Schloß Schönbrunn's** *Weihnachtsmarkt* offers old-fashioned Christmas decorations (open M-F noon-8pm, Sa-Su 10am-8pm). Visit the happy **Spittelberg** market, where artists and university kids hawk offbeat creations (open M-F 2-8pm, Sa-Su and holidays 10am-8pm). The **Trachtenmarkt** shop in Schotteng. near Schottentor offers atmospheric Christmas shopping. Most theaters, opera houses, and concert halls have Christmas programs (see Opera, p. 128 or Theater and Cinema, p. 128). The city also turns the Rathausplatz into an enormous outdoor skating rink in Jan. and Feb.

The climax of the New Year's season is the **Neujahrskonzert** (New Year's concert) by the Viennese Philharmonic, broadcast worldwide. The refrain of the *Radetzkymarsch* by Strauss signals that the new year has truly begun. New Year's also brings a famously flashy **Imperial Ball** in the Hofburg. For those lacking 7-digit incomes, the City of Vienna organizes a huge chain of *Silvester* (New Year's) parties in the Inner City. Follow the **Silvesterpfad,** marked by lights hung over the street, for outdoor karaoke, street waltzing, firecrackers, and hundreds of people drinking champagne in the streets. At midnight, the giant bell of St. Stephen's rings across the country, broadcast by public radio stations.

New Year's is barely over before **Fasching** (Carnival season) arrives in February and spins the city into a bubbly daze of bedlam. These are the weeks of the Viennese waltzing balls. The most famous is the **Wiener Opernball** (Viennese Opera Ball), which draws the world's Princess Stephanies and Donald Trumps, and takes place on a Thursday evening in the beginning of February. Tickets must be reserved years in advance. You don't have to sit out if you can't make the *Opernball*—there's something for everyone. Even the kindergartners in public preschools have *Fasching Krapfen* parties, and McDonald's puts up carnival crepe banners. For a free *Fasching* celebration, join the **carnival parade** that winds its way around the Ring, stopping traffic the day before Lent.

NIGHTLIFE

With one of the highest bar-to-cobblestone ratios in the world, Vienna is a great place to party, whether you're looking for a quiet evening with a glass of wine or a wild night in a disco full of black-clad Euro muscle men and drag queens. The *Heurigen* on the outskirts of Vienna provide a culturally immersive way to spend an evening (see p. 103), but if you're looking for a more urban type of night-wandering, head downtown. Take the subway (U1 or U4) to "Schwedenplatz," which will drop you within blocks of the **Bermuda Dreiecke** (Triangle), so called both for the 3 block triangle it covers and for the tipsy revelers who never make it home. The area is packed with lively, crowded clubs. If your vision isn't foggy yet, head down **Rotenturmstrasse** towards St. Stephen's cathedral or walk around the areas bounded by the Jewish synagogue and Ruprechtskirche. Another good zone to search for nightlife in the inner city is the smooth, dark **Bäckerstraße** and its cellar bars. Slightly outside the Ring, the streets off Burgg. and Stiftg. in the 7th district and the university quarter (8th and 9th districts) have tables in outdoor courtyards and loud, hip bars. They can be a good place to seek refuge when the summer crowd in the Bermuda Triangle feels too pubescent or touristy.

Vienna's kinetic club scene rages every night of the week, later than most bars. DJs spin wax until 4 or even 6am, and some clubs will keep it going after hours until 11am the next morning. One fact of Viennese nightlife: it starts late. If you arrive at some place at 11pm, it will be a scene from a high school dance, full of adolescents toting cell phones and smoking cigarettes. As usual, the best nights are Friday and Saturday, beginning around 1am or so. Cover charges are reasonable, and the theme nights are varied and frenetic enough to please anyone. While techno still rears its digitalized head, house, jungle, and trip-hop have a strong following as well. For the scoop on raves, concerts, and parties, grab the fliers at swank cafes like MAK or Berg das Café, or pick up a copy of the indispensable **Falter** (28AS)—besides some excellent articles in German, it prints listings of everything from opera and theater to punk concerts and updates on the gay/lesbian scene, and will list places that have sprung up too recently for *Let's Go* to review. (Vienna's club turnover is too rapid to keep up with in a guide updated only once a year.) Also, be sure to grab a schedule for the **Nightbus** system, which runs across Vienna all night after the regular public transportation shuts down at midnight (look for a Nightbus marker at your daytime stop to see if it stops there).

BARS

The term "bar" has a loose definition in Vienna. Many restaurants (see **Restaurants,** p. 97) live a Dr. Jekyll-Mr. Hyde dual existence as a place both to eat and to party.

INSIDE THE RING

Cato, I, Tiefer Graben 19 (☎533 4790). Take U3 to "Herreng.," walk down to Strauchg., turn right, and continue on to Tiefer Graben; this tiny place will be on your left. This laid-back bar is super comfortable and you'll be singing songs with the friendly clientele before the end of the evening. Enjoy the music, art-deco decor, and delicious champagne cocktails. Open Su-Th 6pm-2am, F-Sa 6pm-4am.

Santo Spirito, I, Kumpfg. 7 (☎512 9998). From Stephanspl., walk down Singerstr. and turn left onto Kampfg. (5min.). The stereo pumps out Rachmaninoff's second piano concerto while excited patrons co-conduct. Busts on the wall pay homage to famous baton-wavers. Owner vacations in July, otherwise open from 6pm until people leave.

Blue Box, VII Richterg. 8 (☎523 2682). Take U3 to "Neubaug.," turn onto Neubaug., and take your 1st right onto Richterg. Clouds of smoke, blue leather couches, and a deafening bass beat define this popular bar. Party all night and then come back for an excellent breakfast served late, very late (until 5pm). M 6pm-2am, Tu-Th, Su 10am-2am, Fr-Sa 10am-4am.

Club Berlin, I, Gonzag. 12 (☎533 0479). Go downstairs in this house of swank to see Vienna's bold and beautiful wind their way around the partitions in this former wine cellar with great music. Open Su-Tu 6pm-2am, F-Sa 6pm-4am.

Centro, I, Bäckerstr. 1. Behind the Stephansdom, turn right off Rotenturmstr. onto Lugeck, which leads to Bäckerstr. Come and chill among colorful posters in this mellow joint. Open M-Su 11am-4am.

Jazzland, I, Franz-Josefs-Kai 29 (☎533 2575). Near U1/U4 "Schwedenpl." Excellent live jazz of all styles and regions filters through the soothing brick environs for a slightly older clientele. 50AS cover. Open Tu-Sa 7pm-2am. Music 9pm-1am.

Benjamin, I, Salzgries 11-13 (☎533 3349). Just outside of the Triangle area. Go down the steps from *Ruprechtskirche,* left onto Josefs Kai, and left again on Salzgries. Dark and rickety, this is a punk-rocker's heaven. Candles tilt in wax-covered wine bottles while a hard-core but nice student crowd parties on. Great beer–*Budvar* (37AS) and *Kapsreiter* (43AS). Open Su-Th 7pm-2am, F-Sa 7pm-4am.

Café MAK, I, Stubenring 3-5 (☎714 0121), inside the Museum für Angewandte Kunst (see p. 102). This bright cafe is a happening, rowdy bar by night with techno-rave parties on Sa in July. Open Tu-Su 10am-2am.

Zwölf Apostellenkeller, I, Sonnenfelsg. 3 (☎512 6777), behind the Stephansdom. To reach this underground tavern, walk into the archway, take a right, go down the long staircase, and discover grottoes that date back to 1561. One of the best *Weinkeller* (wine cellars) in Vienna and a definite must for catacomb fans. Beer 37AS. *Viertel* of wine from 25AS. Open Aug.-June 4:30pm-midnight.

Esterházykeller, I, Haarhof 1 (☎533 3482), off Naglerg. One of Vienna's least expensive *Weinkeller.* Relaxed cellar bar, popular with local 20- and 30-somethings. Try the *Grüner Veltliner* wine (26AS). Open in summer M-F 11am-11pm; in winter also Sa-Su 4-11pm.

Kaktus, I, Seitenstetteng. 5 (☎533 1938), in the heart of the Triangle. Packed with the bombed and the beautiful. Open Su-Th 6pm-2am, F-Sa 6pm-4am.

OUTSIDE THE RING

Alsergrunder Kulturpark, IX, Alserstr. 4 (☎407 8214). On the old grounds of a turn-of-the-18th-century hospital, Kulturpark is not one bar but many. A young Viennese crowd flocks to the beautifully landscaped grounds for the beer garden, *Heurigen,* champagne bar–the list goes on. All sorts of people and all sorts of nightlife–just about anything you might want for a happening night out. Open Apr.-Oct. daily 4pm-2am.

Chelsea, VIII, (☎407 9309), Lerchenfeldergürtel under the U-Bahn between Thaliastr. and Josefstädterstr. The best place in Vienna for underground music: live bands from across Europe play here (except in summer). Cover 60-200AS. Open daily 7pm-4am.

Objektiv, VII, Kirchbergg. 26 (☎522 7042). Take U2 or U3 to "Volkstheater," walk down Burgg. 2 blocks, and turn right on Kirchbergg. to find one of the most eclectic bars in Vienna, with old stoves and sewing machines as tables and cowboy boots as decorations. A mellow atmosphere, lively local crowd, and cheap drinks top things off. Happy Hour daily 11pm-1am. Open M-Sa 6pm-2am, Su 6pm-1am.

Kunsthalle Café, IV, Treitlstr. 2 (☎586 9864). Inside the bright yellow contemporary art museum, as well as outside on its large rocky terrace, this chill cafe-by-day is filled nightly with students and the bright sounds of funk/jazz/blues. A great place for a chat on a warm summer night. Open 10am-2am or whenever the last person leaves.

Europa, VII, Zollerg. 8 (☎526 3383). Buy a drink and strike a pose. Surrounded by concert posters and funky light fixtures, the hip 20-something crowd hangs out late, especially after a late night's clubbing. Open daily 9am-5am.

Miles Smiles, VIII, Langeg. 51 (☎405 9517). Take U2 to "Lerchenfelderstr." Head down Lerchenfelderstr. and take the 1st right. This place has a cool, if somewhat touristy, atmosphere. The music is post-1955 jazz. Open Su-Th 8pm-2am, F-Sa 8pm-4am.

Eagle Bar, VI, Blümelg. 1 (☎587 2661). Come to scope the scene and be scoped by it at this bar for gay men only. The diverse, young clientele is derived from the leather and/or denim set. Open 9pm-4am.

Das Möbel, VII, Burgg. 10 (☎524 9497). This high-ceilinged cafe also functions as a showcase for furniture designers. At night, the metal couches, car seat chairs, Swiss-army-tables, and other pieces –which rotate every 6 weeks if not bought–are in full use by a hip crowd. **Internet access** 20AS for 30min. Open daily noon-1am, Sa-Su breakfast buffet 10am-4pm.

Flieger, IV, Schleifmühlg. 19 (☎586 7309). One of Vienna's 1st New Wave bars, Flieger's alternative scene is crowded and lively. The Katu drink (33AS), made with cactus juice, is rumored to be "mind-moving." Open M-Th 6pm-2am, F-Su 6pm-4am.

Nightshift, VI, Corneliusg. 8 (☎586 2337). This hard-core joint caters to gay men only, preferably in black leather. This is not a place for the faint of heart (or the straight), as lots of bare chests cruise by. Su-Th 10pm-4am, F-Sa 10pm-5am.

DISCOS AND DANCE CLUBS

U-4, XII, Schönbrunnerstr. 222 (☎815 8307) Take U4 to "Meidling Hauptstr." Packed with all types, this place keeps the music fresh and the party going. U-4 has all the trappings, including 2 dance areas, multiple bars, and rotating theme nights to please a varied clientele. Th Gay Heaven Night. Cover 100AS. Open daily 11pm-5am.

Volksgarten Disco, I, Burgring I (☎533 0518). Take U2 or U3 to Volkstheater. A mix of hip-hop, soul, funk, and house keep this party going all night and into the garden, as it gets packed with local revelers and international party-seekers. Cover 80-180AS. Open Th-Su 10pm-5am.

Flex Halle, I, Donaulände/Augartenbrücke (☎533 7525), near the Schottenring U-Bahn station, seems more dangerous than it actually is. Head towards the river and down a narrow staircase. This small, dark, on-the-water club with neon lights and a slummy feel has live bands and chemically-enhanced excitement. Good dancing. Free **Internet access.** Cover 70-150AS. Open 8pm-4am.

Club Meierei, III, Stadtpark (☎710 8400). Take U4 Stadtpark, "Heumarkt" entrance. Located in the Stadtpark with no neighbors and thus more freedom to party loudly. One of Vienna's hottest clubs—and if it gets too hot you could always step out into the park for some fresh air. Cover 80-100AS. Open W, F and Su 10pm to whenever.

THE REGENBOGENPARADE At the end of June or beginning of July every year, Austrians gather for an afternoon and evening of gay pride in Vienna at the Rainbow Parade, which consists of over 40 floats sponsored by social, political, and commercial organizations from around Austria, as well as the Czech Republic and Slovakia. Everyone from Dykes on Bikes and the Rosa Lila Villa to Jewish Homosexuals and AIDS awareness organizations takes part. The effervescent parade parties its way along the Ringstraße down to Karlspl., where the public celebration concluded—to be continued privately in bars the rest of the night. The Viennese gay community also hosts the annual "Life Ball," the only charity event held in Vienna's *Rathaus,* which raises money for people with AIDS and HIV.

Why Not, I, Tiefer Graben 22 (☎535 1158). The neon interior of this relaxed gay and lesbian bar/disco holds both a chill chatting venue and a hip-hop-happening subterranean black-box dance floor. Saturday is the night to be here, with drink specials for 43AS. Cover 100AS. Open F-Sa 10pm-4am, Su 9pm-2am. Women-only 1 Th per month.

VIENNA

DAYTRIPS FROM VIENNA

STIFT KLOSTERNEUBURG

Easily accessible via bus or S-bahn 40 from Heiligenstadt (15min., every 30min., 19AS), or a 1½hr. walk from Leopoldsberg (see p. 123).

Founded by the Babenberg Leopold III in 1114, the **Chorherrenstift (monastery)** put the small town of Klosterneuburg on the map as the center of medieval Austrian art and culture. In 1133, Leopold elevated the institute to its present monastic status as **Stift Klosterneuburg,** becoming one of the most powerful monasteries in the country. Its origin is more romantic than political. According to legend, Leopold and his wife Agnes were admiring the landscape, when a gust of wind carried away Agnes's veil. Leopold pledged to build a monastery where the veil was found. In 1730, Emperor Karl IV, Maria Theresia's father, moved into Klosterneuburg and began expanding the complex with a **palace** intended to match the grand scale of the monastery and thus symbolize the importance of the *Kaiserreich* (Emperor's kingdom) to the *Gottesreich* (God's kingdom). Only two of the nine projected domes were completed, but it's still damn impressive. Today, the monastery-cum-palace is still functional, but most parts are open to the public. The ornate church contains the renowned Late-Romanesque Verduner Altar, with its elaborate wood and gold detail. (Stiftsplatz 1. Open year-round M-Su 9am-5pm.) To quench your thirst for knowledge, visit the **museum** (open May-Nov. Tu-Su 10am-5pm). Call ahead for a guided tour of the complex. (☎(02243) 411212. Tours every 30min. 9am-noon and 1:30. 60AS, students 30AS.)

MÖDLING AND HEILIGENKREUZ

Trains and S-bahn #1 and 2 make the short journey from Vienna Südbahnhof to Mödling all day long (20min., 38AS; Eurail valid). Buses leave every hour from Südtiroler-Pl. in Vienna. In Mödling, bus #365 connects to Heiligenkreuz (dir.: Hinterbrühl; every 2hr., 19AS).

"Poor I am, and miserable," Beethoven wrote before his arrival in **Mödling.** Seeking physical and psychological rehabilitation, he schlepped all the way to this tranquil "cradle of ideas." He finished *Missa Solemnis* within Mödling's embrace, and his spirits thoroughly improved. A recovering victim of industrialization, Mödling is slowly but surely regaining the charm that drew the likes of Schubert, Wagner, Strauss, Schönberg, and Klimt here. From the train station, turn right up the small hill and left down Hauptstr., which provides delightful meandering, cafes, and shops. Head to Mödling's **tourist office**, Elisabethstr. 2, next to the *Rathaus*, for the lowdown on the city and *Privatzimmer*. (☎(02236) 26727. Open M-F 9am-6pm, Sa 10am-2pm.) When you're through wandering, pick up some picnic supplies and catch a bus into the countryside near Heiligenkreuz.

Heiligenkreuz itself is a both a peaceful village and a harmonious Cistercian monastery that seems to have grown whole from the grassy hills in this remote corner of the Austrian countryside. The bus stops twice in Heiligenkreuz; get off at the second stop to visit the 700-year-old monastic retreat that bears the same name as the village. Founded by Leopold V, notorious for holding Richard the Lionheart for ransom, the monastery was originally intended as a "school of love" and a reformation of the pre-existing Benedictine order. Life at Heiligenkreuz has never been particularly austere, however—visit the *Weinkeller* where the monks still press their own grapes, enjoy beer and bratwurst in the shade of the *Stiftsgasthaus Heiligenkreuz*, or simply stand in the Zen-like quiet of the monastery's blooming central courtyard to experience the serene continuity of centuries. The vaulted chapel houses magnificent stained-glass windows, still intact despite threats of yore from stern church elders that they would put the abbot on a fast of bread and water until they were removed. Visitors can enter the abbey itself only by taking a tour. (Tours M-Sa 10, 11am, 2, 3, and 4pm, Su 11am. 65AS, senior citizens 55AS, students 30AS, children 25AS.)

CARNUNTUM

Carnuntum is accessible by S-bahn S7 from Wien Mitte or Wien Nord (1hr., every 30min., 76AS). The park is a well-marked 10-minute walk from the station. You'll pass a little tourist office booth on the way to the park on Hauptstr. By car from Vienna, take highway A4, exit at Fischamend, and follow road B9 to Petronell-Carnuntum.

By 15 BC, the Romans had conquered the Alps, Dolomites, and Danube river valleys, using the river route to transport soldiers, slaves, and goods through the empire. Of their many outposts, which included Vindobona (Vienna), Iuavum (Salzburg), and Brigantium (Bregenz), Carnuntum was by far the largest and most impressive until conquered by the Germanic Alemanni tribe in the AD 3rd century. Archaeological digs have uncovered houses, public baths, canals, and a temple to the goddess Diana all dating from the first to 3rd centuries. Today, the site is a work-in-progress to discover and preserve that history. Most artifacts are on display in the **Archäologischer Park Carnuntum,** where you can sign up to tour the place or to take part in the digging. (Hauptstr. 465. ☎(02163) 33770; fax 33775; info@carnuntum.co.at; www.carnuntum.co.at. Open Apr.-Nov. M-F 9am-5pm, Sa-Su 9am-6pm. 48AS, students 38AS; guided tours 38AS.)

Twenty kilometers of bike paths lead from the train station through the Heidentor ruins (from 300 BC), an amphitheater, an ancient military camp, and (in nearby Bad Deutsch-Altenburg) the **Archäologisches Museum Carnuntum,** the largest Roman museum in Austria. (Open Jan. 15-Dec. 15 Tu-Su 10am-5pm. 60AS, students 40AS; guided tours 35AS. Combo museum/park ticket 85AS, students 60AS.) Carnuntum hosts annual Roman festivals including the **Roman Athletic Competition** in April, the **Art Carnuntum** fest from July to August with open-air cinema, theater, and concerts (☎(02163) 3400 for information; pb@artcarnuntum.co.at), and a **Roman Christmas market** in December.

STIFT ALTENBURG

Stift Altenburg can be reached by bus from Wien-Mitte directly (7am) or with a change in Horn (5 per day, 160AS). A pleasant option in good weather is to walk along the picturesque 6km path from Horn to the Stift (follow green signs).

The Benedictine abbey **Stift Altenburg**, founded in 1144 by Countess Hildburg von Poigen-Rebgau in memory of her deceased husband, swells with Baroque paintings and sculpture. The abbey was frequently attacked by Hussites and Swedes during the Thirty Years' War, and most of what is visible now dates from after the sacking of the monastery by Swedish soldiers in 1645. Altenburg was subsequently rebuilt under the architect and pupil of Prandtauer, Joseph Munggenast, who replaced most of the Gothic cloister, although remnants of it have been excavated and are visible today. Stift Altenburg is famous not only for its magnificent church buildings, but also for the **library** housed within the abbey, conceived in the Baroque mind as a temple to human wisdom, in playful contrast to the neighboring temple to divine wisdom. Much of the art in the church and library, as well as the ceremonial staircase and intriguing **crypt,** was done by Paul Troger. His sculptures, paintings, and frescoes depict Biblical scenes along with benevolent mythological divinities, and a few jolly skeletons. The abbey underwent extensive restoration after being badly damaged in both world wars. It hosts annual art exhibits and summer concerts given by the **Stift Altenburger Music Akademie.** (Open May-Nov. Tu-Su 9am-noon and 1-5pm. To see the crypt and library, you must take a guided tour 11am, 2, and 4pm. 60AS, students 30AS. Guided tours of the art exhibit 9:30am, 1, and 3pm. 80AS, students 40AS. Combination ticket for both tours 130AS, students 65AS. For more info contact the Stift (☎(02982) 345 121; fax 34 5113; stift.altenburg@wvnet.at). For concert tickets, call (02982) 53080, in winter (011) 586 19 00.)

FARTHER AFIELD

The following cities are a bit farther afield and offer more than the average tourist can take in during a single day, but, if your time and/or money are short, it may make sense for you to tackle them using Vienna as a base. Travel times listed below are for train travel.

EISENSTADT, BURGENLAND

Fans of Haydn and the powerful Eszterházy princes won't want to miss this pleasantly provincial capital of Burgenland, with palaces, concerts, and composer memorabilia on offer (1hr., p. 136).

BADEN BEI WEIN, NIEDERÖSTERREICH

Just beyond the Wienerwald, this perennial spa town has been pampering the rich and famous since Caesar Augustus with its sulfur baths, casino, and rosarium (1hr., p. 283).

MELK, NIEDERÖSTERREICH

Jutting from the steep green hills along the Danube, the Benedictine monastery of Melk is a must-see, not only for its architecture, but also for its thoughtfully curated art exhibits that juxtapose the modern and the medieval—and the views of the town below are just as aesthetically pleasing (1½hr., p. 279).

KREMS/STEIN, NIEDERÖSTERREICH

Neighbors Krems and Stein, also along the Danube, have been politically affiliated for decades, but each retains its own personality: Krems captivates with its pastel Baroque splendor, while Stein charms with its twisting medieval byways—and both are wrapped in vineyard-covered hills that offer wine-tasting cellars with breath-taking views (1hr. by train, but consider taking the DDSG ferry, p. 274).

SALZBURG, SALZBURGERLAND

This heavily touristed powerhouse of sights isn't really a day trip, but if you can't spare the cash or time to stay in town, and have an extra day on your rail pass, before you skip Salzburg altogether consider spending a few hours enjoying Mozart, medieval streets, baroque majesty, and, of course, *The Sound of Music,* on a marathon trip from Vienna (3½hr., p. 215).

BURGENLAND

Just southeast of Vienna is Burgenland, Austria's most scarcely populated province (pop. 70,000) and one of Austria's last territorial acquisitions. Until Burgenland was ceded to Austria in 1921, it was part of Hungary; in fact, it owes its name to three castles that now lie beyond its borders in Hungary. Given its history, it is not surprising that Burgenland has a Hungarian-influenced cuisine and pockets of Hungarian speakers in the more rural parts of the province. Geographically, Burgenland is diverse, with rolling hills and dense woodlands in the west, the Neusiedlersee in the north-east, and the peaks of the Rosaliengebirge on the present Hungarian border. Burgenland's gentle hills and lush river valleys give it the rich wines and *Heurigen* (cozy, vine-hung taverns) that make it world-famous. Because of the seasonal nature of many of Burgenland's delights, it's best to coordinate your visit with one of many festivals that liven up the sleepy towns.

HIGHLIGHTS OF BURGENLAND

Walk in Haydn's footsteps through the sumptuous apartments of the Hungarian Eszterházy family in **Eisenstadt** (see p. 136).

Sample rich new wines in the vineyards of **Rust** (see p. 141).

Take a dip in the *Neusiedlersee*, then watch a floating opera in **Mörbisch** (see p. 143).

EISENSTADT ☎02682

Where I wish to live and die.
—Josef Haydn

Haydn, *Heurigen*, and Huns are the three cultural pillars of Burgenland's tiny provincial capital (pop. 11,000). As court composer for the **Eszterházy** princes, **Josef Haydn** composed some of his greatest melodies here. The town is still basking in his glory. The Eszterházy princes, powerful Hungarian landholders claiming descent from Attila the Hun, are to this day one of the wealthiest families in Europe. The Eszterházys first settled in Eisenstadt when it was part of Hungary and decided to remain there after the change in borders. Today they own many of the region's famed vineyards, whose new wines rival those produced in Bordeaux.

GETTING THERE AND GETTING AROUND

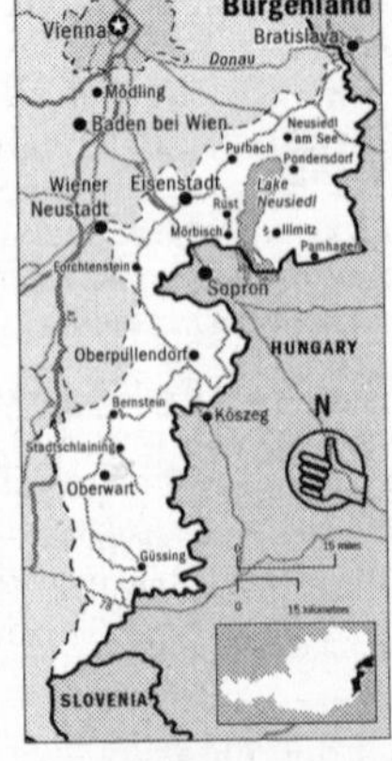

Eisenstadt is southeast of Vienna, just west of Neusiedler See. Getting there by train is a little complicated. One option is to take the S-bahn from the Südbahnhof (1½hr., every hr., 76AS outbound, 95AS inbound back to Vienna) and switch trains in **Neusiedl am See,** but you must be sure to sit in the correct section of the train, since the train splits on its way to Neusiedl am See, and one section heads to Hungary. You may find it more convenient to take a direct **bus** from **Wien Mitte** to Eisenstadt (1½hr., every hr. 6am-8:45pm, 95AS).

Buses run from Eisenstadt to **Rust, Mörbisch,** and **Wiener Neustadt.** The **bus station** (☎2350) is on Dompl. next to the cathedral. Buy your ticket on the bus and tell the bus driver where you're going. To get to Eisenstadt by **car,** take Bundesstr. 16 or Autobahn A2 or A3 south from Vienna (50km). From Wiener Neustadt, take Bundesstr. 153 or Autobahn S4 east. There is an underground parking garage (25AS per hr.) outside the Eszterházy Palace.

ORIENTATION AND PRACTICAL INFORMATION

Eisenstadt is centered around Hauptstr., the city's *Fußgängerzone*. From the train station, follow Bahnstr. (which becomes St. Martinstr. then Fanny Eißlergasse) to the middle of this central area (20min.). From the bus stop, walk half a block to the church. With your back to the church, cross Pfarrg. and walk down tiny Marckingstr. to Hauptstr. Turn left and walk to the end, where Schloß Eszterházy is on your right. The **tourist office** is in the right wing of the castle. The staff has information on accommodations, musical events, guided tours, and *Heurigen* in Eisenstadt and surroundings. For a rural living experience, ask about *Beim Bauern Zur Gast*, which lists winegrowers who rent rooms in their houses. (☎67390; fax 67391; tve.info@bnet.at. Call for hours.) Services in Eisenstadt include: **bike rental** at the train station (☎62637; 150AS per day, 120AS per half-day; with train ticket 100AS, 80AS; mountain bikes 175-200AS; reservations advised); **currency exchange** at the post office or at **Creditanstalt Bankverein** on the corner of St. Martin and Dompl. (open M-Th 8am-1pm and 2-4pm, F 8am-3pm); and **public bathrooms** at Dompl., and Eszterházy Palace. The **post office,** on the corner of Pfarrg. and Semmelweise, has good rates for traveler's checks (☎62271; open M-F 7am-6pm, Sa 7am-1pm). The **postal code** is A-7000.

BURGENLAND

ACCOMMODATIONS AND FOOD

Consider Eisenstadt as a daytrip—with no youth hostel in the vicinity, *Privatzimmer* are the only budget option. Most are on the outer city limits and rent only during July and August. The youth hostels in **Vienna** (see p. 92) and **Neusiedl am See** (see p. 139) are cheaper and only an hour away. What accommodations do exist are packed in July and August, and reservations are a must. At **Gasthaus Kutsenits,** Mattersburgerstr. 30, a clean, quiet room can be yours at a reasonable price if you're willing to walk a kilometer. From Schloß Eszterházy, head down Rusterstr. to Mattersburgerstr. (☎63511. Breakfast included. Singles 250 AS, with shower 350AS; doubles 400AS, with shower 500AS; 50AS supplement for 1-night stays.)

The many **Heurigen** in Eisenstadt offer modest, generally affordable meals with their wines. Another good bet is to wander along Hauptstr., following your nose. **Café Central,** Hauptstr. 40, is a pleasant, unassuming little cafe (named after the famous Viennese haunt) in a shady courtyard off the main street, where a quiet crowd consumes scrumptious baguettes (40AS) and ice cream specialties. (☎75234. Open M-Th 7am-midnight, F-Sa 7am-2am, Su 9am-midnight.) **Fischhandlung Golosetti** (☎62437), in the middle of Joseph-Stanislaus-Albachg. off Hauptpl., offers big, cheap *Schnitzelsemmeln* and other meaty sandwiches for a mere 29AS. You can find a **Spar Markt** at Eszterházystr. 38 and Bahnstr. 16-18, both open M-F 7am-12:30pm and 2:30-6pm, Sa 7am-noon. Another supermarket is **Julius Meinl,** Hauptstr. 13, open M-F 8am-6pm, Sa 7:30am-noon.

SIGHTS AND FESTIVALS

As one might expect, most of the sights in Eisenstadt are directly connected to Haydn or the Eszterházy family, but they're authentic and sincere enough to interest all comers, Haydn fans or no.

THE ESZTERHÁZY PALACE. Built on the footings of the Kanizsai family's 14th-century fortress, the castle-turned-palace now known as **Schloß Eszterházy** acquired its cheerful hue when the Hungarian Eszterházy family showed allegiance to the great Austrian Empress in the 18th century by painting the building *Maria Theresien gelb* (Maria Theresian yellow). More recently, the fabulously wealthy Eszterházys, who still own the building, leased the family home to the Austrian provincial government, allowing the bureaucrats to occupy 40% of the castle while the family retrenched itself in the remaining 60%. When it bought its portion for 125,000AS, the government apparently overlooked the Eszterházys's clause that made the government responsible for renovation and maintenance costs. Rumor has it the government has spent more than 40 million *Schillings* on the upkeep of the Red Salon's silk tapestry alone. In the magnificent **Haydnsaal** (Haydn Hall), the hard-working composer conducted the court orchestra almost every night from 1761 to 1790. Classical musicians consider the Haydnsaal an acoustic mecca. Since the government removed the marble floor and replaced it with a wooden one, the room is so acoustically perfect that seats for concerts in the room are not numbered—supposedly every seat provides the same magnificent sound. More often than not the music of Haydn fills the hall. During tours of the *Schloß*, tourists are encouraged to lift their voices in song in order to test out the hall's sound properties. Even when the music stops, the room is an aristocratic visual symphony of red velvet, gold, monumental oil paintings, and woodwork. *(At the end of Hauptstr. ☎ 719 3000. 50min. tours Easter-Oct. daily every hr. on the hour 9am-5pm; Oct.-Easter M-F 60AS, students and seniors 40AS.)*

HAYDN EVENTS. Catering to the town's Haydn obsession, **Haydnmatinees** (☎ 719 300), held from May to October, feature four fine fellows, bewigged and bejeweled in Baroque costumes of imperial splendor, playing a half-hour of impeccable Haydn. *(Tu and F 11am in the palace. 95AS.)* The palace also hosts **Haydnkonzerte.** *(July-Aug. Th at 8pm; May-June and Sept.-Oct. Sa at 7:30pm. 160-350AS.)* True Haydn enthusiasts can wait for The Big One: the **Internationale Haydntage,** featuring concerts, operas, and large free video screenings of the best of past festival concerts outdoors near the *Schloß*. In 2001, the festival will begin the second week of September. *(Festival office ☎ 618 660; fax 61805; office@hadynfestival.at. Tickets 200-1400AS.)*

THE OLD TOWN. The *Kapellmeister* had a short commute to the concert hall each day: he lived just around the corner. His modest residence is now the **Haydn-Haus,** Haydng. 21, where original manuscripts and other memorabilia are exhibited. *(☎ 626 5229. Open Easter-Oct. daily 9am-noon and 1-5pm. Guided tours by appointment. 30AS, students 15AS. Combination ticket for Haydn-Haus and Landesmuseum 50AS, students 25AS.)* The *maestro* lies buried in the **Bergkirche**. From the palace, make a right on to Eszterházystr. and walk two blocks. Haydn's remains were placed there in 1932 after phrenologists removed his head to search for signs of musical genius on the skull's surface. After being displayed at the Vienna Music Museum for years, Haydn's head was reunited with his body in 1954. Entrance to the *Bergkirche* includes admission to the **Kalvarienberg,** a pilgrimage annex to the church, which illustrates the 14 Stations of the Cross with hand-carved Biblical figures. Stand in the central nave and try to distinguish the real Doric columns from the *trompe l'oeil* paintings. The church's rooftop stations provide a great view of surrounding Burgenland. *(☎ 62638. Open Easter-Oct. daily 9am-noon and 1-5pm. 30AS, students 15AS.)*

JEWISH MUSEUM. Eisenstadt's **Jüdisches Museum** presents a history of Jewish life in Eisenstadt and the Burgenland region. The Eszterházys were known for their hospitality toward Jews, who played a major part in their rise to power. By settling Jews in Eisenstadt, they circumvented the law preventing Christians from lending money with interest. The museum's display is organized according to Jewish holidays and contains religious items dating from the 17th century. The building contains an original private synagogue with a beautiful ark in the style of Empress Josephine as well as Gothic and Oriental murals from the early 1800s. *(Unterbergstr. 6. From the palace, make a right and then another right onto Gloriettealle, then your first left to Unterbergstr. ☎ 65145; info@oejudmus.or.at; www.oejudmus.or.at/oejudmus. Open May-Oct. T-Su 10am-5pm. 50AS; students 40AS.)* Around the corner on Wertheimer-Str., near the hospital, is a **Jewish cemetery** dating back several centuries.

FESTIVALS. Leaving Eisenstadt without sampling the wine would be like leaving Vienna without tasting *Sachertorte.* In early July the *Winzerkirtag Kleinhöflein* floods Hauptpl. with kegs, flasks, and bottles as local wineries attempt to sell their goods. Mid-August brings the Festival of 1000 Wines, when wineries from all over Burgenland crowd the palace's *Orangerie* with their Dionysian delicacies. If you like music with your wine, visit at the end of May when the free, outdoor Eisen-

EISENSTADT'S JEWISH COMMUNITY The history of Jews in Eisenstadt is an extraordinary tale of growth and tragic downfall. As early as 1675, Prince Paul Eszterházy was moved by the plight of the persecuted Jews and decided to shelter them as "Schutzjuden" (protected Jews) on his estates. From 1732 on, the Jewish quarter of Eisenstadt formed the prosperous independent community of "Unterberg-Eisenstadt," which remained unique in Europe until 1938. In that year, the Jews of the Burgenland were among the first to be affected by the deportation orders of the Nazis. Today, only a few Jewish families remain in Eisenstadt.

stadt Fest provides all kinds of music, from classical to rock. At any other time of the year, fresh wine is available straight from the source in the wineries themselves. Most are small and aren't allowed to open for more than three weeks per year to sell their wine. Fear not—the wineries stagger their opening times so that wine is always available. To find out which *Buschenschenken*, or *Schenkhäuser* (wine taverns), are open, ask the tourist office for the schedule or look in the local newspaper. Most of the *Buschenschenken* are clustered in Kleinhöfler-Hauptstr.

THE NEUSIEDLERSEE REGION

Burgenland's major lake, the Neusiedlersee, is but a vestige (320 sq. km) of the water that once blanketed the entire Pannenian Plain. It is so large that you cannot see the opposite shore, but, with no outlets or inlets save underground springs, Austria's only steppe lake never gets deeper than 2m. The water line recedes periodically, exposing thousands of square meters of dry land, and from 1868-1872, the lake dried up entirely. Warm and salty, the lake is a haven for more than 250 species of waterfowl. The marsh reeds (sometimes almost 2m high) that surround the lake shelter many rare animals and plants, including bugs, which can make it unpleasant to swim anywhere other than at designated areas. **Storks,** however, thrive on this vegetation—see if you can spot their chimney-nests, believed to bring good luck. In 1992, the lake and surrounding area was incorporated into the national park **Neusiedlersee-Seewinkel,** in order to preserve this natural wonder for generations of birds.

Humans enjoy the lake as well, with thousands of sun-hungry vacationers visiting its resorts each summer for swimming, sailing, fishing, and cycling. **Cruises** on the Neusiedlersee allow you to travel between Rust, Illmitz, and Mörbisch with your bike for 60AS one-way and 100AS round-trip. **Gangl** runs boats every hour from Illmitz to Mörbisch (☎(02175) 2158 or 2794; May-Sept. 9am-6pm). In Mörbisch, **Schifffahrt Weiss** cruises to Illmitz (☎(02685) 8324; May-Sept. every 30 min. 9am-6pm). For more information about the region, contact the **Neusiedlersee Regionalbüro** at Hauptpl. 1, A-7100 Neusiedl am See (☎8600; fax 860 020; info@neusiedlersee.com; www.neusiedlersee.com).

NEUSIEDL AM SEE ☎02167

Less than an hour from Vienna by express train, Neusiedl am See is the gateway to the Neusiedlersee region. The principal attraction is the lake, not the town, so consider Neusiedl a day at the beach. Proximity to the lake, the array of water sports, and affordable accommodations make Neusiedl a popular destination for families with children.

TRANSPORT AND PRACTICAL INFORMATION. Neusiedl am See's **Hauptbahnhof,** 15 minutes by foot from the town center, is the destination of trains from Vienna and Eisenstadt. (Information and ticket window open 5am-9pm. Eisenstadt 19AS; Vienna 76AS.) By **car** from Vienna, take A4 or route 10 east. From Eisenstadt, take route 50 north and route 51 east. To get to town, take a right on Bahnstr. and follow the road right onto Eisenstädterstr. (which becomes Obere

Hauptstr.) and into Hauptpl. The **bus station,** centrally located on Seestr. 15a, at the end of Untere Hauptstr. (☎2406), offers a **Fahrradbus** (#1813) that carries bikers and bikes to and from Mörbische, Neusiedl, and Illmitz. There's frequent service to **Vienna** (95AS) and **Bruck an der Leitha** (38AS).

The **tourist office,** in the *Rathaus* on Hauptpl., helps with accommodations and offers advice on boat and bike rentals. (☎2229; fax 2637. Open July-Aug. M-F 8am-7pm, Sa 10am-noon and 2-6pm, Su 4-7pm; May-June and Sept. M-F 8am-4:30pm; Oct.-Apr. M-Th 8am-noon and 1-4:30pm, F 8am-1pm.) **Raiffeisbank,** Untere Hauptstr. 3, has the best **currency exchange** rates. (☎2564. Open M-F 8am-12:30pm and 1:30-4pm.) Services include: **bike rental** (70AS per half-day, 90AS per day with train ticket, otherwise for 120AS and 150AS) and **luggage storage** (30AS) at the train station; and **emergency help** (☎133). The **post office,** Untere Hauptstr. 53, is on the corner of Untere Hauptstr. and Lisztg. (Open M-F 8am-noon and 2-6pm.) The **postal code** is A-7100.

ACCOMMODATIONS. Heavy tourist activity, partly generated by Neusiedl's proximity to Vienna, makes finding accommodations tough. **Jugendherberge Neusiedl am See (HI),** Herbergg. 1, sports 86 beds in 21 quads and one double. Follow Wienerstr. and turn left onto Goldbergg. The hostel is on the corner at Herbergg. It's an uphill walk, but don't get discouraged—renovations have equipped the hostel with a sauna and winter greenhouse. There are showers in every room, but bathrooms are in the hall. (☎/fax 2252. Breakfast included. Sheets 20AS. Key deposit 100AS. Reception 8am-2pm and 5-8pm. Reservations strongly recommended. Open Mar.-Oct. 170AS, under 19 150AS.) **Gasthof zur Traube,** Hauptpl. 9, has a cordial staff and pretty pink rooms, family-friendly. (☎2423. Breakfast included. Singles 410AS; doubles 650AS.) **Rathausstüberl,** around the corner from the *Rathaus* on Kircheng., is a sunny 15-room *Pension* with 2 singles and 13 doubles. (☎2883; fax 288307. Breakfast buffet included. Reservations recommended. 270-490AS per person.) The *Pension* also has a restaurant with a lovely shaded courtyard, great wine, and plenty of fresh fish and vegetarian dishes. The *Menü* includes soup, entree, and salad for 75AS. (Open Mar.-Dec. daily 10am-midnight.)

FOOD AND ACTIVITIES. On your way to the beach you can grab a picnic at the **Billa** grocery store on Seestr. (Open M-Th 7:30am-6:30pm, F 7:30am-8pm, Sa 7am-5pm.) **Rauchkuchl,** Obere Hauptstr. 57, offers *Blaufränker* red wine or other homemade specialties as well as the opportunity to hear local dialect (☎2585. Open Tu-Sa 5-11pm).

You're here, you've got your bathing suit and towel, now where's the **beach?** Head to the end of Seestr. (1km), or catch the bus from the *Hauptbahnhof* or Hauptpl. (every hr. until 6pm). The beach is a bit rocky, but pleasant (25AS, children 20AS). The **Segelschule Neusiedl am See** (☎340 044) at the docks on the far right will rent you a sailboard (1hr. 148-160AS, half- or full-day 450-800AS), dinghy (3- to 4-person boat 160AS per hr.), or standard surfboard (400AS for the weekend; open daily 8:30am-6pm). Close by on Seestr., you'll find **paddleboats** (80AS per hr.) and **rowboats** (40AS per hr.) at **Bootsvermietung Leban.**

In August, Neusiedl hosts a **Stadtfest,** during which the *Fußgängerzone* comes to life with countless food booths and modern music bands. Admission is free; call the festival office for more information. (☎3293. Open daily 1-3pm.)

RUST ☎02685

During the summer, tourists inundate this tiny wine capital of Austria to partake of the fruit of the vine. Ever since 1524, when the Emperor granted the wine-growers of Rust the exclusive right to mark the letter "R" on wine barrels, Rust has been synonymous with good—really good—wine. The town is particularly known for sweet dessert wines, called *Ausbruch* (literally "outbreak"). The quantity of desiccated grapes needed for a bottle is astounding, and consequently, so is the price. Wine isn't Rust's only attraction, however. The unspoiled town center with medieval houses and nesting storks and Rust's location on the Neusiedlersee give you something to appreciate while enjoying your fine wine buzz.

ORIENTATION AND PRACTICAL INFORMATION

Rust lies 17km east of Eisenstadt on the Neusiedlersee. Rust does not have a train station, but **Post Buses** run between **Eisenstadt** and Rust several times per day (38AS), and between Rust and **Vienna** (Wien Mitte/Landstr.) four times a day (114AS). The **bus station** is a glorified bus stop located just behind the post office at Franz-Josef-Pl. 14. By **car** from Vienna, take Autobahn A3 to Eisenstadt and then from Eisenstadt take Bundesstr. 52 straight into Rust. To reach the *Fußgängerzone* (whose *Fußgänger* status is sometimes disrupted by the gentle roar of tractors), leave the post office and turn left. You will almost immediately come to the intersection of four streets, with Conradpl. diagonally across the intersection. Walk straight across Conradpl. to the triangular plaza where the *Rathaus* stands. Inside, the **tourist office** hands out maps, plans bicycle tours, and gives information on wine tastings, the beach, and *Privatzimmer*. (☎6574; fax 50210. Open May-Sept. M-F 9am-noon and 2-6pm, Sa 9am-noon, Su 10am-noon; Oct.-Apr. M-F 9am-noon and 1-4pm.) The **Raiffeisenkasse Rust,** Rathauspl. 5, is the best place to **exchange money** (☎607 05; open M-F 8am-noon and 1:30-4pm). The Raiffeisenkasse has a 24-hour **ATM. Reisebüro Blaguss** in the *Rathaus* and **Ruster Freizeitcenter** (☎595) by the beach are open late and provide emergency currency exchange. Call **taxis** at 6576. The **post office,** Franz-Josefs-Pl., exchanges money but not travelers' checks (open M-F 8am-noon and 2-6pm). The **postal code** is A-7071.

BURGENLAND

ACCOMMODATIONS AND FOOD

If you want to stay in Rust, getting a *Privatzimmer* is the way to go. Reservations are strongly recommended for all *Privatzimmer* during festival times (July and August). Some will not accept telephone reservations for a one-night stay, but most won't turn you away at the door if there's a free room. Be warned: prices may rise in the high season. You'll receive a warm welcome at **Gästehaus Ruth,** Dr. Alfred-Ratzg. 1 (☎277 or 6828; fax 6828), where rooms range from 230-280AS. Rust's new **Jugendgästehaus,** administered from Conradpl. 1, but located half a mile away at Ruster Bucht 2 (☎591; fax 5914) sits on the beachfront near tennis courts and bike paths. Dorms cost 160-190AS per night. From April through October, there's always room for tent-dwellers at **Ruster Freizeitcenter,** which offers showers, washing machines, a game room, a playground, and a grocery store. (☎595. Showers included. Reception 7:30am-10pm. 44-55AS, children 16-27AS; tent 38-44AS.) The grounds are only five minutes from the beach, to which guests receive free entrance.

Ubiquitous vineyard-restaurants called *Buschenschenken* offer cheap snacks and superb wine; the tourist office has a complete list. You'll find plenty of good eating options along Rathausstr., though the ravenous should seek out **Zum Alten Haus,** on the corner of Raiffenstr. and Franz Josefpl., which serves up enormous portions of *Schnitzel* and salad for only 85AS (☎230; open Tu-Su 9am-10pm). **Alte Schmiede,** Seezeile 24 (☎6418), roofed with grape vines, serves traditional Austrian food with a Hungarian twist in a lively, friendly atmosphere. **A & O Markt Dreyseitel** on Weinbergg. between Mitterg. and Schubertg. sells the raw materials for a meal. (☎238; open M-F 7am-noon and 3-6pm).

SIGHTS AND ENTERTAINMENT

Wine and storks are the primary reasons to come to Rust, though its *Altstadt* is one of the three in Austria named a "model city" by the Council of Europe (the others are Salzburg and Krems). The award praises both the architectural and natural preservation of this quiet town with elm-shaded lanes.

LOOK WHAT THE STORK BROUGHT Since 1910, Rust's storks have been attracted to the high chimneys of the *Bürger* houses, and by 1960 nearly 40 pairs were nesting in the old city. Soon, however, locals noticed a decline and began to voice their concern over the dwindling number of these endangered birds. In 1987, Rust and the World Wildlife Federation initiated a special program to protect and reestablish the birds. The storks eat mainly frogs, fish, snakes, and beetles—critters found among *Neusiedlersee's* reedy marshes. When the reeds grew too tall, the storks had difficulty finding food. Rust borrowed cattle from another part of Austria and set them in the marshes as natural lawnmowers. Blue placards mark the houses with chimneys that the storks habitually return to nest in. The storks come to Rust at the end of March, and from the end of May you can see the (stork) babies in the nests. The chicks stay home for 2 months before flying away and beginning their adult lives. The storks have also hatched a post office, the **Storks' Post Office,** A-7071 Rust, at the *Rathaus.* Its stork postmark provides funds to support the birds.

WINE ACADEMY. Rust is home to Austria's only **Weinakademie.** The institution offers courses ranging from wine cultivation to basic bartending, and holds wine tours and tastings. *(Hauptstr. 31. ☎6451 or 6853; fax 6431. Open for wine tastings F-Su 2-6pm. 150AS for 10 tastes.)* Many vintners *(Weinbauern)* offer wine tastings and tours of their cellars and vineyards. **Rudolf Beilschmidt,** Weinbergg. 1 (☎326), has tours May through September on Fridays at 5pm. **Weingut Marienhof,** Weinbergg. 16 (☎ 251), conducts tours on Tuesdays from April to September at 6pm for 60AS.

FISCHERKIRCHE. Rust's **Fischerkirche,** around the corner from the tourist office, was begun in the 12th century and is the oldest church in Burgenland. In the 13th century, Queen Mary of Hungary, after being rescued from the Mongols by fishermen, donated the *Marienkapelle,* an interior chapel containing lovely 15th-century sculptures of Madonna. Fortunately, the Romanesque and Gothic sections have survived the ravages of Baroque remodeling fervor. *(Tours by appointment. Call Frau Kummer at ☎550. Open May-Sept. M-Sa 10am-noon and 2:30-6pm, Su 11am-noon and 2-4pm. 10AS, students 5AS.)*

LAKE ACCESS AND ACTIVITIES. Sun worshippers can sit and splash on the south shore of the **Neusiedlersee.** There is a **public beach** complete with showers, lockers, restrooms, phones, water slide, and snack bar. Though the murky waters of the lake daunt some swimmers, the water is actually of drinking quality. The muddy color comes from the shallow, easily disturbed clay bottom. For wimps who remain unconvinced, the beach also has a chlorine pool. Be sure to keep the entrance card—you'll need it to exit the park again. *(☎501. 40AS per person, after 4pm 30AS.)* To reach the beach, walk down Hauptstr., take a left onto Am Seekanal, then a right onto Seepromenade, which cuts through all of the marsh lands (about 7km) surrounding the perimeter of the lake.

If lounging at the beach isn't active enough for you, rent a **boat** from **Family Gmeiner**, next to the beach on the water's edge. **Sailboats** are 60AS per hour or 270AS for 5 hours. **Paddleboats** are 80AS per hour, 325AS for five hours. **Electric boats** are 130AS per hour, 380AS for five hours. The same company runs **Schiffrundfahrten** (boat tours) that can transport you to Illmitz on the opposite shore. *(☎493 or (62683) 55 38). Boats leave Rust Apr.-Oct. Th-Su and holidays at 10am and 4pm and return from Illmitz at 11am and 5pm.)* Besides swimming, boating, and bird-watching, tourists flock to the *Neusiedlersee* area to **bike.** The lake area is criss-crossed with bicycle routes. Many follow the lake shore or wind in and out of the little towns along the Austro-Hungarian border. The route covers 170km, but those out for less intense biking can do a smaller section and then take the bus back, or take the Illmitz boat to the opposite shore and then bicycle back.

DAYTRIP FROM RUST

MÖRBISCH

Buses from Eisenstadt to Mörbisch leave every two hours (38AS). The #1820 bus makes the trip from Rust to Mörbisch in 5 minutes (19AS), or you can bike from Rust along the 6km country lane to Mörbisch. In the summer it's a long, hot 90min. by foot. Blaguss Reisen (☎(01) 501 800) in Vienna arranges a shuttle bus to Mörbisch at 6pm from Wiener Hauptstr. 15, Wien (round-trip 200AS).

The tiny village of Mörbisch lies 5km south of Rust along the *Neusiedlersee*, the last settlement on the western shore before the Hungarian border. The road from Eisenstadt and Rust is lined with *Hüterhütten*, stone huts where young men would spend weeks in solitude, guarding grapes from human and winged trespassers. Mörbisch centers around Hauptstr., where the **tourist office** lies at #23 . Pick up brochures on Mörbisch and the surrounding Burgenland, as well as a list of accommodations. (☎026 8588 56; fax 84309. Open 9am-noon and 1-6pm; Nov.-Feb. M-Th 9am-3pm.) The town has its own beach, which includes a floating theater that hosts an operetta festival each summer—the **Mörbisch Seefestspiele.** Performances float atop the lake most Thursdays and every Friday, Saturday, and Sunday from mid-July to the end of August. Tickets are 250AS to 800AS and can be purchased at the theater ticket office.

There are many *Pensionen* and *Privatzimmer* in Mörbisch. For a sunny room and cheerful surroundings less than 5 minutes from downtown, stay at **Weinhof Schindler,** Kinog. 9. Taste their homegrown wine and grape juice on a seaside terrace. (☎/fax 8318. Breakfast included. Open Apr.-Nov. 300-350AS per person. 15AS surcharge for 1-night stays.)

Mörbisch is truly a wine town, which is never more evident than during the **Weinfesttage** just before the opening of the *Seefestspiele.* The main street becomes one large *Heurige* filled with thirsty Austrians. During the **Weinblutenfest** in mid-June, visitors can ride a horse-drawn carriage from one vineyard to the other, stopping at each to sample the wine (100AS per person).

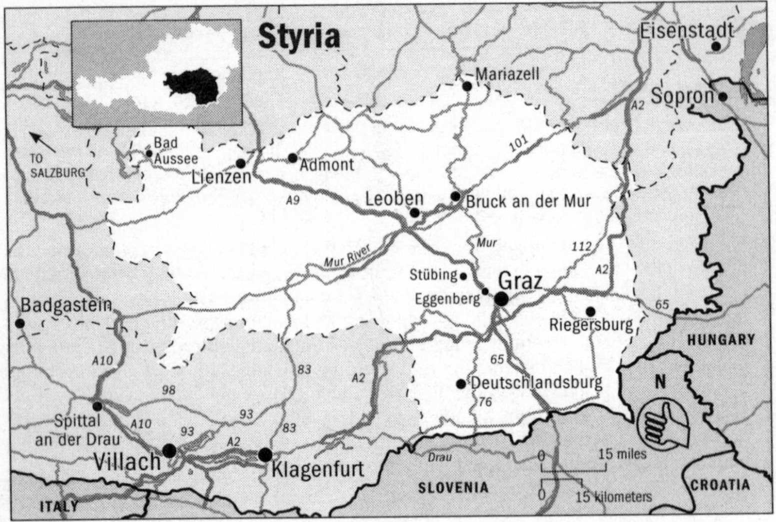

STYRIA

STYRIA (STEIERMARK)

Styria, promoted by tourist offices as "the Green Heart of Austria," is Austria's second largest province (in terms of geography, not population). The province is made up primarily of mountains, which range from craggy, bare peaks in the northwest to gentle, thickly forested slopes in the southeast. Though the region provides striking views and excellent skiing, Styria has been spared the brunt of the tourist incursions, which allows it to preserve many of Austria's folk traditions and ancient forests. Even Styria's gem-like city Graz sits relatively undisturbed by tourists in its setting. The stud farm for Austria's Lipizzaner horses in Styria sets the tone for the province, both refined and virile: Styrians are stubbornly individualistic, with a dialect that few outsiders can understand, gamey local cuisine, and a gruff sense of humor, but the province is also home to many pilgrimage shrines, and delicately crumbling medieval strongholds.

HIGHLIGHTS OF STYRIA

Peruse the collected treasures of **Graz's** Landesmuseum Joanneum (see p. 149).

Besiege the invincible medieval fortress in **Riegersburg** (see p. 153).

Make a pilgrimage to the Alpine village of **Mariazell,** home to some of Austria's finest *Lebkuchen* (gingerbread) bakeries (see p. 157).

GRAZ ☎0316

A fast toe-tapping accordion melody fills the narrow cobblestoned Sporgasse, as locals drink their wine and laughter erupts from a nearby cafe table. An unhurried, Mediterranean air pervades the scene, as the sun sets on the red-tiled roofs and Baroque domes. Deliciously under-touristed, Graz's *Altstadt* rewards the traveller with every turn of its gently winding streets, with every glance up to its graciously worn facade, with every lick of its creamy *gelato*. This second largest of Austria's cities keeps a sweaty and energetic nightlife thanks to its 45,000 students at Karl-Franzens-Universität, where the scientist of the stars, Johannes Kepler, hit the

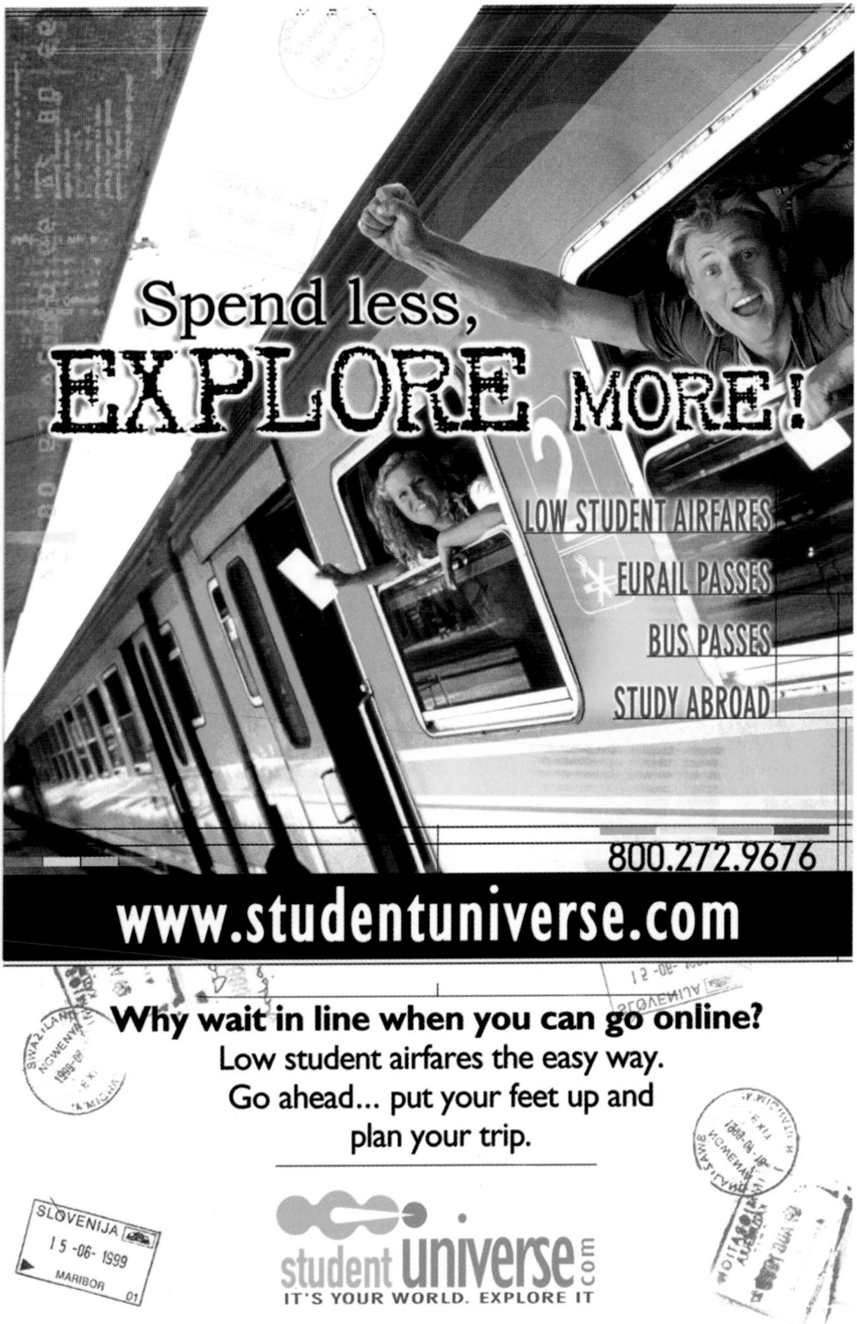
Spend less,
EXPLORE MORE!
LOW STUDENT AIRFARES
EURAIL PASSES
BUS PASSES
STUDY ABROAD
800.272.9676
www.studentuniverse.com
Why wait in line when you can go online?
Low student airfares the easy way.
Go ahead... put your feet up and
plan your trip.
SLOVENIJA
15-06-1999
MARIBOR
student universe.com
IT'S YOUR WORLD. EXPLORE IT

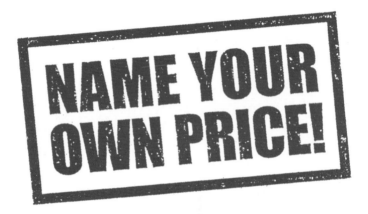

books. When the students aren't around, its renowned music venues attract a whole slew of festivals during July and August.

Since Charlemagne claimed this strategic gateway to Hungary and Slovenia for his empire in the 9th century, Graz has been fought over by Slavs, Frenchmen, and Russians. The ruins of Graz's own mini mountain, the **Schloßberg,** commemorate the turmoil—the stronghold withstood battering at the hands of the Ottoman Turks in the 17th century, Napoleon's armies (3 times) in the 19th-century, and the Soviet Union during WWII. Down below, the city, with its red-tiled roofs, enticing parks, and diverse museums, shows no evidence of the centuries of conflict. Graz is known to the world primarily for the exploits of hometown hero **Arnold Schwarzenegger,** who lived in Graz before he left his family and athletic trainer to become the Terminator. The small pond where Arnold proposed to Maria Shriver is now a pilgrimage site for determined fans, despite the bemused protestations of tourist officials that it's "nothing special."

GETTING THERE AND AROUND

Flights arrive at the **Flughafen Graz,** Flughafenstr. 51, 9km from the city center. Take bus #631 from the airport into town (30min., 6 per day 5:35am-6:20pm, 20AS). **Train lines** converge at the **Hauptbahnhof,** on Europapl., west of the city center. (The *Ostbahnhof* on Conrad-von-Hötzendorf-Str. is mainly a freight station; don't get off there unless you came in a crate.) The **Graz-Köflach Bus** (GKB) departs from Griespl. for West Styria. For the rest of Austria, the **BundesBus** departs from Europapl. 6 (next to the train station) and from Andreas-Hofer-Pl.

Trains: Hauptbahnhof, Europapl. (☎7848, info 1717, info open 7am-9pm). To: **Salzburg** (4¼hr., 10 per day 6:22am-10pm, 430AS); **Linz** (3¾hr., 7 per day 6:22am-6:22pm, 350AS); **Innsbruck** (6¼hr., 8 per day 6:22am-10pm, 560AS); **Vienna** (3¾hr., 17 per day 6:22am-6:22pm, 330AS); **Zurich** (10hr., 4 per day 6:22am-10pm, 1030AS); and **Munich** (6¼ hr., 9 per day 6:22am-6:22pm, 720AS).

Buses: Graz-Köflach Bus (GKB), Köflneherg. 35-41 (☎5987), is open M-F 8am-5pm. The Post Bus office, Andreas-Hofer-Pl. 17, is open M-F 7am-6pm. The **branch** at the *Hauptbahnhof* is open M-F 9am-noon.

Public Transportation: For information on all local buses, trams, and trains, call **Mobil Zentrale,** Schönaug. 6 (☎820 606). Open M-F 8am-5pm. Purchase single tickets (20AS) and 24hr. tickets (42AS) from the driver, booklets of 10 tickets (160AS), or week-tickets (100AS) from any *Tabak*. Tickets are valid for all trams, buses, and the **cable car** that ascends the Schloßberg. Children half-price. 500AS penalty for riding without a ticket. Most tram lines run until 11pm, most bus lines until 9pm.

Taxi: Funktaxi, ☎983. **City-Funk,** ☎878.

Car Rental: Budget, Europapl. 12 (☎716 966; fax 722 074), and at the airport (☎2902, ext. 342).

Automobile Clubs: ÖAMTC, Conrad-von-Hötzendorf-str. 127 (☎504). **ARBÖ,** Kappellenstr. 45 (☎891 217).

Bike Rental: At the train station. 150-200AS per day, 90-160AS with Eurail or valid ticket. Open M-F 6:30am-6pm, Sa 6:30am-4pm, Su 7am-3:30pm. **Bicycle Graz,** Korüsistr. 5 (☎825 713 16), has city bikes for 80AS per day, 150AS per weekend; mountain bikes 150AS, 250AS. Open M-F 7am-1pm and 2-6pm.

STYRIA

ORIENTATION AND PRACTICAL INFORMATION

Graz spreads across the Mur River in the southeast corner of Austria. The city is a gateway to Slovenia (50km south) and Hungary (70km east). Two-thirds of Graz's 5km² area consists of beautiful parks, earning it the nickname "Garden City." **Hauptplatz,** on the corner of Murg. and Sackstr., directly in front of the *Rathaus*, is the center of the city. **Jakominiplatz,** near the Eisernes Tor and 5 minutes from Hauptpl., is the hub of the city's bus and streetcar system. **Herrengasse,** a pedes-

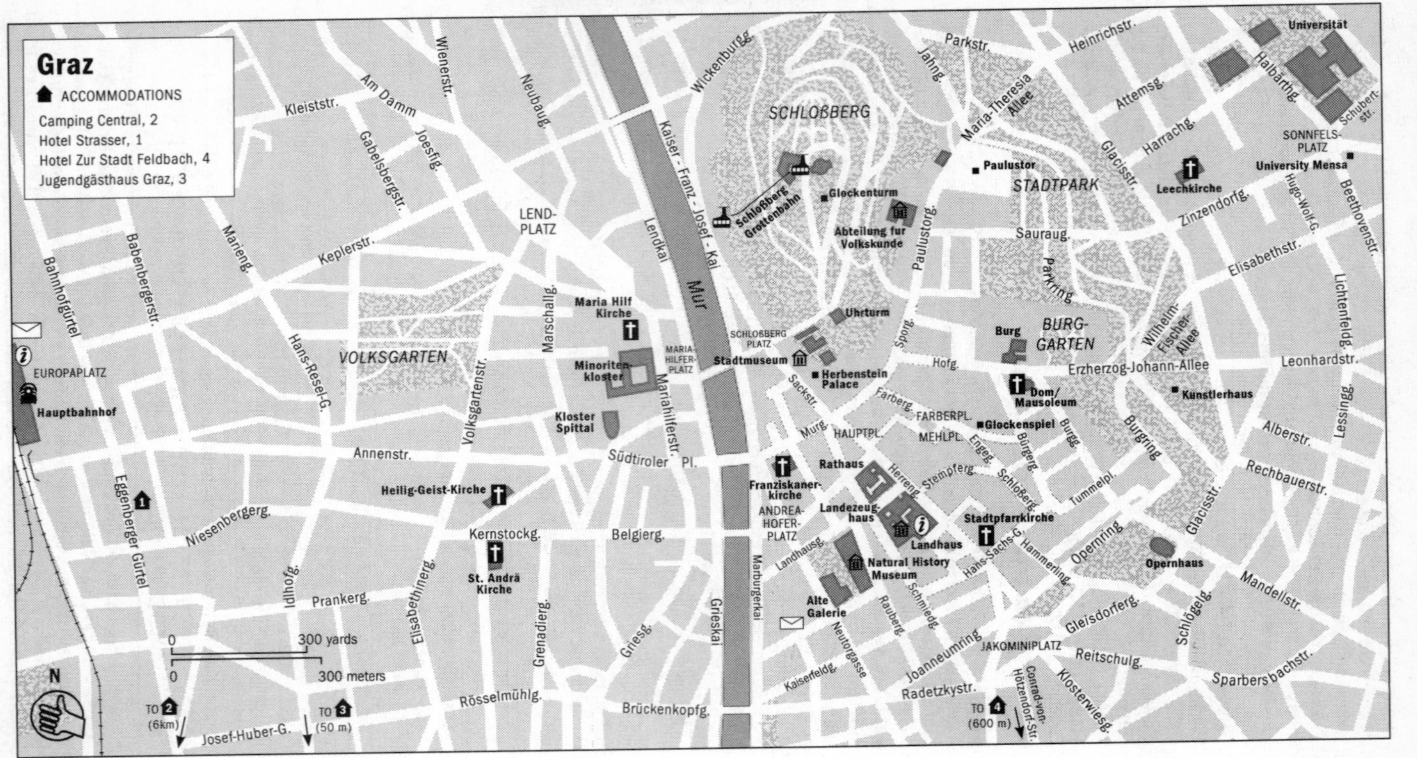
Graz
ACCOMMODATIONS
Camping Central, 2
Hotel Strasser, 1
Hotel Zur Stadt Feldbach, 4
Jugendgästhaus Graz, 3
SCHLOßBERG
STADTPARK
BURG-GARTEN
VOLKSGARTEN
Mur
Kaiser - Franz - Josef - Kai
Lendkai
Marburgerkai
Grieskai
Universität
University Mensa
Leechkirche
Künstlerhaus
Opernhaus
Paulustor
Glockenturm
Abteilung fur Volkskunde
Uhrturm
Herbenstein Palace
Burg
Dom/ Mausoleum
Glockenspiel
Stadtpfarrkirche
Landhaus
Natural History Museum
Rathaus
Landezeug-haus
Alte Galerie
Franziskaner-kirche
Stadtmuseum
Schloßberg Grottenbahn
Maria Hilf Kirche
Minoriten-kloster
Kloster Spittal
Heilig-Geist-Kirche
St. Andrä Kirche
Hauptbahnhof
EUROPAPLATZ
LEND-PLATZ
JAKOMINIPLATZ
ANDREA-HOFER-PLATZ
SCHLOßBERG PLATZ
MARIA-HILFER-PLATZ
SONNFELS-PLATZ
HAUPTPL.
FARBERPL.
MEHLPL.
Beethovenstr.
Lichtenfeldg.
Lessingg.
Leonhardstr.
Elisabethstr.
Hugo-Wolf-G.
Schubert-str.
Halbärthg.
Zinzendorfg.
Harrachg.
Attemsg.
Heinrichstr.
Glacisstr.
Maria-Theresia Allee
Parkstr.
Jahng.
Wickenburgg.
Paulustorg.
Sporg.
Hofg.
Sauraug.
Parkring
Erzherzog-Johann-Allee
Wilhelm-Fischer-Allee
Alberstr.
Rechbauerstr.
Mandellstr.
Sparbersbachstr.
Schlögelg.
Opernring
Burgring
Tummelpl.
Burgg.
Bürgerg.
Schloßberg.
Engeg.
Stempferg.
Herreng.
Farberg.
Sackstr.
Murg.
Hans-Sachs-G.
Hammerling
Gleisdorferg.
Reitschulg.
Klosterwiesg.
Conrad-von-Hötzendorf-Str.
Joanneumring
Schmiedg.
Rauberg.
Neutorgasse
Landhausg.
Kaiserfeldg.
Radetzkystr.
Mariahilferstr.
Südtiroler Pl.
Belgierg.
Griesg.
Brückenkopfg.
Marschallg.
Grenadierg.
Neubaug.
Volksgartenstr.
Kernstockg.
Rösselmühlg.
Wienerstr.
Joesfig.
Am Damm
Gabelsbergstr.
Keplerstr.
Annenstr.
Elisabethinerg.
Prankerg.
Idlhofg.
Kleiststr.
Hans-Resel-G.
Marieng.
Niesenbergerg.
Babenbergerstr.
Eggenberger Gürtel
Bahnhofgürtel
Josef-Huber-G.
TO 4 (600 m)
TO 3 (50 m)
TO 2 (6km)
0
300 yards
0
300 meters
N

trian street lined with cafes, boutiques, and ice cream shops, runs from the Hauptpl. to Jakominipl., forming the heart of the *Fußgängerzone*. The **Universität** is tucked away in the northeast part of Graz, near the posh residential district of St. Leonhard. The **Hauptbahnhof** lies on the other side of the river, a short ride from Hauptpl. on tram #3, 6, or 14. To get to the city center by foot from the train station, follow Annenstr. up and over Hauptbrücke (15min.).

TOURIST SERVICES

Tourist Office: Main office, Herreng. 16 (☎80750; fax 807 5515; info@graztourismus.at; www.graztourismus.at), has free city maps and a walking guide of the city (10AS). Friendly English-speaking staff makes free room reservations. **Tours** of the *Altstadt* in English and German start out front (2½hr., June-Sept. daily 2:30pm; Oct.-May Sa only; 75AS). Open in summer M-F 9am-7pm, Sa 9am-6pm, Su and holidays 10am-3pm; in winter M-F 9am-6pm, Sa 9am-3pm, Su and holidays 10am-3pm. There's a **branch,** (☎716 837), in the *Hauptbahnhof.* Open M-Sa 9am-1pm and 2-6pm.

Consulates: South Africa, Villefortg. 13 (☎322 548). **UK,** Schmiedg. 10 (☎826 105).

FINANCIAL AND COMMUNICATION SERVICES

Currency Exchange: Best rates at the main **post office** (cashier open M-F 7am-5pm, Sa 7am-2pm). Most banks open M-F 8am-noon and 2-4pm. The train station has the longest hours (M 5am-10pm, Tu-Su 5:45pm-10pm).

Bookstores: English Bookshop, Tummelpl. 7 (☎826 266; english.books@aon.net; members.aon.net/english.books), has 2 vast floors of fiction, nonfiction, you name it. Open M-F 9am-6pm, Sa 9am-noon.

Internet Access: A 15min. walk from the center of town, **Jugendgästehaus Graz,** Idlhofg. 74 (see p. 148), has nifty coin-operated machines that cost 5AS for 10min. **Café Zentral,** Andreas-Hofer-Pl. 9 (☎832 468), charges 60AS for 1hr. minimum, divided among as many visits as you want. Open M-Sa 6:30-10pm.

Post Office: Main office, Neutorg. 46. Open M-F 7am-9pm, Sa 8am-2pm. Cashier closes M-F at 5pm. A **branch office,** Europapl. 10, is next to the main train station. M-F 7am-midnight, Sa-Su 8am-10pm. **Postal Code:** A-8010; branch office A-8020.

OTHER SERVICES

Bi-Gay-Lesbian Organizations: Verein Frauenservice Graz (Women's Information Center), Idlhofg. 20 (☎716 022). Office open M, W, F 9am-1pm, Tu 5-7pm. Medical help available W 5-7pm.

Luggage Storage: At station, 30AS per day. Open 6am-midnight. Lockers 30-50AS.

Laundromat: Putzerei Rupp, Jakominstr. 34 (☎821 183), has do-it-yourself (5kg load 75AS, soap 10AS) and professional handling. Open M-F 8am-5pm, Sa 8am-noon.

EMERGENCIES

Emergencies: Police, ☎133, office outside the *Hauptbahnhof* (☎888 2775). **Ambulance,** ☎144.

AIDS Hotline: Steirische AIDS-Hilfe, Schmiedg. 38 (☎815 050). Counseling available W 11am-1pm, F 4-7pm. Blood tests Tu and Th 4:30-7:30pm.

Pharmacy: Bärenapotheke, Herreng. 11 (☎830 267), opposite the tourist office. Open M-F 8am-12:30pm and 2:30-6pm, Sa 8am-noon. AmEx, MC, Visa.

Hospital: Krankenhaus der Elisabethinen, Elisabethinerg. 14 (☎7063).

ACCOMMODATIONS

Sniffing out a cheap bed in Graz may require a bit of detective work, as most budget hotels, guest houses, and pensions run 300-450AS per person, and many are in the boondocks. Luckily, the web of local transport provides a reliable and easy commute to and from the city center. Ask the tourist office about *Privatzimmer* (150-300AS per night), especially in the crowded summer months.

Jugendgästehaus Graz (HI), Idlhofg. 74 (☎714 876; fax 714 87688), 15min. from the train station. Exit the station and cross the street, head right on Eggenberger Gürtel, left on Josef-Huber-G. (after the car dealer), then take the 1st right at Idlhofg. The hostel is behind a parking lot on your right. Buses #31, 32, and 33 run here from Jakominipl. (last bus around midnight). This hotel-quality hostel has its own cafe and restaurant, as well as cheap **Internet** access (5AS for 10min.). Small breakfast included. **Laundry** 40AS, soap 5AS. Reception 7am-11pm. No real curfew; security guard opens the doors every 30min. from 10pm-2am. Key available (300AS deposit). 4- to 6-bed dorms 220AS, singles 320AS, doubles 540AS. Mattress on the floor 155AS.

Hotel Strasser, Eggenberger Gürtel 11 (☎713 977; fax 716 856; hotel.strasser@noten.com), 5min. from the train station. Exit the station, cross the street, and head right on Bahnhofgürtel; the hotel is on the left, across from the Midas station. Big, breezy rooms with big windows and colorful rugs. Top-rate restaurant serves the best cocoa around. Breakfast included. Free parking. Singles 380AS, with shower 460AS; doubles 600AS, 680AS; triples 860AS; quads 1000AS.

Hotel Zur Stadt Feldbach, Conrad-von-Hötzendorf-Str. 58 (☎829 468; fax 829 468-15), 20min. walk south of Jakominipl. From train station take tram #3 or 6 to Hauptpl. or Jakominipl., switch to tram #4 (dir.: Liebnau) or #5 (dir.: Puntigam) to "Jakominigürtel." The hotel is on the right. Breakfast 50AS. 24hr. reception on 2nd floor. Singles 350AS; doubles 500AS, with shower stall, 650AS; triples with shower 800AS.

Camping Central, Martinhofstr. 3 (☎(0676) 378 5102, fax (0316) 697 824). From train station, take tram #3 or 6 to Jakominipl. Then take bus #32 to "Badstraßgang" (20 min.), turn right at the Billa supermarket and walk up the road. This clean campground has a **swimming pool** and miniature golf (25AS, children 20AS). **Laundry** 70AS. Reception 8am-10pm. Open Apr.-Oct. 155AS per person, includes tent site, shower, and use of the swimming pool; additional adults 80AS, children 4-14 50AS. Camper 205AS for 2 people. Tax 5AS.

FOOD

Graz's student community sustains a bonanza of cheap eateries. Inexpensive meals are on Hauptpl. and Lendpl., off Keplerstr. and Lendkai, where concession stands sell *Wurst*, ice cream, beer, and other fast food until late. There are markets along Rösselmühlg., an extension of Josef-Huber-G., and on Jakoministr. directly off Jakominipl. Low-priced student hangouts line Zinzendorfg. near the university. Note that most salads come dressed in the local dark pumpkin-seed oil. There are 4 **outdoor markets** at Kaiser-Josef-Pl. and Lendpl. (M-Sa 8am-1pm), as well as on Hauptpl. and on Jakominipl. (M-F 7am-6pm, Sa 7am-12:30pm) where vendors hawk their fruits and vegetables amid a happy splash of colors. For groceries there are two **Interspars.** One at Lazarett-Gürtel 55, in the enormous City Park shopping mall (☎710 436; open M-F 9am-7:30pm, Sa 8am-5pm). A cheap restaurant is inside (open M-F 7am-7:30pm, Sa 8am-5pm). There is another branch next door to the Mensa (open M-F 8am-1pm and 4-6:30pm, Sa 7:30am-12:30pm).

RESTAURANTS

Gasthaus "Alte Münze", Schloßbergpl. 8 (☎829 151). Sitting on the tranquil Schloßbergplatz, Gasthaus Alt Münze serves scrumptious Styrian specialities (hearty meat-cheese-pasta-combo *Steierpfandl* 95AS). Daily *Menü* 85AS. Open Tu-Su 8am-11pm.

Kebap Haus, Jakoministr. 16 (☎811 006), just south of Jakominipl., dimly lit and crowded, Kebap Haus is a superior Turkish restaurant with famous Falafel (78AS), inexpensive sandwiches on pita (38-52AS), and delicious Mediterranean pizzas (72-89AS). Lunch specials include soup, entree, and salad (85AS). Open M-Sa 11am-midnight.

Mangolds, Griesgasse 11 (☎718 002), serves fresh vegetarian entrees, desserts, and a salad bar in a huge restaurant that's an appealing mixture of Scandinavian design and rustic arts-and-crafts. Open M-F 11am-8pm, Sa 11am-4pm.

Da Vinci, Jakominipl. 19 (☎825 200), keeps the customers happy and the waiters very busy with cheap and incredibly delicious pizzas (85AS). Open daily 11am-1am.

Gastwirtschaft Wartburgasse, Halbärthg. 4 (☎388 750). Antique posters and loud music make this smoky, indoor/outdoor cafe/bar Graz's premier student hangout. Well-made standard dishes make up for the wait. Lunch specials (68-110AS) and pasta, vegetarian, or meat entrees (42-120AS). Open daily 9am-2am.

University Mensa, Sonnenfelspl. 1 (☎323 362), just east of the Stadtpark at the intersection of Zinzendorfg. and Leechg. Take bus #39 to "Uni/Mensa" for the best deal in town. Simple and satisfying *Menüs,* vegetarian *(Vollwert)* or with meat, for 50-56AS. Large *à la carte* selection includes diverse salads (20AS) and pizza (29AS). Continental breakfast 32AS. Open M-F 8:30am-2:30pm.

Calafati, Lissag. 2 (☎916 889), a 3min. walk from the hostel away from the train station. Lunch combos (main course, soup or spring roll, dessert, 50-80AS) make this slightly out-of-the-way Chinese restaurant a bargain. Several vegetarian and take-out options (65-89AS). Lunch specials 11:30am-3pm; dinner 5:30-11:30pm.

SIGHTS

LANDESMUSEUM JOANNEUM. Graz's land museum is Austria's oldest public museum. The holdings are so vast that officials have been forced to house portions in separate museums scattered throughout the city. One ticket, purchased at any of the locations, is valid for the arsenal, the natural history museum, and most of the art museums in the city (70AS, students and seniors 50AS).

THE OLD TOWN. An entertaining way to explore Graz is to use the tourist office's guide, *Old Town Walk* (10AS). The tourist office is in the **Landhaus,** the seat of the provincial government, and a sight in itself. The building was remodeled by architect Domenico dell'Allio in 1557 in Lombard style. Through the arch to the right is a striking Renaissance arcaded stone courtyard, where *Classics in the City* is held (see p. 152). A picture from one of the upper floors is worthwhile.

LANDESZEUGHAUS (PROVINCIAL ARSENAL). On the other side of the tourist office is the fascinating **Landeszeughaus,** built between 1642 and 1644 by Anton Solar. The 1st floor details the history of the arsenal and the Ottoman Turk attacks in a series of placards and displays, with English translations. In 1749, after the Turks had packed their cannon and gone home, the armory was marked for dismantling, but an eloquent protest by the Styrian nobles convinced Empress Maria Theresia to preserve the arsenal as a symbolic gesture. The building, with its massive collection of arms and armor intact, served as a firehouse until 1882, when it first opened as a museum. Today, the 4 story collection includes enough spears, muskets, and armor to outfit 28,000 burly mercenaries. The dim light, and slightly cool air make you wonder whether a ghostly army is not already wearing the standing suits of armor. The full experience is an extravagant spectacle, with thousands of metal barrels and blades spread out (on the ceiling and walls) in abstract geometrical patterns. Allow at least 2 hours to learn the history and peruse the collection. *(Herreng. 16. ☎801 79810. Open Apr.-Oct. M-F 9am-5pm, Sa-Su 9am-1pm. Tours 11am and 3pm, call ahead for English ones; 20AS. Admission with Joanneum ticket.)*

ART MUSEUMS. The Joanneum includes the **Neue Galerie,** housed in the elegant Palais Herberstein at the foot of the Schloßberg, which showcases off-beat, avant-garde works and paintings from the 19th- and 20th-century. *(Sackstr. 16. ☎829 155; fax 815 401. Open M-F 10am-6pm, Sa 10am-1pm. Admission with Joanneum ticket.)* Its counterpart, the **Alte Galerie,** presents a mid-sized collection of Medieval and Baroque art, mostly by Styrian artists. Notable holdings include Lucas Cranach's *Judgment of Paris* and Jan Brueghel's copy of his father's gruesome *Triumph of Death.* *(Neutorg. 45. ☎801 74770. Open Tu-Su 10am-6pm. Tours Su at 11am. Admission with Joanneum ticket. English descriptions available.)* The Alte Galerie shares space with the **Kunstgewerbe,** an exhibition space for late 19th- and 20th-century art and design.

(☎801 74780. Hours vary. Admission with Joanneum ticket.) The **Künstlerhaus,** an independent museum in the Stadtpark, hosts exhibitions ranging from Tibetan artifacts to Secessionist paintings by Klimt. *(Open M-Sa 9am-6pm, Su 9am-noon. 15AS, students free.)*

HISTORY AND SCIENCE MUSEUMS. Next door to the Neue Galerie at the western foot of the Schloßberg is the **Stadtmuseum.** On the third floor, a series of 19th-century drawings of the city are presented alongside modern photographs and a large-scale model circa 1800. *(Sackstr. 18. ☎822 580. Open Tu 10am-9pm, W-Sa 10am-6pm, Su 10am-1pm. 50AS, students and children 30AS.)* Up on the Schloßberg (see below), the **Garnisonsmuseum** exhibits its modest collection of military uniforms and feathered helmets. *(Open Tu-Su 10am-5pm. 20AS, students and children 10AS. Combo ticket including Schloßberg tour 40AS, 20AS.)* The Joanneum's scientific component is the **Natural History Museum,** which encompasses geology, paleontology, mineralogy, zoology, and other -ologies. The museum has a specimen of the largest beetle in the world and a truly splendid collection of minerals and semi-precious stones. Ask in the Geology gallery to leave the museum through the secret coal mine. *(Rauberg. 10. ☎301 74760. Open Tu-Su 9am-4pm. Admission with Joanneum ticket.)*

CHURCHES. Graz has 7 historical churches, each with its own charms. The 13th-century Gothic **Leechkirche,** Zinzendorfg. 5, between the Stadtpark and the university, is the city's oldest structure. The lemon yellow **Stadtpfarrkirche,** diagonally across Herreng. from the Landeszeughaus, was the Abbey Church of the Dominicans in the 16th century. The late-Gothic church suffered severe damage in WWII air raids. When Salzburg artist Albert Birkle designed new stained-glass windows for the church in 1953, one made worldwide news: the left panel behind the high altar portrays the scourging of Christ, silently watched over by two figures bearing a marked resemblance to Hitler and Mussolini. The church holds **organ concerts** *(July 22-Aug.26, Th, 8pm. 60AS, students 40AS).*

On Hofg., opposite the Burggarten and Burgtor stands Graz's **Dom** (cathedral), built in 15th-century Gothic style by Emperor Friedrich III. In 1485, the church mounted a picture of the "Scourges of God" on the south side of the building to remind Christians of the most palpable trinity of the time: the plague, Ottoman invasions, and locusts—a combination that had wiped out 80% of the population 5 years earlier. The Dom holds **free organ concerts** *(every Su 8pm Aug.-Sept.).*

OTHER SIGHTS. Around the corner, on Burgg., the solemn 17th-century Habsburg **Mausoleum** is one of the finest examples of Austrian Mannerism. The domed tomb holds the remains of Ferdinand II in the underground chamber. Cryptic English signs are pasted to the stone walls. Master architect Fischer von Erlach (responsible for much of Vienna's Baroque grandeur) designed the beautiful frescoes upstairs. *(Open M-Sa 10am-12:30pm and 2-4pm. 10AS, children 5AS.)* Down the street, the magnificent **Opernhaus** (Opera House), at Opernring and Burgg., was built in less than 2 years by Viennese theater architects Fellner and Helmer. Contrasting with the elaborate Opernhaus, the nearby gigantic metal statue, **Lichtschwert** (light sword), makes a statement in the name of liberty. The **Glockenspiel,** located just off Engeg. in Glockenspielpl., opens its wooden doors every day at 11am, 3, and 6pm to reveal life-size wooden figures spinning to a slightly out-of-tune folk song. The black-and-gold ball underneath turns to show the phases of the moon.

SCHLOßBERG. North of Herreng. and Hauptpl., the wooded **Schloßberg** (literally "Castle Mountain") rises 123m above Graz. The hill is named for a castle which stood on it from 1125 until 1809, when it was destroyed by Napoleon's troops. Though the castle is almost completely gone, the Schloßberg remains a beautiful city park. From Schloßbergpl., visitors can climb the zigzagging stone steps of the **Schloßbergstiege,** built by Russian prisoners during WWI and traditionally known as the *Russenstiege* (Russian steps) or the *Kriegstiege* (war steps). The path continues through the terraced Herberstein Gardens to the top of the hill. The top of the Schloßberg is a carefully tended park, with sweeping views out over the vast Styrian plain surrounding Graz. Napoleon didn't manage to capture the Schloßberg until *after* he conquered the rest of Austria—he then razed the fortress in an infantile rage. The **Glockenturm** (bell tower), built in 1588, is one of the few castle structures still standing, which the little Emperor spared in return for a sizeable ransom from the citizens of Graz. *(Tower open 9am-5pm, except during guided tours; 15AS, students and children 10AS.)* Its enormous bell ("Liesl") draws a crowd with its 101 clangings daily at 7am, noon, and 7pm. The nearby **Uhrturm** (clocktower) dates from 1265. A guided tour of the Schloßberg includes viewing the Uhrturm clockworks from 1712. *(Tours in German or English Apr.-Oct. every 2hr., meet at Glockenturm, Tu-Su 9am-5pm on the hour; 30AS, students and children 15AS.)*

From Schloßbergpl., the **Schloßberg Passage** burrows into the *Berg*. A network of tunnels was blasted into the hill during WWII to serve as a mass bomb shelter for up to 50,000 civilians. Visitors may walk through the cool, dark main passage and peer down spooky side tunnels. In 2000, one of the side tunnels was fitted with 64 televisions broadcasting from around the world, computers and nifty gadgets such as e-books (appropriately enough the most popular e-book is *Alice in Wonderland*). This **Dom im Berg** (Cathedral in Mountain), as it has been termed, serves as a "presentation site for Styria's creativity and intelligentsia." Email can be checked here too. *(Open 9am-6pm. Tunnel free. Dom im Berg 50AS.)* The **Grazer Schloßberg Grottenbahn** travels for 30 minutes through the mountain past illuminated scenes from fairy tales, history, and literature, including a stuffed dummy Gulliver restrained by dozens of dusty Lilliputian Ken dolls. *(Open daily 10am-6pm; last train at 5:30pm, tickets up to 35AS.)*

PARKS AND GARDENS. Down the hill on the eastern side near the Uhrturm and through the Paulustor arch is the lovely **Stadtpark.** Separating the old city from the university quarter, the gardens attract walkers, sun-bathers, and frisbee players. Graz acquired the ornate central fountain, which has 8 figures holding huge spitting fish, at the 1873 Vienna World's Fair. Paris snatched up the 2 complementary side pieces, now in Pl. de la Concorde. South of the fish fountain, the Stadtpark blends into the **Burggarten,** a bit of carefully pruned greenery complementing what remains of Emperor Friedrich III's 15th-century **Burg.** His cryptic wall inscription "A.E.I.O.U." remains a mystery, varyingly interpreted as *"Austria Erit In Orbe Ultima,"* (Austria is the Ultimate on Earth), or *"Alles Erdreich Ist Österreich Untertan"* (All on Earth is Under Austria). A vague desire for Austria to rule the universe can be intuited. Or a love of vowels. Friedrich's son, Maximilian I, enlarged the building and in 1499 commissioned the Gothic double spiral staircase, predating Watson and Crick by almost 500 years. He also inserted the **Burgtor** (Castle Gate) into the city wall. *(Garden open 7:30am-7pm.)*

ENTERTAINMENT AND FESTIVALS

The cultural magazine *Graz Derzeit*, free at the tourist office, prints a complete daily listing of events with details on prices and locations (www.iic.wifi.at/graz/veranstaltungen/derzeit). Students can check the **student administration office** of the university, which has billboards papered with concert notices, student activity flyers, and carpool advertisements.

OPERA AND THEATRE. For professional music and dance performances, Graz's neo-Baroque **Opernhaus,** at Opernring and Burgg. (☎8008), sells standing-room tickets an hour before curtain call. The program includes operas and ballets of worldwide repute; for many young hopefuls, Graz is considered a stepping stone to an international career. One big show comes each July while the regular companies are on vacation—1999 brought *Stomp*, 2000 *Porgy and Bess*, and in 2001 *Evita* will grace the stage. Tickets cost a pretty penny (130-995AS), but standing-room slots start at 45AS, and student rush tickets cost 150AS. The **Schauspielhaus** (☎8005), the theater on Freiheitspl. off Hofg., sells bargain seats just before showtime. All tickets and performance schedules are available at the **Theaterkasse,** Kaiser-Josef-Pl. 10 (☎8000; open M-F 8am-6:30pm, Sa 8am-1pm), and the **Zentralkartenbüro,** Herreng. 7 (☎830 255).

FESTIVALS. Since 1985, the city has hosted its own summer festival, **Styriarte.** Mostly classical concerts are held daily from late June to late July in the gardens of the Schloß Eggenberg, the large halls of Graz Convention Center, and the squares of the old city. Tickets are available at Palais Attems, Sackstr. 17. (☎825 000; styriarte@mail.styria.co.at; www.styriarte.com. Open M-F 8:30am-12:30pm and 2-6pm, Sa 9am-1pm.) Every summer the **American Institute of Musical Studies** transfers to Graz. Vocal and instrumental students perform works ranging from Broadway to Schönberg on the streets and in concert halls—ask for a schedule at the tourist office. From July to mid-August, **organ concerts** are held every Thursday at the Stadtpfarrkirche and every Sunday at the *Dom* (8pm; 60AS, students 40AS). July and August also bring **Jazz-Sommer Graz** a festival of free concerts by international jazz legends like Art Farmer, Toots Thielemans, and Tommy Flanagan (☎605 311; Th-Sa, 8:30pm at Maria Hilferpl.). The first two weeks of June bring storytellers from afar to **Graz Erzählt,** Europe's largest storytelling festival. From late July to early August, Graz surrenders its streets to **La Strada,** the international festival of puppet and street theatre. In late September and October, the **Steierischer Herbst** (Styrian Autumn) festival celebrates avant-garde art with a month of films, performances, art installations, and parties. Contact the director for details, Sackstr. 17 (☎823 0070; stherbst@ping.at; www.ping.at/members/stherbst).

FILM. The award-winning movie theater **Rechbauerkino,** Rechbauerstr. 6 (☎830 508), occasionally screens un-dubbed arthouse films in English (85AS, children 70AS). The **Royal Kino,** Conrad-von-Hötzendorfstr. 10, a few blocks south of Jakominipl., shows new releases in English, without subtitles (70AS before 6:45pm, 85AS after). In summer, the **Classics in the City Festival** shows free films of great opera performances and serves food in the *Landhaus* courtyard next to the tourist office (July-Aug. daily at 8:30pm, weather permitting).

NIGHTLIFE

The hub of after-hours activity in Graz can be found in the so-called **"Bermuda Dreiecke"** (triangle) an area of the old city behind Hauptpl. and bordered by Mehlpl., Färberg., and Prokopiag., and Puerto Rico. The Triangle's dozens of beer gardens and bars are packed with people all night, every night; sitting in an outdoor cafe until at least 11pm is *de rigueur*, when local ordinance requires that festivities move indoors. Most of the university students prefer to down their beers in the pubs lining Zinzendorfg. and Halbärthg. on the other side of the Stadtpark.

Café Harrach, Harrachg. 26 (☎322 671). At this grad-student hangout, a half-liter of *Gösser* goes for 31AS, but this is wine-drinking country. Almost everyone is throwing back white wine spritzers (27AS). Open July-Sept. M-F 5pm-midnight, Sa-Su 7pm-midnight; Oct.-May M-F 9am-midnight, Sa-Su 7pm-midnight.

Tom's Bierklinik, Färberg. 1 (☎845 174), has the largest stock of international beers in Austria. Go ahead and try prescriptions from Hawaii, Trinidad, or India (all 75AS), or just get a local fix with a glass of the ever-popular *Murauer Pils* (32AS). Walk-in hours M-Sa 8pm-4am.

Kulturhauskeller, Elisabethstr. 30 (☎381 058), underneath the Kulturhaus. A young crowd demands ever louder and more throbbing dance music, but the partying doesn't get started until 11pm on weekends. *Weißbier* 37AS. No shorts or military clothing. 19+. Obligatory coat check and security fee 20AS. Open Tu-Sa 10pm-3:30am.

Triangel, Burgg. 15, below the Kommod bar/restaurant. Vaulted brick ceilings, mirrored arches, and a low-key, well-dressed clientele of trendy twenty-somethings. Open 8pm-4am. Occasional bands, no cover.

DAYTRIPS FROM GRAZ

SCHLOß EGGENBERG

Take tram #1 (dir.: Eggenberg) to "Schloß Eggenberg" (5am-midnight). Cross the street and backtrack ¼ block turning at your first right (Schloßstr.).

To the west of Graz, the grandiose **Schloß Eggenberg,** Eggenberger Allee 90, contrasts sharply with the surrounding shabby suburban neighborhood. Built for Prince Ulrich of Eggenberg, this 5-towered palace now holds an extensive coin museum, an exhibition of artifacts from antiquity, and a prehistoric museum. The guided tour of the elegant **Prunkräume**—filled with 17th-century frescoes, tile ovens, and ornate chandeliers—reveals the convoluted cosmological design of the palace. This microcosm of time has four towers symbolizing the four seasons, 12 gates for the months of the year, and 365 windows for the days. (☎(0316) 583 264. Antiquities and coin collection open Tu-Su 9am-noon and 12:30-5pm; prehistoric museum open Tu-Su 9am-1pm and 1:30-5pm. Museum entrance 120AS including the Prunkräume, otherwise 100AS; groups, children, and students 70AS. Tours in German and English; every hr., 10am-noon and 2-4pm. Tour 20AS, plus entrance to the museums.) Royal blue peacocks wander freely in the game preserve surrounding the palace. (Free with castle entrance, 2AS for gardens only. Open daily 8am-7pm.) Classical concerts are held in the castle's **Planetensaal** (Planet Hall; ☎825 000; Aug.-Sept. M at 8pm; tickets from 130AS).

ÖSTERREICHISCHES FREILICHTMUSEUM

Drivers should take the road to Salzburg and turn off at Gratwein. Trains run to Stübing from Graz every hour (74AS round trip); from the Stübing train station, turn left onto the main road and walk 25-30min. to the museum. Buses run irregularly between Stübing and the museum (4 per day, 15AS), so you're better off walking. The most convenient transport is by bus that runs from Lendplatz in Graz (M-Sa at 9am and 12:30pm) straight to the museum, returning at 1:23pm and 4:40pm (74AS round trip).

The **Österreichisches Freilichtmuseum (Open-air Museum),** in the nearby town of **Stübing,** showcases Austrian farm life as it existed in the not-so-distant past. The museum consists of 90 farmhouses, barns, mills, and storehouses from all over Austria, transported plank-by-plank and lovingly restored, surrounded by woods and grain fields. The tranquility of the surrounding greenery momentarily hides the hard work involved in keeping a farm going. Try your hand at spinning wool or churning butter—you might be inspired to kiss your computer when you get home. If you're accustomed to your food arriving in neat supermarket packaging, the museum will remind you how grain is farmed, cheese made, and bees kept. There are also reconstructions of blacksmithies, water mills, stables, and elaborate birdhouses. A snack bar at the mid-point of the tour serves slices of bread with *Schweineschmalz* (lard), or pastries for the less adventurous (free, but you ought to give a reasonable donation). An exhibit house near the far end of the museum displays pictures and charts of agricultural techniques through the ages. (☎(03124) 53700. Open Apr.-Oct., Tu-Su, 9am-5pm. 75AS, students 40AS, children 30AS. Exhibits in German. English guidebook 30AS.)

RIEGERSBURG ☎03153

A sleepy town buried in the rolling green country east of Graz would have gone unnoticed, untrammeled by tourists, if it weren't for the impressive castle overshadowing it. The hillside town of Riegersburg in Styria is home to one of the finest castles in Austria, never conquered by any enemy. The *Schloß*, and the magnificent hostel inside, balance on the edge of a steep cliff, looking out across vast panoramas of rolling farmland and distant, misty hills.

TRANSPORT AND PRACTICAL INFORMATION. If you've got a **car,** Riegersburg is an easy, 55km trip from Graz. Take A-2 and exit at Ilz. Otherwise, poor train-bus connections necessitate precise planning. Ride the **bus** directly from **Graz** (from Andreas-Hofer-Pl.; 2hr.; M-Sa 12:35pm, M-F 5:30pm, Su 10:45am; round-trip 210AS). Buses from Riegersburg to Graz generally leave at pre-dawn hours (2hr.; M-Sa 5:40 and 6:05am, Su 5:35pm). Or, take the **train** from Graz to **Feldbach** (1hr., every hr. 6:18am-10:43pm, 90AS) and switch to the bus into Riegersburg at the bus depot near the train station (M-F 7 per day, 8:03am-6:20pm, 20min., 20AS). A

100AS ticket purchased on the bus back to Feldbach (M-F, 7 per day 6:50am-5:50pm) is valid for train connections back to Graz (every hr. 4:20am-8:22pm). If necessary, you can always call a **taxi** (☎381) to take you back to Feldbach (170-210AS). If you happen to be in Graz on Friday and would like someone else to handle the transportation issue, reserve a spot on the Graz tourist office's *Castles and Chateaux Tour*, which includes Riegersburg (290AS per person, includes transportation, English-speaking tour guide, and entrance fee). Tour leaves from behind the tourist office on Landhausg. April-Oct. Fridays at 2pm. Inquire at Graz tourist office (see p. 157). The **tourist office,** just up the street toward the castle from the bus stops, can help you find a room (☎8670; open M-Sa 11am-6pm, Su 10am-6pm). **Exchange currency** at the **post office,** Riegersburgstr. 26 (open M-F 8am-noon and 2-6pm, Sa 8am-noon; exchange until 5pm). The **postal code** is A-8333.

ACCOMMODATIONS AND FOOD. One of the compelling reasons to come to Riegersburg is the **Jugendherberge im Cillitor (HI),** Riegersburg 3, which is actually incorporated into the fortress walls. Walk toward the castle, and up the very steep stone path. The hostel entrance is in the archway you pass through as you veer left. This ivy-clad hostel has 14-bed dorms with arrow-slits from which to fight off advancing school groups. Friendly proprietors are always willing to dispense advice on local sights. (☎8217; fax 82174; mobile ☎(0664) 551 3922; oejhu-stmk@oejhv.or.at. Breakfast included; other meals 55-65AS. Hall showers and toilets. Curfew 10pm. Open May-Oct. Dorms 135AS.) At the bottom of Riegersburg's hill, **Lasslhof,** is a yellow hotel with a popular bar/restaurant and a ghastly art collection in the halls between the 2-, 3-, and 4-bed rooms. (☎8201 or 8202. Breakfast included. Reception 8am-10pm. Doubles 360AS, with shower 480AS; triples 540AS, 720AS; quads 720AS-960AS.) At the restaurant downstairs, wolf down *Wienerschnitzel* with potatoes and salad (77AS), or snack on *Frankfurter mit Gulaschsaft* (38AS). Stock up on groceries at **SPAR Market,** across from the start of the stone path (open M-F 7am-noon and 2:45-6:15pm, Sa 7am-12:30pm).

SIGHTS: BURG KRONEGG. Naturally, Riegersburg relies heavily on the revenue from tourists who gawk at the well-preserved remains of **Burg Kronegg,** the town's only man-made attraction. While attackers could never get inside, tourists can, but only after tackling the steep, stone-paved path leading up to the castle. Bring sturdy shoes and bottled water. The path itself is one of the most exciting parts of the visit. Lush vineyards clothe the castle slopes, while tall elegant cypresses peek out from the distance. Benches, stone arches, and monuments provide good excuses to catch your breath. Ask a local to point out the Prince and Princess of Liechtenstein's current residence—note the swimming pool inside the old moat. You might circle the castle and climb up the *Eselstiege* (donkey stairs) instead of walking up the steep slope. Legend claims that this back entrance was built in the 17th century when 2 feuding brothers owned the place, and one closed off the top entrance. Actually, the stairs were laid in the 15th century as a food transportation route before the quarrelsome brothers even had mouths to quarrel with. On your way up, look for an inconspicuous crescent moon carved into the stone wall to mark the highest point reached by invading Turks.

CHANGING HANDS The Burg Kronegg has a complicated history. In the 13th century, the castle consisted of 2 separate fortresses on the plateau: the older Burg Kronegg to the north, and Burg Lichtenegg to the south. In the 17th century, Duchess Elisabeth von Wechsler had the lower castle torn down and Burg Kronegg fortified against the Turks, making it one of the largest and most impregnable strongholds in Austria—108 rooms surrounded by 3km of walls with 5 gates and 2 trenches. The fearsome castle withstood the 1664 Ottoman onslaught, driving back the Turks in the great Battle of Mogersdorf. In 1822, the Princes of Liechtenstein acquired the castle, restored it, and moved in; the Princes still live there today.

The castle itself houses several well-maintained exhibits and museums. The **Burgmuseum** showcases 16 of the castle's 108 rooms, packed with art and self-congratulatory historical notes on the Liechtenstein family (yes, like the country), who bought the castle in 1822 and still own it. The **Weiße Saal** (White Hall), with its stucco ceiling flourishes and crystal chandeliers, lacks only dancers in decolleté gowns waltzing around the floor. The **Hexenzimmer** (Witch Room) contains an eerie collection of portraits of alleged witches (including Katharina "Green Thumb" Pardauff, executed in 1675 for causing flowers to bloom in the middle of winter) and a real iron maiden. There's also Prince Friedrich's (the current owner of the castle) gallery of amateur photography. The **Hexenmuseum** (Witch Museum) spreads over 12 more rooms, with an exhibit on the most expansive witch trial in Styrian history (held between 1673 and 1675). Filled with torture devices, funeral pyres, and other gruesome exhibits, the museum investigates, with historical rigor, the accusation that 95 women and men had caused hail and thunderstorms. (☎82131. Open Apr.-Oct. daily 9am-5pm. Admission to each museum 90AS, students 60AS; combination ticket 130AS, 90AS. 1hr. tours in German throughout the day, 10AS. Exhibits in German with a somewhat helpful English brochure.)

You can best appreciate the castle's beauty from the surrounding network of gravel paths and stone staircases. Take a good look at the elaborate iron pattern covering the well in the castle's second courtyard—it's said that any woman who can spot a horseshoe within the design will find her knight in shining armor within a year. In the shadow of the castle chirps the rather meager **Greifvogelwarte Riegersburg,** showcasing Oct. birds of prey. (Open Apr.-Oct. 10am-5pm; shows with trainers dressed in castle finery M-Sa 11am and 3pm, Su 11am, 2, and 4pm. 60AS, students 30AS.) At one of the many *Buschenschenken* on the hills surrounding the castle, you can sample Schilcher wine, a *rosé* grown from hearty native grapes.

LEOBEN ☎03842

The buckle of Austria's "Iron Belt," Leoben lies between a ring of mountains and the Mur River. With 29,000 people, Leoben is not quite a small town, more of a tiny charmed city. Leoben offers both the benefits of just a little urbanity and splendid outdoors. The elegant town square, replete with ice cream stands, sends off a number of streets that lead the visitor to an ancient church, to Leoben's Gösser beer brewery, and to the idyllic city park, "Am Glacis." Just past the tight streets, however, the town disappears and forest trails take one away from the civilized paved world.

TRANSPORT. The **information counter** at the train station in Leoben can help decipher the snarl of rail lines (☎42545, ext. 390; open M-Sa 6am-8pm, Su 6am-9pm). Trains arrive at the station from **Graz** (every 2hr., 114AS), **Vienna Westbahnhof** (2¼ hr., 8:18am-1:15am, 218AS), **Salzburg** (3½hr., every 2hr., 7:19am-10:41pm, 350AS), and **Klagenfurt** (2hr., every hr. 7:33am-8:46pm, 280AS). From smaller destinations such as **Mariazell,** take the train to **Bruck an der Mur** and then take the train to Leoben (15min., 1-2 per hr. 5:35am-11pm, 40AS). The train station also has **lockers** (20AS) and **luggage storage** (30AS; open 6:45am-9pm). For local connections, the main **bus station** in Leoben is a 10-minute walk from the train station at the corner of Franz-Josef-Str. and Parkstr. Leoben is just minutes from Autobahn A9, which runs south to Graz and northwest to Steyr and Linz; take the Leoben exit.

ORIENTATION AND PRACTICAL INFORMATION. The Mur River surrounds Leoben; from the train station, you must cross it to reach the center of town. **Franz-Josef-Strasse** (the main traffic artery) and **Peter-Tunner-Strasse** run parallel for the length of the town, leading to Hauptpl. and beyond. Reach the first by exiting the train station and crossing the bridge straight ahead. Reach the second by taking a right and then another right after crossing the same bridge. Leoben's **tourist office,** Hauptpl. 12, dispenses a hotel list and a complimentary map, along with information on local events and hikes. Walk straight out of the train station, cross the river, and take your second right onto Franz-Josef-Str. Follow the road past the bus terminal to the main square. The tourist office is on the right. (☎44018; fax 482 181. Open M 7am-5pm, Tu-Th 7am-6:30pm, Fr same hours but closed from 1-3pm, Sa 9am-12:30pm.) Services include: a **parking garage** under Hauptpl. with an entrance on Langg. (5AS per 30min.); free **public restroom** in the garage, accessible from the elevator in the center of Hauptpl; **taxis** at stands on Hauptpl. and the train station; **Stadt Apotheke,** Krotlendorferg. 6, pharmacy not far from the tourist office (☎42451; open M-F 8am-noon and 2:30-6pm, Sa 8am-noon); **hospital** (☎401); **post office** at Erzherzog-Johann-Str. 17 (open M-F 8am-6:30pm, Sa 8am-5pm). The **postal code** is A-8700.

ACCOMMODATIONS. Accommodations are sparse in Leoben, budget accommodations even sparser. During July and August, the **Schulverein der Berg-und-Hüttenschule Leoben,** Max-Tendlerstr. 3, rents out 47 double rooms, some of which can be rented as singles. From the train station walk straight and cross the river. Turn right on Stadtkai until Peter-Tunner-Str., and follow it until Max-Tendlerstr. Turn right and walk to the end (10min.) Rooms are large and plain. (☎44888. Fax 448 883. Breakfast included. 237AS for a single, 414AS for a double.) **Gasthof Altman,** Südbahnhofstr. 32, has 12 doubles and a 3-lane bowling alley in a convenient, albeit busy, location. Exiting the train station, facing away from the tracks, turn left and walk down Südbahnhofstr. for 10min.; Altman will be on your right. Private TV sets, showers, and hardwood floors make Altman more luxurious than most hotels in this price range. The bowling alley and restaurant (meals 60-190AS) fill with locals delighting in beer and bowling pins (☎42216. Breakfast included. Bowling alley open Tu-Sa 10am-midnight, Su 10am-3pm; 10AS for 10min. Free parking. One person 350AS, double 580AS. MC, Visa.)

STYRIA

FOOD. Kirchg. is home to a number of cheap restaurants. In particular **Wirsthaus zur Turmstub'n,** Kirchg. 7-9, serves up reasonably priced Austrian fare, with midday *Menüs* about 75AS. (☎42649. Open Tu-Sa 10am-10pm, Su 10am-5pm.) Across the street from Homanng. 24 is an alley that leads to a set of stairs that climb to **Cafe Vinum** at the top of the tower. They serve only drinks, so sip your wine or espresso while watching lovely Leoben below (open Tu-Su 10am-1am). Dirt-cheap eats are to be had at the **food stand,** across from St. Xaver Church for Würstler or Frankfurter for about 30AS. Another alternative is **La Pizza,** Langg.1, which has large pizzas for 2 (75-120AS) but nowhere to sit—take out a pie to enjoy by the river (☎45347. Open M-F 11am-2pm and 5-10pm, Sa-Su 11am-10pm). Or get some edibles at the **markets** along Franz-Josef-Str., **Billa** supermarket Langg. 5 (open M-W 8am-7pm, Th 7:30am-7pm, F 7:30am-7:30pm, Sa 7:30am-5pm), or the **farmers' market** on Kirchpl. (Tu and F 7am-1pm).

SIGHTS AND ENTERTAINMENT. Most of Leoben's attractions center around **Hauptplatz,** 10min. from the train station (cross the bridge and bear right onto Franz-Josef-Str.). Sights are designated by a square sign with an ostrich eating iron horseshoes, one held daintily between its toes and the other protruding from its beak. This city symbol alludes to Leoben's dependence on the iron trade—in the Middle Ages, ostriches were thought capable of eating and digesting iron. That's a goose, you say? Well, when it was designed, no one in Leoben knew what an ostrich looked like.

Most of the buildings on Hauptpl. are former homes of the **Hammerherren** (Hammer men). The most ornate of the bunch is the 1680 **Hacklhaus,** bearing a dozen statues on its pink facade. Justice holds a sword and a balance, Hope brandishes an anchor, and Wisdom views the world through the mirror in his hand. Now that's wise. Standing guard at the entrance to Hauptpl. are the **Denkmäler und Monumenten** (memorial statues and monuments), beautifully crafted works erected to ward off the fires and plague that devastated much of Styria in the early 18th century. Look for St. Florian the fire-proof and St. Rosalia the plague-resistant. Just outside Hauptpl. is the **Pfarrkirche Franz Xaver,** a rust-colored church whose elaborate interior is dominated by black and gold. Go through the Kreuzgang to see 14 paintings showing Christ from condemnation to crucifixion. The **Schwammerlturm** (Mushroom Tower) guards the bridge over the Mur.

Relax in one of Leoben's well-manicured gardens. A stroll through the **Stadtpark "Am Glacis"** one block past Hauptpl. leads to the **Friedensgedenkstätte** (Peace Memorial), which commemorates the 1797 treaty with Napoleon. The tiny museum showcases an exhibit detailing the political and military events surrounding the treaty—see the very feather pen that Napoleon used to inscribe his signature. (Open May-Sept. daily 9am-1pm and 2-5pm. Free.)

A scenic 30-minute walk along the Mur rewards you with the chance to inspect the **Gösser brewery.** Examine antique brewing machinery, wander around inside the **Göss Abbey** (the oldest abbey in Styria), and swill down a free stein of fresh brew (☎209 05802. Brauhausg. 1. 9am-6pm every Sa and Su 50AS, students 25AS. You can only tour if you arrange ahead of time (it's worth it). The **Stadttheater,** Homanng. 5, is the oldest functioning theater in all of Austria (☎406 2302; box office open M-Sa 9:30am-12:30pm and Th-F 4-6:30pm; theater closed June-Sept.). The city fills the summer void with the **Leobener Kultursommer,** a program of theater, classical, and pop concerts, literary readings, and treasure hunts (June-Sept.). Pick up a free program from the tourist office

To wander away from Leoben take a **hike** with the hiking maps that the tourist office provides. A brief one, that is easy to reach, begins at the Stadtpark. From Mühltalestr., walk toward and up Dirnböckw. Follow the road as it curves until steps leading into the forest appear. When two trails diverge in the woods choose the one leading right and up to arrive at the top of a lush grassy valley. With the mountains in the horizon, at your level, and Leoben below, the view rewards the moderate half-hour hike.

MARIAZELL ☎03882

Tilting precariously on the side of the Alps, the little town of Mariazell, somewhat extravagantly subtitled *Gnadenzentrum Europas* (Europe's Center of Mercy), is both unabashed resort and important pilgrimage site. During the day, the beautiful town is best suited for lazy walks, hikes, a ski in the Bürgeralpe, and a dip in the nearby **Erlaufsee.** The faithful come here to pay homage to a miraculous Madonna made of linden wood, once owned by Magnus, the traveling monk who founded the town by establishing a shrine to the Virgin here in 1157.

GETTING THERE AND AROUND

Mariazell is accessible from St. Pölten by a zippy little mountain train called the **Mariazellerbahn** (2½hr., 7 per day, 5:59am-5:30pm, 150AS). **Buses** connect Mariazell to **Bruck an der Mur** (1¾ hr., 5:45am-6:15pm, 106AS), **Graz** (3hr., 7am-4:50pm), and **Vienna** (3hr., 6:50am-3:50pm, 195AS). The **bus station** is down the steps below the post office near Hauptpl., but for bus information you should inquire in the post office, or ask waiting bus drivers for information on times and rates. To reach Mariazell **by car** from **Vienna,** take Autobahn A-1 west to St. Pölten, and exit onto Rte. 20 south (1hr.). From **Graz,** take Rte. S-35 north to Bruck an der Mur then Rte. S-6 to Rte. 20 north.

ORIENTATION AND PRACTICAL INFORMATION

The **tourist office,** Hauptpl. 13, has information on local skiing, boating, fishing, hiking, transportation, and accommodations, and makes free room reservations. From the train station, facing away from the tracks, turn right on Erlaufseestr., then left up the hill to Wienstr., Mariazell's main road. Follow it to **Hauptpl.** the town center, and look for the green information sign on your right. (☎2366; fax 3945; www.mariazell.org. Open May-Sept. M-F 9am-12:30pm and 2-5:30pm, Sa

9am-12:30pm and 2-4pm; Oct.-Apr. M-F 9am-12:30pm and 2-5pm, Sa 9am-12:30pm; closed Sa. Apr. and Nov.) The **train station,** Erlaufseestr. 19 (☎ 2230), **rents bikes** (100-200AS per day depending on bike type) and **stores luggage** (ask the attendant). Services available include: **lockers** at the bus station (10AS); **currency exchange** or **ATM,** at the Raiffeisenbank, behind and across the street from the tourist office (open M-F 8am-noon and 2pm-4pm, Sa 8am-11am); St. Sebastian **Hospital,** Spitalg. 4 (☎2222). **Internet** access is available at the Internet-Cafe, Hauptpl. 9, though the hostel (see below) gives a cheaper price. (Internet-Cafe ☎3713. Open Th-Tu 8am-11pm, 1AS per minute.) The **post office** is upstairs from the cafe (☎2551, open M-F 8am-noon and 2-6pm, Sa 8-10am). The **postal code** is A-8630.

ACCOMMODATIONS AND FOOD

Mariazell has one hostel and a plethora of *Pension* along Wienerstr.

Jugendgästhäuser (HI), Erlaufseestr. 49 (☎2669), can be reached from the train station by facing away from the tracks, turning left and walking down the street for about 10min. The newly built hostel is wonderfully bright and comfortable with **Internet** access (30AS), and a restaurant. Sports facilities including sauna and tennis courts cost between 40 and 200AS, room with 2-4 beds 270AS, 50AS more for a single.

Pension Zechner, Wienerstr. 25 (☎6040) has rooms with showers, sinks, and a telephone, and many with balconies from which one can admire the sunshine spilling through the hills. Common room with TV and small video library including *Boyz 'n the Hood.* Breakfast included. Singles and doubles available. 290AS per person, 10AS more in winter.

Alpenhaus Ganser, Brünnerweg 4 (☎4685), offers a quiet night on the mountainside. On the way to town from the train station, turn left from Wienerstr. at the tennis courts. It is a 7min. walk around the bend and up 2 sets of stairs to the large, bright-brown Alpenhaus. Uphill and indoors you'll find homemade furniture, hand-carved wood, and fantastic views. Includes a parking garage and sleds that you can ride (in winter) directly to the cable car. A ski trail leads straight to the front door. Breakfast included. May not be open in Nov., call ahead. 180AS per person, 10AS surcharge in winter.

Camping Erlaufsee, (☎2148 or 2116). A small, tidy campsite across the street from the beautiful lake on Erlaufseestr. Equipped with showers (hot water 5AS), toilets, BBQ pits, and activity room. Can be reached by **bus** from the station (15min. 9:10am-3:45pm, 20AS). Open May to mid-Sept. 50AS, children 15 and under 25AS; tent site 40AS.

FOOD

Stüberl Goldener Stiefel, the corner of Wiener-Neustadt-Str. and Dr.-Karl-Lüger-G. (☎2731), has cheap food and occasional live music. Pizza 50-90AS. Open Tu-Su 8:30am-midnight.

Wirtshaus Brauerei, Wienerstr. 5 (☎2523). Occupying what is supposedly the oldest building in town, the brewery celebrates its age with home-brewed beer (37AS) and large pretzels (17AS). While eating your *nudeln*, gaze at the family portraits, and the photos from Kaiser Franz Josef's 1910 visit to Mariazell. Open M-W 10am-11pm, F-Sa 10am-midnight, Su 10am-2pm.

Hotel Goldener Löwe, Hauptpl. 1a (☎ 2444). across from the church, lets you sit on the terrace overlooking Hauptpl. while sipping homemade mead, drink of the gods, Tu-Su 9am-7pm. Besides serving Italian and Austrian dishes, the hotel offers the craft-happy a try at **candle-making** (Sa-Su 3pm) or **gingerbread-baking** (by appointment; 35AS, plus a fee for materials). But the real reason to visit is the **1st-floor men's bathroom**—as you enter, the pissoir lights up by itself. A waterfall runs on the wall, and a map of constellations in the stall helps you ponder your fate. Each stall is also equipped with a 15-minute hourglass. Says a vendor across the street: "I have been to Paris; I have been in the grand hotels of New York City. But never have I seen such a bathroom."

Chen Xinling, Hauptplatz 3 (☎2591), is a good place for find both Chinese and Austrian dishes (around 80AS) if other places in town are closed. Open daily from 11am-11pm.

Billa supermarket, Wienerstr. 4. Open M-F 8am-7pm, Sa 8am-5pm.

SIGHTS AND OUTDOOR ACTIVITIES

CHURCH. This pilgrimage town has welcomed millions of devout Christians over the centuries, all journeying to visit the Madonna within the Basilica, with its black spires visible from any point in town. International crowds file into the church to admire the miraculous Madonna, resting on the Gnadenaltar (Mercy Altar). Empress Maria Theresia, who had her first holy communion in Mariazell, donated the silver and gold grill that encloses the Gnadenaltar. *(☎2595. Church open 6am-7pm. Free tours by appointment through the Superiorat, Kardinal-Tisserant-Pl. 1.)* The church's amazing Schatzkammer (treasure chamber) contains gifts from former pilgrims. *(Open May to late-Oct., Tu-Sa 10am-3pm, Su 11am-4pm. 40AS, students 20AS.)*

OUTDOORS. Located just under the Bürgeralpe and a short jaunt from the Gemeindealpe, Mariazell's mountains are ideal for skiing. A cable car at Wienerstr. 28 zips to the top of the Bürgeralpe. *(☎2555. Every 20min. July-Aug. 8:30am-5:30pm; Apr.-June and Oct.-Nov. 9am-5pm; Sept. 8:30am-5pm. Ascent 75AS, descent 50AS, round-trip 105AS; with guest card or student ID 60AS, 35AS, 70AS.)* Ski lifts and trails line the top. *(1-day pass 280AS, 2-day 530AS.)* For ski information on the Bürgeralpe, Gemeindealpe, Gußwerk, Tribein, and Köcken-Sattel Mountains (no lifts), call the Mariazell tourist office. In the summer wander on Mariazell's hiking trails. You can take the Hans Wertanek Promenade from near the town center to the Erlaufsee (about 5km), or go to the tourist office to get further information about trails.

The **Erlaufsee** is a crystal-clear lake surrounded by a white pebble beach, domineering mountains, and sunbathing Austrians; take the **bus** from the station (15min. 9:10am-3:45pm, 20AS). Toilets and lockers, but not showers, are available. Once at the water's edge, try renting an **electric boat** *(90-120AS for 30min.)* or a **paddle** or **row boat** from Restaurant Herrenhaus *(☎3138; 50-70AS for 30min).*

STYRIA

ADMONT

☎03613

Tiny Admont (pop. 2800), the gateway to the Gesäuse Alpine region, lies on the border between Styria and Upper Austria, along the Enns River. The narrow streets of Admont are perfect for strolls, but even better are the hikes through mountains to other towns in the region. Benedictine monks built an abbey here in the 11th century, and, although fire has repeatedly ravaged the complex, the stubborn friars have refused to let the church go up in smoke.

TRANSPORT AND PRACTICAL INFORMATION. Orient yourself by walking along Hauptstr., the main road, which lies in front of the tourist office. **Trains** run from **Selzthal,** the regional hub to Admont (20min., 5:45am-6:43pm, 40AS). Get to Selzthal from Linz (1¾hr., 5:55am-7:57pm, 198AS; see **Linz,** p. 263) or via Bruck an der Mur (1¾hr., 5:20am-10:47pm, 154AS). The Admont train station desk is open M-Sa 5:30am-7:20pm, Su 7am-7:20pm. **Buses** to Linz depart from the front of the post office and marketplace. The Admont **tourist office** tracks down rooms for free, and offers a free map and activity information. To arrive at the tourist office, exit the post office and immediately head left—the office will be on the right. (☎2164; fax 3648. Open M-F 8am-noon and 2-6pm, Sa 9am-noon; Sept.-May M 8am-noon, Tu-F 8am-noon and 2-5pm.) The **post office** can be reached by exiting the train station, facing away from the rails, turning left and walking for 10min. (☎244 128; open M-F 8am-noon and 2:30-6pm). **Currency exchange** and a 24hr. **ATM** is available at Raiffeisenbank. To get there exit the tourist office and walk away from the post office (☎2132; open M-F 8am-noon and 2:30-4:30pm). For a **pharmacy** exit left out of the post office (open M-F 8am-noon, 2:30-4pm, Sa 8am-noon). For **medical emergencies** call 82431. The **postal code** is A-8911.

ACCOMMODATIONS AND FOOD. The most convincing reason to come to Admont is—honestly—the youth hostel, **Schloß Röthelstein (HI)**, reputedly the most beautiful in Europe. Housed in a restored 330-year-old castle, the hostel offers winter ice skating, a sauna (costs extra), tennis, a soccer field, even a small track. Indoors, the main dining area is a huge hall draped with ivy and chandeliers, and an exquisite *Rittersaal* (knights' hall) functions as a concert hall. The rooms contain bay windows, brass fixtures, wood furniture, private telephones, and elegant lamps. The only challenge is getting here—yes, it *is* that lone castle sitting very high on the very big hill. From the train station, turn left down Bahnhofstr. and left again at the post office. Cross the tracks and continue straight down that road for 25min. (don't turn right at the "Fußweg" sign pointing to the castle, unless you feel mountain-goatish), past the lumberyard. Turn right at the "Schloßherberge Röthelstein" sign and follow the paved road as it curves up and up (about 25min. more). **Taxis** (☎2801 or 2323) from the station run about 70AS. Parking at the hostel. Reception open 7am-midnight. The hostel is often reserved by groups so call ahead. (☎2432; fax 279 583. Breakfast included. 6- to 8-bed dorms 235AS, singles and doubles 340AS per person. Non-members add 40AS.)

If the trek is too intimidating, try a *Privatzimmer*. Several line Paradiesstr., along the route to the hostel and generally run about 180-250AS. Closer to the town center is **Frühstückspension Mafalda,** Bachpromenade 75. At the post office, turn left and cross the rail tracks, then make the next 2 rights and cross the tracks again. Mafalda is right under the tracks, that can be a little too evident come sleepy-time. (☎ 2188. Hall showers and breakfast included. 240AS per person. 50AS surcharge for 1-night stays.) **Gästehaus Burgort,** Sonnenweg 272, is a bit out of the way but amenities and warm owners make it worth the trip. Exit the tourist office and walk left down Hauptstr. Watch out for a sign saying Volkshaus pointing to the right; at the street before it go left and then walk down the right branch. Continue straight at the 4-way intersection and then when the road forks veer left. Continue down Wagnerstr. and then Ennsweg, before going right onto Sonnenweg—the house will be down the street on the left. (☎2259. 230AS for a single, 400AS for a double, 20AS surcharge in winter, 20 percent surcharge for stays of less than three nights.)

The **ADEG supermarket** is on the way to the tourist office (open M-F 7:30am-noon and 3-6pm, Sa 7:30-noon). The Gasthöfe along Hauptpl. provide prepared Austrian fare; check out **Gasthof Zeiser,** Hauptstr. 6, for particularly cheap midday *Menüs* at around 69AS-92AS. (☎2147. Open daily 8am-10pm.)

SIGHTS AND OUTDOOR ACTIVITIES. Aside from its hostel, Admont is best known for its **Benediktinerstift** (Benedictine abbey), founded in 1088 and currently staffed by 29 monks, who also run a high school and a profitable door-making factory. What is most worth visiting is the **library** the monks maintain, which dates from 1776. With pink marble, glimmering statues, and frescoed ceilings, the library is a Baroque masterpiece. Most impressive, however, are the books, thousands of ancient tomes bound in white that make the library seem as sacred as the abbey itself. The **Natural History Museum,** full of bottled snakes and insects and the world's largest collection of flies, is housed in the same building. Next door, a special collection of manuscripts, some as old as the 11th century, are displayed in aesthetically pleasing lucite boxes. (Library and museums open Apr.-Oct. 10am-noon and 2-4pm; Nov.-Mar. Tu-Su 11am-noon and 2-3pm. Combined admission 60AS, students 30AS. English info sheets 5AS.)

It would be a sin to visit Admont without trying one of its hikes. Pick up *wanderkarte* (hiking maps) from the tourist office. Highlights include hiking Mt. Frauenberg (770m, 20-25min. hike) and other towns in the **Gesäuse** region.

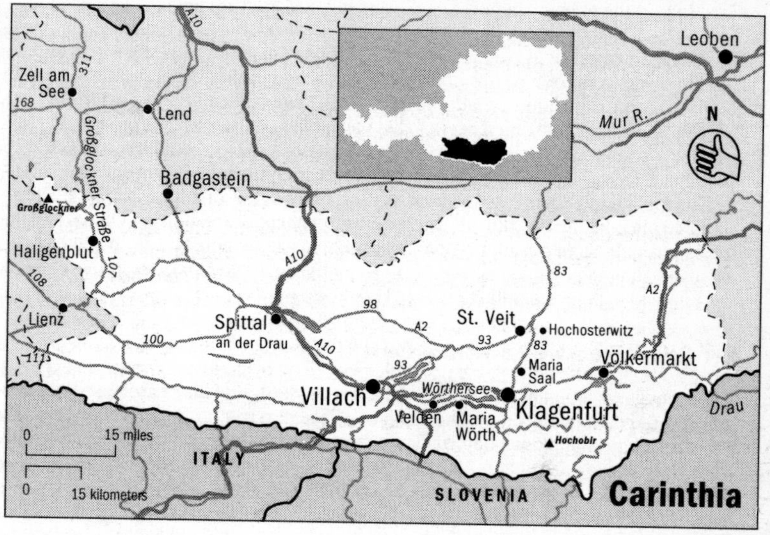

CARINTHIA (KÄRNTEN)

The province of Carinthia covers the southernmost part of Austria. In the west, it juts in between East Tirol and Salzburger Land, reaching into the Hohe Tauern National Park and the Glockner mountain range. The peaks that guard the Italian and Slovenian borders in Carinthia may look severe, but they shield the province from cold northern winds. The sunny climate, Italian architecture, and laid-back atmosphere give Carinthia a Mediterranean feel not unlike Switzerland's Ticino region. Though non-Austrians take little notice of this part of the country, natives consider Carinthia a vacation paradise, thanks to its scenic vistas and relaxing lakesides. There are nearly 200 lakes in Carinthia, including the **Wörthersee, Ossiachersee, Faakersee,** and **Millstättersee.** In summer, the warm water attracts families to the countless lake resorts, which offer an array of recreational activities. If your land-legs are surer than your sea-legs, there are rock faces to tackle all around. Abbeys and castles dot the mountainsides, mute witnesses to Carinthia's distant past. If you'll be in Carinthia for an extended period of time, consider investing in a **Kärnten Card,** good for up to 3 weeks of unlimited local transportation, free admission to most area sights and museums, and discounts on many cable cars, boat cruises, toll roads, stores, and restaurants. The card, available at area tourist offices, is a great deal at 395AS (ages 5-16 170AS).

HIGHLIGHTS OF CARINTHIA

Escape to the warm and seductive **Wörthersee,** home base to many vacationers as well as an Austrian soap opera (see p. 167).

Travel the (mini-)world in Klagenfurt's **Minimundus** amusement park (see p. 166).

Admire the view from the impressive medieval castle in **Hochosterwitz** (see p. 167).

CARINTHIA

KLAGENFURT ☎0463

Situated on the edge of the idyllic Wörthersee, Klagenfurt (pop. 90,000) is a major summertime destination for Austrians. Klagenfurt means "ford of laments," harking back to harsher times when travel across the lake and the surrounding marshes was a matter of life and death. Celts and Romans settled here, and in 1518, Klagenfurt became the administrative and cultural capital of Carinthia. Playfully dubbed "the Austrian Riviera," this easygoing, southernmost provincial capital now attracts thousands of work-weary Austrians who unwind in its beachfront suburbs. Klagenfurt's Wörthersee is the warmest alpine lake in Europe and serves as Europe's largest skating arena in winter. Only 60km north of Italy, the Carinthian capital lives life like its Italian counterparts: locals enjoy casual strolls through a palette of outdoor cafes, Italian Renaissance courtyards, and tree-lined avenues framed by Alpine peaks. More recently the town has been in the news as the home of right-wing politician Jörg Haider (see p. 68).

GETTING THERE AND AROUND

Trains chug to the **Hauptbahnhof** at the intersection of Südbahngürtel and Bahnhofstr. The **Ostbahnhof,** at the intersection of Meißtalerstr. and Rudolfsbahngürtel, is for shipping only. **Buses** depart from opposite the main train station. By **car,** Klagenfurt lies on Autobahn A2 from the west, Rte. 91 from the south, Rte. 70 from the east, and Rte. 83 from the north. From **Vienna** or **Graz,** take Autobahn A2 south to Rte. 70 west.

Trains: Hauptbahnhof (☎1717; open 24hr.). To: **Lienz** (2½hr., 12 per day 6:36am-11:36pm, 200AS); **Salzburg** (3hr., 9 per day 5:34am-7:36pm, 340AS); the **Vienna Südbahnhof** (4¼hr., 12 per day 3:42am-8:30pm, 450AS); **Villach** (30min., every ½hr. 12:16am-11:41pm, 74AS, change trains here for Italy); **Graz** (via Bruck a.d. Mur; 3hr., 12 per day 4:40am-6:50pm, 340AS). Make other connections in Salzburg or Vienna.

Buses: BundesBuses leave for most destinations in Carinthia. To: **Villach** (74AS), **Pörtschach** (54AS), **St. Veit** (45AS), **Friesach** (86AS), and **Graz** (201AS). Ticket window open M-F 7-11am and 11:30am-3pm. Info line (☎581 1350) open M-F 7am-4:30pm. For info on weekends call 066 0518 8. Buy tickets either at the train station ticket window or aboard the bus.

Public Transportation: Klagenfurt's bus system is punctual and comprehensive. The tourist office can provide a *Fahrplan* (bus schedule). The central bus station is at Heiligengeistpl. Single-fare 22AS. Buy individual tickets or a 24hr. pass (40AS) from the driver. *Tabak* kiosks sell cut-rate blocks of tickets. Illegal riders risk a 400AS fine.

Car Rental: Hertz, St. Ruprechterstr. (☎56147); **Avis,** Villacherstr. 1c (☎55938).

Bike Rental: At the *Hauptbahnhof.* 150AS, with that day's train ticket 90AS. **Impulse** (☎516 310) has 9 stations all over town, including the tourist office, across from the train station, and the campground. 90AS for 1 day (students 50AS), 300AS for 1 week. The tourist office distributes the pamphlet *Radwandern,* detailing local bike paths.

ORIENTATION AND PRACTICAL INFORMATION

To reach the town center from the station, follow Bahnhofstr. to Paradeiserg. and turn left. Neuer Platz is two blocks down on the right. **Alterplatz, Neuer Platz,** and **Heiligengeistplatz,** the town's bus center, comprise the 3-ring circus of the city's center. They lie within the **Ring,** the inner district of Klagenfurt, which is also the center of social and commercial activity, bordered by St. Veiter Ring, Völkermarkter Ring, Viktringer Ring, and Villacher Ring. Streets within the Ring generally run in a north-south/east-west grid. The **Lendkanal,** a narrow waterway, and **Villacherstr.** go from the city's center 3km to the Wörthersee.

Tourist Office: Gäste Information (☎537 223; fax 537 295; tourismus@klagenfurt.at; www.info.klagenfurt.at) is on the 1st floor of the *Rathaus* in Neuer Pl. From the station,

go down Bahnhofstr. and left on Paradeiserg., which opens into Neuer Pl. The English-speaking staff supplies colorful brochures and helps find rooms for free. Daily tours of the *Altstadt* July-Aug. 10am (call 2 weeks in advance to arrange a tour in English). Open May-Sept. M-F 8am-8pm, Sa-Su 10am-5pm; Oct.-Apr. M-F 8am-5pm. The **Jugend Info** youth information office, Fleischbankg. 4 (☎1799), focuses on academic, social, and legal issues and has a knowledgeable staff that can recommend entertainment and restaurants as well. Open M-Th 7:30am-4pm, F 7am-12:30pm.

Currency Exchange: Best rates in town are at the main post office (exchange machine 24hr.) and its train station branch.

Luggage Storage: At the train station. 30AS per piece. Lockers 30AS. Open M-Sa 6:30am-10:30pm, Su 7am-10:30pm.

Bi-Gay-Lesbian Organizations: Gay Hot-Line Klagenfurt, Postfach 193 (☎504 690). Hotline open W 7-9pm. **Bella Donna Frauenzentrum** (Women's Center), Villacherring 21-22 (☎511 248). Open M-F 9am-midnight.

Pharmacy: Landschafts-Apotheke, Alterpl. 32. Check local newspaper to find the 24hr. pharmacy.

Hospital: Klagenfurt Krankenhaus, St.-Veiter-Str. 47 (☎538).

Emergencies: Police, ☎133 or ☎5333. **Ambulance,** ☎144. **Medical Assistance,** ☎141.

Post Office: Main post office, Pernhartg. 7, off Neuer Pl. (☎55655). Open M-F 7:30am-6pm, Sa 7:30-11am. **Postal Code:** A-9020.

ACCOMMODATIONS

Though the summer heat dries up the pool of available rooms, Klagenfurt does find ways to compensate: 2 student dorms convert to youth hostels during July and August. Be aware, however, that only Jugendherberge Klagenfurt offers dorm accommodations; for the others, you'll pay considerably more for converted student single or double rooms. The tourist office helps locate rooms for free and distributes the helpful *Hotel Information* (with a city map) and *You are Welcome* pamphlets, in English, as well as the German pamphlets *Ferienwohnungen*, *Ferienhäuser*, and *Privatquartiere*, which list private rooms.

Jugendherberge Klagenfurt, Neckheimg. 6 (☎230 020; fax 230 0202 0), at Universitätstr., is close to the university, a 20min. walk from the Wörthersee, and a 45min. walk from the center of the city. From the train station, take bus #40, 41, or 42 to "Heiligengeistpl." then bus #10 or 11 to "Neckheimg." from stand #2. Buses run about every hour in the evenings (8:30am-11:30pm). Although far from the city center, its proximity to the lake and numerous bars in the nearby university area make up for this inconvenience. Breakfast (7-8am) and sheets included. Kitchen, laundry, and sauna available. Reception 7-9am and 5-10pm. Curfew 10pm; key deposit required. Mostly spacious quads, all rooms have a shower and toilet. Dinner 80AS. 200AS, non-members 240AS. For singles add 100AS; doubles add 50AS.

Jugendgästehaus Kolping, Enzenbergstr. 26 (☎56965; fax 569 6532). From the station, head right down Bahnhofstr., right on Viktringer Ring, left on Völkermarkter Ring, right at Feldmarschall-Conrad-Pl. (which becomes Völkermarkterstr.), and right on Enzenbergstr. (20min.). A student dorm during the year, Kolping welcomes travelers during summer, offering huge rooms with gleaming bathrooms. Students never had it so good. Breakfast included. 24hr. reception. Open early July to early Sept. 276AS per person, 80AS extra for single, 40AS for single-night stay; non-HI members add 50AS.

Pension Klepp, Platzg. 4 (☎32278). Klepp is a 10min. walk from both the station and the city center. From the station, follow Bahnhofstr., take the 3rd right onto Viktringer Ring, then the 2nd right onto Platzg. Clean, spacious rooms with cozy beds. Hall showers and toilets. Be prepared to pay for lodging upon arrival. Singles 250AS; doubles 415AS; triples 600AS.

Jugendheim Mladinski Dom, Mikschallee 4 (☎35651; fax 356 5111). From the train station, turn right on Südbahngürtel, right on St.-Peter-Str., cross Ebentalerstr., follow the road that curves to the left, and take the 1st left. Or take bus #40, 41, or 42 to "Heiligengeistpl.," then bus #70 or 71 (dir.: Ebental) to "Windischkaserne" from stand 13, and continue in the same direction (bus runs M-Sa until 6:50pm). Serves as a dorm for Slovenian students during the school year, converts into a bed-and-breakfast in summer. Breakfast included. Parking available. Reception M-F 6am-midnight, Sa-Su 24hr. Curfew 10pm; key available. Open July 12-Aug. 31. Singles 280AS; doubles 460AS; triples 510AS. Children under 12 130AS, under 6 90AS. 20AS discount after 3 nights.

Klagenfurt-Wörthersee Camping-Strandbad (☎21169; fax 211 6993), on Metnitzstrand off Universitätsstr. From the train station, take bus #40, 41, or 42 to "Heiligengeistpl.," then bus #12 to "Strandbad Klagenfurter See." Turn left immediately upon disembarking and walk 2min. The crowded campsite is on the left, on the edge of the Wörthersee. On-site grocery store, miniature golf, and beach. Showers and beach entry included. Open May-Sept. Mid-June to mid-Aug. 80AS per person, ages 3-14 40AS; large site 100AS; small site 20AS. May to mid-June and late Aug. to Sept. 50AS, ages 3-14 25AS. 12AS tax for persons over 18.

FOOD

You don't have to walk far or look hard to find a cheap place to eat in Klagenfurt, especially in Neuer Pl., Kardinalpl. and along Burgg. The tourist office prints *Sonntagsbraten*, a pamphlet listing the addresses and operating hours of cafes, restaurants, clubs, and bars. **Warning:** With the notable exceptions of Café Musil (listed below) and McDonald's, restaurants are closed on Sunday in Klagenfurt. Every Thursday and Saturday from 8am to noon, the compact **Benediktinerplatz** on the lower west side of the *Altstadt* welcomes a barrage of rickety, wooden stands showcasing fresh fruits and vegetables. There is a **SPAR** Markt, Hermang. just off Heiligengeistpl. (open M-F 8am-6:30pm, Sa 8am-1pm). Another on Bahnhofstr. has a small, cheap restaurant inside. After 3pm, breads and sweets in the Konditorei are half-price (open M-F 7:30am-6:30pm, Sa 7:30am-5pm). There is also a SPAR on Villacherstr., 5min. from the youth hostel.

Rathausstüberl, Pfarrpl. 35 (☎57947), on a cobblestone street right by the Pfarrkirche, serves fresh Carinthian specialties at low prices. *Käsenudel mit grünem Salat* (cheese and potato dumplings with green salad) and other daily specials are 85AS. Italian entrees 65-78AS. Enjoy a couple of beers with the sociable local crowd. English menus available. Open M-F 8:30am-midnight, Sa 8:30am-2pm and 7pm-2am.

Landhaus Restaurant (☎50633), inside the courtyard of the Landhaus on Ursulineng. Savor inexpensive, tastefully presented meals in the shadow of one of Klagenfurt's most distinctive buildings. Tagliatelle 98AS, delightfully sweet *Marillenknödel* 68AS. *Tagesmenü* 75 or 105AS. Open M-Sa 10am-midnight.

Café Musil, 10-Oktoberstr. 14 (☎511 660), is a larger bistro version of the city's most famous cake and coffee connection. Open daily 7am-10pm.

Anni's Café-Konditorei-Imbiße, Feldmarschall-Conrad-Pl. 6 (☎511 835). This everything-in-one cafe is a quick and cheap haven for any meal. Chow down on *Salatschüssel* (a salad concoction; 35-50AS) and *Schinken-Käse Toast* (ham and cheese on toast; 30AS) in the sun-drenched, ivy-enclosed *Gastgarten* out back. Also serves ice cream (7AS), candy, and fresh baked goods (12-28AS). Open M-F 7am-7pm, Sa 7am-1pm.

Arcobaleno, Wienerg. 11, at the corner of Heupl., serves up an unimaginably large variety of authentic Italian gelato for 10AS a scoop. Long lines wait for this tasty treat in almost any weather. Open M-Sa 10:30am-midnight.

Seerestaurant-Strandbad, Strandbad Klagenfurt See (☎261 396), has a salad buffet, snacks, and, from 4:30pm in summer, scrumptious grilled fish or fowl. Try the *Grillhendl* (grilled chicken, 90AS) and enjoy the lake breezes. Open M-Sa 8am-midnight.

SIGHTS AND MUSEUMS

Klagenfurt and its suburbs are home to no fewer than 23 castles and mansions; the tourist office's English brochure *From Castle to Castle* gives a suggested path and details on architecture and operating hours. Another tourist office brochure, the German *Museumswandern*, gives addresses and opening hours for the city's 15 museums and 22 art galleries.

THE OLD TOWN. Get the pamphlet, *A Walk Round Klagenfurt's Old Town*, from the tourist office to explore on your own, or participate in one of several **free guided tours.** *(Tours leave from the front of the Rathaus. July-Aug. M-Sa 10am; usually in German.)* Buildings in this part of town display a strange amalgam of architectural styles: *Biedermeier*, Italian Renaissance, Mannerist, Baroque, and *Jugendstil* façades. Visitors are inspired to look up at the play of architectural styles rather than at the uniform storefronts on the street level. At the edge of Alterpl. stands the 16th-century **Landhaus,** originally an arsenal and later the seat of the provincial diet. The symmetrical towers, staircases, and flanking projections create an elegant courtyard, which is sprinkled with the umbrellas of numerous outdoor cafes. Inside, 665 brilliant coats of arms blanket the walls. Artist Johann Ferdinand Fromiller took nearly 20 years to complete these pieces. Don't let the ceiling's "rounded" edges fool you—the room is perfectly rectangular. *(Open Apr.-Sept. M-F 9am-noon and 12:30-5pm. 10AS, students 5AS.)*

A stroll through Kramerg., one of the oldest streets in Klagenfurt, leads past the bronze statue of the legendary **Wörther-See Manndl,** with his little keg incessantly spilling water into the pool below (see Keg Party, p. 171). Continue on Kramerg.

directly to **Neuer Platz.** Here, merry-go-rounds for the young, cafes for the caffeine-addicted, and soapboxes for the cantankerous are all readily available amid a torrent of motion and activity. Standing proudly over the eastern end, a statue of Empress Maria Theresia glares regally at the skateboarders launching themselves off her pedestal. Compounding the indignity, a 60-ton half-lizard/half-serpent copper creature spits water in her direction. This fountain depicts the **Lindwurm,** Klagenfurt's heraldic beast.

CATHEDRAL. Two blocks south of Neuer Pl., off Karfreitstr., is Klagenfurt's **Domplatz** and **Kathedrale.** Rebuilt after Allied bombing in 1944, the modern exterior of the church and the surrounding square render the church almost indistinguishable from the surroundings. The cathedral's interior, however, is awash with high arches, crystal chandeliers, pink and white floral stucco, and a brilliant gold altar. Other ecclesiastical paraphernalia are on display in the tiny **Diözesanmuseum** next door, including the oldest extant stained-glass window in all Austria—a humble, 800-year-old sliver portraying Mary Magdalene. *(Lidmanskyg. 10. ☎577 084. Open mid-June to mid-Sept. M-Sa 10am-noon and 3-5pm; mid-Sept. to mid-Oct. and May to early June 10am-noon. 30AS, students 15AS, children 15AS.)*

LANDESMUSEUM. One of Klagenfurt's largest museums is the Landesmuseum (Historical Museum), which was Emperor Franz Josef's favorite. It houses the *Lindwurmschädel*, the fossilized rhinoceros skull discovered in AD 1335 that, 3 centuries later, inspired the Lindwurm statue at Neuer Pl. (see above). Other pieces include 18th-century musical instruments and ancient Celtic and Roman artifacts. The Medusas at the corners of the miraculously intact 3rd-century Dionysus mosaics could take on a *Lindwurm* any day. *(Museumg. 2. ☎536 3055 2. Open Tu-Sa 9am-4pm, Su 10am-1pm. 30AS, children 15AS.)*

KÄRNTNER LANDESGALERIE. Two blocks east of Neuer Pl., the Landesgalerie is home to an eccentric collection of 19th- and 20th-century artwork, with a focus on Carinthian Expressionism and well-endowed papier-mâché turkeys. *(Burgg. 8. ☎536 3054 2. Open M-F 9am-6pm, Sa-Su 10am-noon. 20AS, students 5AS.)*

ROBERT MUSIL MUSEUM. Across the street from the train station, this museum honors the work of its namesake, famous for his 3-volume *The Man Without Qualities*, with an archive of his writings, but not much else. *(Bahnhofstr. 50. ☎501 429. Open M-F 10am-5pm, Sa 10am-2pm. 40AS, students 20AS.)*

AMUSEMENT PARK. Eager to see more of the world? Don't miss Klagenfurt's most shameless concession to tourist kitsch, the **Minimundus** park, only minutes from the Wörthersee. If you choose the audio-guide version of the **Minimundus** experience, you'll enter with Louis Armstrong singing *It's a Wonderful World* in the background and the world's most famous monuments at your feet. Artists have created intricately detailed models of over 170 world-famous buildings and sights—all on a 1:25 scale. You'll be on eye level with the Parthenon, Big Ben, the Taj Mahal, and many more. At night, a lighting system illuminates the models. All profits go to the Austrian "Save the Child" society, a fact you can use to soothe your stinging wallet. *(Villacherstr. 241. A short walk from Wörthersee and a bus ride from the city center. From the train station, take bus #40, 41 or 42 to "Heiligengeistpl.," then switch to bus #10, 11, 20, 21, or 22 (dir.: Strandbad) to "Minimundus." ☎211 940. Open July-Aug. Su-Tu and Th-F 9am-7pm, W and Sa 9am-9pm; May-June and Sept. 9am-6pm; Apr. and Oct. 9am-5pm. 120AS, children 6-15 40AS, students and seniors 90AS, groups of 10 or more 90AS per person. English guidebook 35AS, audio-guide 30AS.)*

ZOO. Next door to Minimundus is **Happ's Reptilien Zoo.** To prevent the persecution of the Lindwurm's descendents, the zoo presents exhibits on snakes' environments. Herr Happ has a loose definition of "reptile"—along with puff adders and iguanas, the reptile zoo features spiders, scorpions, rabbits, guinea pigs, and fish. The accident-prone should avoid Saturday's piranha and crocodile feeding. *(☎23425. Open May-Sept. 8am-6pm; Oct.-Apr. 9am-5pm. 75AS, students 65AS, children 35AS.)*

DRAGON'S TALE Once upon a time, the settlement of Klagenfurt was harassed by a most unwelcome winged lizard—the *Lindwurm* (Dragon). This virgin-consuming monster terrorized the area, preventing settlers from draining the marshes. Enter Hercules, monster-slayer, and all-around *Übermensch,* who quickly dispatched the beast and saved the village. Centuries later, the "skull" of the slain beast was found, proving many an old wives' tale about the heroic founding of the town. The overjoyed townspeople commissioned sculptor Ulrich Vogelsang to create an exact likeness of the monster using its "skull" as the model. The statue of the *Lindwurm* on Neuer Platz became the town's symbol, despite that, in 1840, scientists proved the "skull" belonged not to the beast of legend, but to a pre-historic rhino. Klagenfurt's collective heart broke in 1945 when an allied soldier climbed onto the sensitive *Lindwurm's* tail, snapping it in two. The beast has since recovered and terrorizes Klagenfurt once more, albeit with a softer touch—stuffed animals reminiscent of Puff the Magic Dragon are for sale *everywhere.*

OUTDOOR ACTIVITIES

On hot spring and summer days, crowds bask in the sun and loll in the clear water of the nearby Wörthersee. This water-sport haven is Carinthia's warmest, largest, and most popular lake. The two closest **beaches** to Klagenfurt are **Strandbad Klagenfurter See** and **Strandbad Maiernigg.** The former is crowded but near the hostel and easily accessible by public transportation. From the train station, take bus #40, 41, or 42 to "Heiligengeistpl." then bus #10, 11, or 12 to "Strandbad Klagenfurter See." (Both open 8am-8pm. 35AS, children 15AS; after 3pm 20AS, children 7AS. Family card with 1 adult and up to 5 children 50AS, with 2 adults 80AS. Locker key deposit 50AS.) Strandbad Maiernigg is far from the noise and fuss of its busier counterpart, but you'll need a car or a bicycle to get there. From downtown, ride along Villacherstr. until it intersects Wörthersee Süduferstr., and then follow signs to "Wörthersee Süd."

To enjoy the water without getting (too) wet, rent a **rowboat** (30min., 24AS), **paddle boat** (42AS), or **electric boat** (66AS). A *Radwandern* brochure, free at the tourist office, suggests bike tours, including one covering a castle-church circuit. The Karawanken mountains to the south, such as the **Hochobir** (2139m) provide good hiking, but many are accessible only by car. Ask at the tourist office for details.

NIGHTLIFE

The best of Klagenfurt's nightlife rages in the pubs of **Pfarrplatz** and **Herrengasse.** To maximize your entertainment *Schilling*, read the tourist office's *Veranstaltung-Kalender* (calendar of events), available in English. The tourist office has brochures listing concerts, gallery shows, museum exhibits, and plays. Get tickets from **Reisebüro Springer** (☎387 0055). The *Jugendstil* **Stadttheater,** built in 1910, is Klagenfurt's main venue for operas and plays. *(Box office ☎552 660. Open mid-Sept. to mid-June Tu-Sa 9am-noon and 4-6pm. 40-520AS, students and seniors half-price.)*

DAYTRIPS FROM KLAGENFURT

BURG HOCHOSTERWITZ

Hochosterwitz is located just outside the town of Launsdorf, northeast of Klagenfurt and 10km east of St. Veit. Trains run to Launsdorf from Klagenfurt (30min., 10 per day, fewer on weekends, 3:42am-9:20pm, round-trip 120AS). Drivers can take route 83 from Klagenfurt to St. Veit and switch to the district road to Hochosterwitz. From Launsdorf, walk 2km to the base of Hochosterwitz (you can't miss it), and 10min. more to the main parking lot and entrance kiosk.

Dominating the countryside from the top of a steep hill that seems to rise out of nowhere, **Burg Hochosterwitz** is a striking testament to the erstwhile wealth and power of Carinthia's nobility. This is the stuff that medieval dreams were made of—a long, fortified wall winds around the hillside, culminating in a stocky castle with turrets and towers. The sight is made even more impressive by the castle's high elevation above pasturelands and fields of corn and wheat. Even if you don't have the time to visit the castle, the trip is worthwhile for this majestic sight of human and natural creation. It's been around (at least in its present form) since 1571, when German nobleman and governor of Carinthia Georg von Khevenhüller bought the property and made an extensive and costly renovation of the existing castle. Irked by marauding Ottoman Turks, Georg constructed the 14 massive gates that guard the road up to the castle, each with its own nickname and strategically designed shooting apertures. The gates alone took 13 years to build; the church was finished in 1586, although later generations of Khevenhüllers tinkered with the walls and fortifications. The path to the top commands postcard-worthy views at each and every turn, taking in all the neighboring countryside and some of the towns and mountains beyond. (Castle open Apr. and Nov. 9am-5pm; May-Sept. 8am-6pm. 70AS, children 6-15 35AS. English brochure 33AS.) A steep, 30-minute walk along the outer wall takes you up to the top of the hill; a **funicular** also ferries visitors up a nearly vertical track to the top (round-trip 40AS). There's a **restaurant** at the top as well as a small **museum** (same hours as the castle; free with castle admission), filled with old paintings of various Khevenhüllers and a collection of medieval arms. Look for the portrait of the castle's current owner, 80-year-old Max Khevenhüller-Metsch, a descendant of the castle's founder.

WÖRTHERSEE

CARINTHIA

Playfully dubbed the "Austria Riviera," the shores of the Wörthersee, a large, alluring turquoise lake, attract boatloads of Austrian and German tourists in the summer months. Water sports like windsurfing, waterskiing, and parasailing flourish here, as do less rigorous pursuits, such as swimming or the casual cultivation of a beach chair. Several resorts line the lake's shores from popular **Velden** to tranquil **Maria Wörth.** The lake is also in Klagenfurt's back yard (see page p. 162). **Stadtwerke Klagenfurt Wörthersee-und-Lendkanal-Schiffahrt** offers scenic cruises on the lake and short rides down the Klagenfurt canal. The 2-hour **cruise** goes from Klagenfurt as far as Velden, on the opposite shore, and stops at designated docks along the way. (☎21155; fax 211 5515. Round-trip 190AS, advance purchase 170AS.) The Stadtwerke Klagenfurt information center in Heiligengeistpl. sells advance tickets.

VELDEN ☎4272

Although much smaller than Klagenfurt, this one-street town puts all of its energy into summer revelry. In mid-July, the town's main street resounds with the zooming of race cars. Fireworks fly nightly to the tune of Beethoven or the Beatles, depending on the mood. And of course, the beaches are swamped with sun-worshippers, ice cream stands, and souvenir salesmen. The image of Velden would not be complete without the golden *Schloß* (castle), reflecting majestically onto the blue lake. Its attraction to most German-speaking visitors is not its beauty, but rather its fame as the location of the soap opera, "Schloß am Wörthersee."

TRANSPORT AND PRACTICAL INFORMATION. Velden is on the western shore of Wörthersee, and is easily accessible from **Klagenfurt** by train (15min., every 30min-1hr., 56AS). To reach the town center from the train station, turn right on leaving the station, then left onto Birkenallee marked with the sign "Zum See." To find the **tourist office,** Villacherstr. 19, turn right at the end of Birkenallee into Am Cerso, then turn right on Villacherstr. The tourist office is on the left side of the road, in a shiny metal and glass building. A computer will help you find accommodations, and the staff is also willing to help, but cannot make calls to check for vacancies. Free accommodations phone right outside. (☎21030. Open July-Aug. M-F 8am-8pm, Sa 9am-6pm, Su 9am-5pm.)

ACCOMMODATIONS AND FOOD. With no hostel in town, you may want to stay at one of the three in Klagenfurt (15min. by train). But the town does offer a few budget-friendly *Pensions.* **Pension Teppan,** Sternbergstr. 7, has comfy rooms with geranium-covered balconies. From the train station turn right, then left onto Birkenallee (marked with "Zum See" sign). Follow to the end and turn right onto Am Corso. Turn right onto Kirchenpl., which becomes Kirchenstr. Pension Teppan is located where Kirchenstr. meets Sternbergstr. (15min.). The friendly owners will lend bikes for free and offer discounted admission to the beach. Families welcome. Only 10 beds, so call ahead. (☎3169; pension.teppan@carinthia.com. Open Apr.-Sept. Breakfast included. 290-300AS per person.) Restaurants are plentiful on Am Corso and Rosenhtalstr., while snack bars populate the beach front area. **Pizzeria Nuova Italia,** Rosenthalstr. 39, serves scrumptious pizzas (71-150AS) near the lake (☎51274; open daily noon-midnight). For a picnic, try **Billa,** Klagenfurterstr. 12 (open M-F 8am-7pm, Sa 8:30am-1pm).

OUTDOOR ACTIVITIES. Beaches line Seepromenade and Seecorso. The chi-chi plant their umbrellas at **Casinobad** and **Strandclub** (90AS entrance). For less trendy but cheaper alternatives, join the crowd at **Strandbad Wrann** (60AS), **Strandbad Balfon** (55AS) or **Strandbad Leopold** (45AS). Each beach offers their own activities for watery fun. (Rowing boats 40AS per hr. Motorboats 160AS.) There's also windsurfing, waterskiing, and sailing. Inquire for price info. Beachside activities include volleyball, ping-pong, and mini-golf, depending on the beach. On non-beach days, bike along the lake for beautiful views. **Bike rental** at train station is 150AS per day, 90AS with train ticket.

MARIA WÖRTH ☎4273

Recognizable from afar by its distinctive church steeples, the village of Maria Wörth sits on the shores of the Wörthersee. While Velden likes to celebrate summer with a bang, this romantic lakeside village likes to slowly savor the balmy summer days. Tranquil and peaceful, Maria Wörth soothed the nerves of composers Gustav Mahler and Alban Berg. It still draws musical talent to its shores—the Vienna Boys' Choir is rumored to spend their summers here.

TRANSPORT AND PRACTICAL INFORMATION. Maria Wörth lies halfway between Velden and Klagenfurt on the south shore of the lake. Trains don't run on this side of the lake, but you can catch a bus from the bus depot by Klagenfurt's train station. Bus #5310 (dir.:Velden) goes to Maria Wörth (3 times daily except Su; 8am, 10am, noon; 56AS), but check bus schedules first. A much more scenic way of getting to Maria Wörth from Klagenfurt is by boat (45min., boats leave at 10am, noon, 2pm, and 4pm; mid-June to Sept. 9 also at 1pm and 5pm; 55AS; free with Kärnten Card). Boats leave Klagenfurt from the long wooden dock flanked by white banners, past the Strandbad bathing area; purchase tickets at the boat. To reach the **tourist office,** follow the main road away from the shore. The office, on the second floor of the building, offers advice on accommodations and recreation in the area. (☎2557. Open daily 9:30am-12:30pm and 1-5pm.) For a taxi, dial 1712.

ACCOMMODATIONS AND FOOD. Housing in Maria Wörth doesn't come cheap, but the splurge may be worth it if you're traveling with a family and want the Wörthersee resort experience. A waterfront pension will set you back at least 450AS per person; the tourist office has a vast list of accommodations. Some of the better bargains can be found in neighboring Reifnitz, but you'll need to drive there. In Maria Wörth itself, **Pension Watzenig,** St. Anna-Weg 2, is located on a hill above the center of town; walk up the main road inland and turn left at the intersection.

This *Pension* provides access to a private beach, shared with a few other guesthouses, 5 minutes away. (☎2010. Rooms with balcony and TV. 250AS per person; apartments with kitchen 750AS per day.) If you can't stand to be more than a stone's throw from the water, **Pension Beatrice,** right on the waterfront in Dellach, 2km from Maria Wörth, has its own stable of paddle and electric boats (☎3606. Breakfast included. 360-400AS per person). When you get hungry, **Café Primushaus,** beneath the tourist office in Maria Wörth, serves up a large variety of dishes on its outdoor patio like pizzas for 89-105AS or *Schnitzel* with salad for 125AS (☎2500; open daily 9am-10pm).

OUTDOOR ACTIVITIES. Unfortunately, there is no public beach in Maria Wörth; the nearest is in neighboring Reifnitz. To paddle in the Wörthersee's waters, you'll need to either stay at a pension with access to a private beach (not necessarily a pension on the waterfront) or else use the beach at the **Strandrestaurant Ebner,** next to the Hotel Astoria (open 8am-midnight; 50AS, children 25AS; beach chairs 20AS; sun umbrellas 20AS). Boats dock at the shore just beneath the 12th-century **church,** which contains a magnificent 17th-century Baroque altar. Aside from swimming and sunbathing, there are plenty of activities going on in this tiny town. The tourist office can give you a brochure that details who you should contact for boat rental, bike rental, fishing, massages, horseback riding, sailing, diving, and wind-surfing. The **Pyramidenkogel** observation tower (1½hr. from town) looms on the hillside above Maria Wörth. You can climb to its top and survey the Wörthersee and the Karawanken Alps.

THE DRAUTAL

Thanks to its moderate climate and proximity to southern Europe, central Carinthia's Drautal (Drau Valley) feels decidedly un-Teutonic, but it provides access to the traditional Alpine activities and then some. The region offers skiing, hiking, and water sports in highlands and lowlands carved by the **Drau river,** between the Hohe Tauern range and the Villacher Alps. In addition to the transportation hub of Villach and an electronic components industry, the Drautal features a variety of lakeside resorts, including the **Millstättersee, Ossiachersee,** and **Faakersee.** In winter, ice skaters pirouette on the ponds while skiers swoosh down nearby slopes. Between and below the peaks are numerous lakes, streams, and curative warm-water springs.

VILLACH ☎04242

Villach (pop. 55,000) is an attractive city with a divided cultural personality; even the street musicians reveal the influence of neighbors with their traditional Slavic, German, and Italian tunes. An important transportation hub to Italy and Slovenia, Villach is a pleasant place to spend the day, exploring the nearby Mt. Gerlitzen, the castle Schloß Landskron, or the **Ossiachersee** and **Faakersee.**

GETTING THERE AND AROUND

Trains go to **Vienna Südbahnhof** (5hr., 12 per day 1:21am-7:55pm, 470AS); **Klagenfurt** (35min., 43 per day 1:21am-11:40pm, 74AS); and **Graz** (3½hr., 13 per day 4:14am-8:12pm, 380AS). A **free city bus** travels a circuit every 20 minutes (M-F 8:40am-6:20pm, Sa 8:40am-12:20pm). **Ferries** cruise up and down the Drau, from Villach in the east to Weinberg-Bad in the west and back again. Boats depart from the dock beneath the north end of the main bridge. (1½hr. round-trip. Seasonal schedules are complex, but boats usually leave around 10am, 11:50am, 2:30pm, and 4:20pm. 120AS, children ages 6-15 60AS.) A **taxi** stand is located at the *Bahnhof*, or dial 28888 or 23333. You can **rent bikes** at the train station (150-200AS per day, with train ticket or Eurailpass 90-160AS) or at **Das Radl,** Italienstr. 22b (☎26954), in the alley next to the large pink building (120-140AS per day).

KEG PARTY Legend has it that the Wörthersee didn't always exist. Before Austrian soap operas were filmed here and the financially endowed strolled its pristine shores, they say the (then dry) Wörthersee was the site of a "sinful" town. One night a diminutive man—now known as the *Wörthersee Manndl*—entered the town's tavern, which was full of tough guys. Saying that he was sent by the Great Man Upstairs to cure the town's evils, the *Wörthersee Manndl* threatened to release the cork of the keg he carried under his arm and drown everyone with its contents if they didn't follow his commands. The bulky men looked down at the tiny *Manndl*, and his little keg, and laughed heartily into their beers. The unamused *Manndl* promptly popped the cork from the keg. Water flowed out until the men drowned, the tavern was immersed and the town sunk into a silent, watery sleep. But if you happen to cross the Wörthersee by boat at night, they say you can still hear the church bells of the submerged town.

ORIENTATION AND PRACTICAL INFORMATION

Villach sprawls on both sides of the Drau River. The train and bus stations are both on Bahnhofspl., just north of the center of town. Bahnhofstr. leads from the station and over a 9th-century bridge to **Hauptplatz,** the commercial and social heart of the city. Narrow cobblestone paths weave through this area, revealing hidden restaurants and cafes on every corner. Two sweeping arcs of stores flank Hauptpl., closed off at one end by a towering church and by the Drau at the other.

Villach's **tourist office,** Rathauspl., gives advice on attractions and skiing and helps find accommodations for free. From the train station, walk out to Bahnhofstr. over the bridge and through Hauptpl. to Rathauspl. The office is at the far end, on the left. (☎244 440; fax 244 4417. Open in summer M-F 9am-6pm, Sa 9am-noon; in winter M-F 9am-12:30pm and 1:30-5pm.) The **regional tourist office** in St. Ruprecht (☎42000; fax 42777) offers up-to-date ski information. There are **ATMs** throughout the city, including locations on Hauptpl. and in the *Hauptbahnhof.* The station also has 24-hour electronic **lockers** (20-40AS), and a **luggage check** (open 6:30am-8:30pm; 30AS). The local **hospital** is on Dreschnidstr. (☎2080). Dial 20330 to reach the **police** headquarters at Tralteng. 34. **Internet** access is available at **Ken-i-di,** Ledererg. 16 for 60AS per hour (☎21322; open M-F 10am-10pm, Sa-Su 10am-2am). The main **post office,** 8-Mai-Platz 2 also **exchanges currency** (open daily 8am-noon and 2-5pm). The **postal code** is A-9500.

ACCOMMODATIONS AND FOOD

The most reasonably priced establishment in town is **Jugendgästehaus Villach (HI),** Dinzlweg 34. From the train station, walk up Bahnhofstr. and go over the bridge and through Hauptpl. Turn right on Postg., walk through Hans-Gasser-Pl., which merges into Tirolerstr., and bear right at St. Martinstr. Dinzlweg is the first street on the left (30min.). The hostel is tucked away past the tennis courts. This facility, plastered with 1970s neon, has 150 beds in spacious 5-bed dorms, each with its own shower. Disco and free sauna on premises. (☎56368. **Bike rental** 120AS per day. Keys available with ID. Reception 7-10am and 5-10pm. Curfew midnight. Lunch or dinner 80AS each. Breakfast and sheets included. Dorms 190AS.)

There's plenty of affordable food in Villach. **Lederergasse** overflows with small, cheap eateries, while **Hauptplatz** and the sprawling **Kaiser-Josef-Platz** seat swankier patrons. **Basilikum Restaurant and Café,** Windmanng. 30, has courtyard seating and delicious 85AS menüs (☎217 589; open M-Sa 11am-2pm and 5-11pm; closed on holidays). Overlooking the Drau at Nikolaipl. 2, **Konditorei Bernhold** tempts with warm pastries (12-29AS), devilish ice cream concoctions, and a river view worthy of a slowly sipped cappuccino (☎25442; open M-F 7:30am-8pm, Sa 8am-8pm, Su 9:30am-8pm). Picnic supplies wait at **SPAR Markt,** on Hans-Grasser-Pl. and at 10-Oktoberstr. 6 (open M-F 7:30am-6:30pm), or at the **farmer's market** in Burgpl. on Wednesday and Sunday mornings.

SIGHTS AND ENTERTAINMENT

Villach lies off the beaten tourist path for foreigners, but Austrians congregate throughout the lake district in the summer, escaping the city heat of Vienna, Graz, and Salzburg. The attractions here are subtle, but the welcoming atmosphere invites exploration and relaxation.

DOWNTOWN. Any tour of Villach traverses **Hauptplatz,** the 800-year-old commercial heart of the city. The southern end of the square lives in the shadow of the mighty Gothic **St. Jakob-Kirche,** one of Villach's 12 lovely churches. Slightly raised on a stone terrace, this 12th-century church was converted during the Reformation in 1526 and thereby became Austria's first Protestant chapel. An ascent up the church's **Stadtpfarrturm,** the tallest steeple in Carinthia (94m), provides your daily exercise and a view of Villach and its environs. *(Church open July-Aug. M-Th and Sa 10am-6pm, F 10am-9pm, Su noon-6pm; June-Sept. M-Sa 10am-6pm; Oct. and May M-Sa 10am-4pm. Free admission. Steeple 20AS, children 10AS. Free organ concerts June-Aug. Th at 8pm.)*

Villach's **Stadtmuseum,** founded in 1873, exhibits archaeological and mineral displays from six millennia: clocks, hats, 18th-century portraits, and the original gold-on-black Villach coat of arms from 1240. A local tradition required that anyone who wanted to marry must first be able to carry the 90kg statue of Eisner Leonhard around the church. Many honeymoons were ruined by hernias. Right across from the museum is a glass **Holocaust Memorial** almost hidden by the shrubbery. *(Widmanng. 38. ☎205 349. Open May-Oct. daily 10am-4:30pm; Nov.-Apr. M-F 10am-6pm, Sa 10am-noon and 2-5pm. 30AS, students 20AS, children under 15 free.)*

OTHER SIGHTS AND FESTIVALS. Two blocks farther down Peraustr. looms the Baroque **Heilig-Kreuz-Kirche,** the dual-towered pink edifice visible from the city bridge. On the other side of the Drau, the **Villacher Fahrzeugmuseum** is parked at Draupromenade 12. Hundreds of antique automobiles present a rubber-burning ride into the history of transportation. *(☎25530 or 22440; fax 255 3078. Open M-Sa 10am-noon and 2-4pm; mid-June to mid-Sept. M-Sa 9am-5pm, Su 10am-5pm; 60AS, ages 6-14 30AS.)* On the first Saturday in August, the **Villach Kirchtag** (Church Day), held since AD 1225, helps the town celebrate its "birthday" with raucous revelry. *(Entrance to the Altstadt 80AS, 60AS with advance tickets.)*

OUTDOOR ACTIVITIES. Villach lies in a valley between the small but lovely **Ossiachersee** (8km from Villach) and the placid **Faakersee** (10km), so there is plenty of ideal terrain for **swimming, boating,** and **cycling** in easy reach. Trains on the Villach-Ljubljana line stop at Faak am See on the Faakersee, while settlements on the northern shore of the Ossiachersee (i.e., Annenheim, Bodensdorf) lie along the Villach-St. Veit line. The sleek peaks around Villach make for excellent summer **hiking** and winter **skiing,** with a plethora of resorts to woo the winter traveler. A 1-day regional lift ticket valid for 4 areas costs 330AS (children 190AS).

SPITTAL AN DER DRAU ☎4762

At the foot of the Goldeck Mountain, by the Drau river, sits this small city once known for its *Spittal* (hospital). People would travel here from far and wide to find cures for their maladies. They still do, only now laughter is the best medicine at the *Komödienspiele* (comedy play festival) held at *Schloß Porcia*. Self-dubbed the Komödienstadt ("City of Comedy"), Spittal attracts visitors with its care of laughter. Spittal has seen its share of tragedy too, as the ghost at Schloß Porcia will attest. Along with its mascot, the tragi-comedic clown, Pierrot, Spittal embodies a healthy mixture of Mediterranean gaiety and Middle European melancholia.

TRANSPORT AND PRACTICAL INFORMATION. **Trains** run frequently to Spittal an der Drau from **Klagenfurt** (1hr., every half hour, 130AS) and **Villach** (25min., every half hour, 74AS). To reach the town center from the train station, walk down Bahnhofstr. and cut across the park. The creamy white *Schloß Porcia* is at the end of the park and houses the **tourist office,** Burgpl. 1 (☎3420; open July-Aug. M-F 9am-8pm, rest of the year until 6pm, Sa 9am-noon all year). The friendly English-speaking staff will help you find accommodations free of charge. There is **bike rental** at the station (150AS per day, with train ticket 90AS; mountain bike 200-270AS); **ATMs** are on Bahnhofstr. 14 and across Schloß Porcia at Burgpl. 2 and 3.

ACCOMMODATIONS AND FOOD. The **Jugendherberge (HI),** Zur Seilbahn 2, is located at the base of Goldeck Mountain with clean, spacious rooms, all with in-room bathrooms. From the train station turn right, walk past the post office. Continue on Körnerstr, turn right on Ortenburgerstr. and walk under the train tracks, and make the second right onto Wiesenweg (20min.). (☎3252; fax 32524. **Kitchen** available. Restaurant downstairs. Reception 8-9am and 5-7pm. Call ahead. Breakfast 30AS. Dorms 250-350AS.) For a magnificent views try **Jugendherberge Goldeck (HI).** Follow directions for first hostel and take the cable car to the "Mittelstation" half way up the mountain (80AS; last ride up 4:30pm.). This cozy hostel offers a prime location for hiking in the summer and skiing in the winter. Ask the nature-loving staff for more information. (☎2701. Reception 8-9am and 5-9pm, but may vary. Open Dec. 26-Easter and late June-Sept. 20; depending on cable car schedule. Call ahead. Breakfast included. Dorms 200AS.) For a light lunch or ice cream indulgence try **Schloß Café,** Burgpl. 1. Ham and cheese sandwiches go for 36AS; sundaes, for 50-90AS. (☎2890. Open 10am-8pm.) Hungrier folks might enjoy Carinthian specialities like *Käsenudel* (85AS) and savory pizzas (68-150AS) at **Wirthuas Zum Spittl,** Edlingerstr. 1 (☎33960; open daily except W 10am-10pm). **Café-Restaurant Formosa,** Hauptpl. 8, serves filling Chinese dishes like tasty soups (30AS) and a Mittagsmenü (68AS) with meaty and veggie options (☎2113; open daily 11:30am-11pm). Or grab a picnic at **Spar** supermarket inside the Gerngross store, Neuerpl. 1 (☎37115; open M-F 8am-7pm, Sa 7:30am-1pm).

SIGHTS. The rather plain façade of **Schloß Porcia** fails to prepare the eye for the delicate beauty of the Florentine Renaissance style courtyard. During the summers the elegant arcades serve as a backdrop for the light laughter of Spittal's Komödienspiele (see below). The Schloß was built in the 16th century by the Spanish count Gabriel von Salamanca, who was also the Austrian imperial treasurer. It was eventually passed into the hands of the Austro-Italian Porcia family, but at least one Salamanca never left the castle: the ghost of Countess Katherina is said to still inhabit its walls. According to one story, the Countess still laments the death of her beloved son. Another says she's condemned because of her very uncountess-like behavior. She frequently set hounds against her subjects and reportedly murdered one of her maidservants for discovering her hidden stash of money. The Schloß also houses in its upper two floors the **Museum für Volkskultur** (Museum of Folk Art and Tradition). Through creative displays, including a reconstructed classroom circa 1900, this museum recreates Carinthian daily life. The museum ends extravagantly with the richly decorated living room of Count Salamanca. Permanent exhibits with detailed English information. *(☎2890. Open May 15-Oct. 13 daily 9am-6pm. Nov. 1-May 14 M-Th 1-4pm. 45AS; students 20AS.)*

FESTIVALS. During July and August, laughter fills Schloß Porcia's courtyard with the annual **Komödienspiele** (Comedy Play festival). Europe's greatest comedies are performed by the actors of Spittal's own Komödienschule (School of Comedy). Tickets 80-360AS. Students half-price. Box office in Schloß Porcia. Open every performance day 10am-8:30pm. Every odd year on the last weekend in June, Spittal celebrates **Salamancafest.** Sixteenth century garb becomes *de riguer*, drawing the town back to the time of the aristocratic Salamancas who built Schloß Porcia. Food and drink stalls swarm the town center and street musicians lend to the merry atmosphere. The highlight of the festivities, however, isn't so merry. The gruesome death of Countess Katherina's son is reenacted to somehow appease the Countess, whose spectre still haunts the Schloß, mourning the boy's death. Ghostly reasoning or not, it's reason enough to throw a good party.

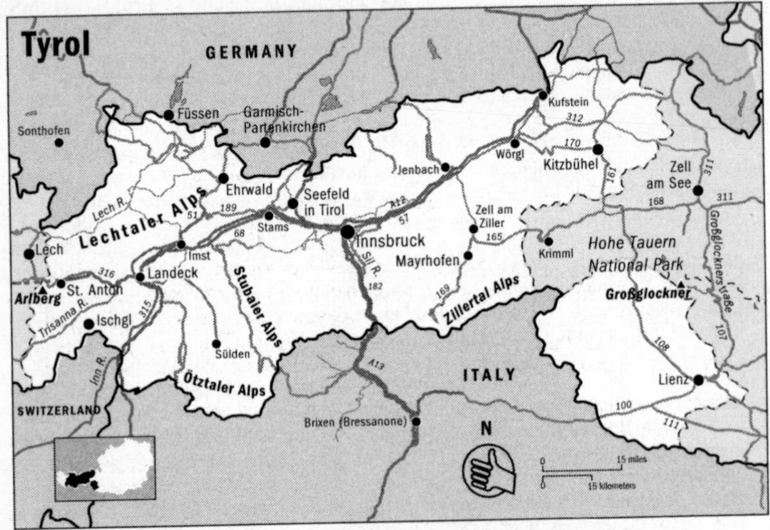

TYROL (TIROL)

Tyrol's mountains overwhelm the average mortal with their superhuman scale and beauty. Stern contours in the Kaisergebirge above St. Johann and Kufstein in the northwest soften slightly into the rounded shapes of the Kitzbühel Alps to the south, but the peaks rise again above the blue-green Zeller See, just over the border in Salzburger Land. This topography has made it impossible for Tyrol to avoid becoming one of *the* mountain playgrounds for the world. Thankfully it is an equal opportunity play place: unsullied, crag-filled valleys like the Ötztal and Zillertal run parallel to valleys finely tuned for the resort fantasies of royals (fantasies that are frequently consummated). But Tyrol doesn't rest on its granite. The urbane capitol city of Innsbruck gives quick explanation for why it was the favorite city of so many Habsburgs in its seamless blend between the gilded houses of the extravagant city, and the snowy mountains that are reflected in those gold surfaces.

HIGHLIGHTS OF TYROL

Get the low down on Alpine hiking during a free hike with **Club Innsbruck** (see p. 183).

Relive your Olympic dreams at the ski jump in **Wilten** (see p. 186) or on the slopes in **Seefeld** (see p. 186).

Use **Sölden** as a base for exploring the dramatic **Ötztal Arena,** (see p. 203).

INNSBRUCK ☎0512

Although the 1964 and 1976 Winter Olympics were held in Innsbruck (pop. 128,000), bringing international recognition to the beautiful mountain city, Innsbruck has too rich a history, and too thriving a cultural life to succumb to ski-resort status. The city's history, is tangible as one strolls past the intricate façades of Baroque buildings, the legacy of the Habsburgs' prolonged stay in the city; since Maximillian I, many a Habsburg called Innsbruck home. Though the Habsburgs are gone, the beauty that drew them here remains: massive, snow-capped peaks are so close they seem to advance down the cobblestoned streets of the *Altstadt* at every turn. If the natural beauty, the history, and the skiing don't tempt you enough, several quiet mountain suburbs offer venues for enjoying Innsbruck without the normal bustle of the city.

GETTING THERE AND AROUND

Flights arrive and depart from the airport, **Flughafen Innsbruck,** Fürstenweg 180 (☎22525), 4km from town. Bus F shuttles to and from the main train station from the airport every 15 minutes (21AS). **Austrian Airlines** and **Swissair,** Fürstenweg 176 (☎1789), have offices in Innsbruck. **Tyrolean Airways** (☎2222) offers regional flights. **Trains** arrive at the **Hauptbahnhof** on Südtirolerpl., which is on bus lines A, D, E, F, J, K, R, S, and #3; the **Westbahnhof** and **Bahnhof Hötting** are cargo stations. **Cars** from the east or west take Autobahn A12. From Vienna take A1 west to Salzburg then A8 west to A12. From the south, take A13 north to A12 west. From Germany and the north, take A95 to Bundesstr. 2 east.

Trains: Hauptbahnhof, Südtirolerpl. (☎1717). Open 24hr. Information open 7:30am-7:30pm. To: **Salzburg** (3hr., 11 per day 2:35am-11:25pm, 360AS); **Vienna Westbahnhof** (7hr., 12 per day 12:39am-11:33pm, 660AS); **Zurich** (4hr., 8 per day 2:38am-11:33pm, 600AS); **Munich** (2hr., 11per day 4:36am-10:54pm, 350AS); **Venice** (7hr., 5 per day 1:42am-17:28pm, 424AS); **Rome** (9½hr., 2 per day 11:28am-10:40pm, 672AS). Connect to **Berlin** from Munich on hourly trains leaving from Munich 5:33am-11:06pm, total Innsbruck-Berlin fare 1642AS.

Buses: BundesBuses (☎503 4382) leave from the station on Sterzingerstr., next to the *Hauptbahnhof* and left of the main entrance for suburban locales.

Public Transportation: The main bus station is in front of the main entrance to the train station. You can purchase single-ride, one-zone tickets (21AS), 24hr. tickets (35AS), 4-ride tickets (61AS), and week-long bus passes (123AS) from any driver or *Tabak.* Punch your ticket when you board the bus or pay a 400AS fine. Most buses stop running around 10:30 or 11:30pm. Check each line for specifics. A free *Nachtbus* service runs every night, heading though Marktpl. at 11:48pm and 1:18am, and by Maria-Theresien-Str. at 11:47pm and 1:17am. Night buses stop at the *Hauptbahnhof*; be sure to check the latest schedules there to avoid missing the bus.

Taxis: Lined up at the main train station (☎25073, 584 912, or 291 537). Approximately 120AS from the airport to the *Altstadt.*

Car Rental: Avis, Salurnerstr. 15 (☎571 754; M-F 8am-6pm, Sa-Su 8am-1pm).

Auto Repairs: ARBÖ (☎123). **ÖAMTC** (☎120).

Hitchhiking: While *Let's Go* doesn't recommend hitching, hitchers have been known to take bus K to "Geyrstr." and go to the Shell gas station by the DEZ store off Geyrstr.

Bike Rental: At the train station (☎503 5395). Open Apr. to early Nov. 150-200AS per day, with Eurail or that day's train ticket 90-160AS. **Sport Neuner,** Salurnerstr. 5 (☎561 501; open M-F 9am-6pm, Sa 9am-noon), near the station, rents mountain bikes. 200AS per day.

ORIENTATION

Most of Innsbruck lies between the **Inn River** on the west and the train tracks on the east. In the middle, the main street is **Maria-Theresien-Straße,** running north and south, somewhat parallel to both the river and the train tracks. Open only to taxis, buses, and trams, and crowded with tourists and cafes, Maria-Theresien-Straße runs between the cobblestoned *Altstadt* (old city) and Maximilianstraße, another big road. Get to the *Altstadt* from the main train station, by taking tram #3 or 6 or bus A, F, or K to "Maria-Theresien-Str.," or exit the train station, turn right until Museumstr.; turn left on that and walk for about 10 minutes. To reach the **university district,** near Innrain, continue down Museumstr. toward the river (curving left

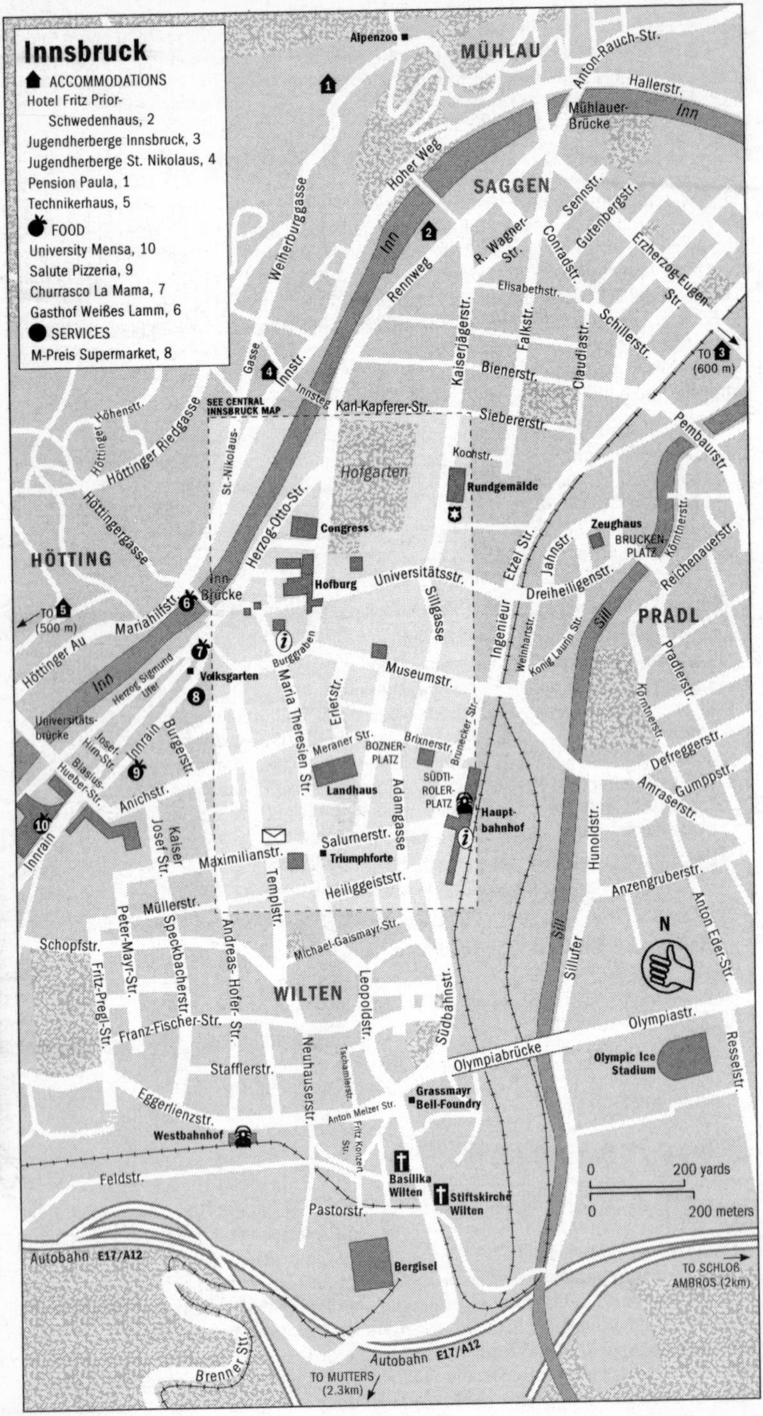

Innsbruck

ACCOMMODATIONS
- Hotel Fritz Prior-Schwedenhaus, 2
- Jugendherberge Innsbruck, 3
- Jugendherberge St. Nikolaus, 4
- Pension Paula, 1
- Technikerhaus, 5

FOOD
- University Mensa, 10
- Salute Pizzeria, 9
- Churrasco La Mama, 7
- Gasthof Weißes Lamm, 6

SERVICES
- M-Preis Supermarket, 8

Alpenzoo
MÜHLAU
Anton-Rauch-Str.
Hallerstr.
Inn
Mühlauer-Brücke
Hoher Weg
SAGGEN
Sennstr.
Gutenbergstr.
Erzherzog-Eugen-Str.
Weiherburggasse
R. Wagner-Str.
Conradstr.
Rennweg
Elisabethstr.
Schillerstr.
Kaiserjägerstr.
Falkstr.
Claudiastr.
TO 3 (600 m)
Gasse
Innstr.
Bienerstr.
Innsteg
Karl-Kapferer-Str.
SEE CENTRAL INNSBRUCK MAP
Siebererstr.
Höhenstr.
Höttinger
Höttinger Riedgasse
St.-Nikolaus-
Kochstr.
Pembaurstr.
Hofgarten
Rundgemälde
Höttingergasse
Herzog-Otto-Str.
Congress
Zeughaus
BRUCKEN-PLATZ
Körnerstr.
Reichenauerstr.
HÖTTING
Inn-Brücke
Hofburg
Universitätsstr.
Etzel Str.
Jahnstr.
Dreiheiligenstr.
TO 5 (500 m)
Mariahilfstr.
Sillgasse
Ingenieur
Weinhartstr.
Konig Laurin Str.
Sill
PRADL
Höttinger Au
Burggraben
Volksgarten
Museumstr.
Pradlerstr.
Herzog Sigmund Ufer
Maria Theresien Str.
Erlerstr.
Brunecker Str.
Universitäts-brücke
Josef-Hirn-Str.
Innrain
Burgerstr.
Meraner Str.
BOZNER-PLATZ
Brixnerstr.
Körnerstr.
Defreggerstr.
Blasius-Hueber-Str.
Anichstr.
Landhaus
Adamgasse
SÜDTI-ROLER-PLATZ
Haupt-bahnhof
Amraserstr.
Gumppstr.
Innrain
Kaiser Josef Str.
Salurnerstr.
Maximilianstr.
Triumphforte
Hunoldstr.
Heiliggeiststr.
Templstr.
Anzengruberstr.
Müllerstr.
Anton Eder-Str.
N
Schopfstr.
Peter-Mayr-Str.
Speckbacherstr.
Andreas-Hofer-Str.
Michael-Gaismayr-Str.
Sillufer
Fritz-Pregl-Str.
WILTEN
Leopoldstr.
Südbahnstr.
Olympiastr.
Franz-Fischer-Str.
Neuhauserstr.
Olympiabrücke
Olympic Ice Stadium
Resselstr.
Stafflerstr.
Tschamlerstr.
Grassmayr Bell-Foundry
Eggerlienzstr.
Anton Melzer Str.
Fritz Konzert Str.
Westbahnhof
Feldstr.
Basilika Wilten
Stiftskirche Wilten
0 200 yards
0 200 meters
Pastorstr.
Autobahn E17/A12
Bergisel
TO SCHLOß AMBROS (2km)
Brenner Str.
Autobahn E17/A12
TO MUTTERS (2.3km)

onto Burggraben, across Maria-Theresien-Str., and onto Marktgraben). The university itself is to the left down Innrain. Most sights are near *Altstadt*. Though Innsbruck is not particularly confusing (for an old, imperial European city), a color map, available at the train station or at tourist offices, is useful.

PRACTICAL INFORMATION

TOURIST SERVICES

Although Innsbruck's myriad tourist offices offer comparable services, the two central offices at Burggraben 3 will probably give the most straightforward information. All offices hawk the **Innsbruck Card,** which gives free access to dozens of local attractions and all public transportation for 24, 48, or 72 hours (230AS, 300AS, 370AS; children 50% off).

Innsbruck Information Office, Burggraben 3 (☎59850; fax 59807; info@innsbruck.tvb.co.at; www.tiscover.com/innsbruck), is on the edge of the *Altstadt* just off the end of Museumstr. on the 3rd floor. Official and not-for-profit, this office has tons of brochures, a city map (10AS), and a helpful staff. Open M-F 8am-6pm, Sa 8am-noon. It's in the same building as **Innsbruck-Information** (☎5356; fax 535 614; ibk.ticket@netway.at), which is a profit-maximizing consortium of local hotels, so arrange tours and concert tickets here but don't expect to reserve budget accommodations. Exchange closes 20min. before office. Open daily 9am-6pm. **Branches** at the train station and major motor exits. **Jugendwarteraum** (☎586 362), in the *Hauptbahnhof* near the lockers, is full of little kids, but gives directions, suggests hostels, and hands out free maps and skiing information. Open M-F 11am-7pm, Sa 10am-1pm. Closed July to mid-Sept.

Österreichischer Alpenverein (ÖAV), Wilhelm-Greil-Str. 15 (☎59547; fax 575 528). The Austrian Alpine Union's main office, provides mountains of information on their huts and hiking opportunities for members. Membership 530AS, ages 18-25 and over 60 390AS, under 18 180AS. Open M-F 9am-1pm and 2-5pm.

Budget Travel: Tiroler Landesreisebüro (☎59885) on Wilhelm-Greil-Str. at Boznerpl. Open M-F 9am-6pm. AmEx, MC, Visa.

Consulate: UK, Matthias-Schmidtstr. 12 (☎588 320). Open M-F 9am-noon.

FINANCIAL AND COMMUNICATION

Currency Exchange: Good rates at **post offices** (see below), and **Innsbruck Information tourist office** (see above). Most **banks** are open M-F 8am-noon and 2:30-4pm.

American Express: Brixnerstr. 3 (☎582 491; fax 573 385). From the station, take a right, then the 1st left. Holds mail. No commission on travelers' checks; small fee for cash. Open M-F 9am-noon and 1-5:30pm.

Bookstores: Buchhandlung Tirolia, Maria-Theresien-Str. 15 (☎59611; fax 582 050). 20 shelves of English language classics, and a nice selection of *Let's Go* titles. Open M-F 9am-6pm, Sa 9am-5pm. **Wagner'she,** Museumstr. 4 (☎595 050; fax 595 0538). Some English-language best sellers, and a respectable collection of English language classics, including *Let's Go*. Open M-F 9am-6pm, Sa 9am-5pm.

Library: Innsbruck Universität Bibliothek, Innrain 50 (☎507 2431), where it crosses Blasius-Heuber-Str. Take bus O, R, or F to "Klinik." Copy machine 1AS per page. Open July-Aug. M-F 8am-8pm, Sa 8am-noon; Sept.-June M-F 8am-10pm, Sa 8am-6pm.

Internet Access: Internet Corner, Bruneckstr. 12 (☎594 27261), across the street from the Hauptbahnhof, charges 1.50AS per min. Open daily 9am-11pm.

Post Office: Maximilianstr. 2 (☎500 7900). Open M-F 7am-11pm, Sa 7am-9pm, Su 8am-9pm. Address *Poste Restante:* Postlagernde Briefe, Hauptpostamt, Maximilianstr. 2, A-6020 Innsbruck. **Branch** next to the station. Open M-F 7am-8pm, Sa 7am-7pm. **Postal Code:** A-6020.

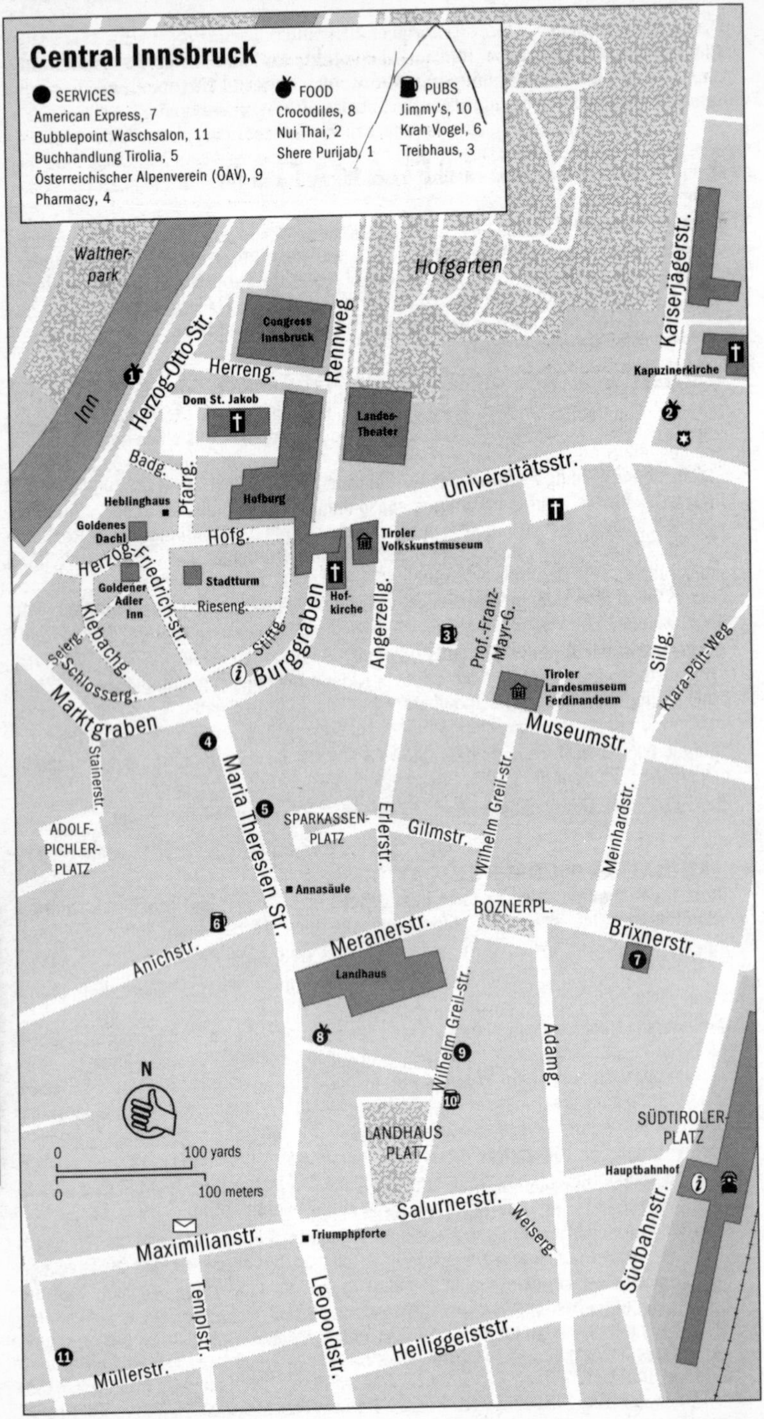

Central Innsbruck

SERVICES
American Express, 7
Bubblepoint Waschsalon, 11
Buchhandlung Tirolia, 5
Österreichischer Alpenverein (ÖAV), 9
Pharmacy, 4

FOOD
Crocodiles, 8
Nui Thai, 2
Shere Purijab, 1

PUBS
Jimmy's, 10
Krah Vogel, 6
Treibhaus, 3

Walther-park
Hofgarten
Inn
Herzog-Otto-Str.
Congress Innsbruck
Rennweg
Herreng.
Kaiserjägerstr.
Kapuzinerkirche
Dom St. Jakob
Landes-Theater
Badg.
Pfarrg.
Universitätsstr.
Heblinghaus
Hofburg
Goldenes Dachl
Hofg.
Tiroler Volkskunstmuseum
Herzog-Friedrich-str.
Stadtturm
Goldener Adler Inn
Rieseng.
Hof-kirche
Angerzellg.
Prof.-Franz-Mayr-G.
Kiebachg.
Seilerg.
Schlosserg.
Stiftg.
Burggraben
Sillg.
Klara-Pölt-Weg
Tiroler Landesmuseum Ferdinandeum
Marktgraben
Museumstr.
Stainerstr.
Maria Theresien Str.
SPARKASSEN-PLATZ
Erlerstr.
Gilmstr.
Wilhelm Greil-str.
Meinhardstr.
ADOLF-PICHLER-PLATZ
Annasäule
BOZNERPL.
Meranerstr.
Brixnerstr.
Anichstr.
Landhaus
Adamg.
N
LANDHAUS PLATZ
SÜDTIROLER-PLATZ
0 100 yards
0 100 meters
Hauptbahnhof
Salurnerstr.
Welserg.
Maximilianstr.
Triumphpforte
Südbahnstr.
Templstr.
Leopoldstr.
Heiliggeiststr.
Müllerstr.

TYROL

LOCAL SERVICES

Bi-Gay-Lesbian Organizations: Homosexuelle Initiative Tirol, Innrain 100 (☎562 403; fax 574 506; hose.tirol@tirol.com). All meetings at 8:30-11:30pm: mixed younger crowd M, lesbian night T, gay night Th, trans-gender night every other F. Call ahead to check about meetings taking place. **Frauenzentrum Innsbruck** (Women's Center), Liebeneggstr. 15 (☎580 839), runs a women's-only cafe for lesbians and straights M,W,F 8pm-midnight, as well as discotheques and poetry readings. Office hours Tu 10am-1pm, Th 2-5pm.

Religious Services: English-language Catholic Mass at the church in Karl-Rahnerpl. on Universitätstr. every Sa at 6pm.

Luggage Storage: Luggage watch for 30AS at the train station. Open July-Aug. 6:30am-midnight; Sept.-June 6:30am-10:30pm.

Lockers: In station for 30-50AS, depending upon size.

Laundromat: Bubblepoint Waschsalon, Andreas-Hofer-Str. 37 (☎565 00714), at the corner of Franz-Fischer-Str. It really tries to be hip, but it's just a laundromat (with a soda machine and a lot of graphics). 7kg washer 55AS, 13kg 120AS, 10 min. in the dryer 10AS. Soap included. Open M-F 8am-10pm, Sa-Su 8am-8pm.

Public Showers: At the train station, near the rest rooms. 30AS.

EMERGENCY

Emergencies: Police, ☎133. Headquarters at Kaiserjägerstr. 8 (☎59000). **Ambulance,** ☎144 or 142. **Fire,** ☎122. **Mountain Rescue,** ☎140

Pharmacy: Apotheke St. Anna, Maris-Theresien-Str. 4 (☎585 847, fax 581 567) is open M-F 8am-6pm, Sa 8am-noon. DC, MC, Visa.

Medical Assistance: University Hospital, Anichstr. 35 (☎5040).

ACCOMMODATIONS

Although 9000 beds are available in Innsbruck and suburban Igls, inexpensive accommodations are scarce in June when only two hostels are open: Jugendherberge Innsbruck and Jugendherberge St. Niklaus. The opening of student dorms to backpackers in July and August alleviates the crush somewhat. Book in advance if possible. Visitors should join the free **Club Innsbruck** by registering at any Innsbruck accommodation (see p. 177). Membership gives discounts on skiing and ski buses (Dec. 21-Apr. 5), bike tours, and the club's hiking program (June-Sept.).

Haus Wolf, Dorfstr. 48 (☎548 673; t.wolf@netway.at; www.myworldprivateweb.at/t.wolf), in Mutters. Exit the main train station through the main exit (over which there is a neon clock) and walk straight to the third traffic island. Catch the Stubaitalbahn to "Mutters" then walk toward the church and turn right on Dorfstr. (30min.). (26AS, week-long ticket 101AS. Last train 10:30pm. Buy tickets from machines on the platform.) Smothered with motherly love, gorgeous mountain views, and a seemingly endless supply of warm bread every morning, the guests of Frau Titti Wolf have the good fortune of enjoying Innsbruck at a distance, in the nearby village of Mutters. Those traveling alone will enjoy the sociable breakfast table. Breakfast and shower included. Singles 170AS; doubles 360AS; triples 540AS.

Hostel Fritz Prior-Schwedenhaus (HI), Rennweg 17b (☎585 814; fax 585 8144; youth.hostel@tirol.com; www.tirol.com/youth-hostel). From the station, take bus C to "Handelsakademie," continue to the end and straight across Rennweg to the river. Or walk right from the station, left on Museumstr., right at the end of the street onto Burggraben, and follow it under the arch and onto Rennweg. Look for "HI" signs near the end (20min.). This 95-bed hostel offers a convenient, leafy location and a view of the Inn River, complete with stained-glass windows and fishtanks. On summer weekdays, you can store your luggage at the front desk any time. Private shower and bathroom included. Breakfast 7-8am, 45AS. Dinner 65AS. Sheets 20AS. **Laundry** 75AS wash and dry. Open July 1-Aug. 31 and Dec. 27-Jan. 5. Reception 7-9am and 5-10:30pm. Reservations honored until 6pm. Lockout 9am-5pm. Curfew 10:30pm; keys with ID deposit. 4-bed dorms 125AS per person, triples 165AS per person, doubles 300AS.

Jugendherberge Innsbruck (HI), Reichenauer Str. 147 (☎346 179 or 346 180; fax 346 17912; yhibk@tirol.com). Take bus R to "König-Laurin-Str." from the train station then bus O to "Jugendherberge" (5min. bus ride). With out-of-fashion modernist architecture and sliding doors, this 178-bed hostel resembles a high-powered corporation. Large lockers in the rooms offset the garish quilts. 3 large lounges with hot plates, TV, and a small library. Breakfast 7-8am (only in summer), 85AS. Showers and sheets included. **Laundry** (45AS) until 10pm. Reception daily 5-10pm, also 3-5pm in July and Aug. Lockout 10am-5pm. Curfew 11pm; key available. Quiet time from 10pm. Phone reservations honored until 6pm. Non-HI-members add 40AS. 6-bed dorms 155AS 1st night, then 125AS; 4-bed dorms 190AS, 160AS; doubles 440AS, 380AS.

Pension Paula, Weiherburgg. 15 (☎292 262; fax 293 017; pensionpaula@telering.at). Take bus K to "St. Nikolaus" then walk uphill. Satisfied guests frequently return to this inn-like home downhill from the Alpenzoo. Views of the river and city center in bright rooms filled with antique furniture; many with balcony. Swap books in the multilingual library. Breakfast included. Reservations recommended in summer. Singles 340AS, with in-room shower 440AS; doubles 560AS, 680AS; triples 750, 920AS.

Technikerhaus, Fischnalerstr. 26 (☎282 110; fax 282 11017). Take bus R to "Unterbergerstr./Technikerhaus," or walk from the train station onto Salurnerstr. Take the 1st right onto Maria-Theresien-Str. then left onto Anichstr. Cross the bridge on Blasius-Hueber-Str., go left on Fürstenweg, and left on Fischnalerstr. Though far from the station, this student-housing complex is near the university and the *Altstadt*. **Restaurant** and 2 TV rooms. Breakfast and showers included. 24hr. reception. Open mid-July through Aug. Make reservations for groups of 3 or more. Singles 298AS, with student ID 280AS; doubles 498AS; triples 708AS.

Haus Kaltenberger, Schulg. 15 (☎548 576), near Haus Wolf. Take the Stubaitalbahn to "Mutters," then walk towards the church, turn right on Dorfstr., and take the 1st left. Well-kept rooms with attractive balconies and mountain views in this comfy house. 2 night min. Shower, but no breakfast included. Singles 220AS, doubles 400AS.

Youth Hostel St. Niklaus (HI), Innstr. 95 (☎286 515; fax 286 51 514; yhniklaus@tirol.com; www.tirol.com/yhniklaus). From the train station take bus K to "Schmelzerg." and cross the street (21AS). If you're in a good mood, the sometimes-crowded rooms with wooden bunkbeds and a sleepover-camp feel are just down from the hostel's sociable restaurant, which proudly serves its *Riesenwiener* (giant *Wienerschnitzl*, 98AS). Breakfast buffet (8-9am) and showers included. **Internet** access 30AS per 15 min. Reception 8-10am and 5-8pm. Wake-up at 8:30am. Lockout 10am-5pm. Curfew 11pm; key available with 200AS or passport deposit. 6-8 bed dorms 180AS 1st night, then 165AS; 4-bed rooms 195AS per person. 3-bed room 205AS per person, doubles 430AS, singles 265-365AS with shower and toilet.

TYROL

Camping Innsbruck Kranebitten, Kranebitter Allee 214 (☎284 180; www.tiscover.som/campinnsbruck). During the day, take bus LK from Bozner Platz (near the Bahnhof) to "Klammstr." (20min.); at night, take bus O to "Lohbachsiedlung" and switch to the LK. Walk downhill to the right, and follow the road. These pleasant grounds in the shadow of a snow-capped mountain include a playground for the kiddos. **Restaurant** open 8am-11am and 4pm-midnight. **Laundry** 50AS. Reception 8am-1pm. If reception is closed, find a site and check in the next morning. 75AS, children under 15 45AS; tents 40AS; cars 40AS. Showers included. Tent rental 75-110AS per person.

FOOD

Most tourists first glimpse cosmopolitan Innsbruck from the glamour of Maria-Theresien-Str. Gawking at the overpriced delis and *Konditoreien* won't fill your stomach, so escape the *Altstadt* and its profiteers by crossing the river to Innstr., in the university district, where you'll uncover ethnic restaurants and *Schnitzel Stuben*. Those looking for cheap or late-hour eats may actually find themselves pleased (and filled) by the cheap, large *kebap* and pizza portions served in and adjacent to the main train station. A few more late-night pizza digs are near the station on Ingenieur-Etzol-Str., but, as always, be careful at night.

Shere Purjab, Innstr. 19 (☎ 282 775), is a small downstairs restaurant serving up some of the cheapest food around. Indian-food takes prominence in the two daily *Menüs* (65-75AS for soup, entree with basmati rice and dessert), but pizzas (60-95AS) and, of course, *Wienerschnitzel* (75AS, with vegetable and dessert) are also cooked up. Open daily 11:30am-2:30pm and 5:50-11pm. AmEx, DC.

Salute Pizzeria, Innrain 35 (☎ 585 818), on the side of the street farthest from the river. This pizzeria is a popular student hangout near the university. Pizza 40-100AS; pasta 60-90AS. Open 11am-midnight.

Churrasco la Mamma, Innrain 2 (☎ 586 398), next to the bridge. Watch the moon rise from the shady terrace next to the river, and fall in love over a plate of spaghetti (82-134AS). Brick-oven pizza 74-112AS. Open 9am-midnight. DC, MC, Visa.

Gasthof Weißes Lamm, Mariahilfstr. 12 (☎ 283 156), on the 2nd floor. This Tyrolean restaurant is deservedly popular with the locals, serving up Alp-sized portions for under 100AS. Window tables offer a pleasant view of the river. Check out the daily *Menüs* (soup, entree, and salad 85-115AS). Open daily except Th 11:30am-2pm and 6-10pm.

Nui Thai, Kaiserjägerstr. 1, (☎ (0676) 412 9111), cooks up a panoply of Thai soups (55-79AS), and dishes from the Wok (102-115AS). Eat your eats in the slick interior, or outside tables, complete with neon chairs. Open M-F 10am-2pm, 5-11pm, Sa 6-11pm.

Crocodiles, Maria-Theresien-Str. 49 (☎ 588 856). This tiny restaurant serves 33 different brick-oven pizzas, including vegetarian options. English menus. Large pizzas 60-90AS, salads 42-84AS. Open M-F 11am-10:30pm, Sa 11am-3pm.

University Mensa, Innrainstr. 52, in the basement of the white building marked "Leopoldino-Francisca." Cheaper eats in Innsbruck would be hard to come by. This student cafeteria is open to the public. 3 daily *Menüs* (soup, entree, and salad 43-55AS). Open M-F 11am-2pm and 5-7pm; less regular hours in summer.

MARKETS

M-Preis Supermarket has the lowest prices around. Branches on the corner of Reichenauerstr. and Andechstr.; on Maximilianstr. by the arch; at Innrain 15; and across from the train station on the corner of Salurnerstr. and Sterzingerstr. Open M-Th 7:30am-6:30pm, F 7:30am-7:30pm, Sa 7:30am-5pm.

Farmer's Markets on Thursdays from 9am-1pm at Franziskanerpl., on Fridays from 9am-2pm at Sparkassenpl., on Saturdays from 8-11:30am at Viktor-Franz-Hess-Str. and 7:30am-1pm at St. Nikolaus-Brunnenpl. **Indoor Farmer's Market,** in the Markthalle near the river at Innrain and Marktgraben. Food, flowers, and other stuff. Open M-F 7am-6:30pm, Sa 7am-1pm.

SIGHTS AND MUSEUMS

If you plan on visiting many museums in Innsbruck in a short amount of time, consider investing in the **Innsbruck Card,** which is available at museums, cable cars, and the tourist office and allows free entry into all museums, cable cars, buses, and trains. (230AS for 24hr., 300AS for 48 hr., 370AS for 72hr.) A 2-hour **bus tour,** including the *Altstadt* and a visit to the ski jump, leaves from the train station (June-Sept. at noon and 2pm, Oct.-May at noon; 160AS, children 70AS).

THE OLD TOWN. Tourists flood the *Altstadt*, a tiny aggregation of old buildings, churches, and museums bordered by the river Inn. Its centerpiece is the **Goldenes Dachl** (Little Golden Roof) on Herzog Friedrichstr., a shiny, shingled balcony built to commemorate the marriage of the Habsburg couple Maximilian I and Bianca, the great-great-great-great-great-great grandparents of Empress Maria Theresia. Beneath the 2,657 shimmering gold squares, Maximilian and his wife kept watch over a crew of jousters and dancers in the square below. Inside the building, the

Maximilianeum Museum commemorates Innsbruck's favorite emperor. Maximilian, who ruled Austria from 1490 to 1519, used his smarts (and well-timed marriages) to create an empire whose size was matched perhaps only by his impressive nose. The museum proper is actually only a video room and a small room with historical stuff; it is best suited for history buffs or those dying to know just what a "Habsburg" is. *(Open May-Sept. 10am-6pm; Oct.-Apr. Tu-Su 10am-12:30pm and 2-5pm. 50AS, students 20AS, seniors 40AS, headphones for commentary included.)*

Many splendid old buildings surround the Goldenes Dachl. Facing the *dachl*, look to the left to see the flush salmon facade of the 15th-century **Helblinghaus** blanketed with a pale green, 18th-century Baroque floral detail. A modest climb up the graffiti-lined staircase of the 15th-century **Stadtturm** (city tower), across from Helbinghaus, yields a modest view of the city, perhaps worth exactly the modest cost of admission. *(Open daily July-Aug. 10am-6pm; Sept.-Oct. and Apr.-June 10am-5pm; Nov.-Mar. 10am-4pm. 30AS, students and children 20AS.)* The 15th-century **Goldener Adler Inn** (Golden Eagle Inn) is a few buildings to the left. Goethe, Heine, Sartre, Mozart, Wagner, Camus, and even Maximilian I ate, drank, and made merry here; you can too if you have 200AS to spare. Innsbruck's most distinctive street is **Maria-Theresien-Straße,** which begins at the edge of the *Altstadt* and runs due south. The street, lined by pastel-colored Baroque buildings, gives a clear view of the snow-capped *Nordkette* mountains. At the beginning of the street stands the **Triumphpforte** (Triumphal Arch) built in 1765 to commemorate the betrothal of Emperor Leopold II. Down the street, the **Annasäule** (Anna Column), erected between 1704 and 1706 by the provincial legislature, commemorates the Tyroleans' victory on St. Anne's Day (July 26, 1703) after a bloody and unsuccessful Bavarian invasion during the War of Spanish Succession.

CATHEDRAL ST. JAKOB. One block behind the Goldenes Dachl rise the twin towers of the Dom St. Jakob (remodeled 1717-1724). The unassuming grey façade conceals a riot of pink and white ornamentation within. *Trompe l'oeil* ceiling murals depict the life of St. James. The cathedral's prized possession is the altar painting of "Our Lady of Succor" by Lucas Cranach the Elder. A 1944 air raid destroyed much of the church, but renovations have restored it to its former grandeur. *(Open daily Apr.-Sept. 8am-7:30pm; Oct.-Mar. 8am-6:30pm. Free.)*

HOFBURG (IMPERIAL PALACE). Behind the Dom St. Jakob and to the right is the entrance to the Hofburg, built in 1460 and completely remodeled in 1754-70 under the direction of Empress Maria Theresia. Imposing furniture and large portraits fill more than 20 sumptuously decorated rooms. Highlights include the dubious "Chinese Room" (whose walls depict "Chinese" people riding tiny elephants hither and thither), and a portrait of Maria's youngest daughter, Marie Antoinette (with head). Around the corner, the cavernous **Gothic Cellar,** a kitchen in Maxmillian's time, is sometimes open for special exhibits. *(☎587 18612. Open daily 9am-5pm. Last entrance 4:30pm. German tours at 11am and 2pm. English guidebook 25AS. Call ahead for English tour. 70AS, students 45AS, youth under 18 30AS, under 14 10AS.)*

TIROLER VOLKSKUNSTMUSEUM (HANDICRAFTS MUSEUM). Across Rennweg sits the Tiroler Volkskunstmuseum. Built between 1553 and 1563 as the "New Abbey," the building was converted into a school in 1785 and a museum in 1929. The exhaustive collection of odd implements, peasant costumes, and period rooms provides a dusty introduction to Tyrolean culture. The most interesting exhibit is a collection of incredibly-detailed *Krippen* (nativity scenes) that depict Jesus and the Wise Men. *(Museum ☎584 302. Open M-Sa 9am-5pm, Su 9am-noon. 60AS, students 35AS, children 20AS.)*

HOFKIRCHE (IMPERIAL CHURCH). The Hofkirche houses an intricate sarcophagus decorated with alabaster scenes from Maximilian I's life and the Schwarze Mander, 28 larger-than-life bronze statues of Habsburg saints and Roman emperors that line the nave. Dürer designed the statues of King Arthur, Theodoric the Ostrogoth, and Count Albrecht of Habsburg who pay their last respects to the emperor. Oddly, Maximilian's final resting place is not in the Hofkirche, but in

Wiener Neustadt, near Vienna. The elegant Silver Chapel holds instead the corpse of Archduke Ferdinand II amidst wallpaper with faded cherubim resembling hard-boiled eggs. *(In the same building as the Volkskunstmuseum. Open daily 9am-5pm.)*

HOFGARTEN (IMPERIAL GARDEN). To get to the lush, manicured **Hofgarten** walk down Museumstr. towards the river, turning right onto Burggraben and continuing as it becomes Rennweg. The Hofgarten is complete with ponds, flower beds, a concert pavilion, and an outdoor chess set with 3ft. tall pieces. It's a lovely spot to escape the crowds of the *Altstadt*.

REGIONAL MUSEUM. The **Tiroler Landesmuseum Ferdinandeum,** showcases the history of Tyrolean art, from medieval altars to modern abstractions. Gothic, Rococo, and Romanesque exhibits on the lower floors quickly give way to modern and interesting *avant-garde* pieces on the upper floors. A small collection of non-local art includes a Schiele, a Klimt, and a pint-sized Rembrandt. *(Museumstr. 15, ☎59489. Open May-Sept. M-W and F-Su 10am-5pm, Th 10am–9pm; Oct.-Apr. Tu-Sa 10am-noon and 2-5pm, Su 10am-1pm.)* The **Zeughaus extension** has scientific and technical stuff, and tries to offer a cultural history of Tyrol. *(Zeughausg. near the train station. ☎587 439. Open May-Sept. F-W 10am-5pm, Th 1am-5pm and 7-9pm; Oct.-Apr. Tu-Sa 10am-noon and 2-5pm, Su 10am-1pm. Combined ticket to both museums 60AS, students 30AS, children 20AS.)*

ALPINE ZOO. Near the Schwedenhaus hostel, across the covered bridge, signs point to the **Alpenzoo,** the highest-altitude zoo in Europe, which houses every vertebrate species indigenous to the Alps. *(A bus to the zoo leaves from across the McDonald's on Maria-Theresien-Str. hourly 10am-5pm; bus fare 20AS, students and children 13AS. ☎292 323, fax 293 089. Open daily summer 9am-6pm; in winter 9am-5pm. 70AS, students and children 35AS.)*

CRYSTAL MUSEUM. Outside the city but well worth seeing is the **Swarovski Kristallwelten,** a multimedia crystal theme-park with a veneer of New Age hokeyness and modern art pretension. Above the underground entrance, the fabulous **Giant,** a mossy face on a hillside, spits water and peers through glowing eyes. Inside, purple walls, moving sculptures, and a stele by Keith Haring are augmented by unusual smells and a heavily synthesized soundtrack. The creator of the Kristallwelten, André Heller, has filled it with homages to Viennese artist Gustav Klimt. *(Take bus #4125 from the bus station to "Waltens." 35min., every 30min. 7:45am-8:22pm, 82AS round-trip. Open daily 9am-6pm. 75AS, students 65AS, children free.)*

OUTDOOR ACTIVITIES

A **Club Innsbruck** membership lets you in on one of the best deals in Austria (see Accommodations). The club's excellent mountain **hiking** program provides guides, transportation, and equipment (including boots) absolutely free to hikers of all ages. Participants assemble in front of the Congress Center (June-Sept. daily at 8:30am), board a bus, and return from the mountain ranges by 4-5pm. The hike isn't strenuous, the views are phenomenal, and the guides are qualified and friendly. Register for Club Innsbruck at any accommodation. Free night-time lantern hikes leave every Thursday at 7:30pm for Gasthof Heiligwasser, just above Igls; enjoy an Alpine hut party once there. If you want to hike on your own, you're better off taking on the gentler mountains in Innsbruck's suburbs (Mutters and Natters), rather than the enormous Nordkette mountains overlooking the city. Ask at the tourist office for maps and information.

The Club Innsbruck membership also significantly simplifies winter **ski excursions;** just hop the complimentary club ski shuttle (schedules at the tourist office) to any suburban cable car (mid-Dec. to mid-Apr.). Membership provides discounts on ski passes. **Innsbruck Gletscher Ski Pass** (available at all cable cars and at Innsbruck-Information offices) is a comprehensive ticket valid for all 62 lifts in the region (3 days 1260AS, 6 days 2270AS; with Club Innsbruck card 1050AS, 1880AS). The tourist office also **rents equipment** on the mountain (downhill approximately 270AS per day; cross-country 160AS). The bus to **Stubaier Gletscherbahn** (for **sum-**

mer skiing) leaves at 7:20 and 8:30am. Take the earlier bus—summer snow is often slushy by noon. In winter, buses also leave at 9:45, 11am, and 5pm (1½hr., last bus back at 4:30pm, round-trip 150AS). One day of winter glacier skiing costs 420AS; summer passes cost 280AS after 8am, 235AS after 11am, and 170AS after 1pm. Both branches of **Innsbruck-Information** offer summer ski packages (599AS including bus, lift, and rental).

For a one-minute thrill, summer and winter **bobsled** rides are available at the Olympic bobsled run in Igls, 5km from Innsbruck. (In summer: ☎378 843; rides W, Th, F at 4 and 6pm, 260AS. In winter: ☎377 525, rides Tu at 10am and Th at 7pm; 390AS). Summer rides, however, are akin to spruced-up *Cool Runnings* carts with wheels. Professionals pilot the four-person sleds. Reservations are necessary.

ENTERTAINMENT

At a corner of the *Hofgarten*, the **Congress Center** and **Tiroler Landestheater** (☎520 744) host a number of festivals and concert series in Innsbruck, starting at 7:30pm. In August, the **Festival of Early Music** features concerts by some of the world's leading soloists on period instruments at the Schloß Ambras, Congress Center, and Hofkirche. (For tickets, call 561 561; fax 535 614.) The Landestheater also presents top-notch plays, operas, and dance most nights of the year. (Concerts 85-590AS, standing room 50AS; plays 70-500AS, standing room 40AS; rush tickets 90AS, available 30min. before the show to anyone under 21 and students under 27.)

The **Tyroler Symphony Orchestra of Innsbruck** plays in the Congress Center, between October and May (☎580 023; tickets 280-440AS; 30% discount for children and students). **Chamber music concerts** (☎ 348 446) cost 160 to 260AS; the same discounts apply. The Spanish Hall at Schloß Ambras holds **classical music concerts** most Tuesday nights in summer (140-600AS, 30% discount for students and children). In late June and mid-July renowned dancers from Paris, New York, and Moscow come to the **International Dance Summer** in the Congress Center to perform in a range of styles (tanzsommer@tirol.com, tickets at Innsbruck Information, Burggraben 3; prices range from 280-880AS; no student tickets).

NIGHTLIFE

Most visitors collapse into bed after a full day of alpine adventure, but there is enough action to keep party-goers from pillows. Nightlife revolves around the **university quarter.** The **Viaduktbogen,** a stretch of theme bars huddled beneath the arches of the railway along Ingenieur-Etzel-Str., contains animated and un-touristy nightlife. For the very latest club and rave events, stop by Treibhaus (see below) and pick up one of the fliers on the grand piano.

Jimmy's, Wilhelm-Greilstr. 17 (☎570 473), by Landhauspl. East meets West beneath the all-seeing eyes of the fluorescent Buddha. Not a cranny left un-chic, nor a nook left un-hip in this trippy bar/cafe which serves up plates "from Africa to Asia." Beer 35-4AS, pasta 48-75AS, "Smiling Buddha" (with rice) 68AS. Open M-F 11am-1am, Sa-Su 7pm-1am. AmEx, MC, Visa.

Treibhaus, Angerzellg. 8 (☎586 874). Turn right on Angerzellg. from Museumstr., then turn right into the alley next to China Restaurant. Innsbruck's favorite alterna-teen hangout has both a well-lit indoor cafe and an outdoor tent. Jazz-oriented, with occasional live music. Food 40-100AS, beer 23-45AS. Food 50-95AS. Open M-F 10am-1am, Sa-Su 10am-1am.

Die Alte Piccolo Bar, Seilerg. 2 (☎582 163). Take the second left after entering the *Altstadt* from Maria-Theresien-Str. This cozy cellar bar attracts a primarily gay male crowd, though women are welcome. Friday and Saturday nights are most popular. Open daily 10pm-4am, except W.

Hofgarten Café (☎588 871), inside the *Hofgarten* park. Follow Burggrabenstr. around under the archway and past Universitätstr., enter the park after passing the Landestheater through the small gateway, and follow the path—you'll hear the crowd. During the day, casual diners sip their beers beneath the big white tent; at night it is a sprawling outdoor affair with networking twenty- and thirty-somethings. Note: the park closes at 10:30pm—use the back entrance to get to the cafe. Snack food 50-100AS, beer 28-48AS, wine spritzers 33AS. Open daily 10am-4am.

Krah Vogel, Anichstr. 12 (☎580 149), off Maria-Theresien-Str. Green-and-orange lanterns illuminate the darkness in this stylish bar/restaurant. A student-age crowd fills up the tables and small garden patio in the back. Ice cream 38-68AS; beer 23-48AS. Open M-Sa 10am-2am, Su 5pm-2am. Kitchen closes at midnight.

DAYTRIPS FROM INNSBRUCK

SCHLOß AMBRAS

The castle stands in a park to the far southeast of Innsbruck and is accessible by tram #6 (dir.: Igls) to "Tummelplatz/Schloß Ambras" (21AS). Follow the signs from the stop. Or, take the shuttle bus that leaves every hour from Maria-Theresien-Str. just opposite McDonalds. (Apr.-Oct hourly from 10am-5pm; Dec.-Mar. daily, except Tuesday, at 2, 3, and 4pm.) Walk from the city only if you have a map since the trail is poorly marked.

One of Innsbruck's most impressive edifices and museums is **Schloß Ambras,** a Renaissance castle built by Archduke Ferdinand of Tyrol in the late 16th century. Its medieval predecessor was a royal hunting lodge, but Ferdinand transformed it into one of the most beautiful Renaissance castles and gardens in Austria. The museum contains an impressive exhibit of good-as-new casts of armor, swords, and lances, ceilings adorned with pagan paintings, works by Velazquez and Titian, as well as Archduke Ferdinand's personal *Wunderkammer* (see Ferdinand's Curio Cabinet, below). The walls of the Spanish Hall, Ambras's most famous room, are covered with mythological scenes and portraits of Tyrol's princes. The castle's gardens, stocked with medicinal plants, are also pleasant for a stroll. (Schloßstr. 20; open Su-M and W-Sa 10am-5pm. 90AS, children and students 50AS; add 30AS for tour. Some parts of the castle may be inaccessible at various times.)

WILTEN

From the Innsbruck train station, take tram #1 or 6 to "Bergisel."

Wilten, the southernmost district of Innsbruck, is perhaps the city's oldest corner, having once served as the site of the Roman camp of Veldidena. It's primarily a residential district with few traces of its distant past, but it has a few notable churches and museums.

BASILICA AND STIFTSKIRCHE WILTEN. Pilgrims traveled to the **Basilika Wilten** on foot in the Middle Ages, but now they arrive in tour buses to inspect its gleaming, gilded rococo interior. The church, with a yellow and white exterior, was built in 1751-56 under the watchful eyes of Maria Theresia, although the sandstone sculpture of Mary and the infant Jesus above the altar dates back to the 14th century. The sides and ceiling of the church bristle with ornate stone and gold details, but nevertheless manages to keep up an airy demeanor. *(Open summers, M-F 8:30am-5pm, Sa 8:30am-noon. Free.)*

Across the street from the *Basilika* stands the **Stiftskirche Wilten,** a church said to have been built upon the site where the giant Haymon fought and killed the giant Thyrsus. The church, with its intricately carved interior and adjoining abbey, holds a treasure trove of decorated rooms, frescoes, a library, and an altar. *(Klosterg. 7. ☎583 048. Admission only with free guided tours, which include the Basilika and meet outside the Stiftskirche. Tours meet July-Sept., M at 4pm, W at 10am, and F at 4pm. English tours by request. Call ahead.)*

BERGISEL MILITARY MUSEUM. Follow the path up the hillside to the **Bergisel-Museum.** The oil paintings and photos commemorate the men who fought under Andreas Hofer in the Tyrolean War of Independence against Bavaria in 1809. Guns, and maps, but the paintings can sometimes be quite moving in their own right, particularly Egger-Lienz's depiction of a bayonet charge in "Die Namenlosen." An upstairs exhibit introduces the 20th century with an exhibit on WW I including modernist paintings and a display of machine guns and flame-throwers. *(☎582 312. Open April-Oct. 9am-5pm. 35AS, children 15AS.)*

BELL FOUNDRY. The **Grassmayr Bell-Foundry,** one block from the *Basilika* towards the city, has been crafting bells for 14 generations, since 1599. In the museum and exhibition rooms, you can watch how these dainty—or behemoth—bells are hand-cast on the premises. Particularly interesting is the section on bells and war, which includes a Nazi-era letter ordering that no more bells shall be cast. *(Leopoldstr. 53. ☎594 1637. Open M-F 9am-6pm, Sa 9am-noon. Castings take place every Friday at 1, 2, and 4pm. Entrance 45AS, children 30AS.)*

OLYMPIC SKI JUMP. From the base of the Bergisel hill, paths also lead up to the **Olympische Sprungschanze** (ski jump), used in the 1964 and 1976 Winter Olympic games. For fear that you'll end up with all the other unfortunate Olympic failures in the graveyard at the bottom of the hill, visitors are not allowed to actually take the plunge—the best you can do is fantasize about weightless flight while taking in the view of the city and outlying mountains.

STAMS

Frequent regional trains that head west towards Landeck stop in Stams (35min., 74AS). By car, take autobahn A12/E60 or highway 171 directly to the abbey.

When you're going for Baroque, you might as well go all out and head for **Stift Stams,** a magnificent onion-domed monastery 40km west of Innsbruck. Founded by the Tyrolean Duke Meinhard II in 1273, the cloisters were completely restyled in the 18th century. The 26 Cistercian monks who reside there allow several guided tours per day through the ornate and majestic **Basilika** and the heavily frescoed **Fürstensaal.** The basilica, restored for its 700th anniversary in 1974, features the Baroque masterwork of local artist Andrä Thamasch. Twelve of his gilded wooden statues line the walls of the **crypt** where Meinhard and his wife, among many others, are buried. A little farther down the nave, Thamasch's modest *Madonna* hangs on the wall—its striking asymmetrical composition makes it unique in its genre. Thamasch died while making it, leaving an empty space for St. John. At the far end of the church, the 14m **tree of life** towers over the altar. Designed by Bartholomäus Steinle in 1613, the tree features 84 golden figures suspended against a blue plaster background, which was added for structural support in the early 1700s. The **Rose Screen,** completed in 1716, is comprised of almost 100 flower bulbs, each laboriously carved from a single piece of iron. Entrance to the cloisters only with the tour. (☎(05263) 56972 or 6242; fax 56974; Jan.-Apr. and Oct-Dec. tours hourly 9-11am; May also at 5pm; June and Sept. also at 1 and 3pm; July and Aug. tours every half hour 9-11am, 1-5pm; 40AS, students 20AS). A **museum,** also within the monastery, has a small collection of religious paraphernalia and art work. (Open mid-June to Sept. Tu-Su 10-11:30am and 1:30-5pm. 40AS, 20AS students; 20AS for those with a basilica entrance ticket.)

TYROL

NEAR INNSBRUCK: SEEFELD IN TIROL ☎05212

After Innsbruck borrowed its smaller neighbor's terrain for skiing events during the 1964 and 1976 Winter Olympics, Seefeld was famous enough to charge high prices for its snowy slopes and lure in the celebrities. To get to the *Fußgängerzone* and the center of town, head down Bahnhofstr. Seefeld's main square, Dorfpl., is on your left at the first major intersection. After Dorfpl., Bahnhofstr. becomes Klosterstr.; the cross-street (the other main arm of the *Fußgängerzone*) is Münchenstr. to the right of the Dorfpl. and Innsbruckstr. to the left.

Trains connect Seefeld to Innsbruck (35min., 5:35am-8:12pm, 47AS). From the station, walk up Bahnhofstr. and past Dorfpl. to the **tourist office,** Klosterstr. 43 to get a list of accommodations. (☎2313; fax 3355; info@seefeld.tirol.at; www.tiscover.com/seefeld. Open mid-June to mid-Sept. and mid-Dec. through Feb. M-Sa 8:30am-6:30pm; mid-Sept. to mid-Dec. and Mar. to mid-June M-Sa 8:30am-12:15pm and 3-6pm). You can **rent bikes** (180AS per day, children 100AS; with train ticket 120AS, 70AS) at the station. For a **snow report,** dial 3790.

Seefeld boasts five-star hotels, but no hostel. *Pensionen* and *Privatzimmer* are the best budget options. Prices for these rooms average 220-320AS in the summer; 50AS more in winter. Make reservations, particularly if traveling alone in high season, since singles are scarce. The entire *Fußgängerzone* is stocked with rows of pricey restaurants, outdoor cafes, and bars, but there are a few good deals. **Restaurant Hiltpolt,** Innsbruckstr. 18, has specials posted outside, such as delicious *Wienerschnitzl* with potato salad (100AS). If you look at the actual menu, or the posh people around you, you may feel out of place; stick to the specials and you'll be all right. (☎2253. Open mid-June-Sept. and Dec.-Mar. noon-2pm and 6-9:30pm.) The **Albrecht Hat's Supermarket,** Innsbruckstr. 24, is located across from Sport Sailer just off Dorfpl. (open M-Sa 8am-12:30pm and 2:30-7:30pm, Su 10am-noon).

The tourist office distributes *Seefeld A-Z,* a listing of the range of summer and winter activities offered in town, as well as season-specific activity calendars. Summer in Seefeld brings a multitude of outdoor activities. The tourist office runs an excellent summer **hiking** program of 4- to 6-hour hikes that wind among the sky-scraping peaks surrounding Seefeld, including the 2569m **Pleisenspitze** and the 2367m **Gehrenspitze.** (Hikes leave mid-June to mid-Sept. Tu and F at 9:30am, W at 8am. Register by 5pm the day before the hike. 65AS with guest card.) The **Kneipp Hiking Society** (☎2263) invites visitors to join its free (with guest card) weekly 3- to 5-hour outings, which depart from the train station Thursdays. To wander on your own, pick up hiking maps at the tourist office (60AS). For cyclists, English language **biking** maps are also available at the tourist office (60AS).

Seefeld offers 2 money-saving ski passes to winter tourists. The **Seefeld Card** is valid for Seefeld, Reith, Mösern, and Neuleutasch (1-day pass 370AS, ages 5-15 220AS, ages 16-17 335AS). The **Happy Ski Pass** is valid for skiing at Seefeld, Reith, Mösern, Neuleutasch, Mittenwald, Garmisch-Zugspitze, Ehrwald, Lermoos, Biberwier, Bichlbach, Berwang, and Heiterwang (pass available for 3-20 days and requires a photograph; 3 days 1030AS, ages 5-15 620AS, ages 16-17 945AS). Twelve different **sports equipment rental shops** lease alpine and cross-country skis, snowboards, and toboggans at standardized rates. (Downhill skis with poles and boots 100-200AS, children 80-130AS; boots 50-100AS; snowboard 200-300AS.) A free **ski bus** runs every 20 minutes (daily 9:20am-4:40pm) between town and the **Rosshütte** and **Gschwandtkopf** ski areas. For those who prefer their skiing on the level, choose from the 100km of *Langlauf* (cross-country) trails (trail map available at the tourist office). **Fun Factory,** Riehlweg 492 (☎5090, fax 5092) offers **snowrafting** (going down the side of a mountain in a rubber boat, 125AS), tobogganing (250AS), and bobsledding (650AS).

EHRWALD ☎05673

Ehrwald (pop. 2,500) is in the Lechtaler Alps, which offers some of the best skiing in the world and the most uninhabited territory in Austria. But Ehrwald has been blessed with more than just beautiful mountains. Other than a few damaged buildings, both World Wars spared the town, and to date nothing has blemished Ehrwald's prized attraction, the majestic **Zugspitze** (2962m, Germany's highest mountain), which draws 400,000 tourists a year. Quieter and cheaper than its neighbors, Ehrwald is more pleasant than nearby German resort towns.

TRANSPORT AND PRACTICAL INFORMATION. All trains to and from Ehrwald must pass through Garmisch-Partenkirchen in Germany, where Ehrwald-bound travelers must switch trains. **Trains** run to **Garmisch-Partenkirchen** (30min., 5:45am-8:04pm, 39AS); **Innsbruck** (2hr., 5:45am-6:57pm, 128AS); **Munich** (2¼hr., 5:45am-6:57pm, 2506AS); and **Salzburg** (4½hr., 6:55am-6:57pm, 450AS). By **car,** Autobahn A12 follows the Inn from Innsbruck to Mötz. Bundesstr. 314 runs north from Mötz to Ehrwald, close to Germany and Garmisch-Partenkirchen. Bundesstr. 198 runs along the Loesach river.

Ehrwald has few street signs. To reach the town center from the train station, cross the tracks onto Bahnhofstr., which then merges with Hauptstr. After about 20 minutes, Hauptstr. veers left and uphill as it becomes Kirchpl. The **tourist office,** Kirchpl. 1, is in the center of town, a few steps beyond the church. (☎20000; fax 3314; ehrwald@zugspitze.tirol.at; www.tiscover.com/ehrwald. Open M-F 8:30am-noon and 1:30-6pm; mid-June to Sept. and mid-Dec. to Feb. also open Sa 9-1pm and Su 9-11am). **Currency exchange** is available at banks (open M-F 8am-noon and 2-4:30pm) and the post office. There is an **ATM** at the **Bank für Tirol und Vorarlberg,** Kirchpl. 21a. **Rent bikes** at Zweirad Zirknitzer, Zugspitzstr. 16, across the tracks and up the hill (☎3219; 90AS per day; mountain bikes 200AS per day, 350AS per weekend; children's bikes 170AS, 320AS). The **post office,** Hauptstr. 5, is on the right about 100m before the town center as you walk from the train station (open M-F 8am-noon and 2-5:30pm). Ehrwald's **postal code** is A-6632.

ACCOMMODATIONS AND FOOD. Ehrwald is filled with fairly inexpensive guest houses. The tourist office has a complete listing of prices and locations. Wherever you stay, be sure to pick up a **guest card** for discounts. **Gästehaus Konrad,** Kirweg 10, is only a few minutes down Hauptstr. from the station toward the town center. After you pass the post office and SPAR market, take the first right onto Kirweg. Konrad is on your right, down a driveway. Each large room has a TV and a painted Alpine scene. Step out onto the balcony for the real thing: a great view of green fields, small villages, and mountains in every direction. (☎2771. Breakfast included. In summer, singles with shower 230-250AS, doubles 460-500AS. In winter, 250AS per person. Surcharges for stays of less than 3 nights.) Camping is available—if you're willing to walk about 25 minutes uphill—at **Camping Dr. Lauth,** Zugspitzstr. 34. Head left out of the train station and immediately turn left. Take the right-hand fork past Zweirad Zirknitzer and continue uphill (ignore the "Leaving Ehrwald" sign). After the road curves left at the Thörleweg intersection, the well-marked campground is on the right. Pitch your tent in the shadow of the Zugspitze. **Restaurant,** and **laundry** (70AS wash and dry). (☎2666; fax 26664; camping-ehrwald@tirol.com; www.camping-ehrwald.at. Reception 24hr. 70AS per person; tent and car 70AS; tax 12.50AS, 17.50 in winter.)

The **Metzgerei Restaurant,** Hauptstr. 15, serves large traditional dishes and vegetarian entrees in its friendly dining room. The *Tiroler Knödel*, two balls of starch laced with ham and served scalding hot over sauerkraut, are a bargain at 55AS. *Tiroler Gröstl* is 89AS. (☎2341. Open 11:30am-8:30pm, limited menu from 2-5pm.) If you're planning a picnic on the summit of the Zugspitze, try the local **SPAR supermarket,** Hauptstr. 1, next to the post office (open M-Th 8am-7pm, F 8am-7:30pm, Sa 7:30am-1pm; July to mid-Sept. and mid-Dec. to Mar. Sa until 6pm).

TYROL

SIGHTS AND ENTERTAINMENT. The **Tiroler Zugspitzbahn** is Ehrwald's leading tourist attraction and greatest feat of engineering. This cable car climbs 2950m to the summit of the Zugspitze in a hold-your-breath (for some, hold-your-lunch) 7 minutes and 12 seconds. The outdoor platforms of the observation station at the ride's end have what some deem the most breathtaking view on the continent. Be sure to bring a sweater, since snow may still be on the ground in the warmer seasons. (☎2309. Open late May to late Oct. and late Nov. to mid-Apr. daily 8:45am-4:45pm. Round-trip 420AS, children 250AS.) The **restaurant** at the summit gives you more food than you could possibly eat for unusually low prices (*Tagesmenü* 85AS). The **Ehrwalder Almbahn** doesn't climb quite so high ("only" 1510m), but the prices don't either (☎2468; May 21-Oct. 18, 8:30am-5:40pm; Dec.-Apr. 8:30am-4pm; 130AS, children 75AS). To reach either cable car, hop on any of the green buses that stop at green "H" signs (every hr., 46AS).

In summer, the Ehrwald tourist office organizes **mountain bike** and **hiking tours** daily. You can book a tour at Bergsport-Total, across the street from the tourist office (free on M, otherwise 180-250AS per person). The tourist office also provides information on hiking, fishing, swimming, boats, skating, climbing, **paragliding,** tennis, **kayaking,** and river rafting in Ehrwald and neighboring areas.

For winter guests, Ehrwald offers the **Happy Ski Pass.** The cheerful little card gives access to 143 lifts, 200km of alpine ski runs, 100km of cross-country trails, and several other winter sports arenas (see Seefeld, p. 186.) Shops in the main square and at lift stations rent skis and equipment (boots, skis, and poles around 350AS per day, 1300AS for 6 days).

KITZBÜHEL

☎05356

When Franz Reischer arrived in Kitzbühel in 1892, his 2m snowshoes and wild ideas about sliding down mountains stirred up a fair amount of skepticism. Two years later the first ski championship was held in town, and everyone wanted a piece of the big-shoe action. The 6 peaks surrounding Kitzbühel were named the "Ski-Circus," and life was never the same. Now the annual **International Hahnenkamm Race,** considered the toughest course in the world, attracts amateurs, professionals, and spectators. Both wealthy vacationers and poor ski-bums can enjoy the town's almost-glitzy center, as well as its opportunities for hiking, biking, and playing in the lake.

GETTING THERE AND AROUND

Kitzbühel has 2 **train stations.** The **Hauptbahnhof**, Bahnhofpl. 1, (☎640 5513 85) and the **Hahnenkamm Bahnhof** are one train stop away from each other. **Buses** stop next to both train stations. Kitzbühel lies on Bundesstr. 161 and is the east terminus of Bundesstr. 170. By **car** from Salzburg, take Bundesstr. 21 south to 312 west; at St. Johann in Tirol, switch to 161 south, which leads straight to Kitzbühel. From Innsbruck, take Autobahn A12 east to Wörgl and switch to either Bundesstr. 312 or Bundesstr. 170.

Trains: From Hauptbahnhof to **Innsbruck** (1-1½hr., 7:21am-11:42pm, 150AS); **Salzburg** (1½hr., 6:25am-8:55pm, 200AS); **Vienna** (6hr., 6:25am-12:47am, 570AS); and **Zell am See** (1hr., 6:25am-8:55pm, 108AS).

Taxis: In front of the Hauptbahnhof, or call 66222 or 66150.

Car Rental: Hertz, Josef-Pirchlstr. 24 (☎64800; fax 72144), at the traffic light on the way into town from the main station. Open M-F 8am-noon and 2-6pm, Sa 9am-noon. 20% discount with valid guest card. AmEx, MC, Visa.

Bike Rental: At the main train station. 180AS per day, with train ticket for that day 120AS. Children 100AS, 70AS. Mountain bike rental at **Stanger Radsport,** Josef-Pirchlstr. 42, for 250AS per day (☎62549, fax 71793; open M-F 8am-noon and 1-6pm, Sa 9am-noon).

Parking: There are 4 lots in Kitzbühel: **Griesgasse, Pfarrau, Hahnenkamm,** and **Kitzbühlerhorn.** The latter 2 are next to the major ski lifts. In winter a free park-and-ride service operates between the lots and lifts. Free parking at the Fleckalmbahn for the cable car (open 8am-6pm). Winter parking at Hahnekamm is 40AS per day.

ORIENTATION AND PRACTICAL INFORMATION

Kitzbühel sits pretty on the hilly banks of the Kitzbüheler Ache River. The town is in the shade of a number of impressive peaks, including the Kitzbüheler Horn (1996m) and the Steinbergkogel (1971m). The tracks connecting the stations form a sort of U around most of the town, and the stations are on opposite sides of the town. To reach the *Fußgängerzone* (pedestrian zone) from the Hauptbahnhof, head straight out the front door down Bahnhofstr. and turn left at the main road. At the traffic light, turn right and follow the road uphill. The city center is a maze of twisting streets; if you get confused, look for the occasional *Zentrum* (center) signs to point you back to the middle. Be sure to pick up a map at the tourist office as soon as you can; especially at night it can be difficult to find one's way.

Tourist Office: Hinterstadt 18 (☎621 550; fax 62307; info@kitzbuehel.com; www.kitzbuehel.com), near the *Rathaus* in the *Fußgängerzone*. Free room reservation service, free telephone at the **electronic accommodations board** (open daily 6am-10pm). Maps and English brochures also available at the board. A **bank** in the office exchanges money in high season. Free (with guest card) **guided walks** in English start at the office May-Oct. M-F at 8:45am. Guided hikes during weekends on demand. Open July-Sept. and mid-Dec. to late Apr. M-F 8:30am-6:30pm, Sa 8:30am-noon and 4-6pm, Su 10am-noon and 4-6pm; Oct. to mid-Dec. and late Apr. to June M-F 8:30am-12:30pm and 2:30-6pm.

Budget Travel: Reisebüro Eurotours, Rathauspl. 5 (☎71304; fax 711 3044), exchanges currency at average rates. Open M-F 8:30am-noon and 3-6:30pm, Sa 8:30am-12:30pm and 4-6:30pm, Su 10am-noon.

Currency Exchange: At banks, travel agencies, and the post office. The post office and most banks have **ATMs** outside.

Luggage Storage: At both stations. 30AS. Open 5am–12:50pm.

Laundromat: Kleider-Fix, Wegscheidg. 5 (☎63520). Wash and dry 180AS; wash only 150AS. Open M-Th 7am-6pm, F 7am-5pm, Sa 9-11am.

Emergencies: Police, ☎133. **Fire,** ☎122. **Medical,** ☎144. **Auto Repair,** ☎123. **Mountain Rescue,** ☎140.

Ski Conditions: ☎181 (German) or ☎182 (English).

Pharmacy: Stadt-Apotheke Vogl, Vorderstadt 15. Open M-F 8am-noon and 2:30-6:15pm, Sa 8am-noon.

Internet: Two terminals at the computer store **Bit and Byte,** Im Gries 1a, provide access for 50AS per half-hour. Open M-F 9am-noon and 2-6pm, Sa 9am-noon.

Post Office: Josef-Pirchlstr. 11 (☎6721), between the stoplight and the *Fußgängerzone*. Bus schedules, fax, and a self-serve copier inside. Open M-F 8am-noon and 2-6pm. **Currency exchange** open M-F 8am-noon and 4-5pm. **Postal Code:** A-6370.

ACCOMMODATIONS

Kitzbühel has almost as many guest beds (7445) as inhabitants (8000), but the only youth hostel is far from town and restricted to groups. *Privatzimmer* and *Pensioner* generally run 200 to 300AS per person; expect to shell out an extra 100AS during the winter. Be sure to call ahead in winter, as the ski races create a huge bed shortage. Cheaper lodging is also available a 6km bus or train ride away in **Kirchberg** (Kirchberg tourist office ☎(05357) 2309). Be sure to ask for your **guest card**—it provides discounts on most local attractions.

Hotel Kaiser, Bahnhofstr. 2 (☎64709), exit Hauptbahnhof facing away from tracks, the hotel will be on left at the end of the street. The native English-speaking owner and staff, all former backpackers, are happy to greet road-weary travelers, and if the hotel's 150 beds are full, the owner Michael will always try to help you find somewhere else to stay at a similar price. School groups often book the hotel, and it is occasionally closed during slow seasons, so call ahead. The hotel has a terrace, billiard table, and an inexpensive bar. **Laundry** 70AS (washed and dried for you). Parking available. 200AS per person in doubles and 4-6 bed dorms, although there may be winter surcharges. Michael offers a special price in Nov.-Dec. for backpackers looking for work in the area: 120AS per person for a 4-6 bed dorm. AmEx, DC, MC, Visa.

Pension Hörl, Josef-Pirchlstr. 60 (☎63144). From the main station, turn left after Hotel Kaiser; Pension Hörl will be on the left. This inexpensive *Pension* is quiet and unassuming with old furnishings and drab balconies. If they don't have an available bed, they'll try to put you up at their nearby **Gästehaus Hörl** (Bahnhofstr. 8). Breakfast included. 190-220AS per person, with private shower 220-240AS. Add 40AS in winter.

Pension Neuhaus "Motorbike," Franz-Reischstr. 23 (☎62200). From the tourist office, turn right, walk through the archway, and follow Franz-Reischstr. to the right. The *Pension* is on the left, near the chairlift with flags fluttering. The proprietors *really* like motorcycles—the dining-room ceiling is covered with biker t-shirts. Breakfast included. Rooms hold up to 6 people. 270-350AS per person. Winter 300-400AS. Prices vary depending on length of stay.

Camping Schwarzsee, Reitherstr. 24 (☎628 060; fax 644 7930; hotel.bruggerhof@camping.netwing.at; www.netwing.at/tirol/kitzbuehel/bruggerhof-camping). Take the train to "Schwarzsee" and follow the train tracks past the bathing areas and around the back of the lake. The campground is behind the Bruggerhof Hotel, and signs point you in the right direction (15 min. walk). Trailer-oriented. Reception 8am-5pm. 95AS per person, ages 2-12 73AS, under 2 free; guest tax 7AS; tents 98AS; caravans 90-100AS; dogs 45AS. Aug. 16-June 83AS per person, all other prices the same.

FOOD

Although many of Kitzbühel's restaurants prepare gourmet delights at astronomical prices, cheaper locales pepper the area surrounding the *Fußgängerzone.* Local specialties include *Tiroler Speckknödel* (bacon-fat dumplings), served either *zu Wasser* (in broth) or *zu Lande* (dry, with salad or sauerkraut); and *Gröstl* (meat and potato hash topped with a fried egg). There is a **SPAR Markt,** on the corner of Ehrenbachg. and Bichlstr. (open M-F 8am-7pm, Sa 7:30am-1pm).

Café-Restaurant Prima, Bichlstr. 22 (☎63885), on the 2nd floor. From the tourist office, walk right and through the arch. Inexpensive meals on a sunny patio or inside at coffeeshop booths. This self-serve chain has a wide selection, including spaghetti (60AS), and *Wienerschnitzel* with soup, salad, and dessert (85AS). Special on some days: pizzas are 52AS between 2 and 5pm. Open 9am-9pm.

Huberbräu-Stüberl, Vorderstadt 18 (☎65677). In the center of town with a terrace that overlooks the street, Huberbräu offers high-quality traditional cuisine at relatively low prices. Besides their *Wienerschnitzel* (98AS) and pizza *margherita* (70AS), check out the filling *Menü*—soup, entree, potato, and dessert for 130AS. Open 9am-midnight.

La Fonda, Hinterstadt 13 (☎73673). This eclectic eatery in the heart of Kitzbühel, down the street from the tourist office, serves cheap, snack-style meals like hamburgers, nachos, and spare ribs. Salads 39-87AS, chicken wings 83AS, Indian chicken curry 81AS. The Tyrol-Mex dishes don't taste quite like the ones they make in Texas, but you can afford to try them anyway—nothing on the menu is over 89AS. Open 4pm-midnight, kitchen opens at 5pm.

SIGHTS AND ENTERTAINMENT

Kitzbühel's church steeples define the town's skyline. The **Pfarrkirche** (parish church) and the **Liebfrauenkirche** (Church of Our Lady) lie in an ivy-cloaked courtyard surrounded by an old cemetery. Between the churches stands the **Ölberg Chapel,** dating from 1450, with frescoes from the late 1500s. The town itself is even older, having celebrated its 700th anniversary in 1971. The local **Heimatmuseum,** Hinterstadt 34, celebrates these years with artifacts in Kitzbühel's oldest house, which dates from the 12th century. Rusty tools from days of yore are displayed, including prehistoric European mining equipment and the first metal bobsled. (☎67274. Open M-Sa 10am-11pm; July 10-Sept. 10 10am-4:30pm. 30AS, with guest card 25% discount, children 10AS.)

At the free **music concerts** in the center of town in July and August, you might find anything from folk harpists to Sousa bands (F 8:30pm, weather permitting). **Casino Kitzbühel** is near the tourist office. (☎62300. Open daily July-Sept. 7pm-late. M ladies' night: free glass of champagne; Tu men's night: free glass of beer. No cover. 18 or older. Semi-formal.) At the end of July, the **Austrian Open** Men's Tennis Championships come to town, drawing such athletes as Austrians Thomas Muster to the Kitzbühel Tennis Club (☎63325; ticket-tennis@kitzbuehel.netwing.at; www.atp-turnier-kitzbuehel.com).

OUTDOOR ACTIVITIES

Few visitors to Kitzbühel remain at ground level for long. The Kitzbühel **ski area,** the "Ski Circus," is one of the finest in the world. Every winter since 1931, Kitzbühel has hosted the **Hahnenkamm Ski Competition,** part of the annual World Cup and considered one of the world's most difficult runs. The competition turns the town into a rollicking 7-day party. (☎73555 for tickets. 50-200AS per day.)

SKIING. The best deal is the **Kitzbüheler Alpen Ski Pass,** which gives access to 260 lifts in 22 villages. *(2200AS, children 1100AS; good for any 6 days of the ski season. Full-season pass 6200AS, children 3100AS.)* A 1-day ski pass *(high season 390-420AS, children 210AS)* grants passage on 64 lifts and shuttle buses that connect them. Lift ticket prices drop after the first day. Tickets for 2 to 14 days are also available, as are tickets for individual lifts, such as the **Gaisberglift** *(60AS, with guest card 50AS, children 30AS)* and **Fleckalmbahn** *(180AS, with guest card 160AS, children 90AS)*. Purchase passes at any of the lifts or at the **Kurhaus Aquarena,** which offers a pool, sauna, and solarium *(☎64385; open daily 9am-8pm; 80AS, with guest card 70AS, children 50AS, 45AS; free entry in winter with ski passes of 2 days or more, in summer with 3-day vacation pass)*.

You can **rent skis** at the Hahnenkamm lift or from virtually any sports shop in the area. Try **Kitzsport Schlechter,** at Jochbergerstr. 7 *(☎220 411; open M-F 8:30am-noon and 2:30-6pm, Sa 8:30am-12:30pm)*. Lessons cost 500AS. Ask at the tourist office about **ski packages:** special low-season deals on lodging, ski passes, and instruction. Week-long packages without instruction start at 3900AS.

HIKING. For summer visitors, more than 70 **hiking trails** snake up the mountains surrounding Kitzbühel. There are a number of low-land hikes that don't require cable cars. Some of the best views are from the **Kampenweg** and **Hochetzkogel** trails, accessible via the Bichlalm bus which leaves daily from various stops in town (every hr. 8am-5:10pm; 26AS, with guest card 20AS). The **Achenpromenade,** taken in the direction of nearby Aurach, is a 1hr., 4km hike suitable for those who want a straight-forward walk. The hike begins at the bridge on Traunsteinerw. and generally follows the river. The **Seidlalmweg,** about 10km long, is a slightly more difficult hiking path. There are a number of ways to hike this trail without going the whole 10km. There are starting points at the Hahnenkammbahn cable car parking lot, and at the parking lot near the Streifalm chair lift.

For those with a bit of cash to burn, cable cars do the climbing for you, and give you open vistas during your whole hike. You can take the **Hahnenkammbahn** *(8am-5:30pm, 180AS up or round-trip, with guest card 160AS, children 90AS)* to the top of one of the most famous ski runs in the world. At the top are 2 restaurants and the **Bergbahn Museum Hahnenkamm** *(☎6957; open daily 10am-4pm; free)*. The **Kitzbüheler Hornbahn lift** ascends to the **Alpenblumengarten,** where more than 120 different types of flowers blossom each spring *(open late-May to mid-Oct. 8:30am-5pm; cable car 90AS per section, children 45AS)*. The smaller **Gaisberg, Resterhöhe,** and **Streiteck** lifts also run in the summer. A 3-day **summer holiday pass** is valid for unlimited use of all cable cars, free Bichlalm bus service, and the Aquarena **pool** *(450AS, children 225AS)*.

Guest card holders can take advantage of the tourist office's **hiking program.** Daily 3- to 5-hour hikes cover over 100 routes and come in 2 flavors: easy and moderate. *(Mid-May to mid-Oct. M-F at 8:45am from the tourist office; call ahead for weekend hikes, minimum 5 people. 90AS, free with guest card, but you pay for cable car rides.)* Individually booked hikes around the mountains are provided by Peter Brandstätter *(☎73323)* and Helmut Mitterer *(☎72246)*.

SWIMMING. The **Schwarzsee**, 2.5km from Kitzbühel, is famed for its healing mud baths. Float in the deep blue water and gaze at the snow-capped mountains high above (see directions to Camping Schwarzsee). *(☎62381. Open 7am-8pm. 40AS, children 30AS; ½day pass after noon 30AS, after 4pm 15AS. 11% discount with guest card. Electric boats rented after 8:30am; 80AS for 30min., 150AS for 1hr.; rowboats 45AS, 85AS.)*

KUFSTEIN

☎05372

Kufstein (pop. 15,000) is a small town with two personalities. One resides in the bustling, snaking streets of the town center and tries to steer the throngs of glassy-eyed English tourists into restaurants, trinket shops, and the city's main attraction: the *Festung* (fortress) which towers above town. The other personality dwells outside the town proper, and beckons to the *Wanderlusters* looking for a hike. Both personalities can be experienced in a day trip from Innsbruck or Kitzbühel.

TRANSPORT AND PRACTICAL INFORMATION. Regular trains run to Kufstein from **Kitzbühel** with a change over in Wörgl (50min., 5:52am-9:29pm, 88AS), and from **Innsbruck** (45min., 127AS). The train station is located on the west bank of the Inn river (ticket office open M 5:25am-8pm, Tu-Sa 5:35am-8pm, Su 7:30am-8:30pm). The **tourist office,** Unterer Stadtpl. 8, just across the river from the train station, distributes free hiking, biking, and skiing maps, as well as a complete list of accommodations and restaurants. (☎ 62207; fax 61455; kufstein@netway.at; www.tiscover.com/kufstein. Open M-F 8:30am-12:30pm and 2-5pm, Sa 9am-noon.) **Exchange currency** at the **post office,** Südtirolerpl. 12 (☎69610; open M-F 8am-noon and 2-6pm; exchange closed at 5pm; right next to the train station). There is an **ATM** in the **Sparkasse** on Südtirolerpl. 12.

ACCOMMODATIONS AND FOOD. Cheap beds are in short supply in Kufstein. A few cozy doubles lie 15 min. out of a town center at **Haus Reheis,** Hugo-Petler-Str. 1 (☎68322; 360AS for doubles without bath, 380AS in winter). Otherwise, try **Camping Kufstein,** Salurnerstr. 36 (☎622 2955; fax 636 894). Shady spots along the river will cost you a mere 50AS (33AS for children; cars 50AS, tent 35AS; showers 15AS; guest tax 7AS; reception daily 8-11am and 6-11pm, open May-Oct.). Surprisingly cheap food is available at the *Imbiße* near the touristy entrance to town around the tourist office, or from restaurant *Menüs*. The **SPAR Supermarket** is on Interer Stadtpl. (open M-F 7:30am-7pm, Sa 7:30am-1pm).

SIGHTS AND OUTDOOR ACTIVITIES. Aside from the incredible surroundings, Kufstein's main attraction is the 13th-century **Festung** (fortress), which raises its crenellated fist high above the river Inn. Climb to the fortress grounds via a medieval *Gangsteig* (covered staircase) or take a short cable car ride. Once you're within the walls of the *Festung*, you're free to walk around the stone ramparts and grassy knolls, many of which provide an excellent view of Kufstein below. Poorly lit archways make you feel like a spelunker. A drafty, drippy rock passage cuts from one side of the fortress to the other and was used as a refuge during both World Wars. At the top of the fortress, the **Heimatmuseum** (regional museum) features a motley mix of prehistoric and early modern artifacts, a room devoted to stuffed birds, as well as a room of sacred art with crushed red velvet wallpaper and a pickled two-headed chicken. (☎602 350. Open daily in summer 9am-5pm, in winter 11am-4pm. Combined entrance to fortress and museum includes cable-car ride, in summer 130AS, students 70AS; winter 110AS, 60AS; guided tours Apr.-Oct.) The *Festung* also houses the 4037 pipes of the **Heldenorgel** (Heroes' Organ), the world's largest open-air organ, which was constructed in 1931 in honor of Austrian soldiers who died in WWI. An exhibit in the fortress near the pipes contains interesting WWI artifacts including uniforms and (inactive) grenades. The organ is played, on the keyboard at the base of the fortress, for all to hear every day at noon and, during July and August, again at 5pm (10AS for auditorium seat; cheapskates can stand a bit outside and hear the pipes nearly as well). To reach some non-man-made heights, take the **Wilder Kaiser Chairlift** high into the mountains (open M-F 8:30am-4:30pm, Sa-Su 8am-4:30pm; round-trip 130AS, children 55AS; ascent only 100AS, 40AS). The tourist office gives away a free map that details hikes ranging in duration from ½hr. to 4hrs.

THE ZILLERTAL VALLEY

Wading between the Tuxer alps, the Zillertaler alps, and the Kitzbühler alps, the Zillertal (Ziller Valley) Alps provide spectacular, affordable, and easily accessible **hiking** and **skiing** away from crowds. The towns in the narrow valley are hugged by mountains on all sides, giving the Zillertal Alps some of the best hiking in western Austria, with more footpaths than roads and more trail guides than police officers.

ORIENTATION AND TRANSPORT. Everyone going into the valley must go through Jenbach, which is at the head of the valley. Trains depart from the Jenbach train station to **Innsbruck** (20min., 12:30am-10:57pm, 70AS), **Wörgl** (20min., 5:11am-12:13am), and **Vienna** (7hr., 5:11am-11:57pm). Traveling south down the valley, Zell am Ziller comes first. At the base of the valley, further south, is Mayrhofen. From Mayrhofen the valley splits into three smaller ones—the narrow *Tuxertal* (Tux valley) leads down to the skiing village of Hintertux. Transportation in the region is simple and convenient, thanks to the **Zillertalbahn** (better known by its nickname, the **Z-bahn**), an efficient network of private buses and trains connecting the villages (☎(05224) 4606). The starting point of the trainline is **Jenbach,** and the terminus is **Mayrhofen** (61AS). You can reach Jenbach from **Innsbruck** (20min., 70AS, Eurail valid). The Z-bahn has 2 types of trains, the **Dampfzug** and the **Triebwagen.** The *Dampfzug* is an old, red steam train targeted at tourists; it costs twice as much and moves half as fast. The Triebwagen and the Z-bahn Autobus have the same rates, and one or the other leaves daily every hour from 6am to 9pm. Getting into the Tuxertal is done by bus, from Mayrhofen. Note that travel on the Z-bahn is not covered by rail passes.

ACCOMMODATIONS. Accommodations in the Zillertal Valley are not a problem. Most towns have a variety of inexpensive rooms for rent—look for *Zimmer Frei* signs hanging from houses. Both Mayrhofen and Zell am Ziller are located as excellent bases for exploring the area. Mountain **huts** also litter the area. The **Kreuzjochhütte** (☎(0664) 382 100) is near Zell am Ziller, and the **Edelhütte** (2238m, ☎(05285) 62168), **Grüne Wand Hütte** (1438m, ☎(0664) 433 2107), **Kasseler Hütte** (2178m, ☎(05285) 63527), and the **Plaüenerhutte** (2373m, ☎(05417) 5167) are near Mayrhofen. Call the huts for prices, hours, and trails leading to their doors.

HIKING AND SKIING. The popular **Z-Hiking Ticket** is valid on all summer lifts in the Zillertal, including those in Zell am Ziller, Fügen, Mayrhofen, Gerlos, and Hintertux (6 days for 490AS, 9 days for 670AS, 12 days for 840AS, children ride free with the purchase of 2 regular tickets). Passes are available at tourist offices, lifts, or railway stations in Zell am Ziller and Mayrhofen. Passes may be used at only one lift per day. Hiking without cable cars is also possible throughout the valley. Hiking between towns in the Zillertal Valley is an option for the hardy traveler. Various trails cross the valley, such as the **Zillerpromenade,** part of which is a 2hr. hike from Zell am Ziller to Mayrhofen.

The Zell am Ziller **ski area** was recently connected to the Gerlos and Königsleiten ski areas, thereby creating the **largest ski zone in the Tyrol.** The Zillertal Super Skipass, covering this mammoth region, is available at any valley lift station and valid on all of the area's 251 lifts (☎71650. 4 days 1270AS, 7 days 1950AS, 10 days 2570AS; including the Hintertux glacier 1470AS, 2330AS, 3090AS; discounts for children). The cost of the lift ticket includes unlimited use of the Z-bahn network. For **summer skiing** head to Hintertux.

ZELL AM ZILLER ☎05282

Zell am Ziller (TSELL am TSILLER; pop. 2,000), 20km south of Jenbach, embodies many of the picture-book images of an Austrian mountain village, with clusters of wooden-shuttered alpine houses surrounded by fields of tall grass and much taller mountains. Founded by monks in the late 8th century—hence the *Zell*, or chapel—

Zell surrendered to materialism in the 1600s when it flourished as a gold-mining town. Today, this beautiful and unassuming village serves the traveler seeking skiing and hiking, *sans* resort-town hype.

TRANSPORT. Zell stands at the north central end of the Zillertal, between Jenbach and Mayrhofen. Those traveling by **ÖBB train** should get off at **Jenbach** and switch to the private **Zillertalbahn** (Z-bahn; ☎2211; Jenbach to Zell am Ziller 54AS; see p. 194), which leaves from the front of the train station. Z-bahn trains and buses leave every hour between about 6am and 8pm for Jenbach or Mayrhofen. If **driving** get to Zell am Ziller from the Inntalautobahn by taking the Zillertal exit, and drive 24km on Zillertal-Bundesstr. 109.

ORIENTATION AND PRACTICAL INFORMATION. The center of town is Dorfplatz, straight out of the train station down Bahnhofstr. In turn, Dorfpl. intersects both of Zell's main streets, Gerlosstr. near the river, and Unterdorfstr. by the railroad tracks. The **tourist office** is at Dorfpl. 3a. From the rail station, head right along Bahnhofstr., and turn right at the end—the office is on your left. Pick up a town map, skiing information, and a pension list if you want to track down a room on your own. The staff will make reservations for free, or you can use the 24hr. accommodation board and computer on the side of the office. (☎2281; fax 228 180; tourist.info.zell@netway.at; www.tiscover.com/zell. Open M-F 8:30am-12:30pm and 2:30-6pm, Sa 9am-noon and 4-6pm; in July-Oct. also Sa 9am-noon and 4-6pm.) Services include: **luggage storage** (30AS) at the train station (daily 8am-noon and 2-5pm); **taxis** ☎2625, 2345, or 2255; **bike rental** at the train station (150AS per day, 90AS children, 180AS mountain bike) or at **SB-Markt Hofer,** Gerlosstr. 30, opposite the campground (☎2220; mountain bikes 170AS per day; open M-F 7am-noon and 2:30-6:15pm); **pharmacy** (☎2641) at Dortpl. 3a, right next to the tourist office. In an **emergency,** dial 133 for mountain rescue or police; for an **ambulance,** dial 144. The **post office** at Unterdorf 2 **exchanges** money and has an **ATM** in front (☎2333; open M-F 8am-noon and 2-6pm; in summer also Sa 9-11am; exchange until 6pm). The **postal code** is A-6280.

ACCOMMODATIONS. Zell am Ziller has no shortage of lodgings. To reach **Haus Huditz,** Karl-Platzer-Weg 1, cross the rail tracks by the tourist office and continue onto Gerlosstr.; bear left onto Gaudergasse (at the Mode Journal building) and look for Karl-Platzer-Weg on the left (10min.). The owner provides beverages, conversation *(auf Deutsch)*, cable TV downstairs, down comforters, and balconies with mountain views, all at a very reasonable price. (☎2228. Breakfast included. Shower 15AS. Singles 200AS 1st night, then 180AS; winter 210AS, 180AS. Doubles 380AS, 340AS; winter 400AS, 350AS.) **Pension Mühlbacher,** Roherstr. 2, which also has an inexpensive restaurant, is a more inn-ish lodging, with breakfast buffet and showers and toilet in the rooms, as well as a TV lounge. (☎2270. Reservations recommended in winter. 270AS summer, 330-340AS winter). **Camping Hofer,** Gerlosstr. 33, offers a space for your tent a few blocks or so from the town center. **Laundry** (80AS), showers, barbecues, free bike tours, weekly hikes, and even a house band round out the offerings. There's a grocery store across the street. (☎2248; fax 22488. Reception 9am-noon and 3-8pm. High-season 65AS per person. Off season 50-55AS. 65-80AS per campsite. Guest tax 12AS.)

FOOD. When you stop for a bite, sample some local specialties. A traditional summer dish is the *Scheiterhaufen*, a monstrous mixture of rolls, apples, eggs, milk, lemon, cinnamon, sugar, butter, and raisins, drizzled with rum. *Zillertaler Krapfen* are sweet, heavy doughnuts, available in every bakery. The cheapest place around is **SB Restaurant Zeller Stuben,** Unterdorf 12, which serves big, buffet-style portions (Spaghetti 60AS, *Gulaschsuppe* 35AS). The less casual restaurant upstairs features 5 daily *Menüs* including soup, entree, and dessert for 90-190AS. (☎2271. Children's and vegetarian menus available. Both restaurants open 11am-9pm.) **Gasthof Kirchenwirt,** Dorfpl. 4, serves up *Zillertaler Kasrahmspätzln*, egg

BRING ON THE BREW The residents of Zell am Ziller celebrate their local brewer on the first weekend in May, when the whole town gets sauced in a 3-day celebration of cold, frothy beverages known as **Gauderfest.** The name is derived from the estate that owns the local private brewery. The Bräumeister's vats, Tyrol's oldest, concoct the beloved and potent Gauderbock especially for the occasion. The festival even has its own jingle: *Gauderwürst und G'selchts mit Kraut,/ hei, wia taut dösmunden,/ und 10 Halbe Bockbier drauf,/ mehr braucht's nit zum G'sundsein!* ("Gauder sausage and smoked pork with sauerkraut, / Hey, how good it tastes,/ and 10 pints of beer to go with it,/ what more could you need for your health!"). The festival's highlight is the **Ranggeln,** traditional wrestling for the title of "Hogmoar." There are also animal fights (attended by a veterinary surgeon) and customary activities like the **Grasausläuten** (ringing bells in order to wake the grass up and make it grow). Revelry continues into the night with Tyrolean folk singing and dancing.

noodles cooked with onions and garnished with cheese, for 70AS (☎2280; open 8am-midnight). Cap off dinner with a visit to **Café-Konditorei Gredler,** Unterdorf 10, where 1995 Confectioner of the Year Tobias Gredler whips up delicate desserts for patrons to enjoy on the riverside patio (☎24890; chocolate-banana cake 34AS, intricate sundaes 40-100AS; open 10am-11pm). The local **SPAR Supermarkt** is around the corner from the tourist office, next to Intersport Strasser (open M-F 7:30am-1pm and 2-6:30pm, Sa 7:30am-12:30pm and 2-5pm).

OUTDOOR ACTIVITIES. Zeller **skiing** comes in 2 packages: **day passes** for shorter visits, valid on the **Kreuzjoch-Rosenalm** and **Gerlosstein-Sonnalm** slopes (1 day 370AS, children 220AS; 2 days 690AS, 420AS; 3 days 990AS, 590AS); and **Super Skipasses** for longer visits (see p. 194). Single tickets are available for non-skiers who tag along to watch (74AS, 120AS roundtrip; children 37AS, 60AS; discount with guest card). Obtain passes at the **Kreuzjoch** (☎71650), **Gerlosstein** (☎2275), or **Ramsberg** (☎2720) cable car stations (all 3 lifts open 8:30am-5pm). **Rent skis** at any of Zell's sporting goods stores. Try **Pendl Sport** at Gerlosstr. 3 (☎2287; open M-F 8am-noon and 2:30-6:30pm, Sa 8am-noon and 3-6pm, Su 9-11am and 4-6pm; DC, MC, Visa). Prices here average 200-300AS per day for equipment rental, with significant discounts for longer rentals. Or, **rent a toboggan** at the Gerlossteinbahn bottom station. (Open M-Sa 7:45am-9:15pm, Su 8:30am-4:30pm. Day rides 65AS, children 33AS, evening rides 70AS, 35AS.)

Register in any town hotel or pension to get a **guest card,** which snags you a free hike led by the tourist office (June-Sept.; register one day in advance at the office). Much hiking around Zell am Ziller is lift-assisted. Two of the three ski lifts in Zell's vicinity offer **alpine hiking:** the **Kreuzjochbahn** (☎71650; open 8:40am-12:15pm and 1-5:10pm; round-trip 182AS, to mid-station 120AS; with guest card 165AS, 108AS) and the **Gerlossteinbahn** (☎2275; open 8:30am-12:20pm and 1-5pm; round-trip 120AS, with guest card 108AS).

TYROL

You can try **paragliding** as well—tandem flights cost 700-1500AS for 5- to 25-minute rides. The term "take-out" will develop a whole new meaning when you trust your life to the paragliding guides at the world's smallest airline, **Pizza-Air,** Zelbergeben 4 (☎22894). For a down-to-earth look at Zell's history, take a tour of the nearby **gold mine.** The journey begins at a petting zoo and adjacent cheese factory before proceeding on a scenic 45min. hike down to the mine entrance. (☎23010; fax 23014. 2hr. tours leave daily on the hr. 9am-4pm. 130AS, children 65AS. Reserve in advance for English tours.)

MAYRHOFEN ☎05285

At the southernmost end of the Zillertal, Mayrhofen is well-positioned for intense outdoor recreation. Four valleys (the **Zillergrund, Stillupgrund, Zemgrund,** and **Tuxertal**) stretch south from the town, providing endless opportunities for hikers and skiers. Proud of their natural splendor but eager to prove their mettle, Mayrhofer residents walk the walk when they're not talking the talk: Mayrhofen native Peter Habeler and fellow Tyrolean Reinhold Messner completed the first oxygen-unaided ascent of Mt. Everest. Habeler now runs the town's alpine school. This isn't some rarefied mountaineer's base-camp, though. Mayrhofen is a polished town with a glut of package tourists who seem to dwindle away as one leaves the town center into the surrounding mountains.

TRANSPORT. Mayrhofen is easily accessible from **Jenbach** (50min., 26 per day 6:00am-9:05pm, 61AS) and **Zell am Ziller** (15min., 26 per day 6:38am-9:52pm, 23AS) by Z-bahn trains and buses. The **train station** lies slightly northeast of town; to reach the center, walk uphill on the main road and turn left at the intersection (☎62362; open M-Sa 7:30am-6:30pm, Su 7:30am-1pm and 1:30-6:30pm).

PRACTICAL INFORMATION. The **tourist office,** Dursterstr. 225, is located inside the massive octagonal information center on a slight hill above the center of town. After entering town from the train station, walk along Hauptstr. in the direction of ascending street numbers, following the green information ("i") signs once you see them. The office dispenses information on outdoor pursuits, tours, and accommodations, and leads free **guided tours,** varying from short walks around town to 5hr. hikes to mountain huts. A 24hr. accommodations board and telephone is outside the office. (☎6760; fax 676 033; mayrhofen@zillertal.tirol.at; www.mayrhofen.com. Tours May-Oct. M-F; call for times and meeting points. Open M-F 8am-6pm, Sa 9am-noon, Su 10am-noon; July-Aug. also Sa 2-6pm.) Services include: **ATM** across the street from the post office at Hypo-Tirol **bank,** Hauptstr. 418; **bike rental** at the train station (150AS, 90AS children, 180AS mountain bike); **luggage storage** at the train station for 30AS per piece (M-Sa 7:30am-6:30pm, Su 7:30am-1pm and 1:30-6:30pm); **Internet access** at Café Tirol, Hauptstr. 448, for 50AS per half-hour (☎62321; daily 10am-10pm); a **pharmacy,** Steinbockapotheke, Hauptstr. 444 (☎62313, fax 62763; open M-F 8am-noon and 2:30-6:30pm, Sa 8am-noon); and **taxis** ☎63364, 63840, and 62260. Emergency telephone numbers include: for **police** ☎133, **fire** ☎122, **mountain rescue** ☎140, and **ambulance** ☎144. The **post office** is located at the intersection of Einfahrt Mitte and Hauptstr. and **exchanges** money (☎623 5111; open M-F 8am-noon and 2-6pm; cashier closes at 5pm). The **postal code** is A-6290.

ACCOMMODATIONS AND FOOD. Finding a budget accommodation in Mayrhofen can be quite difficult, since package groups tend to book up most of the available bed-and-breakfasts. Try your luck at **Pension Fischnaller,** Hauptstr. 410, which occupies a stately house in the center of town. The quiet rooms and elegant furnishings are an oasis of calm in Mayrhofen's busy tourist program. The pension has no sign—ring the bell for service. (☎62347. Breakfast included. In summer 170-240AS per person; in winter 190-260AS. Add 20AS for a single room.) **Haus Woldrich,** Brandbergstr. 355, rents huge rooms, some with a balcony. From the train station, walk up Einfahrt Mitte continuing as it turns into Pfarrer-Krapfstr. until you reach a sign pointing parallel to the road ahead and reading "Brandbergstraße." Turn right and it will be the second house on the left with "Haus Woldrich" painted on the side. (☎62325. In summer 180-240 per person; in winter 220-300AS. Add 30AS for single room.) **Haus Andreas,** Sportplatzstr. 317, about 3 min. from the tourist office, rents out well-lit, clean, comfortable singles and doubles, many with balconies (☎63845; breakfast included; 220-270AS, in winter 230-250AS).

Touristy eateries, most of which are priced better than one might expect, crowd the center of town. **Mo's Esscafé and Musikroom,** Hauptstr. 417, up the street from the post office, tries to bring a piece of Americana to the Austrian Alps. Occasional live music at night. (☎63435. Pizzas 79-105AS, burgers 54-68AS, "Real American Donuts" 15AS. Open Tu-Sa noon-midnight, Su-M 4pm-midnight.) **Café Dengg,** Hauptstr. 412, serves lighter fare and desserts beneath a green awning. (☎64866. Sandwiches 65-78AS, salads 38-97AS, pizzas 88-108AS, *Apfelstrudel* with coffee 49AS. Open M-Sa 10am-11pm.)

OUTDOOR ACTIVITIES. Mayrhofen caters to the year-round sportsperson—endless **hiking** and **skiing** trails in the nearby valleys satisfy mountaineers of all levels. If you plan on doing extensive hiking in the area, it's worth stopping by the tourist office to pick up a detailed map (80-110AS) of routes and mountain huts, which offer both refreshment and lodging. Buses and taxis run frequently up the valleys, to and from the higher alpine zone. The **Z-Hiking-Ticket** simplifies hiking arrangements by giving you free portage on all Zillertal cable cars, buses, and trains, unlimited dips in public swimming pools, as well as reductions on many museums and alpine/paragliding schools (see p. 194).

The first sight that greets many visitors to Mayrhofen is the **Penkenbahn,** with its dangling gondolas passing directly above the town on their way up to the top of the 1850m Penkenberg (☎62277; May 20-Oct. 10. 9am-5pm; 165AS, 150AS with guest card, 90AS children). The Penkenbahn leads to a variety of easy paths. The **Ahornbahn** lift takes passengers to the vicinity of both easy and difficult hikes. From the Ahornbahn mountain station, it is an hour to the Edelhütte mountain hut (☎62168). The Mayrhofen tourist office runs a variety of guided hiking and climbing programs, ranging from leisurely walks to hard-core mountain ascents. A different hike is offered every day, for a fee that ranges from 30-145AS per person.

Paragliders can catch thermals in the surrounding valleys, or take a tandem flight with instructors at **Flugtaxi Mayrhofen** Sportplatzstr. 300 (☎63142; flights from 700AS); or **Stocky-Air** Ramsau 79a (☎3786; 5min. flight 750AS, 15-20min. 1100AS). Opportunities abound for **kayaking, rafting,** and **canyoning** in the white-water; for rafting and canyoning, call **Action Club Zillertal,** Hauptstr. 458 (☎62977); rafting prices start at 395AS, and canyoning prices start at 370AS.

Come winter, **skiers** and **snowboarders** flock to the Ahorn, Penken, and Horberg ski areas above town, all of which are covered by the **Ski Mayrhofen pass** (1 day 370AS, youth 295AS, children 220AS; 3 days 1000AS, 800AS, 600AS). The skipass also entitles you to free transit on the local ski buses. Snow-bunnies can avail themselves of the regional, all-inclusive **Zillertal Super Skipass** (see p. 194). You can **rent skis** at **Intersport,** Hauptstr. 414, for about 200AS per day or 790AS per week (☎62400; open daily 8:30am-6pm).

HINTERTUX ☎05287

At the end of a narrow road that begins at Mayrhofen and winds through the Tuxertal (Tux Valley), tiny Hintertux sits bordered on the sides by mountains and in the front by a breath-taking glacier. But the bus loads of European tourists do not head to Hintertux just for the view; the summer skiing is what draws people up the tiny Tuxertal. Hintertux is the last of five towns in the Tux valley, preceded by Madseit, Juns, Lanersbach, and Vorlanersbach (see hike below for moving up the valley without a bus). Hintertux is expensive, and often a bit difficult to get around, so ski-bums flocking to tackle slopes would do well to arrive early and make a day-trip of it.

To get to Hintertux from Mayrhofen, catch a bus at the **Mayrhofen** train station (45min., 5:55am-5:35pm, 47AS) to the Hintertux tourist office/post office. The **tourist office,** Hintertux 756, has a small kiosk of brochures outside, as well as a free 24hr accommodation phone and computer (☎8506. M-F 8am-noon and 1-6pm, Sa 8am-noon). In the same building as the tourist office is the **post office,** which **exchanges money**. (☎87493. Open M-F 8:30am-noon and 2-5pm). Those planning to make more than a day-trip to Hintertux would be well advised to call the tourist office well in advance: inexpensive accommodations are, unlike 4-star hotels, sorely lacking, and the few *Pensioner* and *Privatzimmer* get booked quickly. Cheaper places to stay are in the towns leading away from the glacier. **Schmittenberghof,** Madseit 220, rents out comfortable doubles and singles, some with balconies, with in-room TVs and hall toilet and shower. Get off the town bus at the "Madseit Gasthof Alte Hütte" stop. (☎87393. Breakfast included. 220AS.) Restaurants in Hintertux tend to be either expensive or closed, at least until July when the owners open for tourists. Pick up some food, and odds and ends at the **Dorfladen** (village store; open M-F 8am-noon, 2-6pm, Sa 8am-noon, 2-5pm).

A great, easy **hiking** trail connects the towns of the Tuxertal. This trail leaves Hintertux from behind the *Thermalbad* parking lot, near the tourist office. Simply keep following the signs that say "Lanersbach." Signs point toward a variety of exits into towns. The scenery ranges from a large rocky outcroppings to verdant river beds, to old men fishing along the trail.

Now to the skiing you came for: during the winter, day passes including the glacier cable car cost 430AS, 350AS for youth (18 or under), and 260AS for children (14 and under). Exclude the glacier cable car and prices drop to 360AS, 290AS, and 215AS. Prices for **summer skiing** are 360AS, 290AS, and 215AS. **Ski rental** is available everywhere in town; **Intersport Hintertux,** Hintertux 783 (☎858 0408) has rental near the glacier cable car.

THE ARLBERG

Half-way between the Bodensee and Innsbruck, the jagged peaks of the Arlberg mountains provide the setting for some of the world's best ski resorts; this is where modern Alpine skiing began. The towns of the Arlberg are generally nestled into small valleys, hugged on either side by inviting mountains, and bedecked with a rushing river. In summer, streams pouring down steep mountainsides create countless waterfalls, providing spectacular **hiking** prospects. Some lifts operate in summer for hiking, but **skiing** remains the area's main draw. With hundreds of miles of ski runs ranging in altitude from 1000 to 3000m, the Arlberg offers unparalleled terrain from December through April. Dauntingly long cross-country trails (up to 42km) link various villages throughout the valleys. All resorts have ski schools in German and English for children, beginners, and proficient skiers. In fact, the world's first ski instructor still lives in Oberlech. The comprehensive **Arlberg Ski Pass** gives access to some of Austria's most lusted-after slopes, including the famed **Valluga** summit. The pass is valid for over 86 mountain railways and ski lifts in St. Anton, St. Jakob, St. Christoph, Lech, Zürs, Klösterle, and Stuben.

On the eastern side of the Arlberg tunnel, you'll find the hub of the region, **St. Anton,** which forms a village along with its distinctly less cosmopolitan cousins **St. Jakob** and **St. Christoph.** The western Arlberg is home to the classy resorts **Lech,** and **Zürs.** In winter, book rooms 6-8 weeks in advance; in the off season, a few days are sufficient.

ST. ANTON AM ARLBERG ☎05446

TYROL

You wouldn't know by looking at it, but little St. Anton is cursed with a split personality. When the sun shines in spring and summer, the town of 2,500 is an alpine postcard incarnate, with cobblestoned streets, *Lederhosen*-ed grandfathers, and lush green mountains. The hiking and relaxing give way, however, once the first snowflake falls, to a cosmopolitan array of European glitterati looking to hit the world-class slopes. Skiing championships enthrall the town in January, and the Isospeed tennis tournament does the same in December. While summer is affordable, save some schillings in winter by staying in nearby **St. Jakob** (5min. by bus).

Be warned that this posh ski town doesn't emerge from spring hibernation until mid-July. If you visit in May or June, you may feel as if you've entered a ghost town—the majority of the hotels and restaurants will be closed or running on reduced hours.

GETTING THERE AND AROUND. St. Anton lies at the bottom of a steep, narrow valley, with neighboring **St. Jakob** and **St. Christoph** (technically part of St. Anton) a few minutes east and west along the valley, respectively. Several major train and bus routes connect St. Anton with major destinations. Train destinations

THE ARLBERG CHANNEL St. Anton's economy depends on its mountain, the Arlberg. Understandably, the town really likes its pet peak. How much? The town has set up a TV channel that provides nothing but live footage of the mountain—hour after hour of trees, rocks, more rocks, and snow. All Arlberg, all the time. Showing up-to-the-minute weather, the channel is ostensibly a service for skiers, but anyone in town can tell you the real reason for it: St. Anton is simply paying high-tech homage to its provider. Twenty-four-hour surveillance replaces burnt offerings—and, anyway, you never know when a mountain might pack up and leave if no one keeps an eye on it.

include: **Innsbruck** (1¼hr., 12:17am-11:14pm, 160AS), **Munich** (4hr., 6:14am-6:04pm, 490AS), **Zurich** (3hr., 5:37am-3:57pm, 500AS), **Vienna Westbahnhof** (6-8hr., 6:14am-11:14pm, 740AS), and **Feldkirch** (45min., 5:37am-11:58pm, 82AS). During late June to Sept. and Dec.-Apr., **buses** run to nearby **Lech** (30min., 8:13am-6:03pm, 46AS), **St. Christoph** (20min., 8:27am-6:37pm, 10AS), and **St. Jakob** (5 min., 8:27am-6:37pm). A *Tageskarte* allows unlimited bus travel between the towns (80AS). Buses stop at the train station.

ORIENTATION AND PRACTICAL INFORMATION. St. Anton has only one main road, which runs the length of the *Fußgängerzone* (the pedestrian zone). To get to the *Fußgängerzone* from the (new) train station, simply walk away from the station, ahead into town. To reach the **tourist office** turn left on the *Fußgängerzone* after exiting the station. The leather-lounge tourist office is off a small square on the left just before the railroad crossing. (☎22690; fax 2532; st.anton@netway.at; www.stantonamarlberg.com. Open July to mid-Sept. M-F 8am-noon and 2-6pm, Sa-Su 10am-noon; May to early June and mid-Sept. to Dec. M-F 8am-noon and 2-6pm; Dec.-Apr. M-F 8:30am-6:30pm, Sa 9am-noon and 1-7pm, Su 10am-noon and 3-6pm.) Services include: **currency exchange** at banks and the post office (avoid automatic exchange machines; banking hours M-F 8am-noon and 2-4:30pm); **bike rental** and advice at **Intersport Alber** in the pedestrian zone (☎3400; fax 3106; 1 day 280AS; prices 20-30AS lower with guest card; open M-F 9am-noon and 2-6pm, Sa 9am-noon); 24hr. **luggage storage** for 30AS at the station; and **taxis** (☎23150, 23860). Dial 2565 for **ski conditions;** for the **police,** dial 133. For an **ambulance,** dial 144. To find the **post office** exit the tourist office, and turn right down the main road, turning right opposite Hotel Schwarzer Adler (open M-F 8am-noon and 2-5:30pm; from Dec.-Apr. also Sa 9-11am). The **postal code** is A-6580.

TYROL

ACCOMMODATIONS. In the summer, affordable accommodations are relatively easy to find. During the ski season, however, prices generally double. If you book far enough in advance (about 2 months), you *may* find relatively cheap housing. During the ski season, accommodations are usually booked around week-long (Sa-Sa) stays. It can be very difficult to get a room for less than one week, except in December and April. One useful resource is the **24-hour electronic accommodation board** outside the tourist office, which lists all *Pensionen*, hotels, and prices, and has a free telephone to call for reservations. **Pension Pepi Eiter** sits to the right on a hill in front of the tourist office. Exit the tourist office facing the main road and walk forward to the sign which has a map of St. Anton. Turn left and take the road leading up the hill. Look carefully for a green sign about 200m up the road, on the left—turn right at the sign, follow the path up the side of Haus Schollberg and up the hill. Pepi Eiter provides luscious beds, light pine rooms, and a chocolate on your nightstand. (☎2550. All rooms with TV. Breakfast and parking included. In summer, singles 220-250AS; doubles 440-500AS. In winter, singles 400-500AS; doubles 800-1000AS. Add 20AS in summer and 50AS in winter for stays shorter than 3 nights.) Your best bet for an affordable winter accommodation is in nearby **St. Jakob** (5min. by free bus). Check the St. Jakob tourist office, or try **Haus Bergwelt,** which has spacious, quiet rooms, some with balconies that look out on grazing cows. (☎2995. All rooms come with shower, bathroom, and TV. Breakfast included. In summer, 200AS per person; in winter, 340-500AS per person.)

FOOD. The *Fußgängerzone* is riddled with pricey, mediocre restaurants. **SportCafé Schneider,** opposite the hulking Sport Hotel, serves up a small selection of soups and sandwiches (38-45AS), spaghetti bolognese (90AS), and ice cream desserts (☎2548; 35-78AS; open 9am-midnight). The **food stand,** just across and facing away from the tourist office, serves up a small selection of *Würst* for prices hovering around 35AS (open M-Sa 11am-4pm). To combat St. Anton's generally high prices, the local supermarkets may be your best bet. The **Nah und Frisch Supermarkt** beckons from the *Fußgängerzone* (open summer M-F 7:30-noon and 3-6pm, Sa 7:30am-noon; winter M-Sa 7am-noon and 2-6:30pm). The local **Spar Markt** is down the main road, 10min. away from the tourist office, just past the *Fußgängerzone* (open M-F 7am-noon and 2-6pm, Sa 7am-12:30pm and 2-6pm).

SKIING. St. Anton's main draw is its exceptional ski slopes and skiing conditions. Ski passes for the Arlberg region are normally sold at the larger hotels, but can also be purchased at the ski lift stations (Galzigbahn, Rendlbahn, St. Christophbahn, and Nasserein-Lift), or at the ticket office in the *Fußgängerzone* behind the Hotel Post. (Half day pass 360AS, children 215AS; 1-day pass 435-485AS, 260-290AS; 6-day pass 2170-2410AS, 1310-1450AS. Discounts of 5-10% available on passes of 6 days or longer for guests staying in St. Anton, St. Jakob, Zürs, or Lech.) Those interested in St. Anton's 4.2km toboggan run should call 23520.

The flurry of construction that St. Anton underwent in 2000 was all in preparation for the **Alpine Ski World Championships** (Jan. 28-Feb. 10, 2001). In preparation, St. Anton shifted the railway line to the other side of town so that skiers will be able to come all the way down the slopes into the town center. All races will finish at a newly built stadium. Non-champion skiers are discouraged from visiting St. Anton during these weeks if they want time on the slopes. Those holding a valid ski-pass will be able to watch the races down the slopes for free. Those who get in town about two months early, from Dec. 1-3, can purchase ski passes for 50% off low-season price. The same deal is offered from Apr. 21-May 1.

HIKING AND CYCLING. In the summer, St. Anton is a quiet haven for hikers. On summer Sundays, the local **hikers** hit the **Wanderwege** with walking sticks and full Tyrolean hiking costume—join them for some spectacular mountain views from trails laden with rushing streams. The tourist office dispenses maps and detailed directions for the myriad trails around St. Anton. Once a week in July, the tourist office sponsors **wildflower hikes.** The office has lists of hikes and a trail map. The **Rosannaschlucht hike** is a three-hour round-trip walk west from the *Fußgängerzone* through the Rosanna gorge, by way of the Rendl cable car station. Near the large map across the street from the tourist office, yellow signs point the way to a variety of walks. The **Leutkircher Hütte** mountain hut is about a three-hour medium-difficulty hike away (☎(05448) 8207; open early July-late Sept.) **Biking** in the Arlberg is arduous but rewarding; 60km of marked mountain bike paths await you, including the popular Ferwall Valley and Moostal trails.

LECH

☎05583

Like its big brother, nearby St. Anton, Lech's livelihood depends on the shivers of joy skiers get when they see piles of pretty snow on pretty mountains. However, it is a different town from St. Anton; the town isn't as overrun with beautiful people, and the beautiful mountains seem much closer. The summer visitor may not get to ski, but upon staying here a night, (s)he gets a free Lech summer card, with unlimited free access to chair lifts, pools, tennis courts, hiking tours, and day-care.

TRANSPORT AND PRACTICAL INFORMATION. During the off season (May-July and Oct.-Dec.), Lech is almost inaccessible by public transportation, with only a few buses each day from nearby **Langen.** In the high skiing and hiking seasons (Dec.-Apr. and June-Sept.), several buses run daily to **St. Anton** (30min., 8:13am-6:03pm, 46AS one-way, day pass 90AS), **Zürs,** and **Langen** (25min., 8:20am-8:30pm, 35AS). There are two main **bus stops** in Lech: one across from the tourist office, and one across from the post office; the terminal stop. Both bus stops are along the town's main road, and Lech lies in between the two stops. *Let's Go* refers to the terminal stop in the directions. From the terminal stop, face away from the bus garage, turn right, and walk for a few minutes to reach the **tourist office.** Hiking maps and English guidebooks are 60AS together. Guided hikes are available. The **24-hour electronic accommodations board** in the foyer has a free phone to make reservations. **Lockers** in the office cost 10AS. (☎21610; fax 3155; lech-info@lech.at; www.lech.at. Open late June to mid-Sept. M-Sa 8am-1pm and 2-7pm, Su 9am-noon and 3-5pm; mid-Sept. to Nov. M-F 9am-noon and 2-5pm, Sa 9am-noon; Dec.-Apr. M-Sa 9am-6pm; May to late June M-F 9am-noon and 2-5pm.) Nearby banks are generally open 8:30am to noon and 2 to 4pm. **Raiffeisenbank,** opposite the church and next to the post office, has an **ATM. Free parking** is available in the Esso garage under the church during the summer season. For ski and road conditions, dial 1515. For the **police,** dial 133; for an **ambulance,** dial 144. Near the bus stop is the **post office** (open M-F 8am-noon and 2-6pm; exchange closes at 5pm). The **postal code** is A-6764.

ACCOMMODATIONS AND FOOD. Guest beds outnumber permanent Lech residents five to one, but when the snowflakes fall the beds fill up and the prices rise. Luckily, the **Jugendheim Stubenbach (HI),** kept discreetly at a distance, caters to the budget traveler. From the bus stop, facing the parking lot, turn left and head down the main road into town, and continue along this road. Take the last fork downhill before leaving Lech, and cross back over the river. Continue for about 15 minutes, curving toward Lech at the tiny white chapel, and then head uphill around Haus Tristeller; the hostel is at the top of the hill, decorated by a large mural of a prophet in mid-revelation. Lovely mountain views come for a bargain price. (☎2419; fax 24194. Breakfast included. Closed Oct., May, and June. 180AS per person, 160AS for 2 nights or more; in winter, 300AS, 280AS.) Those who'd like a private room, or just want to be closer to town, can get to **Haus Brunelle** from the bus stop by facing the parking garage, turning left, and walking down the road past Charly's until #220 appears on the right. (☎2976. Parking available. Open July-Oct. and Nov.-Apr. Breakfast included. In summer, 230AS per person; in winter 320-390AS per person; 10AS surcharge for 1-night stays.)

If you're hungry, **Pizza Charly** will serve you right. Down the main road past the church and just after the bridge, it's underneath the cables of the *Schloßkopfbahn* (where they hang tablecloths in the summer). Pizza (80-130AS) and pasta (84-135AS) are served by the river. (☎2339. Open July to late Apr. daily 11:30am-2pm and 5-10pm.) To flee from Lech's uninspiring restaurants, stock up on the vitals at **SPAR Supermarkt.** To get there, exit the tourist office, facing the river and turn left; it will be on the right (M-F 8am-6:30pm, Sa 8am-5pm, Su 10am-noon).

THE ÖTZTAL

Wending its way between hundreds of sharp 3000m peaks on the Italian border, the Ötztal (Ötz valley) offers some of the wildest and most impressive scenery in the Tyrolean Alps. Tiny farms cling impossibly to the mountainside, as rivulets carve their way through rocks to silt-gray rivers. The 1991 discovery of a frozen man who lived 5000 years ago, nicknamed Ötzi (see Frozen in Time, p. 62), proves that visitors have been enjoying the breathtaking views here for millennia. The area, known as the Ötztal Arena, is Austria's largest skiing and snowboarding center. The four main resorts in the Arena are Sölden, Hochsölden, Vent, and Zwieselstein; each one has a very distinct character. Two major glaciers, the Rettenbach and the Tiefenbach, form the largest interconnected year-round skiing

THREE MEN PLUS BABY During the first week of the new year on Three Kings' Day, troupes of devout Austrian school children go door to door singing the story of Casper, Melchior, and Balthasar in exchange for charity. Donors receive a chalk inscription on their doors worth a year of good luck. The inscriptions read "wx–C+M+B–yz" where w, x, y, and z stand for the digits of that given year in order. So good luck for 2001 is 20–C+M+B–01. Write that on some doors for luck!

area in the Eastern Alps. At the mouth of the valley **Bahnhof Ötztal** sends trains to **Innsbruck** (40min., 6:08am-10:53pm, 88AS) and **St. Anton** (1hr., 5:25am-11:07pm, 108AS). **Buses** ply the 67km route up the Ötztal valley, passing through the main town of Sölden before forking into the narrow Gurgler and Venter ranges. The region is fairly accessible by public transportation, although buses to the more remote towns run on reduced hours in the summer and fall.

SÖLDEN

☎05254

Sitting pretty in a neck of the Ötztal valley 40km south of Bahnhof Ötztal, Sölden's prime location makes it an ideal base for exploring the surrounding villages. Although the town is a major ski resort in winter with slopes for all levels of skiing difficulty, Sölden keeps up a modest appearance; it's the razor-sharp, snow-streaked mountains on either side that really steal the show.

TRANSPORT AND PRACTICAL INFORMATION. **Buses** arrive in the center of town from **Bahnhof Ötztal** (1hr., 7:05am-7:00pm, 78AS) and **Innsbruck** (2hr., 5 per day 8:25am-5:05pm, 142AS) before departing for the higher villages of **Vent** (30min., 8:15am-4:45pm, 46AS) and **Obergurgl** (25min., 7:38am-7:15pm, 33AS). Facing the river, turn left and walk about 100m down the main street, from the bus stop, following the signs with a green-and-white "i," to the **tourist office.** Two free **Internet** terminals are at the tourist office. (☎22120; fax 3131; oetztalarena@netway.at; www.tiscover.at/oetztal-arena. Open M-Sa 8am-6pm, Su 9am-noon and, in summer, 2-6pm.) **Rent bikes** at any one of the 5 sports shops in town (full day 225-250AS, weekend 350-720AS). The **post office** is next to the bus stop (open M-F 8am-noon and 2-6pm; exchange closes at 5pm). The **postal code** is A-6450.

ACCOMMODATIONS AND FOOD. Summer accommodations can be quite affordable in Sölden, but be warned that prices rise steeply in winter as skiers hit the slopes. Check with the tourist office for a list of private accommodations or try **Pension Mina,** Rettenbach 90. Exit the post office facing the main road, turn left, and after crossing the small brook, go uphill a few meters. The *pension* will be on your left. The friendly proprietor offers comfortable rooms with TV, shower, and bathroom. (☎2146. Breakfast included. In summer, 260-290AS per person, in winter 460-490AS. No credit cards.)

There are several restaurants in town, though many close down during the summer season. One of the few budget establishments open year-round is **Café Corso,** by the river across the bridge from the tourist office. (Pizza 89-142AS, pasta 98-148AS. ☎2498; fax 2980. Open noon-midnight daily except W.) Turn left from the post office to get to **SPAR Supermarkt** (M-Sa 8am-noon and 3-6pm).

OUTDOOR ACTIVITIES. The high altitude of Sölden's **skiing** areas (1377-3058m) guarantees snow even in the summer. Slopes of all difficulty levels are spread out over Hochsölden, Gaislachkogl, and the Rettenbach and Tiefenbach glaciers. The **Gaislachkoglbahn** whisks passengers up to the top of the 3058m Gaislachkogl in a twin-cable gondola, is the largest of its kind in the world (open mid-June to mid-Sept., Dec.-May, round-trip 230AS). **Lift tickets** for the 32 cable cars and lifts that serve Sölden's slopes are sold at the Gaislachkoglbahn booth at the southern end of town (420-470AS). There are several ski and snowboard schools in and around Sölden, including **Total Vacancia Sölden** (☎3100; fax 2939) and **Ötztal 2000** (☎220 3500; fax 225 951). Rates hover around 550AS for a 1-day group lesson. Ask at the tourist office about toboggan parties on the 5.5km long toboggan run, which is illuminated along its length in the evening.

In summer, opportunities for **hiking** abound in the surrounding mountains and hills. About 15 hikes can be taken from right next to the post office: a brown sign points the way to *Wanderwege* taking from 1-2½hr. each way. One such sign points to the **Edelweiß Hütte** (☎2647) at 1821m. The tourist office runs two free guided tours every week and sells a book of detailed hiking maps and itineraries (69AS). The **Zirmzapfen Hiking Club** offers a wide-ranging hiking program in summer, with a variety of "themed" hiking weeks, such as Lake Hiking Week (☎2910, www.swi.at/hotel-neue-post-zwieselstein). Those who want some mechanical assistance with their hikes can use the network of cable cars to gain and lose altitude. You can buy lift passes for hikes for 100AS. There are various summer glacier hikes, including one up to the site where Ötzi was discovered (see p. 62), as well as outings to mountain lakes. A newly created High Alpine Panorama Trail offers a wealth of hiking routes that provide unique views of the Ötztal and Stubai Alps. **Cyclists** will enjoy the mountain trails around Sölden, ranging from easy 30-minute outings to the strenuous 70km "Mountain Riders Trail" that runs from Bahnhof Ötztal to the Karlsruher Refuge. A free mountain bike train guide shows you where to ride, including the Stuibenfall waterfall in nearby Umhausen.

DAYTRIP: OBERGURGL. ☎05256

Buses run from Sölden to Obergurgl (25min., 7:38am-7:15pm, 33AS).

Although not blessed with a mellifluous name, tiny Obergurgl, Austria's highest village, is graced with beautiful mountains climbing up in jagged formations around it. Obergurgl proper is little more than a few hotels and guest houses, but you're not likely to stay on the ground long. The **tourist office** is around the corner, in the same building as the bus stop. The staff will help you with accommodations, travel tips, and suggestions for what to do in the magnificent mountains. (☎6466; fax 6353; www.obergurgl.com. Open M-F 8am-6pm, Sa 8am-4pm, Su 9:30am-noon.) In front of the tourist office is a free but slow 24hr. **Internet** terminal. The terminal also helps locate accommodations. For snow information call 6469. Weather permitting, behind the SPAR supermarket, a ski-lift can carry you, white-knuckled, to the top of **Hohe Mut** (2670m), where the stunning view encompasses icy glaciers and the far-off peaks of Italian Tyrol. (Round-trip 130AS. Open 8:30am-4:15pm in summer, 9am-4:15pm in winter.) The trip is worth it: it is a relatively inexpensive ride, and even if you don't plan to hike or ski, the view is wondrous. There are a number of mountain huts in the area, two being the **Lantalereck Hütte** (☎(05250) 233 or (05253) 5396) and the **Lenzenalm Hütte** (☎(05254) 2756). Overnight stays in these huts range from 120-250AS per night. A network of hiking paths covers the mountainsides and woodlands—ask at the tourist office for a map and more information. When the flakes start falling, **skiing** claims Gurgl's heart and soul. You can purchase **lift tickets** at the 2 lift stations (in peak season, 1-day adult pass 460AS; in off-season, 410AS; discounts for children and seniors). Exit the tourist office, turning immediately left on the main road to stock up on vitals at the SPAR Supermarkt (open M-F 8am-noon, 1-6pm; Sa 8am-noon, 1-5pm; Su 8am-noon).

VORARLBERG

At the intersection of 4 nations, the residents of the **Vorarlberg,** Austria's westernmost province, speak like the Swiss, eat like the Germans, ski with Liechtensteiners, but vote Austrian. Visitors should carry a passport at all times; since foreign borders are never more than 2 hours away, a short daytrip can easily become an international excursion. Feldkirch, on the Ill River, lies just minutes from Liechtenstein's border. Bregenz, on the banks of the **Bodensee** (Lake Constance), would be German but for half a dozen kilometers. As a result of its international tendencies, Vorarlberg is well-equipped to welcome visitors from all over the world. Tourism is by far the leading industry, since the mountainous terrain isn't particularly hospitable to agriculture or manufacturing (except chocolate).

From the tranquil Bodensee in the west, Vorarlberg thrusts increasingly upward as you move south and east, climaxing in the massive Arlberg Alps (passable only through the 10km Arlberg Tunnel) at the boundary to Tyrol. Over 1600km of marked hiking paths ranging in altitude from 400 to 3350m crisscross the region, and mountain railways carry hikers to the summits quickly and conveniently. Vorarlberg's 161km network of cycling paths range from leisurely tours through the Bodensee plain to challenging climbs in the Alps. Cycling maps are available at bookstores and tourist offices. For more info, contact the **Vorarlberg Information Office** in Bregenz (☎/fax (05574) 42525; www.vorarlberg-tourism.at).

HIGHLIGHTS OF VORARLBERG

Hike over rolling green pastures to sweet-smelling **Schwarzenberg** (see p. 212).

Wander through the seamless, pastel beauty of **Feldkirch,** the former seat of the Prince of Liechtenstein (see p. 205).

See Puccini performed in the open air at the **Bregenzer Festspiele** (see p. 210).

FELDKIRCH

☎05522

Just minutes from the borders of Switzerland and Liechtenstein, Feldkirch (pop. 28,000) has served for centuries as a hub of trade and transportation. More than in any other city in Vorarlberg, Feldkirch's historic past remains vivid today—the triangular *Altstadt* is a maze of pastel-colored Baroque buildings, lined by arcades that shelter shops and fruit stands. Festivals are complemented by beautiful suburbs that melt away into beautiful forested landscapes.

TRANSPORT AND PRACTICAL INFORMATION. Trains depart from Feldkirch to **Bregenz** (45min., 12:01am-11:01pm, 58AS); **Innsbruck** (2¼hr., 12:20am-11:40pm, 260AS); and **Salzburg** (4hr., 12:20am-10:18pm, 520AS). **Swiss Post Buses** travel from the train station to Buchs and Sargans in Switzerland, with connections to **Liechtenstein** (20min., every 45min., 34AS). For bus info call ☎73974 (open M-Th 8am-12:30pm and 2-4:30pm, F 8am-noon). **City buses** *(Stadtbusse)* connect Feldkirch's various subdivisions (13AS, day pass 25AS). Buses stop at the

VORARLBERG

station and at the main bus stop, which can be reached from the train station by exiting the station, walking away from the tracks, and turning left at the intersection. Hop in a **taxi** outside the station, or call for one (☎1718, 38700 or 84200).

The primary locations of interest in Feldkirch are clustered on the Ill river, in the old city, a confusing warren of streets that makes a map necessary (free at the tourist office). To reach the city center and the **tourist office,** Herreng. 12, walk from the train station to the end of the road, turn left onto Bahnhofstr., and cross via the pedestrian underpass at the first major intersection. Go into the *Bezirkhauptmannschaft* building, and the office is about 50m ahead on the right. The office helps with reservations, hands out historic walking-tour maps and info about cultural events, and sells hiking maps (40AS). (☎73467; fax 79867; tourismus@wtg.feldkirch.com; www.feldkirch.at. Open May-Sept. M-F 9am-6pm, Sa 9am-noon; Oct.-Apr. M-F 8am-noon, 1-5pm, Sa 9am-noon.) The main bus stop has a 24hr. computer that provides information about accommodations, as well as free **Internet** access. **Lockers** (20-30AS) are available at the train station. **Luggage storage** is also available at the station (30AS; 7am-11:30pm). There is a **post office,** and **ATM** on Bahnhofstr., across from the station (open M-F 7am-7pm, Sa 7am-noon). The **postal code** is A-6800.

ACCOMMODATIONS. Feldkirch's youth hostel, **Jugendherberge "Altes Siechenhaus" (HI),** Reichstr. 111, might well be the most historic spot on your visit. Buses #2 and 60 (dir.: "Jugendherberge") run to the hostel from the station (5min.). You can also walk straight out of the station onto the main road, Bahnhofstr. (which becomes Reichstr.), turn right and walk 15 to 20 minutes; a few signs point the way. The hostel is an ancient white, brick-and-wood building on the right of the street, next to a small stone church. This 600-year-old structure served as an infirmary during several plague epidemics. The occasional stone cubby and wooden beam betray the antiquity of this family-oriented hostel with clean rooms and modest beds. (☎73181; fax 79399. Breakfast 50AS. **Laundry** 40AS. Linen 20AS. Oct.-Apr. heating 25AS. Candy, soft drinks, wine, and beer sold at the desk. Wheelchair accessible. Curfew at 10pm; key deposit of 16AS, or ID. Reception M-Sa 7am-10pm, Su 7-10am and 5-10pm. Closed Nov. 20-Dec. 8. Non-HI members add 25AS. Dorms 142AS; double 193AS per person.) If medieval hostelry is not to your taste, take bus #1 or 3 (dir.: Tosters) to "Burgweg" to **Gasthof Löwen,** in a suburb of Feldkirch. From the stop, walk a half-block toward the tall pink-and-white building on Egelseestr. The hotel has simple, quiet rooms. (☎72868; fax 37857. TV, shower, and breakfast included. Singles 310-350AS; doubles 640-700AS.) Campers can pitch their tents at **Waldcamping Feldkirch,** Stadionstr., a large, leafy suburb. To get to the campground, take bus #1 (dir.: "Gisingen" to "Milchhof," and follow the signs; it lies past the soccer field. (☎74308; kkf@montforthaus.feldkirch.com; www.feldkirch.com/kkf/fbg3.htm. **Laundry** available (50AS). Reception 8am-noon and 2-10pm. Sept.-June 55AS, children 28AS, cars 33AS, tents 29-46AS; in July and Aug. 66AS, children 39AS, cars 46AS, tents 37-56AS. MC, Visa.)

FOOD. The *Fußgängerzone* is packed with restaurants and snack bars. **Pizzeria-Trattoria La Taverna,** Vorstadtstr. 18, has authentic Italian dining, with pizzas (85-100AS) and pastas (70-100AS), plus a pretty terrace to eat them on. (☎79293. Open 11:30am-2pm and 5pm-midnight.) The cheapest food in town is likely **Snackman Schnellimbiß,** Bahnhofstr. 25, just in front of the train station. Pick up veggie *kebabs* for 25AS, a hot dog for 32AS, and wash it down with a Capri Sun for 14AS (open M-F 7am-10pm, Sa 7am-5pm). The restaurant inside the huge iron doors of the **Schattenburg** (see Sights, below) serves enormous portions of *Wienerschnitzl* for 139AS, *Apfelstrudel* for 35AS, (open Tu-Sa 11am-2pm, 3-10pm; Su 11am-2pm, 3-9pm). In the center of the *Altstadt*, get picnic supplies at the huge **Interspar Café/Markt,** under Hervis Sport Mode at the top of Johanniterg. off Marktpl. A cooked, half-chicken sells for 49AS (open M-Th 8:30am-7pm, F 8:30am-7:30pm, Sa 8am-7pm). The Marktpl. houses an **outdoor market** (Tu and Sa 8am-1pm).

SIGHTS AND ENTERTAINMENT. Feldkirch's Gothic cathedral, the **St. Nikolaus Kirche,** forms one edge of the *Altstadt* (old town). Mentioned in a manuscript in 1287, the cathedral received a face-lift in 1478 after a series of devastating fires. Today the Dom is a curious amalgam of its facelifts. The modern, geometric stained-glass windows and minimalist stone-cut scenes depicting the life of Jesus, are over a *pietà*, painted in 1521 by Wolf Huber (a master of the Danube School), on the right altar. Frescoes of Feldkirch history and the coats of arms of local potentates adorn the 15th-century **Rathaus** on Schmiedg. At nearby Schloßerg 8 stands the **Palais Liechtenstein,** completed in 1697. The palace once supported the royal seat of the Prince of Liechtenstein, but now houses the city archives and the town library. Its 3rd-floor **art gallery** hosts frequent exhibitions, often free.

At the edges of the *Altstadt*, 3 towers of the original city wall remain: the **Katzenturm,** the **Pulverturm,** and the **Wasserturm.** Just outside the *Altstadt*, one block towards the station on Bahnhofstr., lies the **Kapuzinerkloster** (Capuchin monastery), built in 1605. Hike up the staircase on Burgg. to reach the **Schattenburg,** Feldkirch's most impressive structure, for a fantastic view of the *Altstadt* (castle and cafe open Tu-Su 10am-midnight.) From the early 1200s until 1390, the castle was the seat of the Counts of Montfort, who dominated the Vorarlberg region. The town purchased the castle in 1825 and converted it into the **Feldkirch Heimatmuseum,** where a gaggle of guns and armor bring the Middle Ages into martial relief. (☎71982. Open Tu-Su 9am-noon and 1-5pm. 25AS, youth 15AS, children 5AS.)

Feldkirch's regular **Schubertiade** honors one of Austria's most beloved composers, but will be held in Schwarzenberg in 2001 (see p. 212). (Tickets go on sale 1 year in advance for 300-1400AS. ☎(05576) 72091, fax 75450. Schubertiade GmbH, Villa Rosenthal, Schweizerstr. 1, A-6845 Hohenerns, Postfach 100; info@schubertiade.at, www.schubertiade.at.) From July 7-9, 2001, Feldkirch's annual **wine festival** will intoxicate all those who venture to Marktpl. The circus comes to town toward the last weekend of July, when the annual **Gauklerfestival** (Jester's Festival) looses jugglers, mimes, and clowns from all over the world into the cobblestone streets. The annual **Christmas bazaar** is from Dec. 1-Dec. 24 with crafts, candy canes, crèches, and carols.

BREGENZ

☎05574

Bregenz, the capital city of Vorarlberg, spreads along the eastern coast of the Bodensee (Lake Constance). Separating three countries by only a few kilometers, the lake serves as an international conduit for Swiss, German, and Austrian tourists in search of Alpine and marine getaways. The Celts came here first, then the Romans, who established a camp called Brigantia on the present-day site of the city. Later, Gallus and Columban, Irish missionaries, came upon the vast shimmering lake ringed by mountains and dubbed the locale "Bregenz" (Golden Bowl). The Bowl nowadays fills with fancy Europeans wandering along the gorgeous lakeside or through the historic **Oberstadt**.

GETTING THERE AND AROUND

Trains: Bahnhofstr. (☎67550; 1717 for information). **Trains** to **St. Gallen** (45min., 7:03am-8:40pm, 100AS), **Zurich** (2¼hr., 6:30am-8:40pm, 284AS), **Innsbruck** (2¼hr., 5am-10:14pm, 300AS), **Vienna** (8-10hr., 5am-9:43pm, 810AS), and **Munich** (2½hr., 9:20am-7:20pm, 388AS).

Regional Buses: BundesBuses leave from the train station for the surrounding region.

Public Transportation: 4 bus lines run through the city. 13AS one ride, day pass 25AS.

Taxis: ☎65000, 86688, and 42222.

Car Rental: Hertz, Autolmmler Handels GmbH, Am Brand 2 (☎44995).

Parking: You'll find **free parking** by the *Festspielhaus*. The **Hypobank parking garage** is in the city center (10AS per hour). Metered street parking spaces (5AS per 30min).

PRACTICAL INFORMATION

Tourist Office: Bregenz Tourismus und Stadtmarketing, Bahnhofstr. 14 (☎49590; fax 495 959; tourismus@bregenz.at; www.bregenzat.at). From the train station, face away from the tracks, and turn left; cross the street using the pedestrian underpass and then continue left until the green, glass building. Makes hotel reservations (30AS) and has *Privatzimmer* lists, hiking and city maps, and concert info. Open during the year M-F 9am-noon and 1-6pm, Sa 9am-noon, during the *Festspiele* M-Sa 9am-7pm and Su 4-7pm. The office has a free, if not altogether reliable **Internet** terminal. Free accommodations board with a courtesy phone in the train station.

Consulate: UK, Bundesstr. 110 (☎78586), in neighboring **Lauterach.**

Services at the station: lockers (20-30AS), **luggage storage** (30AS; 6am-9:40pm), **bike rental** (with ticket 120AS, children 70AS; without 180AS, 100AS), an **ATM,** and **public showers** (10AS).

Internet Access: S'Logo, Kirchstr. 47 (☎44191). 1AS per min. Open 5pm-midnight.

Post Office: Seestr. 5 (☎43700; fax 45757). Continue 6 blocks past the tourist office, heading away from the train station; the entrance faces the lake. Open M-F 8am-7pm (cashier closes at 5pm), Sa 8am-2pm. **Postal Code:** A-6900.

ACCOMMODATIONS

Bregenz caters primarily to affluent vacationers, and the prices for even hostel beds is expensive, but backpackers can usually find a comfortable corner. When the *Festspiele* come to town during the last week of July and the first 3 weeks of August, prices rise and reservations are painfully necessary.

Jugendgästehaus (HI), Mehrerauerstr. 3-5 (☎42867; fax 428 6788; bregenz@jgh.at; www.jgh.at). To reach the family-oriented hostel from the train station, cross the bridge that goes over the tracks and out of the station. Then facing away from the tracks, walk left, past the skateboard half-pipe, and look for the big, yellow-brick building immediately on your left. Or take bus #2 from the train station. Though not on the cheap end of HI hostels, offers spic-and-span bunk-bed accommodations in 2-6 person rooms, with bathroom and shower. Also has an **Internet** cafe (40AS per hr.). Sheets, towel, and breakfast included. Reception 7am-10pm. Lockout 10pm. Checkout 10am. Breakfast 6:30-9am. 230AS per person, plus 7AS tax Jan.-Apr and Oct.-Dec., 17AS tax May-Sept. 40AS surcharge for stays under three nights; 30AS surcharge May to mid-Sept.

Pension Gunz, Anton-Schneider-Str. 38 (☎43657), located 2 blocks behind the post office. This homey pension-cum-restaurant serves up tidy rooms, each with shower. Breakfast included. The restaurant serves traditional fare (*Wienerschnitzel* 88AS) as well as vegetarian dishes (70-85AS). Restaurant and reception open 8am-9pm. Singles 340AS; doubles 600AS. 30AS surcharge for 1-night stays. Cash only.

Pension Sonne, Kaiserstr. 8 (☎/fax 42572; g.diem@computer.haus.at). From the station, go right (facing the lake) up Bahnhofstr. into the city, then right on Kaiserstr. Quiet, spacious rooms with wood floors in the heart of the *Fußgängerzone*. All rooms have a sink. Breakfast included. Reception open 7am-10pm. Singles 360AS, with shower 450AS; doubles 600AS, with shower 820AS; triples 870AS, with shower 1080AS. During the *Festspiele*, add 90AS. MC, Visa.

Camping Lamm, Mehrerauerstr. 50-51 (☎71701 or 71745; fax 717 454) is 5min. on foot past the youth hostel. Chock full o' caravans, but there's plenty of room for tents. Open May to mid-Oct. 50AS per person; children 25AS; tents 35-45AS; cars 35AS.

FOOD

Ikaros, Deuringstr. 5 (☎52954). Look for the blue and white-striped awning at the corner of Deuringstr. and Rathausstr. in the *Fußgängerzone*. This exceptional cafe serves up a little taste of the Mediterranean on the Bodensee. A wide variety of Greek dishes, including daily specials (75AS), salads, and warm entrees (55-95AS) are served indoors or on pleasant tables outside. Open M-Sa 10am-1am.

König Pizza und Kebap, Rathausstr. (☎53881), serves up some of the cheapest food in town in a small restaurant that is more attractive than your average *Kebab*-eatery. Eat-in or take-out pizzas (40-90AS), *Dönerkebaps* (40AS), or veggie-*Kebaps* (30AS). Open M-Sa 10am-midnight, Su 6pm-2am.

Zum Goldnen Hirschen, Kirchstr. 8 (☎42815). Look for the wooden building with the small stained-glass windows and a flying gold reindeer over the door. Dark wooden furniture and a timbered interior complements delicious Austrian fare, including vegetarian *Krautspätzle* (85AS) and *Menüs* for 100AS. Open 10am-midnight. AmEx, MC, Visa.

China Restaurant Da-Li, Anton-Schneiderstr. 34 (☎53414), near Pension Gunz, serves up typical Chinese fare, with noodle dishes at 90-110AS and soups 30-50AS. Your best bet is to stop by weekday afternoons for the *Mittagsmenü* with rice, spring roll and entree (65AS), or the lunch buffet (95AS), to be enjoyed in somewhat over-decorated environs. Open daily 11:30am-2:30pm and 5:30-11:30pm.

SPAR Café Restaurant (☎42291, ext. 15) on the 1st floor of the big "GWL" mall building in the *Fußgängerzone*. If Austrian food makes you daydream about fresh vegetables, the self-serve salad and fruit/dessert bars (10AS per 100g) are a godsend. Cafeteria-style entrees 56-98AS. Open M-F 8:30am-5:30pm, Sa 8:30am-3pm. Below the restaurant is the **SPAR Supermarkt.** Open M-F 8am-7pm, Sa 8:30am-5pm.

Farmer's markets fill up Kornmarktstr. every Tuesday and Friday from 8am-noon.

SIGHTS AND OUTDOOR ACTIVITIES

THE OLD TOWN. On the hill above Bregenz looms the **Oberstadt,** or "high city," a once-fortified settlement that contains many of the city's oldest and most attractive buildings. A short hike up Maurachg. from the *Fußgängerzone* brings you to the towering walls, beyond which lie rows of pastel-painted houses that appear just as they might have centuries ago. For lack of building supplies, some of these houses have incorporated fragments of the old city walls in their construction. The major landmark of the *Oberstadt* is the wooden **Martinsturm,** originally built in 1362, which supports Europe's largest onion dome. The 2nd and 3rd floors of the tower house the **Vorarlberg Militärmuseum.** *(☎46632. Open May-Sept. M-Su 9am-8pm. In winter 1-5pm. 10AS, children 7AS.)* Although you can see all of the museum in 10 minutes (20 if you read the German descriptions), you may want to spend more time on the third floor with its sweeping view of the Bodensee and beyond. Next to the tower is the **Martinskirche,** filled with frescoes dating back to the early 14th century. Particularly noteworthy are the depictions of St. Christopher, the Holy Symbol of Grief, and the 18th-century Stations of the Cross. Across Ehregutapl. (with the fountain) from the Martinsturm is **Deuring Schlößchen,** a 17th-century castle that now houses a non-budget hotel.

CHURCHES. Shaded by overhanging trees and vines, Meissnersteige leads down from the corner of the castle to the bottom of the *Oberstadt*. Cross Thalbachg. and hike up Schloßbergstr. to reach **St. Gallus Pfarrkirche,** reputedly founded by medieval Irish missionaries, St. Gallus and St. Columban. The white-stucco sanctuary of the 11th-century church now glows under lavish gold ornamentation and a detailed painted ceiling that dates from 1738. The shepherdess in the altar painting has the face of Empress Maria Theresia, who donated 1500 guilders to the church in 1740. On the opposite side of the *Oberstadt*, the imposing **Herz-Jesu Kirche,** at the corner of Am Brand and Bergmannstr., points its twin steeples to the heavens. Built in 1907 and recently renovated in neo-Gothic style, the huge sanctuary's brick and wood furnishings bring out the Expressionist stained-glass windows.

BREGENZ ART MUSEUM. Walk from the tourist office down the *Fußgängerzone* and away from the train station and you are sure to come across a large, monolithic building, covered with translucent gray tiles, the **Kunsthaus Bregenz,** an avante-garde museum, where exhibits have recently included a video-installation of people making *another* exhibit, as well as a neon-lit "hygiene system" of the future, set to ambient music. *(☎485 940; fax 485 948. Open Tu-W and Fr-Su 10am-6pm, also Th 10am-9pm. 60AS; students 40AS.)*

OUTDOOR ACTIVITIES. There's no better place to stretch one's legs and check out the locals than the **Strandweg** and **Seepromenade,** which follow the curve of the Bodensee from one end of town to the other. All along the waterfront, groomed paths, rose gardens, and strategically placed ice-cream stands surround playgrounds and mini-golf courses. Several sightseeing cruises on the Bodensee depart from the **Hafen** (harbor), Seestr. 4 (☎42868), opposite the post office. Ferries run to the **Blumen Insel Mainau** (Mainau Flower Isle) on the German side of the lake, which features a Baroque castle, an indoor tropical palm house, butterfly house, and gardens rife with orchids, tulips, dahlias, and 1100 kinds of roses. *(Admission to all sights 127AS. Ferries leave Bregenz May-Sept. at 9:20, 10:20, and 11:25am; return from Mainau at 2:50, 4:15, and 4:55pm. Round-trip 293AS; special family rates available.)*

The **Pfänderbahn** cable car leaves from the top of Schillerstr., uphill from the post office, and sways up the **Pfänder** mountain (the tallest peak around the Bodensee) for a panorama spanning from the Black Forest to Switzerland. *(☎421 600. Daily 9am-7pm, every 30min. One-way 70AS, round-trip 125AS. Discounts for seniors and children under 19.)* At the top of the cable car ride, wander with native animals in the free **Alpine Wildlife Park,** or watch **bird flight shows** from May to October. *(Shows daily at 11am and 2:30pm. 45AS, children 24AS.)*

FESTIVALS AND NIGHTLIFE

The concrete monstrosity on the edge of the lake is not a ski ramp gone awry but rather Europe's largest **floating stage** and the centerpiece for the annual **Bregenzer Festspiele.** Every year from mid-July to mid-August, the Vienna Symphony Orchestra and other opera, theater, and chamber music groups come to town, bringing some 180,000 tourists with them. The main events are performances on the floating stage, drawing capacity crowds of 6800. In 2001, the floating opera will be Puccini's *La Bohème*, premiering on July 19th. Also playing will be Carlisle Floyd's *Of Mice and Men*, based on the novella by John Steinbeck, with the performance in English. (Premiere July 18th; runs until Aug. 1. Tickets go on sale in October. 300-1550AS. Students under 26 get 25% off, with the exception of the premiere night. Weekday performances rarely sell out more than a few days before the show. Standing room tickets available. For more info, write to Postfach 311, A-6901 Bregenz; call 4076; ticket@bregenzerfestspiele.com; or look online at www.bregenzerfestspiele.com.)

For late-night entertainment, there are many popular student hangouts on and around Kirchstr. Check out **Uwe's Bier-Bar,** Kirchstr. 25, a popular bar with a mixed crowd. (Beer 39AS. 18+. Open 7pm-1am.)

BREGENZERWALD

Spreading out to the south and east of Bregenz, the Bregenzerwald is home to many small towns and villages that preserve the rustic flavor of Vorarlberg's past. The villages are scattered through wide open pastures and stands of pine trees, coddled by the steeply rising mountainsides; it is not a *wald* (forest) in any real sense. You can explore the Bregenzerwald by taking daytrips into the region from Bregenz, or by staying in Dornbirn or Egg and darting out from there. The peripatetic can walk or bus from town to town staying a night in a few towns.

ORIENTATION AND GETTING AROUND. The Bregenzerwald spreads radially to the south-east from the eastern edge of the *Bodensee*, upon which Bregenz lies. The peaks generally get higher the farther from Bregenz one gets.

Driving from little town to little town is simple because of the low density of roads. Federal road 200 leads from Dornbirn, in a curvy path, generally southeast, with Egg and Au along its path, and Schwarzenberg a bit off. Most towns lie near the few roads in the region, making much of the area rather sparsely populated. Public transportation in the *Bregenzerwald* is based around a regional network of **buses (Netz);** train service in the towns and villages of the Bregenzerwald is rather limited. A few buses to the *Bregenzerwald* region depart from lakeside Bregenz, but Dornbirn is a much better transportation hub: it's only a 15-minute train ride from Bregenz, and bus lines lead from Dornbirn to most *Bregenzerwald* towns. A **Netzticket** allows you unlimited travel by bus and train throughout the *Bregenzerwald* for a given amount of time: one day 90AS, one week 190AS, one month 550AS. For many single trips into the *Bregenzerwald*, a **Tagesticket** (one day ticket) is the most economical option—in fact, the ticket window at the station may just automatically sell you one.

Walking between towns in the Bregenzerwald is not difficult, as the area is more grassy and rolling than it is rugged and mountainous. Signs in many towns point the way to other towns, but be aware that walking between towns frequently entails strolling next to a road, so the gorgeous vistas may be marred by the dissonant rumble of motorcycles. There are, however, less direct trails that go away from the roads; ask tourist offices or consult maps. The town of Schetteregg (8km away from Egg) has a nice concentration of hikes that begin at its parking lot.

ACCOMMODATIONS. Staying in the Bregenzerwald on the cheap is possible in most small towns, though not all. Mountain huts are strewn about the area, and their telephone numbers are available at the tourist office and in the *Kumpass* Bregenzerwald/Westallgäu map/handbook available at newsstands.

DORNBIRN

☎05572

Big ol' Dornbirn is rather unlike its tiny cousins in the Bregenzerwald, with a population of 42,000, and a large, tiled *Fußgängerzone* with a myriad of shops in its Marktplatz. Its bus and train connections make it an appealing transportation hub for Bregenzerwld explorers, and may be right for those who want a base with fewer tourists than nearby Bregenz.

TRANSPORT AND PRACTICAL INFORMATION. Trains depart to **Bregenz** (10-15min., 12:20am-11:29pm, 28AS), **Feldkirch** (30min., 12:20am-11:31pm, 26AS), **Lindau** (20min., 5:29am-6:40pm, 40AS) and **Innsbruck** (2¼hr., 5:09am-9:52pm, 290AS). The station has **lockers** (20AS) and **luggage storage** (30AS; M-Sa 6:30am-9pm, Su 8:30am-9pm). Regional **buses** depart from the parking lot at the side of the train station, and across the street. Line #38 runs to **Schwarzenberg** (7:20am-7:35pm) and line #40 to **Egg** (7:02am-10:35pm). City buses depart from the station and from a traffic island near the center of town.

Exit the train station and walk straight forward on Bahnhofstr. to reach the town center with its big church and Marktplatz. The **tourist office,** Rathauspl. 1, can be reached from the train station by exiting the station, facing away from the tracks, and turning right once you reach Stadtstr. The tourist office has a list of accommodations pasted on the window. (☎22188; fax 31233; www.dornbirn.at. Open M-F 9am-noon, 1-6pm, Sa 9am-noon.) On the way to the town center on Bahnhofstr., on the second floor of a shopping center on the left, there is **Internet** access at Netgate (40AS per 30min., open daily 2pm-1am). An **ATM** is located at the post office and across from the tourist office at **Raiffeisenbank**, which also **changes money** (bank hours M-Th 8am-noon and 2-3:30pm, F 8am-noon, 2-4:30pm). The **post office** is next to the train station and provides currency exchange also (open M-F 8am-7pm, Sa 8am-noon; exchange closes at 5pm). The **postal code** is A-6850.

VORARLBERG

ACCOMMODATIONS AND FOOD. Haus Lerchenmüller, Rohrbach 7, rents our a single and a double room, and is located near the train station. From the station, take the underpass past track 3 and out. Face away from the rails and walk right along the wall, turning left on Förberg., then immediately right, and then immediately right again onto Rohrbach, and walk to the large pink and white house. Rooms come with bathroom, shower, and kitchen access (☎27641; single 250AS; double 500AS). Eateries pepper the town center. **König Kebab** can be found on the way to the town center on Bahnhofstr., after the internet cafe. *Kebabs* are 30-70AS and pizzas 40-90AS (open M-Sa 10am-midnight, Su 4pm-midnight). The huge **EuroSPAR** supermarket sells everything from bananas to flip-flops, and lies behind the church on Mozartstr. (open M-F 8am-7pm, Sa 8am-5pm).

MUSEUMS. The **Stadt Museum,** across from the church in the town center has rotating exhibits on its first floor, and historical artifacts on the floors above dating from 8000BC to the 20th century, including, strangely, a Nazi tea-cup (open Tu-Su 10am-noon and 2-5pm; 30AS, students 15AS, children 10AS). The **Rolls-Royce Museum** displays the largest exhibit of Rolls-Royce cars, engines, and memorabilia in the world. (☎52652; www.rolls-royce-museum.at. Open Apr.-Oct. Tu-Su 10am-6pm, Nov.-Mar. 10am-5pm. 100AS; students 60AS.).

SCHWARZENBERG ☎05512

Schwarzenberg exemplifies the rural and cultural charms of the *Bregenzerwald.* The village sits on a rolling swath of pasture land, near the center of a ring of mountains. The majority of Schwarzenberg's houses are made entirely of wood; when they fall into disrepair, local builders restore them using centuries-old techniques. One can't go far without smelling the pungent scents of wood, fresh-cut grass, and flowers in the colorful window boxes of most houses.

TRANSPORT AND PRACTICAL INFORMATION. Bus #38 runs from Dornbirn. Another option is the 4km walk from Egg, on the sidewalk of the road in-between the two towns. The **tourist office** is located near the town square where the bus from Bregenz stops. Follow the main road downhill from the church and turn right at the *Bäckerei-Konditorei.* The tourist office dispenses maps detailing the many hiking opportunities available in and around Schwarzenberg. (☎3570; fax 2902. Open M-F 8am-noon, 1:30-4:30pm.) The **Raiffeisenbank,** uphill towards the Heimatsmuseum, has an **ATM** (open M-F 8am-noon, 1:30-4pm, Sa 8-11am). A **post office** is near the church and **exchanges money.** (Open M-F 8am-noon and 1:30-5:30pm. Exchange closes at 5pm.) The **postal code** is A-6867.

ACCOMMODATIONS AND FOOD. There are dozens of wooden guest houses in Schwarzenberg and the outlying regions. The tourist office can help find fairly inexpensive private accommodations. **Café Angelikahöhe** (☎2985), offers four double rooms with sink and table for 500AS, though prices go down the longer you stay. Children stay for 50%. Breakfast is included. To reach the pension from the town square, turn left at the *Bäckerei-Konditorei*, go straight, then turn right at the ADEG supermarket. Café Angelikahöhe also serves meals (80-135AS). A sign across from the church points the way (1½hr.) to the **Lustenaur Hütte** (☎(0664) 852 037). Stock up on local produce at **Nah und Frisch/Maria Vögel,** just downhill from the town square (open M-W, F 7:30am-noon, 2:30-6pm, Th and Sa 7:30am-noon).

SIGHTS. Schwarzenberg's man-made attractions include the **Pfarrkirche,** an airy church that features an altar painting by the town's most famous resident, Angelika Kauffmann (1741-1807). Kauffmann was one of the few wealthy female painters of her age. Goethe and Herder were among her friends, and her work received great acclaim in England and Italy. The **Heimatsmuseum,** housed in an old wooden lodge a few minutes' walk up the main road, contains a small permanent collection of her paintings and memorabilia, as well as an interesting exhibit of agricultural and domestic implements from days of yore. (☎2967. Open May-Sept. Tu, Th, and Sa-Su 2-4pm; Oct. Tu and Sa 2-4pm. 35AS, children 10AS.) Schwarzenberg hosts the **Schubertiade** in 2001, a festival of the composer's works (June 13-25 and Aug. 29-Sept. 9, 2001). Purchase tickets at the *Gemeindeamt*, down the hall from the tourist office or see p. 207. Signs in the town center, across from the church, point the way to a variety of hikes and walks.

EGG

☎05512

Little Egg (pop. 3,400), is the main village in the Bregenzerwald. This small, busy hamlet is ideal for those who want to explore the Bregenzerwald while staying in the region. Egg is a 4km walk from nearby Schwarzenberg, and a variety of bus lines service the village. Line #25 goes to Bregenz, #29 to Langeregg and Reifenberg, and line #40 to Dornbirn, Schoppernau and Warth. Buses stop near the post office. Exiting the post office, turn left to reach Egg's **tourist office**, look for the green-and-white "i" sign. The helpful folks there hand out maps, accommodations listings, and offer hiking advice. (☎2426, fax 24266. Open M-F 8am-noon and 2-5pm.) The **Bregenzerwald tourist office,** Loco 613, is located across from the Egg tourist office. Exit the Egg tourist office, cross the street in front of you, and turn left and up the small road with a metal street lamp at its entrance. The office specializes in information on towns and hiking in the Bregenzerwald. (☎2365; fax 3010. Open M-F 8am-noon and 1-5pm.) A bank across the street from the Egg tourist office in the shopping center **exchanges money** and has a **ATM** (open M-F 8am-noon and 1:30-4pm, Sa 8-11am). The **post office** also exchanges money (open M-F 8am-noon and 1:30-5pm; exchange closes at 4:30pm). The **postal code** is A-6863.

The tourist office maintains a list of inexpensive pensions and private rooms. **Haus Fetz,** Mühle 781, rents out comfortable, excitedly decorated rooms, with balconies and in-room toilets and showers. To get to Haus Fetz from the Egg tourist office face the church, and walking down the road towards it, turn right at the first stop sign, and cross the bridge to the right that appears before Gasthof Taube. Bear left, then turn left at the brown sign reading "Haus Fetz." When the road splits, choose the path behind the Sutterlüty building, and look for #781 on the right. (☎2514. Breakfast included. 230AS; 260AS in winter; 20AS surcharge for 1-night stays.) Bounties of the supermarket are at **ADEG,** across the street from the Egg tourist office in the shopping complex. Some of the *Bregenzerwald's* best hikes start off, alas not quite in Egg, but in the parking lot of the nearby village of **Schetteregg;** the tourist office can detail hikes from 1½ to 5 hrs., from forest hikes near streams to treks through mountains.

SALZBURGER LAND

Salzburger Land was not a part of the Hapsburg Empire until 1815, when the Congress of Vienna, while divvying up Europe, stripped the Archbishopric of Salzburg of its autonomy and gave it to the Habsburgs. The area was first united under Roman emperor Claudius in the 1st century, who coveted the region's "white gold". Salzburg's name comes from the German word for salt, *Salz*. Although tourism displaced the salt trade long ago, images of St. Barbara, the patron saint of miners, are everywhere. The provincial capital is, of course, Salzburg, which is famous for just about everything musical, but mostly Mozart and Julie Andrews. The province of Salzburger Land encompasses a slice of the shining lakes and rolling hills of the Salzkammergut in which Hallstatt is the most enticing destination. Though the area lies mostly in the province of Upper Austria the Salzkammergut is accessible primarily through Salzburg and is thus in this chapter. The Salzburger Festspiele, held every July and August, is regarded as one of the premier events of the classical music world (see p. 231). There are many smaller local festivals that pop up throughout the region. Every 3 years on the last Sunday in July (next time in 2001), a mock **Pirates' Battle** is held on the Salzach River at **Oberndorf.** According to the ritual plot, brigands rob a saltboat and then fire on the town of **Laufen,** on the Bavarian side of the river. Eventually, the defeated pirates try to escape. They are arrested and condemned to death, but their sentence is quickly modified to "death by drowning in beer," which signifies the beginning of a lavish feast.

HIGHLIGHTS OF SALZBURGER LAND

Let "Surround Sound" take on a new meaning during **organ concerts** at the Salzburg Cathedral (see p. 232).

See Mozart's relics away from the crowds at **Mozart's residence** (see p. 227).

Venture into the lush **Echental valley** for waterfalls and cliff walks (see p. 237).

SALZBURG

☎0662

While the *Sound of Music* has brought hordes of tourists spinning down Salzburg's main streets, singing songs that were better done by Julie Andrews, Salzburg had much to offer before it was even a gleam in the eye of 20th-Century Fox producers. Wedged between mountains and graced with baroque wonders resulting from Salzburg's position as the ecclesiastical center of Austria, Salzburg offers both spectacular sights and a rich musical culture. Whether it's enthusiastic tourists singing songs, street musicians playing medieval ballads, or a famed soprano bringing the house down with the "Queen of the Night" aria, Salzburg's streets resonate with music. The city's adulation for homegrown genius Wolfgang Amadeus Mozart in particular and classical music in general reaches a deafening roar every summer during the **Salzburger Festspiele** (music festival; p. 231), when financially-endowed admirers the world over come to pay their respects to the musical elite. The *Festspiele* last for 5 weeks, during which time hundreds of operas, concerts, plays, and open-air performances dazzle the fawning fans. Never mind that both Mozart and the von Trapps eventually left, finding Salzburg a bit too stifling (the former fled from the oppressive bourgeois atmosphere and his over-managerial father, the latter from the Nazis)—this little city couldn't keep away its onslaught of visitors even if it wanted to.

GETTING THERE AND AROUND

Salzburg has its own airport—the **Flughafen Salzburg** (☎85800), 4km west of the city center, with frequent connections to **Paris, Amsterdam, Vienna, Innsbruck,** and other major European cities. It is considerably cheaper, however, to fly into **Munich** (see p. 500) and take the train from there. If you do fly into or out of Salzburg, bus #77 (dir.: Bahnhof from the airport, Walserfeld from the train station) circles between the train station and the airport (15min., every 15-30min. 5:32am-11pm, 20AS). A taxi from the airport to the train station should cost roughly 150AS. **Trains** link Salzburg to most major cities. There are 2 train stations in Salzburg: the main passenger hub, the **Hauptbahnhof** on Südtirolerpl., is the first Salzburg stop for trains coming from Vienna, while the Rangier Bahnhof (the 1st stop when coming from Innsbruck) is primarily a cargo station, so don't get off there. **Buses** leave from the bus depot in front of the train station. BundesBuses run throughout the Salzburger Land and Salzkammergut regions (see p. 234).

Motorists coming from Vienna can exit at any of the Salzburg-West exits off Autobahn A1. Among these, the Salzburg-Nord exit is near Itzling and Kasern, and the Salzburg-Süd exit lies south of the city near Schloß Hellbrunn and Untersberg. A8 and E52 lead from the west into Rosenheim and then branch off to Munich and Innsbruck. A10 heads north from Hallein to Salzburg. From the Salzkammergut area, take Grazer Bundesstr. #158. Since public transportation is efficient within the city limits, consider the **Park and Ride** parking lots—park for free when you get off the highway and take the bus into town. The most convenient lot is **Alpensiedlung Süd** on Alpenstr. (exit: Salzburg-Süd), but a bigger lot is open in July and August at the **Salzburger Ausstellungszentrum** (exit: Salzburg-Mitte).

Trains: Hauptbahnhof (☎01717 for information) in Südtirolerpl. To: **Zell am See** (1¾hr., 24 per day 1:36am-9:24pm, 160AS); **Innsbruck** (2hr., every 2hr. 12:39am-9:19pm, 370AS); **Graz** (4½hr., every 2hr. 3am-7:21pm, 430AS); **Vienna** (3½hr., every

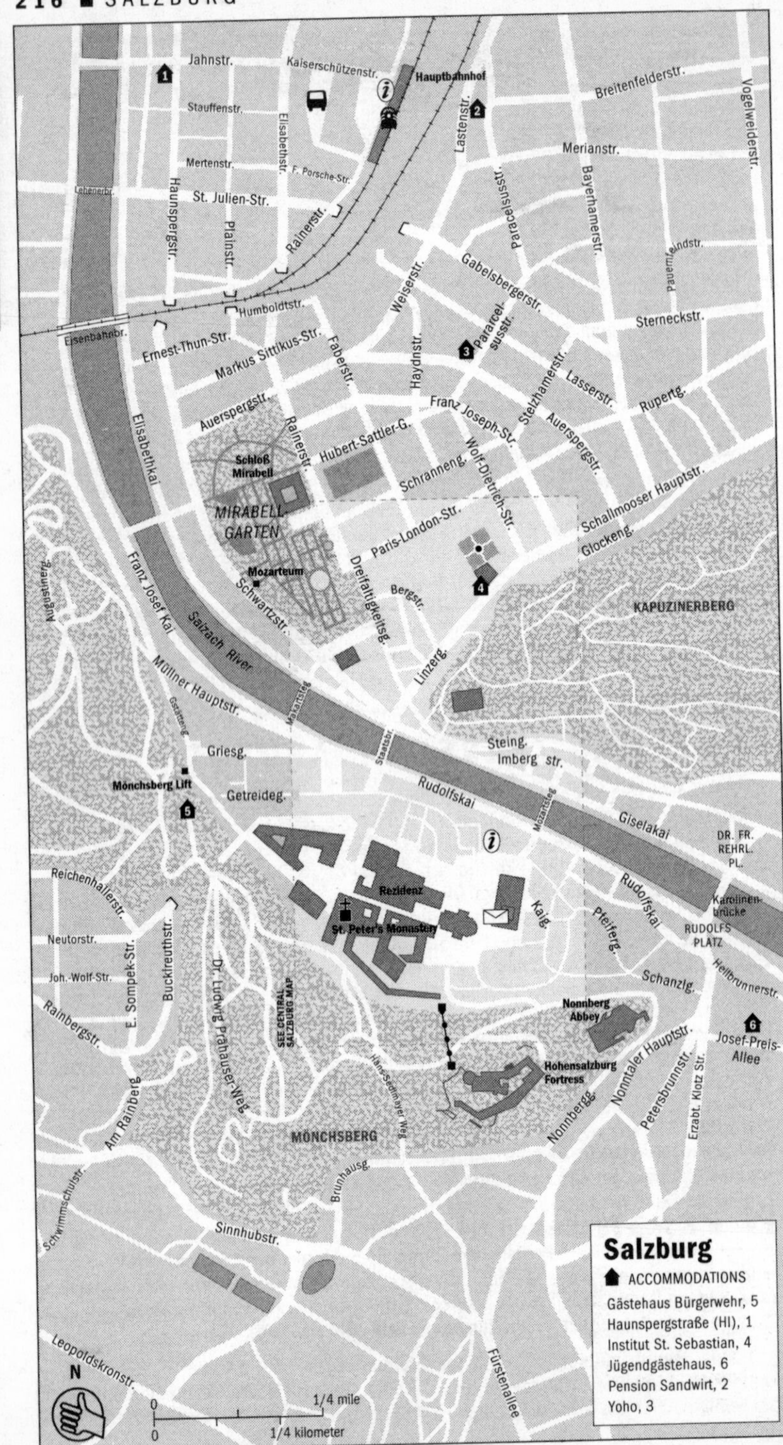

Jahnstr.
Kaiserschützenstr.
Hauptbahnhof
Breitenfelderstr.
Vogelweiderstr.
Stauffenstr.
Elisabethstr.
Lastenstr.
Merianstr.
Mertenstr.
F. Porsche-Str.
Lehenerbr.
St. Julien-Str.
Haunspergstr.
Plainstr.
Rainerstr.
Paracelsusstr.
Bayerhamerstr.
Gabelsbergerstr.
Weiserstr.
Humboldtstr.
Eisenbahnbr.
Ernest-Thun-Str.
Markus Sittikus-Str.
Faberstr.
Haydnstr.
Paracelsusstr.
Sterneckstr.
Stelzhamerstr.
Lasserstr.
Rupertg.
Auerspergstr.
Franz Joseph-Str.
Hubert-Sattler-G.
Elisabethkai
Schloß Mirabell
Schranneng.
Wolf-Dietrich-Str.
Schallmooser Hauptstr.
MIRABELL-GARTEN
Paris-London-Str.
Glockeng.
Mozarteum
Franz Josef Kai
Dreifaltigkeitsg.
Bergstr.
Schwartzstr.
Augustinerg.
KAPUZINERBERG
Salzach River
Linzerg.
Müllner Hauptstr.
Makartsteg
Staatsbr.
Steing.
Imberg str.
Griesg.
Mönchsberg Lift
Getreideg.
Rudolfskai
Mozartsteg
Giselakai
DR. FR. REHRL. PL.
Reichenhallerstr.
Rezidenz
Karolinenbrücke
St. Peter's Monastery
Kaig.
Pfeiferg.
Rudolfskai
RUDOLFS PLATZ
Neutorstr.
Bucklreuthstr.
E. Sompek-Str.
Joh.-Wolf-Str.
Dr. Ludwig Prähauser-Weg
SEE CENTRAL SALZBURG MAP
Schanzlg.
Hellbrunnerstr.
Rainbergstr.
Nonnberg Abbey
Josef-Preis-Allee
Hans-Sedlmayer Weg
Hohensalzburg Fortress
Nonntaler Hauptstr.
Petersbrunnstr.
Erzabt. Klotz Str.
Am Rainberg
MÖNCHSBERG
Nonnbergg.
Schwimmschulstr.
Brunnhausg.
Sinnhubstr.
Leopoldskronstr.
Fürstenallee
N
0
1/4 mile
0
1/4 kilometer
Salzburg
ACCOMMODATIONS
Gästehaus Bürgerwehr, 5
Haunspergstraße (HI), 1
Institut St. Sebastian, 4
Jügendgästehaus, 6
Pension Sandwirt, 2
Yoho, 3

30min. 1:15am-9:32pm, 430AS); **Munich** (2hr., every 30min. 4am-10pm, 316AS); **Zurich** (6hr., 8 per day 12:39am-4:30pm, 888AS); **Budapest** (6½hr., 10 per day 1:16am-8pm, 750AS); **Prague** (7hr., 2 per day, 806AS, connect in Linz); and **Venice** (6hr., 5 per day 4:25am-10:36pm, 560AS). For reservations dial 1700, M-F 7am-6:30pm, Sa 8am-12:30pm. Regular ticket office open 24hr.

Buses: Bus depot (☎(0660) 5188). BundesBuses to **Mondsee** (1hr., every hr. 6:40am-7:20pm, 60AS); **St. Wolfgang** (1½hr., every hr. 6:40am-8:10pm, 90AS); **Bad Ischl** (1½hr., every hr. 6:40am-7:15pm, 100AS); and throughout Salzburger Land. For schedule information, dial 167.

Public Transportation: Get information at the **Lokalbahnhof** (☎872 145), next to the train station. 18 bus lines cut through the city, with central hubs at Hanuschpl. by Makartsteg, Äußerer Stein by Mozartsteg., Mirabellpl., and the *Hauptbahnhof.* Tickets are cheapest from *Tabaks* (1 ride 20AS, day pass 40AS, week 112AS). You can also purchase packs of 5 single-ride tickets from vending machines at bus stops for 75AS or buy single tickets on the bus. Punch your ticket when you board in order to validate it, or suffer a 500AS fine. Buses usually make their last run from downtown to outer destinations at 10:30-11:30pm, earlier for less-frequented routes. Check the schedule posted at stops. **BusTaxi** fills in when the public buses stop running at night. Pick it up at the stop at Hanuschpl. or Theaterg. and tell the driver where you need to go. Every 30min. nightly 11:30pm-1:30am. 35AS for any distance within the city limits.

Parking: Consider the "Park and Ride" option (see above). Otherwise, try **Altstadt-Garage** inside the Mönchsberg (open 24hr.); **Mirabell-Garage** in Mirabellpl. (open 7am-midnight; 28AS per hr.); or **Parkgarage Linzergasse** at Glockeng. off Linzerg. (open 7am-10pm; 20AS per hr. or 160AS for a full day). Other lots are at the airport, Hellbrunn, and Akademiestr. (15AS per hr.). Blue lines on the sidewalk indicate parking is available; buy a ticket for the space from one of the nearby automated machines.

Taxis: (☎8111 or 1716). Stands at Hanuschpl., Residenzpl., and the train station.

Car Rental: Avis, Ferdinand-Porsche-Str. 7 (☎877 278; fax 880 235).

Bike Rental: Climb every mountain and ford every stream with a bicycle from the train station counter #3 (☎888 7316 3). 150AS per day, 90AS with that day's train ticket, 1 week 670AS. Bike paths wind throughout the city; maps at tourist office (84AS).

Hitchhiking: While *Let's Go* does not recommend hitching, hitchers headed to Innsbruck, Munich, or Italy (except Venice), have been seen on bus #77 to the German border. Thumbers bound for Vienna or Venice report taking bus #29 (dir.: Forellenwegsiedlung) to the *Autobahn* entrance at "Schmiedlingerstr." or bus #15 (dir.: Bergheim) to the *Autobahn* entrance at "Grüner Wald."

ORIENTATION

Salzburg, the capital of Salzburger Land, is surrounded by three forested hills. Just a few kilometers from the German border, the city covers both banks of the **Salzach River.** The *Altstadt* (old city) is on the south bank of the river, and the *Neustadt* on the north bank. The *Hauptbahnhof* is on the northern edge of town; buses #1, 5, 6, 51, and 55 connect it to downtown. From the bus, disembark at "Mirabellplatz" in the *Neustadt* or "Mozartsteg," a bridge that leads to Mozartpl. where the main tourist office is. On foot, turn left out of the station onto Reinerstr. and follow it all the way (under the tunnel) to Mirabellpl.

PRACTICAL INFORMATION

TOURIST SERVICES

Tourist Office, Mozartpl. 5 (☎889 8733 0; fax 889 8734 2; tourist@salzburginfo.or.at; www.salzburginfo.or.at), in the *Altstadt.* From the train station, take bus #5, 6, 51, or 55 to "Mozartsteg" then curve around the building into Mozartpl. On foot, turn left on Rainerstr., go to the end, cross Staatsbrücke, then continue along the river's west bank upstream to Mozartsteg. (20min.). The office has free hotel maps (exactly the same as

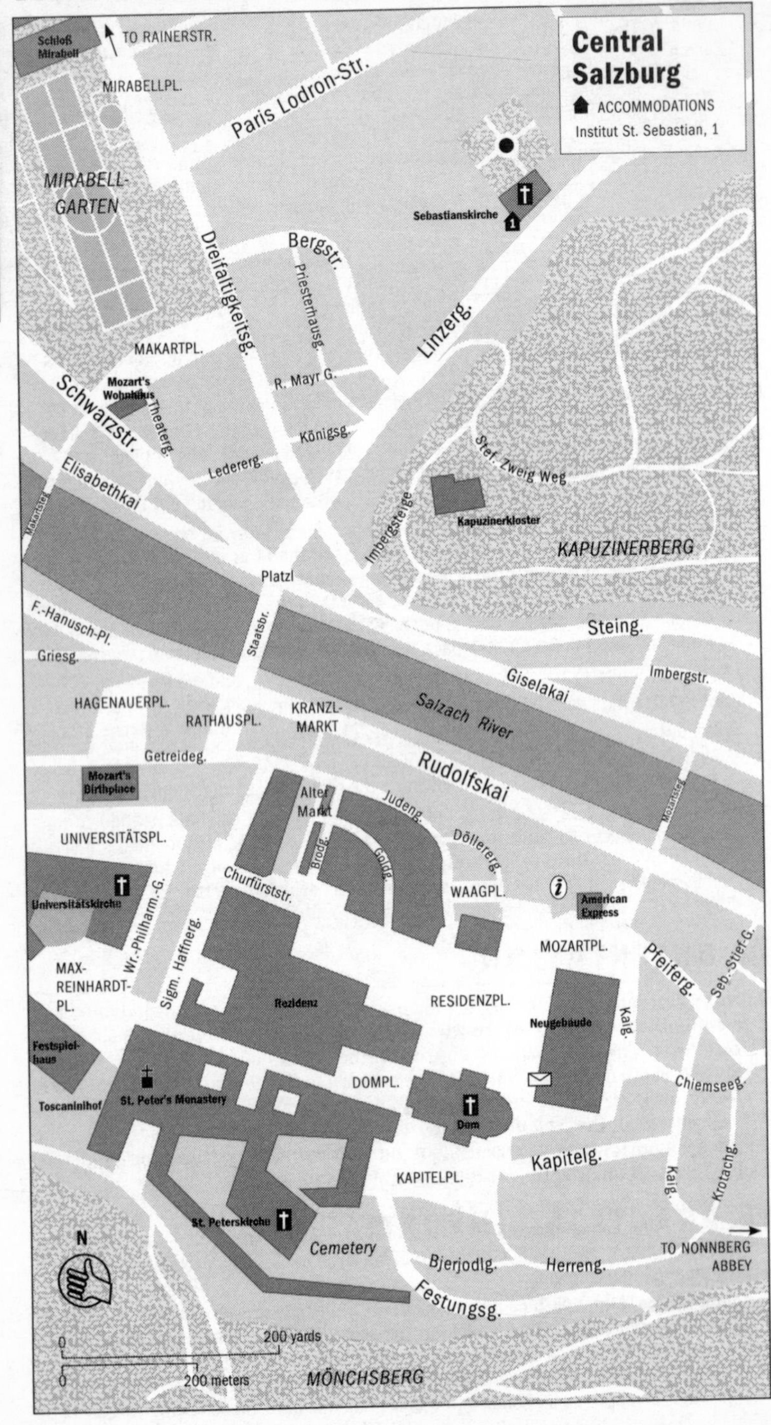
Central Salzburg
ACCOMMODATIONS
Institut St. Sebastian, 1
Schloß Mirabell
TO RAINERSTR.
MIRABELLPL.
Paris Lodron-Str.
MIRABELL-GARTEN
Sebastianskirche
Dreifaltigkeitsg.
Bergstr.
Priesterhausg.
Linzerg.
MAKARTPL.
Mozart's Wohnhaus
Schwarzstr.
Theaterg.
R. Mayr G.
Königsg.
Lederer g.
Elisabethkai
Stef. Zweig Weg
Kapuzinerkloster
Makartsteg
Imbergsteige
KAPUZINERBERG
Platzl
F.-Hanusch-Pl.
Staatsbr.
Steing.
Griesg.
Giselakai
Imbergstr.
HAGENAUERPL.
RATHAUSPL.
KRANZL-MARKT
Salzach River
Getreideg.
Rudolfskai
Mozart's Birthplace
Alter Markt
Judeng.
Mozartsteg
UNIVERSITÄTSPL.
Brodg.
Goldg.
Döllererg.
Churfürststr.
WAAGPL.
American Express
Universitätskirche
Wr.-Philharm.-G.
Sigm. Haffnerg.
MOZARTPL.
Pfeiferg.
Seb.-Stief-G.
MAX-REINHARDT-PL.
Rezidenz
RESIDENZPL.
Neugebäude
Kaig.
Festspielhaus
DOMPL.
Chiemseeg.
Toscaninihof
St. Peter's Monastery
Dom
Kapitelg.
KAPITELPL.
Krotachg.
St. Peterskirche
N
Cemetery
Bierjodlg.
Herreng.
TO NONNBERG ABBEY
Festungsg.
0
200 yards
0
200 meters
MÖNCHSBERG

the 10AS city map), and the **Salzburg Card** (see p. 225). Reservation service 30AS, for 3 or more people 60AS, plus a 7.2% deposit deductible from the 1st night's stay. The overworked staff will tell you which hostels have available rooms. Open July-Aug. 8:30am-8pm; Sept.-June 9am-6pm. There are other **branches** at the **train station** platform #2a (☎889 8734 0; open M-Sa 9:15am-8pm); and the Alpensiedlung Süd **"Park and Ride" lot** (☎889 8736 0). While the office in the *Altstadt* is the largest, the one in the station might have more time to help you out.

Budget Travel: ÖKISTA, Wolf-Dietrich-Str. 31 (☎883 252; fax 883 2522 0; info@oekista.co.at; www.oekista.co.at/oekista), near the International Youth Hotel. Open M-F 9am-5:30pm. **Albatros Travel Service,** Bergstr. 22 (☎881 6710; fax 881 679), answers your travel questions in English. Open M-F 8:15am-6pm.

Consulates: South Africa, Buchenweg 14 (☎/fax 622 035). Open M-F 8am-1pm and 2-5pm. **UK,** Alter Markt 4 (☎848 133; fax 845 563). Open M-F 9am-noon. **US,** Alter Markt 1/3 (☎848 776; fax 849 777), in the *Altstadt*. Open M, W, and F 9am-noon.

FINANCIAL AND COMMUNICATION SERVICES

Currency Exchange: Banks offer better rates for cash than AmEx offices but often charge higher commissions. Banking hours M-F 8am-12:30pm and 2-4:30pm. **Rieger Bank,** at Alter Markt and Getreideg., has extended currency exchange hours. Open July-Aug. M-F 9am-7:30pm, Sa 9am-6pm, Su 10am-5pm; Sept.-June M-F 9am-6pm, Sa 9am-3pm, Su 10am-5pm. The train station's currency exchange is open 7am-9pm. **Panorama Tours** offers cash currency exchange at bank rates with no commission; available only to guests taking their tour (see p. 229).

American Express: Mozartpl. 5, A-5020 (☎8080; fax 808 0178), near the tourist office. Provides all banking services and charges no commission on AmEx checks. Holds mail for check- or card-holders, books tours, and reserves *Festspiele* tickets. Open M-F 9am-5:30pm, Sa 9am-noon.

English-Language Bookstores: American Discount, in a passage in Alter Markt 1 (☎757 541), sells American best-sellers and magazines. **Buchhandlung Motzko Reise,** Elisabethstr. 1 (☎883 311), near the train station, has travel guides and English-language books. Both open M-F 9am-6pm, Sa 9am-5pm.

Internet Access: Cybercafé, Gstätteng. 29 (☎842 6162 2). 80AS per hr. Open W-Su 2-11pm, F-Sa until 1am. **Internet Café,** Mozartpl. 5 (☎844 822). 120AS per hr. Open daily 10am-10pm.

Post Office: At the *Hauptbahnhof* (☎88970). Mail your brown paper packages tied up with string at the main office next to the train station. The office has **currency exchange.** Address *Poste Restante* to Postlagernde Briefe, Bahnhofspostamt, A-5020 Salzburg. Open 6am-11pm. Exchange open M-Th 6am-5pm, F 6am-6pm. **Postal Code:** A-5020.

OTHER SERVICES

Bi-Gay-Lesbian Organizations: Frauenkulturzentrum (Women's/Lesbians' Center), Elisabethstr. 11 (☎871 639). Office and hotlines open M 10am-12:30pm. Runs a **Woman's Café** on the 1st and 3rd F of every month, 8pm-midnight. **Homosexual Initiative of Salzburg** (HOSI), Müllner Hauptstr. 11 (☎435 927), hosts regular workshops and meetings, including a **Café-bar** open F from 9pm and Sa from 8pm.

Luggage Storage: At the train station. Lockers 30-50AS (good for 2 calendar days). Luggage check 30AS per piece per calendar day. Open 6am-10pm.

Laundromat: Norge Exquisit Textil Reinigung, Paris-Lodronstr. 16 (☎876 381), on the corner of Wolf-Dietrich-Str. Self-serve wash and dry 82AS, soap 28AS, (you may not use your own soap); open M-F 7:30am-4pm, Sa 8-10am. Full-serve 185AS; open M-F 7:30am-6pm, Sa 8am-noon.

Public Toilets: In the Festungsbahn lobby (3AS) and at the fish market in Hanuschpl. (2AS). In the *Altstadt* under the archway between Kapitelpl. and Dompl. (7AS).

EMERGENCIES

Emergencies: Police, ☎133. Headquarters at Alpenstr. 90 (non-emergency ☎6383). **Ambulance,** ☎144. **Fire,** ☎122.

Rape Hotline: ☎881 100.

AIDS Hotline: AIDS-Hilfe Salzburg, Gabelsburgerstr. 20 (☎881 488).

Pharmacies: Elisabeth-Apotheke, Elisabethstr. 1 (☎871 484), a few blocks left of the train station. Pharmacies in the city center are open M-F 8am-6pm, Sa 8am-noon; outside the center M-F 8am-12:30pm and 2:30-6pm, Sa 8am-noon. There are always 3 pharmacies open for emergencies; check the list on the door of any closed pharmacy.

Medical Assistance: When the dog bites, when the bee stings, call the **hospital,** Dr. Franz-Rebirl-Pl. 5 (☎65800).

ACCOMMODATIONS

Salzburg has no shortage of hostels—but, then again, it has no shortage of tourists. Most affordable accommodations are on the outskirts of town, easily accessible by local transportation. Ask for the tourist office's list of **private rooms** (separate from the hotel map) or the *Hotel Plan* for information on hostels. The tourist office charges 30AS plus a 7.2% fee to make reservations. From mid-May to mid-September, hostels fill by mid-afternoon—call ahead. During the *Festspiele*, hotels fill months in advance, and most youth hostels and *Gästehäuser* are full days before. At HI hostels there is a 40AS surcharge for non-members. Be wary of hotel hustlers at the station—they are up to no good.

HOSTELS AND DORMITORIES

Gästehaus Bürgerwehr, Mönchsberg 19c (☎841 729), towers over the old town from the top of the Mönchsberg. Take bus #1 (dir.: Maxglan) to "Mönchsberglift," then down the street a few steps and through the stone arch on the left to the Mönchsberglift (elevator), which takes you to the top of the mountain (9am-11pm, round-trip 27AS). At its summit, turn right, climb the steps, and follow signs for "Gästehaus Naturfreundehaus." Get a princely view on a pauper's budget at the most scenic hostel in Salzburg. Only holds 26 in small 2- to 6-bed rooms, so reserve ahead. Genial proprietors also run the terrific restaurant downstairs. Open May to Sept. Fresh-baked breakfast on the terrace (with a magnificent view of Salzburg) 30AS. Showers 10AS per 4min. Sheets 20AS. Reception 8am-9pm. Curfew 1am–hustle up the stairs at a quarter till. Dorms 120AS.

International Youth Hotel (YoHo), Paracelsusstr. 9 (☎879 649 or 83460; fax 878 810), off Franz-Josef-Str. Exit the train station to the left and turn left onto Gabelsbergerstr. through the tunnel. Take the 2nd right onto Paracelsusstr. (7min.). The American and Canadian tourists who have colonized YoHo asked and they receive: there are daily screenings of *The Sound of Music* (at noon). Filled with beer-sipping postcard writers relaxing after the screening and a frat-party atmosphere in the evening, this hostel is a bare-bones, clean place to crash. 24hr. CNN in the bar (beer 25AS). Breakfast 30-55AS. Dinner entrees (including veggie options) 30-75AS. Showers 10AS per 6min. Lockers 10AS. Sleepsacks require 100AS deposit. Reception 8am-noon. "Curfew" 1am (not very strict); quiet time supposedly starts at 10pm. Dorms 150-200AS; doubles 400AS; quads 680AS.

Institut St. Sebastian, Linzerg. 41 (☎871 386; fax 871 3868 5). From the station, take bus #1, 5, 6, 51, or 55 to Mirabellpl. Cross the street and continue in same direction as bus. Turn left onto Bergstr. and left at the end onto Linzerg. The hostel is through the arch on the left just before the church (whose bell tolls early in the morning). Located smack-dab in the middle of the *Neustadt* on the St. Sebastian church grounds. The buildings are a women-only university dorm during the year but accept travelers of either gender in **summer.** Rooftop terrace with postcard views of the city. Only 90 beds, so reserve ahead. Free lockers. Dorm sheets 30AS. **Kitchen** facilities. **Laundry** 40AS. 24hr. reception, but call ahead. No curfew. Dorms only Oct.-June. Dorms 180AS; hotel-like singles 340AS, with shower 390AS; doubles 520AS, 680AS; triples 900AS.

Eduard-Heinrich-Haus (HI), Eduard-Heinrich-Str. 2 (☎625 976; fax 627 980). Take bus #51 (dir.: Salzburg-Süd) to "Polizeidirektion." Cross the street, continue down Billroth-str., and turn left on the Robert-Stolz-Promenade footpath. Walk 200m and take the 1st right; the hostel is the large building up the driveway on the left. Near Salzach Forest with enormous 6- and 7-bed rooms with lockers, **kitchen, laundry** and gym. Showers and breakfast included. **Internet access.** Reception 7-9am and 5-11pm. **Lockout 9am-5pm.** Summer curfew midnight, winter 11pm; key with 300AS deposit. Dorms 186AS.

Haunspergstraße (HI), Haunspergstr. 27 (☎875 030; fax 883 477), near the train station. Walk straight out Kaiserschützenstr. (past the Forum department store), which becomes Jahnstr. Take the 3rd left onto Haunspergstr. This student dorm becomes a hostel in summer. Houses 125 in spacious 2- to 4-bed rooms. Breakfast, shower, and sheets included. **Laundry** 80AS. Reception 7am-2pm and 5pm-midnight. Curfew 11pm. Open July-Aug. Dorms 170AS.

Jugendgästehaus Salzburg (HI), Josef-Preis-Allee 18 (☎842 6700; fax 841 101), southeast of the *Altstadt.* Take bus #5, 51, or 55 to "Justizgebäude," or walk from the tourist office southeast (with traffic) along the river, bear right onto Hellbrunnerstr., turn right onto Petersbrunnstr., then take the 1st left. Rule-oriented hostel with a gaudy color coded interior; boys lodged in the red sector, girls in the blue. School groups make frequent use of the video game room, cafe, and disco. Breakfast, shower, and sheets included. Lunch or dinner 72AS. **Kitchen** facilities available. **Bike rental** 95AS. Handicapped access. Reception M-F 11am-midnight. Curfew midnight. 8-bed dorms 167AS; doubles with shower 267AS per person; quads with shower 217AS per person.

Aigen (HI), Aignerstr. 34 (☎623 248; fax 232 4813). From the station, bus #6 or 51 to "Mozartsteg.," then bus #49 (dir.: Josef-Käut-Str.) to "Finanzamt" and walk 5min. in the same direction as the bus. It's the yellow building on your right. Large hostel with clean, simple 2- to 4-bed dorms. Breakfast, showers, lockers, and sheets included. Reception 7-9am and 5pm-midnight. Curfew midnight. Dorms 180-200AS.

PRIVATZIMMER AND PENSIONEN

Privitazimmer and *Pension* accommodations in the center of the city can be quite expensive, but better quality and lower prices await on the outskirts, and public transportation puts these establishments within minutes of downtown Salzburg. Rooms on **Kasern Berg** are officially out of Salzburg, which means the tourist office can't officially recommend them, but the personable hosts and bargain prices make these *Privatzimmer* a terrific housing option. These are people's homes, so be on your best behavior. All northbound regional trains run to Kasern Berg (generally 4min., every 30min. 6:17am-11:17pm, 20AS, Eurail valid). Get off at the first stop, "Salzburg-Maria Plain," and take the only road uphill. All the Kasern Berg pensions are along this road. If you call in advance, many proprietors will pick you up at the Kasern station. Or, from Mirabellpl., take bus #15 (dir.: Bergheim) to "Kasern" then turn up Söllheimerstr. and hike up the mountain (15min.). By car, exit A1 on "Salzburg Nord." There are rooms in most suburbs of the city as well, some on outlying farms. Camping is a feasible option even for novices, as some of Salzburg's campsites have beds in pre-assembled tents.

Germana Kapeller, Kasern Berg 64 (☎456 671). Hostess Germana speaks perfect English and maintains traditional rooms. She also screens *The Sound of Music* upon group demand (house guests only). Showers and breakfast included. Call ahead. Doubles 400AS; triples 510-600AS.

Haus Christine, Panoramaweg 3 (☎/fax 456 773). On a gravel road set back 16m back from the main Kasern Berg street at the top of the hill, Haus Christine has spacious rooms with a country motif. Friendly family atmosphere. Breakfast is included, and served on glass-enclosed patio overlooking the countryside. Christine will pick you up at the station if you call ahead. 180-200AS per person.

Haus Matilda Lindner, Panoramaweg 5 (☎/fax 456 681). Right next to Haus Christine, Matilda (Christine's sister) offers rooms with balconies for mountain views. Matilda's children give the house a warm atmosphere. Breakfast served in pleasant room which is available for guests' use during the day. Matilda will also pick you up from the station. Families welcome. 170-200AS per person.

Haus Moser, Turnebuhel 1 (☎456 676). Climb up the hidden stairs (very steep) on the right side of Kasern Berg road across from Germana Kapeller. If you're toting a heavy backpack try the driveway entrance at beginning of Kasern Berg road. Signs direct the way. Charming, elderly couple offers comfortable rooms in this dark-timbered home. "Welcome drink," all-you-can-eat breakfast, and shower included. Singles 170-200AS; doubles 340-400AS; triples 510-600AS; quads 700-800AS.

Haus Elisabeth, Rauchenbichlerstr. 18 (☎/fax 450 703). Take bus #51 to "Itzling-Pflanzmann" (last stop), walk up Rauchenbichlerstr. over the footbridge, and continue right along the gravel path. Plush rooms have TVs, balconies, and sweeping views of the city. Breakfast of corn flakes, yogurt, bread, and jam included. Singles with shower 300-330AS; doubles 500-550AS; one 4-person suite with kitchen 1000AS.

Haus Ballwein, Moostr. 69 (☎/fax 824 029). Take bus #1 to "Hanuschpl.," then bus #60—ask the driver to stop at Gsengerweg (*guh-zang-ehr-veg*). This country house has spotless rooms and farmland for a rural reprieve from city tourism, with genial hospitality. Breakfast includes eggs from the farm's own chickens; breakfast included. Rooms with shower 270AS.

Haus Bankhammer, Moostr. 77 (☎/fax 830 067). This grand farmhouse in southern Salzburg has hotel-quality doubles with bath. Breakfast of homemade strawberry-rhubarb jam and fresh milk from the family dairy included. Helga speaks English fluently and will happily do laundry for guests. Rooms 440-500AS.

Haus Rosemarie Seigmann, Kasern Berg 66 (☎450 001). English-speaking Rosemarie tends to bright rooms with comforters and mountain views. Breakfast included. Doubles 380-400AS; triples 510-600AS.

Pension Sandwirt, Lastenstr. 6a (☎/fax 874 351). Exit the main train station from the platform #13 staircase, turn right on the footbridge, turn right at the bottom onto Lastenstr., and go behind the building with the Post sign (3min.). This bed-and-breakfast (not a private home) has rooms a stone's throw away from the train station. Triples and quads have TVs. Breakfast included. **Free laundry.** Singles 300AS; doubles 460AS, with shower 550AS; triples 690AS; quads 880AS.

Haus Mayerhofer, Moosstr. 68c (☎822 479; fax 826 299; cmayerhofen@aon.at; www.members.aon.at/privatzimmer). Take bus #15 or 60 southbound to "Station Firmianstr." (2km from the *Altstadt*). Catering especially to students and young people, friendly hostess Elisabeth offers 3 comfortable rooms. Shower, breakfast buffet, TV room, garden, and parking included. 220-240AS per person.

CAMPING

Camping Stadtblick, Rauchenbichlerstr. 21 (☎450 652; fax 458 018). The brother of the Elisabeth from Haus Elisabeth runs this campground next to Elisabeth's house (see above for directions). By car, take exit "Salzburg-Nord" off A1. Behind a copse of trees with a sweeping view of the city. On-site store. **Laundry** 70AS. Open March 20-Oct. 31. 70AS, *Let's Go* readers 65AS; tent 20AS; bed in a tent 80AS; parking 60AS. 4-person mobile home with refrigerator and stove top, 100AS per person.

FOOD AND DRINK

With countless beer gardens and pastry-shop patios, Salzburg is a great place to eat outdoors. Take advantage of those sunny moments. The local specialty is *Salzburger Nockerl*, a large soufflé of egg whites, sugar, and raspberry filling baked into three mounds that represent the three hills of Salzburg. If you order one be prepared to wait 20-30min. Also make sure you have a friend to share it with—it's huge. Another regional favorite is *Knoblauchsuppe*, a rich cream soup loaded with croutons and pungent garlic—a potent weapon to be used wisely against pesky bunkmates. During the first 2 weeks of September, local cafes dispense *Stürm*, a delicious, cloudy cider (reminiscent, aptly enough, of a storm) that hasn't quite finished fermenting.

There are more of the world-famous **Mozartkugeln** (chocolate "Mozart balls") lining cafe windows than there are notes in all of Mozart's works combined. The *kugeln* are made by covering a hazelnut with marzipan and nougat then dipping it in chocolate. A Salzburg confectioner invented the treats in 1890, but mass production inevitably took over. Although mass-produced *kugeln* wrapped in gold and red are technically *echt* (authentic), try to find the handmade ones wrapped in blue and silver, which are not available anywhere else. Reasonably priced *kugeln* are sold at the **Holzmayr** confectioners (5AS for red, 7AS for blue) or at Konditorei **Fürst** (10AS for blue), both on *Alter Markt*.

In most cases, markets are open weekdays 8am to 6pm, Saturday 8am to noon. Salzburg has many supermarkets on the Mirabellpl. side of the river but very few in the *Altstadt*. **SPAR** is widespread, and a giant **EuroSpar** sprawls next to the train station bus terminal. **Open-air markets** are held on Universitätpl. (M-F 6am-7pm, Sa 6am-1pm) and Mirabellpl. down into Hubert-Sattlerg. (Th 5am-1pm). If you're in town on Saturday morning, you can pick up organic tomatoes and sausage lard at Max Rheinhardtpl. in the *Altstadt*.

Bars, restaurants, and cafes in Salzburg are difficult to define because, more often than not, they become each of those things at different times during the day, serving coffee in the morning, tea in the afternoon, and beer in the evenings.

RESTAURANTS

Restaurant Zur Bürgerwehr-Einkehr, Mönchsberg 19c (☎841 729). Follow the directions to the Bürgerwehr hostel (see p. 220). The mom-and-pop owners of the Bürgerwehr operate this restaurant at the top of the Mönchsberg. Escape the tourist throng below as you recline beneath the terrace's red umbrellas and enjoy the best views in town. This restaurant has one of the most reasonably priced (and tastiest) *Menüs* around. Extraordinary *Gammerknödel* (bacon-filled dumplings with sauerkraut) for just 88AS. Open Apr.-Oct. Sa-Th 11:30am-8:45pm.

Shakespeare, Hubert Sattlerg. 3 (☎879 106), off Mirabellpl. This culturally schizophrenic restaurant serves everything from *Wienerschnitzel* to Greek salad to wonton soup, 36-136AS. Doubles as a bar(d) with hopping **live music,** from tango to *chansons*. Behind the bar is the **Electric Café,** a trip-hop and techno lounge. Restaurant open M-F 11:30am-2:30pm and 6pm-midnight; Sa 6pm-midnight only; Su open from 11am, though the Chinese cook takes Su off. MC, Visa.

Zweltler's, Kaig. 3 (☎840 044), in the *Altstadt*. From Kapitelpl. walk down Kapitelg. onto Kiag. Cozy wooden interior turns into a lively bar as evening turns to night. Good beer complements steak and french fries (180AS). Pasta dishes hover around 100AS. English menu available. Every second W live blues music. Open daily 5pm-midnight.

Il Sole, Gstätteng. (☎843 284), on the right on the Mönchsberg Lift. An unpretentious Italian restaurant popular with the backpacker set. Fairly large pizza from 69AS, savory lasagna 85AS. Open daily 11:30am-2pm and 5:30-11:30pm.

Vegy, Schwarzstr. 21 (☎875 746). From Mirabellpl., walk through the park and turn left onto Schwarzstr. With a kitchen feeling, this little place understands that vegetarian food means more than just cheese. Dozens of filling options to choose from, including a daily *Menü* with soup, coffee, and dessert for 98AS. Open M-F 10:30am-6pm.

Zum Fidelen Affen, Priesterhausg. 8 (☎877 361), off Linzerg. On the occasional warm Salzburg evening sit at one of the outdoor picnic tables, pleasantly crowded with locals and tourists. Drinks 30AS. Full meal of salad and main course 87-110AS. Try the spinach *Spätzle* (doughy dumpling noodles, 88AS) or the beef with onion gravy (89AS). English menu available. Open M-Sa 5pm-11pm.

University Mensa (☎844 9609), across from Sigmund Haffnerg. 16 and through the iron fence. A good deal for penny-pinchers with 2 hot entrees, 1 meat (52AS) and 1 vegetarian (41AS), all served in a lovely courtyard. Valid student ID required (ISIC accepted). Open M-Th 9am-4pm, F 9am-3pm. Get there early, before ravenous students deplete the food supply.

Fischmarkt, at Hanuschpl. in the *Altstadt*. Mammoth trees poke through the roof of this Danish seafood restaurant. Very casual and very packed. Fish sandwiches 50AS; glasses of beer 27AS. The restaurant also sells fresh seafood and seafood salad by the kilogram. Open M-F 8:30am-6:30pm, Sa 8:30am-1pm.

Trzesniewski, Getreideg. 9 (☎840 769), behind the chocolate counter and butcher shop. This constantly packed version of Kafka's favorite hangout in Vienna has a franchise on the ground floor of Mozart's *Geburtshaus*. While indulging in their wonderful (but miniscule) open-faced sandwiches, you can ponder who would roll over in his grave first, Kafka or Mozart. Sandwiches 10AS, but you'll need about 5 to make a good lunch. Open M-F 8:30am-6pm, Sa 8:30am-1pm.

CAFÉS

Café im Künstlerhaus, Hellbrunnerstr. 3 (☎845 601). This low-key cafe is popular with students, artists, and their fans, but thankfully less so with tourists. Treat yourself to a café amaretto or a shot of tequila. Local bands play Tu and Th. Lesbian night Sa. Open M-F 11am-11pm.

Café Tomaselli, Alter Markt 9 (☎844 488), has been a favorite haunt for wealthier Salzburger clientele since 1705. In 1820, Mozart's widow and her second husband came here to write the dead man's bio. Today anyone can sit in its wood-paneled rooms with antique portraits, or find a chair on the balcony overlooking the *Alter Markt*. Coffee (27-37AS) and a mobile dessert counter. English language newspapers available for late afternoon perusal. Open M-Sa 7am-9pm, Su 8am-9pm.

Café Bazar, Schwarzstr. 3 (☎874 278). Enjoy affordable drinks and small meals in this tree-lined garden along the banks of the Salzach away from the crowds of the *Altsadt*, but still providing a view of it. Yogurt with raspberry juice 38AS. Come here for your Turkish coffee fix (38AS). Open mid-July to Aug. M 10am-6pm, Tu-Sa 7:30am-11pm; Sept. to mid-July M-Sa 9:30am-11pm.

Café Glockenspiel, Mozartpl. 1 (☎841 403). Near the tourist office, this place serves incredible ice cream concoctions and fantastic pastries (50-98AS). Sit under the awning or at the tables that spill onto the square to catch the occasional free concert that occurs there. Restaurant upstairs serves filling pasta dishes (100AS). Open M-F 8:30am-9pm, Sa-Su 10am-6pm.

Café Fürst, Brodg. 13 (☎843 759). Trod upon by tourists, Fürst faces off with the equally haughty Café Tomaselli across *Alter Markt*. Specializes in the original *Mozartkugeln* (10AS a pop–savor slowly), but has a vast selection of candies, chocolates, pastries, *torte*, strudels, and cakes. Grab one of the sunny tables outside if you can. Branch in Mirabellpl. Open daily in summer 8am-9pm; in winter 8am-8pm.

Kaffeehäferl, Getreideg. 25 (☎843 249), in the passage across from McDonald's. Unpretentious courtyard cafe provides a needed respite from the tourist rush of Getreideg. The neighboring flower shop adds olfactory pleasure. Quiche Lorraine 48AS; strawberry milkshake 37AS. Open M-Sa 9am-7pm, Su noon-7pm.

BEER GARDENS AND BARS

Munich may be the beer capital of the world, but a good deal of that liquid gold flows south to Austria's *Biergarten* (beer gardens). Alongside Mozart and *The Sound of Music*, beer gardens are an essential part of Salzburg's charm and a must-visit for travelers. Many of the gardens also serve moderately priced meals, but like everything else in Salzburg, they tend to close early. These lager oases cluster in the center of the city by the Salzach River. Nightclubs in the *Altstadt* (especially along Gstätteng. and near Chiemseeg.) generally attract younger types and tourists. For a less juvenile atmosphere, hit the other side of the river—especially along Giselakai and Steing.

Augustiner Bräu, Augustinerg. 4 (☎431 246). From the *Altstadt,* follow the footpath from Hanuschpl. along the river, walking with the current. Go left up the flight of stairs past the Riverside Café, cross Müllner Hauptstr., and walk uphill. Augustinerg. is the 1st left. The brewery, inside the monastery with the big tower, is a Salzburg legend. The great beer brewed by the Müllner Kloster is poured into massive *Steins* from wooden kegs. The outdoor garden holds 1300 people, while the indoor salons seat an additional 1200, creating a rambunctious stadium atmosphere. Different halls attract different crowds, from hard-core Austrians singing German drinking songs to American teenagers. There are bratwurst and salad stands for the hungry. 1 liter 68AS (tip the tap-*meister* 4AS), ½ liter 34AS. Open M-F 3-11pm, Sa-Su 2:30-11pm.

Pub Passage, Rudolfskai 22-26, (☎840 075) under the Radisson Hotel by the Mozartsteg bridge. A shopping promenade for youthful bar-hopping promises late-night parties, though not for the claustrophobic. All these bars are located in the corridors of the "mall" and are open until 2-4am. Though remarkably similar, each bar has its own gimmick: **Tom's Bierklinik,** beers from all over the world; **The Black Lemon,** Latino night every W; **Bräu zum Frommen Hell,** 80s music; and **Hell,** TV sports bar.

Vis à Vis, Rudolfskai 24 (☎841 290), is a lounge cut in the shape of an arched stone tunnel with paisley armchairs, smoking-room couches, and dark-wood coat-racks. A less crowded place than its neighbors for those long night chats. Open Su-Th 8pm-4am, F-Sa 8pm-5am.

Shamrock, Rudolfskai 24 (☎841 610). Up the block from the Pub Passage, this Irish pub has a friendly tucked-in-shirt atmosphere and plenty of room for beer-guzzling groups to mingle. Open M 3pm-2am, Tu-W 3pm-3am, Th-Sa 3pm-4am, Su 2pm-2am.

Zweistein, Giselakai 9 (☎880 201). Wins the prize for funkiest bar in town. Zebra print barstools, inflatable animals, and occasional transvestite performances complement the many exotic drinks. Previously a gay bar, Zweistein now caters to night owls of all orientations. Open M-W 6pm-4am, Th-F 6pm-5am, Sa 2pm-5am, Su 2pm-4am.

Schwarze Katze, Fruhdiele, Auerspergstr. 45 (☎875 405). For those who found a late-night scene in Salzburg and/or got locked out of their hostels, the Black Cat magnanimously opens its doors. Dark, low-key bar/cafe atmosphere guaranteed not to grate on early morning nerves. Open Tu-Sa 4am-noon.

Disco Seven, Gstätteng. 7 (☎844 181). Fun-loving bar with billiard tables and a sweaty dance floor. Drinks half-price W; Sa midnight-1am drinks 20AS. Open daily 11pm-3am.

Frauen Café, Sittikusstr. 17 (☎871 639), is a relaxed venue where lesbians of all stripes come to hang out, drink, and chat. Open W-Sa 8pm-midnight.

SIGHTS

Salzburg is a relatively small town with a disproportionate number of *Sehenswürdigkeiten* (things worth seeing). Whether you're into decadent floral gardens or stoic fortresses, Salzburg's got it. To help bear the financial burden, the tourist office sells the **Salzburg Card,** which grants admission to all museums and sights, as well as unlimited use of public transportation, but is only really a good deal if you plan to cram a great deal of sight-seeing into a short period of time. (24hr. card 225AS, 48hr. 300AS, 72hr. 390AS; ages 7-15 half-price.)

THE ALTSTADT

THE CITY CENTER. In the shadow of the hill-top fortress, arcade passages open up into tiny courtyards filled with geraniums and creeping ivy that lead, in turn, to the tourist-jammed **Getreidegasse.** This winding pathway leading by 17th- and 18th-century facades is one of the best-preserved (and most-visited) streets in Salzburg. Beware of trampling and being trampled by photo-shooting tourists and large tour groups. Many of Getreidegasse's shops have wrought-iron signs dating from the Middle Ages when the illiterate needed pictorial aids to understand which store sold what. Or so they claim. Some suspect a few of these signs are modern tourist revivals…golden arches, for example, don't objectively suggest hamburgers.

MOZART'S BIRTHPLACE. The first place that most visitors rush to in the *Altstadt* is **Mozart's Geburtshaus** (birthplace), on the 2nd floor of Getreideg. 9. The long red and white flag suspended from the roof serves as a beacon for music pilgrims worldwide. Although he eventually settled in Vienna, his birthplace holds the most impressive collection of the child genius's belongings: his first viola and violin, a pair of keyboardish instruments, and a lock of hair purportedly from his noggin. A set of skillful dioramas chronicles previous *Festspiele* productions of Mozart's operas. This museum does tend to get crammed with tourists crowding around the uncarefully curated exhibits, thus blocking the prodigy's relics. For a grander show of Mozart paraphenalia, hop across the river to the Mozart Wohnhaus (see p. 228). *(☎844 313. Open July-Aug. daily, 9am-6:30pm; Sept.-June 9am-5:30pm. In summer show up before 11am to beat the crowds. 70AS, students and seniors 55AS, children 20AS.)*

UNIVERSITY CHURCH. Directly in Mozart's backyard stands the **Universitätskirche,** one of the largest Baroque chapels on the continent, and generally considered Fischer von Erlach's masterpiece. Its distinctive dome stands watch over Universitätspl. and the daily farmer's market. Sculpted clouds coat the nave, with pudgy cherubim (lit by pale natural light from the dome) frolicking all over the immense apse of the church.

FESTSPIELHAUS. Down Wiener-Philharmonikerg. from Universitätspl., the **Festspielhaus,** once the riding school for the archbishops' horses, now houses many of the big-name events of the annual *Festspiele.* It's actually composed of 3 separate performance spaces—the large Opera House, the small Opera House, and an open-air performance space (which appears in *The Sound of Music*). Tours of the opera house are available. *(June-Sept. daily at 9:30am, 2pm, and 3:30pm; Oct.-Dec. and Apr.-May at 2pm. 70AS, children 40AS.)* Opposite the *Festspielhaus*, the **Rupertinum Gallery** hosts temporary exhibits of modern painting, sculpture, and photography in a graceful building remodeled by Friedensreich Hundertwasser *(see p. 119; ☎804 2233 6. Open mid-July to Sept. Su-Tu and Th-Sa 9am-5pm, W 10am-9pm; Oct. to mid-July Tu-Su 10am-5pm, W 10am-9pm. 40AS, students 20AS.)*

MONASTERY AND CHURCH. Down from *Festspielhaus*, the **Toscaninihof,** the courtyard of **St. Peter's Monastery,** hides the stone steps which lead up the Mönchsberg cliffs (**Stiftskirche St. Peter,** within the monastery, began as a Romanesque basilica in the 1100s and still features a marble portal from 1244. In the 18th century, the building was remodeled in Rococo style, with green and pink moldings curling delicately across the graceful ceiling and gilded cherubim blowing golden trumpets. With dozens of signs reading "Caution alarm" and "No cameras," the church struggles to keep at bay the tourists who steal quick photographs of this Fabergé egg turned inside out. *(Open daily 9am-12:15pm and 2:30-6:30pm.)*

PETERSFRIEDHOF (CEMTERY). By continuing through the arch to the right of the church, you'll enter Petersfriedhof, one of the most peaceful places in Salzburg, primarily because tour groups are denied entry. The tiny cemetery is filled with delicate flower-covered graves, some dating back to the 1600s. This secluded spot is a popular subject for romantic painters, and it served as a model for the cemetery where Rolf blew the whistle on the von Trapp family in *The Sound of Music. (Open Apr.-Sept. 6:30am-7pm; Oct.-Mar. 6:30am-6pm.)* Near the far end of the cemetery, against the mountains, is the entrance to the **Katakomben** (catacombs), relatively empty cave-like rooms where Christians allegedly worshipped in secret as early as AD 250. *(☎844 5780. Open in summer Tu-Su 10:30am-4pm; in winter W-Su 10:30am-3:30pm. 12AS.)*

CATHEDRAL. The exit at the opposite end of the cemetery from the Stiftskirche leads into **Kapitelplatz,** home of a giant chess grid, a fountain depicting Poseidon wielding his trident, and a bunch of tradespeople bartering their wares, the platz spreads out in front of one side of Salzburg's immense Baroque **Dom** (cathedral). Archbishop Wolf Dietrich's successor, Markus Sittikus, commissioned the cathedral from Italian architect Santino Solari in 1628. Mozart was christened here in

1756 and later worked at the cathedral as *Konzertmeister* and court organist. The cupola was destroyed during WWII, but was quickly repaired. The church, however, still seems to be collecting donations for the repairs as you cannot leave the church decently without giving at least 10AS. The square leading out of the cathedral, **Domplatz,** features a statue of the Virgin Mary. Around her swarm four lead figures representing Wisdom, Faith, the Church, and the Devil.

ARCHBISHOP'S RESIDENCE. The square on the far side of the cathedral is **Residenzplatz,** named for the magnificent **Residenz** of Salzburg's powerful prince-archbishops. The ecclesiastical elite of Austria have resided here, in the heart of the *Altstadt*, since 1595. With your trusty audio-guide in hand, you can lead yourself through stunning Baroque **Prunkräume** (state rooms), which house an astonishing three-dimensional ceiling fresco by Rottmayr and secret doors. The *Residenz* also houses a gallery (see p. 230). *(☎804 2269 0. Residenz open 10am-5pm. 91AS, students 70AS, audio-guide included.)* Dead-center in Residenzpl. is an immense 15m **fountain**—the largest Baroque fountain in the world—which features amphibious horses charging through the water (note the webbed hooves). Appropriately, *Fiaker* (horse-drawn carriages) congregate near the fountain. *(420AS for 25min.)*

MOZARTPLATZ. Diagonally to the right of Residenzpl. begins yet another square, **Mozartplatz,** which is dominated by the **Neugebäude,** opposite the AmEx office, seat of the city government's bureaucracy. Atop the building, a 35-bell **Glockenspiel** (carillon) rings out a Mozart tune (specified on a notice posted on the corner of the *Residenz*) every day at 7am, 11am, and 6pm, and the tremendous pipe organ atop the Hohensalzburg fortress bellows a response. In the middle of the square is a greening statue of Mozart.

FORTRESS HOHENSALZBURG. **Festung Hohensalzburg** was built between 1077 and 1681 by the ruling archbishops, who used the place as a refuge during the religious wars of the time. Looming over Salzburg from atop Mönchsberg, it is the largest completely preserved castle in Europe because it was never successfully attacked. Nowadays penetrating the castle walls is simply a matter of forking over some shillings. The trail up to the fortress and the **Festungsbahn** (funicular) can be found at the far end of Kapitelpl. The road/stairs require about 20 minutes of uphill walking, while the Festungsbahn takes only a few minutes. Since the ride terminates inside the fortress walls, cable-car tickets include entrance. *(☎842 682. Every 10min. 9am-9pm; Oct.-Apr. 9am-5pm. Ascent 66AS; round-trip 76AS.)* The castle contains a "torture" chamber (though they apparently never had anyone to torture), formidable Gothic state rooms, the fortress organ (nicknamed the "Bull of Salzburg" for its off-key snorting), and an impregnable watchtower that affords an unmatched view of the city and surrounding mountains. You'll also see the archbishop's medieval indoor toilet—a technological marvel of its day. If you pay close attention to the wall carvings in the state rooms and on the exterior, you'll observe turnips everywhere, which was the symbol of archbishop Leonhard von Keutschachs. The **Burgmuseum** inside the fortress displays medieval instruments of torture, including maliciously comical punishment masks and a chastity belt. Nearby the **Rainer Museum** contains objects of war from the 17th century to the present (including the *Anschluß* period). *(☎842 430. Open July-Sept. 8:30am-7pm; Nov.-Mar. 9am-5pm; Apr.-June 9am-6pm. If you walk up, entrance to fortress is 42AS which only allows access to the perimeter of the castle; combo ticket including fortress, castle interiors, and both museums 84AS. If you take the funicular, fortress included in price; castle interior and both museums 42AS.)*

From the fortress many footpaths spread out over the Mönchsberg, all providing bird's-eye views of the city below. After walking over the top of the hills, hikers meander down the leafy trails to the *Altstadt* or descend via the **Mönchsberglift** (elevator) built into the mountain, which opens on Gstätteng. 13. *(Elevator operates daily 9am-11pm. 16AS, round-trip 27AS.)* Down the hill and to the right of the fortress, **Nonnberg Abbey** (where the real Maria von Trapp lived) is still a private monastic complex, but visitors can tour the church, which has Romanesque wall paintings.

BOVINE BEFUDDLEMENT The only time the **Hohensalzburg** fortress was ever under any kind of siege was during the **Peasant Wars** (see Dynastic Austria, p. 63), when the peasants surrounded the fortress in an attempt to starve the archbishop out. When the stubborn archbishop had only one cow left, he painted the remaining beast with different spots on both sides and paraded him back and forth along the castle wall in distinct view of the peasants below. Since the peasants, as the saying goes, were simple-minded folk, they believed that the archbishop had a great reserve of food and decided to give up their embargo.

THE NEUSTADT

MIRABELL PALACE AND GARDENS. On the bus and walking route into town, **Mirabellplatz** holds the marvelous **Schloß Mirabell.** While Archbishop Wolf Dietrich had his own place in the *Residenz* (see p. 227), the supposedly vowed-to-celibacy Wolf had this Renaissance beauty built for his mistress Salome Alt and their 10 children in 1606. He christened the palace "Altenau" in her honor, but when the new archbishop Markus Sittikus imprisoned Wolf Dietrich for arson, Sitkus seized the palace and changed its name to "Mirabell." The castle is now the seat of the city government, and some of the mayor's offices are open for public viewing. The palace hosts classical concerts in the evening, and fans swear that the *Marmorsaal* (Marble Hall) is one of the best concert halls in Europe. It is also a popular place to get married, especially among Japanese couples. *(Open M-F 8am-4pm. Free.)*

Behind the palace, the delicately manicured **Mirabellgarten** is a maze of extravagant seasonal flower beds and groomed shrubs. Students from the nearby Mozarteum often perform here, and Maria von Trapp and her overworked children stopped here for a rousing rendition of "Do-Re-Mi." From the entrance off Mirabellpl., walk up the tiny staircase to see the **Dwarf Garden,** a favorite play area for Salzburg toddlers named for the vertically challenged statues which are slightly more adorable than the von Trapp children. The statues' grotesque marble faces were supposedly modeled after the archbishop's court jesters.

From one of the hedge-enclosed clearings in the *Mirabellgarten*, you can see a tiny wooden, moss-covered shack called the **Zauberflötenhäuschen,** alleged to be where Wolfgang Amadeus composed *The Magic Flute* in just 5 months. It was transplanted from Vienna as a gift to Salzburg's conservatory for young musicians, the **Mozarteum,** which stands back-to-back with the gardens on Schwartzstr. 26-28. The Mozarteum was constructed for the Salzburg Academy of Music and Performing Arts, but there are regular performances in its concert hall (see p. 231). It is also known for its enormous **Mozart Archives** *(☎88940; entrance by appointment).*

MOZART'S RESIDENCE. Just down the street from the Mozarteum stands **Mozarts Wohnhaus,** the composer's residence from 1773 to 1780. At age 17, Mozart moved here with his family from their house in the *Altstadt* where he was born. With smaller crowds than the *Geburtshaus* and much more thoughtfully displayed exhibits, the *Wohnhaus* is the place to go. An audio-guide provides entertaining commentary complete with music samples. A well-presented slide show at the end will have you humming Mozart melodies all day. *(Makartpl. 8. ☎883 4544 0. Open daily 10am-5:30pm. 65AS, students 50AS; audio-guide included.)*

MONASTERY AND CHURCH. At Kapuzinerberg's crest stands the simple **Kapuzinerkloster** (Capuchin Monastery) that Wolf Dietrich built in the late 16th century. Stages of the cross are represented by rubbery mannequins locked behind iron gates. Farther down Linzerg. is the 18th-century **Sebastianskirche.** Its Italian-style graveyard contains the gaudy mausoleum of Wolf Dietrich with an arrogant epitaph commanding all to pray for him or face God's anger. The tombs of Mozart's wife Constanze and father Leopold are also here on the main path leading to the mausoleum. *(From Mirabellgarten or Mozart's Wohnhaus, follow Dreifaltigkeitg. south to its intersection with Linzerg.; head under the stone arch on right side of Linzerg. 14 and follow tiny stone staircase up to Linzerg. 41. Open Apr.-Oct. 9am-7pm, Nov.-Mar. 9am-4pm.)*

MONK-Y BUSINESS Legend has it that the robes of the Kapuzinerkloster's resident monks inspired the world's first cup of cappuccino. A cafe proprietor with an overactive imagination observed the pious gents on a noonday stroll and *voilà*—the world witnessed the birth of a drink with the rich coffee color of the monk's robes topped by white froth hoods. According to this theory, Italy's cappuccino is just a rip-off of the much older *Kapuziner,* still ordered in Austrian cafes today.

THE SOUND OF MUSIC

In 1964, Julie Andrews, Christopher Plummer, and a gaggle of 20th-Century Fox crew members arrived in Salzburg to film *The Sound of Music*, based on the true story of the von Trapp family. Salzburg has never been the same. The city encourages the increased tourism due to the film's popularity (although interestingly enough, many Salzburgers themselves have never seen the film, and most of them who have dislike it). Three official companies run **Sound of Music Tours** in Salzburg. Many hostels and pensions work exclusively with one of the firms and offer discounts to guests. **Salzburg Sightseeing Tours** (☎881 616; fax 878 776) and **Panorama Tours** (☎883 211; fax 871 618; sightseeing@panoramatours.at) operate rival kiosks on Mirabellpl. and run remarkably similar programs. (Tours 400AS. Tours leave from Mirabellpl. daily 9:30am and 2pm.) The renegade **Bob's Special Tours,** Kaig. 19, has no high-profile kiosk, but they do have a minibus. (☎849 511; fax 849 512. 350AS. Tours daily in summer 9am and 2pm; in winter 10am.) The smaller vehicle enables them to tour more of the *Altstadt*, locations that the big tour buses can't reach. All 3 companies offer free pick-up from your hotel, and last 4 hours. The tours are generally worth the money only if you're a big *Sound of Music* fan or if you have a short time in Salzburg and want an overview of the area—the tours venture into the Salzkammergut lake region as well.

If you have the time and enough interest, however, you could rent a bike and do the tour on your own. The film's writers and producers took a great deal of artistic license with the von Trapps' story—many of the events were fabricated for Tinseltown. Though Maria was a nun-apprentice in the film, in reality she merely taught at **Nonnberg Abbey,** high above the city near the Festung (see p. 227). In this abbey, the crew filmed the nuns singing "How Do You Solve A Problem Like Maria?" The little gazebo where Liesl and Rolf unleashed their youthful passion is on the grounds of **Schloß Hellbrunn** (see p. 233). The gazebo is disappointingly small but photogenic (no worries), and the walk back from Hellbrunn to Salzburg's *Altstadt* is lovely on summer afternoons. From the Hellbrun parking lot, head down Hellbrunner Allee. On the way, you'll pass the yellow castle used for the exterior of the von Trapp home (Maria sang "I Have Confidence" in front of the long yellow wall), which is now a dorm for music students at the Mozarteum. Continue along Hellbrunner Allee until it turns into Freisaalweg. At the end of Freisaalweg, turn right on Akadamiestr., which ends at Alpenstr. and the river. The river footpath leads all the way back to Mozartsteg. and Staatsbrücke (1hr.). The back of the von Trapp house (where Maria and the children fell into the water after romping around the city all day) was filmed at the **Schloß Leopoldskron** behind the Mönchberg, now a center for academic studies. Visitors are not welcomed, nor permitted to wander about the grounds, but if you're set on getting a glimpse of the house, take bus #55 to "Pensionistenheim Nonntal," turn left on Sunnhubstr., and left again up Leopoldskroner Allee to the castle. Other filming locations scattered throughout Salzburg include the **Mirabellgarten** (see p. 228) and the **Festspielhaus** (see p. 231).

The von Trapps were married in the church at Nonnberg Abbey, but Hollywood filmed the scene in **Mondsee** instead (see p. 245). The sightseeing tours allow guests to waddle around Mondsee for 45 minutes, but the town is really worth a whole daytrip for its beautiful lake and pastry shops. **Buses** leave the Salzburg train station from the main bus depot (45min., every hr., 60AS). The hills that are alive with the sound of music, inspiring Maria's rapturous twirling in the opening scene, are along the Salzburg-St. Gilgen route near Fusch, but any of the hills in the

Salzkammergut region could fit the bill. For your own re-creational and recreational purposes, try the Untersberg, just south of Salzburg (see p. 233).

To squeeze the last *Groschen* out of starry-eyed tourists, the Stieglkeller hosts a **Sound of Music Dinner Show.** Performers sing your favorite film songs while servers ply you with soup, *Schnitzel* with noodles, and crisp apple strudel. (☎832 029; fax 832 0291 3. May-Oct. show starts at 8:30pm. Show and drink 360AS. Dinner, at 7:30pm, plus the show 520AS. 30% student discount, children under 13 free.)

MUSEUMS

Salzburg's small, specialized museums often get lost in the shadow of the *Festung*, *The Sound of Music*, and the *Festspiele*. The keywords in that sentence are "small" and "specialized." There are also small and specialized private galleries on Sigmund-Haffnerg. that allow budget art viewing.

ART MUSEUMS. The **Museum Carolino Augusteum,** named after Emperor Franz I's widow, Caroline Augusta, houses local Roman and Celtic artifacts on its ground floor, including mosaics and burial remains, naturally preserved thanks to the region's salt. The upper floors feature Gothic and Baroque art. *(Museumpl. 1. ☎841 134. Open Tu-Su 10am-6pm, Th until 8pm. 40AS, students 15AS.)* The **Residenz Gallery,** in the *Residenz*, has exhibits of 16th- to 19th-century art, including some dramatic Dutch works and the rather delightfully sinister Rubens, *Satyr und Mädchen mit Früchtekorb*. *(Residenzpl. 1. ☎840 451. Open Apr.-Sept. 10am-5pm; Oct.-Mar. Su-Tu and Th-Sa 10am-5pm. 50AS, students 40AS.)* Finally, the **Barockmuseum,** in the Orangerie of the Mirabellgarten, pays elaborate tribute to the ornate aesthetic of 17th- and 18th-century Europe. *(☎877 432. Open Tu-Sa 9am-noon and 2-5pm, Su 9am-noon. 40AS, students and seniors 20AS, ages 6-14 free.)*

BEER MUSEUM. Stiegl Brauwelt (Brew World) is Salzburg's own beer museum, attached to the Stiegl brewery just minutes from downtown, with 3 floors showcasing beer-making, the history of brewing, and modern beer culture—including "30 Ways to Open a Beer Bottle" and the wonder of the *Brauwelt*, a 2-story beer-bottle pyramid constructed of 300 Austrian beers. Hop on down to the final hands-on exhibit—the tour concludes with 2 complimentary glasses of Stiegl beer, a *Brezel* (pretzel), and a souvenir beer glass. *(Brauhausstr. 9. Take bus #1 to "Brauhaus" and walk up the street to the giant yellow building. ☎838 71492; www.stiegl.co.at. Open W-Su 10am-4pm. 96AS, students 60AS.)*

OTHER MUSEUMS. The **Haus der Natur,** opposite the Carolino Augusteum, is an enormous museum (80 rooms) with an eclectic collection—from live alligators, and over a dozen giant snakes to huge rock crystals and spinning planets. *(Museumpl. 5. ☎842 653 or 842 322. Open 9am-5pm. 55AS, students 30AS.)* Just inside the main entrance to the *Dom*, the **Dom Museum** houses an unusual collection called the **Kunst- und Wunderkammer** (Art and Curiosity Cabinet) that includes conch shells, mineral formations, and a 2 foot whale's tooth. The archbishop accumulated these curiosities to impress distinguished visitors, as did many of his contemporaries. *(See p. 185; ☎844 189. Open mid-May to mid-Oct. M-Sa 10am-5pm; Su 1pm-5pm. 60AS, students 20AS.)* On Residenzpl., the **Domgrabungsmuseum** displays excavations of the Roman ruins under the cathedral. You'll feel like an archaeologist clambering around in a dig. *(☎845 295. Open May-Oct. W-Su 9am-5pm. 20AS, students 10AS.)* The **Spielzeug Museum,** near the *Festspielhaus*, features 3 floors of puppets, wooden toys, dolls, electric trains, and nifty pre-Lego castle blocks from 1921. *(Bürgerspitalg. 2. ☎847 560. Open Tu-Su 9am-5pm. 30AS, students 10AS. Puppet show Tu-W 3pm.)*

MUSIC AND ENTERTAINMENT

SALZBURG FESTIVAL

Max Reinhardt, Richard Strauss, and Hugo von Hofmannsthal founded the renowned **Salzburger Festspiele** (Festival) in 1920. Every year since, Salzburg has become a musical mecca from late July to the end of August. A few weeks before the festival, visitors strolling along Getreideg. may bump into world-class stars taking a break from rehearsal. On the eve of the festival's opening, over 100 dancers don regional costumes, accessorize with torches, and perform a *Fackeltanz* (torchdance) on Residenzpl. During the festivities themselves, operas, plays, films, concerts, and tourists overrun every available public space. Information and tickets for Festspiele events are available through the **Festspiele Kartenbüro** (ticket office) and **Tageskasse** (daily box office) in Karajanpl., against the mountain and next to the tunnel. (From July1-21, ticket office open M-F 9:30am-noon and 3-5pm. From July 25-Aug., it's open daily at the same times. Box office open M-Sa 9:30am-5pm.) The festival prints a complete program of events that lists all concert locations and dates one year in advance. The booklet is available at any tourist office (10AS). Music fans snap up the best seats months before the festival begins. To **order tickets,** contact *Kartenbüro der Salzburger Festspiele*, Postfach 140, A-5010 Salzburg (☎804 5579; fax 804 5760; info@salzburgfestival.at; www.salzburgfestival.at), no later than the beginning of January. After that, the office publishes a list of **remaining seats,** which generally include some cheap tickets to the operas (around 300AS), concerts (around 100AS), and plays (around 100AS), as well as standing room places (50-100AS). These tickets, however, are gobbled up quickly by subscribers or student groups, leaving very expensive tickets (upwards of 1000AS) and seats at avant-garde modern-music concerts (often as little as 200AS). **Middle-man ticket distributors** sell marked-up cheap tickets, a legal form of scalping—try American Express or Panorama Tours. Those 26 or younger can try for **cheap subscription tickets** (2-4 tickets for 200-300AS each) by writing about 8 months in advance to *Direktion der Salzburger Festspiele*, attn: Ulrich Hauschild, Hofstallg. 1, A-5020 Salzburg.

The powers that be have discontinued hawking last-minute tickets for dress rehearsals to the general public—nowadays, you've got to know somebody to get your hands on one of these tickets. Those without the cunning to back their chair into Placido Domingo thereby causing him to spill his cranberry juice down their newly starched white shirt, leading him to ask how he can ever make it up to them, should take advantage of the **Fest zur Eröffungsfest** (Opening Day Festival), when concerts, shows, and films are either very cheap or free. Folksingers perform in the evenings, and dancers perform the traditional *Fackeltanz* around the horse fountain, literally kicking off the festivities. Tickets for all these events are available on a first-come, first-served basis during the festival's opening week at the box office in the Großes Festspielhaus on Hofstallg. The only other event visitors can always attend without advance tickets is **Jedermann.** The city stages Hugo von Hofmannsthal's modern morality play about the life, love, and death of an immoral man, every year on a stage in front of the cathedral. At the end, people placed in strategic locations throughout the city cry out the eerie word "Jedermann," which echoes all over town. Shouting contests determine which locals win the opportunity to be one of the ghostly criers. Standing-room places for shows are available at the Festspielhaus (60AS).

CONCERTS

MOZARTEUM. Even when the *Festspiele* are not on, many other concerts and events occur around the city. The **Salzburg Academy of Music and Performing Arts** performs a number of concerts on a rotating schedule in the **Mozarteum** (see p. 228). The school often dedicates one cycle of concerts to students and reduces the ticket price to 80AS. For tickets to any of these concerts, contact *Kartenbüro*

Mozarteum, Postfach 156, Theaterg. 2, A-5024 Salzburg (☎873 154; fax 872 996; open M-Th 9am-2pm, F 9am-4pm).

THEMED CONCERTS. For a particularly enchanting (and expensive) evening, attend a **Festungskonzert** (Fortress Concert) in the fortress's ornate *Fürstenzimmer* (Prince's chamber) and *Goldener Saal* (Golden Hall). Concerts occur year-round and may include dinner at the fortress restaurant. Tickets are 360-450AS without dinner, 590-640AS with dinner. You need advanced reservations for concerts. For more information, contact *Festungskonzerte*, Anton-Adlgasserweg 22, A-5020 Salzburg (☎825 858; fax 825 859; www.salzburg.co.at/festungskonzerte; open daily 9am-9pm). A less tourist-oriented activity is the year-round **Salzburger Schloßkonzerte** in Schloß Mirabell (box office in the Schloß Mirabell ☎848 586; fax 844 747; open M-F 9am-5:30pm). For a bit more money and a lot more kitsch, check out the evening **Mozart Serenaden** (Mozart's Serenades) in the Gothic Hall on Burgerstpitalg. 2. (daily 8:30pm in summer, otherwise 7:30pm; 200-420AS). Musicians in traditional garb (knickers, powdered hair, etc.) perform Mozart favorites. For information and tickets, contact *Konzertdirektion Nerat*, A-5020 Salzburg, Lieferinger Hauptstr. 136 (☎436 870; fax 436 970).

CHURCH CONCERTS. The **Dom** also has a concert program in July and August. The church's organ has four separate pipe sections, creating a dramatic "surround sound" effect (concerts Thursday and Friday at 11:15am). Tickets are available at the door (100AS, students 70AS, children free). The church has periodic evening concerts. (280AS, students 180AS, standing room 100AS, children free; Check the door for upcoming programs.) Other churches throughout Salzburg perform wonderful music during services and post information on other concerts, particularly near Easter and Christmas. The **5-Uhr Konzerte** (5 o'clock concerts) held at St. Peter's Monastery are performed by young musicians at rock bottom prices (120AS, students 60AS).

OUTDOOR CONCERTS. In July and August, **outdoor opera** rings out from the historical hedge-theater of Mirabellgarten (330-560AS, students 190AS). Tickets are available from the box office in Schloß Mirabell (☎848 586; fax 844 747; open M-F 9am-5:30pm). In addition, from May through August there are **outdoor performances,** including concerts, folk-singing, and dancing, around the Mirabellgarten. The tourist office has leaflets on scheduled events, but an evening stroll through the park might prove just as enlightening. Listen to the word on the street. Mozartpl. and Kapitelpl. are also popular stops for talented street musicians and touring school bands, and the well-postered Aicher Passage next to Mirabellpl. is a great source of information for other upcoming musical events.

THEATER, MOVIES, AND GAMBLING

Right next to Mirabellgarten at the **Salzburger Marionettentheater,** handmade marionettes perform to recorded *Festspiele* opera. The theater is almost as small as its actors. For more information, contact Marionettentheater, Schwarzstr. 24, A-5020 Salzburg. (Box office open on performance days M-Sa 9am-1pm and 2hr. before curtain. 280-480AS, students 200AS. AmEx, MC, Visa.) Track down English-language **movies** with the film program in the **Das Kino** newspaper. Cinemas rotate a few films each month and often offer films in English with German subtitles. Win enough money to pay off your concert ticket loans at **Casino Salzburg,** located in Schloß Klessheim. Slot machines, blackjack tables, and much more await you. Ask at the tourist office about the free shuttle service from the city center. (☎854 620. Open from 3pm onwards. 18 years or older, semi-formal attire required.)

OUTDOOR ACTIVITIES

If you're sick of the baroque ornamentation and cobblestone streets with which Salzburg assaults its visitors, or if you just want to get your blood pumping, try an adventure tour with **Crocodile Sports,** Gaisbergstr. 34a (☎642 907). Owner and operator Wolfgang will gleefully pick you up from your hotel for a day (or half a day) you'll never forget. Adventures are scheduled throughout the week (so call ahead) and include **canyoning** (590-2790AS), **canoeing** (590-2790AS), **paragliding** (1200AS), and **rafting** (550AS-840AS).

DAYTRIPS FROM SALZBURG

HELLBRUNN AND UNTERSBERG

To reach Hellbrun, take bus #55 (dir.: Anif) to "Hellbrunn" from the train station, Mirabellpl., or Mozartsteg., or walk/bike 1hr. down tree-lined Hellbrunner Allee *(see p. 229).*

Just south of Salzburg lies the unforgettable **Lustschloß Hellbrunn,** a testament to the frivolity that went along with being an archbishop, at least for Wolf Dietrich's nephew, the Archbishop Markus Sittikus. The sprawling estate includes a large palace, fish ponds, trimmed hedge gardens, the "I Am Sixteen, Going On Seventeen" gazebo, and tree-lined footpaths through open grassy fields. The **Steintheater** on the palace grounds is the oldest natural theater north of the Alps. Before entering the gardens with the **Wasserspiele** (literally "water games") you may hear screams of surprised laughter from within. Prepare yourself for an afternoon of wet surprises, including the Neptune grotto and a water-powered dollhouse. Archbishop Markus amused himself by creating elaborate water-powered figurines and a booby-trapped table that could spout water on his drunken guests. If you have to choose between the castle and the *Wasserspiele*, go for the *Wasserspiele*. (☎820 0030. Open July-Aug. 9am-10pm; May-June and Sept. 9am-5:30pm; Apr. and Oct. 9am-4:30pm. Admission only with tour. Castle tour 40AS, students 30AS. *Wasserspiele* tour 80AS, 60AS. Combined tour 100AS, 80AS.)

On the hill above the manicured grounds sits the tiny hunting lodge **Monatsschlößchen** (Little Month Castle), so named because someone bet the archbishop that he couldn't build a castle in a month. As one of the archbishop's many weaknesses was gambling, he accepted the challenge and began spending the church's money on architects, engineers, and laborers who toiled around the clock. He won. The castle now houses the **Folklore and Local History Museum,** which has 3 floors of surprising exhibits, including animals made out of bread, a *papier-mâché*-and-glitter diorama of St. George slaying the dragon, and several *Salzburger Schönperchten*—bizarre 2m hats worn in a traditional Austrian ceremony intended to scare away the demons of winter. (☎820 3722 1. Open mid-Apr. to mid-Oct. 9am-5pm. 20AS, students 10AS.) Near the castle lies the enormous **Hellbrunn Zoo.** The zoo is full of exotic animals and a gross-out masterpiece—the *Hansratte*—a domestic kitchen scene infested with slithery rats. (☎820 176. Open 8:30am-4pm; extended summer hours. 80AS, students 60AS.)

Bus #55 continues south from Hellbrunn to the luscious **Untersberg** peak, where **Charlemagne** supposedly rests deep beneath the ground, prepared to return and reign over Europe when he is needed. Choose between dozens of hikes through color-soaked meadows, with mountains in the distance. The **Eishöhlen** (ice caves) are only a 1½-hour climb from the peak. A **cable car** glides over Salzburg to the summit (☎(06246) 871 217 or 72477; July-Sept. Su-Tu and Th-Sa 8:30am-5:30pm, W 8:30am-8pm; Mar.-June and Oct. 9am-5pm; Dec.-Feb. 10am-4pm; ascent 130AS, descent 110AS, round-trip 215AS; children 75AS, 55AS, 105AS).

HALLEIN-SALZBERGWERK DÜRRNBERG

From Salzberg Hauptbahnhof take Post Bus dir: "Hallein" (1½hr., every 2hr. 7:03am-7:53pm, 94AS). Once there take the cable car (one way 55AS, students 48AS; roundtrip 85AS, 78AS). From the top of the cable car head toward Bad Dürrnberg.

Founded over 2500 years ago by Celts, Hallein was named after the *hall* (salt) that was the source of the fabulous wealth of the Salzburg Prince Archbishops. Without the salt, the archbishops could have afforded few of the baroque masterpieces that the town is so famous for. For 190AS you can visit the underground Salzbergwerk (salt mine) via guided tour. They'll give you a special miner's suit to wear and a ride on a raft across a spooky subterranean lake. You'll see the "Mann in Salz," a prehistoric man found in 1616 so well preserved by the miraculous salt that only his skin is said to have changed color—he's brown now. The 1½ hour tour culminates in a slide down an old-fashioned wooden shaft. (☎ (6245) 852 8515. Open Apr.-Oct. 9am-5pm; Nov.-Mar. 11am-3pm.)

THE SALZKAMMERGUT

Each year in early summer, tourists in the know, bands of Austrian school children, and tour groups of elderly Europeans come to the smooth lakes and furrowed mountains of the Salzkammergut. The wave of visitors breaks at the locally flavored resort towns that speckle the countryside, beneath rolling hills and dark, furry evergreens. The region takes its name from the salt mines that, in their glory days, underwrote Salzburg's architectural treasures. Today, the white gold of the Salzkammergut is no longer salt, but pure sunshine, in the summer, on the sparkling water of the clear lakes and tons of fresh snow in winter. Though technically not in Salzburgerland, Salzburg is the hub for all transportation in the area. If you can only visit one Salzkammergut town make it Hallstatt. After Hallstatt, the choice will depend on what you're looking for, you can find everything from posh spas to rustic hostels. To ensure you're always getting the best deal, pick up the **Salzkammergut Card,** which was introduced to replace individual town cards, and gives 25% discounts on most local sites and attractions. (65AS; available at local tourist offices.) For information on the region contact the **Salzkammergut Regional Tourist Board,** Postfach 65, A-4820 Bad Ischl (☎(6132) 28667; fax (6132) 28667-71; salzkammergut@touristik.at).

GETTING AROUND THE SALZKAMMERGUT. The Salzkammergut is both peacefully remote and easily navigable, with 2000km of footpaths, 12 cable cars and chairlifts, and dozens of hostels to welcome visitors year-round. Within the region, there is a dense network of **buses** that are the most efficient and reliable method of travel into and through the lake region, since the mountainous area is often barren of rail tracks. When traveling by bus, be sure to plan your route in advance, as some connections run infrequently. (Dial 167 from Salzburg for complete schedule information.) **Hitchers** from Salzburg report taking bus #29 to Gnigl and coming into the Salzkammergut at Bad Ischl. *Let's Go* does not recommend hitching. The lake district is apparently one of the rare, refreshing Austrian regions in which hitchhikers can make good time. **Bikers** should check out the 280km **Salzkammergut bike path**, which winds through many of the towns in the region. Contact the Salzkammergut regional tourist office for more information on the route, or consult www.radtouren.at/english. **Hikers** can capitalize on dozens of **cable cars** in the area to gain altitude before setting out on their own, though there are almost always cheaper hikes that can be made without expensive cable cars. Hiking, at all levels, is plentiful in this lush area, and easier than in many more intense Alpine regions. Ask at any tourist office for hiking maps. Reasonably priced **ferries** service each of the larger lakes (railpass discounts on the **Wolfgangsee, Attersee,** and **Traunsee** lines).

ACCOMMODATIONS. Hostels are common throughout the area, but you can often find far superior rooms in private homes and *Pensionen* at just-above-hostel prices. "*Zimmer Frei*" signs peek out from virtually every house (average price is 190-280AS). **Campgrounds** dot the region, but many are trailer-oriented. Away from large towns, many travelers camp discreetly almost anywhere, generally without trouble. At higher elevations there are **alpine huts,** many of which are accesible with light hikes. Contact the **Österreichischer Alpenverein** (Austrian Alpine Club; ☎(0512) 59547), for info and rental. Their central office is in Innsbruck, but locally experienced volunteers staff regional branches.

FUNNY HATS On January 5, the Glöcklerlaufen (running of the figures with special caps) takes place after dark in the Salzkammergut. These *Glöckler* derive their name from the custom of knocking at the door (*glocken* means "to knock") and not from the bells attached to their belts (*Glocke* means "bell"). These caps–reminiscent of stained-glass windows–have an electric light inside; several are on display at the Monats-Schlößchen at Hellbrunn (just outside Salzburg). In return for their New Year's wish, runners are rewarded with a special hole-less doughnut, the *Glöcklerkrapfen*. Although the satisfaction of legions of stained-glass-hat fetishists seems enough, the masked figures also get money and refreshments from the citizenry, which indicates a little about their origin–a long, long time ago, seasonal workers needed such handouts to survive.

HALLSTATT ☎06134

Teetering on the banks of the **Hallstättersee** in a valley surrounded on all sides by the sheer rocky cliffs of the Dachstein mountains, Hallstatt is easily the most beautiful lakeside village in the Salzkammergut, if not all of Austria. It was declared a UNESCO World Cultural Heritage site in 1997. This tiny village of 1400 inhabitants seems to defy gravity, clinging to the face of a stony slope. Halstatt's angle on the mountainside assures that the gorgeous lake dominates the horizon from nearly every vantage point. Over 4 millennia ago, a highly advanced culture thrived in Hallstatt, but they didn't come for the view—Hallstatt was a world-famous settlement back when Rome was still a village, thanks to its "white gold." The salt-rich earth also helped preserve Hallstatt's archaeological treasures, which are so extensive that the pre-historic era in Celtic studies (800-400BC) is dubbed the "Hallstatt era." The tourists come, and the narrow streets are thronged with them, but Hallstatt happily fails to be touristy. Hallstatt merits more than a day-trip; stay the night, or a week, in a room overlooking the clear blue lake.

GETTING THERE AND AROUND

From Salzburg, taking the **bus** (130AS) is the cheapest way to get to Hallstatt, but it requires layovers in both Bad Ischl and Gosaumühle; buses run from Bad Ischl from 6:50am-5:30pm. The **bus stop** is at the edge of downtown on Seestr. near a large sign reading "Lahn." The **train station** is on the side of the lake, but there is no staffed office to help travelers. All trains come from Attnang-Puchheim in the north or Stanach-Irnding in the south. Trains run to **Attnang-Puchheim** (134AS), **Bad Ischl** (38AS), and **Salzburg** via Attnang-Puchheim (210AS). To get from the train station into town take the ferry that leaves after every train and arrives at Landungspl. (10min., 6:55am-6:46pm, 25AS). If you arrive later, stay on the train to the next stop (Obertraun) and take a taxi (150AS) or walk (5km) to the center of Hallstatt. If **driving** from Salzburg or the Salzkammergut towns, take Rte. 158 to Bad Ischl and then Rte. 145 toward Bad Aussee. After Bad Goisern, it's approximately 5km to the narrow road leading along the *Hallstättersee* into Hallstatt. Automobile access to Hallstatt is severely limited. Ample day **parking** lots are available by the tunnels leading into town (free for guests staying in town).

ORIENTATION AND PRACTICAL INFORMATION

Hallstatt is on the *Hallstättersee*, an entrancing oasis at the southern tip of the Salzkammergut. Note when finding an address that street numbers often bounce around randomly. To get to the **tourist office** from the ferry stop, face away from the lake and turn left, walking until Seestr. 169. The office offers free maps and finds vacancies among the plentiful, cheap rooms. (☎8208; fax 8352; hallstatt-info@EUnet.at; www.tiscover.com/hallstatt. Open July-Aug. M-F 9am-5pm, Sa 10am-2pm; Sept.-June M-F 9am-noon and 2-5pm). Services include: **ATM** next to the post office; **public bathrooms** adjacent to the Heimatmuseum; **laundry** at Hotel Grüner Baum, 104 Marktplatz (160AS for washing and drying; inquire at reception); and a **doctor** with an in-house **pharmacy** at Baderplatz 103 (☎8401. Walk in hours M, Th, F, Su 8am-noon, W 5-7pm). The **post office** Seestr. 160 (☎8201), below the tourist office, offers good **currency exchange** rates (open M-Tu and Th-F 8am-noon and 2-6pm, Sa 8-11am; exchange open until 5pm). The **postal code** is A-4830.

ACCOMMODATIONS

Privatzimmer at just-above-hostel prices are prevalent in Hallstatt. The tourist office has an extensive list, but *Let's Go* lists a few of the best and cheapest.

Gästehaus Zur Mühle, Kirchenweg 36 (☎8318). From the tourist office, walk up the hill as if heading toward the Heimatmuseum, then swing right at the end of the *Platz*. The hostel is through the little tunnel on the left, by the cascading waterfall. Close to the city center with pleasant 3- to 18-bed dorms and lots of English-speaking backpackers. Breakfast 40AS. Lunch and dinner available at the restaurant downstairs. Showers and lockers included with deposit of 200AS. Sheets 35AS. Reception 8am-2pm and 4-10pm. Dorms 115AS.

Frühstückspension Sarstein, Gosaumühlstr. 83 (☎8217). From the tourist office turn left on Seestr. and walk for 10min., it will be on the right. Frau Fischer at Sarstein offers the prettiest accommodations in town, vistas of the lake and village, and a beachside lawn for sunning and swimming. Breakfast included. Hall showers 10AS for 10min. and toilets, but a double with both can be had for an extra 100AS per night. 270AS per person for a single or double room, 200AS per person for a triple, with bath 300AS. 20AS surcharge for 1-night stays.

Franziska Zimmerman, Gosaumühlstr. 69 (☎8309) lives up the block toward town from Frau Fischer, Frau Zimmerman's sister, and offers similar (but fewer) accommodations. Frau Zimmerman rents out 2 doubles and a single, all well-furnished and with views of the *Hallstättersee*. Breakfast included. Showers 10AS. Call ahead. Single 220AS, double 420AS. 20AS surcharge for 1-night stays.

Frühstückspension Seethaler, Dr.-F.-Mortonweg 22 (☎8421). Head uphill, bear left, and follow the signs, the pension sits on the hill near the tourist office. All rooms have balconies, most with amazing lake views. 1-4 bed dorms 195AS per person, with in-room shower and toilet 280AS, with kitchen 380AS, 25-50AS surcharge for stays less than 3 nights. Ask about a student deal from Sept.-June.

Camping Klausner-Höll, Lahnstr. 6 (☎8322). Exit the tourist office, walk right on Seestr. for 10min. Breakfast 65-110AS. Showers included. **Laundry** 100AS. Open mid-Apr. to mid-Oct. Gate closed daily noon-2:30pm and 10pm-7am. 55AS plus 10AS tax, children under 14 25AS plus 5AS; tents 45AS; cars 35AS.

FOOD

While rooming in Hallstatt isn't pricey, eating is. The best bet for cheap food is eating the *Menü* at the restaurants below guesthouses. **Gästehaus zum Weißen Lamm,** Dr.-F-Morton Weg 166, across from the Heimatmuseum, serves large, tasty portions. Head downstairs to the "mountain man's cellar" for 2 daily *Menüs* (110 and 120AS) for lunch and dinner, including soup, salad, entree, and dessert (☎8311; open daily 10am-10pm). For cheaper, greasier fare, try **Imbiß Karl Forstinger** on Seestr. near the bus station. (☎6135. Hot dogs and bratwurst 35AS; open daily May-Oct. 10am-6pm). The cheapest fare is at the **Konsum** supermarket across from the main bus stop (open M-F 7:30am-noon and 3-6pm, Sa 7:30am-noon).

SIGHTS AND MUSEUMS

Hallstatt packs some heavy punches for tourists, despite its lean frame. The tourist office sells a 30AS English cultural guide, but exploring the narrow, crooked streets is entertainment in itself. Be sure to get a guest card at your accommodations to secure discounts at many attractions.

CHURCH AND CHARNEL HOUSE. The charnel house next to St. Michael's Chapel at the **Pfarrkirche** offers a fascinating, if macabre, anthropological perspective on the famous prehistoric burial scene in Hallstatt. Within the parish charnel house (*Beinhaus* in German, literally translated as bone-house), rest the bones of villagers from the 16th-century onwards, the latest added in 1995. The Celts buried their dead high in the mountains, but Christians wanted to be buried in the churchyard. Unfortunately, they soon ran out of space on their steep hillside, so after 10 or 20 years, the skull and femurs of the deceased were transferred to the charnel house to make room for more corpses (they're buried vertically as it is). Each of 610 neatly placed skulls was decorated with a wreath of flowers (for females) or ivy (for males) and inscribed with the name of the deceased and the date of death. The skulls were then packed in pyramids resting on a shelf which is supported by their neatly stacked femurs, tibiae, and fibulae. Today, bones are removed and painted only by special request. *(Reach the church from the ferry dock by following the signs reading "K.Kirche." Open May-Sept. daily 10am-6pm. In winter, call the Catholic church at 8279, for an appointment. 10AS, students 5AS.)*

HISTORICAL MUSEUMS. In the mid-19th century, an immense, incredibly well-preserved Iron Age archaeological find was discovered in Hallstatt, revealing a plethora of artifacts, a pauper's grave, and the well-maintained crypts of the ruling class—all circa 1000-500BC. The **Prähistorisches Museum,** across from the tourist office, exhibits some of these treasures, including coiled copper jewelry from the tombs and artifacts from the excavation site on Hallstatt's *Salzberg* (salt mountain). *(☎8208. Open daily Apr. 10am-4pm, May-Sept. 10am-6pm, Oct. 10am-4pm. 50AS, students 25AS, 40AS for groups of 10 or more.)* The price of admission also covers entrance to the tiny **Heimatmuseum** which besides a dusty collection of items of daily living, exhibits such exotica as acquisitions from Guatemala and East Africa, as well as, bizarrely enough, a large array of taxidermically stuffed animals, including a leopard, and a school of fish. Other treasures include swords and a set of biblically themed dioramas. *(Same hours as the Prähistorisches Museum.)*

SALT MINES. The 2500-year-old **Salzbergwerke** are the oldest saltworks in the world, though these days tourists have replaced miners in the tunnels. The surprisingly fascinating guided tours *(1½hr., in English and German)* include a zip down a wooden mining slide on a burlap sack which leads to an eerie lake deep inside the mountain. Be sure to ask for a salt-rock as a souvenir, or pick up the photo taken while you zipped down the slide. *(☎840 046. Open June to mid-Sept. 9:30am-4:30pm; Apr.-May and mid-Sept. to Oct. 9:30am-3pm. 140AS, with guest card 119AS, students 70AS, children under 4 not allowed.)* To reach the salt mines from the tourist office, walk down Seestr. away from the ferry dock and turn right at the bus circle. Follow the black signs with the yellow eyes to the **Salzbergbahn** *(May 29 to Sept. 24 9am-6pm, Sept. 25-Oct. 26 9am-4:30pm, last train runs 30min. before last tour. Rides every 15min. 65AS, round-trip 105AS, children 45AS, 60AS.)*, or take the easy **hike** (see below) to the mines.

OUTDOORS

HIKING. Hallstatt offers some of the most spectacular day hikes in the Salzkammergut, through forests where drops of water cling to the pine needles year-round, thanks to a climate very close to that of a temperate rainforest. The tourist office offers an excellent Dachstein hiking guide (90AS; in English), which details 38 hikes in the area, as well as a mountain bike trail map (35AS). Hike to nearby mountain huts (see guide) or try one of the following short hikes:

Salt mine (Salzbergwerk) hike (45min.). To make this hike, exit the tourist office right on Seestr., turning right at the bus stop and following the "Salzbergwerk" signs—be sure to note that a sign points out when to leave the asphalt trail and go onto the rocky trail.

This simple well-paved hike leads to the salt-mine tour. The hike proceeds mostly in a zig-zag, with each zig and zag giving you a more elevated and astonishing view of Hallstatt. The hike itself feels humid and looks more like a walk through a tropical forest than Austrian woods. Follow the same trail back, or take a cable car. As a 15min. diversion, walk through the marked memorial path, which is not only a resting place for salt barons, but a stroll through a lovely wood.

Waldbachstrub waterfalll hike (1¼hr.) is a light walk along a thundering river and up to a spellbinding waterfall. From the tourist office, turn right on Seestr. toward the bus station, and follow the brown sign reading "Malerweg" near the supermarket, and then continue to follow the subsequent "Malerweg" signs. The Waldbach river's roll will sound through most of the hike. Follow Malerweg straight, crossing over the various bridges, until after about 35min. the "Waldbachstrub" sign appears. Follow it, and be sure to keep to the well-trodden, increasingly steep trail marked by Austrian flags painted on the trees; do not follow the "Gonsteig" signs unless accompanied by a professional guide. Approach the end of the trail carefully, and you will be rewarded with a view of the Waldbachstrub waterfall, whose 2 major sources converge into a huge, beautiful roar. The only way to return is on the same trail that led to the waterfall.

Gonsteig (45min.-1½hr.), is a slippery, nefarious, primitive stairway carved onto the side of the cliff that is the Echental valley's right wall (the valley the Waldbackstrub waterfall is in). For experienced hikers only. Gangstieg is an hour up on the right side, while glacier gardens are about 40min. up on the left, before the mountain tunnel.

WATER SPORTS AND SKIING. For a view of the mountains from below rather than above, try a scenic boat trip around the lake, departing from either ferry landing. *(Schiffrundfarten; ☎8228. May to late Sept. 10:30am-4:45pm. 50min. ride 80AS.)* **Boat rental** costs 160AS per hour for an electric boat, 95AS for a paddle boat, and 75AS for a row boat. from **Hallstatt Schmuck** near the ferry landing by the tourist office. For **wild water canoeing,** contact Gasthof Seewint *(☎8246).* **Swimming** is free at Lahn near the bus station. Winter visitors can take advantage of Hallstatt's **ski bus** *(50AS, contact the tourist office for info),* which runs to the Krippenstein and Dachstein-West Ski areas, leaving Hallstatt several times a day. The tourist office can provide a map for area skiing.

DAYTRIP FROM HALLSTATT

OBERTRAUN AND THE DACHSTEIN CAVES ☎06134

To reach Obertraun from Hallstatt, walk to the Lahn bus station by turning right on Seestr. after the tourist office, where you can catch a bus to Obertraun (10min., 8:35am-4:50pm, 25AS). Stop at the cable car station for the ice caves. Ride the cable car up 1350m to "Schönbergalm" for the ice and mammoth cave. Cable car runs from 8:40am-5:50pm, last trip that arrives in time for a tour at 4:15pm, 170AS roundtrip, children 105AS. The Koppenbrüller cave is a 15min. walk from the bus stop in Obertraun.

At the end of the lake in Obertraun, the prodigious **Dachstein Ice Caves** testify to the geological hyperactivity that forged the region's natural beauty. There are 3 sets of caves: the **Rieseneishöhlen** (Giant Ice Caves) and the **Mammuthöhlen** (Mammoth Caves), even larger than the giant ones; and the **Koppenbrüllerhöhle,** a giant spring in a valley below the village of Obertraun. The ice caves look like some artist's conception of another world, and the eerie light work of the tour makes the huge, strange caves even stranger. Tours are in German, but no narration is needed to wonder at the caves. (☎8400. Open May to mid-Oct. daily 9am-5pm. Admission to either Giant Ice Cave or Mammoth Cave 90AS, children 45AS; combined "Gargantuan Experience" 150AS, 75AS.) The **tourist office** is located in the Gemeindeamt, Obertraun 180 (☎420 8596. Open M-F 8am-noon and 2-5pm; in summer also M-F 5-6pm, and Sa 9am-noon). An **ATM** is across the street at Volksbank. Obertraun's bright yellow **Jugendherberge (HI),** Winkl 26, is a refuge for summer hikers and winter skiers, as well as dozens of school children on class trips.

Rooms are clean and institutional. (☎360. Breakfast included. All rooms have showers. Reception 8am-1pm and 5-7:30pm. 10pm curfew. 4-,6-, and 10- bed dorms, 160AS, under 19 140AS. 12AS tourist tax.)

GMUNDEN ☎07612

Gmunden (pop. 16,000) is the picture of a resort town. Next to the **Traunsee,** the town has an illustrious guest-book and plenty of natural attractions. Posh boutiques and a knack for ceramic work mark the town today, but these dim next to its sunny lakeside beaches and stately mountains.

PRACTICAL INFORMATION AND ACCOMMODATIONS. **Trains** run frequently to Gmunden from **Salzburg** (1½hr., every hr. 3:20am-8:25pm, 160AS) and **Linz** (1hr., every hr. 5:10am-8:29pm, 114AS), both via **Attnang-Puchheim. Buses** connect Gmunden to the rest of the region, including **Grünau,** and depart from the post office. City **buses** provide connections inside the city, and their stops are marked with a green "City-Haltestell" sign. To reach the town center from the station, either turn left and follow Bahnhofstr. down the hill, or else hop on the tram in front of the station (18AS, day pass 22AS). From the tram's Franz-Josef Platz terminal, continue one block and turn left to reach the **tourist office,** Am Graben 2, which provides a list of *Privatzimmern* (210-300AS) and will call to find out if rooms are available. (☎74451. Open Oct.-Apr. M-F 8am-noon and 2-6pm; May-June, Sept. M-F 8am-6pm, Sa 9am-noon; July-Aug. M-F 8am-6pm, Sa-Su 9am-1pm and 5-7pm.) Consider heading to Grünau for the night. The **postal code** is A-4810.

SIGHTS AND OUTDOOR ACTIVITIES. Enjoy the beautiful **Traunsee** by strolling the promenade from the town center to the Habsburg **Villa Toscana,** and over the bridge to the **Seeschloß Ort** (sea castle) which sits like an imperial island. (☎77815. Tours Th and Su 2:30pm; 40AS.)

Gmunden has been a ceramic producing town since the 15th century, which explains the plethora of ceramic shops peeking around every corner. Get deep discounts on ceramic wares at **Gmundner Keramik** on Keramikstr. off Bahnhofstr. by asking the staff for the oh-so-slightly imperfect creations (☎7608. Open M-F 9am-6pm, Sa 9am-1pm). A less orthodox display of ceramics appears at the **Klo and So Museum für Historische Sanitärobjekte,** Pepöckhaus, Traung. 4, a collection of 19th- and 20th-century toilets. The eccentric exhibit includes the early 19th-century chameleon chair with a removable seat, *Biedermeier* wooden boxes, gilded *Jugendstil* toilets adorned with floral and faunal engravings, a *fin de siècle* circular bench draped in red robes with tassels and international specimens including short, blue-tiled Japanese urinals. The *pièce de résistance* is the Habsburg room where you can see Franz-Josef's bedroom john and Sisi's ornate bidet. Be sure to see the letter upstairs from the Japan Toilet Association bestowing the Nishioka prize on the museum for contributing to the "progress of toilet culture throughout the world." There isn't info about the toilets in English, so you are left wondering how one used the pot resting on the elaborate 1m metal structure, or the box covered in knives. (☎794 294. Open May-Oct. Tu-Sa 10am-noon and 2-5pm, Su 10am-noon. 20AS.) Admission to the Klo and So also includes entrance to the **Volkskunde-Ausstellung,** an exhibit of regional folklore in the same building (same hours as Klo and So).

With that big, beautiful Traunsee there, it is natural to want to play in it. For water-skiing, contact **Wasserskiclub Union Traunsee** (☎63602). The sailing information can be found by calling **Segelschule Gmunden** at 75100. **Festwochen Gmunden,** an outdoor concert series, takes place from mid-August to early September (tickets 60-440AS; info ☎70630). From June to August, outdoor concerts are held on the Esplanade or on boats. Get info at the tourist office. **Cruises** around the *Traunsee* on an old paddle steamer leave from the dock near Rathauspl. every 1½ hours (☎65215; daily May-Oct.; 20-85AS).

NEAR GMUNDEN: GRÜNAU ☎07616

Grünau is as far from the resort-ish Gmunden as they come, except when it comes to the gorgeous scenery. Sitting in the middle of the **Totes Gebirge** (Dead Mountains), Grünau is a tiny community with an incredible backyard, ideal for hiking, skiing, boating, fishing, swimming, and relaxing. To get to Grünau, a bus runs frequently from near the **Gmunden** post office (45min., 5:35am-5:20pm, 50AS). A small regional train also runs to Grünau from **Wels** which lies on many train lines (1hr., 6:47am-8:34pm 80AS). Call ahead to the hostel, and one of the staff will pick you up at the station free of charge. Grünau is best experienced from **The Treehouse,** Schindlbachstr. 525, a backpacker's dream resort. This secluded 40-bed lodge seems more like a quality hotel than a hostel (minus a few hundred schillings). Each room has its own bathroom with private shower and goosedown blankets. Once you've settled in, take advantage of its many facilities: tennis court, TV room with over 400 English-language movies, **Internet** access (25AS for 15min.), library, sauna, and basketball hoop (all free of charge, equipment provided), plus 2 bars for nighttime revelry. **Mountain bike** rental costs 70AS per day. The staff will organize adventure tours including **paragliding** (900AS), **canyoning** (650AS), **rafting** (590AS), **bungee jumping** (990AS, only on weekends), a flight over the surrounding mountains (400AS per person, 4 person minimum), and **horseback riding** (100AS per hr.). You can also ask the staff about the **shooting gallery.** For winter visitors, the **ski lift** is a 5-minute walk from the front door, and snow-gear (jackets, snowsuits, gloves, etc.) is provided free of charge. Day ski-lift passes are 250AS, and there is ski and snowboard rental (120AS and 150AS). Guests receive a discount on lift tickets (200AS) and ski and snowboard rental (100AS, 150AS).

Surrounded by mountains and three lakes one can take off on hikes using the free hiking map. The staff will also drop you off at a nearby mountain or lake. Speak to the staff about hiking possibilities. For a short (2hr.) hike, walk to the Kasberg Mountain (1500m) or the Spitzplaneck Mountain (1617m). Old mountain huts lie *en route* and provide a good view of the surrounding peaks. The more adventurous may try the longer, but not-too-difficult hike to Große Priel (2515m). It is often taken as a two-day trek with a mountain hut stay (150AS; ask the Treehouse staff for info) along the way. When back from a wander, the delicious homemade pizzas hit the spot, particularly the House-Haus pizza (75AS). (☎(07616) 8499; treehousehotel@hotmail.com; www.hostels.com/treehouse. Breakfast buffet included. 3-course dinners 90AS. Singles and doubles 200AS per person, triples 190AS, quads 170AS, 6-bed dorm 160AS. MC, Visa, AmEx, and travelers' checks.)

BAD ISCHL ☎06132

Bad Ischl (pop. 15,000) was a salt-mining town for centuries, until a certain Dr. Franz Wirer arrived in 1821 to study the curative properties of the heated brine baths in the area. Pleased with his findings, he began to prescribe brine bath vacations in Bad Ischl for his patients as early as 1822. Archduke Francis Charles and Archduchess Sophia journeyed to Bad Ischl seeking a cure for their state of childlessness and soon managed to produce 3 sons, the so-called **Salt Princes** (one was Franz Josef I, who made Bad Ischl his annual summer residence). Bad Ischl serves two types of budget travelers: those who are willing to splurge and enjoy the pleasures of an affordable resort, and those who wish to simply walk around and relax in an elegant town more substantial than the tiny hamlets in the area.

GETTING THERE AND AROUND

Only 1 **train** comes through the station, running between **Attnang-Puchheim** in the north (1¼hr., 5:05am-8:10pm, 87AS) and **Hallstatt** (30min., 7:07am-6:17pm, 38AS) and **Bad Aussee** (40min., 6:48am-8:19pm, 60AS) in the south. Trains go through these towns to **Vienna** (3¼hr., 400AS), **Linz** (157AS), and **Zell am See** (370AS). **Buses** leave from **Salzburg** (1½hr., every hr. 6:45am-7:15pm, 100AS), and **St. Wolfgang**

(35min., 5:10am-6:20pm, 60AS). **By car,** Bad Ischl lies on Rte. 158 and 145. From **Vienna,** take A-1 West to Rte. 145 at the town of Regau. From **Innsbruck** or **Munich,** take A-1 East past Salzburg and exit onto Rte. 158 near Thalgau. From **Salzburg,** the best way is to take Rte. 158 straight through St. Gilgen and Fuschl.

ORIENTATION AND PRACTICAL INFORMATION

Though it is one of the only towns in the Salzkammergut not on a lake, Bad Ischl lies at the junction of the **Traun** and **Ischl** rivers, which form a horseshoe around the city. Adjacent to the **bus station** (☎23113), the **train station** (☎244 070, desk open M-F 6:30am-6:30pm, Sa 8:05am-5:15pm, Su 10:25am-6:55pm) has **bike rental** (summer only; mountain bikes 150AS per day, 670AS per week; discount with train ticket) at the **luggage storage** window (open M-Sa 8am-5pm, Su 8:30am-2:30pm; 40AS per piece per day; ring for service). **Lockers** (20-30AS) are around the corner. The **tourist office,** Bahnhofstr. 6, can be reached from the station by turning left on Bahnhofstr. and walking for 2min. The office has extensive lists of *Pensionen* and *Privatzimmer*, and an excellent, free map—ask for the detailed one. (☎277 570 or 235 200; fax 277 5777. Open M-F 9am-7pm, Sa 9am-3pm, Su 10am-1pm.) The mustard-colored **post office** is 2min. farther down Bahnhofstr., on the corner of Auböckpl. (Open M-F 8am-noon, 2-6pm, Sa 9-11am. Phone, fax, and **currency exchange** available, currency closes at 5pm.) The **postal code** is A-4820.

ACCOMMODATIONS AND FOOD

Every guest who stays the night in Bad Ischl must pay a *Kurtax*, which entitles you to a guest card (June to mid-Sept. 25-30AS per person per night depending on proximity to the city center; Oct.-May 13-15AS). Bad Ischl's **Jugendgästehaus (HI),** Am Rechenstag 5, is minutes from the *Kaiser*'s summer residence. From the tourist office, walk left on Bahnhofstr., turn right on Kaiser-Franz-Josef-Str., and keep going until you see the *Jugendgästehaus* sign to the left across from the gas station. The hostel offers clean 1- to 5-bed rooms off long corridors. (☎26577; fax 265 7775. Sheets, showers, and breakfast included. Non-HI members pay 40AS surcharge. Reception 8am-1pm and 5-7pm. Quiet hour 10pm; keys available. Reservations recommended. Dorms 155AS.) If the hostel is full, try **Haus Stadt Prag,** Eglmoosg. 9 , which has spacious rooms with balconies. From the train station, go left on Bahnhofstr., right on Kaiser-Franz-Josef-Str., and left on Kreuzpl. Follow until it becomes Salzburgerstr., and bear left on Stiegeng. at the *Goldschmied* sign. Continue along Stiegeng. and up the steps—Haus Stadt Prag is the pink building on your right. (☎/fax 3616. Breakfast included. Singles 280AS, with bath 370AS; doubles 500AS, 700AS; 30AS extra with balcony.)

Restaurants are tucked into every possible niche along Schulg. and the other streets of the pedestrian zone. Cheap eats are available at the various *Imbiße* in town, particularly the **Börni Börges** stand, near the McDonald's on Dr.-Franz-Wirer Str., which serves up various burgers for 28-50AS. Right across from the Stadtpfarrkirche, **Café Ramsauer,** Franz-Josefstr. 8 serves up delicious and reasonably priced cafe fare, on a chandaliered, elegant interior, incongruous with the low prices. (☎22408. Open M-F 9am-8pm; Sa-Su 11am-6pm). Almost as famous as the *Kaiser* himself is the **Konditorei Zauner,** Pfarrg. 7 (☎23522). Established in 1832, this crowded eatery has an international reputation for heavenly sweets and *tortes*. Seat yourself and nosh on extravagant desserts (75-100AS) or gourmet sandwiches (26-42AS). The **Konsum grocery store** is conveniently located at Auböckpl. 12 (open M-F 7:30am-6:30pm, Sa 7:30am-5pm). Browse at the **open air market** held all day every Friday on Salinenpl.

SIGHTS AND OUTDOOR ACTIVITIES

Other than the baths, Bad Ischl's main attraction is what the Habsburgs left behind. Tours leave the **Trinkhalle** 2 blocks left of the tourist office (Su 10am, summer only Th 4pm, 30AS; free with guest card).

VILLAS. In 1854, Austria's last empress, Elisabeth, received the **Kaiservilla** as a wedding present from her mother-in-law. Though his wife didn't care for the place, Emperor Franz Josef made this his summer getaway palace and crammed it with expensive hunter gadgets. Inside, a vast collection of mounted chamois horns looks like the world's most decadent collection of coat hooks. Amidst the animal remains are many interesting relics of Franz Josef's reign, including the desk where he signed the declaration of war against Serbia in 1914 that led to WWI. Entrance is allowed only through a guided tour in German, with English text available. *(☎23241. Open May to mid-Oct. 9-11:45am and 1-4:45pm. 130AS, 120AS with guest card, students 50AS.)* Buy tickets for the tour when you enter the **Kaiserpark** (off Franz-Josef-Str.). Also within the *Kaiserpark*, you'll find the ivy-covered **Marmorschlößl** *(☎24422)*, which houses the **Photo Museum.** Entrance to the Photo Museum requires a pair of fluffy slippers (provided at the front desk) to protect the exquisite wood floors. Habsburg family photos complement temporary exhibitions. *(Open Apr.-Oct. 9:30am-5pm. 15AS, 12AS with guest card, students 10AS.)* The **Lehár Villa,** former home of beloved composer Franz, is worth a quick visit. *(Open May-Sept. daily 9am-noon and 2-5pm. Obligatory tour 55AS; with guest card 45AS; students and children 25AS.)*

PARISH CHURCH AND ORGAN. In the center of town, the **Stadtpfarrkirche** (city parish church) houses the magnificent late-Baroque **Kaiserjubiläumsorgel** (Emperor's Jubilee Organ). Turn left out of the tourist office, then right onto Franz-Josefstr.; the church will be on your left. Played by the likes of organ virtuoso and composer Anton Bruckner, the organ is one of the best in the world. Compact discs of performances are available for 230AS. Check in front of church for organ performance times.

SALBERGWERKE (SALT MINES). A tour through Bad Ischl's Salzbergwerke gets you under the surface of salt mining, literally and figuratively. *(☎200 2631. Open July-Aug. 10am-4:45pm, May 1-end of June and Sept. 1-20 9am-3:45pm. 140AS, with guest card 125AS, children 70AS.)* The mines are outside the city in Perneck and are best reached by car via Grazerstr. to Perneckstr. City bus #8096 also travels to Perneck and leaves from the *Bahnhof (2-5 times daily; last bus 4:15pm; 16AS, day pass 25AS).*

SALT BATHS. Whether or not the **brine baths** that Dr. Wirer talked up really have curative powers, Bad Ischl certainly has a relaxed atmosphere. The bath facilities are mostly in the posh **Kaiser Therme,** a resort across from the tourist office on Bahnhofstr. 1. Splash around in the heated salt baths with whirlpool or consider relaxing in the spacious **sauna.** Release pent-up stress through a **full-body massage** *(284AS for 25min.)*. Mud baths, acupuncture, and other more exotic experiences generally require a doctor's prescription. *(☎233 240; Verwaltung@Kaisertherme.co.at; www.salzkammergut.at/badischl/Kaisertherme. Open M-Sa 9am-9pm, Su 1:30-9pm, last entrance 8pm. 111AS for 3hr., children 57AS. Sauna open Tu-Su 1:30-9pm, Th women only, Tu men only. Combined ticket with pool 153AS for 3hr., children 81AS.)*

HIKING. Hiking paths are shown on a 98AS map available at the tourist office. A good place is around the summit of nearby **Mt. Katrin** (1544m). Get to the **Katrinseilbahn** *(cable car; 100AS. ☎23788)* by taking a city bus from the train station *(last bus 5pm)* or by walking for 15min. to the summit. The **Siriuskogel hike,** however, requires no cable car and rewards you with a wondrous panoramic view of Bad Ischl and environs. To begin the hike from the tourist office, exit the office left, walking toward the train station, continuing along until you have crossed the bridge on the left onto Grazerstr. Turn left onto Siriuskogelgasse, and follow the sign "Zum Siriuskogelgasse." Keep very diligently to the main, trodden trail up the mountain until the top. There you will find the **Gasthaus Siriuskogel.** *(☎25836.*

Be sure to call ahead before taking the stroll to make sure they are open.) The hike up is a pleasant 1hr. trip on a moderately steep forest trail. The view from the Gasthaus is fantastic and best enjoyed with one of the cheap dishes, averaging 50AS. The best way down is the way you came. **Bikers** can get a small trail map (93AS) as well as a trail map of the entire region *(98AS)*. In winter, Bad Ischl maintains an excellent network of **cross-country skiing** trails *(pick up free maps at the tourist office)*.

ENTERTAINMENT

For the low-down around town, pick up the brochure *Bad Ischl Events* from the tourist office. A free outdoor **Kurkonzert** takes place every day except Tuesday at the *Kurpark* along Wienerstr. *(Summer only, 10am and 4pm)*. The exact program of pieces to be performed by the 20-piece *Kurorchestra* is posted weekly on kiosks, in the hotels, and at the *Kurhaus* itself. Every year in mid-August, the **Bad Ischler Stadtfest** brings a weekend of music—classical, pop, jazz, boogie-woogie, oom-pah-pah, etc. Just before the *Stadtfest* on August 15, the Bad Ischlers celebrate Franz Josef's birthday with live music on the Esplanade. From July 11 until August 29, the **Bad Ischl Operetten Festspiele** celebrates the musical talent of operetta composer **Franz Lehár,** who lived in Bad Ischl for 30 years and created *The Merry Widow*, *Gypsy Love*, and *The Land of Smiles*. Tickets are available from *Büro der Operettengemeinde Bad Ischl*, Wiesengerstr. 7, A-4820 Bad Ischl *(☎23839; fax 238 39 39. Open M-Sa 9am-noon and 2-5pm; 200-500AS)*. After June 30, purchase tickets from the Bad Ischl *Kurhaus (☎23766; fax 23384. Open M-F 9am-noon and 3-6pm)*. From April to October, a **flea market** comes to the Esplanade on the first Saturday of the month. Bad Ischl indulges in all sorts of Yuletide festivities, including a **Christkindlmarkt** (Christmas market), Advent caroling in the *Kurhaus*, tours of elaborate **Weihnachtskrippen** (nativity scenes) in the area, and horse-drawn sleigh rides *(Pferdeschliffen)*.

ST. WOLFGANG ☎06138

According to local legend, Bishop Wolfgang of Regensburg hurled his axe into the valley of the **Abersee** in 976AD. Where the axe landed, he built a church, and to protect it, Wolfgang supposedly battled the devil on a rocky outcropping. Once its founder had been canonized for his miraculous feats, the church on the *Abersee* (now the **Wolfgangsee**) became the object of mass pilgrimage. Present-day pilgrims, who come in throngs, are most likely to be the camcorder-and-fanny-pack-toting variety; the pilgrimage site has become a tourist trap. But the tourists are right about something: St. Wolfgang is a great little town to get lost in, and the nearby *Wolfgangsee* and *Schlafberg* provide ample outdoor recreation.

GETTING THERE AND GETTING AROUND

Wolfgang sprawls lazily on the shore of the *Wolfgangsee*, across the water from St. Gilgen. St. Wolfgang has no train station, but **buses** run every hour to **Bad Ischl** (35min., 5:13am-8:08pm, 40AS) and **Salzburg** (1½ hr., 6:45am-7:15pm, 90AS, change at Strobl). A breezy option is the Wolfgangsee **ferry** (☎22320), which runs to nearby **St. Gilgen** (50min., 9:20am-3:20pm, 54AS) and **Strobl** (30min., 8:45am-2:47pm, 40AS) and between St. Wolfgang's 2 ferry landings at St. Wolfgang Markt and the Schafbergbahnhof. (Ferry runs May-Oct. 8:15am-6:15pm. Day passes 200AS, week passes available. Children half price. Eurail valid.) To get to St. Wolfgang from Vienna by car, take A1 West to Mondsee and then head south through St. Lorenz and Scharfling and on to St. Wolfgang. From Salzburg, take Rte. 158 east through Hof, Fuschl, and St. Gilgen.

ORIENTATION AND PRACTICAL INFORMATION

St. Wolfgang, while great to get lost in, can be hard to get around. Street names are very difficult to find, and maps are often not useful—the passing pedestrian is likely to be the best source of directions. A tunnel cuts around the downtown area, with the **bus stop** just outside its western entrance. The **tourist office,** Pilgerstr. 28 is a block or so away. (☎2239; fax 223 981; info@stwolfgang.gv.at; www.salzkammergut.at/wolfgangsee. Open summer M-F 9am-7pm, Sa 9am-noon and 2-6pm, winter M-F 9am-noon and 2-6pm.) Look for a pea-green building on the left, labeled *Marktgemeindeamt*, and pick up the useful **Wolfgangsee Info** pamphlet. An **information kiosk** is farther down the main stretch, by Hotel Peter. Services include: **ATMs** adjacent to the tourist office and in the wall of the **Sparkasse** in Marktpl.; **public bathrooms** at the bus stop and behind the tourist office; **currency exchange** available at the **post office,** around the corner and down the block from the bus stop (☎2201. Open M-F 8am-noon and 2-6pm, Sa 8-11am; exchange open M-F 8am-5pm); and a **pharmacy** near Hotel Peter (M-F 8am-noon, 2-6pm, Sa 8am-noon, Su 9-11am.) The **postal code** is A-5360.

ACCOMMODATIONS AND FOOD

Almost 2000 tourists troop through St. Wolfgang every sunny summer day. The tourist office's brochure lists a canon of hotels, *Pensionen*, and private rooms. Also consider the Berghotel Schafbergspitze in the sights section.

Haus am See, Michael-Pacher-Str. 98 (☎2224), has 50 beds in a rambling old house right on the lake. From the tourist office, simply continue down the main road away from the post office (7min.) until you reach the east entrance of the tunnel; the *Haus* is just beyond, on the right. The bathrooms are not as gorgeous as the view, but the shore access more than compensates. Herr Brosch will even let guests borrow his paddleboat and rowboat. Breakfast included. Hall showers. Parking available. Open May-Oct. Prices depend on balcony and view. Singles 170-280AS; doubles 360-550AS; 2-room quads 800-1000AS. Herr Brosch also runs a **boathouse,** which has the cheapest beds in town. Primitive rooms, but the balcony is literally over the lake and the boathouse has a large, well-kept grass area for picnicking. Beds in singles and doubles start at 150AS.

Gästehaus Raudaschl, Deschbühel Au 41 (☎2561). From the tourist office, continue down the main road, and turn left at Hotel Peter. Climb up the small hill, and it's on the left (5min.). This smaller *pension*, on the way to the major hiking paths, offers a private balcony in each of 7 well-furnished rooms. Breakfast included. Open May-Oct. Singles 230AS, doubles 420AS, with shower 460AS.

Camping Berau, Schwarzenbach 16 (☎2543; camping@berau.at; www.berau.at), rents tents for 60AS. One-time charge of 128AS; 65AS per night, children 45AS.

FOOD

Most of St. Wolfgang's restaurants and *Imbiße* price their wares very competitively. Try any of the snack shacks lining the road from the tourist office into town, where almost nothing is above 55AS. *Konditoreien* also serve up a local specialty—**Schafbergkugeln** (about 23AS), named after the mountain. A variant of the *Mozartkugel*, the *Schafbergkugel* is a tennis-ball-sized hunk of milk chocolate filled with cream, spongecake, nuts, and marzipan. Pick one up at **Bäckerei Gandl,** Im Stöckl 84 (☎2294. Open daily 7am-7pm). Across from the tourist office, the **ADEG** market sells fruits of all kinds and standard groceries (open M-F 7:30am-noon and 2-6pm, Sa 7:30am-6pm).

SIGHTS AND OUTDOOR ACTIVITIES

WALLFAHRTSKIRCHE (PILGRIMAGE CHURCH). St. Wolfgang's main attraction, the **Wallfahrtskirche,** is in the center of town. The church is terrifically ornate, with scarcely an inch outside the pews not intricately decorated. It is worthwhile to just sit down and let your eyes notice the thousands of unexpected details. **Michael Pacher's** altarpiece is the magnificent focal point of the church's interior. Completed by Pacher in 1480, after a decade of labor, the altarpiece opens up like a heavenly closet to expose the coronation of Mary, complete with angels blowing their horns over the virgin. The Schwanthaler Altar is in the middle of the church behind wrought-iron gates. Installed in 1676, the high-Baroque altar was originally made to replace Pacher's one, but the sculptor Thomas Schwanthaler bravely persuaded the abbot to leave Pacher's masterpiece alone. Together the altars almost overwhelm the church—don't miss smaller treasures like Schwanthaler's Rosenkranzaltar (Rose Garland Altar), or the St. Wolfgang memorial room. *(Turn right out of the tourist office and head straight down the road.)*

SCHAFBERGBAHN. St. Wolfgang's other major attraction is the **Schafbergbahn**, a romantic steam engine that laboriously ascends to the summit of Schafberg. The railway was built in 1892, and Hollywood found it charming enough to deserve a cameo in *The Sound of Music*, with the Von Trapp children waving from the windows. From the top, dozens of trails wind down the mountain, leading to such nearby towns as St. Gilgen, Ried, and Falkenstein. Train tickets for the 40-minute ride run as steep as the mountain. *(☎22320. Train runs May-Oct., 1 per hr. 7:15am-6:40pm. Round-trip tickets discounted at 7:15 and 8:10am. Ascent 150AS, children 75AS, half-way 115AS, round-trip 260AS; Eurail valid.)* If you must pay full price, you might as well take advantage of the special deal offered by the **Berghotel Schafbergspitze** *(☎3542; fax 35424)*, a lovely mountain inn peeking over the Schafberg's steepest face. For 550AS per person, you get a round-trip ticket on the railway, a night's lodging in a room (with shower) as well as breakfast. Reserve in advance.

WATER SPORTS. The big, clear *Wolfgangsee* guarantees that water-sport lovers will be kept busy. If you like **swimming,** you can go off the deep end at Strandbad Ried *(☎2587; 40AS, children 20AS)*. Or, if you are willing to do with a small free spot from which to take a dip, exit the tourist office, turn right onto the main road into town, walk for about 15min., and follow the "boot vermietung" sign on the right until the public sea-bath comes into view. Water-skiing is available through Stadler *(☎(0663) 917 9753; 120AS per round)* on the Seepromenade. Rent boats at the beach on Robert-Stolz-Str. across from the tennis courts or in town at the landing near Marktpl. *(Motor boats 30min. 95AS, 1hr. 150AS. Pedal boats 30min, 65AS. Row boats 55AS. Open in summer daily 8am-7pm.)*

OTHER ACTIVITIES. Hiking the mountains at the lake's edge is another possibility. All trails are marked clearly and described in detail in the English *Info* brochure, free at the tourist office. The tourist office also sponsors guides. Hiking maps cost 10AS (small) and 65AS (big). To pass a Friday evening in St. Wolfgang, catch a production of local composer Ralph Benatzky's romantic-comic operetta "White Horse Inn" (a.k.a. *Zum Weißen Rössl*), which became world famous in 1930 *(May, June, and Sept. F 7:30pm; tickets 220-360AS available through the Singspielbüro, ☎2239)*.

MONDSEE ☎06232

The Salzkammergut's warmest lake, the **Mondsee** (Moon Lake), is named for its crescent shape. Water sports are raised to a pinnacle in this stunning locale, taking on almost spiritual dimensions. The town of Mondsee (pop. 3000) lies at the northern tip of the lake and is best enjoyed as a relaxing spot from which to indulge in those distinctly un-relaxing watersports.

GETTING THERE AND AROUND. Mondsee has no train station but is accessible by **bus** from **Salzburg's** main train station (50min., 1 per hr. 6:35am-8:30pm, 60AS). Buses also run 3 times a day from Mondsee to **St. Gilgen** on the *Wolfgangsee* (20min., 8:40am, 12:45pm, and 6:45pm, 29AS). To get to Mondsee by car, take Autobahn A-1, or, for a more scenic drive, take Rte. 158 from Salzburg to St. Gilgen and then Rte. 154 along the edges of the lake to downtown Mondsee.

ORIENTATION AND PRACTICAL INFORMATION. To reach the **tourist office,** Dr.-Franz-Müllerstr. 3, from the bus stop, head up the road past the post office, turn right on Rainerstr., and continue to the end. Turn right again, and the office is on the left. The English-speaking staff gladly gives out every brochure they have and finds accommodations. Their free sightseeing pamphlet details various self-guided tours, hikes and biking tours, a map, and also provides a directory with important phone numbers and recreation information. A box in front of the office is stuffed with maps of Mondsee, available at all hours. (☎2270 or 4270; fax 4470; info@mondsee.org; www.mondsee.org. Open July-Aug. daily 8am-7pm, Sept.-June M-F 8am-noon and 1-5pm.) The **post office,** on Franz-Kreuzbergerstr. to the left and across the street from the bus station, is the most convenient place for **currency exchange** (☎26650. Open M-F 8am-noon and 2-6pm, in summer also open Sa 8-10am; exchange closes at 5pm). There are **ATMs** at the Volksbank by the tourist office and at the Raiffeisenbank on Rainerstr. **Public restrooms** are under the *Rathaus* in Marktpl. The **postal code** is A-5310.

ACCOMMODATIONS AND FOOD. Gasthöfe and hotels crowd the area near Marktpl., and private rooms a little further away, waving red "Zimmer Frei" flags. The **Jugendgästehaus (HI),** Krankenhausstr. 9, has doubles and quads with private showers, as well as one 10-bed dorm. From the bus station, walk up Kreuzbergerstr. toward the post office, turn right on Rainerstr., walk uphill, then go left on Steinbachstr. At the first intersection, go left 10m and then right up narrow Krankenhausstr. Follow the signs to the hostel; it's hidden off a driveway to the left and uphill. The main entrance is below the brown balcony. It's often filled with groups, so call ahead. (☎2418; fax 241 875. Breakfast included; lunch and dinner available in restaurant. Non-members pay 14AS surcharge. Reception M-F 8am-1pm and 5-7pm, Sa, Su 5-7pm. Curfew 10pm; key available. Dorms 135AS; doubles 370-470AS; quads 620-820AS.)

The Marktplatz is brimming with restaurants and *Gasthöfe* serving Austrian and Italian dishes. For delicious coffee and cake (and at better prices than the cookie-cutter cafes in front of the church), head to **Café Übleis,** Badg. 6, right by the tourist office. They specialize in homemade *Mozartkugeln* and ice cream. (☎2433. Open July-Aug. 9am-11pm; Sept.-June 9am-9pm.) **Pizzeria Nudelini,** Marktpl. 5, upstairs in the blue building just down from the church, sells inexpensive, but good Italian-style pizza (68AS for a large cheese) and provides a terrific salad bar (small 38AS, large 58AS; ☎4193. Open Su-W noon-2pm and 5:30-11pm, F-Sa 5:30-11pm). **China Restaurant,** Rainerstr. 13, has a lunch deal for the budget-conscious that includes soup and an entree for 62 to 69AS (☎4468. Open daily 11:30am-2:30pm and 6-11pm; MC, Visa.) **SPAR Markt,** Rainserstr.5, is just past the main square on the way to the hostel (open M-F 7:30am-6:30pm, Sa 7:30am-1pm). A **farmers' market** comes to town every Sa during the summer in Karlsgarten, near the church (8am-noon).

SIGHTS, OUTDOOR ACTIVITIES, AND ENTERTAINMENT. Mondsee is the closest lake resort to Salzburg and one of the least touristed, despite occasional air-conditioned tour buses which rumble in and out the town to see the local **Pfarrkirche,** site of the wedding scene in *The Sound of Music*. The church connects to the authentic remains of a Benedictine monastery dating from 748. The open-air **Freilichtmuseum,** on Hilfbergstr. (behind the church and uphill to the right), features a 500-year-old smokehouse, dairy, and farmhouse all in one. Wander all around playing with myriad antique farm tools and utensils. (Open Apr. Sa,

Su 9am-6pm, May-Sept. daily 9am-6pm, first half of Oct. 9am-5pm, second half of Oct. Sa, Su 9am-5pm. 30AS, seniors 25AS, students 15AS. English info sheet 5SFr.)

In summer, the Mondsee waters buzz with activity. **Alpenseebad,** the public beach is great for swimming with beautiful people, but jumping in at undesignated areas along the shore is forbidden by the lake's wildlife conservation laws (☎2291. Open in fair weather May-Sept. daily 8:30am-7pm; 30AS, children 12AS; after 1:30pm 18AS, 6AS). To go out a little farther, rent a **boat** from Peter Hemetsberger on the shore by the playground, down the street from the tourist office (☎2460 or 4934. Rowboats 75-90AS per hr., paddleboats 100AS, electric boats 130-150AS). Hemetsberger also offers *Seerundfahrten*, boat rides around the lake (40min., boats leave 10:45am, 2, and 3:30pm. Ride 63AS, 1hr. 90AS, 90min. 120AS; children half price). **Water-skiing,** with Wasserskizentrum (☎(0664) 432 3103), costs 130AS per circuit, and 2-person rafting costs 130AS per circuit.

Mondsee holds the **Musiktage,** an annual classical music festival in early September (tickets 100-480AS). Contact the tourist office well in advance for more information. Every year **Hugo von Hofmannsthal's** 1922 morality play, *Jedermann*, is performed (in German) at the open-air **Freilichtbühne** theater every Saturday from mid-July to mid-August (tickets 140-160AS; advance tickets are available at the Salzburger Sparkasse in Marktpl. and at the tourist office).

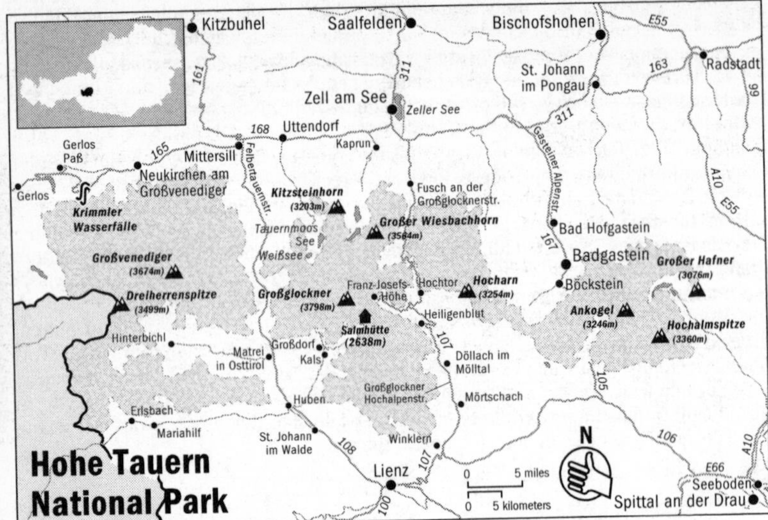

HOHE TAUERN NATIONAL PARK REGION

The enormous **Hohe Tauern** range, part of the Austrian Central Alps, extends well into the provinces of Carinthia, Salzburg, Tyrol, and East Tyrol. All together, the range boasts 246 glaciers and 304 mountains over 3000m. Sheets of ice, grassy heaths, and forested bulwarks partition the Ice-Age valleys. The heart of this Alpine landscape remains largely unspoiled, a fact that prompted conservationists to lobby for the creation of a the **Hohe Tauern National Park.** Between 1958 and 1964, large tracts of mountain land in Salzburg and Carinthia were declared preserves. On October 21, 1971, the provincial government leaders of Carinthia, Salzburg, and Tyrol signed an agreement at Heiligenblut to "conserve for present and future generations the Hohe Tauern as a particularly impressive and varied region of the Austrian Alps." Thus designated, the Hohe Tauern National Park became the largest national park in all of Europe, officially enclosing 29 towns and 60,000 residents, though most of the actual protected park territory is uninhabited.

Appropriately, **Heiligenblut** is the town where the founding papers were signed, because it is the most central town from which to enjoy the splendors of the park. There are a number of other towns that serve as good gateway towns for the park. **Zell am See** and **Lienz,** which lie on either end of the *Großglockerstraße* are the big cities that allow the easiest access, while tiny **Krimml** has its famous waterfalls, and a few places to crash between strenuous hikes.

HIGHLIGHTS OF THE HOHE TAUERN REGION

Make the trip between Lienz and Zell am See, the areas two most exciting cities, on the **Großglocknerstraße,** the world's most exciting highway (see p. 250).

Sleep in the shadow of Austria's mightiest mountain, the Großglockner, in the tiny mountain town of **Heiligenblut** (see p. 252).

Go skiing on the glacier above **Zell am See,** in August (see p. 256).

NATIONAL PARK AND THE GROßGLOCKNERSTRAßE

Unlike national parks in other countries, the Hohe Tauern National Park is not owned by the government, but rather by a consortium of private farmers and members of the **Österreichische Alpenverein** (ÖAV; Austrian Alpine Union). With the exception of the park's mountainous core, many of the alpine meadows and valleys are used for agriculture and forestry. Farmers still herd their cattle over the same 2500m *Tauern* (ice-free mountain paths) once trod by Celts and Romans. The **Glocknergruppe,** in the heart of the park, contains Austria's highest peak, the **Großglockner** (3798m), as well as many alpine lakes and glaciers. The parks ecosystems contains rare trees flowers, marmots, vultures, and lyre-horned ibex (reintroduced into the park in the 1950s and 60s after having been hunted to near extinction). A lazy drive—or a vigorous bike ride—down the *Großglockerstraße*, the paragon of scenic routes, offers a beautiful, if summary, look at the peaks and valleys of the park. Rest stops with picnic tables dot the highway, and provide vistas of valleys that can be explored only by foot.t

GETTING AROUND THE PARK

MOTORIZED TRANSPORT. The park is accessible by car, bus, and, in certain parts, by train. By **car** from Kitzbühel, take Bundesstr. 161 south to 108, which leads through the park. From Zell am See, take Bundesstr. 311 south to 107. From Lienz, take Bundesstr. 107 or 108 north into the park. In case of **breakdown** call the ÖAMTC (☎120). Two **train** lines service towns near the park: a rail line from Zell am See runs west along the northern border of the park, terminating in Krimml (1¾hr., 6:28am-6:49pm, 100AS); another runs south from Salzburg to Badgastein in the southwest corner of the park (1½hr., every 2hr. 7:14am-8:15pm, 170AS).

The park itself is criss-crossed by **bus** lines, which operate on an incredibly complicated timetable, with some buses running infrequently, and other buses changing schedules in early summer. Be sure to ask for specific connections at local tourist offices to avoid getting stranded. Most buses don't have a number but are classified by their end station. Bus routes from all directions go through the center of the park at **Franz-Josefs-Höhe.** From **Zell am See** in the north, the bus goes directly to the Höhe (2hr.; June 19-Oct. 10 daily 10:15am; July 10-Sept. 12 M-F 9:15am and 12:15pm; 145AS). From **Lienz** in the south, take the bus to Heiligenblut and connect to Franz-Josefs-Höhe (1½hr.; buses to Heiligenblut 10am-6:20pm, from Heiligenblut to Franz-Josefs-Höhe 8:40am-4:05pm seasonally, daily at 11am, 107AS total fare). **Return** trips run from Franz-Josefs-Höhe to **Zell am See** (2hr.; July-Sept. M-F 11:45am, 3, and 4pm, Sa-Su 3pm; Sept.-Oct. M-Su 3pm); **Heiligenblut** (30min., 9:30am-4:46pm, Su 4:30pm, 47AS); and **Lienz** (1½hr., daily at 11:50am).

NON-MOTORIZED TRANSPORT. The best **cycling** opportunity in the area is the **Tauernweg** which goes from Krimml to Zell am See (and then keeps going on to Salzburg). Area tourist offices and www.radtouren.at/english have more info on the route. Cyclists can also ride the grueling Großglockerstraße, but be aware that since the National Park is foremost a preserve, cycles are not always allowed.

Hiking trails head out and up into the isolated valleys from every road. In almost every valley there is a mountain hut, offering a place to crash and a base from which to explore. An excellent brochure to have is *Der BundesBus ist Wanderfreundlich* (available at the bus stations in Lienz and Zell am See and the tourist offices in Lienz and Heiligenblut), which contains a schedule of bus departure times, destinations, maps, hiking paths, and other general information. For Anglophones there is a good list and description of hikes on the park's website, but the best idea is to purchase a topographic map of the area and talk to the local tourist office. For safety info and advice on hiking see Essentials p. 28.

ORIENTATION

The center of the park, and BundesBus hub, is **Franz-Josefs-Höhe** and the **Pasterze glacier** (see p. 251), which sits right above the town of Heiligenblut. Despite its name, the Höhe is not a very high spot compared to the 3000m mountains that surround it. Aside from the skiing and hiking on those steep monsters, the main tourist attractions in the park are the **Krimml Waterfalls,** in the northwestern corner, just west of Zell am See, and the **Großglocknerstraße** (Bundesstr. 107), a spectacular high mountain road that runs north/south through the center of the park, between Zell am See and Lienz in the south, through the Franz-Josef-Höhe.

PARK INFORMATION

Due to the park's distribution over 3 different provinces, the network of tourist information is quite decentralized. You can find general information on the park by calling ☎(4875) 5112, emailing nphrt@netway.at, or checking the main website at www.npht.sbg.ac.at, which has an English page. For more specific information you're probably best off talking to the park service branch in whichever province of the park you are visiting. Most of the park falls within Salzburgerland, but the Tyrolean branch is designated as the official headquarters for the entire national park. The **Kärnten (Carinthia) Park Office** is located in Döllach (☎(04825) 6161; hohe.tauern@nationalpark-kaernten.or.at); the **Tyrol office** in Matrei (☎(04875) 5161; npht.tirol@netway.at); and the **Salzburg office** in Neukirchen (☎(06565) 6558; nationalpark@salzburg.or.at). Be aware, however, that the park has small offices scattered throughout the area, and tourist offices in all the towns listed by *Let's Go* are well-acquainted with park information.

ACCOMMODATIONS

If you're interested in coming home to a big city every night, Zell am See and Lienz are good bases for exploring the park. If you would like a smaller mountain town, closer to the park, both Krimml and Heiligenblut serve as convenient places to stay the night. Heiligenblut is more centrally located on the bus line between Zell am See and Lienz (more specifically between Franz-Josef-Höhe and Lienz). If you want to leave all trappings of civilization behind you can stay in the mountain huts that dot the park. A few that are within a day's hike of Heiligenblut, and that provide intimate views of the great Großglockner are the **Salmhütte** (2638m, 5hr. hike from Heiligenblut; ☎(04824) 2089; open July-late Sept.), and the **Glorerhütte** (2642m, 1½hr. from Salmhütte; ☎(0663) 57582; open mid June-mid Oct.). The **Erzherzog-Johann-Hütte,** built in 1880, is, at 3454m, the highest hut in the park, and the closest one to the Großglockner peak (☎(04876) 500 or 444; open July- early-Oct.; only for experienced mountain hikers or guides). For a full list of huts pick up a *Hüttenführer* at any tourist office. For more information on these and other huts contact the ÖAV in Lienz (see p. 260).

THE GROẞGLOCKNERSTRAẞE

Each day more than 3000 visitors pack up their cars for a full-day sail among the Austrian Alps along the breath-taking **Großglocknerstraße,** one of the most beautiful highways in the world. Skirting the country's loftiest mountains, Bundesstr. 107 (its less catchy moniker) winds for 50km amid silent Alpine valleys, meadows of wildflowers, tumbling waterfalls, and huge glaciers between Zell am See and Lienz. The road passes its highest point at **Hochtor,** 2505m above sea level. The slow, steady climb is choked with rubber-neckers and over-ambitious cyclists soaking up the stupefying views. Many of the high-mountains-sweeping-panorama-hairpin-turn-sports-car commercials are filmed here. Switzerland and France used the Großglockner as a model when engineering their own mountain highways.

DRIVING SAFETY TIPS. Many first-time drivers of the Großglocknerstraße are tempted to lean heavily on the brakes, which can lead to brake failure and overheating. Instead, shift to low gear, drive slowly, and never, ever pass anyone.

The trip up to Hochtor takes you from the flora and fauna of Austria into Arctic like environments (never exceeding 50°F even during the hottest summers). Though the highway is officially only the 6.4km stretch from **Bruck an der Großglockner** to **Heiligenblut,** tours generally run from Zell am See or Lienz to the Franz-Josef-Höhe. Total transport time on the Großglockner (with scenic rest stops in between) is 5 hours. Many visitors traverse the Großglocknerstr. in a **tour bus** or **rental car,** neither of which is recommended for those with light pocketbooks or weak stomachs. For budget travelers the **public buses** serve as excellent tour buses, at much lower prices (see p. 249). If you only have one day, resist the urge to disembark at any of the cutesy villages along the way; buses come so infrequently that you'll be stuck in Nowheresdorf for hours. Your time is better spent at the **Franz-Josefs-Höhe,** enjoying the magnificent views. Try to choose a clear day to go—you don't want to pay the entrance fee when viewing conditions are poor. If you are driving you must pay a **toll** at Ferleiten (on the Zell am See side) or Roßbach (on the Heiligenblut side) of 350AS for cars and 230AS for motorcycles. Parking at Franz-Josefs-Höhe is free with your toll receipt. There are also parking and pull-off areas strategically situated at numerous lookout points along the road. The warmer weather from June to September creates the best driving conditions. Be aware that the park forbids traffic from 10pm to 5am. Snowfalls, dumping up to 4m of heavy snow on the road, force the Großglockner to close entirely from October to April. For info on the road conditions call the information office in Heiligenblut (☎(04824) 2212). It is important to note that Großglocknerstr. itself is not part of the National Park, nor under its auspices. Be aware of this when asking park volunteers about the road, or road officers about the park.

ACTIVITIES ALONG THE GROẞGLOCKNERSTRAẞE

FRANZ-JOSEFS-HÖHE. Großglocknerstraße buses from Zell am See, Lienz, and Heiligenblut finish their routes at Franz-Josefs-Höhe, a large observation and tourist center stationed above the Pasterze glacier. Naturally, Franz-Josefs-Höhe is packed with tour buses and camera-toting visitors, but even they can't detract from the sight of the glacier's icy tongue extending down the valley. If the weather's right, you can glimpse the summit of the Großglockner (3797m) peeking through the clouds on the left wall of the valley. Franz-Josefs-Höhe has its own **park office** *(☎(04824) 2727)* at the beginning of the parking area, with its own free mini-museum and Hohe Tauern information center. The office organizes free daily walks around the glacier in July and Aug.; call ahead for times. The staff can also answer questions about the availability and opening times of the mountain huts in the vicinity. *(Open daily 10am-4pm.)* There are several restaurants and snack-bars scattered around Franz-Josefs-Höhe; some of the larger souvenir shops sell inexpensive sandwiches, but the restaurants tend to have prices as high as the altitude.

GLACIER FUNICULAR AND OBSERVATION CENTER. The **Gletscherbahn funicular** ferries you down from Franz-Josefs-Höhe to the glacier itself, where you can walk about 100m across its hard-packed surface *(☎(04824) 2502 or 2288. Funicular runs May 21 to Oct. 10, daily 9am-2pm. Round-trip 98AS, children 55AS.).* Alternately, you can hike down to the bottom yourself (see Hiking, below). Better catch it while you can—the glacier has shrunk 2m in depth in the last few years and will probably continue to shrink unless climate trends dramatically reverse.

Take the *Panoramaweg* near the information office up the hill for a great view (sans a ton of tourists) and walk down it to the **Swarovski Observation Center** for an even better view. The center is a crystal-shaped building that houses

3 floors of binoculars and telescopes for viewing the surrounding terrain. If you're lucky, you might spot some ibex chewing the grass on the mountain behind you. You won't need fancy specs to see the ubiquitous marmots, which are fat, furry, beaver-like rodents who beg crumbs from tourists. You're not supposed to feed them, but try saying no to those cute little noses. *(Open daily 10am-4pm. Free.)*

HIKING. There are infinite opportunities for hikes within the parks. Check the introduction to the park for where to attain further hiking information. There are a number of short hikes in the area of Franz-Josefs-Höhe; the national park office can point you in the right direction, and sells hiking maps (119AS). The professional-level **Glacier Hike** takes about 45 min. one way and can be reached by exiting the National Park office, turning right and descending down the stairs near the cable-car. Be sure you know what you're doing, and stick to the trail. Once at the bottom you can take a look at the glacier and, unusually for the area, stand not on a peak but in a valley. You can also hire a **guide** for hiking, climbing, or ski touring (call the park office in Heiligenblut, ☎(04824) 2700; fax 27004; daily 10am-5pm).

MUSEUMS. The **Glocknerwiesen Museum** is inarguably the Großglocknerstraße's cutest attraction. Located in a small building off the road from Franz-Josefs-Höhe to Heiligenblut (1km before the Guttal intersection) next to the Schoeneck Café, this unmanned museum gives you the low-down on what the birds and the bees have been doing in these mountain pastures for millennia. Exhibits in English and German illustrate the variety of flora, local agricultural techniques, the scents of local flowers, and the erotic trickery employed by blossoms to woo bees. *(Open in "daylight hours," approx. 8am-9pm in summer. Free.)* Coming from Zell am See, you'll pass the **Museum of Alpine Nature** (2300m). The small museum features well-designed nature exhibits, a 25-minute movie (in German), and frightening photos of hikers who forgot to wear sunblock. If you take the bus up here in the summer, you'll have half an hour to roam through the exhibits before the bus leaves for Franz-Josefs-Höhe. *(Open 9am-5pm. Free. English headphones 20AS.)*

HEILIGENBLUT ☎04824

The most convenient and inexpensive accommodations for those wishing to explore Franz-Josefs-Höhe and the Hohe Tauern region can be found in Heiligenblut, a tiny town right in the middle of the Großglocknerstraße, the closest town to the highest mountain in Austria, and a great jumping off point for many hikes in the park. The town's name, which means "holy blood," derives from a legend about a Byzantine general named Briccius who perished nearby in a snowstorm. He carried with him a precious vial supposedly containing a few drops of Christ's blood, now housed in a reliquary in the town church.

TRANSPORT AND PRACTICAL INFORMATION. Heiligenblut can be reached by **bus** from **Franz-Josefs-Höhe** (30min., 9:30am-4:40pm, 47AS), **Zell am See** (2½hr., 3 per day, 145AS), and **Lienz** (1hr., 6 per day, 72AS). The bus stop is in the parking lot in front of Hotel Glocknerhof. The **tourist office,** Hof 4, up the street from the bus stop and Hotel Glocknerhof, dispenses information about accommodations, hiking, sporting activities, and park transportation. (☎200 121; fax 200 143. Open Sept.-June M-F 8:30am-noon and 2:30-6pm, Sa 9am-noon and 4-6pm; July-Aug. M-F 8:30am-6pm). The **post office** is located below the center of town at the bottom of the hill and **exchanges money.** Follow the main road past the chair lift for about 10-15 min. following "Postamt" signs when they appear. (☎2201. Open M-F 8am-noon and 1:30-5pm, Sa 8:30-10:30am. Exchange closed 4pm.) An **ATM** is next to the tourist office at **Raiffeisenbank.**

ACCOMMODATIONS AND FOOD. To reach the **Jugendherberge (HI)**, Hof 36, take the steep path down from the wall behind the bus stop parking lot—the hostel is at the bottom. It offers institutional but pleasant rooms and clean toilets. (☎2259. HI members only, though they might make exceptions, depending on space. Reception May-Sept. 7-10am and 5-10pm. Curfew 10pm, key available. Dorm bed with breakfast 190AS.) **Pension Bergkristall,** has surprisingly luxurious rooms with balconies, TV (and possibly a living room), and is conveniently close to the main lift station. (☎2005; fax 200 533. In summer, 300AS per person with good breakfast; in winter, 280-420AS.)

OUTDOOR ACTIVITIES. In winter, you can ski the slopes of the Hohe Tauern mountains. Ski passes are 340AS per day, children 170AS. You can purchase passes at the lift station past the tourist office. **Bike and ski rental** are available at **Intersport Pichler,** across from the tourist office. (Open M-Sa 9am-6pm, Su 10am-4pm; bikes 220AS per day; ski package 190-300AS per day.) Heiligenblut also provides easy access to the hiking of the National Park. The most satisfying hikes might be to the huts listed in the accommodations introduction to the park. Hiking guides and maps are available throughout town as *Wanderkarte* at kiosks.

ZELL AM SEE ☎06542

Surrounded by a ring of snow-capped mountains that cradle the broad turquoise lake, Zell am See (TSELL am ZAY; pop. 9,700) functions as a year-round resort spot for mountain-happy European tourists. Zell am See's horizon is dominated by 30 peaks over 3000m tall, which belong primarily to the Hohe Tauern range. The town functions as a convenient base from which *Wanderlust*ing tourists explore these peaks on foot or skis. But the town doesn't chase the tourist into the mountains. The cool blue lake calls to those who desire summer rest and relaxation, while visitors to the cobblestoned town center wind through a plethora of shops and cafes during the day, and a maze of bars and dance clubs at night.

GETTING THERE AND AROUND

Zell am See lies at the intersection of Bundesstr. 311 from the north and Bundesstr. 168 from the west. It's also accessible by Bundesstr. 107 from the south, which runs into Bundesstr. 311 north. From **Salzburg,** take Bundesstr. 21 south to 312 south; at Lofer, switch to 311 south to Zell.

Trains: At the intersection of Bahnhofstr. and Salzmannstr. (☎732 14357). Open M 4:50am-7:40pm, Tu-F 6:10am-7:40pm, Sa 6:10am-8:40pm, and Su 7:15am-8:20pm. Trains come from: **Salzburg** (1½hr., 3am-10:05pm, 150AS), **Innsbruck** (2hr., 2am-11:33pm, 260AS), **Vienna** (5hr., 9:21am-11:25pm, 520AS), and **Kitzbühel** (45min., 12:47am-8:31pm, 100AS).

Buses: BundesBus station on Postpl., behind the post office and facing Gartenstr. Buy tickets from the driver, or from the ticket office (☎5444), open M-F 7:30am-1:30pm. Buses run to a variety of local destinations, including **Salzburg** (6:35am-6:50pm) and **Krimml** (1¼hr., 6:02am-9:22pm, 100AS).

Taxis: At the train station, or call 68090 or 74111.

Car Rental: ARAC Inter-Auto, Schmittenstr. 2 (☎74452).

Auto Repairs: ÖAMTC (Austrian Automobile and Touring Club), Loferer Bundesstr. (☎74132). In case of a breakdown, dial 120.

Parking: 24hr. garage at the *Kurcenter* past the post office for 14AS per hr.

Bike Rental: In the station. 180AS per day, with ticket 120AS. Mountain bike 270AS.

ORIENTATION AND PRACTICAL INFORMATION

Zell am See's relative proximity to the German border, Salzburg, Innsbruck, and a wide range of natural attractions makes it a prime destination for international and Austrian tourists alike. Go to the right and up the hill from the train station to reach the *Fußgängerzone.*

Tourist Office: Brucker Bundesstr. 3 (☎770; fax 72032; zell@gold.at; www.zellka-prun.com). From the station, turn right and follow the green "i" sign by the stairs on the left. A nifty computer prints information on accommodations, events, and services in German or English (printer open 8am-midnight). The staff can't make reservations, but they will ferret out vacancies and bury you under brochures. Open July to mid-Sept. and mid-Dec. to Mar. M-F 8am-6pm, Sa 8am-noon and 4-6pm, Su 10am-noon; Apr.-June and Sept. to mid-Dec. M-F 8am-noon and 2-6pm, Sa 9am-noon.

Currency Exchange: At banks or the post office. Almost every bank has an **ATM.**

Luggage Storage: At the train station. 30AS per piece, open M-Sa 6am-8:30pm. 24hr. electronic lockers with accommodations for both bags and skis 40AS.

Internet: Café Estl, Bahnhofstr. 1 (☎72610) near the church, has four terminals downstairs (15AS per 10min.). Open daily 10am-9pm.

Weather conditions: ☎73694.

Emergencies: Police, ☎133. **Mountain rescue,** ☎140.

Post Office: Postpl. 4 (☎73791-0). Open early July to mid-Sept. and late Dec. to Mar. M-F 7:30am-6:30pm, Sa 8-10am; mid-Sept. to late Dec. and Apr. to early July Sa 8-11am. Currency exchange closes at 5pm. **Postal Code:** A-5700.

ACCOMMODATIONS

Zell am See has more than its share of 4-star hotels (and prices), but it has not forgotten the budget traveler. Many affordable accommodations roll out the red carpet for the cost conscious. Ask for a free **guest card** where you are staying, which provides numerous discounts on activities throughout the city.

Pensione Sinilill (Andi's Inn), Thumersbacherstr. 65 (☎73523). Take the BundesBus (dir.: Thumersbach) to "Krankenhaus" (19AS, last bus 7:14pm). Turn left upon exiting the bus, walk about 200m, and look for an old wooden sign on the left side of the street. If you call ahead, Andi will pick you up. On the north shore of the lake, this pension features simple furniture and an easy-going atmosphere. Andi's swimming trophies and stories, and Joy's culinary prowess make for a homey atmosphere. Andi, reared in Zell am See, knows everything about the town and can tell you what's worthwhile. Hall bathrooms and shower. Big breakfast included. 200AS per person in big doubles, though prices go down according to the number of people and duration of stay.

Haus der Jugend (HI), Seespitzstr. 13 (☎57185; fax 571 854; hostel-zell-se@salzburg.co.at). Exit the side of the train station facing the lake ("Zum See"), turn right, and walk along the footpath beside the lake; at the end of the footpath, take a left onto Seespitzstr. (15min.). As the footpath can feel quite deserted at night, you could also take the Stadtbus to "Alpenblick" (19AS). This clean, well-maintained hostel is group oriented, and lies on the lakefront providing large rooms with bath and lakeside terraces. Other goodies include a TV room with VCR, a pinball machine, and a snack shop in the reception area. 106 beds divided into doubles, quads, and 6-bed rooms. Breakfast included. Lunch and dinner each 65AS. 10AS deposit for lockers in some rooms. Reception 7-9am and 4-10pm. Check-out 9am. Lockout noon-4pm. Curfew 10pm, key available on request. Key deposit 300AS or passport. Open Dec.-Oct. Reserve ahead. Dorms 165AS 1st night, then 140AS. MC, Visa.

Haus Haffner, Schmittenstr. 29 (☎72396). Exit the tourist office, turning left on Schmittenstr. (you may wish to use the underground walkway). Walk up Schmittenstr. for about 10 min. and it will be on the left. Rooms are well-furnished, with TV, balcony, and most with shower and toilet. Breakfast included. Singles 220-280AS; doubles 400AS.

Camping Seecamp, Thumersbacherstr. 34 (☎7211; fax 72115), in Zell am See/Prielau, can be reached by BundesBus (dir: Thumersbach) to "Seecamp" (19AS, last bus 7:14pm). Situated on the lakefront, this massive campground has a restaurant, a cafe with terrace, BBQ grills, and even a small shopping market. Showers included. Reception 8am-noon and 2-10pm. Check-out 11am. 89AS per person, ages 2-15 50AS; tents 50AS; cars 30AS; trailers 100AS. Guest tax 9AS for adults. AmEx, MC, Visa.

FOOD

Zell am See lies in the Pinzgau region, where food is prepared to sustain the strenuous labors of hearty farmers. Try the *Brezensuppe* (a clear soup with cheese cubes) as an appetizer and then *Pinzgauer Käsnocken* (homemade noodles and cheese, onions, and chives). Top it all off with *Lebkuchen Parfait* (spice cake parfait), *Blattlkrapfen* (deep-fried stuffed pancakes), or *Germknödeln* (a steamed sweet roll served with poppy seeds, butter, and sugar). The grocery store **SPAR** is at Brucker Bundesstr. 4 (open M-Th 8am-7pm, F 8am-7:30pm, Sa 7:30am-5pm).

Fischrestaurant "Moby Dick," Kreuzg. 16 (☎73320). The great white—with fries. The restaurant smells like what you'd expect, but no matter: the double fishburger with potatoes and salad is only 90AS. Single fishburger 25AS. A few entrees feature fish straight from the lake. Open M-F 9am-6pm, Sa 9am-1pm.

Euro Kebab 2000, across from the train station. Despite its impressive name, serves up the typical cheap *Döner* fare: Kebab in a large roll for 45AS. Open daily 10am-10pm.

Ristorante Pizzeria Giuseppe, Kirchg. 2 (☎72373), in the *Fußgängerzone*. From the station, walk past the church and continue straight. Plenty of vegetarian options, and 33 kinds of beer. English menu. Pasta dishes 78-115AS, pizza 50-125AS, salads 50-93AS. Open Tu-Su 11:30am-11pm. MC, Visa.

Schloß Kammer, Maishofer 22 (☎78202), in the nearby village of Maishofer. Bike up the road past the hospital to a superb restaurant run by the local mayor. Vaulted ceilings, an authentic *Kachelofen* (tiled clay oven), and a large selection of regional dishes. *Fleischknochen* 95AS, *Kaiserschmarr'n* (scrambled pancakes with plum compote for 2) 75AS. Open daily 10am-10pm.

SIGHTS AND OUTDOOR ACTIVITIES

AROUND THE LAKE. Zell's buildings are clustered in the valley of the **Zellersee.** Stroll around the lake or get wet at one of the **beaches: Strandbad Zell am See,** near the center of town (walk toward the lake down Franz-Josef-Str.), complete with platform diving and a waterslide; **Strandbad Seespitz,** by the Haus der Jugend; or **Thumersbacher Strandbad** on the eastern shore. *(All open late May to early Sept. daily 9am-7pm; 40-69AS, generally half-price after 5pm and free after 6pm.)* **Boat tours** around the lake depart from and return to the Zell Esplanade, off Salzmannstr. along the river *(40min., 8 per day 10am-5:30pm, 80AS, ages 6-14 40AS)*. Visit **Edi's Skischule** near the Strandbad Zell am See for **water skiing** *(100AS per round)* and **sailing** *(120AS per hr.)*.

HIKING AND ADVENTURE SPORTS. Independent of the park the Zell am See area provides many opportunities to work those calf muscles. For longer hikes, grab a *Wanderplan* or consider the *Pinzgauer Spaziergang*, a leisurely 7-hour hike. The trail begins at the upper terminal of the Schmittenhöhebahn and is marked "Alpenvereinsweg" #19 or 719. A variety of hikes that do not require cable cars are detailed in the tourist office's free *Wanderkarte*, which includes somewhat skimpy English directions, and a map of the area with trails marked.

Though expensive the **Schmittenhöhebahn** leads to many hikes. The BundesBus *(dir.: Schmittenhöhebahn/Sonnenalmbahn Talstation. 7min., 7:20am-5:50pm, 20AS from post office)* goes to the lift, about 2km north of town on Schmittenstr. *(Mid-July to late-Oct.*

daily every 30min. 8:30am-5pm. 185AS, children 90AS; round-trip 240AS, with guest card 215AS, children 120AS.) The lift station provides several brochures (with English translations) detailing hikes ranging from leisurely strolls to cliff-hangers. In the former category, the **Erlebnisweg Höhenpromenade** *(1 hr. hike)* connects the top stations of the Schmittenhöhe and Sonnkogel lifts. Displays on history, nature, and ecology along the way exercise your mind. Free guided hikes (with purchase of lift ticket) leave from the lower stations *(July-Oct. M-F, with a variety of themes including botanical hikes, forest walks, and children's hikes)*. Contact the Schmittenhöhebahn Aktiengesellschaft *(☎ 789 212)* or the lower station for details.

For rafting *(350-680AS)*, **canyoning** *(550-790AS)*, **paragliding** *(600-700AS)*, and climbing *(490AS)* information, contact **Adventure Service**, Steinerg. 9 *(☎ 73525; fax 74280)*.

SKIING. As you might expect, winter turns Zell am See into a ski resort. The new **Zell/Kaprun Ski Pass** covers both Zell am See and nearby Kaprun; a free bus runs between the two every 20 minutes from late-Dec. to mid-Apr. *(Lift passes: 2 days 740-780AS, students 670-720AS, children 435-480AS.)* One-day passes are available for Zell's Schmittenhöhe lift *(385-430AS, students 350-390AS, children 230-260AS)*. Get a report in German on ski conditions in the Schmittenhöhe area at ☎ 73694; for the Kitzsteinhorn-Kaprun area dial ☎ (06547) 8444. The **Kitzsteinhorn** mountain (3203m) and its glacier in Kaprun also offer **summer skiing.** Get there early on summer days to avoid skiing in slush. A day pass for the mountain costs 270AS, children 145AS. Skis, boots, and poles run 255AS per day and snowboards are 180AS per day; all are available at **Intersport Bruendl** on the glacier *(☎ (06547) 862 1360; office@bruendl.co.at; www.bruendl.co.at. Open 8am-4:30pm)*.

REGIONAL MUSEUM. No visit to Zell am See would be complete without a glimpse of the toilet Franz Josef used when he visited the Schmittenhöhe. This artifact and 4 floors of equally random exhibits (the largest pike ever caught in the lake, Nazi coins, and a floor full of graphic prints) join the erstwhile royal throne in the entertaining **Heimatmuseum** inside the *Vogtturm* (bailiff's tower) on Kreuzg. 2. The tower itself is more than 1000 years old, and its walls have cracked from the vibrations caused by cannon fire through the roof hatches. The cannons were fired not at enemies of old but at oncoming thunderstorms, a practice believed to disperse the clouds. The process continued until the science of meteorology reached Zell sometime in the mid-19th century. *(☎ (0664) 462 6253. Open mid-May to mid-Oct. M-F 2-6pm, Sa 10am-1pm. 25AS, ages 6-16 15AS. English language sheet 3AS.)*

NIGHTLIFE

If all the mountain exercise hasn't worn you out, boogie down at night. Those who want to get really hammered should try the local drinking game **Nageln,** in which drinkers compete to see who can drive a nail into a tree stump first—with the sharp end of a hammer. Somehow, you end up drunk.

Crazy Daisy's Bar, Brucker Bundesstr. 10-12 (☎ 725 1659), is a fun, though touristy joint featuring its own wacky, irreverent t-shirts and the ever-popular aforementioned hammer-in-stump game across from the tourist office. Also serves Mexican and American food. Hamburgers 95AS, burritos 120AS, salads 40-60AS, "breath-killer garlic bread" 30AS. Children's portions available. Open in summer 8pm-1am; in winter 4pm-1am. 2-for-1 happy hour in summer 8-10pm; in winter 4-6pm. MC, Visa.

Pinzgauer Diele, Kircheng. 3 (☎ 2164), has 2 bars and a small dance area guaranteed to get you moving. A mostly under-25 crowd. Mixed drinks 50-95AS, beer 60-75AS. Cover 85AS. Open Su-M and W-Sa 10pm-3am.

Bierstad'l, Kircheng. 1 (☎ 47090). 18-25 yr. olds sample 33 different brews in stock; you'll be on the floor by number 9. Creamy, dark *Hirtl* for 33AS. Open 8:30pm-4am.

Wunderbar, Esplanade 4-6 (☎ 2388; fax 238 8305), at the Grand Hotel, occupies the top floor of a classy waterfront hotel with glass walls and great views, making it quite a romantic spot. Open 7am-2am.

KRIMML

☎06564

From the small mountain town of Krimml, near Zell am See, over 400,000 visitors per year charge up the sloping path to the extraordinary Krimml Waterfalls—a set of three roaring cascades totalling over 400m in height. These waterfalls are usually enjoyed as a daytrip from Zell am See, but the town of Krimml itself might lure you in, providing an overnight base for other hikes or skiing.

TRANSPORT AND PRACTICAL INFORMATION. Krimml is accessible by bus and train. **Buses** are most convenient, since they drop you at the start of the path to the falls (bus stop: Maustelle Ort). Bus lines run from **Zell am See** (1½ hr., 6:02am-9:22am, 110AS) and **Zell am Ziller** (1hr., 3 per day 9:21am-1:26pm, 58AS). The Pinzgauer Lokalbahn **train** comes only from the east, from **Zell am See** (1¾hr., 6:28am-6:49pm, 100AS; a steam train runs on some Sundays, and is 108AS; Eurail valid). The town and **train station** (☎7214; counter open M-F 8:10am-12:45pm and 1:30-3:30pm, Sa 8:10-1:45am) are 3km from the waterfall. The full-service **tourist office** is 2 minutes from the "Krimml Ort" bus stop, down the hill with a 24-hr. accommodation phone and computer. (☎7239 or 6564 (from outside Austria); fax 7550; krimml.info@aon.at; www.salzburg.com/krimml-tourismus. Open M-F 8am-noon and 2:30-5:30pm, Sa 9-11am.) Next door, the **post office** offers good **currency exchange** rates (☎7201; open M-F 8am-noon and 2-5pm). There is a 24-hour **ATM** at **Raiffeisenbank** across from the church.

ACCOMMODATIONS AND FOOD. Large doubles with mountain views are only 220-240AS at **Haus Mühlegg,** Oberkrimml 24 (☎7338). Follow the road past ADEG and the sport shop, and further downhill (5min.); the brown farmhouse is on the right, with flowers on every terrace. Cheap food can be had at the **SPAR,** Oberkrimml 12, down the main road (open M-F 8am-6pm, Sa 8am-noon).

KRIMML WATERFALLS. Dropping a total of 380m, the highest waterfalls in Europe are pleasantly secluded amidst the spindly pines and mountain grasses of the Höhe Tauern National Park. Despite the large number of visitors, the falls retain an unspoiled atmosphere that gets increasingly wild the higher you walk. The path (built in 1900 by the ÖAV or Austrian Alpine Union) that runs just alongside the falls allows for dozens of unusually close and pulse-quickening views of roaring water. Buses to Krimml stop at the waterfalls. To get to the waterfalls from the town and train station either cross the street from the station to catch the bus (10 min., 9:07am-3:07pm, 20AS) to the falls, take a **taxi** (☎7281 or 7223; 50AS) or hike on the foot path. A day pass to park near the entrance to the waterfall hikes costs 90AS for cars and 50AS for motorcycles. Don't forget a raincoat and camera bag; you can't avoid the mist. Entrance to the falls costs 15AS (children 5AS) between 8am and 6pm. The ÖAV/National Park Information stand, next to the ticket booth, offers a variety of maps and English pamphlets and sells a number of German guides (50-180AS) to the flowers, mushrooms, and rocks of the Höhe Tauern. (☎7212. Open May-Oct. M-Sa 11am-4pm. With a minimum of 10 people, the office offers free guided tours of the falls in English if you call in advance.)

The source of the waterfalls is the Krimml "Kees" (glacier), 20km up the valley above the falls. The falls were almost dammed in the 1950s to provide hydroelectric power, but environmentalist pressure and the creation of the Hohe Tauern National Park helped save these marvels. The trail is called the **Wasserfallweg** (4km). The first and most spectacular cascade (150m) is visible shortly past the entrance booth and to the left (incidentally, you might want to pick up picnic foods at the food stand before charging on); it kicks up a huge skirt of spray that douses the rocks, plants, and tourists nearby.

A wide hiking path leads up to the second and third falls, starting past the entrance booth and to the right. Mind your head: signs on the ascent warn German-speakers of possible falling rocks. Even though super-fit Austrian grandmothers appear to handle the climb with ease, it can be tough. It's about 30 minutes

FLOWER COWS Every spring, the local farmers around Krimml set their cattle free to graze on the mountainside. In the fall, they set out to round up the herd. At the end of September, farmers give thanks to the hardy cows who made it back by dressing them up in Carmen Miranda-style flower headdresses and parading them through town at the **Almatriebs-Fest,** which features live music and a farmer's market.

from the first falls to the second and an additional 30 minutes from the second to the third. Next to the second falls, which plunge a mere 100m, is a precipice called **Jägersprung** (hunter's leap). As legend has it, a poacher once jumped from here to the other side of the falls to elude his pursuers—you can judge for yourself how likely this feat is. The third set of falls (140m) is perhaps the most scenic and least cluttered with gawking tourists. There is a jumble of boulders by the side of the river that provide unobstructed views of the falling water.

OTHER ACTIVITIES. Ski passes, available at the tourist office, run 200AS for a full day; youth get 15% off, children 35%. **Ski and boot rental** at **Sport Lachmayer,** are next to ADEG (☎7247, fax 7274-4; open M-F 8am-noon and 2:30-6pm, Sa 8am-noon; full rental 195-275AS per day, 935-1490AS per week; DC, MC, Visa). The 325 km **Tauernweg** bike route begins in Krimml and makes its way to Passau on the Austrian/German border, going along much of the northern border of the park and to Salzburg. For **bike rental** go to the rear of the **ADEG,** in front of the church. (Open M-F 7:30am-noon and 3-6pm, Sa 7:30am-noon. City and mountain bikes 200AS per day, 160AS with guest card.)

LIENZ ☎04852

Lienz is the primary city in East Tyrol (*Osttirol*), a geopolitical oddity: though technically a semi-autonomous, wholly owned subsidiary of the province of Tyrol, the 2 provinces share no common border. Lienz is distinctive for its hybrid Mediterranean personality. Although the Alpine vista and the low-slung houses betray an Austrian heritage, the dusty cobblestone roads, summer heat, and ubiquitous Italian subtitles suggest Northern Italy (just 40km away). Even the weather cooperates—the valley around Lienz registers about 2000 hours of sunshine each year. Proximity to Franz-Josefs-Höhe and Heiligenblut make Lienz a great base for exploring the Hohe Tauern National Park, though in winter the ski-maniacs forget all except the Dolomite slopes nearby.

GET YOUR CITIES STRAIGHT. Lienz is distinct from Linz, an industrial city in northeast Austria. Lienz is pronounced "LEE-ints"; Linz is known as Linz an der Donau. Make the distinction before boarding any trains.

GETTING THERE AND AROUND

Lienz lies at the conjunction of several highways: Bundesstr. 108 from the northwest, 106 and 107 from the northeast, and 100 which runs east and west. By **car** from **Salzburg,** take Autobahn A-10 south to 311, and, just before Zell am See, switch to 107 south to Lienz. From **Innsbruck,** take Autobahn A-12 east to 169 south. At **Zell am Ziller,** switch to 165 east, and at Mittersill take 108 south to Lienz.

Trains: Hauptbahnhof, Bahnhofpl. (☎66060. Train info ☎01717. Information booth open M-F 9am-4:45pm; ticket window open M-Sa 5:15am-6:40pm, Su 8:20am-7:25pm.) Direct trains from **Klagenfurt** (2hr., 6-7 per day 6:36am-7:36pm, 176AS), **Innsbruck** (3hr., 5 per day 7:04am-6:01pm, 165AS), and the **Vienna Südbahnhof** (6hr., 7:04am, 570AS).

Buses: BundesBuses (☎(01) 71101) leave from in front of the *Hauptbahnhof* for destinations throughout the region. (☎64944. Open M-F 7:30am-12:30pm and 1:30-

4:30pm.) To: **Kitzbühel** (2hr., 2-3 per day, 5:45am-5:15pm), **Heiligenblut** (1 hr., 6-9 per day, 72AS) and **Franz-Josefs-Höhe** (3-4 per day, 7:40am-3:05pm), and **Zell am See** (2 per day, 10am-2pm). From July 7-Aug. 23, a **free Stadtbus** circles the city, making fourteen stops before returning to the train station parking lot. (1 per hr. 8am-7pm.)

Taxi: ☎63690, 72606, or 65450.

Parking: At Europapl., 5AS for 45 min.; max. 3hr.

Automobile Association: ÖAMTC, Tirolerstr. 19a (☎63322).

Car Rental: Pontiller Autohaus, Kärtnerstr. 70 (☎62705).

Bike Rental: At the train station. 180AS per day, with train ticket or Eurail 100AS. For children 100AS, 70AS.

ORIENTATION AND PRACTICAL INFORMATION

The **Isel River,** which feeds into the Drau, splits Lienz. From the train station, the centrally located Hauptpl. is across Tirolerstr. and to the left through Boznerpl.

Tourist Office: Europapl. 1 (☎65265; fax 652 652; lienz@netway.at; www.tiscover.com/lienz). From the station, turn left onto Tirolerstr. and right onto Europapl. Courteous staff showers you with brochures (mostly in English), including a list of private accommodations. A 24hr. computer outside, with free phone, hooks visitors up with accommodations as well as information about events and activities. Inquire at the tourist office about **city tours.** Call the **Igelsberg-Stronach Information Center,** (☎04117) for information about **national park tours.**

Currency Exchange: Best rates are in the **post office,** which has an **ATM** in front. Exchange desk open M-F 8am-5pm. Also at the train station and banks.

Luggage Storage: At the train station. 30AS per piece per day. Small lockers 20AS, ski lockers 40AS. (Storage daily 7:30-11:10am and 1:10-6pm; lockers available daily 6am-9:30pm.)

English-Language Books: Two shelves of English best-sellers on the 2nd floor of **Tyrolia Lienz,** Roseng. 3. Open M-F 8am-noon and 2-6pm, Sa 8am-noon. MC, Visa.

Internet Access: Free at the *Öffentliche Bücherei* (public library, ☎63972), inside the *Klosterkirche* at the corner of Mucharg. and Schulstr. Open Tu-F 9am-noon and 3-6pm, Sa 9am-noon.

Pharmacy: Linden Apotheke, Kärntnerstr. 26 (☎633 060) Open M-F 8am-noon and 2-6pm, Sa 8am-noon.

Hospital: Emanuel-von-Hibler-Str. 5 (☎606).

Emergencies: Police, Hauptpl. 5 ☎133. **Fire,** ☎122. **Mountain Rescue,** ☎140. **Ambulance and water rescue,** ☎144. **Roadservice,** ☎120.

Post Office: Boznerpl. 1 (☎66880), on the corner of Hauptpl. across from the train station. Open M-F 7:30am-7pm, cashier until 5pm, Sa 8-11am. **Postal Code:** A-9900.

ACCOMMODATIONS

Even without a youth hostel, Lienz still offers affordable beds, most just beyond Hauptpl. and the town center. Most *Pensionen* and *Privatzimmern* cost 250-300AS per person, and can be found on the list the tourist office maintains.

Bauernhof im Siechenhaus, Kärtnerstr. 39 (☎62188). From the station, turn right onto Tirolerstr., walk across the Isel, take the 1st left, and then an immediate right. Walk 1 block to Kärtnerstr. and turn left. The hostel, adorned with 17th-century frescoes of Lazarus, is on the right. This working farmhouse, with thick, dark wooden beams, served as a home for the sick in the Middle Ages. 200AS per person in doubles and triples.

Haus Obererlacher, Dr.-Karl-Renner-Str. 12 (☎69364). From the tourist office, walk through the archway titled "Altstadt," then turn right until the road, then turn left onto Kärtnerstr. Continue following Kärtnerstr. before turning left on Maximillianstr. Turn right on Marg. Maultaschg., then turn right at the end of the street; the house will be on your left (15 min.). Eight beds in 3 singles, a double, and a triple come with hall showers, toilets, and a better-than-average breakfast. It is a walk, so call ahead. 180AS per person, with 20AS surcharge for single occupancy.

Camping Falken, Eichholz 7 (☎64022; fax 640 226; camping.falken@tirol.com) is across the Drau River near the foot of the Dolomites. From the station, turn left onto Tirolerstr. and left at the ÖAMTC garage, then pass through the tunnel and over the Drau. Follow the road as it curves past the soccer and track facilities, then head left down the small paved footpath through the field. Signs point to the campground on the 15 min. walk. There are plenty of sites here, surrounded by wide fields and mountains, and a ping-pong table, soccer field, and mini-playground. Electricity 30AS. **Showers** (10AS), **laundry** (70AS), and a store. Automobile lockout 1-3pm and 10pm-7am. Reception daily 8-10am and 4-8pm. Reservations recommended July-Aug. Open Dec. 15-Oct. 20. 47-62AS, children 30-45AS; site 65-85AS; guest tax for adults 8AS.

FOOD

Calorie-laden delis, bakeries, and cafes lie in wait in **Hauptplatz** and along **Schweizergasse.** Cheap eats—mostly sausages—await at Lienz's scattered **Imbiße.**

Café Köstl, Kreuzg. 4 (☎62012). A mother-daughter duo prepares some of the cheapest eats in town (entrees from 19AS) in this diner-style restaurant/bakery. Chow down on ham and eggs (49AS), curry *Würstl* (36AS), or pastries (8-17AS). Eat-in or takeout. Open M-Th 7:30am-8pm, F 7:30am-10pm, Sa 7:30am-12:30pm.

Max's Imbiß-Ecke Buffet, (☎72232). Max gives you cheap eats as soon as you step off the train: *Wienerschitzl* with salad (56AS), or *Bratwurst* with roll (28AS). Across the street from the train station. Open M-F 8:30am-6:30pm, Sa 9am-1pm.

Pizzeria-Spaghetteria "Da Franco," Ägidius Peggerstr. (☎69969). Head through Hauptpl. to Johannespl., turn left at Zwergerg., and continue down the small alley. Captained by Franco, a native Italian who decided to try to make it big up north, this restaurant serves terrific potato *gnocchi* (75-89AS) and garlicky-fresh tomato sauce. Pasta dishes and big pizzas 67-115AS; salad 75-115AS. Open in summer 11:30am-2pm and 5:30pm-midnight; in winter 11:30am-2pm and 5pm-midnight. AmEx, MC, Visa.

ADEG Aktiv Markt, in Hauptpl. Open M-F 8am-6:15pm, Sa 8am-12:30pm.

Bauernmarkt (farmer's market), Marktpl. Sa 9am-noon.

OUTDOOR ACTIVITIES AND SIGHTS

HIKING

Besides hiking in the National Park, the Dolomites around Lienz afford the traveller excellent nearby hikes. For lots of information on hikes and on huts contact either the tourist office or Lienz's chapter of the **Österreichischer Alpenverein,** Franz-von-Defreggerstr. 11 (☎72105. Open F 3-6pm). A variety of hikes leave from **Schloß Bruck,** taking from between 1 and 4 hours to complete. Signs on the trail to the castle both point the way and offer length and difficulty information.

Waldehrpfad Hike (1hr.). A level forest hike that is not taxing and wanders by a number of signs offering both description (in German) and the genus and species of various flora along the way. While yet more signs provide environmental info, nearby Liezen often interrupts the view, sometimes peeking through the lovely woods. Follow the signs near the castle reading "Waldehrpfad-Leisach." When signs look ambiguous, take the better-trodden, more direct route. When signs appear pointing towards "Lienz," it is best to follow (you get dropped 20 min. out of town center) or to walk back the way you came—otherwise the hike continues for a little longer, depositing you in nearby Leisach.

The Tristachersee (3hrs. round trip). A 5km hike from Lienz. Cross the bridge by the train station and follow Tristacherstr. The sparkling blue lake is at the base of the Rauchkofel mountain. Couch potatoes can enjoy the lake by riding the free **Bäder- und Freizeitbus** (Bath- and Leisure-Bus) from the *Dolomitenstadion* across the Drau to "Parkhotel Tristachersee" (runs July-Aug., 9 per day 8:53am-6:46pm).

The Hochsteinbahnen chairlifts (☎03975) run from the base station near the castle at the intersection of Iseltaler-Str. and Schloßg., rise 1500m in 2 segments up to the alpine wonderland of **Sternalm** (segment 1 runs sporadically in June; both segment 1 and segment 2 run July to late-Sept.; segment 1 open daily 9am-noon and 1-5pm; segment 2 open 9:15am-12:15pm and 1:15-4:45pm; round-trip for both 100AS, children 50AS; round-trip for either segment 60AS, children 30AS; oneway for either segment 40AS, children 20AS). At the top, the unforgiving Dolomites to the south and the Hohe Tauern to the north appear in spectacular confrontation. From the top you can take the Märchenwanderung (Fairy Tale Hike; 1½hr.), which leads past limestone peaks to the **Hochstein Hütte** (2023m; ☎(0663) 55843), open May-Oct. and from Christmas-Easter; call ahead for prices and availability and for instructions on how to hike there wihout a chair-lift. Also at the summit of the chairlift is the **Moosalm Children's Zoo,** with a menagerie available for petting pleasure (open 10am-5:30pm; free).

SKIING

Lienz serves as an excellent base to attack the **ski** trails of the **Lienzer Dolomiten Complex** (☎63975). During high season from mid-Dec to early Jan and early Feb. to mid-March a one-day ski pass runs 325AS, seniors and youths 280AS, under 15 170AS. ½-day tickets 260AS, 220AS, 130AS. The off-season is from late Nov. to mid-Dec., early Jan. to early Feb., and mid-March to the end of the season, when one day tickets are 295AS, 260AS, 150AS. ½-day tickets are 240AS, 210AS, 120AS. The **Skischule Lienzer Dolomiten** (☎65690) at the Zettersfeld lift offers hour-long private lessons at 450AS for one person, 150AS for each additional person. Group lessons cost 460AS for 4 hours. Private snowboard lessons are also available for 450AS per hour. **Hans Moser und Sohn** (☎69180), at the apex of the Zettersfeld lift, supplies **ski or snowboard rental.** A complete set of downhill equipment, here or elsewhere, runs 210AS per day, children 110AS; a snowboard with boots costs 300AS, 210AS.

MUSEUM

Above Lienz, Schloß Bruck houses the **East Tyrolean Regional Museum,** (☎62580) which exhibits the castle's collection: an eclectic mix of paintings, as well as archaeological and biological artifacts. The castle itself is well kept and a minor work of art in its own right. To get to the castle from the tourist office, exit and turn right on Tirolerstr., following it as it becomes Albin-Eggerstr. and then Iseltalerstr. Signs along the way will direct you to the castle. Open April to November from 10am-6pm.

NIGHTLIFE AND FESTIVALS

Disco-lovers get stoked at the **Stadtkeller-disco,** Tirolerstr. 30, near Europapl. (☎62852. Two bars and dance floor open 9pm-3am; cover 40AS). Across from the Pizzeria Da Franco in the Gastogarden, live jazz and the occasional pianist entertain a youngish crowd at **Türml Nightcafe** (open Tu-Su 5pm-2am). At **Cafe Wha,** Schweizerg. 3, the body-pierced crowd rocks and rolls past the midnight hour, smoking and playing pool (beer 24-35AS; wine 21-25AS; open Tu-Su 6pm-1am).

During the second weekend of August, the sounds of alcohol-induced merriment reverberate across the pastel facades of Lienz's town buildings in celebration of the **Stadtfest** (admission to town center 50AS). The summer months also witness the reaffirmation of Tyrolean culture in a series of Platzkonzerte. Watch as local men dust off their old *Lederhosen* and perform the acclaimed shoe-slapping dance (July-Aug. W and Sa at 8pm, June-Sept. Su at 8pm; free).

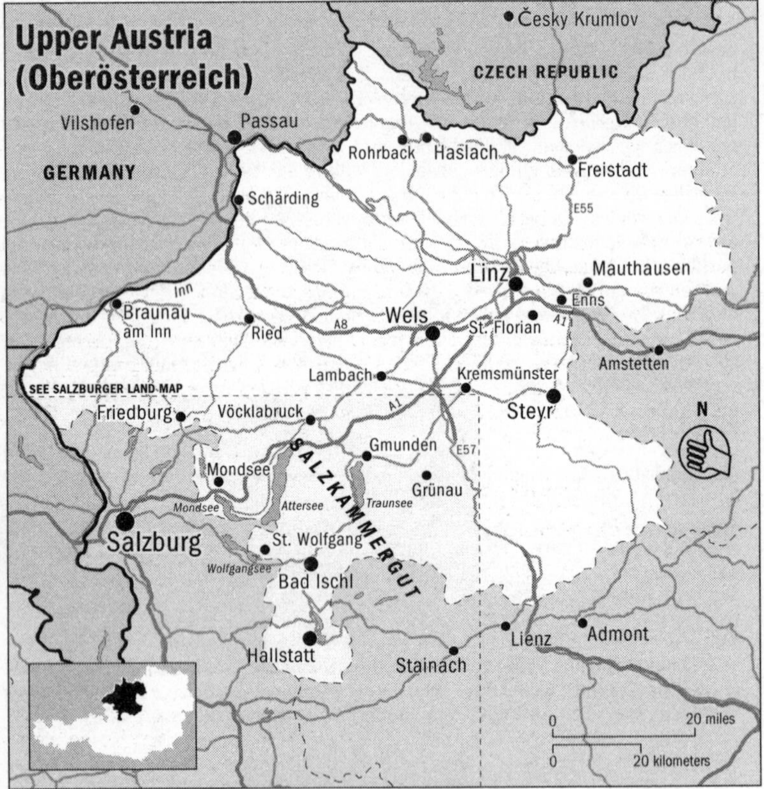

UPPER AUSTRIA (OBERÖSTERREICH)

The province of Oberösterreich (Upper Austria) is comprised of 3 distinct regions: the northeastern corner is known as the **Mühlviertel;** the **Innviertel** covers the western half; and the southwestern corner encompasses the popular resort area, the **Salzkammergut** (which *Let's Go* has placed in the Salzburg chapter because transportation to this region is most convenient from Salzburg). The charming streets of the provincial capital **Linz** mask the city's industrial soul; it is a major center of iron, steel, and chemical production, and home to many Danube port installations. Despite extensive development, the gentle natural beauty of the Danube river valley remains unspoiled. While the mountains here are less rugged than in Tyrol, Salzburg, and Carinthia, the relatively flat terrain in Upper Austria makes for wonderful **bicycling** tours. Well-paved paths, suitable for cyclers of any ability, wind throughout the entire province.

HIGHLIGHTS OF UPPER AUSTRIA

Munch melt-in-your-mouth, jam-saturated **Linzer Torten** while relaxing one of Linz's garden cafes (see p. 265).

Peruse medieval manuscripts at the ornate library in **Kremsmünster** (see p. 270).

Be careful while wandering through rows of cactus at the famous **botanical gardens** in Linz (see p. 267).

LINZ AN DER DONAU ☎0732

Sandwiched between Vienna to the east and Salzburg to the west, Linz (pop. 211,000) suffers from the typical middle-child syndrome—it is not as cosmopolitan as Vienna but not as small-town-charming as Salzburg. As a result, people generally ignore it. Nevertheless, Linz goes to great lengths to stand out from the pack, and the result is a sophisticated yet comfortable old-world town. The third largest city in the country, Linz was once home to Kepler, Mozart, Beethoven, Bruckner, and Hitler (not all at the same time). Technologically, Linz has won its sibling rivalry with Austria's other cities. Sitting on the banks of the blue(ish) Danube, Linz rules magisterially over the industrial sector of Austria. Though the industrial city outskirts aren't particularly scenic, the wealth produced by factories has been used to modernize and gentrify the central city, with exclusive shops, modern art galleries, cyber-cafes, electronic bus stops, and a technology museum that will overload your mental circuits. The trams happily invite passengers to step into the future with "Zukunft. Einsteigen, bitte" written on them. Linz's citizens are friendly (unburdened by the tourist overload of Vienna and Salzburg), and its annual festivals—the classy Brucknerfest and the bedlam nuttiness of the Pflasterspektakel (street performer's fair)—draw artists and crowds from all over the world.

GETTING THERE AND AROUND

Midway between Salzburg and Vienna, and on the rail line between Prague and Graz, Linz is a transportation hub for Austria and much of Eastern Europe. Frequent **trains** connect to major Austrian and European cities. All **buses** come and go from the **Hauptbahnhof,** where schedules are available (bus ticket window open M-F 7am-5:50pm, Sa 7am-1:20pm). **Motorists** arrive via Autobahn West (A1 or E16).

Trains: Hauptbahnhof, Bahnhofpl. (☎1717). To: **Vienna** (2hr., every 30min. 4:43am-9:49pm, 280AS); **Salzburg** (1½hr., every hr. 1:30am-11:13pm, 210AS); **Innsbruck** (3½hr., every 2hr. 12:19am-11:13pm, 490AS); **Munich** (3hr., every 1-2hr. 2:31am-10:29pm, 508AS); and **Prague** (4hr., 2 per day 7:42am-1:38pm, 366AS). The international trains do not run daily, so ask at the train info; better to change trains in Vienna.

Ferries: Wurm & Köck boats connect **Passau** (☎(0851) 929 292; fax 35518), **Linz** (☎(0732) 783 607), and **Krems.** To Passau (5-7hr., depending on current; daily 8am and 2:15pm; 242AS, round-trip 284AS) and Krems (Tu, Th, Su 9am). Boats dock in Linz at the **Donau Schiffstation,** on the south side of the river, and stop at a number of Austrian and Bavarian towns along the way. Discounts for seniors and children under 15. Ferries run late Apr. to Oct.

Public Transportation: Linz's public transport system runs to all corners of the city. Trams start at the *Hauptbahnhof* and run north through the city along Landstr. and Hauptpl. and across Nibelungenbrücke. Several buses criss-cross Linz as well. Nearly all vehicles pass through **Blumauerplatz,** down the block and to the right from the train station. A hub closer to the city center is **Taubenmarkt,** south of Hauptpl. on Landstr. A ticket for 4 stops or less ("Mini") costs 9AS; more than 4 ("Midi") 18AS; and a day ticket ("Maxi") 36AS. Buy tickets from any machine at any bus or streetcar stop and stamp them before boarding; those caught riding without a ticket pay 400AS. The tourist office sells a 48AS combination ticket that includes a day ticket for tram #3 and a round-trip cable car ride to **Pöstlingberg.**

Taxis: At the *Hauptbahnhof,* Blumauerpl., and Hauptpl., (☎ 6969 or 1718).

Parking: Free parking at **Urfahrmarkt** and at Stadion Parkplatz Ziegeleistraße, beginning directly west from the train station.

Bike Rental: At the train station, 150AS per day, with train ticket 90AS. Or at **Oberösterreich Touristic Zentrale,** Kapuzinerstr. 3 (☎311 4967), 15AS per hr., 80AS per day, 120AS for 2 days, 250AS for 5 days, 200AS per weekend. Book in advance.

Automobile Service: ARBÖ, Hatenstr. 6 (☎123), or **ÖAMTC,** Wankmüllerhofstr. 58 (☎120).

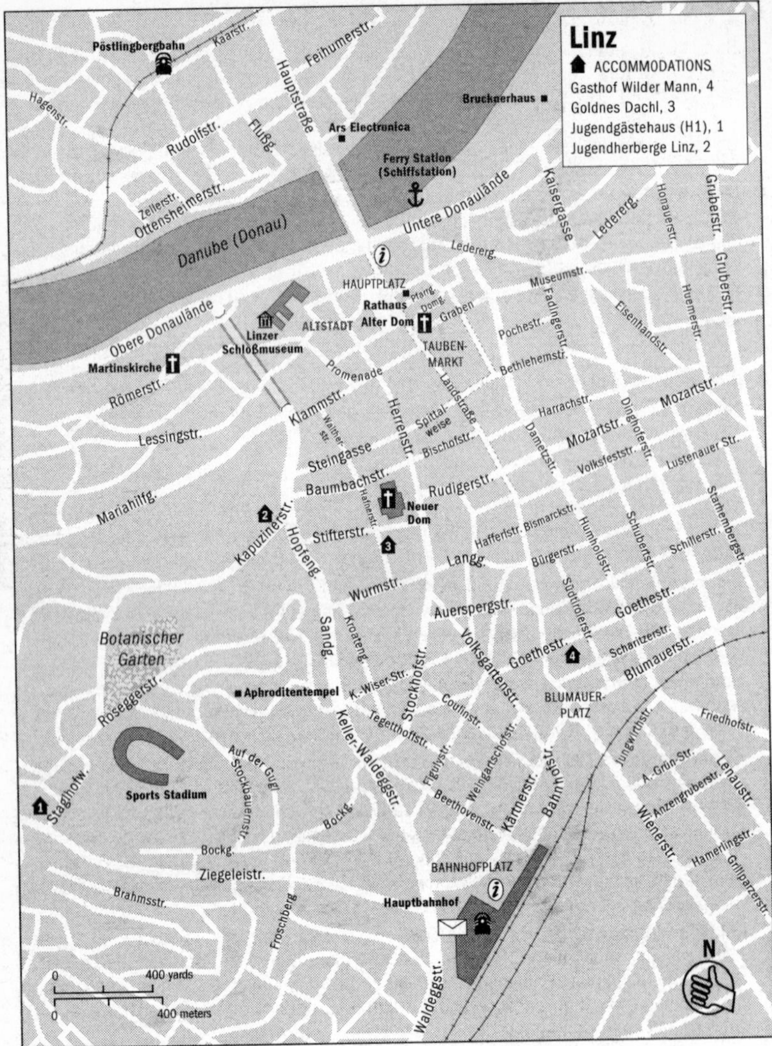

ORIENTATION AND PRACTICAL INFORMATION

Linz straddles the **Danube,** which weaves west to east through the city. Most of the *Altstadt* sights crowd along the southern bank, near the **Nibelungenbrücke.** This pedestrian area includes the huge **Hauptplatz,** just south of the bridge, and extends down **Landstraße,** which ends near the train station. To get to the center of town from the train station take tram #3 to "Hauptplatz" (18AS).

Tourist Office: Hauptpl. 1 (☎707 017, ext. 77; fax 772 873; info.linz@upperaustria.or.at; www.tiscover.com/linz), in the *Rathaus*. The multilingual staff helps find rooms at no charge. Pick up *A Walk Through the Old Quarter* for a summary of the *Altstadt's* main attractions. The tourist office sells the **Linz City Ticket** (299AS) which provides discounts at various sights around the city, including a voucher for a meal up to 150AS and a free ride on the Linz City Express. Open May-Oct. M-F 8am-7pm, Sa 9am-

7pm, Su 10am-7pm; Nov.-Apr. M-F 8am-6pm, Sa 9am-6pm, Su 10am-6pm. There is a tourist info brochure counter in the train station.

Currency Exchange: Banks are open M-W 8am-4:30pm, Th 8am-5:30pm, F 8am-2pm. The **post office** offers better rates for cash. Exchange open M-F 7am-5pm, Sa 8am-1pm. 60AS commission. 24hr. currency exchange machine at the train station.

American Express: Bürgerstr. 14, A-4021 Linz (☎669 013). All travelers' checks cashed, but no currency exchanged. Open M-F 9am-5:30pm, Sa 9am-noon.

Luggage Storage: At the train station, 30AS. Lockers 30-50AS. At tourist office, 10AS.

Bi-Gay-Lesbian Organizations: Homosexuelle Initiative Linz (HOSI), Schubertstr. 36 (☎609 898). Discussion tables Th 8pm at Gasthaus Agathon, Kapuzinerstr. 46. **Frauenbüro,** Klosterstr. 7 (☎772 0185 0).

Internet Access: At the **Ars Electronica Museum** (see p. 267).

English Language Bookstore: Amadeus, 40 Landstr., Decent selection of classics on second floor (each only 30AS!). Open M-F 9:30am-7pm, Sa 9:30-5pm.

Post Office: Bahnhofpl. 11, next to the train and bus stations. Open daily 6am-midnight. Information open M-F 8am-5pm, Sa 8am-4pm. **Postal Code:** A-4020.

UPPER AUSTRIA

ACCOMMODATIONS

Linz suffers from a lack of cheap rooms. The city is just urban enough that locals aren't allowed to rent rooms privately, so it's usually best to stick to the youth hostels and budget hotels. It's a good idea to call ahead everywhere.

Jugendherberge Linz (HI), Kapuzinerstr. 14 (☎782 720 or 778 777), near Hauptpl. This friendly, yellow, no-frills hostel offers the cheapest beds in town in an excellent location. From the train station, take tram #3 to "Taubenmarkt," cross Landstr., walk down Promenade and Klammstr., then turn left on Kapuzinerstr. There are 36 beds in 4- and 6-bed rooms. Reception 8-10am and 5-8pm. No curfew; the key to your free locker opens the front door. Reservations recommended. Breakfast 30AS. Showers and sheets included. **Laundry** 45AS. Dorms 190AS, under 19 160AS. Non-members add 40AS.

Jugendgästehaus (HI), Stanglhofweg 3 (☎664 434; fax 602 164). From the train station, take bus #27 (dir.: Schiffswerft) to "Froschberg." Walk straight on Ziegeleistr., turn right on Roseggerstr., and continue on to Stanglhofweg. This hostel caters to school groups and has little atmosphere otherwise, but rooms are clean and spacious. Parking available. Reception 7:30am-4pm and 6-11pm. Curfew 11pm. Call ahead. Breakfast and sheets included. Private showers and hall toilets. Singles 343AS; doubles 243AS per person; triples 173AS per person. Guest tax 8AS.

Goldenes Dachl, Hafnerstr. 27 (☎775 897). From the train station, take bus #21 to "Auerspergpl." Continue in the same direction along Herrenstr. for half a block, then turn left onto Wurmstr. Hafnerstr. is the 1st right. Large sunny rooms. Only 17 beds. Call ahead, especially if arriving between 2:30pm-5pm or on Su. Singles 310AS; doubles 560-600AS, with shower 620AS.

Gasthof Wilder Mann, Goethestr. 14 (☎656 078). Take tram #3 to "Blumauerpl." Turn left on Landstr., then right on Goethestr. Just 2min. from Blumauerpl., the main transportation hub, this hotel has large, homey rooms, with embroidered drapes and chairs. Restaurant downstairs. Breakfast 50AS. Reception 8am-10pm. Singles 350AS, with shower 420AS; doubles 620AS, 720AS.

Camping Pleschinger See (☎305 314). Take tram #1 or 3 to Rudolfstr. and bus #22 to "Pleschinger See." On the Linz-Vienna biking path on Pleschinger Lake. 45AS. Tents only. Open May to late Sept.

FOOD

Duck into the alleyway restaurants off Hauptpl. and Landstr. to avoid ridiculously inflated prices, or seek out the supermarkets: **Julius Meinl,** Landstr. 50 (open M-F 7:30am-6:30pm, Sa 7:30am-5pm) or **SPAR Markt,** Steing., near the hostels (open M-F

7:30am-7pm). Linz's namesake dessert, the **Linzer Torte,** is rich but worth the price. It's unique for its deceptively dry ingredients—lots of flour and absolutely no cream. The secret is in the red-currant jam filling, which slowly seeps through and moisturizes the dry, crumbly crust. Not all *Linzer Torten* are the same; the best *Torten* sit out for at least 2 days after baking for maximum jam saturation.

Café Traxlmeyer, Promenadestr. 16. (☎773 353). From Hauptpl., head down Schmidttorstr., and turn right on Promenadestr. Chandeliers and marble tables adorn this Viennese-style cafe. For 55AS you can nibble on rolls and jam, sip coffee from your own little pot, flip through newspapers, and watch people play chess throughout the afternoon. *Torten* 24AS. Open M-Sa 8am-10pm.

Mangolds, Hauptpl. 3 (☎785 688), is a paradise for vegetarians. This cafeteria-style restaurant offers only the freshest stuff. Nearly all the vegetables and eggs are 100% organic. Extravagant salad bar (40 different kinds of salad possible) and freshly squeezed fruit and vegetable drinks. Pay by weight–100g for 16AS, 60AS per plate. Open M-F 11am-8pm, Sa 11am-5pm.

Gelbes Krokodil, Dametzstr. 30 (☎784 182), in the Moviemento Theater, pleases a young artsy crowd, which relaxes in the beautiful Gastgarten. Varying menu includes soups (30AS), salads (60-80AS), and vegetarian entrees (80-90AS). Open M-F 11am-midnight, Sa & Su 5pm-midnight. Theater shows international contemporary and classic films. Summer special is a double feature and a drink, for only 120AS.

Levante, Hauptpl. 13 (☎793 430), has crowded outdoor seating on Hauptpl. (look for the bright yellow umbrellas) and authentic Turkish and Greek food at low prices. 35AS sandwiches are a great deal. Open daily 11:30am-11:30pm.

Gasthaus Goldenes Schiff, Ottensheimerstr. 74 (☎739 879), sits on the scenic banks of the Danube. From Hauptpl., cross the bridge, turn left, go around the *Rathaus*, and walk upstream along the river for 7min. Local fisherman sit at wooden tables and drink beer in the *Gastgarten* while eating their 100AS dinners. Good view of Danube Valley. Open W-Su 10am-10pm.

Pizzeria D'Alfredo and **Shalimar,** Bethlehemstr. 38 (☎778 055). Enjoy Italian specialties under a fish-filled net and plant-hung ceiling. Huge selection of large pizzas (85-110AS), pasta dishes (80-95AS), and salads (40-80AS). If you're longing for more Eastern fare and tunes, move to the next room and taste a variety of Pakistani and Indian dishes (80-110AS). Open 11am-2:30pm and 5-11:30pm.

Jindrak Konditorei, Herrenstr. 22 (☎779 258) with other branches throughout Linz. Rumored to serve the best *Linzer Torte* (19.50AS) in Linz. Other mouth-watering sweets and sandwiches line up beneath the glass counters. Open M-Sa 8am-6pm.

SIGHTS AND ENTERTAINMENT

THE OLD TOWN. Start your exploration of Linz at **Hauptplatz,** with the green Pöstlingberg rising majestically in the background. The city constructed the enormous plaza in the 14th and 15th centuries when it grew wealthy from taxing all the salt and iron passing through town. The focus of the square is the marble **Trinity column,** commemorating the city's escape from the horrors of war, famine, the plague, and the 18th century. An octagonal tower and an astronomical clock crown the Baroque **Rathaus.** To date, only 2 people have ever addressed the public from its balcony: Adolf Hitler and Pope John Paul II. Free-spirited star-gazer Johannes Kepler (the fellow who explained the elliptical orbits of the of planets) wrote his major work, *Harmonices Mundi*, while living around the corner at Rathausg. 5. In 1745, Linz's first print shop opened there; today, it houses Onkel Dagobert's Dart Kneipe—a few beers may inspire you to rethink the geometrical harmonies of the dartboard.

CHURCHES. On nearby Domg. stands Linz's twin-towered **Alter Dom** (Old Cathedral), where symphonic composer Anton Bruckner played during his stint as church organist. *(Open daily 7am-noon and 3-7pm.)* To the south, the neo-Gothic **Neuer Dom** (New Cathedral) impresses visitors with the 19th-century hubris necessary to create this Godzilla-scale edifice (the largest in Austria). Its tower could have been the highest in the country, but a strict regulation decreed that no tower could outdo Vienna's Stephansdom. Located to the left of the Schloßmuseum on Röomerstraße, **Martinskirche** wins the prize for the oldest original church in Austria. The central structure erected during the Carolingian period (in the late 8th century) using debris from Roman ruins is still intact.

MUSEUMS. The **Ars Electronica,** just over the bridge from Hauptpl., bills itself as the "museum of the future." It's a bird, it's a plane, it's *you* strapped to the ceiling in a full-body flight simulator that sends you soaring over Upper Austria. After this not-so-natural high, head downstairs to the **CAVE,** an exciting interactive 3-D room that sends you even higher to explore the outer reaches of space. The museum cafe offers **Internet access** for visitors, included in the entrance fee. *(Hauptstr. 2. ☎727 20; info@aec.at; www.aec.at. Open W-Su 10am-6pm. 80AS, students and seniors 40AS.)* The **Neue Galerie,** Blütenstr. 15, on the second floor of the Lentia 2000 shopping center on the north side of the river, has one of Austria's best contemporary art collections. Works by Klimt, Kokoschka, Lieberman, and others line the walls. *(☎707 036 00. Open June-Sept. M-W and F 10am-6pm, Th 10am-10pm, Sa 10am-1pm; Oct.-May M-W and F-Su 10am-6pm, Th 10am-10pm. 60AS, students 30AS.)* The **Linzer Schloßmuseum** presents an eclectic collection of objects from the Middle Ages to the 20th century including one of Beethoven's handsome pianofortes, an early haunting painting by Schiele and a curious 18th-century castle pharmacy. Special exhibits on ground floor every year. *(Tummelpl. 10. ☎774 419. Open Tu-F 9am-5pm, Sa-Su 10am-4pm. 50AS, students 30AS. English brochure available.)*

UPPER AUSTRIA

BOTANICAL GARDEN. For sheer olfactory ecstasy, visit the **Botanischer Garten's** world-famous cactus and orchid collections. The hill where the garden is located was saved from housing developments by grace of the fact that it is hollow—it is the site of an exploded ammunitions plant from WWII. To visit this hothouse take bus #27 (dir: "Chemie") from Taubenmarkt and get off at "Botanischer Garten." *(Rosegerstr. 20. ☎707 018 80. Open daily May-Aug. 7:30am-7:30pm; Sept. and Apr. 8am-7pm; Oct. and Mar. 8am-6pm; Nov.-Feb. 8am-5pm. 10AS, under 18 free.)*

URFAHR AND PÖSTLINGBERG. Cross Nibelungenbrücke to reach the left bank of the Danube. This area, known as **Urfahr,** was a separate city until Linz swallowed it up in the early decades of the 20th century. It boasts some of the oldest buildings in the city and a captivating view of Linz from the apex of the **Pöstlingberg** (537m). To reach the summit, take tram #3 to "Bergbahnhof Urfahr," then either hike ½km up Hagenstr. (off Rudolphstr., which is off Hauptstr. near the bridge) or hop aboard the **Pöstlingbergbahn,** a trolley car that ascends the summit in a scenic 20 minutes. *(☎780 1754 5. Every 20min. M-Sa 5:20am-8pm, Su 11:40am-8pm. 25AS, round-trip 40AS, children half-price.)* The twin-towered **Pöstlingbergkirche,** symbol of the city, stands guard on the crest of the hill. Indulge any lingering childhood fantasies by taking the "magic dragon" train, the **Grottenbahn,** into the fairy-tale caves of Pöstlingberg. *(Open May-Sept. daily 10am-6pm; Apr. and Oct.-Nov. daily 10am-5pm. 50AS, under 15 25AS.)*

NIGHTLIFE AND FESTIVALS

Linzer nightlife is sleepy but does have a pulse, which beats at (yet another) **Bermuda Dreiecke** (Bermuda Triangle), behind the west side of Hauptpl. (head down Hofg. or just follow the crowds of decked-out pub crawlers). Frequented by *Linzers* as well as tourists, this area has the highest nightclub-to-square-meter ratio in the city. In Hauptpl. itself, try **Alte Welt Weinkeller,** Hauptpl. 4 (☎770 053, open daily 7pm-1am; food served 6-11pm), an arcaded, Renaissance-era "wine and culture cellar" where you can soak up wine and spirits. **17er Keller,** Hauptpl. 17 (duck through the archway and enter the steel door on your right), will serve you an

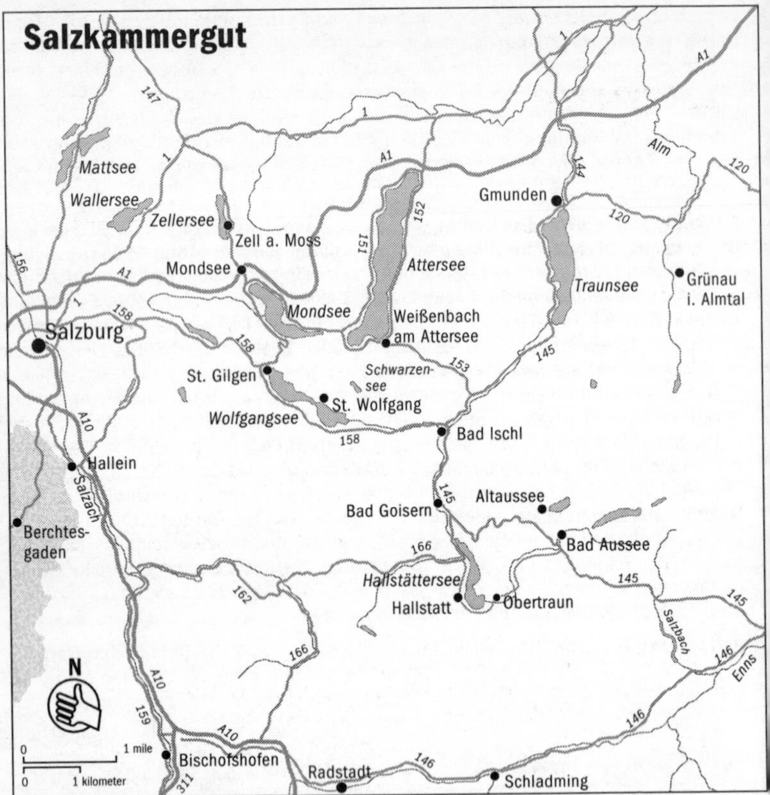

apple-juice-and-cinnamon tequila while you listen to a mix of jazz, funk, blues, and rock (open M-Sa 7pm-1am, Su 7pm-1am). **Coffee Corner Café,** Bethlehemstr. 30, draws a sophisticated, mainly gay and lesbian crowd (☎770 862; open M-Sa 7pm to whenever people go home). Linzers also flock to the other side of the Danube for after-hours entertainment. **Cafe Ex-Blatt,** Waltherstr. 15, covered in old Austrian advertisements and movie posters, attracts a hip retro crowd (☎779 319; open M-F 10pm-2am, Sa-Su 6pm-1am). Grab a bench at **Fischerhäusl,** Flußg. 3, the beer garden on the left as you cross the bridge (☎710 123; open M-F 11am-2pm and 5pm-midnight, Sa-Su 5pm-midnight). Many busy night spots line Landstr.—look between shops for entrances to courtyard *Biergärten.* For dancing, try **My Way,** Goethestr. 51 (☎652 760; open M-Sa 7pm-2am, Su 7pm-midnight).

From mid-Sept. to mid-Oct., the month-long **Brucknerfest** brings a rush of concerts paying homage to native son Anton Bruckner at the **Brucknerhaus** concert hall, an acoustically perfect venue (tickets 220-1100AS, standing room 40-50AS). For tickets, contact *Brucknerhauskasse*, Untere Donaulände 7, A-4010 Linz (☎775 230; fax 761 2201; kassa@liva.co.at; www.brucknerhaus.linz.at). The opening concerts (the end of the 2nd week in Sept.), billed as *Klangwolken* (soundclouds), include spectacular outdoor lasers, a children's show, and a classical evening with Bruckner's Seventh Symphony broadcast live into the surrounding Donaupark to 50,000 fans. During the 3rd weekend of July, the city hosts **Pflasterspektakel,** a free, 3-day, international street performers' festival. Every few steps down Landstr. and Hauptpl., different performers from as far away as New Zealand perform Houdini acts, fire-eating, outdoor theater, bongo concerts, punk rock, and other such feats before the young, funky, social crowd.

DAYTRIPS FROM LINZ

MAUTHAUSEN

*To reach the camp from Linz, take a **train** to Mauthausen (transfer at St. Valentin, 4:43am-11:01pm). A special Oberösterreichischer Verkehrsverbund day pass (102AS) covers the round-trip train ticket from Linz plus all city transportation in Linz and Mauthausen. Beware—the Mauthausen train station is 6km away from the camp, and a bus stops 2km from the camp only twice a day during the week and not at all on weekends. A better option is to store your pack (30AS) at the Mauthausen train station (☎(67238) 2207) and **rent a bicycle** (70AS with train ticket). Go through town and turn right after the Freizeitzentrum. Take the signposted (KZ Mauthausen) Fußweg—for bikes too. You'll pass pastures, fields of hay, and orchards before reaching the bleak walls of the camp. Pick up a map from the train station. By **car,** exit Autobahn A1 (Vienna-Linz) at Enns.*

About half an hour down the Danube from Linz, the remains of a Nazi *Konzentrationslager* (abbreviated KZ; concentration camp) keep their terrible vigil. Unlike other camps in south Germany and Austria, Mauthausen remains intact. Built by Dachau prisoners in 1938, Mauthausen was the central camp for all of Austria and administered 49 subcamps throughout the country. More than 200,000 prisoners passed through Mauthausen, mainly Russian, Italian, and Polish POWs, along with Austrian homosexuals and political criminals, Hungarian and Dutch Jews, Gypsies, and Communists. Mauthausen was infamous for its **Todesstiege** (Staircase of Death), which led to the stone quarry where inmates were forced to work until exhaustion. The steep, even steps currently in place were added for tourists' safety—when the inmates worked here, there was nothing but a stony drop dotted with boulders and jagged rocks. As the prisoners climbed up or down the path, the guards often shoved the last in line so that the entire group fell down the slope, along with the stones they were carrying on their shoulders. The inner part of the camp is now a **museum** (☎(07238) 2269). The barracks, roll-call grounds, cremation ovens, and torture rooms are also accessible. A free brochure or audio-tape tour (in English) walks you through the central part of the camp. There is also an exhibit on the history of the camp and video documentaries in various languages. (Open Apr.-Sept. 8am-6pm; Oct. to mid-Dec. and Feb.-Mar. 8am-4pm. Last entrance 1hr. before closing. 25AS, students and seniors 10AS.)

ST. FLORIAN'S ABBEY

*To reach the abbey from Linz Hauptbahnhof, take the bus (dir.: "St. Florian Stift") to "Kotzmannstr." in downtown St. Florian or "Lagerhaus" (30min., 6:20am-6:35pm, 24AS). Both are a 15min. walk from the abbey. The tourist office, Marktpl. 3 (☎/fax (07224) 5690), has info about the abbey and accommodations (open M-F 9am-1pm). **Tours** of the abbey minus the Kaiserzimmer leave daily. (☎(07224) 890 210). Abbey **open** Apr.-Oct. 60AS, students 55AS, children 20AS. Tours 10, 11am, 2, 3, and 4pm.*

The abbey of St. Florian, 17km from Linz, is Austria's oldest Augustinian monastery. According to legend, the martyr Florian was bound to a millstone and thrown in the Enns river. Although Florian perished, his stone miraculously floated (ouch—the irony) and now serves as the abbey's cornerstone. The complex owes much of its fame to composer Anton Bruckner, who began his career here first as choirboy, then as teacher, and finally as a virtuoso organist and composer. His body is interred beneath the organ, allowing him to vibrate in perpetuity to the sound of his dearly-beloved pipes. The abbey contains the **Altdorfer Gallery,** filled with altarpieces by 15th-century artist Albrecht Altdorfer of Regensburg, an Old Master of the Danube school. Although beautiful works of art with balanced compositions and warm tones, these paintings also contain a hidden political agenda. Notice that Altdorfer paints some of Christ's tormentors as Turks, the sworn enemies of the Austrian Empire. The 14 **Kaiserzimmer** (imperial rooms), built in case of an imperial visit, overwhelm visitors with Baroque splendor. Inside the spectacular, recently renovated church (the only part of the abbey accessible without a tour) sits the enormous aforementioned **Bruckner Organ.** Concerts on the powerful instrument are held from May to October, Sunday to Friday at 2:30pm (20min.; 30AS, students 25AS).

KREMSMÜNSTER

Trains go to Kremsmünster from Linz (45min., every hr., 7:40am-7:35pm, 72AS). From the station, follow Bahnhofstr. as it curves left, then right, then left again, and continue on to Marktpl. The path to the abbey starts at the tourist office, Rathauspl. 1 (☎(07583) 7212; open Tu-F 9am-noon and 3-6pm).

Kremsmünster Abbey, 32km south of Linz, belongs to Austria's oldest order and dates from AD 777 (an auspicious year for an abbey). Some 75 monks still call the abbey home. The abbey owns most of the land in the area, including 3800 hectares of woods and a wine-producing vineyard. Their Borgesian **library,** which has 2 rows of books on every shelf and hidden doors in the bookcases, is Austria's third largest, full of medieval tomes. Visitors are not allowed to handle the books, but guides will take out any volume and page through it for you on request. The **Kaisersaal,** built to receive imperial visitors, is a rich Baroque gallery with marble columns and ceiling frescoes that make the ceilings seem much higher than they actually are. As you walk through, the portraits of the Holy Roman Emperors (from Rudolf of Habsburg to Charles VI) seem to gaze down at you. The abbey's **Kunstsammlung** (art collection) tour covers the library, the *Kaisersaal*, several art galleries, and the **Schatzkammer** (treasury), which shelters a beautifully engraved golden chalice dating from the time of Charlemagne. The monks' collection of exotic animal specimens is on display in the 7-story **Sternwarte.** Also open to visitors is the **Fischkalter,** a series of arcaded pools set with pagan and pastoral statues spouting water. Wooden stag heads with real antlers adorn the room—see if you can find the two with radishes in their mouths. (☎(07583) 527 5216. Open 9am-noon and 1-6pm. Central chapel free. Fischkalter 10AS—enter through the ticket office. 1-hour Kunstsammlung tours Apr.-Oct. at 10, 11am, 2, 3, and 4pm; Nov.-Mar. at 11am and 2pm. 1hr. 55AS, students 30AS. Sternwarte tour May-Oct. 10am, 2, and 4pm. 60AS, students 30AS. Both 1½hr. tours include the Fischkalter. For the student rate, you have to buy tickets to both tours.)

The town of Kremsmünster is filled with twisty medieval streets and daunting, steep stairway paths overgrown with moss and wildflowers. Kremsmünster also claims to be the home of **Europe's first high-rise,** constructed in 1748-1758 as a research center for the natural sciences, with a view as far as the Alps. You'll find fresh fruit at the **open-air market** in Marktpl. (F 1-6pm)..

STEYR

Trains connect Steyr to Linz (45min., every hr. 5:38am-8:54pm, 69AS). To reach the city center from the station, exit the station, turn right and then left on Bahnhofstr. After crossing the river, turn left immediately down Engeg., which leads to Stadtpl.

Steyr is famous as a jewel of medieval city planning. Much of the city looks as it has for the past 500 years, with winding, narrow cobbled alleyways, carved arches, and high stone walls. Two mountain rivers, the **Steyr** and the **Enns,** intersect in the middle of the town, dicing Steyr into three parts. As in Linz, Steyr's comely surface hides the city's industrial identity. The city is well known for its iron trade and holds a unique position in the annals of modern technology—in 1884, Steyr was the first town in Europe to use electric street lighting. Who would have guessed? Now BMW has set up shop in the outskirts of town and Internet start-ups advertise alongside doctors and lawyers.

BAAAHBY, IT'S COLD OUTSIDE! If you're planning a trip to Upper Austria in late spring or early summer, think about some warm clothes. The region receives two blasts of unseasonably cold weather in mid-May and mid-June. Three saints whose holy days fall during the first cold front are known as the *Eisheiligen*, or "ice-saints." They are St. Pankratius (May 12th), St. Bonifatius (May 14th), and St. Sophie (May 15th). A little later, the *Schaffskälte* ("sheep's cold") hits, shortly after the poor animals have been taken up the mountain to higher ground. Only after the June chill ends is the wool shaved off their frisky pink bodies.

The **Stadtplatz,** packed with 15th-century buildings, is the *Altstadt*'s focal point. The 16th-century **Leopoldibrunnen** (Leopold fountain) vies with the Rococo *Rathaus* across the square for the title of ornamental heavyweight champion. Gotthard Hayberger, Steyr's famous mayor, architect, and Renaissance man-about-town, designed the town hall. The former **Marienkirche** (Dominican Church), also crammed onto Stadtpl., was born a Gothic building but grew a Baroque facade in the early 17th century. Most of Steyr's beautiful residences have been transformed into banks or shops with modern interiors hidden behind ornate facades. The major exception is the **Innerberger Stadel.** Now the local **Heimatmuseum,** it contains a plethora of puppets, an extensive stuffed bird collection, and the three Cs of medieval weaponry: crossbows, cannons, and cutlery. (Grünmarkt 26. ☎ 53248. Open Apr.-Oct. Tu-Su 10am-4pm. Free.) Berggasse, one of the numerous narrow lanes typical of Steyr, leads from Stadtpl. up to the pink **Lamberg Schloß,** where the **Schloß Galerie** showcases temporary exhibits (☎ 53222; open Tu-Su 10am-noon and 2-5pm; 25AS, students and children free). If you're not in the museum mood, wander in the palace's green courtyards.

The **tourist office,** Stadtpl. 27, in the *Rathaus*, offers **guided tours** (May-Oct. Sa 2pm) and **headset tours.** Both are 45AS. (☎ 53229; fax 532 2915; steyr-info@ris.at; www.upper.austria.org/regionen/steyr. Open Jan.-Nov. M-F 8:30am-6pm, Sa 9am-5pm, Su 10am-4pm; Dec. M-F 8:30am-6pm, Sa 9am-4pm, Su 10am-3pm.) Steyr hosts a **Musik Festival** from mid-August to mid-September featuring international classical, jazz, and folk. Contact the tourist office for more information.

THE MÜHLVIERTEL

Stretching north and west from Linz, the Mühlviertel's shaded woodland paths and pastures, populated only by the occasional cow, are becoming an increasingly popular hiking area for Austrians. Once upon a time, this region was the stomping ground of pagan Celts. When the Christians stormed in during the Middle Ages, they constructed churches out of the supposedly Celt-proof local granite. This same granite filters the famed mineral-rich waters of the region, considered curative in homeopathic circles.

Although Mühlviertel is part of industrial Upper Austria, it's better known for its rich arts-and-crafts traditions than industrial sprawl. Along the old **Mühlviertel Weberstraße** (Weaver's Road), various textile-oriented towns display their unique methods of linen preparation. Other vacation trails include the **Gotischestraße,** which winds past multitudes of High Gothic architectural wonders, and the **Museumstraße,** which boasts more **Freilichtmuseen** (open-air museums) than you can shake a loom at. These museum villages typically recreate the 15th- and 16th-century peasant lifestyle in a functional hamlet. Poppies are another of the Mühlviertel's big selling points, with products ranging from poppy seed oil and lubricants to mouth-watering poppy seed strudels and poppy-seed-and-honey-filled tarts. Iron from Steiermark (Styria) once flowed through the Mühlviertel on its way to Bohemia along the **Pferdeeisenbahn,** an ancient trade route once traversed by horse-drawn caravans, now an excellent easy hike. Throughout this pastoral countryside, *Bauernhöfe* (farm houses) open their doors to world-weary travelers. For nifty tourist brochures about trails and *Bauernhöfe*, contact the **Mühlviertel Tourist Office,** Blütenstr. 8, A-4040 Linz, Postfach 57 (☎ (0732) 235 020 or 238 155).

FREISTADT ☎ 07942

Freistadt, the largest town in the Mühlviertel, is an idyllic, compact village at the juncture of the **Jaunitz** and **Feldiast** rivers. Due to its strategic location on the *Pferdeeisenbahn* route that connected the Babenberg and Habsburg lands, Freistadt was a stronghold of the medieval salt and iron trade. In 1985, Freistadt received the International Europa Nostra Prize for the finest restoration of a medieval *Altstadt*. Freistadt's pride and joy is the **Freistädter Brauerei,** a community-owned brewery that is still in operation but, unfortunately, no longer open to the public.

TRANSPORT AND PRACTICAL INFORMATION

Freistadt is easily accessible from Linz. The most convenient option is the Post Bus, which leaves from Linz's main train station every 2 hours (6:20am-8:15pm, 78AS) and arrives at Böhmertor in Freistadt, just outside the old city walls, a 2-minute walk to Hauptpl. Trains also run from Linz (5:59am-6:59pm, 78AS), but they arrive at the *Hauptbahnhof*, 3km outside of town. The tiny **tourist office,** Hauptpl. 14, has a free reservations service and provides info about the surrounding Mühlviertel villages (☎/fax 757 00; open May-Sept. M-F 9am-7pm, Sa 9am-12pm; Oct.-Apr. M-F 9am-5pm). The **post office,** Promenade 11 at St. Peterstr., exchanges only hard cash (open M-F 8am-noon and 2-5:30pm, Sa 8-10:30am). The **postal code** is A-4240.

ACCOMMODATIONS AND FOOD

To get to the **Jugendherberge (HI),** Schlosshof 3, from the tourist office, walk around the corner to the red building next to Café Lubinger. The hostel is fairly empty and the owner doesn't have reception hours, so you should call to let them know you're coming. Hand-painted stripes and silly cartoons decorate the walls, and the rooms are very comfortable and clean. There is also a roller skating rink. The accommodating proprietress, Margarete Howel, will wait from 6 to 8pm to give you a key; if no one is there or you don't arrive in time, call her at home at ☎3268. (☎74365. Hall showers and toilets. Breakfast 30AS. Sheets 30AS. **Kitchen** facilities in the youth center below. Dorms 70AS, non-members 90AS.) For a list of pensions and **private rooms,** contact the tourist office.

There are a variety of cheap eats at cozy *Gästehäuser*. Enjoy a *tête-à-tête* at **Café Vis à Vis,** Salzg. 13. It offers the local *Mühlviertel Bauernsalat mit Suppe* (farmer's salad with soup; 60AS), *Freistädter* beer in a garden crowded with young people, and good pizzas (small 63AS, large 90AS; ☎74293; open M-F 9:30am-2am, Sa 5pm-1am). There's also plenty to eat around the Hauptpl. The best ice cream in all of Mühlviertel awaits at **Café Lubiner,** Hauptpl. 10 (soft-serve 12AS, scoops of the hard stuff 7AS each). Try the *Eisschokolade* (48AS) for creamy indulgence. Pastries (25AS) and a great breakfast selection round out the menu. (Open Su-M and W-F 8am-7pm, Sa 8am-6pm.) The most convenient grocery store is **Uni Markt,** Pragerstr. 2, at Froschau behind the Böhmertor side of the *innere Stadt* (open M-F 8am-7pm, Sa 7:30am-12:30pm).

SIGHTS AND OUTDOOR ACTIVITIES

Visitors can wander around Freistadt's well-preserved inner and outer wall fortifications, scan the horizon from its watch tower, feast inside its castle, and swim in the surrounding moat. The tower of Freistadt's remarkable 14th-century castle, the **Bergfried** (50m from the hostel), houses the **Mühlviertler Heimathaus,** a regional museum that displays traditional tools, and period pieces (☎72274; admission with tour only May-Oct. Tu-Sa 10am and 2pm, Su 10am; Nov.-Apr. Tu-F 2pm; 10AS).

Numerous **hiking trails** branch out to amazing Mühlviertel destinations; consider hiking out of town and catching a bus back. Freistadt lies on the Mühlviertel **Museumstraße,** a path linking many of the region's museums, and on the **Pferdeeisenbahn Wanderweg,** a 237km hiking trail along the former medieval trade route. A mildly strenuous 1-hour hike zigzags up Kreuzweg to **Peterskirche.** A large map on the Promenade illustrates other local hiking paths. Get hiking maps (10-35AS), free bus schedules, and biking maps (25AS) at the tourist office.

Each July and August, Freistadt holds a 2-month festival of food and international music, the **Wirthausmusi,** with daily events scattered throughout town. Multicultural meets medieval—or just another excuse to drink *Freistädter* beer?

Lower Austria (Niederösterreich)

LOWER AUSTRIA (NIEDERÖSTERREICH)

The province of Niederösterreich, with its rolling, forested hills carpeted with wildflowers, accounts for a quarter of the nation's land mass—and 60% of its wine production. Rugged castle ruins lurk in the hills above medieval towns, bearing mute witness to the Turkish invasions of yore, while ferry boats languidly navigate the river in the shadows of impressive Baroque edifices that jut from the steep banks above. Hikers and bikers, enjoying the varied terrain, cruise past all of these, frequently on day trips from Vienna. The food's nothing to sneeze at either: local specialties include *Wienerwald* cream strudel, a sinful mixture of flaky crust, curds, raisins, and lemon peel (it tastes *far* better than it sounds).

HIGHLIGHTS OF LOWER AUSTRIA

After a relaxing cruise down the Danube, wander through medieval **Stein** (see p. 277).

Climb up to the ruins of Richard the Lionheart's prison, **Schloß Dürnstein** (see p. 278).

Marvel at **Melk's** big beautiful yellow Benedictine abbey (see p. 279).

Smell the roses, all 20,000 of them, in **Baden's** rosarium (see p. 283).

DANUBE VALLEY (DONAUTAL)

The "Blue Danube" may largely be the invention of Johann Strauss's imagination, but the valley of this mighty, muddy-green river inspired him to create music for good reason. Magnificent castles look down onto the river from hilly perches and lush green vineyards line the banks, producing Austria's best white wine. Romantic villages await at every bend, seemingly unblemished by the rush of industrialization. Glide on a ferry or pedal along its shores—either way, you'll experience the exhilarating, fluid beauty of Austria's most famous river. The **Wachau** region holds the most exemplary bends of the river, those between Melk and Krems—make sure to catch at least this much of the area.

The legendary **Erste Donau Dampfschiffahrts-Gesellschaft** (DDSG—creators of the longest German word in existence, *Donaudampfschifffahrtsgesellschaftkapitänswitwe*, which translates as "the widow of a captain working for the Danube Steamship Company") runs ships every day from May to late October along the Danube. The firm operates an office in **Vienna,** I, Friedrichstr. 7 (☎58 8800; fax 588 80440; info@ddsg-blue-danube.at; www.ddsg-blue-danube.at). Boats go from Vienna to the Wachau region only on Sundays (May 14-Oct.). These trips, complete with didactic commentary, run from Reichsbrücke in Vienna to **Tülln,** and **Krems,** before ending in **Dürnstein** (departing Vienna 8:45am, returning 8:45pm; reservation required; 200AS, round trip 270AS)—note that this ship does not make it as far as Melk, the site of the fantastic monastery.

In fact, the best trip is not this Sunday cruise—much of the early portion of the Sunday ride goes through industrial Vienna. Instead take the ferry that runs every day of the week between the most beautiful towns on the river, those in the Wachau region. Three boats per day leave from Krems and dock at Dürnstein, Spitz, and Melk. From Apr. 22 to Oct. 1 boats leave Krems at 10:15am, 1pm, and 3:45pm, and take 2hr40min to go all the way to Melk (200AS, round-trip 270AS; bike transport is free but call ahead). If you are in Vienna, you can purchase a purchase a **rail/ferry combination,** including train fare from Vienna to the Wachau region, the ferry within the Wachau valley between Krems and Melk, and entrance to the Benedictine abbey of Melk (499AS). Eurail and ISIC holders get a 20% discount on travel, and families may travel for half-price (minimum 1 parent and 1 child ages 6-15; under 6 travel free with a parent). Contact the DDSG or local tourist offices for special ship/bus ticket combinations. Specialty tours include the *Nibelungen*, which sails through areas described in the ancient saga; a summer solstice cruise *(Sonnendfahrt)*, which steams by the Midsummer's Night bonfires in the Wachau valley; and a *Heurigen* ride with a live *Liederabend* (evening song) trio. Other exciting options include a trip past Hundertwasser's most famous monuments on a boat designed by the Austrian eco-architect himself.

Bicyclists should take advantage of the **Danube Cycle Track,** a velocipede's dream. This 305km riverside bike trail goes from Vienna, through the Wachau Valley, and Linz, all the way to Passau, on the German border. It links the Danube villages, and offers captivating views of crumbling castles, latticed vineyards, and medieval towns. Area tourist offices carry the route map. There is also information on the route at www.radtouren.at/english. You can **rent bikes** at almost all train stations, including those at Melk, Spitz, and Krems. One of the most dramatic fortresses on the ride is the 13th-century **Burg Aggstein-Gastein,** formerly inhabited by Scheck von Wald, a robber-baron known to fearful sailors as **Schreckenwalder** (the terror of the woods). The lord was wont to impede the passage of ships with ropes stretched across the Danube and then demand tribute from his ensnared victims.

KREMS AND STEIN ☎02732

Over the river and through the woods, at the head of the Wachau region of the Danube valley, the hybrid town of Krems/Stein is surrounded by lush, green hills covered by terraced vineyards. Historically, Krems and Stein shared a mayor to coordinate trade and military strategy on the critical Danube trading route.

Through the years the two towns have grown into each other's territories. Much of the region's wealth came from the tolls on this riverbend's Danube traders—the Kremser Penny was the first coin minted by the Habsburgs.

The stuccoed walls of **Krems** have pastel charm, channeling wanderers to a relatively modern, shop-filled *Fußgängerzone* (when medieval Stein's your neighbor, Baroque *is* modern). Krems holds most of the sights, ranging from art exhibits to sporting events, but **Stein,** the older half of the duo, has a gorgeous *Altstadt*—its crooked, narrow, cobblestone passages twist and wind back on themselves. In the valley around Krems/Stein, vineyards cultivate 120 different wines. Head for **Kellergasse,** the high street in Stein that lies next to those hills of plenty, where *Heurigen* offer the fruit of these vines as well as great views of the **Stift Göttweig** (abbey) across the Danube. Tour buses often block the entrance to this street leading to the *Heurigen* with good reason—rich wine and the impressive panorama of the valley make it worthwhile for every tourist.

GETTING THERE AND GETTING AROUND

Most visitors arrive on bicycles, but the **train station** is a five-minute walk from Krems's *Fußgängerzone.* To get to the *Fußgängerzone*, exit the front door of the *Bahnhof*, cross Ringstr., and follow Dinstlstr. Regional trains connect Krems to **Vienna** (Spittelau station; 133AS, 8:10am-10:10pm) through Tulln. Travelers to other big cities must change trains in St. Pölten (76AS, 7:30am-10:30pm). In front of the station is a **bus depot.** Both buses and trains leave every 30 minutes for routes to Melk and St. Pölten. Krems lies along the **DDSG ferry** route from **Passau** through **Linz** and **Melk** to **Vienna** (see p. 274). The ferry station is on the riverbank close to Stein and the ÖAMTC campground, near the intersection of Donaulände and Dr.-Karl-Dorreck-Str. To reach Krems from the landing, walk down Donaulände, which becomes Ringstr., then take a left onto Utzstr. To reach Stein, follow Dr.-Karl-Dorreck-Str. and then take a left onto Steiner Landstr.

ORIENTATION AND PRACTICAL INFORMATION

Stein is west of Krems, bracketed by Steiner Kellerg. and Steiner Landstr. The **tourist office** is housed in the Kloster Und at Undstr. 6. From the train station, take a left on Ringstr. and continue (15min.) to Martin-Schmidt-Str. Turn right and follow the street to the end; the office is across the street and to the right. The excellent staff has amassed tons of information on accommodations, sports, and entertainment, as well as the indispensable *Heurigen Kalendar*, which lists the opening times of regional wine taverns. Guided walking tours in several languages leave for Krems or Stein (1½hr., 700AS per group or 35AS per person if more than 20 people show up). They also book hotel reservations. (☎82676; fax 70011; www.tiscover.com/krems. Open Easter-Oct. M-F 9am-7pm, Sa-Su 10am-noon and 1-7pm. In winter M-F 9am-6pm.) Other services include: **Lockers** for 30AS, **luggage storage,** and **bike rental** (☎825 3644; 150AS per day, 120AS per half-day; with train ticket 100AS, 80AS) all at the train station; **ATMs** to be found along shopping streets, **bike rental** at the Donau Campground (see below, half-day 40AS, full-day 60AS) and the train station (90AS per day, with ticket 40AS), **public toilets** at the tourist office and in the *Stadtpark;* and **currency exchange** at the **post office** right off Ringstr. on Brandströmstr. (☎82606; open M-F 8am-noon and 2-6pm, Sa 8-11am). The **postal code** is A-3500.

ACCOMMODATIONS AND FOOD

No matter where you stay, ask your hosts for a **guest card** that grants a number of discounts. The **Jugendherberge Radfahrer (HI),** Ringstr. 77, is a clean, close-quartered hostel accommodating 52 in comfortable 4- and 6-bed rooms. As the name might suggest, it is packed with strong-calved bicycling enthusiasts. Members only. **Lockers** 10AS. Reception 7-9:30am and 5-8pm. Open Apr.-Oct. Call ahead.

Tax, breakfast, bicycle storage, and sheets included. (☎83452; for advance bookings, call the central office in Vienna at 586 4145 or fax at 586 41453. Dorms 180AS. 20AS surcharge on stays less than 3 nights.) Karl and Ingred Hietzgern's **Baroque Bürgerhaus,** Untere Landstr. 53, stands in the *Altstadt* of Krems. From the train station, walk straight ahead, cross Ringstr., continue 2 blocks to Untere Landstr., and turn right. During the Middle Ages, the building was three small houses, which were joined with one facade in the Baroque period. The Hietzgerns have filled the house with *Jugendstil* furniture and hand-painted wood and will happily tell you about anything and everything Kremsian. Open mid-June to mid-September. (☎/fax 76184 or 74036. 2- and 3-bed dorms with shower 310AS; for stays of 3 nights or more 285AS.) Although slightly more expensive, Krems's oldest guesthouse, the centrally located **Hotel-Restaurant "Alte Post,"** Obere Landstr. 32, will host you comfortably amid its dark velvet couches, embroidered curtains, and garden café. Follow directions for *Baroque Bürgerhaus*, but turn left on Untere Landstr., which becomes Obere Landstraße. (☎82276; fax 84396)Singles 350AS, with shower 490AS; doubles 630-830AS. Breakfast included.) In addition, *Privatzimmer* abound on Steiner Landstr. For a more earthy experience, try **ÖAMTC Donau Camping,** Wiedeng. 7, situated on a grassy Danube riverbank near the highway. (☎84455. Reception 7:30-10am and 4:30-7pm. Showers included. Electrical hookup 25AS. Facilities for disabled guests. Open Easter to mid-Oct. 50AS per person plus 10.50AS tax, children 35AS; tents 30-60AS, bring your own; cars 40AS.)

The area around the pedestrian zone in Krems overflows with restaurants and street-side cafés. The famous **Café-Konditorei Hagmann,** Untere Landstr. 8, is known throughout Krems for its outstanding pastries and chocolates, which rival any in Vienna. Try the *Marillenstrudel* (28AS), but beware: you may find yourself returning for breakfast, lunch, and dinner. Grab a *Wachauer Kugel* (ball of chocolate and nougat) for the road. (☎83167, www.hagmann.co.at/konditorei. Open M-F 7am-7pm, Sa 7am-5pm.) **Schwarze Kuchl,** in the same building, offers a salad buffet (small 38AS, large 55AS), assorted goulashes (39-78AS), and bread (☎83128; open M-F 8:30am-7:30pm, Sa 8:30am-2pm). Serving excellent chinese food at rock bottom prices is **China Restaurant** at Obere Landstrasse 5. The lunch Menü is only 60AS, and the convivial atmosphere of the place is worth much more. (☎84183. Open daily 11:30am-2:30pm and 5:30-11:30pm.) At **Heuriger am Rebentor,** Steiner Kellerg. 40 (☎82636), you can sample the strong wines (18AS for a quarter liter) in the vineyard. To round off your decadence, share the cheese platter with a friend (48AS). **Heuriger Hamböck,** Steiner Kellerg. 31, has a charming leafy terrace with a view of the town's spires and a restaurant bedecked with old *Faß* (kegs), presses, and other vineyard tools. The proprietor gives free tours of the cellar, with a tasting. Wine is 22AS a glass; snacks are 30-50AS. (☎84568. Open daily 3pm or until people leave.) The cheapest eats in town are at the **Julius Meinl** supermarket, in front of the train station or on the corner of Gaheisstr. and Obere Landstr. (open M-F 7:30am-6:30pm, Sa 7:30am-5pm).

LITTLE OLD LADIES Lower Austria is packed not only with yellow remnants of the Habsburg days, but also a few reminders of prehistoric times. Krems is one of Austria's top archaeology centers, and its researchers have recently unearthed the remains of a 32,000-year-old hunting community settled in the Danube bend near a place now named Galgenberg. Among the usual shards of bone and clay animal figurines, archaeologists excavated eight pieces of slate that, when fitted together, form a well-endowed female statuette. Fanny von Galgenberg, named for the famous dancer Fanny Elßler, is Austria's oldest known work of art and the world's only known female sculpture from the Aurignae Period. Barely three inches tall and half an inch thick, the figure is engraved with sketches and positioned in a pose that classifies her as part of the archetypal prehistoric Venus figures, like her much younger sister and symbol of fertility, the "Venus of Willendorf," who was found between Krems and Melk.

 SIGHTS

Both Krems and Stein have a plethora of historical attractions, spanning nearly every architectural style to cross the Alps.

THE OLD TOWN. In Stein, fascinating old buildings line **Steiner Landstraße,** a well-preserved vestige of the Middle Ages. Stone steps tucked between streets and houses lead to higher altitudes and impressive views of the town with its onion-domed church and of the flourishing valley. Krems's *Fußgängerzone*, the center of mercantile activity, runs down Obere and Untere Landstr. The entrance to the pedestrian area is marked by the Steiner Tor, one of four medieval city gates flanked by two Gothic towers. Inside the *Tor*, you'll find a refreshing mix of shops, sights, and eateries. Not heavily touristed, this section of town is a great place to meander past the city's architectural treasures. Market places line Obere Landstr., starting with Dominikanerpl., home of the **Dominikanerkirche,** now the Weinstadt Museum. Farther down the pedestrian zone is **Pfarrkirche Platz,** home of the Renaissance **Rathaus** and the **Pfarrkirche** with its piecemeal Romanesque, Gothic, and Baroque architecture. Once there, walk up the hill to the **Piaristenkirche** to see life-sized depictions of Jesus' crucifixion. At the end of the pedestrian zone stands the **Simandlbrunnen,** a fountain depicting a husband kneeling in front of his stern wife. The fountain commemorates the power and influence of women in Krems during the Renaissance, when they succeeded in shutting down the Simandl brotherhood, a fraternity of carousing and late-night debauchery.

WEINSTADT MUSEUM. Built in the Dominikanerkloster, the excellent Weinstadt Museum in Krems features a curious combination of paintings by the world-renowned Baroque artist Marten Johann Schmidt and, in the cloister cellars, archaeological treasures from the Paleolithic Era through the Middle Ages. The changing exhibits cover subjects ranging from local folklore to Apocalyptic art. *(Kornermarkt 14. ☎801 567 or 801 572; fax 801 576. Open Mar.-Nov. Tu 9am-6pm, W-Su 1-6pm. 40AS, students 30AS.)*

KUNSTHALLE KREMS. To enhance Krems' cultural offerings, Kunsthalle Krems has recently opened a new facility on the corner of Steiner Landstr. and Dr.-Karl-Dorreck-Str. From the tourist office, turn right and walk down Undstr., under the overpass, at which point the street becomes Steiner Landstr. The enormous exhibition hall always has fascinating cultural and historical exhibits, often about post-modern or non-European art. *(Steiner Landstr. 8. ☎826 6919; fax 826 6916. Open daily 10am-6pm. 50-100AS, discounts for students and seniors.)*

WINE CELLARS. Above Krems and Stein, the lovely terraced vineyards, where the vines photosynthesize in neat little rows, tempt travelers to seek a bottle of wine and a patch of grass in the sun. Bring a sweater to wear inside the cellars—dry white wines complain if not kept at 10 to 11 degrees Celsius. The **Heurigen** (wine cellars) are not to be missed. Plan carefully, however—the *Heurigen* are only allowed to stay open three weeks every two months from April to October. Better-safe-than-sorry types pick up a schedule from the tourist office; press-your-luck gamblers just stroll down Kellerg. in Stein and hope to happen upon on an open cellar. If you don't have time for *Heurigen*, stop by the city-owned **Weingut Stadt Krems,** on the edge of the pedestrian zone. Go to the end of Obere Landstr., through the gate, and to the right. This winery lacks an attached restaurant, but it does offer free tours of the cellar and bottling center. The free tastings that follow the tour usually seduce visitors into buying a bottle of wine, which runs 40-100AS. *(Stadtgraben 11. ☎80 1440; fax 80 1442. Open for tours M-F 8am-noon and 1-4pm, Sa 8am-noon.)* Those who can still walk straight should lurch down to the historic abbey cellar of **Kloster Und,** by the tourist office. The cellar has all of Austria's regional wines—for 180AS, you get a basket of bread, mineral water to cleanse the palate, and two hours to weave through the selection of more than 100 wines, from the

HOLDING A GRUDGE Upon arriving in the Holy Land during the Third Crusade, England's King Richard the Lionheart threw the Austrian flag to the ground, deeply offending Leopold V, Duke of Austria. Big mistake. When the Holy Roman Emperor was short of cash and ordered Richard captured and held for ransom; Leopold was happy to help out for a cut of the booty. As luck would have it, Richard's ship was wrecked en route to England, and he was forced to cross Austria. Despite Richard's clever disguise (as a peasant), Leopold's men recognized him and locked him up in Dürnstein (giving Robin Hood time to flourish under evil Prince John). For a time, Richard's whereabouts were unknown in England, and a legend arose in the thirteenth-century about how Richard was found: supposedly, Richard's faithful minstrel Blondel wandered through Austria, looking for his master by whistling a tune they had composed together. When the minstrel got to Dürnstein, Richard heard him whistling and whistled back the refrain. England sent representatives with the obscenely large sum of 100,000 Marks for Richard's ransom, of which Leopold garnered 75,000. The pope excommunicated Leopold for imprisoning Richard, but Leopold consoled himself by building (among other things) the town of Wiener Neustadt with his new fortune.

noble Riesling of Wachau to the nutty Neuburger of Burgenland. For those with a smaller appetite or budget, you can try just 6 wines for 70AS. *(Undstr. 6. ☎73073; fax 832 2378. Open March-Dec. 24.)*

FESTIVALS

Krems is a happening festival town, celebrating everything from apricots to wine. Check with the tourist office for exhaustive info. Each year the **Donaufestival**, from mid-June to early July, brings open-air music and dancing, kicking off a summer of cultural activities including theater, circus, symposia, *Lieder*, folk music, even korean drums. From July 15 to August 15, Krems hosts a **Musikfest,** featuring a number of organ, piano, and quartet concerts that take place in the Kunsthalle and various churches. Tickets are available at the tourist office and *Österreichticket* (☎(01) 53601). From August 27 to September 5, Krems hosts the **Lower Austria Wine Fest,** which features wine tastings, culinary specialties, presentations, and folklore. DDSG offers a 40% reduction on ferry rates between Krems and Melk for the occasion. Throughout the year, many **churches** have sacred music and organ concerts, which resonate beautifully within Gothic vaults and are usually free.

DAYTRIP FROM KREMS

DÜRNSTEIN

Trains connect Dürnstein to Krems (every hr. 6am-8pm, 25AS) and Vienna's Franz Josef Bahnhof (every hr., 145AS). To reach town from the train station, descend the hill, turn right, and pass through the underground walkway (5min.). Boats dock at the DDSG ferry station on the Donaupromenade, a riverside road with beaches and bike paths. To reach town from the landing docks, turn right on Donaupromenade and left on Anzugg. which intersects with Hauptstr.

Located a bend or two down the Danube from Krems, among deep green vineyards, Dürnstein is a hilltop medieval village with a mythical charm that attracts tourists and locals alike. The main draw is hiking up to the ruined castle where **Richard the Lionheart** was imprisoned after his capture on the way back from the Third Crusade in 1192 (See Holding a Grudge, below).

Although Richard's capture was the last big splash onto history pages for the Kuenninger dynasty, they continued to prosper on their home turf, building the **Augustiner Chorherrenstift**, an enormous Baroque abbey commissioned by the daughter of the penultimate heir of the family line in 1372 and dedicated to the Virgin Mary. Joseph II dissolved it at the same time he dismantled most of Austria's ecclesiastical institutions and introduced the re-useable coffin, but it has been well-maintained nevertheless. You'll get mesmerizing views from the grandiose blue and white church steeple. Beware the creepy skeletons that guard the elegant interior of the church from all sides. (☎(02711) 375; fax 432. Open Apr.-Oct. 9am-6pm. 25AS, with tour 50AS, tour for students 45AS including glass of wine on Th.)

The **tourist office** is located in a shack in a parking lot down the hill and to the right of the train station. The office and the local *Rathaus* (on Hauptstr.) provide lists of *Privatzimmern* (from 200AS) and open *Heurigen.* (☎(02711) 200. Tourist office open M-F 8am-noon and 1:30-4pm.)

MELK

☎02752

The enormous yellow mass of Melk's monastery floats over dark blue Danube waters and stucco houses of the village below in one of the most surreal vistas you'll find in Austria. Melk's eerie monastery was constructed atop the cliffs in AD 994 as a Babenberg residence, until Margrave Leopold II turned it over to Benedictine Abbot Sigibod, thus founding the Benedictine monastery and, subsequently, the village of Melk. The monastery was a renowned ecclesiastical force in the medieval world, famed for its monumental library and learned monks (who incidentally merited several admiring references in Umberto Eco's novel *The Name of the Rose*). Today, the abbey still wields power as one of few ecclesiastical institutions that report directly to the Pope, with no bishop as middle-man. Melk remains a living monastery, home to 20 monks who toil away, praying, farming, and teaching Austrian youth at the highly scholastic monastery school. Below the abbey, the town is a charming jumble of Renaissance houses, narrow pedestrian zones, cobblestone streets, old towers, and remnants of the medieval city wall. The town, too, remains an active community, rather than an artificial playground for tourists. In the morning, the streets are full of the sounds of residents preparing for their day, greeting even strangers with a friendly "Grüß Gott!'

TRANSPORT AND PRACTICAL INFORMATION

Trains link Melk to **Vienna's Westbahnhof** (1½hr., 156AS) via St. Pölten. Just outside the station's main entrance is the **bus depot.** Bus #1451 chugs from Melk to **Krems** (80AS) and #1538 from Melk to St. Pölten (46AS). Melk is at the end of the **DDSG ferry** route between Vienna and Passau (from Krems 200AS; see p. 274).

Melk's **tourist office,** Babenbergstr. 1, on the corner of Babenbergstr. and Abbe-Stadler-G., has maps and pamphlets on the town's history and athletic activities in the Wachau region. From the train station, walk down Bahnhofstr. and then straight on Bahng. Turn right at Rathauspl. and cross, staying to the right until you hit Abbe-Stadler-G. The office has large **lockers** (10AS) and bike racks, and makes free room reservations. (☎523 0732 or 523 0733; fax 523 0737. Open July-Aug. daily 9am-7pm; Sept.-Oct. and Apr.-June M-F 9am-noon and 2-6pm, Sa 10am-2pm.) **Bike rental** (full-day 150AS, half-day 120AS; with rail ticket 100AS, 80AS), **currency exchange,** and **luggage storage** (30AS) are all available at the train station. The **post office** is at Bahnhofstr. 3 (open M-F 8am-noon and 2-6pm, Sa 8-10am). The **postal code** is A-3390.

ACCOMMODATIONS AND FOOD

To really soak in the cozy atmosphere of Melk, stay in one of the many *Privatzimmer* throughout town or on a country farm. (List available from the tourist office. Prices range from 170-250AS per person. Amenities vary. Breakfast included.) The recently renovated **Jugendherberge,** Abt-Karl-Str. 42, is about a 10-minute walk from the train station (turn right as you exit and follow the green signs). This clean hostel offers 104 beds with checkered sheets in quads with private showers and

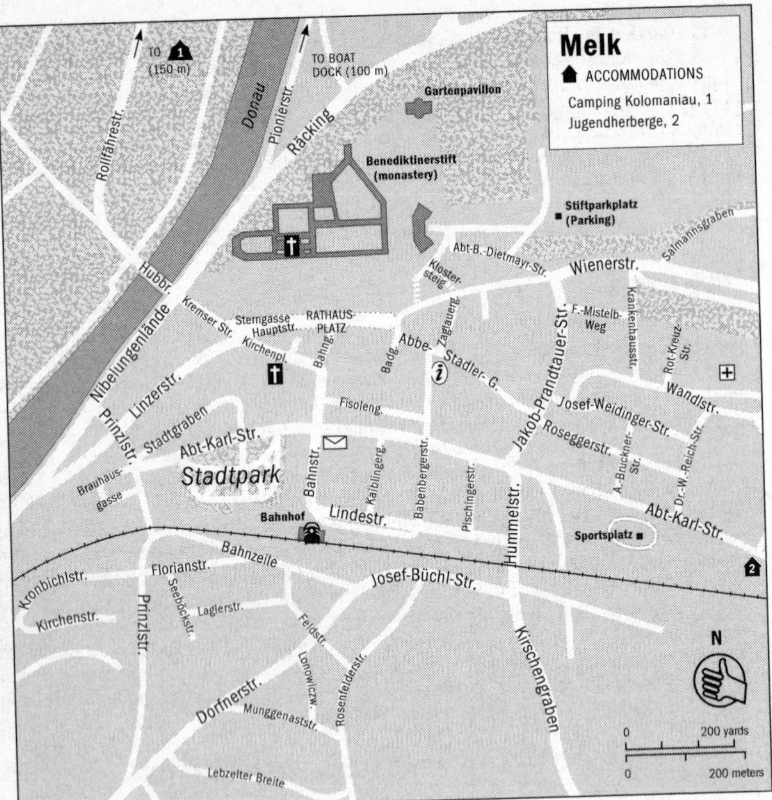

hall toilets. Beware of rampant school groups. (☎52681; fax 54257. Dorms 174.50AS; under 19 140AS. Tax 10.50AS. Breakfast and bicycle storage included. Reception 8-10am and 5-9pm. Open Apr.-Oct.) **Camping Kolomaniau** overlooks the Danube next to the ferry landing. Follow Kremserstr. to the Danube, cross the bridge, and keep right along Rollfährestr. (☎53291. 35AS, children 20AS; tents 35AS; cars 25AS. Tax 10.50AS. Showers 15AS. Reception 8am-midnight.)

Restaurants abound on Rathauspl., but look farther afield for less tourist-oriented joints. A 5-minute walk away from the monastery through Hauptpl. brings you to **Pizzeria "Venezia,"** Linzerstr. 7, where you can choose from 16 lunch *Menü* options ranging from 55 to 85AS. (☎51224. Open daily 11am-2:30pm and 5pm-midnight.) For more regional cuisine, eat with the locals at **Finnis Beis'l,** Sterng. 13 (☎51549), known for its home cooking. From the tourist office, veer right off Hauptpl. onto Sterng. Rustic decor complements the tasty, filling entrees (50-95AS; open Tu-Sa 4pm-midnight). Black lacquered wood and oh-so-chic decor greet you at **Il Palio,** Wienerstr. 3, home of fantastic ice-cream concoctions (☎54732, open daily 9am-midnight). At night, the streets may seem empty, but **"Nostalgiebers 1" Alt Melk,** Wienerstr. 25, certainly won't be. Step into the intimate warmth of deep red velvet curtains, cream-colored walls, and old black-and-white photo portraits and enjoy a *cabernet sauvignon* (28AS) or a milkshake with the genial, mixed-age crowd. (☎4458. Live music 1st and 3rd Th of each month. Open Su-Th 4pm-2am, F-Sa 4pm-4am.) During the day, **SPAR Markt,** Rathauspl. 9, has bread to spread and pears to share (open M and W-F 7am-6pm, Sa 7am-noon).

HIDDEN TREASURE The crown jewel of Melk's *Benediktinerstift* is unquestionably the *Melker Kreuz*, a bejeweled and gilded cross that contains a splinter believed to be a tiny fragment of the cross upon which Jesus was crucified. Crafted in 1363, the cross is two-faced: the "wealthy" side sparkles with diamonds, rubies, emeralds, and fresh water pearls from the Danube, while the "sacred" side depicts the crucified Christ and the four Evangelists at each of its rounded points. On two occasions, the cross has been stolen from the monastery, but each time has made its way back to the abbey by supernatural means (once by sailing itself back on a boat). Legend has it that anyone who opens the cross to look at the relic will be blinded by the holiness of the sight. For those brave (or foolish) enough to try, the cross can only be opened by simultaneously turning the aquamarine stones at the four corners of the cross.

SIGHTS AND OUTDOOR ACTIVITIES

The twin attractions of Melk are the impressive **Benediktinerstift** (Benedictine abbey) and the surrounding Danube countryside, ideal for outdoor activities.

BENEDIKTINERSTIFT. The yellow Benedictine abbey lights up the entire countryside, calling pilgrims to enter God's army, while also commanding fantastic views of the city and the Danube River. The only part open to the general public is the secular wing, where such notables as Emperor Charles VI, Pope Pius VI, and Napoleon took shelter in the imperial chambers. The wing is filled with informative exhibits (mostly in German) and various Baroque optical tricks, including a portrait of Leopold II, whose eyes follow you about the room, and a flat ceiling that appears to be a dome when viewed from the center of the room. Habsburg portraits line cool marble halls: in an act of political deference, royal consort Franz I points to his wife, the reigning Maria Theresa. The stunning abbey library is brimming with sacred and secular texts painstakingly hand-copied by monks. The two highest shelves in the gallery are fake—in typical Baroque fashion, the monks sketched book spines onto the wood to make the collection appear even more formidable. The church itself, maintained by 20 monks, is a Baroque masterpiece. Maria Theresa donated the two skeletons that adorn the side altars—unknown refugees from the catacombs of Rome, lounging in full costume. The centerpiece of the monastery is the Melker Kreuz (Melk Cross)—gold, jewels, the works, all circa 1363 (see Hidden Treasure, above). The monks, who really know their art, keep up with the times, skillfully curating temporary exhibits of contemporary art, and even commissioned artist Peter Bischof to create new murals over weather-ruined frescoes in the interior of the main courtyard. *(Abbey open daily Apr. 15-Nov. 15 9am-6pm. Last entry 1hr. before closing. Audio guide in English 40AS. Guided tours Nov.-Mar. every hour in German, and every day at 3 pm or by arrangement in English. 100AS, students 40AS, tour 30AS extra. Call 523 1252 for more information.)*

CASTLE. Five kilometers out of town is **Schloß Schallaburg,** one of the most magnificent Renaissance castles in central Europe. The castle's architecture is reason enough to visit: Romanesque, Gothic, Renaissance, and Mannerist influences converge in the terra-cotta arcades of the main courtyard. The floor is composed of a 1600-piece **mosaic** depicting mythological figures and gods. *(☎(02754) 6317. Open May-Oct. M-F 9am-5pm, Sa-Su 9am-6pm. 90AS, students 40AS. Call ahead for a tour.)* The castle doubles as the **International Exhibition Center of Lower Austria**, which goes out of its way to bring foreign cultures to life. In 2001, the castle wil show "Tibet: Geheimnisvolle Welt des Alten." *(☎6317. Exhibitions in German.)* Shuttle taxis leave Melk's train station and tourist office daily at 9am, 10am, and noon. The last shuttle taxi back to Melk from castle is 4:25pm (15 min., 30As per person). Or you can hike up to the complex; ask the tourist office for a map from Melk to the palace.

OUTDOOR ACTIVITIES. Hikers can enjoy the network of trails surrounding Melk that wind through tiny villages, farmland, and wooded groves. The tourist office provides a great map, which lists area sights and hiking paths, and handouts on the 10km Leo Böck trail, 6km Seniorenweg, and 15km Schallaburggrundweg. **Cyclists** might enjoy a tour along the Danube toward Willendorf on the former canal-towing path. The 30,000-year-old **Venus of Willendorf,** an 11cm voluptuous stone figure and one of the world's most famous fertility symbols, was discovered there in 1908 (see Little Old Ladies, p. 276). A copy is now on display in Vienna (the original is locked up). For a more sedate option, **ferries** travel to the other side of the Danube to **Arnsdorf,** where the local *jause* (an Austrian version of British high tea), here called *Hauerganse* (vintner's special), will load enough carbos to send you through the vineyards and apricot orchards back to Melk. The ferry returns past the **Heiratswald** (Marriage Woods). Romantic Melk awards a young sapling tree to couples who marry in Melk, which the couple tends for the rest of their lives.

FESTIVAL

The **Sommerspiele Melk** (Melk Summer Festival) comes to town in early July. An open-air stage in front of the monastery's pavilion provides the perfect setting for enjoying world-class theater (in German) on warm summer nights. Tickets (150-350AS) are available at the Melk city hall, theater ticket offices, travel agencies throughout Austria, and the box office next to the monastery after 7:15pm, before performances. (Performances mid-July to mid-Aug. Th-Sa 8:30pm. For more information, call 52307 or fax 523 0727.)

LOWER AUSTRIA

ST. PÖLTEN ☎02742

St. Pölten (pop. 50,000) is one of the few places in Lower Austria not on the Danube, but still worth visiting. There are noticeable fault lines between St. Pölten's industrial heritage and its present bid for tourism, but the town still has much to offer in the form of a shopping-oriented Baroque *Altstadt*, turn-of-the-century *Jugendstil* buildings, and loads of small summer music festivals.

TRANSPORT AND PRACTICAL INFORMATION. The **train station,** on Bahnhofpl. near the pedestrian zone, sends direct trains to **Hütteldorf** and the **Vienna Westbahnhof** 2-3 times per hour (114AS). Right in front of the train station, the **bus** depot runs infrequent buses to **Melk** and **Krems.** A free schedule is available at the bus information booth. Kremsergasse divides the town in half. As you leave the train station and cross Bahnhofpl., Kremserg. is diagonally to your left. Follow it until you hit Riemerpl., and turn right to reach St. Pölten's center, the **Rathausplatz.** The **tourist office** is in the Rathauspassage, the tunnel beneath the *Rathaus.* The staff provides information about St. Pölten, regional events, and the wonders of the surrounding countryside. They'll also give you a room list, lead you on a 1-hour **tour** of the inner city (call up to a week in advance), and rent a **cassette tour** in several languages for 20AS. (☎353 354; fax 333 2819. Open M-F 8am-6pm; April-Oct. M-F 8am-6pm, Sa 9:30am-5pm, Su and holidays 10am-5pm.) There is a free reservations phone next door on the wall of the Reisebüro. Other services include: **currency exchange** at the **Bank Austria**, Rathausg. 2 (☎54919; fax 54575), across the street from the tourist office; **bike rental** at the train station for 150AS, with train ticket 100AS (☎323 3874. Open daily 5:45am-10pm); and **lockers** at the train station available 24 hours a day (30AS). The main **post office,** Bahnhofpl. 1a, is right by the station (open M-F 7am-8pm, Sa 8am-1pm). The **postal code** is A-3100.

ACCOMMODATIONS AND FOOD. St. Pölten works well as a day trip, especially since the town lost its only youth hostel a few years ago. You might consider staying in the hostels in **Krems** (☎(02732) 83452; see p. 274), **Melk** (☎(02752) 2681; see p. 279), or **Vienna** (see p. 92). The tourist office maintains a list of *Privatzimmer*, most of which are outside the city limits.

St. Pölten's local specialties include oysters, fried black pudding, and savory Wachau wine. A comfortable Viennese café with newspapers and lingering guests,

Café Melange, Kremserg. 11, on the second floor, draws a young crowd (☎2393; open M-F 7:30am-6:30pm, Sa 7:30am-5pm). **Café Punschkrapfel,** Domg. 8, is named for its specialty—a small, chocolate, pink-frosted rum cake. Other offerings include fruit frappes (34AS) and a salad buffet (35AS), which taste best in the popular outdoor seating area. (☎6383. Open M-F 7am-7pm, Sa 7am-1pm, 7am-6pm on the first Sa. of the month.) Cheap and healthy fixings await at the **Julius Meinl** supermarket, Kremserg. 21 (open M-F 7:30am-6pm, Sa 7:30am-12:30pm).

SIGHTS. St. Pölten's architecture suffered heavy damage during WWII, and since then, the city has tried very hard to rebuild. Returned to its former glow, the *Altstadt* is adorned with mostly Baroque façades along with a couple of *Jugendstil* gems. The restoration was meticulous and is now so well-maintained that the *Altstadt* looks almost new, as if you were looking at it through eighteenth-century eyes.

The 13th-century **Rathausplatz** at St. Pölten's core, built on the site of a 1st-century Roman settlement, bears witness to this zealous effort. The building at Rathauspl. 2 earned the name **Schubert Haus** due to Franz's frequent visits to the owners, Baron von Münk and family. A neo-Grecian Schubert (bare-chested, no less) conducts above the window above the door. Turn right out of the tourist office onto Rathausg., which becomes Riemerpl. and then Wienerstr., turn right on Ledererg., and follow it past Dr. Karl-Renner-Promenade to see the only *Jugendstil* (Art Nouveau) synagogue in Lower Austria. Architect Joseph Maria Olbrich designed several other *Jugendstil* buildings in St. Pölten's *Altstadt.*

Shopping has been St. Pölten's official pastime since the Romans rolled down **Wienerstraße.** After 1100, the street became the center of the bourgeois-trader settlement established by the Bishop of Passau. **Herrenplatz** has witnessed centuries of haggling at St. Pölten's daily market, inspiring the fountain "The Gossiping Woman." A narrow alley just after Wienerstr. 31 leads to **Domplatz,** which retains much of its charm despite its new-found parking-lot status. The remains of the Roman settlement of Aelium were discovered here when some sewer installers tripped over Roman hypocausts (ancient floor heating systems), and the **Dom** (cathedral) is still intact with the gilded Baroque encrustations, added by Prandtauer when he transformed the original Roman basilica (open daily until 6pm; free). Budget shoppers should check out the **flea market** at *Einkaufszentrum Traisenpark* just outside town on Su, 8am-3pm.

St. Pölten maintains only one major museum, the encyclopedic **Stadtmuseum,** Prandtauerstr. 2, near the Rathaus. It houses a very thorough collection describing St. Pölten from pre-Roman times to the present, containing artifacts ranging from transplanted church pews to *Jugendstil* vases. (☎333 2643 or 2640. Open Tu-Sa 10am-5pm. 20AS, students 10AS.)

FESTIVALS AND PERFORMANCES. The town supports two theaters. **Die Bühne im Hof,** Linzerstr. 18, offers mostly modern theater and dance. (☎352 291; fax 52294. Prices range from 70 to 350AS, depending on what's showing. Students and seniors 50% off.) **The Landeshauptstadt Theater,** Rathauspl. 11, stages traditional opera and ballet. (☎35202, ext. 19. Tickets run 160-290AS, but the box office sells a few standing room tickets for 150AS on evenings of performances.)

Seasonal festivities include the **St. Pöltner Festwoche,** which brings all kinds of events to local theaters and museums at the end of May. The **Donaufestival** from June to early July celebrates dance, theater, and music in the *Festspielhaus*. From the end of September to early October, the Sacred Music Festival features free concerts in various churches. (Information ☎2356; for tickets ☎2122.)

BADEN BEI WIEN ☎02252

Baden is a favorite weekend spot for Viennese and globe-trotters alike to rejuvenate their weary bodies, thanks to the healing effects of Baden's sulfur springs. Since the days of Roman rule, these naturally heated jets of water springing from the ground have been used as therapeutic spas, attracting bathers from all corners of Europe, including Mozart, Schubert, Strauss, and Beethoven. Under imperial patronage in the 19th century, city notables generated magnificent specimens of architecture and art, turning Baden into a wonderland of pastel buildings that also reflect the summer heat, making the relief of a bath even more tempting. As a tribute to the Emperor, the town created a **rosarium,** with over 20,000 roses, extending from the city center to the **Wienerwald** (Vienna Woods; 90,000m^2). Baden's prices are, however, the snakes slithering through this paradisiacal garden; resist temptation by making Baden a daytrip from Vienna, only 26km away.

ORIENTATION AND PRACTICAL INFORMATION. The easiest way to get to Baden is by the Badener Bahn, a **tram** that runs from **Vienna's Karlspl.,** beneath the Opera House, to Baden's **Josefspl.** (60min., every 15min., 5am-10:30pm, 57AS). **Trains** also travel frequently between Vienna's **Südbahnhof** and Josefpl. (outbound from Vienna: 4:40am-11:15pm, inbound: 4:16am-11:43pm, 57AS). By car from the west, take Autobahn West to Bundesstr. 20 at "Alland-Baden-Mödling." From Vienna, take Autobahn South (Süd) and exit at "Baden."

Baden's **tourist office,** Brusattipl. 3 at Leopoldsbad, is accessible from the Josefpl. station. Walk toward the fountain, keep right, and follow Erzherzog-Rainer-Ring to the second left (Brusattiplatz). The tourist office is at the end of the cul-de-sac. The staff speaks some English and has English brochures on request. In the summer, they offer **free tours** of the *Altstadt* (1½hr., M at 2pm and Th at 10am), the wine region (2hr., W at 3pm), wine tastings (Th 4-7pm or by appointment), and guided **hiking** and **mountain-biking** tours (except in Aug.). (☎41833 ext. 57; fax 80733. Open May-Oct. M-Sa 9am-6pm, Su and holidays 9am-12:30pm.) Services include: **bike rental** (50AS) and **luggage storage** (20AS) at the train station; clean, free **public toilets** at Brusattiplatz, the Rosarium, and the train station; **police,** ☎133, and **medical emergency,** ☎144. The **postal code** is A-2500.

LOWER AUSTRIA

ACCOMMODATIONS AND FOOD. If you want to spend the night in Baden despite admonishments from your pocketbook, the tourist office can give you a list of lodgings with prices and descriptions. **Pension Steinkellner,** Am Hang 1, offers decent rooms at reasonable prices in a flower-bedecked building. It's quite a walk from the center of town, up Füsslauerstr. from Josefspl. and right at the fourth stoplight, but the proprietors will pick you up if you call ahead. (☎86226. Breakfast included. Singles 330AS, with shower 340AS; doubles 620AS, with shower 680AS.) Closer to the *Altstadt* is **Pension Wienerstub'n,** Weilburgstrs. 19. (☎48104, fax 418 3512. Breakfast included. Singles 450AS, doubles 650AS.)

Food in Baden is plentiful but, unfortunately, not cheap. **Café Damals,** Rathausg. 3, is in a cool, ivy-hung courtyard facing the Hauptpl. It's a popular place to lunch and linger, but expect to pay at least 80AS for a filling lunch. (☎42686. Open M-F 10am-midnight, Sa 10am-5pm.) If you'd like a side of history with your *Tafelspitz* (boiled beef), head to **Gasthaus zum Reichsapfel,** Spielg. 2. Follow Antong. one block from Theaterpl.; the restaurant is on the corner. As the oldest guesthouse in Baden, it has served hungry wayfarers since the 13th century. Those less interested in the history may still be entertained by the chess, checkers, and collection of *Hagar the Horrible* comic books and *Mad* magazines—in German, of course. (Average meal 90AS. Open Su-M and W-Sa 11am-2pm and 5-11pm.) **Billa,** Wasserg. 14, is a grocery store on the way from the train station to the *Fußgängerzone* (open M-Th 7:30am-6:30pm, F 7:30am-8pm, Sa 7am-5pm). There is a **farmer's market** at Grüner Markt on Brusattipl. (M-F 8am-6pm, Sa 8am-1pm).

SIGHTS. Centered around Hauptpl., Baden's lovely *Fußgängerzone* features the elaborate Dreifaltigkeitsäule (Trinity Column), erected in 1718 to thank God for keeping the plague from Baden, as well as the Rathaus and Franz Josef I's summer home at #17. But the thermal baths that were Baden's biggest attraction in the days of Caesar Augustus still draw in tourists today. Although they smell like sulfur, they're warm, relaxing, and good for you.

The Strandbad, Helenenstr. 19-21, lets you simmer in the hot sulfur thermal pool and cool off in normal chlorinated pools. Kids will get hysterical over the huge water slide and pool—hardly Roman, but definitely fun. (☎48670. Open M-F 8:30am-7:30pm, Sa-Su 8am-6:30pm. M-F 67AS, after 1pm 57AS; Sa-Su 79AS, after 1pm 67AS.) From May until September 28, visit the smaller (but just as toasty) **pool** at Marchetstr. 13, behind the *Kurdirektion* (49AS). The *Kurdirektion* itself, Brusattipl. 4 (☎44531), is the center of all curative spa treatments, housing an indoor thermal pool mainly for patients but open to visitors (72AS). The spa has underwater massage therapy (295AS), sulfur mud baths (305AS), and a basic massage, called the *sport und vital* massage (310AS). A gigantic new spa complex, the **Römertherme Baden,** Brusattiplatz 4, offers even more soothing luxuries all year long. A 2-hour soak costs 110AS for adults, 85AS for students. (☎45030. www.roemertherme.at. Open M noon-10pm, Tu-Su 10am-10pm.)

If you ever tire of soaking, north of Hauptpl. via Maria-Theresa-Gasse lies the **Kurpark.** Set into the southeast edge of the *Wienerwald*, this carefully landscaped, shady garden is studded with statues, among which the imperial court frolicked during the Congress of Vienna in the early 19th century. The delightful **Theresiengarten** within it was laid out in 1792 and the flower clock in the middle of the *Kurpark* grass began ticking in 1929. If you're feeling lucky, visit the **Casino** in the middle of the park. (Opens daily at 3pm. Must be 19 or older. Semi-formal dress required. Free entrance.)

The **Emperor Franz-Josef Museum,** Hochstr. 51, sits atop the Badener Berg at the end of the park (follow signs through the *Sommerarena* along Zöllner and Suckfüllweg) and holds exhibitions of folk art, weapons, religious pieces, and photography. (☎41100. Open Apr.-Oct. Tu-Su and holidays 2-6pm; Nov.-Mar. Tu-Su 11am-5pm.) The **Beethovenhaus,** at Rathausg. 10, is where the composer spent his summers from 1804 to 1825, banging out part of *Missa Solemnis* and much of his *Ninth Symphony*. The museum features the composer's death mask and locks of his hair. (Open Tu-F 4-6pm, Sa-Su and holidays 9-11am and 4-6pm.)

FESTIVALS. Baden hosts a wide range of festivals, most notably the **Beethoven Festival** from mid-September to early October, which features performances by famous Austrian musicians and film screenings at the Stadttheater. For tickets, contact *Kulturamt der Stadtgemeinde Baden*, Hauptpl. 1, A-2500 Baden (☎868 00232; fax 868 00210). From late June to mid-September, the **Sommerarena** in the Kurpark stages magnificent, open-air performances of classic Viennese operettas, including works by Fall and Lehár. For tickets, call 48547, write to *Stadttheater Baden Kartenbüro*, Theaterpl. 7, A-2500 Baden, or stop by the box office in the Stadttheater on Kaiser-Franz-Ring-Str. (Open Tu-Sa 10am-1pm and 5-6:30pm, Su and holidays 10am-noon. 150-500AS, standing room 40AS.) Last-minute tickets, if there are any left, go on sale for half-price 30 minutes before the concert.

Throughout June, Baden blooms with the **Badener Rosentage,** a multi-week celebration of roses at the height of the season. Most activities, including children's theater and puppet shows, are free; they take place throughout the *Badener Rosarium*, where you can also rent boats and float on a shady pond. (Open 9am-7pm. 40AS for 30min., 70AS for 1hr.) World-class **horse racing** occurs near the Casino from June to September, dial 88773 for details. In September, Baden hosts **Grape Cure Week,** a Bacchanalian gathering of local wineries in Hauptpl. selling fresh grapes and grape juice. The theory behind it is that one should irrigate one's system, and the best way to do so is to gobble 1kg of grapes per day. Some take the medicinal philosophy to heart, but for most, it's an excuse to party. For details, stop by one of the *Buschenschanken* (wine taverns). Stands open daily 8am-6pm. First 500 guests get free grape juice.

LIECHTENSTEIN

FACTS AND FIGURES

CAPITAL OF LIECHTENSTEIN: Vaduz

CURRENCY: Swiss Franc

POPULATION: 32,000

MAJOR EXPORTS: Dental products

FORM OF GOVERNMENT: Hereditary constitutional monarchy

LAND AREA: 160km²

LANGUAGE: German

RELIGION: 80% Catholic, 7.4% Protestant

GEOGRAPHY: Flat, river valley in west with two largest towns (Vaduz and Schaan); mountainous terrain in east

A recent Liechtenstein tourist brochure unfortunately mislabeled the already tiny 160km² country as an even tinier 160m². As a matter of fact, this is approximately how much most tourists see of the world's only German-speaking monarchy, as most travelers usually pause only long enough to buy the obligatory postage stamp and hastily record the visit in a passport in the capital city of Vaduz. Liechtenstein is tiny and heavily touristed, but it has some unique characteristics. It has a ruling monarch, Prince Hans Adam II, son of Prince Franz Josef II, who was the first ruler to actually live in Liechtenstein since the present dynasty took control of the country in 1699. Before that, the family ruled Liechtenstein from their estates in the former Czechoslovakia. Liechtenstein's ties to Switzerland were established in 1923 with a customs and monetary union, replacing a similar agreement with the Austro-Hungarian empire that lasted from 1852 to 1919. Yet while Liechtenstein may not have an army or independent foreign representation, it sure has cash.

The tourist business, boosted by some shrewd business decisions made by the last prince, has brought tremendous wealth to the citizens of Liechtenstein. Luxury cars are the transportation of choice for farmers, and the cliff-hanging roads they drive on are the gateways to those places that are truly worth visiting—the unspoiled mountains a world away from the tourist traps below offer hiking and skiing prospects that outweigh the capital's limited charms. The **Liechtenstein Alpine Association** offers free guided full- and half-day hikes every Thursday during the summer, and the Saturday newspaper publishes routes and contact numbers.

HIGHLIGHTS OF LIECHTENSTEIN

Scan the Swiss and Austrian Alps from the Pfälzerhütte, an isolated mountain hut on the sharp ridge above tiny **Malbun** (see p. 289).

Spy on some of the Prince's impressive private art collection at the Staatliche Kunstmuseum in **Vaduz** (see p. 288).

VADUZ AND LOWER LIECHTENSTEIN

The hamlet of Vaduz is Liechtenstein's capital and tourist center. It's not a budget-friendly place and you don't get much for your money. It's a town of tourists traveling in packs, furiously scrambling to find *something* worthy of a photo opportunity. Often, they find nothing more than the mass-produced sculptures sold in front of tourist malls. While campers and bikers might enjoy the surrounding countryside of Lower Liechtenstein (the "lower" refers to the region's elevation rather than a southern position) others should consider heading for the hills in Upper Liechtenstein, and particularly Malbun.

GETTING THERE AND AROUND. Although trains from Austria and Switzerland pass through the country, Liechtenstein itself has no rail system. Instead, it has an efficient and cheap **Post Bus** system that links all 11 villages (short trips 2.40SFr; long trips 3.60SFr students, seniors, and disabled pay half-fare; SwissPass valid). A one-week bus ticket (10SFr, students 5SFr) covers all (and we mean *all*) of Liechtenstein as well as buses to Swiss and Austrian border towns. The pass quickly becomes worthwhile. The principality is a 20-minute bus ride from **Sargans** or **Buchs** in Switzerland and **Feldkirch** in Austria (3.60SFr). While border formalities aren't a problem when going into Switzerland, keep a passport on you while crossing the Austrian border.

PHONE CODE	Liechtenstein uses the Swiss **country code** (41) and international dialing prefix (00). The **city code** is 075 country-wide.

PRACTICAL INFORMATION. Liechtenstein's **national tourist office,** Städtle 37, one block up the hill from the Vaduz Post Bus stop, will stamp your passport with Liechtenstein's bi-colored seal (2SFr or 20AS). It also locates rooms free of charge, makes hotel reservations (2SFr), and distributes free maps and advice on hiking, cycling, and skiing in the area, as well as selling a 15.50SFr hiking map, and a 2.50SFr bike map. (☎232 1443; fax 392 1618; touristinfo@lie-net.li. Open M-F 8am-noon and 1:30-5:30pm, Apr.-Oct. also Sa 10am-noon and 1-4pm, May-Sept. also Su 10am-noon and 1-4pm.) For **currency exchange** at acceptable rates, go to Switzerland. No kidding. **ATMs** are at banks nation-wide. **Lockers** are available at the post office bus stop (5SFr). Biking is a great way to get around the lower country, but can be both difficult and dangerous on mountain roads. **Rent bicycles** (20SFr per day) at **Mellinger AG,** Kirchstr. 10 (☎232 1606; open M-F 8am-noon and 1:30-6pm, and Sa 8am-noon), or at **Rad-Zenter Hermann,** Feldkirchstr. 74 (☎233 3536); it helps to call ahead. For a **taxi,** call ☎373 2952, 392 2222, or 233 3535. For the **police** or **mountain rescue,** call 117. In a **fire,** call 118. In a **medical emergency,** dial 144. For **roadside assistance,** call 140. Liechtenstein's **hospital** can be reached at ☎235 4411. The main **post office** is near the tourist office and has an amazing selection of postage stamps (☎232 2155; open M-F 8am-6pm, Sa 8-11am). The **postal code** is FL-9490.

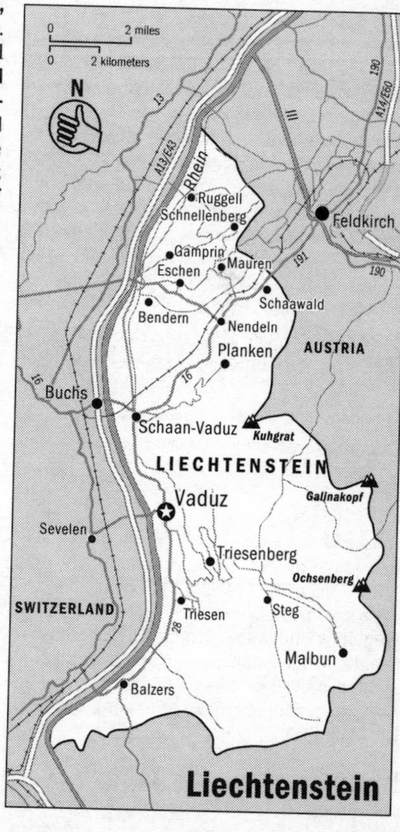

ACCOMMODATIONS AND FOOD. Budget housing options in Vaduz itself are few and far between, but neighboring **Schaan** is more inviting. Budget-friendly **Hotel Post,** facing the back of the Schaan post office (easily accessible by bus #1 from Vaduz), has a friendly staff and plenty of open places in which to relax. Unfortunately it is also near train tracks which can be rather annoying at night. (☎232 1718. Breakfast included. Reception 8am-11pm. Singles 40SFr, with shower 50SFr; doubles 80SFr, with shower 100SFr.) Liechtenstein's sole **Jugendherberge (HI members only),** Untere Rütig. 6, is also in Schaan, and is more institutional and less service-oriented. From Vaduz, take bus #1 (dir.: Schaan) to "Mühleholz," walk toward the intersection with the traffic lights, and turn left down Marianumstr. Walk four to five minutes and follow the signs to this spotless pink hostel, set on the edge of a farm. This hostel serves lone travellers, families, and gaggles of schoolchildren. Be prepared for the bad American rock music piped through all the rooms from 7:30am until 10pm. (☎232 5022; fax 232 5856. Showers and breakfast included. Dinner 12SFr. Laundry 8SFr. Reception 7-9:30am and 5-10pm. Lockout 9:30am-5pm. Curfew 10pm, key available. Open Feb.-Oct. Dorms 26.30SFr; doubles 64.60SFr; family quads 113.20SFr.)

Lower Liechtenstein's 2 peaceful **campgrounds** are easily accessible by Post Bus. For **Camping Bendern,** take bus #50/51 (dir.: Schellenberg) to "Bendern" and walk past the village church (☎373 1211; showers included; 75SFr, 4SFr children tents 4SFr; cars 4SFr; tax 0.30SFr). **Camping Mittagspitze,** between Triesen and Balzers on the road to Sargans, offers gorgeous sites at the foot of the mountain near a cold Alpine brook. (☎392 2686. Shower and pool included. Reception 8:30am-noon and 2-9pm. Open year-round. 8.50SF; tent 5SFr, 0.30SFr tax.)

Eating out cheaply in Liechtenstein is extremely challenging, consider hopping the border to Feldkirch (see p. 206) for a meal. Groceries and a fantastic array of Swiss chocolate are available at **Migros,** Aulestr. 20, across from the tour bus parking lot (open M-F 8am-1pm and 1:30-6:30pm, Sa 8am-4pm, Su 9am-6pm). In the same shopping complex, **Azzuro Pizza** serves take-out pizzas for 7-14SFr and 9SFr kebabs (☎232 48 18; open M-Sa 8am-8pm, Su 9am-5pm).

SIGHTS. 12th-century **Schloß Vaduz,** the regal home of Hans Adam II, Prince of Liechtenstein, presides above the town. Although the interior of the ruler's residence is off-limits to the bourgeois masses, you can hike up to the castle for a closer look and a phenomenal view of the whole country. The 30-min. trail begins down the street from the tourist office, heading away from the post office. (Numerous signs reading "Castle this way: No visit" are only meant to prevent commoners from knocking on the royal front door and inviting themselves inside. Only rich politicians, students with very good university final exams, and retirees are asked to visit the Prince, usually on New Year's Day.) Housed in the same building as the tourist office, the **Liechtenstein Staatliche Kunstmuseum,** Städtle 37 houses two floors of displays. One floor is devoted to temporary exhibits of modern and contemporary art. The other, more impressive floor, contains a colorful selection of mythologically-themed works, with bronze sculptures and pagan paintings, some by Reubens, van Dyck, and Rembrandt. (☎232 2341; fax 232 7864. Open Apr.-Oct. daily 10am-noon, 1:30-5:30pm; Nov.-Mar. 10am-noon, 1:30-5pm. 5SFr, students 3SFr.) Across the street from the tourist office, the monolithic **Kunstmuseum Liechtenstein,** Städtle 32, is slated to open in November 2000 and house the principality's largest art display. (☎235 0300; fax 232 7864. Open Tu-Su 10am-5pm, Th until 8pm. 8SFr, 5SFr students, children, and seniors.)

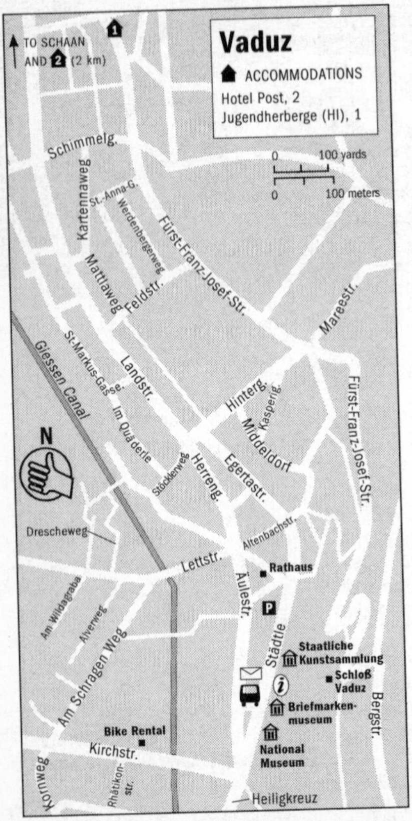

Reproductions of the royal art collection almost inevitably end up on postage stamps in the one-room **Briefmarkenmuseum (Stamp Museum),** Städtle 37, on the other side of the tourist office in one of its 150 pull-out shelves of stamps. (☎232 6105. Open daily Apr.-Oct. 10am-noon and 1:30-5:30pm; Nov.-Mar. 10am-noon and 1:30-5pm. Free.)

UPPER LIECHTENSTEIN

Despite the country's diminutive size, different areas of Liechtenstein have distinct traits, which become more noticeable the higher up you get. These heights are where the real character and beauty of Liechtenstein lie. The roads that snake their way up the mountainsides to tiny villages, such as **Triesenberg** and **Malbun,** allow for spectacular views of the Rhine Valley and the surrounding Alps. Buses make the short run to these towns from Vaduz in under 40 minutes, and the trips are well worth the effort even if you're only spending one day in the country.

TRIESENBERG

The first town up the mountain (serviced by bus #10) is Triesenberg, a town founded in the 13th century by the Walsers, a group of Swiss immigrants forced to flee Valais due to overpopulation, religious intolerance, and natural disaster. The **Walser Heimatmuseum** chronicles the Walsers' religious customs, hut construction, cattle trade, and crafts (☎265 5010; open Tu-F 1:30-5:30pm, Sa 1:30-5pm, June-Aug. also Su 2-5pm; Sept.-May closed Su. 2SFr, children 1SFr). The ultra-friendly **tourist office** (☎262 1926; fax 262 1922) is in the same building as the museum and has the same hours. Signs at the Triesenberg post office point to a variety of walks and hikes. The most stunning **hike** for views of the Rhine Valley begins near Triesenberg. Take bus #30 (20min. dir.: Gaflei, which leaves infrequently but on time) or drive to **Gaflei.** From the parking lot where the bus stops, head toward the gravel path across the street. Look for the trail on the left, and follow signs to "Silum" and then to "Ob. Tunnel, Steg." The level trail wanders through low Alpine forest and meadows. At the end, walk through the tunnel, then down the narrow road to Steg, where bus #10 runs back to Vaduz or Schaan every hour (whole hike 1½hr.).

MALBUN

On the other side of the mountain, secluded Malbun is undoubtedly the hippest place in the principality, harboring approachable people, affordable ski slopes, plenty of hiking, and a **tourist office** (☎263 6577; open May-Oct. and Dec.-Apr. M-F 9am-noon and 1:30-5pm, Sa 9am-noon and 1-4pm). During the winter two chair lifts, four T-bars, and two ski schools service you and not too many other people. (Day pass 33SFr; 6-day pass 136SFr, off-season 129SFr.) Right in the middle of town, **Malbun A.G.** (☎263 9770 or 262 1915) offers 1-day classes (60SFr), 3-day classes (140SFr), and private snowboard lessons (1 day 210SFr). **Malbun Sport** (☎263 3755) rents skis and snowboards. (1-day ski or snowboard rental 30-35SFr, children 13-15SFr; open M-F 8am-6pm, Sa and Su 8am-7pm.) Cross-country skiing is available 2km from Malbun in Steg.

During the summer the #10 bus from Vaduz (40min., 1 per hr. all year, 2.40SFr) is full of hikers heading to Malbun for its mountain **hiking**. The best hike in town is a round-trip hike to **Pfälzerhütte**. The best starting point is from the top of the only chairlift open in the summer, the Sareiserjoch (round-trip 11.70SFr, one-way 7.50SFr; students 9SFr, 5.90SFr; children 6.40SFr, 4.30SFr). This trip up the mountain is worthwhile for the views of the Alps, even if you're not into hiking. For the hike, signs for Pfälzerhütte (be sure to turn left off the main trail after 5 minutes) will lead you over Augustenberg (at 2359m the second highest peak in Liechtenstein). To get back, head toward Gritsch and then Tälihöhi (whole hike 5hr.).

The best place to stay for hiking and skiing access is the superb chalet duo of **Hotel Alpen** and **Hotel Galina.** The friendly young couple that runs these wooden-paneled hotels are experienced sources of info on area outdoor activities. (☎263 1181; fax 263 9446. Open mid-May-Oct. and mid-Dec.-Apr. Reception for both from 7:30am-10pm in Hotel Alpen. In summer singles 40SFr, with shower 70SFr, doubles 50-90SFr, in winter singles 70-90SFr, doubles 140-180SFr. Ask about triples.)

SWITZERLAND

SWISS FRANC	
US$1 = 1.71 (SFR/CHF)	1SFR = US$.58
CDN$1 = 1.15SFR	1SFR = CDN$.87
UK£1 = 2.57SFR	1SFR = UK£.39
IR£1 = 1.98SFR	1SFR = IR£.50
AUS$1 = 1.00SFR	1SFR = AUS$1.00
NZ$1 = .77SFR	1SFR = NZ$1.30
SAR1 = .25SFR	1SFR = SAR4.06
10AS = 1.14SFR	1SFR = AS8.81
1DM = .80SFR	1SFR = DM1.25
1F = .24SFR	1SFR = F4.20
EUR€1 = 1.56AS	1SFR = EUR€.64

PHONE CODES The **country code** for Switzerland is 41. For international calls from Switzerland, add the prefix 00.

The unparalleled natural beauty of Switzerland *(die Schweiz, la Suisse, la Svizzera, Confederatio Helvetica)* seduces hikers, skiers, bikers, paragliders, and scenery gazers from all over the globe to romp about its Alpine playground. Three-fifths of the country is dominated by mountains: the Jura cover the northwest region, bordering France, while the Alps stretch gracefully across the entire lower half of Switzerland, extending into Italy in the south and colliding with Austria in the eastern Rhaetian Alps. The cities that lie around blue lakes make their own claim to fame as international centers of commerce and diplomacy.

The country presents an incredibly unified front to the world—lederhosen and the Ricola man, are frequently allowed to define the country. This front is incredible given the complex, and segmented nature of the country's ethnic landscape. In the battles that made Switzerland, lands that are ethnically Italian, French, and German got thrown together under one big, neutral umbrella that protects them all from the rains of the world. The fundamental differences that the traveler will notice fall primarily along the linguistic faults lines that separate the three regions of the country. These areas retain much of the flavor of their respective national origins.

Switzerland is adept at welcoming tourists to all of these areas with open arms. The Swiss have raised the hospitality industry to an art; service, food, and accommodations are consistently high quality even at the most modest *pensions*. Its efficient and comprehensive public transportation system makes Switzerland an ideal destination for the independent traveler. Although Switzerland is not known for being cheap, the thrifty traveler can always find a bargain. And in Switzerland, the best things— sublime vistas—are priceless.

BUILDING THE SWISS CONFEDERATION:

The Swiss confederation is made up of 23 cantons (states) and 3 half-cantons, from the original three in 1291 (Uri, Schwyz, and Unterwalden). Today, the cantons, clockwise starting with Bern, the capital, are: Bern (incorporated 1353), Lucerne (1332), Obwalden and Nidwalden (1291, originally part of Unterwalden), Zug (1352), Uri (1291), Schwyz (1291), Zurich (1351), Schaffhausen (1501), Thurgau (1803), Appenzell (1501), St. Gallen (1803), Glarus (1352), Graubünden (1803), Ticino (1803), Valais (1815), Geneva (1815), Vaud (1803), Fribourg (1481), Neuchâtel (1815), Jura (1978), Solothurn (1481), Basel (1501), and Aargau (1803).

A BRIEF HISTORY OF SWITZERLAND

FROM CAVE MEN TO CELTS

Before there was cheese, chocolate, and the Swatch watch, there was ice. For hundreds of millennia, Switzerland was blanketed with glaciers several kilometers deep. While evidence of human habitation in the area dates back 350,000 years, only after the last glacial period, 30,000 years ago, did early Swiss stop chasing reindeer through mountain valleys and start establishing permanent settlements. Hunter-gatherer cave-dwelling Stone-Agers traded in their hard rock for heavy metal as Iron Age **Celts** built their houses on stilts near lakes, swamps, and rivers. By 750 BC, Switzerland had become an important center of Celtic culture. The artistic and warlike **Helvetii,** the most prominent Swiss-Celtic tribe, gained notoriety for their (largely unsuccessful) attempts to invade Roman Italy in 222 BC and again as allies of Carthage between 218 and 203 BC (when they assisted Hannibal and his elephants in their famous crossing of the Alps). Their attempts to advance into Gaul in 58 BC were halted by Julius Caesar, who first crushed, then colonized the Helvetians. Romanized between 47 BC and AD 15, they survived as a settled, peaceful, urban civilization for the next two centuries. Helvetian lands extended across the Alpine valleys of central Switzerland, while the east (present-day Graubünden) was populated by the **Rhaeti,** an Etruscan tribe. Rhaetian women, refusing to succumb to Roman conquest, were said to have hurled their own children at attackers in desperation. **Rhaeto-Romansh,** a combination of Roman Latin and the Rhaetian Tuscan dialect, is still spoken in former Rhaetian territories as testimony to their fierce devotion to their ancient culture.

Around AD 250, constant raids from Germanic tribes forced Switzerland to militarize, changing it from a peaceful farming province into an armed frontier. As Roman influence waned in the 5th century, the tribes began to form permanent settlements. **Burgundians** settled the west, merging peacefully with the Romanized Celts and absorbing their culture and language. The more aggressive **Alemanni,** a germanic tribe, foisted their own culture on the Celts of central and northern Switzerland as well as on rival Germanic tribes. They eventually pushed the Burgundians west to the Sarine River, which remains the border between German and French Switzerland. Thus the region now known as Switzerland was divided between the kingdoms that grew out of these various tribes until a series of circumstances, including the childless death of the last of the Burgundian dynasty, lead to their loose union under the **Holy Roman Empire** in 1032.

350,000 BC Paleolithic hunters drop a hand wedge near Basel, giving modern archaeologists proof of their existence.

3000-1800 BC Neolithic Swiss settlers build lake villages.

From 500 BC Celts occupy western Switzerland while Rhaetians settle the east. The Helvetii become a powerful Celtic tribe.

58 BC Caesar defeats Helvetii at Bibracte, beginning Roman rule.

AD 101-150 Celtics, Rhaetians, and Romans peacefully coexist.

260 Germanic tribes attack; Swiss militarize in defense.

500 Barbarians form permanent settlements: Burgundians control the western territories, while the Alemanni dominate central and northeastern Switzerland.

610 Irish monks found the monastery in St. Gallen.

1032 Switzerland is loosely united under the Holy Roman Empire.

SWITZERLAND

AN ALEMANNI LEGACY (1000-1519)

The feisty Alemanni, with their aversion to conformity and centralized government, set the stage for centuries of Swiss individualism. The Alemanni did not establish a strictly democratic society, but their use of a people's assembly and majority rule in making communal decisions was a definite step toward Switzerland's current government. An additional spur to the sentiment of Swiss independence was the fact that the Holy Roman Emperors in this period did not hold centralized control over the patchwork of states nominally under their

1200 Construction of the St. Gotthard Pass opens trade routes through Alpine valleys.

1273 The Swiss nobleman Rudolf of Habsburg becomes Holy Roman Emperor, and attempts to take control of the Forest Cantons.

1291 Rudolf of Habsburg dies. Uri, Schwyz, and Unterwalden sign Everlasting Alliance for mutual protection against enemies–the beginning of the Swiss Confederation.

1315 In the Battle of Morgarten, Swiss defeat the Habsburgs, then renew their alliance at the agreement of Brunnen.

1436 Cultural differences between cantons result in a civil war.

1499 The Swabian War leads to independence from Holy Roman Empire.

1519 Ulrich Zwingli leads religious reform in Zurich.

power, so the individual states exercised a certain amount of autonomy. With this commitment to democratic village life, the descendents of the Alemanni were understandably a bit peeved when Holy Roman Emperor **Rudolf of Habsburg** attempted to take three of their communities (Uri, Schwyz, and Unterwalden—the "Forest Cantons") under his direct control in the late thirteenth century (see Tell-Tale, p. 293). In a secret pact, the three Forest Cantons decided to rebel and signed their **Everlasting Alliance** in 1291—an agreement that obligated the cantons to defend each other from outside attack. The Swiss consider this moment to be the beginning of the Swiss Confederation (which celebrated its 700th anniversary in 1991). The Everlasting Alliance also marked the beginning of 350 years of struggle against the **Habsburg Empire.** In 1315, the Swiss and the Habsburgs duked it out at the Battle of Morgarten. The Swiss emerged victorious, forcing the Habsburgs for the first time to agree to a truce and grant the alliance official recognition, but this was far from the end.

Over the next several centuries, the three-canton core of Switzerland expanded despite conflict between the Everlasting Alliance and the Habsburg Emperors. One by one, Bern, Lucerne, Zurich, Glarus, and Zug jumped on the confederation bandwagon, but a union of such fiercely independent and culturally distinct states made for an uneasy marriage. In the mid-15th century, social tensions between the town and country residents erupted in civil war. The Habsburg emperor Frerick III meddled, allying himself with Zurich, and generally making mischief by causing conflicts in the self-interests of the various cantons. It was only by force of arms (and persistence) that Zurich was forced by the other cantons to drop its alliance and rejoin the confederation. Finally, the Habsburgs pushed their centuries-old conquest of the Swiss to a crisis by enlisting the help of the "Swabian League"– a group of Southern German cities whose motto became "the Swiss, too, must have a master." The **Swabian War** lasted less than nine months in 1499-1500 but the Swiss so decisively repelled the German and Austrian invasion that it brought them virtual independence from the Holy Roman Empire, but domestic struggles continued as cultural and religious differences between the cantons festered.

REFORMATION TO REVOLUTION (1519-1815)

With no strong central government to settle quibbles between cantons of different faith, the Swiss were ill equipped to deal with the major religious reform that transformed Europe in the 16th century. The **Protestant Reformation** rocked Switzerland to its foundations. As Lutheranism swept Northern Europe, radical theologian **Ulrich Zwingli** of Zurich spearheaded his own brand of reform that stressed both the importance of lay people reading scripture and a rejection of the symbols and gestures of Catholicism. In 1523, the city government of Zurich sanctioned Zwingli's proposed *Theses* and strengthened Zwingli's influence within the local government, banning the differently minded Anabaptists and imposing some harsh disciplines on its residents. Meanwhile, in Geneva, French-born lawyer and priest **John Calvin** preached a doctrine of predestination based on a rigid moral framework. For a time he exercised a theocratic sway over Geneva and instituted moral reforms, turning Geneva into a shining exam-

TELL-TALE As part of the Holy Roman Empire, the citizens of the first three Swiss cantons–the Forest Cantons–were willing to recognize the emperor as their overlord, but refused any other feudal obligations. When Emperor Rudolf dispatched deputies to do his dirty work (tax-collecting, fining, jailing), the freemen of the Forest Cantons were less than thrilled. Legend has it that a particularly haughty Habsburg henchman by the name of Gessler demanded that all freemen bow to his hat in homage. The rebellious Swiss descendents of the Alemanni had other ideas. According to the tale, a freeman named William Tell journeyed with his son to the town of Altdorf in canton Uri, where he encountered the knavish Gessler. Tell blatantly ignored Gessler's hallowed hat, which got Gessler's panties in a bunch. Gessler promptly had Tell arrested, and ordered Tell to shoot an arrow through an apple on his son's head. Tell, an expert Swiss marksman, hit the apple and spared his son, then was quick to tell Gessler the next arrow had his name on it. The legend, immortalized in Friedrich Schiller's play in 1804, has come to symbolize the Swiss rough-and-ready mountaineer spirit that vanquishes tyranny in the name of freedom and independence. See Schiller's version of *Wilhelm Tell* during your summer jaunt in Interlaken.

ple of Protestant social control, unsullied by (among other things) the evils of pastry eating, dirty dancing, and sniffing in church. While Zurich and Geneva became strongholds of the Protestant movement, the rural Forest cantons remained loyal to the Catholic Church. They saw the Reformation as a product of wayward-thinking city dwellers. Religious differences combined with tensions between urban and rural cantons resulted in full-fledged battle, climaxing in Zwingli's death and the defeat of the Protestants at Kappel in 1531. The confederation finally interceded in the mid-16th century, granting Protestants freedoms but prohibiting them from imposing their faith on certain others.

1536 John Calvin preaches in Geneva.

Despite religious differences, the confederation remained neutral during the **Thirty Years War,** escaping the devastation wrought on the rest of Central Europe by the conflict of forces with Catholic and Protestant sympathies. The 1648 **Peace of Westphalia** granted the Swiss official neutrality and a multi-national recognition of their independence from the Austrian Habsburg empire.

1531 Catholic and Protestants Swiss duke it out at the Battle of Kappel.

1618-48 The Thirty Years War rages without Switzerland. The Peace of Westphalia gives Switzerland independence from the Austrian Empire, ending 350 years of struggle.

One hundred and fifty years later their independence was tested again by the revolutionary French. Caught up in Revolutionary fervor and perhaps inflamed at the Swiss Guard, who loyally defended King Louis XVI and the royal family until their death, French troops invaded Switzerland in 1798 and, by Napoleon's order, established the **Helvetic Republic.** Napoleon's republic restructured the relationship between the cantons and the federal government, giving more power to the central body. This had not been a popular idea since early spats with the Holy Roman Empire, and the Swiss were not about to simply watch the French install their puppet government. In 1803 the Swiss overthrew Napoleon's regime, leading to brief anarchy. Napoleon's **Mediation Act**

1789 The French Revolution begins.

1793 The Swiss Guardsmen defending Louis XVI are massacred in Paris.

1798-1803 The French invade Switzerland and impose a central government: the Helvetic Republic. The Swiss rebel, and anarchy ensues.

1803 Napoleon's Mediation Act settles strife.

1815 The Congress of Vienna recognizes Swiss neutrality.

settled the whole affair, and established Switzerland as a confederation of 19 cantons (by this time including Basel, Schauffhausen, and Appenzell, who had joined in the 1500s; and St. Gallen, Aargau, Graubünden, Thurgau, Ticino, and Vaud). After Napoleon's defeat at Waterloo, the Congress of Vienna added Geneva, Neuchatel, and the Valais to the Confederation and (again) officially recognized Swiss neutrality.

DIPLOMACY: 1815 TO THE 20TH CENTURY

Neutrality established, Switzerland could turn its attention to domestic issues. Industrial growth brought relative material prosperity, but the era was not exactly golden. The **Federal Pact** of 1815 that replaced Napoleon's decrees once again established Switzerland as a confederation of sovereign states united only for common defense—united foreign policy was still impossible. Because of logistical barriers (each canton had its own laws, currency, postal service, weights, measures, and army—not to mention language and religion) the inhabitants of one canton regarded the inhabitants of others as foreigners. Furthermore, religious differences continued to create increased tension between cantons.

These religious differences led, in 1846, to the formation of a separatist defense league of Catholic cantons known as the **Sonderbund,** composed of Lucerne, Uri, Schwyz, Unterwalden, Zug, Fribourg, and Valais. In July 1847, the **Diet,** a parliamentary body representing the other cantons, declared the Sonderbund incompatible with the Federal Pact and demanded its dissolution. In keeping with the fashion of the time, a civil war broke out. It only lasted 25 days. The Protestant federalist forces were victorious, and the country wrote a new constitution modeled after that of the United States in 1848 (modified in 1874). Finally balancing the age-old conflict between federal and cantonal power, the constitution guaranteed republican and democratic cantonal constitutions and set up an executive body for the first time. The central government then established a free-trade zone and unified postal, currency, and railway systems across all the cantons.

1848 After a 25 day civil war, the winning cantons write a constitution strengthening the central government, and establishing the modern Swiss nation.

SWITZERLAND

Once turmoil had given way to stability, Switzerland cultivated its reputation for resolving international conflicts. The **Geneva Convention of 1864** established international laws for conduct during war. Geneva also became the headquarters for the **International Red Cross.**

1863-4 The first Geneva convention takes place; the Red Cross is established.

1882 The Gotthardbahn (railway across the Alps) is opened.

1914 WWI begins; the Swiss stay out of it.

1920 Switzerland joins the League of Nations after their neutrality is assured.

Not quite free of the tangle of alliances that characterized Europe's turn-of-the-century balance of power, Switzerland's neutrality was tested in both the **Franco-Prussian war** and **World War I** as French- and German-speaking Switzerland claimed different cultural loyalties. In 1920, Geneva welcomed the headquarters of the ill-fated **League of Nations,** solidifying Switzerland's reputation as the center for international diplomacy. At the onset of **World War II,** Switzerland mobilized 20% of the population for a defensive army. Luckily for the Swiss, Hitler's plan to invade Switzerland was thwarted by Allied landings and distractions on the North African front. Both sides found it useful to have Switzerland (and its banks) as neutral territory. While some Jews, escaping Allied prisoners, and other refugees from Nazi Germany found safe haven in Switzerland, the Swiss government, not eager to incur the wrath of the monster that surrounded it,

1939 WWII begins–the Swiss remain neutral, though the threat of a Nazi invasion causes a mobilization of ground troops.

1948 After escaping the war virtually unharmed Switzerland introduces wide-ranging social reforms, including old-age pensions.

1971 Swiss women finally win the right to vote.

1992 Swiss vote against membership in the EEC, the predeccesor to the EU.

1999 Ruth Dreifuss becomes the first female Bundesrat president.

April 18, 1999 Swiss accept a new Federal Constitution (Bundesverfassung).

impeded passage through its territory and assumed the hiding-tortoise position. Aside from some accidental bombings in 1940, 1944, and 1945, Switzerland survived the war unscathed.

As the rest of Europe cleaned up the rubble of two world wars, Switzerland nurtured its already sturdy economy. Zurich emerged as a banking and insurance center, while Geneva invited international organizations, including the World Health Organization, the World Council of Churches, and the World Jewish Congress, to set up shop. Although Geneva became the headquarters for international diplomacy, Switzerland remained independent in its diplomatic relationships declining membership to the United Nations, NATO, and the European Economic Community.

SWITZERLAND TODAY

1999 ELECTIONS. While Austria made international headlines when its far-right, anti-immigrant political party made gains in October 1999 elections (see p. 68), no one seemed to notice when a similar thing happened in Switzerland two weeks later. The far-right **Swiss People's Party** (*Schweizerische Volkspartei*) captured 23 percent of the vote, catapulting from fourth to second among the countries four main parties since the last general elections. The party is strongly anti-immigrant: they rallied behind the cry "Stop Asylum Abuse," an angry response to the thousands of refugees who have poured into Switzerland from Eastern Europe. When the election results came in Jörg Haider of Austria was one of the first to congragulate **Christoph Blocher,** the leader of the People's Party, and a fellow business-maverick-cum-fast-talking-far-right-political-leader. The People's Party jump of 7.9 percentage points since the last elections in 1995 is a particularly astounding change in Switzerland considering that percentage of the vote received by one party has almost never changed more than 1 or 2 percent between elections. It seems that in this election people had become increasingly dissatisfied. The results of the vote bring to light many prominent issues in Switzerland today.

One of the primary reasons for the agitation is the fear of refugees from Eastern Europe taking jobs from Swiss people. One in every five people in Switzerland is foreign and while Switzerland rarely lets these immigrants become citizens (see The Swiss Way or the Highway, below), these extra people seeking jobs have become a target of criticism as unemployment rose in the recent recession. Indicative of the high economic expectations of Switzerland was the panic when the unemployment rate hit a high, in the mid 1990s, of around five percent, which is the standard unemployment in the United States. The question of foreigners has been particularly hot in recent times as Switzerland has taken, proportionately, more Kosovar refugees than any other country. The Swiss have never been welcoming of foreigners, but the recent influx has heightened fears.

The question of foreign workers is intimately tied to the question of Swiss movement toward membership in the **European Union** (EU), a considerable factor in the People's Party success. The People's Party was the only one of the four major parties that did not support Swiss membership in the EU. Among other requirements for EU membership is that all members accept foreign workers from all other EU nations. Switzerland has historically resisted international organizations primarily because they threaten the Swiss people's fierce sense of independence from any outside entanglements (the *Sonderfall Schweiz* or **Swiss Way**). Switzerland is one of the only developed countries that is not a member of the United Nations, even though Geneva houses the organization's European headquarters. In a country that determines many laws through popular referenda, the people are predictably reluctant to give up power to any outside organization.

THE SWISS WAY OR THE HIGHWAY Switzerland is beautiful, but don't plan on staying. Rules for citizenship are some of the toughest in the world. The cantons retain the power to grant Swiss citizenship, and in most cantons applicants for citizenship, on top of a 12-year residency requirement, must be popularly elected by the commune in which they live. For the vote the applicant's picture, economic status (including the applicant's yearly wages), and hobbies are distributed in a pamphlet to the voting public. Sometimes officials will even drop by the applicant's house to examine its cleanliness. All of these requirements have predictably raised questions of Swiss xenophobia in the last year with the rise of the far-right People's Party. The world took notice when, in March, 2000, 56 candidates applied for citizenship in a small town near Lucerne. Of the 56, only eight were accepted, and none of the eight were from the former Yugoslavia, where a majority of the applicants came from. The popular election of Swiss citizens does not occur in cities, but the newly powerful People's Party is proposing this.

During the cold war Switzerland's independence and stability was an economic advantage in a tumultuous Europe, it helped them attain one of the highest standard's of living in the world. But as the waters of stability have flowed in to the rest of Europe, and the continent has become integrated, Switzerland's independence has turned into isolation, and has frequently meant that the nation is excluded from trade deals. The government realized this and offered the people the opportunity to join the **European Economic Area** (EEA) in 1992, the economic forerunner to the EU. The people rejected the government's plan through a referendum in which 80 percent of the people turned out to vote (usual turnout for referenda is 35 percent). This vote precluded the chance of a vote on EU membership.

After the 1992 vote the government initiated bilateral negotiations with the EU to create closer ties and eventually move Switzerland toward membership in the EU. The People's Party was the only political party that did not endorse membership in the EEA in the 1992 referenda and the new bilateral negotiations. By showing such support for the People's Party the Swiss people expressed their own hesitance for the government's move toward **European integration**. The fear that Switzerland was moving toward isolationism after the recent elections, however, were calmed when, in May 2000 two thirds of the people voted to accept the bilateral negotiations between the EU and the Swiss government in a referendum. These results suggest that, while a minority group opposed to integration has grown (the People's Party rise to 23 percent of the vote is still a minority), the group that supports integration has also grown into a strong majority. It is probable that the reason the international response to the People's Party's gains was so quiet is that Switzerland was not a member of an organization like the EU that could publicly castigate the nation for the results.

The election results threaten to shake up the careful political system of consensus that has developed over the last fifty years. The gains of the People's Party led Blocher to request a second seat on the seven-seat Federal Council, the cabinet-like board that is the most powerful political body in the country. For the last fifty years the People's Party has held one seat, while the other 3 parties have each held 2 seats, a political arrangement known as the **magic formula.** This formula was carefully crafted so that the three major languages and two major religions were all fairly represented in Federal Council. Blocher's demands for a second seat threaten the political coalition that has held the divided country in balance.

NAZI GOLD AND OTHER ISSUES. Besides the questions raised in these elections, the other major issue that has dominated Swiss news recently is the question of **Nazi gold.** In the 1990s Swiss banks came under intense scrutiny for their "blind account" policy, which allowed Holocaust victims and Nazi leaders alike to deposit money during WWII. Government investigations are currently reviewing

Switzerland's actions in relation to Nazi assets, treatment of Jewish refugees, and unclaimed accounts. To appease international Jewish groups, the Swiss National Bank has contributed US$69 million to a Special Fund for Holocaust Victims. This crisis has shocked many Swiss into reconsidering their own comfortable idea of the Swiss role in WWII.

While conservative in some respects (women were not allowed to vote in Switzerland until 1971), the Swiss are remarkably progressive in other areas. In 1999, two women were elected to the seven-member Bundesrat (executive authority), one of whom, **Ruth Dreifuss,** will serve a one-year term as president. The Swiss also have instituted a radical drug policy in which drug addicts are not forced to abandon their habit, and heroin may even be prescribed to severe addicts. This controversial policy, aimed at decreasing crime and prostitution associated with drug use, has seen success in the reduction of both crime and hard drug use since 1991. In a recent referendum, the Swiss decided to continue the program.

SWISS GOVERNMENT. Swiss government is based on a three-tiered system of communes, cantons, and confederation. Over 3000 communes (the smallest administrative unit of government) compose the 26 cantons. Each canton has its own constitution, legislature, executive office, and judiciary system. The cantons are in turn incorporated into the Confederation and its two-chamber legislature, the Federal Assembly. One chamber, the National Council, distributes its 200 seats based on population; the other, the Council of States, has 2 representatives from each canton. Decisions of the Federal Assembly take effect only with a majority in both chambers.

The executive branch consists of a group of 7 members—the **Bundesrat (Federal Council)**—elected to 4-year terms by a joint meeting of both legislative chambers. No canton may have more than 1 representative in the Bundesrat at a time. The Bundesrat chooses a president from among its ranks. The president only holds office for 1 year, and the post is more symbolic than functional. **Referenda** and **initiatives** make political decisions a part of the daily life of the Swiss people.

CULTURE AND CUSTOMS

PEOPLE. The Swiss are quite conservative (though their rampant festival scene might convince you otherwise—see **Festival Fever,** p. 300). They are generally very law-abiding, hard-working, and proper. Be punctual and mind your manners: remember to say hello and goodbye to shopkeepers and proprietors of bars and cafes, and always shake hands when being introduced to a Swiss person. The Swiss have an incredibly high standard of living, a life expectancy of 78 years, and virtually no illiteracy. When the dust settled after the Protestant Reformation, Switzerland ended up almost evenly divided between Catholics (46%) and Protestants (44%), though Protestantism has been in slight decline since World War II. The Swiss have been quite tolerant of other religious groups; Geneva, the "City of Peace," shelters various international religious organizations representing 130 faiths, such as the World Council of Churches, the Baha'i International Community, the Lutheran World Federation, the Quaker UN Office, the Christian Children's Fund, and the World Jewish Congress. The Swiss, however, are not known for opening socially to newcomers–their specialized dialects frequently serve as a convenient barrier between Swiss and non-Swiss.

In general, Swiss are active people, encouraged to venture outdoors by the alluring mountain landscape. Skiing and hiking are national pastimes, with more than 40% of the population regularly wandering through the countryside.

LANGUAGE. When in Switzerland, try to speak as the Swiss do (whatever the language happens to be). Less people speak English in Switzerland than in many other European countries because of the number of languages that must be learned to get by within Switzerland. Thus while many speak English, you're always better off trying one of Switzerland's three and a half official federal languages first: German, French, Italian, or Romansh (which is only partially an official federal language). Each language spans a particular geographic region: German is spoken by 64% of the population throughout the bulk of central and

A CRASH COURSE IN SWISS GERMAN

Though you'll most likely never need to speak Swiss German, it is a charming, folksy language that reflects the traditional character of Swiss culture. If you want to pick it up, start with basic practical terms that are nearly the same in all dialects, such as the days of the week: *Mäntig, Zyschtig, Mittwuche, Donschtig, Frytig, Samschtig, Sunntig,* or the months: *Jänner, Horner, März, April, Mei, Brachmonet, Höimonet, Ougschte, Herbstmonet, Wymonet, Wintermonet, Chrischtmonet.* Even if you haven't mastered these tongue-twisters, watch out when buying cereal—be sure to distinguish between *Müesli*, the famous granola, which literally means "little smashed-up things," and *Müsli*, the common misspelling, which means "little mice."

eastern Switzerland. In western Switzerland, French is the language of choice for 19% of the Swiss, while 8% speak Italian, primarily in the southern Ticino region. Romansh is spoken by less than 1% of the population, but it has historical and ethnic significance after having survived for hundreds of years in the isolated mountain valleys of Graubünden (see p. 389). If you don't speak any of these languages, at least greet people with *Grüezi* (pronounced Grew-tsee) and ask *sprechen Sie Englisch, parlez vous anglais*, or *lei parla inglese* (depending on where you are) before pouring out your heart. There is some overlap between languages, and you'll hear people say *merci, ciao*, and *adiö* throughout Switzerland.

In contrast to Germany, where local dialects of German have been looked down on for centuries, German Switzerland celebrates its dialects, known collectively as Swiss German, or *Schwyzertüütsch.* Swiss German is as different from High German as Dutch or Danish, so don't expect to be able to understand it if you speak High German. Linguistically, Swiss German resembles Middle High German, which was spoken in Germany five hundred years ago. Geographic isolation led to the development of highly differentiated dialects in each region with individual peculiarities of pronunciation, grammar, and vocabulary. *Wallisertütsch*, spoken in the southern Valais region, is one of the oldest Swiss German dialects and hence one of the least comprehensible, even to Swiss Germans. On the other hand, *Bärntütsch* and *Züritüütsch*, spoken around Bern and Zurich respectively, are more regular, though there is no written standard of Swiss German. Though words like *chääschüechli* (cheesecake) and *chuchichäschtli* (kitchen cabinets) may sound harsh to Anglophone ears, most German Swiss prefer their dialect to High German. The Swiss identify with their language and will appreciate any effort you make to speak it, so take a breath and practice saying *Ufwiderluege* (goodbye)!

FOOD AND DRINK. Switzerland is not for the lactose intolerant. From rich and varied mountain **cheeses** (see **Say cheese!,** below) to decadent milk chocolate, the Swiss are serious about their dairy products. Even the major Swiss soft drink is a dairy-based beverage, *rivella*, which is recommended for pregnant women. Best of all, these divine bovine goodies are always available for cheap at the local Migros or Co-op. As far as **chocolate** goes, the Swiss have earned bragging rights for their expertise: with the invention of milk chocolate in 1875, Switzerland was poised to rule the world. Switzerland is home to some of the world's largest producers: **Lindt, Suchard,** and **Nestlé.** Visit the Lindt factory in Zurich or the Nestlé factory near Bulle to load up on free samples. **Toblerone,** manufactured in Bern, is an international favorite famous for the bits of nougat in creamy milk chocolate, packaged in a nifty triangular box. Chocolate comes in different percentages of concentration—the higher the percentage, the darker and more bitter the chocolate. The Swiss insist that chocolate is essential to any diet.

So you've had your fill of cheese and chocolate—what's the main course, you ask? It depends on what language your waiter is speaking. Each region is represented, however, in an array of "typical" Swiss dishes, which might include the Zurich speciality, *Geschnetzeltes* (strips of veal stewed in a thick cream sauce), *Luzerner Chugelipastete* (pâté in a pastry shell), *Papet Vaudois* (leeks with sau-

SAY CHEESE! While the words "Swiss cheese" may conjure up images of lunch-boxed sandwiches filled with a hard, oily, holey cheese, Switzerland actually has innumerable varieties, each made from a particular type of milk. Cheese with holes is usually *Emmentaler,* from the valley of the same name near Bern, but nearly every canton and many towns have specialty cheeses. To name a few of the most well-known: *Gruyère* is a stronger and tastier version of *Emmentaler; Appenzeller* is a hard cheese with a sharp tang, sometimes made from sheep's milk instead of cow's milk; *tome* is a generic term for a soft, uncooked cheese similar to French *Chèvre.* In the Italian regions, cheese often resembles the *Parmigiano* from Italy more than the mountain cheeses of the Alpine regions. Cheese in Switzerland is always superb in quality, as Swiss cheese standards are regulated by law, resulting in almost-perfect cheese.

sage from Vaud), *Churer Fleischtorte* (meat pie from Chur), and Bernese salmon. There is usually a bread specific to the region or town. Ask for it by name (e.g. when in St. Gallen, ask for *St. Galler-brot*) at the local market or bakery.

Switzerland's hearty peasant cooking will keep you warm through those frigid Alpine winters. Bernese **Rösti,** a plateful of hash brown potatoes skilleted and occasionally flavored with bacon or cheese, is as prevalent in the German regions as **fondue** (from the French, *fondre*—to "melt") is in the French. Usually a blend of Emmentaler and Gruyère cheeses, white wine, *kirsch,* and spices, fondue is eaten by dunking small cubes of white bread into a *caquelon* (a one-handled pot) kept hot by a small flame. Valaisian **raclette,** is made by cutting a special cheese in half and heating it until it melts; the melted cheese is then scraped onto a baked potato and garnished with meat or vegetables. Fondue and raclette, however, are traditionally wintertime treats. Ordering them in a restaurant on a hot day in July is a dead giveaway that you're a tourist, but these dishes are worth a few odd stares.

The world's chocolate experts would never neglect the lingering sweet-tooth. Indeed, the Swiss are adept at the art of **confectionery.** Among the most tempting cakes are the *Baseler Leckerli* (a kind of gingerbread), *Schaffhauser Zungen, Zuger Kirschtorte,* Engadin nutcakes, the *bagnolet crème* of the Jura (eaten with raspberries and anise seed biscuits), soda rolls, *rissoles* (pear tarts), the nougat and pralines of Geneva, and the *zabaglione* of Ticino. *Vermicelli* (not the Italian pasta but a dessert made of chestnut mousse) is popular all over Switzerland.

The Romans introduced **wine** to the region, but it was not until the 9th century that beer-drinking laity pried it away from the clergy—who used it, of course, for liturgical purposes. By the 19th century, production had grown so indiscriminately, and the results so middling, that consumers went back to drinking beer. But a wine statute in 1953 imposed rigorous quality controls, and since then Swiss wine has regained its reputation. These wines are usually home-pressed blends, comparatively cheap, and delicious.

Each canton has its own local **beer,** a popular beverage in German-speaking Switzerland. Beer is relatively cheap, often less expensive than Coca-Cola. Order *ein helles* for a light beer, *ein dunkles* for a dark one (see Frothy Facts, p. 71).

THE ARTS

While Switzerland is not known abroad for erecting great monuments in the historical canon of the Arts (with a capital "A"), it does have a lively arts scene today, which is visible, for instance, in a day spent viewing contemporary works by young Swiss artists at Zurich's cutting-edge **Kunsthaus** (see p. 349) or a night spent prowling the city's underground music scene.

MODERN MUSIC. The subversive artistic spirit of the late twentieth century has generated a handful of musical groups that have their pulse on the sound of the twenty-first. Most of them produce alternative music aimed at teenagers and twentysomethings, but their liberalism extends to all age groups, particularly in their swinging festivals that heat up the summer nights throughout Switzerland.

FESTIVAL FEVER Back in the 70s, a handful of Swiss hipsters put a new spin on the timeworn tradition of celebrating the harvest or honoring a religious holiday with a rip-roaring raucous festival. What started as a small movement has grown to encompass more than a dozen festivals in nearly every part of the Swiss countryside. Thousands of people flock from festival to festival all summer long, following the sounds of jazz, blues, folk, rock, pop, soul, funk, hip-hop, drum 'n bass, house, and techno. Many of the festivals offer free campsites for all-comers, and have cheap tickets. Check out the University of Geneva's webpage at heiwww.unige.ch/switzerland/culture/events.htm or the Swiss search engine www.music.ch.

Bern, *Gurtenfestival*. This 3-day festival in mid-July attracts 15,000 visitors per day to the Gurten hill above Bern (5min. from town center). Features 2 stages, a half-pipe area, and a DJ area. Maceo Parker a recent guest. (Tickets 59SFr, 89SFr, 129SFr for a 1-, 2-, or 3-day pass. info@gurtenfestival.ch; www.gurtenfestival.ch.)

Winterthur, *Winterthurer Musikfestwochen*. This 17-day festival in late August exhibits over 100 acts from multi-media genres. Open-air festival the last weekend. Much free. (info@musikfestwochen.ch; www.winterthur.musikfestwochen.ch.)

Nyon (near Geneva), *Paléo Festival Nyon*. Switzerland's largest open-air music festival wins the prize for diversity of acts, ranging from electric salsa, hip hop and reggae to trip hop, drum n' bass, and electronic vibes, as well as rock, pop, blues, and even traditional French *chanson*. A free campsite offers sleeps for thousands of festival-goers. (Tickets start at 25SFr per day. paleo@paleo.ch; www.paleo.ch.)

Leysin, *Leysin Alpes Festival*. Billed as "not your average festival," this 3-day fest in mid-August focuses on new up-and-coming groups from "the independent circuit." 2 huge tents showcase hip-hop, badass hardcore, dub, and songwriting acts in comfort, come rain or shine. (Tickets 45SFr per day or 100SFr for three days with advance purchase. Free camping. www.hugo.ch/festival/leysin/.)

St. Gallen, *Open-Air St. Gallen*. This weekend festival in late June combines crowd pleasing favorites like the Counting Crows and many less mainstream bands. (Tickets 144SFr for a 3-day pass. uandermatt@openairsg.ch; www.openairsg.ch.)

Zurich, *Streetparade*. For one day in early August more than 400,000 house and techno fans congregate on the streets of Zurich and stay to party afterwards. No invitation necessary. (www.street-parade.ch.)

Bellinzona (in Canton Ticino), *Bellinzona Blues Festival*. Free piazza performances of blues bands brighten Bellinzona for 3 days in late June. Contact the Bellinzona tourist office for more information (☎825 2131; fax 825 3817.)

Gampel (between Sion and Visp), *Open-Air Gampel* '00 was one of the smaller festivals, but included such big names as Joe Cocker and Chumbawamba. (☎(027) 932 5013; openairgampel@rhone.ch; www.openairgampel.ch.)

A sampling of currently popular bands might feature **Chitty Chitty Bang Bang,** a Franco-Swiss rock foursome which has self-produced two CDs. On another note, **Der Klang** has invented a French *chanson* style which has led them far from the well-trodden tracks of the genre. Popular not only in Switzerland but also in Germany and Japan, **Gotthard's** raw, bluesy vocals, hard-rock rhythms and plentiful solos recall the sound of Bon Jovi. A rock band with folk roots, Geneva's **Polar** has performed with the likes of Massive Attack and Fiona Apple. The phrase "Swiss hip-hop" may incur some skepticism, but Switzerland does "represent" with a handful of groups, including Lausanne's **Legal, Rade,** and **Osez;** Geneva's **Fidel'Escro; CE-2P** from Vevey; and Neuchâtel's **La Sorcellerie.** Crossing over another genre is the jazz musician **Erik Truffaz,** who learned his trumpet skills from the famed Miles Davis. His sound combines jazz with rap and drum 'n bass influences.

20TH CENTURY PAINTING AND SCULPTURE. There are a few early greats among Swiss painters, such as **Urs Graf,** a swashbuckling, soldier-artist-poet skilled in court portraiture, and **Ferdinand Hodler,** an early Symbolist painter who used Swiss landscapes to convey metaphysical messages. But since the 20th cen-

EAT THE MENÜ, BABY! If you're trying to pinch pennies but not starve in the process, eating the *Menü* is the way to go. In Switzerland, a *Menü*, or a *Tagesteller*, much like a *prix-fixe* meal, is a three-course meal served only for lunch. Most *Menüs* cost between 15-20AS for soup, an entree, and dessert (drinks not included). The same meal would cost double for dinner, so get into the habit of eating a large *Menü* lunch to save money and still savor Swiss cuisine. To save even more money carry a water bottle so that you don't have to buy micro-sized drinks at macro-prices, and buy picnic supplies at the supermarket rather than purchasing meals.

tury, Switzerland has been a primary space for liberal experimentation. One of Switzerland's most famous artists is **Paul Klee,** a member of *der Blaue Reiter* (The Blue Rider) school led by **Kandinsky,** and of the Bauhaus faculty. His delicately colored watercolors and oil paintings helped shape the beginnings of abstraction, calling dominant modes of artistic expression into question.

During the World Wars, Switzerland's art scene was energized by an influx of talented refugees, a group of whom produced the **Dada** explosion in Zurich in 1916, including **Hans Arp, Richard Hülsenbeck, Janco, Tristan Tzara,** and **Hugo Ball.** Together they founded the "Cabaret Voltaire" and "Galerie Dada," short-lived centers of Dada activity (see p. 351). The Dada creed was essentially to champion the irrational over the ordered, the mad over the sane, to mock control with chaos. Marginal participants in the Zurich Dada scene later developed into artists in their own right. **Jean Tinguely** created kinetic, mechanized Dada fantasies that celebrated the beauty (and craziness) of motion.

Between and after the wars, Switzerland still attracted liberal artistic thinkers. The **Zurich School of Concrete Art,** which operated primarily between wars, combined elements of Surrealism with ideas from Russian Constructivism in an attempt to work with objects and environments to explore interactions between humans and space. The school includes Paul Klee and **Meret Oppenheim,** a Surrealist famous for her *Fur Cup*. The philosophy guided sculptor **Alberto Giacometti** to play with spatial realities in his creations of the 1930s. Later, Giacometti rejected the premise of Surrealism in order to concentrate on a deep representationalism, creating small, exaggerated, slender figures like *Man Pointing*. After sitting out the Second World War in London and spending time in Prague, Austrian Expressionist painter **Oskar Kokoschka** moved to Switzerland in 1953, settling in Villeneuve. When Kokoschka died in 1980, his widow Olda found herself with an embarrassment of pictures and subsequently founded the Foundation Oskar Kokoschka in the Musée Jenisch in Vevey (see p. 467).

LITERATURE

EARLY EXAMPLES. Though Switzerland is not particularly renowned for its native literary traditions, many famous and talented writers have called Switzerland home, and, perhaps because of its long-standing neutrality, has offered a safe haven from many others fleeing home. Among the former is **Jean-Jacques Rousseau,** best known for his *Social Contract* that inspired the French Revolution. Born in Geneva in 1712, he always proudly recognized his Swiss background—despite the facts that he spent most of his time outside the country and that the Swiss burned his books. A more conventional Swiss resident, **Jacob Burckhardt** promoted a new history of culture and art from his Basel home in the late 19th century. His works include *History of the Italian Renaissance* and *Cicerone: A Guide to the Enjoyment of Italian Art.*

ROMANTICISM. When Romanticism caught on in Swiss literature, **J.J. Bodmer** and **J.J. Breitinger's** advocacy of literature in Swiss German brought them into conflict with many of their German contemporaries, who strove to standardize German through literature. The Swiss-born **Madame de Staël** (née Germaine Necker) was both an important writer in her own right and the driving force behind Romanti-

EXILES AND EMIGRÉS Ever since **Voltaire** came to Geneva in 1755 to do some heavy-duty philosophizing, Switzerland has been the promised land for intellectuals, artists, and soon-to-be-famous personalities. George Gordon, otherwise known as the opium-smoking Romantic **Lord Byron,** quit England in 1816 for Switzerland. Byron wrote "Sonnet on Chillon" while brooding on Lake Geneva; contemporary **Percy Shelley** crafted "Hymn to Beauty" and "Mont Blanc" in the vale of Chamonix. His wife **Mary Wollstonecraft Shelley** came across some ghost stories while in Switzerland, which, heightened by Switzerland's eternal mist and craggy Alps, inspired *Frankenstein.* Speaking of ghosts, such geniuses as **Gogol, Dostoyevsky, Hugo, Hemingway,** and **Fitzgerald** still haunt the Geneva countryside where they wrote when they were in more solid form. **James Joyce** fled to Zurich during WW I and stayed to scribble the greater part of *Ulysses* between 1915 and 1919; WW II drove him to Zurich once again, where he died in 1941.

Other great minds flocked from Germany, Austria, and Italy. **Johann Wolfgang von Goethe** caught his first distant view of Italy from the top of St. Gotthard Pass in the Swiss Alps. **Friedrich Schiller** wrote about the massive church bell in Schaffhausen before penning *Wilhelm Tell.* While on holiday in the Engadin Valley, **Friedrich Nietzsche** went nuts and produced his mountaintop tome *Thus Spoke Zarathustra.* **Richard Wagner** composed most of his major operas during his years with Nietzsche in verdant Switzerland. **Thomas Mann** also found refuge in Switzerland, using one of the Swiss Alps as the setting for his novel *The Magic Mountain.* More recently Switzerland has harbored writers and scientists from the former Eastern bloc, notably Russian author **Alexander Solzhenitsyn** and Czech novelist **Milan Kundera.**

cism's spread from Germany to France. Switzerland produced a few Romantic authors as well, most notably **Gottfried Keller,** who penned a classic 19th-century German *Bildungsroman*, entitled *Der Grüne Heinrich.* **Conrad Ferdinand Meyer** was another highly influential Swiss poet, whose writings, which feature individualistic heroes, effectively unite characteristics of Romanticism and Realism.

20TH CENTURY. Only in the 20th century has Swiss literature come into its own with such greats as **Hermann Hesse,** who received the Nobel Prize for literature in 1946. Hesse's works, including *The Steppenwolf* and *Narcissus and Goldmund*, deal with the crisis of existence and the power of laughter. Another thinker concerned with the crisis of existence on a broad scale, **Carl Gustav Jung** set up a growing psychoanalytic practice in Zurich. He began as an acolyte of Freud but split off by 1915 when he wrote *Symbols of Transformation.* Critics laud **Max Frisch** for his Brechtian style and thoughtful treatment of Nazi Germany; his most widely known works are the play *Andorra* and the novel *Homo Faber*, which was made into a film in the early 1990s. **Friedrich Dürrenmatt** has written a number of cutting, funny plays, most notably *The Visit of the Old Lady* and *The Physicists.* Both Dürrenmatt and Frisch are critical of but loyal to their home country. The novelist **Robert Walser** has been celebrated for his diffuse, existential works, though they were largely ignored until his death in 1956 by an audience expecting clearly defined morals and themes.

RECOMMENDED READING.

Why Switzerland? (1996). Jonathan Steinberg.
Heidi (1902). Johanna Spyri.
Steppenwolf (1927). Hermann Hesse.
A Tramp Abroad (1879). Mark Twain.
Daisy Miller (1878). Henry James.

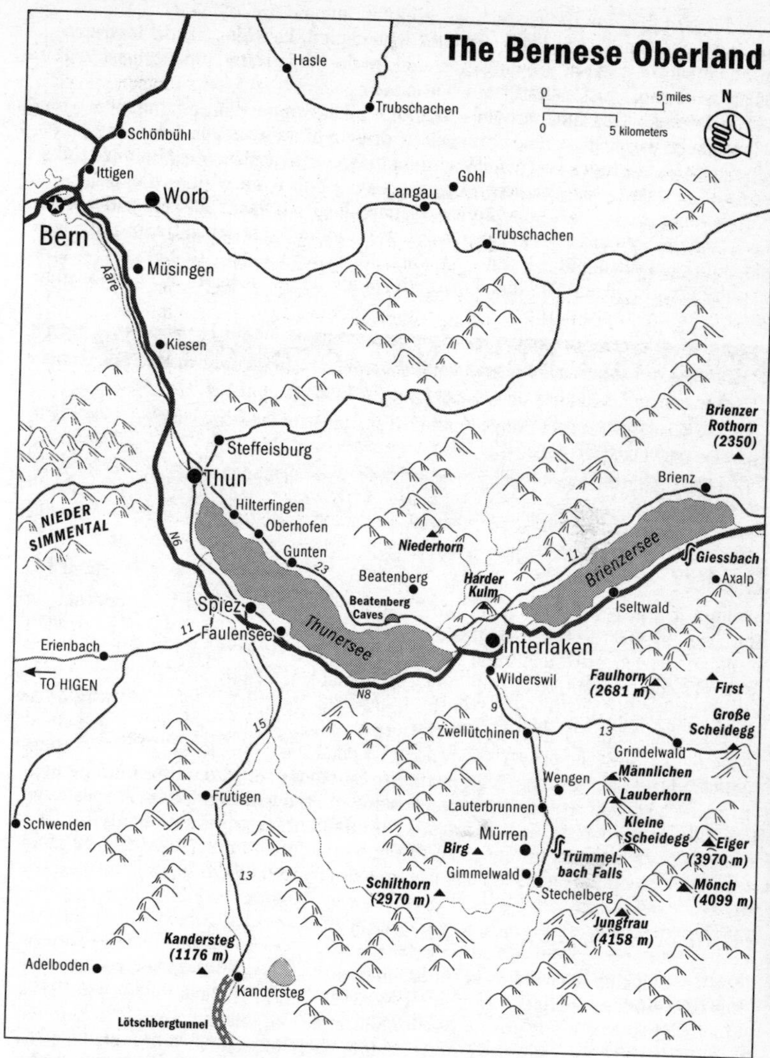

BERNESE OBERLAND

If you made a list of things of which the Swiss are fiercely proud, the Bernese Oberland would be at the top. When WWII threatened to engulf the country, the Swiss army resolved to defend this area to the last. This is partially because the savage mountains made a natural fortress of the area. The jutting peaks that could shelter a country now shelter a pristine and silent wilderness that lends itself to discovery through scenic hikes up the mountains and around the twin lakes, the Thunersee and Brienzersee. In addition to more sedate offerings, the area's opportunities for paragliding, mountaineering, and white-water rafting are virtually unparalleled. The lakeside towns attract a young, international, and rowdy crowd.

Just north of the mountains and lakes is exuberant and fun-loving Bern, the metropolitan heartbeat of the region, and the Swiss capital. Its wide, arcade-lined streets buzz with activity, while glowing green hills in the background hint at the splendor of the wilderness just a short train ride south.

The Bernese Oberland provides copious hiking opportunities, but plan your trips wisely; expensive cable cars quickly drain a hiker's budget. Wherever possible *Let's Go* lists hikes you can do without mechanical assistance. Minimize transportation costs by using a town or village as a hub from which to explore the surrounding area. The 15-day **Berner Oberland Regional Pass** (205SFr; with SwissPass or half-fare card 164SFr) grants 5 days of unlimited regional travel and a 50% discount on the other 10 days. A 7-day variation is available for 165SFr, with 3 days of unlimited travel and 50% discount on the other 4 days. Both are available at train stations or any tourist office.

HIGHLIGHTS OF BERNESE OBERLAND

Speed around the Formula One race car track in **Thun** (see p. 312).

Indulge your Klee fetish in **Bern's** Kunstmuseum, home to the world's largest collection of Klee paintings (see p. 310).

Fly high with **Interlaken's** prime paragliding and skydiving opportunities (see p. 323).

Hike to one of many high-altitude glacial lakes resting above **Kandersteg** (see p. 335).

BERN ☎031

Though it borders *Suisse Romande*, the French-speaking part of the country, Bern belongs to the German-speaking *Deutschschweiz*. The Duke of Zähringen founded Bern in 1191, naming it for his mascot, the bear. The city has been Switzerland's capital since 1848, but don't expect fast tracks, power politics, or men in black—Bern prefers to focus on the lighter things in life. Some old wag once claimed that "Venice is built on water, Bern on wine." While the Bernese seem a bit too sober to merit the proverb, they do appreciate the grape, local Toblerone chocolate, and their sumptuous flower gardens. Situated in a bend of the winding Aare River, Bern's bridges span lush, green banks. Rebuilt in 1405 after a devastating fire, Bern's sandstone and mahogany buildings are dominated mainly by a fat *Bundeshaus* and the stately spire of the Gothic *Münster*. The city itself is an attraction, having been named a world treasure by UNESCO.

GETTING THERE AND AROUND

The **Bern-Belp Airport** (☎960 2111) is 20 minutes from central Bern and is served by Swissair (☎0848 800 700), Crossair (☎960 2121), and Air Engadina (☎960 1211). Direct flights go daily to Basel, Amsterdam, London, Lugano, Brussels, Munich, Paris, Rome, and Vienna. Fifty minutes before each flight, an airport bus that guarantees you'll make your flight runs from the train station in front of the tourist office (10min., 14SFr). If **driving** from Basel or the north, take A2 south to A1. From Lucerne or the east, take 10 west. From Geneva or Lausanne, take E62 east to E27/A12 north. From Thun or the southeast, take A6 north.

TRANSPORTATION

Trains: Bahnhofpl. For rail info, dial 157 2222 (6am-10pm) or 0900 300 300 (24hr., 1.19SFr per min.). The **rail information office** is open M-F 8am-7pm, Sa 9am-5pm. To: **Geneva** (2hr., every 30min. 5:57am-11:24pm, 50SFr); **Lucerne** (1½hr., every hr. 6:43am-11:16pm, 32SFr); **Interlaken** (50min., every hr. 6:20am-11:26pm, 25SFr); **Zurich** (1¼hr., every 30min. 5:52am-11:52pm, 48SFr); **Lausanne** (1¼hr., every 30min. 5:57am-11:24pm, 32SFr); **Basel** (1¼hr., every 30min. 4:48am-11:52pm, 37SFr); **Paris** (4½hr., 4 per day 6:25am-5:03pm, 109SFr); **Munich** (5½hr., 4 per day 5:28am-8:49pm, 123SFr); **Vienna** (10½hr., 4 per day 8:16am-9:16pm, 162SFr);

BERNESE OBERLAND

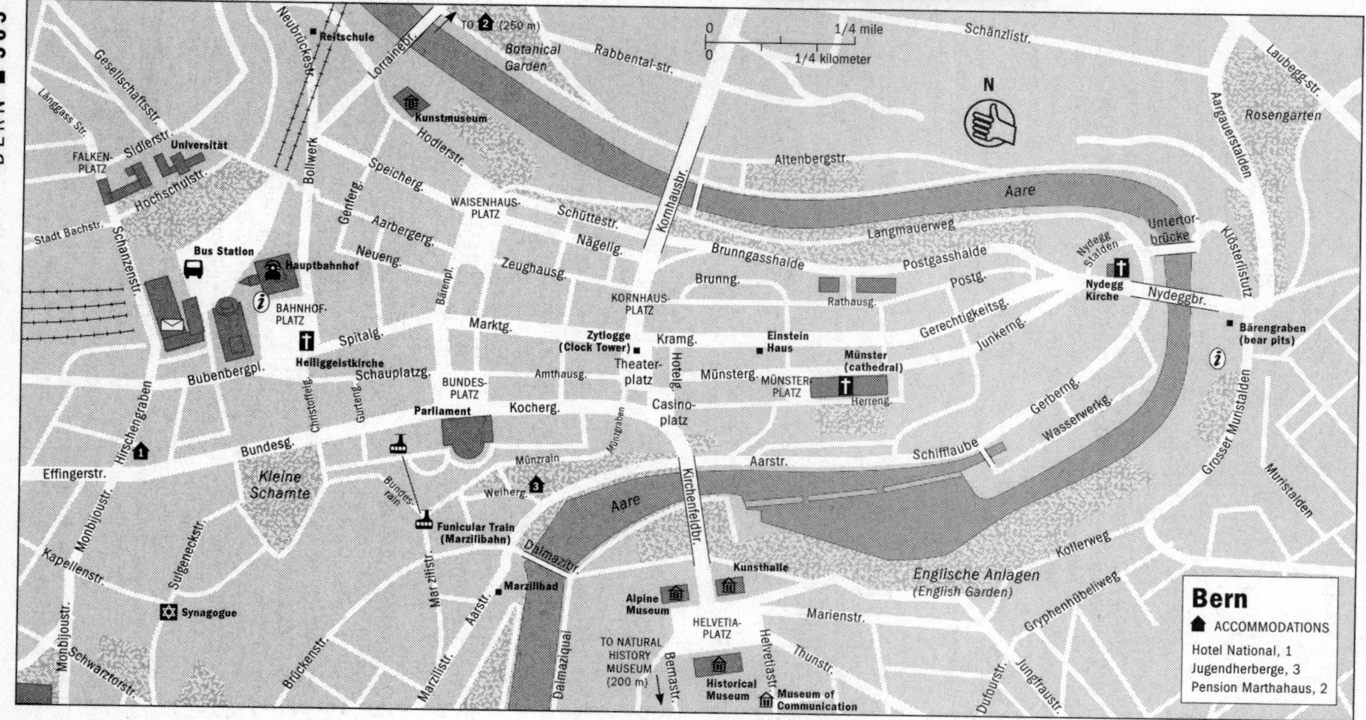

Salzburg (7¼hr., 4 per day 8:16am-9:16pm, 136SFr); **Milan** (3½hr., 13 per day 6:20am-11:26pm, 73SFr); and **Berlin** (8hr., 3 per day 5:28am-7:49pm, 254SFr). Reduce all international fares by 25% for ages 26 and under.

Public Transportation: SVB (☎321 8641; fax 321 8686). A **visitor's card** from the ticket offices downstairs in the station or at the Jurahaus office, Bubenbergpl. 5 (☎321 8631), entitles the holder to unlimited travel on all SVB routes and a 10% discount on city tours. 24hr. pass 6SFr; 48hr. 9SFr; 72hr. 12SFr. This pass is cheaper than the day pass alone (7.50SFr), which is dispensed at automatic vending machines along with one-way tickets (1-6 stops 1.50SFr; 7 or more stops 2.40SFr; SwissPass valid). Buses run 5:45am-11:45pm. **Nightbuses** leave the train station at 12:45, 2, and 3:15am on F-Sa nights, covering major bus and tram lines (5SFr; no reductions). SVB offices in the train station distribute maps and timetables. Open M-W and F 6:30am-7:30pm, Th 6:30am-9pm, Sa 7:30am-6:30pm.

Taxis: Bären-Taxi (☎371 1111) or **NovaTaxi** (☎301 1111). Stands at Bahnhofpl., Waisenhauspl., and Casinopl. Fare: 6.50SFr base; 2.70SFr/km; from 8pm-6am and Su 3SFr per km.

Parking: Bahnhof, entrance at Schanzenbrücke or Stadtbachstr. **Parking Casino,** Kocherg. **City West,** Belpstr., costs 3.20SFr per hr., 28SFr for a day, 12SFr for 2nd and 3rd day. Day-permit parking discs available at the tourist office.

Car Rental: Avis AG, Wabernstr. 41 (☎378 1515). **Hertz AG,** Kochelstr. 1, Casinopl. (☎318 2160). **Europcar,** Laupenstr. 22 (☎381 7555).

Bike Rental: Blubike, Marktg. 27 (☎311 2234), in the Intersport store, loans bikes for free. A 20SFr deposit plus ID are required. Reserve ahead. Open M-W and F 8am-6:30pm, Th 8am-9pm, Sa 8am-4pm. Otherwise, try **Fly-Gepäck** (☎(051) 220 2374) at the station. 26SFr per day, 100SFr per week; mountain bikes 32SFr, 128SF; children's bikes 16SFr, 64SFr. Reservations recommended. Open M-Sa 6:10am-11pm.

ORIENTATION AND PRACTICAL INFORMATION

Most of medieval Bern lies in front of the train station and along the Aare River. Bern's main **train station,** in front of the **tourist office,** is a stressful tangle of essential services and extraneous shops. Check-in, information, buses, luggage watch, bike rental, and a pharmacy are upstairs; tickets, lockers, police, showers, toilets, and currency exchange are downstairs. **Warning:** Like many cities, Bern has a drug community; it tends to congregate around the Parliament park and terraces.

TOURIST SERVICES

Tourist Office: (☎328 1212; fax 312 1233; info@bernetourism.ch; www.bernetourism.ch), on the street level of the station. The office distributes maps and *Bern Aktuell,* a bimonthly guide to events in the city, and makes free room reservations. The 24hr. electronic board outside the office has a free phone line to hotels, computerized receipts, and directions in German, French, and English. **City tours** available by bus, on foot, or by raft. Tours daily in summer, 6-23SFr. Open June-Sept. daily 9am-8:30pm, Oct.-May M-Sa 9am-6:30pm, Su 10am-5pm. **Branch office** at the bear pits, often less crowded than the main office, open June-Sept. daily 9am-5pm; Oct. and Mar.-May 10am-4pm, Nov.-Feb. F-Su 10am-4pm.

Budget Travel: SSR, Rathausg. 64 (☎302 0312; www.ssr.ch). Take bus #12 to "Rathaus." Sells BIJ tickets, ISIC cards, Europass, etc. Open M-W and F 9:30am-6pm, Th 9:30am-8pm, Sa 10am-1pm. **Hang Loose,** Spitalg. 4 (☎313 1818; fax 313 1819; www.hangloose.ch) has BIJ and plane tickets and ISIC cards; matches SSR prices. Open M-F 9am–6pm, Th until 8pm, Sa 9am-noon.

Embassies and consulates: Nearly all foreign embassies in Switzerland are located in Bern, southeast of the Kirchenfeldbrücke. A complete list of consular services can be found in the Essentials section (see p. 7).

COMMUNICATION AND FINANCIAL SERVICES

Currency Exchange: Downstairs in the station. No commission on travelers' checks. Credit card advances on DC, MC, and Visa. Western Union transfers 7am-7pm daily. Open June to mid-Oct. daily 6:30am-9pm; mid-Oct. to May 6:15am-8:45pm.

ATMs at **Credit Suisse** and **Swiss Bank Corp.** Banks open M-W and F 8am-4:30pm, Th 8am-6pm.

Bookstore: Stauffacher, Neueng. 25 (☎311 2411). From Bubenbergpl., turn left on Genferg. to Neueng. 6 floors of books, including English and French. Open M-F 9am-6:30pm, Sa 9am-9pm, Su 8am-4pm.

Libraries: Stadtbibliothek (Municipal and University Library), Münsterg. 61 (☎320 3211), stacks books for the central library of the University of Bern and the city's public library. Lending library open M-F 10am-6pm, Sa 10am-noon. Reading room open M-F 8am-9pm, Sa 8am-noon. **Swiss National Library,** Hallwylstr. 15 (☎332 8911). Lending library and catalog room open M-Tu and Th-F 9am-6pm, W 9am-8pm, Sa 9am-2pm. Reading room open M-Tu and Th-F 8am-6pm, W 8am-8pm, Sa 9am-4pm.

Internet Access: Medienhaus Zeughausg. 14 (☎327 1188), to the right off Waisenhauspl. Free. Open M-F 8am-6pm, Sa 9am-11pm. **Soundwerk Café,** Wasserwerkg. 5. At Aare River, near the bottom of Nydeggbrücke. Free Internet access in a graffiti-covered sound studio. Open M-F 11am-7pm, Sa 11am-4pm. Basement of **JäggiBücher,** Spitalg. on Bubenbergpl. 47-51 (☎320 2020) in Loeb dept. store. 2 computers allow max. 20min. free, 2 more computers cost 5SFr per 30min. Open M-W and F 9am-6:30pm, Th 9am-9pm, Sa 8am-4pm.

Post Office: Schanzenpost 1, next to the train station. Address *Poste Restante* to Postlagernde Briefe, Schanzenpost 3000, Bern 1. Open M-W and F 7:30am-6:30pm, Th 7:30am-8pm, Sa 8am-noon. Express counter M-W and F 6-7:30am and 6:30-10pm, Th 6-7:30am and 8-10pm, Sa 7-8am and noon-6pm, Su 3:30-10pm. **Postal Code:** CH-3000 to CH-3030.

OTHER SERVICES

Bi-Gay-Lesbian Organizations: Homosexuelle Arbeitsgruppe die Schweiz-HACH (Gay Association of Switzerland), c/o Anderland, Mühlenpl. 11, CH-3011. Headquarters of Switzerland's largest gay organization. **Homosexuelle Arbeitsgruppe Bern** (HAB), Mühlenpl. 11, Case Postal 312, CH-3000 Bern 13 (☎311 6353) in Marzilibad, along the Aare. Hosts get-togethers W evenings, with coffee, drinks, and library access. **Schlub** (Gay Students' Organization), c/o Studentinnenschaft, Lercheweg 32, CH-3000 Bern 9 (☎371 0087). **Gay Geneva Evenings** (☎022 320 7265, www.swissgay.ch).

Pharmacy: In the station. Open 6:30am-10pm. **Bären Apotheke,** at the clock tower. Open M 10am-6:30pm, Tu-F 8am-6:30pm, Sa 8am-4pm. AmEx, DC, MC, Visa. For the **24hr. pharmacy on duty,** dial 311 2211.

Luggage Storage: Downstairs in the train station. 24hr. Lockers 3-5SFr. **Luggage watch** at the Fly-Gepäck counter upstairs 5SFr. Open M-Sa 6:10am-11pm.

Lost Property: Downstairs in station, open M-F 8am-noon and 2-6pm. And at Zeughausg. 18 (☎321 5050), open M-W and F 8am-noon, 1-4:30pm, Th 8am-noon, 1-6pm.

Laundromat: Jet Wash, Dammweg 43 (☎078 743 9209). Take bus #20 (dir: Wyler) to "Lorraine." Wash 8kg for 6SFr, 5kg 4SFr; dryers 4SFr. Detergent 1.20SFr. Open M-Sa 7am-9pm, Su 9am-6pm.

Public Showers: At train station. Toilets 1-1.50SFr; showers 10SFr. Open 6am-midnight.

EMERGENCIES

Police, ☎117. **Ambulance,** ☎144. **Doctor,** ☎311 2211.

Rape Crisis Hotline, ☎332 1414.

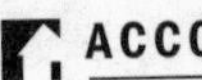

ACCOMMODATIONS

Bern's only hostel is usually reliable for a last-minute bed, but if it's full, cheap accommodations are rare. The tourist office has a list of **private rooms.** Otherwise consider staying in Fribourg (see p. 484), 30 minutes from Bern by train.

Jugendherberge (HI), Weiherg. 4 (☎311 6316; fax 312 5240). From the station cross the tram lines and go down Christoffelg. Take the road through the gates to the left of the Park Café, and follow it down to Weiherg., following the hostel signs. On the banks of the Aare, the hostel has 186 beds. Spacious common areas feature a TV with CNN and life-sized chess on the patio. Reception June-Sept. daily 7-9:30am and 3pm-midnight; Oct.-May 7-9:30am and 5pm-midnight. Closed 2 weeks in Jan. Check-out before 10am. Wheelchair accessible. Reservations by fax only. **Laundry** 6SFr. Breakfast 6SFr. Lunch or dinner 11SFr. 3-night max. stay. Communal hall showers. Dorms 28SFr; overflow mattresses on the floor 14SFr. Tax 1.25SFr. Nonmembers add 5SFr. MC, Visa.

Pension Marthahaus, Wyttenbachstr. 22a (☎332 4135; fax 333 3386; martahaus@bluewin.ch). Take bus #20 (dir: Wyler) to "Gewerbeschule," then the 1st right. Or walk from the station: turn left onto Bollwerk, cross Lorrainebrücke, bear right onto Viktoriarain, then take the 1st left onto Wyttenbachstr. A motherly hostess maintains this comfortable *Pension* in a quiet suburb, offering fresh towels, blankets, TVs (for 3SFr extra), sparkling showers and sinks. **Laundry** 8SFr. Kitchen access. Limited parking. Reception 7:30am-9pm, a porter accommodates latecomers. Checkout 11am. Reservations recommended. Breakfast included. Singles 60SFr, with shower 90SFr; doubles 95SFr, 120SFr; triples 120SFr, 150SFr. Prices drop 5-10SFr in winter. MC, Visa.

Hotel National, Hirschengraben 24 (☎381 1988; fax 381 6878). From the station, cross over the bus stops/tramlines to Bubenberg. on the right. Hirschengraben is the 2nd road downhill. An elegant lobby and rooms furnished with antiques, managed by a gracious staff in a great location. Downstairs restaurant has a 16.50SFr *Menü*. Breakfast included. Reservations recommended in summer. Reception 7am-10:30pm, but the night porter opens the doors for latecomers. Singles 60-80SFr, with shower 85-110SFr; doubles 95-110SFr, 130-150SFr; 3- to 5-person family room 170-260SFr. AmEx, DC, MC, Visa.

Camping Eichholz, Strandweg 49 (☎961 2602). Take tram #9 to "Wabern," backtrack 50m, and take the 1st right. Walk down Eichholzstr. for about 10min.; signs point the way. Riverside location opposite the zoo, within earshot of snuffling boars and drooling bison. Electricity 3SFr. **Laundry** 5SFr. On-site restaurant. Parking available 2-3.20SFr. Showers 1SFr. Open May-Sept. Reserve ahead. 6.90SFr, students 5.50SFr, children 3SFr; tents 5-8.50SFr; 2-bed rooms 15SFr; 3-bed rooms 17SFr; 4-bed rooms 22SFr.

FOOD

Almost every locale ending in "-platz" overflows with cafes and restaurants, though the bigger ones tend to be pricier and more tourist-infested. Try one of Bern's hearty specialties: *Gschnätzlets* (fried veal, beef, or pork), *Suurchabis* (a sauerkraut), or *Gschwellti* (steamed potatoes). The sweet-toothed will savor an airy meringue or home-grown **Toblerone chocolate.**

Café des Pyrenées, Kornhauspl. 17 (☎311 3063). Named after a novel by Swiss author Daniel Himmerberg, this expatriate-style bistro-cafe complete with a small sidewalk terrace is a haven for journalists, office-goers, and busy types. Inventive sandwiches (calamari 6.50SFr) and conservative spaghettis (9.50SFr). The spirits list is extravagant, with 6 types of Spanish brandy. Open M-F 9am-12:30am, Sa 8am-5pm.

Cave 49, Gerechtigkeitsg. 49 (☎312 5592), is a spicy, dimly lit Mediterranean eatery. Enjoy *tortellini alla panno con parmesan* (14.50SFr) or a meaty paprika *chorizo* (6.50SFr). Beers from 2.70SFr. Open Tu-Su 10am-12:30am.

Manora, Bubenbergpl. 5A (☎311 3755), over the tramlines from the station. This self-service chain tends to be crowded, but serves big platefuls that are indisputably nutritious and cheap. Salad bar 4.20-8.90SFr; pasta 8-10SFr; veggie burger plate 9SFr. Open M-Sa 6:30am-11pm, Su 8:30am-11:15pm.

Restaurant Marzilbrücke, Gassstr. 8 (☎311 2780). Turn right from the hostel onto Aarstr. Escape the hostel dinner with a selection of curry dishes (23SFr) or a gourmet Italian pizza (14.50-22.50SFr). The Australian bartender pours a wide selection of wines (4.20-7.50SFr) to the tunes of Peruvian pipes. Open M-Th 11:30am-11:30pm, F 11:30am-12:30am, Sa 4pm-12:30am, Su 10am-11:30pm. Pizzeria open 6-11pm.

Pizza Camargue, Kramg. 42 (☎311 8277). The brick and rippled-plaster dining room is an appropriately oven-like setting for a pizzeria. Try some pizza (14-19SFr), pasta (12.80-20SFr), or lunch *Menüs* (11am-2pm; 12.80-16.80SFr). Open M-W 9am-1am, Th-Sa 9am-2am, Su 11am-midnight.

MARKETS

Migros, Marktg. 46, also has a restaurant and take-away counters, including one with 4.90SFr sandwiches. Open M-W and F 8am-6:30pm, Th 8am-9pm, Sa 7am-4pm.

Reformhaus M. Siegrist, in the Marktg.-Passage (off Marktg.), is a popular health food market. Open M 2-6:30pm, Tu-F 8am-12:15pm and 1:30-6:30pm, Sa 7:45am-1pm.

Fruit and vegetable markets sell fresh produce daily on Bärenpl. (May-Oct. 8am-6pm) and every Tu and Sa on Bundespl. The off-the-wall **onion market,** which takes over the city on the 4th M of Nov., is probably Bern's single best known festival.

SIGHTS AND MUSEUMS

Bern is an easily walkable city. Most of the sights are laid out in a line starting at the Parliament. Several of Bern's museums sit in a compact ring around **Helvetiaplatz** across Kirchenfeldbrücke (accessible by tram #3 or #5).

THE OLD TOWN. Perhaps hearkening back to the flames that set Bern's houses ablaze in 1405, the solid medieval architecture of Bern's *Altstadt* glows red with Swiss flags and geraniums. Behind church spires and government domes, the lush hills along the Aare river create a cooling verdant backdrop. The massive **Bundeshaus,** where the Swiss national government is centered, dominates the Aare. The politicians hide in the **Parlamentsgebäude.** *(☎322 8522. 45min. tour every hr. M-Sa 9-11am and 2-4pm, Su 10-11am and 2-3pm. Free.)*

From the state house, Kockerg. and Herreng. lead to the 15th-century Protestant **Münster** (cathedral). The imagination of the late-Gothic period runs riot in the stern portal sculpture of the Last Judgment, left intact during the Reformation, where the naked damned shuffle off unhappily to Hell on God's left. For a fantastic view of the Aare and beyond, climb the Münster's spire (100m)—it's among the tallest in all of Switzerland. *(Open Easter-Oct. Tu-Sa 10am-5pm, Su 11:30am-5pm; Nov.-Easter Tu-F 10am-noon and 2-4pm, Sa 10am-noon and 2-5pm, Su 11am-2pm. Tower closes 30min. before the church. 3SFr. Free concerts often held Tu at 8pm, early June-Sept.)*

From the Bundeshaus, turn left off Kocherg. at Theaterpl. to reach the 13th-century **Zytglogge** (clock tower). At 4 minutes before the hour, figures on the tower creak to life with a couple of pallid rooster squawks; more entertaining are the fervent oohs and aahs of gathered tourists. *(Tours of the interior June-Sept. daily at 11:30am and 6:3opm, May and Oct. daily at 4:30pm. 6SFr.)* Walking through the city from the clock tower, on the edge of the *Altstadt* the slender, finger-like copper spire of the **Nydegg Kirche** rises from the intersection of Kramg. and Gerechtigkeitsg. The church stands on the remains of the Nydegg imperial fortress that was destroyed in the mid-13th century.

BEAR PITS. Across the Nydeggbrücke lie the **Bärengraben** (bear pits, see Bären Brain, p. 310). The stone-lined pits date back to the 15th century, but they were recently renovated to provide the city's mascots with trees and rocks to clamber over, perhaps to make up in some way for the indignity of having to show off for gawking crowds and screaming kids. On Easter, newborn cubs are displayed in public for the first time. *(Open June-Sept. daily 8am-6pm; Oct.-May daily 8am-dusk. 3SFr to*

BÄREN BRAIN Bern's citizens have got bears on the brain. The city's ursine mascot pervades even the most forsaken alleyways in the form of statuettes, fountains, flags, stained-glass windows, and matchbox covers. The *Bärengraben* are the pits just beyond the center of the city where live bears are kept like some sort of strange totem. Legend has it that Duke Berchtold V of Zähringen, founder of Bern, wanted to name the city after the first animal he caught when hunting on the site of the planned construction. The animal was a you-know-what, and Bern (etymologically derived from *Bären*) was born. The *Bärengraben* themselves weren't built until the Bernese victory at the Battle of Nouana in 1513, when they dragged home a live bear as part of the war booty. A hut was erected for the beast in what is now Bärenplatz (Bear Square) and his descendants have been Bern's collective pets ever since.

feed the bears.) The tourist office at the pits also present **The Bern Show,** a slickly choreographed recap of Bernese history that melds into an overly-indulgent photomontage. *(Every 20min. In German and English, alternately. Free.)* The path snaking up the hill to the left leads to the **Rosengarten;** sit among the blooms and admire one of the best views of Bern's *Altstadt.*

KUNSTMUSEUM. Bern's Kunstmuseum (art museum) sprawls over 3 floors and a couple of buildings, top-heavy with the world's largest Paul Klee collection: 2500 geometrically dreamy works, from his school exercise-books to his largest canvases, along with some works by his chums Kandinsky and Feininger. A smattering of last century's big names are exhibited upstairs: Picasso, Giacometti, Ernst Kirchner, Pollock, and some Dada works by Hans Arp. The museum also has a chic cafe and screens art films. *(Hodlerstr. 8-12, near Lorrainebrücke. ☎311 0944. Open Tu 10am-9pm, W-Su 10am-5pm. Mandatory lockers for bags, 2SFr. Admission 7SFr, students and seniors 5SFr, under 16 free. Extra fees for temporary exhibitions.)*

THE RIVER AARE. Several walkways lead steeply down from the Bundeshaus to the Aare; a cable car assists you on the way up (1SFr). The river itself is ideal for shady walks. On hotter days, locals dive lemming-style from the bridges to take a brisk ride on its swift currents (signs warn that only experienced swimmers should jump in). Along the banks, numerous sets of stone steps invite you to take the plunge. For a more languid afternoon of bathing and basking, the **Marzilibad public pool** lies on the river 3 minutes to the right of the hostel. *(Pool open May-Aug. M-Sa 8:30am-8pm, Sept. M-F 8:30am-7pm, Sa-Su 8:30am-6pm. Lockers and showers available.)*

GARDENS AND ZOO. The **Botanical Gardens** of the University of Bern, Altenbergrain, sprawl down the river at Lorrainebrücke. Exotic plants from Asia, Africa, and the Americas thrive next to native Alpine greenery. *(Take bus # 20 to "Gewerbeschule." ☎631 4944. Park open Mar.-Sept. M-F 7am-6pm, Sa-Su 8am-5:30pm; Oct.-Feb. 8am-5pm daily. Greenhouse open daily 8am-5pm. Free.)* In a towering forest of cedar and pine, the 24-hour park housing the **Dählhölzli Städtischer Tierpark** (Zoo) gives you the chance to animal-watch at night, too. *(Tierparkweg 1. Walk south along the Aare or take bus #19 to "Tierpark". ☎357 1515. Zoo open daily in summer 8am-6:30pm; in winter 9am-5pm. 7SFr, students 5SFr. Parking available.)*

BERNISCHES HISTORISCHE MUSEUM. This collection is so big you won't know where to begin. Luckily, multilingual explanatory notes are available in many rooms of the museum's 7 jam-packed levels. Wide staircases lined with portraits of rotund Bernese citizens lead to evocative exhibits, from the Münster artifacts downstairs to the illuminated manuscripts in the Islamic collection. Niklaus Manuel's wittily macabre *Dance of Death*, in which a jocular skeleton greets representatives of 24 professions, is one of the highlights. Also look out for an eerily grinning William Tell who looks like he's aiming right at you. *(Helvetiapl. 5. ☎350 7711. Open Tu-Su 10am-5pm. 5SFr, students 3SFr, free for those under 17 and school groups. Additional charge for special exhibitions. Free on Saturday.)*

FANCY FOUNTAINS As if bumpy cobblestone streets and happy-go-lucky pedestrians weren't bad enough, motorists in Bern also have to negotiate their way around the 16th-century fountains that squat squarely in the middle of many of the city's *Straßen*. These creations are seen all over Switzerland but the Bernese variety seem especially blinding. Most of the fountains, called *Brunnen*, are attributed to the artist Hans Gieng. Crafted in stone, the *Brunnen* have been restored repeatedly since the mid-1500s to maintain their gaudy color schemes (the city mascot, the bear, shows up in fire-engine red). Highlights include the *Gerechtigkeitsbrunnen* on Gerechtigkeitsg., in which Justice stomps on the Pope, Emperor, Sultan, and Mayor, and the *Kindlifresserbrunnen* ("Child-Devourer Fountain") at Kornhauspl., tastefully translated as the "Ogre Fountain."

SWISS ALPINE MUSEUM. intricate models of Switzerland's most popular mountains give a history of Swiss cartography is this museum of Alpinism. The main floor is an array of topographical maps of the country. The 2nd-floor exhibit on mountain life may be more interesting—check out the devil masks used to protect against threats from the other world. *(Helvetiapl. 4. ☎351 0434. Open mid-May to mid-Oct. M 2-5pm, Tu-Su 10am-5pm; mid-Oct. to mid-May M 2-5pm, Tu-Su 10am-noon and 2-5pm. 5SFr, students and seniors 3SFr.)*

MUSEUM OF NATURAL HISTORY. Most people come to this bright, colorful museum to see Barry, the now-stuffed St. Bernard who saved over 40 people in his lifetime. Some of the other hyper-realistic dioramas, however, get a bit more intense—hyenas feed on zebra corpses, and more dynamic cousins of the *Bärengraben* bears dispute a recently downed moose. Very family and schoolgroup friendly. *(Bernastr. 15, off Helvetiapl. ☎350 7111. Open M 2-5pm, Tu and Th-F 9am-5pm, W 9am-8pm, Sa-Su 10am-5pm. 5SFr, students 3SFr, free on Su.)*

MUSEUM OF COMMUNICATION. This museum looks into how we keep in touch, from tin cans to telnet. Its cheerful, kid-friendly multilingual exhibits and computer touch-screens manage to make mail entertaining. The museum houses the world's largest public display of postage stamps. *(Helvetiastr. 16, behind the history museum. ☎357 5511. Open Tu-Su 10am-5pm. 5SFr, students 3SFr, under 17 free.)*

ALBERT EINSTEIN'S HOUSE. This small apartment where the theory of general relativity was conceived in 1905 is now filled with photos, a few of Einstein's letters, resonating brain waves, and not much else. The museum emphasizes that Albert loved Bern and Bern still loves Albert. *(Kramg. 49. ☎312 0091. Open Feb.-Nov. Tu-F 10am-5pm, Sa 10am-4pm. 3SFr, students and children 2SFr.)*

ENTERTAINMENT

Bern's cultural tastes run the gamut from classical music concerts to late-night café bands. Events are well-publicized on kiosks and bulletin boards. Publications like **Non-Stopp** and **Berner Woche** (the "Going Out" sections of two Bern newspapers) or **Gay Agenda** will be thrust into your hands on street corners.

Operas and ballets are performed at the **Stadttheater,** Kornhauspl. 20 (☎311 0777; summer season runs July to late August; for ticket info, contact *Theaterkasse*, Kornhauspl. 18, CH-3000 Bern 7). The **Berner Altstadtsommer** features free dancing and music concerts, ranging from tango to jazz to funk to choral, in the squares of the *Altstadt*. Bern's **Symphony Orchestra** plays in the fall and winter at the *Konservatorium für Musik* at Kramg. 36 (tickets ☎311 6221). July's **Gurten Festival** (www.gurtenfestival.ch; see Festival Fever, p. 300) has attracted such luminaries as Bob Dylan, Elvis Costello, Björk, and Sinead O'Connor. Jazz-lovers arrive in early May for the **International Jazz Festival** (tickets at any Bankverein Swiss branch). Other festivals include the Bernese Easter-egg market in late March and a notorious **onion market** (see p. 309) on the 4th Monday in November. The orange grove at *Stadgärtnerei Elfnau* (take tram #19 to "Elfnau") has free Sunday concerts in summer. Additionally, **Mahogany Hall,** by the bear pits (Klösterlistutz 18; www.mahogany.ch), is a popular venue for jazz, bluegrass, folk, swing. . . and the list goes on.

From mid-July to mid-August, **OrangeCinema** screens recently released films, including many American ones, in the open air. Tickets are for sale at the tourist office in the train station or at the Orange Shop at Spitalg. 14. For more information, see www.orangecinema.ch.

NIGHTLIFE

The fashionable folk linger in the *Altstadt's* bars and cafés at night. A seedier scene gathers under the gargoyles and graffiti of the Lorrainebrücke, behind and to the left of the station down Bollwerk.

Le Pery Bar, Schmiedenpl. 3 (☎311 5908), off Kornhauspl. This popular nightspot boasts crowds both inside and out, a packed first floor and more relaxed second floor. The Rablaus Restaurant serves lunch and dinner. Bar open M-W 5pm-1:30am, Th 5pm-2:30am, F-Sa 5pm-3:30am.

Art Café, Gurteng. 3 (☎311 4264). A cafe by day and a smoky bar by night, the black and white decor sets a casually trendy tone for wannabe-beautiful people to schmooze and booze. Occasional live acts and DJs. Beers from 3.50SFr. Open M-W 7-12:30am, Th-F 7-2:30am, Sa 8-2:30am, Su 6pm-12:30am.

Klötzlikeller Weine Stube, Gerechtigkeitsg. 62 (☎311 7456). Bern's oldest wine cellar resonates with loud talk and slurred choruses of German drinking songs (wines 3.40-5.20SFr per glass). January and February bring the house specialty, *Treberwurst* (sausage cooked in wine liqueur). Open Tu-Th 4pm-12:30am, F-Sa 4pm-1:30am.

Sous le Pont, from Bollwerk, head left before Lorrainebrücke through the cement park. A den of alternative culture, a fascinating stew of mismatched chairs and mesmerizing Eastern music. Pony-tailed waiters bring 3SFr beers to an unnaturally relaxed, predominantly male, clientele. Open M and Sa after 5pm, Tu-F 11pm-1am.

Reitschule, Bern Neubrückstr. 8 (☎302 8372), left off Bollwerk. A small room painted with bats and buddhas caters to a patchwork crowd of students and loafers. Beers from 3SFr; *Menüs* 5SFr. Open 8pm-whenever.

THE THUNERSEE

As the western member of the pair of lakes that frames Interlaken, the Thunersee's smaller size works to its advantage. The jade-green forests and distant snow-capped Jungfrau peaks seem immediately accessible from the sail-dotted waters of the lake. Its northwestern shores are strewn with castles, enchanting the surrounding towns and cloud-enshrouded peaks.

The Thunersee's three significant towns, **Thun, Spiez,** and **Interlaken,** all lie on the main Bern-Interlaken-Lucerne rail line. **Boats** operated by the BLS shipping company (☎334 5211; www.thunersee.ch) putter to the smaller villages between the Thun and Interlaken West railway stations (June 26-Sept. 26, 2hr., every hr. 8:10am-11:35pm; special evening cruises available from June-Dec. Eurail, Swiss-Pass, and Berner Oberland pass valid). A ferry day-pass good as far as **Brienz** (on the Brienzersee) costs 6.60SFr.

THUN ☎033

Known as the "Gateway to the Bernese Oberland," Thun (pop. 38,000) lies on the banks of the Aare river and the Thunersee. The city's name is derived from the Celtic "dunum," or hill settlement. The town's first settlements date back to 100BC. Graced by nearby castles of every imaginable size and most colors, the quiet, water-laced town confirms the words of Johannes Brahms: "Relaxing in Thun is delightful, and one day will not be enough." Thun is picturesque and historic, but not stodgy. The Selve area offers everything from discothèques and bars to a roller skating rink and a race car track.

GETTING THERE AND AROUND

Trains leave every hour for **Interlaken East** (14.60SFr) and **Interlaken West** (13.60SFr) from 7:45am-9:45pm, every half-hour for **Spiez** (6.20SFr) from 8:45am-10:45pm and every half hour for **Bern** (12.60SFr) from 9:20am-11:19pm. There is a rail **information desk** (open Mar. to mid-Oct. M-F 8am-7:40pm, Sa 8am-5pm; mid-Oct. to Feb. M-F 9am-6:30pm, Sa 9am-4pm). The **boat landing** (☎223 5380) is across the street and to the right of the station. Boats depart for **Interlaken West** (16.60SFr), **Spiez** (8.40SFr), **Faulensee** (9.20SFr), **Hilterfingen** (4.60SFr), and **Oberhofen** (5.40SFr).

ORIENTATION AND PRACTICAL INFORMATION

Thun's main street is the tree-lined boulevard Bälliz. The oldest squares and the castle (all hung with red-and-white flags) lie across the river from the train station on the Aare's north bank. Thun's **tourist office,** Seestr. 2, is outside and to the left of the station. (☎222 2340; fax 222 8323. Open July-Aug. M-F 9am-7pm, Sa 9am-noon and 1-4pm; Sept.-June M-F 9am-noon and 1-6pm, Sa 9am-noon.) The train station has **currency exchange** (open M-Sa 6am-8pm, Su 6:30am-8pm), **bike rental** (27SFr per day; open M-Su 7am-8pm), and **lockers** (3-5SFr). **Taxis** are usually waiting outside the train station, or dial 222 22 22. **Park** at the Parkhaus Aarestr. on Aarestr. (☎222 7826; 1.50SFr per hr.). The **post office** is at Bälliz 60 (open M-W and F 7:30am-6pm, Th 7:30am-7pm, Sa 8:30am-noon). The **postal code** is CH-3601.

ACCOMMODATIONS AND FOOD

The **Herberge zur Schadau** has beds for 20, and includes a recreational room with TV, board games, and a smoky smell. (☎222 5222. Breakfast included. Reception 8am-8pm daily, quiet hours 11pm-7am. 35 SFr per person. No credit cards.) To get to the hostel, exit the train station, turn right and walk 10 minutes down Seestr. **Hotel Metzgern,** Untere Hauptg. 2 has sunny rooms equipped with sinks. From the station, veer left on Bahnhofstr., go straight over two bridges. (☎222 2141; fax 222 2182. Breakfast included. Reception Tu-Th, and Su 8am-11:30pm; F-Sa 8am-12:30am. Singles, doubles, and triples 60SFr per person the 1st night; 55SFr each additional night. Children seven and under are half price. MC, Visa.) Campers should head to **Camping Bettlereiche.** Take bus #1 to "Camping" or turn right from the station and walk 45 minutes down Seestr., which will veer sharply right and turn into Gwattstr. The campsite is crowded with school kids, but it's near the water and surrounded by hills. (☎336 4067; fax 336 4017. Showers included. Reception 8:30am-noon and 2-8:30pm. July-Aug. 16.60SFr for one small tent and one person, 25 SFr for one small tent and two people; Apr.-June and Sept.-Oct. 12.10SFr. MC, Visa.)

Unlike hotel rooms, food in Thun is cheap. Affordable restaurants line Bahnhofstr., and both **Migros** and **Co-op** have markets and restaurants on Allmendstr. straddling the Kuhbrücke. (Both open M-W and F 8am-6:30pm, Th 8am-9pm, Sa 7:30am-4pm, Co-op also Su 7:30am-4pm.) The **Brotbar,** Bälliz 11, is equal parts corner bakery and swanky café. Cross the river at Allmend-Brücke and turn right on Bälliz. Try some *Brötli* (1.70SFr) or hearty potato bread (4.50SFr) while sipping exotic tea (3.80SFr), or a creamy smoothie made from homemade yogurt and fresh fruit (6SFr). (☎222 2221. Open M-W 7am-6:30pm, Th-Sa 7am-12:30am.) For delectable pastries and sandwiches in a comfy corner tea room, try **Confiserie Steinmann,** Bälliz 37, between Brotbar and the post office. Enjoy tarts for 2.40SFr or a mouthwatering *Thuner Leckerli* made from honey, lemon rind, and nuts (6SFr for 5 pieces). (☎222 2047. Open M 1-6:30pm, Tu, W, F 6:45am-6:30pm, Sa 6:45am-4pm.) At the **open-air market** in the *Altstadt*, across the river from the train station, vendors hawk souvenirs, clothes, and fresh produce (open Sa 8am-noon). A **food market** covers Bälliz on Wednesdays and Saturdays from 8am-2pm.

CASTLES

SCHLOß THUN. Thun's centerpiece, this castle presides over the town from the top of the *Altstadt.* The castle houses a historical museum whose upper floors show off a collection of vicious weaponry. The tower was the site of a gruesome fratricide in 1322, when Eberhard of Kyburg unsportingly defenestrated his brother Hartmann. Downstairs in the *Rittersaal* (Knight's Hall) the castle hosts summer classical music concerts June 7-25. *(☎223 2001. From the station, bear left down Bahnhofstr. and go over two bridges, right on Obere Hauptg., left up the Risgässli steps, and left again at the top; follow the signs to Schloß/Museum. Open June-Sept. 10am-6pm; Apr.-May and Oct. 10am-5pm. 6SFr. Students 3SFr, children 1SFr, children under 6 free, family pass for 4 is 12SFr. For concert tickets call 223 2530 or contact the tourist office; tickets 30-50SFr.)*

SCHLOß SCHADAU. The very pink **Schloß Schadau,** in the Walter Hansen Schadaupark, was built in the style of castles in France's Loire Valley. In addition to an extensive gastronomy book collection, the castle houses a fabulous **restaurant.** The lake and its environs have been recreated in the nearby **Wocher Panorama,** Seestr. 45 a full room painting of the area. *(☎223 2462. From the station, turn right and walk about 15 minutes. Panorama open Tu-Su May-Jul. and Sept.-Nov. 10am-5pm. 4SFr, students 3SFr, under 17 free.)*

SCHLOß OBERHOFEN. In neighboring Oberhofen, the 13th-century **Schloß Oberhofen** lures visitors in with its gardens and museum of furniture, and then gives the added bonus of the gorgeous view of the lake. Medieval, Baroque, Renaissance, Louis XVI, and Napoleon III styles mingle freely throughout the castle. There's a lavishly languid Turkish smoking room upstairs and a pallet-furnished cell downstairs, with plenty of wall-mounted antlers in between. *(☎243 1235. Catch bus #21 in front of the train station and take it to "Oberhofen," then head right to the lake, or hike up to the castle. Open mid-May to mid-Nov. daily 10am-noon and 2-5pm. 5SFr, students and seniors 3SFr. Garden open daily May-Oct. 8am-dusk).*

SCHLOß HÜNEGG. The most elaborate of the *Thunersee* castles, its Victorian rooms perpetually remain in an appealing state of lived-in clutter (the cook has left out a bag of flour in the kitchen). The castle grounds, known as **Hünegg Park,** are the dim and leafy home of deer, rabbits, and wild birds *(☎243 1982. Bus #21 runs to Hilterfingen (15min. by foot), where Schloß Hünegg peers over the boat landing. Castle open mid-May to mid-Oct. M-Sa 2-5pm, Su 10am-noon and 2-5pm. 8SFr, students 7SFr.)*

OUTDOOR ACTIVITIES

The popular local **hike** up **Heilingenschwendi,** the hillside above Thun on the lake's north shore, provides a view of the distant Jungfrau mountains (half-day hike). Past the casino and the village of Seematten, turn left, cross the river, and head up through the wooded ridge. Continue farther to the **Dreiländeregg** and **Niesenbänkli** for a panoramic view (3hr.). If you push on to the village of **Schwendi,** near the top, continue hiking a little farther to **Schloß Oberhofen** (see above), where you can catch bus #21 back to town. If the *Schlösser* stifle you, hit the water. The tourist office provides information on **sailing, wind-surfing, river-rafting,** and **boat rental.**

ENTERTAINMENT AND NIGHTLIFE

For late-night partiers and thrill-seekers the Selvereal part of town is the place to be. From the train station, go down Bahnhofstr., turn left on Aarestr. and keep going until it turns into Schiebenstr. and veers left. This strip is home to the **Formula One Thun,** Scheibenstr. 37, indoor race track where you can rent a car, safety equipment, and the track for an exhilarating race. (☎222 8344. Open M 5-10pm, Tu 4-10pm, W-Th 4-11pm, F 4pm-3am, Sa 2pm-3am, Su 2-8pm. For all equipment 25SFr, 17SFr for students who arrive before 6:30pm.) On the same street there are many bars and clubs, including the very fashionable **Orvis Dance Palace,** Scheibenstr. 8, which hosts live DJs spinning techno and house, and has multiple stages to dance on. In a separate room there is food, pool, and a big-screen TV next to a quiet, cool-down bar (beers 4.50SFr). (☎222 2755. Open W 8pm-12:30am, Th 8pm-2:30am, and Fr-Sa 9pm-3:30am; cover W 2SFr, Th 7SFr, Fr-Sa 10SFr.) Nearby **Nachtwerk** has a DJ on each of three floors: techno on the first, hip-hop on the second, and top 40 pop on the third.

Thun's outdoor **festivals** are a bit more tame. On the last Monday and Tuesday in September young cadets shoot it out in the *Altstadt* during the yearly **Ausschiesset** (shoot out). A **William Tell Shoot** honors the cadet who takes the best aim at a model of Gessler (see Tell Tale, p. 293). The *Altstadt* rollicks with merry music during the **Festival of Barrel Organs and Ballad Singers** every July.

NEAR THUN: SPIEZ AND BOLTIGEN

Sleepy Spiez overlooks the *Thunersee.* Its most famous attraction is its castle, **Schloß Spiez,** a medieval fortress with Romanesque, Gothic, and Renaissance flourishes that attest to its colorful history. Trains leave every hour, connecting Spiez with Bern (30min., 17.20SFr), Thun (10min., 6.20SFr), and Interlaken West (20min., 8.60SFr). Boats float to Thun (8.40SFr) and Interlaken (11.40SFr). Spiez's **tourist office,** left as you exit the train station, sells hiking maps and helps find inexpensive rooms. (☎654 2020; fax 654 2192. Open July-Aug. M-F 8am-6pm, Sa 9am-noon; May-June and Sept. M-F 8am-noon and 2-6pm, Sa 9am-noon and 2-4pm; Nov.-Apr. M-F 8am-noon and 2-5pm).

The best place to stay is the **Swiss Adventure Hostel**, in the tiny town of Boltigen (pop. 1500), 45 minutes from Spiez by train (dir.: Zweissimen). Walk straight out of the train station up past the post office and turn right when the street ends. Walk about 150m to the old Hotel Bären, where the hostel is housed. The Adventure Hostel has staked out its place in this quiet valley and building as a restful, crunchier alternative to the partying adventure scene in Interlaken. Because there are no fixed check in times and no lockout you can check in as early as 10am and come and go as you wish. The small adventure company that is run out of this hostel offers the same activities as the Interlaken companies but with a more personal touch: here, after your canyoning trip, you get to eat dinner with your trip leader. The inexpensive, modern rooms are molded into the old hotel without affecting its charm. The hostel offers **Internet access** (12SFr per hr.), **mountain bike rental** (30SFr per day), a cellar **bar,** TV, and a restaurant with breakfast buffet (5SFr) and dinner buffet (15-20SFr) from an accomplished chef. (☎(033) 773 7373; fax 773 7374. 2 free shuttles run to and from Interlaken each day; call for times and availability. 4-10 bed dorms 19SFr per person, quad with shower 25SFr per person, double with shower 34SFr per person, though there are special deals if you do a few adventure activities with them. MC, Visa.)

To see Spiez's castle, bear left on Bahnhofstr. from the station, turn right on Thunstr., and then left on Seestr., or just head towards it—it is visible from anywhere in town. You can stroll through the colorful, walled, lakeside gardens for free. Inside the fortress is a historical museum with enormous bear skins hanging above the mantelpiece, a banquet hall dating from 1614 decorated in Renaissance style, and nearly Mediterranean views of the lake. (☎ 654 1506. Open July-Sept. M 2-6pm, Tu-Su 10am-6pm; Apr.-June and Sept.-Oct. M 2-5pm, Tu-Su 10am-5pm. 4SFr, students 3SFr, children 1SFr.) The castle also hosts classical music concerts from May to June and live theater August (☎654 7018; fax 654 7024).

The mountain piercing the sky above Spiez is the **Niesenberg** (2363m). Hikes on the mountain, while not for beginners, are accessible and wind through the neighboring towns of Niesen, Kulm, and Schwandegg. Pick up hiking maps at tourist offices in Interlaken, Thun, or Spiez. Hiking all the way up or down the mountain is prohibited, but a **funicular** chugs to the top, and the **Lötschberg train** from Spiez (every hr., 7.20SFr round-trip) connects with the funicular at Mülenen. (May-Oct. 8am-5:30pm; 20SFr after 3:50pm, 40SFr before.) The funicular's builders pushed the frontiers of human achievement by building steps alongside the track, which became the **longest flight of steps in the world.** Unfortunately, only professional maintenance teams are allowed to use the steps (all 11,674 of them).

BRIENZ AND THE ROTHORN ☎033

Brienz (pop. 3200) is filled with anachronistic but authentic curiosities, including Switzerland's oldest cog steam railway, an enormous park full of preserved traditional Swiss dwellings, and wood-carvers galore (whatever you ever wanted in wood, you can get it here, even elephant and squirrel bookends). The tempo of life here seems to be cued by the calm, clear waters of the bordering **Brienzersee,** which lies beneath sharp cliffs and dense forests.

TRANSPORT AND PRACTICAL INFORMATION. Brienz makes an ideal daytrip from Interlaken by **train** (20min., 6:10am-9:53pm, 6.20SFr) or **boat** (1¼hr., every hr. 8:20am-5:32pm, 13.20SFr). Cruises on the Brienzersee depart from Interlaken's *Ostbahnhof* (June-Sept. every hr. 9:40am-6:05pm; Apr.-May and Oct. 3 per day, Eurail and SwissPass valid). The station, dock, and Rothorn cog railway terminus occupy the center of town, flanked on Hauptstr. by the post office, banks, and a supermarket. At the west end of town is Brienz-Dorf wharf; at the eastern end you'll find the hostel and campsites. Brienz's **tourist office,** Hauptstr. 143, across and left from the train station, is especially helpful for info on wood-carving cottages. (☎952 8080; fax 952 8088; info@alpenregion.ch. Open July-Aug. M-F 8am-6:30pm, Sa 9am-1pm and 4-6pm, Su 9am-1pm; Sept. to mid-Oct. M-F 8am-noon and 2-6pm, Sa 9am-noon; mid-Oct. to mid-Apr. M-F 8am-noon and 2-6pm; May-June also open Sa 9am-noon.) The train station **rents bicycles** (26SFr per day), **exchanges currency,** and has **lockers** (3-5SFr; all open 6am-11pm). **Park** at the Parkhaus Co-op behind the Co-op on Hauptg. (1½ hour parking limit M-F 7am-7pm, Sa 7am-4pm; unlimited parking M-Sa 7pm-7am, Sa 4pm-7am). The **post office** is next door (☎951 2505; open M-F 7:45am-6pm, Sa 8:30-11am). The **postal code** is CH-3855.

ACCOMMODATIONS AND FOOD. For a place to sleep, cross the tracks at the station to the gravel path by the shore, and walk left (10min.) to find the **Brienz Jugendherberge (HI),** Strandweg 10. The *Lager*-style bunks at this lakeside hostel are pricey, but doorstep access to lake walks compensates. (☎951 1152; fax 951 2260. Breakfast included. Dinner 11.50SFr. **Kitchen** facilities. **Bicycles** 15SFr per day. Reception 7:30-10am and 5-10pm. Open mid-Apr. to mid-Oct. Dorms 25.50SFr; doubles 61SFr.) Inquire at the tourist office about **private rooms. Hotel Sternen am See,** Hauptstr. 92, left from the station on the main road, has a lakeside terrace and offers classes in everything from juggling to jazzercise (15SFr per half day). (☎951 3545. Breakfast included. Reception 8am-8pm. Singles 50-90SFr; doubles 160SFr, triples 160SFr; quads with shower 200SFr. MC, Visa.) For a bed at a higher altitude check out the **Berggasthaus** in Outdoor Activities, below. Two campgrounds lie just past the hostel on the waterfront. The first one, **Camping Seegärtli,** is more secluded and offers free lake-swimming and fresh bread at 8am. (☎951 1351. 15Sfr for parking, reception 8am-7pm; open Apr.-Oct. 15SFr for one tent for one person.) Continue straight on the same road to the larger **Camping Aaregg,** which has an on-site restaurant. (☎951 1843; fax 951 4324. Reception 8am-noon and 2-8pm. Bikes 25SFr per day. Open Apr.-Oct. 14.20SFr per tent.)

Walz Tea Room, Hauptstr. 102 (☎951 1459) has a covered terrace with a spectacular view of the see and the Axalphorn. For those who prefer to dine indoors, huge glass windows provide the same beautiful view (grilled sandwiches 10.50-13SFr, omelettes 9-12SFr). **Steinbock Restaurant,** farther along Hauptstr., has outside tables and a warm wooden interior. (Swiss-style macaroni with apple sauce is 16SFr, veggie dishes, 12-17SFr. ☎951 4055. Open 8am-11pm; AmEx, DC, MC, Visa). A **Co-op** is on Hauptg. across from the station. (Open M-Th 7:45am-12:15pm and 1:30-6:30pm, F 7:45am-12:15pm and 1:30-8pm, Sa 7:4am-4pm. MC, Visa.)

MUSEUMS. The **Freilichtmuseum Ballenberg** (Open-Air Museum), on Lauenenstr. in the nearby town of Ballenberg, is an amazing 80-hectare country park dedicated to the preservation of Swiss heritage. Authentic rural Swiss houses are clumped by geographical region into tiny villages, minus the people. Most of the houses in the park were simply transplanted from their endangered original locations, and many have live exhibitions of traditional trades, such as iron-smithing or cheese-making. (☎952 1030. Open mid-Apr. to Oct. 10am-5pm. 14SFr, with visitor's card 12.60SFr, students 12SFr.) The park is about an hour's walk from the Brienz train station, but a **bus** (every hr. 7:56am-8pm, round-trip 6SFr) connects the two.

If the museum doesn't satisfy your cultural history cravings, Brienz has woodcarvers galore. The largest displays are at the cantonal wood-working schools in town. The **Kantonale Schnitzlerschule** (Wood-Carving School; ☎951 1751) and the **Geigerschule** (Violin-Making School; ☎952 1861) both have display halls about their craft. To reach both, follow the main street away from the station and hostel (15min.), then turn right on Schneeg. Home to 10 students, the *Geigerschule* houses a collection of antique instruments and a showroom of gleaming, finished violins for a mere 5000SFr each. (Both open Sept.-May M-F 8-11am and 2-5pm.; June-Aug. Call for opening hours. Free.) Many local wood-carvers also let you watch them work; contact the tourist office for a list.

OUTDOOR ACTIVITIES. The most accessible mountain in Brienz is the **Rothorn** (2350m) thanks to the **Brienz Rothorn Bahn,** which huffs and puffs its way up the mountain (☎952 2222; www.brienz-rothorn-bahn.ch; June-Oct., every hr., last ascent 4:10pm, last descent 4:55pm). At 107 years old, it is the oldest cog steam railway in Switzerland, and rather pricey (42SFr, round-trip 66SFr; with Bernese Oberland pass 21SFr, 32SFr; with SwissPass 32SFr, 50SFr). Get off at **Planalp,** halfway up the mountain, for medium-range hikes down. Follow the railway down, turning left below Planalp to head through Baalen and Schwanden (3½hr.). From the summit, head east toward the lake and turn right at the Eiseesaltel, continuing down to Hofstetten, Schwanden, and Brienz (4hr.). If you can't bring yourself to leave the summit, check into the **Berggasthaus** (☎951 1221; fax 951 1251. Breakfast included. Reception 7:30am-10pm. Dorms 32SFr; singles 65SFr; doubles 70SFr per person.)

To reach Brienz's lower peak, the **Axalphorn** (2321m), you can take a bus from the station to **Axalp** (8:20am-4:40pm, 8.40SFr) and head up either the east or west ridge (800m, half-day). Bring a map (check the tourist office at Brienz) and some navigational skills, since both paths are indistinct in places.

Boat service gives easy access to the wild, romantic south shore of the Brienzersee. Float 10 minutes from Brienz (5.40SFr) or 1 hour from Interlaken to **Giessbach Falls,** where you can climb along its 14 frothy cascades. The walk up the falls brings you to a palatial hotel (15min.), which is also accessible by cable car from the dock (4.50SFr, round-trip 6SFr). From the hotel, cross the bridge over the falls, but make sure to turn left along the stream to see all the waterfalls. At the top, a ridge walk leads to the right over the lake, and then down to the breezy lakeside village of **Iseltwald**, where you can catch the ferry back to Brienz. (June 18-Sept.10 every hr. 9am-5pm; Sept. 10-Oct. 31, 4 per day 10:20am-5pm; 7.60SFr.)

DAYTRIP FROM BRIENZ: MEIRINGEN

One train connects Meiringen to Brienz (10min., 5:49am-8:57pm 4.40SFr) and Interlaken (30min., every hr. 7:16am-10:35pm, 10SFr), and another to Lucerne (90 min., every hr. 7:04am-7:25pm, 17.20SFr).

When the glaciers receded from the area around Meiringen, they deposited soft limestone that was easily shaped and eroded by the runoff from melting ice. As a result, Meiringen is surrounded by a striking landscape comprised of glacial gorges, steep limestone cliffs, and thunderous waterfalls. The natural drama has served as fodder for many a fertile imagination. The legendary fork-tongued **Tatzelwürmli** is said to inhabit the nearby **Aareschlucht** (Gorge of the Aare), while **Sherlock**

LOCH MEIRINGEN? Meiringen's mythic Gorge of Aare, a narrow mountainside chasm so deep that light barely penetrates its recesses, is said to harbor the fearsome Tatzelwürmli, a scaly Nibelungian worm of monstrous proportions. At the beginning of the 20th century a photographer named Balkin visited Meiringen and "accidentally" snapped photos of what he claimed was the Tatzelwürmli in its natural habitat. Resembling a very fat snake, the *Wurm* was brown with liver spots on its skin, and possessed a forked tongue. Balkin published his film in the *Berlin Illustrated Newspaper*, unleashing a torrent of speculation about the snake-like inhabitant of Meiringen's rocky slopes. Although serious investigations have long since died out, the town still remembers its dragon by means of strange Tatzelwürmli candy, shaped like the beast down to the marzipan tongue, cream belly, and bloody strawberry-candy teeth. Ward off dragon scourges by eating the poor beast in sugary effigy.

Holmes and arch-nemesis Professor Moriarty plunged to their "death" together in the Reichenbach Falls above town.

A series of cave-passageways clinging to the side of the cliff takes you over the water running through the Aareschlucht, which is 200km deep and only one meter wide at points. Follow signs from Bahnhofstr. for the 10-minute walk. (Open Apr.-Nov. 9am-5pm. 6SFr, students 4SFr.) On certain summer nights the gorge is illuminated by floodlights (July-Aug. W and F 9-11pm). In nearby **Rosenlaui** there is another glacial gorge. (Postbus dir.: Schwarzwaldalp. Open May-Oct. 9am-5pm; 6SFr, 4SFr students.) It is a 45-minute round-trip walk through the gorge, but the reward is the view of the giant Rosenlaui glacial valley.

The town has done its best to capitalize on its famous literary connection. The tiny **Sherlock Holmes Museum**, inside the old Anglican church just past the tourist office, blurs fact and fiction, sometimes paying tribute to the exploits of Holmes and sometimes to his creator Sir Arthur Conan Doyle. (☎971 4221. Open May-Sept. Tu-Su 1:30-6pm; Oct.-Apr. by appointment; 3.80SFr, with guest-card 2.80SFr.) If the museum doesn't satisfy your Holmes fetish, you can trek up to the **Reichenbach Falls,** where Holmes plummeted to his fictional death. The highlight may be the ride up to the falls in the 100-year-old wooden open-air funicular. To reach the funicular walk down Bahnhofstr. and turn right on Alpbachstr. (Open mid-May to Sept. 8:15am-5:45pm. One-way 5SFr, round-trip 7SFr.)

During the last week in June and the first week in July, Meiringen hosts **Musikfestwochen,** a classical music festival (☎972 5050, www2.mountain.ch/mufewo; tickets 28-58SFr, students 12-20SFr).

INTERLAKEN ☎033

In AD 1130, two literal-minded Augustinian monks named the land between the **Thunersee** and the **Brienzersee** "Interlaken,"—between lakes. Interlaken lies between the pair of crystal-blue lakes at the foot of the largest mountains in Switzerland: the **Eiger, Mönch,** and **Jungfrau.** With easy access to these adventure playgrounds, Interlaken has earned its rightful place as one of Switzerland's prime tourist attractions. Swiss-German is drowned out by the chorus of English, but the tourism explosion has spurred the development of some of Switzerland's most varied and exciting accommodations. Beneath the enchanting sight of the Jungfrau rising 4158m above the gardens lining Höheweg, Interlaken spreads out around a large central green, the **Höhenmatte,** whose main function seems to be as a landing pad for the hundreds of paragliders that drift down from the skies each day. Interlaken is one of the paragliding capitals of the world (alongside Queensland, New Zealand), thanks to the gentle and stable winds controlled by the mountains rearing up throughout the valley.

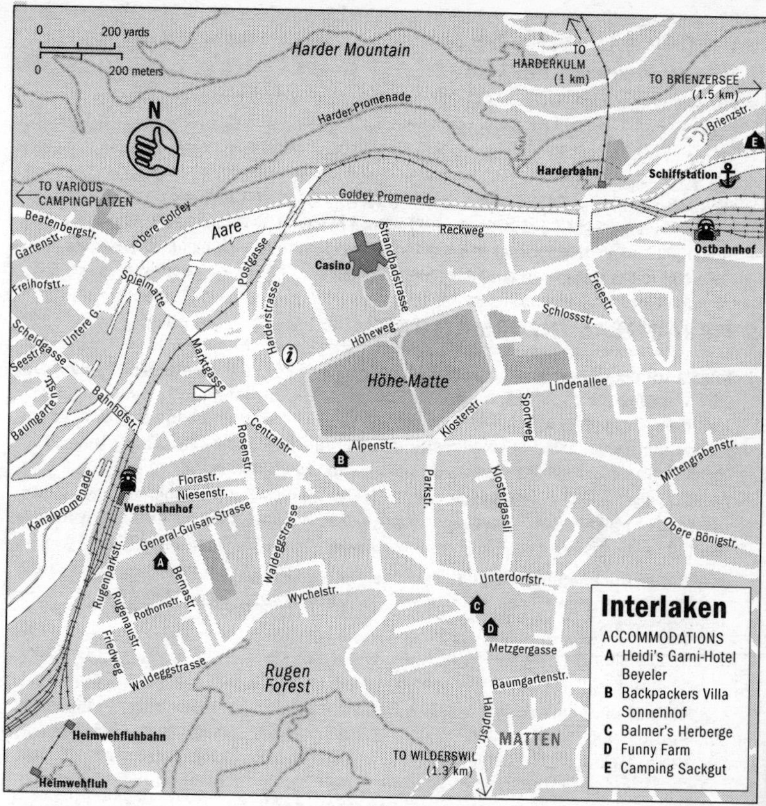

BERNESE OBERLAND

GETTING THERE AND AROUND

By car, Interlaken lies on A6, west on A8, and north on Route 11. The city has 2 train stations. The **Westbahnhof** stands in the center of town bordering the *Thunersee*, near most shops and hotels; trains to Bern, Basel, and other western towns stop here second, and cost slightly less. The **Ostbahnhof,** on the *Brienzersee*, is 10 minutes from the town center by foot or bus (3SFr), and is cheaper for connecting to eastern towns. Both stations have hotel prices posted and direct free phones for reservations. Beware of hostel hustlers at the station; take your time in deciding where to stay—it can make or break your vacation.

Trains: The **Westbahnhof** (☎826 4750) and **Ostbahnhof** (☎828 7319) have trains to: **Bern** (5:34am-10:34pm, 8.60SFr); **Basel** (5:34am-10:34pm, 56SFr); **Zurich** (5:34am-10:34pm, 62SFr); **Geneva** (5:34am-9:40pm, 65SFr); **Lucerne** (5:34am-7:19pm, 27SFr); and **Lugano/Locarno** (5:34am-5:17pm, 72SFr), among others. **Jungfraubahnen,** Harderstr. 14 (☎828 71 11; fax 828 72 64; www.jungfraubahn.ch) runs all trains to the small towns before Jungfrau. SwissPass valid for Wengen, Grindelwald, and Mürren, 25% discount at higher stops. Eurailpass 25% discount on the Jungfraubahnen. Trains to the **mountains** leave every 30min. from June-Sept., and hourly from Sept.-May. from the Ostbahnhof to: **Grindelwald** (6:35am-11:35pm, 9.40SFr), and **Lauterbrunnen** (6:35am-11:32pm, 6.20SFr), and connect to **Mürren** (15.60SFr, 6:35am-4:35pm, change at Lauterbrunnen), **Wengen** (6:35am-11:35pm, 11.80SFr), **Kleine**

Scheidegg (6:35am-5:35pm, 35SFr), and the **Jungfraujoch** (6:35am-3:35pm, 159SFr round-trip, or 120SFr with Good Morning Ticket; see **The Jungfraujoch,** p. 326).

Taxis: Interlaken Ost, ☎822 8080.

Parking: Parking is 2SFr per hr. at the train stations, behind the casino, on Centralstr.

Bike Rental: At either **train station,** 27SFr per day. Open 6am-10pm. **Zumbrunn Velo,** Postg. 4 (☎822 2235), 1 block from the tourist office, towards the train station, has fluorescent city bikes for 8SFr per day, mountain bikes 18SFr. Open Tu-Sa 8am-noon and 1:30-6:30pm. **Intersport Oberland,** Postg. 16 (☎822 0661; fax 822 7307) 20SFr per day, mountain bikes 30SFr, in-line skates 20SFr. Open M-F 8am-noon and 1:30-6:30pm, Sa 8am-noon and 1-4pm. Backpacker's Villa and Balmers also have bike rental, and Backpacker's Villa has motor scooter rental as well (55SFr per day).

PRACTICAL INFORMATION

Tourist Office: Höheweg 37 (☎826 5300; fax 826 5375), in the **Hotel Metropole.** From the Westbahnhof, turn left on Bahnhofpl. and right on Bahnhofstr., which becomes Höheweg. From the Ostbahnhof, turn right as you exit. Free maps and schedules, tickets to the Jungfraujoch and adventure sports. Open July-Aug. M-F 8am-6pm, Sa 9am-noon, Su 5-7pm; Sept.-June M-F 8am-noon and 2-6pm, Sa 9am-noon.

Currency Exchange: Credit Suisse and **Swiss Bank** near the Westbahnhof have **ATMs,** as do both train stations. You'll get average rates on currency exchange in the **train station,** though you might do 1% better in town. (☎826 4736. Open 7am-8pm.)

Bookstore: Buchhandlweg Haupt, Höheweg 11 (☎822 3516). English-language best-sellers, German and French dictionaries, and travel books. Open M-F 8:30am-6:30pm, Sa 8:30am-4pm.

Library: Marktpl. 4 (☎822 0212). Novels in English. Open July-Aug. M, F 4-6pm, W 9-11am and 3-7pm, Sa 10am-noon. Sept.-June M, F 4-6pm.

Laundromat: Self-Service Wash & Dry, Beatenbergstr. 5. Cross the bridge to the left of the Westbahnhof and take the 2nd right on Hauptstr. The manager will do your laundry for 12SFr per load; do it yourself for 10-11SFr. **Backpacker's Villa** has full-service laundry for 12SFr, while **Balmers** has self-service laundry for 8SFr a load.

Snow and Weather Info: For the Jungfrau, call 855 1022.

Late-Night Pharmacy: Call 111. **Grosse Apotheke,** Bahnhofstr. 5A (☎822 7262), is open M-F 7:15am-6:30pm, Sa 7:15am-5pm. AmEx, MC, Visa.

Emergencies: Police, ☎117. **Hospital,** ☎826 2626. **Doctor,** ☎823 2323.

Internet Access: The American expatriate owner of **The Wave,** Rosenstr. 13 (☎823 4032), provides late-night Internet access (14SFr per hr., 11SFr for students). Go right at the main circle between the station and the tourist office. Open M-F 11am-11pm, Sa-Su 2-11pm. The **Backpacker's Villa** has 4 computers (15SFr per hr.). **Balmers** also has Internet on 2 computers for 20SFr per hour.

Post Office: Marktg. 1 (☎224 8950). From the Westbahnhof, go left on Bahnhofpl. Open M-F 7:45am-noon and 1:30-6:15pm, Sa 8:30am-noon. **Postal Code:** CH-3800.

BERNESE OBERLAND

ACCOMMODATIONS AND CAMPING

There are tons of guest beds in Interlaken, but if you want the same adventures with less of a crowd, trek to the **Swiss Adventure Hostel** in Boltigen (see p. 315).

HOSTELS

Backpackers Villa Sonnenhof, Alpenstr. 16 (☎826 7171; fax 826 7172; backpackers@villa.ch; www.villa.ch) diagonally across the Höhenmatte from the tourist office. This central but secluded, remodeled villa (read: mansion) hints at its loftier beginnings 150 years ago. The atmosphere at the hostel is quiet and low-key–the perfect place to crash after a tough day of backpacking. The spacious, airy rooms have beautiful wooden balconies with million-dollar views of the Jungfrau to the south and the Harder

Mann to the north. The friendly young couple who runs the hostel provide tons of services, including TV with CNN, **mountain bike rental** (18SFr per half day), **laundry** (12SFr per load, full service), and **Internet access** (15SFr). Includes breakfast, **kitchen** use, towels, sheets, recreation room, meditation room, lockers, and showers. Call well in advance for reservations. Reception 7:45-11am and 4-9pm. No curfew. 4- to 6-bed room 29SFr per person, triple 33SFr per person, doubles 37SFr per person. 3SFr extra for Jungfrau view, balcony, and in-suite bathroom. AmEx, MC, Visa.

Hotel Alpina, Hauptstr. 44 (☎822 8031; alpina_interlaken@bluewin.ch) has spacious rooms equipped with sinks, TVs, towels, and fluffy, warm comforters—the included breakfast is equally extravagant—all cared for by the motherly Dora. Try to get one of the rooms with balcony views of the mountains. Reception 7am-midnight. No curfew. Closed in November. Reserve a spot by email. Singles and doubles 42SFr.

Balmers Herberge, Hauptstr. 23-25 (☎822 1961; fax 823 3261), in the nearby village of Matten. Take bus #5 from the Westbahnhof to "Hotel Sonne" (2.20SFr) and then backtrack 1min., or walk diagonally across the Höhenmatte from the tourist office and follow signs down Parkstr. from either station. From June to Aug., Balmers runs a shuttle bus from both stations every hr. Sign in, drop off your pack, and return at 5pm when beds are assigned (no reservations). Balmers is Switzerland's oldest private hostel (around since 1945), but it is thoroughly American. Without the paper Swiss flags on the hamburgers and the Rugenbrau beer that flows freely, guests might forget they are in Switzerland. To enjoy the dorms or Balmers **tent** (a huge white circus tent with no insulation a few blocks farther from town), you must value comradeship above comfort. Limited breakfast included. Showers 1SFr per 5min. of hot water. Balmers provides **mountain bike rental** (30SFr per day), nightly movies, TV with CNN and MTV, **Internet access** (20SFr per hr.), a **kitchen** (1SFr per 20min.), **laundry** (8SFr per load), a mini-department store (open 7:30am-9pm), and safety deposit boxes (2SFr). After 9pm, activity shifts underground to the Metro Bar (beers 4.50SFr). Participate with caution: wake-up music starting at 7:30am drives half-conscious guests out by 9:30am, and everyone must re-register each night. In winter, there are **free sleds** and a 20% discount on ski and snowboard rental. No one gets turned away, but it's best to show up early. Reception in summer 6:30am-11pm; in winter 6:30-9am and 4:30-11pm. No curfew. 8-bed dorms and tent 19SFr in summer, 24SFr in winter; 3- or 4-bed room 24SFr in summer, 28SFr per person in winter. Doubles 56SFr in summer, 70SFr in winter. If beds are full, crash on a mattress (13SFr). AmEx, MC, Visa with 5% surcharge.

Funny Farm, (☎(079) 652 6127), behind Hotel Hatterhof, down Hauptstr. from Balmers in the nearby village of Matten. Take bus #5 from the Westbahnhof to "Hotel Sonne" (2.20SFr) and then backtrack 1min., or walk diagonally across the Höhenmatte from the tourist office, then follow signs for Balmer's down Parkstr. More commune than youth hostel, this vast estate is constantly changing according to the interests of the guests. Currently, Funny Farm offers tennis, basketball, volleyball, an archery range, an enormous swimming pool, a sauna and hot tub, an outdoor bar and nightly bonfire, indoor nightclub, and **didgeridoo-making workshops.** Another ephemeral delight is the "Out on the Grass" open-air music festival which will be held in the new amphitheater in July/Aug. 2001. The downside to all this activity is that the owners are frequently not left with time to clean up the place—beware of dust bunnies. Breakfast included. No curfew or lockout. Dorms 25SFr.

Heidi's Garni-Hotel Beyeler, Bernastr. 37 (☎/fax 822 9030). From the Westbahnhof, turn right, go left on Bernastr. (behind the Migros), and walk straight for about 3min. Eccentric fraternal twins Walter and Herbert preside over a rambling old house decorated with sleds, bells, old photographs, and carousel horses. Private rooms with bath have view-laden balconies. Common room with TV and CNN. Sheets and shower included. **Bikes** 25SFr per day. Dorm 20SFr, 2- to 4-bed room 25-30SFr per person, doubles 60-80SFr. Cheaper off-season. Fully-furnished apartments with kitchen, balcony, phone, and TV (2-night min.) doubles 80-90SFr, quad 150SFr. MC, Visa.

Jugendherberge Bönigen (HI), Aareweg 21 (☎822 4353; fax 823 2058), is a 20min. bus ride away from Interlaken. Take the hourly bus #1 or #3 (dir.: Bönigen) to "Lütschinenbrücke". Catering to a younger crowd, this hostel is far removed from the adventure scene in Interlaken. The *Brienzersee* laps at the back doorstep. Try to snag a 6-bed room instead of the 25-bed "Good Morning" dorm on the top floor. Breakfast, showers, sheets, and **kitchen use** included. Lockers 20SFr deposit. Dinner 11.50SFr. **Laundry** 8SFr. **Bike rental** 15SFr per day. Reception 7-10am and 2pm-11:30pm. Reserve at least 2 days in advance June-Aug. Closed mid-Nov. to mid-Dec., and the last two weeks of Jan. 6- and 25-bed dorms 26.70SFr; 4-bed dorms 30.70SFr; doubles 78.40SFr.

CAMPING

Camping Sackgut (☎(079) 656 8958) is closest to town, just across the river from the Ostbahnhof and near the *Brienzersee.* Head toward town, but turn across the 1st bridge and another right on the other side. Reception 9-11am and 4-7pm. Open May-Oct. 7.60SFr; tent 6.50-14.50SFr.

Camping Jungfraublick (☎822 4414; fax 822 1619). Take bus #5 from the Westbahnhof, and continue 5min. past Balmer's on Gsteigstr. This peaceful location has splendid mountain views. Open May-Sept. 12SFr; off-season 7SFr.

Lazy Rancho (☎822 8716; fax 823 1920). Turn left from the station on Bahnhofstr., then left on Seidenfadenstr., right on Steinlerstr. and finally left on Bockstorweg. This spacious, clean campground is equipped with a swimming pool, store, **kitchen,** and **laundry** facilities. Showers 0.50SFr. Open Mar.-Oct. 7-9.50SFr per person; tent site 7-10SFr.

FOOD

Interlaken has a wide range of restaurants, covering the pricey, the scuzzy, and lots of affordable restaurants in between. Generally, the Balmers crowd eats at Balmers (bratwurst, and burgers under 10SFr), the hostel crowd eats at the *Jugendherberge* (11.50SFr), and the Funny Farm folks eat in their renovated cable car, but your tastebuds will be rewarded for venturing outside for a bite. Most of the restaurants listed here are on Marktg. To get there head up Aareckstr., the tiny street left from the station. Follow this street and turn left on Spielmatte. **Migros,** across from the Westbahnhof, also houses a restaurant with giant prancing cows on the ceiling (open M-Th 8am-6:30pm, F 8am-9pm, Sa 7:30am-4pm).

Restaurant Goldener Anker, Marktg. 57 (☎822 1672). This family-run restaurant has many traditional specialties alongside many lowfat and vegetarian dishes. Among other dishes, the California salad (grilled turkey strips on a bed of lettuce and fresh fruit, 14.50SFr) is delicious, and all meals are served with ice water without a request. For dessert they have Crepe Normandy–stuffed with apples and vanilla ice cream (8SFr). The Anker frequently has live bands as well (last year Bob Marley's The Wailers played here). Open M-W and F-Su 10am-12:30am.

Confiserie Schuh (☎822 9441), across from the tourist office, has been an Interlaken landmark since the 19th century. Chocolate boots (from 1.90SFr) and strawberry tarts (4.20SFr) sell like mad in the summer. Open daily 8am-11pm.

Mr. Hong's Chinese Take-Out, Marktg. 48 (☎823 5544). For evenings too beautiful to eat inside, friendly and wise Mr. Hong cooks up a variety of stir-fries to go. Trained in reflexology, Mr. Hong offers up his own holistic philosophy while you wait for your meal. Chomp on mixed veggies (10SFr), sweet and sour chicken (13SFr), or shrimp fried rice (13SFr). Open Apr.-Oct. 11:45am-10pm; Nov.-Mar. 11:45am-9pm.

El Azteca (☎822 7131), on the pedestrian Jungfraustr. towards the station from the tourist office, has a large menu of Mexican and Swiss dishes. The tantalizing options surpass any ordinary taco or burrito, but the best deals are the 4 daily *Menüs,* Mexican, international (15SFr), Swiss (14SFr), and vegetarian (13.50SFr). Open daily in summer 7am-12:30am; in winter closed W 2-6pm. AmEx, MC, Visa.

Hotel Bären, Marktgasse 19 (☎822 7676), serves *Rösti* platters (13-17SFr) and other hearty Swiss dishes to locals and tourists at budget-friendly prices. Open M-Sa 8:30am-12:30am, also open Su in July and August.

OUTDOORS NEAR INTERLAKEN

> Interlaken's adventure sports industry is thrilling and usually death-defying, but accidents do happen. On July 27, 1999, 19 adventure-seeking tourists were killed by a sudden flash flood while canyoning on the Saxeten river. Be aware that you participate in all adventure sports at your own risk.

ADVENTURE SPORTS. Interlaken's steep precipices, raging rivers, and wide-open spaces serve as prime spots for such adrenaline-pumping activities as paragliding, whitewater rafting, bungee jumping, and canyoning (a sport where wet-suited, harnessed future stunt-doubles rappel and swim down a waterfall). Two main companies provide guests with opportunities for these activities. **Alpin Raft** (AR; ☎823 4100; fax 823 4101), the original company, has the wildest guides, and promises that "unlike some first time experiences, this one will be great." **Alpine Center** (AC; ☎823 5523; fax 823 0719), the newest and smallest company, provides the most personal service. All prices include transportation to and from any hostel in Interlaken. Both companies offer **paragliding** (AR/AC 140SFr); **canyoning** (AR 95 SFr, AC 115SFr); **river rafting** (AC 90SFr, AR 95SFr); and **skydiving** (AR/AC 380SFr). Alpin Raft also offers **bungee jumping** (155SFr) and **hang gliding** (AR 155SFr). A number of horse and hiking tours, as well as rock-lessons, are available upon request. Minutes from Interlaken on the Brienzersee, Alpin Raft's **sea-kayaking** provides a strenuous day in the sun and on the water (30SFr).

The independent **Swiss Alpine Guides** (☎822 6000; fax 822 6151) lead full-day **ice-climbing** clinics (May-Oct., 145SFr), as well as full-day **glacier treks** which journey to the icy world on the other side of the Jungfrau (daily in summer; 120SFr). Interlaken's winter activities include skiing, snowboarding, ice canyoning, snow rafting, and glacier skiing. Contact the **tourist office** (☎826 5300) or any of the adventure companies for information.

HIKES FROM INTERLAKEN. The towns closer to the mountains are where the serious hiking starts, but Interlaken has a few good hikes of its own. The most worthwhile hike climbs to the **Harder Kulm** (or Harder Mann, see **Mountain Mann** below). Only the Jungfrau can be seen from Interlaken itself, but from the top of this half-day hike, all 3 peaks are put in front of you for comparison. This view is a striking mountainscape, with the black, triangular face of the Eiger framed by the other two snowy behemoths. The easiest starting point is near the Ostbahnhof. From the Ostbahnhof, head toward town and take the first road bridge right across the river. On the other side, the path has yellow signs (destination: Harderkulm) that later give way to white-red-white *Bergweg* flashes on the rocks. From the top, signs lead back down to the Westbahnhof. A funicular runs from the trailhead near the Ostbahnhof to the top. (2hr. up, 1½hr. down. May-Oct. 12.80SFr, 20SFr round-trip; 25% discount with Eurailpass and SwissPass.)

More horizontal trails lead along the lakes that flank the city. Turn left from the train station, then left before the bridge and follow the canal over to the nature reserve on the shore of the *Thunersee*. The trail winds up the Lombach river, then through pastures at the base of the Harder Kulm back towards town (2hr.).

NIGHTLIFE

If you still have energy at the end of the day there are plenty of options. Even if Interlaken's nightlife heats up during high season it never quite gets red-hot. **Balmer's** (see p. 321) is like a freakin' frat party (beer 4.50SFr; bar open 9pm-1am). When the party dies down there, revelers head to the **Caverne Bar** in the basement of the Mattenhof Hotel, in front of the Funny Farm, where a live reggae band plays W-F. (Beer 3.50SFr; ☎821 6121; open W-Su 10pm-2:30am.)

MOUNTAIN MANN One of the eeriest and most fascinating sights in the Bernese Oberland is the face in the Harder Mountain, called the Harder Mann. His features are the rocky cliffs and a few fortuitously placed trees. On a clear day he is easy to see, a pale triangular face resting against a pillow of trees on one side and a wedge of naked rock on the other. His black moustache has a certain despondent droop, and his deep-socketed eyes have a melancholic, hunted look. He is visible from almost anywhere in town, directly opposite the Jungfrau. The story goes that a strolling monk became possessed and chased a small girl off a cliff. As punishment, he was turned to stone. It might make sense if he hadn't been given the best view in Interlaken, doomed to look at the Jungfrau, Mönch, and Eiger peaks for all eternity, a view for which tourists pay dearly. For the children of Interlaken, there is a happier story: every year the Harder Mann comes down from the mountains to fight off winter. On January 2, they celebrate this fight with wooden Harder Mann masks and a large carnival. Hikers can hike this landmark, but they should not leave the marked paths. Every summer people die attempting to climb roped-off areas.

If you're feeling adventurous, head beyond the hostel confines to one of the local hangouts. **Buddy's,** Höheweg 33, is a small, crowded English-style pub where the beer is cheap (3.50-5SFr; ☎822 7612; open daily from 10am-12:30am). **Johnny's Dancing Club**, Höheweg 92, is located in the basement of the Hotel Carlton is Interlaken's oldest disco (drinks from 6SFr; open Tu-Su 9:30pm-3am). For smoky blues try **Brasserie,** Rosenstr. 17, where live bands play Thursdays with no cover charge. (Beer from 3SFr; ☎822 3225; open M-Sa 8:30am-12:30am, Su 3pm-12:30am.)

For a dose of traditional Swiss culture, see the **Swiss Folklore Show** at the casino for 16SFr (☎827 6100; M 8:30pm and W-Sa July-Aug., sporadically May-Oct.). The other apex of Interlaken's cultural life is the summer production of Friedrich Schiller's **Wilhelm Tell** (in German; English synopsis 2SFr). Lasses with flowing locks and 250 bushy-bearded local men wearing heavy rouge ham up the tale of the Swiss escape from under the Habsburg thumb. The showmanship is complete—20 horses gallop by in every scene, and a vaudeville-like stage around the corner from Balmer's allows the cast to make real bonfires. (Shows late June to mid-July Th 8pm; mid-July to early Sept. Th and Sa 8pm.) Tickets (22-34SFr) are available at Tellbüro, Bahnhofstr. 5A (☎(036) 822 3722; open May-Sept. M-F 8:30-11:30am and 2-5pm; Oct.-Apr. Tu 8-11am and 2-5pm), or at the theater on show nights. Children under 6 are not admitted.

DAYTRIP FROM INTERLAKEN: ST. BEATUS'S CAVES

To get to the caves, walk 15min. uphill from the Sundlauenen Schiffstation, a 30min. boat ride from Interlaken (every hr. 10:30am-5pm), or take bus #21 (7.20SFr round-trip from Interlaken Westbahnhof). You can also walk from Interlaken (2hr.) or Beatenberg (1hr.).

Beneath Beatenberg village, the **Beatushöhlen** (St. Beatus's Caves) riddle the hillside. You can spelunk through 100m of glistening stalactites, waterfalls, and grottoes. At the entrance a wax St. Beatus (the Irish hermit and dragon-slayer) stares down some (also wax) cavemen; at the exit, a sarcastic little dragon bids you "Auf Wiedersehen." Even on hot summer days, the cave stays a cool 8 to 10° C. One-hour tours leave every half-hour from the entrance. Admission includes entry to the **Caving Museum**, 5 minutes downhill. (☎(033) 841 1064. Caves open Apr.-Oct. 10:30am-5pm. Museum Apr.-Oct. Tu-Su noon-5pm. 14SFr, students 12SFr, children 6SFr.) This tiny room chronicles the discovery and mapping of Swiss grottoes.

THE JUNGFRAU REGION

A few miles south of Interlaken, the hitherto middling mountains rear up and become hulking white monsters. Welcome to the Jungfrau Region, home to Europe's largest glacier and many of its steepest crags and highest waterfalls. The

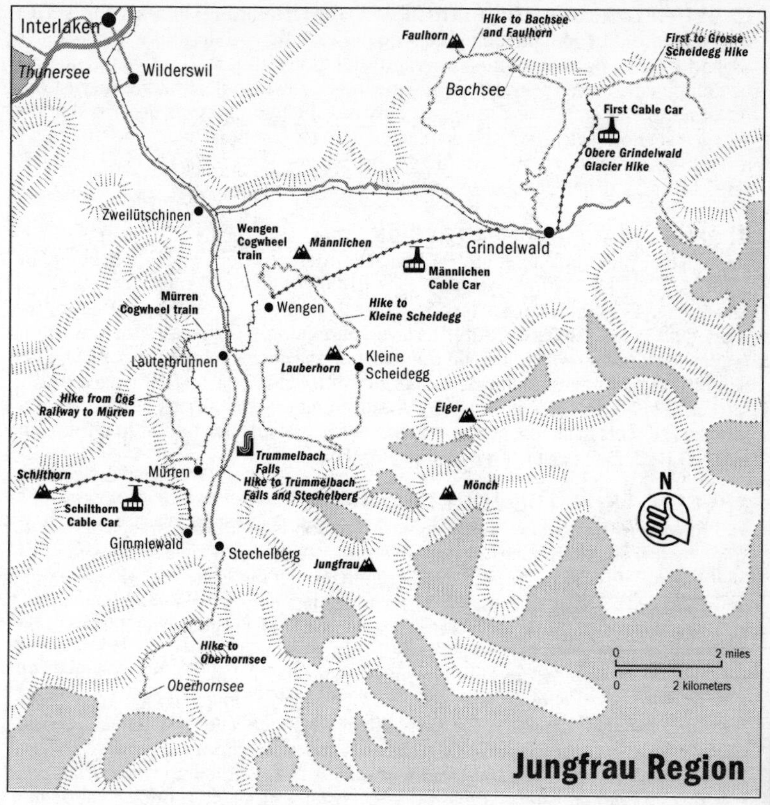

Jungfrau region's list of firsts reflects its irresistible appeal to sportsmen: the first Alpine mountaineering, the first skiing, and the first part of Switzerland opened to tourists. Even with the influx of tourists, the region is astounding for the amount of sheer silence available in the shadow of the snowy peaks and cliff edges. In summer, the Jungfrau region's hundreds of kilometers of hiking blast the senses with spectacular mountain views, wildflower meadows, roaring waterfalls, and pristine forests. The three most famous peaks in the Oberland are the **Jungfrau,** the **Eiger,** and the **Mönch.** In English, that's the Maiden, the Ogre, and the Monk. Natives say that the monk protects the maiden by standing between her and the ogre. Actually, the Jungfrau is 4158m high, so she'd probably kick the Eiger's puny little 3970m butt. On the other side of these giants, a vast glacial region stretches southward, where 6 major glaciers, including the **Grosser Aletschgletscher,** at 45km long the largest in Europe, converge at **Konkordiaplatz.**

ORIENTATION. The region is split into two valleys. The only town in the eastern valley is Grindelwald, which gives access to the glaciers. The other valley—the Lauterbrunnen—holds many smaller towns, including Wengen, Gimmelwald, Murren, and Lauterbrunnen. The 2 valleys are divided by an easily hikeable ridge. On the end of the ridge closer to Interlaken is the Männlichen Peak. At the other end of the ridge, near the Jungfrau is the train town of Kleine Scheidegg. Up above, and on either side of Lauterbrunnen are cliff ledges on which sit the small towns of Wengen, Mürren, and Gimmelwald; all inaccesible by car.

GETTING AROUND AND HIKING. The Jungfraubahn runs all the trains throughout the region, including the cog-railways that go up to the towns above Lauterbrunnen. Because of their proximity, hikes in different towns can frequently be combined—even if you're only staying in one town, look at hiking suggestions for other towns. One hike that moves between the two valleys is described in the Wengen section (see p. 332). If you plan on doing any serious hiking, be sure to get a copy of the *Lauterbrunnen/Jungfrau Region Wanderkarte* (15SFr at any tourist office), which gives an overview of all of the hikes.

SKIING IN THE JUNGFRAU REGION. There are 3 main ski areas in the Jungfrau region, the Mürren-Schilthorn area, the Kleine Scheidegg-Männlichen area, and the Grindelwald-First area, with over 213km of downhill runs between them. The Mürren-Schilthorn area is much smaller than the other two. Day passes for the individual areas are 52SFr. After 2 days you can only get passes for the whole region (all 3 areas) which include transport on the Jungfraubahn. (☎828 7111; fax 828 7264; www.jungfraubahn.ch. Adults 2 days 109SFr, 7 days 278SFr, ages 16-19 2 days 87SFr, 7 days 222, children 6-15 50% discount off adult prices.) There are separate ski schools in almost all the towns. For **snow information** for the Jungfraujoch, dial 855 1022. For a **weather report,** dial 157 4506.

SPECIAL TRIP: THE JUNGFRAUJOCH

The most arresting ascent in the Jungfrau region is up the **Jungfraujoch,** a head-spinning, breath-shortening, 3454m adventure on Europe's highest railway. Chiseled into solid rock, the track tunnels right through the Eiger and Mönch mountains. Its construction was one of the greatest engineering feats of all time, taking 16 years and a work force of 300 men. The line was to have gone even higher to the Jungfrau summit itself (4158m), but by 1912 the project was so over budget that the final 700m were left to hard-core mountaineers. Thanks to the rarefied air's lack of pollution, the top now shelters Europe's highest manned meteorology station and the **Sphinx Laboratory** for the study of cosmic radiation. Half a million visitors per year explore the **Ice Palace** (free), a super-smooth maze cut into the ice. Beware skidding children and blindness due to flash photography. Siberian huskies pull lazy mountaineers across the snow on sleds for 10SFr. Budget sportsmen opt for free "snow-hurtling," i.e. sledding down bunny-level slopes on garbage bags (bring your own bag). If the weather is perfect, try the 30-minute, snowy trek to the **Mönchsjoch** climbing hut. For more passive entertainment, gaze out at the frozen expanse of the **Jungfraufirm glacier** gripping to the backside of the mountain.

Trains start at Interlaken's Ostbahnhof and travel to either Grindelwald or Lauterbrunnen, continuing to **Kleine Scheidegg** and finally to the peak itself. The entire trip costs an enormous sum, but the "Good Morning" ticket makes things cheaper (available for departures at 6:30am from May-Oct., and for departures at 6:35 and 7:35am from Nov.-Apr., returning before noon). All tickets are round-trip, and there is no way down from the top except by train (Eurail and SwissPass 25% off. From Interlaken Ost 150SFr, "Good Morning" ticket 120SFr; Lauterbrunnen 141.20SFr, 102.20SFr; Grindelwald 142SFr, 103SFr; Wengen 130SFr, 91SFr; Murren 160SFr, 121SFr.) Call 855 1022 for a **weather forecast** or use the cable TV broadcast live from the Jungfraujoch and other high-altitude spots (in all tourist offices and big hotels). Bring winter clothing and food—it can be 10°C (50°F) on a July day, and in winter alcohol thermometers crack and car antifreeze freezes.

GRINDELWALD ☎033

Beneath the north face of the Eiger—a rock face that is the apex of any climber's career—crouches Grindelwald, within walking distance of the only glaciers in the Bernese Oberland accessible by foot. It is a cold-weather Shangri-La for outdoorsy folk, though the tourism can become overwhelming. Although it only has 2 streets of any size, Grindelwald is the most developed part of the Jungfrau Region.

TRANSPORT AND PRACTICAL INFORMATION

The Jungfraubahn runs from **Interlaken's** Ostbahnhof (9.40SFr). Trains to **Kleine Scheidegg** (27SFr, 45SFr round-trip; Eurail and SwissPass 25% discount) and the **Jungfraujoch** (round-trip 142SFr, with "Good Morning" ticket 103SFr; Eurail and SwissPass 25% discount) leave from the Grindelwald station. There is also a bus from Balmers (round-trip 15SFr). The **tourist office** is located in the Sport-Zentrum in the middle of town, to the right of the station, and provides chairlift information and a list of free guided excursions. (☎854 121; fax 854 1210; www.grindelwald.ch. Open July-Aug. M-F 8am-7pm, Sa 8am-5pm, Su 9-11am and 3-5pm; Sept.-June M-F 8am-noon and 2-6pm, Sa 8am-noon and 2-5pm). Services in Grindelwald include: **laundry** at **Wash 4 Dry** opposite Hotel Adler on Haupstr. (☎853 1168. 3SFr for washing and 1SFr for 10 minutes of drying); **weather forecast** (☎162); **medical assistance** (☎853 1153); **Internet access** (15SFr per hour) at **Ernst Schudel's,** opposite the tourist office (open daily 9am-noon and 2-6:30pm); **post office**, opposite the station (open M-F 8am-noon and 1:45-6pm, Sa 8-11am). The **postal code** is CH-3818.

ACCOMMODATIONS

Jugendherberge (HI), (☎853 1009; fax 853 5029.) Exit the train station and turn left. Go straight (5-7min.), then cut uphill to the right (8min.) just before "Chalet Alpenblume," and follow the steep trail all the way up the hill. While the hostel is quite a hike from town, the enormous wooden chalet is beautiful. On the inside are dark, wood-paneled living rooms with fireplaces, and many rooms have balconies facing the Eiger. Breakfast included, lunch 8-11SFr, dinner 11.50SFr. Lockers and sheets included. **Mountain bike rental** 15SFr per day. **Laundry** 5SFr. Reception M-Su 7-10am and 3-11pm. No lockout. Dorms in winter 26.30SFr, in summer 29.80SFr; doubles with toilet and shower 48.80SFr, 51.30SFr. Non-members add 5SFr. AmEx, DC, MC.

Mountain Hostel, (☎853 3900; fax 853 4730). Turn right out of the train station, then immediately right on the small trail towards "Grund." Go downhill, bearing right at the Glacier Hotel, to the bottom of the valley where the bright blue hostel sits. Or take the train from Grindelwald to Grund (3.80SFr). Renovated in 1996, the hostel has gleaming 4- and 6-bed dorms and a plush reception area with TVs, table tennis, and billiards. Buffet breakfast included. Sleep sack 5SFr. **Laundry** 12SFr. Outside cooking facilities 0.50SFr. Reception open 8am-noon and 2-9pm. Dorms 32SFr; doubles 84SFr.

Lehmann's Herberge, (☎/fax 853 3141). Follow the main street past the tourist office and look on the right. Verena and Fritz Lehmann run the only hostel in the town itself. Enjoy the comfort of their home as well as their hearty breakfasts, homemade down to the butter and jelly. Breakfast included. Reception 8am-11pm daily. Dorms and doubles 45SFr per person, after 1st night dorms 40SFr.

Gletscherdorf Camping, (☎853 1429; fax 853 3129). From the station, take a right, then the first right downhill after the tourist office, then the third left. The small grounds are the closest campground, and have a phenomenal mountain view. Showers included. Reception 8-10am and 5-8pm daily. 9.10SFr per person, tents 9SFr.

FOOD

Tea Room Riggenburg, (☎853 1059). Follow the main street past the tourist office away from the station. For huge plates of *Rösti,* omelettes, salads, and fresh-baked desserts, hit the tea room. Drink a huge hot cocoa (3.20SFr) or have a slice of vegetable quiche (4.50SFr) on the heated terrace as sparrows dive-bomb for crumbs. Open Tu-Sa 8am-10pm, Su 10am-9pm.

Gepsi Bar, (☎853 2121). The bar is just past the tourist office on the left, and has cheap chicken-, fish-, veggie-, and hamburgers (8.50SFr), and vegetarian *Rösti* (13 SFr). Stop by for Swiss music night on Wednesdays or the Gepsi Toast special on Tuesdays (bread toasted with ham and cheese for just 3 SFr). Thursday is Fellows Night from 9-11pm, when men get a free beer. Entrees start at 8.50SFr, beer at 3.50SFr; the Grindelwald plate goes for 18SFr. Bar open 8:30-11:30pm.

Ye Olde Spotted Cat, (☎853 1234). On Hauptstr. Scratch a few wooden cats' heads while sipping cheap beer (3.50SFr) at this past haunt of Winston Churchill and Field Marshall Montgomery. Open summer 11am-12:30am; winter 3pm-1:30am.

Japanisches Restaurant, (☎853 6066). Tucked away on Hauptstr. farther down from the tourist office. This new establishment stands as a testament to the number of tourists who have made their way to tiny Grindelwald (no it's not for the locals). Their steaming dishes of Japanese noodle dishes (18SFr) may come as a welcome respite from the pounds of *Rösti* and *wurst* you've probably ingested. Open 11:30am-9:30pm daily.

Co-op, on Hauptstr, across from the tourist office. Open M-F 8am-6:30pm, Sa 8am-4pm.

HIKING

Only Zermatt could challenge Grindelwald's claim as Switzerland's premier **hiking** hotspot. The town has nearly everything: easy valley walks, and peaks to challenge top climbers, though for the casual hiker its greatest allure is its proximity to nearby glaciers. While most hikes are possible without the aid of exorbitantly expensive trains and cable cars, these means of transportation allow access to some fantastic hikes. The **First Bahn** leaves from the center of town and climbs the eastern side of the valley (☎854 5051; 28SFr, round-trip 45 SFr; 8:30am-4:30pm). On the other side of the valley is the **Männlichen Gondelbahn,** the longest cable car route in Europe. (☎854 8080. 8am-4pm. 28SFr, round trip 45SFr. 25% discount with SwissPass, 50% with Eurail.) Past the tourist office from the station stands the **Bergführerbüro** (Mountain Guides Office) which sells hiking maps and coordinates rugged activities like glacier walks, ice climbing, and mountaineering. (☎853 5200; fax 853 1222. Open June-Oct. M-Sa 9am-noon and 3-6pm, Su 4-6pm. 1-day activities about 100-400SFr. Reserve ahead for multi-day expeditions.)

Lower Glacier *(Untere Grindelwaldgletscher)*, (4hr. circular hike without the funicular). This hike is moderately steep, becoming steeper the further you go up the trail, although the trail is conquerable in sneakers. The beginning of this hike is close to the center of town; walk up the main street away from station until signs point downhill to "Pfinstegg." You can either walk the first forested section of the trail (1hr.), following signs up to Pfinstegg, or you can take a funicular to the Pfinstegg hut (8am-7pm in the summer. 9.20SFr). From the hut signs lead up the glacier-filled valley to "Stieregg," a hut that offers food to the weary before you turn around.

Upper Glacier *(Obere Grindelwaldgletscher)*. Take the postal bus from Grindelwald (dir.: Grosse Scheidegg) to "Oberslaubkule," and walk uphill to where signs point to "Glecksteinhütte" to the right.

The Faulhorn via the Bachalpsee, (1-7hr). This is the best strenuous hike away from the glaciers. The easiest starting point is near the HI hostel. From the hostel, head uphill on the road (left at the Y) until signs lead upwards to Allflue. To Allflue and slightly beyond is not too exciting forest-hiking, though Allflue provides nice views down into town. From Allflue, go uphill for more than an hour to Waldspitz. The final hike from Waldspitz to Bachsee and the Faulhorn is through beautiful highland meadows with waterfalls and streams meandering through (5hr.). On the way down, head to **Bussalp** (2hr.), where a bus goes back to Grindelwald. For those with a little less stamina and a bit more money, the **First Bahn** goes straight from town to a station only 1 hour away from the Bachsee, knocking 2 to 3 hours off the hike. Another level, easy 1-hour hike offering great views of the glaciers, runs from the top of the First Bahn to Grosse Scheidegg, where you can catch a bus to Grindelwald.

The Männlichen, (1hr.). On the other side of the valley is another easy (though more expensive) hike, reached by the **Männlichen Gondalbahn.** From the Männlichen station, a quick circular hike scales the **Männlichen** peak, which separates Grindelwald and the Lauterbrunnen Valley, before continuing as a flat, 1-hour hike to Kleine

Scheidegg and its intimate views of the Eiger, Mönch, and Jungfrau, where you can catch a train back to Grindelwald. This hike is even easier (and free) as part of the day hike from **Wengen** (see p. 331).

LAUTERBRUNNEN ☎033

The "loud springs" that give Lauterbrunnen its name are the 72 waterfalls that plummet down the sheer walls of the narrow, glacier-cut valley. The town of Lauterbrunnen, which lies in the middle of the valley of the same name, neighbors Switzerland's highest waterfall, the **Staubbach Falls** (280m), which inspired Goethe's poem "Song of the Spirit over the Waterfall" (set to music by Franz Schubert). Mendelssohn composed some of his "Songs without Words" in Lauterbrunnen as well. Lauterbrunnen's extensive accommodations and easy accessibility by car and train make the town an ideal base for hiking and skiing throughout the Jungfrau region, as well as exploring the mountain villages.

TRANSPORT AND PRACTICAL INFORMATION

The Lauterbrunnen **tourist office** is 200m to the left of the train station on the main street. (☎856 8568, fax 856 8569. Open M-F 8am-noon and 2-6pm; July-Aug. also Sa 9am-noon and 1-5pm). **Trains** connect every 30 minutes with **Interlaken Ost** (20min., 6:05am-11:05pm, 6.20SFr), **Wengen** (6:10am-midnight, 5.60SFr), **Kleine Scheidegg** (45min., 7:08am-6:05pm, 25.60SFr), **Jungfraujoch** (4hr., 7:08am-6:05pm, round-trip 141.20SFr, "Good Morning" ticket 102.50SFr), and **Mürren** (20min., 6:10am-midnight, 9.40SFr). Services include: **lockers** (2SFr) and **currency exchange** at the station; **Internet access** at the tourist office (20SFr per hr.); **bike and ski rental** at Crystal Sports (☎856 9090); **medical assistance** (☎856 2626). The **post office** is between the train station and the tourist office (open M-F 7:45-11:45am and 1:45-6pm, Sa 7:45-11am). The **postal code** is CH-3822.

ACCOMMODATIONS AND FOOD

Valley Hostel, (☎855 2008; valleyhostel@bluewin.ch). Head left on the main street, and past the Co-op on the right. The hostel is down a driveway on the left side of the street. Martha, the owner, has smiled and tidied her way into the heart of many a guest, convincing many to stay longer than intended. The large windows allow for breeze to blow over the comfy beds (with fuzzy, cow-patterned sheets) and a view of the Staubbach Falls. Breakfast 8SFr. Showers, sheets, and **kitchen** access included. **Laundry** 8SFr. You can request a fondue (in advance) for 15SFr. Reception 8am-10pm. Dorms 20SFr; 1 double room 50SFr.

Hotel Staubbach, (☎855 5454; hotel@staubbach.ch; www.staubbach.ch). From the station, go left on the main street towards the waterfall (400m); the hotel is on the left. The Staubbach occupies one of the oldest hotels in town, which was lovingly converted by Craig and Corinne Rochinn-Müller into a pleasant and affordable bed and breakfast. The comfortable rooms, most with private bath and shower, have views of the Staubbach Falls. Parking and breakfast buffet included. Reception daily 8am-10pm. Singles 50SFr, with shower 60SFr; doubles 70-120SFr; 3- to 6-bed rooms family suites 35-40SFr per person. 5SFr extra per person in summer for all rooms.

Matratzenlager Stocki, (☎855 1754). Leave the train station's rear exit, descend the steps, cross the river, turn right, and walk 200m. The sign on the house to the right reads *"Massenlager."* This Lauterbrunnen institution is surprisingly tidy given its past incarnation as a barn (which it still closely resembles). The main chamber of the barn has been partitioned into a sleeping area with a long row of mattresses and a spice-stocked kitchen. Reception 10am-6pm. Open Jan.-Oct. Reserve ahead. 13SFr.

Chalet im Rohr, (☎/fax 855 2182). This picture-book chalet, complete with dark wood, intricate carvings, and bright hanging flowers is just below Hotel Staubbach, on the

BERNESE OBERLAND

main street near the church. **Kitchen** facilities 0.50SFr. Parking available. Reception 7am-10pm. 26SFr per person for singles, doubles, triples, and quads.

Camping: Get to **Camping Schützenbach** (☎855 1268; fax 855 1275) by taking a left on the main road and a left over the river by the church, and keep going down the street as it curves sharply to the right (15min.; follow the signs). Reception 10am-noon and 2-7pm. 6SFr; tents 11SFr; dorms 36-44SFr; doubles with sink 64-70SFr; 4-bed "tourist rooms" in barracks-like huts 18-20SFr per person. Or try **Camping Jungfrau** (☎856 20 10; fax 856 20 20). Take the right fork of the main street from the station toward the Staubbach Falls. Reception in summer 8am-9pm; in winter 8am-noon and 2:30-6:30pm. 8-10SFr per person; tents 6-15SFr; dorms 20-22SFr. AmEx, DC, MC, Visa.

For affordable, quality eats hit **Crystal Restaurant** which has *Älpler-Rösti* for 10-12SFr, cheese fondue for 18SFr, and a daily *Menü* for 12SFr that includes salad and an entree (☎856 9090; open 8-11am and 3-9pm daily.) **Horner Bar,** further down the street, has cheap beer (3SFr) and **Internet** access (12SFr per hr.) at one computer (☎855 1673; open 9am-12:30am daily). There's also a disco club upstairs that's open until 2am. There is a **Co-op,** near the post office on the main road (open M-F 8am-noon and 2-6:30pm, Sa 8am-noon and 1:30-4pm).

OUTDOORS

Lauterbrunnen's greatest hike is the flat trail that leads up the valley. The single trail described below can be followed as long as you choose to a number of logical hiking destinations. To get on this trail, follow the right branch of the main road as it leaves town (toward Camping Jungfrau). The road dwindles slowly to a narrow path before becoming a dirt trail through the woods.

HIKE DOWN THE LAUTERBRUNNEN VALLEY. The first, most-touristed segment of the trail leads to the **Trümmelbach Falls,** 10 glacier-bed chutes that gush up to 20,000L of water per second, generating mighty winds and a roaring din (40min.). The chutes of the falls are the only drains for the glacial run-off of the Eiger, Mönch, and Jungfrau glaciers. Explore tunnels and an **underground elevator.** *(Open July-Aug. 8am-6pm; Apr.-June and Sept.-Nov. 9am-5pm. 10SFr; with Jungfrau region visitor's card 9SFr.)* The falls can also be reached by **bus** from Lauterbrunnen *(every hr., 3.20SFr).*

The trail leading to the Trümmelbach Falls is a veritable waterfall parade, passing, in succession, the Staubbach Falls, Spissbach Falls, Agertenbach Falls, and Mümenbach Falls. After the small trail leads off to the left towards the Trümmelbach Falls, the trail becomes noticeably less trafficked as it makes its way toward **Stechelberg,** passing even more waterfalls *(1½hr. from Lauterbrunnen).* Stechelberg, a tiny village with a small grocery store, is the last place to catch a bus back to Lauterbrunnen *(4.40SFr)* before the trail moves on. From Stechelberg, the trail begins to climb, entering the very end of the valley, which is accessible only by dirt road. To stay on the trail, enter Stechelberg and follow its one road to the end. From Stechelberg, the **Schilthorn Bahn cable car** runs to **Gimmelwald** *(7.40SFr),* **Mürren** *(14.40SFr),* **Birg** *(34SFr),* and the **Schilthorn** *(49.60SFr).* The first 2 are free with SwissPass, with Eurail 25% off all 4 destinations. Since Gimmelwald and Mürren are carless by law, leave your car at the parking lot near the cable car *(day 5SFr, week 21SFr, month 30SFr)* or back at Lauterbrunnen.

The next destination on the trail is the 2-building enclave **Trachsellauenen,** 50 minutes from Stechelberg. Trachsellauenen is the departure point for the trail leading into the **nature reserve.** A 2½-hour mountainous hike brings you to the tiny *Oberhornsee,* which sleeps beneath the Tschingel glacier.

BICYCLING. Imboden Bike Adventures, on the main street of Lauterbrunnen, rents out mountain bikes at 20-30SFr per day. On the popular **Mürren Loop,** take your bike for no extra charge on the funicular to Grütschalp *(6.60SFr),* pedal along to Mürren and Gimmelwald, and free-wheel it down to Stechelberg and Lauterbrunnen. *(☎855 2114. Open Tu-Su 9am-noon and 2-9pm.)*

SONGS OF THE WATERFALL From its most famous visitor, J.W. Goethe—who immortalized the valley's Staubbach Falls in his "Gesang der Geisten über den Wassern"—to lesser-known but fiercely loved painters, the Lauterbrunnen Valley has inspired poet and artist alike with its silvery cascades. The last verse of Goethe's poem, possibly the most famous lines in German verse, was set to music by Schubert when he visited the falls. Lord Byron was inspired to write *Manfred* here. Among the many other renowned people who have paid tribute to the Staubbach and Trümmelbach Falls are Caspar Wolf, Albrecht von Haller, Alexandre Calame, Conrad Escher von der Linter, Kaiser Wilhelm, and Napoleon I's wife, Marie Louise von Habsburg, while her husband plotted his comeback in Elba.

WENGEN

☎033

Tiny Wengen (pop. 1,100) occupies a ledge on the cliff-curtained Lauterbrunnental. In rather non-Swiss style, Wengen residents did not try to tame the cliff with a road, so the town is only accessible by train. The only transportation around town is provided by hotel golf carts and a few taxis, but Wengen retains a surprisingly modern feel in spite of the lack of cars. Empty in the summer, Wengen is crowded with out-of-town skiers during the peak winter months. Because Eurail does not cover the train ride to Wengen it is an ideal destination for summer travellers looking for a quiet break from the backpacker social scene of many nearby towns.

TRANSPORT AND PRACTICAL INFORMATION

Wengen is accessible by hourly **trains** from **Interlaken Ost** (45min., 6:35am-11:35pm, 11.80SFr) and **Lauterbrunnen** (15min., 6:10am-midnight, 5.60SFr). After stopping in Wengen the train continues toward **Kleine Scheidegg** (7:25am-6:23pm, 20SFr) and the **Jungfraujoch** (7:20am-6:23pm, 130SFr, morning ticket 91SFr). Leave cars in the Lauterbrunnen **parking garage** (9SFr per day). To reach the **tourist office,** turn right from the station, then immediately left. (☎855 1414; fax 855 3060. Open July-Nov. and Dec.-Apr. 9am-7pm; May-June Tu-Sa 9am-6pm.) Services include: **currency exchange** and hotel reservations at the train station; **pharmacy** (☎855 1246), left out of the station, and 2min. past the tourist office (open M-F 8am-noon and 2-6:30pm, Sa 8am-noon and 2-5pm in the summer, later in the winter); **hospital** (☎826 2626); **Internet access** at the tourist office (20SFr per hr.); **post office** next to the tourist office (open M-F 8am-noon and 3-6pm, Sa 8-noon). The **postal code** is CH-3823.

ACCOMMODATIONS AND FOOD

Hot Chili Peppers, smack dab in the center of town, has a happening bar and a less-than-happening hostel. For a quiet night of sleep turn left from the station and head past the tourist office. This Tex-Mex cafe has spacious rooms above the gigantic bar. Beers are 3.50SFr, house sandwiches 7SFr, and chips 'n' salsa 5SFr. (☎855 5020; chilis@wengen.com. Breakfast 8SFr. Kitchen access included. Reception and restaurant 8:30am-2am. Dorms 24-29SFr; private rooms 44SFr per person, including breakfast.) If Chili Peppers is full, **Eddy's Hostel** provides a no-frills night of sleep in their 3-story bunks with 20 beds to a room. Make a sharp right from the station and walk along the tracks. You will pass Hotel Eden on your right; continue for 50m and then go under the bridge and backtrack to the hotel. Check in at Hotel Eden. (☎855 16 34; fax 855 39 50. Breakfast buffet 15SFr. Reception 7am-10pm. Dorms 26SFr; from Dec.-Apr. 30SFr, including hall shower. 4SFr discount with *Let's Go.*) **Ristorante da Gina** further down the main road from Chili Peppers, with its intimate candle-lit tables and extensive wine selection (from 6SFr per glass) will put even the most weary travelers in a romantic mood. Although most menu items are quite pricey, there are affordable options for the connoisseur (pasta dishes 15-16SFr). The adjoining **da Gina's Pub** has ladies night on Thursdays and happy hour on W, F, and Sa (2-for-1 beers from 9-10pm). Opposite the station is a **Co-op** supermarket (open M, W-F 8am-12:15pm and 2-6:30pm, Tu 8am-12:15pm, Sa 8am-4pm).

OUTDOOR ACTIVITIES

Wengen's elevation from the valley floor puts it close to the tree line and provides spectacular views. The following 7-8 hour **hike** from Wengen traverses the ridge dividing the two valleys of the Jungfrau Region, above the tree line almost the entire time, taking you past the top stations of all the 30-90SFr cable cars and trains for free. Few hikes offer as greatly varied and spectacular a set of views as this one, which can be easily partitioned into shorter hikes.

HIKE TO MÄNNLICHEN AND KLEINE SCHEIDEGG. (7hrs.). The hike begins with an ascent of **Männlichen.** Walk up the main street, away from the tourist office, and towards the end of town; follow signs upward to "Männlichen" (red-and-white marked trail). In the beginning, be careful always to follow the signs to Männlichen up the mountain. Even below the tree line, the trail wanders upwards through a meadowed lane cleared by the cows that will surely accompany you in the early part of the journey. As is true for the whole ascent of Männlichen, there are views of the glacier-laden side of the Jungfrau and the cliff-curtained Lauterbrunnen valley. Towards the top, be sure to turn left when another, unmarked trail merges in. The climb to the Männlichen saddle steeply zigzags upwards for about 3 hours. From the saddle, you can join tourists who took the cable car from Grindelwald for a 15-minute stroll up to the peak, a vertical promontory with a 360° view of the Bernese Oberland. Walk back down to the Männlichen cable car station and restaurant, then follow the signs to **Kleine Scheidegg.** This highly populated trail curves, without climbing, around the contour of the ridge, all the while looking down on the Grindelwald valley and up to the towering Eiger, Mönch, and Jungfrau. You can take the train from Kleine Scheidegg down to Wengen (20SFr) or Grindelwald (27SFr), or you can hike back to Wengen. Cross over the train tracks and follow the red-and-white trail, rather than the tracks. The trail passes the Mönch and Jungfrau as close as is possible on foot, before swinging back towards Wengen (2½hr. downhill).

SKIING. The **Swiss Ski School** (☎/fax 855 2022), by the Co-op 1 minute right of the station, is the cheaper of the town's 2 schools (open late-Dec. to early Apr. Su-F 8:30am-noon, 1-2:30pm, and 3:30-6pm, Sa 9-11am and 4:30-6:30pm). For information on ski passes see p. 326. As you watch golf carts schlepping lazy tourists around, you may find it hard to believe that Wengen attracts the athletically intense to its slopes and trails twice a year. Every January, Wengen hosts the skiing World Cup's longest and most dangerous downhill race, the **Lauberhorn.** Hotels generally won't allow you to book rooms until about a week in advance so that they can guarantee all the racers and support crews a room. The downhill course starts 2315m above Kleine Scheidegg, curls around Wegenalp, and ends at Ziel (1287m) at the eastern end of the village, a drop of nearly 1200m in 2½ min.

MÜRREN ☎033

The quiet, car-free streets of Mürren (pop. 430)—frequented mostly by tractors and bell-clanking herds of cattle—are lined primarily with hotels and guesthouses that sprouted up when Mürren invented slalom skiing. Most people only pass through Mürren on their way to the Schilthorn, the "Magic Mountain," climbed by Hans Castorp in the famous novel by Thomas Mann. However, the challenging hiking, spectacular views, and tranquility of this little ledge make it a worthy detour.

TRANSPORT AND PRACTICAL INFORMATION

Get to Mürren by cogwheel **train** from **Lauterbrunnen** (every 30min. 6:25am-8:30pm, 9.40SFr), or by **cable car** from **Stechelberg** (14.40SFr) or **Gimmelwald** (7.40SFr). Alternatively, **hike** from Gimmelwald (30min. uphill). From the station, the road leading into town forks in two; nearly everything, except the tourist office, is on the lower left fork. The cable car is at the opposite end of town from the train station, on the lower road. The **tourist office,** in the sports center 5 minutes from the station, off the right fork, has information about *Privatzimmer*, hiking trails, and skiing prices. (☎856 8686; fax 856 8696. Open July-Aug. M-F 9am-noon and 1-6:30pm, Sa 1-6:30pm, Su 1-5:30pm; Sept.-May M-F 9am-noon and 2-5pm, June 9am-noon and 2-6:30pm.) The Salomon Station next to the cable car rents **hiking boots** (12SFr per day), mountain **bikes** (35SFr per day) and has **Internet access** (12SFr per hour) on one computer (☎855 2330; open daily 8:30am-5pm). For **medical assistance** call 855 1710; for **police,** ☎856 8081. There are **lockers** at the train station (2SFr), and a **post office** on the station side of the main street (open M-F 8am-noon and 2:30-5:30pm, Sa 8-10:15am). The **postal code** is CH-3825.

ACCOMMODATIONS AND FOOD

Mürren has some good housing options, but head to Gimmelwald for more variety and lower prices (see p. 334). The most traditional Swiss lodgings in town happen to be run by an enthusiastic British woman at the **Chalet Fontana.** The 7 private rooms come with tea and coffee. (☎855 2686; fax 856 8696; chaletfontana@compuserve.com. Reservations recommended. Nov.-Sept. 35-45SFr per person, breakfast included; Oct. 30SFr per person, no breakfast.) More institutional, but still comfortable and airy, is the **Eiger Guesthouse,** right next to the train station. (☎856 5460; fax 856 5461; eigerguesthouse.muerren.ch. Breakfast included. Internet access at the adjoining bar. Reception M-F 8am-11:30pm, Sa-Su 8am-12:30am. 4-bed dorms 39SFr; doubles 100SFr, with shower 120SFr. AmEx, MC, Visa.)

Mürren has a **Co-op** 15min. down the right fork of the town's main walkway which comes in handy for picnics and trips to Gimmelwald (open M, W-F 8am-noon and 1:45-6:30pm, Tu 8am-noon, Sa 8am-noon and 1:45-4pm). Eating out in Mürren is unexpectedly cheap. You can get *raclette* and an unobstructed view of the snow-capped mountains for as little as 11SFr at **Hotel Alpina,** down the left fork of the main road (☎(036) 55 1361). **Singapore Chinese Restaurant,** off the left fork from the train station, speedily serves steaming, spicy Asian food with cheap pan-fried noodles. (*Wonton* noodles 11.50SFr, vegetable fried rice 12.50SFr. ☎856 0110. Open Jul.-Aug. 11am-10pm and Sept.-May noon-9pm.)

HIKING

Mürren's location on the ledge above Lauterbrunnen makes it the ideal starting point for numerous higher-elevation hikes around the Lauterbrunnen Valley. From Mürren (1645m) the trails leading to Gimmelwald, Stechelberg and the Trümmelbach Falls provide unparalleled views of the Eiger, Mönch, and Jungfrau. One trail, easily broken up into smaller segments, goes from the far end of Mürren (the Grütschalp cable car station) to far beyond the end of Gimmelwald, making its way through a dense network of worthwhile stops. Best of all, you don't have to pay anything to appreciate the pastoral views below.

Grütschalp (top of funicular from Lauterbrunnen) to Mürren, (1-2hr.). Starting from Grütschalp a flat, 1-hour hike follows the train tracks to Mürren. A more mountainous, isolated route takes twice as long, and is twice as rewarding. Both trails start across the tracks from the station balcony. The easier trail is marked with a yellow sign to Mürren, while the mountainous hike is demarcated by the red-white-red "Mürren Höhenweg" sign. After an initial steep ascent the trail wanders through buttercup meadows that

BERNESE OBERLAND

stretch before the rising peaks of the Eiger, Mönch, and Jungfrau. When the trail splits, head to "Allmenhubel," then down to Mürren (2hr.).

To Gimmelwald, (2½hrs.). From the far side of Mürren the road leads to Gimmelwald (30min.), or you can take the detour waterfall and cheese route (2½hr.). Turn right before the cable car station, and then right again on the trail that branches off towards **Suppenalp.** On the climb to Suppenalp, be sure to stay essentially parallel to the cable car lines. From the high-altitude valley of Suppenalp, where thin waterfalls pour down luscious green walls, follow the trail that goes back in the opposite direction, under the cable car lines to Shiltalp, where there is an obligatory stop at the hut for fresh, cheap milk (sorry, no skim) and cheese. Go halfway down the hill to Gimmelwald to turn right at the sign for Spielbodenalp. Walk down along the stream where signs point to **Sprutz,** a waterfall that the steep downhill trail ducks behind. From Sprutz the trail descends to Gimmelwald, where cable cars return back to Lauterbrunnen and Mürren.

Stechelberg and Obersteinberg, (1½-5hr.). This hike is a steep descent from the Mountain Hostel in Gimmelwald that gives a great long view of the sheer rock slabs lining the Lauterbrunnen Valley. It's a grand approach to the **Trümmelbach Falls** (1½hr.), with a return possible by cable car (see p. 330). Or, 5 minutes after the river crossing on the Stechelberg path, you can fork right and climb along the flank of the unsettled Lauterbrunnen valley head. The trail reaches the **Obersteinberg hut** (1½hr. more), where you can stay overnight, before continuing on to the **Oberhornsee** (another 2 hr.).

OTHER OUTDOOR ACTIVITIES

UP THE SCHILTORN. The most talked about journey this side of the Lauterbrunnen Valley is the short, albeit expensive, cable car trip to the Schilthorn (2970m) made famous by the alpine exploits of James Bond in *In Her Majesty's Secret Service* (incidentally the worst James Bond film ever). (*☎823 1444. From Mürren 34SFr, round-trip 57SFr; morning ticket 43SFr round-trip.*) At its apex spins the immoderately priced **Piz Gloria Restaurant.** High-altitude restaurants charge snooty prices. Warm up (in summer or winter) with *Glühwein* (mulled wine; 7SFr), and take in the astounding 360° panorama from the Schilthorn station's deck. Bear in mind that there is very little to do at the top when it's cloudy.

BALLOONING, SKIING, AND SNOWBOARDING. Mürren pioneered 2 graceful ways of enjoying the mountains. In 1910 the first Alpine balloon crossing was made from the village, a fact now celebrated annually in mid-August with an **international ballooning week** that fills the skies with big colorful bulbs. The other sport, **slalom skiing,** took off with even more panache. Mürren was the stage for the first major slalom in 1922, the first ski school in 1930, and the first World Championship for downhill slalom in1931. The **ski school** *(☎855 12 47)* has classes for downhill, slalom, and snowboarding. Six half-days of group lessons cost 130SFr. For ski pass information see the Jungfrau Region introduction. The **Inferno Run** seeks volunteers every January (usually for 3 days from the 20th) for the Inferno downhill ski. The **Inferno Triathlon** takes place in August; the torturous Mürren-Schilthorn stretch comes last.

NEAR MÜRREN: GIMMELWALD ☎033

Gimmelwald is little more than a farming town of slightly over 100 people that was stopped in its tracks over 50 years ago when it was generously, though perhaps overcautiously, labeled an avalanche zone. Somehow a number of wonderful lodgings have snuck their way into a few of the old farmhouses. The great lodgings here make for a lively social scene in high season. Gimmelwald still retains the most secluded, rustic feel of any town in the Jungfrau. To get to the town follow the lower road in Mürren downhill for 30min. to Gimmelwald, or take the **cable car** (7.40SFr) from either Mürren or Stechelberg (just up the valley from Lauterbrunnen). Be forewarned that Gimmelwald has **no supermarket,** so stock up in Mürren or Lauterbrunnen, although you can buy fresh-baked bread (2.50-4.50SFr) and fresh milk and yogurt (both 1.20SFr) at Esther's Bed and Breakfast (see below).

Accommodations in Gimmelwald allow you to sleep like a cow or a king—it's your choice. The unifying factors are a fair price and a caring host. All the beds are on one small trail that leads from the bottom of the town road to the top. At the bottom of the trail, next door to the cable car station, the social **Mountain Hostel** is run by a laid-back couple, Petra and Walter, who try to get to know their guests by name. The beds come with a communal **kitchen** and access to life's essentials—fresh bread (3SFr), milk (2SFr), chocolate (2SFr), and **Internet access** (12SFr per hr.). You can reserve a bed, but only after 9:30am on the day you plan to arrive. You can sign up for rooms when the reception is closed—drop your pack, take a hike, and be back for the 6pm check-in. (☎855 1704. Showers 1SFr for 3min. of hot water. Reception 8:30-11am and 5:30-10:30pm. Lockout 9:30-11am. Dorms 17SFr.)

At **Hotel Mittaghorn**, at the top of the trail, you can sample some *Glühwein* (mulled wine) or Heidi cocoa (spiked with peppermint *schnapps*) made by the owner, Walter. In his Edelweiss suspenders, Walter has been presiding over his place for a long time, cooking a 3-course dinner for his guests for only 15SFr. The attic/loft is filled with old, wooden beds that go for 25SFr a night. (☎855 1658. Breakfast 12 SFr. Showers 1SFr for 5min. Order meals in advance. Open Apr.-Nov. Doubles 70-80SFr; triples 100SFr; quads 128SFr. Add 3SFr for a 1-night stay.) Esther at **Esther's Bed and Breakfast** is kept so busy with visitors that she doesn't have time to make breakfast for guests, but does find time to bake the bread and make the fresh milk and cheese that nourish so many of the tourists in the village. (☎855 5488. Kitchen access and shower included. Singles 30SFr; doubles 70-85SFr; triples 90SFr; quads 140SFr.) Esther is also in charge of a barn where you can sleep (breakfast included; 20SFr). The only restaurant in Gimmelwald is in the **Gimmelwald Guest House.** Specialties include bratwurst served with *Rösti* (16.50SFr). Dinner is usually served around 6:45pm.

WESTERN BERNESE OBERLAND

KANDERSTEG ☎033

Kandersteg sits center stage on a natural amphitheater, against a vivid backdrop of jagged cliffs, enormous rock formations, and mountain peaks with glaciers spilling over the top. Short day-hikes lead to isolated glacial lakes, mountain passes with views of the entire Bernese Alps, and some of the largest glaciers in Europe. Slightly out of the way, and noticeably devoid of crowds of English-speaking backpackers, Kandersteg seems to have been overshadowed by towns nearer the Jungfrau, but as far as hiking goes, it outshines them all.

TRANSPORT AND PRACTICAL INFORMATION

Trains connect Kandersteg to **Spiez** (30min., every hr. 5:23am-10:40pm, 15.40SFr) and then **Interlaken Ost** (1hr., 23SFr). One counter at the train station has **bike rentals** (30SFr per day), **currency exchange,** and **luggage storage** (5SFr; open daily 7:10am-7:35pm). Follow the road perpendicular and to the right of the train station about 100m until it meets the main road. Everything is accessible from this point. Turn left to reach the **tourist office,** which has **Internet access** (10SFr per hr.) and **hiking information.** (☎675 8080; fax 675 8081. Open July-Sep. and Jan.-Mar. M-F 8am-noon and 1:30-6pm, Sa 8:30am-noon and 1:30-4:30pm; Oct.-Dec. and Apr.-June M-F 8am-noon and 2-5pm.) Available here as well as at most shops in Kandersteg is the **Kandersteg Wanderkarte** (hiking map; 16.80SFr), an invaluable resource for any hike. Services include: **taxis** (☎671 2377); **medical assistance** (☎675 1424); and a **post office** next to the Co-op (open M-F 8-11:30am and 2:30-6pm, Sa 8-11am). The **postal code** is CH-3718.

ACCOMMODATIONS AND FOOD

Kandersteg isn't particularly prepared for an influx of budget travelers. There are a few options in town, but the best idea might be to make your way up to the many *Berggasthäuser* (mountain guesthouses; see Hiking, below).

Kandersteg International Scout Center, (☎675 8282; fax 675 8289; kandersteg@woulr.scout.org; www.kisc.org). For a wholesome nights sleep catch the bus in front of the train station (5min., every hr. 7:28am-6:38pm, 2SFr) and get off at the "Pfadfinderzentrum" stop, or head down the small road to the right of the train station, turn left after the bridge, and follow the path along the river for 15min. The Center's cheerful, multilingual volunteer staff can reserve you a bed in the chalet, or a place at the campsite. Call at least a week in advance for reservations. Breakfast 6SFr, lunch 10SFr, dinner 12SFr; order meals in advance. Prices include kitchen use. You can also order break, milk, cheese, and other staple items at the reception. Laundry 6SFr. **Internet access** is a shockingly low 8SFr per hr. Reception open 7am-10:30pm daily. Bed in the chalet 16SFr for scouts, 21SFr for non-scouts, campsite 8.50SFr for scouts, 10.50SFr for non-scouts. No credit cards. The Center also organizes a dizzying array of outdoor activities, including **canyoning** (85SFr), rock climbing (20-25SFr per person for a group lesson), river **rafting** (45-68SFr) and **caving** (10SFr per person). The Center can also get you discounts on train rides and nearby tourist attractions.

Hotel National (☎675 1534; fax 675 1737). Turn right on the main road (at the church) and walk 10 to 15 minutes. National has a number of rooms filled with dilapidated old bunk beds. Breakfast 8SFr per person, but the money might be better spent at a bakery in town. Dorms 22SFr, sleepsack 5SFr; doubles 84SFr.

Rendez-vous (☎675 1354; rendez-vous.camping@bluewin.ch). Turn left from the station road, right on the trail just after the tourist office, then follow the camping signs at the top of the road above town. This complex has camping, restaurant, and cheap beds. **Restaurant Rendez-vous** has a room of *Lager* style beds (read: long rows of mattresses) for 29SFr, hearty breakfast included, while **Camping Rendez-vous** on the same spot at the base of the *Öschinensee* chair lift, lets you sleep on the ground; Showers 1SFr for 3min. 7SFr, tent spot 6-12SFr.

When you get hungry, **Hotel Schweizerhof**, on the riverfront in the center of town, is a gastronomic gem. The wooden-shingled pagoda draws you in, only to blow you away with the enormous menu of perfectly cooked dishes . Light summer dishes cost 11.50-15SFr, while the wide range of vegetarian dishes go for 13-15.50SFr. For heartier appetites, there are *Menüs* that include a salad and noodle dish (11.50-25.50SFr). To top it off, try the dessert crepes (5.50-9SFr; ☎675 1919; open daily 9am-10pm). Also near the tourist office, the **Hotel Victorial Ritter** serves an excellent omelette with brie (12SFr) as well as cheap fondue (19.50SFr per person; ☎675 8000. Open daily 9am-midnight). For picnics, the **Co-op** is between the station and the town (open M-F 8am-noon and 1:30-6:30pm, Sa 8am-5pm).

HIKING

The hikes in Kandersteg are among the most exciting and varied in all of Switzerland. Some of the longest glaciers in Europe, most notably the **Kanderfirm,** run along the eastern side of town, and you can hike right to the foot of them. The astoundingly blue **Oeschinensee** is surrounded by steep cliffs that rise to glacial peaks. On the eastern end of the lake, a small mountain **guesthouse** welcomes those seeking to leave the world behind.

Öschinensee, (20min.-1hr20min.). The most easily accessible hiking in Kandersteg traverses the area around the Öschinensee. The quickest hike leads from the top of the **Öschinenseebahn** (9:30am-5pm. 10.40SFr one-way, 14.40SFr round-trip, children 5.20SFr, 7.20SFr), which leaves from Camping Rendez-vous. From the top, a 20-minute trail rolls to the edge of the blue lake bordered on all sides, except for where you stand, by sheer rock walls. If you would rather spend an hour more hiking and save the 13SFr, follow the trail that climbs from the end of the road to Camping Rendez-vous and up to the lake. The low pass which the trail crosses does a terrific job of separating the Öschinensee from civilization below. Right on the shore of the lake stands the **Öschinensee hut,** which makes a perfect base for further exploration, but is also nice enough to warrant staying even if you want to go no further. The 25 *Lager*-style beds adjoin a living room and TV room, and come with a homemade breakfast every morning. (☎675 1119; fax 675 1666. 35-40SFr, doubles 120-160SFr.) Right next to the hut is a small dock with paddle-boats and rowboats that allow you to disturb the perfect calm of the sheltered lake. (Open May-Oct. Paddleboats 22SFr per hr., rowboats 16SFr per hr.)

Blümlisalp Glacier from the Öschinensee, (3-4hr.). The area around the Öschinensee is replete with trails leading to mountain huts. A steep, rocky trail—to be attempted only with hefty boots—shoots upwards from the cabin for 3 hours to **Früdenhorn** hut. (☎675 1433. Open June-Oct. 14.30-23SFr per night, less for children.) A less steep but longer trail enters the uninhabited glacial region between the Kandersteg Valley and the Jungfrau Region. A 4-hr. trek from the Öschinensee brings you to the Blümlisalp hut (same info as for Früdenhorn hut), which cowers beneath the Blümlisalp glacier.

Blausee Hike, (1-2hr.). Two trails lead from Kandersteg to the Blausee: one a challenging series of steep uphills and downhills through the woods (2hr.), the other a flat walk past mountain streams, fields of flowers, and giant moss-covered boulders (1hr.). Both trails begin as one path to the left of the train station (follow the signs) and split into two trails after about 20min. of flat walking. You can also opt to take the bus (10min., hourly 5:23am-9:45pm) to or from the strikingly blue-green Blausee, which is surrounded by a tranquil and well-maintained nature park. At the restaurant on the lake you can sample smoked trout, trout pate, and trout mousse, all products of the on-site trout farm. Lake open 9am-5:30pm daily. Admission 4.50SFr, children 2.40SFr.

Kanderfirm Glacier Hike, (4hr.). For those with insatiable glacial appetites, the hike to the Kanderfirm glacier might prove more satisfying. Take the morning bus to Selden (10SFr; reservations required at the tourist office) and continue on the road until it turns into a trail which, after 2hr., comes to the western edge of the Kanderfirm's icy tongue.

GSTAAD AND SAANEN ☎033

At the juncture of four alpine valleys, Gstaad and its earthier sister, Saanen (combined pop. 6000), are at the heart of Swiss skiing country. The family resemblance of the two towns just five minutes from each other can be seen in the dark wood structures with sloping roofs, but the differences are significant. Saanen inhabits the mountainous scenery with contented ease. Gstaad, however, trades in goats for glitz—its bevy of 5-star hotels and cardigan-draped tourists make it a glamorous anomaly amongst small towns and placid farmland.

TRANSPORT AND PRACTICAL INFORMATION

By **train,** Gstaad is accessible from **Montreux** (1½hr., every hr. 6:12am-9:30pm, 24SFr, round-trip 41SFr) or **Interlaken** (1¾hr., every hr. 7:44am-8:43pm, 32SFr, round-trip 55SFr). From Gstaad station you can reach Saanen by train (5min., every hr. 2.40SFr; from Montreux, it's the stop right before Gstaad) or **post bus** (8min., every hr., M-Sa 6:35am-7:33pm, Su 7:20am-7:33pm, 3SFr). **Buses** also run to **Les Diablerets** (1hr., every hr. 8:27am-3:27pm, 11.80SFr).

The train station in Gstaad has 2-5SFr **lockers, bike rental** (27SFr per day, 21SFr per half-day), **currency exchange,** and a **ski rack.** Gstaad has a very well-organized **tourist office,** just past the railway bridge on the main road to the right of the station. (☎748 8181; for room reservations and package deals, ☎748 8184; fax 748 8183; gst@gstaad.ch; www.gstaad.ch. Open July-Aug. M-F 8:30am-6:30pm, Sa 9am-6pm, Su 10am-noon, 4-6pm; Sept.-June M-F 8:30am-noon and 1:30-6pm, Sa 9am-noon and 3-6pm.) Saanen's main street also has a **tourist office.** (☎ 748 8160; fax 748 8169; saanen@gstaad.ch. Open M-F 8:30am-noon and 2-5pm, Sa 9am-noon and 2-

5pm.) **Internet** access is available at **Kistler Software-Corner** in Gstaad. (☎748 8183. Open Tu-F 8:30am-noon and 2-6:15pm, Sa 8:30am-noon and 2-4pm.) Gstaad's **post office** is next to the train station (open M-F 7:45am-noon and 1:45-6pm, Sa 8:30-noon). For **medical assistance**, call 744 6611. In an **emergency,** dial 117. For **taxis,** dial 744 8080. The **postal code** is CH-3780.

ACCOMMODATIONS

Gstaad proper has few hotels with fewer than 3 stars, but the tourist office publishes a list of budget options, usually far from town. In town, private homes often post signs for rentable rooms, as well. The **Jugendherberge** in Saanen is definitely the most preferable alternative. From Saanen station, turn right on the main street and follow the "youth hostel" signs (10min.). This hostel creaks like your favorite rocking chair but is clean and offers lots of amenities: **bike rental** (15SFr per day, 10SFr per half-day), **laundry** (9SFr), a piano, a TV room, a playground, a library (with English books), and a game room, where you will have to compete with the legions of school groups who descend here on vacation. (☎744 1343; fax 744 5542; saanen@youthhostel.ch; www.youthhostel.ch/saanen. Breakfast and sheets included. Dinner 11.50SFr (order that morning). 5SFr surcharge for non-HI members. Children ages 2-6 half price, under 2 free. Reception 7-10am and 5-10pm. Curfew 10pm, though you can obtain the access code if you'll be out late. Closed Nov. 1-Dec. 25. Phone ahead. Dorms 28-29SFr, singles 43.40SFr; doubles 80SFr; triples and quads also available. AmEx, DC, MC, Visa.) **Camping Bellerive** lies just off the road between Gstaad and Saanen, a 15 minute walk from either. From the Saanen train station, go straight and take a right on the main street. When you get to the freeway intersection, take a right and follow the camping signs. (☎744 6330; fax 744 6345. Check-in 9-10am and 6-7pm, but you can arrive at any time. In summer 6.40SFr, children 3.20SFr. In winter 7.50SFr, 3.20SFr. Tent 5.30SFr. Tax 2.40SFr, children 1.20SFr.) The **Saanen campsite** is on the edge of town. Cross the tracks behind the stations and head left along the river. (☎744 6191; fax 744 6042. Electricity 4SFr. Check-in 6-7pm, but you can arrive at any time. 7.20SFr; tent 7SFr; caravan 11SFr. MC, Visa.)

FOOD

At the **Saanerhof Restaurant,** across the street from the Saanen train station, you can enjoy Swiss specialties (13-21SFr) in a typical ski-lodge atmosphere. (☎744 1515; fax 744 1323. Open M-F 7:30am-11:30pm, Sa, Su 7:30am-12:30am.) Back in Gstaad, budget diners should take advantage of the **Co-op,** left on the main street from the train station (open M-Th 8am-6:30pm, F 8am-8pm, Sa 8am-4:30pm; restaurant open M-Th 8am-6:30pm, F 8am-8pm, Sa 8am-4pm, Su 9am-5pm). In front of the train station, the **Hotel Bernerhof Café** serves up a reasonably priced *menu du midi* (18SFr) and a healthy selection of vegetarian dishes (15-18SFr), along with interesting people-watching (☎748 8844, open Su-Th 6am-11:30pm, F-Sa until 12:30am). For your red-blooded protein fix, slide into soft leather chairs and have a burger and fries with a beer (14-18SFr) or ribs and a salad (16.50SFr) at **Richi's Pub**, just after the church on the main street to the right of the station (☎744 5787; open noon-12:30am).

OUTDOOR ACTIVITIES

ADVENTURE SPORTS. Gstaad and Saanen share a superlative sports scene. Two companies, **Eurotrek** (☎(01) 295 5555) in Gstaad and **Swissraft** (☎744 5080) in Saanen, arrange adventure activities. Both companies do white-water **rafting** (Eurotrek: 98SFr for 3 hr., ages 12-16 70SFr; Swissraft: 99SFr for 3hr.). In July and August, Swissraft also goes **canyoning** (80SFr for 3hr.). You can try **ballooning** with CAST Balloonfahrten (☎744 6259; 390-500SFr) or Hans Büker's Ballonhafen

Gstaad (☎(026) 924 5485; 285-485SFr). To ride air currents up to 2500m, **Paragliding** Gstaad (☎(079) 224 4270; parasport@spectraweb.ch; www.beo.ch/gstaad/paragliding) is another option (190SFr for a tandem flight). To see the countryside with at least your horses' feet planted firmly on the ground, try **horse-trekking** (☎744 2460; 40SFr per half-hour lesson, 60SFr per hourlong lesson) or riding in a horse-drawn cart (☎765 3034; 30min. ride; 25SFr per person). Rounding out your options are 150km of hard-core **mountain-bike** trails; the tourist office publishes a map and guide describing distances and difficulty.

HIKING. The Gstaad tourist office has free hiking maps and descriptions of local hikes of all levels in three languages. A challenging panoramic hike up the **Giferspitz horseshoe** conquers the mountains without skis. Turn right on the main road from Gstaad station, left on the main road just before the river, and take the second big road on the right over the river (with signs to "Bissen"; the turn is 1km from Gstaad). Follow the yellow *Wanderweg* signs for "Wasserngrat" up the hill to the top cable car station (1936m). The fit and adventurous continue up to the **Lauenehorn** (2477m) and, after a rocky scramble, farther to the **Giferspitz** (2541m), Gstaad's tallest peak. The path circles down to Bissen again, but a bus eases the descent (1800m ascent; perfect weather only; allow 1 day). A shorter, more accessible hike starts with a cable car ascent to **Wispile** and a 2-3-hour hike to the Lauensee, a lake and waterfall nature reserve.

SKIING. In winter, Gstaad turns to skiing, with 250km of runs and 69 lifts. Expert skiers will find little to challenge them, but intermediate ones will be very happy. The Top Card ski pass (☎748 8282; fax 748 8260; ski.gstaad@gstaad.ch; www.skigstaad.ch) is 50SFr a day for one sector; a 2-day pass for 90SFr covers all sectors; more limited passes are slightly cheaper. A week of skiing will run about 263SFr, depending on your age. For the dedicated, a season ski pass (890SFr) from the Gstaad region allows skiing in Oberengadin/St. Moritz, Kitzbühel/Tirol, Adelboden-Lenk, Alpes Vaudoises, Ordino-Arcalis, and Pal Arinsal (Andorra). Consult the tourist office for details on heliskiing, snowboarding, curling, and skating. There are 3 snowboarding parks and a glacier for year-round skiing.

SPECIAL EVENTS. The summer brings numerous sporting events to the twin towns. Although Gstaad does not even lie close to an ocean, the **FIVB Women's Beach Volleyball World Tour** rolls through town during the last week of June (admission free, ☎744 0640. In July, the annual **USB Open Tennis Tournament** challenges the green lawns of Wimbledon with grueling clay-court action (July 7-15, 2001). Combining high-culture and grit, the **Gstaad Polo Club** hosts the annual Silver Cup polo tournament in late August.

The musically-minded can partake of the **Menuhin Festival Gstaad,** an annual late-summer event created by virtual Gstaad resident and violinist Yehudi Menuhin (☎748 8333, fax 748 8339; menuhinfestival@gstaad.ch; www.menuhinfestivalgstaad.ch). 2000 performers included pianist Jeremy Manuhin and violinist Sarah Chang. (Tickets 25-125SFr.)

GSTAAR-STRUCK Gsaad has been filled with celebrities since the 1940s. Prince Ranier of Monaco came to the town with his wife, Grace Kelly often. Audrey Hepburn made frequent visits, and Elizabeth Taylor relaxed here with her two-time husband Richard Burton. Not far down the hill, American economist John Kenneth Galbraith spent peaceful winters.

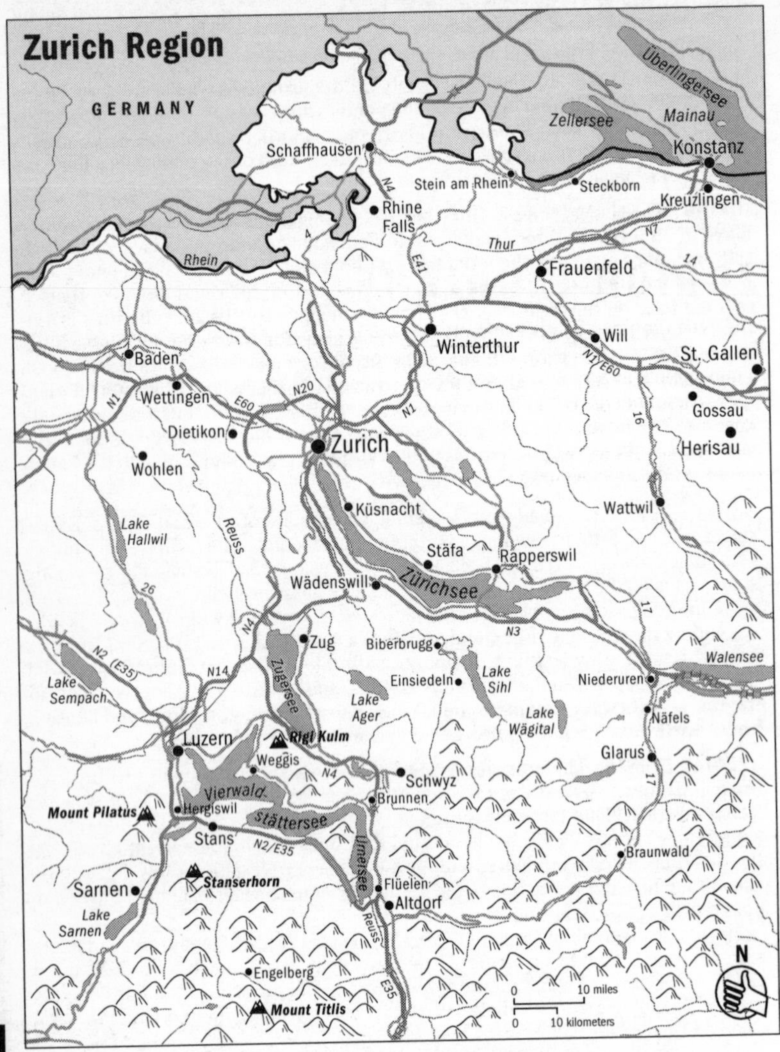

ZURICH AND CENTRAL SWITZERLAND

With more hospitable—though less dramatic—terrain, Central Switzerland is considerably more populated than the mountainous cantons to the south. The higher density of humans brings a greater mass of cultural artifacts. Innovative museums, enchanting castles, and medieval *Altstädte* have been established in Zurich, Lucerne and other towns along the shores of the region's breezy lakes.

HIGHLIGHTS OF ZURICH AND CENTRAL SWITZERLAND

Shock your aesthetics at Zurich's unconventional **Kunstmuseum** (p. 349).

Bathe in multicolored light from the incredible stained-glass windows in Zurich's cathedrals, the **Fraumünster** and the **Grossmünster** (p. 348).

Confront your mortality on the 660-year-old **Kapellbrücke,** Lucerne's famed wooden-roofed bridge (p. 359).

Cruise the **Vierwaldstättersee** from Lucerne to Alpnachstad, where you can ascend the world's steepest cog railway to blue-shadowed **Mt. Pilatus** (p. 361).

ZURICH (ZÜRICH) ☎01

The battalions of briefcase-toting, Armani-suited executives charging daily through the world's largest gold exchange, and fourth-largest stock exchange, pump enough money into the economy to keep Zurich's upper-crust boutiques and posh restaurants thriving. There is, however, more to Zurich than money. The city was once the focal point of the Reformation in German Switzerland, led by the anti-Catholic firebrand Ulrich Zwingli. In the 20th century, however, Zurich's Protestant asceticism succumbed to avant-garde artistic and philosophical radicalism. While James Joyce toiled away at *Ulysses*, the quintessential modernist novel, in one corner of the city, Russian exile Vladimir Lenin read Marx and dreamt of revolution in another. Meanwhile, brouhaha brewed next door as a group of raucous young artists calling themselves the Dadaists founded the seminal proto-performance art collective, the Cabaret Voltaire. A walk through Zurich's *Altstadt* and student quarter will immerse you in the energetic youth counter-culture that spawned these subversive thinkers, only footsteps away from the rabid capitalism of the famous Bahnhofstraße shopping district.

GETTING THERE AND AROUND

Because PTT buses cannot go into Zurich proper, the easiest way into the city is by plane, train, or car. **Kloten Airport** (☎816 2500) is **Swissair's** main hub (☎(084) 8800 700 for general flight information) with daily connections to Frankfurt, Paris, London, and New York. Trains leave every 10 to 20 minutes from the airport for the *Hauptbahnhof* in the city center (5:36am-12:10am; 5.40SFr; Eurail and SwissPass valid), where trains from all over Europe arrive. By **car,** A1 connects Bern, Austria, and southern Switzerland to Zurich. From Basel, A2 connects directly to Zurich. From Geneva, take A1 to Lausanne, A9 to Vevey, and A12 to Zurich.

Trains: Bahnhofpl. To: **Winterthur** (25min., every 15min. 5:21am-12:23am, 10.60SFr); **Lugano** (3hr., every hr. 6:30am-10:07pm, 62SFr); **Lucerne** (1hr., every hr. 6am-12:15am, 22SFr); **Geneva via Bern** (3hr., every hr. 6:28am-11:28pm, 77SFr); **Basel** (1hr., 2-4 per hr. 4:46am-12:03am, 31SFr); **Bern** (1¼hr., 1-2 per hr. 4:46am-12:03am, 48SFr); **Paris** (6-8hr., every hr. 6:37am-10:50pm, 137SFr); **Munich** (4hr., 4 per day 7:33am-5:33pm, 91SFr); **Milan** (4½, every hr. 6:30am-10:59pm, 76SFr); **Vienna** (9hr., 3 per day 7:10am-10:33pm, 131SFr); and **Salzburg** (6hr., 3 per day 7:10am-10:33pm, 102SFr). Reduction for under age 26 on international trains.

Public Transportation: Trams criss-cross the city, originating at the Hauptbahnhof. Long rides (more than 5 stops) cost 3.60SFr (press the blue button on automatic ticket machines), and short rides (less than 5) cost 2.10SFr (yellow button)—the city is small enough that you can avoid long rides for the most part. Buy a 24hr. *Tageskarte,* valid on trams, buses, and ferries, if you plan to ride several times (7.20SFr). Purchase a ticket before boarding and validate it by inserting it into the ticket machine. Policemen won't hesitate to fine you (50SFr) if you try to ride for free. *Tageskarten* are available at the tourist office, hotels, hostels, the automatic ticket machines, or the **Ticketeria** under the train station in Shop-Ville (open M-Sa 6:30am-7pm, Su 7:30am-7pm). The Tickete-

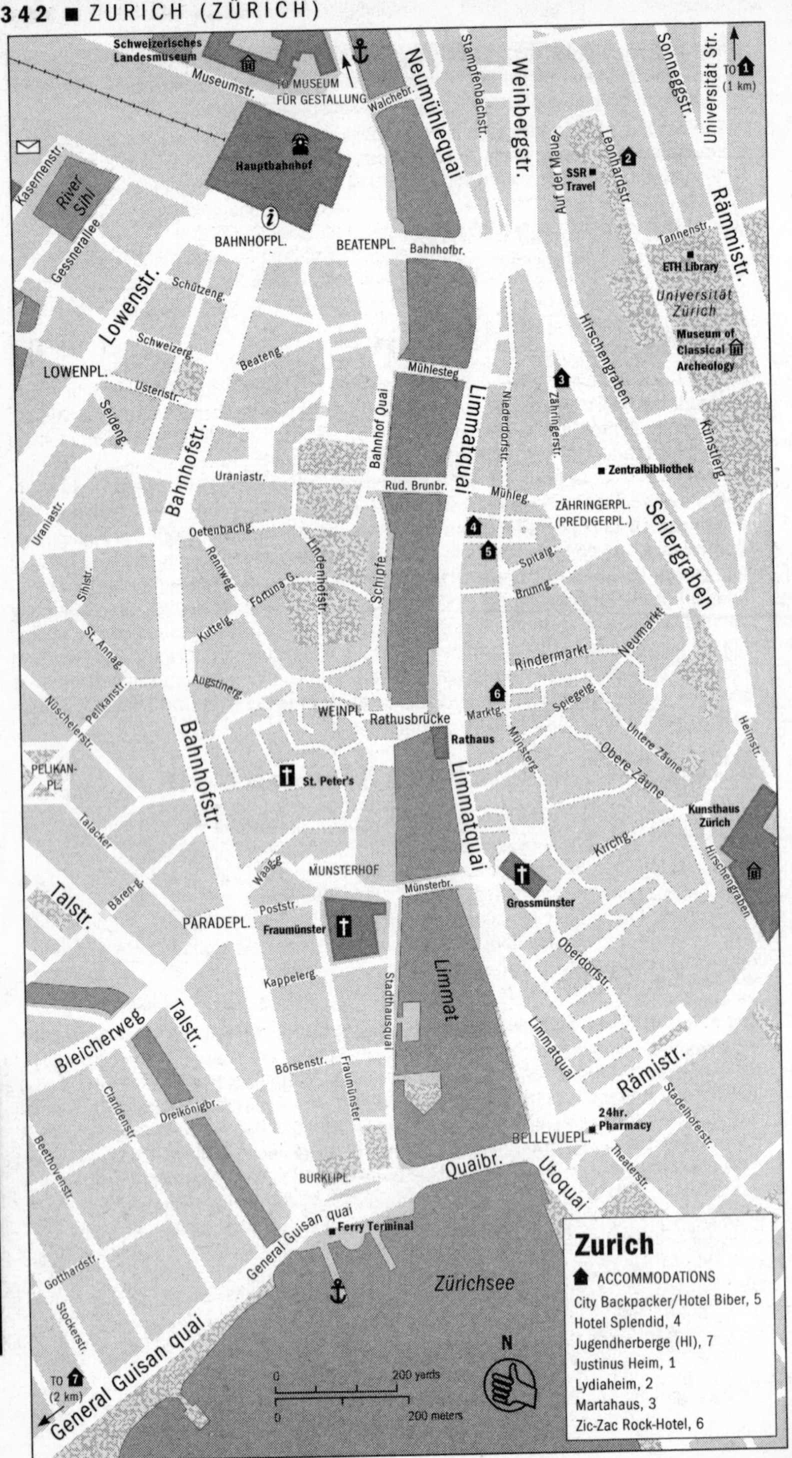

CENTRAL SWITZERLAND

ria also offers 6-day cards (36SFr, under 25 27SFr). All public buses, trams, and trolleys run 5:30am-midnight. Nightbuses run from the center of the city to outlying areas F-Sa at 1,1:30, 2, and 3am.

Ferries: Boats on the **Zürichsee** leave from Bürklipl. and range from a 1½hr. cruise between isolated villages (every 30min. 11am-6:30pm, 5.40SFr, children 2.90SFr) to a "grand tour" (4-5hr., every hr. 9:30am-5:30pm, 20SFr, 10SFr for children). Ferries also leave from the top of the Bahnhofstr. harbor (daily every 30min. 10:05am-9:05pm, 3.60SFr) for a cruise of the Limmat River. The Zürichsee authorities (☎487 1333) offer themed tours—there's even a chance for an "Oldies Night" on the Zürichsee with 50s, 60s, and 70s hits (July-Aug. F 7:30pm, 22SFr). Eurail and *Tageskarte* valid on all boats.

Taxis: Hail a cab or call 444 4444 or 222 2222, or **Taxi for the disabled** (☎272 4242). 6SFr plus 3SFr per km, no tipping.

Car Rental: The best place to rent cars is at the tourist office. They have special deals with agencies. With **Europcar,** at the tourist office (☎214 4000), get a car with unlimited mileage for 109SFr per day, 77SFr for 3+ days. **Branches** at the airport (☎813 2044; fax 813 4900); Josefstr. 53 (☎271 5656); and Lindenstr. 33 (☎383 1747).

Parking: Metropolitan Zurich has many public parking garages, but Zurich police advise parking in the suburbs and taking a tram or train from there for maximum safety and minimum traffic congestion. **Universität Irchel,** near the large park on Winterthurstr. 181, and **Engi-Märt,** Seestr. 25, are suburban lots. City parking costs 2SFr for 1st hr., 2SFr each subsequent 30min.; "Blue-Zone" 24hr. parking 10SFr; 0.50SFr per hr. in the suburbs. In the city, try garages at major department stores: **Jelmoli,** Steinmühlepl., **Migros Limmatplatz,** Limmatstr. 152, and **Globus** at Löwenstr. (All open M-F 7am-7:30pm, Th 7am-10pm, Sa 7am-5pm; 1hr. 2SFr, 2hr. 5SFr.)

Bike Rental: Bike loans are **free** at Globus (☎(079) 336 3610); Enge (☎(079) 336 3612); Oerlikon (☎336 3613); Altstetten (☎336 3614); and Hauptbahnhof (☎323 4858), at the very end of track 18. Passport and 20SFr deposit. Rentals at the baggage counter *(Gepäckexpedition Fly-Gepäck)* in the station cost 27SFr; 7SFr surcharge if you leave it at another station. Open daily 6:45am-7:45pm.

Hitchhiking: Though *Let's Go* does not recommend hitching, hitchers to Basel, Geneva, Paris, or Bonn often take tram #4 to "Werdhölzli" or bus #33 to Pfingstweidstr. Those bound for Lucerne, Italy, and Austria report taking tram #9 or 14 to "Bahnhof Wiedikon" and walk down Schimmelstr. to Silhölzli. For Munich, hitchers have been seen taking tram #14 or 7 to "Milchbuck" and walking to Schaffhauserstr. toward St. Gallen and St. Margarethen, or taking S1 or S8 to Wiedikon and hitch at Seebahnstr. Hitchhiking is illegal on the freeway.

ORIENTATION

Zurich sits in the middle of north-central Switzerland, close to the German border on some of the lowest land in Switzerland. Although the suburbs sprawl for miles, most of the activity within Zurich is confined to a relatively small, walkable area. The **Limmat River** splits the city down the middle on its way to the **Zürichsee.** On the west side of the river is the **Hauptbahnhof** and Bahnhofstraße. Bahnhofstr. begins just outside the *Hauptbahnhof* and runs, parallel to the Limmat River, to the head of the Zürichsee. Halfway down Bahnhofstr. lies **Paradeplatz,** the town center, under which Zurich's banks reputedly keep their gold reserves. **Bürkliplatz** is at the Zürichsee end of Bahnhofstr. From the Platz many grassy quai's surround the lake, providing a spot for sun bathers to relax, and runners not to relax. On the east side of the river is the University district, which stretches above the narrow **Niederdorfstr.** and pulses with bars and hip restaurants (and many hostels). Grand bridges, offering elegant views of the stately old buildings that line the river, bind the two sectors together.

PRACTICAL INFORMATION

TOURIST SERVICES

Tourist Offices: Main office (☎214 4000; fax 215 4044; information@zurichtourism.ch; www.zurichtourism.ch; hotel reservation service ☎215 4040), in the main station. *Über*-friendly and multilingual staff. Concert, movie, and bar information in German and English and copies of *Zürich News,* which prints restaurant and hotel listings. Decipher the German *ZüriTip,* a free entertainment newspaper, for tips on nightlife and alternative culture. Electronic hotel reservation board, at the front of the station, can help you find a room. The reservation desk finds rooms after 10:30am. Open Apr.-Oct. M-F 8:30am-8:30pm, Sa-Su 8:30am-6:30pm; Nov.-Mar. M-F 8:30am-7pm, Sa-Su 8:30am-6:30pm. For bikers and backpackers, the **Touring Club des Schweiz** (TCS), Alfred-Escher-Str. 38 (☎286 8666), offers maps and travel info.

Tours: The tourist office leads frequent, expensive tours: the "Stroll through the Old Town" (2hr., 18SFr, May-Oct. M-F 2:30pm, Sa-Su 10am and 2:30pm); a trolley tour of major sites (2hr., Apr.-Oct. 9:45am, noon, and 2pm; Nov.-Mar. noon and 2pm; 29SFr); and the same tour plus a cable car and boat ride (3hr., April-Oct. 9:30am, 39SFr).

Budget Travel: SSR, Ankerstr. 112 or Leonardstr. 10 (☎297 1111). Open M noon-6pm, Tu-F 10am-6pm. **Branch** office at Bäckerstr. 40 (☎241 1208). Student package tours, STA travel help, ISIC cards. Open M 1:30-6:30pm, Tu-F 10am-6:30pm, Sa 10am-1pm. Also at Oerlikon, open M-F 10am-8pm, Sa 9am-noon. **Globe-Trotter Travel Service AG,** Rennweg 35, 4th floor (☎213 8080; fax 213 8088), specializes in overseas travel. Caters to individual travelers, particularly campers (no package tours), and arranges European transport and accommodations. Student discounts, STA tickets, and ISIC cards available. Open M-W and F 9am-6pm, Th 10am-6pm, Sa 9am-2pm.

Consulates: UK, Minervastr. 117, 8032 Zürich (☎383 6560), near Kreuzpl. Open M-F 9am-noon. For visas and passports, UK citizens should contact the consulate in Geneva. **US Consulary Office,** Dufourstr. 101 (☎422 2566). Visas and passports available only at the embassy in Bern. Open M-F 10am-1pm. **Australian, Canadian, Irish,** and **South African** citizens should contact their embassies in Bern. **New Zealand's** consulate is in Geneva.

FINANCIAL AND COMMUNICATIONS SERVICES

Currency Exchange: At the main train station. Cash advances with DC, MC, and Visa, with photo ID. Open 6:30am-10pm. **Credit Suisse,** Bahnhofstr. 53, 2.50SFr commission. Open M-F 9am-6pm, Th 9am-7pm, Sa 9am-4pm. **Swiss Bank,** Bahnhofstr. 45 and 70, also charges 2.50SFr, and its ATMs take MC and Visa. Branches at Paradepl. and Bellevuepl. (Open M-F 9am-5pm). **ATMs** are all over, but most only take MC.

American Express: Uraniastr. 14, CH-8023 (☎228 7777). Mail held. Travel services. Checks cashed and exchanged, but limited banking. **ATM.** Open M-F 8:30am-6pm.

Internet Access: The **ETH Library,** Ramistr. 101, in the Hauptgebäude, has three free computers. Take tram #6, 9, or 10 to "ETH," enter the large main building and take the elevator to floor H. Open M-F 8:30am-9pm, Sa 9am-2pm. **Internet Café,** Uraniastr. 3 (☎210 3311), in the Urania Parkhaus. 5SFr per 20min. Open M 10am-6pm, Tu-Th 10am-midnight, F-Sa 10am-2am, Su 10am-11pm. At **Cybergate,** at STARS (opposite the Bahnhofpl. tourist office within the station), munch tacos with a cyberjunkie crowd. 15SFr for 1hr. Open daily 11:30am-11pm. Restaurant open M-Sa 11am-midnight, Su 10am-midnight. AmEx, DC, MC, Visa. **Telefon Corner,** downstairs in the station next to Marché Mövenpick, has 6PCs for 5SFr per hour (10SFr deposit required). Open M-F 7am-10:30pm, Sa-Su 9am-9pm.

Bookstores: Just off Bahnhofstr. at Fusslistr. 4, **Orelli Fussli** (☎884 9848; open M-F 9am-8pm, Sa 9am-4pm) is stocked with travel guides, novels, and various genres of books in English. Near the lake, **Payot Libraire,** Bahnhofstr. 9, has a slightly more interesting selection of English books, as well as many travel books. Open M noon-6:30pm, Tu-W and F 9am-6:30pm, Th 9am-8pm, Sa 9am-4pm. Find English-language periodicals at the train station. **Travel Bookshop** and **Travel Maps,** Rindermarkt 20 (☎252 3883) live up to their names. Open M 1-6:30pm, Tu-F 9am-6:30pm, Sa 9am-4pm.

Libraries: Zentralbibliothek, Zähringerpl. 6. (☎268 3100). Open M-F 8am-8pm, Sa 8am-4pm. **Pestalozzi Bibliothek,** Zähringerstr. 17 (☎261 7811), has foreign magazines and newspapers. Open June-Sept. M-F 10am-7pm, Sa 10am-2pm; Oct.-May M-F 10am-7pm, Sa 10am-4pm. Reading room open M-F 9am-8pm, Sa 9am-5pm.

Post Office: Main office, Sihlpost, Kasernestr. 97, just behind the station. Open M-F 7:30am-8pm, Sa 8am-4pm. Address *Poste Restante* to: Sihlpost, Postlagernde Briefe, CH-8021 Zürich. **Branches** throughout the city. **Postal code:** CH-8021.

EMERGENCIES

Emergencies: Police, ☎117. **Fire,** ☎118. **Ambulance,** ☎144.

Medical Emergency: ☎269 6969. **First Aid** ☎361 6161. **24-Hour Pharmacy:** Theaterstr. 14 (☎252 5600), on Bellevuepl.

Rape Crisis Line: ☎291 4646.

OTHER SERVICES

Bi-Gay-Lesbian Organizations: Ask the tourist office for **Zürich Gay Guide,** listing groups, discos, saunas, bars, and restaurants. **Homosexuelle Arbeitsgruppe Zürich (HAZ),** Sihlquai 67, P.O. Box 7088, CH-8023 (☎271 2250), offers a library, meetings, and the free newsletter *InfoSchwül* (open Tu-F 7:30-11pm, Su noon-2pm and 6-11pm). **Frauenzentrum Zürich,** Matteng. 27 (☎272 8503), provides information for lesbians.

Luggage Storage: At the station. Lockers 4SFr and 8SFr per day. Luggage watch 5SFr at the *Gepäck* counter. Open 6am-10:50pm.

Laundromat: Selbstbedienung-Wäscherei (☎242 9914), Müllerstr. 55. Wash and dry 5kg for 10.20SFr. Open daily 6am-11pm.

Public Showers and Toilets: At the train station. Toilets 1-2SFr. Showers 10SFr. Open daily 6am-midnight.

ACCOMMODATIONS AND CAMPING

The few budget accommodations in Zurich are easily accessible via Zurich's public transportation. Reserve at least a day in advance, especially during the summer.

Justinus Heim Zürich, Freudenbergstr. 146 (☎361 3806; fax 362 2982). Take tram #9 or 10 to "Seilbahn Rigiblick" (which passes James Joyce's old house), then take the hillside tram (by the Migros) uphill to the end. Quiet, cheap, private rooms in a residence hall with views of Zurich below. Breakfast and kitchen access included. Reception daily 8am-noon and 5-9pm. Checkout before 10am. Singles 35SFr, with sink 50SFr, with shower 60SFr; doubles 80SFr, 100SFr; triples 120SFr, with shower 140SFr; all rates reduced for multiple week stays.

Martahaus, Zähringerstr. 36 (☎251 4550; fax 251 4540; info@martahaus.ch; www.martahaus.ch). Left out of the station, cross Bahnhofbrücke, and take the 2nd (sharp) right after Limmatquai at the Seilgraben sign. The most comfortable budget accommodations in the *Altstadt.* Partitioned dorms have clean beds, lockers, nightlights, and towels. The dorm room has its own large balcony. Breakfast included. Airport shuttle after 6:20am every hr. 20SFr for one person. 24hr. reception. Dorms 35SFr, singles 70SFr, street-side doubles 98SFR, quiet-side doubles 108SFr, triples 120SFr. AmEx, DC, MC, Visa. The owners of Martahaus also run the nearby **Luther pension,** a women-only residence that shares reception facilities with Martahaus.

Foyer Hottingen Garni, Hottingenstr. 31 (☎256 1919; fax 256 1900; info@foyer-hottingen.ch, www.foyer-hottingen.ch). Take tram #3 (dir.: Kluspl.) to "Hottingerpl." A block from the Kunsthaus, this impeccably clean and newly renovated house has modern facilities and multilingual staff. Only women are allowed in the partitioned dorms during summer, but men and women can rent other rooms. Breakfast and **kitchen** access included. Reception 7am-11pm. Dorms in 11-bed room 30SFr; singles 65SFr, with shower and toilet 95SFr; doubles 100SFr, with shower and toilet 140SFr; triples 130SFr, quads 160SFr; quints 200SFr.

Jugendherberge Zürich (HI), Mutschellenstr. 114 (☎482 3544; fax 480 1727). Take tram #7 (dir.: Wollishofen) to "Morgental" and walk 5min. back toward Zurich along Mutschellenstr. The enormous hostel stays open all day and night to welcome travelers, which may account for the long lines at breakfast, the close quarters, and the bathroom graffiti. Tune in to CNN or watch one of the free nightly movies. **Laundry** 8SFr. Dinner 11.50SFr. Showers, sheets, and breakfast included. Lockers available, but bring your own padlock. **Internet** 1SFr for 6min. 24hr. reception. Check-out before 10am. No lock-out. Dorms 31SFr, 28.50SFr from Nov.-Mar., doubles with toilet and shower 90SFr. Non-members add 5SFr. AmEx, MC, Visa.

The City Backpacker-Hotel Biber, Niederdorfstr. 5 (☎251 9015; fax 251 9024; backpacker@access.ch; www.backpacker.ch/city-backpacker). Cross Bahnhofbrücke in front of the station, then turn right on Niederdorfstr. Spiraling out from the narrow, creaky steps in the traditional *Altstadt* building are the well-used rooms of Biber, which fittingly has a party-happy rooftop deck to complement its prime location for bar-hopping. The hostel's fun location and atmosphere are somewhat balanced by the tiny, tightly-packed rooms. Pick up a free copy of *Swiss Backpacker News* to supplement your itinerary. **Kitchen** access and showers included. Lockers available. Sheets 3SFr, towels 3SFr. **Laundry** 9SFr. **Internet** 10SFr per hr. Reception 8-11am and 3-10pm. Checkout 10am. In summer, 4- to 6-bed dorms 29SFr; singles 65SFr; doubles 88SFr. Key deposit 20SFr. In winter, dorms 27SFr; doubles 88SFr.

Zic-Zac Rock-Hotel, Marktg. 17 (☎261 2181; fax 261 2175; rockhotel@ziczac.ch; www.ziczac.ch). A night in "Pink Floyd" or "Led Zeppelin?" It's possible only at Zic-Zac, Switzerland's first rock 'n' roll hotel. Funky furniture, trendy lighting, and rock 'n' roll superstar names distinguish each room. All rooms have TV, phones, and sinks. Breakfast 4.50SFr. Reception 24hr. Singles 68SFr, with shower 88SFr; doubles 116SFr, 160SFr; studio 160SFr; triples 156SFr, 165SFr; quads with shower 260SFr.

Lydiaheim, Leonardstr. 13 (☎/fax 252 4127). Take tram #6 or 10 to "Haldenegg." Just below the university, this pension offers quiet clean rooms with sinks watched over by guardian nuns. Breakfast and towels included. **Laundry** services. **Kitchen** access. Reception open daily 7am-9pm. Singles 60SFr; doubles 100SFr.

Hotel Splendid, Roseng. 5 off Niederdorfstr. (☎252 5850; fax 262 6140), is a small hotel atop a popular piano bar. Newly renovated rooms are small and eclectically furnished. Showers (included in price) in the hall, sinks in rooms. Convenient for Niederdorfstr. nightlife. Breakfast 9.50SFr. Reception 5:30am-2am. Check-out 11am. Singles 56-70SFr; doubles 93-110SFr. AmEx, DC, MC, Visa.

Camping Seebucht, Seestr. 559 (☎482 1612; fax 482 1660). Take tram #11 to Bürklipl. where you catch bus #161 or 165 to "Stadtgrenze." Scenic lakeside location makes up for the trek. Market, terrace, and cafe on premises. Showers 2SFr. Reception 7:30am-noon and 3-10pm. Open May to late Sept. 8SFr per person; 1.50SFr tax; 5SFr for children ages 4-16. 12SFr per tent, 14SFr per caravan.

FOOD

Zurich's 1300+ restaurants cover every imaginable dietary preference. The cheapest meals in Zurich are available at *Würstli* stands, which sell sausage and bread for 5SFr. For heartier appetites, Zurich prides itself on its *Geschnetzeltes mit Rösti*, slivered veal in cream sauce with hash-brown potatoes. Check out the *Swiss Backpacker News* (available at the tourist office and Hotel Biber) for more info on budget meals in Zurich. Cheap kebab stands and take-away burger joints on Niederdorfstr. offer meals around 6SFr. The **Manor** department store off Bahnhofstr. 75 (corner of Uraniastr.) has a self-service restaurant on the 5th floor (open M-F 9am-8pm, Sa 9am-4pm).

RESTAURANTS

Bodega Española, Münsterg. 15 (☎251 2310). Catalan delights served by charismatic waiters. The delicate-but-filling egg-and-potato tortilla dishes go for 15.50SFr, while the enormous salads are 9.50SFr. Open 10am-12:30am.

Gran-Café, Limmatquai 66 (☎252 3119). Separated from the rushing Limmat river only by the street, you can sit outside and enjoy some of the cheapest (and yet tastiest) meals around (*Menüs* start at 12.80SFr). Save room for the cheap sundaes (5-6SFr). Each day also has a *Menü* (11.80SFr), guaranteed in 7min. or it's free. Start your timers. Open M-F 6am-midnight, Sa-Su 7:30am-midnight.

Hiltl, Sihlstr. 28 (☎227 7000). Trade carrot sticks with the vegetarian elite at this swank restaurant, where the lack of meat makes things surprisingly cheap. Highlights include the all-day salad buffet for 4.60SFr per 100g (15SFr for large salad), and the Indian buffet at night (same price). Open M-Sa 7am-11pm, Su 11am-11pm.

Raclette Stube, Zähringerstr. 16 (☎251 4130). This small, familiy-oriented restaurant opens out onto the street and serves a limited but high-quality menu of classic Swiss fare. Large raclette appetizer 11SFr; fondue 23.50SFr per person; all-you-can-eat raclette 29.50SFr per person. Open daily from 6pm.

Johanniter, Niederdorfstr. 70 (☎251 4600). Of all the Swiss restaurants on Niederdorfstr., Johanniter may be the favorite among locals, with the best food for the least money, all with elegant sidewalk seating. Hearty Swiss *Rösti* and noodle dishes run from 15-18SFr, with plenty to choose from, served late into the night. Open daily 10am-4am, hot food from 11am-3:30am.

Mensa der Universität Zürich, Rämistr. 71 (☎632 6211). Take streetcar #6 to "ETH Zentrum" from Bahnhofpl. or take the red Polybahn uphill from Central Station. Hot dishes 7.50SFr with ISIC card, salad buffet 6SFr. Open July 15-Oct. 21 M-F 11am-2pm; Oct. 22-July 14 M-F and alternate Sa 11am-2:30pm and 5-7:30pm. Mensa B open M-F 6:30am-7:30pm.

Mensa Polyterrasse, behind Rämistr. 101. 10.50-11.30SFr with ISIC. Open M-Sa 11:15am-1:30pm and 5:30-7:15pm. Self-service cafeteria open Oct. 22-July 14 M-F and alternate Sa 11am-2:30pm, July 15-Oct. 21 M-F 7am-5:30pm. Closed during winter vacations.

CAFES

Sprüngli Confiserie Café, Paradepl. (☎224 4711), is a Zurich landmark, founded by one of the original Lindt chocolate makers who sold his shares to his brother. A chocolate heaven, the *Confiserie-Konditorei* concocts exquisite confections and delicious sundaes (8.50-12SFr) with homemade ice cream and sherbet, served on the Bahnhofstr. patio. Lunch *Menüs* 21.50-25.50SFr. Confectionery open M-F 7:30am-8pm, Sa 8am-4pm. Cafe open M-F 7:30am-6:30pm, Sa 7:30am-5pm, Su 10am-5pm.

Zähringer Café, Zähringerpl. 11 (☎252 0500), across the square from the library, at the end of Spitalgasse, above the *Altstadt.* Sip coffee, frappes, or other caffeinated beverages with a hip young crowd. Opens early on weekends so late-night revelers can top off the night with requisite grease (*Rösti* topped with a fried egg 13SFr). Open M 6pm-midnight, Tu-F 8am-midnight, Sa-Su 5am-midnight.

Infinito Espresso Bar, Sihlstr. 20 (☎210 4060), is chic and angular with a broad coffee selection. Espresso from 3SFr, beers from 6SFr, sandwiches and snacks 4-9SFr. Open M and W-F 7am-9pm, Sa 8:30am-5:30pm; July-Aug. M-F 7am-10pm, Sa 8am-8pm.

MARKETS AND BAKERIES

Two bakery chains, **Kleiner** and **Buchmann,** are everywhere in Zurich, offering freshly baked bread, sweets (whole apricot pies around 9SFr), and *Kuchen* (*Bürli* rolls 0.50SFr, *Chäschüechli* 2SFr) for reasonable prices (open M-F 6:30am-6:30pm). The 24-hour **vending machine** in the Shop-Ville beneath the train station has pasta, juice, and other staples, but you may feel uncomfortable heading over there alone at night.

Farmer's Market, at Bürklipl. Fruit, flowers, and veggies. Tu and F 6am-11am.

Co-op Super-Center, straddling the Limmat River next to the train station, is the Co-op to end all Co-ops, visible from almost everywhere. Open M-F 7am-8pm, Sa 7am-4pm.

Migros, Mutschellenstr. 191, near the hostel (open M-F 8am-7pm, Sa 8am-4pm with adjoining restaurant, which is open M-F 7am-7pm, Sa7am-6pm); under the train station in Shop-Ville (open M-F 7am-8pm, Sa-Su 8am-8pm).

SIGHTS

It's virtually inconceivable to start your tour of Zurich anywhere except the stately **Bahnhofstraße.** The famous causeway of capitalism has shoppers peering into the windows of Cartier, Rolex, Chanel, and Armani during the day but falls dead quiet when the shops and banks close at 6pm. At the Zürichsee end of Bahnhofstr., **Bürkliplatz** is a good place to begin exploration of the lake shore. The platz itself hosts a colorful Saturday **market** (May-Oct. 6am-3:30pm). On the other side of the river the pedestrian zone continues on Niederdorfstr. and Munsterg. From Niederdorfstr. turn right onto **Spiegelgasse,** Zurich's memory lane. Commemorative plaques honor Wladimir Illitsch Uljanow (aka "Lenin") at #14, German author Georg Büchner at #12, and "Cabaret Voltaire" (former haunt of Hans Arp, Tristan Tzara, and Hugo Ball) at #3, which is now a funky bar called "Castel Dada" (see Da, Da, Da p. 351, and Nightlife p. 351).

FRAUMÜNSTER. Right off Paradepl., the 13th-century cathedral **Fraumünster** stands on the site of a church founded in the 9th-century by the daughters of the local sovereign. The simplicity of its Gothic lines are offset by the vivid stained-glass chancel windows (installed in 1970) and rose transept window (1978), designed by **Marc Chagall.** Despite his Jewish ancestry, Chagall agreed to design the windows for the Protestant church in the late 1960s. The merging of Old and New Testament stories in the 5 windows reveals Chagall's radical personal interpretation of the texts. The red window on the far left is the Prophet window, next to the blue window depicting Jacob's Ladder. Jesus Christ stands in the top of the green central window, with the yellow Zion window to the right. The blue window on the far right symbolizes the Law, crowned by Moses and the 10 Commandments. A more subdued window called "the heavenly Paradise," designed by Augusto Giacometti in 1930, is hidden in the northern transept. Outside the church on Fraumünsterstr., a mural decorates the Gothic archway in the courtyard, picturing Felix and Regula, the decapitated patron saints of Zurich with their heads in their hands. *(Open May-Sept. 9am-noon and 2-6pm; Oct. 10am-noon and 2-5pm; Nov.-Feb. 10am-noon and 2-5pm, Mar.-Apr. 10am-noon and 2-6pm.)*

GROSSMÜNSTER. This is where Zwingli spearheaded the Reformation in German-speaking Switzerland. The building is primarily Romanesque, with twin Neo-Gothic towers (added in 1786) that have become a symbol of Zurich. The choir is ablaze in color from the blood-red and cobalt-blue stained-glass windows, depicting the Christmas story, which were designed in 1933 by Augusto Giacometti. Below the windows, one of Zwingli's bibles lies in a protected case near the pulpit from which he preached. One of the Romanesque columns presents a legend concerning Charlemagne's horse. While pursuing a stag all the way from Aachen (in northern Germany), the horse is supposed to have stumbled over the graves of Felix and Regula, 3rd-century Christian martyrs, prompting the Holy Roman Emperor to found *Grossmünster*. Venture downstairs to the 12th-century crypt to see Charlemagne's statue and 2m-long sword. If you're feeling active, head up the many twisting stairs to the top of one of the towers for a panoramic view of Zurich. *(Church open Mar. 15-Oct. 9am-6pm; Nov.-Mar. 14 10am-4pm. Tower open Mar.-Oct. daily 1:30-5pm, Oct.-Mar. Sa-Su 1:30-4:30pm. 2SFr for entrance to the tower.)*

ST. PETERSKIRCHE. Because of its claim to the "largest clock face in Europe," St. Peter's Church is a place that attracts "more tourists than the average Zurich sight," a dubious honor. Find it next to the Fraumünster, or just look up. Down

Thermeng. from St. Peter's, recently excavated **Roman baths** dating from the 1st century are visible beneath the iron stairway.

LINDENHOF. This park is the original site of **Turricum,** the namesake and birthplace of Zurich. A great refuge right in the midst of the city, the park has a giant chess board and sweeping views of the river and the *Altstadt.* It attracts locals and tourists alike to lounge and admire the vistas. To find it, follow Strehlg., Rennweg, or Glockeng. uphill to the intersection of the three streets.

AROUND THE UNIVERSITY. Above the town on the *Grossmünster* side of the river, the **University of Zurich** presides over the city. The school—the first in Europe to admit women—was home (briefly) to Einstein and the inventors of the electron microscope. From the university, trams #6, 9, and 10 run uphill to "Zoo" and the **graves** of authors **James Joyce** and **Elias Canetti** in the **Fluntern Cemetery.** The **Zürich Zoo,** beside the cemetery, exhibits over 2000 animal species. *(Zürichbergstr. 221. ☎254 2505. Open Mar.-Oct. 8am-6pm; Nov.-Feb. 8am-5pm. 14SFr, ages 6-16 7SFr.)*

GARDENS AND PARKS. Maintained by the University of Zurich but nowhere near it, University botanical gardens are a verdant oasis, with glass domes housing savanna, sub-tropical, and tropical collections, with human-sized lilies standing outside. Even the horticulturally challenged will enjoy strolling outside through clumps of myrtle and lavender, lounging on the surrounding grassy hills, and watching lily-leaves bob up and down. *(Zollikerstr. 107. To get there, take tram #2 or 4 to "Höschg," take a left onto Hochsg., and follow it to Zollikerstr. ☎385 4411. Open Mar.-Sept. M-F 7am-7pm and Sa-Su 8am-6pm. Free.)* Across the city, the **Stadtgärtnerei** attracts botanists and ornithologists alike to the moist **Palmhouse/Aviary,** which has artificial streams running through it. The Aviary houses 17 species of tropical birds, including 2 fantastically plumed green parrots and a mime bird, all of which are free to whiz around the building, past your shoulder and over your head. *(Sackzeig 25-27. Take tram #3 to "Hubertus" and head down Gutstr. ☎492 1423. Open 9-11:30am and 1:30-4:30pm. Free.)* The lush, perfect-for-a-picnic **Rieterpark,** overlooking the city, creates a romantic backdrop for the **Museum Rietberg** *(take tram #7 to "Museum Rietburg").*

UETLIBERG. The "top of Zurich," this is the king of picnic spots, with a view of Zurich's urban sprawl on one side and the pristine countryside on the other. The flat walk from Uetliberg to Felsenegg is a peaceful escape from the city's hustle and bustle. From Zurich's *Hauptbahnhof,* take the train to "Uetliberg" (15min., every 30min., discount with *Tageskarte*), then follow the yellow signs to Felsenegg (1½hr.). A cable car runs from Felsenegg to Adliswil, where a train returns to Zurich *(buy tickets at any train or cable car station or at most hotels; free with Eurail).* When the weather heats up, visit the bathing parks along the Zürichsee. Strandbad Mythenquai lies along the western shore. *(Take tram #7 to "Brunaustr." and follow the signs. ☎201 0000. Open M-F 9am-8pm, Sa-Su 9am-7:30pm; 5SFr.)*

MUSEUMS

Zurich has channelled much of its banking wealth into its universities and museums, fostering very smart people and outstanding collections. The larger institutions hold the core of the city's artistic and historical wealth, but many of the smaller museums are equally spectacular. The specialized schools of the university open the doors of their museum collections to the public.

ART MUSEUMS

Kunsthaus Zürich, Heimpl. 1 (☎251 6765). Take tram #3, 5, 8, or 9 to "Kunsthaus." The Kunsthaus, which covers Western art from the 15th century on with an undeniable bias in favor of the 20th century, is in itself a compelling reason to come to Zurich. The museum does a wonderful job of mixing in famous locals–Segantini, Hodler, and the Giacomettis (all of them), to name a few–with the international set, so that no element of the exhibition ever grows stale. The Alberto Giacometti loft is particularly well done, with its juxtaposition of the spindly sculptures he became famous for with the not-so-spindly paintings he was doing at the same time. Open Tu-Th 10am-9pm, F-Su 10am-5pm. 4SFr, students and disabled 3SFr. Su free. Added charge for special exhibits.

Museum Rietberg, Gablerstr. 15 (☎202 4528). Take tram #7 to "Museum Rietberg." In confident contrast to the Kunsthaus, Rietberg presents an exquisite collection of Asian, African, and other non-European art, housed in 2 mansions in the Rieter Park (see Gardens and Parks, p. 349). **Park-Villa Rieter** features internationally acclaimed exhibits of Chinese, Japanese, and Indian drawings. **Villa Wesendonck** stores most of the permanent collection of sculptural art from the non-Western world, some of it 2 millennia old. Villa Wesendonck open Tu and Th-Su 10am-5pm, W 10am-8pm. Park-Villa Rieter open Tu-Sa 1-5pm, Su 10am-5pm. Regular admission 5SFr, students 3SFr. Special exhibits and permanent collections 12SFr, students 6SFr.

E.G. Bührle Collection, Zollikerstr. 172 (☎422 0086). Take tram #2 or 4 (dir.: "Tiefenbrunnen") to "Wildbachstr." From Seefeldstr. turn left on Münchaldenstr., walk uphill, and turn right on Zollikerstr. Once the private collection of an industrialist, now exposed to the perusal of the public. It took 20 years for E.G. Bührle to amass his sizable star-studded collection, funded by proceeds of his career. It is fascinating to see one man's perception of art—traditional as it may be—and how his collection and tastes developed over the years. Open Tu and F 2-5pm, W 5-8pm, Su 2-5pm. 9SFr, students 3SFr.

OTHER MUSEUMS

Museum of Classical Archaeology, Rämistr. 73 (☎257 2820). Take tram #6, 9, or 19 to "ETH." As impressive as the collection of Greek and Roman vases and busts filling the first floor lecture hall is, it seems nothing more than a foil for the astonishing basement, which houses replicas of nearly every great statue in the ancient world from 800 BC on. Open Tu-F 1-6pm, Sa-Su 11am-5pm. Free.

Museum für Gestaltung (Design Museum), Ausstellungsstr. 60 (☎446 2211). Take tram #4 or 13 to "Museum für Gestaltung," or walk (5min.) from the main station. This museum consists of enormous spaces adjoined to the School of Design, where varying displays of student work, a collection of vintage advertisement posters, and temporary exhibits on steam shovel art, Buckminister Fuller, or giant corn, vie for attention, with the unifying objective to consider design as it relates to man. Open Tu and Th-F 10am-6pm, W 10am-9pm, Sa-Su 11am-6pm. Hall and gallery 10SFr, students 6SFr.

Lindt and Sprüngli Chocolate Factory, Seestr. 204 (☎716 2233). Take S1 or S8 to "Kilchberg" from the Hauptbahnhof (5.40SFr) or bus #165 to "Kilchberg." From the stop, turn right out of the station, left down the first street, and an immediate right for a 3min. walk straight to the factory. Visitors are welcomed with an open box of Lindt chocolate and a movie about chocolate machines. The chocolate spree ends as visitors leave with free boxes of—what else?—souvenir Lindt chocolate. All exhibits in German. Open W-F 10am-noon and 1-4pm. Free.

Johann Jacobs Museum: Collection on the Cultural History of Coffee, Seefeldquai 17 (☎388 6151). Take tram #2 or 4 to "Feldeggstr." and walk 2min. down Feldeggstr. The museum is on the right at the end of the street. Its presentations commemorate that foundation of modern civilization and kernel of all that is good and right and wholesome in the world: the coffee bean. Visitors peer into display cases to see historical and modern coffee pots. The place is caffeinated down to the bean-patterned rug on the stairs. At the end of the exhibits, enjoy a cuppa joe in the villa's drawing room. All exhibits in German; summaries in English. Open F-Sa 2-5pm, Su 10-5pm. Free.

Schweizerisches Landesmuseum, Museumstr. 2 (☎218 6511 or 218 6565), next to the main train station. The Landesmuseum may be old news for Swiss schoolkids, but it provides fascinating insights into Swiss history. Skip the rather generic first floor of medieval artifacts, but do inspect the castle rooms, which contain 16th-century astrological instruments, Ulrich Zwingli's weapons from the Battle of Kappel in which he died (1531), and a tiny bejeweled clock with a golden skeleton morbidly pointing to the hour. Open Tu-Su 10:30am-5pm, students 5SFr and seniors 3SFr. Special exhibits around 8SFr.

DA, DA, DA The silent walls of Spiegalg. 3 in Zurich's *Altstadt* witnessed one of the most rebellious movements in the history of art and theater. The infamous years between the World Wars offered no lull for the city's citizens, as a group of angry young artists spilled their creativity into the craziest forms of art. The result was Dadaism, an art which refused to be art, and a style whose guiding principle was confusion and paradoxical humor. Dada's aim was to provoke a rude awakening from standardized thought and bourgeois preconceptions. Dada is said to have taken its name either from the French word for "hobby-horse," which Hugo Ball selected by sticking a penknife into a German-French dictionary, or from the refrain of two Romanian founders of the movement, who used to mutter, "Da, da" ("yes, yes" in Romanian). Distinguished painter/sculptor Alberto Giacometti, in a sojourn in Zurich, entered the fray—it is said that one day, he opened the door of Cabaret Voltaire, stepped out, shouted, "Viva Dada!" at the top of his lungs, and disappeared as promenadeurs on the Limmatquai stopped in their tracks. Lenin was also reputedly a fan of Cabaret Voltaire. Today Cabaret Voltaire is preserved in the entrails of the disco/bar Castel Dada (see p. 351).

Museum Bellerive, (☎383 4376). Take tram #4 or 2 (dir.: Tiefenbrunnen) to "Höschg." and walk right to Höschg. #3. Opposite the Zurich Ballet Academy, Museum Bellerive specializes in constantly changing "out-of-the-ordinary" exhibits. The displays may sound tame, but the museum takes them in unexpected directions—past exhibitions included "Made in Japan" (a room full of plastic Japanese meals). "Felt" is coming in 2001. Open Tu-Th 10am-8pm, F 10am-5pm, Sa-Su 11am-5pm. Closes between exhibits, so call ahead.

ENTERTAINMENT AND NIGHTLIFE

For information on after-dark goings-on, check **ZüriTip** or the posters that decorate the streets and cinemas at Bellevuepl. or Hirschenpl. **Niederdorfstr.** rocks as the epicenter of Zurich's nightlife. Due to the number of strip clubs, however, **women may not want to walk alone in this area at night.** On Friday and Saturday nights during the summer, Hirschenpl. on Niederdorfstr. hosts sword-swallowers and other daredevil street performers from around the world. Other hot spots include Münsterg. and Limmatquai, both lined with cafes and bars that overflow with people well into the wee hours of the morning. Beer in Zurich is pricey (from 6SFr), but a number of cheap bars have established themselves on Niederdorfstr. near Muhleg. If all else falls through, go to the cinema. Most movies are screened in English with German and French subtitles (marked E/d/f). Films generally cost 13SFr. After July 18, the **Orange Cinema,** an open-air cinema at Zürichhorn (take tram #4 or 2 to "Fröhlichstr.") attracts huge crowds to its lakefront screenings. To ensure a seat, arrive at least an hour before the 9pm showing (15SFr) or reserve a seat at the open-air ticket counter at the Bellevue tram station. Zurich is full of festivals all year round. The **Zueri-Faescht** (Zurich Festival) will bring an amusement park to the city from July 6-8, 2001. Every August, the *Street Parade* brings together ravers from all over the world for a giant techno party (see Festival Fever, p. 300).

Double-U (W) Bar, Niederdorfstr. 21 (☎251 4144), on the first floor of Hotel Schafli, is a hub of activity, popular even by the high standards of Niederdorfstr. Locals and students crowd the terrace, drinking beer (6.50SFr and up). Open M-Th 2pm-whenever, F-Su 4pm-whenever.

Casa Bar, Münsterg. 30 (☎262 2002), is a tiny, crowded pub with great live jazz. Drink prices hasten poverty (beer from 9.50SFr), but there is no cover. Open daily 7pm-2am.

Castel DADA, Münsterg. 26 (☎266 1010), next to Casa Bar. On the former site of the "Cabaret Voltaire," this lively bar and disco keeps the inner chamber intact. Beers from 6.50SFr. Open Su-Th 6pm-2am, F-Sa 8pm-2am. Disco open until 4am.

Bar Odeon, Limmatquai 2 (☎251 1650), Bellevuepl. Thornton Wilder and Vladimir Lenin used to get sloshed in this posh, artsy joint. Great street-side seating. Beers from 6SFr. During the day, an ebullient crowd sips espresso here. Open 7am-2am, F-Sa 7am-4am.

Oliver Twist, Rindermarkt 6 (☎252 4710) welcomes English-soccer fans in a pub atmosphere that's only somewhat contrived. Beers 7.50SFr and up; mixed drinks from 8.50SFr. Open M-F 11:30am-midnight, Sa 3pm-midnight, Su 4pm-midnight.

Oepfelchammer, Rindermarkt 12 (☎351 2336). This popular Swiss wine bar (3-5SFr per glass) has low ceilings and wooden crossbeams covered with initials and messages from 200 years of merry-making. Those who climb the rafters and drink a free glass of wine from the beams get to engrave their names on the furniture. It's harder than it looks. Open Tu-Sa 11am-midnight; closed for a month in summer.

Barfusser, Spitalg. 14, off Zähringerplatz. (☎251 4064). Europe's oldest gay bar, offers outdoor seating during the day, and drinking into the night (open daily until 2am).

DAYTRIP FROM ZURICH

EINSIEDELN ☎055

Trains leave Zurich for Wädenswil (on their way to Chur) every 20 minutes 6:10am-11:10pm, connecting to Einsiedeln up to a half-hour later (15.40SFr one-way).

Just an hour by train from Zwingli's Protestant pulpit in Zurich, the tiny town of Einsiedeln attracts pilgrims from all over Europe to its spectacular, massive cathedral and legendary Black Madonna. To find the **Klosterkirche** (cathedral), exit the station, cross the street, turn right onto the small lane behind "Doc Holliday's" restaurant, and turn left on Hauptstr. Consecrated in 1735, the cathedral's Milanese exterior with twin lemon-shaped domes dominates the surrounding hills. The Asam brothers dreamed up the interior; its ornate Baroque ceiling overflows with plump, blushing cherubs floating by an overwhelming pastel background of lavender, green, gold, and pink. At 4pm each day (except Sunday) the monks sing *Vespers* and *Salve Regina*, and then recess to the Madonna Chapel to practice their Gregorian chant. Bring coins if you feel inspired to light a candle for meditation (1SFr). The 1m-high **Black Madonna,** resplendent in Royal Spanish attire, against a glowing backdrop of golden clouds, is the cathedral's centerpiece. Years of smoky candlelight and underground storage during the French invasion have darkened the figure. An Austrian craftsman once restored her natural color, but locals, refusing to accept the change in hue, had her painted black again. (Klosterkirche open 5:30am-8:30pm daily.) The **monastery** that stretches back from the cathedral offers 90min. tours of its horse stables and renowned **library** every Saturday at 2pm (18SFr; reserve and buy tickets at the tourist office).

The town's **tourist office** sits below the cathedral at Hauptstr. 85, Klosterpl. (☎418 4488; fax 418 4480; info@einsiedeln.ch). Helpful staff can advise you on hiking opportunities in the lush hills surrounding the cathedral and book tours for you. The gates are usually open, and the pastoral grounds, protected by the crumbling walls of the monastery, are worth a stroll any day. Behind the monastery, short trails lead into the hills where the monastery horses graze.

WINTERTHUR ☎052

Once the country home of eastern Switzerland's wealthy industrialists, Winterthur (VIN-ter-tur) today houses the fruits of their labor. Though Winterthur is overshadowed in all things commercial by its omnipotent neighbor, Zurich, the incredible array of museums in Winterthur—mostly endowed by those deceased wealthy industrialists—make it an excellent daytrip from Zurich (but not on Mondays, when the museums are closed). The town itself has little to offer besides its charming Marktgasse and wealth of culture.

TRANSPORT AND PRACTICAL INFORMATION

Trains run 4 times every hour to Zurich (21.20SFr round trip), and connect there to Basel and Geneva; trains leave twice an hour for St. Gallen (35SFr round trip). Almost all buses to the museums leave from just right of the station.

Winterthur's **tourist office,** within the train station, overflows with excursion ideas and museum info and offers a free hotel reservation service as well as a free, but busy **Internet** terminal (☎267 6700; fax 267 6858; open M-F 8:30am-6:30pm, Sa 8:30am-4pm). On the left side of the station, you'll find **currency exchange** (open daily 6:10am-9pm), **bicycle rental** (27SFr per day; open M-F 7:30am-7:50pm, Sa 7:30am-7pm, Su 8:10am-12:30pm and 2:50-7:30pm), and **luggage storage** (5SFr; same hours as bike rental). The **post office** is opposite the train station (open M-W and F 7:30am-6:30pm, Th 7:30-8pm, Sa 8:30-4pm). The **postal code** is CH-8401.

ACCOMMODATIONS AND FOOD

For some nearly authentic 13th-century castle living, try **Jugendherberge Hegi (HI),** Hegifeldstr. 125, inside the **Schloß Hegi**. To reach the castle, take Post Bus #680 to "Schlossacker." You can also take the train or bus #1 or #5 to "Oberwinterthur Bahnhof." If you're coming from Zurich, take S12 from Zurich's main station (dir.: Seuzach), which stops at Bahnhof Oberwinterthur as well. Exit the station, turn left and continue through the pedestrian underpass, turn left on Hegifeldstr., then walk 10 minutes to the castle, which lies just past the houses. Surrounded by meadows, hedges, and fruit trees (and serenaded by clucking hens and turkeys), the hostel offers no-frills, medieval dwelling. (☎242 3840; fax 242 5830. Kitchen facilities for 1SFr. Sheets included. Reception 7-10am and 5-10pm. Checkout 7-10am. Lockout daily 10am-5pm. Curfew 11pm. Open Mar.-Oct. Dorms 16SFr.)

Most food options are located downtown, near Marktg., which is lined with food stands. The cheapest restaurant food in town is available at the **Migros Restaurant**, on the second floor of Neuweisen, a big mall-like structure (open M-W and F 8:15am-6:30pm, Th 8:15am-9pm, Sa 8am-4pm). Go through the tunnel under the train station and follow the signs. Locals on their lunch break congregate at **Manta Sandwich-Bar,** Untertor 17, near the train station. Filling, gourmet sandwiches (like tomato, mozzarella, and eggplant) go for 5-10SFr. (☎212 4323. Open daily 6am-6:30pm, Sa 6am-4:30pm.) Another local fave, **Pizzeria Pulcinella,** is right off Marktg. on Metzg. (Pizza 14.50-19SFr inside, 3SFr less to take it out. ☎212 9862. Open M-F 11:15am-1:45pm and 5:45-11:30pm, Sa-Su 5:45-10:30pm.) Fruit and vegetable **markets** invade the streets of the *Altstadt* on Tuesdays and Fridays. The **Hegimart** supermarket is conveniently located opposite the Schloß Hegi hostel (open M-F 8:15am-12:15pm and 2:30-6:30pm, Sa 8am-4pm).

SIGHTS

Since museums are Winterthur's biggest draw, there are two things you should get as soon as you arrive. The first is a **Tageskarte** (7.20SFr), which will get you to the museums via public transportation (biking is also a popular option). The second is a **museum pass** (20SFr for 1 day), which will get you into the museums and save you money if you plan on visiting at least 3 of Winterthur's fifteen museums. A brochure covering all of them is available at the tourist office.

OSKAR REINHART COLLECTION. Winterthur's most generous art patron was Oskar Reinhart, as the 2 museums housing his collection demonstrate. The larger of these is the **Museum Oskar Reinhart am Stadtgarten,** in the center of town. Turn right out of the station, then go left on Stadthausstr. for 2 blocks. The museum is focused on the work of Swiss, German, and Austrian painters, particularly portraits. Glass steps lead to the beautifully remodeled fourth floor, which houses temporary exhibits. *(Stadthausstr. 6. ☎267 5172. Open W-Su 10am-5pm, Tu 10am-8pm. 8SFr, students 6SFr.)*

A smaller but more impressive branch of the collection is preserved just outside of town in the **Sammlung Oskar Reinhart am Römerholz.** Take bus #10 to "Haldengut" (departs hourly from the station); turn left off the bus and head up Haldenstr. for a steep 10-minute walk. The museum also sponsors a shuttle service, which runs from the train station to the villa *(every hr., 9:45am-4:45pm, Tu-Sa, 5SFr).* In addition to works by old masters such as Cranach, Holbein, Rubens, El Greco, and Goya, the museum showcases masterpieces by 19th-century European masters, including Cézanne, Manet, Daumier, van Gogh, and Renoir. *(Haldenstr. 95. ☎269 2740. Open Tu-Su 10am-5pm. 8Sfr, students 6SFr.)*

KUNSTMUSEUM. Winterthur's large Kunstmuseum houses some renowned Impressionist pieces, but its specialty is Modernist art by the likes of Klee, Kandinsky, Mondrian, Léger, and Arp. Turn left from the station, right on Museumstr., and left on Lindstr. The collection is displayed in a fittingly modern setting in the newly-built addition. In the summer, temporary exhibits of contemporary art energize the museum. *(Museumstr. 52. ☎267 5162. Open Tu 10am-8pm, W-F 10am-5pm. Prices hover around 10SFr, students 6SFr.)* The **city library** and the **Museum of Natural Science** are in the same building. *(☎267 5166. Library open M 10am-6pm, Tu-F 8am-6pm, Sa 8am-4pm. Natural Science Museum open Tu-Su 10am-5pm.)*

FOTOMUSEUM. Among Winterthur's smaller museums, you'll find the unique Fotomuseum, housed in a former factory. Take bus #2 to "Schleife," walk down Palmstr,. across from the bus stop, for 2 blocks. The museum, which serves as the center of the counter-culture crowd in Winterthur, features exhibitions of photography, lectures, and discussions. *(Grüzenstr. 44. ☎233 6086; www.fotomuseum.ch. Open Tu-F noon-6pm, Sa-Su 11am-5pm. 8SFr, students 5SFr.)*

TECHNORAMA DER SCHWEIZ. The **Swiss Technology Museum,** Technoramastr. 1, is easily reached by taking bus #5 (dir.: Technorama) to the last stop. All displays in this enormous scientific playground are in German, but many of them are self-explanatory and some are beautiful enough to belong in Winterthur's art museums. Try your hand at textile production or water music, or test your hand-eye coordination in the jumbo-jet flight simulator. *(☎243 0505. Open Tu-Su and public holidays 10am-5pm. 16SFr, seniors 14SFr, students 10SFr, ages 6-16 8SFr.)*

STADTKIRCHE. While wandering around the *Altstadt*, visit the **Stadtkirche** (city church) by walking up Untertorstr., just right of the station, for 6 blocks to Obere Kirchg. The church was built in 1180, renovated in the late Gothic style between 1501 and 1515, and now blazes with Alberto Giacometti's stained-glass windows and Paul Zehnder's 1925 murals of brightly colored Bible stories. *(Open daily 10am-4pm.)*

CASTLE MÖRSBURG. If you're up for a jaunt into the country, check out **Castle Mörsburg,** former home of the 13th-century Kyburg dynasty, which now holds 17th- to 19th-century fine art and furniture. Take bus #1 to "Wallrüti," then follow the yellow signs for a 40min. hike through forest, fields, and farms. The fortress is a favorite spot for weekend family hikes and school bike tours. *(☎337 1396. Open Mar.-Oct. Tu-Su 10am-noon and 1:30-5pm; Nov.-Feb. Su 10am-noon and 1:30-5pm. Free.)*

CENTRAL SWITZERLAND

LUCERNE (LUZERN) ☎041

Lucerne just may be the fondue pot at the end of the *Regenbogen* (rainbow)—the Switzerland traveler's dream come true. The city is small but cosmopolitan, ready to satisfy sophisticated culture-lovers and, at the same time, provide a plethora of outdoor opportunities, for the adventurous and less so. Throw in one of the most engaging *Altstädte* in Switzerland, cruises on the placid **Vierwaldstättersee,** and hikes up the queenly peaks of Mt. Pilatus and Rigi Kulm, and you have enough to keep a visitor enthralled for days. Lucerne's position in the heart of Switzerland

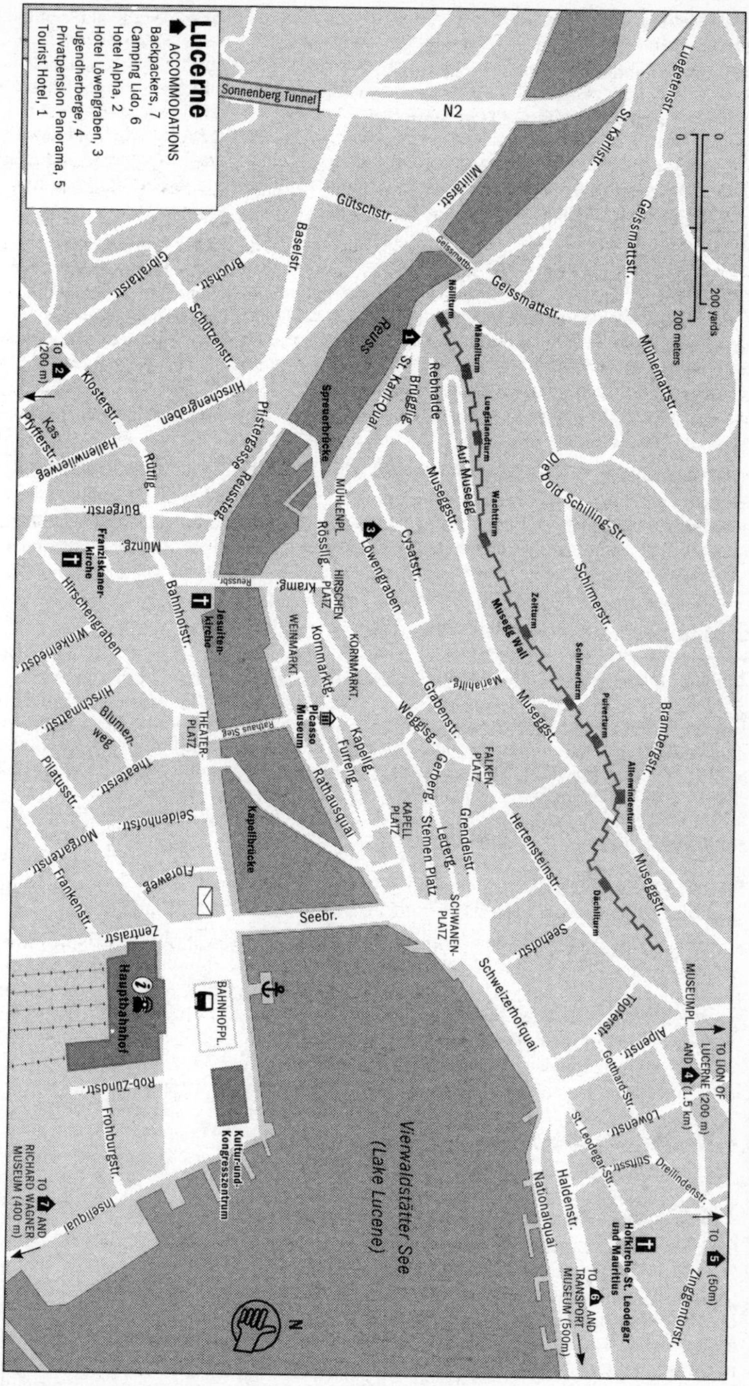

Lucerne

ACCOMMODATIONS
- Backpackers, 7
- Camping Lido, 6
- Hotel Alpha, 2
- Hotel Löwengraben, 3
- Jugendherberge, 4
- Privatpension Panorama, 5
- Tourist Hotel, 1

Vierwaldstätter See (Lake Lucerne)

TO LION OF LUCERNE (200 m) AND 4 (1.5 km)

TO 5 (50m)

TO 6 AND TRANSPORT MUSEUM (500m)

TO 7 AND RICHARD WAGNER MUSEUM (400 m)

TO 2 (200 m)

makes it a daytrip departure point *par excellence* (and the crowds show it). What's more, Lucerne is small enough so that after a few days in the city you'll feel that you've found a home on the road.

GETTING THERE AND AROUND

Trains: Bahnhofpl. (☎157 2222). To: **Basel** (1¼hr., 1-2 per hr. 5:26am-10:54pm, 31SFr); **Bern** (1½hr., every half-hr. to every 3hr. 5:26am-10:54pm, 32SFr); **Geneva** (3hr., every hr. 5:55am-9:57pm, 70SFr); **Interlaken** (2hr., every hr. 6:30am-7:34pm, 26SFr); **Lausanne** (2½hr., every hr. 6:44am-8:54pm, 58SFr); **Lugano** (2¾hr., every hr. 7:18am-8:39pm, 58SFr); **Zurich** (1hr., 2 per hr. 4:59am-11:10pm, 22SFr); and Zurich **airport** (1¼hr., every hr. 4:59am-10:10pm, 26SFr).

Public Transportation: VBL buses depart from in front of the station and provide extensive coverage. With a ho(s)tel stamp on a guest card you can buy a 3-day bus pass for 8SFr at the tourist office. 1 zone 1.70SFr, 2 zones (to the youth hostel) 2.20SFr, 3 zones 2.70SFr. *Tageskarte* (day pass) 10SFr, 2-day pass 15SFr. Free with SwissPass.

Taxis: Cabs congregate in front of the train station, at Schwanpl., at Pilatuspl., and in front of the Municipal Theater. ☎211 1111, 310 1010, or 250 5050.

Car Rental: Hertz, Luzernerstr. 44 (☎420 0277; fax 429 8803), rents Renaults for 73SFr per day.

Parking: Lucerne has many expensive parking garages, including **Bahnhof-Parking,** Bahnhofpl. 2, under the train station, and **City Parking,** Zürichstr. 35. Parking garages run 25-50SFr per day.

Bike Rental: At the **train station,** 27SFr per day. Open M-Sa 7am-7:45pm, Su 9:30am-7pm. Also at the **Backpackers** hostel, 7SFr per day.

ORIENTATION AND PRACTICAL INFORMATION

The **Reuss River** flows through the center of Lucerne, feeding into the Vierwaldstättersee (Lake Lucerne) near the Bahhofplatz. The train station, tourist office, and post office line up along Zentralstr. on the bank south of the Reuss, while the streets of the *Altstadt* twist through the northern bank. The city is connected by the ancient **Kapellbrücke,** which spans the Reuss between Bahnhofstr. on the south bank and Rathausquai on the north.

TOURIST SERVICES

Tourist Office: In the train station (☎227 1717; fax 227 1718; luzern@luzern.org, www.luzern.org). Free city guide (with unwieldy map), and hotel reservation service. Ask about the **Visitor's Card,** which, in conjunction with a hotel or hostel stamp, gives discounts at museums, bars, car rental, stores and more. Open May-Oct. M-F 8:30am-7:30pm, Sa-Su 9am-7:30pm; Nov.-May M-F 8:30am-6pm, Sa 9am-6pm, Su 9am-1pm.

Budget Travel: SSR Reisen, Grabenstr. 8 (☎410 8656). ISIC cards, student travel deals, and discount flights. Open M-W and F 10am-6pm, Th 10am-8pm, Sa 10am-1pm.

Bi-Gay-Lesbian Organizations: Homosexualle Arbeitsgruppen Luzern (HALU), (☎360 1460) publishes a monthly calender of events available at the tourist office. HALU runs **Why Not,** a discussion groups for young gays at W 8 and 11:30pm.

Luggage Storage: Downstairs at the station. **Luggage watch** 5SFr per item. Open 6am-8:45pm. **Lockers** 3-5SFr.

Laundromat: Jet Wasch, Bruchstr. 28 (☎240 0151), off Pilatusstr. past Pilatuspl. from the station. Wash and dry 16SFr. Open May-Oct. M-F 8:30am-12:30pm and 2:30-6:30pm, Sa 9am-1pm; Oct.-Feb. M-F 8:30am-12:30pm, Sa 9am-1pm.

Emergency: Police, ☎117. **Fire,** ☎118. **Ambulance,** ☎144. **Medical Emergency,** ☎111. For the **24hr. pharmacy** on duty, dial 248 8117.

FINANCIAL AND COMMUNICATION SERVICES

Currency Exchange: At the station. Open M-F 7:30am-8pm, Sa-Su 7:30am-7pm. **Migros bank,** Seidenhofstr. 6, off Bahnhofstr. Open M-W and F 9am-5:15pm, Th 9am-6:30pm, Sa 8:15am-noon.

American Express: Schweizerhofquai 4, P.O. Box 2067, CH-6002 (☎410 0077). Mail held and checks cashed for members. Travel services open M-F 8:30am-6pm, Sa 8:30am-noon (Sa in Apr.-Oct. only). **Currency exchange** open M-F 8:30am-noon and 1:30-5pm, Sa 8:30am-noon.

Bookstores: Bücher Brocky, Güterstr.1. From the station take a right onto Iselquai, bear left on Werfstr., then right onto Güterstr. This massive warehouse of books only has a few English shelves, but the selection is quirky and the price is right (1SFr for paperbacks). **Raebes,** (☎229 6020). Turn left from station on Zentralstr. and then walk down Frankenstr. Sophisticated selection of English literature, travel books, maps, and **free Internet** access for customers. Open M 1-6:30pm, Tu-F 8am-6:30pm, Sa 8am-4pm. For English magazines, check out the kiosk in the basement of the train station.

Internet Access: C+A Clothing on Hertensteinstr. at the top of the Altstadt has 2 free, though very busy, terminals on its lower floor. 20 min. time limit. (M-W 9am-6:30pm, Th-F 9am-9pm, Sa 8:30am-4pm). **Parterre,** Mythenstr. 7 (☎210 4093), off Neustadtstr. near Bundespl., is a cool bar with a patio and 3 computers (15SFr per hr.).

Post Office: Main branch near the station on the corner of Bahnhofstr. and Bahnhofpl. Address *Poste Restante* to: Postlagernde Briefe, Hauptpost; CH-6000 Luzern 1. Open M-F 7:30am-6:30pm, Sa 8-noon. **Emergency post** at Luzern 2, behind the main station. **Postal Code:** CH-6000.

ACCOMMODATIONS

Relatively inexpensive beds are available only in limited numbers in Lucerne, so call ahead in order to ensure a roof over your head.

Backpackers, Alpenquai 42 (☎360 0420; fax 360 0442). Turn right from the station on Inseliquai, and follow it through the small industrial area along the lake until it turns into Alpenquai; the hostel is on the right (15min.). Brand-new rooms with balconies and lake or mountain views, plus a comfy dining room with fresh flowers and hundreds of travel books and magazines. Lakeside location puts you next to the grassy lake park and just over a small bridge from a sandy beach. The caring hostess puts a world of information at your feet. The store sells "survival kits" of pasta, sauce, and wine for 8SFr, and many residents take advantage of the two kitchens to cook dinner. Sheets 2-3SFr. **Bike rental** 7SFr per day. **Laundry** 8SFr. Tickets sold for cable cars on all the local mountains. Reception 7:30-10am and 4-11pm. No lockout, and you can store bags here on the day you check out. 2-bed dorms 28SFr, 4-bed dorms 22SFr.

Tourist Hotel Luzern, St. Karliquai 12 (☎410 2474; fax 410 8414; info@touristhotel.ch, www.touristhotel.ch). From the station, walk on Bahnhofstr., along the river, cross over the river at Speurbrucke and then make a left onto St. Karliquai–the hotel is right in front of the old city wall. Cheap, clean rooms with views of the river and Mt. Pilatus in the distance. Very close to the center of the Altstadt. Breakfast included. Free luggage storage. **Laundry** 10SFr. **Bike rental** 15SFr per day. **Internet** access 10SFr per hr. Reception 7am-10:30pm. 11-bed dorm with breakfast 30-33SFr. Quads 43SFr per person, students 39SFr; doubles 98SFr, 99SFr. In winter, rooms 10-15SFr less per person. Add 10SFr per person for private shower. AmEx, MC, Visa.

Jugendherberge (HI), Sedelstr. 12 (☎420 8800; fax 420 5616). During the day, take bus #18 (dri.: "Friedntal") to "Jugendherberge." After 7:30pm, take bus #19 to "Rosenberg" and walk in the direction of the bus, but turn right at the fork. This white-concrete building, near the Rotsee, Lucerne's other lake, has a beautiful valley view you'll have to share with up to 19 fellow travelers. Beds have fresh sheets and night lights. Breakfast buffet, lockers, sheets, and shower included. Dinner 11.50SFr. **Laundry** 12SFr. Reception Apr.-Oct. 7-10am and 2pm-midnight; Nov.-Mar. 7-9:30am and 4pm-midnight. Call ahead in summer. In high season (May-Oct) dorms 30.50SFr, in low season 28SFr; doubles 37.50SFr, 35SFr; doubles with shower 43.50SFr, 41SFr. AmEx, DC, MC, Visa.

Hotel Löwengraben, Löwengraben 18 (☎417 1212; fax 417 1211; hotel@lowengraben.ch, www.lowengraben.ch). From the station, cross Seebrücke. Walk to the end of Schwanenpl. and take a left onto Grendelstr. Follow it uphill and turn onto Löwengraben from Falkenpl.; the hotel will be on your right. Until September 1998, Hotel Löwengraben was a prison providing full services to the miscreants of Luzern. In only 7 months the building was converted into a hostel providing full services to the traveler. Downstairs from the cells is a small food counter, a daytime bar with **Internet** access (15SFr per hr.), an outside patio, and a bar that hosts all-night dance parties (for guests only) every Sa during the summer. Sheets included. Dinner 16.50SFr. 8-bed dorm 19.99SFr, 4-bed dorm 27-31SFr, 3-bed dorm 31-35SFr, double with shower 90SFr, 2-person suites 199SFr.

Privatpension Panorama, Kapuzinerweg 9 (☎420 6701; fax 420 6730; www.pensionpanorama.com). Take bus #7 (dir.: Wesemlin) to "Felsberg" and follow the path downhill. For 8SFr, the owner will pick you up at the station. Clean, spacious rooms on a hill with unbeatable sunset views of Mt. Pilatus or the *Altstadt*. Breakfast, **kitchen** facilities, and limited parking included. **Laundry** 5SF. **Internet** access. Ring the bell or yell for reception. Singles 45SFr, doubles 70-90SFr, "family room" for 4 people 140SFr. Apartment for 2 people 100-120SFr. AmEx, MC, Visa.

Hotel Alpha (☎240 4280; fax 240 9131), at the corner of Pilatusstr. and Zähringerstr. From the station, walk 10min. left down Pilatusstr. This enormous *Pension* is in a residential area just outside the city. The airy rooms are spick-and-span and many have balconies. Breakfast included. Reception daily 7:30am-9:30pm; shorter hours in winter. Singles 60SFr; doubles 92SFr, with shower 110-120SFr; triples without shower 123SFr; quads with shower 156SFr. AmEx, MC, Visa.

Camping: Lido, Lidostr. 8 (☎370 2146; fax 370 2145), 30min. from the station on the Lido beach. Cross the Seebrücke and turn right along the quai, or take bus #2 (dir.: Würzenbach) to "Verkehrshaus." Reception daily 8am-6pm. Open Mar. 15-Oct. 6.50SFr; tent 3SFr; car 5SFr. Showers 0.50SFr per 3min.

FOOD

Markets along the river sell inexpensive fresh goods on Saturday and Tuesday mornings, but the restaurants in supermarkets and department stores offer the cheapest sit-down meals. Just up from Migros, Weggisg. and Rosslig., which form one long street together, are lined with good places to catch a quick bite.

Heini Bakery, Falkenpl. (where Weggisg. meets Hertensteinstr., ☎412 2020), is locally famous for the 20 types of flaky-crusted, densely filling tarts cooked each day. Good for meals or desserts, under 5SFr. Open M-W 7am-6:30pm, Th-F 7am-10pm, Sa 9am-6pm.

Pourquoi Pas, Nationalquai (in front of the Musikpavillon), along the far side of the lake from the station. This is "the little crepe stand that could"–thanks to their quality product and loyal customers. Sugar crepes only 4SFr; for 7.50SFr you can put anything you want on it. 10% discount for Backpacker Luceme guests. Open M-F 11:45am-1:30pm, and 5-8pm, Sa-Su 1pm-whenever.

Kam Tong Chinese Take Away, Inseliquai 8 (☎218 5850), turn right in front of the station and then right on Inselquai to reach this dim, red-papered eatery with cheap but tasty Asian fare. Most meals are from 10-15SFr. Soups 5SFr, vegetable fried rice 10SFr. Open M-W 9am-6:30pm, Th-F 9am-9pm, Sa 9am-4pm.

Ciao Pep, Murbacherstr. 4 (☎228 9050). Turn left on Zentralstr. from the station, then right on Murbacherstr. Munch on panini sandwiches (8.50SFr), pizza (from 14SFr), or pasta (from 12SFr) in a garden setting. Open 7am-12:30am.

Cafeteria Emilio, Grendelstr. 10. (☎410 2810), in the *Altstadt* off Schwanenpl. Locals help themselves to the filling yogurt and *muesli* (7.20SFr), while tourists head for the mini-pizza and salad combo (9SFr) or the tortellini (10.80SFr). Open M, W, and F 6:30am-8pm, Th 6:30am-10pm, Sa 7am-6pm, Su 9am-6pm.

Opus, Bahnhofstr. 16 (☎226 4141). The cheapest restaurant along the expensive quais lining the river in the *Altstadt*. The extra francs are justified by the excellent food, service, and views. Veggie and pasta dishes (from 19SFr); small portions of all dishes available (15SFr). Open M-F 8:30am-12:30am, Sa 8am-12:30am, Su 10am-12:30am.

MARKETS

Migros, at the station, has the best hours of any grocery in town. Open M-W and Sa 6:30am-8pm, Th-F 6:30am-9pm, Su 8am-8pm. Also one at Hertensteinstr. 44. Open M-W 8:30am-6:30pm, Th-F 8:30am-9pm, Sa 8am-4pm. Restaurant has the same hours.

Reformhaus Müller, Weinmarkt 1, sells organic foods. Open M-W and F 9am-12:30pm and 1:30-6:30pm, Th 8:30am-12:30pm and 1:30-6:30pm, Sa 8:30am-4pm.

SIGHTS AND MUSEUMS

THE OLD CITY. The *Altstadt* is famous for its frescoed houses and oriel windows, especially those of the buildings on Hirschenpl. To quickly get into the medieval mood, enter the *Altstadt* through the **Kapellbrücke,** a 660-year-old wooden roofed bridge. It was accidentally set on fire by a barge in 1993, but horrified citizens restored it within a few months. Further down the river, the **Spreuerbrücke** gives an idea of what the Kapellbrücke looked like before the fire. Both bridges have painted triangle ceiling supports; those on the Spreuer allow you to confront your mortality in Kaspar Meglinger's eerie *Totentanz* (Dance of Death) paintings.

On the hills above the river, the **Museggmauer** and its towers are all that remain of the ramparts of the medieval city. After all these years, they still define the city skyline, especially when illuminated at night. Walk up the trail on the far side of the wall to reach the stairs up to the towers and path along the wall. Three of the towers, the Schirmerturm, Männliturm, and Zeitturm, have stairs to the top. The **Zeitturm** (clock tower) provides a particularly pleasing panorama of the city. To find the tower, walk along St. Karliquai, turn right (uphill), and follow the brown castle signs. *(Open 8am-7pm.)*

PICASSO MUSEUM. 200 emotionally charged photographs of Picasso on display at the Picasso Museum present a substantial slice of the great artist's life. In the last few years of Picasso's life, close friend David Duncan captured him delicately sucking the last pieces of fish from a skeleton, trying his foot at ballet, and creating from every angle. By the last picture, showing Picasso's mourning widow, you'll be mourning him, too. *(Am Rhyn Haus, Furreng. 21. From Schwanenpl., take Rathausquai to Furrengasse. ☎410 3533. Open Apr.-Oct. 10am-6pm; Nov.-Mar. 11am-1pm and 2-4pm. 6SFr, with guest card 5SFr, students 3SFr.)*

LÖWENDENKMAL AND GLACIER GARDEN. The city mascot is the dying Lion of Lucerne portrayed in the **Löwendenkmal** (Lion Monument) carved out of a cliff on Denkmalstr. by Danish sculptor Bertel Thorvaldsen. The lion casts his pained eyes over a reflecting pool; Mark Twain described it as "the saddest and most moving piece of rock in the world." The 9m monument honors the Swiss Guard who defended Marie Antoinette to the death at the Tuileries in 1798. From the station, cross Seebrücke to Schwanenplatz, follow Schweizerhofquai to the right, and turn left on Denkmalstr. Up the steps from the monument lies the **Glacier Garden,** a lunar landscape of smooth rocks curved and pot-holed into odd almost-sculptures all accompanied by mood music. There is a kitschy **museum** next to it and the oriental *Spiegellabyrinth* (mirror maze). *(Open Apr.-Oct. 9am-6pm; Nov.-Feb. Tu-Su 10am-5pm; Mar. 10am-5pm daily. 8SFr, with visitors card 6.50SFr, students 6SFr.)*

VERKEHRSHAUS DER SCHWEIZ (TRANSPORT MUSEUM). If you can drive, fly, steer, float, or roll it, it's at the Verkehrshaus der Schweiz. Climb into big-rigs and jet planes or go for a ride in virtual reality, but don't miss the museum's real highlight: the trains. Even the children's train that chugs around the floor is an authentic steam engine. The museum also has a planetarium and screens 7 IMAX shows per day. *(Lidostr. 5. Take bus #6, 8, or 24 to "Verkershaus," or walk along the lake for 15min. ☎370 4444. Open Apr.-Oct. 9am-6pm; Nov.-Mar. 10am-5pm. 18SFr, students 16SFr. Imax 14SFr. Both 28SFr, students 24SFr; 33% discount with Eurail or guestcard.)*

WAGNER MUSEUM. The **Richard Wagner Museum,** Wagner's secluded lakeside home, now exhibits original letters, scores, and instruments. Wagner's years in Lucerne, often known as the "Tribschen years" (1866-1872), were marked by an enormous creative output, as well as private happiness—it was here that he wed Cosima von Bülow. *(Wagnerweg. 27. Take bus #6 or 8 to "Wartegg.," or turn right from the station and walk 25min. along the lake. ☎360 2370. Open mid-Mar. to Nov. Tu-Su 10am-noon and 2-5pm. 5SFr, students and guest card holder 4SFr.)*

NEUES KUNSTMUSEUM. The **Neues Kunstmuseum** (Modern Art Museum) is the newest addition to Lucerne's cultural offerings. Housed within the futuristic Lucerne Culture and Conference Center, the museum is mainly home to temporary exhibits. 2000 saw a smorgasbord of aggressively avant-garde creations. *(Europaplatz 1, next to the train station. ☎226 7800. Open Tu and Th-Su 11am-6pm, W 11am-8pm. 10SFr, students and guest card holders 8SFr.)*

OUTDOOR ACTIVITIES

The cheapest option for getting out on the **Vierwaldstättersee** (Lake Lucerne) is to take one of the **ferries** that service the many tiny villages around the lake. Not only can you enjoy the magnificent scenery in a relaxing way, but you can also disembark at any one of the lakeside villages to explore further. Glass-blowing demonstrations lie in wait at **Hergiswil,** while a short but scenic hike lurks at **Bürgenstock,** ex-US president Jimmy Carter's top choice in Swiss resorts. For an easy walk along the lake, get off the ferry at **Weggis.** The length of the journey determines the fare; consult the Lucerne tourist office for specifics on each town. **SGV** boats leave from the piers in front of the train and bus stations (☎367 6767; SwissPass and Eurail valid). Try to catch one of their 5 steam ships whose internal workings are on display in the middle of the ship. The cruises are actually also passenger ferries that stop at all the lakeside towns, but the tourist office and boat company have put together a yellow pamphlet with possible trips that last from 1-6 hours with no change of boats. These boats can also be used to get to the starting points for the ascents of Rigi, Pilatus, and Stanserhorn (see p. 362). Many of the evening trips are on the water for the sunset—find out the sunset time and check the schedule.

For more vigorous exertion, Lucerne's adventure provider **Outventure** (☎611 1441) will meet you at the Lucerne tourist office to take you **paragliding** (170SFr), **canyoning** (105SFr), or **bungee jumping** (100SFr for a 70m cord; 150SFr for a 130m cord). Book in advance.

NIGHTLIFE

Due to noise regulations, the *Altstadt* falls silent after 7pm. Most of the action moves to Haldenstr. and the streets near the station. The closest bar to town on Haldenstr. is the **Hexenkessel,** Haldenstr. 21, which goes for a mock-pagan look. Replete with broomsticks, it boils Lucerne's twenty-somethings in a 2-story cauldron of loud music and spinning DJs. Saturday night is "Heaven's Gate," while the odd Thursday brings live music. (Obligatory beer 7SFr; no cover. ☎410 9244 or 410 9264. Open 9pm-2:30am.) Down the street lies the bright yellow **Kursaal,** Haldenstr. 6 (☎418 5656), with its ritzy casino offering poker, blackjack, and low-stakes gambling to the masses. Farther down Haldenstr. beneath the Carlton Hotel, **Club 57** is the coolest of the local hangouts. During the week, 57 plays hip world music; on weekends, DJs spin.

Three blocks down Pilatusstr. from the station on Winklereidstr. 24, **Pravda,** is *the* dance club for Lucerners (☎210 2244; open M-Th 10pm-2:30am, F-Sa 10pm-4am). **Cucaracha,** Pilatusstr. 15, has a daily happy hour (5-7:30pm) and offers free Tex Mex snacks with your drink (Coronas 7.50SFr; ☎210 5577; open daily 5pm-12:30am). **Uferlos Bar,** Geissensteinringstr. 14 (☎360 3014 or 360 1460), is a popular gay and lesbian hangout. **Schüür** is hidden beside the train tracks so guests can be as loud as they please at the hippest concerts in town. To get to Schüür, Tribschenstr. 1, follow Zentralstr. alongside the train tracks and turn left onto Lagensandbr. The club is on the left side, on the other end of the bridge. Cheap(er) beers cost 4SFr (☎368 1030; open W-Sa 7pm-4am).

FESTIVALS

Lucerne attracts big names for its summer **Blues Balls Festival** (July 21-29, 2001) and fall **Blues Festival** (Nov. 8-11, 2001). In 2000, Natalie Cole and G. Love and Special Sauce performed on consecutive nights of the former festival. Contact the tourist office or visit www.bluesfestival.ch for more information. August 16 to September 15, 2001 will see the return of the **International Festival of Music.** The festival celebrates primarily classical music, but also features contemporary world music. For tickets or further info, contact: Internationale Musikfestwochen Luzern; Postfach/Hirschmattstr. 13; CH-6002 Luzern (☎210 3562; fax 210 7784; tickets 20-220SFr). The **Nationalquai** is the scene for free summertime **Pavillon Musik** concerts, featuring brass and jazz bands playing Hollywood tunes, Gershwin, and Duke Ellington every other night from June to August. There is a movie every night from mid-July to mid-August with **Open Air Kino Luzern,** at the outdoor theatre in the Seepark near Backpackers Luzern (14SFr)—most movies are in English, so check on any poster in town, or at the tourist office, to see what's playing. Every July elite crews from all over the world row their boats to Lucerne for the **Rowing Regattas** on the Rotsee by the hostel. On Saturdays and Tuesdays from 8am to noon, catch the **flea market** (May-Oct.) along Burgerstr. and Reussteg.

DAYTRIPS FROM LUCERNE

Lucerne's most renowned daytrips are excursions to the mountains that constantly haunt the city's skyline. The trips up to each of the three peaks are as memorable as views from the top. Don't expect to get out into true Swiss countryside on these trips—you'll see few cows—but the routes are well touristed for good reason. The trip up to Pilatus is the most exciting, but the views from Rigi are almost as rewarding. The trip to Stans is for those interested in a bit more solitude for a little less money.

MOUNT PILATUS

The most memorable travel option takes the 1½hr. boat ride from Lucerne to Alpnachstad, ascends with the steepest ***cogwheel train*** *in the world (48° gradient), descends by cable car to Krienz, and takes the bus back to Lucerne (entire trip 77.60SFr, with Eurail or SwissPass 40.60SFr). From June 16 to Sept. 9, the Pilatus Railway (☎(041) 329 1111) offers ½-price fares after 4:30pm from Alpnachstad and Krienz on Th-Sa (29SFr for just the railway and cable car). It is slightly cheaper if you ride the cable car both ways. With a little more time and exercise you can cut down on the price by using your feet. Take the train or boat to Hegiswil and a 3hr.* ***hike*** *up the hillside to Fräkmüntegg, a half-way point on the cable car (22SFr, 25% discount for SwissPass and Eurail). While you miss the cog train, the hike offers constant views back to the lake and Lucerne.*

Like a big gnarly apparition, **Mt. Pilatus** bumps and grinds its way 2132m to the top of Lucerne's southern sky. Standing at the top of this solitary geological mess allows for phenomenal views of the Alps to the south. All of the irregularities allow for numerous quick jaunts to the various craggy promontories rising up around the station and restaurant at the top. The trip up the mountain—which, depending on your route, uses 4 different types of transportation— is at least half the fun.

TELL TALES Mt. Pilatus' imposing facade has haunted the minds of locals for centuries, and, in turn, has spawned numerous myths and legends. The most oft-told legend, and source of the mountain's name, says that the infamous Pontius Pilate was buried on the mountain. It was believed that each year on Good Friday, Pilate would emerge from the grave to wash his bloodied hands in the lake below. According to legend, any attempts to challenge Pilatus' dominion over the mountain brought storms of fury, so climbing the mountain was prohibited. In 1585, a priest and a few townsmen decided to test the story by going into the foothills and creating a ruckus. When there was no retribution the spell was declared broken. Since then, there have been numerous Pilate-sightings (very few have been scientifically documented) so go at your own risk.

RIGI KULM

Trips to Rigi begin with a ferry ride to Vitznau and a cogwheel train ride on the mountain railway to the top. Rigi can also be conquered by foot. It takes 5 hours from Vitznau to the top, and 3 hours from Rigi Kaltbad, where the train can take you. Return down on the train, take the cable car from Rigi Kaltbad to Weggis, and return to Lucerne by boat (round-trip 86SFr, with Eurail and SwissPass 42SFr).

Across the sea from Mt. Pilatus soars the **Rigi Kulm,** which has a view of the lake and its magnificent neighbor. Sunrise on the summit is a Lucerne must; sunsets get good reviews, too (see Mark Twain's 1879 travelogue *A Tramp Abroad*). Staying at **Massenlager Rigi Kulm** on the summit makes early morning viewing possible. Part of Hotel Rigi Kulm, this dormitory has 28 simple bunks. (☎(041) 855 0303; rigi@rigi.ch; www.rigi.ch. Reception open daily 8am-10pm. 25SFr.)

STANSERHORN

A regional train departs approximately every hr. from Lucerne for Stans (15-20min., 7:54am-9:55pm, 6.60SFr), and returns once to three times an hour from Stans (5:30am-9:25pm). Once in Stans, it's a 5 min. walk to the 1893 funicular, which, followed by a cable car, will bring you to the mountain's top (44SFr, 22Sfr with SwissPass or Eurail).

The Stanserhorn (1900m), a grassy mountain located in the village of Stans, suffers from a small inferiority complex to the towering Mt. Pilatus. Nonetheless, the Stanserhorn makes for a pleasurable daytrip from Lucerne, especially since its smaller stature keeps it out of the clouds on days that Pilatus is surrounded. Once atop the mountain, you can view Alpine marmots in their natural habitat (a sign warns you not to whistle—it's the danger call of the furry creatures), or take a number of short hikes to the summit (5-30min., depending on the directness of the path). Pack picnic supplies, which will allow you to skip the overpriced restaurant and enjoy a meal above stunning lake and mountain vistas (on a clear day, you can even see Germany's Black Forest). In addition, there are rotating art exhibits in a room adjacent to the restaurant and welcome center.

SCHWYZ ☎041

To get to the Schwyz station, take the 40min. train ride from Lucerne (12.60SFr). To get downtown, take a 5min. bus ride from the station (2.40SFr) to "Schwyz Postplatz."

One of the 3 original cantons, and the namesake of Switzerland, Schwyz is the home of Switzerland's founding documents. These documents, along with a few historical museums that have sprung up around it, make Schwyz a worthwhile daytrip for a history buff. In the center of town is the **Bundesbriefmuseum** (Museum of Swiss Federal Charter), down Bahnhofstr. from Postplatz. The centerpiece here is the original document from 1291 that shaped the 3 original cantons—Uri, Schwyz, and Unterwalden—into an Eternal Alliance (though at the time it was primarily a mutual defense pact against the Hapsburgs). The seal of Schwyz is missing, but other than that the document is in remarkably good condition, as are the numerous sealed documents around it—later treaties that brought more cantons into the pact and letters from foreign monarchs recognizing the union. (☎819 2064. Open May-Oct. Tu-F 9-11:30am and 1:30-5pm, Sa-Su 9am-5pm; Nov.-Apr. Tu-F 9-11:30am and 1:30-5pm, Sa-Su 1:30-5pm. 4SFr, students 2.50SFr.) Next door, above the Postplatz, the **Forum der Schweizer Geschichte** (Forum of Swiss History) is a brand new museum with 3 floors chronicling Swiss living from the 13th to the 18th century with interactive exhibits (☎819 6011; open Tu-Su 10am-5pm; 5SFr, students 3SFr). If you want to see how they were really living, you can check out **Bethlehem House,** Switzerland's oldest wooden house, built in 1287. Bethlehem House shares the same grounds as the **Ital Reding House,** Schwyz's grandest house, which has an ornately carved interior and is adorned with local art (☎811 4505; both open May-Oct. Tu-F 2-5pm, Sa-Su 10am-noon and 2-5pm; 4SFr admission for each, 2.50SFr for students).

There is no full-fledged tourist office in Schwyz, but there is a counter in the post office, which is not, however, in Postplatz. Turn left on Bahnhofstr. (not at the Bahnhof), where the bus lets you off, and then right on Schmiedg. to reach the **post office/tourist office** (open M-F 7:30am-noon and 1:30-6:30pm, Sa 8-11am).

NEAR LUCERNE

ENGELBERG AND MOUNT TITLIS ☎041

Near the small town of **Engelberg,** south of Lucerne, visitors can ride the world's first revolving cable car to the crest of **Mount Titlis** (3020m), the highest outlook-point in central Switzerland. The panoramic ride gives magnificent views of the crevasses below and peaks above. The top is an active glacial outpost, with an observation deck and restaurant, a glacial grotto, free tube rides down an ice slide, and free guided **glacier hikes** from the top station to the peak of the mountain. (3hr. Tu 9am, late June to mid-Oct. ☎638 0000. Reserve at the tourist office.)

Take the train from Lucerne to Engelberg (1hr., 14.80SFr), and the cable car from Engelberg to Titlis (first ascent from Engelberg 8:30am, last ascent from Engelberg 3:40pm, last descent from Titlis 4:50pm; 73SFr, 58.40 with Eurail and Engelberg guest card, 54.80 with SwissPass). Guided tours are available from Lucerne (including round-trip rail and Titlis fares 85SFr, same discounts). The little village of Engelberg itself is no great shakes, but if you want to stay you can stop over at the family-oriented **Jugendherberge Berghaus (HI),** Dorfstr. 80, just a 10-minute walk out of town. Turn left off Bahnhofstr. onto Dorfstr., and keep walking. (☎637 1292. Non-members add 5SFr. Dinner 11.50SFr. Laundry 7SFr for washer, 10SFr for dryer. Breakfast and sheets included. Reception 8-11am and 5-10:30pm. Checkout 9:30am. Dorms 26SFr 1st night, then 23.50SFr; doubles 64SFr, 59SFr.) Engelberg's **tourist office,** Klosterstr. 3, is a left on Bahnhofstr. from the train station, a right onto Dorfstr., and another right onto Klosterstr. (☎639 7777; fax 637 4156; www.engelberg.ch. Open June 19-Oct. 21 M-Sa 8am-6pm, Su 2-7pm; Oct. 22-Dec. 10 M-Sa 8am-6pm; Dec. 11-Apr. 30 daily 8am-6pm; May 1-June 21 M-Sa 8am-6pm.)

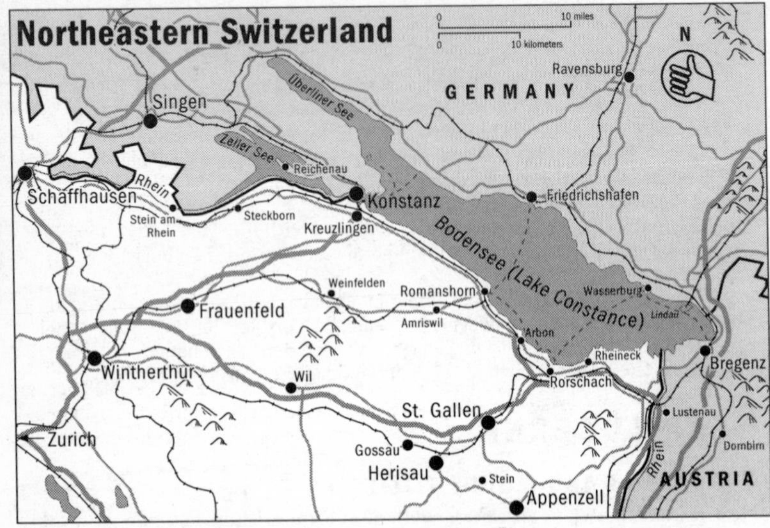

NORTHEASTERN SWITZERLAND

Some of Switzerland's best-preserved towns are found in northeastern Switzerland, which encompasses the cantons of Schaffhausen, St. Gallen, Thurgau, Glarus, and Appenzell. The smaller towns throughout the region are charming: Stein am Rhein has a perfectly intact medieval *Altstadt* (old town) while Appenzell and its surroundings maintain the farmhouses and agriculture lifestyle that made Switzerland. The region is also geographically diverse, from magnificent waterfalls near Schaffhausen to the lofty mountains that surround Appenzell.

HIGHLIGHTS OF NORTHEASTERN SWITZERLAND

St. Gallen's grandiose **Stiftsbibliothek** will knock the socks off even the most Baroque-savvy library lover (p. 371).

Bask in the mist of the **Rheinfalls**, the massive waterfall that Goethe mistook for the source of the ocean (p. 367).

Evade tourist crowds by hiking to the *Wildkirchli*, a 400-year-old chapel built into a cliff face in the mountains around **Appenzell** (p. 374).

SCHAFFHAUSEN ☎052

During WWII, the United States accidentally bombed Schaffhausen due to cartographers' gaffes, making it one of the only Swiss cities to be harmed by the war. In spite of this, Schaffhausen retains an expansive and authentic medieval *Altstadt*, one of the most impressive in all of Switzerland. Gilded bay windows, handmade shopkeepers' signs, and fountains decorate the pedestrian streets and give you a glimpse into Switzerland's past. Schaffhausen's **Munot Fortress,** built in the 1500s, stands tall and valiant above the city. Since no one ever attacked, it proved rather unnecessary, and the citizens apparently used the time spared from military operations to kick back—the local *Falkenbier* is reputedly the best in the canton, and a mug or two of the frothy ferment will put you in an excellent mood to enjoy the ambience and architecture.

GETTING THERE AND AROUND

Schaffhausen is easily accessible by train, bus, and boat. If you're in the mood for exploration, you might consider a **Tageskarte** (27.50SFr), which allows one day of unlimited travel on Bodensee area railways, waterways, and roadways, including those belonging to Schaffhausen, Stein am Rhein, Constance, and St. Gallen. **Trains** arrive in Schaffhausen every hour from **Zurich** (6:57-11:53am; 16.40SFr), **St. Gallen** (8:25am-8:26pm; 29SFr), **Winterthur** (6:11-12:15am; 10SFr), and **Kreuzlingen** (5:52am-8:42pm; 15.40SFr). Numerous **ferries** traverse the Bodensee, departing from Schaffhausen (from Freiepl., below Festung Munot) to **Stein am Rhein** (3 per day, 14.80SFr) and **Konstanz** (4 per day 9:10am-3:35am, 26SFr). **Parking** is available in the parking garage off Rheinstr., in the lots near the cathedral, off Moeratz, and behind the train station.

PRACTICAL INFORMATION

The local **tourist office** looks out onto the lively Fronwagpl. at the head of Vordenstr., to the right. From the train station, head down Schwertstr., the narrow street to the right, and turn right at the fountain in the main square. The office gives city tours in German, French, or English. (☎625 5141; fax 625 5143; info@schaffhausen-tourismus.ch; www.schaffhausen-tourismus.ch. Open May-Oct. M-F 10am-6pm, Sa 10am-4pm, Su 10am-1pm; Nov.-Apr. M-F 9am-12:30pm and 1:30-5pm, Sa 10am-1:30pm. Tours Apr.-Oct. M, W, and F 2:15pm; 1½hr. 10SFr, children 5SFr.) At the station, you can **exchange currency** (M-Sa 7am-7pm, Su 9am-5pm), **rent bikes** (27SFr per day with photo ID, 20SFr with SwissPass; 6SFr extra to return bike at another station), and **store luggage** (5SFr; open M-F 6am-8pm, Sa-Su 8am-8pm). **Lockers** cost 3-5SFr, with 24-hr. access. The **post office** faces the station on Bahnhofstr. (open M-W and F 7:30am-6:30pm, Th 7:30am-9pm, Sa 8am-12:30pm). The **postal code** is CH-8200.

ACCOMMODATIONS AND FOOD

Schaffhausen's **Jugendherberge Belair (HI),** Randenstr. 65, is in the newer (i.e., early 19th-century) section of town. Take bus #6 (dir.: Neuhasen SBB) to "Hallenbad" and find the hostel across the street from the bus stop. Once a villa, the building that now houses the huge hostel is surrounded by shady birch paths and pine-filled glades. Hermann Hesse was frequently a guest of the villa's former owner, and his novel *Rosshalde* is partially set in the house. (☎625 8800; fax 624 5954; schaffhausen@youthhostel.ch. Breakfast, sheets, and showers included. Reception 8-10am and 5:30-10pm. Check-out 9am. Curfew 10:30pm; keys available. Dorms 23SFr, singles 29SFr, doubles 58SFr. Non-members add 5SFr.) For an equally beautiful hostel head to the Rheinfalls (see p. 367). **Camping Rheinwiesen** stands at the edge of the Rhine, 3km from Schaffhausen. Take the train (dir.: Kreuzlingen) to "Langewiesen," where you'll be able to see the campground on the waterfront. (☎659 3300. Open May-Sept.; July-Aug. tents 7.50SFr, adults 6.20SFr, children 3.10SFr.; May-June tents 5.50SFr, adults 4.20SFr, children 2.10SFr.)

The Fronwagpl. comes alive during the day with outdoor cafes, inexpensive food vendors, restaurants, and live entertainment ranging from mimes to fire-breathers. The owner of **Restaurant Thiergarten,** on Münsterplatz across from the Allerheiligen Monastery, adds atmospheric spice to the already tasty menu by serving a different national cuisine each year and decorating to extremes. Past influences include South Africa, the Caribbean, Greece, and Mexico. Bratwurst and *Rösti* for 15SFr are among the permanent Swiss classics. (☎625 3288. Open daily 9am-11pm.) If you're not in the mood to sit around, grab some take-out at **Chinatown,** 36 Vorstadt, a snappy restaurant ideal for those itching to picnic out in the sun, or enjoy the pleasant sidewalk seating (☎624 4677; dishes 14.50SFr and under; open daily 11am-11pm). Schaffhausen's modern **Migros** supermarket, Vorstadt 39, puts up a good medieval front, staking a spot in the Gothic alleys that define Schaffhausen (open M-W and F 8:15am-6:30pm Th 8:15am-8pm, Sa 7:30am-4pm). Stock up on fresh produce at the **farmer's market** at *Johannkirche* (Tu and Sa 7-11am). There's also always **Aperto,** in the train station (open M-Sa 6am-9:30pm, Su 7am-9:30pm), for basic conveniences and foodstuffs.

SIGHTS

Throughout the *Altstadt*, colorful frescoes, fountains, intricate clocks, and woodcarvings transport you into an age of knights, heraldry, and Teutonic bravery. While wandering through the tight streets, keep your eyes trained upwards to see the decorated oriel windows (designed as status symbols) and colorful murals on the medieval buildings. You can review your classical history in the ornate windows on the guild house **Goldener Ochsen,** at the corner of Vorstadt and Löwengässchen, or just enjoy the colorful murals decorating the **Haus zum Ritter,** on Vorderg., which have been called "the most significant Renaissance frescoes north of the Alps."

ALLERHEILIGEN MONASTERY. The medieval wonders continue on the outskirts of the *Altstadt*, in the labyrinthine **Kloster Allerheiligen** (All-Saints Monastery) complex. From the station, take Schwertstr. up to Vorderg., then turn right on Münsterg. The monastery, with its herb garden, enclosed courtyard, and Schiller Bell (the inspiration for Schiller's poem, "Song of the Bell"), is a peaceful refuge from the bustling city. Within the cloister, you'll find the **Museum zum Allerheiligen,** which encompasses a **Natural History Museum** and the **Kunstverein Schaffhausen** (Art Museum). The museum offers an array of exhibits ranging from stuffed boars to modern art. Though most of the displays are not particularly engaging or well-maintained, the museum has an incredible display of Roman artifacts, as well as memorabilia from the 11th-century abbey that stood on the same site, such as a late Gothic refectory and preserved chapels with faded stone tombs, that cannot be depreciated by method of presentation. The highlight is the onyx, a bedazzling hunk of gold, jewels, and a priceless cameo styled in the 1st century AD in Augustan Rome. If you mistakenly believed that Switzerland has always been neutral, check out the military display. In another recess of the museum lie a number of thousand-year-old illuminated manuscripts. *(☎633 0777. Open Tu-Su noon-5pm, Th noon-8pm; 1st Su of each month 11am-5pm. Signs in German only. Free.)*

Attached to the cloister is the **Münsterkirche,** a combination of medieval architecture and 20th-century furnishings, with simple wooden pews set against Cubist stained-glass windows. During the Reformation, Protestants stripped the 11th-century church of ornamentation, leaving the interior cool and white.

HALLEN FÜR NEUE KUNST (HALL FOR MODERN ART). Just across the street from Kloister Allerheiligen, modernity intrudes into Schaffhausen's medieval self-consciousness in the form of the Hallen für Neue Kunst. This old warehouse by the river has been converted into four floors of permanent gallery space for twelve avant-garde artists. Each floor is littered with massive, seemingly indecipherable shapes, colors, and even sounds; the unifying theme is the grand scale on which each piece is executed. *(Baumgartenstr. 23. ☎625 2515. Open May-Oct. Sa 2-5pm, Su 11-5pm; tours Su at 11:30am; 7SFr.)*

MUNOT FORTRESS. Presiding over all this grandeur, old and new, is the 16th-century **Festung Munot,** which offers the most convincing proof of Schaffhausen's medieval past. Reach the fortress by turning right at the head of Schwertstr., then left on Vorderg., continuing all the way up. After climbing the narrow steps leading through the vineyards that carpet the hill from the fortress, you'll enter the cavernous, dimly-lit interior, where skylights cast yellow circles onto the cold, stone floor, conjuring up visions of townsfolk huddling around fires to the thunder of catapults. An observation deck at the top of the tower's steep stone ramps looks out over the sinking wood-shingled roofs that stretch down to the river, the vineyards, and the moat (which has been transformed into an animal husbandry area where deer wander). The vineyards and moat are maintained by a family that lives in the bell tower, continuing the agrarian foundation upon which this erstwhile feudal estate was built. *(Open daily May-Sept. 8am-8pm; Oct.-Apr. 9am-5pm. Free.)*

DAYTRIP FROM SCHAFFHAUSEN

RHEINFALLS

The Rheinfalls are just a 15-minute bus ride from Schaffhausen, in Neuhausen am Rheinfall. Take trolleybus #1, 6, or 9 (dir.: Neuhausen) from the Schaffhausen train station to "Neuhausen Zentrum," then follow signs down the hill to the falls.

The **Rheinfalls** comprise one of Europe's largest sets of waterfalls, though their scope isn't nearly as grand as that designation might lead you to expect. They are, however, majestic enough that Goethe believed them to be the source of the ocean. There are paths all around the falls, or you can take a boat for a closer look from the bottom of the falls. Contact **Werner Mändl** for more information or just look for the boats when you reach the falls. Boats depart every 10 minutes from both the Neuhausen side of the falls (by Schlößli Wörth) and Schloß Laufen. (☎(053) 224 811. May and Sept. 11am-5pm; June-Aug. 10am-6pm; prices from Neuhausen 5.50SFr, children 5-11 3SFr, from Schloß Laufen 6.50SFr, 3.50SFr.) **Rhein Travel,** Schlauchbootfahrten, 8455 Rüdlingen (☎(01) 867 0638), has information about **river rafting.** A bridge over the falls leads to **Schloß Laufen**, from where, for 1SFr, you can follow winding stairs down the steep face of the hill to the foot of the falls.

In the turrets of Schloß Laufen, **Jugendherberge Schloß Laufen am Rheinfalls (HI)** shelters weary backpackers. Take the train to: "Schloß Laufen am Rheinfalls," two stops from Schaffhausen, and then walk up the stairs to the castle and follow the signs for the hostel. From June to October, you can also get to Schloß Laufen by taking PTT bus #S33, which leaves once an hour between 7am-6pm and drops you right at the door of the castle. Simple rooms recall the castle's 15th-century origins and offer splendid views of the Rhine. The hostel fills up quickly; reserve in advance. (☎(052) 659 6152; fax 659 6039. Breakfast included for dorms. Kitchen facilities 2SFr. Reception 8-9:30am and 5-9pm. Dorms 22SFr; quads 29SFr per person. Non-members add 5SFr.) The **Bannerstube** in the castle serves a number of reasonably priced dishes, including delectable salads and the acclaimed *Füürtopf à discretion*, and has a fantastic view of the falls. Soups are 6-8SFr and pasta dishes start at 14SFr. (☎659 6767. Children's menu available. Open daily Apr.-Oct. 11:30am-2pm and 6:30pm-midnight, Oct.-Mar. closed M-Tu.)

STEIN AM RHEIN ☎052

In addition to cobblestone streets and old fountains, the tiny *Altstadt* of Stein am Rhein has more painted surface per cubic meter than any town would know what to do with. Density is what distinguishes Stein am Rhein from other Swiss hamlets, and the small size of the town bespeaks the medieval burghers' efforts to squeeze in as much as possible between the wide river and the immediately adjoining hillside. A port of call for the brightly colored ferries that cruise the lake, Stein am Rhein has nimbly converted its vantage point on the Rhine into an unobtrusive tourist industry, buoyed by the friendliness of all the local proprietors. Unfortunately, Stein am Rhein has sacrificed some of its quiet and charm by allowing cars to course through the *Altstadt*.

YODELING FOREVER Yodeling is usually regarded as part of the picture-book image of Switzerland, alongside holey cheese and numbered bank accounts. For the 100,000+ people who gather every three years at the Federal Yodeling Festival, the traditional Alpine song with alternating high falsetto and low chest notes is more than a cherished tradition; it is a matter of national pride at a time when neutral Switzerland feels increasingly isolated and unloved, its reputation tarnished by allegations of wartime collusion with the Nazis. "We Swiss have had to take a little bit of criticism in the last few years," Swiss Vice President Adolf Ogi said. "But no one has ever criticized us for our yodelers, alphorn blowers and flag swingers," he told a cheering crowd at the 1999 festival in Frauenfeld.

The origins of yodeling are shrouded in antiquity, but its often piercing tones carry long distances and can help lone mountaineers locate each other. In its basic form, "natural yodeling," it has no words and is based on a melody, revolving around six syllables. It has been suggested that yodeling may have started as an imitation of the haunting, echoing sound of the alphorn, another traditional means of communication in the high Alps. The long and somewhat impractical tube-like wooden instrument, up to 13 feet long, has recently enjoyed a revival after coming close to extinction at the beginning of this century. In 2002, the national festival will head to the western city of Fribourg, straddling the language divide between French and German speakers, as wordless yodeling does, according to its enthusiasts. The tradition lives on even among Swiss who have moved away from their home, with participants from as far afield as Canada, New Zealand and South Africa.

TRANSPORT AND PRACTICAL INFORMATION. Trains connect Stein am Rhein to **Schaffhausen** (2 per hr. 5:28am-10:30pm, 6.80SFr), **St. Gallen** (1 per hr. 6:56am-5:56pm, 24SFr), **Winterthur** (1 per hr. 5:07am-11:07pm, 11.80SFr), and **Konstanz** (9.40SFr). **Buses** connect the city to the string of small towns in the area and to Germany. **Boats** depart three times per day (once on Sunday) for **Schaffhausen** (1¼hr., 14.80SFr), **Konstanz** (2½hr., 17.80SFr), and other Bodensee towns, or take a 60-minute cruise on the lake (☎741 2393) for 11SFr (ages 6-16 6SFr).

To reach the city from the station, head straight out of the station onto Bahnhofstr., bear right onto Wagenhauserstr., and left on Charreg., which will take you over a bridge and into the *Rathausplatz* in the center of the *Altstadt*. Rathauspl. becomes Understadt, the town's main drag. **Parking** is available on all streets skirting the Altstadt, and along Hemihoferstr., off Untertor (open 10am-6pm, 1SFr for ½hr.). Stein am Rhein's **tourist office,** Oberstadt. 9, lies on the other side of the *Rathaus* (☎741 2835, fax 741 5146; open M-F 9-11am and 2-5pm). The train station has **currency exchange** and **bike rental** (27SFr per day; open M-F 6:15am-7:35pm, Sa 6:15am-6:35pm, Su 7:15am-7:35pm). There is an **Internet cafe** (which also serves cheap pizza) in **Kiosk Charregass,** Oberstadt 16, a few paces past the tourist office, coming from Rathauspl. (open Tu-Su 10am-11pm; 6SFr for ½hr.). The **post office** is at the train station (open M-F 7:30am-11am and 3-6pm, Sa 8-10:30am). The **postal code** is CH-8260.

ACCOMMODATIONS AND FOOD. The family-oriented **Jugendherberge (HI)** stands at Hemishoferstr. 87. From the train station, take the bus (dir.: Singen) to "Strandbad," and walk straight about 5 min. further. You'll see the flags in front of the hostel across the street. Though the hostel itself is somewhat drab, the staff is helpful and many rooms overlook the Rhine. (☎741 1255; fax 741 5140. Breakfast, sheets, and showers included. Reception 8-9:30am and 5:30-10pm. Curfew 10:30pm; keys available. Open Mar.-Oct. Dorms 23SFr; doubles 29SFr, 3SFr less in the off-season. Non-members add 5SFr.)

Picnickers fill up their baskets at the **Co-op** at the corner of Rathauspl. and Schwarzhorng. (open M-F 8:15am-12:15pm and 2-6:30pm, Sa 8am-4pm). The many outdoor restaurants and cafes around the *Rathausplatz* provide great people-

watching venues. The two young owners of **Restaurant Roten Ochsen,** Rathauspl. 9, are dedicated to preserving the tradition connected with their wooden hall, which has served hungry wanderers for 500 years. Their pride in the establishment is reflected in every mouth-watering 10SFr *Wurst.* (☎741 2328. Open Tu-Sa 10am-11:30pm, Su 10am-6pm.) **The Spaghetteria,** Schifflände 8, sits directly on the Rhine and serves cheap and tasty Italian fare, with pasta dishes from 11SFr. The restaurant also displays the **world's longest piece of spaghetti** at 182.42m. (☎741 2236. Open Mar. 15-Oct. Su-Th 9am-11pm, F-Sa 9am-midnight. Free beer with lunch if you show your *Let's Go.*) **Café "Zur Hoffnung,"** Rathauspl. 21, is chock full of chocolate and luck-bringing Steiner Scherben (☎741 2182; open Tu-Sa 8am-6pm, Su 9am-6pm). For wonderfully smooth, cheap ice cream (1.40SFr per scoop), visit **Il Gelato,** next to the *Rathausplatz* at 12 Understadt (☎741 4748; open Mar.-Oct. daily 10am-9pm).

SIGHTS AND ENTERTAINMENT. Stein am Rhein first came into prominence in the 12th century with the establishment of the **Kloster St. George.** You can reach the Benedictine monastery by heading up Chirchhofplatz from the Rathausplatz. The rooms are wonderfully preserved in their 16th-century state, just as the 5-foot tall monks (judging by the doors) left them, and the cloister exudes a perfect, ascetic peace. Among the ornate wooden engravings, try to find St. George, who slew the dragon and after whom the cloister is named. Less austere than the rest of the monastery is the vibrant *Festsaal*, whose yellow-and-green-tiled floor is off-limits to feet. As there are few lights, try to go when it is bright outside for the best view of the delicate paintings and engravings. (☎741 2142. Open Mar.-Oct. Tu-Su 10am-5pm. 3SFr, students 1.50SFr.) To the right of the monastery, you can admire the exterior of the stately **Rathaus.**

On Untertor, the **Wohnmuseum Lindwurm,** Understadt 18, reconstructs domestic life as it was in the 19th century. This homespun museum is surprisingly large and covers both indoor and outdoor living—live chickens and all. The museum also has information about Stein am Rhein's most dramatic event: the open-air play **"No e Wili,"** which is only performed every 10 years—the next performance is in 2005. (☎741 2512. Open Mar.-Nov., W-M 10am-5pm; 5SFr, 3SFr students.)

A 40-minute hike will take you straight up the mountain to a vantage point from the castle on **Hohenklingen.** To reach this trail, follow Brodlaubeg. out of town until you reach signs that point out the rest of the way. When the trail meets the road near the top, the castle is to the left, with meadows and panoramas to the right.

ST. GALLEN ☎071

Though it lacks the medieval charm of Schaffhausen, St. Gallen's easy access to Zurich, Germany, Austria, the *Bodensee*, and small mountain villages makes it a popular stopover for people moving between these places. The relatively modern *Altstadt* livens up on weekend nights when students from St. Gallen University descend from their hill to party off stress. During the day, St. Gallen has a few cultural gems to share—most notably the venerable grandeur of the *Stiftsbibliothek*, a Baroque library named a World Heritage Treasure by UNESCO.

GETTING THERE AND AROUND

Trains: To: **Zurich** (1hr., 5:10am-10:43pm, 29SFr); **Geneva** (4½hr., 5:10am-8:43pm, 95SFr); **Appenzell** (30min., 5:42am-11:40pm, 1-3 per hr., 10SFr); **Bern** (2½hr., 5:10am-10:43pm, 65SFr); **Lugano** (4hr., 5:10am-8:43pm, 74SFr); and **Munich** (3hr.; 4 per day 8:37am-6:37pm; 63SFr, under 26 49SFr).

Buses: Single fare 2SFr, ages 6-16 1.20SFr, *Tageskarte* (day pass) 7SFr (ages 6-16 5SFr), 6 rides 10SFr. Buy tickets at each stop; multi-fares and *Tageskarten* available at large kiosks or the **VBSG Transit Authority** across from the train station.

Taxis: Sprenger AG, Rohrschacherstr. 281 (☎080 0551 030).

Car Rental: Herold Autovermietung AG, Molkenstr. 7 (☎228 6428; fax 228 6425). 77SFr per day, 195SFr for weekend (3 days).

Parking: Neumarkt Parking Garage, conveniently located near the Neumarkt Supermarket on St. Leonhardstr. 5am-9pm 2SFr per hr.; 9pm-5am 1SFr per hr. Open M-Sa 5am-12:30am. Or park in one of the city's **blue zones** M-F for 5.50SFr per day, free Sa-Su.

PRACTICAL INFORMATION

Tourist Office: Bahnhofpl. 1a (☎227 3737; fax 227 3767; www.st.gallen-bodensee.ch). From the train station, cross the bus stop and pass the fountain on the left; the tourist office is on the right. The staff makes hotel reservations within St. Gallen for free. Maps, brochures, and **city tours** are also available. (Tour June 12-Sept. 28 M, W, and F 2pm. 15SFr, museum admissions and snack included.) Office open M-F 9am-noon and 1-6pm, Sa 9am-noon.

Currency Exchange: At the station. Open M-F 8am-7pm, Sa 8am-5:30pm, Su 1-5:30pm. Also houses **Western Union.**

Luggage Storage: At the train station. Lockers 3-5SFr. Luggage watch 5SFr. Open M-F 7:30am-7:45pm, Sa-Su 9am-noon and 1-6:45pm.

Laundromat: Quick Wash, Rohrschacherstr. 59 (☎245 3173). Take bus #1 to "Stadttheater" and walk for 5min. Wash 6-7.90SFr, dry 1.80-3.80SFr. Open M-Sa 8am-10pm.

Internet Access: Media Lounge, Katerineng. 10 (☎244 3090). With your back to the bus stop at Marktpl., cross at far right into Katerineng. This hip lounge with pop music offers cheap access to your neglected email account. 2SFr minimum; after 10min. 1SFr for 5min., 12SFr for 1hr. Open M-F 9am-9pm, Sa 10am-5pm. For free access, you can trek up to the **St. Gallen University Library,** 50 Dufourstr. (in the middle of campus), where there are four computers in the lobby with access. Take bus #5 to "Universität." Open M-Th 8am-7:45pm, F 8am-6:45pm, Sa 10am-1:45pm.

Post Office: St. Leonhardstr. 45, across the street, to the right of the train station. Open M-W and F 7:30am-6pm, Th 7:30am-8pm, Sa 7:30am-4pm. **Postal Code:** CH-9000.

ACCOMMODATIONS

Jugendherberge St. Gallen (HI), Jüchstr. 25 (☎245 4777; fax 245 4983; stgallen@youthhostel.ch). Right at the train station, you'll find the small Appenzeller/Trogener station with two tracks (#12 and 13). Take the orange train from track #12 (dir.: Trogen) to "Schülerhaus" (trains run once every ½hr., 5:32-11:32am). From the stop, walk uphill on the right, turn left across the train tracks at the sign for the hostel, and walk downhill 2min. Perched on a hill overlooking St. Gallen, this friendly hostel is filled with bright murals and an international student crowd. Though it's a bit of a hike to get here, extra perks include a breakfast room, terrace, barbecue pit, grassy lawn, library, and board games. Fall asleep to the tuneful clanking of Swiss cowbells. Breakfast, shower, and sheets included. Dinner 11.50SFr. Laundry. Parking available. Reception daily 7-10am and 5-10:30pm. Check-out 10am. No lockout. Closed Dec. 17-first week in March. Dorms 24SFr, 6-bed 'family room' with toilet and shower 33SFr per person, singles 58SFr, doubles 66SFr. Non-members add 5SFr.

Hotel Elite, Metzgerg. 9-11 (☎222 1236; fax 222 2177), on the street opposite the bus station. Walk out of the station and bear a diagonal left onto Poststr. Turn left onto Oberer-Graben, and follow it to Marktpl. (on the right). On Marktpl., with your back to the bus station, find Metzgerg. and go straight. This well-scrubbed hotel offers simple, bright rooms with chocolates on the pillows and a convenient location, near the the *Altstadt* and the bus stop at Marktpl. Breakfast included. Doors lock at midnight; ask for keys if you'll be out later. Singles 60-65SFr, with shower 70SFr; doubles (only with shower) 110SFr.

Hotel Weisses Kreuz, Engelg. 9 (☎/fax 223 2843), up the street from the far left of the Marktpl. bus station. Weisses Kreuz sits atop a lively bar run by a cheerful staff. Follow the same directions as to Hotel Elite; Engelg. is one street left from Metzgerg. Scuffed wooden stairs lead up through storage spaces to plain rooms and hall showers in need of some renovation, but beds are clean and the location is great for digging into nightlife in the *Altstadt*. Breakfast and hall showers included. Reception M-Th 6:30am-2pm and 5pm-midnight, F 6:30am-2pm and 5pm-1am, Sa 7:30pm-1am, Su 8am-noon and 6:30-11:30pm. Singles 45SFr; doubles 80SFr, with shower 100SFr.

FOOD

As usual, the cheapest options in town are the markets. There is a **Migros,** St. Leonhardstr., 1 block behind the train station (open M-W and F 8am-6:30pm, Th 8am-9pm, Sa 8am-5pm), with a buffet restaurant in a separate building behind the market, open M-W and F 6:30am-6:30pm, Th 6:30am-9pm, Sa 6:30am-5pm. A **public market,** on Marktpl., bustles with fresh produce, bread, and meat daily 7am-7pm.

Pizzeria Testarossa, Metzgerg. 20 (☎222 0330). A short distance up the street directly across from the Marktpl. bus stop. Secluded on a rooftop patio, choose from delicious vegetarian pizzas (from 13SFR) and "make-your-own-pizza" options. Open Tu-F 10am-midnight, Sa-Su 10am-2pm and 5pm-midnight. AmEx, MC, Visa.

Restaurant Spitalkeller, Spitalg. 10 (☎222 5091). From Marktpl., head down Marktg., left on Spitalg. This smoky, wooden-raftered joint with simple hand-engraved tables is a rustic oasis in the sea of urbanity that surrounds it. Try some hearty Alpine food suited for mountain folks, such as Appenzeller macaroni with sausage or Ticino *Rösti* (with tomatoes and cheese) 12.50SFr. Daily *Menüs* from 10SFr. Open Tu-Sa 8am-midnight.

Christina's, Weberg. 9 (☎223 8808). Wooden tables and colorful walls define this casually chic spot. Veggie dishes from 18.50SFr. Fish and meat dishes from 19SFr. Open Tu-Th 9:30am-11:30pm, F-Sa 9:30am-12:30am, Su 3-11:30pm. AmEx, MC, Visa.

Restaurant Scheitlinsbüchel, Scheitlinsbüchelweg 10 (☎244 6821), stands in a meadow on a hill overlooking the bustle of the city. Running past the house are numerous trails that will take you up to an abbey and into the hills to commune with the cows. Instead of turning left to the youth hostel from the main road, turn right into a small parking lot; as the small road enters the woods, turn left onto the uphill trail; when you reach the road again, go left to reach the farmhouse restaurant where traditional Swiss *Rösti* (from 14.50 SFr) is served on an open patio. (Open Tu-Su 9am-10pm).

SIGHTS

Aside from the aptly named Museumstraße where St. Gallen's four museums reside, St. Gallen's main attractions are centered around the magnificent *Stiftsbibliothek.* From the far left of the station, walk up Bahnhofstr. to Marktpl., then left on Marktg. to reach the abbey.

STIFTSBIBLIOTHEK. Anyone who loves books will marvel at St. Gallen's main attraction, the Stiftsbibliothek, library of the Benedictine abbey at St. Gallen. You'll glide in on huge gray fuzzy slippers (the library provides them and requires visitors to wear them over shoes to protect the beautiful floors), to a chorus of oohs and aahs at the library's lavishly carved and polished exotic wood shelves, filled with rows of gilt-spined books, hundreds of years old. The library maintains a collection of 140,000 volumes and 2000 manuscripts, 500 of which date from before 1200 AD, including 3rd- and 5th-century snippets from Virgil and early Bibles. Although the appearance of the resident death-blackened mummy might indicate otherwise, the *Stiftsbibliothek* is a living, lending library serving scholars from around the globe. Umberto Eco was seen sniffing around here to get inspiration for *The Name of the Rose*, his medieval murder mystery exploring the power of knowledge. *(☎227 3415. Open Apr.-Oct. M-Sa 9am-noon and 1:30-5pm, Su 10am-noon and 1:30-4pm. Open Nov.-Mar. M-Sa 9am-noon and 1:30-4pm. Tours (in German only): Apr., May, and Oct. daily at 2pm, June and Sept. at 10:30am and 2pm, July-Aug. at 10:30am and 2 and 3pm. If you want a tour in English, you must go through the tourist office. 7SFr, students 5SFr.)*

Other, less impressive, attractions of the abbey include the **Kathedrale St. Gallen,** a part of the abbey founded in the 8th century and renovated in the mid-18th. The cathedral has enormous windows that cast light on the golden screen spanning its interior. *(☎227 3388. Open daily 7am-6pm except during Mass.)* The bright abbey courtyard is ideal for a picnic or sunbath. On the far side of the abbey from the library sits the **Evangelical Church of St. Lawrence,** founded in the 9th century. Its small interior (compared to the grand cathedral) showcases castle-like organ pipes and Easter egg wall patterns, while the geometric, blue ceiling calls to mind a starry night. *(Open M-F 9:30-11:30am and 2-4pm.)*

MUSEUMSTRAßE. Two buildings, side by side on this street hold the bulk of St. Gallen's museum-worthy relics. The four-room **Kunstmuseum** *(☎242 0670)* has a small but impressive collection that juxtaposes modern and traditional art. Housed in the same building, the equally minute **Natural History Museum** *(☎242 0670)* rotates various exhibits of Mother Nature's creations, such as the wolf, arranged in thoughtful, interpretative installations. St. Gallen's enormous, slightly disorganized **Historisches Museum** *(☎ 242 0642)* investigates traditional Swiss culture and other native cultures of the world. The local half of the museum displays linen processing, ancient kitchens, a random barber shop, and spiky weapons a tad more formidable than the modern Swiss army knife. The **Ethnology Collection** *(☎242 0643)* provides a tour of various native cultures, carefully avoiding over-interpretation and allowing authentic artifacts to speak for themselves. *(Museumstr. 32-50. From Marktpl., with your back to the bus stop, walk right on Bohl to get to Museumstrasse. All museums open Tu-Sa 10am-noon and 2-5pm, Su 10am-5pm. 10SFr, students 4SFr, one ticket grants admission to all four museums.)*

OTHER SIGHTS. For a nice walk and view of the St. Gallen valley (and perhaps a glimpse of a few endangered species), visit the **Peter and Paul Wildpark,** on Rosenberg in Rotmonten. Take bus #5 (dir.: Rotmonten) to "Sonne" and then walk uphill for about ten minutes. There is a well-tended trail leading through the park, ensuring that you don't miss the ibex, which have returned from near extinction. *(☎222 6792 or 241 5113. Open 24hr. Free.)* For a tamer excursion, explore the campus of the **St. Gallen University.** Take bus #5 (dir.: Rotmonten) to "Universität." The huge park donated to the city in 1963 provides a fantastic view of the city and the Bodensee.

ENTERTAINMENT AND NIGHTLIFE

St. Gallen's *Altstadt* resonates with techno beats and the heavy clink of beer mugs. Cafes and bars in Marktpl. are popular but money-hungry. Head instead for the streets radiating out from Marktpl., which feature cheaper, hole-in-the-wall bars and their tattooed, chained, and bejewelled clientele. Clubs tend to be clustered together, particularly around Goliathg. and Brühlg. Dance clubs aren't good places to drink, as beers are always expensive there.

Filou, Goliathg. 27. (☎245 2125). Follow Goliathg. from Marktpl. to the end, then curve around 200 feet to the right. This smoky bar pumps 80s rock and cheap beer for a twenty-something crowd. Beer guzzlers overflow into the camp-like picnic tables outside. Good luck finding space to dance on the weekend. Open M-Sa 5pm-midnight.

Birreria, Brühlg. 45 (☎223 2533). Over 150 types of beer let you take a barley trip around the globe without moving your lazy gut. Take them away or drink them at the bar. Open M 11am-midnight, Tu-Th 9am-midnight, F-Sa 9am-1:30am.

Ozon, Goliathg. 28 (☎244 8124). Non-stop chrome and mirrors lend the illusion of size to this compact club. If the flashing lights and smoke don't blind you, the prices will (beer from 9SFr). The music selection changes each night, with hip-hop and soul during the week and dance music from the 70s and 80s on the weekend. Cover usually 10SFr. Open Su and Tu-Th 10pm-2am, F-Sa 10pm-3am.

Trichsli Dancing, Brühlg. 18 (☎226 0900). Dance-floor action is projected onto a field of screens. This club features local bands, karaoke, and other theme nights (foxtrot, anyone?). Things gets hopping late at night, so make this your last stop. Su-W no cover, Th-Sa 7-17SFr. Open July-Aug. Th-Tu 10pm-5:30am; Sept.-June 9pm to whenever.

On a more cultured note, the **Stadttheater,** Museumstr. 1 (☎242 0666), housed in a fancy Art Nouveau building, hosts over 200 concerts and dramatic works by renowned artists and musicians year-round. There are several **movie theaters** at Marktpl., the largest being the **Scala Kinocenter and Bar** (☎228 0860) on the Marktplatz, with 5 screens. Every year in late July and early August, the **Open-Air Kino** takes over (www.open-air-kino.ch), screening mostly American films.

For real party animals, St. Gallen's celebration of music and debauchery takes over the fields surrounding the town at the end of June. The **Open Air St. Gallen Music Festival** (see Festival Fever, p. 300) features over 20 live bands. Past headliners have included Metallica, Garbage, Red Hot Chili Peppers, Cypress Hill, the legendary B.B. King, and the Godfather of Soul, James Brown. You must buy a ticket for all 3 days. Tickets run 144SFr, but housing is included if you bring a tent and camp out (showers and toilets available). Otherwise, stay in St. Gallen and take the free shuttle bus from the train station to the concert grounds. It will be coming to town from June 29-July 1, 2001. (☎222 2121; www.openairsg.ch. Box office address: Open Air St. Gallen Festival Boutique, Bahnhofstr. 6, CH-9000, St. Gallen.)

APPENZELL ☎071

Though the smallest canton in Switzerland, Appenzell is world-renowned for its *Appenzeller Käse* (cheese) and its highly conservative people; women weren't allowed to vote until 1991, and the people maintain the traditional Swiss agrarian lifestyle—favorite vocations in the region are still herding animals and hiking. The canton is dotted with tiny villages, but Appenzell town is the regional gathering place for cantonal meetings and various agricultural shows. Outside of the twisting streets and painted wooden barns of Appenzell, people are spread out all over the surrounding countryside, making Appenzell a region best explored on foot. Over the centuries, local herdsmen have developed an extensive and densely concentrated network of trails in the hills and mountains for shepherding their various flocks. These paths are still used for the same purpose; on the trails you will frequently pass herders dressed in traditional garb. The *Gasthäuser* (guesthouses) liberally sprinkled along the trails provide a night's rest and a luxurious respite from Alpine hikes.

TRANSPORT AND PRACTICAL INFORMATION. The rattling but prompt **Appenzellerbahn** chugs between Appenzell and **St. Gallen** twice an hour from 6am-midnight (1hr., 10SFr). From St. Gallen and **Herisau** (an easier connection), there is a regular train to **Zurich** (1hr.). The train from St. Gallen continues on from Appenzell to its last stop in **Wasserauen,** a tiny hamlet that serves as a gateway to the Alpenteil valley, and most of the hiking described below (20min.; 2.40SFr extra). The Appenzell **tourist office,** Hauptg. 4, is next to the *Rathaus*. (☎788 9641; fax 788 9649; infotourismus@ai.ch; www.myappenzellerland.ch. Open May-Oct. M-F 9am-noon and 1:30-6pm, Sa-Su 10am-noon and 2-5pm; Nov.-Apr. M-F 9am-noon and 2-5pm, Sa 2-5pm.) From the train station, walk straight ahead down Bahnhofstr., bearing right as the road curves and intersects Hauptg. The tourist office is to the left of the church. The office makes hotel reservations, sells detailed hiking maps, and gives specific dates for all of Appenzell's farm festivals. The tourist office arranges a free tour of the Appenzeller Alpenbitter factory, which is responsible for production of the region's unique and delicious alcoholic drink (depart from Weissbadstr. 27 on Wednesdays at 10am from mid-June to mid-Oct). The tourist office also has information about **Herr Fässler,** a friendly Swiss farmer and cheesemaker in Grosshütter who loves talking about cheese (mid-June to mid-Sept). For all tourist office-sponsored events, register the day before by 5pm. The **post office** is across the street from the train station (open M-F 7:30am-noon and 1:30-6pm, Sa 8am-noon). The **postal code** is CH-9050.

ACCOMMODATIONS AND FOOD. The ever-present aroma of Appenzeller cheese lingers around **Gasthaus Hof,** on Landsgemeindeplatz in the center of town, a bustling family-run restaurant that provides guest rooms in a separate house. (☎787 2210; fax 787 5883; hotel_hof@hotmail.com. Breakfast included. All private rooms have TVs. Check-in 11am-midnight. Restaurant open 8am-11pm. Dorms 28SFr, lockers 5SFr deposit; singles 65SFr, 95SFr with shower; doubles with shower 130SFr. AmEx, DC, MC, Visa. Reserve one week in advance for private rooms from Aug.-mid-Oct.) Picturesque lodgings await at **Haus Lydia,** Eggerstrandenstr. 53. A staff member will pick you up at the train station if you call ahead. Otherwise, walk 20 minutes from the station on Bahnhofstr. and turn right on Gringelstr., left on Weissbadstr., right on Gaiserstr., and right onto Eggerstrandenstr. Run by a friendly, English-speaking family, Haus Lydia provides large rooms with great pastoral views and a kitchen for guest use. All rooms have private toilets, showers, and TV. When the weather's good, the sons of the owners provide musical entertainment. (☎787 4233; fax 367 2170; haus-lydia@bluewin.ch; www.haus-lydia.ch. Breakfast included. Reserve 2 weeks in advance. Singles 35-40SFr; doubles 75-80SFr.) If you plan on hiking, the **Gasthöfe** (guesthouses) that line the trail are comfortable overnight stops (see Hiking below).

You can get the energy needed for hiking at **Restaurant Traube,** Marktg. 7, near the Landsgemeindeplatz, a classy establishment that serves up Appenzeller specialties by candlelight. (☎787 1407. Meals 9-19SFr; Appenzeller beers 3.50SFr; Open Mar.-Jan. Tu-Su 9am-midnight.) For groceries, try the **Co-op** on Zielstr. To get there, take a right out of the tourist office and turn right at Landsgemeindeplatz onto Zielstr. (open M-Th 8am-6:30pm, F 8am-8pm, Sa 8am-4pm).

SIGHTS. Appenzell's main tourist attration is the **Rathaus,** which houses the museum, town hall, cantonal library, and tourist office. The Großratssaal, with its intricately carved wooden walls and 16th-century frescoes, is particularly remarkable. Inside the *Rathaus* and the adjoining Haus Buherre Hanisefs, the **Museum Appenzell,** Hauptg. 4, chronicles local culture in 6 floors of displays in the wooden-raftered house. A video on lace-making, shown in English and German, is surprisingly captivating, and exposes the realities of idealized traditional Swiss life. (☎788 9631. Open Apr.-Oct. daily 10am-noon and 2-5pm; Nov.-Mar. Tu-Su 2-4pm. 5SFr, students 3SFr.) Next door, the stately **Pfarrkirche St. Mauritius** shows off its Rococo stained-glass windows, gold-filigreed altars, and a magnificent golden chandelier (open daily 9am-7pm).

HIKES IN THE APPENZELL REGION

Deep in the heart of the Alpstein, Appenzell offers great hiking without the temperature extremes of Zermatt or the Ticino region. Ask at the tourist office for *Wandervorschläge: Appenzellerland*, which has a detailed map with all rest areas, or buy a more comprehensive topographical map at a bookstore. Hiking options range from easy walks through the green pastures to strenuous overnight treks. The first hikes listed leave from Appenzell proper and tend to be easier. The second group are more strenuous and rewarding and leave from Wasserauen.

HIKING FROM THE TOWN

Gonterbad (2hr.). An easy and relaxing walk begins in the nearby town of Gonten (10min. by train from Appenzell). Stroll barefoot along a special trail over the meadows to Gonterbad (45min.), where you can rest and wash your feet (towels 2SFr) in the garden of the Bad Gonton hotel and restaurant before heading back to Appenzell (45min.).

Kapellenweg Hike (5hr. round trip). For a moderately difficult hike from Appenzell, try the Kapellenweg, which provides an up-close-and-personal look at local rural life. Cross under the train tracks, take a left, and take a right at the major intersection to get to the beginning of the trail; from there, brown "Kapellenweg" signs point the way. For the first 45min., the trail is flat and winds amongst local farms with requisite tractors, chickens, silos, and farmers hoeing their crops. The rolling green hills dotted with traditional

Appenzeller houses seem to stretch on forever toward the horizon. Don't be surprised when the trail randomly veers off from the paved road at times, leading you through sheep and cow pastures. (Be prepared to hop several wooden fences and shimmy under some barbed wire enclosures.) The trail splits in several places, but all paths eventually lead to the Kapelle Maria (1½hr.) and the larger and more ornate Ahornkapelle (2½hr.). The easiest way to get there is by simply following the paved road the whole way, a route that will take you past a series of small paintings depicting Christ's crucifixion and resurrection. For a more challenging version of the hike (sans paintings, but with chapels), follow the "Kapellenweg" signs that lead uphill into the surrounding woods. Take either trail back to Appenzell.

HIKING FROM WASSERAUEN

For more difficult hikes, the best place to begin is tiny Wasserauen, the last stop on the Appenzeller Bahn (10min. from Appenzell). From there, you can enter the mountains in several ways. The best way to experience the area is to hike between

Though the rewards are great, hiking around Appenzell can be physically strenuous, as the trails wind steeply up and down these mountains. The upper regions of this area tend to stay snow-covered late in the year and some parts are covered year-round. Use caution: do not hike into snowy areas when there is low visibility. It is safest to hike in pairs or groups. If you hike alone, always make sure to let someone know where you're going and when you're planning on coming back. See Wilderness Safety, p. 29 for more information.

the many guesthouses. These guesthouses typically have a restaurant and dorm rooms consisting of mattresses laid side by side on the floor. The first hikes listed leave from the top of **Ebenalp Cable Car,** across the street from the small train station in Wasserauen, which gets you right into the mountains (cable car runs daily from 7:40am-7pm; 22SFr round-trip, 17SFr one-way up, 13SFr down; students and SwissPass or Eurail holders 12SFr round-trip, 9SFr or 6.50SFr one-way). The **Berggasthaus Ebenalp,** 5min. uphill from the top of the cable car, is a good base from which to explore the mountains, with more amenities than other guest houses. (☎799 1194. Breakfast included. Showers 4SFr. Open May-Nov. and winter weekends. Reception 7am-8pm daily. Reserve 2-3 months in advance for Saturday night stays. Dorms 27SFr, sleepsack 5SFr. Singles and doubles with sinks 47SFr per person. AmEx, DC, MC, Visa.) The last two hikes can be done without cable cars.

Wasserauen to Wildkirchli (½hr.). A quick and popular 30min. hike leads down from the Ebenalp (top station) through caves to the **Wildkirchli,** a 400-year-old chapel built into the cliff face and manned until recently by a hermit priest. Just beyond Wildkirchli lies **Berggasthaus Äscher.** At 150 years old, Äscher is the oldest *Gasthaus* in the region. Tucked into the sheer cliff face, one interior wall is actually the rocky mountain slope. (☎799 1142; fax 799 1856; www.aescher-ai.ch. Breakfast included. No showers. Open May-Nov. Dorms 25SFr.)

Ebenalp to Schäfler (1hr.). This steep trail connects the Berggasthaus Ebenalp with its uphill neighbor, the **Berggästhaus Schäfler** (follow the signs to "Schäfler"). The trail begins with a long, gradual ascent up hundreds of wood-and-stone steps cut into the mountain. It descends a bit to the farmhouse Alp Chlus and switchbacks up the steep slope through cow pastures to the Berggästhaus Schäfler. The friendly Dobler family runs this rustic mountain hut perched atop the crest of the ridge. (☎799 1144; www.schaefler.ch. Breakfast included. No showers or running water, but private rooms have porcelain basins and pitchers filled with rainwater. Reception 24hr. Open mid-May to mid-Oct. Reserve up to one month in advance for weekend stays. Dorms 27SFr, one single 40SFr, doubles 80SFr, one quad 33SFr per person. Visa.)

Schäfler to Messmer (1½hr.). This exceedingly steep and rickety downhill trail leads from Berggasthaus Schäfler to **Berggasthhaus Messer.** A couple of sections of the trail have a metal cable to hold onto for balance, but this trail still should not be attempted after rain or snow, since the rocks can get slippery. From Schäfler, follow the signs to "Messmer," which will lead you along a path called the Höheweg for about 30min. The trail then turns left and descends even more steeply, providing a view of the deep blue-green Seealpsee below. A steep uphill climb through cow pastures (10min.) leads to the final destination; the braying of livestock and clanging of cowbells will let you know when you're getting close. (☎799 1255; winter ☎799 1077; www.mesmer.ai. Breakfast included. No showers or running water, but there is a well outside. Reception 24hr. Open July-Oct. Reserve 1-2 months ahead for weekend stays. Dorms 24SFr, 17SFr children under 17.)

Wasserauen to Seealpsee (1hr.) For a more strenuous entry into the mountains from Wasserauen, hike uphill to the Alpine lake **Seealpsee.** Turn left out of the train station and follow the road until it forks. The trail begins at the left fork (just past the Alpenrose). Yellow signs marked *Seealpsee* point out the trail as it rises steeply first through spruce forests lined with waterfalls, and then through high alpine meadows used for cattle grazing (evidenced by the inescapable clanking cow bells). At the top, the trail passes a few farmhouses and ends at **Berggasthaus Seealpsee,** the second of two guesthouses on the trail. The wonderful Dörig-Klossner family, who have run the guesthouse for generations, knows every detail about the surrounding country. Its pristine location near the peaceful waters of the Seealpsee make it a perfect base from which to ascend the surrounding peaks. It's a good place to stop in for advice or for a meal—try the homemade spinach *Spaetzli.* (☎799 1140; fax 799 1820; berggasthaus@seealpsee.ch; www.seealp.ch. Breakfast included. Showers 2SFr. Reception 7:30am-midnight. Reserve 1-2 months in advance for weekend stays. Open Apr.-Nov. Dorms 25SFr, doubles 90SFr. MC, Visa.)

Seealpsee to Säntis (4hr.) The climb to **Säntis** (2503m), the highest mountain in the region, is a good day hike from *Seealpsee.* From *Seealpsee,* hike to **Meglisalp** (1hr.), a cozy cluster of half a dozen farmhouses tucked beneath the peak. Among the farmhouses is **Gasthof Meglisalp,** a great place to stay for a night with the cows and the people who tend them. A local farmer calls out a prayer with a wooden megaphone every night for the neighbors and their cattle, an old Appenzeller tradition. (☎/fax 799 1128; info@meglisalp.ch; www.meglisalp.ch. Breakfast included. Open May-Nov. Reception open 24hr. Reserve 1-2 weeks ahead Sept.-Oct. Dorms 28SFr, singles 48SFr, doubles 96SFr.) To get to Säntis from Meglisalp, head either to *Rotsteinpass* (more difficult) or *Wagenlücke* (easier), and then up to Säntis (both trips 3hrs.). Two guesthouses sit on top of Säntis. The older and more personal house is **Gasthaus Säntis,** which provides a good night's rest before you hike back down. (☎799 1160, winter ☎799 1411. Breakfast included. Dorms 35SFr, singles 54SFr.) There are numerous routes from Säntis back to Wasserauen; the road-weary can take the cable car down from the town of **Schwägalp,** a neighboring town to Appenzell (20-30SFr round-trip; 10-20SFr one-way).

GRAUBÜNDEN

The largest, least populous, and most alpine of the Swiss cantons, Graubünden is made up of remote valleys and snow-clad peaks that are bound to bring out the wild-hearted, lusting-for-life yodeler in everyone. Deep, rugged gorges, forests of larch and fir, and eddying rivers imbue the region with a wildness seldom found in ultra-civilized Switzerland. The area is also a microcosm of Swiss cultural heterogeneity—from valley to valley the language slips from German to Romansh to Italian, with a wide range of dialects in between. Though only 1-2% of the country (and 26% percent of the canton) converses in the ancient Romansh tongue, the language is carefully preserved in schools and books—especially hymnals—and is recognized as an official language, on par with *Schwyzertüütsch* (Swiss-German), Italian, and French.

Graubünden was put on the map in 1864 through the efforts of St. Moritz hotel pioneer Johannes Badrutt. The innkeeper made four British summer visitors an offer they couldn't refuse: if they came in winter and didn't like it, he would pay their travel costs. If they liked it, he'd let them stay as long as they wanted, *for free.* Alas, that was the last of cheap housing in St. Moritz and Davos—the two big resorts—and the little towns in their vicinity. There is, however, more to

Graubünden than the glamorous ski resorts of the Upper Engadine, as travelers willing to go a little farther afield discover. The Swiss National Park in the Lower Engadine is the most tightly protected Alpine landscape in Europe, and one of the most quiet places to hike in Switzerland. Many communities in the area of the park, such as Zuoz, and Scuol are as unspoiled as the landscape.

! Plan your trip to Graubunden carefully. In ski season you probably won't be able to get a room if you don't call ahead. There are no rooms available in May and June when the whole valley shuts down for vacation.

Unfortunately, travel is not cheap in Graubünden. It costs far more to go from Chur to St. Moritz than from Chur to Zurich. If you're planning on moving around much within Graubünden, invest in the **Graubünden Total Regional Pass,** which allows 3, 5,7, or 10 days of free travel in a 10-day period and a 50% discount on other days (140SFr, 190SFr, 240SFr, and 290SFr, respectively). The 10-day pass also grants an eleventh free bonus day. The Regional Pass can only be issued in Switzerland from May to October. It is issued by the **Rhätische Bahn (Viafer Retica** in Romansh), Graubünden's own train company, and is good for trains, buses, and cable cars in the region (SwissPass and Eurail are also valid).

HIGHLIGHTS OF GRAUBÜNDEN

Ascend Munt la Schera's panoramic pedestal in the **Swiss National Park** (see p. 390).

Delve into the psychological underworld of Expressionist Ernst Kirchner at his eponymous museum in **Davos** (see p. 385).

Ski and snowboard for cheap in secluded and spectacular **Arosa** (see p. 381).

Windsurf **Silvaplana's** shimmering lake under high-pressure Alpine winds (see p. 400).

CHUR ☎081

Chur (pop. 32,000) is the capital of Graubünden and, at 5000 years old, probably Switzerland's oldest settlement. Its museums and hip restaurants give the town—situated in the most rural and wild canton—an unexpected cultural and artsy edge. Chur seems to be where all of the canton's outcasts and creative folk congregate. The many sidewalk restaurants and benches in the newer parts of the city near the train station tend to be full most of the day with people who move to the trendy bars at night. For a break from the activity take a walk in Chur's quiet *Altstadt,* whose centerpiece is a cavernous 12th-century cathedral.

TRANSPORT

Chur is the transportation hub for Graubünden. **Trains** connect Chur to: **Zurich** (1½hr., every hr. 4:50am-10:16pm, 38SFr); **Basel** (2¾hr., every hr. 4:50am-10:16pm, 62SFr); **Disentis** (for the **Furka-Oberalp line,** 1¼hr., every hr. 5:47am-10:10pm, 26SFr); **Arosa** (1hr., every hr. 5:35am-11pm, 11.80SFr); **St. Gallen** (1½hr., every hr. 4:50am-10:16pm, 34SFr); and **St. Moritz** (2hr., every hr. 5:10am-10:52pm, 41SFr). Postal buses run to Ticino through **Bellinzona** (2½hr., 5 per day, 84SFr). The train station has **currency exchange, luggage storage** (5SFr), and **bike rental** (26SFr per day, 21SFr per half day at baggage check; open 6am-8pm), and **lockers** (2SFr).

PRACTICAL INFORMATION

Most directions given for Chur are from Postpl., two blocks up Bahnhofstr. from the station. To get to Chur's **tourist office,** Grabenstr. 5, from Postpl., turn left on Grabenstr. The office finds rooms for free. (☎252 1818; fax 252 9076. Open M 1:30-6pm, Tu-F 8:30am-noon and 1:30-6pm, Sa 9am-noon.) Graubünden's **regional tourist office,** Alexanderstr. 24, is located in Chur, and stocks brochures for every city in the canton. From the station, go down Bahnhofstr. and turn left on Alexanderstr. (☎254 2424; fax 254 2400; contact@graubuenden.ch; www.graubuenden.ch. Open M-F 8am-noon and 1:30-5:30pm.)

F. Schuler, Gäuggelistr. 11 has a few **English books** (☎252 1160; open M-F 8am-6pm, Sa-Su 8am-7pm). **The Street Café,** Grabenstr. 47 has **Internet** access for 15SFr per hour (☎253 7914; open 9am-midnight). Slightly cheaper Internet access is a 10-minute walk from town at **Rampa Computers Internet Cafe,** Tittwiesenstr. 60. Walk through the tunnel under the train station, turn right, make a hard left onto Daleurstr., then a quick left onto Tittwiesenstr. (☎284 8928. Open M-F 8am-noon and 1:30-6:30pm. 5SFr for 20min., 12SFr for 1hr.) Do your **laundry** at **Maltesen's Wash Self-Service,** Malteserg. 1 for 9SFr (open M-Sa 9am-midnight, Su noon-midnight). In an **emergency,** dial 117. The **post office** is just left of the train station (open M-F 7:30am-noon and 1:30-6:30pm, Sa 8-noon). Chur's **postal code** is CH-7000.

ACCOMMODATIONS

No luxurious budget accommodations await in Chur; the lack of a youth hostel is sorely felt. The nearest hostel is in **Arosa,** (see p. 381) and there is a nice hotel even closer in **Bad Ragaz,** (see p. 380). There are a few, overpriced and under-cleaned beds in Chur such as those at **Hotel Schweizerhaus,** Kasernenstr. 10. From the Postpl., turn right on Grabenstr. and follow as it becomes Engadinestr. and crosses the bridge; turn right over the bridge, and once you have passed every nudey-bar in Chur, the street turns into Kasernenstr. Iron-spring cots in miniature, poorly-ventilated rooms cost 35SFr per person. (☎252 1096; fax 252 2731. Breakfast included. Reception open 7am-midnight.) The high altitude **Hotel Rosenhügel,** Malixerstr. 32, has scuffed-up rooms but an affable staff. Over the aforementioned bridge, climb Malixerstr. to the hotel on your right (15min. from station). (☎/fax 252 2388. Breakfast and parking included. Reception 8am-midnight. Singles 55SFr; doubles 50SFr per person, with shower 55SFr per person. AmEx, DC, MC, Visa.) **Camp Auchur,** Felsensustr. 61, is a green and grassy campsite on the Rhine. Take bus #2 to "Obere Au" past the sports complex; it's on the left, on the gravel path. Equipped with kiosks and restaurant. (☎284 2283. Electricity 3.30SFr. Showers 0.50SFr. 7.20SFr, tents 6.20-12.50SFr.)

FOOD AND NIGHTLIFE

Chur has a surprising number of trendy eating establishments.

Restaurante Controverse, Steinbruchstr. 2 (☎252 9944), reached by turning left on Grabenstr., which turns into Steinbruchstr., tries very hard to live up to its name with an Art Nouveau decor combined with Louis XIV drapes, black coffee tables, neon lights, and lip-smacking good food. Spaghetti is 10-20SFr and wines 4-8SFr. Open M-Sa 11am-midnight, Su 6-11pm. Closed July 15-Aug. 13.

Valentino's Grill, Untereg. 5 (☎252 7322), is the best budget option. Turn right on Grabenstr. from Postpl., then left through the arches to reach Unterg; continue straight and turn right at the Street Castle sign. Kebabs 7.90-8.90SFr. Falafel with veggies 7SFr. Beer from 3.50SFr. Open every day from 11:30am-1:45pm, in the afternoon on M 5-10pm, Tu-Th 5-11:30pm, F 5pm-midnight, Sa noon-midnight.

Han Kung China Restaurant, Rabeng. 6 (☎252 2458). Follow Poststr. from Postpl., and turn left at St. Martin's Church; in Haus Pestalozza. Although the regular menu is expensive, the filling 3-course lunch specials are 14.50SFr. Open Tu-F 11:45am-2pm.

Restaurant Falken, St. Martinspl. 9 (☎252 2248), is around the corner from the China Restaurant, and has organic, veggie *Menüs* (15.50SFr). Open M-Sa 9am-midnight.

Manor, on Bahnhofstr., has six floors of shopping, including a market with fresh, inexpensive, and tasty breads and sandwiches on the first floor. Open M-Th 8:30am-6:30pm, F 8:30am-9pm, Sa 8am-5pm.

Street Café, Grabenstr. 47 (☎253 7914), is perfect for any drinking needs. Classical statues peer down from the mirrored, red-draped walls providing intimate drinking enclaves within the larger bar; beers start at 3.50SFr. **Internet** access is 15SFr per hour. Open daily 9am-midnight. The **Street Castle** upstairs is a *Ritterstil* (knight-style) chamber where wine flows from the decanter and cask (from 4SFr; cover F-Sa in winter; open July-Apr. Tu-Sa 5pm-midnight; May-June Tu-Sa 7pm-midnight).

SIGHTS

Chur's sights are all within walking distance of the town's center. The highlight is the cavernous 12th-century Romanesque **Dom** (cathedral) at the top of the old town, which displays 8 altarpieces in addition to the **Hochaltar,** a flamboyant 15th-century masterpiece of gold and wood. The crypts, where the Capuchin martyr St. Fidelis is buried, also house the **Dom-Museum,** replete with relics. (☎252 9250. Open Tu-Sa 10am-noon and 2-4pm.) Downhill, the **Martinskirche** counters the cathedral's dusky, lurking presence with understated simplicity: the church's sole decorations are 3 stained-glass windows by Augusto Giacometti. The eerie panels depict the birth of an oddly beefy Christ. Clad in blood-red instead of her usual blue, Mary stares with wide eyes beside her thoroughly befuddled husband.

Chur's **Bündner Kunstmuseum,** Bahnhofstr. 35, at the corner of Bahnhofstr. and Grabenstr., blazes with the art of the 3 Giacomettis: Giovanni, Alberto, and Augusto. Works by Swiss artists Angelika Kauffman and Ferdinand Hodler occupy the ground floor. (☎257 2868. Open Tu-W and F-Su 10am-noon and 2-5pm, Th 10am-noon and 2-8pm. 10SFr, students 7SFr, children under 16 free.) The **Retic Museum,** Quaderstr. 15, houses a collection of tapestries, coins, and archaeological trivia that document the origin of "Rhaetia" and its development into the current Swiss canton of Graubünden. (☎257 2888. Open Tu-Su 10am-noon and 2-5pm. 5SFr, students 2SFr, seniors and groups 3SFr.)

NEAR CHUR

BAD RAGAZ ☎081

A massage at Bad Ragaz's thermal baths may relax your weary muscles, but it will certainly put stress on your wallet. Luckily, a stroll down the wide, tree-lined streets that meander from Bad Ragaz's traffic-free *Bahnhofplatz* may be (almost) as soothing. Bad Ragaz is famous as the home of Heidi, and has thus dubbed itself "Heidiland." Short hikes from the top of mountains serviced by expensive cable cars allow you to explore the area immortalized by Johanna Spyri's beloved tale. A 2-hr. pass to the **Tamina 'Therma** (thermal baths) grants you access to the town spa's 3 pools, waterfalls, watery lounges and grottoes (☎303 2747; open M-Su 7:30am-9pm; 17SFr, solarium costs extra). The **cable car** from Bad Ragaz to Paradiel (26SFr) will take you to the starting point of a 1-hour round-trip **hike** to **Heidi's house.** (☎330 1912. Open Mar.-Nov. 10am-5pm. 5SFr, children 2SFr.)

Bad Ragaz is accessible by train from **St. Gallen** (1¼hr., 27SFr) and **Chur** (15min., 7.40SFr). To reach Bad Ragaz's **tourist office,** Maienfelderstr. 5, turn left on Maienfeldstr. from Bahnhofstr. (☎302 1061; fax 302 6290; info@badragaz-tourismus.ch; www.badragaz-tourismus.ch. Open M-F 9am-6pm, Sa 9am-noon and 1-4pm.) **Currency exchange,** and **bike rental** (27SFr per day) are available inside the train station. For an affordable breath of class and genuine comfort, stay at **Hotel Bergadler,** Bahnhofstr. 29. The grandmotherly owner has made sure that nothing in her house is mass-produced, from the crocheted table covers to the kitschy paintings adorning the walls to the great breakfast served to guests. (☎302 1813, fax 302 4445. Reception open 9am-9pm. Closed Feb. Singles 42.40SFr, with shower 62.40SFr; doubles 84.80, 124.80SFr. MC, Visa.)

AROSA

☎081

The secluded town of Arosa—reached only by a spectacularly scenic 1-hour train ride from Chur—climbs the hillside opposite a panoramic snow-covered mountainscape. Thanks to the "discovery" of the area's stimulating climate in 1888, Arosa has matured from a simple farming village to a full-service tourist depot, with great skiing in winter and hiking in summer. The majority of tourists are down-to-earth German-speaking folk, however, which allows Arosa to avoid the glitz that clings to resorts over the mountain in the Engadine Valley. Its countless peaks, including the 2653m Weisshorn, have been transformed by 15 ski lifts into a skiing paradise that rivals any in Graubünden. The company that owns these lifts has recently established large, well-equipped dormitories that rent cheap, comfortable rooms complete with ski passes, making the area perfect for young budget-conscious skiers and snowboarders. Fortunately for the avid summer hiker, developed ski trails dominate only one side of the valley. On the other side, hiking trails stretch into infinite isolated valleys.

TRANSPORT AND PRACTICAL INFORMATION

Arosa is accessible by **train** only by way of a scenic route from **Chur** (1hr., every hr., 11.80SFr). A **free shuttle bus** (every hr. in summer, every 20min. in winter) transports visitors between the hottest spots in town, including the ski lifts. It also covers the 10-minute walk from the train station to the tourist office (get off at "Casino"). To walk from the train station, turn right out of the station, then right again on Poststr. The **tourist office** arranges hiking trips and ski lessons and makes free hotel reservations. (☎378 7020; fax 378 7021; arosa@arosa.ch; www.arosa.ch. Open Dec. 7-Apr. 13 M-F 9am-6pm, Sa 9am-5:30pm, Su 4-6:30pm; Apr. 14-Dec. 6 M-F 8am-noon and 2-6pm, Sa 9am-1pm; June 29-Aug. 17 also open Sa 2-4pm.) **Parking** is free in summer at the **Parking Garage Obersee,** 2SFr per hour in winter. Beware—a strict traffic ban has been imposed from midnight to 6am every night. The **train station** provides **currency exchange** (M-Sa 6am-9pm, Su 6:30am-9pm), **lockers** (2SFr), and **bike rental** (27SFr per day, 21SFr per half day). In an **emergency,** dial 117. The **post office** offers free **Internet** access and is in Arosa's main square, to the right of the train station (open M-F 7:45am-noon and 1:45-6:30pm, Sa 8-noon). The **postal code** is CH-7050.

ACCOMMODATIONS

Most lodgings in Arosa are near the tourist office. Arriving in town without reservations is a bad idea; reserve well in advance for prime ski-season.

Arosa Bergbahnen, the ski-lift company, runs two dorms that are particularly useful during the winter (to contact both: ☎378 8423; fax 378 8443; flori@arosabergbahnen.ch; www.arosabergbahnen.ch). Rooms come with a ski-lift ticket package.

Haus Florentium is the centerpiece of their development. This enormous former convent, buried in the woods at the top of the town, has been converted to a 150-bed party house complete with large lounging rooms, balconies, and an old chapel-turned-disco. To reach the Haus, follow the cobblestone path down the hill from the tourist office, turn right at the road at the top, left at the gravel path for Pension Suveran, then right at the path in front of the pension. Breakfast included. Dinner 15SFr. Parking 5SFr per day. Dec.-Apr. 1-night stay, 2-day ski pass 150SFr, under 19 138.50SFr; 6-night stay, 7-day ski pass 511SFr, under 19 480SFr. July-Aug., no packages, 36SFr per night, under 19 30SFr.

Haus Bellaval is smaller, but more centrally located. Right above the train station, Belleval offers basic dorms and not much else. Open all year. Breakfast 10SFr. In winter (with lift pass only) 1-night stay, 2-day ski pass 139.50SFr, under 19 128SFr; 6-night stay, 7-day pass 422.50SFr, under 19 392SFr. In summer (with lift pass for two operating hiking lifts) 1-night stay, 2-day pass 53SFr, under 19 40SFr.

Jugendherberge (HI), Seewaldstr. (☎/fax 377 1397; fax 377 1621; jugiarosa@spin.ch), has a friendly, multilingual staff. Go past the tourist office and bear left down the hill (you'll see a sign). It is probably a better choice during the summer, when lifts are not necessary for hiking access (it is also closer to the bottom of the valley where there are more hiking trails). Each dorm has a balcony overlooking either the *Untersee* or the rugged Engadine slopes. Be sure to stock up on 0.50SFr coins for the shower. Sheets and hearty breakfast included. Bag lunch 8.50SFr; dinner 12SFr. Reception 7-10am and 5-10pm. No lockout. Curfew 10pm; key available. Open mid-June to mid-Oct. and mid-Dec. to mid-Apr. Dorms 27SFr; doubles 64SFr.

Pension Suveran (☎377 1969; fax 377 1975) is the quiet, homey, wood-paneled chalet you came to Switzerland to find. Follow directions to Haus Florentium above. Breakfast included. Dinner 15SFr. Closed in Nov. In summer, singles 47SFr, doubles 84SFr. In winter, 58SFr, 106SFr. Add 10SFr per person in winter for stays of less than 3 nights.

Camping Arosa (☎377 1745; fax 377 3005), downhill from the HI hostel, is open year-round in a valley with a brook. Showers (0.50SFr) and cooking facilities. 7.30-8.30SFr per person, children ages 6-12 4SFr; tents 4.50SFr; check-in 4:30-5:30pm.

Mountain Huts: There are a number of huts in the area that are open during both summer and winter seasons. The **Ramozhütte** (SAC; ☎/fax 252 4820) is a 2½-3hr. hike up an isolated valley south of Arosa (24SFr per person, 16SFr SAC members, kitchen facilities available). The **Naturfreundehaus Medergen** (☎377 5215 or (079) 664 8290) has foam mattresses, a kitchen and solar-powered lighting (June-Oct. 40SFr per person, 35SFr youth ages 17-18; Dec.-Apr. 45SFr per person, 45SFr youth; must reserve in advance). It is a 2hr. steep uphill hike from the town of Litzirüti, which is 1hr. downhill by foot (northeast) from Arosa.

FOOD

The best budget eatery in Arosa is **Orelli's Restaurant,** Poststr., down the hill from the tourist office. Hikers young and old chomp happily in this family restaurant decorated with Mickey Mouse and stained glass. Thriftmeisters can eat soup and 4 slices of bread for only 4.80SFr while gazing at the panoramic view. A special vegetarian *Menü* (15-16SFr), salad buffet (8-12SFr), and warm entrees (7.50-17SFr) round out your options. (☎377 1208. Open 7:30am-9pm. Closed May and Nov. MC, Visa.) You'll want to save a few francs for dessert at **Café-Confiserie Kaiser** (☎377 3454), on Poststr. around the downhill bend from Orelli's. This cozy cafe concocts killer confections (meringues 7SFr). The *Menüs* are small but tasty (spaghetti 11SFr, grilled Fleischkäse with Rösti 11SFr). Get groceries at the **Co-op,** before the tourist office on Poststr. (open M-F 8am-12:30pm and 2-6:30pm, Sa 8am-4pm), or **Denner Superdiscount** near the train station (open M-F 8am-12:15pm and 2:30-6:30pm, Sa 8am-12:15pm and 1:15-4pm).

OUTDOOR ACTIVITIES AND ENTERTAINMENT

SKIING. If you're not staying in a dorm with a package ski deal, you can buy separate passes for the 15 **ski lifts and cableways** that hoist skiers to the 70km network of slopes in the **Arosa-Tschuggen ski area.** Ticket offices in Arosa love making passes (all-day passes, morning passes, afternoon passes, 1½-day passes, "choose-your-day" passes, etc. 50SFr per day; 256SFr for 1 week; 385SFr for 2. AmEx, DC, MC, Visa). The smaller Tschuggen-sector day pass is 30SFr. Children under 15 ski for half-price; ages 16-19 and seniors get a 15% discount.

HIKING. When the snow melts, spring uncovers over 200km of flower-covered hiking paths. An **Alpine guide** leads 7- and 9-hour hikes at beginning, intermediate, and advanced levels for only 10-12SFr. (Late June to mid-Oct. Tu-Th. Contact the tourist office for details.) Though not necessary for access to good hiking, two cable cars operate in summer. The **Weisserhornbahn cable car,** above the train station, whisks travelers to the top of the Weisserhorn (every 20min. 24SFr, round-trip 30SFr; 30% off with SwissPass). From the 2653m summit, you can gaze upon all of the Engadine. At the other end of town (accessible by bus) is the **Hörnli-**

LUGE MUCH? Before the advent of spandex uni-suits and titanium, flying down mountains was a very simple affair. As early as 1883, the natives of Arosa found their sleds missing and the hills outside the town sprinkled with the English who came to the town for convalescence. These dashing chaps officially brought the sport of tobogganing to Switzerland in 1883 when they started the Davos Tobogganing Club and inaugurated the famed Cresta Run. Among the many innovations tested on the Arosa hills were iron runners and the head-first plunge technique. A quote from *The Bystander* in 1905 perhaps summed it up best: "tobogganing itself is absurd. It glories in being absurd."

Express (same prices as Weisserhornbahn). A 1½-hour hike follows the ridge between lifts; longer hikes wind into the valleys opposite the town. Most hikes that do not involve cable cars start from the Untersee (at the very end of the street that the hostel is on). A number of hiking maps are available from the Arosa tourist office. The "Arosa und Umgebung" map (10SFr) comes with a list of suggested trails and lengths. Also available at the tourist office is the trail guide booklet "Arosa-Chur-Bündner Herrschaft," published by Kümmerly and Frei.

Alteiner Wasserfällen Hike (2hr.). This hike of easy-to-medium difficulty begins at the Untersee. The trail starts out flat, winding in and out of the Hintern Wald and through fields of wildflowers, before crossing back and forth over a rushing stream several times. At the end of a moderately steep uphill climb, the trail splits, leading to the more impressive Grosser Wasserfall or the Kleiner Wasserfall. Head back along the same path to Arosa. To lengthen the hike, make the steep uphill climb along the trail from the waterfalls to the Atteinsee (5hr. round-trip). This trail also continues on to the other side of the ridge, and to Davos.

Chur hike (5hr.). This difficult hike begins in front of the train station. The trail leads first along the Eichhörnliweg (Squirrel Walk) past Villa Sonnegg to Maran (1hr.) and then continues to Chur, where the train runs back to Arosa.

OTHER ACTIVITIES. For the more sedentary, the Untersee's **free beach** welcomes swimmers and sunbathers, or rent a pedal boat (12SFr per hr., 9SFr per half hr.). The **International Jazz Festival** in late July grants free admission to various local venues. The festival features New Orleans jazz played by American, Swiss, Australian, and English bands. Previous performers include Tuba Fats and Jambalaya. The **Humorfestival** revs up in mid-December with artists from all over the world putting up comedy shows, and skits (tickets 30SFr; available at the tourist office).

DAVOS

☎081

Davos (pop. 12,000) sprawls along the valley floor under 7 mountains laced densely with the wires of chair-lifts and cable cars. Because of its sprawling nature, Davos is not a particularly easy place to get around without a car. This expansive development is a result of Davos' emergence as a health resort and finely tuned ski center that challenges St. Moritz as the resort capital of Graubünden. The influx of tourists in recent decades has given Davos a very impersonal feel, but the thrill of carving your turns down the famed run from Weissfluhgipfel to Kublis (a 2000m vertical drop) may make up for that.

GETTING THERE AND AROUND

Davos is accessible by **train** from **Chur** via **Landquart** (1½hr., every hr. 5:12am-9:25pm, 27SFr) or **Klosters** (8.60SFr) on the Rhätische Bahn lines. The town is divided into two areas, **Davos-Dorf** and **Davos-Platz,** each with its own train station and linked by the long **Promenade.** Davos-Platz is the site of the tourist office, main post office, and most other places of interest to budget travelers. Davos-Dorf is closer to the quiet *Davosersee.* **Buses** (2.50SFr, SwissPass valid) run between the

2 train stations and stop near major hotels and the hostel on the *Davosersee*. For travelers with cars, **parking lots** line the Promenade and Talstr. but be aware that the Promenade traffic is one-way heading west (parking generally 1SFr per hr., free at *Kongresszentrum*). Rent **bikes** at the Davos-Dorf station (27SFr per day).

PRACTICAL INFORMATION

The high-tech main **tourist office,** Promenade 67, in Davos-Platz, caters mostly to those staying in starred hotels. Walk up the hill across the street and to the right of the Davos-Platz train station and then right along the Promenade for 5 minutes. The tourist office is on the left. A smaller **branch office** is across from the Davos-Dorf train station. (☎415 2121; fax 415 2100; davos@davos.ch; www.davos.ch. Both offices open M-F 8:30am-6pm, Sa 8am-5pm; phone lines open 8am-7pm daily.) The train stations **exchange currency, store luggage** (5SFr; Davos-Platz open M-Sa 4:50am-9pm, Su 5:50am-9pm; Davos-Dorf open daily 6:50am-8pm), and rent **lockers** (2SFr). There is **Internet** access at **Expert Roro,** in Davos-Dorf, Promenade 123 (☎420 1111; 5SFr per 20min., 12SFr per hr.; open M 2-6:30pm, Tu-F 8:30am-noon and 2-6:30pm, Sa 8:30am-noon and 2-5pm; AmEx, MC, Visa). Dial 111 for **emergency.** The main **post office** is in Davos-Platz at Promenade 43 (open M-F 7:45am-6pm, Sa 8am-noon). The **postal code** is CH-7270.

ACCOMMODATIONS

In the summer, or for a more relaxing hostel atmosphere, head to Klosters (see p. 386). Wherever you stay, ask for the Davos **visitor's card,** which grants unlimited travel on the city's buses and discounts on attractions.

Jacobshorn ski mountain. The folks here have made their youth-oriented mountain accessible to budget travelers by opening 3 dorm houses for winter thrill-seekers that are sold as a package with their ski passes (passes good only for Jacobshorn mountain; for all 3 houses ☎414 9020, fax 414 9102; hotels@jakobshorn.ch; www.fun-mountain.ch; all 3 open Nov.-May; all credit cards accepted). All 3 houses have essentially the same furnishings: plain white rooms and down quilts to keep you warm.

Snowboarder's Palace, Oberestr. 45-47. Located right above the Davos-Platz tourist office, the Palace has the most authentic ski-lodge appearance, complete with wooden balconies. Breakfast included. Reception open M-F 9-10am and 5-7pm, Sa-Su 8:30-11am and 4:30-8pm. 1-night, 2-day ski pass 110SFr; 6-night, 7-day ski pass 480SFr.

Guest House Bolgenhof, Brämabüelstr. Bland but the closest to town, right beneath the Davos-Platz train station. Breakfast and dinner included. 1-night, 2-day ski-pass 120SFr; 6-night, 7-day ski-pass 540SFr.

Bolgenschanze, Skistr. 1. The most hopping house, conveniently located over the bar where much of the après-ski debauchery occurs. Breakfast and dinner included; must be over 18. 1-night. 2-day ski-pass 130SFr; 6-night, 7-day ski pass 600SFr.

Hotel Montana, Bahnhofstr. Dorf 2 (☎420 1880; fax 420 1881) is for more reclusive types, and in the summer when the big dorms are closed. Just to the left of the Davos-Dorf station. The rooms have peeling paint and stained carpets, but all are equipped with TV and shower or bath. Breakfast 10SFr. Reception open daily 8am-8pm. In summer, 40SFr per person; in winter, 60SFr.

Camping Färich (☎416 1043) in Davos-Dorf is a 4-star facility relatively close to the ski lifts and attractions of the town. Take bus #1 (dir.: Pischa) to "Stilli." 12-22SFr per person, children half-price; tents 6SFr. Open May 18-Sept. 29.

FOOD

Haven't had your *Rösti* fix for the day yet? Visit **Röstizzeria,** in Davos-Dorf, Promenade 128, and satisfy your craving for as little as 14.50SFr in a dining room decorated with carved wood and Japanese fans. There's also pizza from 11SFr. (☎416 3323. Open 6-11pm; AmEx, MC, Visa.) Grab a Bud and a bar stool, American style, at **Café Carlos,** Promenade 58, fittingly in a mall opposite the tourist office in Davos-Platz. This trendy restaurant offers American standards (burgers and sandwiches), and almost everything is under 20SFr. A pianist from Dallas provides live music nightly after 7pm on the leopard-print grand piano. (☎413 1722. Open Tu-Sa 10am-3am. AmEx, MC, Visa.) A **Migros** is located on the Promenade in both Davos-Dorf (open M-F 8:30am-12:30pm and 1:30-6:30pm, Sa 8am-5pm) and Davos-Platz (open M-Th 8:30am-6:30pm, F 8:30am-8pm, Sa 8:30am-5pm). An enormous brand-new **Co-op** is across from the train station (open M-Th 8am-6:30pm, F 8:30am-8pm, Sa 8am-5pm; restaurant open M-Th 8am-6:30pm, F 8am-8pm, Sa 8am-5pm, Su 10am-6pm).

SIGHTS AND OUTDOOR ACTIVITIES

Aside from the skiing, hiking, and museum below, Davos has Europe's largest natural **ice rink** (☎415 3600; 22,000m²), located between Platz and Dorf, which has space for figure skating, ice dancing, hockey, speed skating, and curling (open only in winter; admission 5SFr; skate rental 5.50SFr).

KIRCHNER MUSEUM. The frosted glass structure opposite the Hotel Belvedere on the Promenade, between Dorf and Platz. The museum houses an extensive collection of Ernst Ludwig Kirchner's artwork. This avatar of 20th-century German Expressionism lived in Davos for nearly 20 years before he died here, and is buried in the Davos cemetery. The museum's talented curators oversee an ever-changing exhibition that places Kirchner's work alongside the work of related artists. (☎413 2202. Open Dec. 25-Easter and July 15-Sept. 30 daily 10am-6pm; off season Tu-Su 2-6pm. 8SFr, students and children under 16 5SFr.)

SKIING. Davos provides direct access to 3 mountains—the Parsenn, Jakobshorn, and Schatzalp—and 5 **skiing areas,** covering every degree of difficulty. **Parsenn,** with its long runs and fearsome vertical drops, is the mountain around which Davos built its reputation. Unfortunately, Parsenn's fame has brought the hordes of tourists which can create long lines up to 2 hours long for the main lift. Passes to Parsenn also allow access to 3 other mountains (day pass 54SFr). **Jacobshorn** has found a niche with the younger crowd, especially since the opening of a snowboarding "fun-park" with 2 half pipes. To accommodate younger skiers on tight budgets, combination ski pass and lodging deals (see p. 381) are available (day pass alone 50SFr). The smallest mountain is **Schatzalp** (day pass 26SFr). The **regional ski pass** covers all 7 mountains in the Davos-Klosters area, including unlimited travel on most transport facilities, and doesn't cost much more than individual mountain tickets (2 days 116SFr, 1 week 268SFr). Information and maps are available at the tourist office. In addition to downhill runs, Davos boasts 75km of **cross-country trails** throughout the valley, including a night-lit trail. **The Swiss Ski School of Davos,** Promenade 157 (☎416 2454; fax 416 5951; ssd@bluewin.ch; www.ssd.ch), offers lessons starting at 35SFr for a half-day downhill group lesson and at 55SFr for a half-day group snowboard lesson.

HIKING. One main ski lift on each mountain is open in summer, and many of the area's trails depend on these expensive lifts to bring hikers out of the densely inhabited valley.

Panoramaweg (2hr.). A relatively flat trail that follows the contours of the broad nude hills above town, it offers views of the valley and the southern Swiss Alps. The hike begins from either the top of the Gotschnabahn (from Klosters) or from the "Panoramaweg" stop on the Parsennbahn (which leaves from near the Dorf train station), and traverses the distance in between. There is another cable car in the middle that allows you to shorten the trip (36SFr round-trip, SwissPass, 50% reduction). Other trails leave from the middle stops of the Parsennbahn.

Davos-Platz to Monstein, (5hr.). A more isolated and difficult hike into an adjoining valley that requires no cable car. Take bus #8 from Davos-Platz to Sertig-Dörfli where the hike begins. From Sertig-Dörfli follow signs to "Fenezfurgga," which will take you up past waterfalls and through a valley that divides the Hoch Duncan and the Alpihorn. A wall of cold stone does a good job of helping you feel isolated from the resort world beyond. The trek ends in Monstein, where buses connect to Glaris and then Davos.

KLOSTERS

☎081

Across the Gotschna and Parsenn mountains lies Davos's sister ski resort, Klosters. Though Klosters is but 10 minutes from Davos by train, it is a world removed in atmosphere. While Davos makes an extra effort to be cosmospolitan, Klosters retains much of its rural alpine charm, from the friendly locals to the traditional Engadine-style chalets with their asymmetric roofs. If you don't want the bustle of Davos, peaceful Klosters offers access to the same outdoor activities; most ski packages include mountains from both towns, and Klosters' main ski lift takes you to a mountain pass where you can ski down to either town.

TRANSPORT AND PRACTICAL INFORMATION. Klosters-Platz and Klosters-Dorf are connected to Chur through **Landquart** (1hr., every hr. 5:21am-9:29pm, 19SFr) and **St. Moritz** (2hr., every hr. 5:12am-9:25pm, 34SFr). The same line connects Klosters and **Davos** (30min., every 30min. 5:35am-11:30pm, 8.60SFr). Local buses run between Dorf and Platz and the major ski lifts (1-6 stops 1SFr, 7-10 2SFr, more than 10 3SFr; free with guest card). Like Davos, Klosters is divided into **Klosters-Platz** and **Klosters-Dorf,** connected by a 5-minute bus ride or a 3-minute train ride; most activity occurs in Platz. There are tourist offices in both Platz and Dorf, but the **main tourist office** is in Klosters-Platz. From the train station turn right, turn right again at the Co-op, and cross the street to the building with the "i." The friendly staff can help locate lodgings, suggest hikes, and **exchange currency.** (☎410 2020; fax 410 2010; info@klosters.ch; www.klosters.ch. Open May-Nov. M-F 8:30am-noon and 2-6pm, Sa 8:30am-noon and 2-4pm; Dec.-April M-Sa 8:30am-noon and 2:30-6:30pm, Su 9-11:30am and 3:30-6:30pm.) The Klosters-Platz **train station** provides **currency exchange** (open 6am-8:30pm), **lockers** (2SFr), and **luggage storage** (open 6am-8pm; 5SFr) and **rents scooters** (19SFr per day). Rent **bikes** at **Andrist Sport** on Gotschnastr. (☎410 2080. 38SFr per day; 130SFr for 7 days; open 8am-noon and 2-6:30pm; closed W afternoons; Sa 2-4pm.) There is a **library** with English books on the first floor of the old city hall (Jeuchenhuus) across from the Protestant church. The **post office** is right from the station (open M-F 7:30am-noon and 1:45-6:15pm; Sa 8:30am-noon). The **postal code** is 7250.

ACCOMMODATIONS AND FOOD. **Jugendherberge Soldanella (HI),** Talstr. 73, is run by a friendly and knowledgeable family. Head right from the Klosters-Platz train station, bear left at the rotary, turn right on Talstr., and hike 10 minutes uphill. This massive, renovated chalet with wood paneling, a comfortable reading room, and a flagstone terrace treats guests to a view of the Madrisa and distant glaciers. (☎422 1316; fax 422 5209; klosters@youthhostel.ch; www.youthhostel.ch/klosters. Sheets and breakfast included. 5SFr surcharge for non HI-members. Dinner 11.50SFr. Reception 7-10am and 5-10pm. No lockout or curfew. Closed Easter-early July and mid-Oct. to mid-Dec. Dorms 26.50SFr; doubles 33.50 per person, with sink 37.50SFr. Family rooms 37.50SFr per person. Tourist tax 1.90SFr per day in summer, 2.20SFr in winter; half-price for children ages 2-6. AmEx, MC, DC, Visa.) At **Schweizerhaus** near the Klosters-Dorf train station, you'll find newly remodeled, well-lit rooms close to the smaller Madrisa ski mountain. The young owner is a good source of information for outings. (☎422 1481. Breakfast, sheets, and TV included. Closed May-June and Nov. Dorms 35SFr.) Some great deals await in *Privatzimmer (*private rooms) from 30SFr (list at tourist office). The tourist office also has a list of **mountain huts** in the Klosters area. Two of them, the **Silvrettahütte** (SAC; ☎422 1306; open Mar.-Apr. and July-Oct; breakfast and dinner 28SFr; just breakfast 10SFr; 26SFr, SAC members 17SFr) and the **Vereina-Berghaus**

(☎422 1216 or 422 1197), have shuttle buses (26SFr and 24SFr round-trip, respectively) that transport visitors to and from Klosters.

Gasthaus Casanna, Landstr. 171, is a locally-favored joint offering traditional Swiss dishes (around 12.50SFr), such as delicious homemade *Spätzli* with mushrooms (☎422 1229; fax 422 6278; open M-F 8am-12:30am, Sa 8am-6pm; closed Nov.). The **Co-op** has cheap groceries, and the restaurant upstairs serves *spaghetti Napoli* for 7.50SFr (open M-F 8am-12:30pm and 2-6:30pm, Sa 8am-4pm; restaurant open M-Sa 9am-8pm, Su 10am-8pm).

OUTDOOR ACTIVITIES. Klosters is first and foremost a ski town, though much of its activity revolves around Davos. **Ski passes** for the Klosters-Davos region run 118SFr for 2 days and 273SFr for 6 days (includes public transportation). Klosters does have 2 ski mountains of its own. The **Madrisabahn** leaves from Klosters-Dorf (1-day pass 44SFr, 6-day pass 191SFr). The **Grotschnabahn** ticket also gives access to Parsenn and Strela in Davos and Madrisa in Klosters (1-day pass 55SFr, 6-day pass 246AFr). The **ski school** in Klosters, located in the tourist office, offers ski and snowboard lessons for children and adults (group lessons from 52SFr per day; call 410 2028 the day before to book private lessons).

In the summer, the tourist office has an extensive list of **hiking** suggestions, with exact directions, elevation levels, anticipated times, and a trail map. Summer cable car passes (valid on Grotschna and Madrisabahnen) are also available (6-day pass 120SFr). Got vertigo? Stay close to the luscious green valley floor and make a large loop, going from the Klosters Protestant church up-valley on Monbielstr. to Monbiel. Loop again around toward the left and follow the signs to Pt. 487 and Monbieler Wald. The trail ends at the Alpenrösli restaurant, where you can grab Talstr. back to the hostel. The **Klosters Adventure Program** offers guided hikes and mountain tours, canyoning, horseback riding, river rafting, glacier walks, canoeing, mountain-bike tours, paragliding, and more every weekday mid-June to mid-October (☎325 2444; guided day-hike 30SFr, river rafting 80SFr).

LOWER ENGADINE VALLEY

The Engadine Valley takes its name from the Romansch name *(En)* for the Inn River that flows through the valley and on through Innsbruck, Austria. One transportation line runs from Maloja, at the far west end of the valley, to Scuol on the far east, connecting all towns by train or short bus rides. The region is divided into the Upper and Lower Engadine, divided by the border town of Brail, just west of Zernez and the Swiss National Park.

The Lower Engadine valley represents Graubünden at its purest. Skiing never quite caught on here, and, unaltered by the swift torrent of change brought by the ski industry, the people maintain a strong connection to their land and culture. The Lower Engadine is a stronghold of the **Romansh language,** and nearly every sign is printed in this Latinate relic. The region may not be a skier's paradise, but **hikers** revel in the untouched Alpine ecosystem of the **Swiss National Park** just south of the valley. Regional travel is easy with the **Lower Engadine Regional Pass** that covers all trains and post buses in the area (3 days of 7, 45SFr; 7 days of 14, 65SFr).

THE SWISS NATIONAL PARK

The Swiss National Park offers hikes with views that rival the best hiking areas elsewhere in Switzerland. But the park has one thing that no other areas have: the park's isolation from man-made constructs (including the ubiquitous cowbell) allows hikers to experience the undiluted wildness of the natural terrain. The park became the first national park in the Alps when it was established in 1914. While its size (only 169km^2) pales in comparison to American or Canadian national parks, efforts to protect the ecological balance are far more vigorous than in its North American counterparts. In an effort to minimize disturbance, the park has fewer trails than other mountainous areas in Switzerland, but the lower density of

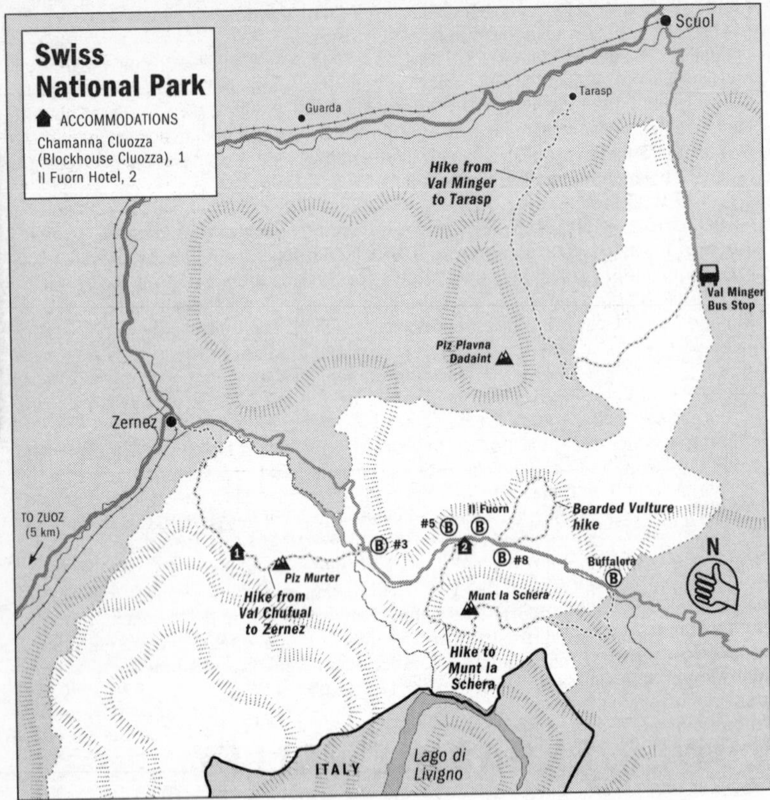

trails in no way limits possibilities for incredible hiking. In fact, the successful conservation movement creates the rare opportunity to hike among marmots, ibexes, eagles, bearded vultures, and other creatures seen nowhere else.

GETTING AROUND THE PARK.

The towns of Scuol, Zernez, and S-chanf lie just north of the park along the same Rhätische Bahn **train** line. **Post Buses** wind along the three major roads that skirt the park. The Ofenpass road goes from Zernez through the middle of the park; there are nine parking lots at regular intervals along the road. **Buses** leave from **Zernez** and stop at these parking places within the park, where the trails start. Roads from S-chanf and Scuol skirt the western and eastern edges of the park, respectively. Both have the same bus setup as the main road, but there are no parking lots along them within the park. The most manageable hike between the villages surrounding the park is the hike from S-chanf to Zernez, using the *Chamanna Cluozza* hut as an overnight resting spot (see Hiking, below).

ORIENTATION AND PRACTICAL INFORMATION

The Swiss National Park is a kidney-shaped area of land stretching from S-chanf in the west to Scuol in the east. These towns are all north of the park; the wilderness extends south from the towns. The landscape consists of thick pine forests, and rocky peaks arrayed around glacial streams. In the middle area of the park is Munt

BUNA SAIRA! Switzerland's oft-forgotten fourth national language, Romansh, is spoken only in the province of Graubünden, where it is an official cantonal language along with German and Italian. Up until about 1850, it was the most spoken language in the canton. By 1880, Romansh speakers dropped to 39.8% of the population, a percentage that kept dropping, then leveled out as the primary language for 23.6% of the residents in Graubünden. In some villages like S-chanf, Romansh speakers are in the majority, and even in large towns like Chur they form a quarter of the population. All Romansh speakers (except toddlers) are fully bilingual with German. Romansh is taught in the schools, and its speakers support five Romansh newspapers and 13 to 14 hours per week of TV broadcast time in Romansh. The language is supported by the Swiss government, but its survival is threatened by the fact that its speakers are divided by at least four major dialects that arose from the mountain isolation of many high-altitude villages. Romansh didn't become a written language until the 16th-century, when people began publishing tracts on preserving Romansh identity. Now, Romansh has a small literature of its own and translations of everything from the Bible to Asterix comics. Maybe when you're traveling through Switzerland, you'll overhear someone calling out, "Bun di!" (hello), "grazia" (thank you), or even "Tge bel che ti es!" (how beautiful you are!).

La Schera, and *Chamanna Cluozza*, the single alpine hut administrated by the park. The alpine grassland of the northern regions is where you're most likely to spot red deer and marmots.

The Swiss National Park is one of the most strictly environmentally regulated nature preserves in the world. Camping and campfires are prohibited, as is collecting flowers and plants. A team of wardens patrols the park at all times, so it's better not to test the rules. The central office of the park is in Zernez (see p. 391). Many landmarks and landforms have Romansh names. The word for "mountain" is *piz*, *val* is "valley," *ova* is "stream," *pra* is "meadow," and *chamanna* means "mountain hut." During June and July, the Park's alpine flora is in full bloom. The best time for birdwatching is mid-June to mid-July; deer, chamois, and ibex are most active in September. The park is closed from Nov.-May.

ACCOMMODATIONS

Many hikes leave from one of the parking places clustered around **Hotel Il Fuorn.** If it's a convenient location you want, Il Fuorn is perfect. Take the bus from Zernez toward Müstair (20 min., every hr. 8:55am-8:20pm, 2.20SFr). The saggy dorm beds in the shack across the road from the main hotel would give even the weariest hiker trouble sleeping. The beds in the hotel are expensive but very comfortable (all the toilets and showers for the dorms are in the main hotel building). The food, while delicious, is pricey (*Spätzle* 19.10SFr, *Rösti* 22.10SFr)—the next building is 10km away, so you're at their mercy. (☎856 1226; fax 856 1801; info@ilfuorn.ch, www.ilfuorn.ch. Breakfast 12SFr. Singles 60SFr, breakfast included. Open May-Oct. Dorms 17SFr.) To save some money get off the bus two stops before Il Fuorn at **Ova Spin,** just outside the western park boundary. With kitchen facilities and a kiosk next door, it will cost you much less to stay and eat there than at Il Fuorn (☎856 1052. 15SFr, best to reserve one week in advance).

If you want to get out into the woods immediately head to one of the **mountain huts** scattered throughout the park. **Chamanna Cluozza,** located in the western block of the park, can only be reached via a three-hour hike from Zernez. (☎856 1235; fax 856 1686. Packed lunches available up on request; open last week of June to mid-October. Beds are 27SFr, 11SFr youth under 20 and students under 26; 58SFr with breakfast and dinner, 42SFR youth and students.) The **Parkhütte Varusch,** located just outside the southwestern border of the park, is a one-hour hike from S-chanf. The solar-powered hut has rooms for 2 to 10 people. (☎854 3122. Breakfast included, lunch and dinner available in restaurant. Open May-Oct.

Dorms 25SFr, doubles 72SFr.) The **Bellavista hut** is a 1½hr. hike from Zernez along the trail to the Murtaröl and the Chamanna Chuozza. It has five beds, a wood stove, a kitchenette, and a knockout view of Zernez and Piz Linard from the front porch. (☎856 1721. Bring your own drinking water. Open May-Oct.; call one week in advance for reservations and to get the key from the owner. 18SFr.) **Camping** is not allowed in the park, but Zernez, Scuol, and S-chanf have campsites right outside the park boundaries (see respective town listings for details).

HIKING

A network of twenty hiking trails runs throughout the park, mostly concentrated in the central 100m² of the park. All trails are clearly marked, and it is against park rules to wander off of the designated trails. Few of the trails are level; most trails in the park involve a lot of climbing, often into areas still covered in snow. Be sure to check in at the **Parkhouse** in Zernez to see which trails are navigable. Their advice is not tempered by paranoia of liability, so when they say a trail is too dangerous, they mean it. An extremely helpful park trail map (scale: 1:45,000) in five languages is available at the Parkhouse in Zernez (14SFr), as well as a written guide to all twenty trails (10SFr). The Parkhouse also sells a geological map and a vegetation map of the park (scale: 1:50,000). The trails that require no mountaineering gear are marked with white-red-white blazes. The Swiss are practically mountain goats, so even some of the non-mountaineering routes can be tricky.

Ova Spin to Il Fuorn (2½hr.). This trail is not hard to find or follow. Take the bus from Zernez to "Ova Spin" and follow the signs to "Il Fuorn." The path begins with a short uphill climb and then passes through the Champlönch meadow, adorned with spectacular wildflowers. Past the meadow is an impressive view of the Val Chavagl, Munt la Schera, and Piz Daint. The trail zig-zags downhill into the forest and crosses the Val Ftur stream (be sure to check out the view of the Val Ftur from the bridge). Then it climbs gradually, finally levelling out into a flat path through the forest. After crossing a massive avalanche chute and passing a renovated 19th-century lime kiln, the hike ends in the meadows surrounding Il Fuorn.

Zernez to Chamanna Cluozza (3hr.). From the Zernez train station, go left on the main road and turn right in, through the meadow behind the Parkhouse. Continue (10min.) until you reach the start of the hike. After a flat walk through a meadow, the path enters the forest, where it turns into a steep uphill climb. When the path splits (approx. 1hr.), take the right fork and grab a drink at the freshwater fountain. Next, the trail traverses a grassy field, where you may be lucky enough to spot red deer grazing. A descent through the woods leads to a meadow and a view of the Piz Linard from the bridge over the Ova da Cluozza. After that, it is just a short climb (80m) to the Chamanna Cluozza.

Zernez to Murtaröl and back (6hr.). This hike begins at the same spot as the Chamanna Cluozza hike and follows the same trail until the path splits (approx. 1hr.); take the left-hand fork. After passing the Bellavista hut (see Accommodations p. 390), the trail goes by a wide avalanche chute. These giant stone walls, built during the 19th century in an effort to prevent avalanches, are still maintained today. The path curves here, leading to a panoramic view of the Val Tantermozza and the mountain chain that surrounds it. At the end of the meadows that follow is the Murtaröl crest (3½hr.) with simultaneous views of the Engadine, Cluozza, and Tantermozza valleys. Sometimes herds of chamois and ibexes are visible from the path along the ridge. The route back to Zernez passes bizarre rock formations and rejoins with the original path at the point where it splits off from the Chamanna Cluozza trail.

Munt la Schera (5hr.). Take the bus from Zernez to Il Fuorn (Parking 6) and head back down the road to Parking 5. Follow the trail originating there toward Alp Buffolora and Munt la Schera. Some trails have viewpoints; this entire trail *is* a viewpoint. The inauspicious beginnings, a gradual 1hr. ascent through the woods, bring you above the tree line where the trail curves around the side of the mountain, with each turn exposing another view of some of Switzerland and Italy's mightiest mountains and lushest val-

MY, WHAT BIG FEET YOU HAVE From the Chamanna Cluozza (with binoculars), you can see the tracks of the theropod, a 4- to 5-m long herbivorous dinosaur that roamed this area over 200 million years ago. The footprints measure 25-30cm across, with a stride of up to 2.2m, similar to those 70-year old Swiss women who pass you by on the trail.

leys. Follow the sign up to **Munt la Schera** to take it all in at once. Take a few deep breaths before heading for the summit. While standing on the flat top of Munt la Schera you may feel you are resting on a pedestal overlooking the entire world. From the top follow signs to "Buffolora." If the view from Munt la Schera doesn't have you singing, the ridge you walk, hemmed by endless meadows, will undoubtedly put you in a mood to do your Julie Andrews routine. The trail quickly descends Munt la Schera, then leisurely winds down to **Buffolora** where buses return to Il Fuorn and Zernez.

Val Minger to Tarasp (5hr.). Take the bus from Scuol (dir.: Scharl) to "Val Minger" (9.40SFr; with Eurail, SwissPass 4SFr). One of the more difficult hikes. From the bus stop, cross the bridge and turn left on the trail, which begins with a slow and steady climb up rocky stream beds. The excitement lies behind you with views of **Piz Pradatsch.** When the trail moves above the tree line it enters a half-pipe shaped valley, at the end of which lies the solitary, majestic **Piz Plavna Dadaint** which pulls you up the valley to the **Sur il Foss pass,** with its uniquely intimate view of nearby mountains. From Sur il Foss you can head around the head of the valley to the **Val dal Botsch pass,** which then leads to Il Fuorn in the center of the park. **This route is only safe in later summer when the snow has melted, and even then should only be attempted with hiking poles and very sturdy boots.** The saner route leads right, toward "Tarasp Fontana." The initial descent can be tricky, depending on recent rock slides, so don't hesitate to use your hands here. The trail passes into a wide rocky plain, bordered by cliffs that create a visual tunnel, training all eyes forward to the mountain range over Scuol, and backward to Piz Nair and the peaks in front of it. The trail heads through the woods to **Tarasp,** where a bus returns to Scuol (every hr. 7:45am-6:30pm).

S-chanf to Alp Trupchun and back (7hr.). From the S-chanf train station, follow the signs to "Alp Trupchun." The path crosses the Inn River and continues along either side of the Ova da Varusch stream. At the bridge, take the higher trail, which climbs to Val da Scrigns steeply before turning left into Val Trupchun. Continue straight down the path (not taking the fork that branches off to the left). As you descend towards the Ova da Trupchun stream, you might spot marmots in some of the forest clearings. After the bridge, the trail rejoins the lower path. The trail is very steep over stony terrain to the Alp Trupchun, which overlooks a basin-shaped valley that is home to deer, ibex, and marmots. Return to S-charf by the same trail, or take the lower path to the right of the Ova da Trupchun.

TOWNS NEAR THE NATIONAL PARK

TRANSPORT HUB: ZERNEZ ☎081

Zernez (pop. 1,000) is the main gateway to the **Swiss National Park,** and home to the headquarters of the park, the **National Parkhouse. Trains** depart from Zernez for **Scuol** (30min., every hr. 5:39am-9:40pm, 11.80SFr) and **Samedan** (30min., every hr. 5:53am-9:04pm, 12.60SFr) with connections to the rest of Switzerland, including **St. Moritz** (45min., 16.40SFr). The **post office** is across the street from the train station (open M-F 8:15-11:45am and 2:15-6pm, Sa 8:15-11am). The **postal code** is 7530.

From the train station, the road to the left that curves through town leads to the **tourist office** (☎856 1300; fax 856 1155; open in summer M-F 8:30am-noon and 2-6:30pm, Sa 9-noon and 2-5pm; in winter M-F 8:30am-noon and 2-5:30pm, Sa 9-11am and 2-4pm.) The same road continues to the **National Parkhouse;** turn right at the T junction. Like the park, the parkhouse is only open June-Oct. It provides information about trail safety and has an extensive selection of maps. (☎856 1378; fax 856

1740; info@nationalpark.ch; www.nationalpark.ch. Open daily in summer 8:30am-6pm.) The Parkhouse also houses a small **museum,** primarily for children, about the park (same hours, 4SFr, children under 16 free). For any emergency outdoor gear at jacked-up prices hit **Sport Sarsura,** right before the tourist office (☎856 1434; open M-F 8am-noon and 2-6:30pm, Sa 8am-noon and 2-5pm). The **Co-op** is across the street (same hours as sports store).

Hotel Bär-Post, left from the main intersection, is a classy hotel that offers less classy rooms in a back building. The dorms are minimal and chilly even in summer; rooms overlook a parking lot. (☎851 5500; fax 851 5599; baer-post@bluewin.ch; www.forum.ch.baer-postzernez.htm. Breakfast 12SFr. Sleep-sack 5SFr. Reception open daily 9am-10pm. Closed Nov. to mid-Dec. Dorms 18SFr. MC, Visa.) The tourist office also provides a list of private rooms (from 20SFr). There is camping at **Camping Cul,** across the train tracks from town, on the river. (☎856 1462. Open May-Oct. 15; reception open July-Aug. 8am-noon and 1-8pm; Sept.-June 8-10am and 6-8pm. 7.90SFr per person, tents 5SFr.) For some of the best pizza (13-18SFr) in Graubünden head to **Grotia Pizzeria Mirta** at the main intersection. (☎856 1735. Open Tu-Su 8am-11:30pm; closed May and Nov. Visa).

SCUOL ☎081

Scuol, (pop. 2,000) the biggest town in the Lower Engadine, is also the closest to a resort in the area, thanks to its spas. The development here, however, has been done in tactful moderation and does not approach the level of commercialization found in ski capitals of the Upper Engadine. Most goods and services are on the main street ("Stradun"), along with a few beautifully grand hotels. Spreading between the Inn River below the town and the rugged peaks above is the *Altstadt*, complete with narrow cobblestone streets and a decidedly old-world feel.

TRANSPORT AND PRACTICAL INFORMATION. The Scuol train station sits at the end of the line from Zernez. Trains depart Scuol every hour (5:25am-10:32pm) for **Zernez** (11.80SFr), **Samedan** (24SFr; for connections to the rest of Switzerland), and **St. Moritz** (26SFr), among other destinations. The train station **changes currency,** and **stores luggage** for 3SFr (open daily 5:15am-9:45pm). From the train station, follow the brown "Centrum" and "i" signs to reach the **tourist office** (☎861 2222; fax 861 2223; info@scuol.ch, www.scuol.ch; open M-F 8am-noon and 2-6:30pm, Sa 10am-noon and 2-6pm, Su 4-6pm). Get **Internet** access at the **Glatscharia,** where you can check email (10SFr per hour) while savoring a bowl of gourmet ice cream (2.50SFr for one scoop, 4.50SFr for two; ☎860 0069; open 2-8pm, closed Tuesdays). Farther down on the left is **Sport Heinrich Scuol,** where you can buy last minute hiking gear before you hit the mountains at high-altitude prices. (☎864 1956. Open in summer M-F 8am-noon and 2-6:30pm, Sa until 5pm; in winter M-F 8am-noon and 1:30-6:30pm, Sa until 6pm.) In an **emergency** dial 117. The **post office** is in the same building as the tourist office (open M-F 7:45am-noon and 1:45-6:15pm, Sa 8:30am-noon). The **postal code** is CH-7550.

ACCOMMODATIONS, FOOD, AND SPA. **Touristenlager Villa à Porta** has simple six-bed rooms in an old building next to the Hotel Filli (check in at the hotel). To get there, head back toward the train station from the tourist office along the main road and turn left down the stairs at the "Restorant Filli 80m" sign. (☎864 9927; fax 864 1336. Breakfast 14SFr. Reservations recommended. Reception open 8am-midnight. 35SFr, 25SFr per person for groups larger than three.) There are 20 or so houses scattered throughout the *Altstadt* that offer **Privatzimmer** (private rooms) for 35-50SFr per person, some including breakfast. The tourist office compiles a list of rooms; call ahead for availability. **Hotel Curuna** is a 15-min walk down the main street from the tourist office. It has spacious double rooms with wooden armchairs and bedframes in a building behind the main hotel. (☎864 1451; fax 864 8470; curuna-scuol@bbluewin.ch. Breakfast included. Reception open 7:30am-midnight. 55SFr per person. MC, Visa.) **Gurlaina Camping** lies on the opposite bank of the Inn River (☎864 1501; fax 864 0760; 8.70SFr, tent 9-11SFr). The chic but mellow **Café Benderer** has delicious coffee (3.30SFr) along with hot sandwiches (8SFr), "Swissbergers" (7.50SFr), and *Rösti* with bratwurst (16.50AFr). (☎864 1533. Open M-F 7:30am-6:30pm, Sa 7:30am-5pm.)

The **Co-op**, on main road, has picnic fixins ready (open M-F 8am-12:15pm and 2-6:30pm, Sa 8am-5pm). The spa **Engadin Bad Scuol** is in the center of town, with an entrance on the main street. The newly renovated complex includes saunas, salt baths, cold and hot water grottoes, and their specialty, the combined Roman-Irish bath—a great way to end a hard day's hike through the wind-chilled Alps (☎861 2000. 25SFr per day. Open daily 8am-10pm, Su 9am-10pm.)

S-CHANF

☎081

The rustic town of S-chanf (pop. 582), with its narrow cobblestone streets and eld-Engadine style houses is a stronghold of local tradition. In most towns in the region Romansch is only a colloquial language; in S-chanf it is the official tongue, spoken in town meetings, schools, and church services. Because S-chanf receives fewer tourists than most towns in the area, it is a peaceful and inexpensive base town from which to explore the National Park.

TRANSPORT AND PRACTICAL INFORMATION. Trains connect S-chanf to **St. Moritz** (change at **Samedan**; 30min., every hr. 8:24am-10:34pm, 10SFr), **Scuol** (1hr., every hr. 6:26am-9:24pm, 18SFr), and **Zernez** (20min., every hr. 5:22am-9:24pm, 7.40SFr). S-chanf connects to the rest of Switzerland through Samedan. **Post Bus** #8 runs from S-chanf into the National Park (10min., 4 per day 8:56am-2:05pm, 2.20SFr). Bus and train tickets are sold at the **post office,** which is down the road to the left of the train station (open M-F 8-11:30am and 2:45-5:15pm, Sa 8:30-10:15am). The **tourist office** is in the Banca Raffeisen office, in the same building as the post office. (☎854 2255; fax 850 1765; infoschanf@datacomm.ch. Open M-Tu and Th-F 8:30-11am and 4-5:30pm, W 8:30-11am.) In an **emergency** dial 117.

ACCOMMODATIONS AND FOOD. Lager Angelini has cheap, clean dorm rooms. Follow the main road from the tourist office past the church, turn left onto the square, take a right after the square, and take a left on the first street, which crosses the river (20min.). (☎854 1360. Reception open 7-10pm. Reserve ahead mid-Dec. to Feb. and Aug. Sleepsack 4SFr. Dorms 22SFr.) **Gasthaus Traube,** run by friendly folks at the more upscale Hotel Aurora, is the perfect place to sink into a down comforter and pillow after a long day. Check in at the Hotel Aurora; take a right out of the tourist office. (☎854 1264; fax 854 2119. Breakfast included. Check in at the Hotel Aurora from 7am-10pm. Singles and doubles are 50SFr per person, with shower 60SFr per person.) Take bus #8 to "Chapella la Resgia" and backtrack along the main road for 20min. to reach **Camping Chapella.** (☎/fax 854 1206. Open May-Oct. and Christmas-Easter. 6SFr, tent 4.50SFr.) **Restaurant Scaletta,** across the street from the tourist office, has a cozy wood interior and typical Swiss specialties (*Rösti* from 15.50-19.50SFr; ☎854 0304; open daily 7am-11pm). **Volg** groceries is down the main street to the right of the tourist office (open M-Tu and Th-F 8am-noon and 2-6:30pm, W 8am-noon, Sa 8am-noon and 2-4pm).

ZUOZ

☎081

Though technically in the Upper Engadine, Zuoz's adherence to architectural and linguistic (Romansh) traditions, as well as the warmth of the citizens, mark it as a Lower Engadine town. Its position on the border of both regions makes it a good central point from which to explore both sides of the Engadine Valley. Burnt to the ground by residents in 1499 to keep it from the Austrians, Zuoz (pop. 1,300) was rebuilt in the early 16th century and remains essentially unchanged today. Ibexes, pinwheels, and flowers float on the whitewashed walls of village houses, and a big carved bear defends the fountains from bloodthirsty Imperial Habsburg troops.

BOYS WILL BE BOYS Zuoz takes pride in its unique holidays and traditional festivals. On March 1, the Chalandamarz engulfs all of Engadine as young boys wander from house to house, ring huge bells, and sing songs to drive off evil spirits and welcome the spring. Originally a pagan fertility rite, the more peculiar San Gian's Day commemorates John the Baptist on July 24, when village boys spritz girls with water from Zuoz's many fountains. The Swiss maidens then flee to their houses and pour buckets of water over the boys' heads. Perhaps there's some Italian blood in this region yet.

TRANSPORT AND PRACTICAL INFORMATION. Zuoz is a short train ride from **St. Moritz** (30min., every hr. 6:53am-9:26pm, 8.60SFr), **Zernez** (20min., every hr. 6:30am-9:10pm, 8SFr), and **Samedan** (20min., same train as St. Moritz, 5.60SFr). The train station provides **luggage storage** (3SFr), **bike rental** (27SFr per day), and **currency exchange** (open M-F 6:10am-6:40pm, Sa 6:10am-6:10pm, Su 8:10am-12:25pm and 1:40-6:10pm). The **tourist office** on Via Maestra provides keys for the church and tower and suggests **hikes.** From the station walk up La Passarella, directly opposite the station. At the top of the pedestrian walkway, turn right on the main street, and the tourist office will be past the main square on your right. (☎854 1510; fax 854 3334; zuoz@spin.ch; www.zuoz.ch. Open July-Aug. and Dec.-Apr. M-F 9am-noon and 3-6pm, Sa 9-11am; May-June and Oct.-Nov. M-F 9am-noon and 3-5pm.) In an **emergency,** dial 117. The **post office** is in the train station (open M-F 8am-noon and 2:15-5:45pm, Sa 8-11am). **The postal code** is CH-7524.

ACCOMMODATIONS AND FOOD. The cheapest lodgings are in the center of town at **Ferienlager Sonder**. Head down Via Maestra from the tourist office and turn right on tiny Chanels at the sign for "Ferienlager" for simple rooms in a 16th-century building. (☎854 0773; fax 854 1439. **Kitchen** use 10SFr; sleep sack 5SFr. Dorms 20SFr.) At the 400-year-old **Chesa Walther** opposite the tourist office, zebra, cougar, and other critter skins adorn the ivy-tangled walls, competing for space with gold-fringed mirrors and antique Graubünden stoves (☎854 1364; partial **kitchen** facilities 5SFr; dorms 35SFr). **Restorant Dorta** cooks up an impressive menu of Engadine specialties, including *Zuozer Krautpizokel* for 22SFr, half portion for 15SFr. (Open Tu 6pm-midnight, W-Su 11:30am-midnight.) Raw materials for a meal await at the **Co-op** opposite the station (open M-F 8am-12:15pm and 2-6:30pm, Sa 8am-5pm) or at **Volg** supermarket next to the tourist office (open M-F 8am-noon and 2-6:30pm, Sa 8am-noon and 2-4pm).

SIGHTS AND OUTDOOR ACTIVITIES. The small **Church San Luzius** on Via Maestra has sweet-smelling pine pews and hymnals in Romansh. Next door is the **prison tower**—preserved as the last wrongdoer left it—filled with blood-curdling, gut-wrenching implements of torture and chilling dungeon cells you can climb into (ask the tourist office for the key).

Zuoz woos **bikers** with 37km of marked trails. For **hikers,** the National Park is right next door, but Zuoz offers a few distinctive hikes of its own. In remembrance of the great artist, the **Via Segantini** leads to views as beautiful as the artist's paintings of glacier-laden mountains such as the 4049m **Piz Bernina.** The path begins just past the Hotel Engiadina, on Via Maestra. Turn right on Chröntschet, then cross the driveway to private houses, which will take you to the gravel path labeled "Via Segantini." The trail requires minimal effort and goes from Zuoz to La Punt (2hr.) and Bever (4hr.), where you can catch a train back to Zuoz.

For a more rugged afternoon, follow the **Ova d'Arpiglia** to a crashing 35m waterfall. To find the trail, turn left from the train station and go through the underpass toward the river. Cross the river on the smaller bridge, turn right after the bike rental, and follow the dirt road heading into the woods. At the first sign head to "Arpiglia," at the second "Mont Seja," and at the third "Sagl d'Arpiglia" which leads along the stream bank and a larch-lined path to the waterfall. The path then climbs steeply to a green meadow to the right of the falls that burgeons with purple wildflowers, known locally as the **"Stairway to Heaven."** Signs point the way from this perfect picnic haven back to Zuoz (round-trip 1½hr.).

UPPER ENGADINE VALLEY

The Engadine Valley is known to the outside world primarily for the skiing in the Upper Engadine, where 350km of ski trails and 60 ski lifts lace the valley and thousands of ski bunnies gather each year. Unlike Zermatt and Grindelwald, where Japanese and American tourists abound, the Upper Engadine attracts mostly German and Swiss visitors to its trails. Connoisseurs rate the downhill skiing in the Upper Engadine just behind the Jungfrau and Matterhorn regions. The trails lead you away from the valley's resort façade and into the Swiss wilderness. With all these mountains there is, of course, great hiking, too. The most unique hiking skirts the melting glaciers flowing down from **Piz Bernina** (at 4049m the highest in the region) and its neighbors. For lowland hikes that don't involve expensive cable cars, Sils is a wonderful starting point.

Ski rental is standard throughout the region (54-60SFr per day, 49-54SFr youth ages 16-20; 29SFr children ages 6-16). **Novices** should head for Zuoz or Corviglia (St. Moritz); **experts** for Diavolezza (Pontresina), Corvatsch (Silvaplana), Piz Nair (St. Moritz), or Piz Lagalb (Pontresina). One-day passes are available for each town (St. Moritz and Celerina are together, as are Sils and Silvaplana). Multiple-day passes are available only for the entire Engadine region—they're not much more expensive and they cover most trains and buses as well (5-day pass 272SFr, youth 245SFr, children 136SFr). Anyone hoping to catch a glimpse of Hollywood should head for **St. Moritz.** Cross-country fanatics should glide to **Pontresina,** where hundreds train for the cruel and unusual **Engadine Ski Marathon,** stretching from Maloja to S-chanf. The race takes place on the second Sunday in March (☎(081) 842 6685 or fax 842 6686 for application/registration; entry fee 70SFr). **Ski schools** in just about every village offer private lessons. For more information on all skiing call or check out the website of Oberengadiner Bergbahn (☎(081) 830 0000; www.skiengadin.ch).

PONTRESINA ☎081

Unlike nearly every other town in the Engadine, Pontresina (pop. 1,900) does not lie on the Inn River. Instead, Pontresina has staked its place—away from the bustle of the rest of the Upper Engadine—in one of the highest wind-sheltered valleys of the region, at the confluence of two major rivers that come tearing down from the mountains above. Its enclosure on 3 sides by mountains (only one of which is used for skiing) makes it a favorite among mountaineering types. Every morning, the famous Diavolezza glacier tour draws hordes of hikers. In winter, Pontresina becomes the cross-country skiing capital of the Upper Engadine, with the youth hostel standing as the capitol building at the intersection of the trails. The hostel is a tourist magnet in the summer as well, providing the cheapest and most accessible lodgings in the region.

TRANSPORT AND PRACTICAL INFORMATION. Trains run to **St. Moritz** (10min., every hr. 5:51am-8:04pm, 4.40SFr) and **Chur** through **Samedan** (2hr., every hr. 5:51am-8:04pm, 41SFr). **Post Buses** connect Pontresina to the villages of the Upper Engadine Valley all the way to **Maloja.** A Post Bus also runs from the left of the train station to the post office, the tourist office, and other important spots in town (every 30min., 6:55am-7:46pm, 2.40SFr). The train station (☎842 6337; open daily 6am-7pm) provides **currency exchange, luggage storage** (3SFr), and **bike rental** (27SFr per day) all at 1 counter (open daily 6:40am-7pm) as well as **lockers** (2SFr).

To get to the town center from the train station, turn right on Via de la Staziun and follow as it winds over 2 rivers, then uphill to the center of town (20min.), or take the Post Bus that departs from the left of the station. The **tourist office** occupies the modern "Rondo" building where the Via de la Staziun meets the town. The office plans free excursions (see p. 397), gives hiking advice, and finds hotel vacancies. (☎838 8300; fax 838 8310; info@pontresina.ch; www.pontresina.com. Open M-F 8:30am-noon and 2-6pm, Sa 8:30am-noon and 3-6pm. From July-Aug. and Dec.-Mar. also open Su 4-6pm.) The **post office,** 10 min. uphill from the tourist office, has free **Internet** access (open M-F 7:45am-noon and 1:45-6:15pm, Sa 8:30am-noon), but there is no time limit, so be prepared to wait a while. The **postal code** is CH-7504.

ACCOMMODATIONS. The **Jugendherberge Tolais (HI),** in the modern, salmon-pink building directly across from the train station, is convenient for early-morning ski ventures and connections throughout the Engadine Valley. The hostel has a restaurant, with great deals for hostelers, as well as table tennis, swings, and a soccer field. (☎842 7223; fax 842 7031, pontresina@youthhostel.ch. Breakfast, lockers, and sheets included. 5SFr charge for non-members. Buffet dinner at 6:30pm 11SFr, mandatory in high season. **Laundry** 8.50SFr. Closed April-May. Reception 7:30-9:30am and 4-10pm. No lockout. Quiet time from 10pm. Christmas-Easter and July-Oct. dorms 30SFr; other times 27.50SFr. AmEx, MC, Visa.) In the heart of town (5min. uphill from the tourist office), **Pension Valtellina** is owned by a gentle Italian grandmother who furnishes her cozy rooms with warm down comforters and pink bathrooms down the hall. (☎842 6406. Breakfast included. Closed June and early Dec. Singles 54-58SFr; doubles 96-98SFr.) The tourist office also has a list of **private rooms** starting at 25SFr per person. **Camping Plauns** offers all the amenities a tent-dweller could hope for. From the trail head just above the train station, walk 3km towards the Bernina Pass to Morteratsch; you can also take the train (dir.: Tirano) to "Morteratsch" (4.40SFr). (☎842 6285, fax 834 5136; a.brueli@bluewin.ch. Open June to mid-Oct. and mid-Dec. to mid-Apr. 7.50SFr; 5.50SFr youth ages 12-15; tents 9SFr.)

FOOD. The **Puntschella Cafe-Restaurant,** is the birthplace of the *Engadiner Torte* (a local delicacy made from candied almonds, raisins, layers of cream and nut puree, and crunchy crust; 4.20SFr). The bakery is filled with a dazzling array of glazed chocolate and fruit delicacies, and the restaurant offers local specialties (entrées 10.50-19.80SFr). Eat on the back terrace while gazing at Piz Bernina. To reach Puntschella, follow Via Maestra uphill from the tourist office and turn right at the "Café Puntschella" sign on Via da Mulin. (☎838 8030. Open in summer 7am-10pm daily, in winter 7am-9pm daily. AmEx, MC, Visa.) Down the hill from the tourist office on Via Maestra (10min. walk or take the bus to "Sportpavillon") you'll find the **Pizzeria Sportpavillon,** looking out on tennis courts and Piz Bernina. The cheerful and efficient waitstaff clad in red bowties and matching suspenders serves pizzas (13.30-19.50SFr, from 10-11pm all pizzas 10SFr) and pasta (13-17SFr; ☎842 6349; open noon-2pm and 6-11pm daily). The **Co-op** resides at the corner of Via Maestra and Via da Mulin (open M-F 8am-12:15pm and 2-6:30pm, Sa 8am-5pm).

SIGHTS. In a well-preserved 17th-century farmhouse, the **Museum Alpin,** Chesa Delnon, up the street to the left of the tourist office, presents life in the Engadine as it used to be: void of high-tech hikers with wimpy polypropylene and full of bearded, pipe-smoking, wool-clad mountaineering men with picks and ropes. Sixty varieties of recorded bird calls arranged by species twitter forth at the touch of a button in the aviary room, also home to 133 stuffed representatives of Engadine fowl. The brilliantly lit mineral collection displays the hidden beauty you've been hiking over. (☎842 7273. Open June-Oct. M-Sa 4-6pm, in bad weather 3-6pm; 5SFr, children 1SFr). At the highest point of the village, the bare exterior of the **church of Santa Maria** conceals a number of well-preserved frescoes, including the **Mary Magdalene cycle** from AD 1495 (open June-Oct. 3:30-5:30pm).

OUTDOOR ACTIVITIES. In winter, Pontresina is a center for **cross-country skiing.** The youth hostel is the *Langlaufzentrum* (cross-country center), and all trails are free for guests. For hikers, the tourist office sells the very helpful "Oberengadia Bergell" (1:50,000) hiking map, which covers the entire Upper Engadine and also includes mountain biking routes (15SFr). In summer there are a number of **hikes** between the **Muottas Maragl cable car** (☎842 8308; one-way 16SFr; base accessible by Post Bus dir: St. Moritz) and the **Piz Languard** and the cable car below it. The level "Hohenweg" rambles above the valley between the cable cars (4hr.). A more demanding route leads from the Muottas Muragl to the **Alp Segantini,** where the painter Giovani Segantini spent his last years (1¼hr.). The trail then climbs to Piz Languard, which offers oft-photographed views up the snaking Morteratsch glacier to the 4049m **Piz Bernina** (3hr.). To reach the Piz Languard more quickly, take the **Alp Languard chairlift** from town (☎842 6255; one-way 15SFr, round-trip 21.50SFr; SwissPass discount). From the top of the lift follow signs to the steep 2½-hour hike to the peak and restaurant.

For more intimate contact with the **glaciers,** there are a number of options. The sedentary traveler can take the train (dir.: Tirano) to "Diavolezza" (6.20SFr) and then the cable car to the top of the **Diavolezza Glacier** (☎842 6419; one-way 19SFr, round-trip 26SFr; with SwissPass 12SFr, 18.20SFr), which sits just above the valley between Piz Palu and Bernina. Bring sunglasses; the snow makes the view from the top nearly blinding to the naked eye. It is possible to hike into the glacial bowl and then down the Morteratsch glacier. The **Mountain Climbing School of Pontresina,** Switzerland's largest, leads the 4-hour hike. (☎838 8333. 22SFr. Hikes daily at noon; meet at the top of the cable car between 10-11:30am.) The other option is to walk up the glacier from the bottom, which is significantly cheaper. Take the train from Pontresina (dir.: Tirano) to "Morteratsch" (4.40SFr) and walk as far up to and alongside the Morteratsch glacier as you desire. From the train stop it is 30min. to the glacier, and 3 hours to the highest hut on the glacier. Signs mark the glacier's recession since the turn of the century along the gushing river created by the melting waters.

Guests of Pontresina—that's you—are entitled to a number of **free sports, tours,** and **excursions,** including free botanical excursions, and free excursions to experience an unforgettable **sunrise** on Piz Lagalb (contact the tourist office for details). For **canyoning**, call Pontresina Events (☎842 7155)

ST. MORITZ ☎081

> In St. Moritz are the hangers-on of the rich...the jewel thieves, the professional backgammon players and general layabouts, as well as the high-class ladies of doubtful virtue (if such a thing still exists)...
>
> —Peter Viertel

Chic, elegant, and exclusive, St. Moritz is one of the most famous ski resorts in the world. Renowned as a playground for the rich and famous, this "Resort at the Top of the World" will convert almost anyone into a (window-)shopper, tempted by Armani, Calvin Klein, and Prada. St. Moritz hosted the Winter Olympics in 1928 and 1948, catapulting itself into the international spotlight. Today, the town offers every winter sport imaginable from world-class skiing and bobsledding to golf, polo, greyhound racing, cricket on the frozen lake, and *Skikjöring*—a sport similar to water skiing in which the water is replaced by snow and the motorboat is replaced by a galloping horse.

GETTING THERE AND AROUND

Trains run every hour to **Chur** (2hr., 41SFr), **Zuoz** (change in Samedan; 30min., 8.60SFr), **Celerina** (5min., 2.40SFr), and **Pontresina** (change in Samedan; 15min., 4.40SFr). Yellow **Post Buses** cover almost all the same routes as the trains. They also provide the only public access to the Engadine Valley west of St. Moritz, since the town is the railway terminus. Buses run every hour to **Silvaplana** (15min., 3.60SFr), **Sils** (20min., 6.20SFr), and **Maloja** (40min., 9SFr), departing from the left of the train station. Two trains leave St. Moritz whose journey are more important than their destinations. From the Engadine Valley to the Matterhorn, the legendary **Glacier Express** covers the 270km to **Zermatt** in a leisurely 8 hours (departing at 9:30am, 147SFr, SwissPass valid, Eurail valid for all but the Brig-Disentis portion of the trip), affording ample time to take in the magnificent Alpine landscapes while crossing 291 bridges and going through 91 tunnels. If you can't sit still for that long, the **Bernina Express** makes the excursion to **Tirano, Italy** (2½hr., every hr., 29SFr, Eurail and SwissPass valid). It's the only Swiss train that crosses the Alps without entering a single tunnel. The **train station** (☎833 5912) provides **currency exchange,** Western Union services, **luggage storage** (3SFr), and **bike rental** (27SFr per day), all at the same counter (open 5:50am-8:10pm), and **lockers** (2SFr). Bikes can also be rented at the youth hostel for 15SFr per day.

PRACTICAL INFORMATION

The resort's **tourist office,** Via Maistra 12, is in the center of town. From the train station, cross the street, climb Truoch Serlas, and take Via Serlas to the left past the post office. As you pass the Badrutt's Palace Hotel on your left, turn right up the Réduit Passage. Emerge from the shopping arcade onto Via Maistra; the tourist office is on the right. The office provides free hotel reservations, skiing info, and advice on hiking in the smaller towns of the Engadine Valley. (☎837 3333; fax 837 3366; information@stmoritz.ch; www.stmoritz.ch. Open July to mid-Sept. and mid-Dec. to Apr. M-F 9am-6:30pm, Sa 9am-6pm, Su 4-6pm; May-June and Nov. M-F 9am-noon and 2-6pm, Sa 9am-noon.) For a **taxi,** call 833 3555. The **Galerie Apotheke** (pharmacy, ☎833 7292) is located next to the Giardino Cafe on Via del Bagn (open M-F 8am-noon and 2-6:30pm, Sa 8am-noon and 2-5pm). In an **emergency,** dial 117. The **post office** is located on Via Serlas on the way to the tourist office and has an **ATM** (open M-F 7:45am-noon and 1:45-6:15pm, Sa 8:30am-noon). **Internet** access is free at the post office, but there are no time limits. Get there early; in the early morning the line is short, but be prepared to wait up to or over an hour in the afternoons. The faster but more expensive option is **Bobby's American Pub,** before the Co-op, on the way to the hostel (17SFr, 3SFr surcharge if you don't buy a drink; open noon-8pm daily). The **postal code** is CH-7500.

ACCOMMODATIONS

With a cappuccino maker in the main lobby, the **Jugendherberge Stille (HI),** Via Surpunt 60, provides welcome luxury after the trek to get there. Because of the thin air in high-altitude St. Moritz and the track down the street, this hostel is a favorite among lithe, spandex-clad Swiss track teams. Follow the signs around the lake to the left of the station (30min.), or take the Post Bus (dir.: Maloja) to "Hotel Sonne" (2.40SFr) and go left on Via Surpunt for 10 minutes. This place is bigger and better than your average hostel with wall-to-wall carpeting, small dorms (max. 4 per room), private showers, a pool table (2SFr), **laundry** (8SFR), table tennis, a game room, and cheap **mountain bike rental** (15SFr per day). (☎833 3969; fax 833 8046, st.moritz@youthhostel.ch; www.youthhostel.ch/st.moritz. Non-members add 5SFr. Sheets, showers, lockers, breakfast, and dinner included—show up before 7:15pm for dinner. Lunch 11SFr. Reception 7-9:45am and 4-9:45pm. No lockout. Curfew midnight; keys available. Quiet hours from 10pm. Dorms from July-Aug. and Dec. 16-Apr. 29 are 43.50SFr, otherwise 41SFr; doubles 112SFr, 107SFr; with shower 135SFr, 127SFr. AmEx, MC, Visa. For more privacy, head next door to the **Sporthotel Stille,** which provides bare, motel-style rooms. (☎833 6948; fax 833 0708; sporthotel.stille.st.moritz@bluewin.ch; www.hostelstille.ch. In summer, singles 65SFr, doubles 110SFr; breakfast included. In winter, no singles, doubles 140SFr; breakfast and dinner included; MC, Visa.) For **camping,** you have two options:

catch the Post Bus (dir.: Sils-Maloja) and push the *halt an* button to request a special stop at "Olympiaschanze," (3SFr) 1 stop after "St. Moritz Bad Signal" (☎833 4090; open May 19-Sept. 27. 4.50-6.50SFr, children half price; tent 5-6SFr); or take a different bus to Silvaplana (10min., every 30min. 7am-9pm, 3.60SFr) and sleep on the beach at **Camping Silvaplana** (☎828 8492; 8SFr; tent 5-7SFr; open mid-May to end of Oct.).

FOOD

If you know where to look, you can eat like a king in St. Moritz without paying 5-star prices. A good place to start is **Restaurant Hauser** on Sonnepl. Walk 1 block down the street that runs straight from the tourist office to take advantage of the diverse, relatively inexpensive menu (Bratwurst and fries 15.50SFr, tofu pad thai 18.50SFr), and a terrace for glitterati gazing. (☎833 4402. Open daily 7:30am-11pm.) **Restaurant Engadinia,** P. da Scoula, is best known for fondue (26.50SFr per person) and "Rösti-pizza" (18.50-19.50SFr). (☎833 3265. Open M-Sa 8:30am-11pm.) Groceries are available at the **Co-op Center,** one square up from the tourist office or at Via dal Bagn 20, the main road between Dorf and Bad, en route to the youth hostel (open M-F 8am-12:15pm and 2-6:30pm, Sa 8am-5pm). The **After Hours** grocery store Via Maistra 2 (☎834 9900), is open 24 hrs. If you're here in late January, sample the culinary delights of the annual week-long **St. Moritz Gourmet Festival.**

SIGHTS AND OUTDOOR ACTIVITIES

MUSEUMS. Follow Via Maistra from the tourist office to Sonnepl., then bear right on Via Somplaz to the **Segantini Museum,** Via Somplaz 30. The museum is two rooms dedicated to the Italian Expressionist painter who spent the last years of his life in nearby Maloja. His work strikes a delicate balance between depicting a fairy-tale Switzerland and the harsh realities of farming life. Save the upstairs *Kuppelsaal*, containing the Alpine trilogy "Birth," "Nature," and "Death," for last. *(☎833 4454. Open June 1-Oct.20 and Dec. 1-Apr. 30 Tu-Su 10am-noon and 3-6pm. 10SFr, students 7SFr.)* The **Engadiner Museum,** Via dal Bagn 39, between Bad and Dorf, gives tourists a sneak-peek at the intricately carved wood interior of those unassuming white houses. The house features tiny gnomish doorways, beautiful and unpronounceable *Chuchichästlis* (cupboards), and a macabre plague-era 4-poster sickbed with a skeleton on the ceiling alongside an inscription that translates as, "As you are, I would like to be" (i.e., still alive). *(☎833 4333. Open June-Oct. M-F 9:30am-noon and 2-5pm, Su 10am-noon; Dec.-Apr. M-F 10am-noon and 2-5pm, Su 10am-noon. Closed in May. 5SFr, students 4SFr, children 2.50SFr.)*

WINTER ACTIVITIES. You've probably heard about St. Moritz's **skiing**—need we say more? *(☎830 0000 for ski packages; day passes 54-60SFr.* *See* p. 395.*)* Each year the **bobsled** run from the '28 and '48 Olympics is rebuilt by 14 skilled laborers with 5000m³ of snow and 4000L of water for the **Olympia Bobrun**. They let you share the fun, but at a rather steep price *(☎830 0200; 200SFr gets you 1 run, 1 drink, and 1 photo; call ahead as slots fill up quickly).*

HIKING. Believe it or not, more guests visit St. Moritz in the summer than in the winter to take advantage of the **hiking.** For a relaxing hike, follow the trail from St. Moritz to **Pontresina** (1½hr.). Go under the train station to "See" exit, and cross the bridge on the other side to find the trailhead. Follow the signs to "Pontresina" from there. The wide gravel trail winds through preserved forest and past the marsh surrounding Staz lake on a level path. In St. Moritz, the flat **Seerundgang** around the San Murezzan lake makes a pleasant stroll on a sunny day. For a more demanding excursion (3hr.), ride from St. Moritz up to **Piz Nair** *(3075m; 21SFr, round-trip 32SFr; under 17 10.50SFr, 16SFr).* After admiring the rooftop view of the Engadine, the most rewarding choice is the steep hike down to **Suvretta Lake** (2580m). On the way down picnics at the isolated lake, in the shadow of majestic **Piz Julier** (3380m), are a must. Follow the Ova da Suvretta back down to the Signalbahn or St. Moritz. Other summer activities in St. Moritz include **river rafting** *(☎833 7714; 75-99SFr per half-day)* and **horseback riding** *(☎833 5733; 45SFr per hr., 80SFr for 2hr.)*.

DAYTRIPS FROM ST. MORITZ

SILVAPLANA ☎081

Silvaplana is a 1hr. hike or 10min. bus ride from St. Moritz (every 30min. 7am-9pm, 3.60SFr).

At the foot of the Julier mountain pass in the magnificent Upper Engadine lake country, Silvaplana (pop. 900) seems to be the meeting place for young thrill-seekers not interested in the flashiness of St. Moritz. Silvaplana's main attraction is the lake, which is usually covered with the brightly-colored sails of windsurfers. The **tourist office,** 1 block up from the bus stop at the corner of Via Maistra and Via dal Farrer, has info on hikes, windsurfing lessons, and rooms (☎838 6000; fax 838 6009; info@silvaplana.ch; www.silvaplana.ch; open M-F 8:30am-noon and 1:30-6pm, Sa 9am-noon and 4-6pm). Get **Internet** access at the Hotel Julier, directly to the left of the tourist office (10SFr per hour; open 7:30am-2am).

All the water activities are based around the campground at the far end of town. The **windsurfing** in Silvaplana is world-famous. Every August, Silvaplana hosts the **Engadine Wind Festival** (Aug. 11-20, 2001; www.silvipana.ch/surf), a nine-day beach bonanza that includes the international **freestyle championships**, the **Surf Marathon,** the **Swiss National and European Windsurfing Championships,** and the town's annual **kite festival**. Silvaplana's hyperactive breezes frolic with kites of the multi-colored, loop-de-looping variety. The folks in Silvaplana invented **kitesurfing,** a sport in which the sail on your windsurfer is replaced by a kite, which allows for jumps 10m in the air (a variation is done on waterskis). Kitesurfing—and its winter equivalent, kitesailing, done on the frozen lake—can be arranged at **Sportzentrum Mulets** or at the **Drachen Atelier,** the store opposite Hotel Julien. (☎828 9767; fax 828 9771; stefan@kitesailing.ch; www.kitesailing.ch; 3hr. group lesson and rental including board, trapeze, kite, and life vest 50SFr; 1-day group lesson and rental 150SFr; 3 days 350SFr; private lessons 100SFr per hour; wetsuit rental 20SFr.) Rent **windsurfers** next to the campground. (☎/fax 828 9229; info@windsurfing-silvaplana.ch; www.windsurfing-silvaplana.ch; 1hr. 25-30SFr, with wetsuit 35-40SFr; 2hr. 35-45SFr, 50-60SFr; 1 day 60-80SFr, 70-90SFr. Group lessons start at 50SFr per hr. Longer lessons advised for novices: 6hr. 180SFr, 12hr. 300SFr. Open June 15-Sept. 15 daily 9am-7pm.)

For **hiking,** Silvaplana's best offerings involve the **Corvatsh cable car,** which provides access to the glaciers around Piz Bernina. The cable car makes 2 stops: the top station has the most breathtaking views, while the middle station allows for an incredible hike. There is a special **Wanderbillet** so you can do both: go all the way to the top for the views, then come halfway down to do the hike (*Wanderbillet* 28SFr, all the way up and down 34SFr; children ages 6-16 half-price). For the hike, walk from the middle station to the hut at Fourcla Surlej and from there down to Pontresina (5hr.). For landlubbers, Silvaplana's **Sportszentrum Mulets** (☎(079) 608 3743) offers tennis (18SFr per hr.), volleyball (free), archery (10SFr per hr.), ping-pong (4SFr per hr.), a weight room (6SFr per day), and soccer (free), (open daily 10am-11pm). In winter, soccer gives way to ice-skating, hockey, and curling.

SILS (SEGL) ☎081

Take a Post Bus from St. Moritz (every 30min. 7:25am-8:25pm, 6SFr).

More than a century ago, **Friedrich Nietzsche** praised Sils (pop. 600) as "the loveliest corner of the Earth," adding, "It is good to live here, in this bracing cold air, where in a wonderful way nature is simultaneously both wildly 'festive' and mysterious—in fact, I like Sils-Maria more than any other place." Sils proves that a lot of people have read Nietzsche since then, as it has become the understated resort getaway for the wealthy in-crowd who want privacy more than St. Moritz-glamour. Fortunately, all this cash has helped preserve, rather than exploit, the tranquil terrain.

Sils has a number of wonderfully rejuvenating **hikes.** A soothing 20min. hike leads to the tip of the tiny forested peninsula just west of town called **Chaste.** Follow the main road toward the lake and at the meadow turn left at the sign for "Chaste." At the tip, you'll discover a stone engraved with one of Nietzsche's sermons. Another easy hike leads from the same spot and goes around the roadless south shore of the lake to the medieval village of **Isola,** set on a small peninsula (45min.), and then on to the town of Maloja (1¾hr.), the source of the Inn River. For a slightly more vertical climb, hike up **Val Fex.** The trail begins opposite the tourist office and winds its way beneath glaciers and 1000m peaks en route to the tiny hamlets of **Platta** (30min.), **Crasta** (50min.), and **Curtins** (1½hr.). Another easy and scenic hike, the **Via Engiadina,** connects Sils with Silvaplana (1½hr.), beginning opposite the tourist office. Strategically-placed rest stops afford views of the nearby mountains and the dazzling blue-green lake below. If you're tired of walking, let **horse-drawn omnibuses** do the work for you. (☎826 5286; Crasta one-way 13SFr, round-trip 19SFr; Platta one-way 10SFr, no round-trip; bus holds 10-15 people.) Sils offers **skiing** from the **Furtschellas cable car,** in conjunction with Silvaplana's slope (day pass 54-60SFr).

After a morning hike, stop by the **Nietzsche House** (halfway between the post office and the tourist office along Sils' main road), where the philosopher spent his summers from 1883 to 1888 (before his final mental breakdown). Exhibitions include his workroom (preserved in its original Spartan decor), Nietzsche-inspired modern art, and two death masks: the genuine one and another his sister had sculpted because she thought the real one was not "impressive" enough. (Open Tu-Su 3-6pm. 4SFr, students 2SFr; guided tours Wednesdays 11:30am-12:30pm, 10SFr per person.) If you think Sils might enchant you as it did Nietzsche, the **tourist office,** down the street to the left from the bus stop, provides hiking and skiing maps, and dirt-cheap **Internet** access (6SFr per hour). They will also call hotels for vacancies. (☎838 5050; fax 838 5059; info@sils.ch; www.sils.ch. Open M-F 8:30am-6pm, Sa 9am-noon and 4-6pm, Dec.-Easter also Su 4-6pm.)

GRAUBÜNDEN

HIKES IN THE BREGAGLIA VALLEY

The Val Bregaglia, which lies between the Engadine and Italy, is a hiker's paradise. Separated from the Engadine by the Maloja Pass, Bregaglia, the local Italian dialect, as well as the slate-roofed houses and milder climate, distinguish Bregaglia from the surrounding area. Within the valley, the landscape varies drastically; wild mountains and steep cliffs are juxtaposed against peaceful chestnut groves. You can get maps for the following hikes in the Upper Engadine towns, but if you are interested in exploring more of the Breglia valley go to the regional tourist office in **Stampa** (bus dir: Chiavenna; 1hr., every hr., 7:36am-8:08pm, 18SFr), where the Bregaglia tourist office is located to the left of the tourist office. (☎822 1555; fax 822 1644; info@bregaglia.ch; www.bregaglia.ch. Open M-F 9-11:30am and 3-5:30pm; July-Sept. also open Sa 9-11:30am.) Two hikes in particular make Bregaglia a worthwhile trip from St. Moritz.

Panorama Hochweg (Sentiero Panoramico) (4½hr.). This pleasantly shaded flat path from Soglio to Casaccia winds through dense greenery along the contour of the mountain, with occasional breaks in the vegetation providing views of the lush valley below. To begin the hike, take the bus from St. Moritz through Sils to Soglio (change in Promontogno, 1½hr., 7:36am-8:08pm, 20SFr, 35SFR round-trip). Take a left on the road to the right of the bus stop, and take a right at the "Casaccia" sign. From there, follow the "Panoramico" and "Casaccia" signs. The path crosses fifteen large waterfalls, each more impressive than the last, as well as numerous smaller mountain streams. After the first hour, it enters a thick pine forest with imposing boulders and a soft red-dirt floor, eventually emerging to a sunny, hilly meadow of wildflowers. After passing stone cottages scattered over the hills, you will reach the peaceful hamlet of Vicosoprano (3 hr.). Although there is no sign in Vicosoprano pointing the way to Casaccia, just continue along the main road to the end of town, where the path resumes. Although the path immediately after Vicosoprano is laced with power lines and passes a noisy power plant, the last 30min. before Casaccia is a peaceful, quiet stroll through woods and flowery meadows. Buses run from Casaccia back to St. Moritz (50min., 9 per day June 24-Oct. 20; 6 per day otherwise; 7:58am-6:58pm).

Historischer Wanderweg (Sentiero Storico) (12hrs.) This flat trail connects all of the towns in the Bregaglia valley from Maloja to Castasegna and can easily be divided into smaller segments, depending on which towns you wish to explore. Overnight accommodations are available in the towns of Casaccia, Vicosoprano, Stampa, Soglio, and Promontogno, making it possible to hike the whole valley in two or three days. The Bregaglia tourist office in Stampa publishes a free map of the trail that comes with a list of historical landmarks and hotels in each of the nine towns.

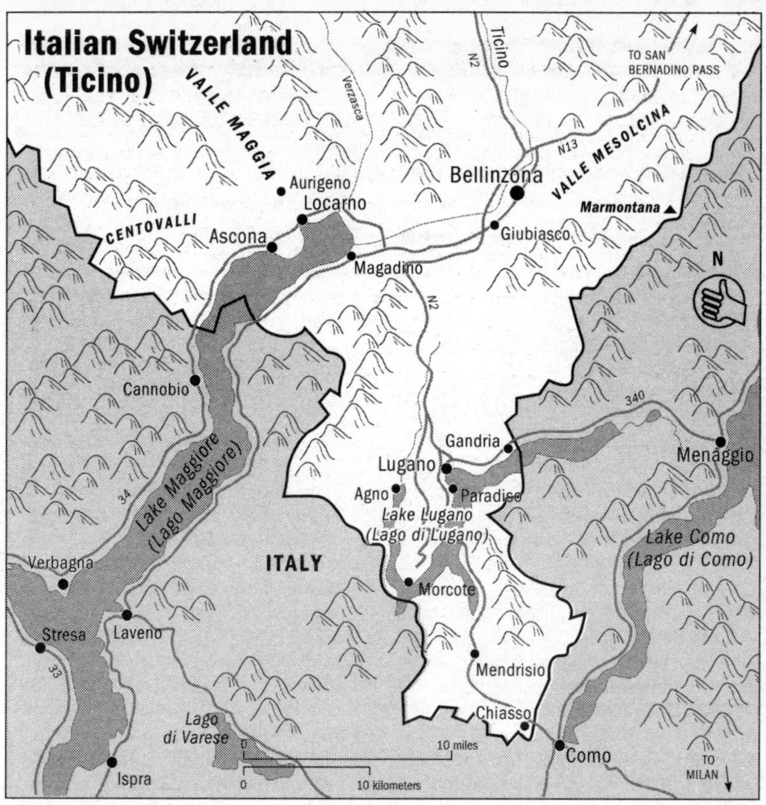

ITALIAN SWITZERLAND (TICINO, TESSIN)

Ever since Switzerland won the Italian-speaking canton of Ticino (Tessin, in German and French) from Italy in 1512, the region has been renowned for its mix of Swiss efficiency and Italian *dolce vita*—no wonder the rest of Switzerland vacations here. The charred-wood chalets of Graubünden and the Bernese Oberland are replaced by jasmine-laced villas painted in the bright colors of Italian *gelato*. Ticino charms with its almost Mediterranean vegetation, emerald-green lakes, and shaded castles. Pastel church façades lead to ancient sanctuaries where faith, not tourism, is still the main draw. Lugano is the financial capital, and thanks to its gardened hostels, also serves as a center for budget travelers. Locarno is the most densely packed city with rewarding sights, and Bellinzona serves as the travel hub for Ticino; most buses and trains pass through the town.

BELLINZONA ☎091

Three medieval castles preside over Bellinzona (pop. 30,000), reminding visitors of days of yore when Bellinzona was a strategic Milanese fort for guarding trade routes through the San Bernadino and St. Gotthard passes. Bellinzona, capital of Ticino, is still an important crossroads for tourists on their way to the lake resorts

HIGHLIGHTS OF TICINO

Marvel at Marianne Werefkin's modern works in the **Museo Comunale d'Arte Moderna** in Ascona (see p. 413).

Make like James Bond and dive off the 255m high Verzasca dam, the **world's highest bungee jump** (see p. 411).

Groove to bass-heavy beats at the **Bellinzona Blues Festival** (see p. 406).

Couldn't crash Cannes? Try the **International Film Festival** in Locarno (see p. 411).

further south. Its central position has bestowed it with a sleek modernity missing in other Ticinese towns, though the villas and vineyards in the surrounding hills cast a pastoral calm over the city, disrupted only once a year by the bass-heavy beats of the Bellinzona Blues Festival.

TRANSPORT AND PRACTICAL INFORMATION

Bellinzona is the main train hub for Ticino. Make connections in Bellinzona to **Basel** (4hr., every 30min. 6:06am-11:35pm, 74SFr); **Lugano** (30min., every 30min. 5:06am-12:36pm, 10.80SFr); **Locarno** (20min., 2 per hr. 5:38am-12:38am, 6.80SFr); **Lucerne** (2¼hr., 6:06am-9:07pm, 52SFr); **Zurich** (2½hr., every 30min. 6:26am-9:07pm, 56SFr); **Milan** (2hr., every hr. 5:07am-1:20am, 54SFr); and **Rome** (7hr., every hr. 5:07am-12:36am, 148SFr). To Milan and Rome, travelers under 27 receive 25% off. Trains to and from **Geneva** require a change in **Domodossola, Italy** (5½hr., 9 per day, 95SFr) or **Olten** (6hr., about 2 per hr. 6:06am-6:26pm, 102SFr). **Post Buses** leave from the station for **Chur** (3 hr., every hr. 6:05am-5:07pm, 52SFr), **San Bernadino** (1¼hr., every hr. 6:05am-9:07pm on weekdays, until 11:07pm on weekends, 30SFr), and elsewhere in eastern Switzerland. **By car,** arrive from the north on N2/E35 or N13/E43; from Lugano or the south on N2/E35 north; from Locarno or the west on Rte. 13 east. For a **taxi,** call 254 444 or 251 151. The train station has **currency exchange, luggage storage** (5SFr at baggage check), **lockers** (3-5SFr), and **bike rental** (at baggage check; 27SFr per day; open 8am-9pm). Public **parking** is available at the train station or in the Colletivo at P. del Sole, off Viale Stazione to the right, down Largo Elvetica (1SFr per 45min.; open 7:30am-10pm).

Bellinzona's **tourist office,** 18 Via Stazione, in the post office building, makes free hotel reservations. From the train station, walk one block left. (☎825 2131; fax 825 3817; bellinzona.turismo@bluewin.ch; www.tourism-ticino.ch. Open M-F 9:30am-6:30pm, Sa 8:30am-12:30pm.) The Castelgrande (see below) has free **Internet** access. The **post office,** on Viale Stazione, is a block left from the station (open M-W, F 7:30am-6:30pm, Th 7:30am-8pm, Sa 9am-2pm). The **postal code** is CH-6500.

ACCOMMODATIONS AND FOOD

Unfortunately, housing options in Bellinzona are bland and overpriced. To reach **Hotel Garni Moderno,** 17b Viale Stazione, turn left from the station, right on Via Claudio Pelladini, and take an immediate right again on Via Cancelliere Molo. All rooms have new carpeting and a sink; half also have balconies. (☎/fax 825 1376. Breakfast included. Reception in the hotel cafe M-Sa 6:30am-10:30pm. Singles 55SFr; doubles 90SFr, 120SFr with shower; triples 120SFr, 150SFr; quads 160SFr, 180SFr. MC, Visa.) If the Garni Moderno is full, **Hotel San Giovanni,** 7 Via San Giovanni, has tidy rooms and an equally convenient location. From the station, turn left on Viale Stazione and right down Scalinata Dionigi Resinelli; continue straight for 100m. (☎/fax 825 1919; ristorantesangiovanni@bluewin.ch. Breakfast included. Parking available. Reception M-Sa 6:15am-midnight, Su 7am-noon. Singles 50SFr, 60SFr with shower; doubles with shower 90SFr. MC, Visa.) Take postal bus #2 to "Arbedo Posta Vecchia" for **Camping Bosco de Molinazzo.** Laundry, swimming pool, and bike rental are all available. (☎829 1118; fax 829 2355. Open Apr. 2-Oct. 17. 7.25SFr, children ages 6-14 half-price; tent 6SFr.)

Those who are nobles in spirit but peasants in pocket head to **Ristorante Inova,** Viale Stazione 5 (on the Piazza Collegiata), in the basement of the Innovazione. The self-serve king offers a wide selection. (Entrees 10-13SFr, salads 4.20-9.90SFr. Open M-W, F 8:30am-6:30pm, Th 8:30am-9pm, Sa 8am-5pm.) Otherwise, fill up on cappuccino (3SFr), *panini* (5SFr), and huge pizza slices (7SFr) at **Peverelli Panetteria Tea Room Pasticceria** in P. Collegiata, off Viale Stazione (open M-F 6:30am-7pm, Sa 6:30am-6pm). **Migros** is in P. del Sole, across from the Castelgrande entrance (supermarket open M-F 8am-6:30pm, Sa 7:30am-5pm; restaurant open M-F 7am-6:30pm, Sa 7am-5pm). The huge **outdoor market** along Viale Stazione lays out everything from fruits and breads to incense and rugs (Sa 7am-noon).

SIGHTS AND ACTIVITIES

CASTLES. Available at the castles and the tourist office, a **"3 Castelli" ticket** (8SFr, students 4SFr) grants entry to all 3 castles. Rising 50m above the P. del Sole on a huge hunk of rock, the oft-renovated **Castelgrande** occupies a site inhabited since the neolithic period (5500-5000 BC) and fortified from the 4th century on. Construction on the current fortress began in the 13th century, with major enlargements in 1473-86. The *bianca* (white) and *nera* (black) towers, rising 27 and 28m high, date from the 13th and 14th centuries. Climb to the top of the Tora Bianca for panoramic views of Bellinzona. The town transformed the castle from 1984-91 in an effort to make it more hospitable to tourists, adding an elevator, an expensive courtyard restaurant, and a concrete and TV-laden **museum** containing scores of wall fragments and old coins. *(The Castelgrande is accessible by the free elevator near P. del Sole or by the winding paths up the hill from P. Collegieta and P. Nosetto. Open 10am-6pm. 4SFr, students 2SFr.)*

Another 90m above Castelgrande, on the opposite hill, the smaller but more satisfyingly dank **Castello di Montebello** offers visitors working drawbridges, ramparts, dungeons, and views as far as Lake Maggiore on a clear day. The tower and former residential quarters now house a mildly interesting **archaeological and civic museum** containing vases, jewelry, and ceramics, as well as ancient bric-a-brac of ceremonial and military arms. *(The castle can be reached on foot from Piazza Collegiata up the slippery mossy steps of Sallita alla Motta or by bus from Viale Stazione. ☎825 1342. Open Tu-Su 10am-6pm, closed in January. Museum 2SFr, students 1SFr.)* Worth a look but not the walk, the **Castello di Corbaro** (230m above city level), the smallest of Bellinzona's 3 castles, surveys the Ticinese mountains. The Duke of Milan had the place slapped together in 6 months after the battle of Giornico—it now hosts temporary art exhibits in its **Belvedere Museum.** *(Take the road from Castello di Montebello or Via Ospedale. ☎825 5906. Open Apr.-Oct. Tu-Su 10am-6pm. Museum 4SFr, students 2SFr.)*

CHURCHES. Tucked away among villas and hotels, a number of notable churches grace Bellinzona. On the P. Collegiata at the end of the Viale Stazione, the **Chiesa Collegiata dei SS Pietro e Stefano** shows off an early Renaissance facade flanked by trumpeting heralds. The breathtakingly ornate stone interior features numerous paintings and frescoes (attributed to Simone Peterzano), overhung by a gilded canopy. Other interesting features are the pulpit in "scagliola" (a painted plaster imitation of marble) that dates from 1784 and the holy water stoup that is also known as the "Fontana Trivulziana" after a nobleman from Messocco who owned it in the 15th century.

The 16th-century **Chiesa di San Biagio** flaunts a gigantic painting of St. Christopher on its exterior and a flock of saints on its columned interior. On the south and west walls are tombstones and a beautifully carved granite font. *(From the train station, walk 15 minutes to the left or take bus #4 to "Cimiterio;" cross under the railroad tracks, turn left up the stairs, turn left again, and follow the tracks 50m. Open 9-11am.)* Across from the Chiesa di San Biagio is the **Villa dei Cedri,** which houses the **Civica Galleria d'Arte** collections. Focusing on the "figurative" art of Switzerland and Italy at the turn of the century, realism and symbolism intermingle in the exhibits. The modern collection might be too esoteric for all but the biggest fans of the period, but the small surrounding park is peaceful and shaded. *(☎821 8520. Grounds open Apr. 1-Sept. 30 8am-8pm, Oct. 1-Mar. 31 9am-5pm. Museum open Tu-Sa 10am-noon and 2-5pm, Su 10am-5pm. 8SFr, free for children and students with I.D.)*

WALKING. The Ticino River is perfect for idle strollers out for balmy breezes and mountain scenery. For a 45-minute hike with grand views of Sasso Corbaro and the valley, take a short post bus ride to Monti di Ravecchia. The trail begins at the hospital parking lot and follows an ancient mule path, leading to now-deserted **Prada,** an ancient trading post possibly dating to pre-Roman times.

MUSIC FESTIVALS AND NIGHTLIFE. The annual **Blues Festival** draws drawls from across southern America in late June (tentatively scheduled for June 28-30, 2001). Previous performers include Luther Allison and Joe Louis Walker. The 1st night is free and the other 2 are 10SFr each. Opera lovers with a bit of extra cash will relish the blockbuster productions of the Bellinzona **Open Air Opera** (July 20-31, 2001). *Aida* will be the main presentation this year. Prices range from 60-140SFr; contact the tourist office or **Ticket Corner** (☎0848 800 800; www.ticketcorner.ch).

LOCARNO ☎091

On the shores of **Lago Maggiore,** Locarno (pop. 30,000) basks in near-Mediterranean breezes and bright Italian sun. This relatively unspoiled resort town has a tropical feeling, perhaps because it gets over 2200 hours of sunlight per year—the most in all of Switzerland. During its world-famous **film festival** each August, Locarno swells with people enjoying balmy evenings of *al fresco* dining beneath palm trees. All this worldly languor coexists in relative peace with the piety of the worshipers in the churches of the **Città Vecchia** (old city). In addition to its self-contained charms, Locarno lies at the foot of the Ticinese hills and serves as an excellent starting point for mountain hikes along the **Verzasca** and **Maggia valleys** or regional skiing.

GETTING THERE AND AROUND

By car, Locarno is accessible from motorway N2, which extends from Basel to Chiasso (exit: Bellinzona-Süd).

Trains: P. Stazione (☎743 6564). To: **Bellinzona** (20min., every 30min. 5:30am-1:09am, 6.80SFr), connecting north to **Lucerne** (3hr., every 30min. 6:06am-12:36am, 56SFr) and **Zurich** (2¾hr., every hr. 6:26am-9:07pm, 60SFr). Trains go south to **Lugano** (45min., every 30min. 5:07am-12:36am, 16.40SFr) and **Milan** (2½hr., several per day 6:30am-8:30pm, 63SFr). For **Zermatt** (4hr., 88SFr), **Montreux** (4¾hr., 74SFr), or **Geneva** (5¾hr., 91SFr), change trains in **Domodossola, Italy** (1¾hr., 2 per hr. 6:05am-7:20pm, 41SFr).

Buses: Buses depart from the train station or from the lakeside Piazza Grande to nearby towns such as **Ascona** (#31, 20 min., every 15 min. 6:25am-12:02am) and **Minusio** (5min., every 15min. 5:04am-11:46pm). Buses also run regularly through the **San Bernadino Pass** to Eastern Switzerland.

Ferries: Navigazione Lago Maggiore, 1 Largo Zorzi (☎751 1865), conducts tours of the entire lake, all the way into Italy. A full day on the Swiss side of the lake costs 10SFr. Sail to **Ascona** (1hr., 6 per day, day pass 11SFr) or the Island of **Brissago** (1¼hr., 9 per day, day pass 20SFr, ages 6-16 receive 50% discounts). A "holiday" card for all of the *Lago Maggiore* and 50% off on the *Lago di Lugano* is 33SFr for 1 day, 54SFr for 3, and 72SFr for 7.

Car Rental: Hertz SA, Garage Stamini SA, Via Sempione 12, Muralto (☎743 5050).

Taxi: Chauffered comfort is only a phone call away at ☎743 1133.

Parking: Metered public parking on Via della Posta and major streets (1SFr per ½hr.). At the same rates, the 24hr. parking garage, **Autosilo Largo SA** (☎751 9613), beneath the *Kursaal,* is accessible from Via Cattori (open 8am-10pm).

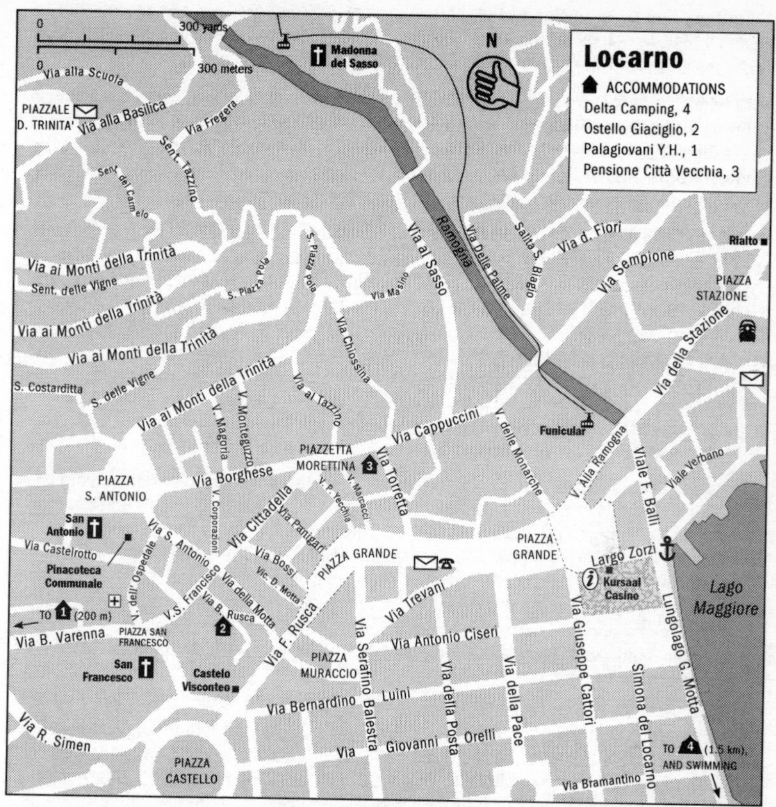

Bike Rental: At the train station. Bikes 27SFr per day, 21SFr per half day. Open 10am-9pm. Call 743 6564 to reserve a bike. 6SFr fee for returning a bike to another station. At the youth hostel, 20 mountain bikes available for 15SFr per day, 10SFr per half-day.

ORIENTATION AND PRACTICAL INFORMATION

Piazza Grande, home of the International Film Festival, is Locarno's anchor, with the town's social life centering around its arcades. Just above P. Grande, the *Città Vecchia* is home to 16th- and 17th-century architecture, as well as luxurious, yet economical accommodations. **Via Ramogna** connects the Piazza to the train station. **Via Rusca** extends from the other side of the Piazza to the Castello Visconteo. South of the Piazza lies the residential district, containing many vacation homes.

Tourist Office: Largo Zorzi (☎791 0091; fax 751 9070; buongiorno@maggiore.ch; www.maggiore.ch), on P. Grande. From the main exit of the train station, walk diagonally to the right, cross Via della Stazione, and continue through the pedestrian walkway (Via alla Ramogna). As you come out, cross Largo Zorzi to your left; the tourist office is in the same building as the *Kursaal* (casino). Office makes hotel reservations for free. Pick up a free map of Locarno and browse the many brochures. The office also organizes **bus excursions** around *Lago Maggiore* and beyond. City tours in English leave the tourist office Apr.-Oct. M at 9:45am, 8SFr. Open July 19-Aug. 15 M-F 9am-6pm, Sa 10am-4pm, Su 10am-noon and 1-3pm; mid-Mar.-July 19 and Aug. 15 to mid-Oct. closes at 4pm on Sa; mid-Oct. to mid-Mar., closed Sa-Su.

Currency Exchange: Try any one of the banks lining P. Grande or the train station. Banks open M-F 9am-4pm, station open 6:30am-8:30pm. Western Union at station open M-Sa 8am-6pm. **ATMs** (which accept MC and Visa) at the station and post office.

Luggage Storage: At the train station, 5SFr. Open 6:50am-8:30pm. **Lockers** 3-5SFr.

Bookstore: Fantasia Cartoleria Libreria, 32 P. Grande, next to the Co-op. English books, travel books, and maps. Open M-F 8am-6:30pm, Sa 8:30am-5pm.

Internet Access: Visitors' Center booth on Viale Balli (☎/fax 751 8408), across the street and 25m uphill from the ferry dock (12SFr per hour). Open June-Oct. 7am-8pm.

Emergencies: Police, ☎117. **Fire,** ☎118. **Road info,** ☎163. **Weather,** ☎162. **Medical Assistance,** ☎111. **Ambulance,** ☎144.

Post Office: P. Grande. Open M-F 7:30am-6:30pm, Sa 8:30am-2pm. **Postal Code:** CH-6600.

ACCOMMODATIONS

A display board outside the train station allows free phone calls to most of the city's hotels and pensions. Reserve everywhere a week in advance during high-season (Mar.-Oct.); book a year ahead for a bed during the film festival.

Pensione Città Vecchia, 13 Via Toretta (☎/fax 751 4554; cittavecchia@datacomm.ch; www.cittavecchia.ch). From P. Grande, turn right on Via Toretta (*not* vigola Toretta; look for a brown sign with the *alberghi* on it) and continue to the top. With the best prices in town and a location to match, the *pensione* is usually full. The co-ed rooms and bathrooms are simple but clean. The talkative owner makes recommendations about what's doin' in Locarno. Tiny breakfast and sheets (included for singles and doubles) 5SFr each. Phones open 8am-9pm; check-in 1-6pm; reservations 1-9pm; call ahead if arriving after 6pm. Open Mar.-Oct. Dorms 22-24SFr; singles 33-35SFr; doubles 64-76SFr per person.

Ostello Giaciglio, 7 Via Rusca (☎751 3064; fax 752 3837). Walk to the end of the P. Grande, turn right onto Via della Motta, and then take the left fork onto Via B. Rusca. Check in across the street at the Hotel Sempione. Black-and-white-checked dorms off marble-floored hallways. **Kitchen** facilities available. Breakfast 10SFr. Rowdy high-school groups tend to take over July-Aug., so call a week ahead for reservations. Reception 7:30am-9pm. 27SFr per person, sleepsack 3SFr. AmEx, MC, Visa.

Palagiovani Youth Hostel (HI), 18 Via Varenna (☎756 1500; fax 756 1501; locarno@youthhostel.ch; www.youthhostel.ch). From station, turn left, follow Via alla Romogna to P. Grande, and turn right on Via della Motta. Take the left fork (Via B. Rusca) past P.S. Francesco, then take Via Varenna to hostel (HI signs point the way from Via Varenna on). High hedges and floral bushes conceal an institutional, hospital-like establishment. 2- to 6- bed rooms, most with balconies, sinks, and lockers. Several rooms have **kitchenettes** at no extra charge. Sheets and breakfast included. Lunch and dinner 11.50SFr each. **Laundry** 6SFr. Towels 1.50SFr. Mountain **bikes** 15SFr per day, 10SFr for half day. Reception in summer 8-10am and 3-11:30pm; in winter 8-10am and 3-10:30pm. Dorms 31SFr, with shower and bathroom 38SFr; doubles 66SFr, 88SFr (subtract 2.50SFr in low season).

Delta Camping, 7 Via Respini (☎751 6081; fax 751 2243; info@campingdelta.com; www.campingdelta.com). A 30min. walk along the lakeside to the right from the tourist office (turn left at the info map) brings you to campstyles of the rich and famous. A reservation fee of 100SFr is required July-Aug., 50SFr of which is returned upon arrival at the site. Shaded by birch trees and adjacent to a golf course and rocky beach; a restaurant (entrees 9.50-18.50SFr), supermarket, workout room, certified diving instructors, and **bike rental** (20SFr per day, 12SFr per half day) are on site. Reception 8am-noon and 3-7pm. Of the 250 plots on this 5-star site, 35 have private, fenced-off gardens. 12.20SFr, 7.20SFr kids ages 3-15, garden plots 20-30SFr; June and Sept. 13.20SFr, 7.20SFr, 25-30SFr; July-Aug. 19.20SFr, 7.20SFr, 36-46SFr.

FOOD

Though most of Locarno's restaurants are pricey, many offer *panini*, pasta, and pizza in the 10-20SFr range, leaving ample funds for that nectar of the gods, *gelato*.

Ristorante Debarcadero (☎751 0555) on Largo Zorzi by the ferry dock. One of the very few spots on the lake that's affordable and not attached to a hotel. A young crowd enjoys pizza (10.50-18SFr), frappes (7SFr), and beer (tap 3.60SFr, bottled 5-6SFr), all accompanied by Top 40 selections. Open 8:30am-midnight.

Gelateria Fiordipanna, Piazzetta F. Franzoni (☎751 4124), on Via della Stazione between P. Grande and the station. The gelato experience of a lifetime, specializing in massive bowls of ice cream packed chock-full with fresh fruit and topped with triumphant whipped-cream cupolas. Each elaborate masterpiece is big enough to be a meal in itself. Ice cream bowls 9.50-11.50SFr, frappes 7SFr. Open Apr.-Oct. 9am-11pm.

Contrada, 26 P. Grande (☎751 4815). Ideal for those with a fetish for felines, this restaurant is a shrine to cuddly cats, which are artistically rendered in every medium on the walls of this satisfyingly quirky establishment. The covered terrace is ideal for people-watching. Pizzas and pasta (10.50-19SFr). AmEx, MC, Visa.

Inova, 1 Via della Stazione (☎743 7676), left as you exit the station. This huge, self-serve restaurant brings affordable, balanced meals to your fingertips: breakfast 5.20SFr, salad bar 4.90-9.90SFr, pasta buffet 8.50-9.90SFr, meaty menus 14.90SFr. Open M-Sa 7:30am-10pm, Su 8am-10pm.

MARKETS

Supermarkets: Aperto, at the station (open 6am-10pm); **Migros,** P. Grande (open M-Sa 9am-7pm).

Farmers' Markets (all in nearby Italian towns accessible by ferry): **Cannobio** (Su mornings; ferries at 9, 9:15, 10, 10:30, and 11am, and 4:20 and 5:15pm; 1hr., round-trip 21SFr); **Luino** (W; ferries at same times as Cannibio ferry and 1:10pm, 1½hr., 23SFr); and **Intra** (Sa; ferries at 9, 9:15, and 10:30am, 2½hr., 27SFr). Bring your passport.

ITALIAN SWITZERLAND

SIGHTS AND MUSEUMS

MADONNA DEL SASSO. For centuries, visitors have journeyed to Locarno solely to see the church of Madonna del Sasso (Madonna of the Rock), founded over 500 years ago when a Franciscan monk had a vision telling him to build a church high above the city. Its orange-yellow hue renders it immediately recognizable from anywhere in town. The church is accessible by a **funicular** that leaves every 15 minutes from a small station just left of the McDonald's (6SFr round trip, 4.50SFr with SwissPass). The true budget traveler will make the 20-minute walk up the smooth stones of the Via al Sasso (off the Via Cappuccini in the *Città Vecchia*), accompanied by capricious lizards scuttling across the path. Funicular riders will miss the sequence of life-size wooden niche statues that line the trail, depicting scenes from Christ's passion, including a *Pietà*, a Pentecost, and a 1650 Last Supper. The **sanctuary** itself envelopes the visitor with gilded carvings, frescoes, and statuary. Hundreds of silver heart-shaped medallions on the walls commemorate acts of God witnessed by worshipers who have made pilgrimages here over the years. Some of the hearts are accompanied by paintings and embroideries in silk.

The museum next door, in the oldest part of the complex, houses a collection of ancient reliquaries and pilgrims' souvenirs. But the highlight is definitely the 2nd floor collection of disaster paintings—near drownings, fires, attempted murders, battles, carriage and train accidents, and lightning strikes—all commissioned by survivors of the events thanking the Madonna for answering their prayers and intervening to save their lives. Miniature body parts commemorate physical healings. *(Grounds open daily 7am-7pm. Museum open Apr.-Oct. M-F 2-5pm, Su 10am-noon and 2-5pm. 2.50SFr, students 1.50SFr. English guidebooks at the entrance are free.)*

CHIESA SAN FRANCESCO. The church that houses the monastic order that founded the Madonna del Sasso rests in more modest surroundings within the city. Founded by the Franciscans shortly after the death of St. Francis of Assisi in the 13th century, the church displays a number of all-but-faded frescoes beneath its sagging roof. Built from stones scavenged from a demolished castle, the exterior bears incongruous inscriptions from the material's original incarnation. Similarly, a vanished cemetery once surrounded the building; of which the only remnant is a curious skull-and-crossbones from the Orelli family monument, now used as an entrance stone in the courtyard in front of the church. *(From P. Grande, turn right on Via B. Rusca and left on Via S. Francesca.)*

OTHER CHURCHES. The cavernous **Chiesa San Antonio** presides over the outskirts of the *Città Vecchia.* Built between 1668 and 1674, its pastel interior is still fairly well-preserved. Circular patches of sunlight illuminate a large fresco depicting Christ being taken off the cross and massive, intricately-carved altars. The church hosts organ concerts year-round; contact the tourist office for the monthly schedule. The small cultural museum in the **Pinacoteca Communale,** across the way, is housed in a renovated palace, where breezy balconies connect the exhibit rooms. The museum hosts changing exhibitions of lesser-known artists. *(Follow Via Marcacci from the P. Grande, and turn left on Via Borghese; San Antonio will be one block up from P. San Antonio. ☎ 756 3185. Open Tu-Su 10am-6pm. 7SFr, students 5SFr, under 17 1SFr.)*

CASTLE AND ARCHAEOLOGICAL MUSEUM. Down the Via F. Rusca from the P. Grande, the **Castello Visconteo** gazes on Locarno. After learning about the history of Locarno, wander through dungeons and up towers where soldiers poured boiling oil on attackers. The medieval castle, constructed between the 13th and 15th centuries, houses the **Museo Civico e Archeologico,** which exhibits Roman glassware, pottery, and coins. *(☎ 756 3180. Open May-Dec. Tu-Su 10am-6pm. 10SFr, students 5SFr.)*

OUTDOOR ACTIVITIES

ON THE LAKE. The deep blue water of the Lago Maggiore is a delight to the eyes, but if you want more immediate contact with the lake, a **ferry** ride to points on both the Swiss and Italian shores is an excellent idea (see p. 406). The tropical **Isole di Brissago** is especially popular for its **botanical gardens,** which were cultivated in 1885 by a utopian-minded baroness hoping to create an earthly paradise. Exotic plants from Asia, the Americas, Australia, and Africa intermingle with delicate stands of bamboo concealing splendidly colored exotic birds. *(☎ 791 4361 or 791 4362; fax 791 0763; dic-ibrissago.amministrazione@tinet.ch; www.isolebrissago.ch. Free guided tour daily at 2:30pm. English guide 2SFr. Open Apr.-Oct., 9am-6pm. Admission 6SFr, 3SFr kids ages 6-16.)* To power your own way around the lake, you can **rent** your own boat from **Brusa Marco** along the water towards Delta Camping *(☎ (079) 214 6257; pedal boats 14-18SFr for 1hr., 8-12SFr for 30min.; motor boats 40SFr, 25SFr).* To cool off, don your swimsuit and head to the **Piscina Lido,** near Camping Delta, for a dip in a pool or the lake *(☎ 751 4408; open 9am-7:30pm; 6SFr, students 4SFr).* 2 minutes farther along the lake at **Bagno Pubblico La Lanca,** you can swim in the lake with swans and ducks for a few francs less *(☎ 751 4408; open 10am-7:30pm; 3SFr, 1.50SFr kids ages 6-15).* Or, seek out a stretch of the **Fiume Maggia,** the rock-strewn artery that feeds into the lake, for free bathing.

VAL VERZASCA HIKE. To escape the city, head out on Post Bus #630.55 to **Sonogno** *(1hr. 10min., 16.40SFr, 32SFr round-trip)* and hike amid the extraordinary peaks at the end of **Val Verzasca** (valley). From the bus stop, take the 1st left and follow the yellow signs to **Lavertezzo.** The trail is marked by yellow signs with directions and town names, and white-red-white blazes. Pass through cool, shady glens and rocky riverbeds as you follow the Verzasca river through the valley. Close to **Lavertezzo,** the river eases its rapid pace, making swimming possible, but pick your swimming hole carefully, as the water can be colder than you think and the undercurrents strong. Climb the **Ponte dei Salti,** a vaulted stone bridge built at the end of the Middle Ages, and gaze into the clear green ponds. You can finish at any point on the hike by meeting the Post Bus that stops along the valley.

ADVENTURE SPORTS. The Verzasca Dam has allowed scores of visitors dizzying adrenaline rushes courtesy of its famous **bungee jump,** the highest in the world. The 255m jump, conquered with such panache by James Bond in *Goldeneye*, costs 244SFr the 1st time (with training, drink, and diploma) and 195SFr for subsequent leaps. You can even jump at night. Contact **Trekking Team** *(☎ 0 848 808 007; info@trekking.ch; www.trekking.ch; Open Apr.-Oct.).* They also offer **canyoning** *(125-165SFr),* **cave exploration** *(98SFr adults, 68SFr kids, 48SFr students),* and a 70m bungee jump *(125SFr first time, then 100SFr)* in **Centovalli** *(package price for both bungee jumps: 345SFr).* The **Visitors Center** on Vaile Bali *(☎/fax 751 8408; info@visitorscenter.ch; www.visitorscenter.ch),* across the street and 25m uphill from the ferry dock, books the above activities with Trekking Team, as well as **skydiving** *(385SFr for a jump from 3500m with 30 seconds of free-fall),* **paragliding** *(185SFr),* **windsurfing lessons** *(60SFr for hour),* **waterskiing and wakeboarding** *(25SFr for 10 min.),* **bike tours** *(48SFr, 39SFr with your own bike),* **rock climbing** *(195SFr per day),* **rafting** *(40-95SFr),* and **sailing lessons** *(180-220SFr, min. 3 people).*

ITALIAN SWITZERLAND

NIGHTLIFE AND FESTIVALS

In spite of its infantilizing *Lion King* theme, the lakeside **Simba Bar** appeals to Locarno's hottest and hippest with its mesmerizing neon aquarium, sparkly hanging mirrors, and rainbow-hued mosaic bar. To get there head toward Camping Delta. Beer is 4SFr. (☎ 752 3388. 18 and older. DJ nightly after 8pm. Open 5pm-1am.) High-rollers lay down their chips at the gold-tinged **Kursaal** (casino) next to the tourist office (open Su-Th noon-2am, F-Sa noon-4am; must be over 20; proper attire required: no shorts or T-shirts). The **Katjaboat,** a little yellow vessel that departs in front of the Hotel Rosa, down the Via Verbano from the ferry dock, offers a light-hearted serving of romantic cheesiness. For only the price of a drink (minimum 5SFr, beer 6SFr, wine 10SFr), the young-at-heart enjoy a 20-minute mini-tour of the lake to wonderfully sappy piped-in music. (☎ (079) 686 3990. Boat runs 10am-1am, though its schedule tends to be as free-spirited as its atmosphere.) Catch recent American and Italian movies (14SFr, 10SFr on Mondays) at the **Cinema Rex** on Via Bossi next to the Co-op, just off P. Grande, or nurse a long drink at one of the numerous outdoor cafes along P. Grande.

For 11 days at the beginning of every August, everything in Locarno halts for the **International Film Festival,** one of the most important movie premiere events in the world. Unlike Cannes, no invitations are required. Over 150,000 big screen enthusiasts descend upon the town for the spectacle—book your room 6 months to a year ahead to stand a chance. The famous centerpiece of the festival is a giant 26m by 14m outdoor screen set up in Piazza Grande for big name premieres by the likes of Jean Luc Goddard, Woody Allen, Spike Lee, and Bernardo Bertolucci. Smaller screens throughout the city highlight young filmmakers and groundbreaking experimentation. (For more info, write to: International Film Festival, Via Luini 3a, CH-6601 Locarno; ☎ 756 2121; fax 756 2149; info@pardo.ch; www.pardo.ch.)

In the 2nd half of July, Locarno teams up with Ascona to host **Ticino Musica,** a festival of classical music focusing on young musicians and students, featuring concerts, operas, and master classes at several venues. Tickets are available at either tourist office or at the door of any event. (☎ 980 0970; fax 980 0971; games@bluewin.ch; www.ticinomusica.com.)

NEAR LOCARNO: AURIGENO

From the train station in Locarno, take bus #10 (dir.: Valle Maggia) to "Ronchini" (25min., every hr. 5:30am-11:35pm, 6.80SFr). Cross the street and turn right from the bus stop, then follow the hostel signs into the forest (15min.). When you get to the paved street, turn right. The hostel is right behind the church. The path can be difficult to follow so you may want to call ahead.

Hidden among chestnut trees, waterfalls, and dozens of lakes in Ticino's largest valley, Valle Maggia, is the village of Aurigeno. Come to Aurigeno to take a "vacation from your vacation" at **Baracca Backpacker** (☎(079) 207 1554), a tiny hostel with lots to offer. It has only 10 beds, but unlimited access to the peaceful outdoors and a home-like atmosphere. Beo the bird noisily greets each new arrival, and the youthful couple who run the hostel provide fresh herbs for cooking, and a wood-working shop for tinkering. While you're escaping from civilization, use the **kitchen, rent a bike** (10SFr per day), or explore the **hiking, climbing,** and **swimming** possibilities in the area. Reception 9-11am and 5-10pm. Open Apr.-Oct. Sleepsack 2SFr per day. Dorms 25SFr.

ASCONA ☎091

In his memoirs of Ascona (pop. 5,000), *The First Step into Wonderland*, Jacob Flach effuses, "Here lies a piece of the Mediterranean Sea embedded in rough mountains, a sun-bathed, blooming cape of the Côte d'Azure, a mile of the Riviera beach sprinkled with azaleas and carnations, and a good dose of the blue sky!" While they may not be as eloquent as Flach, the German-speaking Swiss who spend their summer vacations in this supremely romantic resort village on the shores of Lake Maggiore definitely share his love for it. In addition to enjoying Ascona's tropical sunshine and sparkling water, history buffs can trace the steps of the leftist thinkers and Bohemian artists who tried to establish Utopia on the mountain above, hopefully titled **Monte Verità,** around the turn of the century. Due to the lack of cheap beds Ascona might be best enjoyed as a daytrip from Locarno.

TRANSPORT AND PRACTICAL INFORMATION

Reach Ascona by **bus** #31 from **Locarno** (15min., every 15min. 6:23am-midnight, 2.40SFr) or by **ferry** (1hr., 10 per day, day pass 11SFr). The **tourist office,** in the Casa Serodine behind the Chiesa SS Pietro e Paolo, **exchanges currency** at standard rates. (☎791 0091; fax 751 9070; buongiorno@maggiore.ch; www.maggiore.ch. Open Mar. 20-Oct. 20 M-F 9am-6pm, Sa 10am-4pm; Oct. 21-Mar. 19 M-F 9am-noon and 1:30-5:30pm.) **Guided tours** of Ascona (in German and English) leave from the office (Mar.-Nov., Tu 10am, 1hr., 8SFr). For a **taxi,** call 791 4646 or 791 4141. For **parking,** try the **Autosilo** at the corner of Via Papio and Via Buonamno. **Rent bikes** at **Cicli Sport Shop,** Via Circonvallazione 14 (☎791 7627). From the bus stop, head down Via Papio and turn right in front of Migros. (25SFr per day. Open M, W-F 9am-12:30pm and 2-6:30pm, Tu closed, Sa 9am-noon and 1:30-5pm.) The **post office,** at the corner just uphill from the bus stop at the intersection of Via Papio, Via Borge, and Via Locarno, has an **ATM** (open M-F 7:30am-noon and 1:45-6pm, Sa 8:30-noon). The **postal code** is CH-6612.

ACCOMMODATIONS AND FOOD

Very few of Ascona's many beds fall into a budget price range, which might drive you to sleep in Locarno. Otherwise, try the rooms above the **Ristorante Verbano,** Via Borgo, near the modern art museum, left from the post office (☎791 1274; breakfast included; 45SFr per person). A free hotel reservation board hangs at the bus stop—another option is to ask the tourist office for a list of **camere private** (private rooms; 35-70SFr per person).

Grab a bite to eat at **Otello** on Via Papio 8, just downhill from the bus stop. Their specialty is crêpes (from 7SFr), but they also have gnocchi (11.50-15SFr), pasta dishes (12-19SFr), and polenta dishes (13.50-22SFr). Occasionally, you can hear New Orleans jazz from the bandstand on the terrace in back. (☎791 3307. Open 7:30am-midnight; hot food 11:30am-11:30pm. MC, Visa.) **Ristorante La Torre,** Piazza Motta 61, offers prime views of the lake, but is famous for its whimsically decorated bowls of gelato (9.90SFr). Live piano music daily June-Sept. 6:30-11:30pm. Pizza and pasta starting at 11.80SFr. (☎791 5455. Open Mar.-Oct. and Dec. 27-Jan.6

PARADISE LOST Around the turn of the last century, a distinctly left-of-center collection of anarchists, agrarians, artists, philosophers, vegetarians, and writers sought Utopia on the banks of the *Lago Maggiore*. Political refugees, including Russian anarchist Michail Bakunin, sought refuge in Ascona in the late 1800s. In 1889, the Locarnese philosopher Alfredo Pioda proposed the establishment of a lay convent for international intellectuals to be named "fraternitas" on La Monescia, the hill behind Ascona. Though his vision never came to fruition, thinkers seeking connections between humankind, nature, the world, and the universe came to La Monescia anyway. The hill was renamed "Monte Verità" ("mount of truth") by Henri Oeden-Koven and Uda Hoffman, a pair of free spirits who founded a vegetarian and naturalistic community there in 1900. Meanwhile, Ascona's reputation as a cultural center for the elite continued to grow, drawing the likes of D.H. Lawrence, James Joyce, Hermann Hesse, and Karl Jung (and, in the 20s and 30s, members of the German avant-garde and Dadaists like Klee, Arp, and Segal). The **Museo Casa Anatta** (anatta means "soul" in Sanskrit) preserves the Utopian ideals that flourished during Monte Verità's heyday.

9:30am-1am; closed Nov. 2-Dec. 22; in Jan. and Feb. closed M-Tu.) You can't miss the **Co-op's** orange sign down Via Papio from the bus stop or the **Migros** farther down the same street (both open M-F 8am-12:30pm and 2-6:30pm, Sa 8am-5pm). A **market** spills onto the P.G. Motta along the lake every Tuesday from 10am-5pm.

 SIGHTS

The Post Bus stop at the corner of Via Borgo and Via Papio, at the edge of the old city, leaves you within walking distance of all the sights and the waterfront.

THE OLD CITY. From the bus stop, turning right on the Via Collegio before the Pontifico Papio takes you into the heart of the *Città Vecchia*, with its narrow, banner-hung streets and wrought-iron balconies. Turn right again at the end of the street to find the **Chiesa SS Pietro e Paolo,** whose slender, stone clock tower marks Ascona along the lake. The frescoes inside date from the 15th century. At the edge of the *Città Vecchia*, 1 block downhill from the bus stop on Via delle Cappelle, the *pesca*-hued 15th-century courtyard of the **Collegio Pontifico Papio** is framed by banana trees and adorned with the coat of arms of many a departed collegiate administrator. Presiding over the still-operating Superior private school (est. 1399), the adjacent church of **Santa Maria della Misericordia** spruces up its dim interior with 15th-century frescoes by Seregnesi and Antonio da Tradate and a brand-new organ.

MUSEUMS. The rich stucco of the **Casa Serodine,** the building that now houses the tourist office, is all that remains of what was once a Renaissance artist colony. Today, private galleries line the winding streets, promoting such artists as Marc Chagall and Georges Braque. Down Via Borgo just before the waterfront, the **Museo Comunale d'Arte Moderna** has an extensive permanent collection that includes works by Klee, Utrillo, Amiet, and Jawlensky, as well as moving and evocative temperas by Russian Marianne Werefkin that depict religious

s and scenes of rural Ticino. *(34 Via Borgo. ☎780 5100. Open Mar.-Dec. Tu-Sa 10am-noon and 3-6pm, Su 4-6pm. 5SFr, students and seniors 3SFr.)*

The **Museo Casa Anatta,** a shrine to all things alternative, immortalizes the dashed dreams of Utopia (unfortunately without English labeling). Walk up the hilly Strada della Collina from the bus stop (15min.). This facinating museum contains photos of a 1930s nudist colony in Brissago, anarchist Ernsy Frick's collection of mystical minerals, and the costumes and crowns worn by members of the "individualistic cooperative" during their ritualistic dances in the woods. One room is dedicated to Otto Gross, a schizophrenic man who started the short-lived University for the Emanciaption of Man here at the height of the movement. Don't miss the miniature model of one Utopian (male) anarchitect's proposed Temple to the Land of Fidus, in which men would pass from the Room of Ambition to the Room of Love and worship a statue of the Woman of the Earth. *(☎ 791 0327. Open Apr.-June and Sept.-Oct. Tu-Su 2:30-6pm; July-Aug. Tu-Su 3-7pm. 6SFr, students 4SFr.)*

WATERFRONT SIGHTS. Heading down Via Borgo from the bus stop brings you to the shores of the lake, where there are countless chic terrace restaurants. To the left along the water from Via Borgo, at the end of Piazza G. Motta, the sole remaining tower of the 13th-century **Castello del Ghiriglion,** 26 P.G. Motto, has been reborn as a hotel and expensive restaurant. Further along the waterfront, just past the Eden Roc hotel, the **Museo Epper** hosts temporary exhibitions of 20th-century art. *(14 Via Albarelle. ☎ 791 1942. Open Apr.- June and Sept.-Oct. Tu-F 10am-noon and 3-6pm, Su 3-6pm; July-Aug. Tu-F 10am-noon and 8-10pm, Sa-Su 8-10pm. Free.)* You can tour the *Lago Maggiore* by **renting a boat.** Zandonella, along the water near the Via Borgo, is one good place to start. (☎ 791 3825. Pedal boats 10SFr for 30min., 16SFr for 1hr.; motor boats 27SFr, 44SFr.)

FESTIVALS AND NIGHTLIFE

In late June and early July, Ascona sets up the bandstands and claps its hands to the beat of the **New Orleans Music Festival** (www.jazzscona.ch). Musicians play jazz, gospel, soul, blues, and even zydeco on the waterfront and in local cafes. If you're around in August, consider stopping by for the **International Horse Jumping Competition,** or the **International Music Weeks** of classical music (late Aug. to mid-Oct.). Locarno's discotheque crowd flocks to Ascona's subterranean dance club, **Cincilla,** Via Moscia 6, which is located with several other bars and clubs beneath mysterious arcades beside *Lago Maggiore* to the right of Via Borgo. (Open 10pm-5am. Must be 18.) On rainy nights, catch a flick at the **Cinema Otello,** next to the restaurant of the same name on the Via Papio (☎ 791 0323; 14SFr, movies in English with German or Italian subtitles).

LUGANO ☎ 091

Lugano, Switzerland's third-largest banking center, rests in the crevassed valley between San Salvatore and Monte Brè. Warmed by a Mediterranean climate, Lugano's shady streets are lined with tiles, climbing vines, and wildflowers. Lugano draws plenty of visitors with its seamless blend of religious beauty, artistic flair, and natural spectacle, though it remains slightly less colorful or lively than nearby Locarno. Traveleres flock to Lugano's 2 extraordinary youth hostels in town, both built from luxury villas, with swimming pools and magnificent gardens.

GETTING THERE AND AROUND

The small **Lugano-Agno Airport** services Crossair flights from Basel, Bern, Geneva, London, Nice, Rome, and Zurich. Trains connect the Lugano train station to the airport (every 20min., 4.40SFr). A **shuttle** (☎ (079) 221 4243) runs from the station (every hr. 7:40am-8pm) to the airport (8SFr), town center (10SFr), or other locations upon request (13SFr). To reach Lugano by **car,** take Rte. N2/E35.

Trains: P. della Stazione. Most destinations connect through **Bellinzona** (30min., every 30 min. 5:06am-12:36am, 10.80SFr). To: **Locarno** (1hr., every 30min. 5:37am-12:04am, 16.40SFr); **Basel** (5hr., every 30 min. 5:04am-10:40pm, 81SFr); **Bern** (through Lucerne; 5hr., every hr. 5:05am-8:15pm, 77SFr); **Geneva** (through Lucerne, 7¼hr., 105SFr); **Zurich** (3½hr., every hr. 5:57am-8:39pm, 62SFr); and **Milan** (1½hr., every hr. 5:36am-9:48pm, 14SFr).

Public Transportation: Buses run from the neighboring towns to the center of Lugano and also traverse the city. Schedules and ticket machines at each stop. 1.20-1.90SFr per ride, 24hr. "Carta Giorno" (day pass) 5SFr. SwissPass valid.

Taxis: ☎ 922 8833 or 922 0222.

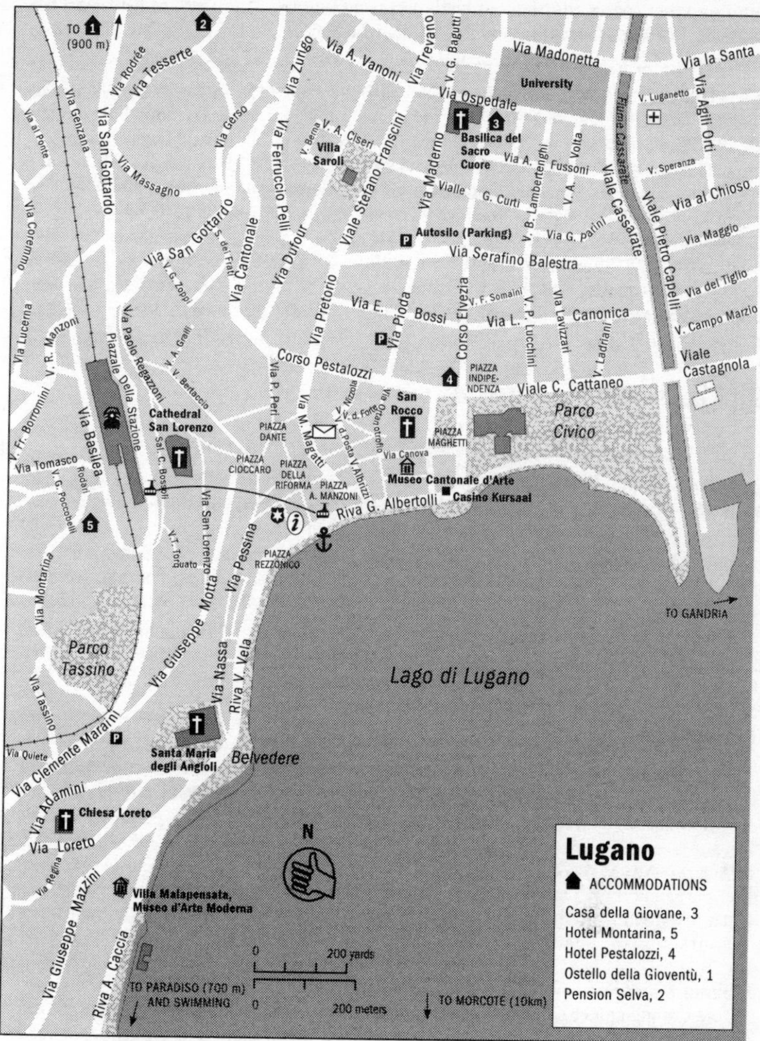

Car Rental: Avis, 8 Via C. Maraini (☎913 4151). **Hertz,** 13 Via San Gottardo (☎923 4675). **Europcar,** 24 Via M. Boglia, Garage Cassarate (☎971 0101).

Parking: Autosilo Balestra, off Via Pioda, on Via S. Balestra, charges 1SFr for 1hr., 4SFr for 3, 25SFr for 12. Overnight parking 6SFr. Open 24hr.

Bike Rental: At the baggage check in the station (☎923 6691). 27SFr per day. 6SFr to return at another station. Open 8am-6pm.

ORIENTATION AND PRACTICAL INFORMATION

The 15min. downhill walk form the train station to the arcaded **Piazza della Riforma,** the town's center, winds through Lugano's large pedestrian zone. For those who would rather avoid the walk, a **cable car** runs between the train station and the waterfront **Piazza Cioccaro** (0.90SFr, 5:20am-11:50pm).

Tourist Office: (☎913 3232; fax 922 7653; info@lugano-tourism.ch; www.lugano-tourism.ch) in the Palazzo Civico, Riva Albertolli, at the corner of P. Rezzonico. From the station, cross the footbridge labeled "Centro" and proceed down Via Cattedrale straight through P. Cioccaro as it turns into Via Pessina. Turn left on Via dei Pesci and left on Riva Via Vela, which becomes Riva Giocondo Albertolli. The office is just past the fountain on the left, across the street from the ferry launch. Pick up free maps and make hotel reservations (4SFr). The tourist office also offers a free **guided city walk** in English Apr.-Oct. at 9:30am M, starting at Chiesa degli Angioli. Open Apr.-Oct. M-F 9am-6:30pm, Sa 9am-12:30pm and 1:30-5pm, Su 10am-2pm; Nov.-Mar. M-F 9am-12:30pm and 1:30-5:30pm.

Consulates: UK, 22 Via Sarengo (☎950 0606). Open M-F 10am-noon.

Currency Exchange: In the train station, ☎923 9326. Open M-Sa 7:10am-7:45pm, Su 8am-7:45pm. Banks open M-F 8:30am-6:30pm.

Luggage Storage: Lockers at the train station. 3-5SFr. Open 24hr.

Lost Property: Check the *Fundbureau* of the Polizei Communale, on the P. Riforma, on the other side of the same building as the tourist office. ☎800 7109. Open M-Sa 10am-4pm.

Internet Access: Biblio-Café Tra, 3 Via A. Vanoni (☎923 2305). From P. Dante, head down the Via Pretorio (15 min.) and turn left on Via A. Vanoni. Open M-Th 9am-midnight, F 9am-1am, Sa 5pm-1am. 8SFr per hr.

Bookstore: Melisa, 4 Via Vegezzi (☎923 8341), across from post office, stocks English-language books downstairs. Open M-F 8am-12:30pm and 1:30-6:30pm, Sa 8:30am-12:30pm and 1:30-5pm. Open continually through lunch May-Sept. AmEx, MC, Visa.

Library: Biblioteca Cantonale, 6 Viale Cattaneo (☎911 5350). From the tourist office turn left and walk along the waterfront; library is in the Parco Civico, just before Fiume Cassarante canal. Open M-F 9am-7pm, Sa 9am-noon and 2-5pm; July-Aug. closed on Sa.

Medical Services: ☎111. **First Aid,** ☎805 6111.

Emergencies: Police, ☎117. **Ambulance,** ☎144. **Fire,** ☎118.

Post Office: Via della Posta, 2 blocks up from the lake near Via al Forte. Open M-F 7:30am-6:15pm, Sa 8am-2pm. Travelers' checks cashed. Telephones, telegraphs, and faxes at the Via Magatti entrance to the PTT building. **Postal Code:** CH-6900.

ACCOMMODATIONS

Lugano's hostels are practically as nice as the luxury hotels that line the lakesides, for a fraction of the price.

Hotel Montarina, 1 Via Montarina (☎966 7272; fax 966 0017; info@montarina.ch; www.montarina.ch), just behind the train station. Walk 200m to the right from the station, cross the tracks, and walk 1min. uphill. Converted from a luxury villa, this palm-tree-enveloped independent hostel attracts young families and students with its **swimming pool,** well-groomed grounds, ping-pong, chandeliered reading room, and terrace with a view. The dorms get rowdy in summer, when vacationing youth party hard. **Laundry** (4SFr, soap 1.50SFr). Good cheap coffee (1SFr). Buffet breakfast 12SFr. Sheets 4SFr. Parking available. Reception 8am-10pm. Open Mar.-Oct. In July and Aug. call 2 weeks in advance for reservations. Dorms 25SFr; singles 50-65SFr; doubles 100SFr, 120SFr with bath.

Ostello della Gioventù (HI), Lugano-Savosa, 13 Via Cantonale (☎966 2728; fax 968 2363). Note: there are 2 streets called Via Cantonale, one in downtown Lugano and one in Savosa, where the hostel is. Take bus #5 (walk 350m in to the left of the station and cross the street to get to the bus stop) to "Crocifisso" (6th stop), and then backtrack a bit and turn left up Via Cantonale. A former luxury villa, this sprawling hostel has secluded gardens a **pool** with a waterslide, and a decidedly elegant atmosphere. The family, who has run the hostel for over 50 years, takes obvious pride in their establishment. Apartments available for families (7-day min. stay; 100-170SFr per day). Breakfast 7SFr. 1SFr for **kitchen** use (after 7pm only). **Laundry** 5SFr. Reception 7am-12:30pm and 3-10pm. Curfew 10pm; keys available on request. Reserve ahead. Open mid-Mar. to Oct. Dorms 23SFr; singles 35SFr, with kitchenette 45SFr; doubles 56SFr, 70SFr. Price drops after 4 nights.

Casa della Giovane, 34 Corso Elvezia (☎911 6646; fax 911 6640), across the street from Basilica Sacro Cuore. Take bus #9 (dir: Ospedale; leaves opposite train station) to "Corso Elvezia." This modern peach and blue building has bright, immaculate rooms for **women only.** Giovane can feel more like a convent than a hostel. The beautiful rooftop terrace, though, has views of the lake and mountains and allows for some serious tanning. Breakfast 4.50SFr. Lunch or dinner 12SFr. **Laundry** 5SFr. Reception 7am-11pm. Under age 18, curfew 9:30pm; ages 18 and up M-Th 11:15pm, F-Su 2am. Reserve ahead. 4-bed dorms 20SFr; singles 50SFr; doubles 60SFr (breakfast included).

Pensione Selva, 36 Via Tesserete (☎923 6017; fax 923 6009). Take bus #9 (dir: Ospedale; leaves opposite the station) to "Sassa," then walk along Via Gottardo for 250m and turn right on Via Tesserete. A path overhung with grapes leads to the cozy *pensione* with an outdoor **pool** and terrace. Reception 8am-midnight. Singles 55SFr, with shower 78SFr; doubles 101SFr, 138SFr. Closed in Nov.

Albergo Pestalozzi, 9 P. Indipendenza (☎921 4646; fax 922 2045; pestalo@bluewin.ch), on the main *piazza* away from the waterfront, 2 blocks up from the casino. Although the rooms have odd color schemes, the location can't be beat. Breakfast included. Lunch or dinner 13-18SFr. Reception 6am-11pm. Reserve ahead. Higher prices give toilet, shower, and bath. Singles 56-96SFr; doubles 96-144SFr; triples 47-70SFr per person. MC, Visa.

Camping: There are 5 campsites, all in **Agno.** Check with the tourist office for a complete list. For **La Palma** (☎605 2561; fax 604 5438) or **Eurocampo** (☎605 2114; fax 605 3187), take the Ferrovia-Lugano-Ponte-Tresa (FLP) train to Agno (4.40SFr). From the station, turn left, then left again on Via Molinazzo. La Palma 7SFr, Eurocampo 7.50SFr; tents 6-10SFr. All sites have showers. Open Apr.-Oct.

ITALIAN SWITZERLAND

FOOD

Lugano's many outdoor restaurants and cafes pay homage to the canton's Italian heritage, serving up plates of *penne* and *gnocchi* and freshly spun pizzas. Lugano's specialty is (visibly) sausage. For some quick *al fresco* shopping and eating, **Via Pessina,** off P. Riforma, livens up at midday with outdoor sandwich and fruit shops. **Salumeria,** 12 Via Pessina, is one of the better ones—you can buy some of the sausage there too. The **Migros,** 15 Via Pretoria, is 2 blocks left of the post office, down Via Pretorio in the center of town, and offers fresh pasta and delicious *ciabatta* (a crusty Italian bread). The food court on the ground floor saves the near-penniless with huge slices of pizza (from 2.50SFr) and sandwiches (from 2.30SFr). Open M-F 8am-6:30pm, Sa 7:30am-5pm. Aperto, in the station, is open 6am-10pm. There is a **public market** on P. della Riforma that sells seafood and produce and yummy veggie sandwiches (4SFr; open Tu and F 7am-noon.)

La Tinèra, 2 Via dei Gorini (☎923 5219), behind Credit Suisse in P. della Riforma. Tucked away in an alley off a cobblestone road, this romantically low-lit underground restaurant has great daily specials (12-18SFr). Try the sausage with *risotto* (13SFr). Open M-Sa 8:30am-3pm and 5:30-11pm. AmEx, MC, Visa.

Ristorante Cantinone, (☎923 1068) P. Cioccaro, behind P. Dante. This popular establishment has the weighty reputation for dishing out the best pizza in town under its pink-and-white striped umbrellas. Try the Tuscan pizza with apples and nuts (15SFr). Pizza and pasta 11.50-19SFr. Salads 7-16SFr. Open 9am-midnight. AmEx, MC, Visa.

Gelateria Arcobaleno, 2 Via Marconi (☎922 6218), 10 min. to the left of the tourist office along the waterfront. Dishes out the most creative and unusual gelato desserts in town, as well as lowfat yogurt gelato. Menu highlights include gelato spaghetti (9SFr), gelato pizza (9SFr), and the Indonesia, a pineapple filled with gelato yogurt, fruit, and whipped cream (11SFr). Open Su-Th 8:30am-midnight, F 8:30am-1am.

Pestalozzi, 9 P. Indipendenza (☎921 4646), in the hotel. This non-alcoholic restaurant offers well-balanced, veggie-friendly menus (9.50-16SFr) including tofu burgers. *Lasagne bolognese* and mixed salad 9.50SFr. Open 11am-9:30pm. MC, Visa.

Taqueria El Chilichil, Corsa Pestalozzi 12 (☎922 8226), down the Corsa Pestalozzi from the P. Indipendenza. Had enough Italian food? This lively taqueria provides a welcome change of pace, serving up entrees like tacos, burritos, and quesadillas (4.50-7.50SFr), as well as Mexican beer (6SFr) and margaritas (7SFr, pitcher 20SFr). Open M-Th 11:30am-11pm, F 11:30am-midnight, Sa-Su 7pm-midnight.

Ristorante Inova, on the 3rd floor of Innovazione Department Store in P. Dante. Budget eaters can't beat these self-serve victuals. Salad bar (4.30-9.90SFr), pasta bar (7.50-9SFr per plate), and other warm daily specials (10-14SFr). Open M-Sa 7:30am-10pm, Su 10am-10pm.

SIGHTS

CHURCHES. The frescoes of the 16th-century **Cattedrale San Lorenzo,** just below the train station, gleam with colors that are still vivid, despite their advanced age. The frescos on the west wall date from the 13th-century. The most spectacular fresco in Lugano is Bernardio Luini's gargantuan **Crucifixion** which was painted in 1529, in the **Chiesa Santa Maria degli Angioli,** to the right of the tourist office on the waterfront. Two blocks to the left of the P. della Riforma, in the Piazza Maghetti, the small but densely decorated 14th-century **Chiesa San Rocco** houses an ornate Madonna altarpiece and gruesome Discopli frescoes of saints being flayed alive and shot with arrows. The national monument **Basilica Sacro Cuore,** on Corso Elevezia across from the Casa della Giovane, is more sparing in its ornamentation, but the painted angels seem to fly right off the walls. Frescoes ringing the altar feature hikers walking alongside the disciples.

ART MUSEUMS. Aside from the churches, Lugano's best known cultural attractions are its art museums—past and present (see **Art for Art's Sake?,** p. 419). The largest and most fun museum is the **Museo Cantonale d'Arte,** which has a permanent collection of 19th- and 20th-century art, including works by Swiss artists Vela, Ciseri, Franzoni, and Klee, and temporary modern art exhibits as well. The first and second floors are highly entertaining and feel, in places, like mirrored halls in an amusement park. The third floor, however, is a more sedate collection of pencil drawings. *(10 Via Canova, across from the Chiesa San Rocco. ☎910 4780. Open Tu 2-5pm, W-Su 10am-5pm. Special exhibits 10SFr, students 7SFr; permanent collection 7SFr, students 5SFr.)*

The **Museo d'Arte Moderna,** Villa Malpensata, 10 min. to the right of the tourist office, has a decent collection of European and American 20th-century art, as well as annual retrospectives and special exhibitions. *(5 riva Caccia. ☎944 4370. Open only for special exhibitions, Tu-Su 9am-7pm. 10SFr, 8SFr for students, 5SFr youth ages 14-18, free for children under 14.)* An elegant lakeside villa houses the **Museo delle Culture Extraeuropee.** The masks, statues, and shields from distant lands stand out against the villa's marble floors and wall paintings. *(324 Via Cortivo. On the footpath to Gandria in the Villa Heleneum. ☎971 7353. Open Mar. 5-Oct. 31 W-Su 10am-5pm. 5SFr, students 3SFr.)*

OUTDOOR ACTIVITIES

PARKS AND GARDENS. Lugano's waterfront parks are ideal places for introspection or play. The **Belvedere,** on quai riva Caccia, is an enormous sculpture garden with an emphasis on modernist metalwork. On sunny afternoons, enthusiasts gather there for open-air chess tournaments. The garden stretches along the lakeside promenade to the right of the tourist office toward Paradiso. In the other direction, the less whimsical but more serene **Parco Civico** is brightened by flower

ART FOR ART'S SAKE? The **Thyssen-Bornemisza Gallery** once housed one of the most outstanding private collections in Europe, until the owner (a fantastically rich old Baron) and his young Spanish wife (a former beauty queen) started looking around for a new home for all of those Rembrandts, Dürers, Van Goghs, and Kandinskys. In the international bidding war that ensued, the collection moved into the hands of the Spanish government for a while to up the ante. Spain became attached to the paintings, so the Baron talked them into building a museum and paying him a cool US$350 million for the stash. The gallery in Lugano, still maintained by the very piqued Swiss, is open out of sheer stubbornness, with lackluster modern art on display. *(Take bus #1 (dir.: Castagnola) to "Villa Favorita" or catch a ferry to Castagnola. Open Apr.-Oct. F-Su 10am-5pm. 10SFr, students 6SFr.)*

beds along the water and trees that reach down with willowy, long arms to touch the lake. Backpackers have been known to crash here (illegally). *(Open Mar. 1-Oct. 31 6:30am-11:30pm; Nov. 1-Feb. 28 7am-9pm.)*

BOATING. To enjoy the lake, try a **ferry ride.** The dock for the **Societa Navigazione del Lago di Lugano** *(☎923 1779; lake.lugano@bluewin.ch)* is to the left of the tourist office. Various tours of the lagoon-like Lake Lugano offer glimpses of the tiny, unspoiled towns along the shore, including **Gandria** *(10.80SFr, round-trip 18SFr)*, **Morcote** *(15.40SFr, 25.60SFr)*, and **Paradiso** *(2.80SFr, 4.80SFr)*. A "grand tour" of the lake in English (3½hr.) is 30.60SFr; 58SFr gets you 7 days of unlimited lake travel. SwissPass is valid on all boats; Eurail is not. Conduct your own tours by **renting a boat.** Various points on the lake rent pedal boats *(7SFr for 30min.)*. **Rent a Boat Saladin** *(☎923 5733)*, to the right of the tourist office, provides motor boats at 40SFr per hour, 25SFr per half hour *(no license required; open 8am-9pm)*. Instead of more *gelato*, cool off at the **Bagno Pubblico** on riva Caccia towards Paradiso. *(☎994 2035. Lake swimming 4SFr, children 2SFr. Open May 13-June 30 and Aug. 14-Sept. 13 9:30am-6:30pm; July 1-Aug. 15 9:30am-8pm.)*

HIKING. Though the tops of the Ticinese mountains are cluttered with tourists, the unhampered views stretch into Italy. The tourist office and Hotel Montarina both have topographical maps and trail guides. The cheapest and most rewarding hike goes to **Monte Boglio,** a 5-hr. round-trip that can be extended over two days by staying at the Pairolhütte (ask at hostels or tourist office for more information). **Monte Brè** (933m) and **Monte San Salvatore** (912m), are both accessible mountains thanks to the funiculars that go to the top. Monte Brè's **funicular** is down the river to the left of the tourist office (☎971 3171; 13SFr, round-trip 19SFr; ages 6-16 6.50SFr, 9.50SFr). The San Salvatore funicular is 20 minutes from the tourist office, down the river to the right in Paradiso (☎985 2828, 12SFr, round-trip 18SFr; ages 6-16 6SFr, 9SFr). With a 13th-century church teetering on craggy cliffs that extend to the water, San Salvatore is easily the more striking of the pair. Hike down from the peak through chestnut forests to **Morcote,** on the shore, where you can catch a ferry back to Lugano (15.40SFr, SwissPass valid, Eurail not valid). The walk from the summit takes about 3½ hours.

ADVENTURE SPORTS. Travelers feeling the uncontrollable urge to throw themselves off cliffs should seek relief with the **ASBEST Adventure Company,** Via Basilea 28, CH-6903 Lugano (☎966 1114; fax 966 1213; info@asbest.ch; www.asbest.ch), based in the Hotel Continental. In the winter, **snowshoe** and **ski** (full-day 90SFr) or **tandem paraglide** over icy crags (165SFr). **Canyoning** (from 90SFr) and **river-diving** (90SFr) are nice in Ticino because the water isn't as cold as the numbing mountain Alpine glacier streams. Or choose between **rock-climbing** (90SFr) and **mountain biking** (35SFr). AmEx, MC, Visa.

NIGHTLIFE AND FESTIVALS

The arcades of the town *piazze* fill at night with people taking a *passaggio*, or a stroll around the city center in their best duds. The outdoor cafes of P. della Riforma are especially lively. Poker and slot machines will swallow your cash at the **Casino** to the left of the tourist office (☎923 3224; slots open noon-4am, tables open M-Sa 9pm-3am, Su 4-7pm; disco open W-Su 11pm-4am; min. age 20). On the way to the casino, stop in at the **Pave Pub,** riva Albertolli 1, a self-proclaimed *museo di birra* (beer museum), offering 50 different beers with a lakeside view of the fountains and a decidedly un-museum like liveliness (☎922 0770; beers start at 4-5SFr; open 11am-1am). For a change of pace head down the Via Pretorio from P. Dante and turn left on Via A. Vanoni for the **Biblio-Café Tra,** 3 Via Vanoni. This laid-back cafe evokes a bit of leftist Spain with bossa nova and battered wood tables. Locals and subversives consume 3.40SFr beers. **Internet** access 8SFr per hour. (☎923 2305. Open M-Th 9am-midnight, F 9am-1am, Sa 5pm-1am.) The Latin American **Mango Club,** 8 P. Dante, mixes live salsa and techno for a sweaty good time (☎922 9438; open from 11pm until last person leaves).

Festivals liven up the lakefront in Lugano even more. During the first 2 weekends in July, Lugano's **Jazz Festival** heats up at no charge. Previous performers include Miles Davis and Bobby McFerrin. The looser **Blues to Bop Festival** (also free) celebrates R&B, blues, and gospel at the end of August, hosting international singers and local amateurs. The festive season wraps up with the **Wine Harvest Festival** in late September and early October, drowning those faded summer memories. From the end of June to early August, **Cinema al Lago** shows international films on the beach nightly at 9:45pm. A huge screen is installed at water level on the lake (☎921 4664; 14SFr, under 17 11SFr).

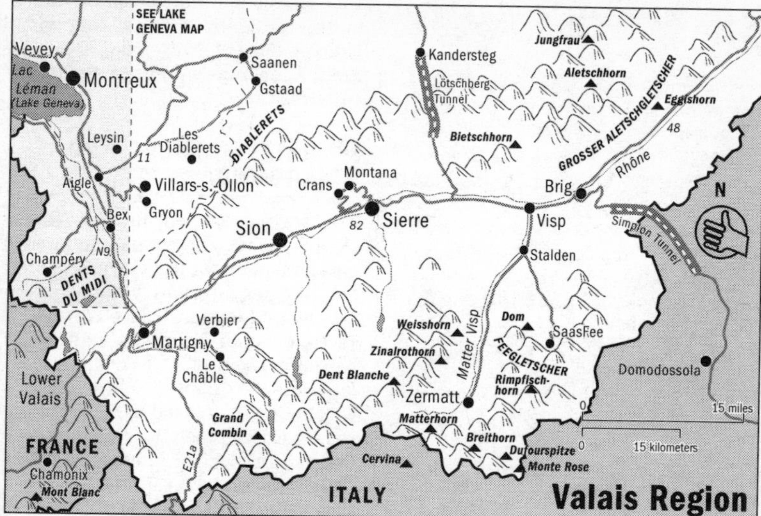

VALAIS (WALLIS)

The territory bounded by Canton Valais occupies the deep, wide glacier cleft shaved by the Rhône river. The clefts of the valley divide the land linguistically. In the west, Martigny and Sion are Francophone; in Brig and Zermatt Swiss-German dominates. Whatever the language, though, the towns share a common industry of getting people up and down the snow covered peaks that surround them, whether on skis or by foot. Though the high mountain resorts can be over-touristed, the inherent drama of the region's spectacular peaks and hulking glaciers still inspires strings of superlatives or awe-struck silence. Zermatt unquestionably has the most to offer for both skiing and hiking and should be the first stop for anyone pressed for time. Beware that Eurail is not valid on the BVZ train line, which services many of the towns in the area.

HIGHLIGHTS OF VALAIS

From **Zermatt,** ski Europe's longest ski run, or hike off in any direction for stunning views of the Matterhorn (see p. 421).

Ski in the summer sun on the slopes of **Saas Fe** (see p. 429).

Need something to contemplate while skiing? Load up on beautiful images at the Foundationi Pierre Gianadda's world-renowned art museum in **Martigny** (see p. 433).

ZERMATT AND THE MATTERHORN ☎027

A trick of the valley blocks out the great Alpine summits that ring Zermatt, allowing the Matterhorn (4478m) to rise alone above the town. Instantly recognizable and stamped on everything from scarves to pencils by Zermatt's merchants of kitsch, the peak still causes you to catch your breath whenever you look up. At dawn it blazes bright orange; some days—some weeks—it is swathed in clouds, completely hidden from view. The main road, Bahnhofstraße, is populated in equal measure by ruddy hiker/skier tourists and their more sedate shopping bagladen counterparts. But a short hike or cable car ride takes you away from all of

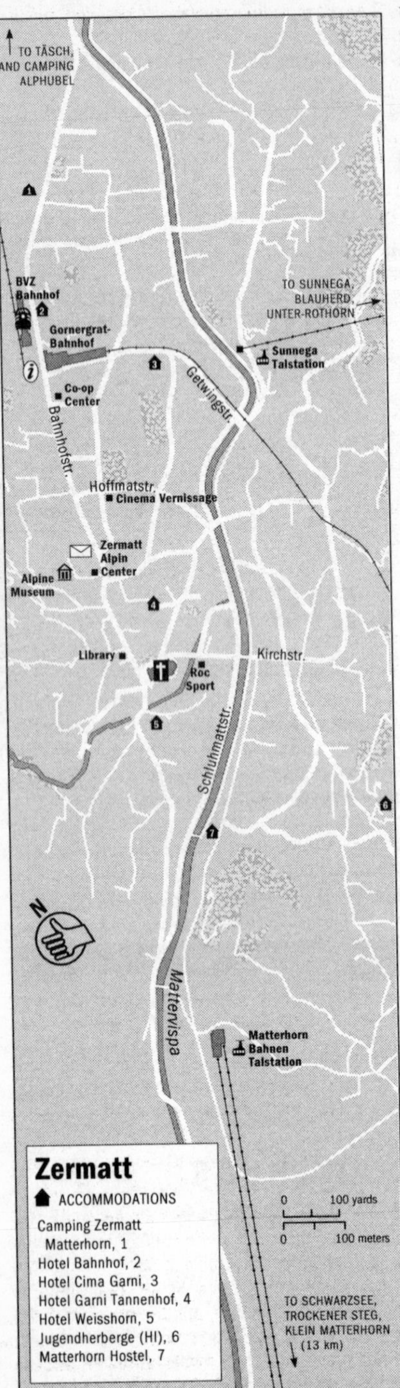

this, to lonely Alpine meadows and splintered icefalls. The hiking and skiing—some of Switzerland's best—are the real reason to make the trek to Zermatt.

GETTING THERE AND AROUND

To preserve the Alpine air from exhaust fumes, Zermatt has outlawed cars and buses; locals in toy-like electric buggies alternately dodge and target pedestrians. The town of **Täsch,** one stop before Zermatt, has **parking garages** for 10SFr per day; the large, outdoor lot by the rail station is 5-6.50SFr per day (and has a reservation board for hotels in Zermatt). Zermatt is only accessible by the **BVZ (Brig-Visp-Zermatt)** rail line (Swiss-Pass valid, **Eurail not valid**).

Trains: (☎966 4711). To get to Zermatt, jump on the BVZ at **Brig** (1½hr., 38SFr, round-trip 63SFr), **Visp** (if coming from Lausanne or Sion; 35SFr, round-trip 58SFr), **Stalden-Saas** (if coming from Saas Fee; 1hr., 23.60SFr, round-trip 31SFr), or **Täsch** (every 20min., 7.40SFr). Trains leave Zermatt for **Brig** from 6am-9:10pm and **Täsch** until 11:10pm. The station has a free phone to Zermatt's hotels, **lockers** (2-5SFr, open 5:45am-8pm), and **hotel taxis,** waiting to round up guests after each train arrives.

ORIENTATION AND PRACTICAL INFORMATION

Zermatt is not the easiest town to navigate, because the place has made it into the 21st century without having street names—instead streets are known for the buildings that stand on them (the names that *Let's Go* uses). Supposedly, the town is instituting names and putting up signs soon, but until then the best way to find your way around is by asking people. The problem is alleviated slightly by the fact that many tourist spots lie on the same street as the tourist office.

Tourist Office: Bahnhofpl. (☎967 0181; fax 967 0185; zermatt@wallis.ch; www.zermatt.ch), in the station

VALAIS

complex. Free booklets *Prato Borni* and *Zermatt* provide excruciatingly detailed practical info for getting around the city. A *Wanderkarte* (hiking map) costs 24.90SFr. Open mid-June to mid-Oct. M-F 8:30am-6pm, Sa 8:30am-7pm, Su 9:30am-noon and 4-7pm; mid-Oct. to mid-June M-Sa 8:30am-noon and 1:30-7pm.

Bike and Ski Rental: Roc Sport (☎967 4340) on Kirchstr. Go left at the church. Mountain bikes 35SFr per day, 25SFr per half-day. Open M-Sa 8am-noon and 2:30-7pm, Su 8am-noon and 3:30-6:30pm. Its outlet, **Julen Sport** (☎967 4340) on Hoffmattstr., has skis but no bikes. Open M-Sa 8:30am-noon, 2-7pm. AmEx, DC, MC, Visa. Otherwise, try **Slalom Sport** (☎966 2366) on Kirchstr. Open M-Sa 8am-noon and 2-7pm, Su 8am-noon and 4-6:30pm. Or **Bayard Sports** (☎966 4960) directly across from the station. Open M-Sa 8am-noon and 2-7pm.

Currency Exchange: Zermatt Tours, next to the tourist office. No commission. Open July 1-Sept. 30 and Dec. 20-Apr. 25 M-Sa 8:30am-noon and 2-6pm, Su 9am-noon and 3-6pm; Oct. 1-Dec. 19 and Apr. 26-June 30 M-F 8:30am-noon and 2-6pm, Sa 8:30am-noon and 2:30-6pm. **Banks** are generally open M-F 9am-noon and 2:30-6pm.

Laundry: Waschsalon Doli (☎967 5100) behind Swiss Souvenirs and across from the train station.

English-Language Library: In the English Church on the hill behind the post office. Small collection of used novels loaned on the honor system. (Open M-Tu and Th-F 4-10pm.)

Weather Conditions: Dial 162 or check the window of the *Bergführerbüro.* **Winter Avalanche Information,** ☎187.

Pharmacy: Pharmacie Internationale Zermatt (☎966 2727), Bahnhofstr. to right of station. Open M-Sa 8:30am-noon and 2-6:30pm; Su 11am-noon and 5-6pm. Emergency service for 10SFr surcharge.

Internet Access: Get your email fix at **Matterhorn Hostel** for 10SFr per hr. **Hotel Post** (☎967 1932), down Bahnhofstr. to the right of the station, charges 1SFr for 3min., 2SFr for 8 min., 3 SFr for 20 min.

Emergencies: Police, ☎117. **Fire,** ☎118. **Ambulance,** ☎671 212. **24hr. Alpine Rescue,** ☎1414.

Post Office: Bahnhofstr., in Arcade Mont-Cervin, 5min. to the right of the station. **ATM.** Open M-F 8:30am-noon and 1:45-6pm, Sat 8:30am-noon. **Postal Code:** CH-3920.

VALAIS

ACCOMMODATIONS

Climbers, hikers, and snowboarders buoy up the demand for budget beds in Zermatt. Finding a dorm bed on the spot can be a squeeze July through August, Christmas and New Year's, and mid-February through mid-March. Many hotels in winter and all chalets in summer only accept bookings for a week at a time. In desperation, some campers are tempted to park their bods illegally in the wide-open spaces above town—this practice can incur fines between 50 and 100SFr.

Hotel Bahnhof (☎967 2406; fax 967 7216; Hotel_Bahnhof@hotmail.com), on Bahnhofstr., 1min. to the left of the station. Renovated rooms provide hotel housing at hostel rates. Try to get one of the rooms with a view of the Matterhorn. **Laundry** 3SFr. No breakfast, but one of the few places with a **kitchen** and large dining room. Open mid-Dec. to mid-Oct. Reception 8am-around 8pm. Dorms 30SFr; 4-bed rooms with private showers 40SFr; singles 52SFr, with shower 56SFr; doubles 82-88SFr. MC, Visa.

The Matterhorn Hostel (☎968 1919, fax 968 1915; info@matterhornhostel.com), is a 12min. walk from the station. Turn right on Bahnhofstr., left at the church, and take the first right after the river onto Schluhmattstr. Hostel is 400m up the street. The graffiti might be part of the decor of this young, independent hostel, but the rest of the mess is probably not there for aesthetic effect. The service is a bit slow, and the beds aren't too comfortable, but the hostel draws a fun crowd of outdoor types. Breakfast 6SFr. Dinner 12SFr *Menü* or à la carte (10-20SFr) in summer. Sheets 3.50SFr. **Internet access** 10SFr per hr. Coin-operated **laundry** 2-8SFr for wash and dry. The bar outside serves beer for 3SFr. TV room, games, no curfew. Reception 7:30-11am and 4-10pm. Metal bunks 24-29SFr in summer, 29SFr in winter. AmEx, MC, Visa.

Jugendherberge (HI), Winkelmatten (☎967 2320; fax 967 5306; zermatt@youthhostel.ch), is a 15min. hike from the station, the last part up a steep hill. Turn right along Bahnhofstr. and left at the church. Cross the river, take the second street to the right (at the Jugendherberge sign), and select the left fork in front of Hotel Rhodania. A fully loaded, if predictably institutional hostel, where you get all the goodies...for a higher price. Unobstructed views of the Matterhorn from bedroom windows, friendly staff, giant outdoor chess set, ping-pong, and foosball await. Breakfast, sleepsack, showers, and **dinner** (kosher and vegetarian available) included. Laundry 8-16SFr per load. Closed May and late Oct. to mid-Dec. Reception 7-10am and 4-10pm in summer, 6:30-9:30am and 4-11pm in winter. Dorms 36SFr, 46SFr in July and Aug., one double 98SFr, 103SFr. AmEx, DC, MC, Visa.

Hotel Weisshorn, Bahnhofstr. (☎967 1112; fax 967 3839; anfrage@holidaynet.ch). From the train station, turn right along Bahnhofstr. The hotel is 30m past the church. Low, paneled ceilings, winding staircases, and cushy beds draw guests to this hotel. While it is the most affordable of the tourist-magnet hotels, rates vary depending on season. Breakfast included. Reception 7am-10pm. Reservations up to two months in advance necessary in winter high season. Singles 46-56SFr, with private shower, TV, and phone 65-77SFr; doubles 84-106SFr, 110-144SFr; triples 58.50-70.50SFr per person. MC, Visa.

VALAIS

Hotel Garni Tannenhof (☎967 3188; fax 967 3173; hotel-tannenhof@rhone.ch). From the station, turn right on Bahnhofstr., walk 300m, turn left at Bayard Sports and then take the first right. Features retro rugs, leather chairs, and a solicitous staff, not to mention the excellent breakfast. Every room comes with a radio and telephone. Breakfast included. Reception 7am-7pm. Reserve at least 1 month in advance in winter, 2-3 weeks in summer. Closed Oct. 20-Dec. 5. Singles 45-55SFr; with private shower 60-80SFr; doubles 90-100SFr, 110-130SFr; triples 35-40SFr per person. AmEx, DC, Visa.

Hotel Cima Garni (☎967 2337; fax 967 5539), 250m up the street that leads straight out of the station; behind Swiss Souvenirs. This bed and breakfast blends a standard Swiss exterior (red shutters on brown building) with an interior of brown, orange, and yellow. The pine paneling is so shiny you can almost smell the polish. Clean, bright rooms sport Matterhorn paintings and varying color schemes. Breakfast included. Singles and doubles 50-65SFr per person in summer, 65-90SFr in winter. Visa.

Camping Matterhorn Zermatt, Bahnhofstr. (☎/fax 967 3921), is 5min. to the left of the train station. Though the mountains are pretty, the spotty, grass-covered area looks onto train tracks. Showers included. June 10-Oct.11. Reception 8:30-9:30am and 5:30-7pm. 9SFr, children 6SFr.

Camping Alphubel (☎967 3635), in Täsch. Since Zermatt is car-free, caravaners and motorists can park their vehicles and stay here. From the station, cross the parking lot and turn right in front of the tourist offices past the river, then right across the railroad tracks. Showers included. Open May to mid-Oct. Reception 8am-8pm. 4.50SFr, ages 6-16 2.50SFr; tent 5SFr; car 5SFr; caravan 6SFr.

Mountain Huts: The tourist office has a list of private huts in the Zermatt area. They offer a good deal for serious climbers and hikers; they are all a full day's hike from Zermatt. All huts are open July-Aug., are accessible to walkers if there's no snow, and include breakfast unless otherwise noted. Try **Schönbielhütte** (2694m; ☎967 1354; 35.50SFr), **Rothornhütte** (3177m; ☎967 2043; 32SFr; see the Grandchild Hike p. 428), the crowded **Gandegghütte** (3029m; ☎(079) 607 8868, fax (027) 967 2112; anfrage@holiday.ch; 25 SFr; no breakfast), or **Hörnlihütte** (3260m; ☎967 2264; 43SFr; see Hörnli Hike p. 427).

FOOD AND NIGHTLIFE

Rather than charging the usual inflated Alpine prices, a number of the cafes along Bahnhofstr. leave both your wallet and your stomach full. After dark, revellers flood the streets, paying visits to the bars that fuel Zermatt's après-ski party scene. For groceries, the **Co-op Center** is across from the station (open M-Sa 8:30am-12:15pm and 1:45-6:30pm).

RESTAURANTS

Café-Konditorei Hörnli (☎967 4457), Bahnhofstr., across from Hoffmattstr, is a relaxed, quiet little place, lit by tiny futuristic lamps where you can relax and recharge in air-conditioned bliss. Breakfast 6-14SFr, salads 8.50SFr, sweet crêpes 4-7.50SFr, delectable ice cream concoctions 5-9SFr. The bakery downstairs has a mouth-watering selection of everything nice. Be sure to try the fresher-than-fresh apple strudel (2.20SFr). Cafe open 7:30am-7pm (open until 10pm from mid-July to mid-Aug.), bakery open M-Sa 7:30am-noon and 2-6:30pm.

Pöstli "Brown Cow" Pub (☎967 1932), Bahnhofstr., past the post office in the Great Swiss Disaster complex at the Hotel de la Post. The clientele of lively English-speaking locals comes for the whimsical cow-pattern decor (even painted on the metal ceiling fans) and back-to-basics, greasy-spoon food. Potato skins 9.50SFr, or sadistically chomp on a burger, 11-15SFr. Heineken 3.40SFr. Open 8am-midnight. Be sure to check out the other bars, restaurants, and clubs in the Great Swiss Disaster complex while you're there, but the food and drinks at the Brown Cow are by far the cheapest.

Walliserkanne (☎966 4610), Bahnhofstr., next to the post office. Although its atmosphere is somewhat lacking, Walliserkanne offers filling Swiss fare including *Käsespätzle* (homemade pasta with cheese, 16.50SFr), *Käseschnitte mit Schinken and Tomate* (toasted cheese with ham and tomato, 16SFr), and fresh strawberries in whipped cream (9SFr), as well as pizza and pasta (14-19.50SFr). Open 11:30am-2pm and 6-10pm. Pizzeria downstairs open 11:30am-11pm. AmEx, DC, MC, Visa.

Café du Pont (☎967 4343), 7min. from the station on Bahnhofstr., next to Hotel Weisshorn. Zermatt's oldest restaurant tends to attract a similarly aged clientele. Gain new appreciation for your youth while browsing through the multilingual menus burnt into slabs of wood hanging on the wall, then decide between stick-to-your-ribs Swiss dishes like *raclette* (7.50SFr), *Rösti* (11-15SFr), and *fondue du Pont* (22SFr). Sandwiches 6.50SFr. Open June-Oct. and Dec.-Apr. daily 9am-11pm; food served 11am-10pm.

BARS

The Pipe Surfer's Cantina, (☎213 3807; www.gozermatt.com/bars+clubs). Go right on Bahnhofstr. from the station, then left at the church onto Kirchstr. For those craving a sunny tropical climate, the Pipe is the next best thing. This randomly placed surf bar is the nightly site of the craziest beach party in the Alps. Owner Nikk, generous with the free shots (stop by in the afternoon for a 2-for-1 coupon or get one at the HI hostel), keeps customers rolling with his hilarious wisecracks. Also a place to load up on outdoor advice–the staff are all experts. Don't leave without downing a shot of Moo, the made-on-the-premises caramel vodka (5SFr). Frozen margaritas 6SFr, beer 3.50SFr. Food on the weekends. Special Bum's Play plate includes beer and entree; giros 11SFr, kebabs 8SFr. Open daily 3:30pm-2:30am.

The North Wall Bar (☎967 2863). Head over the river on Kirchstr. and take the second right en route to the youth hostel. No frills, 100%-English-speaking climbers' haunt where skiing and mountaineering videos play every evening alongside the dart games. This is the place to scrounge a job in Zermatt–from the staff, who also give hiking advice. The kitchen will serve you "the hottest pizza in the Alps" (10SFr, plus 1SFr for fancy topping like mussels, corn, broccoli, or egg). Beer 4.50SFr for 0.5L. Open mid-June to Sept. and mid-Dec. to Apr. 6:30pm-12:30am, pizza served until 10pm.

Grampi's Pub (☎967 7788), Bahnhofstr., across from Pöstli Pub. This centrally located bar thumps with pop dance music every night. Draft beer 3.80SFr for 0.25L; bottled beer 4.50-7SFr; long drinks 11-13SFr. Open 8:45am-3am, downstairs bar until 4am (DJ 9pm-3:30am), upstairs Italian restaurant 6pm-2:30am.

OUTDOOR ACTIVITIES

The building right from the station, past the post office is the Zermatt Alpin Center, which houses both the **Bergführerbüro** (Guide's Office; ☎966 2460, fax 966 2469; alpincenter@zermatt.ch, www.zermatt.ch/alpincenter) and the **Skischulbüro** (Ski School Office; ☎967 2466; skischule.zermatt@spectraweb.ch). In this building you can pick up detailed 4-day weather forecasts every morning, ski passes, and guided climbing expeditions (see below for more). Both offices are open July-Sept. M-F 8:30am-noon and 4-7pm, Sa 4-7pm, Su 10am-noon and 4-7pm.

SKIING

73 lifts, 14,200m of combined elevation, and 245km of prepared runs make Zermatt one of the world's best-equipped ski centers. Serious skiers will find real challenges here, as well as **Europe's longest run**—the 13km trail from Klein Matterhorn to Zermatt. The town also has more **summer ski trails** than any other Alpine ski resort—36 sq. km of year-round runs between 2900 and 3900m. In the summer, the **Skischulbüro** (see above for info) offers group classes for skiing and snowboarding (either activity: 1 day 40SFr, 5 days 200SFr). Individual ski/snowboard lessons are 80SFr for 1hr., 210SFr for 3 hr. **Ski and boot rental** is standard throughout the area, as is snowboard rental: 50SFr for 1 day, 200SFr for 7. Finding a reliable sports store is not a problem (most shops open daily 8am-noon and 2-7pm). Zermatt's **ski passes** operate on a regional system during the **summer** (from the end of April to October). You can buy passes for any of the regions (Matterhorn complex, Gornergrat complex, and Sunnegga complex), but you can only buy passes for the individual regions for one day at a time. The Matterhorn region costs 77SFr for 1 day. The Klein Matterhorn/Trockener Steg sub-region is now combined with Italy's Mt. Cervinia (1 day 62SFr). From November to the end of April, you have to buy a combined pass for all 3 regions, and you can buy it for any number of days (1 day 62SFr, 7 days 324SFr).

CLIMBING

Two companies lead expeditions up into the snowy regions above Zermatt. The **Bergführerbüro** sends groups up the Breithorn (120SFr), Pollux (230SFr), and Castor (240SFr) every day during the summer (see above for hours). These prices do not include equipment, hut accommodations, or lifts to the departure points. The other company is the **Freeride Film Factory** (☎213 3807; nikk@rhone.ch), which is run out of the Pipe Surfer's Cantina. Freeride offers custom hiking and climbing expeditions for lower prices than the Ski School (150-200SFr), and all of their guides speak English. They also give you a videotape of your expedition. For equipment rental, see hiking below. Just so you know, climbing the Matterhorn is expensive and requires a guide, perfect physical condition, a 4am start, and extensive rock-climbing experience (at least PD+).

HIKING

Outstanding walks into the world of glaciers and high mountains leave from Zermatt in every direction. Although these paths are well-maintained and marked, a proper topographic map is essential for safety and adds to your appreciation of the mountains. Lifts and railways to the south and east are also valuable hiking tools; they can save you difficult climbs and precious energy. SwissPasses will win you a 25% discount on many of these lifts, but **Eurail** is generally not valid. Prudent walkers should come prepared (see Essentials: Health, p. 20). Zermatt is particularly prone to sudden electrical storms, and you may need to dive for cover. Check the weather forecast in the Bergführerbüro before leaving. To rent hiking boots, try **Matterhorn Sport,** Bahnhofstr. (☎967 2956), which also rents out climbing equipment; **Glacier Sport,** Bahnhofstr. (☎968 1300) across from Walliserkanne; or **Burgena Sport,** Bahnhofstr. (☎967 2794) next to Grampi's pub. (1-day rentals are 14SFr; 7 days 52SFr; 14 days 80SFr. All stores open daily 8am-noon and 2-7pm.)

MONTE ROSA CONQUERS CELEBRITIES The Monte Rosa has a long and illustrious career with glitterati. Leonardi DaVinci, staring up at it from the Italian side, thought it the highest mountain on earth. Among its unlikely conquerors have been Pope Pius XI, who pioneered a new route to the Grenzensattel in 1889 before donning the papal robes. A youthful Winston Churchill climbed the Rosa in 1894 before bringing peace to the free world.

While many hikes test even the strongest outdoorsperson, there are plenty of hikes for people at any fitness level. The hiking around Zermatt can be divided into four main geographical areas. To the immediate **southeast** from Zermatt is the Gornergrat. Behind the Gornergrat are the **Monte Rosa** (4634m) and the **Liskamm** (4527m), the second and third highest mountains in Switzerland, respectively. From this area, framed by woods and reflected in lakes, the Matterhorn takes on its most familiar angle. A cog railway winds up to the peak of the Gornergrat to make views more accessible. Directly **south** from Zermatt, in between the town and the mountain, is the Schwarzsee. From the lake, the Matterhorn parades the pyramidal west face. This direction is the way to wilderness—steep icefalls peel off the **Breithorn** (4164m), and below the icefalls are the glacier-scoured, sun-bleached boulder fields and Zermatt's most well-known hike to the Hörnlihutte. Compared to the well-trodden highways south of Zermatt, the slopes of the Sunnegga-Roth side to the **north** are much better-known during ski season. Rockier and steeper, these difficult paths lead to proper summits rather than scenic huts or viewpoints. On the Kalbematten side, **west** of Zermatt, the mountains are savage, spiky pinnacles. The **Zinalrothorn** (4221m), **Obergabelhorn** (4063m), and **Dent Blanche** (4357m) are some of the toughest climbs around.

VALAIS

Hörnlihütte Hike (5hrs. each way without cable car, 2hrs. each way with). Very few climbers in the world are experienced enough to be able to reach the top of the Matterhorn. However, if you love pushing yourself to the physical max, you can get almost the same adrenaline rush as they do by struggling up to the **Hörnlihütte.** This serves as the base camp for the normal route up the Matterhorn and is a good platform for vicariously watching brightly colored dots claw their way upward along the ridge. The 1600m ascent to the hut is for the fit and well-booted only (a good walking stick or ski pole is also recommended); a **cable car** from the far end of town to the **Schwarzsee** (2552m) saves you 900m of climbing (20.50SFr; round-trip 33SFr; open May 2-Oct. 8, 8:10am-6:40pm). If you elect to walk the whole way, leave Zermatt along the left bank of the Matter Vispa, as for the Granny hike below. About 2km or so from Zermatt, a wide track marked "Zum See, Schwarzsee und Hörnlihütte" heads down and left across the river. Follow the 3-hour path as it zigzags steeply up to the tiny lake, the Schwarzsee, and admire the monstrous Gorner gorges on the left. On the lake there is a chapel, built in an act of piety by a group of climbers when their prayers were answered and the clouds miraculously lifted from the snowstorm they were stuck in. From the Schwarzsee the path becomes rockier and wilder as it joins the true northeast ridge of the Matterhorn, climbing gently at first but ending in a merciless, exposed *arête* (sharp ridge) by the buildings at Hörnli (Schwarzsee to Hörnli takes about 2hr.). Be aware that **casual hikers *cannot* continue above the hut.** More than 500 people have died in the kilometers above this point, as a sobering walk around Zermatt's cemeteries will prove. To descend a different way, bear right at the *Schwarzsee* to the Furgg cable car terminus and follow the path down to town. The path traverses a steep cliff but is stable underfoot and has even closer views of the gorges carved by the **Gornergletscher.**

The Gornergrat (numerous hikes possible). Because the Gornergrat provides the hands-down best view of the Matternorn, it swarms with as many as 5,000 visitors per day. The crowds come on the train, which departs opposite Zermatt's main station (7am-11pm), making its way to the **Gornergrat** (3090m; 38SFr, round-trip 63SFr) by way of **Riffelalp** (2211m; 17.20SFr, 32SFr), **Riffelberg** (2582m; 27SFr, 46SF) and **Rotenboden** (2815m; 34SFr, 58SFr), before ending at the Gornergrat. From each of these stations there are wonderful hikes. From the Gornergrat itself hikes continue on down to the wide, flat **Gornergletscher** and along the ridge toward the **Stockhorn** (3532m). You can either walk to the Stockhorn, or take the cable car that traverses the distance (12SFr each way). In the other direction from Stockhorn is **Rotenboden.** From Rotenboden you can divert to the Monte Rosa hut (5hr. to the hut and back), following the glacier. Each destination provides a closer encounter with the ice but loses a fraction of the panorama that makes the Gornergrat so special. You can also get off the train at the **Riffelalp** station and descend to Zermatt by following the side of the mountain around to the *Grünsee,* facing the snout of the **Findelngletscher,** then crossing the river and returning to Zermatt by way of the **Moosjesee** and the **Leisee,** 2 small pools that provide a beautiful foreground to the Matterhorn.

Granny Hike; to Zmutt (1hr.). This, the easiest hike of them all, offers the most dramatic encounter with the Matterhorn's north face. The path to **Zmutt** is wide, clear, well-marked and completely flat. From Zermatt, follow Bahnhofstr. past the church, then follow the sign to the right. Climb the steady slope through the Arolla pines to the weathered chalets of the hamlet of Zmutt. The path levels out as it continues through the meadows above a small reservoir, granting views of the Hörnli ridge and the Matterhorn. As you go on, the Matterhorn's north wall, which drops 200m with an average gradient well over 45°, comes into breathtaking view.

Grandchild Hike (10hrs. round trip). If you want to make the Granny hike more challenging (well worth the extra effort, since the views get exponentially better as you ascend), continue on to the **Schönbielhütte** (2694m, 4hr. from Zmutt). The hike becomes more difficult as it ascends past lakes and waterfalls at the outlet of the rock-strewn **Zmuttgletscher** and follows the lateral ridge to the Schönbielhütte, an ideal spot for lunchtime carbo-loading of pasta or *Rösti*, or an overnight stop. On the return journey, the valley frames the Rimpfischhorn (4199m) and Strahlhorn (4190m). The full-day hike is 25km, covering 1050m of gentle elevation.

VALAIS

Sunnegga-Rothorn Hike. Once you've had enough Matterhorn-chasing, try this difficult hike, which starts from the Zermatt station. Head down to the river beside the Gornergratbahn, cross it, turn left, then hop on the Sunnegga-Rothorn railway and lift as far as **Blauherd** (2560m; 25SFr, round-trip 34SFr). From the station a wide path gently circles the **Unterrothorn**'s right flank to a mountain pass at 2981m. From the pass take the series of zigzags on the right (some offering fixed handrails) up to the **Oberrothorn** (3415m).

The Triple-T Hike. A similarly un-Matterhorn-related hike of medium difficulty is that from **Tuftern** (2339m) to **Täschalp** (2650m) to **Täsch** (1449m; 6hrs.). From Tuftern, take the high-mountain trail (under "Unter Gattla") to reach Täschalp. From Täschalp the trail goes upwards to the Täsch hut (2701m, ☎967 3913, 38SFr including breakfast) and then gradually back down to Täsch. From Täsch, you can either hike back up to Zermatt or take the train (10 min., every 20min. 6:25am-11:30pm, train runs May 28-Oct. 10, 7.40SFr).

OTHER ACTIVITIES

Zermatt doesn't have much going for it when it rains. The posher hotels have **swimming pools;** Hotel Christiania has the biggest one. Follow the right bank of the river to the left past the Rothorn/Sunnegga cable railway station. (Hotel ☎967 1907. 10SFr, children 6SFr. Open July-Sept. M, W, and F-Su 8-10:30am and 1:30-7:30pm, Th 1:30-7:30pm.) For an additional 10SFr, you can work up a sweat in the sauna. Other hotels offer massages for those weary hiking muscles. Another rainy day refuge is the **Alpine Museum** near the post office. Here, the courage of those adventurers who first conquered regional peaks with (by modern standards) absurd equipment is proven by paraphernalia of their not-so-fortunate comrades: broken ropes, mangled shoes, and bashed-in lanterns found with corpses, sometimes months after tragic falls. Special attention is given to the first ascent of the Matterhorn. Over half of the expedition was killed on July 14, 1865, on the way back down. A haunting photograph is all that remains of one such victim, Lord Alfred Douglas (the love of Oscar Wilde's life), whose remains were never found. Recovered remains of victims of the Matterhorn are buried in the cemetery, next to the church with picks and ropes defiantly carved into their graves. (☎967 4100. Open June-Sept. 10am-noon and 4-6pm; Dec.-May M-F and Su 4:30-6:30pm. Closed Nov.-Oct. 5SFr, students 3SFr, children under 16 1SFr. Guide in English 1SFr.)

The **Cinema Vernissage** (☎ 967 6636), next to Julen Sports on Hoffmattstr., has 2 or 3 screenings nightly, Monday to Saturday, of nearly new releases, usually in English. In the latter half of July, films are shown at the **open air cinema** (10-15SFr; cafe open M-Sa 5pm-midnight; AmEx, DC, MC, Visa). Elaborating on Zermatt's favorite topic, early July brings the **Mountain Film Festival** (☎967 6636, fax 967 6801; www.vermissage-zermatt.ch), during which films about, well, the mountains, receive their due in open air. August 15 brings the **Alpine Folklore Parade,** when locals take a break from their mountain chores and dust off their alphorns and lederhosen. The Roman Catholic church sporadically hosts **classical music concerts** (25SFr) throughout the month, and at the end of August, runners in the **Matterhornlauf** climb 1001m from Zermatt to the *Schwarzsee* at the foot of the Matterhorn.

SAAS FEE ☎027

Saas Fee occupies one of Switzerland's most dramatic sites, and is nicknamed "the pearl of the alps" because of the way it rests in a hanging valley above the Saastal, beneath thirteen 4000m peaks, including the **Dom** (4545m). The glacial ice of the **Feegletscher** comes so low that you can visit the frozen giant on a 30-minute evening stroll. To protect all this Alpine glory, the entire resort town is closed to cars, giving electrically powered mini-vans and trucks free run of the rambling streets. The town is not nearly as tourist-choked as Zermatt, but then it's not nearly as interesting. A similar abundance of knee-high socks and sleek neon suits, however, proves that Saas Fee's main draw is also the outdoor scene. Town officials prohibit disturbing "the fairy-like charm of Saas Fee" after 10pm (noisemakers fined 200SFr). The raucous silence of the encroaching glacier will have to do. Keep in mind that lifts, restaurants, and hotels shut down for maintenance, renovations, and vacations for townspeople from early May to mid-June.

GETTING THERE AND AROUND

A **post bus** runs (every hr. 5:35am-7:35pm) to **Brig** (1¼hr., 17.20SFr, round-trip 32SFr); and **Visp** (50min., 14.60SFr, 29.20SFr), where trains connects to Lausanne, Sion, and the rest of Valais; **Stalden Saas** (40min., 11.80SFr, 23.60SFr), which connects to Zermatt for another 30SFr; and **Saas Grund** (10min., 3SFr, 6SFr). Reserve a seat on all buses starting at Saas Fee at least 2 hours before departure. Dial 958 1145 or drop by the bus station (open 7:30am-12:35pm and 1:15-6.35pm). Drivers can **park** in the lot across the street and to the right of the tourist office (1 day 13SFr, in summer 11SFr; with guest card after 2nd day 9SFr, 7.50SFr).

ORIENTATION AND PRACTICAL INFORMATION

The **tourist office,** opposite the bus station, dispenses seasonal information, hiking advice, guides, and reasonably useful town maps. (☎958 1858; direct reservations 958 1868; fax 958 1860; to@saas-fee.ch; www.saas-fee.ch. Open July to mid-Sept. and mid-Dec. to mid-Apr. M-F 8:30am-noon and 2-6:30pm, Sa 8am-7pm, Su 9am-noon and 3-6pm; mid-Sept. to mid-Dec. and mid-Apr. to June M-Sa 8:30am-noon and 2-6pm, Su 10am-noon and 4-6pm.) In an **emergency,** dial 117. In an after-hours emergency, call the **pharmacist** at 957 4417 or (079) 417 6718. During business hours, visit **Vallesia Apotheke,** farther up the main street to your right outside the tourist office (☎957 2618. Open M-Sa 8:30am-noon and 2-6:30pm). **Internet access** is available at Hotel Dom on the main street (☎957 5101. 10SFr per ½hr., 18SFr per hr.). For a **weather report,** dial 162. The bus depot has small **lockers** (2SFr) and houses the **post office** with public **fax** and **ATM** (open M-F 8:15am-noon and 2-6pm, Sa 8:15am-noon). The **postal code** is CH-3906.

ACCOMMODATIONS

Travelers willing to sacrifice comfort can find bargains in hotel basements. The cheapest is **Hotel Garni Imseng.** From the station, head down the main street, left of the tourist office, then turn left and pass the church. Next to the 3-star hotel's bakery, rows of 7 bunks are stacked 3 high, like filing cabinets, with no space between rows. The whole thing looks suspiciously like a boiler room, but at least you'll wake to the smell of fresh bread, and you just might have the 21 beds to yourself. The doubles in the hotel have TVs and leather couches upstairs, but will cost you twice as much. (☎958 1258; fax 958 1255; www.kisswiss.com/0864-4963. Breakfast 15SFr. Reception 8:30am-noon and 2-7pm. Kitchen facilities and ski and bike storage included. Dorm 20SFr. Sheets 5SFr. Doubles 80SFr.) Across the street from Garni Imseng, **Hotel Garni Feehof** doubles the price but lifts quality of life exponentially. Warm, wooden, and wonderful, nearly all the creaky pine rooms have balconies and deliciously soft beds with enormous marshmallow-like down comforters. (☎957 2308; fax 957 2309. Reception 9-11am and 3-6:30pm. In winter, reserve 2 weeks in advance. Breakfast and shower included. Singles 48-52SFr in summer, 45-66SFr in winter.)

One of the town's better values is **Pension Garni Mascotte** and its two sister chalets, **Alba** and **Albana.** Head down the road opposite the station, just left of the tourist office. At the main street, turn right and continue up the hill for 200m; Mascotte is on the left. (☎957 2724; fax 957 1216. Albana's rooms have shower and toilet. Breakfast included. Add 10SFr for half-pension. **Laundry** facilities, ski storage, and TV lounge. Open mid-Dec. to Apr. and July-Sept. Alba dorms 27-30SFr. Albana 5-bed dorms 28-33SFr; 4-bed dorms 30-35SFr; 2-bed dorms 38-48SFr. Smarter rooms in Mascotte 45-55SFr.) An alternative to staying the night in Saas Fee proper is a night in a **mountain hut,** where breakfast is always included. The **Mischabelhütte** (3329m; ☎957 1117; 33SFr, dinner included), **Hoh-saas** (3098m; ☎957 1713; 36SFr), and **Weissmieshütte** (2726m; ☎957 2554; 30SFr), above Saas Grund are all accessible from July to September. The Saas Fee tourist office (see Practical Information, above) and Bergführerbüro (see hiking, below) have further details.

FOOD

In Saas Fee, where there's a hotel, there's a restaurant. **Spaghetteria da Rasso,** 2 minutes to the left of the pharmacy under the Hotel Britania, has a shady terrace, wooden gnomes, and occasional accordionists that attract quite a crowd. (☎957 1526. Open June-Sept. 10am-11:30pm; Oct.-Dec. F-Sa 10am-11:30pm; winter Tu-Su 10am-11:30pm. AmEx, MC, Visa.) Though it's certainly not difficult to find Swiss specialties around town, the **Restaurant Chämi-Stube,** on the main street near the church, is a large, family-owned establishment, candle-lit, and quiet. (☎957 1747. Bratwurst and *Rösti* 15SFr, a rather alcoholic Valaisian fondue 22SFr, and *Apfelstrudel mit Vanillesauce* 5SFr. Open 9am-midnight.) Hungry shoppers can choose between 3 **supermarkets** in small Saas Fee, and all 3 have the same hours: M-F 8:30am-12:15pm and 2:15-6:30pm, Sa 8:30am-12:15pm and 2:15-5pm. Near the tourist office and Pension Mascotte is the **Supermarkt.** A small **Konsum** Center stands next to the ski school across from the Alpine guide picture board. The pick of the lot, though, is the new **Migros,** just down the hill from the church.

OUTDOOR ACTIVITIES

SKIING

During the **summer,** two cable cars to **Felskinn** (3000m) and an underground funicular, the "Metro Alpin," to **Mittelallanin** (3500m) enable summer **skiers** to enjoy 20km of runs and a stupendous Alpine view (round-trip to Mittelallanin, 7:30am-3:45pm, 58SFr; to Felskinn, 7:30am-4pm, 30SFr, closed May 8-June 30). In winter, an immense network of lifts opens (day ski passes 58SFr, children 35SFr; 6 days 270SFr, 162SFr; 13 days 480SFr, 288SFr). For those still disinclined toward inclines, the **Ski School,** across the street from the church, offers group skiing or snowboarding lessons from mid-December to April. (☎957 2348; www.saas-fee.ch/skischool. Skiing 45SFr for 3 hr., 168SFr for 1 week; snowboarding 45SFr for 2 hr., 1 week 153SFr. Slight reductions available in late Jan. Open M-F 8:30-noon and 2:30-6pm, Sa-Su 4-6pm.) In Saas Fee, if a store doesn't sell stuffed marmots, it **rents skis.** Stores in the **Swiss Rent-A-Sport System** (look for the black and red logo) offer 3 grades of equipment (skis 28-50SFr per day, 6 days 105-180SFr; snowboards 28-38SFr, 80-105SFr; boots 15-19SFr, 52-77SFr). The *über*-organized can call ahead and have equipment set aside for their arrival; call or fax the main Swiss Rent-A-Sport outlet in town, **Anthamatten Sport Mode,** across from the Spaghetteria (☎958 1918; fax 957 1970; open Mar.-Dec. 8:30am-noon and 1:30-6:30pm, Jan.-Apr. 8:30am-6:30pm).

HIKING

The **Bergführerbüro** (Mountain Guides Office), in the same building as the ski school, leads climbs to a number of 4000m summits for both amateurs and experts (☎957 4464. Closed May and June. Open M-Sa 9:30am-noon and 3-6pm). Day tours run anywhere from 130 to 395SFr per person. **Hikers** have 280km of marked trails from which to choose. Casual strollers can head out of town along the main street and through the athletic facilities, turning right at the fork towards the stream. An easy path leads up to a water mill powered by rushing rapids and the Café Gletscher Grotto. A **Saas Valley Hiking Pass** (149SFr, family rate 299SFr) provides access for 1 week to all cable cars and post buses in the valley and entrance to the ice pavilion at **Mittelallanin,** the **Bielen Recreation Center,** and other museums. The pass is available at the tourist office or any cable car station. Most lifts close from May to early June and from mid-October to mid-December, when bad weather renders many hikes impassable.

VALAIS

Mischabelhütte Hike (full day hike). For a hard, steep trek, hike up to the **Mischabelhütte** (3329m), which has the single best panorama of the Saas Fee natural amphitheatre accessible to walkers. From the pharmacy on the main street, turn right after the church and take the right fork 100m farther on. Check for snow cover before you leave, however–the last part of the hike is rocky and highly unpleasant with any hint of ice (1550m ascent).

Glacier Hike (half day hike). A lovely half-day walk begins with a cable-car ride to **Plattjen** (2570m). For picture-perfect views of the Dom and Lezspitze, a path leads to the right and zigzags left after 5 minutes. From the top it descends for 15 minutes, then heads left around the amphitheatre, spiralling slowly down below the **Feegletscher.** The view opens up as you drop down to the **Gletschersee** (1910m) at the glacier tip. The path then gently follows the left bank of the outlet stream back to Saas Fee.

Hannig Hike (2hr20min.). This easy walk from the church to Hannig begins flat (30 min.) and gets steeper as you get deeper into the woods. Follow the "Hannig" signs all the way. On the way up, you'll have close encounters with goats and pigs as you pass through the small farms on the hill. Make a stop at the Mannigalp hut for fresh milk and cheese from the cows and goats you met on the way up. After an hour, the path splits into the Hannig trail and the longer, more scenic Hannig Waldweg trail. When you reach the restaurant at the top, you can either continue on the trail toward Melchbode and back to Saas Fee or take the **Sonnenbahn Hannig** cable car (14SFr adults, 7SFr children, 25% discount with SwissPass), which will drop you off at the Spaghetteria.

OTHER ACTIVITIES

On rainy days, you can amuse yourself at the **Bielen Recreation Center,** next to the bus station. The complex has an expensive but excellent **swimming pool** and **jacuzzi.** (☎957 2475. Open June 1-9pm, July-Oct. 10am-9pm. 12SFr, with guest card 10SFr; children 7SFr, 6SFr.) The Mountain Guide Office organizes an outing to a nearby gorge every Monday and Friday that is accessible all year long, even in bad weather. Kids as young as 10 can scuttle along water-carved rock faces, aided by safety equipment (65SFr).

For two weeks in mid-August, Saas Fee hosts the **Musica Romantica** classical music festival with artists from all over Europe (60SFr symphony concert ticket, 38SFr recital ticket, 230SFr weeklong ticket, 50% discount for children under 16). Contact the tourist office for a list of performers and to purchase tickets.

SION ☎027

Sion is big and modern enough to have made 3 consecutive bids for the Winter Olympics. Sion's accesibility and central location also make the town useful as a base for exploring all of Walais. But, given the lack of excitement off its slopes,Sion was predictably rejected on each of its 3 bids.

GETTING THERE AND AROUND. Trains pass every 30 minutes in each direction along the Rhône Valley, going west to **Martigny** (15min., 4:55am-10:53pm, 8.60SFr), **Aigle** (35min., 4:55am-10:53pm, 17.20SFr), **Montreux** (50min., 4:55am-10:53pm, 23SFr), and **Lausanne** (1¼hr., 4:55am-10:53pm, 30SFr); and east (6:04am-1:03am) to **Sierre** (10min., 5.60SFr) and **Brig** (30-45min., 17.20SFr), where you connect to **Zermatt** (49.60SFr) and **Saas Fee** (29.20SFr). The **train station** (☎329 2227) provides **currency exchange** (open 6am-8:30pm), **lockers** (3-5SFr), **luggage storage** (5SFr for 24hr.; open 6:30am-8pm), **bike rental** (27SFr per day; reserve in advance), and a **rail information** office (open M-F 9am-noon and 1:30-6:30pm, Sa 8:30am-noon and 1:30-5pm). Just outside, Switzerland's largest **Post Bus station** congests the square with a blur of yellow buses.

VALAIS

ORIENTATION AND PRACTICAL INFORMATION. To get to the **tourist office,** pl. de la Planta, from the train station, walk directly up av. de la Gare, and turn right on rue de Lausanne. (☎322 8586; fax 322 1882; info@siontourism.ch; www.siontourism.ch. Open July 15-Aug. 15 M-F 8:30am-6pm, Sa 10am-4pm; Aug. 16-July 14 M-Sa 8:30am-noon and 1:30-5:30pm.) The office provides free room reservations, a ticket corner (☎322 8593) for tickets to any event from Sion to Geneva, and 2-hour **guided tours** (July-Aug. Tu and Th 4pm, additional group tours on request; 8SFr, children and students 5SFr). Services include: **Internet access** at **Quanna,** in the train station (☎321 1060. Open M-Th 11am-11pm, F 11am-midnight, Sa 10am-midnight, Su noon-11pm; 10SFr per hr.); **taxi,** ☎322 3232. In an **emercency** call 117. The **post office,** pl. de la Gare, is to the left of the train station (open M-F 7:30am-6:15pm, Sa 8:15am-noon). The **postal code** is CH-1950.

ACCOMMODATIONS. Sion's budget accommodations are less than desireable, but adequate. Built in 1991, the **Auberge de Jeunesse (HI),** av. de l'Industrie 2, is vast and impersonal, with clean bathrooms, little balconies, and lockers in every room. From the station, walk left and down the stairs to rue de la Blancherie; continue left underneath the train tracks. Although it's big, the hostel can often be fully booked by marauding school groups in July and August. The next closest HI hostel is in Montreux, so call ahead. (☎323 7470; fax 323 7438. Breakfast included. Dinner 11.50SFr if you reserve it. **Kitchen** facilities 2SFr. Reception 7:30-9:30am and 5-10pm, until 9pm from Dec.-Apr. Curfew 10:30pm; keys on request. Lockout 9:30am-5pm. 5SFr surcharge for non-HI members. 4-bed dorms 26.80SFr; 2-bed dorms 30.30-33.80SFr. AmEx, MC, Visa.) Staying anywhere else will give your wallet a painful sting. Desperate travelers seeking a cheap bed can try some of the villages outside Sion. The tourist office's booklet *Sion* gives details. (In **Pont-de-la-Morge** singles run 35-40SFr, doubles 68-80SFr; in **Saint-Léonard** 50-70SFr, 70-90SFr. Post Buses run to both towns.) **Camping Les Iles,** rte d'Aproz, is a 5-star riverside site. Take a very short ride on Post Bus #2 to Aproz. (☎346 4347; fax 346 6847. Open Jan.-Oct. 9.20SFr, tents 9SFr; in off-season 7.60SFr, tents 6SFr.)

AT&T Direct® Service

The easy way to call home from anywhere.

AT&T Access Numbers

Austria ●	**0800-200-288**	**France**	**0800-99-00-11**
Belarus ×	**8 ♦ 800-101**	**Gambia ●**	**00111**
Belgium ●	**0-800-100-10**	**Germany**	**0800-2255-288**
Bosnia ▲	**00-800-0010**	**Ghana**	**0191**
Bulgaria ▲	00-800-0010	Gibraltar	8800
Cyprus ●	080-900-10	**Greece ●**	**00-800-1311**
Czech Rep. ▲	**00-42-000-101**	**Hungary ●**	**06-800-01111**
Denmark	**8001-0010**	**Iceland ●**	**800-9001**
Egypt ● (Cairo) ‡	**510-0200**	**Ireland ✓**	**1-800-550-000**
Finland ●	0800-110-015	**Israel**	**1-800-94-94-949**

Italy ● 172-1011	**Russia (Moscow)** ▶▲●755-5042
Luxembourg ✚ ..800-2-0111	**(St. Petersbg.)** ▶▲● ..325-5042
Macedonia ● ..99-800-4288	**Slovakia** ▲ ..00-42-100-101
Malta.......... 0800-890-110	**South Africa** ..0800-99-0123
Monaco ● 800-90-288	**Spain** 900-99-00-11
Morocco........002-11-0011	**Sweden** 020-799-111
Netherlands ●...0800-022-9111	**Switzerland** ● 0800-89-0011
Norway 800-190-11	**Turkey** ● 00-800-12277
Poland ▲● ..00-800-111-1111	**Ukraine** ▲..........8◆100-11
Portugal ▲ 800-800-128	U.A. Emirates●......800-121
Romania ●......01-800-4288	**U.K.**............0800-89-0011

FOR EASY CALLING WORLDWIDE

1. Just dial the AT&T Access Number for the country you are calling from. *2.* Dial the phone number you're calling. *3.* Dial your card number.

For access numbers not listed ask any operator for **AT&T Direct**® Service.

In the U.S. call 1-800-331-1140 for a wallet guide listing all worldwide AT&T Access Numbers.

Visit our Web site at: **www.att.com/traveler**

Bold-faced countries permit country-to-country calling outside the U.S.

- ● Public phones require coin or card deposit to place call.
- ▲ May not be available from every phone/payphone.
- ✚ Public phones and select hotels.
- ◆ Await second dial tone.
- ▶ Additional charges apply when calling from outside the city.
- † Outside of Cairo, dial "02" first.
- ✖ Not available from public phones or all areas.
- ✔ Use U.K. access number in N. Ireland.

When placing an international call ***from*** the U.S., dial 1 800 CALL ATT.

EMEA

© 8/00 AT&T

FOOD. The streets of the *vieille ville* are lined with cafes and restaurants. Unlike most of them, the **Café des Châteaux,** rue des Châteaux 3, is unpretentious and affordable. To get there, exit the tourist office and go left down rue de Lausanne, left on rue du Grant-Pont, and right on rue des Châteaux. (Salads 5-14SFr, fondue 19-22SFr, *escargots* 13SFr. ☎372 1396. Open 8am-midnight, closed Wednesdays.) For cheap and filling Turkish delights, turn right at the end of rue du Midi and grab a kebab (6-9.50SFr), veggie falafel (8SFr) or baklava (1.50SFr) at **Snack Istanbul** (☎323 7905. Open M-Sa 9am-9:30pm, Su noon-9:30pm). Picnics await immediate assembly at **Migros** supermarket and restaurant (main courses 8-15SFr) in the Centre Commercial Metropole on av. de France, 1 block left from the station (open M 1-6:30pm, Tu-Th 8:15am-6:30pm, F 8:15am-7:30pm, Sa 8am-5pm). A **produce market** occupies the pl. de la Planta every Friday from 8:30am to 6pm.

SIGHTS AND ENTERTAINMENT. None of Sion's sights are anything to write home about. The most exciting event is the **Tibor Varga Festival,** which lasts from July to September and brings major orchestras. (☎323 4317, fax 323 4662; festivargasion@vtx.ch; www.festival-varga.ch; tickets 20-80SFr, available through the tourist office ticket corner). Summer evenings bring **free concerts** of classical music through the **Academie de Musique** (☎322 6652).

Sion's other favorite pastime is wine-tasting. Most cafes have white-washed terraces where patrons sip *Valais Fendant* or *Johannisberg-Tavillon*, the leading labels in town. Consult the tourist office for organized **wine-tasting excursions** and a list of local cellars. A long-distance path through the vineyards, *le chemin du vignoble*, passes close to Sion and through tasting territory. Always call before you arrive at a *cave*, and try to rustle up a group if you want the proprietor to be more welcoming. One *centre de dégustation* is **Les Celliers de Champsec,** av. Grand-Champsec 30, just across the river (☎203 4131; fax 203 4707; open M 2-6:30pm, Tu-F 10am-noon and 2-6:30pm, Sa 10am-noon and 2-5pm).

The few museums center around the castles that tower over the town: the bishop's house, the towering **Château de Tourbillon,** is on one hill; the chapter's seat, the **Château de Valère,** on another; and the municipal powerhouse, the **Château de la Majorie et du Vidomnat,** downtown.

The Château de la Majorie et du Vidomnat is home to the **Musée des Beaux-Arts,** Pl. de la Majorie. Fans of Valaisian art will enjoy the scenes of rural life; even the uninitiated will enjoy the experimental 8-piece metal sculpture suspended from the ceiling of the stark Jesuit chapel (open only during temporary exhibits)—from the right viewpoint, it resolves into a seamless crystal circle. (☎606 4670. Open Tu-Su 10am-noon and 2-6pm. 5SFr, students 2.50SFr.) Up the hill to the right from the Château de la Majorie, the world's oldest working organ (c.1390-1430) still pipes among the faded murals of the **Basilisque du Château de Valère.** Every Saturday at 4pm in July and August the pipes are full with the sounds of the annual festival of ancient organ music (20SFr, students 10SFr).

MARTIGNY ☎027

Strategically located at the foot of the Grand St. Bernard Pass, French-speaking Martigny (pop. 15,000) was established by Roman Emperor Claudius during the first century AD to control trade routes between Switzerland and Italy, making it the oldest town in Valais. A medieval castle towers over the suburban town, its slack posture mirroring the valley's trees, beaten into tilted poses by the whipping winds. Rather than resting on its Roman laurels or wallowing in its medieval splendor, however, Martigny is definitely living in the new. Thanks in large part to the **Fondation Gianadda,** Martigny is a major center for modern art and classical music. For the more adventurous, Martigny provides access to **Mont Blanc,** at 4807m, the highest mountain in the Alps, which straddles the French and Italian borders.

GETTING THERE AND AROUND. Frequent **trains** run west to **Lausanne** (30-60min., every 30min. 5:10am-11:27pm, 23SFr); **Montreux** (30min., every 30min. 5:10am-11:27pm, 14.60SFr); and **Aigle** (20min., every 30min. 5:10am-11:27pm, 9.40SFr); and east to **Sion** (15min., 3 per hr. 6:08am-12:48am, 8.60SFr). Two private lines leave for **Orsières,** where you can change for **Aosta** in Italy via the **St. Bernard Pass** (2hr., 6 per day 8:10am-5:38pm, 31.40SFr); and for **Châtelard** where you can change for **Chamonix** in France, a starting point for the 10- to 14-day Mont Blanc circuit (1¾hr., every hr. 6:41am-7:52pm, 30SFr). **Buses** run to **Champex** and the **Col de la Forclaz pass,** starting points for Mont Blanc. The train station (open 6:15am-8pm) provides **currency exchange, lockers** (3-5SFr), **luggage storage** (5SFr), **bike rental** (27SFr per day, 21SFr per half-day), and a **rail information** office (open M-F 9am-noon and 1:30-6pm, Sa 9am-noon and 1:30-5pm).

ORIENTATION AND PRACTICAL INFORMATION. Martigny's **tourist office,** pl. Centrale 9, is straight down av. de la Gare at the far corner of pl. Centrale (☎721 2220; fax 721 2224. Open July-Aug. M-F 9am-6pm, Sa 9am-noon and 2-6pm, Su 10am-noon and 4-6pm; Sept.-June M-F 9am-noon and 1:30-6pm, Sa 9am-noon). For a **taxi,** call 722 2200 or 722 2117. Get **Internet** access (12SFr per hr.; 6SFr an hr. for youth under 18) at Le Coin Internet at the Casino, halfway between the station and pl. Centrale on rue de la Gare (☎722 1393; open M-Sa 6:30am-midnight, Su 9am-11pm). The **hospital** (☎603 9000) has a switchboard that connects you to the late-night doctor and pharmacy. **Pharmacie Centrale** (emergency ☎722 5556) is part of Migros supercenter at pl. du Manoir 5. In an **emergency,** dial 117. The **post office,** av. de la Gare 32, between the station and the tourist office, has a public fax and an **ATM** (☎722 2672; open M-F 7:30am-noon and 1:30-6:30pm, Sa 8am-noon). The postal code is CH-1920.

VALAIS

ACCOMMODATIONS. Since travelers in Martigny are mainly business types, budget pickings are slim. The town does have the unique **Le Ranch El Capio,** on Autoroute N9 (Sion-Simplon), or a 30-minute walk from the train station: turn left and walk to Rue Simplar, left again until the Aoste-Chamonin Autoroute overpass, left up the highway, then right toward Sion, and continue straight on until you see signs to the left. This ranch is the real deal; meals are eaten overlooking the livestock and orchards. Service, however, can move as slowly as the mules in the corral. Giddy-up, Herr Kuhboy. (☎723 2783. Breakfast 6SFr, lunch 14SFr, dinner 12SFr. 4- to 6-bed rooms and singles for 26.50SFr per person.) **Les 3 Chemins de Fer** is directly across the street from the train station. It rents out a few spartan rooms to those who would rather not fight Martigny's whipping winds to reach El Capio. (☎722 2296. Breakfast consists of croissant and coffee. Rooms have showers, toilets, kitchenettes, TV. Reception 7am-10pm daily. Singles 50SFr, doubles 40SFr per person. MC, Visa.) **Camping Les Neuvilles,** rue du Levant 68, packs its shaded plot with motor homes. From the station, head straight on av. de la Gare, take the second left on av. des Neuvilles, and turn right onto rue du Levant. Amenities include playgrounds, a store, **laundry** machines, a **sauna,** a solarium, and miniature golf. (☎722 4544. Shower included. Reception July-Aug. 8am-noon and 1:30-10pm. 6.80SFr, tents 7.50SFr, 4-person bungalow 80SFr, 3-night minimum, Sept.-June 63SFr. Dorm beds 20.60SFr.)

FOOD. Cafes crowd Martigny's tree-lined pl. Centrale, some with *Menüs* in the 15-25SFr range. **Crêperie Le Rustique,** av. de la Gare 44, lives up to its name with a dark wood interior with nature scenes painted on stucco. Enjoy savory crêpes (9.50-13.50SFr) or sweet ones (4.50-9.50SFr), and wash them down with a 3.50SFr mug of cider. (☎722 8833. Open M-F 8am-11pm, Sa 10:30am-midnight, Su 3:30-11pm.) For cheaper fare, **Lords' Sandwiches,** av. du Grand-St.-Bernard 15, serves 36 kinds of sandwiches (3.80-11.70SFr), including a bacon burger with fries, and the Zeus, an overstuffed roast beef sandwich. (☎723 3598. Open M-Th 7am-10:30pm, F

7am-midnight, Sa 8:30am-midnight, Su 3-10:30pm.) For straightforward Italian food, locals recommend **Pizzeria au Grotto,** rue du Rhône 3, off rue Marc-Morand to the left of pl. Centrale. The Grotto has pizzas (8-17SFr) and pasta entrees for 10-20SFr (☎722 0246; open 8am-midnight. MC, Visa).

The immense **Migros** supermarket at pl. du Manoir 5, just off pl. Centrale, has 18 different boutiques, a restaurant, and moving sidewalks (supermarket open M-Th 8:15am-6:30pm, F 8:15am-8pm, Sa 8am-5pm; restaurant open M-Th 7:30am-6:30pm, F 7:30am-8pm, Sa 7:30am-5pm). Down rue de la Poste from the post office, a **Co-op** offers similar services (open M-Th 8:15am-6:30pm, F 8:15am-8pm, Sa 8am-5pm). Stroll down av. de la Gare on Thursday mornings to buy edible and wearable goods at the **public market** (open 7:30am-noon).

SIGHTS. Martigny's most engaging attraction is the **Fondation Pierre Gianadda,** Rue du Forum 59. Head down the rue Hôtel-de-Ville behind the tourist office and follow the signs. The permanent collection includes works by Cézanne, Van Gogh, Ensor, Van Dongen, and Picasso, while the central atrium hosts blockbuster international traveling exhibitions—on the plate for 2001 are Russian icons from January to June and Picasso from June to November. The exhibits tend to overshadow the rest of the foundation, including the mildly interesting **Gallo-Roman Museum,** which showcases classical works like the Octoduran bronzes discovered in Martigny and a 3-horned bronze bull's head. Downstairs, the more entertaining **Automobile Museum** exhibits more than 50 vintage cars—Bugattis, gleaming early Peugots, and a Rolls Royce Silver Ghost—built between 1897 and 1939, all in working condition. The garden surrounding the Fondation is populated with excellent modern sculptures, including some by Brancusi, Miró, and Rodin. Especially amusing are the bronze sculptures of giant body parts by Cesar. Admission to the illuminated park is free on summer nights. (☎722 3978; fax 722 3163; info@gianadda.ch; www.gianadda.ch. Open Feb.-June 10am-6pm, June-Oct. 9am-7pm, Oct.-Feb. 10am-noon and 1:30-6pm. Guided tours in French W at 8pm or by prior arrangement. Wheelchair accessible. 12SFr, students 5SFr, family ticket 25SFr.) The foundation hosts classical music concerts, many in conjunction with the **Festival Tibor Varga** and the **Montreux Voice and Music Festival** (see p. 466).

The tourist office leads 1½-hour **guided tours** of Martigny, including the Fondation (July-Aug. 10am, 3pm; by appointment the rest of the year; 14SFr, students 7SFr, family ticket 30SFr). If you want to explore on your own, the ever-helpful office distributes a brochure that will guide you on a walking tour of Martigny's Roman ruins *(promenade archéologique)*. Past the railroad tracks, remnants of a Roman road point toward Britannia and, through the pass, Roma. Nearby, the grassy 4th-century **Amphithéâtre Romain** is the spectacular setting for the final contest of the Valais **cow fighting** season (see Bovine Battle below). 50m away from the Fondation, signs lead to the remains of a temple to the **sun god Mithra** dating from the 3rd century AD (now under an apartment building). **Le Château de la Bâtiaz,** the ruins of a 13th-century castle that once belonged to the bishops of Sion, overlooks Martigny from the hill. From the station, head along av. de la Gare, and turn right at pl. Centrale along rue Marc-Morand. Climb the massive stone tower extending over an outcropping of bare rock for a bird's-eye perspective of the flat Rhône floodplain. (Open mid-June to mid-Oct. M and W 10am-7pm, Th-Su 10am-10pm. 5SFr adults, 2.50SFr children ages 10-16.)

FESTIVALS. Martigny hosts the **Foire du Valais,** the trade fair of Valais, in the blue and yellow convention center from Sept.28-Oct.7 (5-10SFr). Local businesses and farmers offer their wares, from shoes to marble sculptures. The final Sunday brings all-day **cow fighting.** The event is a must-see if you are in southern Switzerland. The **Foire du Lard** (Bacon Fair) has overtaken the pl. Centrale every first Monday in December since the Middle Ages. Traditionally, Valais mountain folk descended on Martigny to stock up on pork products for the winter. Now the festival has expanded to a large open-air market—though the theme is still "pig."

BOVINE BATTLE The fighting cows of Valais have been, since medieval times, the privilege of the rich, the spectacle of the poor, and the lifelong devotion of breeders. Valais and cows go way back: the first Swiss-domesticated cows (little neolithic specimens) were found in Valais, near Martigny. Since then, the highest reverence has been accorded to the *Heren* strain, valued for its fine milk and meat, and particularly mountain-adapted nature. Such vigor is not only a matter of physique–*Heren* females have an aggressive streak that reveals itself in their violent, profound eyes, hot blood, and savage aspect. For hundreds of years, breeders have raised cows in hopes of achieving success at the annual cow fights *(Combats de Reines)*, which began to be institutionalized in 1923. When facing off, the combatants (called *lutteuses*, or wrestlers) exhibit a veritable repertoire of well-documented moves and behaviors, from preliminary head movements and *escarpier* (pawing the ground), to head-on and lateral attacks. After a mighty struggle, whichever animal is not lying on the ground recieves an extra-special bell and some salt from her owner, along with the distinction of being *la reine*, the queen, the true honor every virtuous cow is after.

VERBIER ☎027

Although it may seem to be a typical mountain town, Verbier (pop. 2,500) is sleek and modern compared to the artificially rustic decor of many other ski towns. Cobblestones are nowhere to be found along the winding streets, and the countless multi-star hotels and sports stores are streamlined, shiny derivations of the classic chalet design. The slopes are the big story in Verbier; its entire transportation system seems designed to churn Rayban-wearing ski and snowboard enthusiasts from one cable car to another. Other sports thrive as well, casting an athletic glow over the town and pushing the envelope of the edgy and the extreme. Verbier's ongoing expansion up the mountain only accentuates the sense of a town literally on the move. Note that in May and June, everything (hotels, shops, restaurants, cable cars, etc.) closes, and the streets are virtually silent.

TRANSPORT. Getting to Verbier is a 2-step process—from Martigny to Le Châble, then from Le Châble to Verbier. Martigny lies on the high-speed train line that connects the Lake Geneva cities (Montreux, Lausanne) to Sion and Brig. The **St. Bernard Express** runs trains to **Le Châble** (30min., every hr. 7:12am-8:07pm, 9.40SFr, Eurail and SwissPass valid). You can take the **Post Bus** (25min., every hr. 6:55am-8pm, 5SFr) or the **cable car** (10min., runs nonstop June 23-Aug. 27 8:45am-4:50pm, 7SFr, round-trip 10SF) to Verbier, depending on when you arrive in Le Châble. The **last bus** from Verbier to Le Châble leaves at 7pm. In the winter, a bus goes **directly** from Martigny to Verbier, but reservations are crucial, as there is only 1 bus on Friday evenings, and 3 on Saturdays. **Téléverbier** offers **free local bus** service throughout the town.

ORIENTATION AND PRACTICAL INFORMATION. The **tourist office,** pl. Centrale, publishes the amazingly informative booklet *Le Guide* in 4 languages. From the cable car, head down rue de Médran. (☎775 3888; fax 775 3889; verbiertourism@verbier.ch; www.verbier.ch. Open M-F 8am-noon and 2-6:30pm, Sa 9am-noon and 4-6:30pm, Su 9am-noon in May-June and Sept.-Nov; extended winter hours.) **Bike rental** is available at Ski Service, on the rue de Médran off pl. Centrale (☎771 6770, fax 771 6771. 25SFr for half-day, 35SFr for 1 day). For a **taxi,** dial 771 7771 or 771 3465. Check your **email** at Harold's, on the pl. Centrale near the rue de Médran. (☎771 6243. Open 11am-1:30am, closed M and W during the summer. 20SFr per hour.) The station at Le Châble offers **currency exchange,** or try the **ATM** at the Banque Cantonale du Valais, on pl. Centrale across from and to the right of the tourist office. In an **emergency,** call the **police** at 117 or the **hospital** at 771 6677. The **pharmacy** is to the right of the tourist office. (☎771 6622; fax 771 5188; emergency ☎771 2122. Open M-Sa 8:30am-12:15pm and 2:30-6:30pm, Su 10am-12:15pm and 5-6:30pm. AmEx, DC, MC, Visa.) The **post office** is just off pl. Centrale on rue de la Poste (open M-F 9am-noon and 3-6pm, Sa 9-noon) and also serves as the Post Bus station. The **postal code** is CH-1936.

ACCOMMODATIONS. **The Bunker** caters to the young snowboarder crowd during the winter. As the name suggests, the hostel is in the bomb shelter (see **Bombs Away** below) beneath the city's sports center (a 10min. walk down rue de la Poste from the bus station). Although the concrete walls and steel vault doors have been painted bright pink, the place still retains that military feel, with no windows and up to 45 cramped beds (3-story bunks separated by fireproof curtains) per room. Nonetheless, the frigid Bunker boasts an impressive list of perks: lockers, a shuttle bus to the ski lifts, a lounge with cable TV and VCR, and free access to the ice skating rinks, indoor and outdoor pools, and beach volleyball courts at the sports centre. (☎771 6602; fax 771 6603; sleep@thebunker.ch; www.thebunker.ch. Breakfast included. Closed May to mid-June. No curfew, no lockout. 21-25SFr plus 25SFr deposit for standard military issue sheets and blanket and a room key. AmEx, MC, Visa.) The Bunker offers ski and snowboard specials (incl. lodging, ski pass, meals, and access to the centre's facilities) starting at 495SFr per week. For those who prefer the more traditional hostel arrangement, the brand-new **summer house** at the sports centre has sunny rooms that overlook the pool, kitchen facilities, and cable TV. (☎771 6602; fax 771 6603. Open mid-June to Oct. Dorms 21SFr, doubles 35SFr. AmEx, MC, Visa.)

The **Hotel Rosablanche,** rue de la Barmette off rue de Médran near pl. Centrale, has spartan rooms and a miniature golf course. (☎771 5555; fax 771 7055. Breakfast included. Reception 8am-11:30pm. Singles and doubles 45SFr per person, 58SFr with shower. Open July-Oct. AmEx, Visa.) Hotels are somewhat cheaper in Le Châble, so making the short commute isn't a bad idea. For the truly motivated, **Auberge de la Jeunesse (HI)** (☎776 1898; fax 776 1312) is a bus ride away from Le Châble in **Bruson** (10min., every hr. 7:10am-6:15pm, 3SFr). Though it doesn't offer meals, the 40 beds are only 10SFr (15SFr in high season). In winter, there's a **campsite** (☎776 2051) outside Le Châble.

FOOD. Though Verbier is well on its way to major-ski-resort status, many of its restaurants are laid back and budget friendly; the influx of young, adventurous internationals keeps the nightlife jumping and accessible to Anglophones. Restaurants, bars, and clubs pack the pl. Centrale and the roads radiating from it. **Le Crok No Name Bar,** up rue des Creux from pl. Centrale, draws hip locals and sportsters alike with the easy funk of its multi-colored tile exterior, terra-cotta bar, and long leather couches. Frequent concerts (rock, funk, jazz) accompany creative *panini* sandwiches that cost 7.50SFr. (☎771 6934. Open July-Apr. 10am-2pm, May-June M,W-Th 5:30-10pm, F-Sa 5:30-1:45am.) **Le Monde des Crêpes,** down rue de la Poste from pl. Centrale, puts an alternative twist on the traditional crêperie. (Savory crêpes 5.90-9.70SFr, dessert crêpes 5.40-11.80SFr, cider 2.70SFr. ☎771 6402. Open M-Th 9-11:30am, F-Sa 9:30-11:30am, 2:30-6pm.)

For excellent Italian specialties, hike up the rue des Creux from pl. Centrale to the **Pizzeria Al Capone.** Shorten the walk by taking the Téléverbier bus to "Brunnet." Diners get an eyeful of snow-capped peaks and neon paragliders. (Pizzas 13-18SFr, gnocchi 18-19SFr, *plats du jour* 20-22SFr. ☎771 6774. Open daily 9am-midnight. Call in advance for dinner reservations during the high season.) **Le Caveau,** to the right of the tourist office, serves up plenty of Swiss and local specialties through its wine-cask entrance. The subtly-lit interior, like much else in Verbier, is traditional with a touch of modern wackiness. Try the hot goat cheese over a salad (15SFr), or the *assiette du jour* for 17- 20SFr. (☎771 2226. Open noon-2pm, 6:30-10pm.) For picknickers, **Denner superdiscount** is down rue de Verbier from pl. Centrale (open M-F 8:30am-12:15pm and 2:30-6:30pm, Sa 8:30am-12:15pm and 2-5pm), and the **Co-op** is down rue de la Poste (open M-W and F 8:30am-12:15pm and 2:30-6:30pm, Th 8:30am-12:15pm, Sa 8:30am-12:15pm and 2:30-5pm).

BOMBS AWAY Switzerland may be a neutral country, but that doesn't mean its citizens are unprepared for an attack. Every Swiss household must either build its own bomb shelter or pay a yearly fee to reserve one bed per person at a community one. You never know when those shelters will come in handy: in the winter of 1998, hundreds of Verbier residents crowded in to the local bomb-shelter (today's hostel, the Bunker) to seek shelter from a deadly avalanche.

OUTDOOR ACTIVITIES AND ENTERTAINMENT. Verbier has a total of 400km of **ski** runs; its best runs are on the **Mont Fort glacier** (3329m), which offers skiing and snowboarding Nov.-Apr. A behemoth of a cable car, the **Téléjumbo** can carry 150 passengers at a time to the glacier via Col des Gentianes (also the site of a snowboard half-pipe). From the Médran cable car station (up the rue de Médran from the tourist office), another cable car runs through Les Ruinettes to **Attelas** (2193m), and further to **Mont Gelë** (3023m). Ski pass prices and cable car schedules are complicated, based on the length and area of validity—make sure to pick up the pertinent info at the tourist or Téléverbier offices. (2-day pass for the 4-valley region and Mont Fort 112SFr; for the Verbier slopes only, 98SFr. 3-day passes 162SFr. Photo ID required. Non-skier day pass 37SFr, 22SFr. Ages 17-20 15% reduction, seniors and ages 7-16 40% reduction.) Rental shops in Verbier abound; **Ski Service,** down rue de Médran between pl. Centrale and the cable station, operates through the Rent-A-Sport system. (Skis 28SFr per day, snowboards 38SFr, boots 15SFr. ☎771 6770; fax 771 6771. Open 10am-12:30pm and 3-6:30pm. AmEx, MC, Visa.) The tourist office makes recommendations to would-be skiers based on skill level; they do the same for the summer **hiking trails** in the area.

Adventure opportunities don't melt with the snow. **La Maison du Sport** (☎775 3363) offers multi-day, guided excursions, hikes, and courses on everything from canyoning to ice climbing. There are plenty of opportunities to join the flock of **paragliders** who dot the skies above Verbier. **Max Biplace** (☎771 5555 or (079) 219 3655) offers tandem flights—book them at La Fantastique (☎771 4141). The **Centre de Parapente,** near the Centre Polysportif (☎771 6818), also offers tandem paragliding (150SFr) and hanggliding (250SFr). The multi-level **Centre Polysportif** (☎771 6601), downhill from pl. Centrale on rue de la Poste, has a **swimming pool** (7SFr, 5SFr children ages 6-16), **ice-skating** (6SFr, 4SFr; skate rentals 6SFr, 5SFr), **squash** (12-14SFr per 30min.), and **tennis** (23SFr per hour; open 10am-9pm; outdoor pool closes at 7pm). From March 24-25, 2001, Verbier will host an international snowboard freeride contest (www.xtreme-snowboard.com).

Every summer Verbier draws an impressive array of performers to its **classical musical festival** (in 2001, July 21-Aug. 6). Recent attendees include James Levine, Evgeny Kissin, Sir Neville Marriner, and the Emerson Quartet. Tickets range from 30-115SFr and are available from the ticket corner next to the Médran cable car station (☎771 8282; www.verbierfestival.com), though free events are posted each day of the festival.

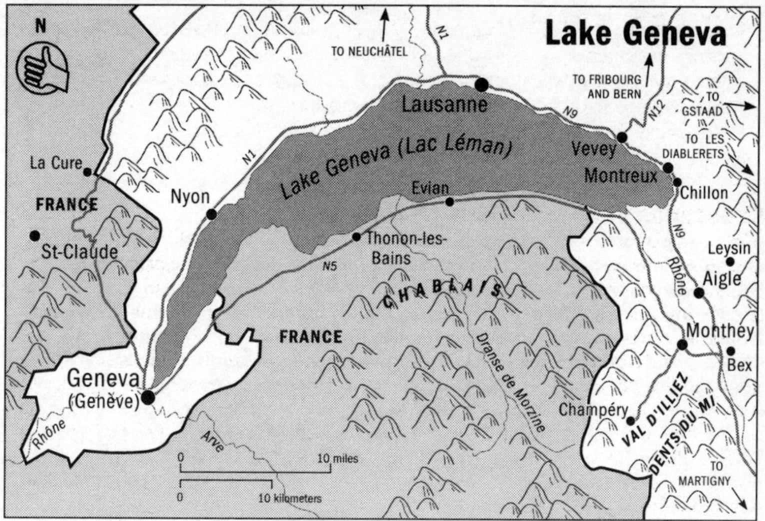

LAKE GENEVA REGION (LAC LÉMAN)

All around Lac Léman, hills dotted by villas or festooned with the terraced garlands of ripening grapes seem tame and settled . . . then the haze clears and the rough-hewn mountain peaks behind the hills become visible. In that moment, the lake discards its cultivated prettiness and urbanity for the energizing promise of unpopulated wilderness and wide lonely expanses. Many travelers suffer financial anxiety when they consider venturing into the prosperous Lake Geneva region, since high prices are the general rule in Geneva, Lausanne, and Montreux, but courageous adventurers discover that the towns along the lake abound with at least three of Switzerland's cheapest commodities: peace and quiet is just a short stroll along the tree-lined quay or up into the vine-laced hills, chocolate is available for a pittance nearly everywhere, and the unforgettable views are, as always, free.

HIGHLIGHTS OF LAKE GENEVA

Get lost in **Geneva's** charming and historic vieille ville, then follow the music down to Carouge, a village to the south with a long history of parties (see p. 453).

Follow in the footsteps of T.S. Eliot, Dickens, and Henry James down **Lausanne's** beautiful lakeside streets, and feel like a resort-goer of the 1920s (see p. 454).

Get inspired by radically different art at the **Collection de l'Art Brut** in Montreux, then visit the chilling **Chateau Chillon** with its dungeon for radicals (see p. 462).

GENEVA (GENÈVE, GENF) ☎022

Step onto one of Geneva's lakeside quays, and you'll be confronted instantly by bankers barking into cellular phones, students strolling hand-in-hand, and families just enjoying the shore. There is no typical resident of this small (pop. 178,000) city: commerce plays its part in shaping the local character, but so do art, music,

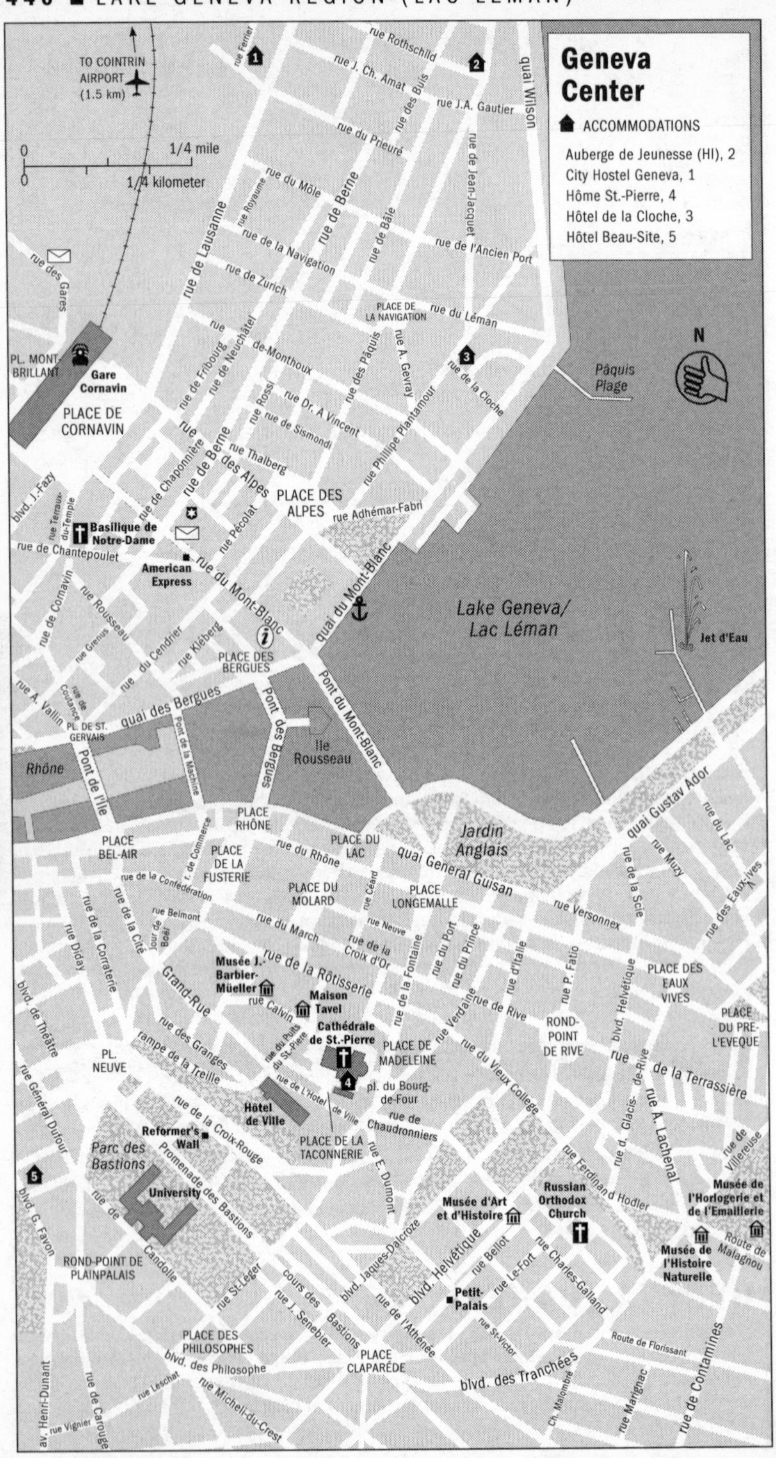
Geneva Center
ACCOMMODATIONS
Auberge de Jeunesse (HI), 2
City Hostel Geneva, 1
Hôme St.-Pierre, 4
Hôtel de la Cloche, 3
Hôtel Beau-Site, 5
TO COINTRIN AIRPORT (1.5 km)
1/4 mile
1/4 kilometer
N
Gare Cornavin
PLACE DE CORNAVIN
PL. MONT-BRILLANT
Basilique de Notre-Dame
American Express
PLACE DES ALPES
PLACE DES BERGUES
Lake Geneva/ Lac Léman
Jet d'Eau
Pâquis Plage
Ile Rousseau
Rhône
Jardin Anglais
PLACE BEL-AIR
PLACE RHÔNE
PLACE DE LA FUSTERIE
PLACE DU LAC
PLACE DU MOLARD
PLACE LONGEMALLE
PLACE DES EAUX VIVES
PLACE DU PRE-L'EVEQUE
ROND-POINT DE RIVE
Musée J.-Barbier-Müeller
Maison Tavel
Cathédrale de St.-Pierre
PLACE DE MADELEINE
pl. du Bourg-de-Four
Hôtel de Ville
PLACE DE LA TACONNERIE
PL. NEUVE
Reformer's Wall
Parc des Bastions
University
ROND-POINT DE PLAINPALAIS
Musée d'Art et d'Histoire
Russian Orthodox Church
Musée de l'Horlogerie et de l'Emaillerie
Musée de l'Histoire Naturelle
Petit-Palais
PLACE DES PHILOSOPHES
PLACE CLAPARÉDE
quai Wilson
quai du Mont-Blanc
quai des Bergues
quai General Guisan
quai Gustav Ador
Pont du Mont-Blanc
Pont des Bergues
Pont de l'Ile
rue de Lausanne
rue de Berne
rue du Mont-Blanc
rue des Alpes
Grand-Rue
rue du Rhône
rue de la Rôtisserie
rue de Rive
blvd. Helvétique
blvd. des Tranchées
blvd. des Philosophe
rue de Candolle
rue de la Croix-Rouge
Promenade des Bastions
rue de Contamines
rue de la Terrassière

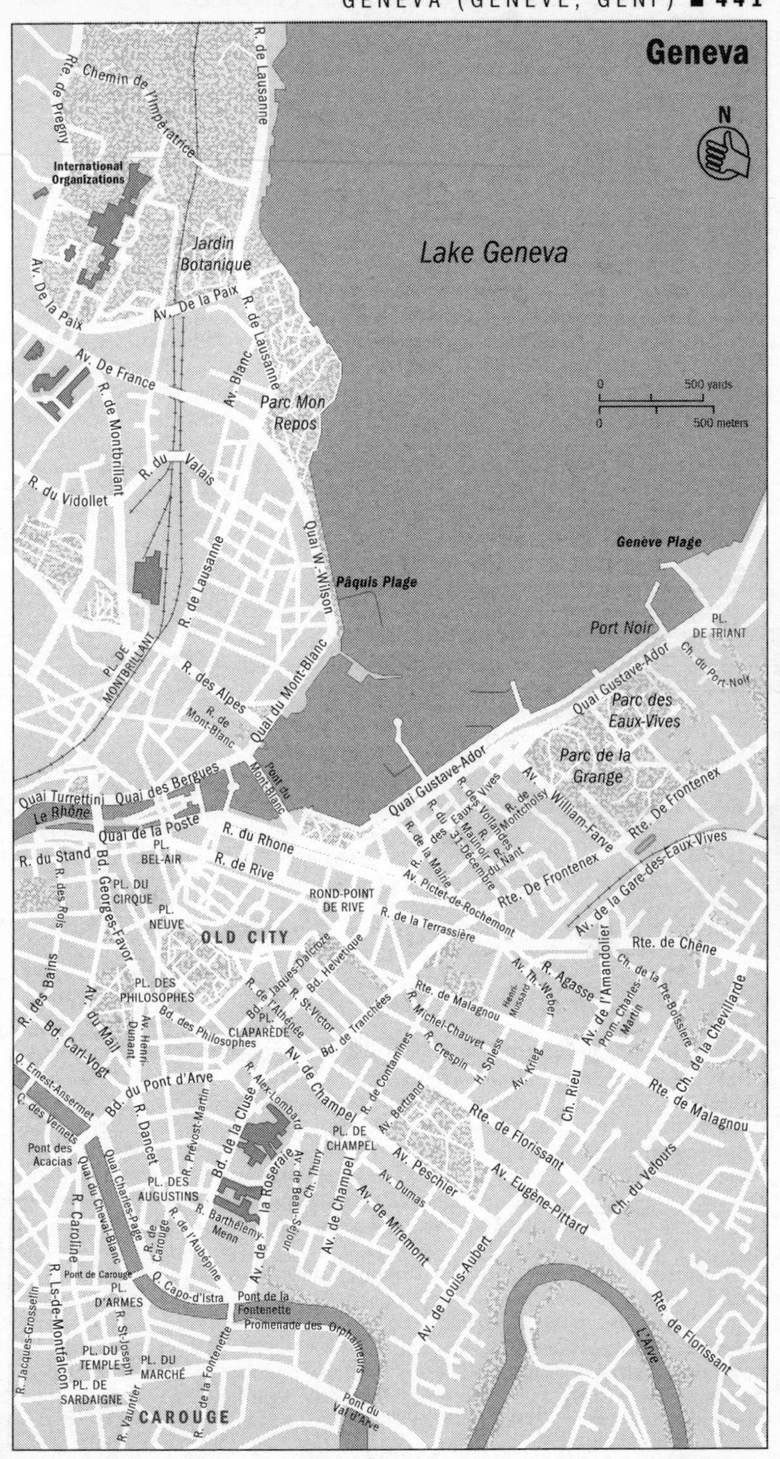
Geneva
N
Lake Geneva
0 500 yards
0 500 meters
International Organizations
Jardin Botanique
Parc Mon Repos
Pâquis Plage
Genève Plage
Port Noir
Parc des Eaux-Vives
Parc de la Grange
OLD CITY
CAROUGE
Rte. de Pregny
Chemin de l'Impératrice
R. de Lausanne
Av. De la Paix
Av. De France
R. de Montbrillant
Av. Blanc
R. du Valais
R. du Vidollet
Quai W.-Wilson
PL. DE MONTBRILLANT
R. des Alpes
R. de Mont-Blanc
Quai du Mont-Blanc
Pont du Mont-Blanc
Quai des Bergues
Quai Turrettini
Le Rhône
Quai de la Poste
PL. BEL-AIR
R. du Rhone
R. de Rive
R. du Stand
Bd. Georges-Favor
R. des Rois
PL. DU CIRQUE
PL. NEUVE
ROND-POINT DE RIVE
Quai Gustave-Ador
PL. DE TRIANT
Ch. du Port-Noir
Av. William-Favre
Rte. De Frontenex
Av. de la Gare-des-Eaux-Vives
Rte. de Chêne
R. de la Terrassière
Av. Pictet-de-Rochemont
R. de la Mairie
R. des Eaux-Vives
R. du 31-Décembre
R. des Vollandes
R. Maunoir
R. du Nant
R. de Montchoisy
R. des Bains
Av. du Mail
Bd. Carl-Vogt
PL. DES PHILOSOPHES
Bd. des Philosophes
Av. Henri-Dunant
PL. CLAPARÈDE
Bd. Jacques-Dalcroze
R. de l'Athénée
Bd. Helvetique
R. St-Victor
Bd. de Tranchées
Rte. de Malagnou
R. Michel-Chauvet
R. Crespin
H. Spiess
Henri Mussard
Av. Th.-Weber
R. Agasse
Av. de l'Amandolier
Prom. Charles-Martin
Ch. de la Pte-Boissière
Ch. de la Chevillarde
Av. Krieg
Ch. Rieu
Rte. de Malagnou
Q. Ernest-Ansermet
C. des Vernets
Bd. du Pont d'Arve
R. Dancet
R. Prévost-Martin
Bd. de la Cluse
R. Alex-Lombard
Av. de Champel
R. de Contamines
Av. Bertrand
Rte. de Florissant
PL. DE CHAMPEL
Av. Peschier
Av. Eugène-Pittard
Ch. du Velours
Pont des Acacias
Quai du Cheval-Blanc
Quai Charles-Page
R. Caroline
PL. DES AUGUSTINS
R. Barthélemy-Menn
R. de Carouge
R. de l'Aubépine
Av. de la Roseraie
Av. de Beau-Séjour
Ch. Thury
Av. de Champel
Av. Dumas
Av. de Miremont
Av. de Louis-Aubert
Pont de Carouge
PL. D'ARMES
R. Ls-de-Montfalcon
R. Jacques-Grosselin
R. St-Joseph
Q. Capo-d'Istra
Pont de la Fontenette
Promenade des Orphelins
Rte. de Florissant
L'Arve
PL. DU TEMPLE
PL. DU MARCHÉ
PL. DE SARDAIGNE
R. Vautier
R. de la Fontenette
Pont du Val d'Arve

scholarship, and—don't forget—tourism. Part of Geneva's malleable identity comes from its strongly international component: only one-third of the city's residents are natives of the canton. Isolated from the rest of Switzerland both ideologically and geographically (the city rests in the lower western corner of the nation), the Genevan sense of independence is perhaps the one theme uniting the city's wildly diverse group of citizens.

Geneva's citizens have a long and belligerent tradition of doing battle to protect their political and religious independence. Medieval Geneva fended off constant attacks, protecting its strategic site where the Rhône River flows out of Lake Geneva. In 1536, however, Geneva openly welcomed the Protestant Reformation. The townspeople voted to convert *en masse* and invited an unknown 25-year-old, John Calvin, to their cathedral. His fiery sermons from Geneva's pulpit between 1536 and 1564 brought in waves of persecuted French and Italian refugees to the "Rome of Protestants." Geneva then waged a hard-won battle for freedom from the Catholic House of Savoy, whose duke sought to crush both Protestantism and Genevan democracy (see Soup's On, p. 443, and Prison is a Holy Place, p. 466).

Unfortunately, over the next 150 years, the zeal of the Reformists occasionally took the form of authoritarian rule within the city walls, exemplified by the burning of Calvin's detractors and the burning of Rousseau's books. But Geneva's cosmopolitanism eventually won out, and the city became a gathering place for aesthetes and free thinkers. Voltaire lived and worked in the Geneva area for 23 years, and his compatriot Madame de Staël later held her salons in nearby Coppet. In the early 19th century, mountain-loving romantics Shelley and Byron found inspiration in the city's surroundings. Mary Wollstonecraft Shelley created Dr. Frankenstein's monster here, and George Eliot set up house in Geneva, the home town of her hero, Rousseau. One of Geneva's most famous political refugees was Lenin, who sat around here from 1903 to 1905 and again in 1908 before being quietly shipped back to Moscow in a sealed train by Western leaders hoping to disrupt the turn-of-the-century Russian government.

Neon-topped temples to international commerce intermingle with the serious business of world affairs. Under the inspiration of native Henri Dunant, the **International Committee of the Red Cross** established itself in Geneva in 1864, and nations from around the world signed the peace-keeping First Geneva Convention in the same year. In 1919, Geneva's selection as the site for the League of Nations confirmed the city's reputation as a center for both international organizations and arbitrations. Geneva still retains the European office of the **United Nations** and dozens of other international bodies ranging from the Center for European Nuclear Research to the World Council of Churches.

GETTING THERE AND GETTING AROUND

Geneva's **Cointrin Airport** is a **Swissair** hub, with direct flights to New York, Paris, London, Amsterdam, and Rome. To reach the city from the arrivals hall, go up a level and head outside to catch bus #10 to town (15min., every 6min., 2.20SFr). The ticket dispenser requires exact change—large bills can be broken at the changeomat behind the escalator. For a shorter trip to Gare Cornavin, take the train (6min., every 10 min., 4.80SFr). Geneva has two rail stations. **Gare Cornavin** is the primary station and departure point for all major Swiss and foreign cities. The second station, the tiny **Gare des Eaux-Vives** on the eastern edge of the city, connects to France's regional rail lines.

By **car,** Geneva is more accessible from France than from the rest of Switzerland. To drive to Geneva from the west, take A40 which continues on to Lausanne and Montreux. From the south take N201 north. From the north, take A40 from France and within Switzerland. From the east, take A40 west. N1 is the best way to reach Geneva from Lausanne or Montreux. Don't go crazy looking for the route numbers—they're not all that visible; just follow the signs for Geneva. Hugely popular **ferries** (CGN; ☎ 741 5231) connect Geneva to Lausanne and Montreux, depart-

SOUP'S ON Before it became part of the Swiss Confederation, Geneva warded off almost-constant attack from the French House of Savoy. After sporadically battling for over 200 years, the city finally triumphed due to Swiss practicality. On the night of December 11, 1602, Savoyard soldiers attempted to scale the city walls. A lone housewife saw the attack and proceeded to dump a pot of boiling soup on the soldiers' heads, buying enough time to sound the city's alarm. Each year, the **Festival of the Escalade** celebrates this event, as costumed citizens reenact the battle and children eat chocolate *marmites* (pots) filled with marzipan vegetables.

ing from quai du Mont-Blanc. A round-trip ticket (47-57SFr, ages 16-25 half-off, seniors 20% discount) includes the option of returning to Geneva by train.

Flights: Cointrin Airport (☎717 7111, flight information ☎799 3111; fax 798 4377) is a hub for **Swissair** (☎(0848) 800 700). Several direct flights per day to New York, Paris, London, Amsterdam, and Rome. **Air France** (☎827 8787) has 7 per day to Paris, and **British Airways** (☎(0848) 801 010) has 7 per day to London.

Trains: All trains run approximately 4:30am-1am. There are two stations:

Gare Cornavin, pl. Cornavin, is the main station. To: **Lausanne** (40min., every 10-20min., 20SFr); **Bern** (2hr., every hr., 40SFr); **Zurich** (3½hr., every hr., 77SFr); **Basel** (3hr., every hr., 72SFr); **Montreux** (1hr., 2 per hr., 29SFr); **Interlaken** (3hr., every hr., 65SFr); **Paris** (3hr.40min., 8 per day, 196SFr, under 26 166SFr); **Milan** (4hr., 10 per day, 164SFr, under 26 132SFr); and **Vienna** (10-12hr., 2 per day, 361SFr). To book a seat on long-distance or international trains, join the throng at reservation and information (open M-F 8:30am-7pm, Sa 9am-5pm).

Gare des Eaux-Vives (☎736 1620), on av. de la Gare des Eaux-Vives (Tram #12, "Amandoliers SNCF") connects to France's regional rail lines through **Annecy** (1½hr., 6 per day, 14SFr) or **Chamonix** (2½hr., 4 per day, 24SFr). The ticket machine at the station does not return change. Ticket office (Gare des Eaux-Vives) open M-F 9am-6pm, Sa 11am-5:45pm.

Public Transportation: Geneva has an efficient bus and tram network. **Transport Publics Genevois** (☎308 3434), next to the tourist office in Gare Cornavin, provides a free map of local bus routes called *Le Réseau;* the timetables cost a few francs. Open 6:15am-8pm. 2.20SFr 1hr. of unlimited travel on any bus; 3 stops or fewer 1.50SFr. Full-day passes 5SFr for 1 zone, 8.50SFr for 4. SwissPass valid on all buses; Eurail not valid. Buses run roughly 5:30am-midnight. Noctambus (3SFr, 1:30-4:30am) runs when the others don't. Buy multi-fare and day tickets at the train station, others at automatic vendors at every stop. Stamp multi-use tickets before boarding or risk 60SFr fines.

Taxis: Taxi-Phone (☎331 4133). 6.30SFr plus 2.70SFr per km. Taxi from airport to city 25-30SFr., max. 4 passengers (15-20min.).

Car Rental: Avis, rue de Lausanne 44 (☎731 9009). **Europcar,** rue de Lausanne 37 (☎732 5252; fax 738 1780). **Budget,** rue de Zurich 36 (☎900 2400), is the cheapest: rentals start at 86SFr per day. All have offices at Cointrin, but check for airport surcharges (around 11%).

Parking: On-street 1SFr per hr. The garage (☎736 6630) under Cornavin station (enter at pl. Cornavin) is 2SFr for 1hr., 3SFr for 2. **Garage Les Alpes,** rue Thalberg, is 2SFr per hr. weekdays, 1SFr per hr. nights and weekends. Digital boards on highways list several car-parks and the number of vacant spaces.

Bike Rental: Geneva is pedal-happy with well-marked bike paths and special traffic lights for spoked traffic. For routes, get *Itineraires cyclables* or *Tours de ville avec les vélos de location* from the tourist office. Behind the station, **Genève Roule,** pl. Montbrillant 17 (☎/fax 740 1343), has 5 free bikes available (sponsored by the Red Cross). A 50SFr deposit is required; hefty fine if bike is lost or stolen. Slightly nicer neon bikes start at 5SFr per day. Open 7:30am-9:30pm.

Hitchhiking: *Let's Go* does not recommend hitchhiking. Hitchers say, however, that Switzerland is one of the safer countries in Europe in which to hail a ride. Those headed to Germany or northern Switzerland take bus #4 to "Jardin Botanique." Those headed to France take bus #4 to "Palettes," then line D to "St. Julien."

ORIENTATION

Geneva began as a fortified city on a hill, and the historic *vieille ville*'s labyrinthine cobbled streets and quiet squares around John Calvin's **Cathédrale de St-Pierre** still occupy the heart of the urban landscape. Across the Rhône River to the north, billionaires' banks and five-star hotels gradually give way to lakeside promenades. Farther north, another hill holds the U.N., Red Cross, and W.T.O., as well as rolling green parkland. Across the Arve river to the south lies the village of Carouge, home to many student bars and clubs (take tram #12 to "pl. du Marché").

Be sure to carry your passport with you at all times; the French border is never more than a few minutes away and buses frequently cross it. City buses provide swift service, with major hubs at the Gare Cornavin, Rd.-Pt. de Plainpalais, and pl. Bel Air (near the *ponts de l'Ile*); trips that stay within zone 10 (most of the city) officially cost 2.20SFr, but ticket purchasing is largely on the honor system and some devious backpackers try to get away with riding for free. Be warned, however: those caught without a ticket face a 60SFr fine, and playing confused anglophone will probably not work. Much of this city can be walked in good weather.

PRACTICAL INFORMATION

TOURIST AND FINANCIAL SERVICES

Tourist Offices: At information offices (marked by a blue lower-case "i" sign), the free must-haves are the city map and the booklet *Info Jeunes/Young People*. The **main office,** rue du Mont-Blanc 18 (☎909 7000; fax 909 7011; info@geneve-tourisme.ch; www.geneve-tourisme.ch), lies 5min. away from Cornavin towards the pont du Mont-Blanc, within the Central Post Office Building. English-speaking staff books hotel rooms (5SFr fee), offers **walking tours,** and provides information on anything from local events to vegetarian and kosher restaurants. The office maintains a free direct phone line to Geneva hotels in Gare Cornavin, as well as a board listing budget accommodations. Open July-Aug. 9am-6pm; Sept.-June M-Sa 9am-6pm. During the summer, head for the magic bus, Geneva's **Centre d'Accueil et de Renseignements** (CAR; ☎731 4647), parked in place Mont-Blanc, by the Metro Shopping entrance to Cornavin Station. This office-in-a-bus is geared towards young people and posts a daily updated list of musical and theatrical performances. Open June 15-Sept. 15 9am-11pm.

Consulates: Australia, chemin des Fins 2 (☎799 9100; fax 799 9178). **Canada,** av. de l'Ariana 5 (☎919 9200; fax 919 9277). **New Zealand,** chemin des Fins 2 (☎929 0350; fax 929 0377). **South Africa,** rue de Rhône 65 (☎849 5454; fax 849 5438). **UK,** rue de Vermont 37 (☎918 2426; fax 918 2322). **US,** World Trade Center Bldg. #2 (☎798 1605; recorded information ☎798 1615). Call to schedule appointments.

Budget Travel: SSR, rue Vignier 3 (☎329 9734 or 329 9733; www.ssr.ch), off av. Henri-Dunant near Plaine de Plainpalais by the Forget-Me-Not Hotel, offers youth and student fares. Open M-F 9:15am-6pm, Sa 9am-noon. AmEx, MC, Visa.

FINANCIAL SERVICES AND COMMUNICATIONS

Currency Exchange: ATMs, which offer the best rates, are easy to find in Geneva. There is one at Gare Cornavin, in the entrance to the pharmacy. For traditional service, **Gare Cornavin** has good rates and no commission on travelers' checks, advances cash on credit cards (min. 200SFr), and arranges Western Union transfers. Open Nov. 1-Mar. 31 6:45am-8pm, Apr. 1-Oct. 31 6:45am-9:30pm. Western Union desk open 7am-7pm.

American Express: rue du Mont-Blanc 7, P.O. Box 1032, CH-1211 Geneva 01 (☎731 7600; fax 732 7211). Mail held 2-3 months; arrangements can be made for over a year. All banking services; reasonable exchange rates. Hotel and train (30SFr) reservations and tickets for city tours and excursions. Open in summer M-F 8:30am-6pm, Sa 9am-noon; in winter M-F 8:30am-5:30pm, Sa 9am-noon.

English-Language Bookstores: ELM (English Language and Media) Video and Books, rue Versonnex 5 (☎736 0945; fax 786 1429), has a quality range of new books in

English and a book-ordering service. Open M-F 9am-6:30pm, Sa 10am-5pm. AmEx, DC, MC, Visa. The adjoining video store (☎736 0222) rents videos in English (from 5.50SFr), but you must be a member. Open M-F 9am-8pm, Sa 10am-7pm. **Book Worm,** rue Sismondi 5 (☎/fax 731 8765), near the train station off rue de Berne. Two long-haired chihuahuas keep watch over this genteel store of used books and classic English-language videos (4-5SFr for 2 days). Tea room serves tea with a biscuit (2.50SFr), lunch (F-Su 12:30-2:30pm, 14.50SFr), and desserts (6SFr). Open Tu-Sa noon-8pm, Su 12-6pm. AmEx, MC, Visa. **Librairie des Amateurs,** Grand Rue 15 (☎732 8097), in the *vieille ville.* Classy secondhand dealer. Open M 2-6:30pm, Tu-F 11am-6:30pm, Sa 2pm-5pm. **Payot Libraire,** rue de Chantepoulet 5 (☎731 8950), is Geneva's largest chain of bookstores, with an amazingly broad and well-selected stock of English-language books. Open M 1-6:30pm, Tu, W, F 9am-6:30pm, Th 9am-8pm, Sa 9am-5pm. AmEx, DC, MC, Visa.

Library: American Library, rue de-Monthoux 3 (☎732 8097), at Emmanuel Church. 20,000 titles. 1-month membership (25SFr) allows you to borrow books (6 max.) for 2 weeks and offers a small but eclectic collection of books on tape (3SFr). Open Tu and F 12:30-5pm, W 2-7pm, Th 2-5pm, Sa 10am-4pm, Su 11am-12:30pm.

Internet Access: Open Vidéo Club, rue Chantepoulet, has 12 PCs available, along with a wide selection of American videos. Internet 5SFr per hr. Open M-Th 9:30a,-3am, F9:30am-5am, Sa 11am-5am, Su 3pm-1am. **Point 6,** rue de Vieux-Billard 7a, off rue des Bains (☎800 2600), rents spots at the screen for 6SFr per hr, 4SFr for a half-hour. Open M-Tu, Th noon-midnight, W 10am-midnight, F noon-2am, Sa 10am-2am, Su 10am-10pm. **Funet Discount Internet Café,** rue de Lausanne 44 (☎738 5000; fax 738 5021). Turn left on rue de Lausanne from Gare Cornavin and walk 5min. to find 7 PCs loaded with the latest netware. 15min. for 5SFr; 30min. 7SFr; 1hr. 12SFr. Open M-F 9am-9:30pm, Sa-Su noon-9:30pm. Copier available. MC, Visa. Internet access also available in some hostels as well as in the artists' colony (see p. 450).

Post Office: Poste Centrale, rue de Mont-Blanc 18, a block from Gare Cornavin in the stately Hôtel des Postes. Open M-F 7:30am-6pm, Sa 8:30-noon. Address *Poste Restante* to DONALDSON, Lou, Genève 1 Mont-Blanc, CH-1211, Geneva. Another branch is located behind the train station at rue des gares 10-16. 24-hr. self-service; counters open M-F 7am-10:45pm, Sa 7am-8pm, Su noon-8pm.

OTHER SERVICES

Bi-Gay-Lesbian Organizations: Diologai, rue de la Navigation 11-13. (☎906 4040; www.hivnet.ch/diologai.) From Gare Cornavin, turn left and walk 5min. down rue de Lausanne; turn right onto rue de la Navigation. Resource group with programs from support groups to outdoor activities. Publishes *Diologai,* a guide to French-speaking Switzerland's gay scene. Mostly male, but women welcome. **360°,** 25 rue de Lausanne (☎740 0071), publishes a magazine, *360°*, and maintains an office at 2 pl. Grenus (☎ (087) 887 9360) with walk-in hours on Su from 4-9pm. Open 10am-7pm. **Gay International Group** (GIG; ☎(087) 880 3002; taped message 789 1869) is for international gay visitors or semi-permanents in Geneva, including Anglophones. Communal meals every 6 weeks. **Centre Femmes Natalie Barney** (women only), 19 Chemin Chateau Bloch (☎797 2714), offers similar services to Dialogai, but is smaller and lesbian-oriented. 24hr. answering machine with events listing; live phone answering W 6-8pm.

Travelers with Disabilities: CCIPH (Centre de Coordination et d'Information pour Personnes Handicapées), 28 Bld. du Pont d'Arve (☎809 5398). The tourist office also provides a free guide to the city for disabled visitors, called *Guide à l'Usage des Personnes Handicapées,* which includes oversized maps.

Luggage Storage: Gare Cornavin. 3-10SFr per day. Open 4:30am-12:45am. Lockers 3-5SFr.

Lost Property: rue des Glacis de Rive 7 (☎787 6000). Open M-F 7:30am-4pm.

Laundromat: Lavseul, rue de-Monthoux 29 (☎735 9051 or 732 6146). 5SFr to wash, 1SFr for10 min. to dry. Open 7am-midnight.

Public Showers: Point d'Eau, rue Chandieu 4 (☎734 2240). Take bus #8 to "Canonnière" and turn right onto rue de Vermont; it's on the left. **Free** hot showers and personal hygiene center for the ripe backpacker. Open M-F 3-7pm, Sa 10am-2pm. Additional location at rue de Fronteneux 48, open M-F 9am-noon.

EMERGENCIES

Emergencies: Police, rue de Berne 6 (☎117, non-emergency ☎715 3850), next to post office. **Fire,** ☎118. **Ambulance,** ☎144.

Rape Crisis Hotline: Viol-Secours (☎345 2020). Open M 2-6pm, Tu 3-6pm, W 4-8pm, Th 9am-1pm, F 2-5pm.

Late-Night Pharmacy: Every night a changing set of 4 pharmacies stays open late (9 or 11pm). Consult *Genève Agenda* for addresses and phone numbers. The pharmacy at the train station has the longest regular hours.

Medical Assistance: Hôpital Cantonal, rue Micheli-du-Crest 24 (☎372 3311). Bus #1 or 5 or tram #12. Door #2 is for emergency care, Door #3 for consultations. For information on walk-in clinics call the **Association des Médecins** (☎320 8420).

ACCOMMODATIONS AND CAMPING

Geneva is one of the most cosmopolitan cities in the world, and its 5-star hotel system is geared more toward the international banker or diplomat than the friendly budget traveler. Luckily, the seasonal influx of university students and interns has created a second network of decently-priced hostels, pensions, and university dorms moonlighting as summer hotels. The indispensable *Info Jeunes* lists about 50 options; we list the highlights below. The tourist office publishes *Budget Hotels*, stretching definitions a bit to include rooms at 120SFr per person. Even for the shortest stays, reservations are a must. For longer stays, check *Tribune de Genève*'s weekly supplement of apartment classifieds or the tourist office's board.

City Hostel Geneva, rue Ferrier 2 (☎901 1500, fax 901 1560, info@cityhostel.ch, www.cityhostel.ch). From the station, turn left on rue de Lausanne, walk 5 min., turn left onto rue de Prieuré, and right onto rue Ferrier. This newly-opened hostel has one major advantage: location, location, location. Small dormitory rooms and disorganized staff more than compensated for by the hostel's proximity to the station, waterfront, and restaurants. Kitchen facilities, TV room, a book exchange, a comprehensive listing of markets in Geneva, and **Internet** access (7SFr per hr.), all help to lighten the atmosphere. No curfew or lockout. Reception 8-11:30am and 3-10pm, checkout 10am. All rooms have sinks. Linens 3SFr. Single-sex, 4-bed dorms 24SFr; singles 50SFr, doubles 70SFr.

Auberge de Jeunesse (HI), rue Rothschild 28-30 (☎732 6260; fax 738 3987; booking@yh.geneva.ch; www.yh-geneva.ch). Walk 10min. left from the station down rue de Lausanne, then right on rue Rothschild. Take bus #1 from the station (dir.: Wilson) to the end of the line. Don't expect atmosphere; do expect a comfortable last-minute bunk and a ton of people to meet. Check-in lines can be long. Amenities include a sizable lobby, restaurant (dinner 11.50SFr, with dessert and drink 14SFr), **kitchen** facilities, TV room with CNN, library, 3 **Internet** stations (7SFr per hr.) and snack bar. Breakfast, hall showers, sheets, and lockers included. **Laundry** 6SFr. Special facilities for disabled guests. 5-night max. stay. Reception June-Sept. 6:30-10am and 2pm-1am; Oct-May 6:30-10am and 4pm-midnight. Reservations wise. Lockout in summer 10am-4pm, in winter 10am-5pm. Curfew midnight. Dorms 24SFr; doubles 65SFr with toilet, 75SFr with toilet and shower; quads 105SFr. MC, Visa.

Hôme St-Pierre, cours St-Pierre 4 (☎310 3707; fax 310 1727; homestpierre@freesurf.ch). Take bus #5 to "pl. Neuve" or walk 15min. from the train station: cross the Rhône at pont du Mont-Blanc, then go up rue de la Fontaine to pl. du Bourg-de-Four. Look to the right. Mere seconds from the west entrance of the cathedral, this **women's only** 150-year-old "home" has comfortable beds, a large **kitchen,** and a dining room. Enjoy the music of the *vieille ville* (including a church bell serenade every 15min.), spectacular rooftop views, and a convivial atmosphere. Laundry 7SFr. Reception M-Sa

9am-noon and 4-8pm, Su 9am-noon. No lockout or curfew. Popular, so reserve ahead. Breakfast (M-Sa) 5SFr. Showers and lockers included. Dorms 23SFr; singles 36-45SFr; doubles 50-60SFr. MC, Visa.

Cité Universitaire, av. Miremont 46 (☎839 2211; fax 839 2223). From the station, find the #3 bus in front of the "Le Popeye" restaurant. Take it to the last stop; the Cité Universitaire will be directly on your right. This institutional college housing in a modern tower block has TV rooms, newspapers, restaurant, **disco** (all-night dancing Th and Sa, free to residents), ping-pong, tennis courts, small grocery shop, and some great views. Hall showers included. Reception M-F 8am-noon and 2-10pm, Sa 8am-noon and 6-10pm, Su 9am-11am and 6-10pm. Lockout 11am-6pm and curfew 11pm, both for dorms only. Checkout 10am. 4 dorms (July-Sept. only) 17SFr, including lockers; singles 38SFr; doubles 55SFr; studios with kitchenette and bathroom 68SFr. AmEx, MC, Visa.

Hôtel de la Cloche, rue de la Cloche 6 (☎732 9481; fax 738 1612), off quai du Mont-Blanc across from the Noga Hilton. A converted mansion, each room has a chandelier and a TV; some have antique mirrors and balconies. Ask for a room with a view of the lake. Showers included. Breakfast 5SFr, included with some rooms. Reception 8am-midnight. Reserve 2-3 weeks in advance in summer. Singles 55SFr; doubles 80SFr; triples 85SFr, or 100SFr, with toilet and shower; quad 140SFr, with toilet and shower. Prices go down 5-10SFr in winter. AmEx, MC, Visa.

Hôtel Beau-Site, pl. du Cirque 3 (☎328 1008; fax 329 2364; hotelbeausite@swissonline.ch; www.hotel-beau-site.ch). Take bus #1 or 4 to "Cirque," or walk from the station: turn right on blvd. Fazy, cross the Rhône at pont de la Coulouvrenière, and follow blvd. Georges-Favon to pl. du Cirque (20min.) Paneled rooms with quilt-covered beds and semi-antique furniture–some even have marble fireplaces. Reception 7am-11pm; call if you'll be arriving later. Checkout 11:15am. Call ahead for availability. Breakfast included; free coffee and tea in lobby 10am-10pm. All rooms with sink and radio, some have TVs. 10% student discount. Singles 60SFr, with shower 70SFr, with bath and toilet 85SFr; doubles 82SFr, 90SFr, 110SFr; triples 100SFr, with shower 110SFr; quads 110SFr, with shower 115SFr. AmEx, MC, Visa.

Camping Pointe-à-la-Bise, Chemin de la Bise, (☎752 1296). Take bus #9 to "Rive" then bus E (north) to "Bise" (about 7km). Reception 8am-noon and 4-8pm. Open Apr.-Oct. 6SFr per person. No tents provided, but beds are 18SFr each.

Camping d'Hermance, rue du Nord 44 (☎751 1483). Take bus E north, 14km out of town. 1 person 10SFr, 2 17SFr. Open all day. Consult *Info Jeunes* (at the tourist office) for a comprehensive list of additional locations.

FOOD

It's true that you can find anything from sushi to *paella* in Geneva, but you'll generally need a banker's salary to foot the bill. Many supermarkets also have cafeterias with some of the best deals available, and *Info Jeunes* lists university cafeterias that won't tax your wallet.

Boulangeries and *pâtisseries* offer unparalleled opportunities for gourmet food at budget prices—6SFr goes a long way when you combine a fresh loaf of bread with an avocado and tomatoes from Migros or Co-op. For dining out, there are extensive options in the *vieille ville* near the Cathedral, from *créperies* to sidewalk cafes. You'll often have to splurge a bit and pay for the location. In the area called *Les Paquîs*, bordered by the rue de Lausanne and Gare Cornavin on one side and the Quais Mont-Blanc and Wilson on the other, almost any sort of ethnic food is available. Kebab stands are interspersed with Brazilian cafes, and the colorful neighborhood offers more reasonable prices than most Genevan restaurants. To the south, the village of Carouge is known for its lively student population as well as its cozy pizzerias and funky, chic brasseries. Dining on the waterfront or in immediately surrounding areas will definitely cost you, but it's possible just to enjoy an after-dinner ice cream cone at a lakeside cafe instead. Around pl. du Cirque and plaine de Plainpalais, are a number of cheap, student-oriented "tea rooms," offering bakery and traditional fare at reasonable prices.

Le Rozzel, Grand-Rue 18 (☎312 4272). Take bus #5 to pl. Neuve, then walk up the hill past the cathedral on rue Jean-Calvin to Grand-Rue. This Breton-style *crêperie* with outdoor seating on the most elegant street in the *vieille ville* serves large dinner crêpes (7-17SFr), dessert crêpes (5-12SFr), and sangria (5SFr). *Menü* available for 19SFr. Open M-F 8am-10pm, Sa 10am-10pm. AmEx, MC, Visa.

Restaurant Manora, rue de Cornavin 4 (☎909 4410), 3min. from the station on the right, in the Placette department store. This huge self-serve restaurant with a fresh, varied, high-quality selection offers salads (from 4.20SFr), fruit tarts (3.20SFr), entrees cooked on the spot (from 11SFr), and maybe the only free water in all of Geneva. Wheelchair accessible. Open M-Sa 7am-9pm, Su 9am-9pm.

La Crise, rue de Chantepoulet 13 (☎738 0264). From the station, turn right on rue de Cornavin and left on rue de Chantepoulet. Watch the owner, Mme. LeParc, cook your food in this tiny, veggie-friendly restaurant. Healthy portions, slender prices: quiche and veggies 8.50SFr; soup 3.50SFr; beer or wine 3SFr; plat du jour with soup and salad 14SFr. A *Menü* offers awesome deals. Open M-F 6am-8pm, Sa 6am-3pm.

Chez Ma Cousine, rue de Bourg-Four 6, in the *vieille ville.* The sign above this small but popular restaurant implores you: "On y mange de poulet," "Let's eat chicken." It's perfectly cooked, served with fries and salad for the low price of 12.90SFr. Salads also available at the same price, mixed with—of course—chicken. Desserts 5.50-8.50SFr. Open M-F 7am-midnight, Sa 11am-midnight, Su 11am-11pm.

Auberge de Saviese, rue des Pâquis 20 (☎732 8330; fax 784 3623). Take bus #1 to "Monthoux." From Gare Cornavin, turn left onto rue de Lausanne, then right on rue de Zurich, until you hit rue des Pâquis. Share coffee (1.90SFr) with locals breakfasting behind newspapers. In addition to lunch *plat du jour,* the menu features an excellent *fondue au cognac* (19.50SFr), *raclette* with all the trimmings (30SFr), and classic regional perch (27SFr). Open M-F 9am-10:30pm, Sa-Su 6-11pm. AmEx, DC, MC, Visa.

Les Armures, rue du Puits-St-Pierre 1 (☎310 3442; fax 818 7113), 30 seconds from the main entrance to the cathedral, in the Hotel Les Armures. One small step up in price, one giant leap up in atmosphere. Wear clean socks. A huge plaque announces that President Clinton ate here, and for a small splurge you can too. Good-sized fondue 22-25SFr; pizza 13.50-16SFr. Open noon-3pm, 6pm-midnight. AmEx, DC, MC, Visa.

MARKETS

Co-op, Migros, Grand Passage, and **Orient Express** branches are ubiquitous in Geneva. On Sundays, the few options include Gare Cornavin's **Aperto** (open daily 6am-10pm) and scattered neighborhood groceries and bakeries. Exquisite Swiss chocolate is sold in any supermarket, but the specialty store *par excellence* is **Chocolats Micheli,** rue Micheli-du-Crest 1 (☎329 9006), which produces confectionery works of art (open Tu-F 8am-6:30pm, Sa 8am-5pm).

Co-op (☎310 7711), on the corner of rue du Commerce and rue du Rhône, in the Centre Rhône Fusterie. The restaurant on floor one has *Menüs* from 9.50SFr and salads for 2.30SFr per 100g, plus a sizeable wine gallery. Open M 9am-6:45pm, Tu, W, and F 8:30am-6:45pm, Th 8:30am-8pm, Sa 8:30am-5pm. MC, Visa.

Les Halles du Molard, 48 rue de Rhône, on the pl. du Molard, offers an array of gourmet delights, including fresh produce, a *fromagerie*, and still-swimming seafood. Open M-W and F 7:30am-6:45pm, Th 7:30am-8pm, Sa 8am-5:45pm.

Marché des Eaux-Vives, bd. Helvétique, between cours de Rive and rue du Rhône. Huge dairy, vegetable, and flower market. Open W and Sa 8am-1pm.

Public Markets: There are fresh fruits and cheese on **rue de Coutance,** M-Sa 8am-6pm. A produce market is located on **Rd-Pt. de Plainpalais** Tuesday and Friday mornings, and Su 8am-6pm. In Carouge, the **pl. du Marché** offers a market W and Sa 8am-1pm. The **pl. de la Navigation** has markets Th and F 8am-1pm.

SIGHTS

For centuries Geneva was tightly constrained by a belt of fortified walls and trenches. By the mid-19th century when they were finally removed, the city's most interesting historical sites were already established in a dense, easily walkable space. The tourist office offers 2-hour **walking tours** during the summer. *(June 14-Oct. 2, M-F 10am. Sa 10am throughout the year. 12SFr, students and seniors 8SFr, children 6SFr.)* Qualified guides lead tours on all things *Genevois:* the Reformation, internationalism, the Red Cross, the *vieille ville,* and the city's museums. Recordings of the tours are available in winter, and a portable cassette player will walk you through 2000 years of Geneva's history for 10SFr plus a 50SFr deposit.

CATHEDRAL. The *vieille ville*'s **Cathédrale de St-Pierre,** the navel of the early Protestant world, is as austerely pure as on the day that Calvin stripped the place of its catholic embellishment. From its altar, Calvin preached to full houses from 1536 to 1564; today you can gawk at (but not sit in) his chair. The brightly painted **Maccabean Chapel,** restored in flamboyant style, gives an idea of how the cathedral walls might have looked pre-Reformation. Look out for the stunning organ, a massive silvery construction with a powerful sound. The 157-step **north tower** provides a commanding view of the old town's winding streets and flower-bedecked homes. *(Open June-Sept. M-Sa 9am-7pm, Su 11:30am-7pm; Oct.-May M-Sa 10am-noon and 2-5pm, Su 11am-12:30pm and 1:30-5pm. Closed Su mornings for services. Tower closes 30min. earlier and costs 3SFr July-Aug. Bell-ringing Sa afternoon and free organ recital Sa 6pm.)* The ruins of a Roman sanctuary, a 4th-century basilica, and a 6th-century church rest in an **archaeological site** below the cathedral. *(Open June-Sept. Tu-Sa 11am-5pm, Su 10am-5pm; Oct.-May Tu-Sa 2-5pm, Su 10am-noon and 2-5pm. 5SFr, students 3SFr.)*

OLD CITY. Surrounding the cathedral are medieval townhouses and burger-scaled mansions that make up Geneva's *vieille ville.* One minute from the west end sits **Maison Tavel,** Geneva's oldest civilian medieval building, a posh fortified urban palace. The fourteenth-century structure now houses a municipal history **museum** by the same name (see p. 451). The **Old Arsenal** a few steps away has 5 cannons and a mural depicting the arrival of Huguenot refugees—and Julius Caesar. Across the street is the **Hôtel de Ville** (town hall), whose components date from the 15th through 17th centuries. It was here that world leaders met on August 22, 1864 to sign the **Geneva Convention,** governing conduct during war and still in effect today.

The **Grand-Rue,** which begins at the *Hôtel de Ville,* is crammed with clustered medieval workshops and 18th-century mansions, often featuring hastily added third or fourth floors, the makeshift result of the real estate boom following the influx of French Huguenots after Louis XIV repealed the Edict of Nantes. Plaques commemorating famous residents abound, including one at #40 marking the birthplace of philosopher **Jean-Jacques Rousseau.** Antique shops and art galleries line the Grand-Rue, and nighttime brings live jazz to the restaurants and cafes.

Heading away from the *vieille ville* on rue de Chaudronniers brings you to the glittering domes of the **Russian Orthodox Church,** rue Toepffer, next to the Musée d'Art et d'Histoire. Step inside for the hauntingly lovely ikons, stained glass, and heavy incense-weighted air. Photography, short skirts, and shorts are not allowed.

WATERFRONT. Descending from the cathedral toward the lake is akin to walking forward 600 years. The streets widen, buses scuttle back and forth, and every corner sports a chic boutique or watch shop. On the waterfront, the **Jet d'Eau,** down quai Gustave-Ardor, spews a spectacular plume of water 140m into the air. The sight is a self-consciously invented tourist spectacle, originally inspired by a faulty piping jet. As the world's highest fountain, it keeps about 7 tons of water aloft at any given time from March to October.

The floral clock in the nearby **Jardin Anglais** pays homage to Geneva's watch industry with over 6,500 plants and has the world's largest second hand (2.5m). The clock is probably Geneva's most overrated attraction and was once the city's most hazardous. Almost a meter had to be cut away from the clock because tour-

ARTAMIS: GUERRILLA ARTIST COLONY What do you do when you're a young artist in Geneva and have no place to work? If there's 300 others like you, you shut down the tourist industry until the city gives you a place of your own. That's what happened in the summer of 1996 when a group of artists staged a sit-in demonstration at place du Bourg-de-Four just below the Cathédrale de St-Pierre. They ripped up pavement, built bonfires, and confused the hell out of tourists for six days until the city capitulated and granted them a no-rent lease for an abandoned industrial park on the left bank, now called Artamis (☎320 3930; www.artamis.org, artamis@artamis.org). You'll find it at 14 quai de Rhône, on the #2 and 10 bus lines ("Palladium"). Rising from the wreckage of an old factory, this ten-building complex displays high-quality graffiti and houses a mix of thriving art workshops, theaters, and fund-raising facilities as well as some of the best deals in town. There's an Internet cafe (5SFr per hr.), a movie theater (2SFr), and bars. Electronic music enthusiasts should stop by the Database Building, a recording studio where many of the top house and jungle DJs in the area come to experiment and exchange ideas. Some of their efforts are put on Internet stream radio at www.basic.ch. All facilities and the main phone line (with information on performances and events) are open 4pm to 2am.

ists, intent on taking the perfect photo, continually backed into unfortunate encounters with oncoming traffic.

The rose-lined quays lead to two fun-parks. On the north shore, **Pâquis Plage,** at quai du Mont-Blanc 30, is popular with the *Genevois*. *(☎732 2974. 2SFr; open 9am-8:30pm.)* Farther from the city center on the south shore, **Genève Plage** *(☎734 2682)* offers a giant waterslide, an Olympic-sized pool, volleyball tournaments, and topless sunbathing for 5SFr. The source of these waters, the Rhône, was consecrated by the pope during a particularly bad outbreak of the bubonic plague as a "burial" ground. As you frolic in the lake, be reverent or revolted accordingly.

Ferry tours leave from quai du Mont-Blanc for panoramic views of Geneva. Cruises narrated in English are provided by **Swiss Boat** *(☎732 4747. 35min. 8SFr, children 5SFr; 1hr. 12SFr, 7SFr; 2hr. 20SFr, 15SFr)* and **Mouettes Genevoises** *(☎732 2944. 45min. 8SFr, children 5SFr, seniors 6 SFr; 2hr. 12SFr, 7SFr, 8SFr)*. **CGN** *(☎741 5231 or 741 5235)* has been sending cruises to lakeside towns, including Lausanne, Montreux, and the stupendous Château de Chillon, for the past 125 years *(round-trip 33-50SFr, Eurail and SwissPass valid)*. *Les Heures Bleues* provides more details.

PARKS AND GARDENS. Geneva is a city bedecked with sumptuous gardens. Strategically scattered throughout the city, you'll be sure to find one by wandering a few blocks in any direction. Below the cathedral on the Rue de la Croix-Rouge, the **Parc des Bastions'** leisurely loveliness stretches from the Place Neuve to the Place des Philosophes. On one flank, **Le Mur des Réformateurs** (Reformers' Wall) displays a sprawling collection of bas-relief narrative panels, an array of multilingual inscriptions, and the towering figures of the Reformers themselves. As the largest statues (Knox, Beze, Calvin, and Farel) jostle each other sternly for "leader of the Protestant pack" bragging rights, Cromwell and Rhode Island's Roger Williams trail behind. The imposing campus of **Geneva University** sits opposite the wall, with sunbathers in between.

Strolling north along the river quais brings you to the lush **Parc Mon-Repos** (off av. de France) and **La Perle du Lac** *(off av. de la Paix)*, where panting joggers and playful kids stream along curvy paths painted with an impossibly varied palette of floral hues. At the **Jardin Botanique,** opposite the World Trade Organization, basilica-shaped greenhouses grow a collection of rare plants whose aromas waft across rue de Lausanne. *(Open Apr.-Sept. 8am-7:30pm; Oct.-Mar. 9:30am-5pm. Free.)* Venturing a little farther (and farther uphill) brings you to **Parc de l'Ariana,** where you can stroll the impressive grounds surrounding the United Nations building and the Ariana pottery museum (see p. 453).

On the opposite (south) side of the lake, past the Jet d'Eau on quai Gustave-Ador you'll find **Parc la Grange,** which features a garden of 40,000 roses, at their peak bloom in June. Next to la Grange, **Parc des Eaux-Vives** is the perfect spot for a picnic or an impromptu frisbee game.

INTERNATIONAL HILL. Spectacular views of Lac Léman with Mont-Blanc in the background can be found in the series of garden-parks up the hill behind the train station (see **Jardin Botaniqe** and **Parc de l'Ariana** above). The **Museum of the History of Science** (see p. 452) lives in one and the **World Trade Organization** (WTO) lies in another farther north. For even better vistas, climb higher to Geneva's international city, where embassies and multilateral organizations abound. The best one to visit is the **International Red Cross,** which contains its own museum (see p. 451). In the Red Cross's shadow stands the European headquarters of the **United Nations,** housed in the building that sheltered the now defunct League of Nations. The guided tour of the UN is quite dull, despite some art (typical title: "Peace: There is Room for All") donated by all the countries of the world and an opportunity to sign "The Golden Book of Peace." *(Open July 9am-6pm; Apr.-June and Aug.-Oct. 10am-noon and 2-4pm; Nov.-Mar. M-F 10am-noon and 2-4pm. 8.50SFr, seniors and students 6.50SFr, children 4SFr, children under 6 free. For information, contact the Visitors' Service ☎907 4560 or ☎907 4896, which also conducts 1hr. tours in any of 15 languages when a sizable group requests them.)* The constant traffic of international diplomats (often in handsome non-Western dress) provides more excitement than anything the tour guides have to say. There's also a not-so-subtle display of Cold War one-upmanship: the armillary sphere depicting the heavens and donated by the US stands next to a monument dedicated to the "conquest of space" donated by the former USSR.

MUSEUMS

Geneva is home to many exceptional museums, usually housed in splendid surroundings, whether architectural or natural. Fortunately, a good number of them are free; unfortunately, the most interesting aren't.

RED CROSS MUSEUM. Check your ironic detachment at the door of the **International Red Cross and Red Crescent Museum,** lest it be ripped forcibly from you during a powerful tour of the best museum in Geneva. Built into a hillside and towering over the nearby UN, the museum employs images, both still photographs and wartime film-clip montages, rather than rhetoric, to drive home its emotional narrative of historic humanitarianism. The stark, unadorned glass and steel building houses a maze of provocative graphics and audiovisual displays all through the narrative lens of the life of Henry Dunant, the Red Cross's founder. Dostoyevsky's keynote words: "Each of us is responsible to all others for everything," resonate much more after a visit here. 7 million POW records, including de Gaulle's, from WWI, reside here. Displays in English, French, and German. *(Av. de la Paix 17. Take bus #8, F, V or Z to "Appia" or "Ariana." ☎748 9525 or 748 9506. Open Su-M and W-Sa 10am-5pm. 10SFr, students and seniors 5SFr, under 12 free. Self-guided audio tours 5SFr.)*

ART MUSEUMS. If you visit just one art museum in Geneva, the **Petit-Palais** should be it. This beautiful mansion contains paintings, sculptures, and drawings by Picasso, Renoir, Gauguin, Cézanne, and Chagall. The inventive basement *salles* present themed exhibitions: the influence of primitive art on modern aesthetes, the nude female form, and radiant meditations on nature. *(Terrasse St-Victor 2, off bd. Helvétique. Take bus #17 to "Petit Palais" or #1, 3, or 5 to "Claparède." ☎346 1433. Open M-F 10am-6pm, Sa-Su 10am-5pm. 10SFr, students and seniors 5SFr, children under 12 free. V.)*

For a more historically comprehensive overview, visit the **Musée d'Art et d'Histoire,** where you'll find a high quality collection of art and artifacts ranging from an open Egyptian sarcophagus with an unwrapped mummy to contemporary art. The spacious central courtyard juxtaposes a traditional fountain with modern metal sculpture and stone panels excavated from Greco-Roman ruins. *(rue Charles-Galland*

2. Take bus #3, 5, 6, or 8 to "Athenée," or bus #17 to "St. Antoine." ☎418 2600. Open Tu-Su 10am-5pm. Museum free; temporary exhibit rates vary.)

If you're looking for the cutting-edge and avant-garde, look no further than the **Musée d'Art Moderne et Contemporaire**. The brochure asks, "Do you know the art of your own era?", implying that you will after a visit here. The museum displays a huge diversity of works, from Minimalist paintings to video art and landscape photographs. *(Rue des Vieux-Grenadiers 10. Take bus #3: "Cirque," walk down the av. de Mail, and turn right on rue des Vieux-Grenadiers. ☎320 6122. Open Tu noon-9pm, W-Su noon-6pm. 9SFr, 6SFr for 13-18-year olds, students, teachers, artists and retirees; free for children under 12, scholars, students of art, art history, or architecture, the unemployed, and invalids. Mandatory lockers 2SFr.)* MAMCO also houses the **Jean Tua Car and Cycle Museum,** with its collection of 70 cars as well as motorcycles and bicycles, most dating back to before 1939. *(Rue des Bains 28-30. Take bus #1 to "Bains," by rue des Vieux-Grenadiers. ☎321 3637. Open W-Su 2-6pm. 8SFr, students 6SFr, children 4SFr.)*

The **Musée Barbier-Mueller** has 3 floors of what the ethnocentric once called primitive art, including one of the most respected collections of African art in the world. The museum encompasses time periods as distant as early European and regions as far-flung as southern Africa. Photographs of the objects in their original settings put the frequently changing exhibitions in context. *(Rue Jean-Calvin 10. From the Grand Rue in the vieille ville, turn onto rue de la Pélisserie and left on rue Jean-Calvin. ☎312 0270; musee@barbier-mueller.ch. Open 11am-5pm. 5SFr, children under 12, senior citizens, students and the unemployed 3SFr.)*

HISTORICAL MUSEUMS. You can ponder the nature of humanity as you browse the varied collection at the **Musée d'Ethnographie,** which includes Japanese Samurai armor, Australian aboriginal paintings, and a shrunken Bolivian mummy. Don't miss the exhibits from Uzbekistan and Turkey. *(Carl-Vogt 65-67. Take bus #1 or 4 to "Bains." Head down rue de Bains past the automobile museum and turn left onto bd. Carl-Vogt. Bd. Open Tu-Su 10am-5pm. Permanent exhibits free. Temporary exhibits ☎418 45 50; www.ville-ge.ch/musinfo/ethg/index.htm. 5SFr, students 3SFr, children free.)*

Pack rats will find a museum after their own hearts at **Maison Tavel,** next to the Hôtel de Ville. This house stores everything that the city couldn't bear to throw away, including the 1799 guillotine from pl. Neuve, a collection of medieval front doors, and a vast zinc and copper model of 1850 Geneva that took 18 years to build. Guidebooks in 6 languages available at the entrance. *(Rue du Puits-St-Pierre 6. ☎310 2900. Open Tu-Su 10am-5pm. Free, except for temporary exhibits.)*

MUSÉE D'HISTOIRE DES SCIENCES. At the other end of the academic spectrum, the Musée d'Histoire des Sciences (Museum of the History of Science), housed in an elegant *palazzo* facing the lake, showcases esoteric scientific gear. Downstairs starts sensibly enough with sundials, astrolabes, globes, and a telescope or two, but upstairs gets odder and bloodier with amputation saws, a wax model of a syphilis patient's erupting facial sores, skull drills, and the gruesomely crude tools of early gynecology and obstetrics. Exhibits in French. *(Take bus #4 or 44 to "Sécheron." Villa Bartholoni, rue de Lausanne 128, in the park at La Perle de Lac. ☎731 6985; http://mah.ville-ge.ch. Open W-M 1-5pm. Free.)*

MUSÉE DE L'HORLOGERIE ET L'ÉMAILLERIE. The Musée de l'Horlogerie et L'Émaillerie (Museum of Watches and Enameling), is a feast for the ears and eyes. Stroll to the rhythms of hundreds of still-functioning antique horologic masterpieces, a complex beat punctuated every few minutes by chimes, bells, cuckoos, or clockwork musical interludes. Fingernail-sized wonders, free-standing giants, and 80s swatches compete to be the first to ring before the hour and confuse wrist-watched tourists. *(Route de Malagnou 15. Take bus #1, 6, or 8 to "Museum." ☎418 6470. Open W-M 10am-5pm. Museum free; temporary exhibits 5SFr, students 3SFr, under 15 free.)*

CHÂTEAU DE PENTHES (SWISS GUARD MUSEUM). Military history buffs will enjoy a rare treat at **Château de Penthes** (Museum of the Swiss Abroad), an ivy-cloaked chateau that features a small collection focused on the world-famous, flamboyantly dressed Swiss Guard. Stroll the surrounding parks—Lac Léman doesn't look quite as languid from anywhere else. *(Chemin de l'Impératrice 18. Take bus V or Z to "Penthes." ☎ 734 9021 or 734 4091. Open Tu-Su 10am-noon and 2-6pm. Guides in French, English, and German. Grounds open 9am-7pm. 5SFr, students and children 1.50SFr.)*

MUSÉE ARIANA (CERAMICS MUSEUM). The mind-numbingly complete collection of ceramics at Musée Ariana calls to mind all the knick-knacks collecting dust on your grandmother's shelves. The collection resides in a late-nineteenth-century monumental medley of colored marble that combines neo-Baroque and neo-Classical elements in cheerful tackiness. *(Av. de la Paix 10. Take bus #8 or 18 to "Appia" or U-2 to "Ariana." ☎ 418 5450; www.mah.ville-ge.ch. Open Su-M and W-Sa 10am-5pm. Free.)*

VOLTAIRE MUSEUM. Finally, Voltaire devotees can find their niche at the **Institut et Musée Voltaire,** an eighteenth-century mansion (Voltaire's home from 1755-1760) overflowing with Voltaire memorabilia. The museum's collection consists mainly of printed matter, manuscripts, and iconographical documents. Particularly diverting are Huber's cartoons of the *philosophe*, Frederick of Prussia's sycophantic letters, and Voltaire's cantankerous replies to Rousseau. Some paintings and sculptures, including works by Houdon. *(Rue des Délices 25. Take bus #6 or 26 to "Prairie" or #7, 11, or 27 (dir.: Lignon) to "Délices." ☎ 344 7133. Open M-F 2-5pm. Free.)*

ENTERTAINMENT AND NIGHTLIFE

There is enough to do in Geneva to keep even the most sophisticated traveler happy. *Genève Agenda*, available at the tourist office, is your guide to fun, with listings ranging from festivals to movies (be warned—a movie runs about 16SFr).

FESTIVALS

Summer days bring festivals, free open-air concerts, and **free organ music** in Cathédrale de St-Pierre (Sa 6pm, June-Sept.; carillon performances Sa 5pm). In July and August, the **Cinelac** turns Genève Plage into an open-air cinema that screens mostly American films. Call 840 0404 or check out www.cinelac.ch for more information. Admission is generally 16SFr. Check the listings in *Genève Agenda* for indoor cinemas (films marked "v.o." are in their original language with French and sometimes German subtitles while "st. ang." means that the film has English subtitles). There's also the biggest celebration of **American Independence Day** outside the US on July 4 and the **Fêtes de Genève** in early August filled with international music and artistic celebration culminates in a spectacular fireworks display. **La Bâtie Festival,** a performing arts festival traditionally held late August to early September, draws Swiss music-lovers for a 2-week orgy of cabaret, theater, and concerts by experimental rock and folk acts. Many events are free; students pay half-price for the others (regular prices 10-32SFr). For information, call 908 6950 or batie@world.com.ch. **Free jazz concerts** take place in July and August at the *Théâtre de Verdure* in Parc de la Grange. Most parks offer free concerts; check at the tourist office for information. The best party in Geneva is **L'Escalade,** commemorating the dramatic repulsion of invading Savoyard troops (see Soup's On, p. 443). The revelry lasts a full weekend and takes place in early December.

CAFES, BARS, AND NIGHTCLUBS

Some of the main areas for Geneva nightlife include: **La Jonction,** at the junction of the Rhône and Arve rivers, accessible by the #2, #10-20, and the D buses (stop: Jonction), is home to Artamis (see p. 450), and to casual bars and concert venues for rockers and ravers. **Pl. Bourg-de-Four,** in the *vieille ville* below the Cathedral, attracts students and professionals to its charming terraces and old-world atmosphere. **Place du Molard,** on the right bank by the pont du Mont-Blanc, offers terrace cafes as well as big, loud bars and clubs, catering to a crowd that takes partying seriously. **Les Paquîs,** near the Gare Cornavin and the pl. de la Navigtion, is the city's red-light district, but also appeals to a less fleshly hunger with its wide array of rowdy, low-lit bars, many of them ethnically themed. **Carouge,** across the river Arve, is a student-friendly locus of nightlife activity, the same place dissidents headed to party during Calvin's purification of the city. Some of Geneva's most popular nightlife is semi-underground. **Squats** have become a popular housing option for counter-cultural young people who don't wish to support The Man by paying rent. The authorities are quite aware of their existence, but rarely break up the parties. Information is generally spread through (surprise!) word-of-mouth, but one of the more official squats is **Le Rhino,** on Blvd. des Philosophes between Plainpalais and pl. Claparède. It's unmistakable with its red banners, which denounce tenancy and capitalism and ask in English, "Do you speak Rhino?"

Au Chat Noir, rue Vautier 13, Carouge (☎343 4998). Take tram #12 to "pl. du Marché," off the far left end of the square. The upside-down car hanging from the ceiling is a puzzle, but the sensuously curved old bar and dark red curtains set the mood in this popular venue for jazz, funk, rock, salsa, and sax-moaning blues. Live concerts every night. (Showtime 9:30pm, 15SFr cover.) Keeps the party going until quite late with loud music and a more-than-festive atmosphere. Beers 5SFr, sangria 10-12SFr. Open M-Th 6pm-4am, F 6pm-5am, Sa 9pm-5am, Su 9pm-4am.

La Clémence, pl. du Bourg-de-Four 20 (☎312 2498). Generations of students have eaten at this famous, chic bar, named after the big bell atop the Cathédrale de St-Pierre. Tables overflow into the square come nightfall. Teen-idol waiters tend to a chatty clientele of students and young professionals. Come for breakfast (croissant 1.20SFr, coffee 2.70SFr) or beer (4-8SFr). Open M-Th 7am-12:30am, F-Sa 7am-1:30am.

L'Usine, pl. des Volantaires 4 (☎781 4057; kab@usine.ch). Located near La Jonction (Take the #2, #10, #29, or D bus to "Bel-Air"), L'Usine is one of the hippest, most cutting-edge nightspots around. Disco, techno, hardcore metal and drum n' bass are just a few of the many musical varieties represented, in the warehouse-like building with multiple venues inside. Shows begin anywhere from 7 to 11pm, and cover ranges from 5 to 20SFr. Look out for concert schedules throughout Geneva, or just ask around for more information.

Flanagan's, rue du Cheval-Blanc 4 (☎310 1314), off Grand Rue in the *vieille ville*. Friendly bartenders pull a good beer in this Irish cellar bar. Chat merrily in your mother tongue amid dusty, liquor-inspired memorabilia. Pint o' Guinness 8SFr; 6SFr during happy hour, 5-8pm daily. Live music Th-Sa 10am-2am. Open 4pm-2am.

Sunset Café, rue de la Navigation (☎906 4047), next to Dialogai. A single strand of red lights traverses this sophisticated little cafe. Fresh flowers brighten the red walls and curtains, and salsa music accompanies your gourmet nibblings (gazpacho 6SFr, carpaccio with apples and salad 10SFr). Gay-friendly. Open W-Su 5pm-midnight.

LAUSANNE ☎021

Two thousand years ago, Romans came to the little town of Lausanne on the shores of Lac Léman and found it so enticing that they stayed until the collapse of their empire. Later, the city inspired a different sort of *roman* with the arrival of Dickens and Thackeray. T.S. Eliot managed to create the apotheosis of high Modernist pessimism here, writing *The Wasteland* near the placid Ouchy shoreline and the medieval labyrinth of the *vieille ville* (old city). Today, Lausanne's unique museums, distinctive neighborhoods, varied festivals, and magnificent parks make it well worth a stay.

GETTING THERE AND AROUND

Trains: pl. de la Gare 9 (☎157 2222; costs 1.19SFr per min.). To: Montreux (20min., every 30min. 5:45am-11:57pm, 9.40SFr); Geneva (50min., every 30min. 4:20am-12:46am, 20SFr); Basel (2½hr., 2 per hr. 5:21am-9:10pm, 62SFr); Zurich (2½hr., 3 per hr. 5:21am-10:25pm, 67SFr); and Paris (4hr., 4 per day 7:36am-5:52pm, 93SFr).

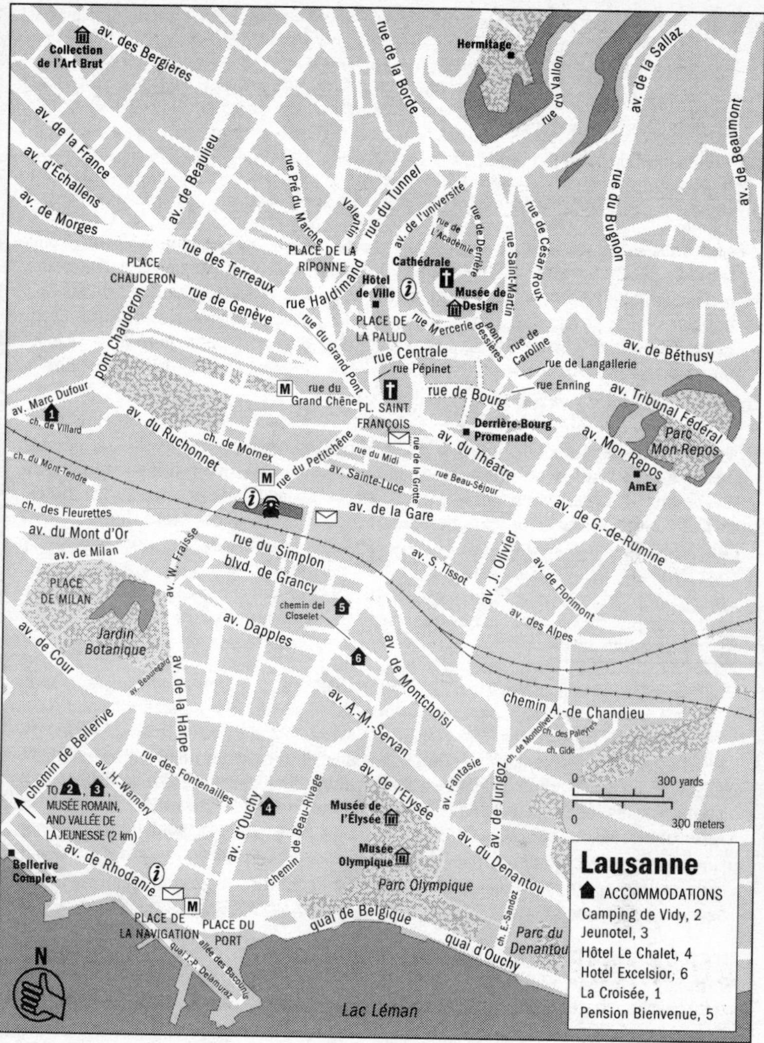

Public Transportation: The 5-stop **Métro Ouchy** runs from the *vieille ville* to the Ouchy waterfront. The **Métro Ouest** runs from the center of town west to the University of Lausanne and the Federal Institute of Technology. Both Métros run approximately M-Sa 5am-midnight, Su 6am-midnight. Buses cross the city roughly 6am-midnight (check bus stops for specific lines). Exact change needed. 3-stop ticket 1.30SFr; 1hr. pass 2.20SFr; 24hr. pass 6.50SFr; ages 6-16 0.70SFr, 1.30SFr, 3.50SFr. Métro free with SwissPass or Lausanne Pass, but not with Eurail. A day pass is a great investment if you plan to explore more than one part of this unbelievably steep city.

Ferries: CGN, av. de Rhodanie 17 (☎614 0404). To: **Montreux** (1½hr., 4 per day last ferry 6:05pm, one-way 19.40SFr, round-trip 32SFr); **Geneva** (3½hr., 4 per day last ferry 5:15pm, one-way 33SFr, round-trip 48SFr); **Evian** (last ferry 12:15am, one-way 15.20SFr, round-trip 24SFr). Purchase tickets at dock. Eurail and SwissPass valid. Open M-F 8am-7:30pm. Ferries run more often in July-Aug.

Taxis: Available at rue Madeleine 1, pl. St. François, Place de la Navigation, and in front of the station. Or call the **taxibus** (☎(0800) 080 0312) or **taxiphone** (☎(0800) 801 802). For 24hr. service call (0800) 810 810.

Car Rental: Avis, av. de la Gare 50 (☎340 7200; fax 340 7209). **Hertz,** pl. du Tunnel 17 (☎312 5311). **Europcar,** av. Ruchonnet 2 (☎323 9152).

Parking: Parking Simplon-Gare, rue du Simplon 2 (☎617 6744), behind the station (entrance on Blvd. de Grancy), costs 1SFr for 25min, 1SFr for 1hr.40min overnight. Open M-F 8am-7pm, Sa 8am-5pm. On city streets, white zones may indicate unlimited parking, rare red zones allow 15hr. parking, blue zones 1½hr. To park on the street, pick up a parking disc from the tourist office. Set the present time and the maximum stay time, and leave the disc displayed on the dashboard.

Bike Rental: (☎(0512) 242 162), at the baggage check in the station. Rentals 27SFr per day, 21SFr per half-day. 5SFr off with Eurail or SwissPass. Return bikes at another station for an additional 7SFr. Open M-Sa 6:40am-7:30pm, Su 8am-7:30pm.

ORIENTATION AND PRACTICAL INFORMATION

Two-dimensional maps of Lausanne are confusing because the city was built on a number of steep hills now connected via vaulted bridges over valleys below. The easiest way to explore the unbelievably steep city of Lausanne is on the **Métro Ouchy,** a five-stop subway system which covers a short physical distance but relieves tourists from tough climbs. The Métro's Lausanne-CFF stop is directly across from the train station and can take you either down to Ouchy, which is the neighborhood on the waterfront, or up to the *vieille ville.* Buses #1, 3, and 5 serve the train station. Most buses are routed to pl. St. François, in the center of the city.

LAKE GENEVA

TOURIST SERVICES

Tourist Office: Main office (☎613 7373 or 613 7321; information@lausanne-tourisme.ch; www.lausanne.tourisme.ch) in the main hall of the train station. Open 9am-7pm. **Branch office** across from Place de la Navigation (M: Ouchy or bus #2: Ouchy). Pick up the *Plan Officiel* (a map and public transportation guide) and *Welcome to Lausanne* (booklet listing cheap hotels and private rooms) for free. The staff sells **Lausanne Passes** (see Lausanne Pass, p. 459) and makes hotel reservations for 3% of the rate. Wheelchair accessible. Open Apr.-Sept. 8am-9pm, Oct.-Mar. 9am-6pm.

Budget Travel: SSR Travel, blvd. de Grancy 20 (☎617 5627; fax 616 5077; www.ssr.ch/ssr), 2 streets downhill from the station past the overpass; turn right. Books student tickets and organizes group travel. Open M-F 9:15am-6pm, Sa 9am-noon.

FINANCIAL AND COMMUNICATION SERVICES

Currency Exchange: At the station (☎312 3824). Good rates. No commission on travelers' checks. Western Union transfers 7am-6:30pm. Cash advances with AmEx, DC, MC, Visa. Open 6:30am-7:30pm.

American Express: av. Mon Répos 14 (☎310 1900; fax 310 1919), across from parking garage. Cashes travelers' checks, sells airline tickets, and holds mail for 2 months. Travel services open M-F 8:30am-5:30pm; financial office open 2-5:30pm.

Bookstore: Payot Libraire, pl. Pépinet 4 (☎341 3131; fax 341 3345). Large Anglophone section with contemporary and classic fiction, some nonfiction, and plenty of *Let's Go.* Open M 1-6:30pm, Tu-F 8:30am-6:30pm, Sa 8:30am-5pm.

Library: Cantonal and University Palais de Rumine, pl. de la Riponne 6 (☎316 7880; www.unil.ch/BCU). Open for borrowing M-F 10am-6pm, Sa 9am-noon. Reading room open M-F 8am-10pm, Sa 8am-5pm. Borrowing card free with ID.

Internet Access: Quanta, av. de la Gare, next to McDonald's and the Métro Lausanne-CFF stop, and across from the train station. 4SFr for 30 min. Open M-Th 11am-midnight, F 11am-1am, Sa 10am-1am, Su noon-midnight.

Post Office: Centre Postal, av. de la Gare 43bis (☎344 3513), on the right as you exit the station. Address *Poste Restante* to: 1000 Lausanne 1 Cases, CH-1001, Lausanne.

Open M-F 7:30am-noon and 1:30-6:30pm, Sa 8am-noon. Express mail M-F noon-1:30pm and 6:30-10pm, Sa noon-4pm, Su noon-10pm. To dispatch your postcard from the site where, in 1783-1793, Edward Gibbon wrote his *Decline and Fall of the Roman Empire,* visit **Poste St. François,** 15 pl. St.-François (☎344 3831). Open M-F 7:30am-5:30pm, Sa 8am-noon. **Postal Code:** CH-1002.

OTHER SERVICES

Laundromat: Quick Wash, bd. de Grancy 44 (☎079 449 3761), 2 streets downhill behind the train station; turn right. Wash and dry around 12-14SFr. Open M and W-Su 9am-8:30pm, Tu noon-8:30pm.

Luggage Storage: At the train station. Lockers 3SFr and 5SFr per day. Open 24hr.

Lost Property: pl. Chauderon 7 on the lower level (☎315 3386). Open M-F 8am-12:15pm and 1:45-6pm, Sa 8am-noon.

24-Hour Pharmacy: Dial 111 to find out which pharmacy is open all night; they rotate weekly. **24hr. medical service,** at the hospital (☎314 11 11).

EMERGENCIES

Emergency: Police, ☎117. **Fire,** ☎118. **Ambulance,** ☎144.

Crisis Line, ☎143.

ACCOMMODATIONS

As the home of the world's oldest hotel school, Lausanne has a well-deserved reputation for service-industry excellence. It's a good idea to pick up the tourist office's list of cheap hotels, private boarding houses, and family *pensions* since innumerable festivals, conferences, and congresses can make housing scarce. The owners of these establishments generally prefer stays of at least three nights and often as long as a month. Travelers looking for apartments to rent can turn to the local paper *24 Heures*, which carries regular listings, or to the notice boards of big department stores.

La Croisée, av. Marc Dufour 15, (☎321 0909) is reachable by a 15-min (600m) walk from the train station (up av. du Ruchonnet, continue as it turns into av. Marc Dufour); or by bus #4 (take Métro Ouchy from the station stop to the Lausanne-Flon stop at the top; walk up to Pl. St.-François and catch the #4 (dir: Maladière) from the other side of the street. Ride the #4 bus until the Pont Marc Dufour stop, then walk back for about 2 min. to La Croisée. This youth hostel and 2-star hotel is located in a former church building right near the station and is convenient both to the waterfront and the *vieille ville.* Sparkling clean, with stunning views of Lake Geneva, all the rooms have individuality and charm unseen at other hostels. Offering game and TV rooms, a welcoming terrace, and a cafeteria space, La Croisée has amenities to satisfy even the weariest of backpackers. Some hall showers and bathrooms; some are within rooms. Special rates for extended stays. Breakfast included; dinner ranges up to 17SFr. Children stay at a discount 30-100%. No curfew. Reservations wise. Spacious 4- to 12-bed dormitories 30-40SFr per person, singles 90SFr; doubles 130SFr; one beautiful triple/quad 65SFr per person if there are 3 people, 55SFr per person if there are 4.

Jeunotel (HI), Chemin du Bois-de-vaux 36 (☎626 0222; fax 626 0226). Take bus #2 (dir.: Bourdonnette) to "Bois-de-Vaux." Cross the street and follow the signs. This large and gleaming hostel with the cleanliness of a hospital ward is down a long concrete driveway on your right just past the *Musée Romain de Lausanne-Vidy.* Courtyards with ping pong tables, a bar and a restaurant within the complex, and a mostly young backpacker crowd enliven its concrete sterility. Wheelchair accessible. Reservations wise in the summer. 24-hr. reception year-round. Dorms 25-32SFr; singles 58SFr, with shower 82SFr; doubles 88SFr, with shower 104SFr; triples and quads 35SFr per person. Monthly rates available. AmEx, DC, MC, Visa.

Pension Bienvenue, rue du Simplon 2 (☎616 2980), 5min. from the train station. Turn right along av. de la Gare, right on av. d'Ouchy, right after the bridge. Or, more quickly, exit out the back entrance of the station, cross the street, and turn left onto rue du Simplon. The pension is 2 blocks on the left side of the street. **Women only.** This 25-room *pension* has communal TV rooms, **laundry, kitchen,** a piano, and free breakfast. The social atmosphere is a tranquil respite; but, unfortunately, city noise is all too close. Hall showers and bathrooms only. Reception 8-11:30am and 5-9pm. Singles 45SFr; doubles 80SFr. Special rates for extended stays.

Hotel "Le Chalet," av. d'Ouchy 49 (☎616 5206). Take Métro Ouchy to "Jordils" or bus #2 (dir.: Bourdonnette) to "Jordils." Built in 1877, this chalet has been run by the same charmingly eccentric matron since 1940. Each room has a sink and balcony. Occasionally *literati* visit the hotel hoping to commune with the spirit of longtime guest August Strindberg in the evergreen garden. Hall showers. Breakfast 9SFr. Reception 8am-9pm. Singles 49-62SFr; doubles 88SFr; 1 'family room' triple 99SFr.

Hotel Excelsior, chemin du Closelet 6 (☎616 8451; fax 616 8458; excelsior@fastnet.ch), 5min. from the train station. Turn right along av. de la Gare, right on av. d'Ouchy, and left after the bridge on Closelet. In the middle of a renovation, Excelsior's spacious rooms balance the cramped, run-down hallways and some shared bathrooms. Parking 10 SFr. Reception 8am-10pm every day. Singles 60SFr, with breakfast 66SFr, with bathroom, shower, and TV 83SFr, and breakfast 89SFr; doubles 88, 98, 120, 130SFr. AmEx, MC, Visa.

Camping de Vidy, chemin du Camping 3 (☎622 5000; fax 622 5001; www.campinglausannevidy.ch). Take bus #2 from M: Ouchy (dir.: Bourdonnette) to "Bois-de-Vaux." Cross the street and go down chemin du Bois-de-Vaux past Jeunotel and under the overpass. The office is straight ahead across rte. de Vidy. Restaurant (May-Sept. 8am-midnight), supermarket, playground, near a swimming **pool.** Reception 8am-12:30pm and 5-8pm. Showers included. Electricity 3SFr. Wheelchair accessible. Open year-round. 6.50SFr, students and ages 6-15 6SFr; tents 7-11SFr; 1- to 2-person bungalow 54SFr; 3- to 4-person bungalow 86SFr. Tax 1.20SFr per tent, 1.30SFr per vehicle. Cash only.

FOOD

No visit to Lausanne is complete without a taste of Lac Léman's famous perch or *papet vaudois* (a local delicacy made of leeks, potatoes, cabbage and sausage). Restaurants, cafes, and bars cluster around pl. St.-François and the *vieille ville;* while *boulangeries* sell cheap sandwiches on every street. Surprisingly fresh fare and crusty bread await at Métro stations. Numerous groceries, frequent markets, and an abundance of parks make for affordable and pleasant picnics. For crepes, ice cream, and other sweet fares, there are a number of stands on the Ouchy waterfront, which are generally open from the morning well into the evening.

Le Barbare, Escaliers du Marché 27 (☎312 2132), at the top of steps off the far right of the pl. de la Palud. Stop by for lunch or a mid-afternoon treat after climbing up to the Cathedral. Sandwiches 4.50SFr, omelettes 7-9SFr. Try the *Chocolate Maison Viennois avec Chantilly,* a rich chocolate drink (4.90SFr). Open M-Sa 8:30am-midnight.

Manora, pl. St-François 17 (☎320 9293), beneath Zürich Bank sign. Proffering "the longest buffet in Lausanne," this chain restaurant offers fresh food at very reasonable prices. Hot food 11am-10pm. Buffet 10:45am-10:30pm. Open 7am-10:30pm.

Ma-Jong, Escalier du Grand Pont 3 (☎329 0525). From the Lausanne-Flon Métro stop, walk up the incline; Ma-Jong will be on the left. Cafeteria-style, pan-Asian dining in a black-and-white room that's almost stylish in its plainness. Specials from pad Thai to roast duck are available for 14SFr (with salad and sometimes rice). Dim sum and sushi also offered. Take-out or eat-in. Open M-Th 9am-10:30pm, F-Sa 9am-midnight.

Crêperie La Chandeleur, rue Mercerie 9 (☎312 8419). From pl. St.-François head down the rue Pépinet to the pl. de la Palud; rue Mercier is off the pl. de la Palud. Enjoy custom-made crepes in a tea-room atmosphere, whether traditional (butter, sugar, or honey 4-8SFr), sugar-deprived (ice cream 7-10SFr), or gourmet (*flambées,* with choice of liqueur 8-11SFr). Open Tu-Th 11am-10pm, F-Sa 11am-11:30pm. DC, MC, Visa.

Au Couscous, rue Enning 2 (☎321 3840). From pl. St.-François, head away from the Zurich Bank sign and turn left up the hill, then right on rue de Bourg; it's at the end. Inside, a North African theme prevails with red tablecloths, a mosaic-tiled floor, and sequined pillows. Extensive, veggie-friendly menu (14-24SFr). Couscous is the real specialty (25-32SFr), but the informative menu contains other Tunisian delicacies. Open M-Th 11:30am-2:30pm and 6pm-1am, F 11:30am-2:30pm and 6pm-2am, Sa 6pm-2am, Su 6pm-1am.

MARKETS

Migros, 2 av. de Rhodanie (☎613 2660), 30 seconds to the right of the Ouchy stop on the Métro or bus #2 stop "Pl. du Navigation," plus several other locations throughout the city. M 9am-9:45pm, Tu-Su 8am-9:45pm.

Co-op, (☎616 4066). From the train station, head downhill past the overpass; turn right on blvd. de Grancy. Open M-F 8am-7pm, Sa 8am-5pm.

Produce markets, at the pl. de la Palud and the rue de Bourg behind the pl. St.-François. W and Sa mornings.

SIGHTS AND MUSEUMS

A Lausanne tourist brochure makes the odd statement that "in Lausanne, people are consuming culture as others swallow vitamins." Perhaps something was lost in the translation, but nevertheless, 650,000 visitors flock to Lausanne's lovely *vieille ville* and museums each year. For multi-day visits, the **Lausanne Pass** is a great deal, entitling visitors to museum discounts and free public transportation in and around Lausanne (15SFr for 2 days).

THE OLD CITY AND THE OLD OLD CITY. The medieval town center is known as the *vieille ville*, but the true old city is on the waterfront, where archaeological digs have unearthed 2000-year-old remains of the *Vicus de Lousonna*. You can stroll through it and see the foundations of a temple, the remains of a basilica, a forum, a few villas, and the traces of a complete Gallo-Roman colony. *(Take bus #2 to "Bois-de-Vaux" and follow signs.)* History buffs may enjoy poking around the **Musée Romain de Lausanne-Vidy,** Chemin du Bois-de-Vaux 24, next door to the hostel, the excavation site of a Roman house whose wall murals still retain their bright colors. The two floors hold many finds from the site. All explanations are only in French, so it may be a waste of time for non-francophones. *(☎652 1084. Open Tu-W and F-Su 11am-6pm, Th 11am-8pm. Wheelchair accessible. 4SFr, students free.)*

Vidy, as the colony was known, gradually decayed as Rome waned, and the town's inhabitants moved up to the more easily defended hills of the *cité*. The population grew and built up the town, making it the largest in the area by the time the Gothic **Cathédrale** was consecrated in 1275 under Holy Roman Emperor Rudolph and Pope Gregory X. Take bus #16 to "Cathédrale" or climb 2 series of medieval, covered stairs to the hilltop, where the cathedral's huge wooden doors open up into the hushed, vaulted space illuminated by flashes of stained glass. Lausanne is one of the last towns in Switzerland to retain a night watchman who cries the hour from 10pm to 2am. *(Cathedral open July to mid-Sept. M-F 7am-7pm, Sa-Su 8am-7pm; mid-Sept. to June closes at 5:30pm. Church services Su 10am and 8:15pm. Free guided tours July to mid-Sept. at 10:30, 11:15am, 3, and 3:45pm.)*

Below the cathedral, the Renaissance **Hôtel de Ville** (city hall), on the pl. de la Palud, with its bronze dragon roof, serves as a meeting point for guided **tours** of the town. *(Tours M-Sa 10am and 3pm. 10SFr, students free, English available.)* Also below the cathedral is the pl. de la Riponne, presided over by the majestic **Palais de la Rumine,** which houses the Cantonal and University Library, as well as several small archaeological and zoological museums. *(Palais de la Rumine open M-F 7am-10pm, Sa 7am-5pm, museums have more limited hours.)*

ART MUSEUMS. The **Collection de l'Art Brut** is an utterly original gallery filled with disturbing and beautiful sculptures, drawings, and paintings by artists on the fringe—institutionalized schizophrenics, poor and uneducated peasants, and convicted criminals. Nearly as fascinating as the works are the biographies of their tortured creators, displayed in English and French and often accompanied by intense photographed portraits. From a prison cell wall painstakingly carved with a broken spoon to intricate junk and sea-shell masks, this collection of obsessions started by radical primitivist Jean Dubuffet ranks as Lausanne's most satisfying collection. Don't miss the unforgettable new Robert Darger room, which portrays the fantasy world of a part-time janitor from Chicago who created his own alternate universe on paper. *(Av. Bergières 11. Take bus #2 or 3 to "Jomini," the museum is across the street. ☎ 647 5435. Open Tu-Su 11am-1pm and 2-6pm, in July-Aug. M 11am-1pm and 2-6pm. 6SFr, students and seniors 4SFr, under 15 free.)*

On a more conventional note, the **Musée de l'Elysée** houses an engaging series of diverse exhibits and photographic archives, ranging from 1820 prints to contemporary artistic endeavors in film. The basement's resonant tile and hushed atmosphere make the images even more haunting. *(Av. de l'Elysée 18. Take bus #2 to "Croix d'Ouchy" and go downhill, then left on av. de l'Elysée. ☎ 617 4821; www.elysee.ch. Open Tu-W and F-Su 10am-6pm, Th 10am-9pm. Archives open Th by appointment. 5SFr, students 2.50SFr.)* North of the *vieille ville*, the **Hermitage** is a magnificent house given over to temporary exhibitions that vary from single artists and special themes to individual public and private collections. Call ahead for a schedule, since the museum closes between shows. *(Rte. du Signal 2. Bus #16 to "Hermitage" stops infrequently out front. ☎ 320 5001. Open Tu-W and F-Su 10am-6pm, Th 10am-9pm. 13SFr, students 5SFr, seniors 10SFr, under 19 free. AmEx, MC, Visa.)*

DESIGN MUSEUM. Museum of Design and Contemporary Applied Arts, pl. de la Cathédrale 6. This newly opened museum, formerly dedicated to the decorative arts, houses a well-chosen collection of modern, cutting-edge pieces. The basement has an anachronistic selection of Egyptian art, while the main floors host temporary exhibits. 2000 saw an out-there display of all things inflatable, including one designer's vision of a home that could fit in your pocket! *(Take bus #16 to "Cathédrale." The museum is next to the cathedral. ☎ 315 2530, mu.dac@lausanne.ch. Open Tu 11am-9pm, W-Su 11am-6pm. 6SFr, 4SFr for students and seniors.)*

LAKE GENEVA

OLYMPIC MUSEUM. The **Musée Olympique** is a high-tech temple to modern Olympians with a smaller exhibit dedicated to the ancient games. An extensive video collection allows visitors to relive any requested highlight since the games were first filmed. The bilingual English/French displays of medals, mementos, and equipment arranged around the central spiral ramp swarm with kids. Wheelchair accessible via av. de l'Elysée. *(Quai d'Ouchy 1. Take bus #2 or Métro: "Ouchy." ☎ 621 65 11; www.museum.olympic.org. Open May-Sept. M-W and F-Su 9am-6pm, Th 9am-8pm; Oct.-Apr. Tu-W and F-Su 9am-6pm, Th 9am-8pm. 14SFr, students and seniors 9SFr, ages 10-18 7SFr, families 34SFr max. MC, Visa. The idyllic grounds are a better deal for free.)*

WATERFRONT. A sign along the waterfront declares Ouchy to be "a free and independent community," and indeed its slower tempo, indulgent hotels, and eco-modern sculptures strikingly set it apart from the *vieille ville*. Ouchy's main promenades, the **quai de Belgique** and **place de la Navigation,** are both excellent spots to exercise those calf muscles. The local word is that Lausanne's women have the best-looking legs in Switzerland, the hard-won prize of a life spent hiking the city's hills. You can see more of Ouchy's inhabitants at the **Bellerive Complex,** a beach park where locals set their children loose on spotless, activity-filled lawns while both genders go topless and take in some sun. *(Take bus #2 to "Bellerive" or walk down av. de Rhodanie from Ouchy. Open mid-May to early-Sept. daily from 9:30am until dark or rain. 4.50SFr, students and seniors 3SFr, under 17 2SFr. 0.50SFr discount after 5pm.)*

PARKS AND GARDENS. The Bellerive Beach is just one of Lausanne's many natural oases. At the **Vallée de la Jeunesse** rose garden, an unassuming path of wildflowers bends to reveal a spectacular display of 1000 bushes arranged in a terraced semi-circle around a fountain to the tune of thousands of birds. More exotic birds trill from the aviaries of the downtown **Parc du Mon-Repos.** Centering around a small chateau where Voltaire wrote from 1755 to 1757, the park includes venerable trees, an orange grove, and a small stone temple. The region's propensity to bloom is channeled at the **Derrière-Bourg Promenade,** where flowers depict events from the canton's history. Those more inclined to stroll can explore gorgeous shore-line trails between Ouchy and **Lutry,** a medieval village 4km away; tired feet can ride back to the *quai* on bus #9.

The **Botanical Garden of Lausanne** is in one section of pl. de Milan-Montriond Park, just up the hill from the bus #1 stop "Beauregard." A wandering path takes you past rose bushes, herbs, and signs describing the local fauna, but the observation spot atop a hill next to the gardens steals the show with its unobstructed panorama of the lake. A sign names each peak visible across the water and the date on which they were first conquered by climbers. The surrounding neighborhood is charming and peacefully untouristed. *(Av. de Cour 14bis. ☎616 2409. Park open Mar., Apr., Oct. 10am-5:30pm; May-Sept. 10am-6:30pm.)*

ENTERTAINMENT AND NIGHTLIFE

For every exhibit in Lausanne's museums, there are several performances in progress on stage and screen: the **Béjart Ballet, Lausanne Chamber Orchestra, Cinémathèque Suisse, Municipal Theatre, Opera House,** and **Vidy Theatre** reflect Lausanne's thriving cultural life. The tourist office publishes *Momento*, a monthly update and schedule of the most significant events, and posters on the streets and in *tabacs* should clue you in on everything else. For information, reservations, and tickets, call *Billetel* (☎310 1650). The **Festival de la Cité** (July 7-14, 2000) brings the *vieille ville* to life with free theater and dance events. Swiss craftwork fills the **Marché des Artisans** in pl. de la Palud from 10am to 7pm on the first Friday of every month from March to December. **Lunapark** (amusement park) sets up rides and carnival games at Bellerive annually from mid-May to mid-June. As for nightlife, you can't heave a brick in the pl. St.-François without putting it through the window of a cabaret or hitting the bouncer of a night-club. *Lausannois* party-goers inhabit the bars until 1am (2am on weekends) and dance at the clubs till 4am. The hard-core then head over to the bar in the train station, which opens at 5am.

The Mad, rte. de Genève 23 (☎312 2919, info 312 1122). Go left as you exit the Lausanne-Flon Métro stop, then walk 3min. down rte. de Genève. On a street lined with clubs, The Mad sticks out—that might have something to do with the large pink condom that graces its exterior—a 5-floor warehouse discotheque splashed with bright colors and the slogan "Mad But Not Mad" crawling up it. World-class DJs spin trance W, house Th, and progressive stuff F-Sa. Gay night Su. Beer 7.50SFr, mixed drinks 14SFr. Open Tu-Su 11pm-5am. Cover 20SFr F-Sa before midnight, 25SFr after midnight.

Dolce Vita, rue César Roux 30 (☎311 4019). From pont Bessières, head up rue Caroline past the large crossroads. This funky room with frequent live shows of rap, indie, world music, and blistering acid jazz also hosts a rock festival every April. Beer 4-5SFr. Happy hours W-Th and Su 10pm-midnight (beer 2SFr). Open Su and W 10pm-2am, F-Sa 10pm-4am; in summer also Th 10pm-3am. Weekend cover 5-25SFr.

Bleu Lézard, rue Enning 10 (☎321 3830). From pl. St-François turn left to rue de Bourg, then head right past Au Couscous. Yuppie types crowd this bistro. Decor by local artists. Beer 3.20SFr, mixed drinks 3.30SFr-9SFr. Vegetarian dishes 15SFr-30SFr. Bar hours: Tu, Th 8pm-2am, W, Su 8pm-1am, F-Sa 6:30pm-3am. Hot food: M-Sa 11:30am-2pm and 6:30-10:30pm, Su 10am-5pm and 6:30-10:30pm.

Au Lapin Vert, (☎312 1317), on ruelle du Lapin Vert, off rue de l'Académie behind the cathedral. This upscale version of a hole-in-the-wall pub blasts English rock at mellow students and young professionals. Beer 3.50SF, mixed drinks 9-10SFr. Open Su-Th 8pm-2am, F-Sa 8pm-3am.

D! Club, ruelle de Grand Pont, is Lausanne's other hot discotheque. Go left out of the Lausanne-Flon Metro stop, walk under Rue de Grand Point bridge, and turn left. 10SFr cover. Open Th 11:30pm-4am, F-Sa 11:30pm-5am, Su 10pm-2am.

Ouchy White Horse Pub, av d'Ouchy 66 (☎616 7575). The equestrian theme works strangely with the bright plaster molding and neon-filled jars. Beer on tap 5-7SFr per pint. *Tapas* 4.80-8.50SFr. Hamburger, fries, and coke 13SFr. Open 7am-1:30am. Kitchen closes 12:30am. AmEx, DC, MC, Visa.

MONTREUX ☎021

Arriving in Montreux, the traveler gets a sense of a resort well past its heyday—one that could've been frequented by the elegant, Jazz-Age characters of F. Scott Fitzgerald. The grand hotels and promenade along the lakefront still emanate wealth and prestige, faded though it may be, and if you arrive in early July, you will undoubtedly notice the strains of jazz emerging from every corner. The annual **Montreux Jazz Festival** is not just a celebration of music but an on-going, city-wide, all-ages party. Luminaries ranging from Freddie Mercury to Alanis Morissette, and most famously, Miles Davis have dropped in, echoing the city's reputation in the past couple of centuries as a magnet for the famous (just a few of its illustrious guests: Sarah Bernhardt, Victor Hugo, and Fitzgerald himself). Even further back in the area's literary tradition lies the visit of Lord Byron to the disturbingly beautiful **Château de Chillon,** a medieval fortress with its own checkered history.

GETTING THERE AND AROUND

Trains: (☎963 4515) on av. des Alpes. To: **Geneva** (1hr., every 30min. 5:39am-11:39pm, 29SFr); **Lausanne** (20min., every 5-25min. 5:31am-12:09pm, 9.40SFr); **Bern** (1½hr., every hr. 5:39am-10:39pm, 40SFr). Direct trains also go to **Martigny, Aigle, Sion,** and **Brig** and (literally) through the mountains to **Gstaad.**

Public Transportation: Buy tickets at the back of the bus or multi-use tickets at the tourist office. A very helpful map, available at the tourist office in several languages, divides the area into zones; your fare will depend on the number of zones you cross to reach your destination. 1 zone 2SFr, juniors (6-20 years) 1.50SFr; 2 zones 2.60SFr, 1.80SFr; 3 zones 3.30SFr, 2.30SFr; 4 zones 4SFr, 2.80SFr. Day-pass 7.50SFr, 5SFr; available at tourist office. SwissPass valid. Special late-night buses run during the Jazz Festival, tickets 2-4SFr (buy at the back of the bus); SwissPass valid.

Boats: CGN, (☎963 4655), on quai du Débarcadère next to the tourist office. To: **Lausanne** (1½hr., 6 per day, 33SFr); **Geneva** (5hr., 4 per day, 52SFr); **Vevey** (25min., 6 per day, 13.60SFr); shorter rides to **Villeneuve** and **Château de Chillon.** Buy tickets at the quay, tourist office, or on board. Eurail and SwissPass valid.

Bike Rental: At the baggage check in the train station. 27SFr per day, 21SFr per half-day; 7SFr charge to return bikes to other stations (including Martigny, Aigle, and Sion) by prior arrangement. Open 6:30am-8:30pm. AmEx, MC, Visa.

ORIENTATION AND PRACTICAL INFORMATION

Montreux and its surroundings rise rapidly from the eastern shores of Lake Geneva to the edge of the Alps at Les-Roches-de-Naye Jardin. Luckily for those backpackers who are running out of steam, the train station is within easy walking distance of most city sights. Hiking up rue du Marché will bring you to the *vieille ville,* of interest for the views as much as for the architecture.

Tourist Office: pl. du Débarcadère (☎962 8484 or 963 8113; fax 963 7895; tourism@montreux.ch; www.montreux.ch). Descend the stairs opposite the station called the "Escaliers de Jacobi" and head left on Grand Rue; the office is on the right. The harried staff shares the office with desks for festival tickets and bus and train information. Free hotel reservation service within Montreux. The free photocopied map does not have all of Montreux's street names, so grab the excellent **free map** from **Union de Banques Suisses,** av. de Casino 41. Tourist office open mid-June to mid-Sept. daily 8:30am-7pm; late Sept. through early June M-F 8:30am-5pm, Sa-Su 10am-3pm.

Luggage Storage: At the station. Lockers 3-5SFr, open 6:30am-8:45pm. Luggage watch 5SFr per bag. Open daily 6:30am-8:45pm.

Budget Travel: SSR Travel, av. des Alpes 25 (☎961 2300; fax 961 2306). Open M-F 9:15am-12:30pm and 1:30-6pm, Sa 9:30am-12:30pm.

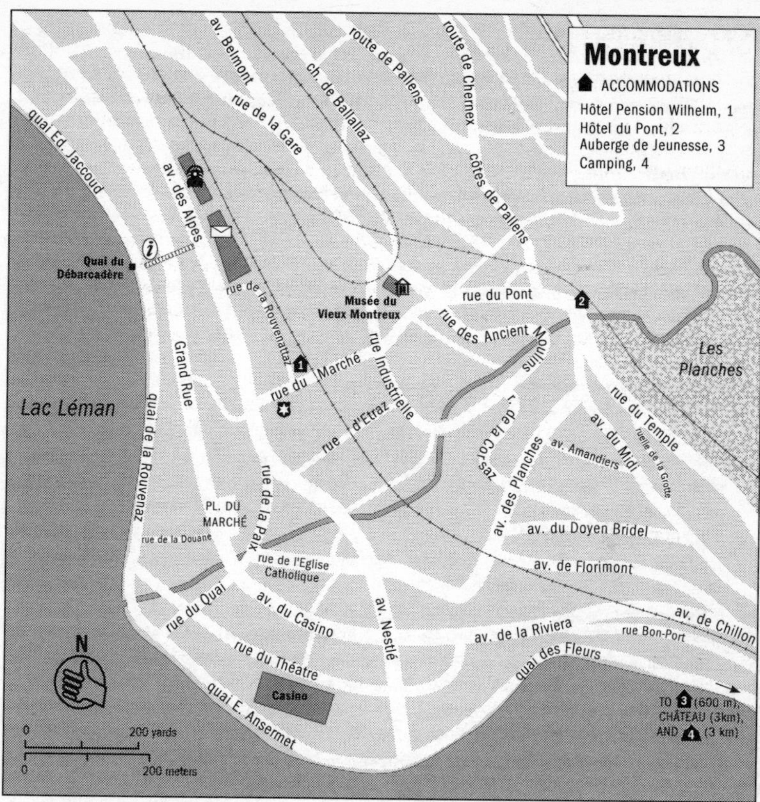

Currency Exchange: Good rates and no commission at the station. Western Union transfers and credit card advances. Open 6:45am-8:45pm. Banks in Montreux are generally open M-F 8:30am-4:30pm. Some close for lunch, but the one by the station does not.

Bookstore: Payot Libraire, av. du Casino 42 (☎963 0607). The friendly staff helps you through their multi-lingual stock. Open M 10:30am-12:30pm and 1:30-6:30pm, Tu-F 8:30am-12:30pm and 1:30-6:30pm, Sa 9am-5pm. AmEx, DC, MC, Visa.

Internet Access: Internet Palace, Grand Rue 100 (☎962 1093; internet.palace@montreux-palace.com; www.montreux-palace.com), next to the Montreux Palace. 20SFr per hr., students 15SFr; 30min. 11SFr, 7.50SFr. Open M-Sa noon-9pm.

Laundromat: Salon-Lavoir, rue Industrielle 30. Open M-Sa 7am-7pm. 5SFr per load.

Jazz Hotline: ☎983 8282. Open May through the end of the festival.

Late-Night Pharmacy: ☎962 7700.

Emergencies: Police, ☎117. **Fire,** ☎118. **Ambulance,** ☎144. **Hospital,** ☎966 6666.

Post Office: Av. des Alpes 70. Left as you exit the station. Address *Poste Restante* to: Montreux 1, CH-1820 Montreux. Open M-F 7:30am-6pm, Sa 8am-noon. **Postal Code:** CH-1820.

ACCOMMODATIONS

Cheap rooms are scarce in Montreux and almost non-existent during the jazz festival. Hotels and hostels are often fully booked before May. Revelers frequently stash their bags in the train station lockers and crash on the lakefront, but the police will move lakeside sleepers out at 7am. Ask at the tourist office for the lists of *Pensions et Petits Hôtels* or studio apartments available during the festival. If you still can't find a room, try the hostel in Vevey. Otherwise, take bus #1 to "Villeneuve," 5km away, where there are a handful of budget hotels, or consider commuting from Lausanne or Martigny.

Auberge de Jeunesse Montreux (HI), passage de l'Auberge 8 (☎963 4934; fax 963 2729). Take bus #1 on Grand Rue (dir.: Villeneuve) to "Territet." Head up the street, take the 1st right (rue du Bocherex), and go down the stairs (passage de l'Auberge). Or, walk 20min. along the lake past the Montreux Tennis Club. Clean, spacious, and family-owned, this modern hostel offers many conveniences, including a waterfront location and dining room. But light sleepers beware: noisy train tracks run nearby. Breakfast and linens included. Dinner 11.50SFr. Lockers 2SFr deposit. TV room. Free (non-affiliated) parking nearby. Reception Apr.-Sept. 7-10am and 4-11pm; Oct.-Mar. 7:30-9:30am and 5-10pm. Lockout 10am-4pm. Check-out 9:30am in winter, 10am in summer. Curfew midnight; keys available with a passport deposit. Wheelchair accessible. Non-members add 5SFr per night. 112 beds in 6- or 8-bed dorms. Dorms 29SFr, doubles 38SFr, with shower and bathroom 42SFr. Prices drop 2SFr in low season. AmEx, DC, MC, Visa.

Hôtel Pension Wilhelm, rue du Marché 13-15 (☎963 1431; fax 963 3285). From the station, take a left on av. des Alpes, walk up 3 min. and take a left on rue du Marché, uphill past the police station. All rooms have sinks. Breakfast included. Reception daily 7am-midnight. Closed Oct.-Feb., though it is possible to stay in winter if you call ahead. Doubles 100SFr, with shower and toilet 120SFr; single occupancy 65SFr, in off season 55SFr. Cash or travelers' checks only.

Hôtel du Pont, rue du Pont 12 (☎/fax 963 2249), at the top of the *vieille ville*. From the station, go left 800m on av. des Alpes (3min.) then left up rue du Marché. Continue uphill until it becomes rue du Pont; the hotel is on the left (enter through the cafe). Bright, nicely sized rooms with bathrooms and TVs. Breakfast included. Dinner 14.80SFr. Reception M 7am-3pm, Tu-F 7am-midnight, Sa-Su 8:30am-midnight. Singles, doubles, and triples 60SFr per person. AmEx, MC, Visa.

Camping: Les Horizons Bleus (☎960 1547). Take bus #1 to "Villeneuve." From the bus stop, follow the lake to the left (5min.) to this lakeside site. Showers included. Electricity 3.50SFr. Discount in winter. Reception 9am-12:30pm and 4-9pm. 7SFr per person, ages 6-16 4SFr; 6-12SFr per tent; tax 0.50SFr.

FOOD

Montreux is very pricey and most establishments are well-touristed; for lakeside dining, pack a picnic. Markets with reasonable prices abound on the Grand Rue and av. de Casino.

Le Zodiac, av. de Casino 50 (☎963 2424). Provides an air-conditioned respite from the often sweltering lakefront. Cafe fare is typical and well-priced: sandwiches 4.50-8SFr. Open M-F 6:45am-7pm, Sa 7:30am-6:30pm.

Babette's, Grand Rue 60 (☎963 7796), downstairs from the station to the left. Similar to Zodiac but with less seating. This casual restaurant serves crêpes of all types for lunch (10-13.50SFr) and dessert (6-8.50SFr). Sandwiches to go at the outside counter 5-13SFr. Open 7am-7pm.

The White Horse, 28 Grand Rue (☎963 1592). A sign on the door declares this an "authentic" English pub. It's not, but the food is good and the atmosphere friendly, from the francophone staff to the fuzzy white dog who snores at customers' feet. Sandwiches 7-9SFr; salads 6-8SFr; pizza 9.50SFr; beer 4-8.50SFr per pint. Pinball, darts, foosball, and arcade games in back. Open M-Sa 10am-1am, Su 3pm-midnight.

Restaurant Le Palais "Hoggar," quai E. Ansermet 14 (☎963 1271), next to the Hostellerie du Lac. The prices may look exorbitant compared to the other selections in *Let's Go* (appetizers 8-18SFr, curry from 21.50SFr), but the views from the blue-tile and wrought-iron terrace compensate. Open Feb.-Dec. daily 11am-10pm. AmEx, DC, V.

La Locanda, av. du Casino 44 (☎963 2933), is a small restaurant with cozy decor. Large pizzas 15-20SFr; salads 16SFr and up. Open M-Tu and Th-Sa 11:30am-2:30pm and 6pm-midnight. AmEx, MC, Visa.

Marché de Montreux, place du Marché. Covered outdoor market of food goods. Every Friday 7am-3pm. Also look for the **flea market** at this site.

Co-op, Grand Rue 80. Open M-F 8am-12:15pm and 2-6:30pm, Sa 8am-5pm.

SIGHTS AND MUSEUMS

The Montreux-Vevey **museum passport** (15SFr), available at the tourist office, covers entry to 10 museums and is a deal if you plan to visit at least 3.

THE OLD TOWN AND HISTORY MUSEUM. From the museum, the *vieille ville* is just a few minutes up the rue du Pont. A refreshing world away from the craziness of the waterfront, the rue de Temple offers pure views and a quiet walk to the stone church **Église de Montreux.** The **Musée du Vieux-Montreux,** on the outskirts of the *vieille ville*, chronicles Montreux's history from Roman times through its "colonization" by the resort industry in the late 19th century. The two things that make it worth a visit are the view from the outside and the list of the city's "illustrious guests" from over the years. *(Rue de la Gare 40. ☎963 1353. Open Apr.-Oct. 10am-noon and 2-5pm. 6SFr, students and seniors 4SFr, under 17 free.)*

CHÂTEAU DE CHILLON. The gloomy **Château de Chillon** is not only the main sightseeing draw in Montreux, but also one of Switzerland's most visited attractions. Built on an island in the 13th century, Chillon is a fortress with all the comforts of home: prison cells, a torture chamber, an armory, and booby-traps to fend off attackers who get past the moat. Viewing these vestiges of the past is not the only thing that will send a chill down your spine; so will the story of François de Bonivard, a priest who spent 4 years chained to a pillar in the dungeon of Chillon in the 16th century for aiding the Reformation in Geneva. He was freed by Protestant soldiers who in 1536 seized Montreux from the Catholic Duke of Savoy. Besides inspiring the title of a bus stop in Montreux, Bonivard's captivity also served as inspiration for writings by the ubiquitous Rousseau, Victor Hugo, and most famously, Lord Byron. Byron's poem, "The Prisoner of Chillon," on sale at the gift shop for a big markup, tells a romanticized version of Bonivard's plight. In the château you can see where Byron etched his name into a pillar, presumably to empathise with poor François. Spend some time wandering through the castle's 28 accessible rooms, and don't forget to look out on the sparkling lake. *(Take the CGN ferry from the quai de Débarcadère (13SFr, ages 16-25 5.50SFr) or bus #1 to "Chillon" from anywhere on Grand Rue or av. de Casino (2.60SFr, juniors 1.80SFr). ☎966 8910; fax 966 8912; www.chillon.ch. Open Apr.-Sept. 9am-6pm; Mar. and Oct. 9:30am-5pm; Nov.-Feb. 10am-4pm; 7SFr, students 5.50SFr, ages 6-16 3.50SFr.)*

MUSIC FESTIVALS

The **Montreux Jazz Festival,** world-famous for exceptional musical talent and one of the biggest parties in Europe, pushes everything in the town aside for 15 days starting the first Friday in July. Headliners in 2000 included B.B. King, Taj Mahal, Lou Reed, and D'Angelo. Demand has sent ticket prices into the stratosphere: individual tickets range from 59-99SFr. Standing room tickets range from 39-69SFr. Write to the tourist office well in advance for information and tickets. The easiest way to purchase tickets in advance is on the website, www.montreuxjazz.com. The **jazz hotline** in Montreux, run by the **Jazz Boutique** ticket sellers at Grand Rue 100, is active from mid-March through the summer (☎963 8282; Su-F 10am-12:30pm and 2-6:30pm, Sa 10am-5pm). The **postal address** for ticket orders is Grand Rue 100, CP1325, CH-1820 Montreux. In Switzerland, you can buy tickets from **Ticket Corner** (☎848 8008 00) and at the **Congress Center** in Montreux. Many events sell out before July, some as early as January. If you can find a room but no

PRISON IS A HOLY PLACE

Eternal Spirit of the chainless Mind
Brightest in dungeons, Liberty! thou art;
For there thy habitation is the heart–
The heart which love of thee alone can bind;
And when thy sons to fetters are consigned–
To fetters, and the damp vault's dayless gloom,
Their country conquers with their martyrdom
And Freedom's fare finds wings on every wind.
Chillon! thy prison is a holy place
And thy sad floor an altar–for 'twas trod,
Until his very steps have left a trace
Worn, as if thy cold pavement were a sod,
By Bonivard! –May none those marks efface!
For they appeal from tyranny to God.

—**Lord Byron,** excerpt from "The Prisoner of Chillon"

tickets, come anyway for the **Jazz Off,** 500 hours of free, open-air concerts by new bands and established musicians. The 1999 festival also added a free, open-to-the-public solo jazz piano competition.

From August to early September, the **Montreux Voice and Music Festival** takes over with operas, symphonies, and classical recitals performed by musicians from as far away as Moscow and Memphis. Tickets to concerts in Montreux and Chillon range from 10SFr for any student ticket to 40SFr for all concerts at Chillon, up to 160 SFr for big names. Contact the Office of the Classical Music Festival, to the left of the Casino, at rue du Théâtre 5, 1st Floor, Case Postale 353, CH-1820 Montreux 2. (☎966 8025; fax 963 2506; courrier@montreux-festival.com; www.montreux-festival.com. Office open M-F 10am-1pm and 2-7pm, Sa 10am-1pm. Open for extended hours two or three weeks before the festival begins.)

 NIGHTLIFE

Montreux caters to all tastes and personalities, from carefree campers to 5-star fops. Don't worry about finding the "place to be" in this town—if you're by the water, especially in early July, you're there.

Casino de Montreux, rue du Théâtre 9 (☎962 8383). From av. du Casino, turn on rue Igor Stravinsky toward the lake. The casino draws mobs of quarter-jingling tourists to its flashy slot machines. The charm of the original 1881 casino (which helped launch the careers of Stravinsky and fellow composer Ernest Ansemet) is largely gone, but it's still worth stopping by to cap off a day of languid indolence with slots, video poker (M-F 3pm-4am, Sa-Su noon-4am), and *boule,* a roulette variant (8pm-2am). Dance club downstairs (M-Sa 10pm-4am).

Duke's Jazz Bar, Grand Rue 97 (☎962 5070), 50m down Grand Rue toward Vevey past the Auditorium Stravinsky. Enter through the posh Royal Plaza Inter-Continental Hotel. As a venue for the Montreux Jazz Festival, this high-class establishment bursts at the seams for 2½ weeks in July. After performing, artists often stay to hang out. Celebrate with 295SFr champagne or stick to the impressive 6-7.50SFr range of beers. Open Su-Th 6pm-1am, F-Sa 6pm-2am (though the party never ends during the festival).

Rock Café, rue de l'Auberge 5 (☎963 8888), up the stairs from the youth hostel. Its name and guitar-art may aspire to imitate the Hard Rock, but this neighborhood bar can't escape its more down-to-earth, "grungy" style. Loud music, young crowd, billiard room, video games, darts, and pinball. Beer 6SFr per pint; choose among bottles from 8 countries. Open Su-Th 5pm-midnight, F-Sa 5pm-2am. AmEx, DC, V.

VEVEY

☎021

Vevey experienced its heyday as a resort town back in the 19th century, when hordes of upper-class English made it a virtual colony of the Queen's empire, placing it in countless novels of society. The upside to its decline in the 20th century is that Vevey has avoided the 5-star stratification of nearby Montreux. Charlie Chaplin fled here from McCarthyism in 1953 and Jean-Jacques Rousseau, Victor Hugo, Fyodor Dostoevsky, Henry James, Le Corbusier, and Graham Greene have all worked within Vevey's borders. Vevey remains handsome and well-preserved, its friendly residents creating a serene community along the shore of Lake Geneva.

TRANSPORTATION AND PRACTICAL INFORMATION

There are 3 ways to reach Vevey from Montreux: take **bus** #1 to "Vevey" (20min., every 10min., 2.60SFr, 1.80SFr for juniors); ride the **train** (5min., every 15-30min., 3SFr); or cruise over on a **boat** (20min., 5 per day, 8SFr, 6SFr for seniors). The **tourist office** is at Grand-Place 29 (☎922 2020; fax 922 2024; veveytourism@vevey.ch; www.montreux-vevey.com). To get there from the station, cross pl. de la Gare, go past av. de la Gare, and turn left on av. Paul Cérésole. At the end of the road, cut across the parking lot toward the columned arcade; the office is inside. (Open late June-late Aug. M-F 8:30am-6pm, Sa 8:30am-5pm, Su 9am-5pm; Sept. to mid-June M-F 8:30am-noon and 1:30-6pm, Sa 8:30am-noon.) **Lockers** (3-5SFr) and **bike rental** (city bike 26SFr per day and 20SFr per half-day; mountain bike 32SFr, 25SFr; open 7:30am-7:30pm) are available at the train station. **Internet** access at Cyberworld, rue de Torrent 4/6 (15SFr per hr; ☎923 7833; open M-Sa 11am-midnight, Su 1pm-midnight). In an **emergency,** ☎117, **fire** ☎118, **ambulance** ☎144. The **post office** is across pl. de la Gare (open M-W, and F 7:30am-6pm, Th 7:30am-7pm, Sa 8:30am-noon) and has a 24hr. **ATM.** The **postal code** is CH-1800.

ACCOMMODATIONS AND FOOD

Overlooking Grand-Place just off the waterfront is the **Riviera Lodge,** pl. du Marché 5, which has sixty beds in bright, shiny rooms and attractively modern, lavish facilities. On the 4th floor, the reception desk, manned by a friendly, multilingual staff, shares space with a terrace, a spotless **kitchen, laundry facilities** (up to 7SFr), **Internet** access, and several common rooms. Guests receive a free pass for discounts and free activities in the Montreux-Vevey region, such as a ride up the Vevey funicular. (☎923 8040; fax 923 8041; rivieralodge@bluewin.ch; www.rivieralodge.ch. Breakfast 7SFr. Sheets 5SFr. Reception 8am-noon and 5-8pm, extended during peak summer season. Call if arriving later. 4-, 6-, or 8-bed dorms 22SFr; doubles 70SFr.) Many family homes also house travelers; one is **Pension Bürgle,** rue Louis-Meyer 16, just off Grand-Place. The rooms are large; many have sinks, balconies and TVs. Hallway bathrooms and showers. (☎/fax 921 4023; www.vevey.ch/tourisme/pension-burgle.htm. Breakfast included. Dinner 12SFr. Reception 7am-11pm. Payment for 1st night required for reservations. 40SFr per person.)

For cheap, fresh food, check out the comprehensive **produce** (and **flea**) **market** at the Grand-Place (pl. du Marché; Tu and Sa mornings 8:30am-noon). Do-it-yourself fare at **Migros** (open M 9am-6:30pm, Tu-W 8am-6:30pm, Th 8am-8pm, F 8am-6:30pm, Sa 7:30am-5pm; restaurant opens 30min. earlier M-F) and **Co-op** (same hours), across av. Paul Cérésole off Grand-Place. Cafe-restaurants with *Menüs* for at least 12-15SFr line Grand-Place, but food is cheaper away from the lakefront. Next to the train station stands an **Aperto convenience store** (open 6am-9:30pm).

MUSEUMS

Though not as thrilling as Montreux's *Château de Chillon*, the museums of Vevey are distinctive and well put-together. For an excellent deal, pick up a **Montreux-Vevey Museum Passport** (15SFr), which grants entrance to 10 museums in the two

THE PASSING OF A GIANT On July 8, 1991, at the Montreux Jazz Festival, the great jazz trumpeter Miles Davis played his last live performance. An historic concert, Davis played in the style that launched his early career. Davis was a bona fide jazz hero, pioneering the "fusion" of jazz and rock and the invention, with Gil Evans, of "cool" jazz. In their revolutionary collaboration, Davis and Evans broke away from the frenetic scale structure of be-bop improvisation. Davis's smooth, modal improvisations, heard on such albums as *Kind of Blue*, influenced a whole generation of artists, including John Coltrane and Bill Evans. Although other artists expanded and developed modal jazz, Davis moved on and never looked back, abandoning some of his most-loved works for over 20 years until Quincy Jones stepped in. Jones had long wanted to do a concert to revive Davis's early material. When Davis finally agreed, the two performed together at Montreux, playing songs that hadn't been heard live for a generation. Jones has said that he had never seen Davis as pleased and as connected with the audience in any other concert. Several weeks later, Davis fell ill, and died of pneumonia on September 28, 1991.

towns. Many of Vevey's museums can be reached on a stroll by the lake towards the neighboring town of Tour-de-Peilz.

Musée Jenisch, Av. de la Gare 2 (☎921 2950), displays well-curated, temporary exhibits and a room of spontaneous, spry watercolors and pastels by adopted citizen Oskar Kokoschka—he lived in nearby Villeneuve for the last 25 years of his life. Tours available. Open Tu-Su Mar.-Oct. 11am-5:30pm; Nov.-Feb. 2-5:30pm. 8-12SFr, half-price for students.

Swiss Museum of Games (☎944 4050). At the end of the quai in the 13th-century Savoy Château de la Tour-de-Peilzis. A shrine to the twin ideals of skill and chance with its display of ancient chess pieces, cardboard Cold War games, and Nintendo. Multilingual exhibits wax philosophical on the sociology of games (calling flirtation a 'game' along with cow-tipping in the American suburbs), but it's more fun just to play with the toys. Open Tu-Su 2-6pm. 6SFr, students and seniors 3SFr, under 16 free. Tours 10SFr, students and seniors 7SFr, children under 16 3.50SFr.

Alimentarium/Food Museum, (☎924 4111), on the corner of rue du Léman and quai Perdonnet. This unlikely interesting museum tells the story of food from its production in the sun to its processing in the human body. Food processing machinery, Nestlé commercials, and human-sized hamster wheels are some of the highlights of this child-friendly museum. Open Apr.-Oct. Tu-Su 10am-5pm; Nov.-Mar. Tu-F 10am-noon and 2-5pm, Sa-Su 10am-5pm. 6SFr, students and seniors 4SFr, children ages 6-16 are free.

Swiss Camera Museum, Ruelle des Anciens-Fossés 6 (☎925 2140), is near the tourist office. 3 floors are filled with historic photographic equipment from daguerreotypes to early spy cameras. Though there are several hands-on exhibits, the more technical explanations can be hard to handle without a good knowledge of French. Open Tu-Su Apr.-Oct. 11am-5:30pm; Nov.-Mar. 2-5:30pm. 5SFr, students 4SFr, children free. Tours 3SFr.

NIGHTLIFE AND FESTIVALS

Cross the square from the station to the post office and follow the underpass (passage St. Antoine) across the tracks. At the top of the stairs, in Vevey's industrial area, signs hang for **Les Temps Modernes,** rue des Deux Gares 6 (☎922 3439). A factory-turned-cafe, record store, and dance studio, it has become a cultural junction for local artists. Live jazz and rock (W-Sa) jolt the central stage area. (Salads 5-14SFr. *Plats du jour* 13-16SFr. Beers 5SFr; 1SFr more during performances. Open M-Tu 8am-midnight, W-Th 8:30am-1am, F 8:30am-2am, Sa 5pm-2am.)

Right behind the Riviera Lodge on rue de Torrent 9, the **National** offers a dual experience, with a relaxed, romantic candlelit terrace and a packed basement with a DJ and dancing. (Open M-Th 11am-midnight, F-Sa 11am-2am, Su 4pm-midnight.) Across the street from the National at rue de Torrent 4-6, lies **Vertigo** where dizziness-inducing drinks are served in a fashionable bar atmosphere.

The **Folklore Market** (in pl. du Marché; open July and Aug.) allows you to sample all the local wine you can hold for only the price of the first glass, sometimes as low as 4SFr. Year-round, the **Winetrain** winds its way through 8km of villages and vineyards in Lavaux (every hr. from Vevey station; round-trip up to 10SFr, children 5SFr, SwissPass and Eurail valid.) The tourist office has a list of tasting venues, a map with directions to the wine centers, and a guide to six nearby hiking tours.

In July and August, an **open-air cinema** at pl. Scanavin brings classical and current flicks to Vevey. The summertime **International Comedy Film Festival,** dedicated to former resident Charlie Chaplin, features official competitions during the day and more accessible screenings at night. The **Theatre of Vevey,** rue de Théâtre 4 (☎923 6055), produces live theatre in Vevey.

AIGLE

☎024

Most travelers who zip through the rail hub of Aigle (pop. 7,500) barely notice it from the train window, but this tiny town with an impressive 12th-century château is well-known to locals for its excellent white wines and indulgent, vine-laced beauty. Cradled at the meeting point of several mountain valleys, Aigle is an important transport junction for many of the Alpine resort towns hidden deep in the Vaud Alps (*Alpes Vaudoises*).

TRANSPORT AND PRACTICAL INFORMATION. The quickest train connections are to **Montreux** (10min., 2 per hr. 6:17am-12:29am, 5SFr) and **Lausanne** (30min., 2 per hr. 5:45am-11:57pm, 13.60SFr). A **cog railway** from Aigle services **Les Diablerets** (50min., every hr. 6:22am-9:34pm, 10SFr) and **Leysin** (30min., every hr. 6:04am-10:38pm; SwissPass valid). A **bus** connects Aigle and **Villars** (30min., every hr. 7:05am-8:38pm, 8SFr), where another cog railway (dir.: Bex) runs to **Gryon** (15min., 3SFr, Eurail and SwissPass valid). The resourceful and patient folks at the **tourist office,** 10 min. up the street that leads straight out of the train station, have loads of quality information. (☎466 3000; fax 466 3003; info@alp3000.ch; www.alp3000.ch. Open M-Th 7:30am-noon and 1:30-5:30pm, F 7:30am-noon and 1:30-5pm.) There is an **ATM** at UBS bank, just before the tourist office on the main street. On the way to the ATM you'll pass the **post office** (open M-F 7:30am-6pm and Sa 8am-noon). The **postal code** for Aigle is CH-1860.

ACCOMMODATIONS AND FOOD. You will know the moment you step into **Hôtel des Messageries,** that the owner's favorite color is pink. To get there go down the main street straight out of the train station, take a right on Rue du Rhône, and then take a left on Rue de Midi. (☎466 2060; fax 466 6258. Breakfast included. Singles and doubles 45SFr per person, 50SFr with shower.) **Camping des Farrettes** (☎466 1964) is open year-round.

The funkiest restaurant in town is **Le Medieval Pizzeria,** located on the rue du Bourg (the pedestrian street that intersects with the main road after you pass the UBS ATM coming from the train station). Munch on one of eighteen kinds of pizza (8-16SFr) while sitting under the perilously spiky wrought-iron chandelier suspended amidst the daggers and chains hanging from the walls, with a similarly interestingly clad crowd. (☎466 2881. Open Su-Th 7am-11:30pm, F 7am-1:30am, Sa 7am-2am.) On Friday and Saturday nights, Le Medieval turns into a nightclub (beer 2.50-4.50SFr), with a live DJ after 9pm. The interior of the **Buffet de la Gare** isn't quite so exciting, but the food is good, cheap (*Menüs* 15SFr) and served quickly. (☎466 2661. Open Tu-F 6:30am-11pm, Sa-Su 8am-11pm.) **Confiserie Hedinger,** before the tourist office on the main street, peddles out-of-this-world chocolates, truffles, and other mouthwatering treats—all made on-site. (Chocolate goods 3.80-5SFr per 100g, strawberry torts 2.40SFr. ☎466 2143. Open 7am-6:30pm, closed Mondays.) Picnickers should head to the **Coop,** turning left after Hôtel Le Suisse (open M 9am-12:15pm and 1:30-6:30pm, Tu-F 7:45am-12:15pm and 1:30-6:30pm, Sa 7:45am-5pm), or **Denner Super Discount,** turning right off the main road after the church (open M-W 8:30am-noon and 1-6:30pm, Th-F until 6pm, Sa 8am-5pm).

SIGHTS. Aigle's main attraction is a 12th-century castle, the **Château d'Aigle,** nestled among the vineyards on the edge of town. At the fascinating wine museum inside, learn everything you ever wanted to know and more about the nectar of the gods: how it's been made, transported, stored, drunk and celebrated throughout the centuries. (☎466 2130. Open Apr.-June and Sept.-Oct. Th-Su 10am-12:30pm and 2-6pm, July-Aug. 10am-6pm daily. 7SFr adult 5SFr students and children ages 6-16; visit with wine-tasting and souvenir glass (min. 10 people) is 14SFr per person.) Aigle hosts its own annual wine-tasting festival. For 10SFr, each person gets a glass and can go from *cave* to *cave* sampling all of the local wines. For info about the festival and other wine-tasting opportunities contact the Association Vinicole Aigle, Av. Margencel 9. (☎466 2451; fax 466 6215; vinicole@aigle.ch.)

LES DIABLERETS ☎024

There may be only five lifts open on Les Diablerets' glacier in July and August, but that's five more than almost anywhere else in Switzerland, and the snow is 100% guaranteed. Come winter, the town (pop. 1,300) stresses substance over the snootier stylings of local rivals Gstaad, Crans-Montana, and Verbier. The result: a younger, more sports-driven crowd. Snowboarders will appreciate the respect they receive, and hikers can putter about peacefully on the varied terrain.

TRANSPORT AND PRACTICAL INFORMATION

Three public transport services connect Les Diablerets to the rest of Switzerland: the **train** down to **Aigle** (50min., every hr. 6:27am-9:28pm, 10SFr); the **Post Bus** over the mountains to **Gstaad** (via the Col du Pillon, in summer 5 per day 9:39am-5pm, 11.80SFr); and the **BVB bus** to the mountain town of **Juillet** (via Col de la Croix, 35min., 3 per day 10am-5:05pm, 10.80SFr). In summer, local buses are the only way to reach the Diablerets glacier **cable cars.** The first bus leaves at 9:39am and the last returns at 4:50pm, so plan accordingly or be ready for a 45-min. walk.

The **tourist office,** rue de la Gare, in a chalet down the road to the right of the station, publishes a devilishly impressive range of literature, including a list of activities and events. (☎492 3358; fax 492 2348; info@diablerts.ch; www.diablerets.ch. Open July 3-Aug. 29 and mid-Dec. to Apr. 8:30am-6pm; June 1-July 2 and low season M-Sa 8:30am-12:30pm and 2-6pm, Su 9am-12:30pm.) Services include: **taxis** ☎(079) 205 0555; **emergencies** ☎492 3283; **ambulance,** ☎494 5030; **police,** ☎492 2488; **post office,** right out of the train station (open M-F 8am-noon and 2:30-6pm, Sa 7:45-10:45am). The **postal code** is CH-1865.

ACCOMMODATIONS

The cheapest accommodations are on the outskirts of town.

Les Diablotins, rte du Pillon, (☎492 3633; fax 492 2355; diablotins@freesurf.ch; www.diablotins.ch) is a big modern block popular with young snowboarding groups. From the station, turn right, bend left around the hairpin turn, and turn left along rte du Pillon at the top of the hill. Avoid the ensuing 20-minute uphill walk by calling from the station; the hostel will send a minibus. 2-to 5-bed rooms are in good shape (all have private sinks and most have balconies) in spite of the thousands of schoolkids that tramp through the halls and shared showers each year. This large institution has 4 dining halls, several lounges, and a bar and **disco**—all segregated by age and noise-tolerance levels. Breakfast included. Dinner 16SFr. Reception 8am-8pm. Reserve one week ahead in winter. Jan. 6-Jan. 19 and Apr.-Christmas 33-47SFr, youth 18 and under 38-40SFr; Christmas-New Year's and Feb. 10-Mar. 3 44-58SFr, youth 37-49SFr; Jan. 9-Feb. 10 and Mar. 3-Apr. 16 40-54SFr, youth 34-46SFr. Price drops 3-4SFr after 4 nights. AmEx, MC, Visa.

James' B Organization (☎492 3481; fax 492 3482; gaz@swissonline.ch; www.jamesb.ch). Down the rue de la Gare past the Coop, is another mecca for hardcore snowboarders. Every summer James' B hosts a massive snowboard and skateboard camp to which young enthusiasts from all over Europe flock *en masse*. Closed mid-May to mid-June. Singles 40-50SFr, doubles 40-50SFr per person.

Camping La Murée, (☎492 2199). Take the Aigle train one stop to "Vers l'Église," go left past the post office and church, and cross the railroad tracks and the river to get to this quiet site in a tiny valley town. Showers included. Reception 6-7pm. 6.50SFr in the summer, 6SFr in winter; children ages 6-18 3.80SFr, tents 12.50-39SFr.

FOOD

At **Le Muguet,** opposite the tourist office, try a dessert crepe (5-9.50SFr) with *chocolat viennois* (3.80SFr), or a dish of *chantilly crême* (1.50SFr). Cross the channel for their sandwiches (3.50-8SFr) and tea. (☎492 2642. Open 6:30am-7pm; food served until 6pm. MC, Visa.) Just after the hairpin curve on route de Colde la Croix, **Pizzeria Locanda Livia** serves 24 kinds of pizza (13-19.50SFr, 4SFr less for miniature version), including a 4-cheese pizza with gruyère called *rêve de souris*—mouse's dream. (☎492 3280. Open 11:30am-2pm and 6:30-10pm. Closed Wednesdays. AmEx, MC, Visa.) Right from the station along rue de la Gare, **Pam Super Discount** stocks the cheapest groceries (open M 7:30am-12:15pm, Tu-F 7:30am-12:15pm and 2-6:30pm, Sa 7:30am-12:15pm and 2-6pm).

OUTDOOR ACTIVITIES

SKIING. Les Diablerets' year-round **skiing** just got better with the 1999 addition of a new **cable car,** which goes from the Col du Pillon above the village to Cabane, then to the glacier at Scex-Rouge. Diablerets day passes, combined Diablerets/Villars passes, Alpes Vaudoises transportation and lift passes, and other **ski passes** are for sale at the departure point of the cable car. Book special hotel deals that include stay-and-ski passes, a fondue evening, tobogganing, curling, skating, and babysitting services at the tourist office. **Jacky Sports,** near the tourist office, rents **ski equipment.** (☎492 3218; www.swissrent.ch. Open 9am-noon, 2-6pm; in high season M-F 8:30am-noon and 2-6:30pm, Sa-Su 8:30am-6:30pm. Skis 28-50SFr per day, snowboards 28-38SFr, boots 15-19SFr; special rates for multi-day rentals; AmEx, DC, MC, Visa.) The **ski and snowboard school**, in the tourist office, offers lessons (☎492 2002; 6 days 125SFr, children 117SFr).

HIKING AND BIKING. Jacky Sports also rents **mountain bikes** (35SFr per day, 5 days 110SFr). One full-day circuit, also possible on foot, leaves from the tourist office. Head around the hairpin turn at the junction with Col du Pillon road. Climb upwards to **La Ville** and its view of the Diablerets glacier spilling high above the village. Turn right along the valley wall to Métraille and La Crua, and begin a long descent to the crag-cradled Lac Retaud and Col du Pillon before free-wheeling back to Les Diablerets. (Attempt only in good weather.) For a good hike that can be done in several segments to suit ability, turn right across the river at the pharmacy, then right again so that you are facing the Sommet des Diablerets (3209m) and the glacier. The sides of the valley close in as you continue the level riverside walk, which deposits you on the stage of a rugged 200m-high amphitheater at **Creux de Champ** (1hr., 160m ascent). The path starts to climb steeply up the sides to the Refuge de Pierredar at 2278m (3hr. above Les Diablerets, 1110m ascent). The agile can then push on up to **Scex Rouge** (2971m), the cable car terminus on the glacier, which affords an unforgettable alpine view (full day hike, high summer and perfect weather only; guide recommended for later sections of the hike).

ADVENTURE SPORTS. For the daredevils in the house Les Diablerets's adventure sports awaken the death wish within. **Mountain Evasion** is anything but; they organize **canyoning** (80-160SFr), ice canyoning (65SFr), glacier bivouacs (120SFr), **rappelling** (85SFr), **dirt bike** riding (35-150SFr), and guided hiking and mountain biking (50-120SFr), not to mention **luging** (16SFr, 36SFR for a nighttime descent with fondue). (☎/fax 492 1232; mountain-evasion@bluewin.ch. Winter office in the Maison du Tourisme, summer office in a little wooden shack along the river. At the pharmacy turn right across the river, then left onto the Chemin de Vernex. Open 5:30am-6:30pm. MC.) Left from the train station and past the post office along rue de la Gare, Centre ParAdventure offers **paragliding** (60-150SFr), **canyoning** (80SFr), and the mudbiking. (☎492 2382; fax 435 2582; paradventure@bluewin.ch. Open 9-9:30am and 5:30-6:30pm.) The **New Devil School of Snowboarding** has entered its bid for the town's corniest name pun. (☎492 3717; fax 492 2348. Open 8:30am-6:30pm. 45min lesson 45SFr, 90min lesson 80SFr.)

LEYSIN ☎024

In this laid-back town where people show up to work in sweats and flannels, the locals aren't so local. Leysin is full of ex-roaming backpackers who came, saw, and stayed on to bolster the outdoor industry, find Swiss spouses, and teach at the clutch of American and Japanese colleges in the area. The town offers long views of the mountain-girded Rhône Valley and the distant shores of Lac Léman.

TRANSPORT AND PRACTICAL INFORMATION

The only way to reach Leysin by public transport is the **cog railway** from Aigle. The railway leisurely chugs passengers to the top of the steep climb (30min., every hr. 6:04am-10:38pm; SwissPass valid). There are 4 stops: Leysin-Village (8SFr), Versmont, Feydey (9.40SFr), and Grand-Hôtel (10SFr). There is a free hourly **shuttle** to help you up and down the hillside, including a stop at the hostel (runs June 20-Sept. 18 and Dec.16-Apr.16). The **tourist office,** located in the Centre Sportif just up the road to the left from pl. du Marché, provides **hiking maps.** (☎494 2244; fax 494 1616; tourism@leysin.ch; www.leysin.ch. Open M-F 8am-9pm, Sa-Su 9am-9pm.) Services include: **ATM** at the **Banque Cantonal Vaudous** just below Hefti Sports; **taxis,** dial 493 2293 or 494 2555; **bike rental** at the station for 27SFr; **Pharmacie Leysin** on pl. du Marché (☎493 4500. Open M-F 8:30-noon and 2-6:30pm; Sa 9am-12:30pm and 2-5pm); **post office** in Leysin-Village on rue du Village (☎494 1205. Open M-F 8-11am and 2:30-6pm, Sa 8:30-11am.) For a **snow report**, call 494 1301, for **police** ☎493 4541; in an **emergency,** dial 117. The **postal code** is CH-1854.

ACCOMMODATION

Hiking Sheep Guesthouse, Villa La Joux (☎/fax 494 3535; hikingsheep@leysin.net; www.leysin.net/hikingsheep). Take the cog rail to "Grand Hôtel" and turn left on the gravel road, or catch the shuttle in high season. Less than 50km from the nearest hiking and skiing the Sheep has shining wooden bunks, a convivial dining room, breathtaking balconies, and pristine **kitchen** facilities. Friendly owner Gérard goes the extra mile for his guests, supplying satellite TV, log fires, BBQs, cooking lessons, game and meditation rooms, **Internet** access, **laundry** (10SFr), mountain bike rentals (35SFr per day, 25 SFr per half-day), *jai alai,* volleyball, badminton, afternoon hiking tours, and life advice. Buffet breakfast 8SFr, English breakfast 10SFr. Sheets included. Reception open 8-10am and 5-10pm. No curfew or lockout. Check-out 10:30am. June 15-Dec. 15 dorms 26SFr, doubles 66SFr; Dec. 16-June 14 dorms 30SFr, doubles 70SFr; for children subtract about 1SFr. MC, Visa.)

Hotel Bel-Air, (☎494 1339; fax 494 1369) has simple rooms and tranquil views. Breakfast included. Singles 45SFr; doubles 90SFr, with shower 105SFr. AmEx, Visa.

Hotel La Paix, on av. Rollier, (☎/fax 494 1375), is opposite the "Versmont" train stop. Narrow hallways connect old-fashioned rooms with fading prints of *belle epoque* Leysin. Breakfast included. Lunch or dinner 16SFr. Reception 8am-8pm. Singles 48SFr, with shower 54-58SFr; doubles with shower 108SFr. AmEx, MC, Visa.

Camping Semiramis (☎494 3939; fax 494 2121) is a large grassy field at the foot of a hill near an evergreen forest. From Leysin-Village station, walk left on rue de Village, then right on rue du Suchet past the post office. Showers included. 5.80SFr in summer, 6.20SFr in winter, children 3SFr, 5SFr; tents 3-4SFr. AmEx, DC, MC, Visa.

FOOD

L'Horizon (☎494 1505) is a local fave. A level 15-minute walk from the Hiking Sheep gets you to the source of excellent fondue (18-19SFr). Try the local valley delicacy, *Williamine,* a pear schnapps. Open 10:30am-10pm; closes at 6 pm Su and M.

La Prafandaz, a longer walk from the Hiking Sheep past more cows (signs point the way), is a slightly off-the-wall chalet decorated with a ticking-udder cow clock and ample evidence of the owner's love of mushrooms—he makes his own sauce from hand-picked specimens. The house specialty, *les rosettes*, consists of meat, vegetables, or salmon rolled into home-made pasta, grilled, and smothered in a rich, bubbling sauce for 18SFr. Open 10:30am-10pm. Closed Tuesdays.

La Grotta (☎494 1532), rewards a stroll to the Feydey district. Hearty Italian food (pizzas 10-18SFr, pastas 12-20SFr), and the added attraction of the owner's Swatch collection—a dazzling expo of all the editions since 1983, including special music alarm, beeper, and ski-pass versions. Open Tu-Su 8:30am-midnight.

La Nonna Restaurant Pizzeria (☎494 2194), above the Centre Sportif. The giant cactus and fishing nets suggest a bit of an identity crisis, but the slightly cheaper food convinces doubters. *Menüs* 15-20SFr, pasta 14-22SFr, 19 exotic pizzas (many vegetarian) 12-19SFr. Open 7:30am-11pm, kitchen serves food 10:30am-2pm and 6-10:30pm.

Co-op, just off the big bend in rue Favez, below pl. du Marché and the Centre Sportif. Open M-F 8am-noon and 2-6:30pm, Sa 8am-noon and 2-5pm.

OUTDOOR ACTIVITIES

A **Leysin Holiday Card** (distributed after 1 night at any hotel or hostel) grants a 10-50% discount at any of Leysin's sports centers, cable cars, and ski lifts. For guided **hiking** and **adventure sports** contact the **Swiss Climbing Club** (☎494 1846, fax 494 3375; eal@leysin.net; www.leysin.net). The most unusual **hike** is **La Via Ferrata** (the "iron path"), a series of metal safety cables, steps, and rungs that ascends **La Tour d'Aï** (Leysin's highest peak at 2331m), accommodating all levels of hikers. The 2½-hour hike from the village winds past a cheese farm full of bovine beauties into steep wildflower fields; (small) signs point out the **Via Ferrata.** The necessary gear (16SFr) is available from **Hefti Sports,** 2 minutes from the Centre Sportif on pl. du Marché. (☎494 1677. Open M-Sa 8:30am-noon and 2-6:30pm, Su 10am-noon and 3-6pm.) Hefti Sports also rents **ski equipment** (skis and boots 43SFr per day, 31 per half-day boots, snowboards 43SFr per day, 31SFr per half-day). 1-day **ski passes** average 40SFr, children 25SFr; weekly passes are available.

There are two sports centers in the village. **Centre Sportif,** in the Place Large, has squash and tennis courts, **pools** and Turkish bath (☎494 2244; o.t.leysin@pingnet.ch; www.leysin.ch. Open M-F 8am-9pm, Sa-Su 9am-9pm; pools have slightly shorter hours). Downhill near the campsite, the **Ice Skating Sports Centre** (☎494 2442) offers what the name suggests (7SFr, students and children 4.50SFr; skate rental 4SFr, 3SFr). For **paragliding,** call **École Parapante** (☎494 2602 or (079) 638 2602).

GRYON

☎024

The tiny town of Gryon has experienced a population boom in recent years—from 800 to 1,000. Rather than risk a greater unemployment rate as a result of this 25% increase, the proud locals have an ordinance which allows only one child from each family to stay in the town. The kids have a tendency to come back though, drawn to Gryon's virtually untouched, tranquil setting in the mountains, within reach of the Dents du Midi and the Les Diablerets glacier. The neighboring town of **Villars** (45min. on foot uphill) is bigger, busier, packed with hotels, and at the foot of 120km of ski runs. Gryon offers peace, relaxation, and a history older than Switzerland (dating back to 1189). There are only two ways to reach Gryon: by **cog railway** from Bex (30min., every hr., 5.60SFr, Eurail and SwissPass valid), which lies on the main rail line connecting the Lake Geneva cities (Geneva, Lausanne, Montreux) to Aigle, Martigny, and Sion, or by **foot** from Villars (one stop further on the cog rail; 45min. walk from the hostel). **Buses** connect Villars, through Col de la Croix to Les Diablerets (35min., 3 per day 9:02am-4:20pm, 10.80SFr runs July 2-Sept. 18) and another to Aigle (30min., every hr. 6:15am-7:45pm, 8SFr). The **tourist office** is uphill on the route de Villars, about 10 minutes from the hostel (☎498 1422; fax 498 2622. Open M-Sa 8am-noon and 2-6pm, Su 9am-noon, 4-6pm).

Gryon's main draw for world-weary travelers is its hostel, the **Swiss Alp Retreat,** housed in the Chalet Martin. From the station, take a right and follow the signs to the hostel. The Swiss Alp retreat has taken the "hostel" concept to a whole new level. Owners Bertrand and Robyn (and a super-friendly young staff) manage with a cooperative style that's a little different—expect communal kitchen facilities, co-ed dorms, and no formal reception. New arrivals are immediately sucked into the bohemian, Anglophone-with-any-accent backpacker crowd. Happy to "take a vacation from their vacation," world travelers passing through Gryon have been known to stay…and stay. In the 7 years it took for the hostel to grow from 4 beds to 87, 10 couples who met at the Chalet Martin have gotten married. The hostel's amenities include discounted **ski rentals, Internet access** (10SFr per hour), **video rental** (2SFr) from a small but entertaining collection, and **laundry** (3-5SFr), and a pool of possible future spouses. The main chalet has recently been renovated to feature homey common rooms and funky wood-framed showers. Chalet Martin's real attraction, however, is its prime location for taking advantage of the surrounding outdoors. The hostel has daily sign-ups for **cheese farm tours, paragliding, thermal baths** (in Villars), and various excursions (like a ski trip to Zermatt). They also lend out maps to hikers and provide a 60% discount on ski rentals all year. (☎/fax 498 3321; chaletmartin@yahoo.com; www.gryon.com. No meals, but large kitchen facilities available. Call ahead. Check-in 9am-9pm. Dorms in summer 25SFr for a one-night stay; 20SFr per night for a two-night stay; 15SFr per night for a three-night stay; 100SFr per week; in winter prices 3SFr more. Overflow mattresses possible.)

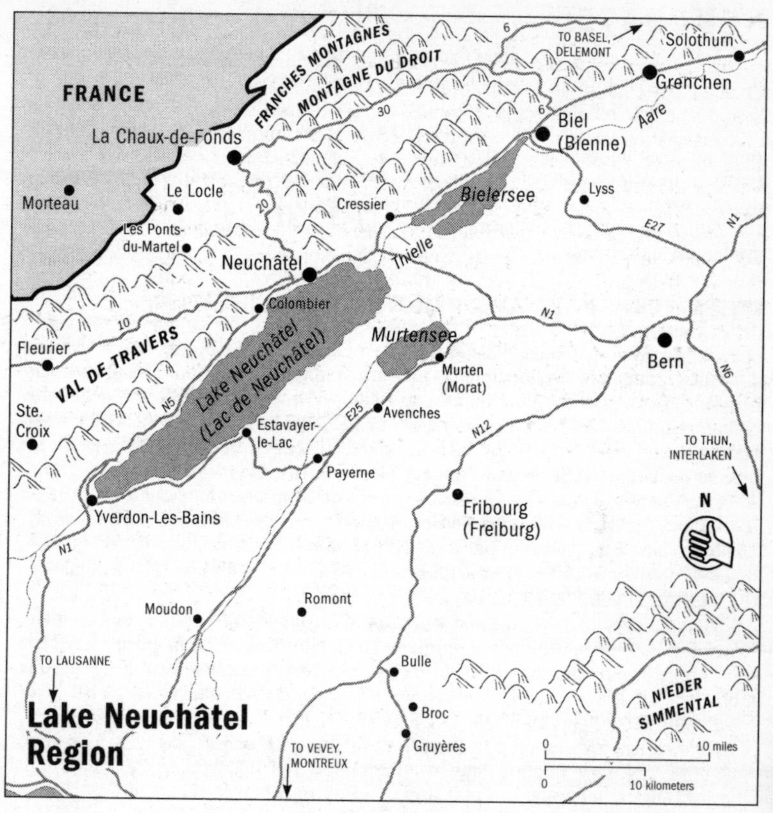

LAKE NEUCHÂTEL REGION

The aqua hues of Lake Neuchâtel and the verdant Jura mountains imbue the Lake Neuchâtel region with intimate charm. In connection with the upcoming National Exhibition (a celebration of all things, SwissExpo '02, May 15-Oct. 20, 2002), the Three-Lake Region of **Lake Neuchâtel, Bielersee**, and **Murtensee** is attempting to establish itself as the new tourist hotspot in Switzerland. Their hope is that winter-time thrill-seekers will flock to Lake Neuchâtel with the same enthusiasm as the nature-lovers who enjoy its mild climate the rest of the year.

HIGHLIGHTS OF LAKE NEUCHÂTEL

Experience **Neuchâtel's** lively cafe culture, relax on a lakeside promenade, and catch a bird's-eye view from the *Tour des Prisons* (see p. 477).

Stroll through the lush vineyards of **Cressier** and sample the new wine with some fresh local cheese (see p. 479).

Hike from **Biel** along mossy cliffs to legendary Taubenloch, then enjoy a 3-course meal at Eau-Berge du Taubenloch while baby goats gambol about your feet (see p. 483).

Unwind at the Musée International d'Horlogerie in **La Chaux-de-Fonds** (see p. 481).

NEUCHÂTEL

☎032

Neuchâtel sits perched on the edge of its eponymous lake, with its glorious edifices looking as if they might melt right into the turquoise water. Alexandre Dumas once said that Neuchâtel appeared to be carved out of butter. Although he was no doubt referring to the unique yellow stone that characterizes the city's architecture, the comment could easily be mistaken for a reference to the calorie-laden treats in local *pâtisseries*. *Neuchâteloise* cuisine prides itself on its distinctive quality, especially in fondue, sausages, and fresh fish from the lake and nearby rivers. The town also offers winding streets with both a sense of history, and a young, student-oriented flair.

TRANSPORT AND PRACTICAL INFORMATION

Neuchâtel sits atop a long, oval-shaped lake near the French border and the rolling Jura mountains. The city centers on pl. Pury, a major square and the hub of every bus line. **Trains** connect Neuchâtel to **Basel** (1¾hr. via Biel/Bienne, every hr. 5:39am-10pm, 37SFr); **Bern** (45min., every hr. 5:06am-12:15am, 17.20SFr); **Interlaken** (2hr. via Bern, every hr. 5:37am-10:13pm, 42SFr); **Geneva** (1½hr., every hr. 5:55am-11:01pm, 42SFr); and **Fribourg** (1hr. via Ins, every hr. 5:06am-10:13pm, 19SFr). A series of stairs leads down to the shore from the station, and bus #6 goes to pl. Pury, the central **bus stop. Ferries** provide service to **Murten** (1¾hr., 3 per day, 15.40SFr) and **Biel** (2¼hr., 3 per day, 24SFr), departing from the Port de la Ville, just behind the post office, free with Eurail or SwissPass. **Bike rental** is available at the baggage check (27SFr per day).

From pl. Pury, face the lake and walk 2 blocks to the left to find the **tourist office,** Hôtel des Postes (in the same building as the post office). City maps are free, and the deluge of brochures will fit the needs of everyone. A useful regional **biking** guide is 5SFr. Also available is *La Route du Vignoble Neuchâteloise*, a list of all local vineyards. (☎889 6890; fax 889 6296; tourisme.neuchatelois@ne.ch; www.ne.ch/tourism. Open mid-June to mid-Sept. M-F 9am-6:30pm, Sa 9am-5pm, Su 2-5pm; late Sept. to early June M-F 9am-noon and 1:30-5:30pm, Sa 9am-noon.) The **post office** occupies the rest of the building (open M-F 7:30am-6:30pm, Sa 8am-noon). **Internet access** is available at Mouse Killer, av. de Premier Mars 6 (☎724 3479), at 10SFr per hour. For the **police,** ☎117; for the **hospital,** ☎722 9111. The **postal code** is CH-2001.

ACCOMMODATIONS

Even if the **Oasis Neuchâtel,** rue du Suchiez 35, weren't the only hostel in town, it would still be a good place to stay. From the station, take bus #6 to "pl. Pury," then find bus #1 (dir.: Cormondrèche) in front of the main kiosk in Pl. Pury. Take it to "Vauseyon." Walk back towards town a few steps, then take the stairs marked "Escalièrs de Suchiez" all the way up. The hostel will be at the top, marked by a sign and yellow happy faces. Perched on a hilltop, this exotically decorated, quirky house offers 38 beds, table tennis, darts, a BBQ, and an eco-friendly, multilingual atmosphere. The thin walls, however, let in a lot of noise, particularly when there are school groups. Beware that it's a long walk after the buses stop running at night. (☎731 3190; fax 730 3709. Reception 8-10am and 5-9pm. No curfew. Reservations recommended July-Aug. Breakfast, shower, and sheets included. Free on your birthday! 4- to 6-bed dorms 23SFr; doubles 56SFr; 2- to 4-person garden teepee in summer 20SFr per person.) If Oasis is full, check the *Hôtel Restaurant* guide for cheap options in nearby towns, or try the Auberge de Jeunesse in La Chaux-de-Fonds, which often has room (see p. 481). The closest **campground** is in Columbier: **Camping Colombier** is on the lakefront. (☎841 2446. Open Mar.-Oct. 25SFr for 2 people, 23SFr for 2 people on foot with a tent, 31 SFr for 2 people with car or caravan; no tents provided. July-Aug. 15 add 2SFr.)

FOOD

Neuchâtel may live off tourists in July and August, but the rest of the year it's a university town, which means that there is good, cheap food. **Crêperie Chez Bach et Buck,** av. du Premier-Mars 22, 5min. down the street from the tourist office, counters its friendly, laid-back atmosphere with an intensely detailed list of choices. Enjoy amazing sugar crepes with fruit or ice cream for 2.70-6.80SFr, or savory crepes with meat or cheese for 2.50-9.80SFr. (☎725 6353. Crepes served M-Th 11:30am-2pm and 5:30-10pm, F-Sa 11:30am-2pm and 5:30-11:30pm, Su 6-10pm.) At **A.R. Knecht Boulangerie et Pâtisserie,** pl. des Halles 6, on the left facing away from the lake, locals munch croissants stuffed with spiced ham (1.70SFr), lacy fruit tarts (3.10SFr), and the house specialty *pain noix* for 3.10SFr. (☎725 1321. Open Tu-Sa 6am-6:30pm.) Further up the pl. des Halles, the unassuming bistro **Appareils de Chauffage et de Cuisine** serves up a well-endowed *plat du jour* consisting of meat or fish, vegetables, and bread to the strains of subdued, cool jazz (☎721 4396; open M-Th 7am-1am, F-Sa 7am-2am, Su 7pm-1am). This cafe is the main source of income for the **Centre d'Art Neuchâtel (CAN)** next door, an experimental art center perpetually on the brink of financial collapse (☎724 0160; www.can.ch/can). In the town center, **Migros,** rue de l'Hôpital 12, has groceries (open M 1:15-6:30pm, Tu-W 8am-6:30pm, Th 8am-8pm, F 7:30am-6:30pm, Sa 7:30am-5pm). There's an **Aperto** in the station (☎721 20 41; open 6am-10pm).

SIGHTS

Neuchâtel's cultural offerings are packed, for the most part, into a tight, easily walkable area. You can traverse the town in minutes, unless it happens to be the last weekend in September when the 3-day **Fête des Vendanges** (Wine Festival) is going on, in which case it may take hours to wade through throngs of drunks enjoying parades, jazz concerts, and wine feasts. A Swiss museum passport, available at many museums, costs 30SFr and grants you free admission to most museums in Neuchâtel, La Chaux-de-Fonds, and neighbor La Locle. Neuchâtel's small but respected archaeological museum began the process of moving to nearby Hauterive in 1999, to repoen in 2001.

THE OLD TOWN. The heart of town is the *vieille ville*, which is dominated by a cobble-stone marketplace (pl. des Halles), 1 block to the right of pl. Pury, home of the thrice-weekly market *(T, Th, and Sa 6:30am-noon).* Get an overview of the entire city with a **guided tour.** *(During the summer only; check at the tourist office for specific times and departure locations. 8SFr, under 13 3SFr.)* The tourist office also displays several "Promenades" or walks that you can do by yourself—the routes are well marked.

CHURCHES, CASTLES, AND DUNGEONS. From the pl. des Halles, turn left onto the rue de Chateau (marked by the red-faced clock, the **Tour de Piesse**) and climb the stairs on your right to reach both the **Collégiale** (a church) and the **chateau** which gives the town its name. Begun in the 12th century, construction of the church took so long to complete that architectural styles changed from Romanesque to Gothic. The golden stars and blue skies of the vaulted ceiling arch harmoniously over stained-glass windows and faded wall murals reinstalled after all the iconoclastic fervor of the Reformation died down. The gaudy **Cenotaph,** a sculptural composition of the Counts of Neuchâtel from 1372 on, was covered during the Reformation to prevent destruction and has been covered again for restoration scheduled for completion by mid-2000. *(Church open Oct.-Mar. 9am-6:30pm, April-Sept. 9am-8pm; free concerts the last Friday of every month; free.)* Next door, the 12th-century chateau served as the seat of the Count of Neuchâtel during the Middle Ages. Look for splotches of red on the old outside walls, remnants of a disastrous fire in 1415 that literally baked the yellow stone. Today the bureaucrats of the cantonal government sit behind the striped shutters and flower boxes. The interior can be seen only on free but dull guided tours (in English) which meet in the courtyard.

(Tours Apr.-Sept. M-F every hr. on the hr. 10am-noon and 2-4pm, Sa 10-11am and 2-4pm, Su 2-4pm.) A small cloister garden connects the chateau to the **Tour des Prisons** (Prison Tower) on rue Jehanne-de-Hochberg. The 125-step ascent allows you to examine the tiny wooden cells used until 1848 and enjoy a magnificent view from the top. *(Open Apr.-Sept. 8am-6pm. 1SFr, coins only.)*

MUSÉE D'ART ET D'HISTOIRE. The Musée d'Art et d'Histoire (Museum of Art and History), which houses an eclectic collection of paintings, coins, weapons, and textiles, tells the history of Neuchâtel mostly in French, *mais oui*. There are pecial presentations by the curatorial staff on Tuesdays at 12:15 and 1:15. The uncanny 18th-century automatons created by Jacquet-Droz are the museum's pride and joy; 2 barefoot boys in velvet coats scribble away while a lady plays the harpsichord. Performances are on the first Sunday of each month at 2, 3, and 4pm. Upstairs, the Art Nouveau decorations of the cupola include oil paintings (one of which portrays Neuchâtel as the "Intellectual Life"), stained glass, and sculpted angels that literally fly out of the walls. *(From pl. des Halles, walk toward the lake and turn left onto esplanade Léopold-Robert 1. ☎717 7920; fax 717 7929. Open Tu-Su 10am-5pm. Open M from Easter to Pentecost. 7SFr, students 4SFr, under 17 and Th free.)*

MUSÉE D'HISTOIRE NATURELLE. The Musée d'Histoire Naturelle (Museum of Natural History) sits atop the rue des Terreaux, to the left off rue de l'Hôpital. This spunkier version of the standard natural history museum displays examples of Switzerland's animals, stuffed and mounted in surprisingly entertaining dioramas of their natural environment. *(Turn right from the pl. des Halles onto the Croix du Marché, which becomes rue de l'Hôpital. Open Tu-Su 10am-5pm. 6SFr, students 3SFr, free W.)*

HÔTEL DU PEYROU. Further along rue de l'Hôpital, elegant gates and 2 alluring sphinxes invite a stroll into place du Peyrou. The crunchy gravel walks of the formal garden lead to the Hôtel du Peyrou, the one-time home of Jean-Jacques Rousseau's friend and publisher, Pierre-Alexandre du Peyrou.

OTHER SIGHTS. Neuchâtel's other attractions cater to the sense of taste. Visitors can sample chocolates at the **Wodey-Suchard Chocolate Factory,** directly behind the pl. Pury. *(Rue du Seyon 5. Open M 11am-6:30pm, Tu-F 6:30am-6:30pm, Sa 6:30am-5pm).* Venture out to nearby Cressier (see p. 479) for **wine tasting** in leafy vineyards. Hard-core cheese enthusiasts can pilgrimage out to the **Fromagerie Les Martel** (cheese factory) in neighboring Les Ponts-de-Martel for a tour and demonstration. *(Major Benoit 25, Les Ponts-de-Martel. 40min. bus ride from train station. ☎937 1666. Open 8am-noon, 5-7pm. Free.)* The tourist office has copious brochures advertising many similar excursions from Neuchâtel.

NIGHTLIFE

The university crowd makes the nightlife in Neuchâtel predictably lively; the city is famous among regional club-goers for its techno DJs. Opposite Crêperie Bach et Buck, the **Casino de la Rotonde,** Foubourg du Lac 14 (☎724 4848), has 2 dance clubs specializing in jungle (beers 3-5SFr; admission from 10SFr; open F-Su 10pm-4am.) Just behind the casino stands the **Bar Au 21,** Foubourg de Lac 23 (☎725 8198). Nurture beers (2.50-4.50SFr) or long drinks (6-8SFr) under Pink Floyd posters, or play pinball and foosball with a clientele generally younger than the club's name suggests. (M-Th 7am-1am, F 7am-2am, Sa 5pm-2am, Su 5pm-1am.)

The popular **Shakespeare Pub,** rue des Terreaux 7, across from the Musée d'Histoire, caters to a somewhat older, blue-collar crowd. Medieval timbers and stone walls loom over a 3-story pit lit by a combo of disco lights and British street lamps. Dance music tends toward Prince. Beers go for 4-5SFr., long drinks for 8.50-13.50SFr. Prices go up after 1am. (Open Tu-Su 8:30pm-4am. Men pay 13SFr to get in with one drink voucher on weekends.) Consume beer (7SFr), burgers (7-8SFr), and/or pizza (7-12SFr) all night long at the **Garbo** bar-discoteque, rue de Chavannes 5 and 7, 1 block to the left of the Shakespeare Pub. Walk in past the mylar-wrapped walls and foam space rocks for karaoke Tu-Th and blistering techno F-Sa (☎724 3181; www.garbo.ch. Open 10pm-6am.)

DAYTRIPS FROM NEUCHÂTEL

CRESSIER

☎032

Trains make the 10min. trip from Neuchâtel to Cressier (every hr. 5:39-11:22pm, 3.60SFr).

The sleepy medieval wine-making hamlet of Cressier presents a perfect opportunity for a day trip, or even just a mid-afternoon's respite from city life. Built around a tiny chateau that today houses the local government, the medieval village packs no less than 7 **caves** (wine cellars) where friendly local vintners are glad to offer tours of their facilities and answer questions about grapes. The finale, of course, is *la dégustation*, sampling wines poured by the hands that make them. Simply ask the vintner: *"Deguster du vin, s'il vous plaît?"* Choose from *chasselas, pinot noir*, or *l'oeil-de-perdrix*, or leave it to the expert *("Votre choix")*, to receive a glass of Cressier wine, straight from the vineyard's barrels.

Many *caves* line the one and only main street. Of note is the particularly traditional and congenial *cave* of **Jean-Paul Ruedin,** rte. de Troub 4, just around the corner from the train station. Jean-Paul is the 14th Ruedin son to operate the family vineyards since Jacques Ruedin first planted the grapes in 1614. The *cave* Ruedin, whose white wine *(vin blanc)* has been honored by the *Gerle d'Or* for the past serveral years, exudes a laid-back, philosophical attitude towards their craft; as the door declares, *"Aimer le vin c'est aimer la vie"*—"To love wine is to love life." (☎757 1151. Open Tu-F 8am-noon and 1:30-5:30pm, Sa 9-11:30am.) For an especially varied vineyard visit, attend a *dégustation extraordinaire* hosted by the **Maison Vallier,** 1 rue Vallier (behind and to the left of the chateau), Friday evenings from 5-7:30pm, where various vintners present their wares (Apr.-Oct.).

Though sampling is encouraged, it is considered impolite not to buy afterwards. The cheapest bottles start around 9SFr, to which 4SFr can add a fresh baguette, cheese, and chocolate from the **Co-op** next to the church on rue Gustave Jeanneret (open M-Tu and Th-F 7:45am-12:15pm and 2-6:30pm, W 7:45am-12:15pm, Sa 7:45am-12:15pm and 1:30-6pm). Take your bounty with you on a 10min. stroll up into the vineyards for panoramic views of the valley by following the yellow *tourisme pédestre* signs off rue de Chateau. A little extra effort brings you to the tiny town of **Combe,** where the tinkling of cowbells accompanies the lake view.

For a splurge, you can enjoy farm fresh regional delicacies at **La Croix Blanche,** rue de Neuchâtel 12, across from Jean Ruedin, including local trout (15SFr) and fondue (18.50SFr). Upstairs, the restaurant's hotel offers spacious singles for 70SFr or doubles for 100SFr, shower, TV, and breakfast included. Hotel guests also get special lunch and dinner of regional delicacies and "surprises of the owner" for 20SFr. Reception hours vary; arrangements can be made at the cafe. (☎757 1166. Open M-Tu, Th-Su 7-11:30am and 7pm-midnight. AmEx, MC, Visa.) A few doors down, the **Hôtel de la Couronne,** rue de Neuchâtel 2 (☎757 1458; fax (038) 473 201) serves a range of fresh fish (22-24SFr). Upstairs, the attic features half-timbered walls with showers in the rooms. (Singles 60SFr; doubles 90SFr. Reception at the bar. Restaurant open Tu-Th 8am-2pm and 4-11:30pm, F 8am-2pm and 4pm-12:30am, Su 9am-4pm.)

YVERDON-LES-BAINS

☎024

What's in a name? In the case of Yverdon-les-Bains, it's the essence of the town's existence, the **thermal baths** for which it is named. When Roman settlers discovered the source of the hot springs some 1500 years ago, they began cultivating the curative powers of the mineral-rich waters to ease all manner of ailments. People still come here for the baths, but the city also possesses a small but charming Altstadt, a 13th-century château, and some neolithic ruins attesting to the longevity of the locale's appeal.

TRANSPORT AND PRACTICAL INFORMATION. Trains run from Yverdon directly to Neuchâtel (25min., every hr. 5:33am-11:33pm, 11.80SFr), Geneva (50min., every hr. 6:19am-11:25pm, 29SFr); Lausanne (30min., every hr. 6:25am-

11:25pm, 12.60SFr); and Basel (2hr., every hr. 5:33am-9:33pm, 48SFr). The train station is located at ave. de la Gare 1 (☎425 2115; open 6am-10pm). The **tourist office,** on pl. Pestalozzi in the *centre ville*, a 3-minute walk straight ahead from the station, calls itself the office of "thermalisme" (in reference to the thermal baths). The tourist office resides in the Hôtel de Ville, an 18th-century structure next to the château. (☎423 6290, fax 426 1122, www.yverdon-les-bains.ch/tourisme. Open Apr.-Oct. M-F 8:30am-noon and 1:30-6pm; Nov.-Mar. M-F 8:30am-noon and 1:30-5:30pm; June-Sept. also Sa 9am-noon; July-Aug. M-F 8:30am-6pm.)

ACCOMMODATIONS AND FOOD. The tourist office can provide information on a number of reasonably-prices hotels in Yverdon, but unfortunately, the most affordable accommodations are outside the *centre ville*, well after the medieval facades have melted into 20th-century suburbia. The **Gîte du Passant (HI),** rue de Parc 14, is a 56-bed establishment reminiscent of summer camp, with small but cheery rooms right by the river, and a big grassy lawn. From the station, take an instant right, walk alongside the river, cross the bridge at the av. des Sports, and head down the riverside path for 5-10min. The hostel is past the police station. (☎425 1233; fax 426 0096. Reception daily 7-9:30am and 5-10:30pm. Breakfast and shower included. Dorms 22SFr the first night; 20SFr subsequent nights.) Nearby on the riverside lies the **Hôtel du Lac,** rue des Cygnes 25, features clean, simple, rooms with sinks, managed by a warm and welcoming staff. (☎425 2307; fax 426 6636. Reception M-F 7:30am-11pm, Sa 8:30am-2pm. Hall showers. Singles 40SFr, doubles 70SFr, triples 90SFr. AmEx, MC, Visa.) **Boulangeries** and cafes cluster in the colorful streets radiating from the *centre ville;* most feature regional specialties (like perch or **papet vaudois,** made of sausage and vegetables).

SIGHTS. The **Centre Thermal,** off ave. des Bains, and its glitzy adjoining hotel, entice visitors with 4 pools and therapeutic treatments ranging from electrotherapy to massage. Although the clientele tends toward an older crowd, the center also offers recreational activities for sprightlier guests. A word to the wise—plug your nose, since the healing powers of the springs come at the price of their sulfurous stench. To get there from the train station, head left down the av. de la Gare to the av. Haldimand then follow the signs, or take bus #2 or #3 to "Prairie" and continue down the av. des Bains. Take a right onto rue d'Entremonts and follow the signs from there. (☎423 0232. Open M-F 8am-10pm; Sa-Su 9am-8pm. Last entry one hour before closing. Admission to the baths 13SFr, ages 3-16 8SFr, other facilities charge separately.)

Though Yverdon sits on the southwestern shore of Lake Neuchâtel, the only good way to get close to the water is to picnic on the narrow strip of beach, and enjoy the velodrome-like effect of the surrounding hills. Head down rue des Pecheurs behind and to the left of the station and turn right on av. des Sports. Follow alongside the stadium and after it, take a left. The beach will be in front of you. Nearby is a forested area containing 47 **standing stones,** a sort of neolithic mini-Stonehenge dating back to 4,000 BC. Yverdon's aesthetic appeal is concentrated in the *centre ville*, a smallish square flanked by the **Savoy château** to the left and the 18th-century Baroque church on the right. The château was built in 1260 by the Dukes of Savoy to protect Yverdon on the east, a role fulfilled in part by the lake on the north and the river Thiele on the west (though you'd never know it from its rather anemic size today). The square, 4-towered edifice houses a museum containing prehistoric artifacts as well as items from Yverdon's days as the Roman camp of **Eburondunum.** (☎425 9310. Museum open Oct.-May Tu-Su 2-5pm; June-Sept. Tu-Su 10am-noon and 2-5pm. 8SFr, students and seniors 7SFr, children 4SFr.) The chateau is also home to the **Musée de la Mode** (Fashion Museum), featuring temporary exhibits on fashion. 2000's theme was "The Ball of the Century." (☎425 9310. 4Sfr, free for children).

For a total change of pace, visit the inexplicable **Maison d'Ailleurs** (Museum of the Elsewhere), across pl. Pestalozzi from the tourist office. The science fiction lover will find a lot to pore over here; temporary exhibits are quite comprehensive (in 2000, they featured illustrations from science fiction novels, with interactive exhibits). One floor houses a library devoted to the genre. (Pl. Pestalozzi 14. ☎ 024 425 6438; www.ailleurs.ch. Open W-Su 2-6pm. 5 Sfr, students 4SFr.)

LA CHAUX-DE-FONDS ☎ 032

Sprawling, lakeless, and largely devoid of medieval charm, La Chaux-de-Fonds seems an unlikely attraction amid the more scenic *villes* in the mountains of French Switzerland. But the city, birthplace of the architect **Le Corbusier** and auto magnate **Louis Chevrolet,** magnetizes visitors by means of time and technology. A major historic watchmaking center, the town showcases a museum exploring "man and time," the best horological gallery in Switzerland. Dubbed Europe's highest city thanks to its 1000m altitude, La Chaux-de-Fonds is a comfortable home base for skiers and mountain bikers wanting to explore mountain trails.

TRANSPORT AND PRACTICAL INFORMATION

Trains arrive from Neuchâtel (40min., every hour 5:04am-11:21pm, 10SFr). The **tourist office,** Pl. le Corbusier 1, occupies the ground floor of Espacité, a giant silver and red building. From the station, walk straight 1 block, then turn on av. Léopold-Robert. Ride the elevator (free) to the 14th floor for a panoramic view of the area after picking up a 2SFr city map and free info on activities. The office can also help you with information about several self-guided walking tours that visit Le Corbusier's creations. (☎ 919 6895; fax 919 6297; tourisme.montagnes@ne.ch, www.ne.ch/tourisme. Open June 15-Sept. 15 M-F 9am-6:30pm, Sa 10am-4pm; Sept. 15-June 15 M-F 9am-noon and 1:30-5:30pm, Sa 9am-noon.)

ACCOMMODATIONS AND FOOD

The dim but very clean **Auberge de Jeunesse (HI),** rue du Doubs 34 (☎ 968 4315; fax 968 2518), is at the corner of rue du Stand behind an iron gate. Take bus #4 (dir. L'Hôpital) to "Stavay-Mollondin," walk a block, then turn right on rue du Stand. The 80 beds are rarely full. (**Laundry** 6SFr, but no dryers. Dinner 11.50SFr. Reception 7:30-9:30am and 5-10pm in winter, until 10:30pm in summer. No lockout. Wheelchair accessible. Breakfast and sheets included. Hall showers only. Dorms 24SFr, doubles 31SFr. 4-6 bed "family" rooms 24SFr per person, with sink 26SFr. Subtract 2.50SFr in off-season. Non-members add 5SFr. AmEx, DC, MC, Visa.)

Cheap food is most easily obtained in megastores like the **Co-op Super Centre** on rue du Modulor, left off av. Léopold-Robert before the tourist office (open M 1:30-6:30pm, Tu, W, F 8am-6:30pm, Th 8am-8pm, Sa 8am-5pm) or the *plats du jour (*6-10SFr) at the **Migros** restaurant two blocks right of the station on the 4th floor of the Metropole Center (M 1-6:30pm, Tu-W, F 11am-6:30pm, Th 11am-8pm, Sa 11am-5pm). **Le P'tit Paris,** rue du Progrès 4, is a student-crowded cafe with vaulted ceilings and live jazz in the musty **Paris Cave** in back. Continue down the road from the tourist office, turn left on rue du Stand, then right on rue du Progrès. Indulge in a shrimp cocktail for 8SFr or beer for 2.60SFr. (☎ (039) 286 533. Concerts 10-15SFr. Open M-Th 8am-midnight, F 8am-2am, Sa 9am-2am, Su 4pm-midnight.)

SIGHTS AND OUTDOOR ACTIVITIES

The fascinating **Musée International d'Horlogerie,** Rue des Musées 29, in the Parc des Musées, chronicles humanity's quest to measure the great continuum, from Stonehenge to the atomic clock. From the station, turn right on the rue des Musées and follow it to the right of the Metropole Center. Here, the vast and the minuscule unite. Dardi's astrarium and Ducommun's planetarium illustrate the rigidly timed dance of the planets in the Ptolemian and Copernican systems. Sleek cylindrical and spherical display cases rise eerily from the floors and hang from the ceiling like space-age stalagmites and stalactites, accompanied by exhibits in English,

German, and French. Dominating one corner of the park outside, the **carillon,** an artistic conglomeration of steel pipes and colored slats, measures time to the hundredth of a second and emits acoustically precise musical ditties in sync with carefully orchestrated panel movements every 15 minutes. (☎967 6861; fax 967 6889. Open June-Sept. Tu-Su 10am-5pm; Oct.-May 10am-noon and 2-5pm. 8SFr, students 4SFr; free Su 10am-noon.)

Next door, the **Musée des Beaux-Arts,** Rue des Musées 33, looks like a cross between a pseudo-Roman bath and a parking garage. The sparse collections of not-so-great 19th- and 20th-century Swiss derivatives of French schools aren't really worth the effort. But there are 2 pockets of dense excellence: a room of Le Corbusier paintings wild with color and chaos that contrast startlingly with the functional straight lines of his architecture, and another filled with recently bequeathed paintings, including works by Van Gogh, Gauguin, Renoir, and Courbet. (☎913 0444; fax 913 6193. Open Tu and Th-Su 10am-noon and 2-5pm. W 10am-noon and 2-8pm. 6SFr, 8SFr for temporary exhibits, students 3SFr, 4SFr. W free.)

For a literal taste of history, investigate the **Musée Paysan et Artisanal** (Museum of Farming and Crafts), Crêters 148. Take Bus #3 (dir.: Les Foulets) to "Polyexpo." This authentic 16th-century farmhouse reconstructs the home, workshop, sausages, and general lifestyle of the medieval peasant family. It illustrates how the confinement of long Jura winters gave rise to the region's watchmaking obsession. (☎926 7189. Open May-Oct. Tu-Sa 2-5pm, Su 10am-noon and 2-5pm; Nov.-Apr. W, Sa-Su 2-5pm. 3SFr, students 2SFr.)

Skiers can take a regional train to **Tête de Ran** (1422m), in **Les Hauts-Geneveys** (☎853 1151), for downhill or cross-country (lift tickets 15SFr per day), or a bus to **La-Vue-des-Alpes** (☎853 3018), which offers night-skiing and ski lessons. (Buses run 3-4 times per day W and Sa-Su 9:15am-5:15pm. Reservations necessary at ☎926 1275.) In summer, bikers and hikers enjoy well-marked trails (**rent bikes** at the station, but ask the tourist office for trail maps and bike rental information.)

NIGHTLIFE

If you're feeling restless at night, take a 20-minute stroll under the stars from the hostel to the very edge of town to the **Bikini Test,** La Joux-Perret 3 (☎ 968 0666). From the hostel, walk downhill 7 blocks to rue de la Serre, then turn left and go around the Place des Lilas. The street becomes rue du College. Head for the music. Converted from a late medieval barn, the discoteque sports murals of monsters and musicians cavorting on a lunar landscape. Inside, robot gargoyles glare down on the 2nd story loft as the DJ mixes salsa with techno. Kids dance and drink away (beer 3-5SFr) while smoke of various persuasions drifts by. Downstairs, the chill-out room shows shark movies and Monty Python clips. For a closer nightspot, try the popular **Dublins,** 32a rue Docteur Coutery. Walk 3 blocks left from the hostel, then left and downhill. On weekends, rowdy 20-somethings turn out for 2.50SFr beers, spilling out into the cobblestones beyond the pub doors. (☎914 1118. Open M-Sa 8:30am-11:15pm.)

BIEL (BIENNE) ☎032

In 1765, Rousseau spent what he called the happiest moments of his life in Biel. However, little of the fortified town remains unchanged by the tumultuous years that followed the philosopher's sojourn. In 1798, Biel was overrun by Napoleon's armies, laying the foundation for the city's present bilingualism (60% speak French, 40% German). Industrial parks for Rolex and Omega now overpower the vestiges of the *Altstadt* Rousseau loved, but Biel is still attractive for its proximity to Lac Bienne (Bielersee) and surrounding hills. Since few budget accommodations grace Biel, consider making it a daytrip from Solothurn, Neuchâtel, or Bern.

TRANSPORT AND PRACTICAL INFORMATION. Trains run to Biel from **Solothurn** (20min., every hr. 5:42am-12:15am, 8.60SFr); **Bern** (30min., every 30min. 5:37am-12:02am, 11.80SFr); and **Neuchâtel** (20min., 2 per hour 5:39am-midnight,

MAN AND MACHINE Born Charles Edouard Jeanneret-Gris in 1887, **Le Corbusier,** architect, city planner, and painter, is a monumental presence in 20th-century art. This son of a La-Chaux-de-Fonds watchmaker rebelled against the inertia of 19th-century nationalism and historicism, seeking pure, precise forms motivated by function rather than cultural reference. He designed in glass and reinforced concrete, a revolutionary choice of material that countless others repeated throughout the 20th century. He was also infatuated with iconic machines of modernity, like the automobile and the airplane, and believed that houses and cities should be designed and organized like machines in their economy of structure and efficient use. As he said in *Toward a New Architecture,* "the house is a machine for living."

10SFr). The Biel **tourist office** is just outside the train station at Bahnhofpl. (☎ 322 7575; fax 323 7757. Open M-F 8am-12:30pm and 1:30-6pm; May-Oct. also Sa 9am-3pm.) The train station **exchanges currency** (M-F 6am-8pm, Sa-Su 7am-7pm), **rents bikes** (mountain bike 27SFr), rents **lockers** (3-5SFr; open 5am-12:30am), and **stores luggage** (5SFr per day; open 7am-9pm). **Internet access** is available at Migros, Freierstr. 3, in the Take-Away section, on two coin-operated PCs for 5SFr/hr. For the **police,** ☎ 117; for the **ambulance,** ☎ 144. The **post office** is just left of the train station (☎ 321 1840; open M-F 7:30am-6:30pm, Sa 7:30am-1pm).

FOOD AND ACCOMMODATIONS. If you do decide to stay in Biel, there is the **Lago Lodge,** Uferweg 5, Nidau, which bills itself as a "hostel, bistro, and brewery at Lake Biel." Just steps away from the Bielersee's shores: take a left out of the train station, follow the street as it curves around, rurn right onto rue des Bains and follow it to the water. Turn left at the ferries and cross the river Thiele and take an immediate left; Lago Lodge will be on your right (10 min. walk). The Lodge offers a prime location, clean spacious rooms, and a convivial atmosphere to a crowd of young backpackers. (☎ 331 3732, fax 331 3733; lagolodge@access.ch, www.backpacker.ch/lagolodge. Reception 7am-noon and 3-11pm. Laundry 5SFr. **Internet access,** kitchen facilities, and breakfast available. Linens 5SFr extra. Dorms 20SFr, 4-6 bedrooms 25SFr, doubles 70SFr.)

For picnic supplies, there is always the **Aperto** in the station (open 6am-10pm), the **Co-op City Centre,** on Nidaug. (open M-W, F 8am-7pm, Th 8am-9pm, Sa 7:30-4pm), or **Migros,** Freierstr. 3, 1 block straight ahead from the station (open M-F 7:30am-7pm, Sa 7:30am-4pm). In front of Migros, numerous cafes and restaurants in the *Zentralplatz (Place Centrale)* satisfy those post-hike munchies.

HIKING. The 2 best **hikes** from Biel pass through magnificent gorges: the walk to **Twannbachschlucht** leads to mountaintop fields ripe for picnics, while the trek to **Taubenloch** threads through a rugged canyon and its canopy forest.

Twannbachschlucht (3hr.) To get to Twannbachschlucht, take bus #11 from the train station to "Magglingen/FuniMacolin," then take the rail car from Biel to Magglingen (every 15min 5:55am-11:55pm; 4.20SFr, SwissPass valid.) From this vantage point, 3 different paths lead to Twannberg, the starting point of the Twannbachschlucht hike. The trail follows a ridge above Lake Biel and passes through dense forest and flower-filled meadows, ending in the picture-book town of Twann at the bottom of the gorge. Return to Biel by train (10min., every hr. 6:01am-11:46pm, 3.60SFr) or lake ferry (6.80SFr, 7 per day, Eurail not valid), or move on to Neuchâtel.

Taubenloch (40min.) Taubenloch is a less ambitious hike, though its more dynamic terrain makes it perhaps more rewarding. Buses #1, 2, and 3 run to "Taubenloch" where you can enter the canyon through the **Zum Wilden Mann** restaurant's garden (2SFr suggested donation). Legend has it that a beautiful maiden nicknamed "Die Taube" ("The Dove") threw herself to her death here to escape an enamored tyrant. The well-traveled and well-cleared trail hugs the edges of 30m drops of sheer rock walls carved eons ago by the rushing rapids below. Waterfalls plunge past mossy cliffs, illuminated by the sunlit green canopy above. Many hikers turn back at the water treatment plant, but hungrier souls who press on just a few minutes will find the **Eau-Berge du Taubenloch** restaurant at Frinvillier 2535. Fill up on a delicious three-course *Menü* for under 15SFr while the owner's baby goats and friendly dog romp around your feet. (☎/fax 358 1132. Open Feb. to mid-Dec., Tu-Sa 9am-11pm, Su 9am-7pm.) The walk back from Frinvillier to Biel takes about 1 hour.

ENTERTAINMENT. A **boat tour** of the lake provides a leisurely introduction to the city. To reach the harbor and beach from the train station, turn left at Bahnhofpl., follow the road around to the left, and look for the brown-and-white signs for *Schiffländle* and *Débarcadère*. Boat tours range from 13.60SFr (Biel-Twann, 30min.) to 45SFr (Biel-Murten, 3hr. and Biel-Solothurn, 2½hr.) round-trip. In early July, an **open-air cinema** called "Yellow Movie Nights" runs mostly American recent releases in **Schloßpark Nidau**. Tickets (15SFr) are on sale at the tourist office.

FRIBOURG (FREIBURG) ☎026

Modern Fribourg stretches in front of the train station with a mix of stores and concrete apartment buildings, while its truly charming *vieille ville*, established on the banks of the Sarine by the Zähringen dynasty in 1157, stretches down the wooded hills of the gorge to the river. The contrast is stark, and is only one of the dichotomies that characterize Fribourg's multi-faceted personality. Young Swiss are drawn to Fribourg by both the university and the siren call of lakes and mountains. The town has a penchant for modern art, open-air shopping, and fine dining, but its most distinctive attractions are quiet remnants of medieval religious fervor. Fribourg was an isolated bastion of Catholicism during the Reformation; even the local brew, Cardinal beer, celebrates a 19th-century bishop. Meanwhile, Fribourg bridges the Swiss linguistic divide: 30% of the population firmly count themselves *Freiburger*; the remaining 70% *Fribourgeois*.

TRANSPORT AND PRACTICAL INFORMATION

Fribourg sits on the main rail line between Zurich and Geneva. **Trains** leave for **Bern** (25min., every 30min. 6:14am-12:16am, 11.80SFr); **Lausanne** (50min., every 30min. 6:20am-11:47pm, 23SFr); **Basel** (1¾hr., every 30min. 6:14am-11:16pm, 48SFr); **Neuchâtel** (1hr., every hr. 5:46am-9:46pm, 19SFr); and **Interlaken** (1½hr., every hr. 6:42am-9:46pm, 35SFr). For a **taxi,** dial (079) 219 4610. Fribourg's **tourist office,** av. de la Gare 1, 100m to the right of the station door, makes hotel reservations for a 3SFr fee, often refunded by the hotel. (☎321 3175; fax 322 3527; info@Fribourg-Tourism.ch; www.FribourgTourism.ch. Open M-F 9am-12:30pm and 1:30-6pm, Sa 9am-12:30pm and 1:30-4pm; closed Sa afternoons Oct.-May.) **Exchange currency** at the train station (open 6am-8:30pm) or at one of the many banks lining rue du Romont. **Lockers** (3-5SFr, open 5:10am-12:45am), **luggage watch** (open 7am-7:55pm; 5SFr per item), and **bike rental** (20SFr per day, ID deposit) are available at the station. Dial 117 for the **police** and 112 for general **emergencies. Internet access** is available at **Cyber Atlantis,** 18 rue de Lausanne, for 10SFr per hr. (open M 4-6:30pm, Tu-Fr noon-6:30pm, Sa 10am-4pm). The **post office,** av. de Tivoli, is the skyscraper to the left of the station (open M-W 7:30am-6:15pm, Th 7:30am-8pm, Sa 8-noon). The **postal code** is CH-1700.

ACCOMMODATIONS AND FOOD

Fribourg's **Auberge de Jeunesse** stands at rue de l'Hôpital 2. Head left out the train station and walk past the overpass, across av. de Tivoli, past the post office, onto the narrow rue du Criblet, left at the playground, and up the path to the hostel. The building will be on your right; watch for it, there are few signs. The hostel is a converted hospital, with long, quiet corridors. (☎323 1916; fax 323 1940. Breakfast, sheets, and showers included. Lunch and dinner 11.50SFr. Lockers, **laundry,**

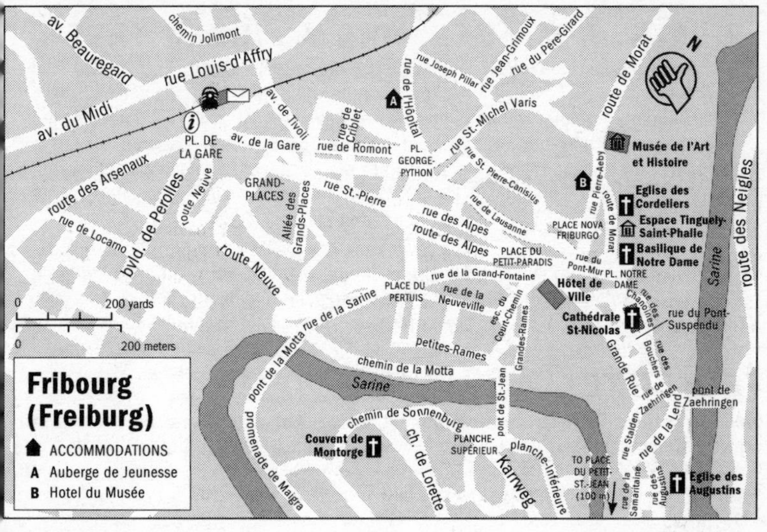

kitchen, and ping-pong tables available. Reception 7:30-9:30am and 6-10pm. Open Feb.-Nov. Reservations recommended. Dorms 26.45SFr. Non-members add 5SFr.) **Hotel du Musée,** rue Pierre Aeby 11, is above a Chinese restaurant: the reception is within the dining room. From the station, follow av. de la Gare to rue de Romont to rue de Lausanne and turn left at the end of rue de Lausanne, by pl. Nova-Friburgo. The large, well-furnished rooms are carpeted. (☎/fax 322 3209. Breakfast 5SFr. Open M-Th 10am-2:30pm and 5pm-11:30pm, F-Sa 10am-2:30pm and 5pm-midnight. Reserve 2-3 days ahead. Singles 40-45SFr, with shower 50-55SFr; doubles 80-90SFr, 90-100SFr. AmEx, MC, Visa.) From the station, campers can catch a GFM bus to "Marly," where **Camping La Follaz** has lakeside plots and showers. (☎436 2495. Reception 9am-8pm. Open Apr. 1 to Oct. 15. 5.20SFr per person, tents for 1-2 people 5SFr, for 4-6 7SFr.)

Small cafes selling quasi-Italian or German Swiss dishes populate almost every main street in the *vieille ville,* as well as rue de Romont. For a plethora of kebab places, check out Blvd. des Perolles, and other streets around the station. **Bindella Ristorante Bar,** rue de Lausanne 38 , cooks inventive, high-quality pasta (from 11.50SFr) and pizza dishes in a low-lit interior. Your taste buds will thank you for a small monetary splurge. Come hear free live jazz on the last Thursday of every month at 8:30pm. (☎322 4905. Open M-Sa 11:30am-2:30pm, and 6-11pm.) An airier Mediterranean design brightens the **Restaurant des Marechaux,** rue des Chanoines 9, food served 6-11pm, to the side of the cathedral. Feast on Greek *spanakopita* with *tzatziki* (9SFr) or various *souvlaki* (19-25SFr) in this veggie-friendly establishment, overlooking the gorge. (☎322 3333. Open 5pm-midnight.) **Perriard Boulangerie,** rue de Lausanne 61, will satisfy your sweet-tooth with a variety of pastries and confectionery delights, such as *noisettines* for 2SFr and breads for 1-3SFr; (☎322 3489; open Tu-F 7:30am-7pm, Sa 7:30am-6pm, Su 8am-6pm). A **produce market** stands in pl. Georges Python between rue de Romont and rue de Lausanne (T, W 7am-noon) or in pl. Hôtel de Ville (Sa 7am-noon). The virtually inseparable supermarket twins, **Co-op** and **Migros,** share the same street (respectively, 6a and 2 rue St.-Pierre, by Grand-Places) and the same hours (open M-W, F 8am-7pm, Th 8am-9pm, Sa 8am-4pm). This Co-op has a restaurant but the Migros does not. Head to the **Migros** at Pérolles Centre, Blvd. de Pérolles 21 (near the station), for their second-floor restaurant and large grocery with the same hours as above. Along the side of La Placette Shopping Mall (the 1st building on rue de Romont) there is a

DEATH, A MAIDEN, AND A LINDEN TREE

Once upon a time (June 22, 1476) in a land far, far away (Fribourg), there lived an old man named Nicholas who declared that he would give his daughter Beatrice's hand in marriage to the man who proved himself most valiant on the battlefield. As the knights went off to fight Charles the Bold in Murten, Beatrice waved a linden branch at Rudolphe, her childhood love. Determined to win her hand, Rudolphe proved himself the bravest knight on the battlefield–at the cost of a mortal wound. Undaunted, he ran back to Fribourg, waving a linden branch and shouting "Victory!" When he finally reached Beatrice's balcony in pl. Hôtel de Ville, he collapsed. Beatrice ran to her love, who could say only "Homeland! Love! To Heaven!" before dying in her arms. The town planted the linden branch as a relic of the victory in the square. In 1984, a traffic accident uprooted the tree, but the town salvaged a shoot and replanted it in the original spot, where it flourishes today. In memory of the battle and of Rudolphe's plight, runners from Murten and Fribourg race between the two cities every October.

Manora self-service restaurant with meat, fruit, salad, and dessert kiosks that produce a fine meal for 8-15SFr (open M-Sa 7am-10pm, Su 9am-10pm).

SIGHTS AND MUSEUMS

Fribourg's beautiful churches, monasteries, and convents naturally lend themselves to a walking tour.

THE OLD TOWN. From the station, head down rue de Romont, past pl. Georges Python, and along rue de Lausanne and its pink-bannered open-air shopping galleries. Rue de Lausanne empties into pl. Nova-Friburgo, a busy intersection with a fine view of the **Hôtel de Ville** and its fanciful clock tower. Pantaloon-clad Renaissance automatons regularly chime in the hours. A fountain of St. George dominates the courtyard below, and gives unexpected showers to visitors and the commemorative **Morat Linden Tree** in heavy winds (see Death, a Maiden, and a Linden Tree, p. 486).

MUSÉE D'ART ET D'HISTOIRE. Off pl. Nova-Friburgo, rue Pierre Aeby leads to the **Musée d'Art et d'Histoire** (Museum of Art and History). Skip the 18th-century portraiture—the haunting historical artifacts are the meat of the collection. Look for the Hans Geiler wood carvings and the gleefully macabre, bejeweled skeleton of St. Felix, ca.1755. *(Rue de Morat 12. ☎305 5140. Open Tu-W and F-Su 11am-5pm, Th 11am-8pm. Free; special exhibits 6-10SFr, student discount.)*

JEAN TINGUELY-NIKI DE SAINT PHALLE MUSEUM. On the other side of the Église des Cordeliers from the Musée d'Art et d'Histoire, the **Espace Jean Tinguely-Niki de Saint Phalle** showcases the work of avant-garde Fribourg native Tinguely and his wife, Saint-Phalle. Tinguely's work features bizarre, massive machines made out of rusty metal, while Saint-Phalle's work uses brilliant colors in curvaceous sculpture. *(Rue de Morat 2. ☎305 5170. Open W, F-Su 11am-6pm, Th 11am-8pm. 5 SFr, 3SFr for students, free for children under 16.)*

MONASTERY AND CHURCHES. From the museum, backtrack on rue. de Morat to the **Église des Cordeliers,** part of a Franciscan monastery. The unassuming facade masks a colorful interior, featuring vividly animated paintings framed by pastel marble, and an elaborate altar that lies in star-studded darkness. *(Open Apr.-Sept. 7:30am-7pm; Oct.-Mar. 7:30am-6pm.)* Farther down the road is the **Basilique de Notre-Dame,** whose dim, incense-laden atmosphere contrasts sharply with the bright, ornate Église des Cordeliers. Across pl. Notre-Dame rises the bell tower of the **Cathédrale St.-Nicolas,** the focal point of Fribourg. It took over 200 years to erect the Gothic columns, now smoke-blackened, that shoot upwards into pointed arches and elegant stained-glass windows. View the town from the 76m, 368-step **tower.** *(Cathedral open M-Sa 7:30am-7pm, Su 8:30am-9:30pm. Free. Tower open June-Oct. M-*

Sa 10am-noon and 2-5:15pm, Su 2-5:15pm. 3SFr, students 2SFr, children 1SFr.) From the cathedral, head downhill, from rue des Chanoines to rue des Bouchers, take a left onto rue de Zaehringen and a left onto Stalden. Take the steps of Stalden down, until you hit Passage des Augustins. A left turn there will lead you to the rue des Augustins and its highlight, the 13th-century **Église des Augustins.** Although only order members have complete access to the monastery, visitors can examine the monastery's huge, eagle-topped altarpiece. Two tiny chapels sit high on the hill above town. The postage-stamp sized **Chapelle de St. Jost** is closed to the public, but the **Chapelle de Lorette,** housing an illuminated statue of the Virgin Mary, welcomes visitors. *(Open Mar.1-Oct. 31 T, Th, Sa-Su.)*

FESTIVALS AND NIGHTLIFE

Fribourg's university, music conservatory, art groups, and civic institutions host several festivals throughout the year, including a **Carnival** (a Mardi Gras type party in the *vieille ville* February 23-27, 2001), an **International Film Festival** (March 11-18, 2001), an **International Guitar Festival** (late March to early April), an **International Jazz Festival** (mid-July), and the **Belluard Bollwerk International** festival, a gathering of musicians, dancers, critics, scholars and just about anyone else involved in the arts in late June to mid-July (☎469 0900; www.belluard.ch). **Open-air cinema** runs from mid-July to mid-August, screening many American films (get advance tickets from the tourist office). The above is just a primer; the tourist office can provide more information on festival-laden Fribourg.

If you're not partying in the streets, try **Café Belvedere,** Grand Rue 36, at the top of Stalden, which resembles a 3-D M.C. Escher drawing, with comfortably worn couches perfect for intimate conversation. Alterna-intellectuals lounge on terraces overlooking the gorge, sampling the wine or beer of the month (3.50-5SFr) while listening to the pleasantly dippy music. *Menüs* feature salads, pasta, and various fowl for 11.50-13.50SFr. (☎323 4407. Open M-Tu 11:30am-11:30pm, W-Th 11:30am-12:30am, F 11:30am-3am, Sa 10:30am-3am, Su noon-midnight.)

DAYTRIPS FROM FRIBOURG

GRUYÈRES ☎026

To get to Gruyères, buy a tichet at the GFM booths in the bus station in Fribourg, directly behind the train station. A 20-minute bus ride will land you in Bulle, where you can catch a train to Gruyères (20min., 16.40SFr, round-trip 26SFr). The last departure from Gruyères is at 8:17pm, though a bus departs 9:25pm. Buses and trains run approx. every hour.

Tiny Gruyères (pop. 1,412) carries a weighty reputation for its cheese. Unfortunately, the whole town is painfully conscious of it. The local tourist industry goes to absurd extremes (strategically placed milk cows, locals in dubiously medieval garb chirping the virtues of their wares, and suspiciously artificial-smelling smoke permeating a castle whose hearths have been bare and unlit for years), but the towering beauty of the surrounding mountains overcomes the kitsch. A château filled with contemporary art and the milky calm of working cheese dairies make this eccentric town well worth a daytrip. Follow the signs from the station, and at the top of a (steep) series of hills and stairs you'll find the **tourist office** (☎921 1030, fax 921 3850; www.gruyeres.ch. Open June-Aug. M-F 8am-5:30pm, Sa-Su 9am-5pm; Sept.-May M-F 8am-noon and 1:30-5pm, Sa-Su Apr. and Oct. 9am-5pm).

The **La Maison du Gruyère,** cheese factory *par excellence*, is located directly across from the train station. Newly renovated, it draws in crowds with a souvenir market, cheesemaking demonstrations, and its own classic Swiss restaurant. (☎921 8400, www.lamaisondugruyere.ch. Open daily Apr.-Sept. 8am-7pm; Oct.-Mar. 8am-6pm. Cheesemaking 8am-4pm daily. 5SFr, family rate 10SFr.) The truly lactose-devoted can take a GFM bus to "Moléson-sur-Gruyères" to the **Fromagerie d'Alpage.** An anachronistic phenomenon, this 17th-century factory makes cheese

GOT MILK? Before most kids hear of watch-making or political neutrality, they know about Swiss cheese. These children are frequently misguided, though. The 84,000 tons of cheese Switzerland produces annually don't only consist of the familiar, hole-ridden variety. While most of it (56,500 tons) is the recognizable Emmental, 22,000 tons is Gruyère, a nutty-tasting cousin without any holes to speak of. The region has been making cheese since the 12th century, though today's dairy artisans operate in modern facilities amid expansive cow pastures. Two varieties of cows contribute their milk to the effort: *tachettée rouge* (red) and *noir* (black). Each animal produces around 30 kilos of milk each day, which is transported to the *fromagerie* (cheese factory). Workers process 3 million kilos a year by pouring it into large vats, where it is centrifuged, matured with bacteria, congealed with natural enzymes into a yogurt-like consistency, and heated to get rid of excess liquid (which is saved to feed pigs). Each cheese round is then pressed into shape for 18 hours until it reaches 800 kilos per cm^2, before it is stamped for quality and authenticity.

the old-fashioned way, over a huge cauldron on the fireplace. (☎921 1044. Open daily 9:30am-7pm, with demonstrations at 10am and 3pm, May-Oct.)

Gruyères's only major street, which is lined by flowerbox-adorned old houses, leads even further uphill to the absolutely beautiful and bizarre **Château de Gruyères.** The striking château exterior competes for your eyes' attention with the Dent-de-Broc mountains that rise up all around it. Inside, the château's eccentricity is matched only by that of the town itslef.

The castle was home to a series of earls from the 12th through the 16th centuries. After the dynasty ended, it was in the hands of local county governments and private families, until it was restored by the government in 1938. Don't expect to be taken back to its earliest days when you walk in—the mismatched decor of each room reflects many different eras: medieval tapestries are juxtaposed with Louis XV chairs, and one room houses **Franz Lizst's** pianoforte (yup, he lived here too). Only the dungeons remain of the original feudal castle; the living quarters burned to the ground in 1493 and were rebuilt as the first Renaissance castle in the Northern Alps. Adding to the anachronistic confusion, the castle is also now home to the **International Center of Fantastic Art,** a collection that roams freely between the erotic, the demonic, and the grotesque, and is scattered throughout the castle. (☎921 2102. Open June-Sept. 9am-7pm, Mar.-May and Oct. 9am-noon and 1-5pm; Nov.-Feb. M-F 9:30am-noon and 1:30-4pm, Sa 10:30am-noon and 1:30-5pm. 5SFr, students 2SFr, essential English guide 0.50SFr.) Historical tapestries are displayed upstairs. Both the château and *vieille ville* are reliably flooded with more tourists than locals and cows combined. The gravel path around the castle and a short walk downhill to the right of the main street provide some relief from souvenir shops and bring those magnificent mountains a little closer. When hunger strikes, a meal of Gruyères cheese fondue can prove a budget buster (20-40SFr), but the region's other specialty, *la double-crème de la Gruyère avec fraises* (strawberries in clotted cream), is deliciously affordable (10-13SFr).

MURTEN (MORAT) ☎032

Murten is accessible ***by train*** *from Fribourg (26min., every hr. 5:41am-12:27am, 10SFr); Neuchâtel (30min. via Ins, every hr. 5:12am-10:13pm, 10.80SFr); and Bern (45min. via Lyss, every hr. 5:47am-10:27pm, 11.80SFr).* ***LNM ferries*** *run from Neuchâtel (105min., 5 per day 9:45am-5pm, 15.40SFr), and offer lake cruises (13.20SFr; 4-5 per day 7:55am-6:35pm; ☎(032) 725 4012).*

A small village that maintains a relatively low quaintness-to-souvenir-shop ratio, Murten makes for a leisurely daytrip. The lakeside town maintains an amicable bilingualism, despite the predominance of German over the 12% French-speaking minority (who call the town "Morat"). Only at the end of the town's main street do the 2 languages literally go their separate ways: the road splits into Französischkirchg. on the left and Deutschkirchg. on the right. Murten/Morat, surrounded by

POISON VERT Though the Swiss drinking age is only 16, and beer is cheaper than Coca-Cola, there is one guilty pleasure the Swiss no longer enjoy. *Absinthe,* a potent anise-flavored liquor, has been banned in the country since 1912. Absinthe is the product of 5 herbs (Wermmtkraut, Melisse, Fenchelsamen, Anis, and Stem-Anis) which are combined with alcohol, fermented, and heated. A French doctor first brought the elixir to Switzerland for medicinal use; when he died, the recipe he left with his housekeeper gained popularity as an *aperitif,* reaching its prime in the late 19th century. The liquor, dubbed *le poison vert* ("the green poison"), was a bit too potent, perhaps—it was blamed for hallucinations, epileptic incidents, and poisonings. In the infamous 1905 Commugny murders, an allegedly absinthe-induced stupor drove a man to kill his wife and children. Soon after, absinthe was banned for consumption in Switzerland and France. A weaker derivative, *Ricard,* is served in restaurants; for the real deal, head to the Czech Republic.

its medieval *Ringmauer/ramparts*, overlooks the pale blue **Murtensee/Lac de Morat.** This high-altitude town has a bloody history: Charles the Bold, Duke of Burgundy, was defeated in 1476 by an army of the old Swiss Confederacy in what came to be known as the Battle of Murten (See Death, a Maiden, and a Linden Tree, p. 486); Napoleon defeated a similar contingency in 1798, laying the foundation for Murten's French-speaking community.

The train station (☎670 2646), in the same tiny square as the post office, **changes currency, rents bikes** (26-32SFr per day), and has small **lockers** (2SFr). Turn right from the station to find a **Co-op** grocery store halfway up Bahnhofstr. with a cafeteria upstairs (entrees 9.90-10.90SFr; open M-Th 8am-7pm, F 8am-8pm, Sa 7:30am-4pm). At the end of Hauptg., the **tourist office,** Kirchg. 6, is on the left (☎670 5112; fax 670 4983; open M-F 9am-noon and 2-6pm, Sa 9am-noon).

As Bahnhofstr. curves uphill, it leads to the swaying lindens that mark the entrance to the **Schloß/Château,** with its imposing square tower. Now the home of several administrative offices, the château also hosts occasional dramatic productions. The main street, Hauptstr. (to the right of the château), catches the eye with numerous flags blazoned with the cantonal symbol, the lion, hung from its arcades. Turn right off Hauptg. to Deutschkirchg. to climb up to the **ramparts** for views of the red-clay-tiled roofs below and the lake beyond. Ascending to the second level of the ramparts yields postcard-perfect views of the Murtensee. On the other side of the ivy-covered walls is the **Stadtgraben**—gardens rife with roses, pink honeysuckle, and multicolored lupins.

The *Stadtgraben* path descends the ramparts and ends at the linden tree park. Follow Lausannestr. in the opposite direction and obey the signs to reach the town's old mill, now the **Murten Historisches Museum.** The museum's collection, with signs mostly in German and French, may not be thrilling enough to warrant an extensive visit, but you may enjoy the neolithic remains or the bottles of Murten's famously strong and famously psychedelic *absinthe* (see Poison Vert, p. 489). (☎670 3100. Open May-Sept. Tu-Su 10am-noon and 2-5pm; Oct.-Dec. and Mar.-Apr. Tu-Su 2-5pm; Jan.-Feb. Sa-Su 2-5pm. 6SFr, seniors 5SFr, students 3SFr.)

NORTHWESTERN SWITZERLAND

The cantons of Basel (-Stadt and -Land), Solothurn, and Aargau, in northwest Switzerland are gently beautiful. Their subtle charms include excellent museums, a rich Humanist tradition, and charming old town centers. It's a difficult region to avoid, since Basel is a major transportation hub for travel to and from Germany and France. Despite their proximity to France and French-speaking Switzerland, the cantons of northwestern Switzerland are German-speaking. Most towns have French variants of their names, but don't let that confuse you.

HIGHLIGHTS OF NORTHWEST SWITZERLAND

Pick Picasso's brain at two collections of the artist's work in **Basel** (see p. 494).

Forget *Mardi Gras*—catch **Fasnacht** fever in Basel (see p. 490).

Stomp through Roman sewers in **Augusta Raurica** (see p. 497).

BASEL (BÂLE) ☎061

Situated on the Rhine near France and Germany, Switzerland's third largest city is home to a large medieval quarter as well as one of the oldest universities in Switzerland—a school whose graduates include Erasmus of Rotterdam, Bernoulli, and Nietzsche. The kids keep Basel young, and the biggest party of them all, Basel's *Fasnacht*, rivals the New Orleans *Mardi Gras;* residents have a mad carnival before the onset of Lent. The murmur of the Rhine wending its way to Germany accompanies riverside walks. On the left bank, the *Münster* presides over the *Altstadt* in a towering conglomeration of red sandstone, stained glass, and sprouting spires. The most outstanding attractions of Basel are the 30 museums in the hilly streets of the elegant St. Alban district. Basel takes great pride in its cultural heritage; as you wander the streets you'll encounter art from Roman times to the 20th century, serenaded by student musicians on every street corner.

GETTING THERE AND AROUND

The **Euroairport** (☎267 9025) serves continental Europe, though most trans-continental flights are routed through Zurich. Shuttle buses run passengers between the airport and the SBB train station (M-F 7:30am-6:45pm, Sa 11am-5:15pm). Basel stands at the crossroads of Switzerland, France, and Germany and accordingly has **3 train stations:** the French SNCF station is next door to the Swiss SBB station in Centralbahnpl., and trains from Germany arrive at the DB station (Badische Bahnhof). City trams to the town center depart from the SBB station (M-F every 5min., Sa-Su every 15min.). **Buses** to Swiss, French, and German cities depart from their respective train stations. If **driving** from France, take A35, E25, or E60; from Germany, E35 or A5; from within Switzerland, take Rte. 2 north.

Trains: SBB station (☎157 2222; 1.19SFr per min.), on Centralbahnpl. **SNCF station** on Centralbahnpl. **DB station** (☎690 1111), across the Rhine down Greifeng. From the SBB station to: **Zurich** (1hr., every 15-30min. 4:45am-12:03am, 31SFr); **Geneva** (3hr., every hr. 4:41am-9:53pm, 72SFr); **Lausanne** (2½hr., every hr. 4:41am-9:53pm, 62SFr); **Bern** (1¼hr., every hr. 4:41am-12:03am, 37SFr); **Salzburg** (via Zurich, 7hr., 5 per day 5:51am-9:01pm, 127SFr); **Vienna** (via Zurich, 10-12hr., 5 per day 5:51am-9:01pm, 156SFr). To **Paris** (5-6hr., 12 per day 5:51am-12:28am, 70SFr); **Munich** (via

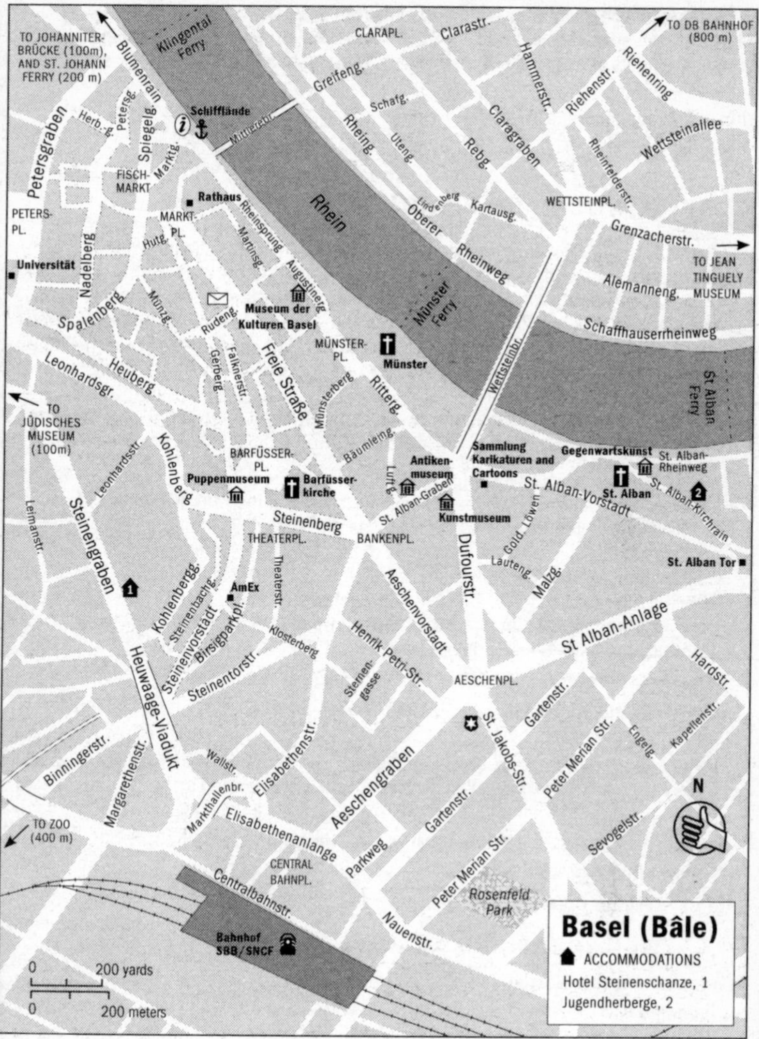

Zurich or Karlsruhe, 5¼hr., every hr. 7:05am-8:13pm, 114-122SFr); **Milan** (via Lucerne or Bern, 4½-6hr., every hr. 5:54am-10:13pm, 159SFr). Make international connections at the French (SNCF) or German (DB) stations. 25% discount on international trips for travelers age 16-25.

Ferries: There are 4 **ferries** cross the Rhine: the **Vogel Gryff** at Klingental; the **Leu** below the Münster terrace; the **Wild Maa** at St. Alban; and the **Ueli** at St. Johann. In summer, boats run 9am-7pm; in winter 11am-5pm. Rhine **cruises** depart from the *Schiffstation* next to the tourist office (☎639 9500; 4 per day May-Oct. 13; station open M-F 9am-12:15pm and 1-7pm, Sa 11am-4pm, Su 8am-3pm). Enjoy "Samba Night" or one of the other special Rhine cruises (varying times and prices; check at the station). Round-trip to Rheinfelden 53SFr, to Waldhaus 27SFr. Tickets available 30min. before departure.

Public Transportation: Trams and buses run reliably from 6am-midnight. Most sights are within zone #10. 1-zone tickets 2.80SFr, day ticket 7.80SFr; ages 6-16 half-price. Automatic vendors at all stops sell tram tickets. Maps at tourist office or train station.

Taxis: In front of the train station, or call 271 1111, 633 3333, or 271 2222.

Parking: Jelmoli, Rebg. 20; **Bahnhof SBB,** Güterstr. 2.50SFr per hr.

Bike Rental: At train stations. 27SFr per day. Open daily 6am-9:40pm.

ORIENTATION AND PRACTICAL INFORMATION

Basel sits in the northwest corner of Switzerland, so close to France that the *Tour de France* sometimes traverses the city. Groß-Basel (Greater Basel), where most sights are located, lies on the left bank of the Rhine; Klein-Basel (Lesser Basel) occupies the right bank. Pick up a city map (0.50SFr) and other useful publications at either of the 2 tourist offices. To reach **Marktplatz** on foot from the SBB and SNCF stations, cross the Centralbahnpl., go left on Elisabethenanlage, right down Elisabethenstr., and left on Freie Str. (20min.) From the DB station, follow Rosentalstr. (which becomes Clarastr. and then Greifeng.) over the Mittlere Rheinbrücke and around to the left on Eiseng. (15min.).

Tourist Office: Basel Tourismus, Schifflände 5 (☎268 6868; fax 268 6870; info@baseltourismus.ch, www.baseltourismus.ch). From the SBB station, take tram #1 to "Schifflände." The office is on the river, near the Mittlere Rheinbrücke. Lists of hotels, restaurants, museums, events, and tours of Basel and the surrounding area. Open M-F 8:30am-6pm. A **bus tour** of the city leaves from the SBB station (May-Oct. at 10am; 20SFr, 10SFr for children). There is a **branch office** (☎271 3684; fax 272 9342; hotel@messebasel.ch) at the SBB station. Open M-F 8:30am-7pm, Sa 8:30am-12:30pm and 1:30-6pm, Su 10am-2pm.

Currency Exchange: At any bank or the SBB station bureau (open 6am-9pm).

Luggage Storage: At all stations. Lockers 3-5SFr, 24hr. access. Storage 5SFr per day, open 6:30am-10pm.

Bookstores: Buchhandlung Bider und Tanner, Bankenpl., Aeschenvorstadt 2 (☎206 9999), is Basel's travel bookshop, with a room of well-selected English-language books. Open M-W and F 8:15am-6:30pm, Th 8:15am-9pm, Sa 8:15am-5pm.

Emergencies: Police, ☎117. **Medical,** ☎144. **Hospital,** ☎265 2525.

Hotlines: Helping Hand, ☎143.

Bi-Gay-Lesbian Organizations: Arcados, Rheing. 69 (☎681 3132; fax 681 6656; info@arcados.com; www.arcados.com), at Clarapl. has oodles of information on bars, restaurants and hangouts. Open Tu-F 12-7pm, Sa 11am-4pm.

Internet Access: Domino, Steinenvorstadt 54. Arcade with an Internet coffee-bar upstairs, 10SFr per hr., 12SFr per hr. after 6pm. Open M-Th 9am-midnight, F-Sa 9am-1am (Sa 10am-1am in summer), Su 1pm-midnight. Must be 18 years old.

Post Office: Rüdeng 1. Take tram #1 or 8 to "Marktpl." and walk 1 block back away from the river. Open M-W and F 7:30am-6:30pm, Th 7:30am-8pm, Sa 8am-noon. **Poste Restante address:** *Postlagernde Briefe*, Rüdengasse, CH-4001 Basel 1. **Postal Codes:** CH-4000 to CH-4059.

ACCOMMODATIONS

Basel's biggest shortcoming is its lack of cheap lodgings. Call ahead to ensure a spot in the hostel.

Jugendherberge (HI), St. Alban-Kirchrain 10 (☎272 0572; fax 272 0833; basel@youthhostel.ch; www.youthhostel.ch/basel). Take tram #2 to "Kunstmuseum" and turn right on St.-Alban-Vorstadt, then left at the church. Or walk 10-15min. from the SBB station down Aeschengraben to St. Alban Anlage. At the tower, follow the signs down the hill. Near a calm stretch of the river, this curious old building is a mecca for skyscraper-weary travelers. The efficient institutional setup has lockers for every bunk, wheelchair access, TV, phones, and a day-pass for public transportation. Non-members add 5SFr. Breakfast, showers, and sheets included. Dinner and lunch 11.50SFr. **Laundry** 7SFr. Reception 7-10am and 2pm-midnight. (2pm-11pm from Nov.-Feb.) Check-out 7-10am. Dorms 29-31SFr; singles 79SFr; doubles 98SFr. Reduce by 2.50SFr Jan. 1-Feb. 19 and Nov.-Dec. MC, Visa.

Hotel-Pension Steinenschanze, Steinengraben 69 (☎272 5353; fax 272 4573). From the SBB station, turn left on Centralbahnstr. and follow signs for Heuwaage (5min.) Under the large bridge, go up the ramp to Steinengraben and turn left. Advantages abound in this 3-star hotel: rooms with phone, radio, TV, private bathrooms, and balconies over the hotel garden or the street. Breakfast included. Daytime luggage storage. 24hr. reception. 3-night max. stay for students. Singles 110-180SFr, under 25 with ISIC 60SFr; doubles with shower 160-250SFr, 100SFr. AmEx, DC, MC, Visa.

Camping: Camp Waldhort, Heideweg 16 (☎711 6429), in Reinach. Take tram #11 to "Landhof." Backtrack 200m toward Basel, cross the main street, and follow the signs. Beautiful location far from Basel but in a residential area. Reception 7am-12:30pm and 2-10pm. 7SFr; tents 10SFr. Open Mar.-Oct.

FOOD

With all the students about, relatively cheap eateries are numerous. Barfüsserpl., Marktpl., and the streets connecting them are especially full of restaurants. Your cheapest bet for a meal lies at one of the many food stands in this area, where Swiss classics and falafel sandwiches prevail.

Zum Schnabel, Trillengässlein 2 (☎261 4909). From Marktpl., walk one block on Hutg. (by EPA) to Spalenberg., then turn left onto Schnabelg. In this corner terrace, Italian-speaking servers present well-prepared German dishes. 12.80SFr buys bratwurst with *Rösti,* and a salad. Pasta 12.80-19.80SFr. Open M-Th 8am-midnight, Sa-Su 8am-1am. AmEx, DC, MC, Visa.

Café Gleich, Steinenvorstadt 23 (☎281 8286). This casual restaurant serves an array of vegetarian dishes to locals. Salads range from 6.40SFr-16.50SFr, omelettes 13-17SFr, plats du jour 15.60-21.50SFr. Open M-F 9am-9:30pm.

Hirscheneck, Lindenberg 23 (☎692 7333). Cross Wettsteinbrücke and take the first left onto Kartansgasse. An unabashedly left-of-center restaurant-bar where dreadlocks, piercings, and the hammer and sickle prevail. Features at least 2 vegetarian and organically grown dishes every day. *Menü* 11.50-16.50SFr. Open M-Sa 2pm-midnight, Su 10am-midnight. Kitchen open M-Sa 6:30-10:30pm, Su 10am-4pm.

Café Barfi, Leonhardsberg 4 (☎261 7038), to the right of Gerberg. from Marktpl. The proprietor serves up mostly Italian dishes with some surprises, like *samosas* (5.50SFr). Outdoor diners enjoy accordion serenades. Daily *Menü* 16.50-17.50SFr. Open M-Sa 10am-11pm. MC, Visa.

Manor, Greifeng. 22, and **Pfauen,** Freie Strasse 75, both offer good, cheap self-service restaurants. Both open M-W, F 8:30-6:30pm, Th 8:30am-9pm, Sa 8am-5pm.

MARKETS

Migros, SBB station, open M-F 6am-10pm, Sa-Su 7:30am-10pm. Also at Steinenvorstadt and Clarapl. 17, both open M-W and F 8am-6:30pm, Th 8am-9pm, Sa 7:30am-5pm.

Public market, on Marktpl. Fresh fruits, vegetables, and baked goods every weekday morning. Open until 6:30pm on M, W, and F; Tu, Th, and Sa until 1:30pm.

SIGHTS AND HIKING

Basel's easy-to-use pedestrian tourist signs will help you negotiate your way around the city's curving, interlacing streets, perhaps better than any map can.

Marktpl., which sits near the river at the culminating point of Freie Str. and other major shopping avenues, is the center of the *Altstadt* (old town).

THE OLD TOWN. The very red **Rathaus,** erected in the early 1500s to celebrate Basel's entry into the Swiss Confederation, brightens Marktpl. with its blinding facade adorned with gold and green statues. *(Guided guided tours Tu 2:30pm; meet in the courtyard. 10SFr, children 5SFr.)* Behind the Marktpl., tread softly on the **Mittlere Rheinbrücke,** which is 775 years old. Built in 1225, the bridge connects Groß-Basel to Klein-Basel. A block away from Marktpl. in the heart of the *Altstadt*, a colorful Gothic fountain livens up the **Fischmarkt.** Leading off of Fischmarkt, the tiny **Elftausendjungfern-Gässlein** (Lane of 11,000 Virgins) is famous for St. Ursula's pilgrimage of girls to the Holy Land during the Children's Crusade. The medieval practice of gaining indulgences by walking this lane is now defunct, but people still stagger through after overindulging at nearby bars. For a contrasting aesthetic, walk from Marktpl. toward Barfüsserpl. onto Theaterpl., where the spectacular **Jean Tinguely Fountain,** also known as the **Fasnachtsbrunnen,** captures a moment of modern chaos as iron sculptures parodying human foibles spew water.

CATHEDRAL. Behind Marktpl. along the Rhein, the **Münster,** Basel's medieval treasure, stands on the site of an ancient Celtic settlement and a Roman fort. The red sandstone facade features hundreds of figures in various acts of piety ranging from trumpet-playing to dragon-slaying. Behind the altar, gilt Latin inscriptions memorialize the life of Erasmus, the renowned scholar and staunch Catholic who remained loyal to his faith even after his beloved Basel joined the Reformation in 1529. When he died, the city set aside dogma to give him a proper Catholic burial in its Protestant cathedral. Bernoulli, the mathematician who discovered the math behind flight, also rests in the cloister. The **tower** provides the city's best view of the Rhine, Klein-Basel, and Black Forest. *(Open Easter-Oct.15 M-F 10am-5pm, Sa 10am-4pm, Su 1-5pm; Oct. 16-Easter M-Sa 11am-4pm, Su 2-4pm. Free. Tower closes 30min. before the church. 3SFr. Due to recent suicides, you can't go up alone.)*

UNIVERSITY QUARTER. Head down one of the tiny alleys off Fischmarkt to reach Petersgraben, which leads to the Peterspl. and the University quarter. The **University of Basel,** founded in 1406, is Switzerland's oldest university. Its library houses rare volumes from Erasmus, Luther, and Zwingli. The grounds are ideal for picnicking, napping, or reading Kant. Bargain-hunters flock here every Saturday morning for the **flea market,** which starts at 9am and goes until early afternoon. Around the corner from the university library, the 700-year-old **Spalentor** (gate tower), one of the original city wall's 3 remaining towers and one of the most impressive gates in Switzerland, marks the edge of the *Altstadt*.

ZOO. The **Zoologischer Garten,** one of the best zoos in Europe, is a 10-minute walk down Steinenvorstadt from Barfüsserpl. Follow signs along the wooden path, or take tram #1 or 8 to "Zoo Bachletten." The zoo is famous for successfully breeding several endangered species, and the gardens are as much of an attraction as the animals. Restaurants, picnic areas, and ice cream vendors abound. *(Binningerstr. 40. ☎295 3535. Open daily May-Aug. 8am-6:30pm; Sept.-Oct. and Mar.-Apr. 8am-6pm; Nov.-Feb. 8am-5:30pm. 12SFr, students and seniors 10SFr, ages 6-16 5SFr.)*

HIKING. 1200km of yellow *Wanderweg* marked trails crisscross the countryside around Basel. Take Bus #70 to "Reigoldswil" where the **Gondelbahn** goes to the Jura mountain peak, "Wasserfallen" (937m). From the peak you can hike to Waldenburg (2½-3hr.), or to Jägerwegli (1½-2hr).

MUSEUMS

Basel's 30 museums may seem overwhelming, but they are worth the time it takes to explore them. The **Kunstmuseum** is deservedly the most famous, but many esoteric galleries are also fascinating. Subjects range from medieval medicine to mechanized mannequins. Pick up the comprehensive museum guide at the tourist

COCK-EYED DRAGON The city of Basel has two emblems: a bishop's *crozier* (staff), strange because the city threw out its bishop when it joined the Reformation in 1529, and a heraldic creature called a cockatrice or basilisk (Basel-isk), strange because it's part dragon and part rooster. These monsters were believed to have come from a hen's egg hatched by a serpent (often on a heap of dung), and a glance from their eyes was supposed to cause sudden death. As a result, in 1474, the citizens of Basel brought forth what may have been the world's first and only public trial and execution of a chicken. The hapless bird allegedly laid an egg on a dung heap, a crime for which it was tried, convicted, and beheaded. The egg was ceremonially burnt.

office, or visit the website, www.museembasel.ch. A **Swiss Museum Pass,** valid for one month (all over Switzerland at participating museums) costs 30SFr.

KUNSTMUSEUM (MUSEUM OF FINE ARTS). begun in 1661, the Kunstmuseum was the first independent public gallery in Switzerland. A formidable slab and marble structure, the *Kunstmuseum* houses extensive, outstanding compilations of old and new masters. The Picasso collection was acquired when a resoundingly affirmative electoral referendum persuaded the city government to grant the museum money to buy two. Touched by such enthusiasm, the artist himself donated 4 more. *(St. Alban-Graben 16. Accessible by tram #2. ☎206 6262. Tu and Th-Su 10am-5pm, W 10am-7pm. Combined ticket with Museum für Gegenwartskunst 7SFr, students 5SFr. Special exhibition rates. Free first Su of every month.)*

FONDATION BEYELER. The Beyeler is one of Europe's finest private art collections. It's hard to think of a major artist who is not represented here: Picasso, Matisse, Cézanne, Lichtenstein begin the list. The outdoor lily-pond is only matched by a Monet version within. *(Baselstr. 101, Riehen. Take tram #6 (dir.: "Riechen Girenze") to "Riehendorf" then walk straight for 5min. ☎645 9700. Open 10am-6pm, W 10am-8pm. 12SFr, students 9SFr.)*

MUSEUM FÜR GEGENWARTSKUNST (MODERN ART). Find most of Basel's really modern art at this museum, between the youth hostel and the Rhine, which is largely composed of temporary exhibition spaces. *(St. Alban-Rheinweg 60. ☎272 8183. Open Tu-Su 11am-5pm. Combined ticket with Kunstmuseum 7SFr, students 5SFr. Special exhibition rates. Free first Su of every month.)*

MUSEUM JEAN TINGUELY. Everything rattles and shakes in this intriguing homage to the Swiss sculptor's vision of metal and movement. Tinguely's massive "Grosse Méta Maxi-Maxi Utopia" allows visitors to climb over and experience his crazy futuristic vision. *(Grenzacherstr. 210. Take tram #2 or 15 to "Wettsteinpl." and bus #31 (dir.: "Habermatten") to "Museum Tinguely." ☎681 9320. Open W- Su 11am-7pm. 7SFr, students 5SFr.)*

PAPIERMÜHLE (PAPER MILL). A quick float down the river past the hostel brings you to the Papiermühle, a restored medieval mill with a noisy water wheel which continues to mash rags so that visitors can make their own paper. Try writing with a quill or typesetting a souvenir. The main exhibit is a fun, well-presented love-letter to the written (or printed) word, from the Rosetta Stone to the Gutenberg press. *(St. Alban-Tal 37. ☎272 9652. Open Tu-Su 2-5pm. 9SFr, students 6SFr. Family ticket 22SFr.)*

ETHNOLOGY AND NATURAL HISTORY MUSEUMS. A mansion topped by Neoclassical friezes houses the **Museum der Kulturen Basel,** and its excellent collection of non-Western art. In the same building, the **Naturhistorisches Museum** has engaging exhibits of woolly mammoths and inventive displays of model animals against their own skeletal images. *(Augusting. 2. ☎266 5500. Both museums open Tu-Su 10am-5pm. 6SFr, under 13 4SFr. Special rates for temporary exhibitions. Free first Su of every month.)*

BARFÜSSKIRCHE (FRANCISCAN CHURCH). The church collection includes stained glass windows emblazoned with cantonal coats-of-arms, stunning iconography, and the oldest *crozier* city banner. The interior is an old church with pink stone columns and huge windows veiled in transparent linen. Downstairs, re-created rooms showcase medieval and Renaissance furnishings. *(Steinenberg 4, on Barfüsserpl. ☎271 0505. Open M and W-Su 10am-5pm. 5SFr, students and seniors 3SFr, free on the 1st of the month and for under age 16.)*

OTHER MUSEUMS. The German sketches in the **Sammlung Karikaturen and Cartoons** possess a universally expressive wit, plus inclusions from the 20th-century funnies like *Peanuts* and *Calvin and Hobbes*. *(St. Alban-Vorstadt 28. ☎271 1336. Open W and Sa 2-5:30pm, Su 10am-5:30pm. 6SFr, students 3SFr.)* You'll do best to stick to the lower floors of the **Antikenmuseum** *(Museum of Ancient Art; St. Alban-Rheinweg 60. ☎271 2202. Open Tu-Su 10am-5pm. 5SFr, students 3SFr. Free first Su of every month.)* The **Jüdisches Museum der Schweiz** (Jewish Museum) contains small, well-organized exhibits on the law, the Jewish year, and Jewish life. *(Kornhausg. 8. Take bus #37 to "Lyss." ☎261 9514. Open M and W 2-5pm, Su 11am-5pm. Free.)* The **Puppenmuseum (Toy Museum) Basel** holds 4 floors of toys, densely packed into dark display cases. *(Steinenvorstadt 1. ☎225 9595. Open M-W and F-Su 11am-5pm, Th 11am-8pm. 7SFr, students 5SFr, under 16 free.)*

ENTERTAINMENT AND NIGHTLIFE

FESTIVALS. In a year-round party town, Basel's carnival, or **Fasnacht,** still manages to distinguish itself as fun fun fun. The festivities commence the Monday before Lent with the *Morgestraich*, which has occurred every year for the last 600, a not-to-be-missed, 4am parade that ends precisely 72 hours later (March 5-7 in 2001). Fife and drum music plays to revelers in brilliant masks that lampoon the year's local scandals. The goal is to scare away winter (it rarely succeeds). The 32rd annual **ART fair** will draw masses of modern art-lovers to the city from June 13-18, 2001. The tourist office provides lists in English of Basel's other cultural offerings, including concerts, ballets, gallery exhibits, fairs, and other happenings.

BARS AND NIGHTCLUBS. A university town through and through, Basel's nightlife reflects the influence of student patrons. Start bar-hopping at **Barfüsserplatz,** where students sit at outdoor tables and drink wine on the steps of the Barfüsserkirche. When the bars close, kids in black often head for after-hours clubs. Most places have a 21+ policy, but the crowds get younger on weekends. The two most popular local beers are **Warteck** and **Cardinal.**

Atlantis, Klosterberg 10 (☎228 9696). From Bankenpl., it's off Elisabethenstr. to the right. Big. Hot. Smoky. Loud. Raucous. This multi-level, sophisticated bar sways to reggae, jazz, and funk. Bands play every night the Italian soccer team does not. Concerts 10-23SFr. Open M-Th 11am-2am, F 11am-4am, Sa 5pm-4am (kitchen open 11am-2pm and 6pm-2am).

Brauerei Fischerstube, Rheing. 45 (☎692 6635). Cross Mittlere Rheinbrücke and take the 1st right. This old-school *Biergarten* is adjacent to Basel's only brewery, crafting 4 of the best beers in town. The delectably sharp *Hell Spezial* goes well with the homemade pretzels. *Bier* 2.50SFr-5.90SFr. Open M-Th 10am-midnight, F-Sa 10am-1am, Su 5pm-midnight. MC, Visa.

Babalabar, Gerberg. 74 (☎261 4849), to the left off Gerberg. from Barfüsserpl., is a dark, modern dance club for beautiful people. Go for techno nights or samba rhythms from the Latin-crazy DJ. Cover Su-Th 5SFr, F-Sa 10SFr. Open in summer M 9pm-2am, Tu-Su 10pm-morning.

Pickwick Pub, Steinenvorstadt 13 (☎281 8687), near Barfüsserpl. This English-style pub, draped in football memorabilia, hosts a salt-of-the-earth crowd of students and adults alike. Bartenders are happy to go the extra mile. Beers from 3.80SFr. Open Su-W 11am-midnight, Th 11am-1am, F-Sa 11am-3am.

Dupf, Rebg. 43 (☎692 0011). Cross Weittsteinbr. and turn left onto Rebg. This chic, well-coiffed gay and lesbian bar welcomes a mixed crowd. Beers from 3.80SFr. Open daily 5pm-whenever, summer 4pm-whenever.

Elle et Lui, Rebg. 39 (☎691 5479). Dupf's younger, bohemian next-door neighbor, Elle et Lui, caters to gay and lesbian clientele of all ages and tastes. Open daily 6pm-3am.

DAYTRIP FROM BASEL

AUGUSTA RAURICA

Take the hourly regional train (dir.: Laufenberg) 3 stops to "Kaiseraugst" (15min., 4.80SFr). In addition, a ferry runs from Schifflände, by the Basel tourist office, to Kaiseraugst (☎639 9500; 2hr., 4 per day, May 1-Oct. 17, 19.20SFr, round-trip 35SFr, ages 6-16 half-price).

The twin towns of **Kaiseraugst** and **Augst** will take you farther back than medieval Basel. Founded in 43 BC, **Augusta Raurica,** the oldest Roman colony on the Rhine, grew into an opulent trading center by the 2nd century. After destruction at the hands of the Alemanni in the late 3rd century, the Romans built an adjacent fortress. Ongoing excavations continue to uncover temples, baths, and workshops. Most of the attractions are in Augst, clustered around the small **Roman Museum** (☎816 2222; fax 816 2261), a 10-minute walk from the station. Plenty of signs point the way, but be sure not to miss the left turn onto Giebenacherstr. You can visit Switzerland's first Christian church (the Baptistery), the remains of Roman baths, and many other artifacts of settlement throughout the ages. Though its exhibit on Roman gastronomy (featuring a continuous video of 2 people eating) has a mesmerizing juvenile appeal, more entertaining is a ramble through the fields to the **Roman Farm Animal Park,** where bullying pigs and selfish donkeys butt heads. (Sites and museum open Mar.-Oct. M 1-5pm, Tu-Su 10am-5pm; Nov.-Feb. Tu-Su 10am-noon and 1:30-5pm. Museum 5SFr, students 3SFr; parks free.) You can also stomp through the cold, dark, damp **Roman cellars** and **sewers** dating from 43 BC. The museum staff is happy to recommend walks around the former colony.

SOLOTHURN ☎032

Sandwiched snugly between the Jura Mountains and the Aare River, Solothurn compactly captures the best of Switzerland in its enchanting *Altstadt.* The city's charm rubs off on its inhabitants—the friendliness of shopkeepers and restaurateurs is palpable. Annual film, classical music, and literature festivals attest to the town's love affair with culture; citizens of Solothurn unleash their rambunctious side during their rowdy Winter Carnival. Though Solothurn lacks the major museums and historical sights that would attract tourists for long visits, the Jura mountains offer endless biking and hiking prospects.

TRANSPORT AND PRACTICAL INFORMATION. **Trains** leave Solothurn's main station at Hauptbahnhof for **Basel** (1hr., every hr. 5:39am-11:14pm, 25SFr), **Neuchâtel** (45min., every hr. 5:42am-11:12pm, 18SFr), and **Bern** (40min., every 30min. 5:18am-11:20pm, 13SFr). For hiking tips, a map, or free room reservations, head to the **tourist office,** Hauptg. 69. From the train station, walk through the underpass toward the *Zentrum* and follow Hauptbahnhofstr. across Kreuzackerbrücke up Kroneng. The office is left of the cathedral. (☎626 4646; fax 626 4647; info@solothurn-city.ch, www.solothurn-city.ch. Open M-F 8:30am-noon and 1:30-6pm, Sa 9am-noon.) **Exchange currency** or **rent bikes** (26SFr per day, mountain bike 32SFr per day) at the **train station** (both open M-F 6:10am-8:50pm, Sa-Su 6:30am-8:50pm). For **taxis,** dial 622 6666 or 622 2222. **Lockers** (3-5SFr, 24hr.) and **luggage storage** (5SFr; 6:10am-8:50pm) are at the station. For the **police,** ☎117; in case of **fire,** ☎118; for the **hospital,** ☎627 3121. For the **post office,** go past the hostel on Postpl., turn left off Kreuzackerbrücke, and onto Landhausquai (☎625 2929; open M-F 7:30am-6pm, Sa 8-noon). The **postal code** is CH-4500.

ACCOMMODATIONS AND FOOD. Overlooking the Aare river on the edge of the *Altstadt*, the **Jugendherberge "Am Land" (HI),** Landhausquai 23, is a slick, high-tech vision of glass and steel incongruously framed by the exterior of a 1642 schoolhouse. From the train station, walk over Kreuzackerbrücke and take the first left onto Landhausquai. Picture windows overlooking the river and chrome track lighting keep the place well lit. Amenities include a pool table, roof terrace, and music room, but get to like your bunkmates, because beds are close together in the dorms. (☎623 1706; fax 623 1639. Lunch and dinner 11.50SFr. Breakfast and sheets included. Reception 7:30-10am and 4:30-10:30pm. Non-members add 5SFr. 9-bed dorms 25.50SFr; 6-bed dorms 26.50SFr; 5-bed dorms with sink 29SFr; triples with toilet and shower 37SFr per person; doubles 42SFr per person. Sur-tax 1SFr if under 16, 2SFr if over. Major credit cards.) The **Hotel Kreuz,** Kreuzg. 4, offers more privacy but less newness. Go left off Kreuzackerbrücke before the hostel. Paper-thin walls and concerts in the second-floor bar don't make Kreuz the quietest of hotels. (☎622 2020; fax 621 5232; kreuz@soluet.ch. Breakfast and hall showers included. Reception M-Th 9am-11:30pm, F 9am-12:30am, Sa-Su 2-11:30pm. Spartan singles 48-58SFr; doubles 82-87SFr. Prices drop for multiple nights.)

In the *Altstadt*, sounds of chatter and clinking silverware from the numerous affordable cafes and restaurants waft through the air. The **Taverna Amphorea,** Hauptg. 51, down the street from the tourist office towards Marktpl., exudes a Mediterranean sense of relaxation while dishing up large portions of vegetarian-friendly Greek and Middle Eastern specialties for under 25SFr (☎623 6763; open Tu and Th 11am-11:30pm, W 9am-11:30pm, F 11am-12:30am, Sa 9am-12:30am). From Marktpl., turn left on Hauptg., then left on Stalden to find the **Sandwich House,** Stalden 9, which puts a techno twist on the friendly neighborhood deli. Survey an astounding array of edible things to put between two halves of a fresh roll, made to order for 4.50-16SFr (☎/fax 623 33 78; open M-W and F 8:30am-6:30pm, Th 8:30am-9pm, Sa 11am-5pm, Su 1:30-5:30pm). Stock up on foodstuffs at the **Manora** grocery store/self-service restaurant at Gurzelng. 18 to the left off Marktpl. (open M-W and F 9am-6:30pm, Th 9am-9pm, Sa 8am-5pm), or try the **farmer's market** at Marktpl. (W and Sa 8am-noon). There is an Aperto at the train station (open M-Sa 6am-10pm, Su 7am-10pm). **Co-op** and **Migros** are outside old city walls behind the post office (both open M-W and F 8am-6:30pm, Th 8am-9pm, Sa 7:30am-5pm).

SIGHTS. Solothurn's well-preserved Baroque architecture is enough to justify a visit to the city. The **Red Tower** on the Marktpl. sports several clock faces and a macabre little skeleton. Built in 1762-73 by a Ticino architect, the cheerful Italianate architecture of the **Kathedrale St. Ursen** greets visitors with bubbling fountains as they cross the Kreuzackerbrücke. The cathedral, frothily adorned with golden sunbursts, is dedicated to St. Ursus, the patron saint of Solothurn, who lost his head here during Roman times for refusing to worship Roman gods. Its **tower** provides the *Altstadt's* best view. (☎622 3753. Church open 8am-noon and 2-7pm. Oct.-Easter closes at 6pm. Tower 2.50SFr.)

For anyone who played with little toy soldiers, the **Museum Altes Zeughaus** blows them up to their full size. Housed in a 1609 arsenal, the museum holds row after row of gory instruments of death, from medieval daggers to WWII artillery. (Zeughauspl. 1, to the left of the cathedral. ☎623 3528. Open May-Oct. Tu-Su 10am-noon and 2-5pm; Nov.-Apr. Tu-F 2-5pm, Sa-Su 10am-noon and 2-5pm. 6SFr, students 4SFr.) On the fringes of town, the staid **Kunstmuseum** has an extensive collection of post-1850 Swiss works. The temporary exhibits (recently, elegantly stoic Indonesian statues) tend to be more stimulating than the permanent collection. (Werkhofstr. 30. ☎622 2307. Open Tu-F 10am-noon and 2-5pm, Sa-Su 10am-5pm. Free, but it is worth a donation to see the Jean Tinguely collection box in action.)

Schloß Waldegg, the local castle, is surrounded by wheat fields and tree-lined walks that contrast nicely with its ruler-perfect formal French gardens. The panorama of the Jura mountains outside the castle is more enjoyable than the museum inside, which can't decide whether to preserve the neoclassical decor from, or share it with visitors. (Take bus #4 to "St. Niklaus" and walk 10min. up Riedholzstr. Open Apr.-Oct. Tu-Th, Sa 2-5pm, Su 10am-noon and 2-5pm; Nov.-Mar. Sa-Su 10am-noon and 2-5pm. Wheelchair accessible. Parking available. 6SFr, students 4SFr.)

OUTDOOR ACTIVITIES. The Jura mountains over Solothurn encourage fans of Mother Nature to get up close and personal. Marked **hiking** and **biking** trails lead through the Jura to nearby Altreu (2hr.), where the oldest and best-known stork colony in Switzerland rests and poops. The trek to the **Weissenstein Alpine Center** is more challenging and rewarding. (2hr. Trail head at the corner of Wengisteinstr. and Verenawegstr.; follow the yellow signs to Weissenstein.) Take the chairlift (13SFr, students 6.50SFr) down from Weissenstein and hop on a train (4.40SFr) in Oberdorf to return. **Boat tours** leave Solothurn for Biel and from there to Murten or Neuchâtel. (2½hr., 26SFr, round-trip 45SFr. SwissPass valid. Ferries run early May to mid-Oct.) In the winter, **cross-country skiing** dominates the athletic scene. Weissenstein (1280m) has 7km of trails and chairlifts for downhill skiing on 2 small slopes best suited to beginners.

ENTERTAINMENT AND NIGHTLIFE. Various **festivals** enliven Solothurn. In 2001, the **Swiss Film Festival** will bring celluloid lovers to the city January 23-28. The **Chesslete** (Feb. 22-28, 2001)—festivities intended to drive away winter—is a week-long topsy-turvy carnival. The festivities include fantastical masks, raucous *Guggenmusik*, and re-naming the town "Honolulu." Swiss writers gather to read, drink, and sit on panels during the annual **literature festival** (May 25-27 in 2001). Solothurn fans of classical music and opera enjoy the **Classic: Open Air Fest** in July (www.classic-openair.ch). The city's other big event is the **Jazz am Märetplatz** festival, August 23-25, 2001. Concerts fill the Marktpl. for those three days, attracting jazz aficionados from far and wide.

Nightlife in Solothurn does not exist outside of the Thursday-Saturday window. Hipsters find each other on weekends for live rock and funk at the **Creep Club,** Dammstr. 59 (☎621 2060; creep@solnet.ch, www.solnet.ch/creep). Continue down the river past the post office and turn right on Dammstr. For dance music there's **Kofmehl Fabrik,** Gibelinstr. (☎623 5060, info-line ☎621 2062, info@kofmehl.net), on the outskirts of town. From Creep Club, go to the end of Dammstr., turn left on Segelzstr., and right on Gibelinstr. Amidst fields and cows, this former metal factory is decked out in trippy graffiti and holds occasional movie nights. If you hit Solothurn in the middle of summer, check out **Yellow Movie Nights,** an open-air cinema, screening mostly American new releases for 2 weeks, late July to early Aug. (Information ☎0848 333 123, or at www.helloyellow.ch).

MUNICH (MÜNCHEN)

The capital and cultural center of Bavaria, Munich is a sprawling, relatively liberal metropolis in the midst of solidly conservative southern Germany. Munich's sensual merriment is most obvious during the wild *Fasching* (Jan. 7-Feb. 27, 2001) and the legendary *Oktoberfest* (Sept. 22-Oct. 7, 2001). Since the Bavarian Golden Age of the 18th and 19th centuries and the devastation of WWII (when less than 3% of the city was left intact), Munich has proved resilient, and today basks in Western German postwar economic glory. World-class museums, handsome parks and architecture, and a rambunctious arts scene create a city of astonishing vitality.

PHONE CODES	The city code for Munich is 089. If calling Austria or Switzerland dial 01149 to get out of Germany; then dial 43 (Austria) or 41 (Switzerland) before dialing the number.

GETTING THERE AND AROUND

Flights: Flughafen München (☎975 2131 3). S-Bahn #8 connects the airport to the Hauptbahnhof every 20min. DM15.20 or 8 strips on the *Streifenkarte*. A **Lufthansa shuttle bus** runs the same route with a pickup at the Nordfriedhof U-Bahn stop in Schwabing. Buses leave from Arnulfstr., on the northern side of the train station, every 20min. 6:50am-7:50pm, and return from Terminal A *(Zentralbereich)* and Terminal D every 20min. 7:55am-8:55pm. DM16, round-trip DM26.

Trains: The **Hauptbahnhof** (☎223 3125 6, info ☎ (0180) 599 6633). To: **Innsbruck** (2hr., every hr., DM48, DM37); **Salzburg** (1¾hr., every hr., DM41, DM30); **Vienna** (5hr., every hr., DM106, DM82); **Zürich** (5hr., every 2 hr., DM110, DM85); **Berlin** (7½hr., 2 per hr., DM277, youth DM222); Station open 6am-10:30pm.

Public Transportation: MVV runs Su-Th 5am-12:30am, F-Sa 5am-2am. Eurail, InterRail, and DeutscheBahn passes valid on the S-Bahn only. Buy tickets at blue *MVV-Fahrausweise* machines and validate them in the "E" boxes before entering the platform. Transit maps are at the tourist office, EurAide, and MVV counters in the train station. A *Streifenkarte* (11-strip ticket) costs DM16 and can be used by more than 1 person. **Single ride** DM3.80 or 2 strips; **Kurzstrecke** (short trip) tickets DM1.90 or 1 strip, valid for 2 stops on the U- or S-Bahn, or 4 stops on a streetcar or bus. **Single-Tageskarte** (single-day ticket) DM9, valid for 1 day. **Partner-Tageskarte** (DM14) can be used by 2 adults, 4 children under 18, and a dog.

Taxis: Taxi-Zentrale (☎21611 or 19410) in front of the station and throughout the city.

Car Rental: Swing, Schellingstr. 139 (☎523 2005), rents from DM45 per day. **Avis** (☎550 1212), **Europcar/National** (☎550 1341), **Hertz** (☎550 2256), and **Sixt Budget** (☎550 2447) have offices upstairs in the station. Prices from DM130 per day.

Bike Rental: Radius Bikes (☎596 113), in the Hauptbahnhof, behind the lockers opposite tracks #30-31. From DM5 per hr., DM25 per day, DM75 per week. Deposit DM100, passport, or credit card. Students and Eurail holders receive a 10% discount. Open daily May to mid-Oct. 10am-6pm.

Hitchhiking: *Let's Go* does not recommend hitchhiking. For ride-sharing check the bulletin boards in the **Mensa,** Leopoldstr. 13. Hitchers have been known to try *Autobahn* on-ramps; standing behind the blue sign with the white auto incurs a fine. To: **Salzburg,** take U1 or 2 to "Karl-Preis-Platz"; **Bodensee** and **Switzerland,** take U4 or 5 to "Heimeranpl.," then bus #33 to "Siegenburger Str."

ORIENTATION

Munich's center is encircled by the main **Ring** and quartered by two thoroughfares which cross at the **Marienplatz** and meet the traffic rings at **Karlsplatz** (a.k.a.

Stachus) in the west, **Isartorplatz** in the east, **Odeonsplatz** in the north, and **Sendlinger Tor** in the south. The **Hauptbahnhof** is west of Karlspl. East of the Isartor, the **Isar** flows south-north by the city center. To get to Marienpl. from the station, go straight on Bayerstr. to Karlspl. and continue through Karlstor to Neuhauser Str., which becomes Kaufingerstr. before it reaches Marienpl. Or, take S1-8 (two stops from the Hauptbahnhof, dir.: Ostbahnhof) to Marienpl.

PRACTICAL INFORMATION

Tourist Offices: EurAide in English (☎593 889; www.euraide.de), along track #11 (room 3) of the Hauptbahnhof. Open June-Oktoberfest daily 7:45am-noon and 1-6pm; Oct.-Apr. M-F 8am-noon and 1-4pm, Sa 8am-noon; May daily 7:45am-noon and 1-4:30pm. **Fremdenverkehrsamt** (☎233 3025 7; www.munich-tourist.de), in front of the train station is much more busy. Books rooms for free with 10-15% deposit. Purchase the **München Welcome Card** here (see **Public Transportation,** above).

Budget Travel: Council Travel, Adalbertstr. 32 (☎388 3897 0), near the university. Open M-F 10am-1pm and 2-6:30pm, Sa 10am-3pm. **DER Reisebüro** (☎551 4020 0; www.der.de) in the Hauptbahnhof. Open M-F 9:30am-6pm and Sa 10am-1pm.

Currency Exchange: ReiseBank (☎551 0837) has a branch in front of the main entrance to the train station on Bahnhofpl. (open daily 6am-11pm), and another around the corner from EurAide at track #11 (open M-Sa 7:30am-7:15pm, Su 9:30am-12:30pm and 1-4:45pm). Western Union services available.

American Express: Promenadepl. 6 (☎290 900; 24hr. ☎ (0130) 853 100), in Hotel Bayerischer Hof. Open M-F 9am-5:30pm, Sa 9:30am-12:30pm. **Branch** at Kaufingerstr. 24 (☎228 0138 7), by the Frauenkirche. Open M-F 9am-6pm, Sa 10am-2pm.

Internet Access: Times Square Internet Café, Bayerstr. 10a, on the south side of the train station. DM4.50 per 15min. **Internet-Café,** Nymphenburger Str. 145, on the corner of Landshuter Allee. U1 to "Rotkreuzplatz." Free with pasta (DM5.30-7.50) or pizza (DM5.50-8.50); otherwise, DM5 per 30min. Open daily 11am-4am.

Bookstores: Anglia English Bookshop, Schellingstr. 3 (☎ 283 642), offers reams of English-language books in a gloriously chaotic atmosphere. U-Bahn #3 or 6 to "Universität." Open M-F 9am-6:30pm, Sa 10am-2pm.

Post Office: Across from the Hauptbahnhof on Bahnhofpl. Open M-F 7am-8pm, Sa 8am-4pm, Su 9am-3pm. Address mail to be held: *Postlagernde Briefe* für Kathryn SCHULTZ, Hauptpostamt, München **80335,** Germany.

Luggage Storage: At the **train station** (*Gepäckaufbewahrung*). Open M-F 6:30am-11pm, Sa-Su 7:30am-10pm. DM4 per piece per day. Lockers in the main hall and opposite tracks #16, 24, and 28-36. DM2-4 per 24hr.

Bisexual, Gay and Lesbian Resources: Gay services information (☎260 3056). **Lesbian information** and the **LeTra Lesbentraum,** Angertorstr. 3 (☎725 4272). Phones staffed M and W 2:30-5pm; Tu 10:30am-1pm; Th 7-9pm.

Ticket Agencies: To order **tickets by phone** call **München Ticket** (☎548 1818 1).

Laundromat: City SB-Waschcenter, Paul-Heyse-Str. 21. From the station, turn right on Bayerstr., then left on Paul-Heyse-Str. Wash DM6, dry DM1 per 10min. Open daily 7am-11pm. **Münz Waschsalon,** Amalienstr. 61, near the university. Wash DM6.20, soap DM1, dry DM1 per 10min. Open M-F 8am-6:30pm, Sa 8am-1pm.

Emergency: Police, ☎110. **Ambulance** and **Fire,** ☎112. **Medical,** ☎594 475.

Pharmacy: Bahnhof-Apotheke, Bahnhofpl. 2 (☎594 119), outside the train station. Open M-F 8am-6:30pm, Sa 8am-2pm. Call 594 475 for 24hr. service (in German).

Medical Assistance: Klinikum Rechts der Isar, across the river on Ismaninger Str. U4 or 5 to "Max-Weber-Platz." UK and US consulates carry lists of English-speaking doctors.

ACCOMMODATIONS AND CAMPING

Munich accommodations are usually seedy, expensive, or booked solid; during Oktoberfest, only the last category exists. In summer, call before noon or book a few weeks ahead. If planning an extended stay, try bargaining with a *Pension* owner. Remember: **Bavarian HI hostels do not accept guests over age 26.** Don't even think of sleeping in public areas, including the Hauptbahnhof; police patrol frequently all night long.

Euro Youth Hotel, Senefelderstr. 5 (☎599 0881 1; www.euro-youth-hotel.de). From the Bahnhofspl. exit of the Hauptbahnhof, make a right on Bayerstr. and a left on Senefelderstr. Offers a friendly and well-informed English-speaking staff loaded with brochures. 24hr. reception. No curfew or lockout. Breakfast buffet DM7.90. Laundry DM6. Dorms DM29; doubles DM42, with shower, telephone, and breakfast DM60; triples and quads DM36. Also inquire about their new location on S6, with close to 1000 beds and shuttle service to and from the airport, scheduled to open April 2001.

Jugendlager Kapuzinerhölzl ("The Tent"), In den Kirschen 30 (☎141 4300; www.the-tent.de). Streetcar #17 from the Hauptbahnhof (dir.: Amalienburgstr.) to "Botanischer Garten"; go straight on Franz-Schrank-Str. and left at In den Kirschen. Sleep under a big circus tent on a wooden floor. Laundry DM4. Internet DM2 per 15min. Free city tours (W 9am). Passport required as deposit. Open mid-June to Aug. DM15 for foam pad, blankets, bathrooms, shower (not necessarily warm), breakfast, and enthusiastic management; beds DM19. **Camping** DM8 per person; DM8 per site.

Jugendherberge Pullach Burg Schwaneck (HI), Burgweg 4-6 (☎793 0643), in a castle 12km outside the city center. S7 (dir.: Wolfratshausen) to "Pullach." Exit the station on the Munich side and walk toward the soccer field down Margarethenstr.; follow signs (8min.). Clean rooms with green furniture are quiet and well-kept. Breakfast included. Dinner DM8. Reception 4-11pm. Curfew 11:30pm. Dorms DM23; singles DM37.50; doubles DM35.50 per person; quads DM26 per person.

Jugendherberge München (HI), Wendl-Dietrich-Str. 20 (☎131 156; jhmuenchen@djh-bayern.de). U1 (dir.: Westfriedhof) to "Rotkreuzpl." Go down Wendl-Dietrich-Str. to the left of the *Schwestern Schule* building; the entrance is on the right. The most "central" HI hostel, 3km from the city. Safes available. Breakfast and sheets included. Bike rental DM24. Mandatory DM20 key deposit. Reception 24hr. Check-in after 11am, but lines form before 9am. Reservations only accepted a week in advance; if you get one, arrive by 6pm or call ahead. Men-only dorm DM25; coed dorms DM30.

4 you münchen, Hirtenstr. 18 (☎552 1660; www.the4you.de), near the Hauptbahnhof. Exit at Arnulfstr., go left, right onto Pfefferstr., then left on Hirtenstr. Ecological youth hostel. Breakfast buffet DM8. Sheets DM5. Key deposit DM20. Dorms DM26-32; singles DM56; doubles DM40. Over 27 15% surcharge. In adjoining hotel, singles with bath DM79; doubles with bath DM129; extra bed DM49.

Jugendgästehaus Thalkirchen (HI), Miesingstr. 4 (☎723 6550). U1 or 2 to "Sendlinger Tor," then U3 (dir.: Fürstenrieder West) to "Thalkirchen." Take the Thalkirchnerpl. exit and follow Schäftlarnstr. toward Innsbruck and bear right, then go down Frauenbergstr. and left on Münchner Str. Breakfast and sheets included. Laundry DM10. Reception 7am-1am. Check-in 2-6pm. Curfew 1am. Dorms DM37.50; singles DM42.50.

CVJM Jugendgästehaus, Landwehrstr. 13 (☎552 1410; fax 550 4282; info@cvjm-muenchen.org). Take the Bayerstr. exit from the train station, head down Goethestr. or Schillerstr. and take the 2nd left onto Landwehrstr. Breakfast included. Reception 8am-12:30am. Curfew 12:30am-7am. Reservations can be made a year ahead. Closed during Easter and Dec. 20-Jan. 7. Singles DM53; doubles DM90; triples DM126. Rates lower Dec.-Feb., higher during Oktoberfest. Over 26 16% surcharge.

Hotel Helvetia, Schillerstr. 6 (☎590 6850; hotel-helvetia@t-online.de), next to Vereinsbank, to the right of the station. Friendliest hotel in Munich. Beautiful, newly-renovated rooms with oriental rugs, most with phones. Breakfast included. Singles DM55-65; doubles DM72-95, with shower DM99-115; triples DM105-126.

Hotel Kurpfalz, Schwanthaler Str. 121 (☎540 98 60; www.munich-hotels.com). Exit the station on Bayerstr., turn right and walk 5-6 blocks down Bayerstr., veer left onto Holzapfelstr., and make a right onto Schwanthaler Str. (10min.). Or, take streetcar #18 or 19 to "Holzapfelstr." Free email; Internet surfing DM5 per 30min. Singles from DM89; doubles from DM109; triples (doubles with cots) DM165.

Hotel-Pension Utzelmann, Pettenkoferstr. 6 (☎594 889). From the station, walk 4 blocks down Schillerstr. and go left on Pettenkofer. Nostalgic, elegant rooms with upholstered furniture and oriental rugs. Breakfast included. Reception 7am-10pm. Singles DM55, with shower DM95, with bath DM130; doubles DM98, DM115, DM150; triples DM140, DM160, DM180; quads DM170, with shower DM190.

Pension Locarno, Bahnhofspl. 5 (☎555 164; www.deutschland-hotel.de/muc/locarno.htm). From the station's main entrance walk left across Bahnhofspl. and look for the "Pension" sign. Plain, newly furnished and carpeted rooms, all with TV and phone. Reception Su-M 7:30am-midnight, Tu-Sa 7:30am-5am. Singles DM55-75; doubles DM85; triples DM125; quads DM140.

Pension Hungaria, Briennerstr. 42 (☎521 558). From the train station, go left onto Dachauer Str., right on Augustenstr., and across and to the right on Briennerstr.; it's the 2nd building to your left (10min.). Or U1 to "Stiglmaierpl."; take the Briennerstr./Volkstheater exit, and it's on the next corner at Augustenstr. Oriental rugs, comfortable furnishings, and a small travel library adorn this cozy pension. Breakfast included. Showers DM3. 24hr. reception 2 floors up. Singles DM60-65; doubles DM85-90; triples DM110; quads DM130. Oktoberfest surcharge DM10 per room.

Pension Schillerhof, Schillerstr. 21 (☎594 270; www.hotel-schillerhof.de). Exit onto Bahnhofpl. from the station, turn right, and walk 2 blocks down Schillerstr. Breakfast included. Reception 6am-10pm. Reservations can be made online. Singles DM60-80; doubles DM90-120; extra bed DM20. Oktoberfest surcharge DM25-40 per person.

Pension Central, Bayerstr. 55 (☎543 9846). Go right out the Bayerstr. exit of the station. Although the exterior may not please the eyes, you can't judge a book by its cover. Reception 24hr. Singles DM65, with bath DM75; doubles DM95, DM110-120; triples DM120; quads DM160-180; quints DM200-220.

Pension Frank, Schellingstr. 24 (☎281 451; www.pension-frank.de). U3 or 6 to "Universität." Take the Schellingstr. exit, then the first right onto Schellingstr. Fabulous location for cafe and bookstore aficionados. Breakfast included. Reception 7:30am-10pm. Check-out 11am. Dorms DM40; singles DM55-65; doubles DM95.

Pension am Kaiserplatz, Kaiserpl. 12 (☎349 190). Near tons of nightlife–good location if you doubt your sense of direction after a couple of beers. U3 or 6 to "Münchener Freiheit." Take the escalator to Herzogstr., then go left 3 blocks to Viktoriastr. Take a left at Viktoriastr.; it's at the end of the street on the right (10min.). Breakfast included. Reception 7am-9pm. Dorms DM40; singles DM59; doubles DM89, with shower DM99-105; each additional person DM40.

Pension Geiger, Steinheilstr. 1 (☎521 556). U2 to "Theresienstr." Exit on Augustenstr. S.O. and walk down Theresienstr. toward Kopierladen München. Take a right on Enhuberstr. and a left on Steinheilstr.; enter through the double doors on the right. Family-run in a quiet neighborhood. Showers DM2. Reception (2 floors up) 8am-9pm. Arrive by 6pm or call. Closed Dec. 24-Jan. 31. Singles DM55-DM80; doubles DM98-DM108.

Campingplatz Thalkirchen, Zentralländstr. 49 (☎723 1707). U1 or 2 to "Sendlinger Tor," then #3 to "Thalkirchen," and change to bus #57 (20min.). From the bus stop, cross the street on the left and take a right onto the footpath next to the road. Well-run, crowded grounds with jogging and bike paths. Jogging and bike paths. Showers DM2. Laundry. Curfew 11pm. Open mid-Mar. to late Oct. DM8.40 per person, DM2.50 per child under 14; DM5.50-7 per tent; DM8.50 per car.

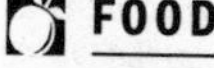

FOOD

The **Viktualienmarkt,** south of Marienpl., is Munich's gastronomic center. (Open M-F 10am-8pm, Sa 8am-4pm.) To sink your fangs into an authentic Bavarian lunch, grab a *Brez'n* (pretzel) and spread it with *Leberwurst* or cheese (DM5-6). The university district off **Ludwigstraße** is unpretentiously hip. Many reasonably-priced restaurants and cafes cluster on **Schellingstr., Amalienstr.,** and **Türkenstr.** Ride U3 or

6 to "Universität." *Munich Found* (DM4) and *Prinz* (DM5) list restaurants, cafes, and bars. Fruit and vegetable **markets** are held throughout the city, many on Bayerstr. **Plus supermarket,** Schellingstr. 38 (open M-F 8:30am-7pm, Sa 8am-3pm) and **A&P Tengelmann,** in the Karlspl. subway station, meet **grocery** needs. From the Hauptbahnhof, walk east on Bayerstr., make a right onto Sonnenstr., and enter the U-Bahn after Schlosserstr. (Open M-F 8:30am-8pm, Sa 8am-4pm.)

Marché, Neuhauser Str., between Karlspl. and Marienpl. The top floor of this monstrous eatery offers cafeteria-style, make-your-own-meal displays. Great vegetarian selections. You'll get a stamp for each item you take; pay on the way out. And, by the way, don't lost that card! If you do, you'll either pay DM100 or spend the day washing dishes. Top floor open 11am-10pm, bottom floor open 8am-11pm.

Weißes Bräuhaus, Tal 7, across from McDonalds at the end of Marienpl. Brimming with traditional Bavarian dishes (DM8.90-25). Open daily 7:30am-midnight.

News Bar, Amalienstr. 55, at the corner of Schellingstr. Trendy cafe serving large portions at reasonable prices. Crepes DM12-14. Open daily 7:30am-2am.

Beim Sedlmayr, Westenriederstr. 14, off the Viktualienmarkt. Anyone craving *Weißwurst* (DM7) will love this slice of Bavaria. Specials DM7-27. Beer DM5.70 for 0.5L. Open daily 9am-10pm. Kitchen open M-F 11am-9pm, Sa 8am-4pm.

Gollier, Gollierstr. 83. U4 or 5 or S7 or 27 to "Heimeranpl.," then walk 2 blocks north on Garmischer Str. and turn left on Gollierstr. Delicious vegetarian fare (DM6-19). Open M-F noon-3pm and 5pm-midnight, Sa 5pm-midnight, Su 10am-midnight.

SIGHTS AND MUSEUMS

MARIENPLATZ AND ENVIRONS. Marienplatz is the social nexus of Munich, marked by a number of monuments. An ornate 17th-century column dedicated to the Virgin Mary, the **Mariensäule** commemorates the fact that the Swedes did not destroy the city during the Thirty Years War. At the neo-Gothic **Neues Rathaus,** the **Glockenspiel** chimes with a display of jousting knights and dancing coopers. *(Daily 11am, noon, and 5pm.)* At bedtime (9pm), a mechanical watchman marches out and the Guardian Angel escorts the *Münchner Kindl* (Munich Child, the town's symbol) to bed. *(Tower open M-F 9am-7pm, Sa-Su 10am-7pm. DM3, under 18 DM1.50.)* The **Altes Rathaus** tower, to the right of the Neues Rathaus, displays all of Munich's coats of arms since its inception as a city, except the swastika-bearing one from the Nazi era. One block toward the Hauptbahnhof on Kaufingerstr., the onion-domed towers of the 15th-century **Frauenkirche** are among Munich's most notable landmarks. *(Open Apr.-Oct. M-Sa 10am-5pm. DM4, students DM2.)*

SOUTH OF MARIENPLATZ. The golden interior of the 11th-century **Peterskirche,** just south of Marienpl., was Baroquified in the 18th century. Over 300 steps scale the tower, dubbed "*Alter Peter*" by locals. *(Rindermarkt and Peterspl. Open M-Sa 9am-5pm, Su 10am-7pm. DM2.50, students DM1.50.)* Mad King Ludwig (of castle fame) rests with 40-odd other Wittelsbachs in the crypt of the 16th-century Jesuit **Michaelskirche.** *(On Neuhauser Str. Crypt open M-F 9:30am-4:30pm, Sa 9:30am-2:30pm. DM2, students and under 16 DM1.)* Farther south along Sendlinger Str. lies the Rococo **Asamkirche,** named after the Asam brothers, who promised God to build the church if they survived a shipwreck. *(Sendlinger Str. 32. Tours June-Sept. Sa at noon. DM5.)*

RESIDENZ. Down the pedestrian zone from Odeonspl., the richly decorated **Residenz** (Palace) forms the material vestiges of the Wittelsbach dynasty. The grounds now house several museums, a beautifully landscaped **Hofgarten,** and a bejeweled **Schatzkammer,** or treasury. *(Open Apr. to mid-Oct. M-W and F-Su 9am-6pm, Th 9am-8pm; late Oct. to Mar. daily 10am-4pm. Last admission 1 hr. before closing. DM8; students, seniors, and groups DM6, children under 15 free with adult.)* The **Residenzmuseum** comprises the former Wittelsbach apartments and State Rooms, a collection of European porcelain, and a 17th-century court chapel. German tours of the Residenzmuseum meet just outside the museum entrance. The walls of the **Ahnengalerie,** hung with 120 "family portraits," trace the royal lineage in an unusual manner. *(Max-Joseph-Platz 3.*

U3-6 to Odeonspl. Same hours as Schatzkammer. DM8, students and children DM6. Residenzmuseum tours Su and W 11am, Tu and Sa 2pm. DM8, Su DM10. Combination ticket to Schatzkammer and Residenzmuseum DM14, students and seniors DM11.)

SCHLOSS NYMPHENBURG. After 10 years of trying for an heir, Ludwig I celebrated the birth of his son Maximilian in 1662 by erecting an elaborate summer playground. Check out the "Gallery of Beauties"—whenever a woman caught Ludwig's fancy, he would have her portrait painted. A few lakes and four manors also inhabit the palace grounds. *(Streetcar #17, dir.: Amalienburgstr. Palace open Apr. to mid-Oct. M-W and F-Su 9am-6pm, Th 9am-8pm; late Oct. to Mar. daily 10am-4pm. Schloß DM7, students DM5; entire complex DM15, students DM12. Grounds open until 9:30pm. Free.)*

ENGLISCHER GARTEN. On sunny days, all of Munich flocks here to bike, fly kites, play badminton, or ride horseback. The grounds contain a Japanese tea house, Chinese pagoda, and Greek temple, as well as nude sunbathing areas, marked "FKK" on signs and maps. Nudity + lots of *Bratwurst* and *Bier* = consider yourself warned. Head to the bridge on Prinzregentenstr., near the Staatsgalerie Moderner Kunst, to watch Müncheners surf the rapids of the artificial Eisbach river.

MUSEUMS. Munich is a supreme museum city, and many of the city's offerings would require days for exhaustive perusal. A day pass (DM30) to all of Munich's museums is sold at the tourist office and at many larger museums.

Deutsches Museum, Museumsinsel 1. S1-8: Isartor, or streetcar #18 to "Deutsches Museum." One of the world's best science and technology museums. Fascinating exhibits include the work bench upon which Otto Hahn split his first atom, and labyrinthine mining tunnels. Open daily 9am-5pm. DM12, students DM5.

Alte Pinakothek, Barerstr. 27. Commissioned by King Ludwig I, the last of the passionate Wittelsbacher art collectors, this world-renowned hall houses Munich's most precious collection–including works by Titian, da Vinci, Raphael, Dürer, Rembrandt, and Rubens. Open Tu and W-Su 10am-5pm, Th 10am-8pm. DM7, students DM4; combination ticket for the Alte and the Neue Pinakothek DM12, students DM6.

Glyptothek, Königspl. 3. Features 2400-year-old pediment figures from the Temple of Aphaea as well as Etruscan and Roman sculptures. Open Tu-W and F-Su 10am-5pm, Th 10am-8pm. DM6, students DM3.50. Tours Th at 6pm; free. Combination ticket for the Glyptothek and the Antikensammlung DM10, students DM5.

Neue Pinakothek, Barerstr. 29, next to the Alte Pinakothek. Sleek space for 18th- to 20th-century works by van Gogh, Klimt, Cézanne, and Manet. Open W and F-M 10am-5pm, Th 10am-8pm. Same prices as Alte Pinakothek.

BMW Museum, Petuelring 130. U3 to "Olympiazentrum." The ultimate driving museum features a fetching display of past, present, and future products of Bavaria's second-favorite export. Open daily 9am-5pm. Last entry 4pm. DM5.50, students DM4.

ZAM: Zentrum für Aussergewöhnliche Museen, (Center for Unusual Museums), Westenriederstr. 41. S1-8: Isartor, or streetcar #17 or 18. Holds such treasures as the Padlock Museum, the Museum of Easter Rabbits, and the Chamberpot Museum. Open daily 10am-6pm. DM8, students and children DM5.

ENTERTAINMENT AND NIGHTLIFE

Munich's cultural cachet rivals the world's best. Theater offerings range from dramatic classics at the **Residenztheater** and **Volkstheater** to comic opera at the **Staattheater am Gärtnerplatz** to experimental works at the **Theater im Marstall** in Nymphenburg (standing tickets around DM10). Scores of small fringe theaters, cabaret stages, art cinemas, and artsy pubs cluster in **Schwabing.** Munich's July **opera festival** is held in the **Bayerische Staatsoper,** Maximilianstr. 11 (☎21 85 19 30 or ☎21 85 19 19); take U3-6 to "Odeonspl." or streetcar #19 to "Nationaltheater." Standing and student tickets (DM7-20) to the numerous operas and ballets are sold at Maximilianstr. 11 (☎26 46 20), behind the opera house, or 1 hour before performances at the side entrance on Maximilianstr. (Box office open M-F 10am-6pm, Sa 10am-1pm. No performances Aug. to mid-Sept.) The opera festival is accompanied by a concert series in the Nymphenburg and Schleißheim palaces. The *Monatsprogramm* (DM2.50) lists schedules for all of Munich's stages, museums, and festivals.

Munich throws together Bavarian *Gemütlichkeit* and trendy cliquishness, the latter represented by *Schicki-Mickis*—club-going, coiffed and scented specimens of both sexes. A nighttime odyssey begins at one of Munich's beer gardens or beer halls; the alcohol keeps flowing at cafes and bars, which, except for Friday and Saturday nights, shut off their taps at 1am. Then the discos and dance clubs, sedate before midnight, suddenly spark and throb relentlessly until 4am. The trendy bars, cafes, cabarets, and discos plugged into **Leopoldstr.** in **Schwabing** attract tourists from all over Europe. **Münchener Freiheit** is the most famous (and most touristy) bar/cafe district. Pick up *Munich Found*, *in München*, or *Prinz* at any newsstand to find out what's up. Munich's homosexual scene centers in the **"Golden Triangle"** stretching from south of the Sendlinger Tor through the Viktualienmarkt/Gärtnerpl. to the Isartor. Pick up *Rosa Seiten* at **Max&Milian Bookstore,** Ickstattstr. 2 (open M-F 10:30am-2pm and 3:30-8pm, Sa 11am-4pm), or at any other gay locale for listings of gay nightlife and services.

Kunstpark Ost, Grafinger Str. 6. U5 or S1-8 to "Ostbahnhof"; follow signs for the "Kunstpark Ost" exit, turn right onto Friedenstr. and then left onto Grafinger Str. This huge complex with 40 different venues swarms with young people dancing the night away. Try the psychedelic-trance **Natraj Temple** (open F-Sa), the alternative cocktail and disco joint **K41** (open nightly), the very chill cigars and drinks mecca **Cohibar** (open W-Sa), or the risqué South American rock bar **Titty Twister** (open W-Sa).

Nachtwerk and Club, Landesberger Str. 185. Streetcar #18 or 19 or bus #83 to "Lautensackstr." The older, larger **Nachtwerk** spins mainstream dance tunes in a packed warehouse. Its little sister **Club** offers rock, trip-hop, house, acid jazz, and rare grooves. Cover for both DM10. Open daily 10pm-4am.

Master's Home, Frauenstr. 11. U3 or 6 or S1-8 to Marienpl. A tremendous stuffed peacock greets visitors to the subterranean bar and *faux* private home. Mixed drinks DM11.50. Open daily 6:30pm-3am.

BEER, BEER, AND MORE BEER

To most visitors, Munich means beer. There are four main types of beer served in Munich: **Helles** and **Dunkles,** delicious light and dark beers; **Weißbier,** a cloudy blond wheat beer; and **Radler** ("cyclist's brew"), half beer and half lemon soda. The six great Munich labels are *Augustiner*, *Hacker-Pschorr*, *Hofbräu*, *Löwenbräu*, *Paulaner*, and *Spaten-Franziskaner;* most restaurants will serve only one. Munich's beer typically has a 3.5% alcohol content. The longest beer festival in the world is Munich's **Oktoberfest** (Sept. 22-Oct. 7, 2001), at **Theresienwiese** (U4 or 5).

Hirschgarten, Hirschgarten 1. U1 to "Rotkreuzpl.," then streetcar #12 to "Romanpl." The largest beer garden in Europe (seating 9000) is boisterous and pleasant, but somewhat remote. *Maß* DM9.30. Open daily 9am-midnight; kitchen open until 10pm.

Augustinerkeller, Arnulfstr. 52, at Zirkus-Krone-Str. S1-8 to "Hackerbrücke." Founded in 1824, Augustiner is viewed by most Müncheners as the finest beer garden in town. *Maß* DM10.50. Open daily 10:30am-midnight or 1am.

Hofbräuhaus, Am Platzl 9, 2 blocks from Marienpl. In 1589, Bavarian Duke Wilhelm the Pious founded the Hofbräuhaus for the worship of Germany's most revered beverages. Many tables are reserved for locals, and a good number of *Müncheners* keep their personal steins in the beer hall's safe. To avoid tourists, go in the early afternoon. 15,000-30,000L of beer are sold per day. *Maß* DM11.40. Open daily 9am-midnight.

Am Seehaus, Kleinhesselohe 3. U6 to "Dietlindenstr.," then bus #44 (dir.: Giesing) to "Osterwaldstr." On the Kleinhesseloher See in the Englischer Garten. Beloved by locals for the lack of tourists. *Maß* (DM11). Open M-F 11am-midnight, Sa-Su 10am-midnight. Beer garden closes at 11pm.

APPENDIX

CLIMATE

AVG TEMP	JANUARY		APRIL		JULY		OCTOBER	
	°C	°F	°C	°F	°C	°F	°C	°F
Geneva	0	32	9.5	49	19.5	67	10	50
Interlaken	0	32	10	50	19.5	67	11	51
Zurich	-1	30	8	47	18	64	8	47
Innsbruck	-2.5	28	9.5	49	18	64	9.5	49
Salzburg	-1.5	29	8	47	18	64	9	48
Vienna	-1	30	10	50	20	68	11	51
Munich	.5	33	9	48	19	66	11	51

Although Austria and Switzerland are on about the same latitude as Newfoundland, their climates are considerably milder than one might expect. In general, winters are cold and snowy enough for skiing, while summers are warm enough for outdoor cafés. July is usually the hottest month and February the coldest, with temperatures down to -10°C (5°F). Summer temperatures can reach 38°C (100°F) for brief periods, although summer evenings are usually cool. Mountainous areas of Austria and Switzerland are, understandably, cooler and wetter the higher you get; as a rule, temperatures decrease about 1.7°C (3°F) with each additional 300m elevation. Snow cover lasts from late December to March in the valleys, from November to May at about 1800m, and stays year-round above 2500m. There are occasional summer snowfalls in many mountainous towns. Switzerland's lake areas, in the temperate swath of plain that extends across from Lake Constance in the northeast through Zurich and Bern down to Geneva, are very wet all year–don't forget your umbrella. For up-to-date weather and temperature information on a particular city, check www.weatherlabs.com.

TIME ZONES

Switzerland and Austria both use Central European time (abbreviated MEZ in German), which is 6 hours later than Eastern Standard Time and 1 hour later than Greenwich Mean Time. It is 9 hours earlier than Eastern Australia Time and 11 hours earlier than New Zealand Time. Austria and Switzerland use the 24-hour clock for all official purposes, so 19:30pm is the same as 7.30.

HOLIDAYS AND FESTIVALS

The *International Herald-Tribune* lists national holidays in each daily edition, though the listing on www.holidayfestival.com is more complete and useful. If you plan your itinerary around these dates, you can encounter the festivals that entice you and circumvent the crowds visiting the ones that don't. This information is also valuable when determining when to arrive where—many services shut down on holidays and could leave you strapped for food and money in the event of an ill-timed arrival. Note also that in Austria, the first Saturday of every month is *Langer Samstag* (long Saturday); most stores stay open until 5pm. In small towns, stores are often closed from noon Saturday until 8am Monday, remember when stocking up on food for weekends. Check the individual town listings and the index for information on the festivals below.

BOTH COUNTRIES

DATE	FESTIVAL	REGION
January 1	New Years	National
April 13	Good Friday	National
April 16	Easter Monday	National
May 24	Ascension	National
June 4	Whit Monday	National
December 25	Christmas	National

AUSTRIA

DATE	FESTIVAL	REGION
January 6	Epiphany	National
June 14	Corpus Christi Day	National
May 1	Labor Day	National
Late July to Late August	Salzburg Music Festival	Salzburg
August 15	Feast of the Assumption	National
October 26	Austrian National Day	National
November 1	All Saints' Day	National
December 8	Feast of the Immaculate Conception	National
December 26	Boxing Day	National

SWITZERLAND

DATE	FESTIVAL	REGION
January 2	Berchtold's Day	National
Early March	Fasnacht (Carnival)	Basel, Luzern
Mid July	International Jazz Festival	Montreux
August 1	Swiss National Day	National
December 26	St.Stephen's Day	National

MEASUREMENTS

Austria and Switzerland use the metric system. Unconventional local units for measuring wine or beer are explained in the text when necessary. Note that gallons in the U.S. are not identical to those across the Atlantic; one U.S. gallon equals 0.83 Imperial gallons.

MEASUREMENT CONVERSIONS

1 inch (in.) = 25.4 millimeters (mm)	1 millimeter (mm) = 0.039 in.
1 foot (ft.) = 0.30 m	1 meter (m) = 3.28 ft.
1 yard (yd.) = 0.914m	1 meter (m) = 1.09 yd.
1 mile = 1.61km	1 kilometer (km) = 0.62 mi.
1 ounce (oz.) = 28.35g	1 gram (g) = 0.035 oz.
1 pound (lb.) = 0.454kg	1 kilogram (kg) = 2.202 lb.
1 fluid ounce (fl. oz.) = 29.57ml	1 milliliter (ml) = 0.034 fl. oz.
1 gallon (gal.) = 3.785L	1 liter (L) = 0.264 gal.
1 acre (ac.) = 0.405ha	1 hectare (ha) = 2.47 ac.
1 square mile (sq. mi.) = 2.59km^2	1 square kilometer (km^2) = 0.386 sq. mi.

DISTANCE (IN KM)

Distances may vary depending on the type of transportation used and the route traveled. In certain cases, traveling through a neighboring country such as Germany or Italy can be the fastest route.

	Basel	Bern	Geneva	Graz	Innsbruck	Interlaken	Linz	Locarno	Lugano	Salzburg	Vienna	Zermatt
Basel												
Bern	71											
Geneva	187	129										
Graz	597	610	718									
Innsbruck	290	303	418	307								
Interlaken	98	43	230	581	278							
Linz	509	536	658	158	245	517						
Locarno	180	135	204	520	235	92	478					
Lugano	201	158	219	512	233	114	476	21				
Salzburg	410	433	554	200	137	412	108	370	369			
Vienna	658	684	801	138	383	661	151	615	608	249		
Zermatt	169	105	126	602	311	72	555	82	95	447	694	
Zurich	76	98	224	525	216	92	443	135	153	102	591	159

CITY PHONE CODES

CITY TELEPHONE CODES			
Basel	061	**Linz**	0732
Bern	031	**Lucerne**	041
Bregenz	05574	**Interlaken**	036
Geneva	022	**Innsbruck**	0512
Graz	0316	**Lugano**	091
Linz	0732	**Salzburg**	0662
Innsbruck	0512	**Vienna**	01
Lausanne	021	**Zermatt**	027
Liechtenstein	075	**Zurich**	01

LANGUAGE

Confronted with Switzerland's four official languages and the countless dialects of German spoken throughout Austria and Switzerland, many travelers feel somewhat intimidated by the thought of communicating. Each of the following phrasebooks is designed to help you master your most urgent communicative needs in each of the major languages spoken in Austria and Switzerland. Each phrasebook is preceded by a pronunciation guide. Don't be afraid to attempt to use the phrases listed; with a little practice, they'll roll off your tongue.

The first, perhaps most helpful phrase a traveler should learn is "Sprechen Sie Englisch?," "Parlez-vous anglais?," or "Lei parla inglese?" (for use in the appropriate regions). Even if the person you ask doesn't speak English, he/she will appreciate your attempt to speak their language. Most younger Austrian and Swiss urbanites speak at least a smattering of English—usually much more—thanks to the establishment of English as a requirement for high school diplomas. Outside of cities and among older residents, however, the English proficiency becomes less reliable and you may have to rely on phrasebooks or an impromptu translation by the local tourist office.

If you're unsure in a foreign vocabulary, it's best to err on the side of formality. For example, it never hurts to use titles like *Herr* (Mr.) or *Frau* (Mrs.), the Italian terms *Signore* and *Signora*, or the French equivalents *Monsieur* and *Madame*

(Mrs.). *Fräulein,* on the other hand, is a loaded word and should be avoided by shakier German speakers, since it sometimes carries class connotations. When in doubt, use the formal pronoun (*Sie* in German, *Vous* in French, *Lei* in Italian) with the plural form of the verb. People will let you know when it's time to switch to more familiar language.

GERMAN PRONUNCIATION

Once you learn a few rules of German pronunciation, you should be able to sound out even the longest compound noun. Consonants are the same as in English, with the exception of C (pronounced *K*); J (pronounced *Y*); K (always pronounced, even before N); P (nearly always pronounced, even before F); QU (pronounced *KV*); S (pronounced *Z* at the beginning of a word); V (pronounced *F*); W (pronounced *V*); Z (pronounced *TS*). The ß, or *ess-tsett,* is simply a double S. Pronounce SCH as *SH.* In Austria, R is rolled in the front of the mouth, while CH is pronounced in Switzerland with the hoarse, throat-clearing sound that people often erroneously associate with German. Vowels are as follows: A as in "father"; E as the *A* in "hay" or the indistinct vowel sound in "uh"; I as the *ee* in "cheese"; O as in "oh"; U as in "fondue"; Y as the *oo* in "boot"; AU as in "sauerkraut"; EU as the oi in "boil." With EI and IE, pronounce the last letter as a long English vowel—*heisse* is HY-ssuh; *viele* is FEEL-uh.

FRENCH PRONUNCIATION

French pronunciation is more difficult than German, as many of the letters in a word are silent. Do not pronounce any final consonants except L, F, or C; an E on the end of the word, however, means that you should pronounce the final consonant sound, e.g., *muet* is mew-AY but *muette* is mew-ET. This rule also applies to plural nouns—don't pronounce the final S. J is like the S in "pleasure." R is rolled in the front of the mouth even more than in Austria. C sounds like *K* before A, O, and U; like *S* before E and I. A *ç* always sounds like *S.* Vowels are short and precise: A as the *O* in "mom"; E as in "help" (é becomes the a in "hay"); I as the *ee* in "creep"; *O* as in "oh." UI sounds like the word "whee." U is a short, clipped *oo* sound; hold your lips as if you were about to say "ooh," but say *ee* instead. OU is a straight *oo* sound. With few exceptions, all syllables receive equal emphasis.

ITALIAN PRONUNCIATION

Italian pronounciation isn't too complicated. There are 7 vowel sounds in standard Italian: A as in "father," I as the *ee* in "cheese," U as the *oo* in "droop," E either as *ay* in "bay" or *eh* in "set," and O both as *oh* in "bone" and *o* as in "off." Save for a few quirks, Italian consonants are easy. H is always silent, R is always rolled. C and G: are hard before a, o, or u, as in "cat" and "goose," but they soften into ch and j sounds, respectively, when followed by i or e, as in English "cheese" and "jeep" or Italian *ciao* (chow), "goodbye," and *gelato* (jeh-LAH-toh), "ice cream." CH and GH are pronounced like K and G before I and E, as in *chianti* (ky-AHN-tee), the Tuscan wine, and *spaghetti* (spah-GEHT-tee), the pasta. Pronounce GN like the NI in "onion," as in *bagno* (BAHN-yoh), the bathroom. GLI is like the LLI in *million,* so *sbagliato* ("wrong") is said "zbal-YAH-toh." When followed by A, O, or U, SC is pronounced as *SK. Scusi* ("excuse me") yields "SKOO-zee." When followed by an E or I, SC is pronounced SH as in *sciopero* (SHOH-pair-oh), "strike."

USEFUL PHRASES

ENGLISH	GERMAN	FRENCH	ITALIAN
Hello.	Hallo	Bonjour	Ciao
Excuse me/sorry	Entschuldigung.	Excusez-moi.	Scusi/Mi dispiace
Could you please help me?	Können Sie mir bitte helfen?	Est-ce que vous pouvez m'aider?	Potrebbe aiutarmi?
Good day	Guten Tag/Grüss Gott (Gruezi/Gruessach)	Bonjour.	Buongiorno
Good morning.	Guten Morgen	Bonjour.	Buonagiorno.
Good evening.	Guten Abend.	Bonsoir.	Buona sera.
Good night.	Gute Nacht	Bonne nuit.	Buona notte.
Good-bye.	Tschüß! (informal); Auf Wiedersehen! (formal)	Au revoir.	Arrivederci/ ArrivederLa
yes/no/maybe	ja/nein/vielleicht	oui/non/peut-être	sì/ no/forse
Please	Bitte	S'il vous plaît	Per favore/Per piacere
Thank you	Danke	Merci	Grazie
You're welcome.	Bitte.	De rien.	Prego.
Who?	Wer?	Qui?	Chi?
What?	Was?	Comment?	Cosa?
Where?	Wo?	Où?	Dovè?
When (what time)?	Wann?	Quand?	Quando?
Why?	Warum?	Pourquoi?	Perche?
My name is...	Ich heisse...	Je m'appelle...	Mi chiamo...
What is your name?	Wie heissen Sie?	Comment vous appellez-vous?	Come ti chiami?
Where are you from?	Woher kommen Sie?	Vous venez-d'où?	Di dove sei?
I'm from ...	Ich komme aus...	Je viens de...	Sono di...
How are you?	Wie geht's?	Comment ça va?	Come sta (formal)/stai?
I'm fine.	Es geht mir gut.	Ça va bien.	Sto bene.
I'm not feeling well.	Mir ist schlecht.	J'ai mal/Je suis blessé.	Sto male.
I have a headache.	Ich habe Kopfweh.	J'ai mal à la tête.	Ho un mal di testa.
I need a doctor.	Ich brauche einen Arzt.	J'ai besoin d'un médecin.	Ho bisogno di un medico.
Leave me alone.	Lass mich in Ruhe.	Laissez-moi tranquille.	Lasciame in pace!
I'll call the police.	Ich rufe die Polizei an.	J'appelle la police.	Telefono all polizia!
Help!	Hilfe!	Au secours!/Aidez-moi, s'il vous plaît.	Aiuto!
Stop/Enough!	Halt!/Genug!	Arrête!	Ferma!/Basta!
Do you speak English?	Sprechen Sie Englisch?	Parlez-vous anglais?	Lei parla inglese?
I can't speak . . .	Ich kann kein Deutsch.	Je ne parle pas français.	Non parlo italiano
I don't understand.	Ich verstehe nicht.	Je ne comprends pas.	Non capisco
I understand	Ich verstehe.	Je comprends.	Ho capito
Please speak slowly.	Sprechen Sie bitte langsam.	S'il vous plaît, parlez moins vite.	Parla piu lentamente, per favore.
Excuse me?	Wie, bitte?	Pardon?	Come?
Please repeat.	Bitte widerholen sie.	Répétez, s'il vous plaît.	Potrebbe ripetere?
I would like...	Ich möchte...	Je voudrais...	Vorrei...
I'm looking for...	Ich suche...	Je cherche...	Trovo...
How much does that cost?	Wieviel kostet das?	Ça coûte combien?	Quanto costa?
Where can I buy something to eat/to drink?	Wo kann ich etwas zu essen kaufen/zu trinken kaufen?	Où est-ce que je peux acheter quelquechose à manger/à boire?	Dove posso comprare qualcosa da bere o mangiare?
OK.	In Ordnung.	D'accord.	D'accordo.

I don't know.	Ich weiss nicht	Je ne sais pas.	Boh./Non lo so.
Where is the toilet?	Wo ist die Toilette?	Où sont les toilettes?	Dov'è il gabinetto?
Please	Bitte	S'il vous plait	Per favore
How do you say that in German?/French?...	Wie sagt man das auf Deutsch?	Comment ça se dit en français?	Come si dice...?
What does this mean?	Was bedeutet das?	Qu'est-ce que ça veut dire?	Cosa vuol dire questo?
Where is the phone?	Wo ist das Telefon?	Où est le téléphone?	Dov'è il telefono?
I am a student (male/female).	Ich bin Student/Studentin.	Je suis étudiant(e).	Sono studente/studentessa.
student discounts	Studentenermässigungen	tarifs réduits pour les étudiants	sconto studentesco
No problem	Kein Problem	Ce n'est pas grave.	Va bene.

DIRECTIONS AND TRANSPORTATION

ENGLISH	GERMAN	FRENCH	ITALIAN
(to the) right	rechts	à droite	a destra
(to the) left	links	à gauche	a sinistra
straight ahead	geradeaus	tout droite	sempre diritto
here	hier	ici	qui/qua
there	da	lá-bas	li/lâ
far	fern	près de	lontano
near	nah	loin	vicino
east/west	Ost/West	est/ouest	ovest/este
north/south	Nord/Süd	nord/sud	nord/sud
I would like a ticket to...	Ich möchte eine Fahrkarte nach...	Je voudrais un billet à...	Vorrei un biglietto per...
Where is this train going?	Wohin fährt dieser Zug?	Quelle est la destination de la train?	Dove va questo treno?
Which bus goes to...	Welcher Bus fährt nach...?	Quel bus va â...?	Qual' autobus va a...?
When does the train leave?	Wann fährt der Zug ab?	Quand est-ce que le train port?	A che ora parte il treno?
Please stop.	Bitte halten Sie.	Arretez, s'il vous plait.	Ferma, per favore.
Where is...?	Wo ist...?	Où est...?	Dov'è...?
the train station?	der Bahnhof?	la gare?	la stazione?
the tourist office?	das Touristbüro?	le bureau de tourisme?	l'ufficio turistico?
the post office?	die Post?	la poste?	l'ufficio postale?
the old town?	die Altstadt?	la vieille ville?	il centro storico?
the hostel?	die Jugendherberge?	l'auberge de jeunesse?	il ostello?
a grocery store?	ein Supermarkt?	le supermarché?	il supermercato?
the bus stop?	die Haltestelle?	l'arrêt d'autobus?	la fermata del' autobus?
one-way	einfache Fahrt	un billet aller-simple	solo andata
round-trip	hin- und zurück	aller-retour	andata e ritorno

TIMES AND HOURS

ENGLISH	GERMAN	FRENCH	ITALIAN
At what time...?	Um wieviel Uhr...?	À quelle heure?	A che ora...?
What time is it?	Wie spät ist es?	Quelle heure est-il?	Che ore sono?
It is 5 o'clock.	Es ist 5 Uhr.	Il est 5 heures.	Sono le cinque.
It's early.	Es ist früh.	Il est tôt.	in anticipo/presto
It's late.	Es ist spät.	Il est tard.	in ritardo/tardi
opening hours	die Öffnungszeiten	Les heures d'ouverture	orari
daily	täglich	chacque jour	quotidiano

weekly	wochentlich	chacque semaines	settimanale
monthly	monatlich	chacque mois	mensile
today	heute	aujourd'hui	oggi
tomorrow	morgen	demain	domani
yesterday	gestern	hier	ieri
now	jetzt	maintenant	adesso/ora
immediately	sofort	tout-de-suite	subito
always	immer	toujours	sempre
except	ohne	sauf	ecceto
January	Januar	janvier	gennato
February	Februar	février	febbraio
March	März	mars	marzo
April	April	avril	aprile
May	Mai	mai	maggio
June	Juni	juin	guigno
July	Juli	juillet	luglio
August	August	août	novembre
September	September	septembre	settembre
October	October	octobre	ottobre
November	November	novembre	novembre
December	December	decembre	dicembre
open	geöffnet	ouvert	aperto
closed	geschlossen	fermé	chiuso
morning	der Morgen	le matin	mattina
afternoon	der Nachmittag	l'après-midi	pomeriggio
evening	der Abend	le soir	sera
night	die Nacht	la nuit	notte
break time, rest day	die Ruhepause, der Ruhetag	fermeture	riposo
Monday	Montag	lundi	lunedi
Tuesday	Dienstag	mardi	martedi
Wednesday	Mittwoch	mercredi	mercoledi
Thursday	Donnerstag	jeudi	giovedi
Friday	Freitag	vendredi	venerdi
Saturday	Samstag	samedi	sabato
Sunday	Sonntag	dimanche	domenica
holidays	ferien	jours fériés (j.f.)	giorni festivi

NUMBERS

NO.	GERMAN	FRENCH	ITALIAN
0	null	zéro	zero
1	eins	un	uno
2	zwei or zwoh	deux	due
3	drei	trois	tre
4	vier	quatre	quattro
5	fünf	cinq	cinque
6	sechs	six	sei
7	sieben	sept	sette
8	acht	huit	otto
9	neun	neuf	nove
10	zehn	dix	dieci
11	elf	onze	undici

12	zwölf	douze	dodici
13	dreizehn	treize	tredici
14	vierzehn	quatorze	quattordici
15	fünfzehn	quinze	quindici
16	sechzehn	seize	seidici
17	siebzehn	dix-sept	diciasette
18	achtzehn	dix-huit	diciotto
19	neunzehn	dix-neuf	dicianove
20	zwanzig	vingt	venti
21	einund-zwanzig	vingt et un	ventuno
30	dreißig	trente	trenta
40	vierzig	quarante	quaranta
50	fünfzig	cinquante	cinquanta
60	sechzig	soixante	sessanta
70	siebzig	soixante-dix	settanta
80	achtzig	quatre-vingt	ottanta
90	neunzig	quatre-vingt-dix	novanta
100	(ein)hundert	cent	cento
101	hunderteins	cent-et-un	centouno
1000	(ein)tausend	mille	mille

FOOD AND RESTAURANTS

ENGLISH	GERMAN	FRENCH	ITALIAN
restaurant	das Restaurant	un restaurant	il ristorante
bar	die Bar	un Bar	il Bar
meal	das Mahl	le repas	pasto
water	das Wasser	l'eau	l'acqua
breakfast	das Frühstück	le petit déjeuner	la (prima) colazione
lunch	das Mittagessen	le déjeuner	il pranzo
dinner/supper	das Abendessen	le dîner/le souper	la cena
to snack	naschen	le goûter	Mangiare tavela calda
I am thirsty	Ich habe Durst	J'ai faim.	Ho sed.
I am hungry	Ich habe Hunger	J'ai soif.	Ho fame.
waiter(ess)	Kellner(in)/Herr Ober	serveur/euse	cameriere/a
Check, please.	Die Rechnung, bitte.	L'addition, s'il vous plaît.	Mi dà il conto per favore-servizio
Service included.	Bedienung inklusiv.	Service compris.	Servizio compresso.
I would like...	Ich hätte gern...	Je voudrais...	Vorrei
It tastes good.	Es schmeckt gut.	Ça a un bon gout.	Tutto bene.
Do you have vegetarian food?	Haben Sie vegetarisches Essen?	Avez-vous de la nourriture vegetarienne?	Hai qualcosa vegeteríana da mangiare?
I am diabetic.	Ich bin Diabetiker.	Je suis diabétique.	Sono diabetico.
tea	das Tee	le thé	il tè
hot chocolate	heisse Schokolade	le chocolat chaud	una cioccolata
milk	das Milch	le lait	la latte
coffee	das Kaffee	le café	il café
beer	das Bier	la bière	la bierra
wine	der Wein	le vin	il vino
tap water	das Leitungswasser	de l'eau de robinet	acqua di rubinetto
bread	das Brot	le pain	il pane
vegetables	die Gemüse	le légume	le verdure
meat	das Fleisch	la viande	le carne
sausage	die Wurst	le saucisson	la salsiccia

chicken	das Huhn	le poulet	il pollo
pork	das Schweinfleisch	le porc	il maiale
beef	das Rindfleisch	le bœuf	la bistecca
cheese	der Käse	le fromage	il formagio
pasta	die Nudeln	les pâtes	pasta
potatoes	die Kartoffeln	la pomme de terre	la patate
dessert	der Nachtisch	le dessert	il dolce
jelly	die Marmelade	la gelée	la gelatina

MISCELLANEOUS WORDS

ENGLISH	GERMAN	FRENCH	ITALIAN
a single room	ein Einzelzimmer	une chambre simple	una camera singola
money	das Geld	l'argent	i soldi
exchange	wechseln	echanger	cambio
hospital	das Krankenhaus	un hôpital	ospedale
sick	krank	malade	ammalato/a
smoking	raucher	fumer	fumare
good/bad	gut/schlecht	bon/mauvais	buono/cattivo
happy/sad	glücklich/traurig	heureur/triste	felice/triste
hot/cold	heiß/kalt	chaud/froid	caldo/freddo
big/small	groß/klein	grand/petit	piccolo/grande
full/empty	voll/ leer	plein/vide	pieno/vuoto
dangerous	gefährlich	dangereux	pericoloso
safe	ungefährlich	sûr	sicuro
Caution!	Achtung!/Vorsicht!	Attention!	Attenzione!
Fire!	Feuer!	Feu!	Fuoco!
You're cute.	Du bist süß.	Tu'es mignon/ne.	Sei belino/a
May I buy you a drink?	Darf ich dir ein Getränk kaufen?	Je peux t'offrir quelquechose?	Posso offrirle qualcosa da bere?
Would you buy me a drink?	Wurdest Du mir ein Getränk kaufen?	Tu m'offre quelquechose?	Può offrirmi qualcosa da bere?
My father is a policeman.	Mein Vater ist Polizist.	Mon père est policier.	Il mio padre è polizia.
Quick! Throw me the ladder!	Schnell! Wirf mir den Leiter zu!	Vite! Jetez-moi l'échelle!	Pronto! Buttame la scala!

INDEX

INDEX

C

N

O

T

U

INDEX

Will you have enough stories to tell your grandchildren?